ARCHBOLD

2004

AUSTRALIA
LBC Information Services
Sydney

CANADA and USA
Carswell
Toronto

HONG KONG
Sweet & Maxwell Asia

NEW ZEALAND
Brookers
Wellington

A CIP catalogue record for this book is available from the British Library

ISBN 0421 859 30X

No natural forests were destroyed to make this product; only farmed
timber was used and replanted

ISBN 0-421-85930-X

9 780421 859302

© Sweet & Maxwell Limited
2004

ARCHBOLD

MAGISTRATES' COURTS CRIMINAL PRACTICE

2004

LONDON
SWEET & MAXWELL
2004

Published in 2004 by Sweet & Maxwell Limited of
100 Avenue Road,
London NW3 3PF
www.sweetandmaxwell.co.uk
Typeset by Sweet & Maxwell Ltd, 100 Avenue Road, London, NW3 3PF

Printed and bound in England by
William Clowes Ltd, Beccles, Suffolk

PREFACE

The publication of this book represents the birth of a new work which we hope will prove hugely useful to those who work in the magistrates' courts. *Archbold Criminal Pleading, Evidence & Practice* has been the leading guide to criminal pleading, evidence and practice in the Crown Court for some150 years before the Crown Court was created. Practitioners will be well aware that the pressure has been on the authors of *Archbold* to limit the size (and weight) of their authoritative work. They have not been able to focus on summary trial issues. The publishers have long envisaged a companion book which would complement *Archbold Crown* by providing the legal support needed by practitioners in the magistrates' court. A team of writers, all of whom have a wealth of relevant experience, have therefore developed this complementary text, under the co-ordinating guidance of an academic general editor. The creation of such a text is no easy task: and the writing team have had many discussions along the way about the practical and legal issues facing those working in a magistrates' court and how best to explain them. We hope that readers will let us know what they think. We are particularly interested in whether readers think we have achieved the correct balance. Is the balance between statutory materials and expert commentary helpful? And the balance between sections: which are too long and which too short? Are there matters which should be here which aren't? Particularly challenging have been the host of offences which may be charged: inevitably all cannot be described and analysed. Please email your comments to the address at the bottom of this page.

There will never be a right time to launch a book such as this, and practitioners in the criminal courts are only too aware that this is a time of great change: see the *Courts Act* 2003, the *Extradition Act* 2003, the *Sex Offences Act* 2003, not to mention the *Criminal Justice Act* 2003. ... But because this is a time of change, perhaps this is all the more reason for publishing this new book now and most certainly all the more reason for us to welcome comment. We are already working on a supplement and next year's edition.

The authors, Barbara Barnes, Robert Brown, Jeremy Coleman, Gaynor Houghton-Jones and Kevin McCormac, have all worked fantastically hard to meet tough deadlines. Whilst the team of writers deserve full credit for their individual chapters, we all wish to pay tribute to two research assistants who worked hard to launch the book. Megan Addis, who worked on the project for three months in the summer of 2003, and Louise Cowen, who supported the main authors for an eight month period, both contributed hugely to the writing of the original drafts and researching statutory and case law materials. We all are grateful to Megan and Louise for their professional approach to the launch of this project. We would also like to thank Shanta Deonarine and Michael Seath for their contribution to the flow charts in Chapter 34 and Joanna McCormac for her review of the sentencing chapters. Mistakes remain the responsibility of the individual authors.

Nothing would have happened without the team at Sweet and Maxwell. Tania Quan's inspiration and determination made us all persevere with what seemed like a daunting project; Nicky Meech and Johanna Whelehan kept chasing our flagging authors with a remarkable blend of encouragement and discipline!

Nicky Padfield
General Editor
Fitzwilliam College, Cambridge CB3 0DG   Email: crime@thomson.com

July 2004

FOREWORD

The criminal jurisdiction of the magistrates' court and its overall responsibilities has increased enormously over the past few years, and this trend is set to continue. Long gone are the days when an untrained bench assisted by a legally qualified clerk was deemed sufficient to be able properly to discharge their judicial functions. The complexities of modern society, the proliferation of new offences, additional alternatives to custodial sentences and the frequent changes in practice and procedure imposed by Parliament on an almost annual basis present a constant stream of new challenges which, welcome or unwelcome, are a reality which must be faced and absorbed by bench and practitioner alike.

Some of these challenges can be met by effective use of training, mentoring and assessment to enable justice in the summary jurisdiction to be informed, efficient and geographically consistent. The Judicial Studies Board is currently playing an important role in this field, which is to be greatly expanded in the short and medium term.

Additionally, the availability of an authoritative and comprehensive text dealing with the practice, procedures and law pertinent to the magistrates' court is essential to all those involved in making the system effective, be they practitioners, prosecuting (or defence) authorities, magistrates and those responsible for advising them in the administration of their courts. It is here that Archbold Magistrates' Court Criminal Practice is invaluable.

For the first time there is a single volume work dedicated entirely to the criminal jurisdiction of the magistrates' and youth courts. The very size of the volume evidences the weight and detail of essential reference in this field. Particularly to be welcomed is the layout — structured as it is in chronological order, providing step by step guidance through procedures and then dealing comprehensively with specific offences and sentences, and including procedural checklists, flowcharts and diagrams where necessary to deal with procedurally complex matters.

The extensive coverage (where relevant) of the *Criminal Justice Act* 2003, the *Sexual Offences Act* 2003, dealing with mentally disordered offenders, extradition and Youth Courts will provide a welcome relief to those concerned to understand these vital but often daunting topics.

I have little doubt that this book will take its place alongside its (currently) more famous sister as an indispensable work of reference and practice. I welcome it with enthusiasm.

His Honour Judge William Rose

August 2004

CONTENTS

Part I: Pre-trial Issues

CHAPTER 1: CRIMINAL INVESTIGATIONS

CHAPTER 2: CONSTITUTION AND JURISDICTION

CHAPTER 3: EXTRADITION

CHAPTER 4: COMMENCEMENT OF PROCEEDINGS

CHAPTER 5: BAIL

CONTENTS

CONTENTS

CONTENTS

CONTENTS

CONTENTS

ABBREVIATIONS

ASBO	Anti-Social Behaviour Order
CCSU	Council of Civil Service Unions
CDRO	Criminal Defence Representation Order
CJA	Criminal Justice Act
CJCSA	Criminal Justice and Court Services Act
CJPOA	Criminal Justice and Public Order Act
CLA	Criminal Law Act
CPIA	Criminal Procedure and Investigations Act
CPS	Crown Prosecution Service
CRO	Community Rehabilitation Order
CYPA	Children and Young Persons Act
DCW	Designated Case Worker
DTTO	Drug Treatment and Testing Order
FACT	Federation against Copyright Theft
ISSP	Intensive Supervision and Surveillance Program
JOPI	Joint Operational Instructions
MDO	Mentally Disordered Offenders
PACE	Police and Criminal Evidence Act 1984
PCC(S)A	Powers of Criminal Courts (Sentencing) Act
POCA	Protection of Children Act
PSR	Pre-sentence Report
RIPA	Regulation of Investigatory Powers Act
RTA	Road Traffic Act
SOA	Sexual Offences Act
SSR	Specific Sentence Report
YJCEA	Youth Justice and Criminal Evidence Act
YOT	Youth Offending Team

TABLE OF STATUTES

*[References to repealed sections are omitted, except in cases where the old law is discussed. A paragraph reference in heavy type thus, **3–68** indicates the paragraph in which the text of an enactment is printed.]*

TABLE OF STATUTORY INSTRUMENTS

*[References to repealed sections are omitted, except in cases where the old law is discussed. A paragraph reference in heavy type thus, **3–68** indicates the paragraph in which the text of an enactment is printed.]*

xlvii

Table of Statutory Instruments

TABLE OF CASES

TABLE OF CASES

Table of Cases

TABLE OF EUROPEAN CASES

Part I

Pre-Trial Issues

CHAPTER 1

CRIMINAL INVESTIGATIONS

I. INTRODUCTION

The law governing the powers of the police in the conduct of criminal investigations **1–1** is primarily contained in the *Police and Criminal Evidence Act* 1984. The police also retain common law powers and additional powers have been enacted subsequently especially in the *Police Act* 1997 and the *Criminal Justice and Police Act* 2001. Further amendments are made by the *Criminal Justice Act* 2003, when in force. The Act is supplemented by a series of Codes of Practice.

A. POLICE AND CRIMINAL EVIDENCE ACT 1984 (PACE) AND CODES OF PRACTICE

Police and Criminal Evidence Act 1984, s.66

Codes of practice

66.—(1) The Secretary of State shall issue codes of practice in connection with— **1–2**
    (a) the exercise by police officers of statutory powers—
        (i) to search a person without first arresting him;
    or
        (ii) to search a vehicle without making an arrest;
    (b) the detention, treatment, questioning and identification of persons by police officers;
    (c) searches of premises by police officers; and
    (d) the seizure of property found by police officers on persons or premises.
    (2) Codes shall (in particular) include provision in connection with the exercise by police officers of powers under section 63B above.

Under ss.66 and 67 of the *Police and Criminal Evidence Act* 1984, the Secretary of **1–3** State for the Home Office has the power to issue codes of practice. The Code issued in relation to s.63B of the Act refers to the power of the police to take samples from persons in police detention to ascertain whether there is any Class A drugs in their body.

There are six main Codes of Practice. The most recent versions were issued on April **1–4** 1, 2003, with further modifications in 2004.
    A. Code of Practice for the Exercise by Police Officers of Statutory Powers of Stop and Search

B. Code of Practice for the Searching of Premises by Police Officers and the Seizure of Property found by Police Officers

C. Code of Practice for Detention, Treatment and Questioning of Persons by Police Officers

D. Code of Practice for the Identification of Persons by Police Officers

E. Code of Practice on Tape Recording of Interviews with Suspects

F. Code of Practice on Visual Recording of Interviews with Suspects

(1) Status of the codes Police and Criminal Evidence Act 1984, ss.60, 66, 67

1–4.1   The Codes are admissible in evidence and the court may take account of any relevant provision. They are issued as Statutory Instruments. Section 11 of the *Criminal Justice Act* 2003 amends s.67 of the *Police and Criminal Evidence Act* 1984 and provides for the procedure for the making and revision of codes. A consultation process must occur with the police, members of the legal profession and other such persons as are thought fit.

In *R. v McCay* (1990) 91 Cr.App.R. 84, the Court of Appeal referred to Code D as having the full authority of Parliament but the correctness of this decision has been doubted: [1990] Crim.L.R. 340. In *R. v Quinn* [1995] 1 Cr.App.R. 480, Code D was referred to as a "statutory code". They are codes of practice designed to regulate the conduct of persons charged with the duty of investigating offences by providing a structure within which the checks and controls of the Act operate.

1–5   Annexes elaborate upon aspects of the Codes and must be observed. Notes for guidance advise upon the application of the Codes and Annexes but do not have the binding effect of the codes themselves although they are there to be followed.

The Codes and the guidance encapsulate the principles of the European Convention of Human Rights and must be observed by Police Officers who are defined as a public authority: s.6 of the *Human Rights Act* 1998. Proceedings may be taken against a Police Force if their officers are found to have acted in breach of Convention rights.

Articles 5, 6, 8 and 14 are particularly relevant to the exercise of police powers.

Article 5 protects the right to liberty and security. The Article states that everyone has a right to liberty and security of the person and they should not be deprived of their liberty except in the circumstances specified by the Article and in accordance with procedures prescribed by law. Paragraph 5(1)(c) sets out the arrest condition:—

> "The lawful arrest or detention of a person effected for the purpose of bringing him before the competent legal authority on reasonable suspicion of having committed an offence or when it is reasonably considered necessary to prevent his committing an offence or fleeing after having done so."

Article 5(2) requires that everyone shall be informed promptly, in a language which he understands of the reasons for his arrest and of any charge against him.

Article 5(4) and (5) gives a right to speedy challenge of the legality of the arrest or detention and a right to compensation if the arrest or detention is in contravention of the Article. Article 6 protects the right to a fair and public trial and guarantees minimum rights to any person charged with a criminal offence. Article 8 sets out the right to respect for private and family life. Article 14 provides a prohibition of discrimination in the enjoyment of the Convention Rights.

Copies of the Codes should be available at Police Stations for public consultation and for reference for police officers and detained persons.

(2) Application of the Codes

1–6   Police officers and persons with a duty to investigate and charge offences are bound by the Codes.

Police and Criminal Evidence Act 1984, s.67

Codes of Practice—supplementary

67.—(1–7D) *Provisions for the issue and review of codes of practice (as amended by* section 11 of the *Criminal Justice Act* 2003).

(8) *Repealed*

(9) Persons other than police officers who are charged with the duty of investigating offences or charging offenders shall in the discharge of that duty have regard to any relevant provision of such a code.

(9A) persons on whom powers are conferred by—

    (a) any designation under section 38 or 39 of the *Police Reform Act* 2002 (police powers for police authority employees)

    (b) any accreditation under section 41 of that Act (accreditation under community safety accreditation schemes)

shall have regard to any relevant provision of a code of practice to which this section applies in the exercise or performance of the powers and duties conferred or imposed on them by that designation or accreditation.

(10) A failure on the part—

    (a) of a police officer to comply with any provision of such a code; or

    (b) of any person other than a police officer who is charged with the duty of investigating offences or charging offenders to have regard to any relevant provision of such a code in the discharge of that duty, or

    (c) of a person designated under section 38 or 39 or accredited under section 41 of the *Police Reform Act* 2002 to have regard to any relevant provision of such a code in the exercise or performance of the powers and duties conferred or imposed on him by that designation or accreditiation,

shall not of itself render him liable to any criminal or civil proceedings.

(11) In all criminal and civil proceedings any such code shall be admissible in evidence; and if any provision of such a code appears to the court or tribunal conducting the proceedings to be relevant to any question arising in the proceedings it shall be taken into account in determining that question.

(12) *Courts martial etc.*

[This section is printed as amended by the *Police and Magistrates' Courts Act* 1994, s.37(1) (a), *Police Act* 1996, Sch.9, the *Criminal Justice and Police Act* 2001, s.7, and the *Police Reform Act* 2002, Schs 7 and 8.]

Questions may arise as to whether a person is bound by the Codes. Case law indicates **1–7** that the Court will consider whether a duty exists either in common law, statute or contract. A store detective has been held to have a duty to investigate incidents (*R. v Bayliss* (1993) 157 J.P. 1062) but a headteacher has not (*DPP v G, The Times* November 24, 1997). An inspector of the RSPCA may be bound (*RSPCA v Eager* [1995] Crim.L.R. 59) as was an officer of the Federation Against Copyright Theft (*Joy v FACT* [1993] Crim.L.R. 588). Both officers of Customs and Excise and officers of the Serious Fraud Office have been held to be bound by the Codes: *R. v Okafor*, (1994) 99 Cr.App.R. 97; *R. v Director of SFO Ex p. Saunders* [1988] Crim.L.R. 837.

Where the Code refers to duties to be carried out by police officers at a police station it may be impractical for investigators who are not police officers to comply with those requirements. A Social Security investigator was held not to be in breach of the Code in failing to advise of the right to free legal advice on interview. This provision of the Code was held only to apply to investigators at the police station where the free Legal Aid representation scheme applied and a duty solicitor could be called: *R. (Social Security Secretary) v South Central Division Magistrates, The Daily Telegraph*, November 28, 2000, DC.

The codes are admissible in evidence in all criminal and civil proceedings. Breach of the Codes is not an offence and there is no individual legal liability attaching to a constable for non-compliance but the admissibility of evidence obtained in breach of the Codes may be excluded by the Court under *PACE* 1984, s.76 (confessions) or s.78 (Unfair evidence), see Chapter 21.

Breach of a Code does not lead to evidence automatically being excluded: *R. v Haynes* (2004) 148 S.J. 181.

B. STOP AND SEARCH

(1) Introduction

1–8 Section 1 of the *Police and Criminal Evidence Act* 1984 gives the police power to stop and search in England and Wales. Other statutory powers of stop and search also exist,*e.g. Firearms Act* 1968, s.47(3), *Misuse of Drugs Act* 1971, s.23(2) and *Terrorism Act* 2000, s.44. Under s.60 of the *Criminal Justice and Public Order Act* 1994, extended powers of search were introduced. Even where consent to a search is given, a statutory power of search must exist and the Code will still apply.

General

1–9 Code A sets out the principles governing the power of the police to stop and search persons and vehicles. Under s.117 of the *Police and Criminal Evidence Act* 1984, officers are permitted to use "reasonable force" if necessary in the exercise of this and other powers conferred under the Act.

(2) Reasonable Grounds for Suspecting

1–10 When exercising the power to stop and search persons or vehicles a constable must have reasonable grounds for suspecting that stolen or prohibited articles will be found. The existence of a reasonable suspicion is crucial to the existence of the power to stop and search.

"Reasonable suspicion" is not defined in the Act. Code A, paras 1.6 and 1.7 provide guidance on what amounts to a reasonable suspicion. There must be an objective basis for the suspicion based on facts, information or intelligence which are relevant to the likelihood of finding prohibited articles or stolen property: para.A:2.2. A reasonable suspicion cannot be based only on personal factors relevant to the suspect (*e.g.* age, appearance or known record). There must also be reliable supporting intelligence or information or some specific behaviour by the person concerned giving rise to the suspicion. A reasonable suspicion cannot be based on generalisations or stereotypical images of certain groups or categories of people as more likely to be involved in criminal activity.

The Code states that "where there is reliable information or intelligence that members of a group or gang carry knives unlawfully or weapons or controlled drugs and wear a distinctive item of clothing or other means of identification to indicate their membership of the group or gang" then that distinctive item of clothing or other means of identification may provide reasonable grounds to stop and search a person: para.A:2.3. This recent addition to the code implies that mere identifiable membership of a group or gang is sufficient to found a reasonable suspicion. The Code states that the item of clothing or means of identification may of itself provide reasonable grounds to stop and search a person, not that such clothing or identification may support a reasonable suspicion that the person is carrying prohibited items or stolen property.

(3) Power of constable to stop and search persons and vehicles

Police and Criminal Evidence Act 1984, s.1

Power of constable to stop and search persons, vehicles etc

1–11 **1.**—(1) A constable may exercise any power conferred by this section—

  (a) in any place to which at the time when he proposes to exercise the power the public or any section of the public has access, on payment or otherwise, as of right or by virtue of express or implied permission; or

    (b) in any other place to which people have ready access at the time when he proposes to exercise the power but which is not a dwelling.

(2) Subject to subsection (3) to (5) below, a constable—

    (a) may search—

        (i)   any person or vehicle;

        (ii) anything which is in or on a vehicle,

    for stolen or prohibited articles [or any article to which subsection (8A) below applies]; and

    (b) may detain a person or vehicle for the purpose of such a search.

(3) This section does not give a constable power to search a person or vehicle or anything in or on a vehicle unless he has reasonable grounds for suspecting that he will find stolen or prohibited articles [or any article to which subsection (8A) below applies].

(4) If a person is in a garden or yard occupied with and used for the purposes of a dwelling or on other land so occupied and used, a constable may not search him in the exercise of the power conferred by this section unless the constable has reasonable grounds for believing—

    (a) that he does not reside in the dwelling; and

    (b) that he is not in the place in question with the express or implied permission of a person who resides in the dwelling.

(5) If a vehicle is in a garden or yard occupied with and used for the purposes of a dwelling or on other land so occupied and used, a constable may not search the vehicle or anything in or on it in the exercise of the power conferred by this section unless he has reasonable grounds for believing—

    (a) that the person in charge of the vehicle does not reside in the dwelling; and

    (b) that the vehicle is not in the place in question with the express or implied permission of a person who resides in the dwelling.

(6) If in the course of such a search a constable discovers an article which he has reason- **1–12** able grounds for suspecting to be a stolen or prohibited article [or an article to which subsection (8A) below applies], he may seize it.

(7) An article is prohibited for the purposes of this Part of this Act if it is—

    (a) an offensive weapon; or

    (b) an article—

        (i)   made or adapted for use in the course of or in connection with an offence to which this sub-paragraph applies; or

        (ii) intended by the person having it with him for such use by him or by some other person.

(8) The offences to which subsection (7)(b)(i) above applies are—

    (a) burglary;

    (b) theft;

    (c) offences under section 12 of the *Theft Act* 1968 (taking motor vehicle or other conveyance without authority); and

    (d) offences under section 15 of that Act (obtaining property by deception) and

    (e) offences under section 1 of the *Criminal Damage Act* 1971 (destroying or damaging property).

(8A) This subsection applies to any article in relation to which a person has committed, or is committing or is going to commit an offence under section 139 of the *Criminal Justice Act* 1988.

(9) In this Part of this Act "offensive weapon" means any article—

    (a) made or adapted for use for causing injury to persons; or

    (b) intended by the person having it with him for such use by him or by some other person.

[This section is printed as amended by the *Criminal Justice Act* 1988, s.140 and the *Criminal Justice Act* 2003, s.1.]

The term "constable" covers every police officer of whatever rank: *Lewis v Cattle* **1–13** (1938) 2 K.B. 454.

This section confers the power on police to stop and search anyone who is found in a public place or in a place accessible from a public area. It does not entitle searches to be carried out in private dwellings but it does cover people found in yards or gardens of dwellings if it is believed that they do not have permission to be there.

Section 139 of the *Criminal Justice Act* 1988 refers to unlawful possession of a bladed article.

(4) Provisions relating to search under s.1

Police and Criminal Evidence Act 1984, s.2

Provisions relating to search under s.1 and other powers

1–14

    2.—(1) A constable who detains a person or vehicle in the exercise—
      (a) of the power conferred by section 1 above; or
      (b) of any other power—
         (i) to search a person without first arresting him; or
        (ii) to search a vehicle without making an arrest,
      need not conduct a search if it appears to him subsequently—
         (i) that no search is required; or
        (ii) that a search is impracticable.

    (2) If a constable contemplates a search, other than a search of an unattended vehicle, in the exercise—
      (a) of the power conferred by section 1 above; or
      (b) of any other power, except the power conferred by section 6 below and the power conferred by section 27(2) of the *Aviation Security Act* 1982—
         (i) to search a person without first arresting him; or
        (ii) to search a vehicle without making an arrest,
      it shall be his duty, subject to subsection (4) below, to take reasonable steps before he commences the search to bring to the attention of the appropriate person—
         (i) if the constable is not in uniform, documentary evidence that he is a constable; and
        (ii) whether he is in uniform or not, the matters specified in subsection (3) below;
      and the constable shall not commence the search until he has performed that duty.

1–15

    (3) The matters referred to in subsection (2)(ii) above are—
      (a) the constable's name and the name of the police station to which he is attached;
      (b) the object of the proposed search;
      (c) the constable's grounds for proposing to make it; and
      (d) the effect of section 3(7) or (8) below, as may be appropriate.

    (4) A constable need not bring the effect of section 3(7) or (8) below to the attention of the appropriate person if it appears to the constable that it will not be practicable to make the record in section 3(1) below.

    (5) In this section "the appropriate person" means—
      (a) if the constable proposes to search a person, that person; and
      (b) if he proposes to search a vehicle, or anything in or on a vehicle, the person in charge of the vehicle.

    (6) On completing a search of an unattended vehicle or anything in or on such a vehicle in the exercise of any such power as is mentioned in subsection (2) above a constable shall leave a notice—
      (a) stating that he has searched it;
      (b) giving the name of the police station to which he is attached;
      (c) stating that an application for compensation for any damage caused by the search may be made to that police station; and
      (d) stating the effect of section 3(8) below.

    (7) The constable shall leave the notice inside the vehicle unless it is not reasonably practicable to do so without damaging the vehicle.

    (8) The time for which a person or vehicle may be detained for the purposes of such a

search is such time as is reasonably required to permit a search to be carried out either at the place where the person or vehicle was first detained or nearby.

(9) Neither the power conferred by section 1 above nor any other power to detain and search a person without first arresting him or to detain and search a vehicle without making an arrest is to be construed—

(a) as authorising a constable to require a person to remove any of his clothing in public other than an outer coat, jacket or gloves; or

(b) as authorising a constable not in uniform to stop a vehicle.

(10) This section and section 1 above apply to vessels, aircraft and hovercraft as they apply to vehicles.

Section 6 of the Act confers defined powers of stop and search on constables employed **1–16** in undertakings related to railways, road and water transport and docks and harbours etc. Searches may be carried out on vehicles before they leave the goods areas of the relevant premises. The *Aviation Security Act* 1982 confers powers to stop and search persons and vehicles leaving a cargo area of an aerodrome.

Under the Code a constable may stop and question a suspect and then has a discretion not to proceed with a search if it is unnecessary or impracticable. If the search is to proceed the officer has a duty to comply with the requirements of this section, providing the information specified. All these details must be recorded in writing and the person involved has a right to be given a copy of this record either in person or if the search was of an unattended vehicle the record must be left with the vehicle. Any failure to comply with the section means a Constable is not acting in the execution of his duty and a search will not be lawful: *Osman v DPP* (1999) 163 J.P. 725, DC.

(5) Duty to make records concerning searches

Police and Criminal Evidence Act 1984, s.3

Duty to make records concerning searches

3.—(1) Where a constable has carried out a search in the exercise of any such power as is **1–17** mentioned in section 2(1) above, other than a search—

(a) under section 6 below; or

(b) under section 27(2) of the *Aviation Security Act* 1982,

he shall make a record of it in writing unless it is not practicable to do so.

(2) If—

(a) a constable is required by subsection (1) above to make a record of a search; but

(b) it is not practicable to make the record on the spot,

he shall make it as soon as practicable after the completion of the search.

(3) The record of a search of a person shall include a note of his name, if the constable knows it, but a constable may not detain a person to find out his name.

(4) If a constable does not know the name of a person whom he has searched, the record of the search shall include a note otherwise describing that person.

(5) The record of a search of a vehicle shall include a note describing the vehicle.

(6) The record of a search of a person or a vehicle—   **1–18**

(a) shall state—

(i)   the object of the search;

(ii) the grounds for making it;

(iii) the date and time when it was made;

(iv) the place where it was made;

(v)   whether anything, and if so what, was found;

(vi) whether any, and if so what, injury to a person or damage to property appears to the constable to have resulted from the search; and

(b) shall identify the constable making it.

(7) If a constable who conducted a search of a person made a record of it, the person who was searched shall be entitled to a copy of the record if he asks for one before the end of the period specified in subsection (9) below.

(8) If—

    (a) the owner of a vehicle which has been searched or the person who was in charge of the vehicle at the time when it was searched asks for a copy of the record of the search before the end of the period specified in subsection (9) below; and

    (b) the constable who conducted the search made a record of it,

the person who made the request shall be entitled to a copy.

(9) The period mentioned in subsections (7) and (8) above is the period of 12 months beginning with the date on which the search was made.

(10) The requirements imposed by this section with regard to records of searches of vehicles shall apply also to records of searches of vessels, aircraft and hovercraft.

1–19   This section does not cover searches carried out by constables on the premises of statutory undertakings or at airports, above.

The written record should be made contemporaneously or as soon as possible after the event. The searched persons name or description, including ethnicity will be included as will details of any searched vehicle. The police have no power to require the name or to detain a person in order to ascertain his or her name so a visual description is the alternative.

The record of a search of a person or of a vehicle must include the object of the search; the grounds for making it; the date and time when it was made; the place where it was made; whether anything, and if so what, was found; whether any, and if so what, injury to a person or damage to property appears to the constable to have resulted from the search.

(6) Road checks

Police and Criminal Evidence Act 1984, s.4

Road checks

1–20   **4.**—(1) This section shall have effect in relation to the conduct of road checks by police officers for the purpose of ascertaining whether a vehicle is carrying—

    (a) a person who has committed an offence other than a road traffic offence or a [vehicle] excise offence;

    (b) a person who is a witness to such an offence;

    (c) a person intending to commit such an offence; or

    (d) a person who is unlawfully at large.

(2) For the purposes of this section a road check consists of the exercise in a locality of the power conferred by section 163 of the *Road Traffic Act* 1988 in such a way as to stop during the period for which its exercise in that way in that locality continues all vehicles or vehicles selected by any criterion.

(3) Subject to subsection (5) below, there may only be such a road check if a police officer of the rank of superintendent or above authorises it in writing.

(4) An officer may only authorise a road check under subsection (3) above—

    (a) for the purpose specified in subsection (1)(a) above, if he has reasonable grounds—

        (i) for believing that the offence is a serious arrestable offence; and

        (ii) for suspecting that the person is, or is about to be, in the locality in which vehicles would be stopped if the road check were authorised;

    (b) for the purpose specified in subsection (1)(b) above, if he has reasonable grounds for believing that the offence is a serious arrestable offence;

    (c) for the purpose specified in subsection (1)(c) above, if he has reasonable grounds—

        (i) for believing that the offence would be a serious arrestable offence; and

        (ii) for suspecting that the person is, or is about to be, in the locality in which vehicles would be stopped if the road check were authorised;

    (d) for the purpose specified in subsection (1)(d) above, if he has reasonable grounds for suspecting that the person is, or is about to be, in that locality.

1–21   (5) An officer below the rank of superintendent may authorise such a road check if it appears to him that it is required as a matter of urgency for one of the purposes specified in subsection (1) above.

(6) If an authorisation is given under subsection (5) above, it shall be the duty of the officer who gives it—

(a) to make a written record of the time at which he gives it; and

(b) to cause an officer of the rank of superintendent or above to be informed that it has been given.

(7) The duties imposed by subsection (6) above shall be performed as soon as it is practicable to do so.

(8) An officer to whom a report is made under subsection (6) above may, in writing, authorise the road check to continue.

(9) If such an officer considers that the road check should not continue, he shall record in writing—

(a) the fact that it took place; and

(b) the purpose for which it took place.

(10) An officer giving an authorisation under this section shall specify the locality in which vehicles are to be stopped.

(11) An officer giving an authorisation under this section, other than an authorisation under subsection (5) above—

(a) shall specify a period, not exceeding seven days, during which the road check may continue; and

(b) may direct that the road check—

(i) shall be continuous; or

(ii) shall be conducted at specified times,

during that period.

(12) If it appears to an officer of the rank of superintendent or above that a road check **1–22** ought to continue beyond the period for which it has been authorised he may, from time to time, in writing specify a further period, not exceeding seven days, during which it may continue.

(13) Every written authorisation shall specify—

(a) the name of the officer giving it;

(b) the purpose of the road check; and

(c) the locality in which vehicles are to be stopped.

(14) The duties to specify the purposes of a road check imposed by subss.(9) and (13) above include duties to specify any relevant serious arrestable offence.

(15) Where a vehicle is stopped in a road check, the person in charge of the vehicle at the time when it is stopped shall be entitled to obtain a written statement of the purpose of the road check if he applies for such a statement not later than the end of the period of twelve months from the day on which the vehicle was stopped.

(16) Nothing in this section affects the exercise by police officers of any power to stop vehicles for purposes other than those specified in subsection (1) above.

[This section is printed as amended by the *Road Traffic (Consequential Provisions) Act* 1988, Sch.3 and the *Vehicle Excise and Registration Act* 1994, Sch.3.]

Road Traffic Act 1988, s.163

Power of police to stop vehicles

163.—(1) A person driving a mechanically propelled vehicle on a road must stop the vehicle **1–23** on being required to do so by a constable in uniform.

(2) A person riding a cycle on a road must stop the cycle on being required to do so by a constable in uniform.

(3) If a person fails to comply with this section he is guilty of an offence.

(4) A constable in uniform may arrest a person without warrant if he has reasonable cause to suspect that the person has committed an offence under this section.

[This section is printed as amended by the *Road Traffic Act* 1991, Sch.4 and the *Police Reform Act* 2002, s.49(1).]

Section 4 extends the power to stop vehicles on the road to enable searches to be made. A Constable in uniform has power under the *Road Traffic Act* 1988, s.163 to stop vehicles. Section 4 allows for the power under s.163 to be used for a specified time, not exceeding seven days, in a specified locality for the purposes of carrying out searches of vehicles under s.1. There is no requirement for a reasonable suspicion to attach to the individual vehicles that are stopped but *PACE* 1984, ss.1 and 2 must still be complied with as any search is carried out. The checks must be authorised by a senior officer unless it is a matter of urgency. The authorisation may only be given if the authorising officer has reasonable grounds for believing the matters listed in s.4(4).

Serious arrestable offences are defined in *PACE* 1984, s.116.

The reasons for the search and the results of it must be documented.

(7) Power to stop and search in anticipation of violence

Criminal Justice and Public Order Act 1994, s.60

Powers to stop and search in anticipation of violence

1–24   **60.**—(1) If a police officer of or above the rank of inspector reasonably believes—

     (a) that incidents involving serious violence may take place in any locality in his police area, and that it is expedient to give an authorisation under this section to prevent their occurrence, or

     (b) that persons are carrying dangerous instruments or offensive weapons in any locality in his police area without good reason,

he may give an authorisation that the powers conferred by this section are to be exercisable at any place within that locality for a specified period not exceeding 24 hours.

(3) If it appears to an officer of or above the rank of superintendent that it is expedient to do so, having regard to offences which have, or are reasonably suspected to have, been committed in connection with any activity falling within the authorisation, he may direct that the authorisation shall continue in being for a further 24 hours.

(3A) If an inspector gives an authorisation under subsection (1) he must, as soon as it is practicable to do so, cause an officer of or above the rank of superintendent to be informed.

(4) This section confers on any constable in uniform power—

     (a) to stop any pedestrian and search him or anything carried by him for offensive weapons or dangerous instruments;

     (b) to stop any vehicle and search the vehicle, its driver and any passenger for offensive weapons or dangerous instruments.

(5) A constable may, in the exercise of the powers conferred by subsection (4) above, stop any person or vehicle and make any search he thinks fit whether or not he has any grounds for suspecting that the person or vehicle is carrying weapons or articles of that kind.

(6) If in the course of a search under this section a constable discovers a dangerous instrument or an article which he has reasonable grounds for suspecting to be an offensive weapon, he may seize it.

(7) This section applies (with the necessary modifications) to ships, aircraft and hovercraft as it applies to vehicles.

(8) A person who fails

     (a) to stop, or to stop a vehicle,

when required to do so by a constable in the exercise of his powers under this section shall be liable on summary conviction to imprisonment for a term not exceeding one month or to a fine not exceeding level 3 on the standard scale or both.

(9) Any authorisation under this section shall be in writing signed by the officer giving it and shall specify the grounds on which it is given and the locality in which and the period during which the powers conferred by this section are exercisable and a direction under subsection (3) above shall also be given in writing or, where that is not practicable, recorded in writing as soon as it is practicable to do so.

1–25   (9A) The preceding provisions of this section, so far as they relate to an authorisation by a member of the British Transport Police Force (including one who for the time being has the same powers and privileges as a member of a police force for a police area), shall have effect as if the references to a locality in his police area were references to any locality in or in the vicinity of any policed premises, or to the whole or any part of any such premises.

(10) Where a vehicle is stopped by a constable under this section, the driver shall be entitled to obtain a written statement that the vehicle was stopped under the powers

conferred by this section if he applies for such a statement not later than the end of the period of twelve months from the day on which the vehicle was stopped as respects a pedestrian who is stopped and searched under this section.

(10A) A person who is searched by a constable under this section shall be entitled to obtain a written statement that he was searched under the powers conferred by this section if he applies for such a statement not later than the end of the period of twelve months from the day on which he was searched.

(11) In this section—

"British Transport Police Force" means the constables appointed under section 53 of the *British Transport Commission Act* 1949;

"dangerous instruments" means instruments which have a blade or are sharply pointed;

"offensive weapon" has the meaning given by section 1(9) of the *Police and Criminal Evidence Act* 1984 or, in relation to Scotland, section 47(4) of the *Criminal Law (Consolidation) (Scotland) Act* 1995; and

"policed premises", in relation to England and Wales, has the meaning given by section 53(3) of the *British Transport Commission Act* 1949 and, in relation to Scotland, means those places where members of the British Transport Police Force have the powers, protection and privileges of a constable under section 53(4)(a) of that Act (as it relates to Scotland);

"vehicle" includes a caravan as defined in section 29(1) of the *Caravan Sites and Control of Development Act* 1960.

(11A) For the purposes of this section, a person carries a dangerous instrument or an offensive weapon if he has it in his possession.

(12) The powers conferred by this section are in addition to and not in derogation of, any power otherwise conferred.

[This section is printed as amended by the *Knives Act* 1997, s.8, the *Crime and Disorder Act* 1998, s.25 and the *Anti-Terrorism, Crime and Security Act* 2001, Sch. 7.]

1–26 This section allows for random stop and search powers to be exercised by any police constable in uniform in any locality where an authorisation has been given. This is a temporary extension of police powers available in the specific situations outlined. The Notes for Guidance state that the authorisation given under the section must have an objective basis such as intelligence or information about a history of violence at a particular location or an increase in crime involving weapons in the area. The authorising officer must determine the geographical area that constitutes a "locality". The power can be authorised for 24 hours and extended for a further 24 hours if the conditions of the section. are met.

The power of search is limited to offensive weapons or dangerous instruments that have a blade or are sharply pointed. Unlike the power to stop and search in s.1 of the *Police and Criminal Evidence Act* 1984 a constable in uniform may exercise the powers conferred under s.60(4) if he or she thinks fit, regardless of whether there are any grounds for suspecting that the person or vehicle is carrying offensive weapons or dangerous articles. If during the course of a search under this section a constable discovers a dangerous instrument or an article which he or she has reasonable grounds for suspecting to be an offensive weapon, it may be seized. Items seized may be retained in accordance with s.60A of *PACE* 1984 and regulations made by the Secretary of State. Section 2 of *PACE* 1984 applies with the requirements to explain and record the searches.

(8) Power to require removal of disguises

Criminal Justice and Public Order Act 1994, s.60AA

Powers to require removal of disguises

1–27 **60AA.**—(1) Where—

(a) an authorisation under section 60 is for the time being in force in relation to any locality for any period, or

(b) an authorisation under subsection (3) that the powers conferred by subsection (2) shall be exercisable at any place in a locality is in force for any period, those powers shall be exercisable at any place in that locality at any time in that period.

(2) This subsection confers power on any constable in uniform—

(a) to require any person to remove any item which the constable reasonably believes that person is wearing wholly or mainly for the purpose of concealing his identity;

(b) to seize any item which the constable reasonably believes any person intends to wear wholly or mainly for that purpose.

(3) If a police officer of or above the rank of inspector reasonably believes—

(a) that activities may take place in any locality in his police area that are likely (if they take place) to involve the commission of offences, and

(b) that it is expedient, in order to prevent or control the activities, to give an authorisation under this subsection,

he may give an authorisation that the powers conferred by this section shall be exercisable at any place within that locality for a specified period not exceeding twenty-four hours.

(4) If it appears to an officer of or above the rank of superintendent that it is expedient to do so, having regard to offences which—

(a) have been committed in connection with the activities in respect of which the authorisation was given, or

(b) are reasonably suspected to have been so committed,

he may direct that the authorisation shall continue in force for a further twenty-four hours.

(5) If an inspector gives an authorisation under subsection (3), he must, as soon as it is practicable to do so, cause an officer of or above the rank of superintendent to be informed.

(6) Any authorisation under this section—

(a) shall be in writing and signed by the officer giving it; and

(b) shall specify—

(i) the grounds on which it is given;

(ii) the locality in which the powers conferred by this section are exercisable;

(iii) the period during which those powers are exercisable;

and a direction under subsection (4) shall also be given in writing or, where that is not practicable, recorded in writing as soon as it is practicable to do so.

1–28　　(7) A person who fails to remove an item worn by him when required to do so by a constable in the exercise of his power under this section shall be liable, on summary conviction, to imprisonment for a term not exceeding one month or to a fine not exceeding level 3 on the standard scale or both.

(8) The preceding provisions of this section, so far as they relate to an authorisation by a member of the British Transport Police Force (including one who for the time being has the same powers and privileges as a member of a police force for a police area), shall have effect as if references to a locality or to a locality in his police area were references to any locality in or in the vicinity of any policed premises, or to the whole or any part of any such premises.

(9) In this section "British Transport Police Force" and "policed premises" each has the same meaning as in section 60.

(10) The powers conferred by this section are in addition to, and not in derogation of, any power otherwise conferred.

(11) This section does not extend to Scotland.

[This section is printed as amended by the *Anti-terrorism, Crime and Security Act* 2001, s.94(1).]

1–29　　At any time that an authorisation or extended authorisation is in force under s.60 of *PACE* 1984, a constable in uniform may require disguises or masks to be removed or seized. This power is designed to prevent offenders from avoiding prosecution by concealing their identity. An authorisation for the use of these powers on a free-standing basis can also be made if a senior officer reasonably believes that activities may take place that would involve the commission of offences and that it is expedient in order to prevent or control such activities that the powers should be authorised. The power may last for 24 hours and be extended for a further 24 hours if the specific conditions are met.

A constable in uniform must also have a reasonable belief that the mask, *etc.* is being worn to conceal identity before exercising the power to require removal or to seize the item so there must be an objective basis for use of the power.

The authorisation itself must be properly documented but the exercise of this power has not been held to be a search so the requirements of s.2 of *PACE* 1984 do not apply: *DPP v Amery* [2002] Crim.L.R. 142.

Failure to remove an item on being required to do so is an arrestable offence under sch.1A of *PACE* 1984.

C. ENTRY, SEARCH AND SEIZURE

(1) Introduction

The power of a police officer to enter private property is governed by statute and **1–30** common law. Entry must be gained either with the consent of the occupier or under the authorisation of a warrant or other legal power. Otherwise the entry will be an actionable trespass: *Entick v Carrington* (1765) 19 State Tr. 1029.

The powers of a constable to enter and search premises prior to the arrest of any suspect are codified in the *Police and Criminal Evidence Act* 1984 and the Codes of Practice. The only common law power of entry retained by the Act is under s.17(6) of *PACE* 1984 which allows a constable to enter premises to deal with or prevent a breach of the peace.

Other powers of entry are covered in specific statutes; *e.g. Theft Act* 1968, s.26, *Misuse of Drugs Act* 1971, s.23. Other investigating officers such as Customs and Excise officers and local government officers have powers of entry and search under relevant legislation.

General

Where an officer wishes to gain entry to premises for the purposes of a search and he **1–31** believes consent is either unforthcoming or impracticable, application will be made to a magistrate or district judge for a search warrant. The warrant from the court will authorise the officer to enter and search named premises for specific items. Such applications will be made in writing generally in standard format and will be signed and substantiated on oath or affirmation. The application can be made to the magistrate or district judge in court, in the retiring room or, in urgent situations, out of hours to the magistrate or district judge at home. The requirements of s.8 of *PACE* 1984 must be fully complied with and the principles of the European Convention on Human Rights must be considered, particularly Art.8 which provides the right to respect for privacy and family life. The granting authority must be satisfied that the issue of a warrant is a proportional step and that the infringement of Art.8 rights is in accordance with the law and necessary in a democratic society in the interests of national security, public safety or the economic well-being of the country, for the prevention of disorder or crime, for the protection of health and morals or for the protection of the rights and freedom of others.

A search of premises has been held to be an interference with Art.8 rights (see *Funke v France* (1993)16 E.H.R.R. 297; *Chappell v UK* (1987) 12 E.H.R.R. 1) and justification for the infringement is necessary. The prevention of crime or the protection of others would form the required qualification on the enjoyment of the right to privacy. Questions of proportionality must also be considered not only in the issue of the warrant but also the way in which it is to be executed. Magistrates may inquire into the nature of the premises and whether families and neighbours will be treated with respect and sensitivity within the remit of the warrant.

The power under s.8 was described by a Court as "draconian", consequently requiring the magistrate or district judge to satisfy themselves that there are reasonable grounds for believing the various matters set out in the information which justify the issue of a warrant. The fact that the applicant officer believes it is not enough: *R. v*

Guildhall Magistrates Ex p. Primlaks Holdings Co (1989) 89 Cr.App.R. 215. It has also been suggested that magistrates should be provided with a checklist to remind them of the contents of s.8 when warrants are being applied for so their minds may be directed to the relevant issues: *R. v The Chesterfield Justices Ex p. Bramley* [2000] 1 Cr.App.R. 486.

(2) Warrant to enter and search premises

Police and Criminal Evidence Act 1984, s.8

Power of justice of the peace to authorise entry and search of premises

1–32   **8.**—(1) If on an application made by a constable a justice of the peace is satisfied that there are reasonable grounds for believing—

    (a) that a serious arrestable offence has been committed; and

    (b) that there is material on premises specified in the application which is likely to be of substantial value (whether by itself or together with other material) to the investigation of the offence; and

    (c) that the material is likely to be relevant evidence; and

    (d) that it does not consist of or include items subject to legal privilege, excluded material or special procedure material; and

    (e) that any of the conditions specified in subsection (3) below applies,

he may issue a warrant authorising a constable to enter and search the premises.

(2) A constable may seize and retain anything for which a search has been authorised under subsection (1) above.

(3) The conditions mentioned in subsection (1)(e) above are—

    (a) that it is not practicable to communicate with any person entitled to grant entry to the premises;

    (b) that it is practicable to communicate with a person entitled to grant entry to the premises but it is not practicable to communicate with any person entitled to grant access to the evidence;

    (c) that entry to the premises will not be granted unless a warrant is produced;

    (d) that the purpose of a search may be frustrated or seriously prejudiced unless a constable arriving at the premises can secure immediate entry to them.

(4) In this Act "relevant evidence", in relation to an offence, means anything that would be admissible in evidence at a trial for the offence.

(5) The power to issue a warrant conferred by this section is in addition to any such power otherwise conferred.

(6) This sections applies in relation to a relevant offence (as defined in section 28D(4) of the *Immigration Act* 1971) as it applies in relation to a serious arrestable offence.

[This section is printed as amended by the *Immigration and Asylum Act* 1999, Sch.14.]

1–33   This section confers on district judges and magistrates the power to authorise constables to enter and search premises

Before a warrant to enter and search premises may be issued the district judge or magistrate before whom the information is laid must satisfy themselves that there are reasonable grounds for believing that the conditions set out in the section exist. This means they must;

    a. Identify the serious arrestable offence—see s.116 of *PACE* 1984.

    b. Check details of the address or location to be searched, which can include premises and vehicles. In the case of multi-occupancy premises such as hostels or offices care must to be taken to clarify the parameter of the search.

    c. Check the list and specification of the items being sought and confirm that they are likely to be of substantial value to the investigation.

    d. Check why these items would be relevant evidence and admissible in evidence at the trial and confirm that the items being sought are not subject to legal privilege or in any other way confidential. (A search of business or office premises—

especially a lawyers office may give rise to immediate concerns under this provision).

The officer may be questioned to ascertain this information and a record of any **1–34** answers should be appended to the information. It may be difficult for a magistrate or district judge to ascertain whether materials sought are subject to legal privilege, excluded materials or special procedure material although definitions of these items are included in the Act. If there is any doubt the application should be refused because the proper procedure would be for the application to be made to a circuit judge under s.9 and Sch.1, *PACE* 1984. The safeguards at the Crown Court are much greater than under s.8 as the judge may hold an inter partes hearing relating to the material and can make orders to produce such items.

A warrant issued in Scotland for a search for protected material can still be endorsed under s.4 of the *Summary Jurisdiction (Process) Act* 1881 as the provisions of *PACE* 1984 cover only the issue of a warrant and not its endorsement which is a separate act; *R. Manchester Stipendiary Magistrate and the Lord Advocate Ex p. Granada Television Ltd* (2001) 1 A.C. 300.

The information should also disclose the condition met that justifies the issue of a warrant usually that the purpose of a search will be frustrated if consent to enter were requested. A constable is not obliged to try all other methods of entry in order to prove that consent is not practicable: *R. v Billericay Justices Ex p. Dobbyn* [1991] Crim.L.R. 472.

A warrant may not be required if consent is given to enter and search but such **1–35** consent should be recorded in writing and the terms of the Code still apply.

An officer conducting a search under the warrant is limited to seizing only the items covered by s.8: *R. v Chief Constable of Warwickshire Constabulary Ex p. Fitzpatrick* [1998] 1 All E.R. 65. All documents or items found can be scrutinised to determine whether they are subject to legal privilege or otherwise excluded or special procedure material but such sifting must take place on the premises, unless s.50 of the Criminal Justice and Police Act 2001 applies, see below. The officer is not entitled to bag items up and take them away to be looked through but at the same time the claim that items are privileged does not have to be taken at face value: *R. v Chesterfield Justices Ex p. Bramley* (above).

Serious arrestable offence

Police and Criminal Evidence Act 1984, s.116

Meaning of "serious arrestable offence"

116.—(1) This section has effect for determining whether an offence is a serious arrestable of- **1–36** fence for the purposes of this Act.

(2) The following arrestable offences are always serious—

    (a) an offence (whether at common law or under any enactment) specified in Part I of Schedule 5 to this Act; and

    (b) an offence under an enactment specified in Part II of that Schedule; and

    (c) any offence which is specified in paragraph 1 of Schedule 2 to the *Proceeds of Crime Act* 2002 (drug trafficking offences),

    (d) any offence under section 327, 328 or 329 of that Act (certain money laundering offences).

(3) Subject to subsection (4) below, any other arrestable offence is serious only if its commission—

    (a) has led to any of the consequences specified in subsection (6) below; or

    (b) is intended or is likely to lead to any of those consequences.

(4) An arrestable offence which consists of making a threat is serious if carrying out the threat would be likely to lead to any of the consequences specified in subsection (6) below.

(6) The consequences mentioned in subsections (3) and (4) above are

    (a) serious harm to the security of the State or to public order;

(b) serious interference with the administration of justice or with the investigation of offences or of a particular offence;

(c) the death of any person;

(d) serious injury to any person;

(e) substantial financial gain to any person; and

(f) serious financial loss to any person.

(7) Loss is serious for the purposes of this section if, having regard to all the circumstances, it is serious for the person who suffers it.

(8) In this section "injury" includes any disease and any impairment of a person's physical or mental condition

[This section is printed with subs.(2) as amended by *Proceeds of Crime Act* 2002, s.458 from July 24, 2002.]

SCHEDULE 5

Serious Arrestable Offences

Part 1

Offences mentioned in s.116(2)(A)

1–37

(a) Treason

(b) Murder

(c) Manslaughter

(d) Rape

(e) Kidnapping

(f) Incest with a girl under the age of 13

(g) Buggery with a person under the age of 16

(h) Indecent assault which constitutes an act of gross indecency

(i) An offence under section 170 of the *Customs and Excise Management Act* 1979 of being knowingly concerned, in relation to any goods, in any fraudulent evasion or attempt at evasion of a prohibition in force with respect to the goods under section 42 of the *Customs Consolidation Act* 1876 (prohibition on importing indecent or obscene articles).

Part II

Offences mentioned in s.116(2)(B)

1–38

(a) Section 2 of the *Explosive Substances Act* 1883 (causing explosion likely to endanger life or property).

(b) Section 5 of the *Sexual Offences Act* 1956 (intercourse with a girl under the age of 13)

(c) Section 16 of the *Firearms Act* 1968 (possession of firearms with intent to injure)

(d) Section 17(1) of the *Firearms Act* 1968 (use of firearms and imitation firearms to resist arrest)

(e) Section 18 of the *Firearms* 1968 (carrying firearms with criminal intent)

(f) Section 1 of the *Taking of Hostages Act* 1982 (hostage taking)

(g) Section 1 of the *Aviation Security Act* 1982 (hi-jacking)

(h) Section 134 of the *Criminal Justice Act* 1988 (torture)

(i) Section 1 of the *Road Traffic Act* 1988 (causing death by dangerous driving)

(j) Section 3A of the *Road Traffic Act* 1988 (causing death by careless driving when under the influence of drink or drugs)

(k) Section 1 of the *Aviation and Maritime Security Act* 1990 (endangering safety at aerodromes)

(l) Section 9 of the *Aviation and Maritime Security Act* 1990 (hijacking of ships)

(m) Section 10 of the *Aviation and Maritime Security Act* 1990 (seizing or exercising control of fixed platforms)

(n) Section 1 of the *Protection of Children Act* 1978 (indecent photographs and pseudo-photographs of children)

    (o) Article 4 of the *Channel Tunnel (Security) Order* 1994 No.570 (hijacking of channel tunnel trains)

    (p) Article 5 of the *Channel Tunnel (Security) Order* 1994 no.570(seizing or exercising control of the channel tunnel system)

    (q) Section 2 of the *Obscene Publications Act* 1959 (publication of obscene matter)

Section 116 determines whether an arrestable offence is a "serious arrestable offence" for the purposes of the Act. Certain offences are always serious, such as murder; other arrestable offences will be serious if it has led to serious consequences or was intended to lead to serious consequences as defined in subs.(6).

The fact that an offence is a "serious arrestable offence" gives the police extra powers in relation to it under several sections of the Act.

An arrestable offence is one to which the powers of summary arrest conferred by s.24 of the *Police and Criminal Evidence Act* 1984 apply.

(3) Excluded material

Police and Criminal Evidence Act 1984, ss.10–14

Meaning of "items subject to legal privilege"

    10.—(1) Subject to subsection (2) below, in this Act "items subject to legal privilege" means—   **1–39**

        (a) communications between a professional legal adviser and his client or any person representing his client made in connection with the giving of legal advice to the client;

        (b) communications between a professional legal adviser and his client or any person representing his client or between such an adviser or his client or any such representative and any other person made in connection with or in contemplation of legal proceedings and for the purposes of such proceedings; and

        (c) items enclosed with or referred to in such communications and made—

            (i) in connection with the giving of legal advice; or

            (ii) in connection with or in contemplation of legal proceedings and for the purposes of such proceedings, when they are in the possession of a person who is entitled to possession of them.

    (2) Items held with the intention of furthering a criminal purpose are not items subject to legal privilege.

Any item to be protected under this section must consist of a communication or items **1–40** connected with a communication. Records of a conveyancing transaction including details of the financing are not privileged but correspondence between the solicitor and his client about the conveyance could be privileged if the letters contained advice: *R. v Crown Court at Inner London Sessions Ex p. Baines and Baines* (1988) Q.B. 579. Attendance notes of a solicitor on his client were held not to be privileged as they simply provided a record of time and did not amount to the giving of legal advice: *R. v Crown Court at Manchester Ex p. Rogers* (1999) 4 All E.R. 35. A completed application form for legal aid was held to be privileged as being made in contemplation of legal proceedings: *R. v Crown Court at Snaresbrook Ex p. DPP* (1988) Q.B. 532.

Where a scientist carried out tests on a blood sample provided by the defence it was held that the sample was an item made for the purposes of legal proceedings and so was covered by s.10: *R. v R* (1994) 4 All E.R. 260.

In *R. v Central Criminal Court Ex p. Francis and Francis* (1989) A.C. 346, it was held that communications made between a lawyer and his client in the furtherance of a criminal purpose could not be protected by legal privilege (following the leading case in common law, *R. v Cox and Railton* (1884) 14 Q.B.D. 153). Legal privilege could not extend to cover such advice irrespective of the innocence of the lawyer and s.10 was interpreted widely to remove that privilege no matter which party had the intention of furthering a criminal purpose. In Francis the documents in dispute were to be used in the furtherance of money laundering by drug traffickers.

Although legal privilege does not attach to such documents they could still be special **1–41** procedure material if there exists an express or implied undertaking to hold them in confidence: See s.14 and *R. v Guildhall Magistrates Court Ex p. Primlak Holdings* (1989) 89 Cr.App.R. 215.

Meaning of "excluded material"

1–42   **11.**—(1) Subject to the following provisions of this section, in this Act "excluded material" means—

       (a) personal records which a person has acquired or created in the course of any trade, business, profession or other occupation or for the purposes of any paid or unpaid office and which he holds in confidence;

       (b) human tissue or tissue fluid which has been taken for the purposes of diagnosis or medical treatment and which a person holds in confidence;

       (c) journalistic material which a person holds in confidence and which consists—

          (i) of documents; or

          (ii) of records other than documents.

(2) A person holds material other than journalistic material in confidence for the purposes of this section if he holds it subject—

       (a) to an express or implied undertaking to hold it in confidence; or

       (b) to a restriction on disclosure or an obligation of secrecy contained in any enactment, including an enactment contained in an Act passed after this Act.

(3) A person holds journalistic material in confidence for the purposes of this section if—

       (a) he holds it subject to such an undertaking, restriction or obligation; and

       (b) it has been continuously held (by one or more persons) subject to such an undertaking, restriction or obligation since it was first acquired or created for the purposes of journalism.

Meaning of "personal records"

1–43   **12.** In this Part of this Act "personal records" means documentary and other records concerning an individual (whether living or dead) who can be identified from them and relating—

       (a) to his physical or mental health;

       (b) to spiritual counselling or assistance given or to be given to him; or

       (c) to counselling or assistance given or to be given to him, for the purposes of his personal welfare, by any voluntary organisation or by any individual who—

          (i) by reason of his office or occupation has responsibilities for his personal welfare; or

          (ii) by reason of an order of a court has responsibilities for his supervision.

Hospital records of admission to or discharge from hospital can fall under the definition of 'personal records' because they relate to a person's physical or mental health. *R. v Cardiff Crown Court Ex p. Kellam, The Times*, May 3, 1993, DC.

Meaning of "journalistic material"

1–44   **13.**—(1) Subject to subsection (2) below, in this Act "journalistic material" means material acquired or created for the purposes of journalism.

(2) Material is only journalistic material for the purposes of this Act if it is in the possession of a person who acquired or created it for the purposes of journalism.

(3) A person who receives material from someone who intends that the recipient shall use it for the purposes of journalism is to be taken to have acquired it for those purposes.

Meaning of "special procedure material"

1–45   **14.**—(1) In this Act "special procedure material" means—

       (a) material to which subsection (2) below applies; and

       (b) journalistic material, other than excluded material.

(2) Subject to the following provisions of this section, this subsection applies to material, other than items subject to legal privilege and excluded material, in the possession of a person who—

       (a) acquired or created it in the course of any trade, business, profession or other occupation or for the purpose of any paid or unpaid office; and

(b) holds it subject—
    (i) to an express or implied undertaking to hold it in confidence; or
    (ii) to a restriction or obligation such as is mentioned in section 11(2)(b) above.
  (3) Where material is acquired—
    (a) by an employee from his employer and in the course of his employment; or
    (b) by a company from an associated company,
it is only special procedure material if it was special procedure material immediately before the acquisition.
  (4) Where material is created by an employee in the course of his employment, it is only special procedure material if it would have been special procedure material had his employer created it.
  (5) Where material is created by a company on behalf of an associated company, it is only special procedure material if it would have been special procedure material had the associated company created it.
  (6) A company is to be treated as another's associated company for the purposes of this section if it would be so treated under section 302 of the *Income and Corporation Taxes Act* 1970.

1–46 Frequent applications are made to search for and seize "special procedure material". This includes records held by solicitors and accountants or banks and building societies and also films or photographs held by the media.

In *R. v Leeds Magistrates Court Ex p. Dumbleton* [1993] Crim.L.R. 866 it was held that the protection of special procedure material could not attach to forged documents as they could not have been acquired or created in the course of the profession of a solicitor. The Court also said that there could be no confidence in iniquity so the documents could not fall under the protection of s.12.

(4) Safeguards

Police and Criminal Evidence Act 1984, s.15

Search warrants—safeguards

1–47 **15.**—(1) This section and section 16 below have effect in relation to the issue to constables under any enactment, including an enactment contained in an Act passed after this Act, of warrants to enter and search premises; and an entry on or search of premises under a warrant is unlawful unless it complies with this section and section 16 below.
  (2) Where a constable applies for any such warrant, it shall be his duty—
    (a) to state—
      (i) the ground on which he makes the application; and
      (ii) the enactment under which the warrant would be issued;
    (b) to specify the premises which it is desired to enter and search; and
    (c) to identify, so far as is practicable, the articles or persons to be sought.
  (3) An application for such a warrant shall be made *ex parte* and supported by an information in writing.
  (4) The constable shall answer on oath any question that the justice of the peace or judge hearing the application asks him.
  (5) A warrant shall authorise an entry on one occasion only.
  (6) A warrant—
    (a) shall specify—
      (i) the name of the person who applies for it;
      (ii) the date on which it is issued;
      (iii) the enactment under which it is issued; and
      (iv) the premises to be searched; and
    (b) shall identify, so far as is practicable, the articles or persons to be sought.
  (7) Two copies shall be made of a warrant.
  (8) The copies shall be clearly certified as copies.

1–48 Both the information and the warrants must be signed and dated by the person granting the application. The time of the application will also be noted on the documents so that time limits can be observed. The information is lodged with the Court and the original warrant and copies are taken by the officer.

Sometimes requests are made for copies of informations as well as warrants. Such copies can be provided to other Courts or to legal representatives if the Court is satisfied of the reason why the information is required. There are issues about the protection of informants so disclosure of the information may not be automatic to the individual whose premises were searched.

(5) Execution of the warrant

Police and Criminal Evidence Act 1984, s.16

Execution of warrants.

1–49
16.—(1) A warrant to enter and search premises may be executed by any constable.

(2) Such a warrant may authorise persons to accompany any constable who is executing it.

[(2A) A person so authorised has the same powers as the constable whom he accompanies in respect of

    (a) the execution of the warrant, and

    (b) the seizure of anything to which the warrant relates.

(2B) But he may exercise those powers only in the company, and under the supervision of the constable.]

(3) Entry and search under a warrant must be within one month from the date of its issue.

(4) Entry and search under a warrant must be at a reasonable hour unless it appears to the constable executing it that the purpose of a search may be frustrated on an entry at a reasonable hour.

(5) Where the occupier of premises which are to be entered and searched is present at the time when a constable seeks to execute a warrant to enter and search them, the constable—

    (a) shall identify himself to the occupier and, if not in uniform, shall produce to him documentary evidence that he is a constable;

    (b) shall produce the warrant to him; and

    (c) shall supply him with a copy of it.

(6) Where—

    (a) the occupier of such premises is not present at the time when a constable seeks to execute such a warrant; but

    (b) some other person who appears to the constable to be in charge of the premises is present,

subsection (5) above shall have effect as if any reference to the occupier were a reference to that other person.

(7) If there is no person present who appears to the constable to be in charge of the premises, he shall leave a copy of the warrant in a prominent place on the premises.

1–50
(8) A search under a warrant may only be a search to the extent required for the purpose for which the warrant was issued.

(9) A constable executing a warrant shall make an endorsement on it stating—

    (a) whether the articles or persons sought were found; and

    (b) whether any articles were seized, other than articles which were sought.

(10) A warrant which—

    (a) has been executed; or

    (b) has not been executed within the time authorised for its execution,

shall be returned—

        (i) if it was issued by a justice of the peace, to the chief executive to the justices for the petty sessions area for which he acts; and

        (ii) if it was issued by a judge, to the appropriate officer of the court from which he issued it.

(11) A warrant which is returned under subsection (10) above shall be retained for 12 months from its return—

(a) by the chief executive to the justices, if it was returned under paragraph (i) of that subsection; and

(b) by the appropriate officer, if it was returned under paragraph (ii).

(12) If during the period for which a warrant is to be retained the occupier of the premises to which it relates asks to inspect it, he shall be allowed to do so.

[This section is printed with the amendments inserted by s.2 of the *Criminal Justice Act* 2003.]

The police may execute the warrant and there is power (inserted by the *Criminal*   **1–51**
Justice Act 2003) for members of other agencies involved in the investigations leading to the issue of the warrant to execute it and seize items. Such authorised persons must observe the Codes of Practice. Officers of other agencies may be authorised to accompany the police but the number should be restricted and those persons must not exceed their authority: *R. v Reading Justices, Chief Constable of Avon and Somerset and Intervention Board for Agricultural Produce Ex p. South West Meat Ltd* [1992] Crim.L.R. 672.

It was held not to be in the public interest for members of the media to accompany officers when executing search warrants. Only in exceptional circumstances could such attendance be justified for the purposes of immediate publicity of the search: *R. v Marylebone Magistrates Court Ex p. Amdrell Ltd* (1998) 162 J.P. 719, DC.

As soon as possible after entry and before search the officer should identify himself   **1–52**
and if not in uniform a warrant card should be produced for inspection. The original search warrant itself should also be produced and be made available for inspection. The procedure relating to the warrant must comply with both ss.15 and 16 or the entry and search will be unlawful: *R. v Longman* [1988] 1 W.L.R. 619, CA.

The endorsed warrant will be returned to the Court and kept with the information for at least 12 months.

(6) Entry to arrest

Police and Criminal Evidence Act 1984, s.17

Entry for purpose of arrest etc.

17.—(1) Subject to the following provisions of this section, and without, prejudice to any   **1–53**
other enactment, a constable may enter and search any premises for the purpose—

(a) of executing—

(i) a warrant of arrest issued in connection with or arising out of criminal proceedings; or

(ii) a warrant of commitment issued under section 76 of the *Magistrates' Courts Act* 1980;

(b) of arresting a person for an arrestable offence;

(c) of arresting a person for an offence under—

(i) section 1 (prohibition of uniforms in connection with political objects) of the *Public Order Act* 1936;

(ii) any enactment contained in section 6 to 8 or 10 of the *Criminal Law Act* 1977 (offences relating to entering and remaining on property);

(iii) section 4 of the *Public Order Act* 1986 (fear or provocation of violence);

[(iiia) section 163 of the *Road Traffic Act* 1988 (failure to stop when required to do so by a constable in uniform);]

(iv) section 76 of the *Criminal Justice and Public Order Act* 1994 (failure to comply with interim possession order);

(ca) of arresting, in pursuance of section 32(1A) of the *Children and Young Persons Act* 1969, any child or young person who has been remanded or committed to local authority accommodation under section 23(1) of that Act;

(cb) of recapturing any person who is, or is deemed for any purpose to be, unlawfully at large while liable to be detained—

(i) in a prison, remand centre, young offender institution or secure training centre, or

> (ii) in pursuance of section 92 of the *Powers of Criminal Courts (Sentencing) Act* 2000 (dealing with children and young persons guilty of grave crimes), in any other place;
>
> (d) of recapturing any person whatever who is unlawfully at large and whom he is pursuing; or
>
> (e) of saving life or limb or preventing serious damage to property.

1–54   (2) Except for the purpose specified in paragraph (e) of subsection (1) above, the powers of entry and search conferred by this section—

> (a) are only exercisable if the constable has reasonable grounds for believing that the person whom he is seeking is on the premises; and
>
> (b) are limited, in relation to premises consisting of two or more separate dwellings, to powers to enter and search—
>
> > (i) any parts of the premises which the occupiers of any dwelling comprised in the premises use in common with the occupiers of any other such dwelling; and
> >
> > (ii) any such dwelling in which the constable has reasonable grounds for believing that the person whom he is seeking may be.

(3) The powers of entry and search conferred by this section are only exercisable for the purposes specified in subsection (1)(c)(ii) or (iv) above by a constable in uniform.

(4) The power of search conferred by this section is only a power to search to the extent that is reasonably required for the purpose for which the power of entry is exercised.

(5) Subject to subsection (6) below, all the rules of common law under which a constable has power to enter premises without a warrant are hereby abolished.

(6) Nothing in subsection (5) above affects any power of entry to deal with or prevent a breach of the peace.

[This section is printed as amended by the *Public Order Act* 1986, Schs 2 and 3, the *Criminal Justice and Public Order Act* 1994, Sch.10, the *Prisoners (Return to Custody) Act* 1995, s.2, the *Powers of Criminal Courts (Sentencing) Act* 2000, Sch.9 and the *Police Reform Act* 2002, s.49.]

1–55   This section empowers a constable to enter and search premises in the absence of the consent of the occupier and without a warrant but the terms of the section must be complied with. The right of entry is to enable warrants of arrest or warrants of commitment for non-payment of fines to be executed or for suspects to be arrested for the listed offences. An officer can only use these powers of entry and search if he has reasonable grounds for believing that the person he is seeking is on the premises. In order to be satisfied that an officer is acting in the execution of his duty the officer should give his reason for entry to the occupier even where consent to the original entry may have been given: *Riley v DPP* (1990) 91 Cr.App.R. 14. If no reasons are given the officer must show that it was impossible, impracticable or undesirable to do so: *O'Loughlin v Chief Constable of Essex* [1998] 1 W.L.R. 374. It matters not that no eventual charge was preferred against the person sought, but the officer must have reasonable grounds for the belief that a suspect for an arrestable offence is on the premises: *Kynaston v DPP* (1988) 87 Cr.App.R. 200.

Entry to recapture a person who is unlawfully at large is provided for but there is the added condition that the officer must be in pursuit of the suspect at the time. A patient who absconded from a psychiatric hospital was held to be unlawfully at large but officers were not entitled to use the power under this subsection because they simply went to her home address suspecting she would be there and did not actually engage in a pursuit. The Court held that a chase of some description, even if short and of small distance was envisaged by the term "pursuit": *D'Souza v DPP* (1993) 96 Cr.App.R. 278.

The officer does not need to be in uniform unless the offence for which arrest is sought relates to unlawfully entering and remaining on property or failing to comply with an interim possession order.

The common law power of entry to deal with a breach of the peace is preserved.

Under s.117 of the *Police and Criminal Evidence Act* 1984 reasonable force may be used in effecting the entry.

Police and Criminal Evidence Act 1984, s.18

Entry and search after arrest

18.—(1) Subject to the following provisions of this section, a constable may enter and search **1–56** any premises occupied or controlled by a person who is under arrest for an arrestable offence, if he has reasonable grounds for suspecting that there is on the premises evidence, other than items subject to legal privilege, that relates—

    (a) to that offence; or

    (b) to some other arrestable offence which is connected with or similar to that offence.

(2) A constable may seize and retain anything for which he may search under subsection (1) above.

(3) The power to search conferred by subsection (1) above is only a power to search to the extent that is reasonably required for the purpose of discovering such evidence.

(4) Subject to subsection (5) below, the powers conferred by this section may not be exercised unless an officer of the rank of inspector or above has authorised them in writing.

(5) A constable may conduct a search under subsection (1) above—

    (a) before the person is taken to a police station [or released on bail under section 30A]; and

    (b) without obtaining an authorisation under subsection (4) above.

if the condition in subsection (5A) is satisfied

[(5A) The condition is that the presence of the person at a place (other than a police station) is necessary for the effective investigation of the offence.]

(6) If a constable conducts a search by virtue of subsection (5) above, he shall inform an officer of the rank of inspector or above that he has made the search as soon as practicable after he has made it.

(7) An officer who—

    (a) authorises a search; or

    (b) is informed of a search under subsection (6) above, shall make a record in writing—

        (i) of the grounds for the search; and

        (ii) of the nature of the evidence that was sought.

(8) If the person who was in occupation or control of the premises at the time of the search is in police detention at the time the record is top be made, the officer shall make the record as part of his custody record.

[This section is printed as amended by the *Police Reform Act* 2002, Sch.7 and the *Criminal Justice Act* 2003, Sch.1, printed in square brackets.]

When a constable has authorisation under this section and proposes to enter premises by force he still has a duty to inform the occupier, as far as it is practicable to do so, of the reasons why he is doing so: *Linehan v DPP* [2000] Crim.L.R. 861.

(7) General power of seizure

Police and Criminal Evidence Act 1984, s.19

General power of seizure etc.

19.—(1) The powers conferred by subsections (2), (3) and (4) below are exercisable by a con- **1–57** stable who is lawfully on any premises.

(2) The constable may seize anything which is on the premises if he has reasonable grounds for believing—

    (a) that it has been obtained in consequence of the commission of an offence; and

    (b) that it is necessary to seize it in order to prevent it being concealed, lost, damaged, altered or destroyed.

(3) The constable may seize anything which is on the premises if he has reasonable grounds for believing—

    (a) that it is evidence in relation to an offence which he is investigating or any other offence; and

(b) that it is necessary to seize it in order to prevent the evidence being concealed, lost, altered or destroyed.

(4) The constable may require any information which is [stored in any electronic form] and is accessible from the premises to be produced in a form in which it can be taken away and in which it is visible and legible or [from which it can readily be produced in a visible and legible form] if he has reasonable grounds for believing—

    (a) that—

        (i) it is evidence in relation to an offence which he is investigating or any other offence; or

        (ii) it has been obtained in consequence of the commission of an offence; and

    (b) that it is necessary to do so in order to prevent it being concealed, lost, tampered with or destroyed.

(5) The powers conferred by this section are in addition to any power otherwise conferred.

(6) No power of seizure conferred on a constable under any enactment (including an enactment contained in an Act passed after this Act) is to be taken to authorise the seizure of an item which the constable exercising the power has reasonable grounds for believing to be subject to legal privilege.

[This section is printed as amended by the *Criminal Justice and Police Act* 2001, Sch.2, Pt 2, para.13(2)(a).]

1–58   Once an officer has lawfully gained access to premises he then has a power of seizure under this section. Unlike s.17 where common law powers of entry are abolished except for breach of the peace, this section preserves common law powers of seizure under subs.(5). This interpretation was confirmed in *Cowan v Condon* [2000] 1 W.L.R. 254 where the Court held that the common law power of search and seizure in relation to vehicles was not revoked by *PACE* 1984. Vehicles fell within the definition of premises in the Act (see s.23) and the officer had power to seize 'anything' on the premises. This was not restricted to the contents of the premises but could include seizing the 'premises' themselves if they were not immoveable.

Specific powers of seizure under other statutes still apply, *e.g.* s.26(3) of the *Theft Act* 1968.

The powers under ss.18 and 19 are restricted to domestic offences but the preserved common law powers of search and seizure were held to apply to extradition crimes. Article 8 rights to privacy under ECHR were not violated because such search was lawful and proportionate to the legitimate aim of preventing crime: *R. (Rottman) v Commr. Of Police of the Metropolis* [2002] 2 W.L.R. 1315.

(8) Power to seize computerised information

Police and Criminal Evidence Act 1984, s.20

Extension of powers of seizure to computerised information

1–59   **20.**—(1) Every power of seizure which is conferred by an enactment to which this section applies on a constable who has entered premises in the exercise of a power conferred by an enactment shall be construed as including a power to require any information stored in any electronic form and accessible from the premises to be produced in a form in which it can be taken away and in which it is visible and legible or from which it can readily be produced in a visible and legible form.

(2) This section applies—

    (a) to any enactment contained in an Act passed before this Act;

    (b) to sections 8 and 18 above;

    (c) to paragraph 13 of Schedule 1 to this Act; and

    (d) to any enactment contained in an Act passed after this Act.

[This section is printed as amended by the *Criminal Justice and Police Act* 2001, Sch.2.]

(9) Access to and copying of things seized

Police and Criminal Evidence Act 1984, s.21

Access and copying

21.—(1) A constable who seizes anything in the exercise of a power conferred by any enact- **1–60**
ment, including an enactment contained in an Act passed after this Act, shall, if so requested by a
person showing himself—

    (a) to be the occupier of premises on which it was seized; or

    (b) to have had custody or control of it immediately before the seizure,

provide that person with a record of what he seized.

(2) The officer shall provide the record within a reasonable time from the making of the
request for it.

(3) Subject to subsection (8) below, if a request for permission to be granted access to
anything which—

    (a) has been seized by a constable; and

    (b) is retained by the police for the purpose of investigating an offence,

is made to the officer in charge of the investigation by a person who had custody or control of
the thing immediately before it was so seized or by someone acting on behalf of such a person,
the officer shall allow the person who made the request access to it under the supervision of a
constable.

(4) Subject to subsection (8) below, if a request for a photograph or copy of any such
thing is made to the officer in charge of the investigation by a person who had custody or
control of the thing immediately before it was so seized, or by someone acting on behalf of
such a person, the officer shall—

    (a) allow the person who made the request access to it under the supervision of a
        constable for the purpose of photographing or copying it; or

    (b) photograph or copy it, or cause it to be photographed or copied.

(5) A constable may also photograph or copy, or have photographed or copied, anything
which he has power to seize, without a request being made under subsection (4) above.

(6) Where anything is photographed or copied under subsection (4)(b) above, the
photograph or copy shall be supplied to the person who made the request.

(7) The photograph or copy shall be so supplied within a reasonable time from the
making of the request.

(8) There is no duty under this section to grant access to, or to supply a photograph or
copy of, anything if the officer in charge of the investigation for the purposes of which it
was seized has reasonable grounds for believing that to do so would prejudice—

    (a) that investigation;

    (b) the investigation of an offence other than the offence for the purposes of
        investigating which the thing was seized; or

    (c) any criminal proceedings which may be brought as a result of—

        (i) the investigation of which he is in charge; or

        (ii) any such investigation as is mentioned in paragraph (b) above.

(9) The references to a constable in subsections (1), (2), (3)(a) and (5) include a person
authorised under section 16(2) to accompany a constable executing a warrant.

[This section is printed as amended by the *Criminal Justice Act* 2003, Sch.1.]

A refusal to grant access under s.21(8) should be challenged by way of judicial review: **1–61**
Allen v Chief Constable of Cheshire Constabulary, The Times, July 16, 1988.

Where company documents have been seized the person who had control immediately before the seizure has right of access. This right is vested in the company and
not the directors or former directors: *Re DPR Futures Ltd* [1989] 1 W.L.R. 778.

This section applies to proceedings under the *Proceeds of Crime Act* 1995 when
there is an investigation into whether a person has benefited from any criminal conduct
or there is an investigation into the extent or whereabouts of the proceeds of any criminal conduct. Such proceedings are defined in s.15(2) of the *Proceeds of Crime Act* 1995
as being an investigation of, or in connection with an offence.

(10) Retention of seized information

Police and Criminal Evidence Act 1984, s.22

Retention

1–62   **22.**—(1) Subject to subsection (4) below, anything which has been seized by a constable or taken away by a constable following a requirement made by virtue of section 19 or 20 above may be retained so long as is necessary in all the circumstances.

(2) Without prejudice to the generality of subsection (1) above—

    (a) anything seized for the purposes of a criminal investigation may be retained, except as provided by subsection (4) below—

        (i) for use as evidence at a trial for an offence; or

        (ii) for forensic examination or for investigation in connection with an offence; and

    (b) anything may be retained in order to establish its lawful owner, where there are reasonable grounds for believing that it has been obtained in consequence of the commission of an offence.

(3) Nothing seized on the ground that it may be used—

    (a) to cause physical injury to any person;

    (b) to damage property;

    (c) to interfere with evidence; or

    (d) to assist in escape from police detention or lawful custody,

may be retained when the person from whom it was seized is no longer in police detention or the custody of a court or is in the custody of a court but has been released on bail.

(4) Nothing may be retained for either of the purposes mentioned in subsection (2)(a) above if a photograph or copy would be sufficient for that purpose.

(5) Nothing in this section affects any power of a court to make an order under section 1 of the *Police (Property) Act* 1897.

(6) This section also applies to anything retained by the police under section 28H(5) of the *Immigration Act* 1971.

(7) The reference in subsection (1) to anything seized by a constable includes anything seized by a person authorised under section 16(2) to accompany a constable executing a warrant.

[This section is printed as amended by the *Immigration and Asylum Act* 1999, Sch.14 and the *Criminal Justice Act* 2003, Sch.1.]

1–63   The police are not entitled to retain property where the seizure was not in compliance with ss.15 and 16 of the *Police and Criminal Evidence Act* 1984 and so was unlawful. This section only applies to property which is lawfully in the possession of the police: *R. v Chief Constable of Lancashire Ex p. Parker* (1993) 97 Cr.App.R. 90.

The system for recovery of property retained by the police was considered in *R. v Southampton Justices Ex p. Newman*, (1989) 88 Cr.App.R. 202. Documents had been seized from the defendant's home on his arrest by officers of Customs and Excise. He applied to the court for an order under s.48 of the *Magistrates' Courts Act* 1980 for the return of this property. The magistrates held that s.48 did not apply because it referred to the return of property 'taken from the accused'. They interpreted this to mean that only property actually taken from the defendant's person and not from his home at the time of arrest could be covered by the section. The Court conceded that this left the defendant with no direct remedy as although the *Police and Criminal Evidence Act* 1984, ss.17 and 19 applied to Customs Officers by virtue of the *PACE (Application to Customs and Excise) Order* 1985, (SI 1985/1800), s.22 did not and neither did the *Police Property Act* 1897. It was suggested that the court has an inherent power to control the proceedings so it might in these circumstances adjourn or refuse to proceed if it thought it in the interests of justice that the documents should be returned to the defendant to enable him to prepare his defence.

1–64   The provisions of the *Police Property Act* 1897, whereby application may be made to the magistrates court for the return of property in police possession to the owner or any person as the court thinks meet are preserved. (See Chapter 15, Regulatory Offences—Police).

(11) Additional powers of seizure from premises

The powers of seizure under *PACE* 1984 are considerably extended under the pro- **1–65** visions of the *Criminal Justice and Police Act* 2001. The amendments are intended to modernise the law in relation to information held on computers and material that is stored by other methods of new technology. It was also prompted by the difficulties highlighted in *R. v The Chesterfield Justices Ex p. Bramley* [2000] 1 Cr.App.R. 486 where an officer was faced with a large amount of items and could not decide immediately on their relevance or indeed whether they were covered by legal privilege. The legislation entitles an officer to remove such items for scrutiny. The following provisions are listed and came into force on April 1, 2003.

Criminal Justice and Police Act 2001, s.50

Additional powers of seizure from premises
    50.—(1) Where—   **1–66**
     (a) a person who is lawfully on any premises finds anything on those premises that he has reasonable grounds for believing may be or may contain something for which he is authorised to search on those premises,
     (b) a power of seizure to which this section applies or the power conferred by subsection (2) would entitle him, if he found it, to seize whatever it is that he has grounds for believing that thing to be or to contain, and
     (c) in all the circumstances, it is not reasonably practicable for it to be determined, on those premises—
       (i) whether what he has found is something that he is entitled to seize, or
       (ii) the extent to which what he has found contains something that he is entitled to seize,
    that person's powers of seizure shall include power under this section to seize so much of what he has found as it is necessary to remove from the premises to enable that to be determined.
    (2) Where—
     (a) a person who is lawfully on any premises finds anything on those premises ("the seizable property") which he would be entitled to seize but for its being comprised in something else that he has (apart from this subsection) no power to seize,
     (b) the power under which that person would have power to seize the seizable property is a power to which this section applies, and
     (c) in all the circumstances it is not reasonably practicable for the seizable property to be separated, on those premises, from that in which it is comprised,
    that person's powers of seizure shall include power under this section to seize both the seizable property and that from which it is not reasonably practicable to separate it.

    (3) The factors to be taken into account in considering, for the purposes of this section, **1–67** whether or not it is reasonably practicable on particular premises for something to be determined, or for something to be separated from something else, shall be confined to the following—
     (a) how long it would take to carry out the determination or separation on those premises;
     (b) the number of persons that would be required to carry out that determination or separation on those premises within a reasonable period;
     (c) whether the determination or separation would (or would if carried out on those premises) involve damage to property;
     (d) the apparatus or equipment that it would be necessary or appropriate to use for the carrying out of the determination or separation; and
     (e) in the case of separation, whether the separation—
       (i) would be likely, or
       (ii) if carried out by the only means that are reasonably practicable on those premises, would be likely,
    to prejudice the use of some or all of the separated seizable property for a purpose for which something seized under the power in question is capable of being used.

(4) Section 19(6) of the 1984 Act and Article 21(6) of the *Police and Criminal Evidence (Northern Ireland) Order* 1989 (S.I. 1989 No. 1341 (N.I. 12)) (powers of seizure not to include power to seize anything that a person has reasonable grounds for believing is legally privileged) shall not apply to the power of seizure conferred by subsection (2).

(5) This section applies to each of the powers of seizure specified in Part 1 of Schedule 1.

(6) Without prejudice to any power conferred by this section to take a copy of any document, nothing in this section, so far as it has effect by reference to the power to take copies of documents under section 28(2)(b) of the *Competition Act* 1998, shall be taken to confer any power to seize any document.

(12) Additional powers of seizure from the person

Criminal Justice and Police Act 2001, s.51

Additional powers of seizure from the person

1–68　　　**51.**—(1) Where—

  (a) a person carrying out a lawful search of any person finds something that he has reasonable grounds for believing may be or may contain something for which he is authorised to search,

  (b) a power of seizure to which this section applies or the power conferred by subsection (2) would entitle him, if he found it, to seize whatever it is that he has grounds for believing that thing to be or to contain, and

  (c) in all the circumstances it is not reasonably practicable for it to be determined, at the time and place of the search—

    (i) whether what he has found is something that he is entitled to seize, or

    (ii) the extent to which what he has found contains something that he is entitled to seize,

  that person's powers of seizure shall include power under this section to seize so much of what he has found as it is necessary to remove from that place to enable that to be determined.

(2) Where—

  (a) a person carrying out a lawful search of any person finds something ("the seizable property") which he would be entitled to seize but for its being comprised in something else that he has (apart from this subsection) no power to seize,

  (b) the power under which that person would have power to seize the seizable property is a power to which this section applies, and

  (c) in all the circumstances it is not reasonably practicable for the seizable property to be separated, at the time and place of the search, from that in which it is comprised,

that person's powers of seizure shall include power under this section to seize both the seizable property and that from which it is not reasonably practicable to separate it.

1–69　　　(3) The factors to be taken into account in considering, for the purposes of this section, whether or not it is reasonably practicable, at the time and place of a search, for something to be determined, or for something to be separated from something else, shall be confined to the following—

  (a) how long it would take to carry out the determination or separation at that time and place;

  (b) the number of persons that would be required to carry out that determination or separation at that time and place within a reasonable period;

  (c) whether the determination or separation would (or would if carried out at that time and place) involve damage to property;

  (d) the apparatus or equipment that it would be necessary or appropriate to use for the carrying out of the determination or separation; and

  (e) in the case of separation, whether the separation—

    (i) would be likely, or

    (ii) if carried out by the only means that are reasonably practicable at that time and place, would be likely,

  to prejudice the use of some or all of the separated seizable property for a purpose for which something seized under the power in question is capable of being used.

(4) Section 19(6) of the 1984 Act and Article 21(6) of the *Police and Criminal Evidence (Northern Ireland) Order* 1989 (S.I. 1989 No. 1341 (N.I. 12)) (powers of seizure not to include power to seize anything a person has reasonable grounds for believing is legally privileged) shall not apply to the power of seizure conferred by subsection (2).

(5) This section applies to each of the powers of seizure specified in Part 2 of Schedule 1.

(13) Procedure for exercise of additional powers

Criminal Justice and Police Act 2001, s.52

Notice of exercise of power under s.50 or 51

52.—(1) Where a person exercises a power of seizure conferred by section 50, it shall (subject **1–70** to subsections (2) and (3)) be his duty, on doing so, to give to the occupier of the premises a written notice—

    (a) specifying what has been seized in reliance on the powers conferred by that section;

    (b) specifying the grounds on which those powers have been exercised;

    (c) setting out the effect of subsections 59 to 61;

    (d) specifying the name and address of the person to whom notice of an application under section 59(2) to the appropriate judicial authority in respect of any of the seized property must be given; and

    (e) specifying the name and address of the person to whom an application may be made to be allowed to attend the initial examination required by any arrangements made for the purposes of section 53(2).

(2) Where it appears to the person exercising on any premises a power of seizure conferred by section 50—

    (a) that the occupier of the premises is not present on the premises at the time of the exercise of the power, but

    (b) that there is some other person present on the premises who is in charge of the premises,

subsection (1) of this section shall have effect as if it required the notice under that subsection to be given to that other person.

(3) Where it appears to the person exercising a power of seizure conferred by section 50 that there is no one present on the premises to whom he may give a notice for the purposes of complying with subsection (1) of this section, he shall, before leaving the premises, instead of complying with that subsection, attach a notice such as is mentioned in that subsection in a prominent place to the premises.

(4) Where a person exercises a power of seizure conferred by section 51 it shall be his **1–71** duty, on doing so, to give a written notice to the person from whom the seizure is made—

    (a) specifying what has been seized in reliance on the powers conferred by that section;

    (b) specifying the grounds on which those powers have been exercised;

    (c) setting out the effect of subsections 59 to 61;

    (d) specifying the name and address of the person to whom notice of any application under section 59(2) to the appropriate judicial authority in respect of any of the seized property must be given; and

    (e) specifying the name and address of the person to whom an application may be made to be allowed to attend the initial examination required by any arrangements made for the purposes of section 53(2).

(5) The Secretary of State may by regulations made by statutory instrument, after consultation with the Scottish Ministers, provide that a person who exercises a power of seizure conferred by section 50 shall be required to give a notice such as is mentioned in subsection (1) of this section to any person, or send it to any place, described in the regulations.

(6) Regulations under subsection (5) may make different provision for different cases.

(7) A statutory instrument containing regulations under subsection (5) shall be subject to

annulment in pursuance of a resolution of either House of Parliament.

(14) Return or retention of seized property

Criminal Justice and Police Act 2001, ss.53–58

Examination and return of property seized under s.50 or 51

1–72   **53.**—(1) This section applies where anything has been seized under a power conferred by section 50 or 51.

(2) It shall be the duty of the person for the time being in possession of the seized property in consequence of the exercise of that power to secure that there are arrangements in force which (subject to section 61) ensure—

    (a) that an initial examination of the property is carried out as soon as reasonably practicable after the seizure;

    (b) that that examination is confined to whatever is necessary for determining how much of the property falls within subsection (3);

    (c) that anything which is found, on that examination, not to fall within subsection (3) is separated from the rest of the seized property and is returned as soon as reasonably practicable after the examination of all the seized property has been completed; and

    (d) that, until the initial examination of all the seized property has been completed and anything which does not fall within subsection (3) has been returned, the seized property is kept separate from anything seized under any other power.

(3) The seized property falls within this subsection to the extent only—

    (a) that it is property for which the person seizing it had power to search when he made the seizure but is not property the return of which is required by section 54;

    (b) that it is property the retention of which is authorised by section 56; or

    (c) that it is something which, in all the circumstances, it will not be reasonably practicable, following the examination, to separate from property falling within paragraph (a) or (b).

(4) In determining for the purposes of this section the earliest practicable time for the carrying out of an initial examination of the seized property, due regard shall be had to the desirability of allowing the person from whom it was seized, or a person with an interest in that property, an opportunity of being present or (if he chooses) of being represented at the examination.

(5) In this section, references to whether or not it is reasonably practicable to separate part of the seized property from the rest of it are references to whether or not it is reasonably practicable to do so without prejudicing the use of the rest of that property, or a part of it, for purposes for which (disregarding the part to be separated) the use of the whole or of a part of the rest of the property, if retained, would be lawful.

Obligation to return items subject to legal privilege

1–73   **54.**—(1) If, at any time after a seizure of anything has been made in exercise of a power of seizure to which this section applies—

    (a) it appears to the person for the time being having possession of the seized property in consequence of the seizure that the property—

        (i) is an item subject to legal privilege, or

        (ii) has such an item comprised in it,

    and

    (b) in a case where the item is comprised in something else which has been lawfully seized, it is not comprised in property falling within subsection (2),

it shall be the duty of that person to secure that the item is returned as soon as reasonably practicable after the seizure.

(2) Property in which an item subject to legal privilege is comprised falls within this subsection if—

    (a) the whole or a part of the rest of the property is property falling within subsection (3) or property the retention of which is authorised by section 56; and

    (b) in all the circumstances, it is not reasonably practicable for that item to be separated from the rest of that property (or, as the case may be, from that part of it) without prejudicing the use of the rest of that property, or that part of it, for purposes for which (disregarding that item) its use, if retained, would be lawful.

(3) Property falls within this subsection to the extent that it is property for which the person seizing it had power to search when he made the seizure, but is not property which is required to be returned under this section or section 55.

(4) This section applies—

- (a) to the powers of seizure conferred by sections 50 and 51;
- (b) to each of the powers of seizure specified in Parts 1 and 2 of Schedule 1; and
- (c) to any power of seizure (not falling within paragraph (a) or (b)) conferred on a constable by or under any enactment, including an enactment passed after this Act.

Obligation to return excluded and special procedure material

55.—(1) If, at any time after a seizure of anything has been made in exercise of a power to **1–74** which this section applies—

- (a) it appears to the person for the time being having possession of the seized property in consequence of the seizure that the property—
  - (i) is excluded material or special procedure material, or
  - (ii) has any excluded material or any special procedure material comprised in it,
- (b) its retention is not authorised by section 56, and
- (c) in a case where the material is comprised in something else which has been lawfully seized, it is not comprised in property falling within subsection (2) or (3),

it shall be the duty of that person to secure that the item is returned as soon as reasonably practicable after the seizure.

(2) Property in which any excluded material or special procedure material is comprised falls within this subsection if—

- (a) the whole or a part of the rest of the property is property for which the person seizing it had power to search when he made the seizure but is not property the return of which is required by this section or section 54; and
- (b) in all the circumstances, it is not reasonably practicable for that material to be separated from the rest of that property (or, as the case may be, from that part of it) without prejudicing the use of the rest of that property, or that part of it, for purposes for which (disregarding that material) its use, if retained, would be lawful.

(3) Property in which any excluded material or special procedure material is comprised falls within this subsection if—

- (a) the whole or a part of the rest of the property is property the retention of which is authorised by section 56; and
- (b) in all the circumstances, it is not reasonably practicable for that material to be separated from the rest of that property (or, as the case may be, from that part of it) without prejudicing the use of the rest of that property, or that part of it, for purposes for which (disregarding that material) its use, if retained, would be lawful.

(4) This section applies (subject to subsection (5)) to each of the powers of seizure speci- **1–75** fied in Part 3 of Schedule 1.

(5) In its application to the powers of seizure conferred by—

- (b) section 56(5) of the *Drug Trafficking Act* 1994,
- (c) Article 51(5) of the *Proceeds of Crime (Northern Ireland) Order* 1996 (S.I. 1996 No. 1299 (N.I. 6)),[and]
- [(d) section 352(4) of the *Proceeds of Crime Act* 2002,]

this section shall have effect with the omission of every reference to special procedure material.

(6) In this section, except in its application to—

- (a) the power of seizure conferred by section 8(2) of the 1984 Act,
- (b) the power of seizure conferred by Article 10(2) of the *Police and Criminal Evidence (Northern Ireland) Order* 1989 (S.I. 1989 No. 1341 (N.I. 12)),
- (c) each of the powers of seizure conferred by the provisions of paragraphs 1and 3 of Schedule 5 to the *Terrorism Act* 2000, and

(d) the power of seizure conferred by paragraphs 15 and 19 of Schedule 5 to that Act of 2000, so far only as the power in question is conferred by reference to paragraph 1 of that Schedule,

"special procedure material" means special procedure material consisting of documents or records other than documents.

Property seized by constables etc

1–76   **56.**—(1) The retention of—

(a) property seized on any premises by a constable who was lawfully on the premises,

(b) property seized on any premises by a relevant person who was on the premises accompanied by a constable, and

(c) property seized by a constable carrying out a lawful search of any person,

is authorised by this section if the property falls within subsection (2) or (3).

(2) Property falls within this subsection to the extent that there are reasonable grounds for believing—

(a) that it is property obtained in consequence of the commission of an offence; and

(b) that it is necessary for it to be retained in order to prevent its being concealed, lost, damaged, altered or destroyed.

(3) Property falls within this subsection to the extent that there are reasonable grounds for believing—

(a) that it is evidence in relation to any offence; and

(b) that it is necessary for it to be retained in order to prevent its being concealed, lost, altered or destroyed.

(4) Nothing in this section authorises the retention (except in pursuance of section 54(2)) of anything at any time when its return is required by section 54.

(5) In subsection (1)(b) the reference to a relevant person's being on any premises accompanied by a constable is a reference only to a person who was so on the premises under the authority of—

(a) a warrant under section 448 of the *Companies Act* 1985 authorising him to exercise together with a constable the powers conferred by subsection (3) of that section;

(b) a warrant under Article 441 of the *Companies (Northern Ireland) Order* 1986 (S.I. 1986 No. 1032 (N.I. 6)) authorising him to exercise together with a constable the powers conferred by paragraph (3) of that Article.

Retention of seized items

1–77   **57.**—(1) This section has effect in relation to the following provisions (which are about the retention of items which have been seized and are referred to in this section as "the relevant provisions")—

(a) section 22 of the 1984 Act;

(b) Article 24 of the *Police and Criminal Evidence (Northern Ireland) Order* 1989 (S.I. 1989 No. 1341 (N.I. 12));

(c) section 20CC(3) of the *Taxes Management Act* 1970;

(d) paragraph 4 of Schedule 9 to the *Weights and Measures (Northern Ireland) Order* 1981 (S.I. 1981 No. 231 (N.I. 10));

(f) section 448(6) of the *Companies Act* 1985;

(g) paragraph 4 of Schedule 8 to the *Weights and Measures Act* 1985;

(i) Article 441(6) of the *Companies (Northern Ireland) Order* 1986;

[...]

(k) section 40(4) of the *Human Fertilisation and Embryology Act* 1990;

(l) section 5(4) of the *Knives Act* 1997;

(m) paragraph 7(2) of Schedule 9 to the *Data Protection Act* 1998;

(n) section 28(7) of the *Competition Act* 1998;

(o) section 176(8) of the *Financial Services and Markets Act* 2000;

(p) paragraph 7(2) of Schedule 3 to the *Freedom of Information Act* 2000.

(2) The relevant provisions shall apply in relation to any property seized in exercise of a power conferred by section 50 or 51 as if the property had been seized under the power of seizure by reference to which the power under that section was exercised in relation to that property.

(3) Nothing in any of sections 53 to 56 authorises the retention of any property at any

time when its retention would not (apart from the provisions of this Part) be authorised by the relevant provisions.

(4) Nothing in any of the relevant provisions authorises the retention of anything after an obligation to return it has arisen under this Part.

Person to whom seized property is to be returned

1–78

58.—(1) Where—

(a) anything has been seized in exercise of any power of seizure, and

(b) there is an obligation under this Part for the whole or any part of the seized property to be returned,

the obligation to return it shall (subject to the following provisions of this section) be an obligation to return it to the person from whom it was seized.

(2) Where—

(a) any person is obliged under this Part to return anything that has been seized to the person from whom it was seized, and

(b) the person under that obligation is satisfied that some other person has a better right to that thing than the person from whom it was seized,

his duty to return it shall, instead, be a duty to return it to that other person or, as the case may be, to the person appearing to him to have the best right to the thing in question.

(3) Where different persons claim to be entitled to the return of anything that is required to be returned under this Part, that thing may be retained for as long as is reasonably necessary for the determination in accordance with subsection (2) of the person to whom it must be returned.

(4) References in this Part to the person from whom something has been seized, in relation to a case in which the power of seizure was exercisable by reason of that thing's having been found on any premises, are references to the occupier of the premises at the time of the seizure.

(5) References in this section to the occupier of any premises at the time of a seizure, in relation to a case in which—

(a) a notice in connection with the entry or search of the premises in question, or with the seizure, was given to a person appearing in the occupier's absence to be in charge of the premises, and

(b) it is practicable, for the purpose of returning something that has been seized, to identify that person but not to identify the occupier of the premises,

are references to that person.

(15) Application for return of property

Criminal Justice and Police Act 2001, s.59

Application to the appropriate judicial authority

59.—(1) This section applies where anything has been seized in exercise, or purported **1–79** exercise, of a relevant power of seizure.

(2) Any person with a relevant interest in the seized property may apply to the appropriate judicial authority, on one or more of the grounds mentioned in subsection (3), for the return of the whole or a part of the seized property.

(3) Those grounds are—

(a) that there was no power to make the seizure;

(b) that the seized property is or contains an item subject to legal privilege that is not comprised in property falling within section 54(2);

(c) that the seized property is or contains any excluded material or special procedure material which—

(i) has been seized under a power to which section 55 applies;

(ii) is not comprised in property falling within section 55(2) or (3); and

(iii) is not property the retention of which is authorised by section 56;

(d) that the seized property is or contains something seized under section 50 or 51 which does not fall within section 53(3);

and subsections (5) and (6) of section 55 shall apply for the purposes of paragraph (c) as they apply for the purposes of that section.

(4) Subject to subsection (6), the appropriate judicial authority, on an application under subsection (2), shall—

    (a) if satisfied as to any of the matters mentioned in subsection (3), order the return of so much of the seized property as is property in relation to which the authority is so satisfied; and

    (b) to the extent that that authority is not so satisfied, dismiss the application.

(5) The appropriate judicial authority—

    (a) on an application under subsection (2),

    (b) on an application made by the person for the time being having possession of anything in consequence of its seizure under a relevant power of seizure, or

    (c) on an application made—

        (i) by a person with a relevant interest in anything seized under section 50 or 51, and

        (ii) on the grounds that the requirements of section 53(2) have not been or are not being complied with,

    may give such directions as the authority thinks fit as to the examination, retention, separation or return of the whole or any part of the seized property.

(6) On any application under this section, the appropriate judicial authority may authorise the retention of any property which—

    (a) has been seized in exercise, or purported exercise, of a relevant power of seizure, and

    (b) would otherwise fall to be returned,

if that authority is satisfied that the retention of the property is justified on grounds falling within subsection (7).

1–80   (7) Those grounds are that (if the property were returned) it would immediately become appropriate—

    (a) to issue, on the application of the person who is in possession of the property at the time of the application under this section, a warrant in pursuance of which, or of the exercise of which, it would be lawful to seize the property; or

    (b) to make an order under—

        (i) paragraph 4 of Schedule 1 to the 1984 Act,

        (ii) paragraph 4 of Schedule 1 to the *Police and Criminal Evidence (Northern Ireland) Order* 1989 (S.I. 1989 No. 1341 (N.I. 12)),

        (iii) section 20BA of the *Taxes Management Act* 1970, or

        (iv) paragraph 5 of Schedule 5 to the *Terrorism Act* 2000,

    under which the property would fall to be delivered up or produced to the person mentioned in paragraph (a).

(8) Where any property which has been seized in exercise, or purported exercise, of a relevant power of seizure has parts ("part A" and "part B") comprised in it such that—

    (a) it would be inappropriate, if the property were returned, to take any action such as is mentioned in subsection (7) in relation to part A,

    (b) it would (or would but for the facts mentioned in paragraph (a)) be appropriate, if the property were returned, to take such action in relation to part B, and

    (c) in all the circumstances, it is not reasonably practicable to separate part A from part B without prejudicing the use of part B for purposes for which it is lawful to use property seized under the power in question,

the facts mentioned in paragraph (a) shall not be taken into account by the appropriate judicial authority in deciding whether the retention of the property is justified on grounds falling within subsection (7).

(9) If a person fails to comply with any order or direction made or given by a judge of the Crown Court in exercise of any jurisdiction under this section—

    (a) the authority may deal with him as if he had committed a contempt of the Crown Court; and

    (b) any enactment relating to contempt of the Crown Court shall have effect in relation to the failure as if it were such a contempt.

(10) The relevant powers of seizure for the purposes of this section are—

    (a) the powers of seizure conferred by sections 50 and 51;

    (b) each of the powers of seizure specified in Parts 1 and 2 of Schedule 1; and

(c) any power of seizure (not falling within paragraph (a) or (b)) conferred on a constable by or under any enactment, including an enactment passed after this Act.

(11) References in this section to a person with a relevant interest in seized property are references to—

(a) the person from whom it was seized;

(b) any person with an interest in the property; or

(c) any person, not falling within paragraph (a) or (b), who had custody or control of the property immediately before the seizure.

(12) For the purposes of subsection (11)(b), the persons who have an interest in seized property shall, in the case of property which is or contains an item subject to legal privilege, be taken to include the person in whose favour that privilege is conferred.

(16) Interception of communications and surveillance

Police Act 1997, ss.91–108 and Regulation of Investigatory Powers Act 2000, ss.5–11

Part III of the *Police Act* 1997, ss.91–108, contains the statutory framework for the **1–81** authorisation of entry or interference with property or wireless telegraphy. Apparatus and devices can be installed in premises for the purposes of covert surveillance under the authorisation of the *Regulation of Investigatory Powers Act* 2000. The Act (*RIPA*) provides a statutory framework for the installation of surveillance equipment with a system of authorisations and supervision by various commissioners and tribunals.

Under s.93 of the *Police Act* 1997, entry to the premises can be gained to maintain or retrieve the equipment used. The covert entry can be authorised for the police, customs officers and others. *RIPA* was brought in following the case of *R. v Khan (Sultan)* [1997] A.C. 558, where the lack of regulation of covert activities was bemoaned by the House of Lords. Mr Khan applied to the European Court of Human Rights following his unsuccessful appeal to the House of Lords complaining that his right to privacy under Art.8 had been interfered with by the bugging and also that he had not had a fair trial under Art.6 because the evidence had been unlawfully obtained. It was held that the covert bugging of the defendant was in breach of his Art.8 rights. This interference was not "in accordance with the law" as the regulations for use of surveillance were only included in Home Office guidance and not statute. However, the way in which the evidence was obtained did not affect the fairness of the trial under Art.6 as the admissibility of the evidence was suitably controlled in domestic law by the *Police and Criminal Evidence Act* 1984, s.78: *Khan v UK* (2001) 31 E.H.R.R. 45.

The provisions of the two Acts do not refer to the admissibility of evidence obtained by covert surveillance but they do provide the required framework of law and the activities of the police can be measured against this to judge if their conduct affects the fairness of the proceedings.

In respect of the *Police Act* 1997 a Code of Practice has been issued—*Police Act 1997 (Authorisation of Action in Respect of Property) (Code of Practice) Order* 1998 SI 1998/3240.

Existing police powers continue to apply to surveillance that is not covert and does **1–82** not involve interference with property or wireless telegraphy. This could cover situations where filming or taping is undertaken in public places or with the consent of the owner of premises. (See *Home Office Circular "Guidelines on the Use of Equipment in Police Surveillance Operations"* 1984.)

D. Arrest and Detention

(1) Introduction

The word arrest carries its normal meaning of checking or hindering the motion or **1–83** action of a thing or person. An arrest can be effected by touching or seizing a person to restrain them. A person may also effectively be arrested by being told an arrest is happening but if mere words are used they must be calculated to bring to the defendant's notice the fact that he was under compulsion and thereafter that he submitted to that compulsion. An officer should use very clear words such as "I arrest you": *Alderson v Booth* [1969] 2 All E.R. 271. Whether or not a person has been arrested depends not on the legality of the arrest but whether he has been deprived of his liberty to go where he pleases: *Spicer v Holt* [1976] 3 All E.R. 171.

General

1–84   Powers of arrest, whether by police or any other persons are governed by statute and common law. Any arrest has to have a legal basis or it may amount to a criminal offence or give rise to civil liability. An arrest may take place without a warrant in situations of urgency or immediacy but in other cases a warrant is required from the Court which authorises an arrest in specific circumstances. The statutory provisions are—

1. Arrest without a warrant under *PACE* 1984, ss.24–23.
2. Arrest without a warrant in specific statutes preserved by *PACE* 1984, s.26(2) and Schedule 2.
3. Arrest without a warrant under statutes brought in subsequent to *PACE* 1984, *e.g. Public Order Act* 1986.
4. Arrest with a warrant issued by a magistrate or district judge—s.1, *Magistrates' Courts Act* 1980.
5. Arrest with or without a warrant under *Criminal Justice and Public Order Act* 1994, P10. (Cross-border enforcement).
6. Common law power of arrest for breach of the peace preserved by *PACE* 1984.

1–85   Powers of arrest are also governed by Art.5, ECHR. For an arrest or detention to be ECHR compliant it must be lawful, in accordance with procedures prescribed by law and the grounds for the arrest must fall within the provisions of Art.5 paras (1)(a)–(f).

Article 5 is to be narrowly construed as providing an exhaustive list of the circumstances in which a person can be deprived of their liberty: *Winterwerp v Netherlands* [1979] 2 E.H.R.R. 387. Any arrest must be in accordance with the national law and procedure but the European Court themselves will interpret and apply the relevant domestic law, taking into account the margin of appreciation, in deciding whether Art.5 is violated: *Benham v UK* [1996] 22 E.H.R.R. 293. Whether the domestic law on which the arrest or detention is based is accessible and precise has been held to determine whether it is lawful or not: *Zamir v UK* [1985] 40 D.R. 42. The law relating to arrest and detention for breach of the peace was considered by the European Court in the case of *Steel v UK* [1998] 28 E.H.R.R. 602 and the domestic law was held to be "formulated with the degree of precision required by the Convention".

Code C of the Codes of Practice covers the detention, treatment and questioning of persons by police officers. Most of the provisions relate to detention at the Police Station but mention is made in the Notes of Guidance about the procedural requirements on arrest. See C:10A *et seq.* On arrest, a person may be conveyed to a police station or released on street bail to attend a police station later.

(2) Reasonable Grounds for Suspecting

1–86   Under Art.5(1)(c) of the ECHR there is a requirement for reasonable suspicion to found the basis for arrest and detention, see *Fox, Campbell and Hartley v UK* [1990] 13 E.H.R.R. 157; *Murray v UK* [1996] 19 E.H.R.R. 193. The Court will expect the existence of facts or information which would satisfy an objective observer that the person concerned may have committed the offence.

The test for determining whether reasonable grounds for the suspicion to justify an arrest existed is partly subjective, in that the arresting officer must have formed a genuine suspicion that the person being arrested was guilty of an offence. The test is also partly objective, as there had to have been reasonable grounds for forming such a suspicion.

Refusal to answer questions may increase an officer's suspicion but it cannot alone amount to a reasonable suspicion that an offence has been committed because citizens are not under a general legal duty to answer police questions: *Rice v Connolly* [1966] 2 Q.B. 414.

With regard to reasonable grounds for suspecting that an arrestable offence has been committed, the officer need not have a specific statutory provision in mind, or mentally identify specific offences with technicality or precision. The officer must reasonably suspect the existence of facts amounting to an arrestable offence of a kind that the officer has in mind: *Chapman v DPP* (1989) 89 Cr.App.R. 190, DC.

(3) Arrest without warrant for an arrestable offence

Police and Criminal Evidence Act 1984, s.24

Arrest without warrant for arrestable offences

24.—(1) The powers of summary arrest conferred by the following subsections shall apply— **1–87**
    (a) to offences for which the sentence is fixed by law;
    (b) to offences for which a person of 21 [18] years of age or over (not previously convicted) may be sentenced to imprisonment for a term of five years (or might be so sentenced but for the restrictions imposed by section 33 of the *Magistrates' Courts Act* 1980); and
    (c) to the offences listed in Schedule 1A,
and in this Act "arrestable offence" means any such offence.

(2) [Schedule 1A (which lists the offences referred to in subsection (1)(c)) shall have effect.]

(3) Without prejudice to section 2 of the *Criminal Attempts Act* 1981, the powers of summary arrest conferred by the following subsections shall also apply to the offences of—
    (a) conspiring to commit any of the offences listed in Schedule 1A;
    (b) attempting to commit any such offence other than [one which is a summary offence];
    (c) inciting, aiding, abetting, counselling or procuring the commission of any such offence;
and such offences are also arrestable offences for the purposes of this Act.

(4) Any person may arrest without a warrant—
    (a) anyone who is in the act of committing an arrestable offence;
    (b) anyone whom he has reasonable grounds for suspecting to be committing such an offence.

(5) Where an arrestable offence has been committed, any person may arrest without a warrant—
    (a) anyone who is guilty of the offence;
    (b) anyone whom he has reasonable grounds for suspecting to be guilty of it.

(6) Where a constable has reasonable grounds for suspecting that an arrestable offence has been committed, he may arrest without a warrant anyone whom he has reasonable grounds for suspecting to be guilty of the offence.

(7) A constable may arrest without a warrant—
    (a) anyone who is about to commit an arrestable offence;
    (b) anyone whom he has reasonable grounds for suspecting to be about to commit an arrestable offence.

[This section is printed as amended or repealed in part by the *Sexual Offences Act* **1–88**
1956, s.5(3), the *Criminal Justice Act* 1988, s.170(1),(2) and Sch.15, para.98 and Sch.16, the *Official Secrets Act* 1989, s.11(1), the *Football (Offences) Act* 1991, s.5(1), the *Criminal Justice and Public Order Act* 1994, s.85(1) and (2), 155, 166(4) and 167(7), the *Offensive Weapons Act* 1996, s.1(1), the *Protection from Harassment Act* 1997, s.2(3), the *Crime and Disorder Act* 1998, ss.27(1), 32(2) and 84(2), the *Football (Disorder) Act* 2000, s.81 and Sch.12, para.13, the *Criminal Justice and Public Order Act 2001*, ss.12(6), 46(6) and 71 and the *Anti-terrorism, Crime and Security Act* 2001, ss.82(1) and 94(3) and as from a day to be appointed by the *Criminal Justice and Court Services Act* 2000, s.74 and Sch.7, para.77 and the *Police Reform Act* 2002, s.48 and the

Criminal Justice Act 2003, s.3 which amends Sch.1A to the *Police and Criminal Evidence Act* 1984—prospective amendments shown in square brackets.]

[This section is printed as amended by the *Police Reform Act* 2002.]

1–89 Section 33 of the *Magistrates' Courts Act* 1980 provides for certain either way offences to be triable summarily only with limited penalties because of the low value involved, *e.g.* criminal damage offences. The offences listed in Schedule 1A are:

Police and Criminal Evidence Act, Sch.1A

"SCHEDULE 1A

SPECIFIC OFFENCES WHICH ARE ARRESTABLE OFFENCES

Customs and Excise Acts

1–90 1. An offence for which a person may be arrested under the customs and excise Acts (within the meaning of the *Customs and Excise Management Act* 1979).

Official Secrets Act 1920

1–90.1 2. An offence under the *Official Secrets Act* 1920 which is not an arrestable offence by virtue of the term of imprisonment for which a person may be sentenced in respect of them.

Criminal Justice Act 1925

2ZA. An offence under section 36 of the *Criminal Justice Act* 1925 (untrue statement for procuring a passport).

Prevention of Crime Act 1953

1–91 3. An offence under section 1(1) of the *Prevention of Crime Act* 1953 (prohibition of carrying offensive weapons without lawful authority or excuse).

Sexual Offences Act 1956

4. An offence under—

(a) section 22 of the *Sexual Offences Act* 1956 (causing prostitution of women; or

(b) section 23 of that Act (procuration of girl under 21).

Obscene Publications Act 1959

5. An offence under section 2 of the *Obscene Publications Act* 1959 (publication of obscene matter).

Theft Act 1968

1–92 6. An offence under—

(a) section 12(1) of the *Theft Act* 1968 (taking motor vehicle or other conveyance without authority etc.); or

(b) section 25(1) of that Act (going equipped for stealing *etc.*).

Misuse of Drugs Act 1971

6A. An offence under section 5(2) of the *Misuse of Drugs Act* 1971 (having possession of a controlled drug) in respect of cannabis resin (within the meaning of that Act).

Theft Act 1978

7. An offence under section 3 of the *Theft Act* 1978 (making off without payment). *Protection of Children Act* 1978

Protection of Children Act 1978

8 An offence under section 1 of the *Protection of Children Act* 1978 (indecent photographs and pseudo-photographs of children).

Wildlife and Countryside Act 1981

1–93 9. An offence under section 1(1) or (2) or 6 of the *Wildlife and Countryside Act* 1981 (taking, possessing, selling etc. of wild birds) in respect of a bird included in Schedule 1 to that Act or any part of, or anything derived from, such a bird.

10. An offence under—

(a) section 1(5) of the *Wildlife and Countryside Act* 1981 (disturbance of wild birds);
(b) section 9 or 13(1)(a) or (2) of that Act (taking, possessing, selling etc. of wild animals or plants); or
(c) section 14 of that Act (introduction of new species etc.).

Civil Aviation Act 1982

11. An offence under section 39(1) of the *Civil Aviation Act* 1982 (trespass on aerodrome).

Aviation Security Act 1982

12. An offence under section 21C(1) or 21D(1) of the *Aviation Security Act* 1982 (unauthorised presence in a restricted zone or on an aircraft).

Sexual Offences Act 1985

13. An offence under section 1 of the *Sexual Offences Act* 1985 (kerb-crawling).   **1–94**

Public Order Act 1986

14. An offence under section 19 of the *Public Order Act* 1986 (publishing etc. material likely to stir up racial or religious hatred).

Criminal Justice Act 1988

15. An offence under—
(a) section 139(1) of the *Criminal Justice Act* 1988 (offence of having article with a blade or point in public place); or
(b) section 139A(1) or (2) of that Act (offence of having article with a blade or point or offensive weapon on school premises).

Road Traffic Act 1988

16. An offence under section 103(1)(b) of the *Road Traffic Act* 1988 (driving while disqualified).

17. An offence under subsection (4) of section 170 of the *Road Traffic Act* 1988 (fail- **1–95** ure to stop and report an accident) in respect of an accident to which that section applies by virtue of subsection (1)(a) of that section (accidents causing personal injury).

17A. An offence under section 174 of the *Road Traffic Act* 1988 (false statements and withholding material information).

Official Secrets Act 1989

18. An offence under any provision of the *Official Secrets Act* 1989 other than subsection (1), (4) or (5) of section 8 of that Act.

Football Spectators Act 1989

19. An offence under section 14J or 21C of the *Football Spectators Act* 1989 (failing to comply with requirements imposed by or under a banning order or a notice under section 21B).

Football (Offences) Act 1991

20. An offence under any provision of the *Football (Offences) Act* 1991.

Criminal Justice and Public Order Act 1994

21. An offence under—   **1–96**
(a) section 60AA(7) of the *Criminal Justice and Public Order Act* 1994 (failing to comply with requirement to remove disguise);
(b) section 166 of that Act (sale of tickets by unauthorised persons).
(c) section 167 of that Act (touting for car hire services).

Police Act 1996

22. An offence under section 89(1) of the *Police Act* 1996 (assaulting a police officer in the execution of his duty or a person assisting such an officer).

Protection from Harassment Act 1997

23. An offence under section 2 of the *Protection from Harassment Act* 1997 (harassment).

Crime and Disorder Act 1998

24. An offence falling within section 32(1)(a) of the *Crime and Disorder Act* 1998 (racially or religiously aggravated harassment).

Criminal Justice and Police Act 2001

25. An offence under—

(a) section 12(4) of the *Criminal Justice and Police Act* 2001 (failure to comply with requirements imposed by constable in relation to consumption of alcohol in public place); or

(b) section 46 of that Act (placing of advertisements in relation to prostitution)."conspiracy and aiding, abetting, counselling or procuring of the listed Schedule 1A offences are also arrestable under this section.

1–97   [Paragraphs 2ZA, 6A and 17A were inserted under s.3 of the *Criminal Justice Act* 2003, enacted in January 2004.]

1–98   Powers of arrest are available to effect a citizen's arrest under this section as it refers to any person, but powers of arrest granted to police constables are much wider. A citizen has power to make an arrest only when an arrestable offence is in the process of being committed or when such an offence has been committed. The citizen must have reasonable grounds for suspecting the person he arrests of committing the offence or being guilty of having committed it. For a police officer he needs only have reasonable grounds to suspect that an arrestable offence has been committed before arresting without warrant any person whom he has reasonable grounds for suspecting of being guilty of it. The circumstances then allowing for citizen's arrest are more restricted depending on the fact that an arrestable offence has actually been committed. If a defendant is at trial acquitted of an offence then the citizen's arrest is invalidated because no arrestable offence was committed: *R. v Self* [1992] 3 All E.R. 476; *Walters v W. H. Smith & Sons Ltd* [1914] 1 K.B. 595.

For police officers to exercise their powers there must objective justification for their belief that the conditions of s.24(6) are met. There must be evidence that the officer did in fact at the time of arrest have reasonable grounds for suspecting an arrestable offence had been committed and reasonable grounds for suspecting the person he was arresting for being guilty of the offence. In the case of *Chapman v DPP* (1989) 89 Cr.App.R. 190, a constable was told by a colleague that he had been assaulted. The officers gave chase to the suspect and followed him to a nearby flat. On seeking entry the officer said that he wished to arrest the suspect for "assault". Entry was denied and the occupant of the premises was charged with assaulting the officer in the execution of his duty. The difficulty was that assault is not an arrestable offence so the powers of s.24 (6) were not engaged. The Court held that it must be shown at the time of arrest that the officer had the required suspicion or belief in his mind and it could not be construed retrospectively. In the absence of actual suspicion and belief relating to an arrestable offence there was no power of arrest. This strict interpretation of the section has been re-considered in more recent cases. In *R.v Chalkley and Jeffries* [1998] 2 Cr.App.R. 79, it was held that a collateral motive for an arrest on otherwise good and stated grounds did not necessarily make the arrest unlawful. Here the defendants were arrested on suspicion of credit card frauds but whilst they were being detained the police entered the premises of one to install covert bugging devices to assist in the investigation into more serious armed robbery offences. The arrest was challenged as unlawful because there was an ulterior motive but the court held that as the motive was a desire to investigate and put a stop to other far more serious crime the lawfulness of the arrest, which was properly founded according to s.24(6) was not impugned. In *Hough v Chief Constable of Staffordshire* [2001] EWCA Civ 39 it was held that information held on a police computer was likely to constitute sufficient objective justification to found a reasonable suspicion for an arrest even though it transpired that the information was incorrect. The Court said that it depended on the circumstances of the arrest and in particular the urgency of the situation whether a duty arose for an officer to make additional inquiries before a reasonable suspicion could be founded.

(4) Arrest for a non-arrestable offence subject to the general arrest conditions

Police and Criminal Evidence Act 1984, s.25

General arrest conditions

25.—(1) Where a constable has reasonable grounds for suspecting that any offence which is **1–99** not an arrestable offence has been committed or attempted, or is being committed or attempted, he may arrest the relevant person if it appears to him that service of a summons is impracticable or inappropriate because any of the general arrest conditions is satisfied.

(2) In this section "the relevant person" means any person whom the constable has reasonable grounds to suspect of having committed or having attempted to commit the offence or of being in the course of committing or attempting to commit it.

(3) The general arrest conditions are—

    (a) that the name of the relevant person is unknown to, and cannot be readily ascertained by, the constable;

    (b) that the constable has reasonable grounds for doubting whether a name furnished by the relevant person as his name is his real name;

    (c) that—

        (i) the relevant person has failed to furnish a satisfactory address for service; or

        (ii) the constable has reasonable grounds for doubting whether an address furnished by the relevant person is a satisfactory address for service;

    (d) that the constable has reasonable grounds for believing that arrest is necessary to prevent the relevant person—

        (i) causing physical injury to himself or any other person;

        (ii) suffering physical injury;

        (iii) causing loss of or damage to property;

        (iv) committing an offence against public decency; or

        (v) causing an unlawful obstruction of the highway;

    (e) that the constable has reasonable grounds for believing that arrest is necessary to protect a child or other vulnerable person from the relevant person.

(4) For the purposes of subsection (3) above an address is a satisfactory address for service if it appears to the constable—

    (a) that the relevant person will be at it for a sufficiently long period for it to be possible to serve him with a summons; or

    (b) that some other person specified by the relevant person will accept service of a summons for the relevant person at it.

(5) Nothing in subsection (3)(d) above authorises the arrest of a person under subparagraph (iv) of that paragraph except where members of the public going about their normal business cannot reasonably be expected to avoid the person to be arrested.

(6) This section shall not prejudice any power of arrest conferred apart from this section.

This section gives powers to a constable to arrest a suspect in the case of offences **1–100** which are not arrestable. These offences will by their nature be less serious and only become arrestable if the special conditions listed apply. The process is in two stages and the Courts have held that the relevant condition must be in the officer's mind at the time of arrest and that there should be evidence of this. In *Edwards v DPP* (1993) 97 Cr.App.R. 301 an officer purported to arrest a defendant for obstruction. This is not an arrestable offence and at the time of arrest no mention was made of s.25 or the relevant conditions. The defendant could have been arrested for more serious offences under the *Misuse of Drugs Act* 1971 but the officer chose to tell him it was for 'obstruction' and the arrest was held invalid as not complying with s.25. An example of how the prodcedure should be properly followed is found in *Nicholas v Parsonage* [1987] R.T.R. 199 where the defendant was stopped by police for riding his bicycle dangerously. The officers asked for his name and address and he refused to tell them.

He was warned he could be arrested and he was asked again. Again he refused and tried to cycle off. He then assaulted an officer who restrained him. The court held that the conditions of s.25 were met and the arrest was lawful.

Section 25(6) preserves the common law power to arrest for breach of the peace: *Albert v Lavin* [1981] 3 All E.R. 878.

(5) Other statutory powers of arrest without warrant

Police and Criminal Evidence Act 1984, s.26

Repeal of statutory powers of arrest without warrant or order

1–101   **26.**—(1) Subject to subsection (2) below, so much of any Act (including a local Act) passed before this Act as enables a constable—

     (a) to arrest a person for an offence without a warrant; or

     (b) to arrest a person otherwise than for an offence without a warrant or an order of a court,

shall cease to have effect.

     (2) Nothing in subsection (1) above affects the enactments specified in Schedule 2 to this Act.

This section abolished all previous powers of arrest without a warrant except those listed in Sch.2. The common law powers for arrest for breach of the peace are preserved in other sections. Legislation has been brought in after *PACE* 1984 where powers of arrest without warrant are included in the specific acts, *e.g. Public Order Act* 1986. These powers are covered under the specific offences section.

(6) Arrest with a Warrant issued by a Magistrate or District Judge

1–102   Application may be made to a magistrate or district judge under the *Magistrates' Courts Act* 1980, s.1 for a warrant of arrest, see §§ 4–61—4–67.

(7) Information to be given on arrest

Police and Criminal Evidence Act 1984, s.28

Information to be given on arrest

1–103   **28.**—(1) Subject to subsection (5) below, where a person is arrested, otherwise than by being informed that he is under arrest, the arrest is not lawful unless the person arrested is informed that he is under arrest as soon as is practicable after his arrest.

     (2) Where a person is arrested by a constable, subsection (1) above applies regardless of whether the fact of the arrest is obvious.

     (3) Subject to subsection (5) below, no arrest is lawful unless the person arrested is informed of the ground for the arrest at the time of, or as soon as is practicable after, the arrest.

     (4) Where a person is arrested by a constable, subsection (3) above applies regardless of whether the ground for the arrest is obvious.

     (5) Nothing in this section is to be taken to require a person to be informed—

     (a) that he is under arrest; or

     (b) of the ground for the arrest,

if it was not reasonably practicable for him to be so informed by reason of his having escaped from arrest before the information could be given.

1–104   An arrest is unlawful unless at the time of the arrest or as soon as practicable after the arrest, the arrested person is informed that he is under arrest and of the ground of arrest.

Article 5(2) of the ECHR requires that any person who is arrested shall be informed promptly, in a language which he understands of the reasons for his arrest and of any charge against him. The person arrested should be told in simple, non-technical language, the essential legal and factual ground for his arrest so as to be able, if he sees fit, to apply to a court to challenge its lawfulness: *Fox, Campbell and Hartley v UK* (above) and see also *Taylor v Chief Constable of Thames Valley Police, The Times,* July 13, 2004.

Where a person is being arrested under s.25 he must be told both the offence for which he is being arrested and the general arrest condition to justify the arrest. "At the time of arrest" covers the short but reasonable time around the arrest both before and after the actual moment of arrest. *Nicholas v Parsonage* (above) followed in *Mullady v DPP* [1997] C.O.D. 422.

Where a defendant was caught in a car by an automatic locking device set as a trap **1–105** by the police, it was held that he was arrested at the time he was locked in. Officers arrived on the scene shortly after and informed him of his arrest and the ground of it which was held to be as soon as was practicable after the arrest: *Dawes v DPP* [1995] 1 Cr.App.R. 65.

It has been held to be sufficient to tell a person they were arrested for "unlawful possession"; *Abbassy v Commissioner of the Metropolitan Police* (1990) 90 Cr.App.R. 250, but insufficient to say 'Theft of cheques' when the offences involved the theft of a cheque book and cheques in it and the subsequent dishonest encashment of one cheque to almost empty the account with additional evidence that the defendant had been at the victim's house and been seen at his bank at the relevant times: *Wilson v Chief Constable of Lancashire* [2002] 99 1 L.S.G. 19.

Where a person is not informed of the reasons for his arrest at the time, the arrest is unlawful but this can be cured by his being informed of the full reasons at the Police Station: *R. v Kulynycz* [1971] 1 Q.B. 367.

If a person has hearing difficulties or cannot speak English then the duty on the ar- **1–106** resting officer is to take whatever action a reasonable person would have done in the circumstances to convey the fact of and reasons for arrest: *Wheatley v Lodge* [1971] 1 W.L.R. 29.

The suspect must be informed of the true nature of the investigations and an arrest was held to be unlawful when the defendant was arrested for offences of assault and theft and questioned on that basis when the police already had sufficient evidence to arrest him for robbery and manslaughter but chose not to do so whilst he gave compromising answers in relation to the lesser charges: *R. v Kirk* [2000] 1 Cr.App.R. 400.

There are many occasions when because of the nature of the physical arrest it is not practicable to inform the person detained of the reasons for the arrest at the time. The officer then has a duty to maintain the arrest and inform of the reasons as soon as is practicable thereafter. A lawful arrest will not be made unlawful retrospectively where because of a struggle on arrest the reasons could not be given. If it is impracticable to give the reasons at the time of arrest a failure to do so later at the police station does not invalidate the arrest: *DPP v Hawkins* [1988] 3 All E.R. 1949.

On arrest there is also a duty to caution in accordance with Code C para.10 either **1–107** immediately prior to arrest or on arrest. Para.10.1 explains when the caution must be given if there are grounds to suspect an offence may have been committed. Questions may be put to establish identity or ownership of items or in furtherance of the conduct of a search but once there are grounds to suspect an offence the person must be cautioned before any further questions about his involvement in the offence are put.

The requirement of cautioning before questioning does not extend to the asking of routine questions designed to establish ownership of an item. In *R. v Senior* (2004) 148 S.J. 300 it was held that it was not necessary to caution a suspect before asking questions about the ownership of a suitcase known to contain drugs. Such a question had no element of surprise or unfairness but once a person identified himself as the owner the caution should be given.

The words of the caution are;—

> "You do not have to say anything. But it may harm your defence if you do not mention when questioned something which you later rely on in court. Anything you do say may be given in evidence."

Minor deviations are not a breach of the code as long as the sense of it is preserved.

(8) Use of force in making arrest

Police and Criminal Evidence Act 1984, s.117

Power of constable to use reasonable force

1–108   **117.** Where any provision of this Act—
  (a) confers a power on a constable; and
  (b) does not provide that the power may only be exercised with the consent of some person, other than a police officer,
the officer may use reasonable force, if necessary, in the exercise of the power.

This section together with s.17 gives the police power to enter premises with the use of reason able force to arrest for an arrestable offence. When exercising these powers the officer must give the reasons why he is doing so unless it is impossible, impracticable or undesirable to do so in the circumstances: *O'Loughlin v Chief Constable of Essex* [1998] 1 W.L.R. 374.

(9) Voluntary attendance at police station

Police and Criminal Evidence Act 1984, s.29

Voluntary attendance at police station etc

1–109   **29.** Where for the purpose of assisting with an investigation a person attends voluntarily at a police station or at any other place where a constable is present or accompanies a constable to a police station or any such other place without having been arrested—
  (a) he shall be entitled to leave at will unless he is placed under arrest;
  (b) he shall be informed at once that he is under arrest if a decision is taken by a constable to prevent him from leaving at will.

(10) Arrest elsewhere than at police station

1–110   Section 4 of the *Criminal Justice Act* 2003 introduces a scheme of "street bail" which allows for police officers to arrest a person on the street or elsewhere and then to grant bail without the need to escort them to a police station. No conditions may be imposed on the bail and the person involved is under a duty to attend later at a police station. Written notice must be given before the person is released which records the offence for which he has been arrested and the grounds of arrest. Failure to answer to street bail may lead to arrest without warrant. Section 4 amends s.30 of the *Police and Criminal Justice Act* 1984 and adds ss.30A–30D to cover the arrangements for "street bail".

Police and Criminal Evidence Act 1984, ss.30–30D

Arrest elsewhere than at police station

     30.—(1) Subsection (1A) [applies where a person is, at any place other than a police station—
  (a) arrested by a constable for an offence,or
  (b) taken into custody by a constable after being arrested for an offence by a person other than a constable.
(1A) The person must be taken by a constable to a police station as soon as practicable after the arrest.]

(1B) Subsection (1A) [has effect subject to section 30A (release on bail) and subsection (7) (release without bail)].

(2) Subject to subsections (3) and (5) below, the police station to which an arrested person is taken under subsection (1A) above shall be a designated police station.

(3) A constable to whom this subsection applies may take an arrested person to any police station unless it appears to the constable that it may be necessary to keep the arrested person in police detention for more than six hours.

(4) Subsection (3) above applies—

    (a) to a constable who is working in a locality covered by a police station which is not a designated police station; and

    (b) to a constable belonging to a body of constables maintained by an authority other than a police authority.

(5) Any constable may take an arrested person to any police station if—

    (a) either of the following conditions is satisfied—

        (i) the constable has arrested him without the assistance of any other constable and no other constable is available to assist him;

        (ii) the constable has taken him into custody from a person other than a constable without the assistance of any other constable and no other constable is available to assist him; and

    (b) it appears to the constable that he will be unable to take the arrested person to a designated police station without the arrested person injuring himself, the constable or some other person.

(6) If the first police station to which an arrested person is taken after his arrest is not a designated police station, he shall be taken to a designated police station not more than six hours after his arrival at the first police station unless he is released previously.

[(7) A person arrested by a constable at any place other than a police station must be released without bail if the condition in subsection (7A) is satisfied.

(7A) The condition is that, at any time before the person arrested reaches a police station, a constable is satisfied that there are no grounds for keeping him under arrest or releasing him on bail under section 30A.]

(8) A constable who releases a person under subsection (7) above shall record the fact that he has done so.

(9) The constable shall make the record as soon as is practicable after the release.

[(10) Nothing in subsection (1A) or in section 30A prevents a constable delaying taking a person to a police station or releasing him on bail if the condition in subsection (10A) is satisfied.

(10A) The condition is that the presence of the person at a place (other than a police station) is necessary in order to carry out such investigations as it is reasonable to carry out immediately.

(11) Where there is any such delay the reasons for the delay must be recorded when the person first arrives at the police station or (as the case may be) is released on bail.]

(12) Nothing in subsection (1A) above shall be taken to affect—

    (a) paragraphs 16(3) or 18(1) of Schedule 2 to the *Immigration Act* 1971;

    (b) section 34(1) of the *Criminal Justice Act* 1972; or

    (c) any provision of the *Terrorism Act* 2000.

(13) Nothing in subsection (10) above shall be taken to affect paragraph 18(3) of Schedule 2 to the *Immigration Act* 1971.

[This section is printed as amended by the *Prevention of Terrorism (Temporary Provisions) Act* 1989, Sch.8 and the *Terrorism Act* 2000, s.125. The amendments of the *Criminal Justice Act* 2003 appear in square brackets. They were brought into force on January 29, 2004.]

Bail elsewhere than at police station

    30A.—(1) A constable may release on bail a person who is arrested or taken into custody in the circumstances mentioned in section 30(1).   **1–111**

(2) A person may be released on bail under subsection (1) at any time before he arrives at a police station.

(3) A person released on bail under subsection (1) must be required to attend a police station.

(4) No other requirement may be imposed on the person as a condition of bail.

(5) The police station which the person is required to attend may be any police station.

[Section 30A was inserted by the *Criminal Justice Act* 2003, s.4 and came into force in January 2004.

Bail under section 30A: notices

    30B.—(1) Where a constable grants bail to a person under section 30A, he must give that person a notice in writing before he is released.   **1–112**

(2) The notice must state—

    (a) the offence for which he was arrested, and

    (b) the ground on which he was arrested.

(3) The notice must inform him that he is required to attend a police station.

(4) It may also specify the police station which he is required to attend and the time when he is required to attend.

(5) If the notice does not include the information mentioned in subsection (4), the person must subsequently be given a further notice in writing which contains that information.

(6) The person may be required to attend a different police station from that specified in the notice under subsection (1) or (5) or to attend at a different time.

(7) He must be given notice in writing of any such change as is mentioned in subsection (6) but more than one such notice may be given to him.

[Section 30B was inserted by the *Criminal Justice Act* 2003, s.4 and came into force in January 2004.

Bail under section 30A: supplemental

1–112.1   **30C.**—(1) A person who has been required to attend a police station is not required to do so if he is given notice in writing that his attendance is no longer required.

(2) If a person is required to attend a police station which is not a designated police station he must be—

    (a) released, or

    (b) taken to a designated police station,

not more than six hours after his arrival.

(3) Nothing in the *Bail Act* 1976 applies in relation to bail under section 30A.

(4) Nothing in section 30A or 30B or in this section prevents the re-arrest without a warrant of a person released on bail under section 30A if new evidence justifying a further arrest has come to light since his release.

[Section 30C was inserted by the *Criminal Justice Act* 2003, s.4 and came into force in January 2004.

Failure to answer to bail under section 30A

1–112.2   **30D.**—(1) A constable may arrest without a warrant a person who—

    (a) has been released on bail under section 30A subject to a requirement to attend a specified police station, but

    (b) fails to attend the police station at the specified time.

(2) A person arrested under subsection (1) must be taken to a police station (which may be the specified police station or any other police station) as soon as practicable after the arrest.

(3) In subsection (1), "specified" means specified in a notice under subsection (1) or (5) of section 30B or, if notice of change has been given under subsection (7) of that section, in that notice.

(4) For the purposes of—

    (a) section 30 (subject to the obligation in subsection (2)), and

    (b) section 31,

an arrest under this section is to be treated as an arrest for an offence.

[Section 30D was inserted by the *Criminal Justice Act* 2003, s.4 and came into force in January 2004.

The *Immigration Act* 1971 allows Customs Officers to take into detention from on board a ship or aircraft a person whom they wish to examine under the Schedule pending a decision as to whether leave to enter should be given or refused. An immigration officer can also require the captain of the vessel to prevent the person from disembarking.

Section 34 of the *Criminal Justice Act* 1972 empowers a constable to take a person to an approved treatment centre for alcoholics on arrest for an offence of being drunk under s.12 of the *Licensing Act* 1964 or drunk and disorderly under s.91(1) of the *Criminal Justice Act* 1967.

A private person making an arrest should take a defendant to a police constable as soon as possible although it is acceptable for a shoplifter to be taken to the shop manager initially for a decision to prosecute: *John Lewis & Co v Tims* [1952] 1 All E.R. 1203. Failure by a constable to take a person to the Police Station as soon as practicable could affect the fairness of proceedings and evidence could then be excluded under s.78, *PACE* 1984: *R. v Kerawalla* [1991] Crim.L.R. 451. The Courts have held that the power under subs.(10) must not be abused and where a search was undertaken before taking the suspect to the police station and whilst the search was underway questions were put to the suspect without the protection afforded by Codes of Practice, the evidence obtained in this way was excluded for unfairness: *R. v Khan* [1993] Crim.L.R. 54; *R. v Raphie* [1996] Crim.L.R. 812.

(11) Arrest for further offence

Police and Criminal Evidence Act 1984, s.31

Arrest for further offence
1–113

31. Where—
   (a) a person—
      (i)   has been arrested for an offence; and
      (ii) is at a police station in consequence of that arrest; and
   (b) it appears to a constable that, if he were released from that arrest, he would be liable to arrest for some other offence,
he shall be arrested for that other offence.

The purpose of this section is to prevent the release and re-arrest of a suspect that would result in an artificial extension of the detention periods regulated by s.41, *PACE* 1984 *et seq*. There is no requirement that the further arrest should occur as soon as practicable only that it must be done before expiry of the relevant detention period: *R. v Samuel* [1988] Q.B. 615.

(12) Search following arrest

Police and Criminal Evidence Act 1984, s.32

Search upon arrest
1–114

32.—(1) A constable may search an arrested person, in any case where the person to be searched has been arrested at a place other than a police station, if the constable has reasonable grounds for believing that the arrested person may present a danger to himself or others.
   (2) Subject to subsections (3) to (5) below, a constable shall also have power in any such case—
   (a) to search the arrested person for anything—
      (i)   which he might use to assist him to escape from lawful custody; or
      (ii) which might be evidence relating to an offence; and
   (b) to enter and search any premises in which he was when arrested or immediately before he was arrested for evidence relating to the offence for which he has been arrested.
   (3) The power to search conferred by subsection (2) above is only a power to search to the extent that is reasonably required for the purpose of discovering any such thing or any such evidence.
   (4) The powers conferred by this section to search a person are not to be construed as authorising a constable to require a person to remove any of his clothing in public other than an outer coat, jacket or gloves but they do authorise a search of a person's mouth.
   (5) A constable may not search a person in the exercise of the power conferred by subsection (2)(a) above unless he has reasonable grounds for believing that the person to be searched may have concealed on him anything for which a search is permitted under that paragraph.
   (6) A constable may not search premises in the exercise of the power conferred by

subsection (2)(b) above unless he has reasonable grounds for believing that there is evidence for which a search is permitted under that paragraph on the premises.

(7) In so far as the power of search conferred by subsection (2)(b) above relates to premises consisting of two or more separate dwellings, it is limited to a power to search—

(a) any dwelling in which the arrest took place or in which the person arrested was immediately before his arrest; and

(b) any parts of the premises which the occupier of any such dwelling uses in common with the occupiers of any other dwellings comprised in the premises.

(8) A constable searching a person in the exercise of the power conferred by subsection (1). above may seize and retain anything he finds, if he has reasonable grounds for believing that the person searched might use it to cause physical injury to himself or to any other person.

(9) A constable searching a person in the exercise of the power conferred by subsection (2)(a) above may seize and retain anything he finds, other than an item subject to legal privilege, if he has reasonable grounds for believing—

(a) that he might use it to assist him to escape from lawful custody; or

(b) that it is evidence of an offence or has been obtained in consequence of the commission of an offence.

(10) Nothing in this section shall be taken to affect the power conferred by section 43 of the *Terrorism Act* 2000.

[This section is printed as amended by the *Prevention of Terrorism (Temporary Provisions) Act* 1989, Sch.8, the *Criminal Justice and Public Order Act* 1994, s.59 and the *Terrorism Act* 2000, s.125.]

1–115   Code B of the Codes of Practice applies to searches carried out under this section.

All searches must be founded on a reasonable suspicion.The search must take place at the time of arrest and not hours later: *R. v Badham* [1987] Crim.L.R. 202.

The conditions of the section must be complied with. Where a person was arrested on suspected burglary and was asked by the police to hand over his car keys it was held that this request was beyond their powers under the section because the keys were not "evidence relating to an offence", in this case the burglary: *R. v Churchill* [1989] Crim.L.R. 226. The search is limited to the extent reasonably required to find the items or evidence mentioned in subs.(2) and it will be a question of fact whether that was the genuine reason why officers made their entry. If this is challenged and the search is found to be unlawful the question of fairness and admissibility of evidence will arise under s.78, *PACE* 1984: *R. v Beckford* (1991) 94 Cr.App.R. 43.

This power to search is complemented by the power under s.18, *PACE* 1984 to search premises after arrest for an arrestable offence, which is slightly wider in scope. A search under s.18 can be undertaken where the person arrested was still at the police station whereas under s.32 the search is envisaged as taking place at the time of arrest and at the premises where he was arrested or where he had been immediately before his arrest. See *R. (on the application of Rottman) v Commissioner of the Metropolitan Police* [2002] 2 All E.R. 865.

Detention after Arrest

1–116   The Act and Codes provide a framework regulating the detention of suspects in police custody. Reasons for detention must be given and the length of time that a person may be detained is limited and subject to review. Rights of the suspect are protected covering the conduct of searches and the taking of forensic samples. A custody officer is appointed at designated police stations with specific duties and responsibilities for detained persons. A person is in detention when he or she is arrested for an offence and taken to a police station or when he attends voluntarily at a police station and is then arrested: s.118, *PACE* 1984. The time for recording detention starts to run from arrival at the police station or from 24 hours after arrest, whichever is earlier: s.41, *PACE* 1984. The timetable for review is as follows:—

6 hours	First review by police
+ 9 hours	Second review by police
+ 9 hours	Further review by police
24 hours	Charge required UNLESS
+ 12 hours	Authorised by senior officer. Then charge required UNLESS
36 hours	Application to court for warrant of further detention
+ 36 hours	Further detention order by court
+ 36 hours	Extension of further detention ordered by court BUT
96 hours	Maximum length of detention allowed before charge.

Longer periods of detention may be authorised under counter–terrorism provisions, see *Terrorism Act* 2000.

Police and Criminal Evidence Act 1984, s.34

Limitations on police detention

34.—(1) A person arrested for an offence shall not be kept in police detention except in accordance with the provisions of this Part of this Act.

(2) Subject to subsection (3) below, if at any time a custody officer—

(a) becomes aware, in relation to any person in police detention, that the grounds for the detention of that person have ceased to apply; and

(b) is not aware of any other grounds on which the continued detention of that person could be justified under the provisions of this Part of this Act,

it shall be the duty of the custody officer, subject to subsection (4) below, to order his immediate release from custody.

(3) No person in police detention shall be released except on the authority of a custody officer at the police station where his detention was authorised or, if it was authorised at more than one station, a custody officer at the station where it was last authorised.

(4) A person who appears to the custody officer to have been unlawfully at large when he was arrested is not to be released under subsection (2) above.

(5) A person whose release is ordered under subsection (2) above shall be released without bail unless it appears to the custody officer—

(a) that there is need for further investigation of any matter in connection with which he was detained at any time during the period of his detention; or

(b) that, in respect of any such matter, proceedings may be taken against him or he may be reprimanded or warned under section 65 of the *Crime and Disorder Act* 1998

and, if it so appears, he shall be released on bail.

(6) For the purposes of this Part of this Act a person arrested under section 6(5) of the *Road Traffic Act* 1988 [or section 30(2) of the *Transport and Works Act* 1992] is arrested for an offence.

(7) For the purposes of this Part a person who

(a) attends a police station to answer to bail granted under section 30A,

(b) returns to a police station to answer to bail granted under this part, or

(c) is arrested under section 30D or section 46A

is to be treated as arrested for an offence and that offence is the offence in connection with which he was granted bail.

[This section is printed as amended by the *Road Traffic (Consequential Provisions) Act* 1988, Sch.3, the *Criminal Justice and Public Order Act* 1994, s.29 and the *Criminal Justice and Court Services Act* 2000, s.56. Subsection 6(5) is printed as amended by the *Police Reform Act* 2002, s.53(1).]

The reference to s.65 of the *Crime and Disorder Act* 1998 in subs.(5)(b) relates to **1-117** the system of court diversion for children and young persons, see Part V.

The *Road Traffic Act* 1988 gives an officer power to arrest without warrant anyone who has provided a positive breath test at the roadside or who has failed to provide a specimen but the officer has reasonable cause to suspect that the person has alcohol his body. Section 46A gives power for a constable to arrest without warrant any person who has failed to answer their police bail back to the police station. In these situations an offence may not have been committed but this section means the defendant may be treated as if it had.

Article 5(3) requires that everyone arrested or detained shall be brought "promptly" before a judge or other judicial officer. The provisions of *PACE* 1984, ss.41–46 provide for the right for prompt appearance before a court to be safeguarded. The European Court is reluctant to lay down specific time frames as a minimum requirement but detention for over four days under the *Prevention of Terrorism (Temporary Provisions) Act* 1984 was held to be in breach of the Article: *Brogan v UK* [1988] 11 E.H.R.R. 117.

A person is in police detention after he has been taken to the police station, or if he attended there voluntarily, after he has been arrested. See s.118 of *PACE* 1984.

Police and Criminal Evidence Act 1984, s.35

Designated police stations

1–118　　**35.**—(1) The chief officer of police for each police area shall designate the police stations in his area which, subject to sections 30(3) and (5), 30A(5) and 30D(2) above, are to be the stations in that area to be used for the purpose of detaining arrested persons.

(2) A chief officer's duty under subsection (1) above is to designate police stations appearing to him to provide enough accommodation for that purpose.

(2A) The Chief Constable of the British Transport Police Force may designate police stations which (in addition to those designated under subsection (1) above) may be used for the purpose of detaining arrested persons.

(3) Without prejudice to section 12 of the *Interpretation Act* 1978 (continuity of duties) a chief officer—

　(a) may designate a station which was not previously designated; and

　(b) may direct that a designation of a station previously made shall cease to operate.

(4) In this Act "designated police station" means a police station for the time being designated under this section.

[This section is printed as amended by the *Anti-terrorism, Crime and Security Act* 2001, Sch.7 and the *Criminal Justice Act* 2003, Sch.1.]

Police and Criminal Evidence Act 1984, s.36

Custody officers at police stations

1–119　　**36.**—(1) One or more custody officers shall be appointed for each designated police station.

(2) A custody officer for a police station designated under section 35(1) above shall be appointed—

　(a) by the chief officer of police for the area in which the designated police station is situated; or

　(b) by such other police officer as the chief officer of police for that area may direct.

(2A) A custody officer for a police station designated under section 35(2A) above shall be appointed—

　(a) by the Chief Constable of the British Transport Police Force; or

　(b) by such other member of that Force as that Chief Constable may direct.

(3) No officer may be appointed a custody officer unless he is of at least the rank of sergeant.

(4) An officer of any rank may perform the functions of a custody officer at a designated police station if a custody officer is not readily available to perform them.

(5) Subject to the following provisions of this section and to section 39(2) below, none of the functions of a custody officer in relation to a person shall be performed by an officer who at the time when the function falls to be performed is involved in the investigation of an offence for which that person is in police detention at that time.

(6) Nothing in subsection (5) above is to be taken to prevent a custody officer—

　(a) performing any function assigned to custody officers—

   (i) by this Act; or

   (ii) by a code of practice issued under this Act;

  (b) carrying out the duty imposed on custody officers by section 39 below;

  (c) doing anything in connection with the identification of a suspect; or

  (d) doing anything under sections 7 and 8 of the *Road Traffic Act* 1988.

 (7) Where an arrested person is taken to a police station which is not a designated police station, the functions in relation to him which at a designated police station would be the functions of a custody officer shall be performed—

  (a) by an officer who is not involved in the investigation of an offence for which he is in police detention, if such an officer is readily available; and

  (b) if no such officer is readily available, by the officer who took him to the station or any other officer.

 (7A) Subject to subsection (7B), subsection (7) applies where a person attends a police station which is not a designated station to answer to bail granted under section 30A as it applies where a person is taken to such a station.

 (7B) Where subsection (7) applies because of subsection (7A), the reference in subsection (7)(b) to the officer who took him to the station is to be read as a reference to the officer who granted him bail.

 (8) References to a custody officer in the following provisions of this Act include references to an officer other than a custody officer who is performing the functions of a custody officer by virtue of subsection (4) or (7) above.

 (9) Where by virtue of subsection (7) above an officer of a force maintained by a police authority who took an arrested person to a police station is to perform the functions of a custody officer in relation to him, the officer shall inform an officer who—

  (a) is attached to a designated police station; and

  (b) is of at least the rank of inspector,

that he is to do so.

 (10) The duty imposed by subsection (9) above shall be performed as soon as it is practicable to perform it.

[This section is printed as amended by the *Road Traffic (Consequential Provisions) Act* 1988, Sch.3 and the *Criminal Justice Act* 2003, Sch.1.]

 Sections 7 and 8 of the *Road Traffic Act* 1988 give the power to a constable to **1–120** require specimens of breath or blood for analysis in road traffic investigations. The custody officer may perform these functions.

 The Chief Constable has a duty to appoint at least one custody officer (of at least the rank of sergeant) for each designated station but there is not a requirement to ensure that a custody officer will always be available at a designated station to perform the duties of the custody officer: *Vince v Chief Constable of Dorset Police* [1993] 1 W.L.R. 415, CA (Civ. Div.).

 The functions of the investigating officer and the custody officer are to be kept separate under subs.(5). This provision was not breached where the custody officer who was acting in co-operation with the investigating officers, placed the defendants in a bugged cell. The bugging of the cell was held not to be an oppressive or unfair method of obtaining the relevant evidence: *Bailey and Smith* (1993) 97 Cr.App.R. 365.

 For the duties of a custody officer in general see ss.37–38, *PACE* 1984, see Chapter 4.

Police and Criminal Evidence Act 1984, s.39

Responsibilities in relation to persons detained

 39.—(1) Subject to subsections (2) and (4) below, it shall be the duty of the custody officer at a **1–121** police station to ensure—

  (a) that all persons in police detention at that station are treated in accordance with this Act and any code of practice issued under it and relating to the treatment of persons in police detention; and

  (b) that all matters relating to such persons which are required by this Act or by such codes of practice to be recorded are recorded in the custody records relating to such persons.

(2) If the custody officer, in accordance with any code of practice issued under this Act, transfers or permits the transfer of a person in police detention—

(a) to the custody of a police officer investigating an offence for which that person is in police detention; or

(b) to the custody of an officer who has charge of that person outside the police station,

the custody officer shall cease in relation to that person to be subject to the duty imposed on him by subsection (1)(a) above; and it shall be the duty of the officer to whom the transfer is made to ensure that he is treated in accordance with the provisions of this Act and of any such codes of practice as are mentioned in subsection (1) above.

(3) If the person detained is subsequently returned to the custody of the custody officer, it shall be the duty of the officer investigating the offence to report to the custody officer as to the manner in which this section and the codes of practice have been complied with while that person was in his custody.

(4) If an arrested juvenile is transferred to the care of a local authority in pursuance of arrangements made under section 38(6) above, the custody officer shall cease in relation to that person to be subject to the duty imposed on him by subsection (1) above.

(5) Repealed.

(6) Where—

(a) an officer of higher rank than the custody officer gives directions relating to a person in police detention; and

(b) the directions are at variance—

　(i) with any decision made or action taken by the custody officer in the performance of a duty imposed on him under this Part of this Act; or

　(ii) with any decision or action which would but for the directions have been made or taken by him in the performance of such a duty,

the custody officer shall refer the matter at once to an officer of the rank of superintendent or above who is responsible for the police station for which the custody officer is acting as custody officer.

[This section is printed as amended by the *Children Act* 1989, Schs 13 and 15.] For the treatment of juveniles, see Part V.

(13) Review of detention

Police and Criminal Evidence Act 1984, s.40

Review of police detention

1–122　　　**40.**—(1) Reviews of the detention of each person in police detention in connection with the investigation of an offence shall be carried out periodically in accordance with the following provisions of this section—

(a) in the case of a person who has been arrested and charged, by the custody officer; and

(b) in the case of a person who has been arrested but not charged, by an officer of at least the rank of inspector who has not been directly involved in the investigation.

(2) The officer to whom it falls to carry out a review is referred to in this section as a "review officer".

(3) Subject to subsection (4) below—

(a) the first review shall be not later than six hours after the detention was first authorised;

(b) the second review shall be not later than nine hours after the first;

(c) subsequent reviews shall be at intervals of not more than nine hours.

(4) A review may be postponed—

(a) if, having regard to all the circumstances prevailing at the latest time for it specified in subsection (3) above, it is not practicable to carry out the review at that time;

(b) without prejudice to the generality of paragraph (a) above—

　(i) if at that time the person in detention is being questioned by a police officer and the review officer is satisfied that an interruption of the questioning for the purpose of carrying out the review would prejudice the investigation in connection with which he is being questioned; or

    (ii) if at that time no review officer is readily available.

(5) If a review is postponed under subsection (4) above it shall be carried out as soon as practicable after the latest time specified for it in subsection (3) above.

(6) If a review is carried out after postponement under subsection (4) above, the fact that it was so carried out shall not affect any requirement of this section as to the time at which any subsequent review is to be carried out.

(7) The review officer shall record the reasons for any postponement of a review in the custody record.

(8) Subject to subsection (9) below, where the person whose detention is under review has not been charged before the time of the review, section 37(1) to (6) above shall have effect in relation to him, but with the modifications specified in subsection (8A).

[(8A) The modifications are—   **1–123**

    (a) the substitution of references to the person whose detention is under review for references to the person arrested;

    (b) the substitution of references to the review officer for references to the custody officer; and

    (c) in subsection (6), the insertion of the following paragraph after paragraph (a)—

    '(aa) asleep;'.]

(9) Where a person has been kept in police detention by virtue of section 37(9) above, section 37(1) to (6) shall not have effect in relation to him but it shall be the duty of the review officer to determine whether he is yet in a fit state.

(10) Where the person whose detention is under review has been charged before the time of the review, section 38(1) to (6B) above shall have effect in relation to him, but with the modifications specified in subsection (10A).

[(10A) The modifications are—

    (a) the substitution of a reference to the person whose detention is under review for any reference to the person arrested or to the person charged; and

    (b) in subsection (5), the insertion of the following paragraph after paragraph (a)—

    '(aa) asleep;'.]

(11) Where—

    (a) an officer of higher rank than the review officer gives directions relating to a person in police detention; and

    (b) the directions are at variance—

        (i) with any decision made or action taken by the review officer in the performance of a duty imposed on him under this Part of this Act; or

        (ii) with any decision or action which would but for the directions have been made or taken by him in the performance of such a duty.

the review officer shall refer the matter at once to an officer of the rank of superintendent or above who is responsible for the police station for which the review officer is acting as review officer in connection with the detention.

(12) Before determining whether to authorise a person's continued detention the review officer shall give—

    (a) that person (unless he is asleep); or

    (b) any solicitor representing him who is available at the time of the review,

an opportunity to make representations to him about the detention.

(13) Subject to subsection (14) below, the person whose detention is under review or his solicitor may make representations under subsection (12) above either orally or in writing.

(14) The review officer may refuse to hear oral representations from the person whose detention is under review if he considers that he is unfit to make such representations by reason of his condition or behaviour.

[This section is printed with amendments of the *Police Reform Act* 2002, s.108 included in square brackets. These provisions come into force on a date to be appointed.]

Review before charge is carried out by an Inspector but after charge by the custody **1–124** sergeant whose has general precharge duties including a duty to determine whether to charge a person in detention or to detain him further to obtain the evidence to charge him. Further duties under the section flow from the decision he makes. The review provisions work in conjunction with the duty to charge within time limits (*q.v.*)

Amendments inserted in *PACE* 1984 by the *Criminal Justice and Police Act* 2001 provide for reviews to be carried out by telephone (s.40A) and video-conferencing: s.45.

Section 6 of the *Criminal Justice Act* 2003 substitutes s.40A to allow for a review to be carried out by means of a discussion, conducted by telephone, with one or more persons at the police station where the arrested person is held. This does not apply though if the review could be carried out using video-conferencing facilities. The section came into force on January 29, 2004 and is dependent on equipment being available and regulations authorising its use.

(14) Time limit

Police and Criminal Evidence Act 1984, s.41

Limits on period of detention without charge

1–125   **41.**—(1) Subject to the following provisions of this section and to subsections 42 and 43 below, a person shall not be kept in police detention for more than 24 hours without being charged.

(2) The time from which the period of detention of a person is to be calculated (in this Act referred to as "the relevant time")—

 (a) in the case of a person to whom this paragraph applies, shall be—
  (i) the time at which that person arrives at the relevant police station; or
  (ii) the time 24 hours after the time of that person's arrest,
  whichever is the earlier;

 (b) in the case of a person arrested outside England and Wales, shall be—
  (i) the time at which that person arrives at the first police station to which he is taken in the police area in England or Wales in which the offence for which he was arrested is being investigated; or
  (ii) the time 24 hours after the time of that person's entry into England and Wales,
  whichever is the earlier;

 (c) in the case of a person who—
  (i) attends voluntarily at a police station; or
  (ii) accompanies a constable to a police station without having been arrested,
  and is arrested at the police station, the time of his arrest;

 (ca) in the case of a person who attends a police station to answer to bail granted under section 30A, the time when he arrives at the police station.

 (d) in any other case, except where subsection (5) below applies, shall be the time at which the person arrested arrives at the first police station to which he is taken after his arrest.

(3) Subsection (2)(a) above applies to a person if—

 (a) his arrest is sought in one police area in England and Wales;
 (b) he is arrested in another police area; and
 (c) he is not questioned in the area in which he is arrested in order to obtain evidence in relation to an offence for which he is arrested;

and in sub-paragraph (i) of that paragraph "the relevant police station" means the first police station to which he is taken in the police area in which his arrest was sought.

(4) Subsection (2) above shall have effect in relation to a person arrested under section 31 above as if every reference in it to his arrest or his being arrested were a reference to his arrest or his being arrested for the offence for which he was originally arrested.

1–126   (5) If—

 (a) a person is in police detention in a police area in England and Wales ("the first area"); and
 (b) his arrest for an offence is sought in some other police area in England and Wales ("the second area"); and

(c) he is taken to the second area for the purposes of investigating that offence, without being questioned in the first area in order to obtain evidence in relation to it,

the relevant time shall be—

> (i) the time 24 hours after he leaves the place where he is detained in the first area; or
>
> (ii) the time at which he arrives at the first police station to which he is taken in the second area,

whichever is the earlier.

(6) When a person who is in police detention is removed to hospital because he is in need of medical treatment, any time during which he is being questioned in hospital or on the way there or back by a police officer for the purpose of obtaining evidence relating to an offence shall be included in any period which falls to be calculated for the purposes of this Part of this Act, but any other time while he is in hospital or on his way there or back shall not be so included.

(7) Subject to subsection (8) below, a person who at the expiry of 24 hours after the relevant time is in police detention and has not been charged shall be released at that time either on bail or without bail.

(8) Subsection (7) above does not apply to a person whose detention for more than 24 hours after the relevant time has been authorised or is otherwise permitted in accordance with sections 42 or 43 below.

(9) A person released under subsection (7) above shall not be re-arrested without a warrant for the offence for which he was previously arrested unless new evidence justifying a further arrest has come to light since his release but this subsection does not prevent an arrest under section 46A below.

[This section is printed as amended by the *Criminal Justice and Public Order Act* 1994, s.29 and the *Criminal Justice Act* 2003, Sch.1.]

Police and Criminal Evidence Act 1984, ss.42–44

Authorisation of continued detention

42.—(1) Where a police officer of the rank of superintendent or above who is responsible for **1–127** the police station at which a person is detained has reasonable grounds for believing that—

> (a) the detention of that person without charge is necessary to secure or preserve evidence relating to an offence for which he is under arrest or to obtain such evidence by questioning him;
>
> (b) [an offence for which he is under arrest is an arrestable offence; and]
>
> (c) the investigation is being conducted diligently and expeditiously.

he may authorise the keeping of that person in police detention for a period expiring at or before 36 hours after the relevant time.

(2) Where an officer such as is mentioned in subsection (1) above has authorised the keeping of a person in police detention for a period expiring less than 36 hours after the relevant time, such an officer may authorise the keeping of that person in police detention for a further period expiring not more than 36 hours after that time if the conditions specified in subsection (1) above are still satisfied when he gives the authorisation.

(3) If it is proposed to transfer a person in police detention to another police area, the officer determining whether or not to authorise keeping him in detention under subsection (1) above shall have regard to the distance and the time the journey would take.

(4) No authorisation under subsection (1) above shall be given in respect of any person—

> (a) more than 24 hours after the relevant time; or
>
> (b) before the second review of his detention under section 40 above has been carried out.

(5) Where an officer authorises the keeping of a person in police detention under subsection (1) above, it shall be his duty—

> (a) to inform that person of the grounds for his continued detention; and
>
> (b) to record the grounds in that person's custody record.

(6) Before determining whether to authorise the keeping of a person in detention under subsection (1) or (2) above, an officer shall give—

> (a) that person; or

(b) any solicitor representing him who is available at the time when it falls to the officer to determine whether to give the authorisation,

an opportunity to make representations to him about the detention.

(7) Subject to subsection (8) below, the person in detention or his solicitor may make representations under subsection (6) above either orally or in writing.

(8) The officer to whom it falls to determine whether to give the authorisation may refuse to hear oral representations from the person in detention if he considers that he is unfit to make such representations by reason of his condition or behaviour.

(9) Where—

(a) an officer authorises the keeping of a person in detention under subsection (1) above; and

(b) at the time of the authorisation he has not yet exercised a right conferred on him by section 56 or 58 below,

the officer—

    (i) shall inform him of that right;

    (ii) shall decide whether he should be permitted to exercise it;

    (iii) shall record the decision in his custody record; and

    (iv) if the decision is to refuse to permit the exercise of the right, shall also record the grounds for the decision in that record.

(10) Where an officer has authorised the keeping of a person who has not been charged in detention under subsection (1) or (2) above, he shall be released from detention, either on bail or without bail, not later than 36 hours after the relevant time, unless—

(a) he has been charged with an offence; or

(b) his continued detention is authorised or otherwise permitted in accordance with section 43 below.

(11) A person released under subsection (10) above shall not be re-arrested without a warrant for the offence for which he was previously arrested unless new evidence justifying a further arrest has come to light since his release but this subsection does not prevent an arrest under section 46A below.

[This section is printed as amended by the *Criminal Justice and Public Order Act* 1994, s.29. Subsection (1)(b) was substituted by the *Criminal Justice Act* 2003, s.7, and came into force in January 2004.]

The power to extend detention applies to all arrestable offences. An arrestable offence is defined in s.24, *PACE* 1984 and Sch.1A.

These provisions permit detention without charge for 24 hours from arrest or arrival at the police station, which ever is earlier. Section 41 gives details as to how the time should be computed. Section 42 permits a senior officer to authorise continued detention on the grounds given for a further 12 hours making a total of 36 hours detention without charge. The authorisation to extend the detention must be given within the first 24-hour period but after the second review which must occur at the latest 15 hours after the detention was first authorised. If authorisation is given then for a period of less than the 12 hours allowed it may be further extended up to the maximum of 12 hours as long as any authorisation is made during the currency of the extended period of detention: *R. v Taylor (Leroy)* [1991] Crim.L.R. 541. After 36 hours the person must be released from detention and at that stage he can either be bailed to return to the police station or simply released. If he is not bailed or released he must be charged or application for further detention in custody can be made to a Court under s.43, *PACE* 1984.

Warrants of further detention.

1–128   **43.**—(1) Where, on an application on oath made by a constable and supported by an information, a magistrates' court is satisfied that there are reasonable grounds for believing that the further detention of the person to whom the application relates is justified, it may issue a warrant of further detention authorising the keeping of that person in police detention.

(2) A court may not hear an application for a warrant of further detention unless the person to whom the application relates—

(a) has been furnished with a copy of the information; and

(b) has been brought before the court for the hearing.

(3) The person to whom the application relates shall be entitled to be legally represented at the hearing and, if he is not so represented but wishes to be so represented—

    (a) the court shall adjourn the hearing to enable him to obtain representation; and

    (b) he may be kept in police detention during the adjournment.

(4) A person's further detention is only justified for the purposes of this section or section 44 below if—

    (a) his detention without charge is necessary to secure or preserve evidence relating to an offence for which he is under arrest or to obtain such evidence by questioning him;

    (b) an offence for which he is under arrest is a serious arrestable offence; and

    (c) the investigation is being conducted diligently and expeditiously.

(5) Subject to subsection (7) below, an application for a warrant of further detention may be made—

    (a) at any time before the expiry of 36 hours after the relevant time; or

    (b) in a case where—

        (i) it is not practicable for the magistrates' court to which the application will be made to sit at the expiry of 36 hours after the relevant time; but

        (ii) the court will sit during the 6 hours following the end of that period,

    at any time before the expiry of the said 6 hours.

(6) In a case to which subsection (5)(b) above applies—

    (a) the person to whom the application relates may be kept in police detention until the application is heard; and

    (b) the custody officer shall make a note in that person's custody record—

        (i) of the fact that he was kept in police detention for more than 36 hours after the relevant time; and

        (ii) of the reason why he was so kept.

(7) If—

    (a) an application for a warrant of further detention is made after the expiry of 36 hours after the relevant time; and

    (b) it appears to the magistrates' court that it would have been reasonable for the police to make it before the expiry of that period,

the court shall dismiss the application.

(8) Where on an application such as is mentioned in subsection (1) above a magistrates' court is not satisfied that there are reasonable grounds for believing that the further detention of the person to whom the application relates is justified, it shall be its duty—

    (a) to refuse the application; or

    (b) to adjourn the hearing of it until a time not later than 36 hours after the relevant time.

(9) The person to whom the application relates may be kept in police detention during the adjournment.

(10) A warrant of further detention shall—

    (a) state the time at which it is issued;

    (b) authorise the keeping in police detention of the person to whom it relates for the period stated in it.

(11) Subject to subsection (12) below, the period stated in a warrant of further detention shall be such period as the magistrates' court thinks fit, having regard to the evidence before it.

(12) The period shall not be longer than 36 hours.

(13) If it is proposed to transfer a person in police detention to a police area other than that in which he is detained when the application for a warrant of further detention is made, the court hearing the application shall have regard to the distance and the time the journey would take.

(14) Any information submitted in support of an application under this section shall state—

    (a) the nature of the offence for which the person to whom the application relates has been arrested;

    (b) the general nature of the evidence on which that person was arrested;

    (c) what inquiries relating to the offence have been made by the police and what further inquiries are proposed by them;

(d) the reasons for believing the continued detention of that person to be necessary for the purposes of such further inquiries.

(15) Where an application under this section is refused, the person to whom the application relates shall forthwith be charged or, subject to subsection (16) below, released, either on bail or without bail.

(16) A person need not be released under subsection (15) above—

(a) before the expiry of 24 hours after the relevant time; or

(b) before the expiry of any longer period for which his continued detention is or has been authorised under section 42 above.

(17) Where an application under this section is refused, no further application shall be made under this section in respect of the person to whom the refusal relates, unless supported by evidence which has come to light since the refusal.

(18) Where a warrant of further detention is issued, the person to whom it relates shall be released from police detention, either on bail or without bail, upon or before the expiry of the warrant unless he is charged.

(19) A person released under subsection (18) above shall not be re-arrested without a warrant for the offence for which he was previously arrested unless new evidence justifying a further arrest has come to light since his release; but this subsection does not prevent an arrest under section 46A below.

The maximum length of time for detention authorised by the police is 36 hours. If more time is required before a person can be charged application on a sworn information may be made to a court for a warrant of further detention. The application should be made within court sitting hours if at all possible but the period of detention of 36 hours may sometimes expire at a weekend or other time when a court is not sitting. The time limits should be closely monitored and if the application will need to be made out of court sitting hours the justices' clerk should be notified in advance as a bench must be convened and legal representation for the person detained must be provided. There is also a period of six hours grace if it is impracticable to convene a court within the 36 hours. The court must be satisfied that the grounds of s.43(4) are made out and further detention may be ordered for as long as the court thinks fit up to a maximum of 36 hours. Application may be made on a sworn information to the court to extend a warrant of further detention for up to another 36 hours. The longest period of detention in total must not exceed 96 hours from when it first started to run.

Extension of warrants of further detention.

1–129
44.—(1) On an application on oath made by a constable and supported by an information a magistrates' court may extend a warrant of further detention issued under section 43 above if it is satisfied that there are reasonable grounds for believing that the further detention of the person to whom the application relates is justified.

(2) Subject to subsection (3) below, the period for which a warrant of further detention may be extended shall be such period as the court thinks fit, having regard to the evidence before it.

(3) The period shall not—

(a) be longer than 36 hours; or

(b) end later than 96 hours after the relevant time.

(4) Where a warrant of further detention has been extended under subsection (1) above, or further extended under this subsection, for a period ending before 96 hours after the relevant time, on an application such as is mentioned in that subsection a magistrates' court may further extend the warrant if it is satisfied as there mentioned; and subsections (2) and (3) above apply to such further extensions as they apply to extensions under subsection (1) above.

(5) A warrant of further detention shall, if extended or further extended under this section, be endorsed with a note of the period of the extension.

(6) Subsections (2), (3) and (14) of section 43 above shall apply to an application made under this section as they apply to an application made under that section.

(7) Where an application under this section is refused, the person to whom the application relates shall forthwith be charged or, subject to subsection (8) below, released, either on bail or without bail.

(8) A person need not be released under subsection (7) above before the expiry of any period for which a warrant of further detention issued in relation to him has been extended or further extended on an earlier application made under this section.

E. QUESTIONING AND TREATMENT OF DETAINED PERSONS

(1) Search of detained persons

The police have powers to search persons in detention and to seize and retain **1–130** anything found on them. Such personal searches are not only undertaken to discover, identify and look for evidence but also to remove anything that may be used to cause harm to people or property or assist escape. During detention the police may take fingerprint evidence and also intimate and non-intimate samples for forensic purposes and to obtain a DNA profile. The conduct of searches is regulated by the act and Code C.

Police and Criminal Evidence Act 1984, s.54

Searches of detained persons
54.—(1) The custody officer at a police station shall ascertain everything which a person has with him when he is—
  (a) brought to the station after being arrested elsewhere or after being committed to custody by an order or sentence of a court; or
  (b) arrested at the station or detained there, as a person falling within section 34(7), under section 37 above.
  [(2) The custody officer may record or cause to be recorded all or any of the things which he ascertains under subsection (1).
  (2A) In the case of an arrested person, any such record may be made as part of his custody record.]
  (3) Subject to subsection (4) below, a custody officer may seize and retain any such thing or cause any such thing to be seized and retained.
  (4) Clothes and personal effects may only be seized if the custody officer—
  (a) believes that the person from whom they are seized may use them—
    (i)   to cause physical injury to himself or any other person;
    (ii) to damage property;
    (iii) to interfere with evidence; or
    (iv) to assist him to escape; or
  (b) has reasonable grounds for believing that they may be evidence relating to an offence.
  (5) Where anything is seized, the person from whom it is seized shall be told the reason for the seizure unless he is—
  (a) violent or likely to become violent; or
  (b) incapable of understanding what is said to him.
  (6) Subject to subsection (7) below, a person may be searched if the custody officer considers it necessary to enable him to carry out his duty under subsection (1) above and to the extent that the custody officer considers necessary for that purpose.
  (6A) A person who is in custody at a police station or is in police detention otherwise than at a police station may at any time be searched in order to ascertain whether he has with him anything which he could use for any of the purposes specified in subsection (4)(a) above.
  (6B) Subject to subsection (6C) below, a constable may seize and retain, or cause to be seized and retained, anything found on such a search.
  (6C) A constable may only seize clothes and personal effects in the circumstances specified in subsection (4) above.
  (7) An intimate search may not be conducted under this section.
  (8) A search under this section shall be carried out by a constable.
  (9) The constable carrying out a search shall be of the same sex as the person searched.

[This section is printed with amendments by the *Criminal Justice Act* 1988, s.147

and the *Criminal Justice and Public Order Act* 1994, Sch.10. The amendments of the *Criminal Justice Act* 2003, s.8 are printed in square brackets and came into force in January 2004.]

1–131　The requirement to record property found on a detained person is removed leaving a discretion to do so.

An intimate search is defined in s.65 as a physical examination of body orifices other than the mouth. See also s.62, § 1–139, below.

(2) Searches and examination to ascertain identity

Police and Criminal Evidence Act 1984, s.54A

Searches and examination to ascertain identity

1–132　**54A.**—(1) If an officer of at least the rank of inspector authorises it, a person who is detained in a police station may be searched or examined, or both—

> (a) for the purpose of ascertaining whether he has any mark that would tend to identify him as a person involved in the commission of an offence; or
>
> (b) for the purpose of facilitating the ascertainment of his identity.

(2) An officer may only give an authorisation under subsection (1) for the purpose mentioned in paragraph (a) of that subsection if—

> (a) the appropriate consent to a search or examination that would reveal whether the mark in question exists has been withheld; or
>
> (b) it is not practicable to obtain such consent.

(3) An officer may only give an authorisation under subsection (1) in a case in which subsection (2) does not apply if—

> (a) the person in question has refused to identify himself; or
>
> (b) the officer has reasonable grounds for suspecting that that person is not who he claims to be.

(4) An officer may give an authorisation under subsection (1) orally or in writing but, if he gives it orally, he shall confirm it in writing as soon as is practicable.

(5) Any identifying mark found on a search or examination under this section may be photographed—

> (a) with the appropriate consent; or
>
> (b) if the appropriate consent is withheld or it is not practicable to obtain it, without it.

(6) Where a search or examination may be carried out under this section, or a photograph may be taken under this section, the only persons entitled to carry out the search or examination, or to take the photograph, are constables.

(7) A person may not under this section carry out a search or examination of a person of the opposite sex or take a photograph of any part of the body of a person of the opposite sex.

(8) An intimate search may not be carried out under this section.

(9) A photograph taken under this section—

> (a) may be used by, or disclosed to, any person for any purpose related to the prevention or detection of crime, the investigation of an offence or the conduct of a prosecution; and
>
> (b) after being so used or disclosed, may be retained but may not be used or disclosed except for a purpose so related.

1–133　(10) In subsection (9)—

> (a) the reference to crime includes a reference to any conduct which—
>
> > (i) constitutes one or more criminal offences (whether under the law of a part of the United Kingdom or of a country or territory outside the United Kingdom); or
> >
> > (ii) is, or corresponds to, any conduct which, if it all took place in any one part of the United Kingdom, would constitute one or more criminal offences;
> >
> > and
>
> (b) the references to an investigation and to a prosecution include references, respectively, to any investigation outside the United Kingdom of any crime or

suspected crime and to a prosecution brought in respect of any crime in a country or territory outside the United Kingdom.

(11) In this section—

(a) references to ascertaining a person's identity include references to showing that he is not a particular person; and

(b) references to taking a photograph include references to using any process by means of which a visual image may be produced, and references to photographing a person shall be construed accordingly.

(12) In this section "mark" includes features and injuries; and a mark is an identifying mark for the purposes of this section if its existence in any person's case facilitates the ascertainment of his identity or his identification as a person involved in the commission of an offence.

[This section is printed as inserted by the *Anti-terrorism, Crime and Security Act* 2001, s.90(1) and amended by the *Police Reform Act* 2002, s.107(1).]

Appropriate consent is defined in s.65 as being the consent of the person to be **1–134** searched if they are over 17 years of age; the consent of the person himself and that of his parent or guardian where the person to be searched is aged 14 to 16; and the consent of the parent or guardian of the person to be searched where the person is 13 years of age or less.

(3) Fingerprinting, DNA profiling and samples

Police and Criminal Evidence Act 1984, s.61

Finger-printing

61.—(1) Except as provided by this section no person's fingerprints may be taken without the **1–135** appropriate consent.

(2) Consent to the taking of a person's fingerprints must be in writing if it is given at a time when he is at a police station.

[(3) The fingerprints of a person detained at a police station may be taken without the appropriate consent if—

(a) he is detained in consequence of his arrest for a recordable offence ;and

(b) he has not had his fingerprints taken in the course of the investigation of the offence by the police.]

(3A) [Where a person mentioned in paragraph (a) of subsection (3) or (4) has already had his fingerprints taken in the course of the investigation of the offence by the police] that fact shall be disregarded for the purposes of that subsection if—

(a) the fingerprints taken on the previous occasion do not constitute a complete set of his fingerprints; or

(b) some or all of the fingerprints taken on the previous occasion are not of sufficient quality to allow satisfactory analysis, comparison or matching (whether in the case in question or generally).

[(4) The fingerprints of a person detained at a police station may be taken without the **1–136** appropriate consent if—

(a) he has been charged with a recordable offence or informed that he will be reported for such an offence; and

(b) he has not had his fingerprints taken in the course of the investigation of the offence by the police.]

(4A) The fingerprints of a person who has answered to bail at a court or police station may be taken without the appropriate consent at the court or station if—

(a) the court, or

(b) an officer of at least the rank of inspector,

authorises them to be taken.

(4B) A court or officer may only give an authorisation under subsection (4A) if—

(a) the person who has answered to bail has answered to it for a person whose fingerprints were taken on a previous occasion and there are reasonable grounds for believing that he is not the same person; or

(b) the person who has answered to bail claims to be a different person from a person whose fingerprints were taken on a previous occasion.

1–137   (5) An officer may give an authorisation under [subsection (4A)] above orally or in writing but, if he gives it orally, he shall confirm it in writing as soon as is practicable.

(6) Any person's fingerprints may be taken without the appropriate consent if

     (a) he has been convicted of a recordable offence;

     (b) he has been given a caution in respect of a recordable offence which, at the time of the caution, he has admitted; or

     (c) he has been warned or reprimanded under section 65 of the *Crime and Disorder Act* 1998 for a recordable offence.

(7) In a case where by virtue of [subsection (3), (4) or (6)] above a person's fingerprints are taken without the appropriate consent—

     (a) he shall be told the reason before his fingerprints are taken; and

     (b) the reason shall be recorded as soon as is practicable after the fingerprints are taken.

(7A) If a person's fingerprints are taken at a police station, whether with or without the appropriate consent—

     (a) before the fingerprints are taken, an officer shall inform him that they may be the subject of a speculative search; and

     (b) the fact that the person has been informed of this possibility shall be recorded as soon as is practicable after the fingerprints have been taken.

(8) If he is detained at a police station when the fingerprints are taken, the reason for taking them and, in the case falling within subsection (7A) above, the fact referred to in paragraph (b) of that subsection shall be recorded on his custody record.

(8B) The power to take the fingerprints of a person detained at a police station without the appropriate consent shall be exercisable by any constable.

(9) Nothing in this section—

     [(a) *affects any power conferred by* paragraph 18(2) of Schedule 2 to the *Immigration Act* 1971; *or*]

     (b) applies to a person arrested or detained under the terrorism provisions.

[This section is printed as amended by the *Prevention of Terrorism (Temporary Provisions) Act* 1989, Sch.8, the *Criminal Justice and Public Order Act* 1994, Sch.10, the *Police Reform Act* 2002, Sch.7 and the *Criminal Justice and Police Act* 2001, s.78. The words in square brackets are provisions that are prospectively to be included under the *Criminal Justice and Police Act* 2001, s.78(2) and the words in italics in square brackets are inserted as amended by the *Immigration and Asylum Act* 1999, s.169(1). The sections in square brackets are amendments included in the *Criminal Justice Act* 2003, s.9 which came into force in April 2004.]

1–138   Fingerprints are defined in s.65 as a record in any form and produced by any method, of the skin pattern and other physical characteristics or features of a person's fingers or either of his palms.

Appropriate consent is that of the person to be fingerprinted himself, or in the case of a youth aged 14–16 his consent and that of his parent or guardian and in the case of a youth under the age of 14 the consent of his parent or guardian.

Fingerprints after conviction can be taken under s.27 of *PACE* 1984. The conditions are that the person to be fingerprinted must have been convicted of a recordable offence; he must not have been in police detention at any time for the offence and must not have had prints taken in the course of the investigation or since the conviction. The omission to take prints can be rectified by a requirement for the person to attend and give his prints at the police station within one month after the date of conviction.

Failure to comply with the requirement can lead to arrest.

A person may be identified by fingerprints alone, see Chapter 21, generally for the effect of fingerprint evidence).

A person is detained at a police station and so prints can be taken, when he is held there temporarily having been remanded in custody by the magistrates court: *R. v Seymour* [1995] 9 *Archbold News* 1, CA.

Intimate searches and samples

Police and Criminal Evidence Act 1984, s.55

Intimate searches

55.—(1) Subject to the following provisions of this section, if an officer of at least the rank of **1–139**
inspector has reasonable grounds for believing—

    (a) that a person who has been arrested and is in police detention may have concealed on him anything which—

        (i) he could use to cause physical injury to himself or others; and

        (ii) he might so use while he is in police detention or in the custody of a court;
or

    (b) that such a person—

        (i) may have a Class A drug concealed on him; and

        (ii) was in possession of it with the appropriate criminal intent before his arrest,

he may authorise an intimate search of that person.

(2) An officer may not authorise an intimate search of a person for anything unless he has reasonable grounds for believing that it cannot be found without his being intimately searched.

(3) An officer may give an authorisation under subsection (1) above orally or in writing but, if he gives it orally, he shall confirm it in writing as soon as is practicable.

(4) An intimate search which is only a drug offence search shall be by way of examination by a suitably qualified person.

(5) Except as provided by subsection (4) above, an intimate search shall be by way of examination by a suitably qualified person unless an officer of at least the rank of [superintendent] considers that this is not practicable.

(6) An intimate search which is not carried out as mentioned in subsection (5) above shall be carried out by a constable.

(7) A constable may not carry out an intimate search of a person of the opposite sex.

(8) No intimate search may be carried out except—

    (a) at a police station;

    (b) at a hospital;

    (c) at a registered medical practitioner's surgery; or

    (d) at some other place used for medical purposes.

(9) An intimate search which is only a drug offence search may not be carried out at a police station.

(10) If an intimate search of a person is carried out, the custody record relating to him shall state—

    (a) which parts of his body were searched; and

    (b) why they were searched.

(11) The information required to be recorded by subsection (10) above shall be recorded as soon as practicable after the completion of the search.

(12) The custody officer at a police station may seize and retain anything which is found on an intimate search of a person, or cause any such thing to be seized and retained—

    (a) if he believes that the person from whom it is seized may use it—

        (i) to cause physical injury to himself or any other person;

        (ii) to damage property;

        (iii) to interfere with evidence; or

        (iv) to assist him to escape; or

    (b) if he has reasonable grounds for believing that it may be evidence relating to an offence.

(13) Where anything is seized under this section, the person from whom it is seized shall be told the reason for the seizure unless he is—

    (a) violent or likely to become violent; or

    (b) incapable of understanding what is said to him.

(14) Every annual report—

    (a) under section 22 of the *Police Act* 1996; or

(b) made by the Commissioner of Police of the Metropolis,

shall contain information about searches under this section which have been carried out in the area to which the report relates during the period to which it relates.

(14A) Every annual report under section 57 of the *Police Act* 1997 (reports by Director General of the National Crime Squad) shall contain information about searches authorised under this section by members of the National Crime Squad during the period to which the report relates.

(15) The information about such searches shall include—

(a) the total number of searches;

(b) the number of searches conducted by way of examination by a suitably qualified person;

(c) the number of searches not so conducted but conducted in the presence of such a person; and

(d) the result of the searches carried out.

(16) The information shall also include, as separate items—

(a) the total number of drug offence searches; and

(b) the result of those searches.

(17) In this section—

"the appropriate criminal intent" means an intent to commit an offence under—

(a) section 5(3) of the *Misuse of Drugs Act* 1971 (possession of controlled drug with intent to supply to another); or

(b) section 68(2) of the *Customs and Excise Management Act* 1979 (exportation etc. with intent to evade a prohibition or restriction);

"Class A drug" has the meaning assigned to it by section 2(1)(b) of the *Misuse of Drugs Act* 1971;

"drug offence search" means an intimate search for a Class A drug which an officer has authorised by virtue of subsection (1)(b) above; and

"suitably qualified person" means—

(a) a registered medical practitioner; or

(b) a registered nurse.

[This section is printed as amended by the *Criminal Justice Act* 1988, Sch.15, the *Police Act* 1996, Sch.7 and the *Police Act* 1997, Sch. 9. The word in square brackets in subss.(1) and (5) are printed as prospectively amended by the *Criminal Justice and Police Act* 2001, s.79.]

1–140   An intimate search is physical examination of body orifices other than the mouth, see *PACE* 1984, s.65. The code of practice for the Detention, Treatment and Questioning of Persons, Code C; Annex A gives specific guidance on the conduct of intimate searches. Customs Officers have power to conduct intimate searches only under s.55(1)(a) SI 1985/1800.

Police and Criminal Evidence Act, s.62

Intimate samples

1–141   **62.**—(1) Subject to section 63B below an intimate sample may be taken from a person in police detention only—

(a) if a police officer of at least the rank of inspector authorises it to be taken; and

(b) if the appropriate consent is given.

(1A) An intimate sample may be taken from a person who is not in police detention but from whom, in the course of the investigation of an offence, two or more non-intimate samples suitable for the same means of analysis have been taken which have proved insufficient—

(a) if a police officer of at least the rank of inspector authorises it to be taken; and

(b) if the appropriate consent is given.

(2) An officer may only give an authorisation under subsection (1) or (1A) above if he has reasonable grounds—

(a) for suspecting the involvement of the person from whom the sample is to be taken in a recordable offence; and

(b) for believing that the sample will tend to confirm or disprove his involvement.

(3) An officer may give an authorisation under subsection (1) or (1A) above orally or in writing but, if he gives it orally, he shall confirm it in writing as soon as is practicable.

(4) The appropriate consent must be given in writing.

(5) Where—

(a) an authorisation has been given; and

(b) it is proposed that an intimate sample shall be taken in pursuance of the authorisation,

an officer shall inform the person from whom the sample is to be taken—

(i) of the giving of the authorisation; and

(ii) of the grounds for giving it.

(6) The duty imposed by subsection (5)(ii) above includes a duty to state the nature of the offence in which it is suspected that the person from whom the sample is to be taken has been involved.

(7) If an intimate sample is taken from a person—

(a) the authorisation by virtue of which it was taken;

(b) the grounds for giving the authorisation; and

(c) the fact that the appropriate consent was given,

shall be recorded as soon as is practicable after the sample is taken.

(7A) If an intimate sample is taken from a person at a police station—

(a) before the sample is taken, an officer shall inform him that it may be the subject of a speculative search; and

(b) the fact that the person has been informed of this possibility shall be recorded as soon as practicable after the sample has been taken.

(8) If an intimate sample is taken from a person detained at a police station, the matters required to be recorded by subsection (7) or (7A) above shall be recorded in his custody record.

(9) In the case of an intimate sample which is a dental impression, the sample may be taken from a person only by a registered dentist.

(9A) In the case of any other form of intimate sample, except in the case of a sample of urine, the sample may be taken from a person only by—

(a) a registered medical practitioner; or

(b) a registered health care professional.

(10) Where the appropriate consent to the taking of an intimate sample from a person was refused without good cause, in any proceedings against that person for an offence—

(a) the court, in determining—

(i) whether to commit that person for trial; or

(ii) whether there is a case to answer; and

(aa) a judge, in deciding whether to grant an application made by the accused under—

(i) section 6 of the *Criminal Justice Act* 1987 (application for dismissal of charge of serious fraud in respect of which notice of transfer has been given under section 4 of that Act); or

(ii) paragraph 5 of Schedule 6 to the *Criminal Justice Act* 1991 (application for dismissal of charge of violent or sexual offence involving child in respect of which notice of transfer has been given under section 53 of that Act; and.

(b) the court or jury, in determining whether that person is guilty of the offence charged,

may draw such inferences from the refusal as appear proper.

(11) Nothing in this section applies to the taking of a specimen for the purposes of any of the provisions of sections 4 to 11 of the *Road Traffic Act* 1988 or of sections 26 to 38 of the *Transport and Works Act* 1992.

(12) Nothing in this section, except as provided in section 15(11) and (12) of, and paragraph 7(6A) and (6B) of Schedule 5 to, the *Prevention of Terrorism (Temporary Provisions) Act* 1989, applies to a person arrested or detained under the terrorism provisions. In relation to the taking of an intimate sample from a person where a person is detained under the *Prevention of Terrorism (Temporary Provisions) Act* 1989, Schedule 5, any examining officer, constable or prison officer, or any other person authorised by the Secretary of State, may take all such steps as may be reasonably necessary for photographing, measuring or otherwise identifying him.

Intimate samples

1–142   Intimate samples are defined in s.65 as a sample of blood, semen or any other tissue fluid, urine or pubic hair; a dental impression; a swab taken from a person's body orifice other than the mouth. For appropriate consent, see § 1–139, above.

Authorisation does not have to be sought before consent but if authorisation were granted first any subsequent consent given may be on a dubious basis: *R. v Butt* (unreported). An analysis of the result of intimate samples taken under the provisions of this section in the course of an investigation can be used in proceedings for a separate investigation into a different offence: *R. v Kelt* [1994] 2 All E.R. 780.

Other samples

Police and Criminal Evidence Act 1984, s.63

Other samples

1–143   **63.**—(1) Except as provided by this section, a non-intimate sample may not be taken from a person without the appropriate consent.

(2) Consent to the taking of a non-intimate sample must be given in writing.

[(2A) A non-intimate sample may be taken from a person without the appropriate consent if two conditions are satisfied.

(2B) The first is that the person is in police detention in consequence of his arrest for a recordable offence.

(2C) The second is that—

     (a) he has not had a non-intimate sample of the same type and from the same part of the body taken in the course of the investigation of the offence by the police, or

     (b) he has had such a sample taken but it proved insufficient.]

(3) A non-intimate sample may be taken from a person without the appropriate consent if—

     (a) he is being held in custody by the police on the authority of a court; and

     (b) an officer of at least the rank of *superintendent* authorises it to be taken without the appropriate consent.

(3A) A non-intimate sample may be taken from a person (whether or not he is in police detention or held in custody by the police on the authority of a court) without the appropriate consent if—

     (a) he has been charged with a recordable offence or informed that he will be reported for such an offence; and

     (b) either he has not had a non-intimate sample taken from him in the course of the investigation of the offence by the police or he had a non-intimate sample taken from him but either it was not suitable for the same means of analysis or, though so suitable, the sample proved insufficient.

(3B) A non-intimate sample may be taken from a person without the appropriate consent if he has been convicted of a recordable offence.

(3C) A non-intimate sample may also be taken from a person without the appropriate consent if he is a person to whom section 2 of the *Criminal Evidence (Amendment) Act 1997* applies (persons detained following acquittal on grounds of insanity or finding of unfitness to plead).

(4) An officer may only give an authorisation under subsection (3) above if he has reasonable grounds—

     (a) for suspecting the involvement of the person from whom the sample is to be taken in a recordable offence; and

     (b) for believing that the sample will tend to confirm or disprove his involvement.

1–144   (5) An officer may give an authorisation under subsection (3) above orally or in writing but, if he gives it orally, he shall confirm it in writing as soon as is practicable.

(5A) An officer shall not give an authorisation under subsection (3) above for the taking from any person of a non-intimate sample consisting of a skin impression if—

     (a) a skin impression of the same part of the body has already been taken from that person in the course of the investigation of the offence; and

(b) the impression previously taken is not one that has proved insufficient.

(6) Where—

    (a) an authorisation has been given; and

    (b) it is proposed that a non-intimate sample shall be taken in pursuance of the authorisation,

an officer shall inform the person from whom the sample is to be taken—

      (i) of the giving of the authorisation; and

      (ii) of the grounds for giving it.

(7) The duty imposed by subsection (6)(ii) above includes a duty to state the nature of the offence in which it is suspected that the person from whom the sample is to be taken has been involved.

(8) If a non-intimate sample is taken from a person by virtue of subsection (3) above—

    (a) the authorisation by virtue of which it was taken; and

    (b) the grounds for giving the authorisation,

shall be recorded as soon as is practicable after the sample is taken.

(8A) In a case where by virtue of subsection (2A), (3A), (3B) or (3C) above a sample is taken from a person without the appropriate consent—

    (a) he shall be told the reason before the sample is taken; and

    (b) the reason shall be recorded as soon as practicable after the sample is taken.

(8B) If a non-intimate sample is taken from a person at a police station, whether with or without the appropriate consent—

    (a) before the sample is taken, an officer shall inform him that it may be the subject of a speculative search; and

    (b) the fact that the person has been informed of this possibility shall be recorded as soon as practicable after the sample has been taken.

(9) If a non-intimate sample is taken from a person detained at a police station, the matters required to be recorded by subsection (8) or (8A) or (8B) above shall be recorded in his custody record.   **1–145**

(9ZA) The power to take a non-intimate sample from a person without the appropriate consent shall be exercisable by any constable.

(9A) Subsection (3B) above shall not apply to any person convicted before 10th April 1995 unless he is a person to whom section 1 of the *Criminal Evidence (Amendment) Act* 1997 applies (persons imprisoned or detained by virtue of pre-existing conviction for sexual offence etc).

(10) Nothing in this section applies to a person arrested or detained under the terrorism provisions word substituted by *Criminal Justice and Police Act* 2001, Part 3 section 80(1).

[This section is printed as amended by the *Criminal Justice and Public Order Act* 1994, s.55 and Sch.10, the *Criminal Evidence (Amendment) Act* 1997, ss.1 and 2, the *Criminal Justice and Police Act* 2001, s.80 and the *Police Reform Act* 2002, Sch.7. The word in italics in subs.(3) is not yet in force and neither are the amendments to subss.(9A) and (10). The words in square brackets are amendments included in the *Criminal Justice Act* 2003, s.10 which came into force in April 2004.]

Non-intimate samples include saliva, skin impressions, mouth swabs, hair (other than pubic hair) and samples from under the nails: s.65 of *PACE* 1984.

Supplementary provisions

Police and Criminal Evidence Act 1984, s.63A

Fingerprints and samples: supplementary provisions

63A—(1) Where a person has been arrested on suspicion of being involved in a recordable   **1–146** offence or has been charged with such an offence or has been informed that he will be reported for such an offence, fingerprints or samples or the information derived from samples taken under any power conferred by this Part of this Act from the person may be checked against—

    (a) other fingerprints or samples to which the person seeking to check has access and which are held by or on behalf of any one or more relevant law-enforcement authorities or which are held in connection with or as a result of an investigation of an offence;

(b) information derived from other samples if the information is contained in records to which the person seeking to check has access and which are held as mentioned in paragraph (a) above.

(1A) In subsection (1) above "relevant law-enforcement authority" means—
  (a) a police force;
  (b) the National Criminal Intelligence Service;
  (c) the National Crime Squad;
  (d) a public authority (not falling within paragraphs (a) to (c)) with functions in any part of the British Islands which consist of or include the investigation of crimes or the charging of offenders;
  (e) any person with functions in any country or territory outside the United Kingdom which—
    (i) correspond to those of a police force; or
    (ii) otherwise consist of or include the investigation of conduct contrary to the law of that country or territory, or the apprehension of persons guilty of such conduct;
  (f) any person with functions under any international agreement which consist of or include the investigation of conduct which is—
    (i) unlawful under the law of one or more places,
    (ii) prohibited by such an agreement, or
    (iii) contrary to international law, or the apprehension of persons guilty of such conduct.

(1B) The reference in subsection (1A) above to a police force is a reference to any of the following—
  (a) any police force maintained under section 2 of the *Police Act* 1996 (police forces in England and Wales outside London);
  (b) the metropolitan police force;
  (c) the City of London police force;
  (d) any police force maintained under or by virtue of section 1 of the *Police (Scotland) Act* 1967;
  (e) the Police Service of Northern Ireland;
  (f) the Police Service of Northern Ireland Reserve;
  (g) the Ministry of Defence Police;
  (h) the Royal Navy Regulating Branch;
  (i) the Royal Military Police;
  (j) the Royal Air Force Police;
  (k) the Royal Marines Police;
  (l) the British Transport Police;
  (m) the States of Jersey Police Force;
  (n) the salaried police force of the Island of Guernsey;
  (o) the Isle of Man Constabulary.

1–147   (1C) Where—
  (a) fingerprints or samples have been taken from any person in connection with the investigation of an offence but otherwise than in circumstances to which subsection (1) above applies, and
  (b) that person has given his consent in writing to the use in a speculative search of the fingerprints or of the samples and of information derived from them,

the fingerprints or, as the case may be, those samples and that information may be checked against any of the fingerprints, samples or information mentioned in paragraph (a) or (b) of that subsection.

(1D) A consent given for the purposes of subsection (1C) above shall not be capable of being withdrawn.

(2) Where a sample of hair er than public hair is to be taken the sample may be taken either by cutting hairs or by plucking hairs with their roots so long as no more are plucked than the person taking the sample reasonably considers to be necessary for a sufficient sample.

(3) Where any power to take a sample is exercisable in relation to a person the sample may be taken in a prison or other institution to which the *Prison Act* 1952 applies.

(3A) Where—

    (a) the power to take a non-intimate sample under section 63(3B) above is exercisable in relation to any person who is detained under Part III of the *Mental Health Act* 1983 in pursuance of—

        (i) a hospital order or interim hospital order made following his conviction for the recordable offence in question, or

        (ii) a transfer direction given at a time when he was detained in pursuance of any sentence or order imposed following that conviction, or

    (b) the power to take a non-intimate sample under section 63(3C) above is exercisable in relation to any person,

the sample may be taken in the hospital in which he is detained under that Part of that Act.

Expressions used in this subsection and in the *Mental Health Act* 1983 have the same meaning as in that Act.

(3B) Where the power to take a non-intimate sample under section 63(3B) above is exercisable in relation to a person detained in pursuance of directions of the Secretary of State under section 92 of the *Powers of Criminal Courts (Sentencing) Act* 2000 the sample may be taken at the place where he is so detained.

(4) Any constable may, within the allowed period, require a person who is neither in police detention nor held in custody by the police on the authority of a court to attend a police station in order to have a sample taken where—

    (a) the person has been charged with a recordable offence or informed that he will be reported for such an offence and either he has not had a sample taken from him in the course of the investigation of the offence by the police or he has had a sample so taken from him but either it was not suitable for the same means of analysis or, though so suitable, the sample proved insufficient; or

    (b) the person has been convicted of a recordable offence and either he has not had a sample taken from him since the conviction or he has had a sample taken from him (before or after his conviction) but either it was not suitable for the same means of analysis or, though so suitable, the sample proved insufficient.

(5) The period allowed for requiring a person to attend a police station for the purpose specified in subsection (4) above is— **1–148**

    (a) in the case of a person falling within paragraph (a), one month beginning with the date of the charge or of his being informed as mentioned in that paragraph or one month beginning with the date on which the appropriate officer is informed of the fact that the sample is not suitable for the same means of analysis or has proved insufficient, as the case may be;

    (b) in the case of a person falling within paragraph (b), one month beginning with the date of the conviction or one month beginning with the date on which the appropriate officer is informed of the fact that the sample is not suitable for the same means of analysis or has proved insufficient, as the case may be.

(6) A requirement under subsection (4) above—

    (a) shall give the person at least 7 days within which he must so attend; and

    (b) may direct him to attend at a specified time of day or between specified times of day.

(7) Any constable may arrest without a warrant a person who has failed to comply with a requirement under subsection (4) above.

(8) In this section "the appropriate officer" is—

    (a) in the case of a person falling within subsection (4)(a), the officer investigating the offence with which that person has been charged or as to which he was informed that he would be reported;

    (b) in the case of a person falling within subsection (4)(b), the officer in charge of the police station from which the investigation of the offence of which he was convicted was conducted.

[This section is printed as amended by the *Criminal Justice and Public Order Act* 1994, s.56, the *Criminal Procedure and Investigations Act* 1996, s.64, the *Criminal Evidence (Amendment) Act* 1997, ss.3 and 4, the *Powers of Criminal Courts (Sentencing) Act* 2000, Sch.9 and the *Criminal Justice and Police Act* 2001, s.81.]

1–149   Detention under s.92 of the *Powers of Criminal Courts (Sentencing) Act* 2000 relates to offenders under the age of 18 convicted of murder or other serious offences who are ordered to be detained at her Majesty' pleasure or other specified period.

A recordable offence is one to which regulations in s.27 apply. The *National Police Records (Recordable Offences) Regulations* 2000, SI 2000/1139 provide for the recording in national police records of convictions for and cautions reprimands and warnings given for any offence punishable with imprisonment and any other offence listed in the schedule to the regulations.

This section allows for the checking of fingerprints and samples through several databases as an aid to detection.

Testing for the presence of Class A drugs

1–150   The *Criminal Justice and Police Act* 2001 amended *PACE* 1984 to give powers to the police to test detained persons aged 18 or over for drugs. The power attaches to specified trigger offences only and relates to Class A drugs. The police must have reasonable grounds to suspect that the person's offending is contributed to or caused by a drug habit before requesting that a sample be given. Once a sample has been taken it can be used to inform bail and sentencing decisions. More generally the information may be used to guide supervision whilst in detention and to identify the need for treatment and advice on drug abuse.

Failure to give a sample without good cause is an offence punishable with three months imprisonment or a fine at Level 4.

Police and Criminal Evidence Act 1984, s.63B

Testing for presence of Class A drugs

63B.—(1) A sample of urine or a non-intimate sample may be taken from a person in police detention for the purpose of ascertaining whether he has any specified Class A drug in his body if the following conditions are met.

(2) The first condition is—

(a) that the person concerned has been charged with a trigger offence; or

(b) that the person concerned has been charged with an offence and a police officer of at least the rank of inspector, who has reasonable grounds for suspecting that the misuse by that person of any specified Class A drug caused or contributed to the offence, has authorised the sample to be taken.

(3) The second condition is that the person concerned has attained the age of 18.

(4) The third condition is that a police officer has requested the person concerned to give the sample.

(5) Before requesting the person concerned to give a sample, an officer must—

(a) warn him that if, when so requested, he fails without good cause to do so he may be liable to prosecution, and

(b) in a case within subsection (2)(b) above, inform him of the giving of the authorisation and of the grounds in question.

(6) A sample may be taken under this section only by a person prescribed by regulations made by the Secretary of State by statutory instrument.

No regulations shall be made under this subsection unless a draft has been laid before, and approved by resolution of, each House of Parliament.

(7) Information obtained from a sample taken under this section may be disclosed—

(a) for the purpose of informing any decision about granting bail in criminal proceedings (within the meaning of the *Bail Act* 1976) to the person concerned;

(b) where the person concerned is in police detention or is remanded in or committed to custody by an order of a court or has been granted such bail, for the purpose of informing any decision about his supervision;

(c) where the person concerned is convicted of an offence, for the purpose of informing any decision about the appropriate sentence to be passed by a court and any decision about his supervision or release;

(d) for the purpose of ensuring that appropriate advice and treatment is made available to the person concerned.

(8) A person who fails without good cause to give any sample which may be taken from him under this section shall be guilty of an offence.

The trigger offences are listed in Sch.6 of the *Criminal Justice and Court Services* **1–151**
Act 2000. They are offences under the *Theft Act* 1968, s.1 (Theft), s.8 (burglary), s.9
(Robbery), s.10 (aggravated burglary), s.12 (taking a motor vehicle without consent),s.12A
(aggravated vehicle taking), s.15 (obtaining property by deception), s.25 (going equipped
for theft etc); and offences under the *Misuse of Drugs Act* 1971 if they are in respect of
a Class A drug; s.4 (restriction on production and supply of controlled drugs), s.5(2)
(possession of a controlled drug) and s.5(3) (possession of a controlled drug with intent
to supply). Section 22 of the *Theft Act* 1968 (handling stolen goods) and ss.3 and 4 of
the *Vagrancy Act* 1824 (begging) and attempts to commit para.1 offences are also bigger offences by virtue of SI 2004/1892, with effect from July 27, 2004.

Information from the samples is relevant to bail decisions, sentencing and treatment.

This section is presently in force in the police areas of Nottinghamshire, Staffordshire, and the Metropolitan Police District (SI 2001/2232), Bedfordshire, Devon and
Cornwall, Lancashire, Merseyside, South Yorkshire and North Wales (SI 2002/1149)
and Avon and Somerset, Greater Manchester, Thames Valley and West Yorkshire. (SI
2002/862.) The *Police and Criminal Evidence Act 1984 (Drug Testing of Persons in
Police Detention) (Prescribed persons) Regulations* 2001 SI 2001/2645 lists the relevant persons.

Police and Criminal Evidence Act 1984, s.63C

Testing for presence of Class A drugs: supplementary.

63C.—(1) A person guilty of an offence under section 63B above shall be liable on summary **1–152**
conviction to imprisonment for a term not exceeding three months, or to a fine not exceeding
level 4 on the standard scale, or to both.

(2) A police officer may give an authorisation under section 63B above orally or in writing but, if he gives it orally, he shall confirm it in writing as soon as is practicable.

(3) If a sample is taken under section 63B above by virtue of an authorisation, the authorisation and the grounds for the suspicion shall be recorded as soon as is practicable after the sample is taken.

(4) If the sample is taken from a person detained at a police station, the matters required
to be recorded by subsection (3) above shall be recorded in his custody record.

(5) Subsections (11) and (12) of section 62 above apply for the purposes of section 63B
above as they do for the purposes of that section; and section 63B above does not prejudice the generality of section 62 and 63 above.

(6) In section 63B above—

"Class A drug" and "misuse" have the same meanings as in the *Misuse of Drugs Act*
1971;

"specified"(in relation to a Class A drug) and "trigger offence" have the same meanings as
in Part III of the *Criminal Justice and Court Services Act* 2000.

[This section is printed as inserted by the *Criminal Justice and Police Act* 2001,
s.57.]

Destruction of fingerprints and samples

Police and Criminal Evidence Act 1984, s.64

Destruction of fingerprints and samples

64.—(1A) Where— **1–153**

(a) fingerprints or samples are taken from a person in connection with the investigation of an offence, and

(b) subsection (3) below does not require them to be destroyed, the fingerprints or samples may be retained after they have fulfilled the purposes for which they were taken but shall not be used by any person except for purposes related to the prevention or detection of crime, the investigation of an offence or the conduct of a prosecution.

(1B) In subsection (1A) above—

(a) the reference to using a fingerprint includes a reference to allowing any check to be made against it under section 63A(1) or (1C) above and to disclosing it to any person;

(b) the reference to using a sample includes a reference to allowing any check to be made under section 63A(1) or (1C) above against it or against information derived from it and to disclosing it or any such information to any person;

(c) the reference to crime includes a reference to any conduct which—

    (i) constitutes one or more criminal offences (whether under the law of a part of the United Kingdom or of a country or territory outside the United Kingdom); or

    (ii) is, or corresponds to, any conduct which, if it all took place in any one part of the United Kingdom, would constitute one or more criminal offences;

    and

(d) the references to an investigation and to a prosecution include references, respectively, to any investigation outside the United Kingdom of any crime or suspected crime and to a prosecution brought in respect of any crime in a country or territory outside the United Kingdom.

(3) If—

(a) fingerprints or samples are taken from a person in connection with the investigation of an offence; and

(b) that person is not suspected of having committed the offence,

they must, except as provided in the following provisions of this section, be destroyed as soon as they have fulfilled the purpose for which they were taken.

1–154   (3AA) Samples and fingerprints are not required to be destroyed under subsection (3) above if—

(a) they were taken for the purposes of the investigation of an offence of which a person has been convicted; and

(b) a sample or, as the case may be, fingerprint was also taken from the convicted person for the purposes of that investigation.

(3AB) Subject to subsection (3AC) below, where a person is entitled under subsection (3) above to the destruction of any fingerprint or sample taken from him (or would be but for subsection (3AA) above), neither the fingerprint nor the sample, nor any information derived from the sample, shall be used—

(a) in evidence against the person who is or would be entitled to the destruction of that fingerprint or sample; or

(b) for the purposes of the investigation of any offence;

and subsection (1B) above applies for the purposes of this subsection as it applies for the purposes of subsection (1A) above.

(3AC) Where a person from whom a fingerprint or sample has been taken consents in writing to its retention—

(a) that sample need not be destroyed under subsection (3) above;

(b) subsection (3AB) above shall not restrict the use that may be made of the fingerprint or sample or, in the case of a sample, of any information derived from it; and

(c) that consent shall be treated as comprising a consent for the purposes of section 63A(1C) above;

and a consent given for the purpose of this subsection shall not be capable of being withdrawn.

(3AD) For the purposes of subsection (3AC) above it shall be immaterial whether the consent is given at, before or after the time when the entitlement to the destruction of the fingerprint or sample arises.

(4) Repealed.

(5) If fingerprints are destroyed—

(a) any copies of the fingerprints shall also be destroyed; and

(b) any chief officer of police controlling access to computer data relating to the fingerprints shall make access to the data impossible, as soon as it is practicable to do so.

(6) A person who asks to be allowed to witness the destruction of his fingerprints or copies of them shall have a right to witness it.

(6A) If—

(a) subsection (5)(b) above falls to be complied with; and

(b) the person to whose fingerprints the data relate asks for a certificate that it has been complied with,

such a certificate shall be issued to him, not later than the end of the period of three months beginning with the day on which he asks for it, by the responsible chief officer of police or a person authorised by him or on his behalf for the purposes of this section.

(6B) In this section—

"the responsible chief officer of police" means the chief officer of police in whose police area the computer data were put on to the computer.

(7) Nothing in this section—   **1–155**

(a) affects any power conferred by paragraph 18(2) of Schedule 2 to the *Immigration Act* 1971 or section 20 of the *Immigration and Asylum Act* 1999 (disclosure of police information to the Secretary of State for use for immigration purposes); or

(b) applies to a person arrested or detained under the terrorism provisions.

[This section is printed as amended by the *Criminal Justice Act* 1988, s.148, the *Criminal Justice and Public Order Act* 1994, s.57, the *Police Act* 1996, Sch.7 and the *Criminal Justice and Public Order Act* 2001, ss.82, 137.]

This section has been amended by s.82 of the *Criminal Justice and Police Act* 2001 **1–156** so that it is no longer required to destroy fingerprints and samples and now fingerprints and samples lawfully taken in the course of one investigation can be used in other investigations. The only situation where a request can be made for destruction is by a person who provides prints or a sample and who is not suspected of an offence. This section applies to DNA samples: *R. v Nathaniel* [1995] 2 Cr.App.R. 565.

Fingerprints and samples have been held to be personal and so Art.8 rights to privacy are engaged. The interference of retaining such evidence was held not to be substantial and was also justified under Art.8(2) as being necessary for the prevention of crime and the action was proportionate: *R. (on the application of Marper) v Chief Constable of South Yorkshire* [2003] 1 All E.R. 148.

Previously there was an obligation to destroy such samples etc. but where use was made of samples which should have been destroyed this was held not to vitiate the evidence but to raise the issue of fairness and admissibility under s.78, *PACE* 1984 which was for the trial court to decide. This reasoning must still apply to any samples or prints which are improperly retained under this section: *Att.-Gen.'s Reference (No. 3 of 1999)* [2001] 2 W.L.R. 56.

Photographing of suspects

Police and Criminal Evidence Act 1984, s.64A

Photographing of suspects etc

64A.—(1) A person who is detained at a police station may be photographed—   **1–157**

(a) with the appropriate consent; or

(b) if the appropriate consent is withheld or it is not practicable to obtain it, without it.

(2) A person proposing to take a photograph of any person under this section—

(a) may, for the purpose of doing so, require the removal of any item or substance worn on or over the whole or any part of the head or face of the person to be photographed; and

(b) if the requirement is not complied with, may remove the item or substance himself.

(3) Where a photograph may be taken under this section, the only persons entitled to take the photograph are constables.

(4) A photograph taken under this section—

(a) may be used by, or disclosed to, any person for any purpose related to the prevention or detection of crime, the investigation of an offence or the conduct of a prosecution; and

(b) after being so used or disclosed, may be retained but may not be used or disclosed except for a purpose so related.

(5) In subsection (4)—

(a) the reference to crime includes a reference to any conduct which—

(i) constitutes one or more criminal offences (whether under the law of a part of the United Kingdom or of a country or territory outside the United Kingdom); or

(ii) is, or corresponds to, any conduct which, if it all took place in any one part of the United Kingdom, would constitute one or more criminal offences; and

(b) the references to an investigation and to a prosecution include references, respectively, to any investigation outside the United Kingdom of any crime or suspected crime and to a prosecution brought in respect of any crime in a country or territory outside the United Kingdom.

(6) References in this section to taking a photograph include references to using any process by means of which a visual image may be produced; and references to photographing a person shall be construed accordingly.

[This section is printed as amended by the *Anti-terrorism, Crime and Security Act* 2001, s.92 and the *Police Reform Act* 2002, Sch.7.]

(4) Tape recording of interviews

Police and Criminal Evidence Act 1984, s.60

Tape-recording of interviews

1–158   **60.**—(1) It shall be the duty of the Secretary of State—

(a) to issue a code of practice in connection with the tape-recording of interviews of persons suspected of the commission of criminal offences which are held by police officers at police stations; and

(b) to make an order requiring the tape-recording of interviews of persons suspected of the commission of criminal offences, or of such descriptions of criminal offences as may be specified in the order, which are so held, in accordance with the code as it has effect for the time being.

(2) An order under subsection (1) above shall be made by statutory instrument and shall be subject to annulment in pursuance of a resolution of either House of Parliament.

PACE 1984 Code E is the relevant code for the Tape Recording of Interviews with Suspects. The relevant order by the Secretary of State has been made for all police areas and now all interviews of those suspected of the commission of indictable offences must be tape recorded at police stations. The only exemption is for terrorism offences.

In addition a Practice Direction has been issued about the tape recording of police interviews in relation to the preparation for proceedings in the Crown Court which may also assist for magistrates court proceedings. Guidance was also given in the case of *R. v Rampling* [1987] Crim.L.R. 823. See *Archbold Crown* for details—§ 15–228.

Equipment is available for tapes to be played in the magistrates' courts and either full or edited transcripts may be adduced as evidence by the interviewing officer.

Several Home Office Circulars have been published with further guidance for police officers on the operation of the tape recording of interviews. See Home Office Circulars 76/1988, 26/1995 and 47/1995.

(5) Visual recording of interviews

Police and Criminal Evidence Act 1984, s.60A

Visual recording of interviews

1–159   **60A.**—(1) The Secretary of State shall have power—

(a) to issue a code of practice for the visual recording of interviews held by police officers at police stations; and

(b) to make an order requiring the visual recording of interviews so held, and requiring the visual recording to be in accordance with the code for the time being in force under this section.

(2) A requirement imposed by an order under this section may be imposed in relation to such cases or police stations in such areas, or both, as may be specified or described in the order.

(3) An order under subsection (1) above shall be made by statutory instrument and shall be subject to annulment in pursuance of a resolution of either House of Parliament.

(4) In this section—

(a) references to any interview are references to an interview of a person suspected of a criminal offence; and

(b) references to a visual recording include references to a visual recording in which an audio recording is comprised.

Orders allow for visual recording of interviews at the following police stations; Basingstoke, Portsmouth, Southampton, Chatham, Gravesend, Tonbridge, Bromley, Collingdale, Edmonton, Redditch, Telford, Worcester, Harlow, Colchester and Southend. (SI 2002/1069, 2002/2527)

PACE 1984 Code F is the Code of Practice covering the Visual Recording of Interviews with Suspects.

(6) Right to have someone informed when arrested

Police and Criminal Evidence Act 1984, s.56

Right to have someone informed when arrested

56.—(1) Where a person has been arrested and is being held in custody in a police station or **1–160** other premises, he shall be entitled, if he so requests, to have one friend or relative or other person who is known to him or who is likely to take an interest in his welfare told, as soon as is practicable except to the extent that delay is permitted by this section, that he has been arrested and is being detained there.

(2) Delay is only permitted—

(a) in the case of a person who is in police detention for a serious arrestable offence; and

(b) if an officer of at least the rank of [superintendent] authorises it.

(3) In any case the person in custody must be permitted to exercise the right conferred by subsection (1) above within 36 hours from the relevant time, as defined in section 41(2) above.

(4) An officer may give an authorisation under subsection (2) above orally or in writing but, if he gives it orally, he shall confirm it in writing as soon as is practicable.

(5) Subject to subsection (5A) below an officer may only authorise delay where he has reasonable grounds for believing that telling the named person of the arrest—

(a) will lead to interference with or harm to evidence connected with a serious arrestable offence or interference with or physical injury to other persons; or

(b) will lead to the alerting of other persons suspected of having committed such an offence but not yet arrested for it; or

(c) will hinder the recovery of any property obtained as a result of such an offence.

(5A) An officer may also authorise delay where he has reasonable grounds for believing that—

(a) the person detained for the serious arrestable offence has benefited from his criminal conduct, and

(b) the recovery of the value of the property constituting the benefit will be hindered by telling the named person of the arrest.

(5B) For the purposes of subsection (5A) above the question whether a person has benefited from his criminal conduct is to be decided in accordance with Part 2 of the *Proceeds of Crime Act* 2002.

(6) If a delay is authorised—

(a) the detained person shall be told the reason for it; and

(b) the reason shall be noted on his custody record.

(7) The duties imposed by subsection (6) above shall be performed as soon as is practicable.

(8) The rights conferred by this section on a person detained at a police station or other premises are exercisable whenever he is transferred from one place to another; and this section applies to each subsequent occasion on which they are exercisable as it applies to the first such occasion.

(9) There may be no further delay in permitting the exercise of the right conferred by subsection (1) above once the reason for authorising delay ceases to subsist.

(10) Nothing in this section applies to a person arrested or detained under the terrorism provisions.

[This section is printed as amended by the *Drug Trafficking Offences Act* 1986, s.32, the *Criminal Justice Act* 1988, s.99 and the *Terrorism Act* 2000, s.125. The word in square brackets in subs.(2)(b) is inserted by the *Criminal Justice and Police Act* 2001, s.74 from a date to be appointed. Subsection (5A) is substituted by subss.(5A) and (5B) by the *Proceeds of Crime Act* 2002, s.456 from March 24, 2003.]

1–161   A serious arrestable offence is defined in s.116 of *PACE* 1984.

The code of Practice for the Detention, Treatment and Questioning of persons by Police officers—Code C deals with the right of a person detained at the police station not to be held incommunicado (Para.C5) and Annex B deals with the delay in notifying arrest or allowing access to legal advice.

(7) Right of access to a solicitor

Police and Criminal Evidence Act 1984, s.58

Access to legal advice

1–162   58.—(1) A person arrested and held in custody in a police station or other premises shall be entitled, if he so requests, to consult a solicitor privately at any time.

(2) Subject to subsection (3) below, a request under subsection (1) above and the time at which it was made shall be recorded in the custody record.

(3) Such a request need not be recorded in the custody record of a person who makes it at a time while he is at a court after being charged with an offence.

(4) If a person makes such a request, he must be permitted to consult a solicitor as soon as is practicable except to the extent that delay is permitted by this section.

(5) In any case he must be permitted to consult a solicitor within 36 hours from the relevant time, as defined in section 41(2) above.

(6) Delay in compliance with a request is only permitted—

(a) in the case of a person who is in police detention for a serious arrestable offence; and

(b) if an officer of at least the rank of superintendent authorises it.

(7) An officer may give an authorisation under subsection (6) above orally or in writing but, if he gives it orally, he shall confirm it in writing as soon as is practicable.

(8) Subject to subsection (8A) below an officer may only authorise delay where he has reasonable grounds for believing that the exercise of the right conferred by subsection (1) above at the time when the person detained desires to exercise it—

(a) will lead to interference with or harm to evidence connected with a serious arrestable offence or interference with or physical injury to other persons; or

(b) will lead to the alerting of other persons suspected of having committed such an offence but not yet arrested for it; or

(c) will hinder the recovery of any property obtained as a result of such an offence.

(8A) An officer may also authorise delay where he has reasonable grounds for believing that—

(a) the person detained for the serious arrestable offence has benefited from his criminal conduct, and

(b) the recovery of the value of the property constituting the benefit will be hindered by the exercise of the right conferred by subsection (1) above.

(8B) For the purposes of subsection (8A) above the question whether a person has benefited from his criminal conduct is to be decided in accordance with Part 2 of the *Proceeds of Crime Act* 2002.

(9) If delay is authorised—

    (a) the detained person shall be told the reason for it; and

    (b) the reason shall be noted on his custody record.

(10) The duties imposed by subsection (9) above shall be performed as soon as is practicable.

(11) There may be no further delay in permitting the exercise of the right conferred by subsection (1) above once the reason for authorising delay ceases to subsist.

(12) Nothing in this section applies to a person arrested or detained under the terrorism provisions.

[This section is printed as amended by the *Drug Trafficking Offences Act* 1986, s.32, the *Criminal Justice Act* 1988, s.99 and the *Terrorism Act* 2000, s.125. Subsection (8A) is substituted by subss.(8A) and (8B) of the *Proceeds of Crime Act* 2002, s.456, from March 24, 2003.]

Under the Code of Practice for the Detention, Treatment and Questioning of **1–163** Persons—Code C the obligation to inform of the right to consult a solicitor only applies to persons under arrest at a police station or in police detention elsewhere. This right does not extend to persons arrested and detained by an officer before arriving at the police station .It does not extend to persons remanded in custody at a magistrates court but they have a right of access to a solicitor at common law upon request and as soon as is reasonably practicable: *R. v Chief Constable of South Wales Ex p. Merrick* [1994] 1 W.L.R. 663.

Access to legal advice may only be delayed for up to 36 hours from the relevant time **1–164** and only if a person is detained for a serious arrestable offence and such delay is authorised by an officer of at least the rank of superintendent. The relevant time as defined in s.41(2) is the time at which the person arrives at the police station where he is detained or the time 24 hours after the time of the person's arrest, whichever is the earlier. Section 58(8) specifies the grounds upon which delay may be permitted.

A different regime applies to those detained on terrorist charges.

Code C and Annex B thereto deal with the right to a lawyer and the reasons for denying access. It will be a rare and unusual case when the conditions of s.58(8) are met. The situation was considered in detail in the case of *R. v Samuel* [1988] Q.B. 615. The right of access to legal advice was described by the court as "one of the most important and fundamental rights of a citizen" which was not to be lightly denied. Access to a solicitor can only be refused for the reasons given in s.58(8) when the officer believes that a solicitor will effectively commit a criminal offence by interfering with evidence or witnesses or alerting other suspects or hindering the recovery of property. To justify such belief very specific evidence about the detained person and the actual solicitor involved is required. The court also considered the scenario of a solicitor being used unwittingly by a defendant to act as described under the subsection and said that a very sophisticated and manipulative defendant would be the only type who could hoodwink a professional solicitor to that extent, so very strong and specific evidence about the specific detained person would be required.

See also *R. v Silcott, Braithwaite and Raghip, The Times*, December 9, 1991.   **1–165**

A blanket ban cannot be put on suspect solicitors but the Chief Constable may under Code C, para.6 advise that a certain solicitor may hinder an investigation and then the appropriate officer in the case can decide if he should be excluded: *R. v Thompson and the Chief Constable of Northumbria* [2001] 1 W.L.R. 1342.

Where there is a breach of s.58 and access is denied wrongfully, issues about admis- **1–166** sibility of evidence will need to be considered under *PACE* 1984, ss.76 and 78, see Chapter 21. A breach of s.58 does not mean that the evidence will be automatically rejected. This is a matter for the court to decide in each individual case.

Lack of legal representation was held not to fall within the unfairness of s.78 when the defendant had been arrested and convicted previously and was aware of his rights on arrest: *R. v Dunford* (1990) 1 Cr.App.R. 150. The presence of a solicitor's clerk rather than a solicitor at interview was held not to amount to a breach of s.58 that could justify exclusion of evidence under s.78: *R. v Dunn* (1990) 1 Cr.App.R. 237.

An arrested person cannot justify his failure to provide a specimen under s.7 of the *Road Traffic Act* 1988 on the ground that he wished to have access to a solicitor under this section: *DPP v Billington* (1988) 87 Cr.App.R. 68.

1–167   Article 6 of the European Convention on Human Rights protects the right to a fair trial and Art.6(3) requires that an accused be allowed the benefit of legal advice in the initial stages of interrogation as he has the right to adequate time and facilities for the preparation of his defence: *Murray v UK* (1996) 22 E.H.R.R. 29. If an accused's right to exercise his defence rights has been infringed, it is not necessary to prove that the interference had a prejudicial effect on the course of the trial, so where confidentiality of a conference with a lawyer was not ensured this was held to be a violation of Art.6 invalidating a conviction: *Brennan v UK* (2002) 34 E.H.R.R. 18. The court will consider whether the infringement has a real possibility of prejudicing the defence right to prepare the case and the taking of defence instructions through a wicket of a cell door and the giving of instructions over the telephone in the presence of an officer were held not to violate Art.6(3)(b): *R. (M) v Commissioner of Metropolitan Police*; *R. (La Rose) v the same* [2002] Crim.L.R. 215.

1–168   The concept of "equality of arms" under Art.6 imposes on the state a positive obligation to ensure that the defence does not act under a disadvantage in comparison to the prosecution: *Patanki and Dunshirn v Austria* [1963] 6 V.B. 714. The duty under s.58 and the Codes are the measures in place to try to meet that obligation.

CHAPTER 2

CONSTITUTION AND JURISDICTION

I. INTRODUCTION

The magistrates' court is a creature of statute and although the office of justice of the **2–1** peace dates back to the 14th century the powers of the present day magistrate are based on more recent Acts of Parliament. The relevant statutes are the *Magistrates' Courts Act* 1980 which essentially outlines the jurisdiction and powers of the court and the *Justices of the Peace Act* 1997 which provides for the appointment of magistrates, justices' clerks and district judges and the administration of the court. The *Criminal Justice Act* 2003 and the *Courts Act* 2003 provide for amendments to the administration and powers of magistrates courts.

Magistrates' Courts Act 1980, s.148

"Magistrates' court"

148.—(1) In this Act the expression "magistrates' court" means any justice or justices of the **2–2** peace acting under any enactment or by virtue of his or their commission or under the common law.

(2) Except where the contrary is expressed, anything authorised or required by this Act to be done by, to or before the magistrates' court by, to or before which any other thing was done, or is to be done, may be done by, to or before any magistrates' court acting for the same petty sessions area as that court.

A magistrates' court has no jurisdiction unless it is specifically conferred by statute. It is an inferior court and has no inherent jurisdiction. It is not a court of record so transcripts are not taken. The legal Adviser may take a manual note of proceedings but this is not a verbatim record. The final record of all decisions and adjudications is the court register which is generally computer generated and stored. Decisions of the magistrates' courts are subject to appeal to the Crown Court on fact and by way of case stated or judicial review to the High Court on cases of law or mixed fact and law, see Chapter 22.

A magistrates' court normally comprises of a district judge or magistrates. A district judge will sit alone and magistrates will sit in benches of not less than two or more than three magistrates: *Magistrates' Courts Act* 1980, s.121; *Justices of the Peace (Size and Chairmanship of Bench) Rules* 2002. Normally there are three magistrates and objection may be taken to less than that number particularly when trials are to be heard. The problem with a bench of only two is the potential for disagreement. Some exceptions apply where magistrates may sit alone to conduct committals or to adjourn cases and also to give directions in early administrative hearings: *Magistrates' Courts Act* 1980, s.4, 10; *Crime and Disorder Act* 1998, ss.49 and 50.

II. JUDGES OF THE MAGISTRATES' COURTS

2–3   The jurisdiction of the magistrates' courts may be exercised by magistrates or district judges (magistrates' courts) sitting in court with the justices' clerk or a qualified legal adviser.

Magistrates, otherwise known as Justices of the Peace, are part-time unpaid volunteers and district judges are lawyers appointed to a full-time salaried post.

(1) Justices of the Peace

Justices of the Peace Act 1997, ss.5, 6

Appointment and removal of justices of the peace

2–4   **5.**—(1) Subject to the following provisions of this Act, justices of the peace for any commission area shall be appointed by the Lord Chancellor by instrument on behalf and in the name of Her Majesty and a justice so appointed may be removed from office in like manner.

(2) Subsection (1) above—

(a) does not apply to [District Judges (Magistrates' Courts).]

Residence qualification

2–5   **6.**—(1) Subject to the provisions of this section, a person shall not be appointed as a justice of the peace for a commission area in accordance with section 5 above, nor act as a justice of the peace by virtue of any such appointment, unless he resides in or within 15 miles of that area.

(1A) If a person who is the Lord Mayor or an alderman of the City of London is appointed in accordance with section 5 above as a justice of the peace for a commission area including the City of London, subsection (1) above shall not apply in relation to his appointment as a justice of the peace for that area so long as he holds either of those offices.

(2) If the Lord Chancellor is of the opinion that it is in the public interest for a person to act as a justice of the peace for a particular area though not qualified to do so under subsection (1) above, he may direct that, so long as any conditions specified in the direction are satisfied, that subsection shall not apply in relation to that person's appointment as a justice of the peace for the area so specified.

(3) Where a person appointed as a justice of the peace for a commission area in accordance with section 5 above is not qualified under the preceding provisions of this section to act by virtue of the appointment, he shall be removed from office as a justice of the peace in accordance with that section if the Lord Chancellor is of the opinion that the appointment ought not to continue having regard to the probable duration and other circumstances of the lack of qualification.

(4) No act or appointment shall be invalidated by reason only of the disqualification or lack of qualification under this section of the person acting or appointed.

[These sections are printed as amended by the *Access to Justice Act* 1999, Schs 10, 11 and 15.]

2–6   The residence qualification is designed to ensure that local justice is meted out by magistrates who will have some knowledge of the area in which they sit. Exception is made for the City of London where historically Aldermen and the Lord Mayor sit as magistrates by virtue of their office.

Justices of the Peace, also referred to as magistrates, do not receive a salary for their work but they may claim expenses for travel, subsistence and financial loss: *Justices of the Peace Act* 1997, s.10. No legal qualification is needed but conversely, there is no bar to barristers or solicitors holding office as a magistrate. Training is organised by the Magistrates' Courts Committee and the justices' clerk has responsibility for ensuring that appropriate training is delivered. In order to take the chair in court, a magistrate must have successfully completed a chairmanship training course as approved by the Lord Chancellor in accordance with the *Justices of the Peace (Size and Chairmanship of the Bench) Rules* 2002. This consists of formal training sessions and appraised sittings in the chair. All magistrates are formally appraised on a continuing basis.

Magistrates are addressed in Court through the Chairman as 'Sir' or 'Madam' and collectively as 'Your Worships'.

(2) District Judges (Magistrates' Courts)

Justices of the Peace Act 1997, ss.10A, 10C, 10D, 10E(1)

Appointment and Tenure

10A.—(1) Her Majesty may, on the recommendation of the Lord Chancellor, appoint a **2–7** person who has a 7 year general qualification (within the meaning of section 71 of the *Courts and Legal Services Act* 1990) to be a District Judge (Magistrates' Courts).

(2) The Lord Chancellor—

    (a) shall designate one of the District Judges (Magistrates' Courts) to be the Senior District Judge (Chief Magistrate); and

    (b) may designate another of them to be his deputy.

(3) A District Judge (Magistrates' Courts) may not be removed from office except by the Lord Chancellor on the ground of incapacity or misbehaviour.

(4) The Lord Chancellor may pay to a District Judge (Magistrates' Courts) (in addition to the salary charged on and paid out of the Consolidated Fund under section 9 of the *Administration of Justice Act* 1973) such allowances as he may, with the approval of the Treasury, determine.

Status

10C.—(1) A District Judge (Magistrates' Courts) shall by virtue of his office be a justice of the **2–8** peace for every commission area.

(2) Where any enactment makes provision defining the powers of any person or court by reference to the area for which a person is a justice of the peace, the provision shall have effect where that person is a District Judge (Magistrates' Courts) as if it defined the powers by reference to the area for which he is for the time being acting as a justice of the peace.

(3) A District Judge (Magistrates' Courts) shall sit at such court-houses, on such days and at such times, as may be determined by, or in accordance with, directions given by the Lord Chancellor from time to time.

(4) References in any enactment, instrument or other document to a district judge or deputy district judge do not include a District Judge (Magistrates' Courts).

Power to discharge functions exercisable by two justices

10D.—(1) A District Judge (Magistrates' Courts), sitting in a place appointed for the purpose, **2–9** shall have power—

    (a) to do any act; and

    (b) to exercise alone any jurisdiction,

which can be done or exercised by two justices, including any act or jurisdiction expressly required to be done or exercised by justices sitting or acting in petty sessions.

(2) Subsection (1) above does not apply where the law under which the act or jurisdiction can be done or exercised was made after 2nd August 1858 and contains express provision contrary to that subsection.

(3) Any statutory provision auxiliary to the jurisdiction exercisable by two justices of the peace shall apply also to the jurisdiction of a District Judge (Magistrates' Courts).

(4) [Licensing]

(5) Any authority or requirement in any enactment for persons to be summoned or to

appear at petty sessions in any case shall include authority or a requirement in such a case for persons to be summoned or to appear before a District Judge (Magistrates' Courts) at the place appointed for his sitting.

(6) [Family Proceedings]

Disapplication of restrictions

2–10   **10E.**—(1) Nothing in the *Magistrates' Courts Act* 1980—

(a) requiring a magistrates' court to be composed of two or more justices or to sit in a petty sessional court-house or an occasional court-house; or

(b) limiting the powers of a magistrates' court when composed of a single justice or when sitting elsewhere than in a petty sessional court-house,

shall apply to any District Judge (Magistrates' Courts) sitting in a place appointed for the purpose.

(2) [Family Proceedings]

[These sections are reprinted as amended by the *Access to Justice Act* 1999, s.78.]

District judges (magistrates' courts) are professional, salaried members of the judiciary. Until 1997 they were called stipendiary magistrates and were appointed to particular commission areas generally within large metropolitan areas such as London, Manchester and Leeds. The *Justices of the Peace Act* 1997, s.10A changed the description of the judicial office to district judge (magistrates' courts) and established a national bench led by the senior district judge (chief magistrate). The district judge will usually still be assigned to a commission area but may be directed by the Department for Constitutional Affairs through the senior district judge to sit at any court in England and Wales as required: *Access to Justice Act* 1999, s.78.

2–11   The district judge retains the jurisdiction of the Petty Sessions area no matter where he might sit and can be accommodated in any court within the commission area to deal with cases arising from their own petty sessions area. Unlike magistrates, a district judge (magistrates' court) will always sit alone in all criminal proceedings: *Justices of the Peace Act* 1997, s.10D(b).

The Judicial Studies Board is responsible for training district judges and delivers induction and continuing training. Certain district judges are designated by the Lord Chancellor or the senior district judge to deal with particular types of specialist work such as youth court cases, extradition and applications for warrants of further detention under the *Terrorism Act* 2000.

A district judge is addressed as 'Sir' or 'Madam'.

(3) Justices' clerks

2–12   The justices' clerk and legal advisers give advice on law, practice and procedure to the magistrates and district judges.

Justices of the Peace Act 1997, ss.42(1), (2), 43, 45, 48

Appointment and removal of justices' clerks

42.—(1) Justices' clerks shall be appointed by the magistrates' courts committee; and a magistrates' courts committee may appoint more than one justices' clerk for any petty sessions area.

(2) A person may not be appointed as justices' clerk unless—

(a) the magistrates' courts committee have submitted to the Lord Chancellor, in accordance with regulations, an application for approval of one or more persons offering themselves for the appointment;

(b) the Lord Chancellor has approved one or more of those persons; and

(c) the person appointed is a person so approved.

Qualifications for appointment as justices' clerk

2–13   **43.** No person shall be appointed as justices' clerk unless either—

(a) at the time of appointment—

(i) he has a 5 year magistrates' courts qualification (within the meaning of section 71 of the *Courts and Legal Services Act* 1990); or

(ii) he is a barrister or solicitor and has served for not less than five years as assistant to a justices' clerk; or

(b) he then is or has previously been a justices' clerk.

General powers and duties of justices' clerks

45.—(1) Rules made in accordance with section 144 of the *Magistrates' Courts Act* 1980 **2–14** may (except to the extent that any enactment passed after this Act otherwise directs) make provision enabling things authorised to be done by, to or before a single justice of the peace to be done instead by, to or before a justices' clerk.

(2) Such rules may also make provision enabling things authorised to be done by, to or before a justices' clerk (whether by virtue of subsection (1) above or otherwise) to be done instead by, to or before a person appointed by a magistrates' courts committee to assist him.

(3) Any enactment (including any enactment contained in this Act) or any rule of law which—

(a) regulates the exercise of any jurisdiction or powers of justices of the peace; or

(b) relates to things done in the exercise or purported exercise of any such jurisdiction or powers,

shall apply in relation to the exercise or purported exercise of any such jurisdiction or powers by the clerk to any justices by virtue of subsection (1) above as if he were one of those justices.

(4) The functions of a justices' clerk include giving advice to the justices to whom he is clerk, at their request, about [matters of law (including procedure and practice)] on questions arising in connection with the discharge of their functions, including questions arising when the clerk is not personally attending on them.

(5) The powers of a justices' clerk include, at any time when he thinks he should do so, bringing to the attention of those justices any point of matters of law [including procedure and practice] that is or may be involved in any question so arising.

(6) For the purposes of subsections (4) and (5) above the functions of justices of the peace do not include functions as a judge of the Crown Court.

(7) Subsections (4) and (5) above—

(a) apply in relation to any of the justices to whom the justices' clerk is clerk as they apply in relation to all of them; and

(b) do not define or in any respect limit—

(i) the powers and duties of a justices' clerk; or

(ii) the matters on which justices may obtain assistance from their clerk.

Independence of justices' clerks and staff exercising legal functions

48.—(1) When exercising any legal function— **2–15**

(a) a justices' clerk shall not be subject to the direction of the justices' chief executive or any other person or body; and

(b) a member of the staff of a magistrates' courts committee shall not be subject to the direction of any person or body other than a justices' clerk.

(2) In subsection (1) "legal function" means—

(a) any function exercisable by one or more justices of the peace; or

(b) a function specified in section 45(4) or (5) above.

[These sections are reprinted as amended by the *Access to Justice Act* 1999, s.89.]

The role of the justices' clerk is to advise the magistrates on the law, practice and **2–16** procedure. These areas often overlap so advice is required on issues of mixed fact and law. The justices' clerk manages a team of legal advisers to whom powers are delegated to give legal advice to district judges and magistrates both in and out of Court. Most legal advisers are solicitors or barristers and others hold recognised Court Clerk qualifications. The magistrate is not obliged to accept the advice and it is the bench, not the legal adviser who is the ultimate decision maker on questions of law and fact. However it is accepted practice that they should do so, see *Jones v Nicks* [1977] R.T.R. 72 when the Bench acted against the advice of the legal adviser and accepted that the adverse effect on employment was a special reason not to endorse a driving licence. On appeal, it was held that the legal adviser had correctly explained the law to them and their decision against this advice was a nullity. Any magistrate will ignore legal advice at their peril for if a decision is made unsupported by the advice of the legal adviser, they could be held liable for errors affecting the liberty of the subject, *etc*. The *Practice Direction (Criminal Proceedings: Consolidation)* [2002] 1 W.L.R. 2870 gives detailed explanation of the role of the legal adviser including the method in which advice should be tendered.

Legal advisers are required under the *Practice Direction (Criminal Proceedings: Consolidation)* to advise on questions of law (including Human Rights) questions of mixed law and fact, matters of practice and procedure, other issues relevant to the matter before the court and structured decision making. The Legal Adviser will also assist the court in drawing up and recording the reasons for decisions. At all times the Legal Adviser must exercise care not to trespass on the judicial responsibility of the bench by usurping its functions.

2–17   The legal adviser's role is to advise on these matters only and they must not appear to be trying to influence the magistrate's factual decisions: *Stafford Justices Ex p. Ross* [1962] 1 W.L.R. 456. In this case the clerk to the justices was seen to pass a note to the magistrates which contained an argument on the facts pointing to the guilt of the accused. The conviction was quashed on appeal as it was held that the clerk was attempting to influence the decision of the magistrates on matters of fact. The legal adviser has a duty to ensure that every case is conducted fairly and that responsibility may incorporate assisting unrepresented defendants, taking notes of the evidence as a reminder and also asking questions of witnesses and parties to clarify evidence or issues in the case.

The legal adviser should not retire with the magistrates as a matter of course when they consider their verdict. If once the magistrates leave court, the legal adviser becomes aware that there is a point of law upon which they might require assistance then an approach may be made to the magistrates in the retiring room, see *Uxbridge Justices Ex p. Smith* (1985) 149 J.P. 620, where counsel for the defence referred to a passage in a legal text book as support for his submission. The Bench retired and the legal adviser took the opportunity of reading the passage in full and then informed counsel that she was going to see the magistrates in the retiring room to advise them of her view on the law. On appeal the court held that in the absence of any indication or suspicion that the legal adviser had taken part in deciding questions of fact or the verdict, she was just carrying out her responsibility to advise the bench on the law. In *Consett Justices Ex p. Postal Bingo Ltd* [1967] 2 Q.B. 9, the interventions of the justices' clerk were even more marked but nevertheless on appeal the court held that he was acting in accordance with his duties to advise the bench. The case involved a complex matter of mixed law and fact. The justices' clerk went out with the magistrates to the retiring room together with his assistant and stayed there for over two hours of deliberations. The High Court held that the bench were entitled to his advice on 'entangled questions of law and fact' and that his presence on their retirement did not invalidate the decision. In *R. v Eccles Justices Ex p. Fitzpatrick* (1989) 89 Cr.App.R. 324, the clerk initially refused to allow the defendant to apply to the magistrates to change his plea and then went out to join the bench in the retiring room for about 25 minutes without being requested to do so. After a guilty plea was entered the clerk left court again with the bench and stayed in the retiring room with them for 30 minutes. The magistrates' decision to commit the defendant to the Crown Court for sentence was quashed on appeal. It was held that the clerk should not retire with the magistrates unless clearly requested to do so. In the absence of any dispute on the law the magistrates did not need the advice of their clerk and his querying the motives behind a request to have the plea put again was improper. There was a reasonable suspicion of interference by the clerk which made the process unsafe.

2–18   The law has moved on since these cases and it is doubtful that such a wide interpretation would now be given to the advisory role of the justices' clerk. The *Human Rights Act* 1998 has had an impact on the transparency of communications between magistrates and legal advisers as expressed in the *Practice Direction (Criminal Proceedings: Consolidation)*. The courts will be expected to limit and explain all consultations that take place out of court so that justice is seen to be done and Art.6 of the ECHR is observed.

Legal advice should be given in open court. Where advice is given in the retiring room without having been previously canvassed in open court it will be given on a provisional basis only to the magistrates. The substance of the advice should be repeated in open court allowing the parties to make representations and then the advice will be stated in open court with amendments as required.

Where the defendant is unrepresented the legal adviser is under a duty to assist both the defendant and the court. This will consist of explaining procedures to the defendant and where evidence is given in a trial, identifying the points in issue and ensuring appropriate questions are put to witnesses and assisting the defendant to give evidence if they so wish so that opportunity is provided to put the defence case fully: *R. v Chichester Justices Ex p. DPP* (1993) 157 J.P. 1049.

Under the *Justices' Clerks Rules* 1999, r.2, justices' clerks may perform tasks which are authorised to be done by, to or before a single magistrate. The powers are specified in the Schedule to the Rules and include the issue of summonses, allowing agreed adjournments, granting criminal defence representation orders and the giving of directions in trials. The justices' clerk may delegate these powers to the legal advisers. In practice this means that the legal adviser will often deal with cases whilst the Bench retire to consider other matters. The justices' clerk may also sit alone to conduct early administrative hearings where the powers allow for pleas to be taken; remands on agreed bail and directions relating to trials to be given: *Crime and Disorder Act* 1998, s.50.

III. SITTING OF THE MAGISTRATES' COURTS

Magistrates' Courts Act 1980, s.121

Constitution and place of sitting of court

121.—(1) A magistrates' court shall not try an information summarily or hear a complaint **2–19** except when composed of at least 2 justices unless the trial or hearing is one that by virtue of any enactment may take place before a single justice.

(2) A magistrates' court shall not hold an inquiry into the means of an offender for the purposes of section 82 above or determine under that section at a hearing at which the offender is not present whether to issue a warrant of commitment except when composed of at least 2 justices.

(3) A magistrates' court shall not—
    (a) try summarily an information for an indictable offence or hear a complaint except when sitting in a petty-sessional court-house;
    (b) try an information for a summary offence or hold an inquiry into the means of an offender for the purposes of section 82 above, or impose imprisonment, except when sitting in a petty-sessional court-house or an occasional court-house.

(4) Subject to the provisions of any enactment to the contrary, where a magistrates' court is required by this section to sit in a petty-sessional or occasional court-house, it shall sit in open court.

(5) A magistrates' court composed of a single justice, or sitting in an occasional court-house, shall not impose imprisonment for a period exceeding 14 days or order a person to pay more than £1.

(6) Subject to the provisions of subsection (7) below, the justices composing the court before which any proceedings take place shall be present during the whole of the proceedings; but if during the course of the proceedings any justice absents himself, he shall cease to act further therein and, if the remaining justices are enough to satisfy the requirements of the preceding provisions of this section, the proceedings may continue before a court composed of those justices.

(7) Where the trial of an information is adjourned after the accused has been convicted and before he is sentenced or otherwise dealt with, the court which sentences or deals with him need not be composed of the same justices as that which convicted him; but, where

among the justices composing the court which sentences or deals with an offender there are any who were not sitting when he was convicted, the court which sentences or deals with the offender shall before doing so make such inquiry into the facts and circumstances of the case as will enable the justices who were not sitting when the offender was convicted to be fully acquainted with those facts and circumstances.

(8) This section shall have effect subject to the provisions of this Act relating to [family proceedings].

[This section is reprinted as amended by the *Children Act* 1989, Sch.11, para.8(c).]

The minimum number of magistrates to hear a trial is two and it cannot be more than three: *Justices of the Peace (Size and Chairmanship of Bench) Rules* 1995.

Magistrates' Courts Act 1980, s.147

Occasional court-house

2–20　　　**147.**—(1) The justices acting for a petty sessions area may appoint as an occasional court-house any place that is not a petty-sessional court-house.

(2) A place appointed as an occasional court-house after 31st May 1953 shall not be used as such unless public notice has been given that it has been appointed.

(3) There may be more than one occasional court-house for each petty sessions area; and an occasional court-house may be outside the petty sessions area in which it is appointed, and if so shall be deemed to be in that area for the purpose of the jurisdiction of the justices acting for that area.

The powers of the court when sitting in an occasional court-house are limited by s.121 of the *Magistrates' Courts Act* 1980 (above). Licensed premises cannot be used as petty sessional court-houses or occasional court-houses: *Licensing Act* 1964, s.190.

IV. IMPARTIALITY OF MAGISTRATES

A. GENERAL

2–21　　A magistrate is disqualified from sitting or adjudicating on a case if
　　(a) a statutory disqualification applies;
　　(b) he would be a judge in his own cause;
　　(c) there is evidence of actual bias; or
　　(d) there is evidence of apparent bias.

Where a defendant demonstrates partiality or prejudice on the part of a judge there are irresistible grounds for objecting to the trial of the case by that judge.

Article 6 of ECHR guarantees a right to a fair and public hearing by "an independent and impartial tribunal". This includes the concept of subjective and objective impartiality. The subjective test is on the basis of the personal conviction of the particular judge and the objective test is ascertaining whether the judge offers guarantees sufficient to rule out any legitimate doubt as to the judge's impartiality: *Hauschildt v Denmark* [1990] 12 E.H.R.R. 266.

If a magistrate is disqualified he should declare an interest and withdraw from court. It is possible for the interest to be declared and the parties to waive any objection on the basis of bias.

B. STATUTORY DISQUALIFICATION

Justices of the Peace Act 1997, s.66

Disqualification in certain cases of justices who are members of local authorities

2–22　　　**66.**—(1) A justice of the peace who is a member of a local authority shall not act as a member of the Crown Court or of a magistrates' court in any proceedings brought by or against, or by way of appeal from a decision of, the authority, any committee or officer of the authority or in the case of a local authority which are operating executive arrangements the executive of that authority or any person acting on behalf of that executive.

(2) For the purposes of subsection (1) above—

    (a) any reference to a committee of a local authority includes a joint committee, joint board, joint authority or other combined body of which that authority is a member or on which it is represented; and

    (b) any reference to an officer of a local authority refers to a person employed or appointed by the authority, or by a committee of the authority, in the capacity in which he is employed or appointed to act.

(3) A justice of the peace who is a member of the Common Council of the City of London shall not act as a member of the Crown Court or of a magistrates' court in any proceedings brought by or against, or by way of appeal from a decision of, the Corporation of the City or the Common Council or any committee or officer of the Corporation or Common Council.

(4) Subsection (2) above applies for the purposes of subsection (3) above with the substitution, for references to a local authority, of references to the Corporation or the Common Council.

(5) Nothing in this section prevents a justice from acting in any proceedings by reason only of their being brought by a police officer.

(6) No act shall be invalidated by reason only of the disqualification under this section of the person acting.

(7) In this section "local authority" means—

    (a) a local authority within the meaning of the *Local Government Act* 1972 or the *Local Government (Scotland) Act* 1973;

    (b) a police authority established under section 3 of the *Police Act* 1996;

  (bza) the Metropolitan Police Authority;

  (ba) the Service Authority for the National Criminal Intelligence Service;

  (bb) the Service Authority for the National Crime Squad;

    (c) a joint authority established by Part IV of the *Local Government Act* 1985;

  (cc) the London Fire and Emergency Planning Authority;

    (d) a housing action trust established under Part III of the *Housing Act* 1988;

    (e) the Broads Authority; and

    (f) a National Park authority.

(8) In this section "executive" and "executive arrangements" have the same meaning as in Part II of the *Local Government Act* 2000.

A "local authority" means a London borough council, a district council, a county **2–23** council, a parish council or a community council: *Local Government Act* 1972, s.270.

A magistrate who is a local councillor should not sit in court when the local authority is bringing a prosecution. He should declare an interest and withdraw from court. The case can continue with two magistrates sitting.

Justices of the Peace Act 1997, s.67

Justices not disqualified by reason of liability to local taxation.

    67. A justice of the peace may perform any act in the execution of his office as such a justice **2–24** in relation to the laws concerning—

    (a) rates leviable by a rating authority;

    (b) community charges of a charging authority;

    (c) council tax set by a billing authority; or

    (d) the non-domestic rate of a special authority within the meaning of section 144(6) of the *Local Government Finance Act* 1988,

even though he is rated to or chargeable with any rates falling within paragraph (a) above or is liable, or would but for any enactment or anything provided or done under any enactment be liable, to pay an amount in respect of any charge, tax or rate falling within paragraphs (b) to (d) above in the area affected by the act in question.

C. Party to a Case

It is one of the most fundamental principles of justice that a person cannot be a judge **2–25** in his own cause: *Dimes v Proprietors of Grand Junction Canal* (1852) 3 H.L. Cas. 759.

Once it is shown that a magistrate is a party to a case or has an interest in the subject matter of the case he is disqualified without the need for any investigation into any actual bias. A direct pecuniary interest or proprietary interest in the outcome of a case acts as an automatic disqualification and an assumption of bias: *R. v Bow Street Magistrates Ex p. Pinochet Ugarte* [1999] 1 All E.R. 577.

D. ACTUAL BIAS

2–26   It is rare that actual bias is shown, but where it is the magistrate must disqualify himself: *R. v Gough* [1993] 1 A.C. 646.

E. APPARENT BIAS

2–27   A judge is not disqualified from trying a case because he expresses a personal view before the start of a case which touches upon issues of law and practice which then arise in the case: *R. v Browne, The Times*, August 23, 1997.

In *Incal v Turkey* (2000) 29 E.H.R.R. 449, the European Court of Human Rights summarised the convention jurisprudence. It held that in order to establish whether a tribunal is independent regard must be had to the manner of appointment of its members and their terms of office, the existence of safeguards against outside pressure and the question whether it presents an appearance of impartiality. There are two tests as to the condition of impartiality: the first consists of trying to determine the personal conviction of a particular judge in a given case (the subjective approach) and the second in ascertaining whether the judge offered guarantees sufficient to exclude any legitimate doubt in this respect (the objective approach). Appearances may be important but what is at stake is the confidence which the courts in a democratic society must inspire in the public and with regard to the criminal courts, in the defendant. In deciding whether there is a legitimate reason to fear that a particular court lacks independence or impartiality, the perspective of the defendant is important, what is decisive however is whether his doubts as to the impartiality of the tribunal are objectively justified.

The law was reviewed in detail in *R. v Gough* [1993] 1 A.C. 646 which concerned a claim of apparent bias by a juror who was the neighbour of the defendant's brother. The court went on to consider the authorities on apparent bias and sought to identify the test to be applied. In the case of magistrates it was said that the court should consider if there was a real danger of bias on the part of the magistrate in the sense that he might unfairly regard with favour or disfavour the case of a party before him. The test of bias is whether there is a real risk that the defendant might have been denied a fair trial.

2–28   In *R. v Bow Street Magistrate Ex p. Pinochet Ugarte (No.2)* [1999] 1 All E.R. 577; [1999] 2 W.L.R. 272, HL, a member of the tribunal dealing with the applicant's case was connected to a charity called Amnesty International, which had intervened in the case. It was held on appeal that it is an automatic disqualification if a judge acts in his own cause. The court was reluctant to extend the ambit of automatic disqualification to cover the present case but it was a fundamental principle that justice should not only be done, but be seen to be done. The judge's connection with a party to the case disqualified him from hearing the case.

There are many ways in which apparent bias might be claimed and it will depend on the circumstances of each case whether there is a risk that requires disqualification.

A remark by a magistrate that it was not the practice of the court to describe police officers as liars was held to amount to apparent bias as it demonstrated a strong reaction in favour of the police witnesses: *R. v Highgate Justices Ex p. Riley* [1996] R.T.R. 150. The fact that solicitors representing a party in proceedings also advised the judge about personal matters did not mean that he would necessarily be biased in their favour and did not require him to disqualify himself after the connection had been disclosed: *Taylor v Lawrence* [2002] 2 All E.R. 353.

The magistrates must also be seen to be giving their clear and undivided attention to **2–29** the proceedings. Apparently falling asleep,dealing with other paperwork or reading other documents during a trial have all resulted in convictions being quashed as unsafe; *R. v Weston-super-Mare Justices Ex p. Taylor* [1981] Crim.L.R. 179; *R. v Marylebone Stipendiary Magistrate Ex p. Perry* [1992] Crim.L.R. 514; and *R. v South Worcestershire Justices Ex p. Daniels* [1997] 161 J.P. 121.

The test for apparent bias for a magistrate also applies to justices' clerks because they are part of the judicial process in the magistrates' courts: *R. v Gough* (above).

V. RIGHTS OF AUDIENCE AND COURT DRESS

Defendants in person barristers and solicitors with rights conferred by the *Courts* **2–30** *and Legal Services Act* 1990 may address the Court.

Magistrates' Courts Act 1980, s.122

Appearance by counsel or solicitor
   122.—(1) A party to any proceedings before a magistrates' court may be represented by a legal representative.
   (2) Subject to subsection (3) below, an absent party so represented shall be deemed not to be absent.
   (3) Appearance of a party by a legal representative shall not satisfy any provision of any enactment or any condition of a recognizance expressly requiring his presence.

[This section is printed as amended by the *Courts and Legal Services Act* 1990, Sch.18.]

Barristers and solicitors regularly appear in the magistrates' courts to represent **2–31** defendants. A defendant may not be in court, either because he is ill or has been removed for misconduct or he may simply choose not to attend. It is possible for the proceedings to continue with the lawyer acting in the interests of the absent defendant. Lawyers will also represent bodies corporate and enter pleas on their behalf without the need for company officers to be present.

In certain instances, statute requires that the defendant be present in court. Where a defendant has been released on bail to appear before the court, it is not sufficient for his legal representative to attend at court, bail must be answered in person as there is a duty to surrender to the custody of the court: *Bail Act* 1976, s.3. Bail may only be enlarged in absence if there is a reasonable cause for the failure to surrender. There are further specific provisions which require the defendant's presence even when represented, *e.g.* plea before venue should be dealt with in the presence of the accused unless he is removed from court because of his disorderly conduct: s.17B of the *Magistrates' Courts Act* 1980; committal for trial to the Crown Court s.6(2) of the *Magistrates' Courts Act* 1980 which requires the court to commit the accused for trial and the *Magistrates' Courts Rules* 1981, rr.6 and 7 which require the charge on which the defendant is to be committed to be read to him as part of the process. Under s.51 of the *Crime and Disorder Act* 1998, a person may only be sent for trial when he 'appears' or is 'brought before the court'. Community penalties may be imposed only in the defendant's presence because of the legal requirement on the court to explain to the offender in ordinary language the effect of the order and the consequences of breach (see *Powers of Criminal Courts (Sentencing) Act* 2000). Similarly there is a legal requirement to explain to an offender the reasons why the court is imposing a custodial sentence: *Powers of Criminal Courts (Sentencing) Act* 2000, s.79.

Rights of audience are conferred by ss.27 and 28 of the *Courts and Legal Services Act* 1990. Duly qualified barristers and solicitors have a right of audience under these provisions. The court may also grant an individual right of audience to specified persons for specific proceedings under s.27(2)(c) of the Act. This discretion extends to any person in any proceedings: *R. v Southwark Crown Court Ex p. Tawfick, The Times*, December 1, 1994.

Professional Codes of Conduct dictate the dress code for courts. Although wigs and gowns are not worn in the magistrates' court, a smart standard of dress is expected of all professionals appearing before the court.

VI. ADMINISTRATION OF THE MAGISTRATES' COURTS

2-32   The administration and management of the magistrates' courts are the responsibility of Magistrates' Courts Committees or in the case of London the Greater London Magistrates' Courts Authority. The Committee membership consists of Justices of the Peace. They employ a Justices' Chief Executive to run the courts of a commission area and also the justices' clerks who hold operational responsibility for the courts as well as being the legal adviser to the magistrates.

The administration of the magistrates' court will be subject to change under the *Courts Act* 2003, which is not yet in force. This Act also affects the appointment process of magistrates or 'lay justices' who will be assigned to 'local justice areas'.

Under the unified courts system, Magistrates' Courts Committees will be abolished and courts boards, covering Crown Courts, county courts and magistrates' courts will have the duty to scrutinise, review and make recommendations about the way in which the Lord Chancellor is discharging his general duty of ensuring that courts are run efficiently and effectively.

VII. GENERAL JURISDICTION

2-33   The organisation of the magistrates' courts is presently based on the division of England and Wales into geographical areas known as commission areas, for the purposes of identifying where magistrates may sit and dispense justice. These areas are further divided into petty sessional areas. The jurisdiction and consequently the powers of the magistrates are also limited by the nature of the offence charged and the location where the offence is committed. All these restrictions are contained in the relevant statutes: *Justices of the Peace Act* 1997 and the *Magistrates' Courts Act* 1980.

This will be amended by the *Courts Act* 2003, when in force, which introduces a commission of the peace for the whole of England and Wales and divides that into local justice areas under ss.7 and 8.

(1) Commission areas

Justices of the Peace Act 1997, s.1

Commission areas

2-34   **1.**—(1) England and Wales shall be divided into areas for each of which there shall be a commission of the peace.

(2) The areas shall be as specified by the Lord Chancellor by order made by statutory instrument; but a commission area may not consist of an area partly within and partly outside Greater London.

(3) An area for which there is a commission of the peace shall be known as a commission area.

[This section is printed as amended by the *Access to Justice Act* 1999, s.74.]

On appointment a magistrate will be assigned to a specific commission area which relates to the residential qualification explained above. A magistrate for any commission area may also sit in any commission area which adjoins the commission area for which he is a magistrate: *Justices of the Peace Act* 1997, s.68. This allows for judicial resources to be effectively utilised within neighbouring areas if there is any particular pressure of work in one commission area.

District judges (magistrates' courts) are also appointed to Commission Areas but they may be required to sit in other areas in England and Wales.

Justices of the Peace Act 1997, s.4

Petty sessions areas

4.—(1) England and Wales shall also be divided into areas known as petty sessions areas.　　**2–35**

(2) The areas and their names shall be as specified by the Lord Chancellor by order made by statutory instrument.

(3) Each petty sessions area shall consist of either—

(a) the whole of a commission area; or

(b) an area wholly included within a commission area.

[This section is printed as amended by the *Access to Justice Act* 1999, s.75.]

(2) Jurisdiction for Offences

Magistrates' Courts Act 1980, s.2

Jurisdiction to deal with charges

2.—(1) A magistrates' court for a commission area shall have jurisdiction to try all summary　**2–36** offences committed within the commission area.

(2) Where a person charged with a summary offence appears or is brought before a magistrates' court in answer to a summons issued under paragraph (b) of section 1(2) above, or under a warrant issued under that paragraph, the court shall have jurisdiction to try the offence.

(3) A magistrates' court for a commission area shall have jurisdiction as examining justices over any offence committed by a person who appears or is brought before the court, whether or not the offence was committed within the commission area.

(4) Subject to sections 18 to 22 below and any other enactment (wherever contained) relating to the mode of trial of offences triable either way, a magistrates' court shall have jurisdiction to try summarily an offence triable either way in any case in which under subsection (3) above it would have jurisdiction as examining justices.

(5) A magistrates' court shall, in the exercise of its powers under section 24 below, have jurisdiction to try summarily an indictable offence in any case in which under subsection (3) above it would have jurisdiction as examining justices.

(6) A magistrates' court for any area by which a person is tried for an offence shall have jurisdiction to try him for any summary offence for which he could be tried by a magistrates' court for any other area.

(7) Nothing in this section shall affect any jurisdiction over offences conferred on a magistrates' court by any enactment not contained in this Act.

Once a defendant has been brought before a court in a petty sessions area under the　**2–37** relevant legal process the magistrates have power to proceed to trial in respect of a summary offence if it is alleged to have been committed within their commission area. This ensures that less serious offences (*e.g.* road traffic offences) are dealt with expeditiously in the locality in which they are committed. For either way offences no such geographical limitation applies and magistrates have jurisdiction to deal with either way offences no matter where they are alleged to have been committed.

Where a person is being tried summarily at the magistrates' court, the court also has jurisdiction to deal with any summary offences alleged to have been committed by that person even if they were perpetrated outside of the commission area: s.2(6). This allows for outstanding cases to be consolidated but only if the substantive offence remains to be dealt with in the magistrates' court: *R. v Croydon Magistrates' Court Ex p. Morgan* (1998) 162 J.P. 521.

Magistrates' Courts Act 1980, s.3(1)–(3)

Offences committed on boundaries, etc.

3.—(1) Where an offence has been committed on the boundary between two or more areas　**2–38** to which this section applies, or within 500 yards of such a boundary, or in any harbour, river, arm of the sea or other water lying between two or more such areas, the offence may be treated for the purposes of the preceding provisions of this Act as having been committed in any of those areas.

(2) An offence begun in one area to which this section applies and completed in another may be treated for the purposes of the preceding provisions of this Act as having been wholly committed in either.

(3) Where an offence has been committed on any person, or on or in respect of any property, in or on a vehicle or vessel engaged on any journey or voyage through two or more areas to which this section applies, the offence may be treated for the purposes of the preceding provisions of this Act as having been committed in any of those areas; and where the side or any part of a road or any water along which the vehicle or vessel passed in the course of the journey or voyage forms the boundary between two or more areas to which this section applies, the offence may be treated for the purposes of the preceding provisions of this Act as having been committed in any of those areas.

This section recognises the mobility of crime and would apply to driving offences including a course of dangerous driving undertaken over a stretch of road spanning more than one commission area or indeed to offences committed on moving vehicles as a journey is made which crosses boundaries.

VIII. TERRITORIAL JURISDICTION

A. Introduction

2–39   Generally, the courts are not concerned with conduct which occurs overseas: *Cox v Army Council* [1963] A.C. 48.

Criminal offences may have a foreign element and in such cases the court will investigate the parliamentary intention in defining offences when deciding on any geographical limitation. In the absence of clear words to the contrary parliament is presumed not to have intended to make conduct occurring outside the territorial jurisdiction of the Crown a criminal offence triable in an English court: *Air India v Wiggins* (1980) 71 Cr.App.R. 213. In the case of blackmail where the letter making the demand was posted in England the offence was held to be triable in England although the letter was directed to the intended victim abroad: *Treacey v DPP* [1971] A.C. 537, HL.

Certain offences may be prosecuted in this country even where the offence was committed abroad, *e.g.* murder abroad by a British subject: *Offences against the Person Act* 1861, s.9; and terrorist acts committed in certain foreign countries: *Suppression of Terrorism Act* 1978, s.4.

2–40   There is provision for offenders to be extradited to England and Wales from foreign countries for offences committed here and similarly offenders may be extradited out of this jurisdiction if they are found in England and Wales and are subject to trial abroad. The complexities of international crime were recognised by the *Criminal Justice Act* 1993 which extends and clarifies the jurisdiction of the criminal courts in the UK in relation to crimes with a foreign element. See further *Archbold Crown*, §§ 2–37 *et seq.*

B. Embassies and Consulates

2–41   The building occupied by a foreign embassy or consulate and the land upon which it stands remain the territory of the United Kingdom but diplomatic and consular premises are inviolable. The consent of the head of the mission is required before the local investigating authorities may gain entry. This can present problems in the magistrates' court when diplomatic representatives or their staff commit criminal offences. Vehicles bearing diplomatic plates can incur parking tickets or other road traffic violations. Before these offences can be successfully prosecuted there must be effective service of a summons or enforcement notice at the diplomatic premises. In such cases the prosecution may choose not to proceed. For more serious offences warrants of entry or arrest can only be executed with official consent from the Embassy authorities.

C. Ships

English courts have jurisdiction in respect of offences committed on board United **2–42** Kingdom ships if the defendant is a British citizen and is charged with having committed the offence on board any United Kingdom ship on the high seas, or in any foreign port or harbour, or on board any foreign ship to which he does not belong: *Merchant Shipping Act* 1995, s.281(a). If the defendant is not a British citizen English courts have jurisdiction if he is charged with having committed an offence on board any United Kingdom ship on the high seas: *Merchant Shipping Act* 1995, s.281(b). Section 3(A) of the *Magistrates' Courts Act* 1980 makes it clear that ss.280, 281 and 282 of the *Merchant Shipping Act* 1995 apply generally to offences under the law of England and Wales and not simply to specific offences under the Act.

D. Aircraft

Offences committed on aeroplanes are covered by specific statutes (see Regulatory **2–43** Offences—Airports and Aeroplanes) and the court has jurisdiction over any offences committed in the aircraft whilst it is in flight over the United Kingdom. Under s.92 of the *Civil Aviation Act* 1982, any act or omission taking place on board an aeroplane while on flight elsewhere than in or over the United Kingdom, if it constitutes an offence if committed on land, will be an offence in the air. Foreign aircraft are not affected by this Act unless the next landing of the aircraft is in the UK and where the vessel is registered elsewhere than the UK that the offence would constitute a criminal offence in the country of registration. The consent of the DPP is needed to prosecute offences committed on aircraft when not over UK airspace: s.92(2).

IX. SOVEREIGN AND DIPLOMATIC IMMUNITY

Diplomatic agents enjoy immunity from the criminal jurisdiction of the state of resi- **2–44** dence: *Diplomatic Relations Act* 1964, Sch.1, Art.31.

Members of diplomatic, administrative and technical staff of a mission and members of their families forming part of their household and domestic service staff are exempt from criminal proceedings: *Diplomatic Relations Act* 1964, Sch.1, Art.37. Private servants of members of the mission rather than servants of the mission itself enjoy no such immunity. Members of the families of diplomatic staff and members of the technical and administrative staff and their families who are British nationals or permanent residents do not enjoy immunity from criminal jurisdiction.

Where the question as to whether a defendant is entitled to diplomatic immunity under the *Diplomatic Relations Act* 1964 arises, a certificate issued by or under the authority of the Secretary of State is conclusive evidence: *Diplomatic Relations Act* 1964, s.4. In *R. v Secretary of State for Foreign and Commonwealth Affairs Ex p. Trawnik, The Times*, April 18, 1985, the court held in a case of state immunity that a minister's certificate could not be challenged by way of judicial review except on the ground that it was a nullity or was issued beyond the scope of the minister's statutory power.

Diplomatic privilege cannot be pleaded successfully unless the Foreign and Com- **2–45** monwealth Office has been notified of the entry of the individual into the United Kingdom in accordance with the Vienna Convention on Diplomatic Relations, Art.10 even though Art.10 is not reproduced in the Schedule to the *Diplomatic Relations Act* 1964: *R. v Lambeth JJ Ex p. Yusufu* [1985] Crim.L.R. 510.

It is possible for the immunity to be waived. Waiver must be made on by or on behalf of the representative of the country concerned and cannot be made by the defendant. Until such a waiver is made the proceedings are without jurisdiction and are void: *R. v Madan* [1961] Crim.L.R. 253.

X. CHILDREN AND YOUNG PERSONS

Under s.68 of the *Criminal Justice Act* 1991 the magistrates' courts have jurisdiction **2–46** in respect of summary and indictable offences only where the offender is aged 18 years and over. Offenders under the age of 18 years are dealt with by the youth court.

The magistrates' court has power to deal with young people under the age of 18 in restricted circumstances.

a) If a person aged 17 or under appears alone before a magistrates' court, unless there is an adult co-defendant, the case must be adjourned to a youth court (*Children and Young Persons Act* 1933, s.46). The defendant may be remanded either on bail, in custody if aged 17 or to local authority accommodation if younger. A young person aged 15 or 16 can also be remanded to secure accommodation. Youth courts rarely sit on Saturdays or Bank Holidays so the youth will be produced at the adult court and will be remanded under this section to the next convenient youth court.

b) If a young person aged under 18 is jointly charged with an adult the magistrates' court (as opposed to the youth court) may deal with him: *Children and Young Persons Act* 1933, s.46. If the adult elects or is committed for jury trial at the Crown Court, the magistrates may commit the young person for trial at the Crown Court if it is in the interests of justice to do so: *Magistrates' Courts Act* 1980, s.24. If the adult consents to summary trial and pleads not guilty then the magistrates can direct that the young person be tried jointly with the adult. The court also has discretion to sever the co-defendants if it is in the interests of justice and may remit the young person to a youth court for trial: *Magistrates' Courts Act* 1980, s.29. Factors to consider are the age and plea of the young person and the advisability of duplication of trials.

c) The magistrates' court must remit a young person who is convicted of a joint charge with an adult to the youth court for sentence unless satisfied it would be undesirable to do so. The appropriate youth court will be the court acting for the same PSA as the adult court or the youth court that has jurisdiction for the area where the young person resides: *Powers of Criminal Courts (Sentencing) Act* 2000, subss.8(1) and (2). The circumstances in which a magistrates' court may find it undesirable to remit the young person are set out in section 8 of the Act. Instead of remittal the court may make a referral order if the case falls within the relevant conditions. The magistrates' court has power to sentence a young person on conviction in a joint matter with an adult if the court is of the opinion that the case is one which can properly be dealt with by means of an absolute or conditional discharge, a fine not exceeding £250 in the case of a young person aged 10–13 inclusive or £1,000 for a young person aged 14–17, or an order for the offender's parent or guardian to enter into a recognisance to take proper care of him and exercise proper control over him: *Powers of Criminal Courts (Sentencing) Act* 2000, subss.8(6)–(8).

2–48   A co-defendant who is a young person may become an adult during the process of the case. If he was 17 at the time of commission of the offence but reaches 18 before the first court appearance the adult court has jurisdiction and may hear the case. His young age should be taken into account on sentencing. If he appears as a youth co-defendant and reaches the age of 18 by the date of conviction, then he should be treated by the adult court as if he were still a young person with the restrictions on sentencing powers applying.

In *R. v Ghafoor* [2002] Crim.L.R. 739, the defendant was 17 at the time of commission of an offence of rioting but was 18 by the time he was convicted. On appeal his sentence of four and a half years detention in a Young Offenders Institution was reduced to 18 months on the basis that taking his age into account at the time of the offence, this period of detention was equal to the length of any detention and training order that could properly have been imposed in the youth court. The relevant age for determining sentencing powers was the age at the time of the offence.

EXTRADITION

I. INTRODUCTION

Extradition is the handing over by one country of a person who is alleged to have **3–1** committed a crime or who has been convicted of a criminal offence to another country which has jurisdiction to deal with the crime.

Throughout the centuries it has been traditional for states to grant asylum to fugitives **3–2** from other countries. It also became established that countries would not give asylum to those who had committed crimes unless it was considered that those crimes were political in nature. Treaties between countries exist to facilitate the return of those who have committed or are alleged to have committed serious offences.

The United Kingdom seeks extradition from elsewhere while other countries seek extradition from this country.

Bow Street Magistrates' Court in Central London, being the office of the senior district judge (chief magistrate) and those other district judges designated to hear extradition proceedings, is the centre for outward extradition in England and Wales.

This section is concerned with magistrates' courts proceedings for outward extradi- **3–3** tion only. The proceedings are now covered by the *Extradition Act* 2003. All statutory references are to that Act.

There will be a number of cases already in the system which will follow the previous legislation but these will soon be completed and any new application will be made under this Act. Some case law arising from earlier legislation has been included as it may still give guidance in certain circumstances.

The Act categorises the United Kingdom's extradition partners into two. The Secre- **3–4** tary of State for the Home Office designates countries into each category. These categories may change. A country may migrate from category two to category one. No country may be designated under Part 1 where the death penalty would be available if the person were found guilty: s.1(3).

The difference in procedure between the two categories is that the Secretary of State **3–5** for the Home Office still has a role to play so far as Category 2 countries are concerned whereas the Act introduces a fast track procedure in Pt 1 initially for EU member states and Gibraltar without the need for any intervention by the Secretary of State at any stage. A check will need to be made to ascertain which countries have been designated to which category at any particular time. In addition the designation of category two countries may give special terms, for example, the USA does not have to provide *prima facie* evidence.

A request may be withdrawn and the person discharged.

II. JURISDICTION

3–6   Extradition proceedings are dealt with by district judges who have been designated by the Lord Chancellor for that purpose: ss.67 and 137. Jurisdiction lies with the designated judge as opposed to the area or courthouse. The judge will normally sit at Bow Street Magistrates' Court but can sit elsewhere. A magistrate may deal with an application for a provisional warrant but arrangements are in place at Bow Street for such applications to be made there both in and out of normal court hours.

III. ARREST

3–7   The subject of an extradition request will normally be arrested on a warrant. The type of warrant will differ according to which part of the Act applies to the requesting state. The warrant may be a Part 1 warrant (European Arrest Warrant), or a Part 2 Provisional or certified warrant. Part 3 warrants refer to incoming extradition and are not dealt with here.

(1) Part 1 Warrant

3–8   This has commonly been called the European Arrest Warrant. The provisions are contained in s.2 of the Act.

Extradition Act 2003, s.2

Part 1 warrant and certificate

2.—(1) This section applies if the designated authority receives a Part 1 warrant in respect of a person.

(2) A Part 1 warrant is an arrest warrant which is issued by a judicial authority of a category 1 territory and which contains—

     (a) the statement referred to in subsection (3) and the information referred to in subsection (4), or

     (b) the statement referred to in subsection (5) and the information referred to in subsection (6).

(3) The statement is one that—

     (a) the person in respect of whom the Part 1 warrant is issued is accused in the category 1 territory of the commission of an offence specified in the warrant, and

     (b) the Part 1 warrant is issued with a view to his arrest and extradition to the category 1 territory for the purpose of being prosecuted for the offence.

3–9   4) The information is—

     (a) particulars of the person's identity;

     (b) particulars of any other warrant issued in the category 1 territory for the person's arrest in respect of the offence;

     (c) particulars of the circumstances in which the person is alleged to have committed the offence, including the conduct alleged to constitute the offence, the time and place at which he is alleged to have committed the offence and any provision of the law of the category 1 territory under which the conduct is alleged to constitute an offence;

     (d) particulars of the sentence which may be imposed under the law of the category 1 territory in respect of the offence if the person is convicted of it.

(5) The statement is one that—

     (a) the person in respect of whom the Part 1 warrant is issued is alleged to be unlawfully at large after conviction of an offence specified in the warrant by a court in the category 1 territory, and

     (b) the Part 1 warrant is issued with a view to his arrest and extradition to the category 1 territory for the purpose of being sentenced for the offence or of serving a sentence of imprisonment or another form of detention imposed in respect of the offence.

3–10   (6) The information is—

(a) particulars of the person's identity;

(b) particulars of the conviction;

(c) particulars of any other warrant issued in the category 1 territory for the person's arrest in respect of the offence;

(d) particulars of the sentence which may be imposed under the law of the category 1 territory in respect of the offence, if the person has not been sentenced for the offence;

(e) particulars of the sentence which has been imposed under the law of the category 1 territory in respect of the offence, if the person has been sentenced for the offence.

(7) The designated authority may issue a certificate under this section if it believes that the authority which issued the Part 1 warrant has the function of issuing arrest warrants in the category 1 territory.

(8) A certificate under this section must certify that the authority which issued the Part 1 warrant has the function of issuing arrest warrants in the category 1 territory.

(9) The designated authority is the authority designated for the purposes of this Part by order made by the Secretary of State.

(10) An order made under subsection (9) may—

(a) designate more than one authority;

(b) designate different authorities for different parts of the United Kingdom.

3–11 A warrant is issued in the requesting State and sent to the UK for execution. It must have been issued by a judicial authority and will state whether the person to be arrested is to be prosecuted or has been convicted. It will give details of identity, particulars of the offence, how it was committed or the fact of a conviction, the possible or actual sentence together with details of any other outstanding warrants. The designated authority for England and Wales is the National Criminal Intelligence Service. That authority will certify whether the judicial authority has the function of issuing arrest warrants in the requesting country.

The transitional provisions provide that an Art. 95 alert is to be treated as a Pt 1 warrant: s.212.

3–12 Where a person is unlawfully at large from serving a sentence in a country other than the convicting country under special arrangements for the transfer of prisoners a warrant may be issued by either the convicting country or the country where he is serving the sentence: s.63.

Once the certificate has been issued by the designated authority a police or customs officer may execute the foreign warrant against a member of the public and, may do so, even if the warrant is not in his possession. There are also provisions for service personnel to be arrested by service policemen: s.3.

In cases of urgency a person may be arrested without warrant. This is called a provisional arrest and may take place where an officer has reasonable grounds for believing that a Pt 1 warrant has been or will be issued: s.5.

Extradition Act 2003, s.5(1), (2)

Provisional arrest

3–13 5.—(1) A constable, a customs officer or a service policeman may arrest a person without a warrant if he has reasonable grounds for believing—

(a) that a Part 1 warrant has been or will be issued in respect of the person by an authority of a category 1 territory, and

(b) that the authority has the function of issuing arrest warrants in the category 1 territory.

(2) A constable or a customs officer may arrest a person under subsection (1) in any part of the United Kingdom.

(2) Part 2 Warrants

3–14 A warrant may be a provisional or certified warrant.

A certified warrant will be considered where a certificate has been sent from the Secretary of State to a designated district judge. The certificate will be issued where a category two country requests the extradition of someone either alleged to have committed an offence or who has been convicted of an offence and provides valid supporting documentation through the diplomatic channels to the Secretary of State. It is a matter for the Secretary of State whether the documents sent to him as the formal requisition comply with requirements: *R. v Governor of Brixton Prison Ex p. Cuoghi, The Times*, May 12, 1998.

Extradition Act 2003, ss.70, 71(1)–(7)

Extradition request and certificate

3–15   **70.**—(1) The Secretary of State must issue a certificate under this section if he receives a valid request for the extradition to a category 2 territory of a person who is in the United Kingdom.

(2) But subsection (1) does not apply if the Secretary of State decides under section 126 that the request is not to be proceeded with.

(3) A request for a person's extradition is valid if—

(a) it contains the statement referred to in subsection (4), and

(b) it is made in the approved way.

(4) The statement is one that the person—

(a) is accused in the category 2 territory of the commission of an offence specified in the request, or

(b) is alleged to be unlawfully at large after conviction by a court in the category 2 territory of an offence specified in the request.

(5) A request for extradition to a category 2 territory which is a British overseas territory is made in the approved way if it is made by or on behalf of the person administering the territory.

3–16   —(6) A request for extradition to a category 2 territory which is the Hong Kong Special Administrative Region of the People's Republic of China is made in the approved way if it is made by or on behalf of the government of the Region.

(7) A request for extradition to any other category 2 territory is made in the approved way if it is made—

(a) by an authority of the territory which the Secretary of State believes has the function of making requests for extradition in that territory, or

(b) by a person recognised by the Secretary of State as a diplomatic or consular representative of the territory.

(8) A certificate under this section must certify that the request is made in the approved way.

(9) If a certificate is issued under this section the Secretary of State must send these documents to the appropriate judge—

(a) the request;

(b) the certificate;

(c) a copy of any relevant Order in Council.

3–17   The Secretary of State may choose not to issue a certificate if there are competing claims. He may defer the claim: s.126.

Upon receipt of the relevant documentation a designated judge may issue a warrant of arrest with or without bail: s.71.

Arrest warrant following extradition request

3–18   **71.**—(1) This section applies if the Secretary of State sends documents to the appropriate judge under section 70.

(2) The judge may issue a warrant for the arrest of the person whose extradition is requested if the judge has reasonable grounds for believing that—

(a) the offence in respect of which extradition is requested is an extradition offence, and

(b) there is evidence falling within subsection (3).

(3) The evidence is—

(a) evidence that would justify the issue of a warrant for the arrest of a person accused of the offence within the judge's jurisdiction, if the person whose extradition is requested is accused of the commission of the offence;

(b) evidence that would justify the issue of a warrant for the arrest of a person unlawfully at large after conviction of the offence within the judge's jurisdiction, if the person whose extradition is requested is alleged to be unlawfully at large after conviction of the offence.

(4) But if the category 2 territory to which extradition is requested is designated for the purposes of this section by order made by the Secretary of State, subsections (2) and (3) have effect as if "evidence" read "information".

(5) A warrant issued under this section may—

(a) be executed by any person to whom it is directed or by any constable or customs officer;

(b) be executed even if neither the warrant nor a copy of it is in the possession of the person executing it at the time of the arrest.

(6) If a warrant issued under this section in respect of a person is directed to a service policeman, it may be executed in any place where the service policeman would have power to arrest the person under the appropriate service law if the person had committed an offence under that law.

(7) In any other case, a warrant issued under this section may be executed in any part of the United Kingdom.

3–19 The designated district judge must be satisfied that the offence is an extradition offence and that a warrant for similar circumstances in the UK would be justified. The warrant may be executed even if it is not in the possession of the arresting officer.

A provisional warrant may be issued under s.73 as a preliminary step at a time when no formal request for extradition has been made.

Extradition Act 2003, s.73(1)–(7)

Provisional warrant

3–20 **73.**—(1) This section applies if a justice of the peace is satisfied on information in writing and on oath that a person within subsection (2)—

(a) is or is believed to be in the United Kingdom, or

(b) is or is believed to be on his way to the United Kingdom.

(2) A person is within this subsection if—

(a) he is accused in a category 2 territory of the commission of an offence, or

(b) he is alleged to be unlawfully at large after conviction of an offence by a court in a category 2 territory.

(3) The justice may issue a warrant for the arrest of the person (a provisional warrant) if he has reasonable grounds for believing that—

(a) the offence of which the person is accused or has been convicted is an extradition offence, and

(b) there is written evidence falling within subsection (4).

3–21 (4) The evidence is—

(a) evidence that would justify the issue of a warrant for the arrest of a person accused of the offence within the justice's jurisdiction, if the person in respect of whom the warrant is sought is accused of the commission of the offence;

(b) evidence that would justify the issue of a warrant for the arrest of a person unlawfully at large after conviction of the offence within the justice's jurisdiction, if the person in respect of whom the warrant is sought is alleged to be unlawfully at large after conviction of the offence.

(5) But if the category 2 territory is designated for the purposes of this section by order made by the Secretary of State, subsections (3) and (4) have effect as if "evidence" read "information".

(6) A provisional warrant may—

(a) be executed by any person to whom it is directed or by any constable or customs officer;

(b) be executed even if neither the warrant nor a copy of it is in the possession of the person executing it at the time of the arrest.

(7) If a warrant issued under this section in respect of a person is directed to a service policeman, it may be executed in any place where the service policeman would have power to arrest the person under the appropriate service law if the person had committed an offence under that law.

3–22   It is quite common for this type of warrant to be sought where it is deemed urgent. Many people wanted for extradition crimes are found to be in transit or about to leave the country or are on their way to this country and there is no time for a formal request under s.70. Information is often received from Interpol through police channels pending receipt of a formal extradition request and supporting documentation. The information should state that extradition will be sought and give sufficient facts about the person, the offence and the possible penalty.

Although an application may be made to a magistrate, applications are generally dealt with at Bow Street Magistrates' Court by a designated judge. The police will make contact with the justices' clerk or one of the legal advisers who will check the information for any defects and either draft a warrant for the judge's consideration or check a warrant which has already been prepared by the police. The practice of the legal adviser checking the process was approved in *R. v Governor of Pentonville Prison Ex p. Osman (No.3)* [1990] 1 All E.R. 999.

The judge must be satisfied on the written information that the allegation would amount to an extradition offence and that a warrant is justified. In *R. v Evans Ex p. Pinochet Ugarte, The Times*, November 3, 1998, a second provisional warrant was issued on the same information when the first warrant, having been issued in a very tight timescale, was found to be defective. That practice was upheld although Lord Bingham C.J. stated that it was unusual and generally undesirable.

3–23   The case of *R. v Bow Street Magistrates' Court Ex p. Allison, The Times*, June 5, 1997 defined an urgent case as one that is urgent at the time of the issue of the warrant, regardless of the cause of the urgency. In that case the person, who had been in custody awaiting extradition to the USA for other offences, was likely to be released very soon and was liable to abscond.

If a person is on his way, the judge should be satisfied that he has actually boarded a flight to this country and that there are no stops en route where he might get off.

The warrant may be executed even if it is not in the possession of the arresting officer. Premises may be entered and searched to facilitate an arrest. Upon arrest the person and the premises where the person was found or had recently been at, may be searched for evidence relating to the offence or the identity of the person: ss.161, 162 and 163.

3–24   After arrest the police also have powers under Pt 4 of the Act in relation to entry and search of premises, seizure of material, the taking of photographs, fingerprints and other samples: ss.164–168. Codes of Practice are in existence.

The warrant may be issued with or without bail. Where the police bail the person, a police officer will liaise with the court to take account of the court lists and statutory time limits. The Secretary of State will be informed because where the person is arrested on a provisional warrant the court will need the Secretary of State's order before it can proceed. It should be noted that the judge must receive the certificate and supporting documentation within 45 days from the date of arrest (or any longer period agreed with a particular state) otherwise the person may be discharged.

IV. REPRESENTATION

3–25   The requesting state will in most cases be represented by the Crown Prosecution Service which acts as an agent. Many of its powers, being peculiar to the law of England and Wales, for example discontinuance, do not apply in extradition matters. The requesting state may alternatively instruct a firm of solicitors.

The person arrested may instruct solicitors and may apply for a legal representation order. In *R. v Bow Street Magistrates' Court Ex p. Shayler* [1999] 1 All E.R. 98 (albeit a potential inward extradition) the refusal of legal aid at the stage that a warrant had been issued but not executed was upheld.

V. PROCEDURE

(1) First appearance before the court

Once a person is arrested he must be brought before a designated judge as soon as **3–26** practicable except in the case where a person has been provisionally arrested under s.5 when he must be brought before the judge within 48 hours: ss.4, 6 and 72.

In each case a copy of the warrant must be given to the person arrested as soon as practicable after arrest. Failure to do so may result in the person's discharge.

The prosecutor will prepare "charges" in the form of offences known to the law of England and Wales but they have no formal status. They are there to assist the judge: *R. v Bow Street Magistrates' Court Ex p. Kline*, unreported, June 30, 1999.

The judge will want to establish identity and whether the person will consent to **3–27** extradition. If consent is not forthcoming the judge must fix the date of the extradition hearing and timetable the rest of the proceedings. He may remand the person in custody or bail: ss.8, 71. The presumption of bail applies: s.198.

Identity

The question of identity must be established on a balance of probabilities: ss.7, 78.   **3–28**

The defendant may admit that he is the person concerned. If identification is in dispute, however, evidence must be brought before the court. Photographic or video evidence may be submitted: *Bradshar, Re*, unreported, February 28, 1984; *R. v Governor of Pentonville Prison Ex p. Rodriguez, The Times*, November 29, 1984, DC; *R. v Governor of Pentonville Prison Ex p. Voets* [1986] 2 All E.R. 630.

A passport linking the fugitive to the papers was approved in *Khan, Re*, unreported, **3–28.1** June 30, 1995. Evidence of what was said at the time of arrest has also been approved: *R. v Governor of Pentonville Prison Ex p. Boettcher*, unreported, April 28, 1993. In that case the fugitive had given his name, address and date of birth as contained in the papers and had remarked that the alleged assault was against his girlfriend.

In *Osawe v Government of H.M. Prison Brixton*, unreported, July 28, 2003, fingerprints and photographs overruled the fact that the person's name was different from that on the papers. In *Artan Brahja v 1) the Governor of H.M Prison Brixton 2) the Government of Italy* [2003] EWHC 509 Admin, it was held, where details on the person's driving licence were different, that minor discrepancies were not sufficient to raise doubts over identity.

If there is insufficient evidence to show that the person is the one to whom the warrant refers he must be discharged.

An unusual name, date of birth, abode and passport number even if the latter is found in papers relating to a co-defendant is sufficient evidence for identification: *Savvas v Govt. of Italy* [2004] EWHC 1233.

Consent to extradition

The court must inform the person of his right to consent to extradition and the fact **3–29** that consent will be irrevocable: ss.7 and 45 for Pt 1 cases and ss.127 and 128 for Pt 2 cases. They are in similar terms.

If the person wishes to consent there is no reason why the judge cannot proceed to order extradition or in Pt 2 cases forward the case to the Secretary of State for his decision. The person must either be legally represented or has been offered legal aid but has refused or failed to apply or it has been refused or withdrawn. The consent must be recorded in writing. This is intended to provide a speedy process and protection is afforded through legal advice.

Where consent is not forthcoming, the judge will set the hearing date. In Pt 1 proceedings the time limit set in s.8 is 21 days from the date of arrest but there is provision for a later date to be fixed if it is in the interests of justice. Subsequently the hearing may be adjourned further. The judge is expected to manage the progress of the case to ensure there is no undue delay. The person will either be remanded in custody or on bail.

3–30 So far as Pt 2 proceedings are concerned the judge will proceed to timetable the case in accordance with the statutory time limits. Where the arrest is under a certified warrant the hearing date must not be later than two months from the date that the person first appears before the court although this period may be extended if the interests of justice so require: s.75. Where the arrest is under a provisional warrant, a hearing must be fixed within two months from the date that the certificate from the Secretary of State is due to be received by the court.

(2) The extradition hearing

3–31 Extradition proceedings are classified as a type of summary proceeding. They are criminal proceedings for the purposes of legal representation under the *Access to Justice Act* 1999. The general right to bail under the *Bail Act* 1976 applies.

Extradition Act 2003, ss.9(1), (4), (5), 77(1), (4), (5)

Judge's powers at extradition hearing
    9. & 77.—(1) In England and Wales, at the extradition hearing the appropriate judge has the same powers (as nearly as may be) as a magistrates' court would have if the proceedings were the summary trial of an information against the person in respect of whom the Part I warrant was issued.
    (4) If the judge adjourns the extradition hearing he must remand the person in custody or on bail.
    (5) If the judge remands the person in custody he may later grant bail.

3–32 The extradition hearing will be conducted as if it were a summary trial but no plea is taken as the person is not being tried in this country. The advocate for the requesting country will open the case and deal with preliminary matters. He will then introduce his evidence which will normally be in statement form and will be read. Any oral evidence will be taken in the form of a deposition. If identity or consent has not been determined before, the judge will deal with those matters at that stage.

In Pt 2 cases the judge must ensure he has
— the certificate from the Secretary of State
— particulars of the person whose extradition is requested
— particulars of the offence specified in the offence
— an arrest warrant issued in the requesting state or a certificate of conviction from the requesting state and details of the sentence, if any.
He must satisfy himself that the documents have been served upon the person: s.78.

Extradition Act 2003, s.78

Initial stages of extradition hearing
3–33   **78.**—(1) This section applies if a person alleged to be the person whose extradition is requested appears or is brought before the appropriate judge for the extradition hearing.
    (2) The judge must decide whether the documents sent to him by the Secretary of State consist of (or include)—
      (a) the documents referred to in section 70(9);
      (b) particulars of the person whose extradition is requested;
      (c) particulars of the offence specified in the request;
      (d) in the case of a person accused of an offence, a warrant for his arrest issued in the category 2 territory;
      (e) in the case of a person alleged to be unlawfully at large after conviction of an of-

fence, a certificate issued in the category 2 territory of the conviction and (if he has been sentenced) of the sentence.

(3) If the judge decides the question in subsection (2) in the negative he must order the person's discharge.

(4) If the judge decides that question in the affirmative he must decide whether—   **3–34**
  (a) the person appearing or brought before him is the person whose extradition is requested;
  (b) the offence specified in the request is an extradition offence;
  (c) copies of the documents sent to the judge by the Secretary of State have been served on the person.

(5) The judge must decide the question in subsection (4)(a) on a balance of probabilities.

(6) If the judge decides any of the questions in subsection (4) in the negative he must order the person's discharge.

(7) If the judge decides those questions in the affirmative he must proceed under section 79.

(8) The reference in subsection (2)(d) to a warrant for a person's arrest includes a reference to a judicial document authorising his arrest.

The judge must decide whether the offence is an extradition offence and whether extradition is barred within the terms of the Act.

(a) *Extradition offence*

The Act differentiates between those convicted of offences and sentenced and those **3–35** who are merely accused of committing offences.

Offenders who have been sentenced

Part 1 cases are dealt with under s.65.   **3–36**

Extradition Act 2003, s.65

Extradition offences: person sentenced for offence

65.—(1) This section applies in relation to conduct of a person if—
  (a) he is alleged to be unlawfully at large after conviction by a court in a category 1 territory of an offence constituted by the conduct, and
  (b) he has been sentenced for the offence.

(2) The conduct constitutes an extradition offence in relation to the category 1 territory if these conditions are satisfied—
  (a) the conduct occurs in the category 1 territory and no part of it occurs in the United Kingdom;
  (b) a certificate issued by an appropriate authority of the category 1 territory shows that the conduct falls within the European framework list;
  (c) the certificate shows that a sentence of imprisonment or another form of detention for a term of 12 months or a greater punishment has been imposed in the category 1 territory in respect of the conduct.

(3) The conduct also constitutes an extradition offence in relation to the category 1 territory if these conditions are satisfied—
  (a) the conduct occurs in the category 1 territory;
  (b) the conduct would constitute an offence under the law of the relevant part of the United Kingdom if it occurred in that part of the United Kingdom;
  (c) a sentence of imprisonment or another form of detention for a term of 4 months or a greater punishment has been imposed in the category 1 territory in respect of the conduct.

(4) The conduct also constitutes an extradition offence in relation to the category 1 terri- **3–37** tory if these conditions are satisfied—
  (a) the conduct occurs outside the category 1 territory;
  (b) a sentence of imprisonment or another form of detention for a term of 4 months

or a greater punishment has been imposed in the category 1 territory in respect of the conduct;

(c) in corresponding circumstances equivalent conduct would constitute an extra-territorial offence under the law of the relevant part of the United Kingdom punishable with imprisonment or another form of detention for a term of 12 months or a greater punishment.

(5) The conduct also constitutes an extradition offence in relation to the category 1 territory if these conditions are satisfied—

(a) the conduct occurs outside the category 1 territory and no part of it occurs in the United Kingdom;

(b) the conduct would constitute an offence under the law of the relevant part of the United Kingdom punishable with imprisonment or another form of detention for a term of 12 months or a greater punishment if it occurred in that part of the United Kingdom;

(c) a sentence of imprisonment or another form of detention for a term of 4 months or a greater punishment has been imposed in the category 1 territory in respect of the conduct.

3–38   (6) The conduct also constitutes an extradition offence in relation to the category 1 territory if these conditions are satisfied—

(a) the conduct occurs outside the category 1 territory and no part of it occurs in the United Kingdom;

(b) a sentence of imprisonment or another form of detention for a term of 4 months or a greater punishment has been imposed in the category 1 territory in respect of the conduct;

(c) the conduct constitutes or if committed in the United Kingdom would constitute an offence mentioned in subsection (7).

3–39   (7) The offences are—

(a) an offence under section 51 or 58 of the *International Criminal Court Act* 2001 (genocide, crimes against humanity and war crimes);

(b) an offence under section 52 or 59 of that Act (conduct ancillary to genocide etc committed outside the jurisdiction);

(c) an ancillary offence, as defined in section 55 or 62 of that Act, in relation to an offence falling within paragraph (a) or (b);

(d) an offence under section 1 of the *International Criminal Court (Scotland) Act* 2001 (genocide, crimes against humanity and war crimes);

(e) an offence under section 2 of that Act (conduct ancillary to genocide etc committed outside the jurisdiction);

(f) an ancillary offence, as defined in section 7 of that Act, in relation to an offence falling within paragraph (d) or (e).

(8) For the purposes of subsections (3)(b), (4)(c) and (5)(b)—

(a) if the conduct relates to a tax or duty, it is immaterial that the law of the relevant part of the United Kingdom does not impose the same kind of tax or duty or does not contain rules of the same kind as those of the law of the category 1 territory;

(b) if the conduct relates to customs or exchange, it is immaterial that the law of the relevant part of the United Kingdom does not contain rules of the same kind as those of the law of the category 1 territory.

(9) This section applies for the purposes of this Part.

3–40   The definition of an extradition offence where a person has been sentenced depends upon whether the conduct has occurred within or outside the territory of the requesting state.

Where the conduct has occurred in the territory of the requesting state, it is an extradition offence if it is certified as conduct within the European framework list and he has been sentenced to a minimum of twelve months imprisonment or detention or it is an offence also within the UK and a sentence of four months or more imprisonment or detention has been imposed.

Where the conduct has occurred outside the territory of the requesting state, it is an extradition offence if a minimum four month sentence of imprisonment or detention has been imposed and the conduct amounts to an extra-territorial offence in the UK punishable with a minimum of 12 months or the conduct amounts to an offence punishable with a minimum of 12 months in UK and a minimum of four months has been imposed in the requesting state or a minimum sentence of four months has been imposed in the requesting state and the offence is one of genocide, crimes of humanity or war crimes or an ancillary offence.

Part 2 cases are dealt with under s.138.   **3–41**

Extradition Act 2003, s.138

Extradition offences: person sentenced for offence

138.—(1) This section applies in relation to conduct of a person if—

    (a) he is alleged to be unlawfully at large after conviction by a court in a category 2 territory of an offence constituted by the conduct, and

    (b) he has been sentenced for the offence.

(2) The conduct constitutes an extradition offence in relation to the category 2 territory if these conditions are satisfied—

    (a) the conduct occurs in the category 2 territory;

    (b) the conduct would constitute an offence under the law of the relevant part of the United Kingdom punishable with imprisonment or another form of detention for a term of 12 months or a greater punishment if it occurred in that part of the United Kingdom;

    (c) a sentence of imprisonment or another form of detention for a term of 4 months or a greater punishment has been imposed in the category 2 territory in respect of the conduct.

(3) The conduct also constitutes an extradition offence in relation to the category 2 territory if these conditions are satisfied—

    (a) the conduct occurs outside the category 2 territory;

    (b) a sentence of imprisonment or another form of detention for a term of 4 months or a greater punishment has been imposed in the category 2 territory in respect of the conduct;

    (c) in corresponding circumstances equivalent conduct would constitute an extra-territorial offence under the law of the relevant part of the United Kingdom punishable with imprisonment or another form of detention for a term of 12 months or a greater punishment.

(4) The conduct also constitutes an extradition offence in relation to the category 2 ter- **3–42** ritory if these conditions are satisfied—

    (a) the conduct occurs outside the category 2 territory and no part of it occurs in the United Kingdom;

    (b) the conduct would constitute an offence under the law of the relevant part of the United Kingdom punishable with imprisonment or another form of detention for a term of 12 months or a greater punishment if it occurred in that part of the United Kingdom;

    (c) a sentence of imprisonment or another form of detention for a term of 4 months or a greater punishment has been imposed in the category 2 territory in respect of the conduct.

(5) The conduct also constitutes an extradition offence in relation to the category 2 territory if these conditions are satisfied—

    (a) the conduct occurs outside the category 2 territory and no part of it occurs in the United Kingdom;

    (b) a sentence of imprisonment or another form of detention for a term of 4 months or a greater punishment has been imposed in the category 2 territory in respect of the conduct;

    (c) the conduct constitutes or if committed in the United Kingdom would constitute an offence mentioned in subsection (6).

(6) The offences are—

    (a) an offence under section 51 or 58 of the *International Criminal Court Act* 2001 (genocide, crimes against humanity and war crimes);

    (b) an offence under section 52 or 59 of that Act (conduct ancillary to genocide etc committed outside the jurisdiction);

    (c) an ancillary offence, as defined in section 55 or 62 of that Act, in relation to an offence falling within paragraph (a) or (b);

    (d) an offence under section 1 of the *International Criminal Court (Scotland) Act* 2001(genocide, crimes against humanity and war crimes);

    (e) an offence under section 2 of that Act (conduct ancillary to genocide etc committed outside the jurisdiction);

    (f) an ancillary offence, as defined in section 7 of that Act, in relation to an offence falling within paragraph (d) or (e).

3–43   (7) If the conduct constitutes an offence under the military law of the category 2 territory but does not constitute an offence under the general criminal law of the relevant part of the United Kingdom it does not constitute an extradition offence; and subsections (1) to (6) have effect subject to this.

    (8) The relevant part of the United Kingdom is the part of the United Kingdom in which—

    (a) the extradition hearing took place, if the question of whether conduct constitutes an extradition offence is to be decided by the Secretary of State;

    (b) proceedings in which it is necessary to decide that question are taking place, in any other case.

    (9) Subsections (1) to (7) apply for the purposes of this Part.

3–44   Here conduct will amount to an extradition offence if it:

    1) occurs in the requesting state, the conduct would constitute an offence in England and Wales punishable with a minimum of 12 months imprisonment or detention and a minimum of four months imprisonment or detention has been imposed

    2) occurs outside the requesting state and a minimum of four months imprisonment or detention has been imposed in the requesting state and the conduct would constitute an extra territorial offence under the law of England and Wales punishable with a minimum of 12 months imprisonment or detention

    3) occurs outside the requesting state and no part of it has occurred within the UK and it would constitute an offence in England and Wales punishable with a minimum of 12 months imprisonment or detention and a minimum sentence of four months imprisonment or detention has been imposed in the requesting state

    4) occurs outside the requesting state and no part occurs within the UK, a minimum of four months imprisonment or detention has been imposed in the requesting state and the conduct if committed in the UK would constitute an offence of genocide, crimes against humanity and war crimes or ancillary offences.

Those accused of crimes or unlawfully at large after conviction but before sentence

3–45   Part 1 cases are dealt with under s.64.

Extradition Act 2003, s.64

Extradition offences: person not sentenced for offence

    64.—(1) This section applies in relation to conduct of a person if—

    (a) he is accused in a category 1 territory of the commission of an offence constituted by the conduct, or

    (b) he is alleged to be unlawfully at large after conviction by a court in a category 1 territory of an offence constituted by the conduct and he has not been sentenced for the offence.

    (2) The conduct constitutes an extradition offence in relation to the category 1 territory if these conditions are satisfied—

(a) the conduct occurs in the category 1 territory and no part of it occurs in the United Kingdom;

(b) a certificate issued by an appropriate authority of the category 1 territory shows that the conduct falls within the European framework list;

(c) the certificate shows that the conduct is punishable under the law of the category 1 territory with imprisonment or another form of detention for a term of 3 years or a greater punishment.

(3) The conduct also constitutes an extradition offence in relation to the category 1 territory if these conditions are satisfied— **3–46**

(a) the conduct occurs in the category 1 territory;

(b) the conduct would constitute an offence under the law of the relevant part of the United Kingdom if it occurred in that part of the United Kingdom;

(c) the conduct is punishable under the law of the category 1 territory with imprisonment or another form of detention for a term of 12 months or a greater punishment (however it is described in that law).

(4) The conduct also constitutes an extradition offence in relation to the category 1 territory if these conditions are satisfied—

(a) the conduct occurs outside the category 1 territory;

(b) the conduct is punishable under the law of the category 1 territory with imprisonment or another form of detention for a term of 12 months or a greater punishment (however it is described in that law);

(c) in corresponding circumstances equivalent conduct would constitute an extraterritorial offence under the law of the relevant part of the United Kingdom punishable with imprisonment or another form of detention for a term of 12 months or a greater punishment.

(5) The conduct also constitutes an extradition offence in relation to the category 1 territory if these conditions are satisfied—

(a) the conduct occurs outside the category 1 territory and no part of it occurs in the United Kingdom;

(b) the conduct would constitute an offence under the law of the relevant part of the United Kingdom punishable with imprisonment or another form of detention for a term of 12 months or a greater punishment if it occurred in that part of the United Kingdom;

(c) the conduct is so punishable under the law of the category 1 territory (however it is described in that law).

(6) The conduct also constitutes an extradition offence in relation to the category 1 territory if these conditions are satisfied— **3–47**

(a) the conduct occurs outside the category 1 territory and no part of it occurs in the United Kingdom;

(b) the conduct is punishable under the law of the category 1 territory with imprisonment or another form of detention for a term of 12 months or a greater punishment (however it is described in that law);

(c) the conduct constitutes or if committed in the United Kingdom would constitute an offence mentioned in subsection (7).

(7) The offences are—

(a) an offence under section 51 or 58 of the *International Criminal Court Act* 2001 (genocide, crimes against humanity and war crimes);

(b) an offence under section 52 or 59 of that Act (conduct ancillary to genocide etc committed outside the jurisdiction);

(c) an ancillary offence, as defined in section 55 or 62 of that Act, in relation to an offence falling within paragraph (a) or (b);

(d) an offence under section 1 of the *International Criminal Court (Scotland) Act* 2001 (genocide, crimes against humanity and war crimes);

(e) an offence under section 2 of that Act (conduct ancillary to genocide etc committed outside the jurisdiction);

(f) an ancillary offence, as defined in section 7 of that Act, in relation to an offence falling within paragraph (d) or (e).

(8) For the purposes of subsections (3)(b), (4)(c) and (5)(b)—

(a) if the conduct relates to a tax or duty, it is immaterial that the law of the relevant part of the United Kingdom does not impose the same kind of tax or duty or does not contain rules of the same kind as those of the law of the category 1 territory;

  (b) if the conduct relates to customs or exchange, it is immaterial that the law of the relevant part of the United Kingdom does not contain rules of the same kind as those of the law of the category 1 territory.

(9) This section applies for the purposes of this Part.

3–48   For conduct to amount to an extradition offence it must either:

  1) occur in the requesting state with no part occurring within the UK and is punishable with a minimum of three years imprisonment or detention or

  2) occur in the requesting state and is punishable by a minimum of twelve months imprisonment or detention and would constitute an offence in the UK if committed there or

  3) occur outside the requesting state and is punishable with a minimum of 12 months imprisonment or detention and would be an extra territorial offence under UK law punishable with a minimum of 12 months imprisonment or detention or

  4) occur outside the requesting state with no part of it occurring within the UK and would be an offence in the UK punishable with a minimum of 12 months imprisonment or detention and is similarly punishable in the requesting state or

  5) occur outside the requesting state with no part of it occurring within the UK and is punishable with a minimum of 12 months imprisonment or detention and would also be an offence of genocide, war crimes or crimes against humanity or ancillary crimes if committed in the UK

3–49   Pt 2 cases are dealt with under s.137.

Extradition Act 2003, s.137

Extradition offences: person not sentenced for offence

3–50   **137.**—(1) This section applies in relation to conduct of a person if—

  (a) he is accused in a category 2 territory of the commission of an offence constituted by the conduct, or

  (b) he is alleged to be unlawfully at large after conviction by a court in a category 2 territory of an offence constituted by the conduct and he has not been sentenced for the offence.

(2) The conduct constitutes an extradition offence in relation to the category 2 territory if these conditions are satisfied—

  (a) the conduct occurs in the category 2 territory;

  (b) the conduct would constitute an offence under the law of the relevant part of the United Kingdom punishable with imprisonment or another form of detention for a term of 12 months or a greater punishment if it occurred in that part of the United Kingdom;

  (c) the conduct is so punishable under the law of the category 2 territory (however it is described in that law).

(3) The conduct also constitutes an extradition offence in relation to the category 2 territory if these conditions are satisfied—

  (a) the conduct occurs outside the category 2 territory;

  (b) the conduct is punishable under the law of the category 2 territory with imprisonment or another form of detention for a term of 12 months or a greater punishment (however it is described in that law);

  (c) in corresponding circumstances equivalent conduct would constitute an extraterritorial offence under the law of the relevant part of the United Kingdom punishable with imprisonment or another form of detention for a term of 12 months or a greater punishment.

(4) The conduct also constitutes an extradition offence in relation to the category 2 territory if these conditions are satisfied—

  (a) the conduct occurs outside the category 2 territory and no part of it occurs in the United Kingdom;

(b) the conduct would constitute an offence under the law of the relevant part of the United Kingdom punishable with imprisonment or another form of detention for a term of 12 months or a greater punishment if it occurred in that part of the United Kingdom;

(c) the conduct is so punishable under the law of the category 2 territory (however it is described in that law).

(5) The conduct also constitutes an extradition offence in relation to the category 2 ter- **3–51**
ritory if these conditions are satisfied—

(a) the conduct occurs outside the category 2 territory and no part of it occurs in the United Kingdom;

(b) the conduct is punishable under the law of the category 2 territory with imprisonment for a term of 12 months or another form of detention or a greater punishment (however it is described in that law);

(c) the conduct constitutes or if committed in the United Kingdom would constitute an offence mentioned in subsection (6).

(6) The offences are—

(a) an offence under section 51 or 58 of the *International Criminal Court Act* 2001 (genocide, crimes against humanity and war crimes);

(b) an offence under section 52 or 59 of that Act (conduct ancillary to genocide etc committed outside the jurisdiction);

(c) an ancillary offence, as defined in section 55 or 62 of that Act, in relation to an offence falling within paragraph (a) or (b);

(d) an offence under section 1 of the *International Criminal Court (Scotland) Act* 2001 (genocide, crimes against humanity and war crimes);

(e) an offence under section 2 of that Act (conduct ancillary to genocide etc committed outside the jurisdiction);

(f) an ancillary offence, as defined in section 7 of that Act, in relation to an offence falling within paragraph (d) or (e).

(7) If the conduct constitutes an offence under the military law of the category 2 territory but does not constitute an offence under the general criminal law of the relevant part of the United Kingdom it does not constitute an extradition offence; and subsections (1) to (6) have effect subject to this.

(8) The relevant part of the United Kingdom is the part of the United Kingdom in which—

(a) the extradition hearing took place, if the question of whether conduct constitutes an extradition offence is to be decided by the Secretary of State;

(b) proceedings in which it is necessary to decide that question are taking place, in any other case.

(9) Subsections (1) to (7) apply for the purposes of this Part.

Conduct constitutes an extradition offence if it: **3–52**

1) occurs in the category 2 state and is punishable there with a minimum of 12 months imprisonment or detention and it also constitutes an offence in the UK similarly punishable

2) occurs outside the category 2 state, is punishable with a minimum of 12 months imprisonment or detention and would also be an extra-territorial offence in the UK similarly punishable

3) occurs outside the category 2 state and no part of it occurred in the UK, is punishable with a minimum of 12 months imprisonment or detention and is an offence in the UK similarly punishable

4) occurs outside the category 2 state and no part occurred in the UK, is punishable with a minimum of 12 months imprisonment or detention and the offence if committed in the UK would be one of genocide, crimes against humanity or war crimes or ancillary crimes.

It is not an extradition offence if it is an offence under the military law of the category 2 state but is not an offence under UK law.

(b) *Restrictions or bars to extradition ss.11–25, 79, 95, 96*

Extradition will not be ordered where any of the following bars are found to apply: **3–53**

— Double jeopardy
— Extraneous considerations
— Passage of time
— Age (Pt 1 only)
— Hostage-taking considerations
— Speciality (Pt 1 only)
— The person's earlier extradition to the UK from another country (Pt 1 only)

Double jeopardy: ss.12, 80

3–54   No-one should be extradited if he would be entitled to be discharged within the UK because of a previous acquittal or conviction.

The plea of *autrefois convict* or *acquit* arises only in relation to being tried for a crime. If a person has been discharged in previous extradition proceedings he can face further extradition proceedings on the same charges again: *Rees v Secretary of State for the Home Dept* [1986] 2 All E.R. 321.

The *Criminal Justice Act* 2003, when implemented, will have a bearing on extradition proceedings in so far as it applies to acquittals on indictment. It provides for the possibility of a retrial in certain circumstances where there is new and compelling evidence and it is in the interests of justice that the crime is reinvestigated.

3–55   An acquittal of a co-accused is not a matter which the court should take into account: *Rottman v Governor of H.M. Prison Brixton* [2003] EWHC 496.

Extraneous considerations: ss.13, 81

3–56   If it appears that a person will be prosecuted, prejudiced in his trial, punished or detained on the grounds of race, religion, nationality, gender, sexual orientation or political opinion the judge will refuse extradition.

Passage of time: ss.14, 82

3–57   Where a lengthy period of time has elapsed between the commission of the offence or being unlawfully at large and the extradition the court is entitled to consider whether it would be unjust or oppressive to extradite him.

The issue is whether the person is able to have a fair trial after the particular period of time has elapsed. In *Re Woodcock* [2003] EWHC Admin 2668, it was stated that the test to be applied was, having regard to the passage of time, whether it would be unjust to return the person for trial, not whether it would be unjust to try the accused. In carrying out that exercise the court had to have regard to whatever safeguards might exist in the domestic law of the requesting state to ensure that the accused would not be subjected to an unjust trial there. The domestic court would have a clearer picture of what evidence was available and the issues likely to arise and would be in a better position to decide whether a fair trial was possible. In *Daley v Governor of H.M. Prison Brixton*, unreported, June 25, 2003, a nine year delay was held to be oppressive where no previous attempt had been made for extradition.

Age: s.15

3–58   A person under the age of criminal responsibility had the offence occurred within England and Wales will not be extradited. Youths will be brought before designated judges on extradition matters and will not be taken to a Youth court.

Hostage-taking considerations: ss.16, 83

3–59   Where communication between the person and the appropriate consular authorities would not be possible and the conduct constitutes an offence or an attempt to commit an offence under s.1 of the *Taking of Hostages Act* 1982 extradition is barred.

Speciality: s.17

The rule of speciality limits the offences for which the person may be tried in the **3–60** country requesting extradition. In Pt 1 extradition is barred unless arrangements have been made with the country concerned. Extradition is limited to those offences upon which a person has been extradited, those which are disclosed from the same facts, those to which consent has been given by a judge and those which are not punishable by imprisonment or detention. If the offence does not fall within the exceptions he must be given an opportunity to leave the country within 45 days from the date of his arrival. It does not apply if the person has consented to extradition or has waived his rights. A certificate issued by the Secretary of State is conclusive proof that there are arrangements between the UK and the other country.

Earlier extradition to United Kingdom from another country: s.18

A person cannot be extradited where the consent of the first country is necessary **3–61** before he is extradited to another country and that consent has not been given: s.96.

In Pt 2 cases, it is for the Secretary of State to decide the issue of speciality as well as other matters which might render extradition inappropriate.

(c) *Other considerations*

Convictions in absence: ss.20, 86

A person who has been convicted in his absence is protected by the terms of the Act. **3–62** In Pt 1 cases the judge must decide whether the person absented himself from the trial deliberately. If he decides in the affirmative then he must decide whether the extradition would be compatible with the *Human Rights Act* 1998, s.21. If the extradition is not compatible then the person must be discharged.

If the judge decides that the person had not deliberately absented himself he must go on to decide whether the person would be entitled to a retrial or an appeal which would be heard as a retrial and that the person would be entitled to defend himself and to examine witnesses in person or through legal assistance of his own choosing and for that legal assistance to be free if he could not pay. If the person is not so entitled he must be discharged.

In Pt 2 cases it is for the judge to decide whether, on the evidence supplied to him, a case to answer has been made out as if it were a summary trial against the person in this country: s.84. In *Lodhi v 1) Governor of H.M. Prison Brixton 2) Government of the United Arab Emirates* [2001] EWCA Admin 178, it was stated that a person whose extradition was sought should be treated as a person accused rather than *autrefois convict* where he had been convicted in his absence but where the conviction would be set aside on his return. Under the former legislation it was stated in *Re Togyer, The Times*, July 12, 2003 that it is not wrong to order the extradition of a person convicted in his absence where he had chosen not to take part in those proceedings and where, despite the low monetary value of the offence, his criminal record meant that the offence could not be treated as trivial.

An accusation must be made in good faith: *Ingrid Sutej v (1) Governor of H.M.* **3–63** *Prison Holloway (2) Government of Switzerland* [2003] EWHC 1940 Admin; *Gulay Asliturk v Government of Turkey* [2002] EWHC 2326.

See § 3–70 below.

Domestic charges: ss.22, 88

Domestic charges take precedence and the extradition proceedings must be **3–64** adjourned until their conclusion.

Persons serving sentences: ss.23, 89

3–65   Where a person for whom an extradition warrant has been issued is found to be serving a sentence in the UK the extradition hearing may be adjourned until the sentence has been served.

Competing claims: ss.24, 90

3–66   Other claims may be deferred.

Physical or mental condition: ss.24, 90

3–67   Medical evidence may be introduced to show that it would be unjust or oppressive to extradite the person on the grounds of his physical or mental condition whereupon the judge may order his discharge. In *R. v Secretary of State for the Home Department*, unreported, March 14, 2003,, it was stated that the question of mental fitness to stand trial as opposed to be extradited was a matter for the requesting state.

Human Rights: s.87

3–68   There is a positive duty to consider whether the person's extradition would be compatible with ECHR. In *Re Al-Fawwaz* [2001] 1 W.L.R. 1234, it was held that the use of evidence from an anonymous witness did not deprive him of a fair trial within the terms of Art.6.

Asylum Claim: ss.39, 40, 121

3–69   Where the person makes an application for asylum during the course of the proceedings there is no need for the proceedings to be adjourned but the person cannot be extradited until the asylum claim is finally determined.

VI. EVIDENCE

3–70   The evidence brought before the judge under Pt 1 will be that sufficient under the terms of the Act for the judge to make an extradition order. The court will also hear representations. In *Re Evans* [1994] 1 W.L.R. 1006, under the former legislation, it was held that a person who was the subject of extradition proceedings could not call evidence to show that the conduct alleged did not amount to an extradition offence because it was not criminal in Sweden.

     The evidence necessary for an extradition order under Pt 2 for most of the category 2 countries will be that which is sufficient for a case to be answered: *Re Nielson* [1984] 2 All E.R. 81, HL; *United States Government v McCaffery* [1984] 1 W.L.R. 867, HL; *R. v Parekh* [1988] Crim.L.R. 832. The offender's evidence may be heard: *Re Gross* [1998] 3 All E.R. 624.

     In these circumstances the test in *R. v Galbraith*—see Part 3 below—will be used. That was commended by the House of Lords in *Alves v DPP* [1992] 4 All E.R. 787. The UK government has agreed to dispense with the *prima facie* rule for certain countries, *e.g.* USA. Designation orders will need to be checked.

3–71   The court may receive properly authenticated evidence in the form of statements or affidavits received from the requesting state. It can also receive statements made in this country as well as hear evidence on oath or affirmation. Formal admissions may also be made.

Extradition Act 2003, ss.202, 205(1)–(2)

Receivable documents

3–72   **202.**—(1) A Part 1 warrant may be received in evidence in proceedings under this Act.

(2) Any other document issued in a category 1 territory may be received in evidence in proceedings under this Act if it is duly authenticated.

(3) A document issued in a category 2 territory may be received in evidence in proceedings under this Act if it is duly authenticated.

(4) A document issued in a category 1 or category 2 territory is duly authenticated if (and only if) one of these applies—

(a) it purports to be signed by a judge, magistrate or other judicial authority of the territory;

(b) it purports to be authenticated by the oath or affirmation of a witness.

(5) Subsections (2) and (3) do not prevent a document that is not duly authenticated from being received in evidence in proceedings under this Act.

Written statements and admissions

205.—(1) The provisions mentioned in subsection (2) apply in relation to proceedings under **3–73** this Act as they apply in relation to proceedings for an offence.

(2) The provisions are—

(a) section 9 of the *Criminal Justice Act* 1967 (proof by written statement in criminal proceedings);

(b) section 10 of the *Criminal Justice Act* 1967 (proof by formal admission in criminal proceedings);

Extradition proceedings are not a trial on the merits, however most of the rules **3–74** governing admissibility of evidence in England and Wales will apply.

Those termed rules of law, *e.g.* hearsay, will apply whereas those termed rules of practice, *e.g.*, refreshing memory, will not: *R. v Governor of Gloucester Prison Ex p. Miller* [1979] 2 All E.R. 1103.

The meaning of "accused person" was considered in *Re Ismail* [1999] A.C. 320. The House of Lords stated that it is more than mere suspicion that an individual has committed an offence and courts ought to adopt a purposive interpretation.

> "It is necessary for our courts to adopt a cosmopolitan approach to the question whether as a matter of substance rather than form the requirement of there being an "accused" person is satisfied…the Divisional court in this case posed the right test by addressing the broad question whether the competent authorities in the foreign jurisdiction had taken a step which can fairly be described as the commencement of a prosecution. But in the light of the diversity of cases which may come before the courts it is right to emphasise that ultimately the question whether a person is "accused" …will require an intense focus on the particular facts of each case".

Where a person has not been convicted the provisions covering documentary evi- **3–75** dence are found in s.84.

Extradition Act 2003, s.84(1)–(7)

Case where person has not been convicted

84.—(1) If the judge is required to proceed under this section he must decide whether there is evidence which would be sufficient to make a case requiring an answer by the person if the proceedings were the summary trial of an information against him.

(2) In deciding the question in subsection (1) the judge may treat a statement made by a person in a document as admissible evidence of a fact if—

(a) the statement is made by the person to a police officer or another person charged with the duty of investigating offences or charging offenders, and

(b) direct oral evidence by the person of the fact would be admissible.

(3) In deciding whether to treat a statement made by a person in a document as admissible evidence of a fact, the judge must in particular have regard—

(a) to the nature and source of the document;

(b) to whether or not, having regard to the nature and source of the document and to any other circumstances that appear to the judge to be relevant, it is likely that the document is authentic;

(c) to the extent to which the statement appears to supply evidence which would not be readily available if the statement were not treated as being admissible evidence of the fact;

(d) to the relevance of the evidence that the statement appears to supply to any issue likely to have to be determined by the judge in deciding the question in subsection (1);

(e) to any risk that the admission or exclusion of the statement will result in unfairness to the person whose extradition is sought, having regard in particular to whether it is likely to be possible to controvert the statement if the person making it does not attend to give oral evidence in the proceedings.

(4) A summary in a document of a statement made by a person must be treated as a statement made by the person in the document for the purposes of subsection (2).

(5) If the judge decides the question in subsection (1) in the negative he must order the person's discharge.

(6) If the judge decides that question in the affirmative he must proceed under section 87.

(7) If the judge is required to proceed under this section and the category 2 territory to which extradition is requested is designated for the purposes of this section by order made by the Secretary of State—

(a) the judge must not decide under subsection (1), and

(b) he must proceed under section 87.

3–76   Where the person has been convicted in his absence the evidential requirements are found in s.86.

Extradition Act 2003, s.86(1)–(7)

Conviction in person's absence

86.—(1) If the judge is required to proceed under this section he must decide whether there is evidence which would be sufficient to make a case requiring an answer by the person if the proceedings were the summary trial of an information against him.

(2) In deciding the question in subsection (1) the judge may treat a statement made by a person in a document as admissible evidence of a fact if—

(a) the statement is made by the person to a police officer or another person charged with the duty of investigating offences or charging offenders, and

(b) direct oral evidence by the person of the fact would be admissible.

(3) In deciding whether to treat a statement made by a person in a document as admissible evidence of a fact, the judge must in particular have regard—

(a) to the nature and source of the document;

(b) to whether or not, having regard to the nature and source of the document and to any other circumstances that appear to the judge to be relevant, it is likely that the document is authentic;

(c) to the extent to which the statement appears to supply evidence which would not be readily available if the statement were not treated as being admissible evidence of the fact;

(d) to the relevance of the evidence that the statement appears to supply to any issue likely to have to be determined by the judge in deciding the question in subsection (1);

(e) to any risk that the admission or exclusion of the statement will result in unfairness to the person whose extradition is sought, having regard in particular to whether it is likely to be possible to controvert the statement if the person making it does not attend to give oral evidence in the proceedings.

(4) A summary in a document of a statement made by a person must be treated as a statement made by the person in the document for the purposes of subsection (2).

(5) If the judge decides the question in subsection (1) in the negative he must order the person's discharge.

(6) If the judge decides that question in the affirmative he must proceed under section 87.

(7) If the judge is required to proceed under this section and the category 2 territory to which extradition is requested is designated for the purposes of this section by order made by the Secretary of State—

(a) the judge must not decide under subsection (1), and

(b) he must proceed under section 87.

In *Ginova v Government of the Czech Republic* [2003] EWHC 2187, unreported, **3–77** July 23, 2003, it was said that the burden of proof on the requesting state to show that a person was unlawfully at large was proof beyond reasonable doubt.

Where authentication of documents is required it is not necessary for each and every statement on oath to be certificated: *Oskar v Government of Australia* (1988) A.C. 366. It is sufficient to have a certificate which sufficiently identifies all the statements which it certifies. In that case the statements were all tied together.

In *Lodhi* above it was said that statements in English made by a non-English speaker had to be accompanied by a signature to a document written in his own language coupled with an attested translation of his signed affidavit into English.

It has been held that an affidavit is a document containing evidence whereas a deposition is a document recording evidence and both are admissible: *Fernandez v Government of Singapore* [1971] 2 All E.R. 691.

In *Orechovsky v Government of Slovakia* [2003] EWHC 2758, unreported, **3–78** November 5, 2003, it was held that the court could consider articles drawn from the internet concerning human rights abuse in the requesting state. The court was not restricted to hearing evidence in the strict sense.

There is no right of access to unused material: *R. v Governor of Pentonville prison Ex p. Lee* [1993] 3 All E.R. 504. This was approved in *Lodhi v Governor of H.M. Prison Brixton* [2001] EHWC Admin 178. In *Kashamu*, unreported, October 6, 2000, the extradition order was quashed on the grounds that the extradition proceedings were unfair as a result of the non-disclosure of crucial evidence. The position of disclosure is unresolved but the court must ensure that the proceedings are fair: Art.6, ECHR.

The *Police and Criminal Evidence Act* 1984 does not strictly apply to extradition proceedings as a person has not been arrested for an offence. Case law has, however, confirmed that s.78 of that Act does apply: *R. v Governor of Pentonville Prison Ex p. Walters* [1987] Crim.L.R. 577; *R. v Governor of Pentonville Prison Ex p. Chinoy* [1992] 1 All E.R. 317; *R. v Governor of Brixton Prison Ex p. Levin* [1997] 3 W.L.R. 117. In the latter case Lord Hoffman stated that extradition proceedings were criminal proceedings but of a very special kind. He confirmed that s.78 applied. He said:

> "The question is, therefore, whether the admission of the evidence would have such an adverse effect on the fairness of the decision to… extradite the accused for trial, even if the trial is a fair one… It would undermine the effectiveness of international treaty obligations if the courts were to superimpose discretions based on local notions of fairness upon the ordinary rules of admissibility. I do not wish to exclude the possibility that the discretion may be used in extradition proceedings founded upon evidence which, although technically admissible, has been obtained in a way which outrages civilised values. But such cases are also likely to be very rare."

In *R. (Saifi) v Governor of Brixton Prison* [2001] 1 W.L.R. 1134, Rose L.J., in **3–79** rejecting a burden of proof test for s.78, stated that—

> "Under s.78 any circumstance which can reasonably have a bearing on fairness should be considered. The weight to be attached to an individual circumstance may increase or decrease because of the presence of other related or unrelated circumstances. The preponderance of all the circumstances may show that the admission of the evidence would have such an adverse effect on fairness as to require its exclusion."

Evidence of identity is admissible—see § 3–27 above. In the case of *Anthony*, June 27, 1995, it was stated that when there is an issue as to whether the person brought before the magistrate is the person requested by the foreign state, that is a question which is fundamental to the jurisdiction of the magistrate.

The burden of proof is in accordance with the person being accused of a summary offence. The judge will weigh up the evidence but will not weigh the evidence: *R. v*

Governor of Pentonville Prison Ex p. Osman [1989] 3 All E.R. 701,

> "... it was the magistrate's duty to consider the evidence as a whole, and to reject any evidence which he considered worthless. In that sense was his duty to weigh up the evidence. But it was not his duty to weigh the evidence. He was neither entitled nor obliged to determine the amount of weight to be attached to any evidence, or to compare one witness with another. That would be for the jury at the trial. It follows that the magistrate was not concerned with the inconsistencies or contradictions in...evidence, unless they were such as to justify rejecting or eliminating his evidence altogether ... As a working guide, we could not do better than adopt the language of the magistrate ... substituting "consider" for "weigh"."

VII. THE DECISION

3–80 In Pt 1 cases, the judge will make an extradition order or will discharge the person. If there is no appeal the extradition will then take place within ten days unless a later date is agreed: ss.35, 46. In Pt 2 cases the judge will either commit the person in custody or on bail to await the Secretary of State's decision on extradition or will discharge him.

In *R. v Bow Street Magistrates' Court Ex p. Allison, The Times,* June 2, 1998, it was held that there is no legal duty to give reasons but stated that in matters of such importance, in almost every case the judge should explain briefly the reasons for his conclusions. It is the practice at Bow Street to give reasons for the decision either immediately at the close of the proceedings in court, or, if the case has been a complicated or lengthy one, at an adjourned hearing. Normally the reasons are reduced to writing and supplied to the parties. In the *Pinochet* case they were also supplied to the press.

If a person has been ordered to be extradited under Pt 1 and he is serving a sentence in this country the judge may make the order subject to a condition that extradition is not to take place unless he has received an undertaking on behalf of the requesting state that the person will be returned to the UK to serve the remainder of his sentence on the conclusion either of the proceedings or the sentence to be served there: s.52.

3–81 Where a person has been discharged and an appeal is pending then he will be remanded in custody or on bail pending the conclusion of the appeal: s.30.

VIII. CHALLENGING THE DECISION

3–82 An appeal may be made by the requesting state against discharge and by the person concerned against the order for extradition.

In Pt 1 cases the appeal is to the High court on a question of law and fact: s.26. The High Court may allow or dismiss the appeal: s.27. In Pt 2 cases no appeal from a committal order by the judge shall lie until the Secretary of State has made his decision: s.103.

An appeal will lie from the High court to the House of Lords: s.32 and in certain instances the House may remit the case back to the district judge.

Extradition Act 2003, ss.26, 27

Appeal against extradition order

3–83 **26.**—(1) If the appropriate judge orders a person's extradition under this Part, the person may appeal to the High Court against the order.

(2) But subsection (1) does not apply if the order is made under section 46 or 48.

(3) An appeal under this section may be brought on a question of law or fact.

(4) Notice of an appeal under this section must be given in accordance with rules of court before the end of the permitted period, which is 7 days starting with the day on which the order is made.

Court's powers on appeal under s.26

3–84 **27.**—(1) On an appeal under section 26 the High Court may—
(a) allow the appeal;

(b) dismiss the appeal.

(2) The court may allow the appeal only if the conditions in subsection (3) or the conditions in subsection (4) are satisfied.

(3) The conditions are that—

(a) the appropriate judge ought to have decided a question before him at the extradition hearing differently;

(b) if he had decided the question in the way he ought to have done, he would have been required to order the person's discharge.

(4) The conditions are that—

(a) an issue is raised that was not raised at the extradition hearing or evidence is available that was not available at the extradition hearing;

(b) the issue or evidence would have resulted in the appropriate judge deciding a question before him at the extradition hearing differently;

(c) if he had decided the question in that way, he would have been required to order the person's discharge.

(5) If the court allows the appeal it must—

(a) order the person's discharge;

(b) quash the order for his extradition.

The High Court may allow the appeal only if it believes that the judge should have decided a question before him differently and that difference would have led to the person's discharge. Its powers are to dismiss the application or to quash the extradition order and discharge the person.

Extradition Act 2003, s.28

Appeal against discharge at extradition hearing

28.—(1) If the judge orders a person's discharge at the extradition hearing the authority **3–85** which issued the Part 1 warrant may appeal to the High Court against the relevant decision.

(2) But subsection (1) does not apply if the order for the person's discharge was under section 41.

(3) The relevant decision is the decision which resulted in the order for the person's discharge.

(4) An appeal under this section may be brought on a question of law or fact.

(5) Notice of an appeal under this section must be given in accordance with rules of court before the end of the permitted period, which is 7 days starting with the day on which the order for the person's discharge is made.

The requesting state may appeal against discharge within seven days on a question of law or fact. On appeal the High Court may allow the appeal if the judge ought to have decided a question differently and that would not have led to the person's discharge or a new issue has been raised or new evidence is available and that if heard by the judge would not have led to the person's discharge.

Extradition Act 2003, s.29

Court's powers on appeal under s.28

29.—(1) On an appeal under section 28 the High Court may—   **3–86**

(a) allow the appeal;

(b) dismiss the appeal.

(2) The court may allow the appeal only if the conditions in subsection (3) or the conditions in subsection (4) are satisfied.

(3) The conditions are that—

(a) the judge ought to have decided the relevant question differently;

(b) if he had decided the question in the way he ought to have done, he would not have been required to order the person's discharge.

(4) The conditions are that—

(a) an issue is raised that was not raised at the extradition hearing or evidence is available that was not available at the extradition hearing;

(b) the issue or evidence would have resulted in the judge deciding the relevant question differently;

(c) if he had decided the question in that way, he would not have been required to order the person's discharge.

(5) If the court allows the appeal it must—

(a) quash the order discharging the person;

(b) remit the case to the judge;

(c) direct him to proceed as he would have been required to do if he had decided the relevant question differently at the extradition hearing.

(6) A question is the relevant question if the judge's decision on it resulted in the order for the person's discharge.

The specific procedure for Pt 2 cases is contained in the following provisions

Extradition Act 2003, ss.103–106

Appeal where case sent to Secretary of State

3–87   **103.**—(1) If the judge sends a case to the Secretary of State under this Part for his decision whether a person is to be extradited, the person may appeal to the High Court against the relevant decision.

(2) But subsection (1) does not apply if the person consented to his extradition under section 127 before his case was sent to the Secretary of State.

(3) The relevant decision is the decision that resulted in the case being sent to the Secretary of State.

(4) An appeal under this section may be brought on a question of law or fact.

(5) If an appeal is brought under this section before the Secretary of State has decided whether the person is to be extradited the appeal must not be heard until after the Secretary of State has made his decision.

(6) If the Secretary of State orders the person's discharge the appeal must not be proceeded with.

(7) No appeal may be brought under this section if the Secretary of State has ordered the person's discharge.

(8) If notice of an appeal under section 110 against the decision which resulted in the order for the person's discharge is given in accordance with subsection (5) of that section—

(a) subsections (6) and (7) do not apply;

(b) no appeal may be brought under this section if the High Court has made its decision on the appeal.

(9) Notice of an appeal under this section must be given in accordance with rules of court before the end of the permitted period, which is 14 days starting with the day on which the Secretary of State informs the person under section 100(1) or (4) of the order he has made in respect of the person.

Court's powers on appeal under s.103

3–88   **104.**—(1) On an appeal under section 103 the High Court may—

(a) allow the appeal;

(b) direct the judge to decide again a question (or questions) which he decided at the extradition hearing;

(c) dismiss the appeal.

(2) The court may allow the appeal only if the conditions in subsection (3) or the conditions in subsection (4) are satisfied.

(3) The conditions are that—

(a) the judge ought to have decided a question before him at the extradition hearing differently;

(b) if he had decided the question in the way he ought to have done, he would have been required to order the person's discharge.

(4) The conditions are that—

(a) an issue is raised that was not raised at the extradition hearing or evidence is available that was not available at the extradition hearing;

(b) the issue or evidence would have resulted in the judge deciding a question before him at the extradition hearing differently;

(c) if he had decided the question in that way, he would have been required to order the person's discharge.

(5) If the court allows the appeal it must—

(a) order the person's discharge;

(b) quash the order for his extradition.

(6) If the judge comes to a different decision on any question that is the subject of a
direction under subsection (1)(b) he must order the person's discharge.

(7) If the judge comes to the same decision as he did at the extradition hearing on the
question that is (or all the questions that are) the subject of a direction under subsection
(1)(b) the appeal must be taken to have been dismissed by a decision of the High Court.

Appeal against discharge at extradition hearing

105.—(1) If at the extradition hearing the judge orders a person's discharge, an appeal to **3–89**
the High Court may be brought on behalf of the category 2 territory against the relevant
decision.

(2) But subsection (1) does not apply if the order for the person's discharge was under
section 122.

(3) The relevant decision is the decision which resulted in the order for the person's
discharge.

(4) An appeal under this section may be brought on a question of law or fact.

(5) Notice of an appeal under this section must be given in accordance with rules of
court before the end of the permitted period, which is 14 days starting with the day on
which the order for the person's discharge is made.

Court's powers on appeal under section105

106.—(1) On an appeal under section 105 the High Court may—   **3–90**

(a) allow the appeal;

(b) direct the judge to decide the relevant question again;

(c) dismiss the appeal.

(2) A question is the relevant question if the judge's decision on it resulted in the order
for the person's discharge.

(3) The court may allow the appeal only if the conditions in subsection (4) or the conditions in subsection (5) are satisfied.

(4) The conditions are that—

(a) the judge ought to have decided the relevant question differently;

(b) if he had decided the question in the way he ought to have done, he would not
have been required to order the person's discharge.

(5) The conditions are that—

(a) an issue is raised that was not raised at the extradition hearing or evidence is
available that was not available at the extradition hearing;

(b) the issue or evidence would have resulted in the judge deciding the relevant
question differently;

(c) if he had decided the question in that way, he would not have been required to
order the person's discharge.

(6) If the court allows the appeal it must—

(a) quash the order discharging the person;

(b) remit the case to the judge;

(c) direct him to proceed as he would have been required to do if he had decided
the relevant question differently at the extradition hearing.

(7) If the court makes a direction under subsection (1)(b) and the judge decides the relevant question differently he must proceed as he would have been required to do if he had
decided that question differently at the extradition hearing.

(8) If the court makes a direction under subsection (1)(b) and the judge does not decide
the relevant question differently the appeal must be taken to have been dismissed by a decision of the High Court.

IX. COSTS

Where extradition has been ordered costs may be awarded under s.60 for category 1   **3–91**
cases and s.133 for category 2.

Extradition Act 2003, ss.60(2), (4), 133(2), (6)

Costs where extradition ordered

60. & 133.—(2) ... the appropriate judge may make such order as he considers just and reasonable with regard to the costs to be paid by the person.

(4) An order for costs under this section—

(a) must specify their amount;

(b) may name the person to whom they are to be paid.

3–92 Where extradition is ordered, the person may be ordered to pay a specific sum of costs which is considered just and reasonable.

Where the person has been discharged or taken to be discharged, costs may be ordered under s.61 for category 1 cases and s.134 for category 2.

Extradition Act 2003, ss.61(2), (5)–(8), 134(2), (5)–(8)

61. & 134.—(2) .... an order under subsection (5) in favour of the person may be made by—

(a) the appropriate judge, if the order for the person's discharge is made by him;

(5) An order under this subsection in favour of a person is an order for a payment of the appropriate amount to be made to the person out of money provided by Parliament.

(6) The appropriate amount is such amount as the judge or court making the order under subsection (5) considers reasonably sufficient to compensate the person in whose favour the order is made for any expenses properly incurred by him in the proceedings under this Part.

(7) But if the judge or court making an order under subsection (5) is of the opinion that there are circumstances which make it inappropriate that the person in whose favour the order is made should recover the full amount mentioned in subsection (6), the judge or court must—

(a) assess what amount would in his or its opinion be just and reasonable;

(b) specify that amount in the order as the appropriate amount.

(8) Unless subsection (7) applies, the appropriate amount—

(a) must be specified in the order, if the court considers it appropriate for it to be so specified and the person in whose favour the order is made agrees the amount;

(b) must be determined in accordance with regulations made by the Lord Chancellor for the purposes of this section, in any other case.

3–93 Here there are three options:

1) where the judge considers that a person should not receive all his costs he should specify the amount of costs ordered

2) where the judge considers that the person should receive all his costs he may specify the sum where the sum is agreed by the person

3) where the judge considers that the person should receive all his costs he may order that they may be taxed by the determining officer: s.62.

X. POST EXTRADITION

3–94 Under Pt 1 where the extradition order has been made with consent, then, if a request is made by the requesting state for extradition on another offence, the judge will hold a hearing to determine whether the offence is an extradition offence and whether he would order extradition if he had proceeded in the normal way: s.55. In Pt 2 cases that is a matter for the Secretary of State.

CHAPTER 4

COMMENCEMENT OF PROCEEDINGS

I. PROSECUTION OF OFFENCES

Introduction

A prosecution consists of the institution and pursuance of legal proceedings against **4–1** named persons or bodies. When a decision is made to prosecute a criminal case it will generally be started in the magistrates' court. Cases may be commenced in a variety of ways and by a number of different people, including private individuals, corporations and representatives of statutory organisations such as the police.

General

The Crown Prosecution Service on behalf of the police prosecutes the majority of **4–2** cases in the magistrates' courts. Prosecutions are also brought by public authorities such as the Serious Fraud Office or Customs and Excise. Government departments and local authorities are also empowered by specific statutes to institute and carry on prosecutions of certain offences.

The named individual who commences the prosecuting process may be described as the prosecutor, even if little or no role is taken by them personally in the subsequent court proceedings. Where the prosecution begins with the accused being charged at the police station, a police officer will commence the prosecution by signing the charge sheet. Where the prosecution begins with the laying of an information before a magistrate, the person who laid the information commences the prosecution. The prosecution may then be taken over from the individual prosecutor by the relevant prosecuting body which in the case of the police officers will be the Crown Prosecution Service. Examples of prosecutions brought by Government Departments are offences under the *Vehicle Excise Registration Act* 1994 prosecuted by the Secretary of State for Transport and also television licence offences which are prosecuted on behalf of the Secretary of State for the Home Office. A private individual either acting alone or on behalf of a body corporate may also prosecute a case through the criminal courts by applying to the court for a summons to commence the proceedings.

Anyone who appears in the magistrates' court to commence or carry on a prosecu- **4–3** tion will either be a private individual or a corporation both of whom may instruct a legal representative at their own expense or they will be an individual employed by an public authority which is publicly funded with statutory powers to conduct prosecutions. Public authorities may also instruct lawyers as agents to conduct prosecutions.

Prosecution of Offences Act 1985, s.1(1), (6)–(7)

The Crown Prosecution Service

1.—(1) There shall be a prosecuting service for England and Wales (to be known as the **4–4** "Crown Prosecution Service") consisting of—

(a) the Director of Public Prosecutions, who shall be head of the Service;

(b) the Chief Crown Prosecutors, designated under subsection (4) below, each of whom shall be the member of the Service responsible to the Director for supervising the operation of the Service in his area; and

(c) the other staff appointed by the Director under this section.

(6) Without prejudice to any functions which may have been assigned to him in his capacity as a member of the Service, every Crown Prosecutor shall have all the powers of the Director as to the institution and conduct of proceedings but shall exercise those powers under the direction of the Director.

(7) Where any enactment (whenever passed)—

(a) prevents any step from being taken without the consent of the Director or without his consent or the consent of another; or

(b) requires any step to be taken by or in relation to the Director;

any consent given by or, as the case may be, step taken by or in relation to, a Crown Prosecutor shall be treated, for the purposes of that enactment, as given by or, as the case may be, taken by or in relation to the Director.

[This section is printed as amended by the *Courts and Legal Services Act* 1990, Sch.10 and the *Access to Justice Act* 1999, Sch.15.]

4–5   The *Prosecution of Offences Act* 1985 established the Crown Prosecution Service (CPS) in England and Wales. The Director of Public Prosecutions is the head of the service and the prosecutor who conducts the case will either be a lawyer employed directly by the CPS or an appointed and approved solicitor or barrister who will act as agent. Such agents are subject to instructions from the CPS throughout the progress of the case including when matters arise in court. The CPS also employs designated caseworkers who are not legally qualified but who have limited rights of audience under s.7A of the *Prosecution of Offences Act* 1985. They deal with criminal proceedings other than trials and act as prosecutor in early first hearing cases when pleas of guilty are anticipated.

Prosecution of Offences Act 1985, s.3

Functions of the Director

4–6   **3.**—(1) The Director shall discharge his functions under this or any other enactment under the superintendence of the Attorney General.

(2) It shall be the duty of the Director, subject to any provisions contained in the *Criminal Justice Act* 1987—

(a) to take over the conduct of all criminal proceedings, other than specified proceedings, instituted on behalf of a police force (whether by a member of that force or by any other person);

(b) to institute and have the conduct of criminal proceedings in any case where it appears to him that—

(i) the importance or difficulty of the case makes it appropriate that proceedings should be instituted by him; or

(ii) it is otherwise appropriate for proceedings to be instituted by him;

(c) to take over the conduct of all binding over proceedings instituted on behalf of a police force (whether by a member of that force or by any other person);

(d) to take over the conduct of all proceedings begun by summons issued under section 3 of the *Obscene Publications Act* 1959 (forfeiture of obscene articles);

(e) to give, to such extent as he considers appropriate, advice to police forces on all matters relating to criminal offences;

(f) (Appeals).

(g) to discharge such other functions as may from time to time be assigned to him by the Attorney-General in pursuance of this paragraph.

(3) In this section—

"police force" means any police force maintained by a police authority under the *Police Act* 1996 [, the National Crime Squad] and any other body of constables for the time being specified by order made by the Secretary of State for the purposes of this section; and

"specified proceedings" means proceedings which fall within any category for the time being specified by order made by the Attorney General for the purposes of this section.

(4) The power to make orders under subsection (3) above shall be exercisable by statutory instrument subject to annulment in pursuance of a resolution of either House of
Parliament.

[This section is printed as amended by the *Criminal Justice Act* 1987, Sch.2, the *Police Act* 1996, Sch.7 and the *Police Act* 1997, Sch.9. Section 3(2) is set out as
prospectively to be amended by the *Immigration and Asylum Act* 1999, s.164 and
subs.(2)(ba) as amended prospectively by the *Police Reform Act* 2002, Sch.7.]

The Director of Public Prosecutions is in charge of the CPS but he is accountable to **4–7**
the Attorney-General who is a Law Officer of government. The appointment to
Attorney-General is political and the incumbent will usually be a member of the House
of Commons. One of the responsibilities of the office is to prosecute in important criminal cases. The Solicitor-General is another Law Officer who is the subordinate of the
Attorney-General and in effect acts as his deputy.

The DPP must take over all prosecutions commenced by a Police Force as defined in
s.3(3) of the Act. SI 1985/1956 lists the specified bodies of constables as follows:

   British Transport Police,
   City of London Police,
   Dover Harbour Board Police,
   Falmouth Docks Police,
   Felixstowe Dock and Railway Company Police,
   Manchester Dock Police Force,
   Mersey Tunnel Law Enforcement Officers,
   Metropolitan Police Force,
   Milford Docks Police Force,
   Ministry of Defence Police,
   Port of Bristol Police,
   Port of Liverpool Police,
   Port of London Authority Police,
   Royal Parks Constabulary (England),
   Tees and Hartlepool Port Authority Harbour Police,
   United Kingdom Atomic Energy Authority Constabulary.

All prosecutions commenced by these forces will be taken over by the DPP.

The DPP has no duty to take over specified proceedings. These proceedings are **4–8**
defined in the *Prosecution of Offences Act 1985 (Specified Proceedings Order)* 1999
(SI 1999/904).

The offences listed are;

 1) Fixed Penalty Offences (s.51 and Sch.3 of the *Road Traffic Offenders Act* 1988)
 2) Using or keeping an unlicensed vehicle on a public road (Road tax) (s.29 of the
   Vehicle Excise and Registration Act 1994)
 3) Road traffic offences. (Specified sections of the *Road Traffic Offenders Act* 1988)
 4) Road traffic regulations offences. (Specified sections of the *Road Traffic Regulation Act* 1984)
 5) *Royal and Other Parks and Gardens Regulations* 1977.

Proceedings under these provisions will not be conducted by the CPS. The prosecuting police force will take responsibility for their prosecution. The offences cease to be
"specified proceedings" once a summons has been served unless the necessary documents to enable the case to be dealt with on a written plea of guilty are also served on
the offender with the summons. Proceedings also cease to be specified once the court
starts to receive evidence but information provided to the court where a written plea of
guilty has been entered is not treated as evidence for these purposes.

In practice this means that the court may deal with "specified proceedings" where written pleas are received to the listed offences in the absence of the CPS. The court will be assisted by the presence of a representative of the relevant police force.

Prosecution of Offences Act 1985, ss.5, 6

Conduct of prosecutions on behalf of the Service

4–8.1   **5.**—(1) The Director may at any time appoint a person who is not a Crown Prosecutor but [who has a general qualification (within the meaning of section 71 of the *Courts and Legal Services Act* 1990)] to institute or take over the conduct of such criminal proceedings as the Director may assign to him.

(2) Any person conducting proceedings assigned to him under this section shall have all the powers of a Crown Prosecutor but shall exercise those powers subject to any instructions given to him by a Crown Prosecutor.

[This section is printed as amended by the *Courts and Legal Services Act* 1990, Sch.10.]

This section allows agents to act for the CPS. The agent must be a barrister or solicitor from a list approved by the CPS. Individual cases will then be sent to the agent or they may be instructed to deal with all cases listed in the Court on any particular day. The agent will only act in the case in accordance with instructions from the CPS.

Prosecutions instituted and conducted otherwise than by the Service

4–9   **6.**—(1) Subject to subsection (2) below, nothing in this Part shall preclude any person from instituting any criminal proceedings or conducting any criminal proceedings to which the Director's duty to take over the conduct of proceedings does not apply.

(2) Where criminal proceedings are instituted in circumstances in which the Director is not under a duty to take over their conduct, he may nevertheless do so at any stage.

It is open to private individuals to take out criminal prosecutions and the DPP may take the prosecution over at any time. The DPP may also take over specified proceedings as mentioned above.

4–10   With the number of bodies authorised under statute to conduct prosecutions, there are occasions when issues may arise over who should take responsibility for a prosecution.

In *R. v Ealing JJ Ex p. Dixon* [1989] 2 All E.R. 1050, the court held that the police have no power to entrust the conduct of criminal proceedings to anyone other than the Crown Prosecution Service. In this case the police charged the defendants for offences against the *Copyright Act* 1956. They were assisted in the investigation by representatives of the Federation Against Copyright Theft who were present when a search warrant was executed and the defendants were charged. A police officer signed the charge sheet as did the FACT representative. When the case came to court a solicitor instructed by FACT purported to prosecute the case. On application by the defence the court agreed that FACT had no standing to prosecute the case as it had been commenced by the police with the charging process and so would have to be taken over by the CPS under ss.3 and 6 of the *Prosecution of Offences Act* 1985. The approach of the court was upheld by the High Court on appeal. A private prosecutor was not permitted to take over a prosecution when a defendant had been arrested and charged by the police.

On the other hand in the Divisional Court in *R. v Stafford Magistrates' Courts Ex p. Commissioners of Customs and Excise* [1991] 2 Q.B. 339, Watkins L.J. was of the view that the case of *Dixon* was wrongly decided. In the Stafford case a customs officer arrested an individual without a warrant and took him to the police station to be charged by the custody officer under s.37 of the *Police and Criminal Evidence Act* 1984. At the committal proceedings the court ruled that the proceedings had been instituted on behalf of the police force and so could only be conducted by the Crown Prosecution Service. On appeal it was held that the police were not deemed to have started the proceedings. The prosecution was not surrendered by Customs and Excise simply because the police formally charged the suspect. The prosecution could only be said to have been brought by the police when they investigated the matter, arrested the suspect and brought him to custody.

In *R. v Tower Bridge Metropolitan Stipendiary Magistrate Ex p. Chaudhry* **4–11** [1994] R.T.R. 113 the Court considered the propriety of a private individual applying to take out a prosecution when proceedings had already been instituted by the CPS. The defendant was summonsed by the CPS for an offence of driving without due care following an incident which resulted in a fatal accident. The mother of the motor cyclist who was killed applied to the magistrates court for a summons against the defendant for causing death by dangerous driving. The court refused to issue the summons. On appeal the Divisional Court held that the magistrate was right to have regard to all relevant circumstances, including the fact that the CPS had already taken out a prosecution, when considering whether to issue a summons. In the absence of special circumstances the Court said that magistrates should be slow to issue a private summons when the defendant was already subject to informations laid by the Crown.

All agencies responsible in various circumstances for prosecuting offences are encouraged to work in partnership and in view of the criticism of *Dixon* in the Stafford case it may be that the Courts will take a more flexible view of the role of various prosecutors in ensuring that offenders are brought to justice.

An example of the entitlement of bodies other than the CPS to prosecute offences **4–12** may be found in s.222 of the *Local Government Act* 1972 which gives powers of prosecution to local authorities where they consider it "expedient for the promotion or protection of the interests of the inhabitants of their area". Other enactments such as the *Road Traffic Offenders Act* 1988 also prescribe specific offences for which local authorities may institute proceedings. In *Middlesbrough Borough Council v Safeer* [2002] 1 Cr.App.R. 23, the defendants were prosecuted by Middlesborough Borough Council for using a vehicle without insurance. The Crown Court allowed an appeal on the basis that s.4 provided an exhaustive list of offences which did not include no insurance and the council could not rely on s.222 of the *Local Government Act* 1972 to prosecute that offence. On further appeal the Administrative Court held that the express powers of prosecution listed in s.4 did not preclude a prosecution for offences which fell within the ambit of s.222. The defendant was also prosecuted by the Council for plying for hire as a hackney carriage without a licence in addition to having no insurance. The Administrative Court decided that in view of the council's responsibility to regulate hackney carriages and the fact that it could not licence a hackney carriage if there was no insurance policy in place, the power to prosecute for no insurance did fall within the scope of s.222.

Decision to prosecute

Not every criminal offence will automatically be prosecuted. Prosecutors retain a **4–13** discretion to prosecute which should be exercised in acordance with published guidelines.

Prosecution of Offences Act 1985, s.10

Guidelines for Crown Prosecutors

 10.—(1) The Director shall issue a Code for Crown Prosecutors giving guidance on general principles to be applied by them—

   (a) in determining, in any case—

     (i) whether proceedings for an offence should be instituted or, where proceedings have been instituted, whether they should be discontinued; or

     (ii) what charges should be preferred; and

   (b) in considering, in any case, representations to be made by them to any magistrates' court about the mode of trial suitable for that case.

 (2) The Director may from time to time make alterations in the Code.

 (3) The provisions of the Code shall be set out in the Director's report under section 9

of this Act for the year in which the Code is issued; and any alteration in the Code shall be set out in his report under that section for the year in which the alteration is made.

The most recent version of the Code was published in 2000. The Code is designed to ensure that fair and consistent decisions on prosecutions are made. The Code is published so that the principles applied by the CPS in exercising its functions are known to everyone involved in the Criminal Justice System whether professionals or members of the public. The duty of the CPS is expressed as being to ensure that "the right person is prosecuted for the right offence" and that all relevant facts are given to the court. The CPS also has a duty to review each case on a continuing basis to test the progress of the case against the Code.

4–14   The Code sets out two stages in the decision to prosecute: the evidential test and the public interest test.

The evidential test must be satisfied for every case and then the public interest test will be considered. If the evidential test is not met then the prosecution will not proceed, no matter how serious the charge may be. If the evidential test is passed the case must still be tested against the public interest criteria.

The Evidential Test

The Prosecutor must be satisfied that there is sufficient evidence to provide a "realistic prospect of conviction". This is an objective test based on whether a jury or bench, properly directed, is more likely than not to convict on the charge. The Prosecutor must decide whether the evidence is admissible and reliable. By asking these questions the strength of the prosecution case can be assessed.

4–15   **The Public Interest Test**

This test recognises the fact that there exists no rule of law that requires suspected criminal offences to be prosecuted automatically. Even if there is enough evidence to justify a prosecution the public interest in pursuing a prosecution must be considered. The Code lists some of the common factors which weigh both in favour of and against prosecution. Factors in favour are aggravating circumstances of offences including the fact that conviction might lead to a significant sentence; that violence or a weapon was used during the offence; that the offence was likely to be repeated by the offender as a pattern of offences or that the offence is prevalent. Factors against prosecution include the fact that a nominal penalty is likely to be imposed; that the prosecution is likely to have a deleterious effect on the victim's physical or mental health or that the defendant is elderly at the time of the offence or was suffering from mental or physical ill health. At all times the serious nature of the offence will be borne in mind. These lists of factors are not exhaustive and the balancing exercise must be carefully performed by the Prosecutor.

In addition the Code provides that Prosecutors must take into account the views of the victims and the consequences to them of deciding not to prosecute.

In cases involving youths the prosecutor must consider the welfare of the youth when deciding whether to prosecute. The gravity of the offence will be relevant and whether a reprimand or final warning has previously been received by the youth.

In the case of adults a Prosecutor may decide that a police caution would provide a suitable alternative to prosecution and the case may be referred back to the Police who administer cautions when offences are admitted.

The Code also gives guidance on the selection of charges, mode of trial and the acceptance of guilty pleas (which may be accepted if the court will still be able to impose a sentence that matches the seriousness of the offence and should not be accepted solely for purposes of convenience) and re-starting prosecutions.

4–16   If a decision not to prosecute was reached in breach of the Code, that decision may be subject to judicial review. The Administrative Court has the power to remit the case to the DPP for further consideration. In *R. v DPP Ex p. C* (1995) 159 J.P. 227 it was held that the application of the code to the decision not to prosecute was flawed in that the evidential test was not properly considered in relation to the charges brought. The case was remitted to the DPP for fresh consideration.

In *R. v Chief Constable of Kent Ex p. L* and *R. v DPP Ex p. B* (1991) 93 Cr.App.R. 416 the court held that it would only intervene in decisions to prosecute where it could be shown that the decision in question was made outside the settled policy or guidelines. These two cases involved youths one of whom was prosecuted when the defence argued that the criteria for a caution were met and another where the defence argued that it was not in the interests of justice to prosecute although there was no admission of guilt. Watkins L.J. said that it was difficult to envisage a circumstance which would allow a decision to prosecute or continue proceedings to be challenged unless it could be shown, in the case of a youth, that the decision maker had acted with total disregard to the policy, or had acted contrary to it, by failing to inquire into the circumstances and background of the person, previous convictions and general character. The Court held that both decisions of the CPS to prosecute were subject to judicial review but in the instant cases disregard of policy had not been established.

Powers and duties of the prosecution

The Prosecutor has the duty of prosecuting the case at court, taking it through the **4–17** preliminary stages of pre-trial hearings to calling evidence at trial and assisting with information at time of sentence. Full consideration of the duties are covered in the relevant sections, see Chapters 19 and 21 in this work.

Cases in which consent to prosecute is required

Following a decision to prosecute, some charges may require consent to be obtained **4–18** for the prosecution to be pursued.

Prosecution of Offences Act 1985, s.25

Consents to prosecutions etc.

25.—(1) This section applies to any enactment which prohibits the institution or carrying on of proceedings for any offence except—

    (a) with the consent (however expressed) of a Law Officer of the Crown or the Director; or

    (b) where the proceedings are instituted or carried on by or on behalf of a Law Officer of the Crown or the Director;

and so applies whether or not there are other exceptions to the prohibition (and in particular whether or not the consent is an alternative to the consent of any other authority or person).

    (2) An enactment to which this section applies—

    (a) shall not prevent the arrest without warrant, or the issue or execution of a warrant for the arrest, of a person for any offence, or the remand in custody or on bail of a person charged with any offence; and

    (b) shall be subject to any enactment concerning the apprehension or detention of children or young persons.

    (3) In this section "enactment" includes any provision having effect under or by virtue of any Act; and this section applies to enactments whenever passed or made.

The most common offences requiring consent are—   **4–19**

DPP Consent

    Child abduction and kidnapping (*Child Abduction Act* 1984)

    Conspiracy (s.4 of the *Criminal Law Act* 1977)

    Health and safety at work (s.38 of the *Health and Safety at Work Act* 1974— consent of the DPP or an inspector of the Environment Agency)

    Some sexual offences (s.8 of the *Sexual Offences Act* 1956)

    Theft or damage to property belonging to a husband or wife by a spouse (s.30 of the *Theft Act* 1968)

Attorney-General's consent

    Conspiracy (s.4 of the *Criminal Law Act* 1977 where the substantive offence requires consent from the Att.-Gen. to prosecute)

Contempt of court (s.7 of the *Contempt of Court Act* 1981—contempt in publications)

Corruption of public servants (s.4 of the *Public Bodies Corrupt Practices Act* 1889)

Customs proceedings (s.147 of the *Customs and Excise Management Act* 1979 where offences are tried summarily and were instituted initially in the name of the Att.-Gen.)

Explosive offences (s.7of the *Explosive Substances Act* 1883)

Highways offences (s.312 of the *Highways Act* 1980—the Att.-Gen. must consent to any prosecution covered in this section other than one taken out by a person aggrieved or a highway authority or council having an interest in the enforcement of the Act)

Hi-jacking (s.8 of the *Aviation Security Act* 1982)

Public Health Offences (s.298 of the *Public Health Act* 1936 and s.64 of the *Public Health (Control Of Diseases) Act* 1984—consent needed for prosecutions other than by a party aggrieved or a council or body whose function it is to enforce the Act)

Trespassing on foreign missions (s.9 of the *Criminal Law Act* 1977)

4–20　Commissioners for Customs and Excise consent:

Proceedings under the Customs and Excise Acts may only be instituted by order of the Commissioners and are commenced in the name of an officer (s.145 of the *Customs and Excise Management Act* 1979) but note such consent is not required where any person has been arrested for an offence for which he is liable to arrest by customs officers or police under this act and the Court may proceed to deal with the case although not instituted by order of the Commissioners, s.145(6) of the *Customs and Excise Management Act* 1979. This allows Courts to deal with such offences as being knowingly concerned in the fraudulent evasion of the prohibition on the importation of controlled drugs or conspiracy to commit that offence without the need for consent.

The consent will need to be produced in court following the first appearance but it is not required for the preliminary actions of arrest and charge. Where consent to prosecute is required by statute that consent must be given or the case will be a nullity.

Most cases requiring consent are serious in nature so will usually not give rise to summonses being issued but where authority to prosecute is required, the person before whom an information is laid should be satisfied that such authority has been obtained before issuing the summons.

Prosecution of Offences Act 1985, s.26

Consents to be admissible in evidence

4–21　　26. Any document purporting to be the consent of a Law Officer of the Crown, the Director or a Crown Prosecutor for, or to—

　　(a) the institution of any criminal proceedings; or

　　(b) the institution of criminal proceedings in any particular form;

and to be signed by a Law Officer of the Crown, the Director or, as the case may be, a Crown Prosecutor shall be admissible as prima facie evidence without further proof.

The relevant consent to prosecute is proved by the production of a document that meets the requirements of s.26. At the hearing it will be presumed that authority was given and the prosecutor need not take any further steps unless the defence objects. Such an objection should be made before the close of the prosecution case. In the case of *Price v Humphries* [1958] 2 All E.R. 725 the court held that proof of consent was a formal matter and the Prosecution was to be allowed to re-open it's case to produce the consent when late objection to the failure to produce it was taken by the defence.

If the defence requests proof of compliance with s.26 the prosecution must produce evidence that they have satisfied the statutory requirements as to consent. If such evidence is not forthcoming the justices are entitled to hold that there is no case to answer:

Anderton v Frost [1984] R.T.R. 106 where computer generated informations named the Chief Constable as the informant the court held that the CPS had to prove in each case that the Chief Constable himself either laid the information or else had given written authority in each individual case to the officers concerned.

The court has to decide what evidence it would wish to hear to be able to determine **4–22** whether the consent was properly given and certified. It would appear difficult to challenge the validity of a certificate without challenging the "bona fides" of the officer or process concerned.

Where a certificate has been overlooked or a defective one is produced, a correct certificate may be produced subsequent to the laying of an information where the lawfulness of the process is challenged: *R. v Clerkenwell Metropolitan Stipendiary Magistrate Ex p. DPP* [1984] 2 W.L.R. 244. The information alleged offences under the *Gas Act* 1972 which were subject to a six month time-limit. A certificate signed by the Secretary of State confirmed that the informations were laid in time. The prosecutions were brought outside of the six month time-limit but within three months of the relevant information coming to the notice of the Secretary of State. The certificate did not include this explanation but the Divisional Court held that the certificate was conclusive evidence that the informations were laid in time.

II. CHARGING OF OFFENCES

Introduction

In criminal proceedings, a person suspected of committing an offence may attend **4–23** voluntarily at a police station or he may be arrested and taken to a police station. Once arrested, suspects may be detained for investigations to be carried out to determine if there is sufficient evidence to bring a charge. Those charged with an offence are either then bailed from the police station to attend at court or are brought to court in custody. The charge sheet which accompanies them gives information about the defendant, including his name, address, date of birth and ethnic origin together with details of the offence, the time of charge and release and any bail conditions: *R. v Manchester Stipendiary Magistrate Ex p. Hill* [1983] 1 A.C. 328.

General

The process of charging offences and the powers and duties of police officers to **4–24** charge offenders are found in the *Police and Criminal Evidence Act* 1984. Under this statute Codes of Conduct for police officers have also been drawn up which set out procedures to be followed during investigations.

The responsibility of deciding whether or not a person should be charged rests with the custody officer at the station where the suspect is being detained: *Police and Criminal Evidence Act* 1984, s.37(7).

Once a police officer has charged a suspect the prosecution commences. The Director of Public Prosecutions will take over the proceedings from the police unless that responsibility is assigned to another person (*q.v. Prosecution of Offences Act* 1985, s.6)

In *Ealing Justices Ex p. Dixon* [1990] 2 Q.B. 91, DC, the court held that a police **4–25** officer acting as custody officer pursuant to ss.37 and 38, *PACE* 1984 had no power to charge a person or perform the other duties imposed by those sections on behalf of a private individual; and where a custody officer did charge someone, the DPP was bound to take over the conduct of the proceedings by virtue of s.3(2) of the *Prosecution of Offences Act* 1985 because they had been "instituted on behalf of a police force".

In *R. v Stafford JJ Ex p. Customs and Excise Commissioners* [1991] 2 Q.B. 339 the Divisional Court declined to follow *Dixon* stating that it was wrongly decided: see above. Watkins L.J. considered that s.6 of the *Prosecution of Offences Act* 1985 envisaged persons other than the DPP might institute proceedings and prosecute offences. The view expressed in *Ex p. Dixon* would lead to the conclusion that a person such as a customs officer who investigated the commission of an offence, arrested a person and took him to a police station to be charged, surrenders the prosecution of the offence to the DPP. In *Dixon* the charging by the police officer was deemed to have the effect of assigning to the police and CPS the duty of prosecuting the case to the exclusion of any other interested party. Conversely in the Stafford case it was held that proceedings could only be said to have been instituted on behalf of the police force and therefore restricted to prosecution by the CPS when it was the police who had investigated, arrested and brought the accused person to the custody officer.

The charging process

Police and Criminal Evidence Act 1984, ss.37–37D

Duties of custody officer before charge

4–26   37.—(1) Where—

    (a) a person is arrested for an offence—

      (i) without a warrant; or

      (ii) under a warrant not endorsed for bail,[...]

    [...]the custody officer at each police station where he is detained after his arrest shall determine whether he has before him sufficient evidence to charge that person with the offence for which he was arrested and may detain him at the police station for such period as is necessary to enable him to do so.

(2) If the custody officer determines that he does not have such evidence before him, the person arrested shall be released either on bail or without bail, unless the custody officer has reasonable grounds for believing that his detention without being charged is necessary to secure or preserve evidence relating to an offence for which he is under arrest or to obtain such evidence by questioning him.

(3) If the custody officer has reasonable grounds for so believing, he may authorise the person arrested to be kept in police detention.

(4) Where a custody officer authorises a person who has not been charged to be kept in police detention, he shall, as soon as is practicable, make a written record of the grounds for the detention.

(5) Subject to subsection (6) below, the written record shall be made in the presence of the person arrested who shall at that time be informed by the custody officer of the grounds for his detention.

(6) Subsection (5) above shall not apply where the person arrested is, at the time when the written record is made—

    (a) incapable of understanding what is said to him;

    (b) violent or likely to become violent; or

    (c) in urgent need of medical attention.

(7) Subject to section 41(7) below, if the custody officer determines that he has before him sufficient evidence to charge the person arrested with the offence for which he was arrested, the person arrested—

    (a) shall be released without charge and on bail for the purpose of enabling the Director of Public Prosecutions to make a decision under section 37B below,

    (b) shall be released without charge and on bail but not for that purpose,.

    (c) shall be released without charge and without bail, or

    (d) shall be charged.

(7A) The decision as to how a person is to be dealt with under subsection (7) above shall be that of the custody officer.

(7B) Where a person is released under subsection (7)(a) above, it shall be the duty of the custody officer to inform him that he is being released to enable the Director of Public Prosecutions to make a decision under section 37B below.

(8) Where—

    (a) a person is released under subsection (7)(b) or (c) above; and

    (b) at the time of his release a decision whether he should be prosecuted for the offence for which he was arrested has not been taken, it shall be the duty of the custody officer so to inform him.

(9) If the person arrested is not in a fit state to be dealt with under subsection (7) above, he may be kept in police detention until he is.

(10) The duty imposed on the custody officer under subsection (1) above shall be carried out by him as soon as practicable after the person arrested arrives at the police station or, in the case of a person arrested at the police station, as soon as practicable after the arrest.

(15) In this Part of this Act—

　　"arrested juvenile" means a person arrested with or without a warrant who appears to be under the age of 17;

　　"endorsed for bail" means endorsed with a direction for bail in accordance with section 117(2) of the *Magistrates' Courts Act* 1980.

[This section is printed as amended by the *Children Act* 1989, Schs 13 and 15, the *Criminal Justice Act* 1991, s.72 and the *Criminal Justice and Public Order Act* 1994, s.29 and Sch.11, and the *Criminal Justice Act* 2003, s.28 and Sch.2.]

Guidance

37A.—(1) The Director of Public Prosecutions may issue guidance—　　**4–27**

　　(a) for the purpose of enabling custody officers to decide how persons should be dealt with under section 37(7) above or 37C(2) below, and

　　(b) as to the information to be sent to the Director of Public Prosecutions under section 37B(1) below.

(2) The Director of Public Prosecutions may from time to time revise guidance issued under this section.

(3) Custody officers are to have regard to guidance under this section in deciding how persons should be dealt with under section 37(7) above or 37C(2) below.

(4) A report under section 9 of the *Prosecution of Offences Act* 1985 (report by DPP to Attorney General) must set out the provisions of any guidance issued, and any revisions to guidance made, in the year to which the report relates.

(5) The Director of Public Prosecutions must publish in such manner as he thinks fit—

　　(a) any guidance issued under this section, and

　　(b) any revisions made to such guidance.

(6) Guidance under this section may make different provision for different cases, circumstances or areas.

Consultation with the Director of Public Prosecutions

37B.—(1) Where a person is released on bail under section 37(7)(a) above, an officer involved　**4–27.1** in the investigation of the offence shall, as soon as is practicable, send to the Director of Public Prosecutions such information as may be specified in guidance under section 37A above.

(2) The Director of Public Prosecutions shall decide whether there is sufficient evidence to charge the person with an offence.

(3) If he decides that there is sufficient evidence to charge the person with an offence, he shall decide—

　　(a) whether or not the person should be charged and, if so, the offence with which he should be charged, and

　　(b) whether or not the person should be given a caution and, if so, the offence in respect of which he should be given a caution.

(4) The Director of Public Prosecutions shall give written notice of his decision to an officer involved in the investigation of the offence.

(5) If his decision is—

　　(a) that there is not sufficient evidence to charge the person with an offence, or

　　(b) that there is sufficient evidence to charge the person with an offence but that the person should not be charged with an offence or given a caution in respect of an offence,

a custody officer shall give the person notice in writing that he is not to be prosecuted.

(6) If the decision of the Director of Public Prosecutions is that the person should be charged with an offence, or given a caution in respect of an offence, the person shall be charged or cautioned accordingly.

(7) But if his decision is that the person should be given a caution in respect of the offence and it proves not to be possible to give the person such a caution, he shall instead be charged with the offence.

(9) In this section "caution" includes—

    (a) a conditional caution within the meaning of Part 3 of the *Criminal Justice Act* 2003, and

    (b) a warning or reprimand under section 65 of the *Crime and Disorder Act* 1998.

Breach of bail following release under section 37(7)(a)

4–27.2   **37C.**—(1) This section applies where—

    (a) a person released on bail under section 37(7)(a) above or subsection (2)(b) below is arrested under section 46A below in respect of that bail, and

    (b) at the time of his detention following that arrest at the police station mentioned in section 46A(2) below, notice under section 37B(4) above has not been given.

(2) The person arrested—

    (a) shall be charged, or

    (b) shall be released without charge, either on bail or without bail.

(3) The decision as to how a person is to be dealt with under subsection (2) above shall be that of a custody officer.

(4) A person released on bail under subsection (2)(b) above shall be released on bail subject to the same conditions (if any) which applied immediately before his arrest.

Release under section 37(7)(a): further provision

4–27.3   **37D.**—(1) Where a person is released on bail under section 37(7)(a) or section 37C(2)(b) above, a custody officer may subsequently appoint a different time, or an additional time, at which the person is to attend at the police station to answer bail.

(2) The custody officer shall give the person notice in writing of the exercise of the power under subsection (1).

(3) The exercise of the power under subsection (1) shall not affect the conditions (if any) to which bail is subject.

(4) Where a person released on bail under section 37(7)(a) or *37C(2)(b)* above returns to a police station to answer bail or is otherwise in police detention at a police station, he may be kept in police detention to enable him to be dealt with in accordance with section 37B or *37C* above or to enable the power under subsection (1) above to be exercised.

(5) If the person is not in a fit state to enable him to be so dealt with or to enable that power to be exercised, he may be kept in police detention until he is.

(6) Where a person is kept in police detention by virtue of subsection (4) or (5) above, section 37(1) to (3) and (7) above (and section 40(8) below so far as it relates to section 37(1) to (3)) shall not apply to the offence in connection with which he was released on bail under section 37(7)(a) or 37C(2)(b) above.

[Sections 37A to 37D were inserted into *PACE* 1984 by the *Criminal Justice Act* 2003, s.28 and Sch.2, in force from January 29, 2004.]

4–28   Section 37 has been amended by s.28 and Sch.2 of the *Criminal Justice Act* 2003 which were brought into force in January and July 2004 (SI 2004/81 and SI 2004/1629). Schedule 2 introduces a power for custody officers to release a person on bail in order to consult with the DPP as to whether that person should be charged. Sections 37A and 37B which have been inserted into *PACE* 1984 provide for the DPP to issue guidance on the exercise of the power to bail pending consultation and also allow for the DPP to consider the sufficiency of the evidence and advise on any charge or caution, including a conditional caution.

The custody sergeant may decide himself on the basis of the evidence presented by the arresting officer whether to charge a suspect and for what offence. He may also order that a suspect be detained whilst he reaches the decision whether to charge. The custody sergeant must address his mind to each individual offence as to the sufficiency of the evidence but he is not obliged to investigate the lawfulness of the arrest which he may assume to be lawful: *DPP v L* [1999] Crim.L.R. 752, DC.

The periods of detention are specified in the Act. Even if there is not sufficient evidence to charge, detention may be ordered to protect evidence or elicit evidence by further questioning. Once the decision is made that there is sufficient evidence the suspect must be charged or released without charge, although he can at this stage be bailed to return to the police station at a later date whilst inquiries are still ongoing.

The Codes of Practice apply to these procedures. Code C governs the detention, treatment and questioning of persons by police officers.

The custody officer has power to grant unconditional or conditional bail under s.47 **4–29** of *PACE* 1984 when exercising his power to release suspects under s.38. The provisions of the *Bail Act* 1976 apply, see Chapter 5. The officer may impose similar conditions of bail as the court except those requiring residence in a Bail Hostel, co-operation with report writers or attendance at lawyers interviews. The officer may also entertain applications to vary bail conditions made by him. Section 41(7) limits the time of detention without charge to 24 hours initially. The suspect, if not charged must then be released on bail or he may be released from detention with no direction about bail and therefore no legal duty to return to the police station. The period of detention may also be extended. When a person fails to answer police bail he may be arrested without a warrant: ss.37C and 37D, and 46A, *PACE* 1984.

Police and Criminal Evidence Act 1984, s.38

Duties of custody officer after charge

38.—(1) Where a person arrested for an offence otherwise than under a warrant endorsed   **4–30** for bail is charged with an offence, the custody officer shall, subject to section 25 of the *Criminal Justice and Public Order Act* 1994, order his release from police detention, either on bail or without bail, unless—

    (a) if the person arrested is not an arrested juvenile—

        (i) his name or address cannot be ascertained or the custody officer has reasonable grounds for doubting whether a name or address furnished by him as his name or address is his real name or address;

       (ii) the custody officer has reasonable grounds for believing that the person arrested will fail to appear in court to answer to bail;

      (iii) in the case of a person arrested for an imprisonable offence, the custody officer has reasonable grounds for believing that the detention of the person arrested is necessary to prevent him from committing an offence;

     (iiia) in the case of a person who has attained the age of 18, the custody officer has reasonable grounds for believing that the detention of the person is necessary to enable a sample to be taken from him under section 63B below,

      (iv) in the case of a person arrested for an offence which is not an imprisonable offence, the custody officer has reasonable grounds for believing that the detention of the person arrested is necessary to prevent him from causing physical injury to any other person or from causing loss of or damage to property;

       (v) the custody officer has reasonable grounds for believing that the detention of the person arrested is necessary to prevent him from interfering with the administration of justice or with the investigation of offences or of a particular offence; or

      (vi) the custody officer has reasonable grounds for believing that the detention of the person arrested is necessary for his own protection;

    (b) if he is an arrested juvenile—

        (i) any of the requirements of paragraph (a) above is satisfied; or

       (ii) the custody officer has reasonable grounds for believing that he ought to be detained in his own interests.

(2) If the release of a person arrested is not required by subsection (1) above, the custody officer may authorise him to be kept in police detention [but may not authorise a person to be kept in police detention by virtue of subsection (1)(a)(iiia) after the end of the period of six hours beginning when he was charged with the offence].

(2A) The custody officer, in taking the decisions required by subsection (1)(a) and (b) above (except (a)(i) and (vi) and (b)(ii)), shall have regard to the same considerations as those which a court is required to have regard to in taking the corresponding decisions under paragraph 2 of Part I of Schedule 1 to the *Bail Act* 1976.

(3) Where a custody officer authorises a person who has been charged to be kept in police detention, he shall, as soon as practicable, make a written record of the grounds for the detention.

4–31   (4) Subject to subsection (5) below, the written record shall be made in the presence of the person charged who shall at that time be informed by the custody officer of the grounds for his detention.

(5) Subsection (4) above shall not apply where the person charged is, at the time when the written record is made—

     (a) incapable of understanding what is said to him;

     (b) violent or likely to become violent; or

     (c) in urgent need of medical attention.

(6) Where a custody officer authorises an arrested juvenile to be kept in police detention under subsection (1) above, the custody officer shall, unless he certifies—

     (a) that, by reason of such circumstances as are specified in the certificate, it is impracticable for him to do so; or

     (b) in the case of an arrested juvenile who has attained the age of 12 years, that no secure accommodation is available and that keeping him in other local authority accommodation would not be adequate to protect the public from serious harm from him,

secure that the arrested juvenile is moved to local authority accommodation.

(6A) In this section—

     'local authority accommodation' means accommodation provided by or on behalf of a local authority (within the meaning of the *Children Act* 1989);

     'secure accommodation' means accommodation provided for the purpose of restricting liberty;

     'sexual offence' and 'violent offence' have the same meanings as in the *Powers of Criminal Courts (Sentencing) Act* 2000;

and any reference, in relation to an arrested juvenile charged with a violent or sexual offence, to protecting the public from serious harm from him shall be construed as a reference to protecting members of the public from death or serious personal injury, whether physical or psychological, occasioned by further such offences committed by him.

(6B) Where an arrested juvenile is moved to local authority accommodation under subsection (6) above, it shall be lawful for any person acting on behalf of the authority to detain him.

(7) A certificate made under subsection (6) above in respect of an arrested juvenile shall be produced to the court before which he is first brought thereafter.

(7A) In this section "imprisonable offence" has the same meaning as in Schedule 1 to the *Bail Act* 1976.

(8) In this Part of this Act "local authority" has the same meaning as in the *Children and Young Persons Act* 1969.

[This section is printed as amended by the *Children Act* 1989, Sch.13, the *Criminal Justice Act* 1991, s.9, the *Criminal Justice and Public Order Act* 1994, s.28 and Sch.10, the *Powers of Criminal Courts (Sentencing) Act* 2000, Sch.9 and the *Criminal Justice and Court Services Act* 2000, s.57]

4–32   Once a suspect is charged the custody sergeant will decide whether to detain him in custody to appear at court or to release him on bail with or without conditions for appearance at court at a later date. The custody sergeant is bound by the provisions of the *Bail Act* 1976, see Chapter 5.

Section 25 of the *Criminal Justice and Public Order Act* 1994 reverses the presumption of bail for serious offences in that it provides that in cases of murder, attempted murder, manslaughter, rape and attempted rape, if the defendant has previously been convicted of any such offence or culpable homicide and in the case of culpable homicide or manslaughter has served a custodial sentence then bail shall only be granted if the custody sergeant is satisfied that there are exceptional circumstances to justify the granting of bail.

Section 63B of *PACE* 1984 gives power for samples to be taken from a person in po- **4–33**
lice detention for the purpose of ascertaining whether the person has a Class A drug in
his body. A period of six hours is deemed sufficient time to arrange for the sample to be
taken. Section 63B is not yet nationally in force but applies in certain areas.

Young persons may also be detained but the police have an over-riding duty to
transfer young persons aged between 10 and 17 to local authority accommodation.

Pursuant to para.16 of Code C of the Codes of Practice, when a person is charged
with an offence at a police station he must be cautioned and given written notice of the
charge, which shows the particulars of the offence stated in simple language and the
precise offence in law with which he is charged.

Detention after charge

Police and Criminal Evidence Act 1984, s.46

Detention after charge
    46.—(1) Where a person—   **4–34**
        (a) is charged with an offence; and
        (b) after being charged—
                (i)   is kept in police detention; or
                (ii) is detained by a local authority in pursuance of arrangements made under
                      section 38(6) above,
        he shall be brought before a magistrates' court in accordance with the provisions of
        this section.

    (2) If he is to be brought before a magistrates' court for the petty sessions area in which
the police station at which he was charged is situated, he shall be brought before such a
court as soon as is practicable and in any event not later than the first sitting after he is
charged with the offence.

    (3) If no magistrates' court for that area is due to sit either on the day on which he is
charged or on the next day, the custody officer for the police station at which he was
charged shall inform the justices' chief executive for the area that there is a person in the
area to whom subsection (2) above applies.

    (4) If the person charged is to be brought before a magistrates' court for a petty sessions
area other than that in which the police station at which he was charged is situated, he
shall be removed to that area as soon as is practicable and brought before such a court as
soon as is practicable after his arrival in the area and in any event not later than the first
sitting of a magistrates' court for that area after his arrival in the area.

    (5) If no magistrates' court for that area is due to sit either on the day on which he ar-
rives in the area or on the next day—
        (a) he shall be taken to a police station in the area; and
        (b) the custody officer at that station shall inform the justices' chief executive for the
            area that there is a person in the area to whom subsection (4) applies.

    (6) Subject to subsection (8) below, where the justices' chief executive for a petty sessions
area has been informed—
        (a) under subsection (3) above that there is a person in the area to whom subsection
            (2) above applies; or
        (b) under subsection (5) above that there is a person in the area to whom subsection
            (4) above applies,
the justices' chief executive shall arrange for a magistrates' court to sit not later than the day next
following the relevant day.

    (7) In this section "the relevant day"—
        (a) in relation to a person who is to be brought before a magistrates' court for
            the petty sessions area in which the police station at which he was charged is
            situated, means the day on which he was charged; and
        (b) in relation to a person who is to be brought before a magistrates' court for
            any other petty sessions area, means the day on which he arrives in the area.

    (8) Where the day next following the relevant day is Christmas Day, Good Friday or a
Sunday, the duty of the [justices' chief executive] under subsection (6) above is a duty to ar-

range for a magistrates' court to sit not later than the first day after the relevant day which is not one of those days.

(9) Nothing in this section requires a person who is in hospital to be brought before a court if he is not well enough.

[This section is printed as amended by the *Access to Justice Act* 1999, s.90.]

4–35   The police have a duty under this section to produce a defendant from custody to court as soon as practicable after charge. Most magistrates' courts are open from Monday to Friday so defendants can be produced either on the day of charge or the following day. Many courts are also open on Saturdays and Bank Holidays and on those days may deal with work for other courts in their area that are not open. If a need arises for a court to sit on any other day, the Justices' Chief Executive for the area must put arrangements in place to provide a court. It is not lawful for a policy to be promoted by a body responsible for running the magistrates court to restrict the convening of courts to weekdays only: *R. v Avon Magistrates' Courts Committee Ex p. Broome* (1988) 152 J.P. 529.

A Court may decide to convene on any day of the year: s.153 of the *Magistrates' Courts Act* 1980.

III. INFORMATIONS

Introduction

4–36   An information is the statement by which a person authorised to issue a summons or warrant is informed of an allegation of an offence: *R. v Hughes* (1879) 43 J.P. 556. The laying of an information is an administrative act performed by the prosecutor, the purpose of which is to obtain either a summons requiring the person to appear before the court or a warrant for the arrest of the person. The issue of warrants and summonses is provided for in the *Magistrates' Courts Act* 1980 and the *Magistrates' Courts Rules* 1981.

In s.29 of the *Criminal Justice Act* 2003 a new method of instituting proceedings is to be introduced. This will allow for the public prosecutor to institute criminal proceedings by issuing a "written charge" and a "requisition" requiring a person to appear before the magistrates' court. The police and the CPS are amongst the list of bodies defined as public prosecutors. The public prosecutors will not have the power to lay an information for the purposes of obtaining a summons but will instead institute and issue the proceedings themselves.

General

4–37   In addition to those persons who attend at a police station voluntarily or those who are arrested by the police and brought to the police station and then to court there are circumstances where individuals are at liberty but the prosecuting authorities wish to secure their presence at court to answer to allegations of criminal conduct. In order to get them to court, an information may be laid before the court or an authorised officer and application may be made by the person laying the information for a warrant for the defendant to be brought to court or a summons requiring him to appear before the court. This process differs from the charging process as the defendant is not detained at a police station whilst the charge is investigated and drawn up. The evidence relating to the offence is considered by a judicial authority and under the *Magistrates' Courts Act* 1980, a district judge or magistrate may issue a warrant of arrest or summons and the justices' clerk or court officer who has delegated authority may also issue summonses.

The information will usually be made in writing by the informant and it will detail the nature of the alleged offence and the circumstances giving rise to it. This provides the evidence on which a warrant or summons will be issued.

The information is laid when it is received at the office of the justice's chief executive for the relevant area: *Hill v Anderton* [1982] 2 All E.R. 963.

Magistrates' Courts Rules 1981, r.4

Information and complaint

4.—(1) An information may be laid or complaint made by the prosecutor or complainant in **4–38** person or by his counsel or solicitor or other person authorised in that behalf.

(2) Subject to any provision of the Act of 1980 and any other enactment, an information or complaint need not be in writing or on oath.

(3) It shall not be necessary in an information or complaint to specify or negative an exception, exemption, proviso, excuse or qualification, whether or not it accompanies the description of the offence or matter of complaint contained in the enactment creating the offence or on which the complaint is founded.

An individual may lay an information or complaint orally or in writing. If a warrant is sought the information will be submitted in writing. The detail of the information may often be limited to a brief statement of the offence alleged to have been committed with minimal explanation of the surrounding circumstances. An information may not be laid by an unincorporated association such as a police force because the definition of "person" in the *Interpretation Act* 1978 as "a body of persons whether corporate or un-incorporated" was not intended to apply to the laying of informations: *Rubin v DPP* [1990] 2 Q.B. 80. In that case an information purported to have been laid by the Thames Valley Police. Watkins L.J. rejected the argument that "the police" could be regarded as the prosecutor. He said:—

> When the police bring a prosecution it has to be commenced by an information which has been laid by a member of the force; that is to say, by that member who reported the offence and the person accused of committing it or by the chief constable himself of some other member of the force authorised by him to lay an information.

In this particular case the information was held not to be invalid because the identity of the informant was easily discovered and the defendant had not been misled.

In *Ealing Justices Ex p. Dixon* [1990] 2 Q.B. 91, Woolf L.J. observed that it was preferable for an individual to lay an information even when the prosecutor was essentially an organisation such as the Federation Against Copyright Theft.

Form and content

An information or complaint must comply with the requirements of Rule 4 of the **4–39** *Magistrates' Courts Rules* 1981. It need not be in writing or on oath unless specifically required to be so by statute. The court should be informed of the precise nature of the offence alleged, including details of the date and place of the offence, the activity which is alleged to amount to an offence and the provision of statute (or common law) which makes the conduct an offence. Separate offences should be individually described but that may be done within a single information provided the details of each offence are clearly identifiable.

Duplicity

Magistrates' Court Rules 1981, r.12

Information to be for one offence only

12.—(1) Subject to any Act passed after 2nd October 1848, a magistrates' court shall not **4–40** proceed to the trial of an information that charges more than one offence.

(2) Nothing in this rule shall prohibit 2 or more informations being set out in one document.

(3) If, notwithstanding paragraph (1) above, it appears to the court at any stage in the trial of an information that the information charges more than one offence, the court shall call upon the prosecutor to elect on which offence he desires the court to proceed, where-upon the offence or offences on which the prosecutor does not wish to proceed shall be

struck out of the information; and the court shall then proceed to try that information afresh.

(4) If a prosecutor who is called upon to make an election under paragraph (3) above fails to do so, the court shall dismiss the information.

(5) Where, after an offence has or offences have been struck out of the information under paragraph (3) above, the accused requests an adjournment and it appears to the court that he has been unfairly prejudiced, it shall adjourn the trial.

An information should charge only one offence. A charge is duplicitous when it alleges facts constituting two different activities. This rule does not apply to complaints which may be more general but which can be the basis of several matters.

Where offences are expressed in statute as disjunctive activities, the particular informations must be carefully drafted to identify the precise offence that it is alleged has been committed. In a prosecution for being in charge of a vehicle when unfit through drink or drugs it was held that this was not bad for duplicity because the information revealed one charge only, that of being in charge when unfit and the fact that the incapability was caused by either drink or drugs did not make the information duplicitous: *Thomson v Knights* [1947] 1 All E.R. 112. This approach was confirmed in *R. v Clow* [1965] 1 Q.B. 598 in relation to an information alleging causing death by driving "at speed and in a manner dangerous to the public". The charge was held not to be bad for duplicity because it related to one single incident of causing death and although they could be separate offences it was permissible to charge them conjunctively.

4–41   In the case of a charge under the betting and gaming legislation a charge was held to be bad for duplicity when the information and charges referred to an offence of admitting a young person apparently under the age of 18 on to licensed betting premises and also to allowing such a person to remain on such premises. These offences were held to constitute two separate incidents that should have been covered by separate informations and charges: *Mallon v Allon* [1964] 1 Q.B. 385

A single document may have a preamble containing particulars common to a number of otherwise separate allegations without infringing the rule against duplicity: *DPP v Shah* [1984] 2 All E.R. 528. Thus several informations may be contained within one document provided the separate offences are identified therein.

If more than one offence is charged in the alternative, it is not correct and the magistrate should ask the prosecutor upon which offence he wishes to proceed. So a charge of being concerned in the management of premises used for the purpose of smoking cannabis or for the purpose of dealing in cannabis was bad for duplicity and the prosecution must identify the specific charge to be pursued: *Fox v Dingley, Ware v Fox* [1967] 1 All E.R. 100. If the prosecution fails to choose, then the magistrate should dismiss the information.

Statement of Offence

Magistrates' Courts Rules 1981 r.100

Statement of offence

4–42   100.—(1) Every information, summons, warrant or other document laid, issued or made for the purposes of, or in connection with, any proceedings before a magistrates' court for an offence shall be sufficient if it describes the specific offence with which the accused is charged, or of which he is convicted, in ordinary language avoiding as far as possible the use of technical terms and without necessarily stating all the elements of the offence, and gives such particulars as may be necessary for giving reasonable information of the nature of the charge.

(2) If the offence charged is one created by or under any Act, the description of the offence shall contain a reference to the section of the Act, or, as the case may be, the rule, order, regulation, byelaw or other instrument creating the offence.

An information must disclose an offence at law. If it does not it is void *ab initio* and may be dismissed. A charge laid under the *Poaching Prevention Act* 1862 referred to introductory and consequential matters but failed to include the actual offence under the section and was held void: *Garman v Plaice* [1969] 1 All E.R. 62.

Under Art.6(3) of the European Convention on Human Rights every person charged **4–43** with an offence has the right to be informed promptly, in a language that he understands, and in detail, of the nature and cause of the accusation. The purpose of this right is to provide the accused with the information needed to prepare a defence. Thus the information required must be more specific than the grounds of arrest required under Art.5(2) of the Convention.

The information must give sufficient particulars of the offence being charged which includes details of the legislative provisions, *i.e.* the Act, Schedule, regulations or rules which create the offence; reasonable information about the nature of the charge and elements of the offence alleged to have been committed and clear information about the place and date of the alleged offence: *Atterton v Brown* [1945] K.B. 122; *Stephenson v Johnson* [1954] 1 W.L.R. 375; *R. v Abergavenny J Ex p. Barratt* [1994] R.T.R. 98.

A magistrate may not reconsider an application which has already been rejected by a fellow magistrate if there has been no material change to the substance of the information: *R. v Worthing JJ* [1981] Crim.L.R. 778.

Joint offenders

An information may charge two or more defendants with having jointly committed **4–44** an offence: *R. v Lipscombe Ex p. Biggins* (1862) 26 J.P. 244.

Time-limit

A statutory time limit applies to the initiation of summary offences which ensures **4–45** prompt prosecution action and discourages delay.

Magistrates' Courts Act 1980, s.127

Limitation of time

127.—(1) Except as otherwise expressly provided by any enactment and subject to subsection **4–46** (2) below, a magistrates' court shall not try an information or hear a complaint unless the information was laid, or the complaint made, within 6 months from the time when the offence was committed, or the matter of complaint arose.

(2) Nothing in—

    (a) subsection (1) above; or

    (b) subject to subsection (4) below, any other enactment (however framed or worded) which, as regards any offence to which it applies, would but for this section impose a time-limit on the power of a magistrates' court to try an information summarily or impose a limitation on the time for taking summary proceedings,

shall apply in relation to any indictable offence.

(3) Without prejudice to the generality of paragraph (b) of subsection (2) above, that paragraph includes enactments which impose a time-limit that applies only in certain circumstances (for example, where the proceedings are not instituted by or with the consent of the Director of Public Prosecutions or some other specified authority).

(4) Where, as regards any indictable offence, there is imposed by any enactment (however framed or worked, and whether falling within subsection (2) (b) above or not) a limitation on the time for taking proceedings on indictment for that offence no summary proceedings for that offence shall be taken after the latest time for taking proceedings on indictment.

Informations or complaints relating to summary only matters must be laid within six **4–47** months of the offence alleged. Other statutes may expressly provide for different time limits. When calculating computation of time general principles apply which are usually considered in civil rather than criminal case law.

The purpose of the time limit is to ensure that summary offences are charged and tried as soon as reasonably practicable after their commission. This principle was confirmed and elaborated upon in the case of *R. v Scunthorpe Justices Ex p. McPhee and Gallagher* (1998) 162 J.P. 635.

When time is computed the day of the offence is excluded: *Stewart v Chapman* [1951] 2 K.B. 792. For periods calculated in months, the period ends at midnight on the day in the subsequent month that bears the same number as the day of the earlier month or the preceding number if no such number appears in the subsequent month: *Dodds v Walker* [1981] 1 W.L.R. 1027, HL.

For an offence taking place continuously or intermittently over a period of time, the period runs from each day on which the offence is committed. There is no jurisdiction to hear an information in respect of offences alleged to have been committed more than six months prior to the date of the information: *R. v Chertsey Justices Ex p. Franks* [1961] 2 Q.B. 152.

If it is unclear whether an information has been laid within the requisite time the defendant is entitled to the benefit of the doubt: *Lloyd v Young* (1963) 107 S.J. 631 [1963] Crim.L.R. 703. It is important that the summons should clearly show the date when the information was laid so there is no doubt that the time limit was observed.

4–48 Delay in the laying of an information, although strictly within the time limits, is a factor which may be taken into account by the magistrate in deciding whether to issue a summons. A magistrate is entitled to inquire into the reasons for the delay in laying an information even when the statutory time limit has not been breached: *R. v Clerk to the Medway JJ Ex p. Department of Health and Social Security* [1986] Crim.L.R. 686; *Wei Hai Restaurant Ltd v Kingston upon Hull City Council* (2002) 166 J.P. 185.

In the *Scunthorpe Justices* case (see above) the defendant was charged with robbery. He tendered pleas to common assault and theft which the CPS were willing to accept. The court refused to allow the charge to be amended on the basis that the six month time-limit in respect of the assault charge had expired. On appeal the Court recognised that the purpose of the time limit was to expedite the trial of summary matters but the court held that a charge could be amended to include a summary matter even if the limit had run out provided the new offence arose out of the same misdoing as the original charge and it was in the interests of justice to amend: *R. v Scunthorpe Justices Ex p. McPhee and Gallagher* (1998) 162 J.P. 635.

In the case of *Manchester Stipendiary Magistrate Ex p. Hill* [1983] 1 A.C. 328 the House of Lords considered in detail the process of laying informations before the magistrates. It was held that the information was laid and time stopped running on the offence when the information was received at the office of the justices' clerk. The receipt of the information was a "ministerial" act that can be performed by any member of staff and the information did not need to have been considered personally by the justices' clerk at that stage.

IV. ISSUING A WARRANT OR SUMMONS

General

4–49 An information may give rise to a summons or a warrant. Upon the laying of an information a district judge or magistrate or other authorised person may issue a summons requiring the person named in the information to appear before the court. A district judge or magistrate in addition has power to issue a warrant of arrest to bring the person named in the information before a magistrates' court. The applicant should have due regard to s.1 of the *Magistrates' Courts Act* 1980 which sets out the conditions which must be met before a warrant of arrest may issue. The person hearing the application has a discretion to refuse a warrant if a summons would be equally effective.

Magistrates' Courts Act 1980, s.1

Issue of summons to accused or warrant for his arrest

4–50   **1.**—(1) Upon an information being laid before a justice of the peace for an area to which this section applies that any person has, or is suspected of having, committed an offence, the justice may, in any of the events mentioned in subsection (2) below, but subject to subsections (3) to (5) below.—

 (a) issue a summons directed to that person requiring him to appear before a magistrates' court for the area to answer to the information, or

 (b) issue a warrant to arrest that person and bring him before a magistrates' court for the area or such magistrates' court as is provided in subsection (5) below

(2) A justice of the peace for an area to which this section applies may issue a summons or warrant under this section—

 (a) if the offence was committed or is suspected to have been committed within the area, or

 (b) if it appears to the justice necessary or expedient, with a view to the better administration of justice, that the person charged should be tried jointly with, or in the same place as, some other person who is charged with an offence, and who is in custody, or is being or is to be proceeded against, within the area, or

 (c) if the person charged resides or is, or is believed to reside or be, within the area, or

 (d) if under any enactment a magistrates' court for the area has jurisdiction to try the offence, or

 (e) if the offence was committed outside England and Wales and, where it is an offence exclusively punishable on summary conviction, if a magistrates' court for the area would have jurisdiction to try the offence if the offender were before it.

(3) No warrant shall be issued under this section unless the information is in writing.

(4) No warrant shall be issued under this section for the arrest of any person who has attained the age of 18 unless—

 (a) the offence to which the warrant relates is an indictable offence or is punishable with imprisonment,or

 (b) the person's address is not sufficiently established for a summons to be served on him.

(5) Where the offence charged is not an indictable offence—

 (a) no summons shall be issued by virtue only of paragraph (c) of subsection (2) above, and

 (b) any warrant issued by virtue only of that paragraph shall require the person charged to be brought before a magistrates' court having jurisdiction to try the offence …

(6) Where the offence charged is an indictable offence, a warrant under this section may be issued at any time notwithstanding that a summons has previously been issued.

(7) A justice of the peace may issue a summons or warrant under this section upon an information being laid before him notwithstanding any enactment requiring the information to be laid before two or more justices.

(8) The areas to which this section applies are commission areas.

[This section is printed as amended by the *Criminal Justice Act* 1991, Sch.8 and s.31 of the *Criminal Justice Act* 2003.]

4–51   The issuing of a summons has been described as a "judicial function" performed by the magistrate or justices' clerk or person authorised by the justices' clerk pursuant to the *Justices' Clerks Rules* 1999. In *Gateshead Justices Ex p. Tesco Stores Ltd* [1981] Q.B. 470 the applicant's summary convictions were quashed because the informations had been processed by assistants in the clerk's office who issued the summonses without referring them to a justice or a justices' clerk. The granting of summonses is more than a rubber-stamping exercise. The person considering the issue of the summons must be authorised to do so and must scrutinise the information to satisfy themselves that the requirements are met and that a summons may properly be granted.

Form and content of summons

Magistrates' Courts Rules 1981, r.98

Form of summons

4–52   **98.**—(1) A summons shall be signed by the justice issuing it or state his name and be authenticated by the signature of the clerk of a magistrates' court.

(2) A summons requiring a person to appear before a magistrates' court to answer to an information or complaint shall state shortly the matter of the information or complaint and shall state the time and place at which the defendant is required by the summons to appear.

(3) A single summons may be issued against a person in respect of several informations or complaints; but the summons shall state the matter of each information or complaint separately and shall have effect as several summonses, each issued in respect of one information or complaint.

(4) In this rule where a signature is required, an electronic signature incorporated into the document shall satisfy this requirement.

A summons must be signed by the person issuing it whether that is a district judge, magistrate, justices' clerk or authorised assistant. Alternatively the summons may be marked with the name of the person who granted it either in the form of a rubber stamp or electronic signature. The summons must state the time and place at which the person named in the summons is to appear.

There remains a discretion to issue the summons even if the information discloses an offence at law and is laid within the time-limits. The person considering the information must apply his mind to the contents and make a judicial decision whether to issue the summons. Application may be refused if it is vexatious or oppressive.

4–53   The proposed defendant has no right to be heard when a summons is applied for but the court has a discretion to allow him to attend: *R. v West London JJ Ex p. Klahn* [1979] 1 W.L.R. 933. The person considering the issuing of a summons is entitled to make inquiries beyond the information, but is not under any duty to do so: *R. v Clerk to the Bradford JJ Ex p. Sykes* (1999) 163 J.P. 224.

The decision whether to issue a summons is subject to judicial review by the Administrative Court: *R. v Horseferry Road JJ Ex p. Independent Broadcasting Authority* [1986] 2 All E.R. 666. The High Court may quash a summons where it was issued in abuse of the process of the court and the allegations made were vexatious and oppressive: *R. v Bury JJ Ex p. Anderson* [1987] Crim.L.R. 638. Likewise, the reviewing court may compel the issue of a summons unreasonably refused.

Effect of defective summons

Magistrates' Courts Act 1980, s.123

Defect in process
4–54   **123.**—(1) No objection shall be allowed to any information or complaint, or to any summons or warrant to procure the presence of the defendant, for any defect in it in substance or in form, or for any variance between it and the evidence adduced on behalf of the prosecutor or complainant at the hearing of the information or complaint.

(2) If it appears to a magistrates' court that any variance between a summons or warrant and the evidence adduced on behalf of the prosecutor or complainant is such that the defendant has been misled by the variance, the court shall, on the application of the defendant, adjourn the hearing.

An irregularity or illegality in the mode of bringing a defendant before the court, if not objected to at the hearing, does not invalidate the conviction: *Gray v Customs Commissioners* (1884) 48 J.P. 343.

4–55   Although no objection is allowed to any information or complaint, or to any summons or warrant, for any defect in its substance or form, if the magistrate considers that any variance between a summons or warrant and the evidence adduced on behalf of the prosecutor or complainant is such that the defendant has been misled by that variance, the court must on the application of the defendant, adjourn the hearing. The effect of s.123(2) is that a summons can be amended: *Meek v Powell* [1952] 1 All E.R. 347.

The amendment of an information by a magistrates' court is subject to judicial review and is liable to be quashed: *R. v Greater Manchester JJ Ex p. Aldi GmbH & Co KG* (1995) 159 J.P. 717; *Marco (Croydon) Ltd v Metropolitan Police* [1984] R.T.R. 24.

A summons may be amended even if by the time the case comes before the court and the application to amend is made the six months' time limit for laying an information in s.127 of the *Magistrates' Courts Act* 1980 has expired: *R v Newcastle JJ Ex p. Bryce* [1976] R.T.R. 325; *R. v Sandwell J Ex p. West Midlands Passenger Transport Board* [1979] Crim.L.R. 56.

The Divisional Court in *R. v Scunthorpe JJ Ex p. McPhee and Gallagher* (1998) **4–56** 162 J.P. 635 enunciated the principles.

The power to amend and adjourn under s.123(2) is available until the case is ended and the magistrates are "functus officio", so it is possible for a case to be adjourned after conviction and the charge amended before sentence: see *Allan v Wiseman* [1975] Crim.L.R. 37 where the defendant's name was amended on the charge after conviction but before the case was ended.

Service of summons

Magistrates' Courts Rules 1981, r.99

Service of summons, etc.

99.—(1) Service of a summons issued by a justice of the peace on a person other than a **4–57** corporation may be effected—

   (a) by delivering it to the person to whom it is directed; or
   (b) by leaving it for him with some person at his last known or usual place of abode; or
   (c) by sending it by post in a letter addressed to him at his last known or usual place of abode.

(3) Service for the purposes of the Act of 1980 of a summons issued by a justice of the peace on a corporation may be effected by delivering it at, or sending it by post to, the registered office of the corporation, if that office is in the United Kingdom, or, if there is no registered office in the United Kingdom, any place in the United Kingdom where the corporation trades or conducts its business.

(4) Paragraph (3) shall have effect in relation to a document (other than a summons) issued by a justice of the peace as it has effect in relation to a summons so issued, but with the substitution of references to England and Wales for the references to the United Kingdom.

(5) Any summons or other document served in manner authorised by the preceding provisions of this rule shall, for the purposes of any enactment other than the Act of 1980 or these *Rules* requiring a summons or other document to be served in any particular manner, be deemed to have been as effectively served as if it had been served in that manner; and nothing in this rule shall render invalid the service of a summons or other document in that manner.

(6) Sub-paragraph (c) of paragraph (1) shall not authorise the service by post of—

   (a) a summons requiring the attendance of any person to give evidence or produce a document or thing; or
   (b) (Child Maintenance summons)

(7) (Maintenance summons—civil proceedings)

(8) Where this rule or any other of these *Rules* provides that a summons or other document may be sent by post to a person's last known or usual place of abode that rule shall have effect as if it provided also for the summons or other document to be sent in the manner specified in the rule to an address given by that person for that purpose.

(9) This rule shall not apply to a judgment summons.

Most summonses from the magistrates' court are sent by post to the last known **4–58** address. If the summons is returned as undeliverable by the Post Office, then recorded delivery or personal service can be directed.

If a person voluntarily attends the court, that attendance cures any want of process or any irregularity in service: *R. v Hughes* (1879) L.R. 4 Q.B.D. 614. However where a person attends before a magistrate to draw attention to the irregularity and then withdraws from the case such conduct does not amount to an appearance so as to waive irregularity in service: *Pearks, Gunston & Tee Ltd v Richardson* [1902] 1 K.B. 91.

Where the person appears before the magistrates' court he should be informed of the irregularity or omission and of the right to object because without that knowledge there can be no waiver: *R. v Essex Justices Ex p. Perkins* [1927] 2 K.B. 475.

Criminal Justice (International Co-operation) Act 1990, s.2

Service of United Kingdom process overseas

4–59   **2.**—(1) Process of the following descriptions, that is to say—

(a) a summons requiring a person charged with an offence to appear before a court in the United Kingdom; and

(b) a summons or order requiring a person to attend before a court in the United Kingdom for the purpose of giving evidence in criminal proceedings,

may be issued or made notwithstanding that the person in question is outside the United Kingdom and may be served outside the United Kingdom in accordance with arrangements made by the Secretary of State.

(2) In relation to Scotland subsection (1) above applies to any document which may competently be served on any accused person or on any person who may give evidence in criminal proceedings.

(3) Service of any process outside the United Kingdom by virtue of this section shall not impose any obligation under the law of any part of the United Kingdom to comply with it and accordingly failure to do so shall not constitute contempt of any court or be a ground for issuing a warrant to secure the attendance of the person in question or, in Scotland, for imposing any penalty.

(4) Subsection (3) above is without prejudice to the service of any process (with the usual consequences for non-compliance) on the person in question if subsequently effected in the United Kingdom.

4–60   The arrangements made by the Secretary of State for the Home Office require the summons and supporting documentation to be sent to the Judicial Co-operation Unit of the Home Office who then forward this to the appropriate authority in the country where the person concerned is residing.

Summonses are generally issued for minor offences which are summary only and not imprisonable (*e.g.* most road traffic offences) where the name and address of the defendant are known. The police may apply for a summons for more serious offences, *e.g.* criminal damage or assault but usually only if the name of the defendant is known and he has a fixed address. If the information discloses more serious offences which are imprisonable and there are doubts over the whereabouts of the defendant or the likelihood of his answering a summons, a warrant may issue.

V. WARRANT OF ARREST

4–61   A warrant is the authority for the arrest of a person in certain defined circumstances, issued either at the start of proceedings, or to secure attendance as they progress.

Magistrates' Courts Act 1980, s.1

4–62   See § 4–50 above for the wording of the section. The recent amendment by s.31 of the *Criminal Justice Act* 2003 removes the requirement for the written information to be substantiated on oath.

This section gives the Court the power to ensure the attendance at court of defendants to answer to charges disclosed in an information. A warrant issued under s.1 is referred to as a "first instance" warrant as it is the first step taken to bring a defendant to court who has not otherwise appeared to answer the charge. Applications for warrants under s.1 are made by individual police officers. The information will be in writing on a standard form and has to be signed by the officer. The information will outline the details of the offence and give the name and address (where known) of the person to be arrested. The information will be checked by court staff to ensure that the offence is indictable or punishable with imprisonment and if it is not the warrant will only issue if the address of the defendant is not known. The application will be dealt with either in court or in the retiring rooms as they are *ex parte* applications. In cases of urgency it may also be possible for application to be made out of hours to a district judge or magistrate at home.

The court will consider whether the warrant should be backed for bail or not but as a warrant will be issued in preference to a summons this would indicate that bail may not be appropriate: s.117 of the *Magistrates' Courts Act* 1980.

Magistrates' Courts Act 1980, s.13

Non-appearance of accused: issue of warrant

13.—(1) Subject to the provisions of this section, where the court, instead of proceeding in **4–63** the absence of the accused, adjourns or further adjourns the trial, the court may, issue a warrant for his arrest.

(2) Where a summons has been issued, the court shall not issue a warrant under this section unless the condition in subsection (2A) below or that in subsection (2B) below is fulfilled.

(2A) The condition in this subsection is that it is proved to the satisfaction of the court, on oath or in such other manner as may be prescribed, that the summons was served on the accused within what appears to the court to be a reasonable time before the trial or adjourned trial.

(2B) The condition in this subsection is that—

(a) the adjournment now being made is a second or subsequent adjournment of the trial.

(b) the accused was present on the last (or only) occasion when the trial was adjourned, and

(c) on that occasion the court determined the time for the hearing at which the adjournment is now being made.

(3) A warrant for the arrest of any person who has attained the age of 18 shall not be issued under this section unless—

(a) the offence to which the warrant relates is punishable with imprisonment, or

(b) the court, having convicted the accused, proposes to impose a disqualification on him.

(3A) A warrant for the arrest of any person who has not attained the age of 18 shall not be issued under this section unless—

(a) the offence to which the warrant relates is punishable in the case of a person who has attained the age of 18, with imprisonment, or

(b) the court, having convicted the accused, proposes to impose a disqualification on him.

(4) This section shall not apply to an adjournment on the occasion of the accused's conviction in his absence under subsection (5) of section 12 above or to an adjournment required by subsection (9) of that section…

(5) Where the court adjourns the trial—

(a) after having, either on that or on a previous occasion, received any evidence or convicted the accused without hearing evidence on his pleading guilty under section 9(3) above; or

(b) after having on a previous occasion convicted the accused without hearing evidence on his pleading guilty under 12(5) above,

the court shall not issue a warrant under this section unless it thinks it undesirable, by reason of the gravity of the offence, to continue the trial in the absence of the accused.

[This section is printed as amended by the *Criminal Justice Act* 1991, Sch.8, the *Criminal Justice and Public Order Act* 1994, Sch.5, the *Criminal Procedure and Investigations Act* 1996, s.48, the *Magistrates' Courts (Procedure) Act* 1998, s.3 and the *Criminal Justice Act* 2003, s.31, which came into force in July 2004.]

The requirement for the information to be substantiated on oath is to be removed. The new requirement is substituted that the offence is punishable with imprisonment for a person who has attained the age of 18.

This section gives power for the court to issue a warrant during the proceedings if the defendant fails to attend at court. It is most commonly used in road traffic matters.

In such cases the court will first ensure that the summons has been properly served and that the defendant has had reasonable time to attend at court. If so satisfied the court may then proceed with the case in the absence of the defendant. If the case is proved the court may wish to disqualify the defendant from driving. If the court does not wish to disqualify and sentence him in absence the case may be adjourned and a notice sent to the defendant requiring him to attend. If he fails to attend after the adjournment notice is sent a warrant may be issued under this section. A warrant may also issue after a written plea of guilty has been received and the court wishes to impose a disqualification in the defendant's presence.

The court will need to consider whether a s.13 warrant should be backed for bail and will take into account the defendants attendance record and the gravity of the offence: s.117 of the *Magistrates' Courts Act* 1980.

Statutory declarations

4–64   The court may not always issue a warrant for the arrest of a defendant who fails to attend court. There is a discretion for the court to proceed with the case in the absence of the defendant under s.11 of the *Magistrates' Courts Act* 1980. The Act provides a safeguard for the absent defendant by allowing for proceedings commenced by way of summons to be invalidated when the defendant makes and serves a statutory declaration to the effect that he did not attend court because he was unaware of the court hearing date.

Magistrates' Courts Act 1980, s.14

Proceedings invalid where accused did not know of them

4–65   **14.**—(1) Where a summons has been issued under section 1 above and a magistrates' court has begun to try the information to which the summons relates, then, if—

    (a) the accused, at any time during or after the trial, makes a statutory declaration that he did not know of the summons or the proceedings until a date specified in the declaration, being a date after the court has begun to try the information; and

    (b) within 21 days of that date the declaration is served on the justices' chief executive for the court,

without prejudice to the validity of the information, the summons and all subsequent proceedings shall be void.

    (2) For the purposes of subsection (1) above a statutory declaration shall be deemed to be duly served on the [justices' chief executive] if it is delivered to him, or left at his office, or is sent in a registered letter or by the recorded delivery service addressed to him at his office.

    (3) If on the application of the accused it appears to a magistrates' court (which for this purpose may be composed of a single justice) that it was not reasonable to expect the accused to serve such a statutory declaration as is mentioned in subsection (1) above within the period allowed by that subsection, the court may accept service of such a declaration by the accused after that period has expired; and a statutory declaration accepted under this subsection shall be deemed to have been served as required by that subsection.

    (4) Where any proceedings have become void by virtue of subsection (1) above, the information shall not be tried again by any of the same justices.

[This section is printed as amended by the *Access to Justice Act* 1999, Sch.13.]

4–66   In proceedings in the magistrates' court, particularly those commenced by way of summons, the prosecution may present the case in the absence of the defendant if the court is satisfied that the summons has been properly served.

Many cases are dealt with in this way, *e.g.* road traffic cases, but caution must be exercised and the seriousness of the offence will be taken into account. See also the guidelines in *R.v Jones* in § 7–12. The prosecution evidence is heard, which usually consists of statements from prosecution witnesses which have been served under s.9 of the *Criminal Justice Act* 1967 and the court will go on to acquit or convict the defendant. If convicted, an adjournment notice may be sent to the defendant requiring his presence for sentencing and if he fails to answer to the notice a warrant may be issued for his arrest. The court may also proceed to sentence in absence.

The first a defendant may know about the proceedings is when an adjournment notice or notice of fine is received or a warrant is executed. It is then open to the defendant to make a statutory declaration under this section that he knew nothing of the proceedings and if that declaration is served on the court then the proceedings are invalidated. The additional requirement is that the declaration should be served on the court within 21 days of the date when the proceedings first came to the notice of the defendant but the court does have a discretion to accept service outside of the 21 day limit if it is not reasonable to expect the defendant to serve the declaration within that time.

Defendants will often make such declarations at court but it is possible for them to be made before a solicitor, etc. It is not necessary for the declaration to be made before the court where the proceedings took place but this will often be the case.

The effect of accepting service of the declaration is that the summons and all proceed- **4–67** ings based on it will be void but the information is not affected: *Singh v DPP* [1999] Crim.L.R. 914. The Court will expunge the conviction and penalty from the records. The Prosecution has the right to re-institute proceedings using the original information and if present in court at the time when the statutory declaration is made and served, application may be made by the prosecution to re-issue the summons immediately and serve it personally on the defendant. Proceedings will then start again but must be tried before a fresh bench.

A defendant who knowingly and wilfully makes a false statement relating to his knowledge of the proceedings under this section may be prosecuted for perjury under s.5 of the *Perjury Act* 1911 and the applicant will be given a warning to this effect when the declaration is made.

BAIL

I. INTRODUCTION

Cases in the magistrates' court are not always concluded at the first hearing. The **5–1** *Magistrates' Courts Act* 1980 confers powers of adjournment in several different circumstances and also gives the court power on adjournment to remand the accused either in custody or on bail during the period of any adjournment: s.128 *Magistrates' Courts Act* 1980.

Any decision to remand a person in criminal proceedings must be made in accordance with the provisions of the *Bail Act* 1976. The Act has been extensively amended by the *Magistrates' Courts Act* 1980, the *Criminal Justice Acts* of 1988 and 1991, the *Criminal Justice and Public Order Act* 1994 and the *Crime and Disorder Act* 1998. It is also amended by the *Criminal Justice Act* 2003, ss.13–21. Sections 13, parts of s.15, sections 16, 17, 19, 20 and 21 came into force in April 2004.

(1) General

Under the *Bail Act* 1976 there is a general presumption that bail will be granted. **5–2** s.4(1). Bail can only be withheld if the exceptions to bail, listed in Sch.1 to the Act, apply. When the court finds the exceptions to apply they must explain their reasons. The question of bail must be considered every time that an accused person appears before the court; s.4(2). When the accused appears in answer to bail or is brought before the court in custody and the case is to be adjourned, the court will invite the prosecution to make representations on bail. The prosecution may object to bail and explain the reasons why (Sch.1 exceptions) or propose conditional or unconditional bail. The defence may then make an application for bail, arguing that either the exceptions are not made out or that the objections can be addressed by the imposition of conditions. The court has an inquisitorial role in bail proceedings and may ask questions of both parties to ensure that it has the required information to enable a proper decision on bail to be made. Also, notwithstanding any agreement reached by the prosecution and defence, it is the decision of the court whether bail should be granted and with what conditions.

The presumption of bail has been affected by the *Criminal Justice and Public Order Act* 1994 which requires that in respect of some specified serious offences, bail shall only be granted if there are exceptional circumstances to justify it.

The *Bail Act* 1976 must be applied so as to be compatible with Art.5 of the European Convention on Human Rights which secures the right to liberty. No person shall be deprived of their liberty save in specified circumstances and in accordance with a procedure prescribed by law. Article 5(1)(c) allows for detention in order to bring a person before a competent legal authority on reasonable suspicion of having committed a crime.

5–3   In relation to bail decisions the European Court has said domestic courts must, "examine all the facts arguing for and against the existence of a genuine requirement of public interest justifying...a departure from the rule of respect for individual liberty and set them out in their decisions on applications for release": *Wemhoff v Germany* [1979] 1 E.H.R.R. 55.

Case law also requires that the court must consider if there are "relevant and sufficient reasons" to justify detention and these reasons must be given: *Letellier v France* [1992] 14 E.H.R.R. 83. This was held to require the exercise of a judicial discretion in reaching bail decisions which cannot be restricted by law: *CC v UK* (1999) E.H.R.L.R. 210.

II. COURT BAIL

A. GENERAL RIGHT TO BAIL

Bail Act 1976, s.1

Meaning of "bail in criminal proceedings"

5–4   **1.**—(1) In this Act "bail in criminal proceedings" means—
         (a) bail grantable in or in connection with proceedings for an offence to a person who is accused or convicted of the offence, or
         (b) bail grantable in connection with an offence to a person who is under arrest for the offence or for whose arrest for the offence a warrant (endorsed for bail) is being issued.

     (2) In this Act "bail" means bail grantable under the law (including common law) for the time being in force.

     (3) Except as provided by section 13(3) of this Act, this section does not apply to bail in or in connection with proceedings outside England and Wales.

     (4) Repealed.

     (5) This section applies—
         (a) Whether the offence was committed in England or Wales or elsewhere, and
         (b) whether it is an offence under the law of England and Wales, or of any other country or territory.

     (6) Bail in criminal proceedings shall be granted (and in particular shall be granted unconditionally or conditionally) in accordance with this Act.

[This section is reprinted as amended by the *Criminal Justice and Public Order Act* 1994, Sch.11, para.2]

Bail Act 1976, s.2

Other definitions

5–5   **2.**—(1) In this Act, unless the context otherwise requires, "conviction" includes—
         (a) a finding of guilt,

(b) a finding that a person is not guilty by reason of insanity,

(c) a finding under section 11(1) of the *Powers of Criminal Courts (Sentencing) Act* 2000 (remand for medical examination) that the person in question did the act or made the omission charged, and

(d) a conviction of an offence for which an order is made placing the offender on probation or discharging him absolutely or conditionally,

and "convicted" shall be construed accordingly.

(2) In this Act, unless the context otherwise requires—

"bail hostel" means premises for the accommodation of persons remanded on bail,

"child" means a person under the age of fourteen,

"court" includes a judge of a court, or a justice of the peace and, in the case of a specified court, includes a judge or (as the case may be) justice having powers to act in connection with proceedings before that court,

"Courts-Martial Appeal rules" means rules made under section 49 of the *Courts-Martial (Appeals) Act* 1968,

"Crown Court rules" means rules made under section 15 of the *Courts Act* 1971,

"magistrates' courts rules" means rules made under section 15 of the *Justices of the Peace Act* 1949.

"offence" includes an alleged offence,

["probation hostel" means premises for the accommodation of persons who may be required to reside there by a probation order,]

"proceedings against a fugitive offender" means proceedings under the *Extradition Act* 1989 or section 2(1) or 4(3) of the *Backing of Warrants (Republic of Ireland) Act* 1965,

"Supreme Court rules" means rules made under section 99 of the *Supreme Court of Judicature (Consolidation) Act* 1925,

"surrender to custody" means, in relation to a person released on bail, surrendering himself into the custody of the court or of the constable (according to the requirements of the grant of bail) at the time and place for the time being appointed for him to do so,

"vary", in relation to bail, means imposing further conditions after bail is granted, or varying or rescinding conditions,

"young person" means a person who has attained the age of fourteen and is under the age of seventeen.

(3) Where an enactment (whenever passed) which relates to bail in criminal proceedings refers to the person bailed appearing before a court it is to be construed unless the context otherwise requires as referring to his surrendering himself into the custody of the court.

(4) Any reference in this Act to any other enactment is a reference thereto as amended, and includes a reference thereto as extended or applied, by or under any other enactment, including this Act.

[This section is reprinted as amended by the *Powers of Criminal Courts (Sentencing) Act* 2000, Sch.9, para.(3)(b).]

The definition of the term "surrender to custody" has been considered in case law. **5–6** Attendance by a defendant at court and "overtly subjecting himself to the court's directions" by appearance at an arraignment in the Crown Court was held to be a surrender to custody sufficient to relieve a surety of his obligations: *R. v Central Criminal Court Ex p. Guney* [1995] 2 All E.R. 577 (Bingham L.J. dissenting). Reporting to a court official in accordance with published instructions was held to be a surrender to custody for the purposes of s.2(2) so that no offence was committed under s.6 of failing to surrender but departure from court later in the morning and without waiting for the case to be called on did engage the powers of s.7 and a warrant for arrest could be issued. Once a defendant has surrendered he is under an implied obligation not to leave the court without consent and court officials would be wise to make it clear that a person who reports to them must not leave the court without being given permission to do so: *DPP v Richards* [1988] Q.B. 701. The question of whether a person has surrendered to custody depends on the facts of the case and not the precise nature of the constraints placed upon them. The fact that there are no security officers or gaolers present in court to restrain the defendant physically does not mean that a defendant cannot surrender to custody. A defendant who left the court after being sentenced to imprisonment rather than wait for the security officers to arrive was held to be unlawfully at large. The argument that he had never surrendered to custody because there was no person there to whose direct control he could submit and so he could not be at large was dismissed by the court on appeal: *R. v Rumble (Jonathan Mark)* [2003] EWCA Crim 770.

Simply arriving at court at the time and place directed is not sufficient. There must be some statement or conduct signifying an indication of acceptance of the court's control: *R. v Reader* (1987) 84 Cr.App.R. 294

Bail Act 1976, s.3

General provisions

5–7   **3.**—(1) A person granted bail in criminal proceedings shall be under a duty to surrender to custody, and that duty is enforceable in accordance with section 6 of this Act.

(2) No recognizance for his surrender to custody shall be taken from him.

(3) Except as provided by this section—

     (a) no security for his surrender to custody shall be taken from him,

     (b) he shall not be required to provide a surety or sureties for his surrender to custody, and

     (c) no other requirement shall be imposed on him as a condition of bail.

(4) He may be required, before release on bail, to provide a surety or sureties to secure his surrender to custody.

(5) He may be required, before release on bail, to give security for his surrender to custody.

The security may be given by him or on his behalf.

(6) He may be required to comply, before release on bail or later, with such requirements as appear to the court to be necessary

     (a) to secure that he surrenders to custody,

     (b) to secure that he does not commit an offence while on bail,

     (c) to secure that he does not interfere with witnesses or otherwise obstruct the course of justice whether in relation to himself or any other person,

     (ca) for his own protection or, if he is a child or young person, for his own welfare or in his own interests

     (d) to secure that he makes himself available for the purpose of enabling inquiries or a report to be made to assist the court in dealing with him for the offence.

     (e) to secure that before the time appointed for him to surrender to custody, he attends an interview with an authorised advocate or authorised litigator, as defined by section 119(1) of the *Courts and Legal Services Act* 1990;

and, in any Act, "the normal powers to impose conditions of bail" means the powers to impose conditions under paragraph (a), (b) or (c) or (ca) above.

5–8   (6ZAA) Subject to section 3AA below, if he is a child or young person he may be required to comply with requirements imposed for the purpose of securing the electronic monitoring of his compliance with any other requirement imposed on him as a condition of bail.

(6ZA) Where he is required under subsection (6) above to reside in a bail hostel or probation hostel, he may also be required to comply with the rules of the hostel.

(6A) In the case of a person accused of murder the court granting bail shall, unless it considers that satisfactory reports on his mental condition have already been obtained, impose as conditions of bail—

     (a) a requirement that the accused shall undergo examination by two medical practitioners, for the purpose of enabling such reports to be prepared; and

     (b) a requirement that he shall for that purpose attend such an institution or place as the court directs and comply with any other directions which may be given to him for that purpose by either of those practitioners.

(6B) Of the medical practitioners referred to in subsection (6A) above at least one shall be practitioner approved for the purposes of section 12 of the *Mental Health Act* 1983.

[(6C) Subsection (6D) below applies where—

(a) the court has been notified by the Secretary of State that arrangements for conducting a relevant assessment or, as the case may be, providing relevant follow-up have been made for the petty sessions area in which it appears to the court that the person referred to in subsection (6D) would reside if granted bail; and

(b) the notice has not been withdrawn.

(6D) In the case of a person ("P")—

(a) in relation to whom paragraphs (a) to (c) of paragraph 6B(1) of Part 1 of Schedule 1 to this Act apply;

(b) who, after analysis of the sample referred to in paragraph (b) of that paragraph, has been offered a relevant assessment or, if a relevant assessment has been carried out, has had relevant follow-up proposed to him; and

(c) who has agreed to undergo the relevant assessment or, as the case may be, to participate in the relevant follow-up,

the court, if it grants bail, shall impose as a condition of bail that P both undergo the relevant assessment and participate in any relevant follow-up proposed to him or, if a relevant assessment has been carried out, that P participate in the relevant follow-up.

(6E) In subsections (6C) and *(6D)* above—

(a) "relevant assessment" means an assessment conducted by a suitably qualified person of whether P is dependent upon or has a propensity to misuse any specified Class A drugs;

(b) "relevant follow-up" means, in a case where the person who conducted the relevant assessment believes P to have such a dependency or propensity, such further assessment, and such assistance or treatment (or both) in connection with the dependency or propensity, as the person who conducted the relevant assessment (or conducts any later assessment) considers to be appropriate in P's case,

and in paragraph (a) above "Class A drug" and "misuse" have the same meaning as in the *Misuse of Drugs Act* 1971, and "specified" (in relation to a Class A drug) has the same meaning as in Part 3 of the *Criminal Justice and Court Services Act* 2000.

(6F) In subsection (6E)(a) above, "suitably qualified person" means a person who has **5–9** such qualifications or experience as are from time to time specified by the Secretary of State for the purposes of this subsection.]

(7) If a parent or guardian of a child or young person consents to be surety for the child or young person for the purposes of this subsection, the parent or guardian may be required to secure that the child or young person complies with any requirement imposed on him by virtue of subsection (6)[, (6ZAA)] or (6A) above, but—

(a) no requirement shall be imposed on the parent or the guardian of a young person by virtue of this subsection where it appears that the young person will attain the age of seventeen before the time to be appointed for him to surrender to custody; and

(b) the parent or guardian shall not be required to secure compliance with any requirement to which his consent does not extend and shall not, in respect of those requirements to which his consent does extend, be bound in a sum greater than £50.

(8) Where a court has granted bail in criminal proceedings that court or, where that court has committed a person on bail to the Crown Court for trial or to be sentenced or otherwise dealt with, that court or the Crown Court may on application—

(a) by or on behalf of the person to whom bail was granted, or

(b) by the prosecutor or a constable,

vary the conditions of bail or impose conditions in respect of bail which has been granted unconditionally.

(8A) Where a notice of transfer is given under a relevant transfer provision, subsection (8) above shall have effect in relation to a person in relation to whose case the notice is given as if he has been committed on bail on the Crown Court for trial.

(8B) Subsection (8) above applies where a court has sent a person on bail to the Crown Court for trial under section 51 of the *Crime and Disorder Act* 1998 as it applies where a court has committed a person on bail to the Crown Court for trial.

(9) This section is subject to subsection (3) of section 11 of the *Powers of Criminal Courts (Sentencing) Act* 2000 (conditions of bail on remand for medical examination).

(10) This section is subject, in its application to bail granted by a constable, to section 3A of this Act.

(10) In subsection (8A) above "relevant transfer provision" means—

    (a) section 4 of the *Criminal Justice Act* 1987, or

    (b) section 53 of the *Criminal Justice Act* 1991.

[This section is reprinted as amended by the *Criminal Justice and Police Act* 2001, s.131(3) and by the *Criminal Justice Act* 2003, s.13 which came into force in April 2004.]

5–10   For the definition of failing to surrender see § 5–6 above. Section 6 provides for the offence of failing to surrender to custody. Under s.3 pre or post-release requirements or conditions may be attached to bail.

The amendments to s.3(6) provide for conditions to be imposed for an adult defendant's own protection, or for a child or young person, their own interests or welfare. Previously this was an exception to bail only and not grounds for imposing conditions.

Securities and sureties are pre-release conditions. A security is a sum of money or other valuable that the person bailed must deposit with the court before he can be released on bail. The asset will be returned when the case is completed but will be forfeited if the defendant fails to answer his bail: s.5 of the *Bail Act* 1976. It is easier for a court to accept cash or some other asset that is realisable and not affected by rights of third parties. A security may be deposited by the defendant or someone else on his behalf. Where a defendant deposited the title deeds to his house the court was not obliged to notify his mother who had a registered charge on the property but the security could only extend to the amount of the son's beneficial interest in the house: *R. (Stevens) v Truro Magistrates' Court* [2002] 1 W.L.R. 144.

A surety is provided by someone other than the defendant. The surety enters into an undertaking that if the defendant fails to surrender to custody the surety will then forfeit the amount of money in which he has stood as surety and if the money cannot be paid the surety may be committed to prison in default: s.8 of the *Bail Act* 1976, s.120 of the *Magistrates' Courts Act* 1980. A surety may be taken in court or elsewhere, *e.g.* at a police station. The surety may agree to stand as surety until the next appointed court date or it may be made to be continuous to a certain event, *e.g.* committal to the Crown Court or first appearance at the Crown Court. A continuous surety is not obliged to attend at court in all the interim hearings for his surety to be taken again provided that the date to which he has agreed to stand as surety is clear.

Where the defendant is a child or young person and a parent or guardian stands as surety, the court may require the parent or guardian to ensure that the child or young person complies with any condition imposed: *Bail Act* 1976, s.3(7) (above). A condition under s.3(7) can only be imposed with the parent or guardian's consent and the sum may not exceed £50.

5–11   In all cases where bail is granted, whether the offence involved is imprisonable or non-imprisonable, the power to impose conditions under s.3 applies. Bail can only be withheld and a person remanded in custody on the grounds set out in the *Bail Act* 1976 (Schs 1 and 2) which differ in relation to imprisonable and non-imprisonable offences. Refusal to consent to a condition of bail is not an exception to the right to bail in either case so a defendant cannot be remanded in custody for that reason: *R. v Bournemouth Justices Ex p. Cross, Griffen and Pamment*, 89 Cr.App.R. 90.

Section 3(3)(c) and (6) restrict the conditions that may be imposed where bail is granted.

When considering the imposition of conditions the court does not have to be satisfied that there are substantial grounds for believing that the instances listed in s.3(6) would occur. It is sufficient if the court "perceived a real and not fanciful risk" that the defendant may not surrender to custody, or may commit offences or interfere with witnesses or obstruct justice or not attend for reports or interviews. Conditions may then be necessary to address the risk.The test is more rigorous when the defendant is being refused bail and deprived of his liberty: *R. v Mansfield Justices Ex p. Sharkey* [1985] 1 Q.B. 613.

Section 3A of the *Bail Act* 1976 relates to the granting of bail by the custody officer at **5–12** a police station and gives the power to impose conditions on police bail. Conditions can only be imposed by the police where they appear necessary in order to prevent a failure to surrender, or the commission of further offences or the interference with witnesses or the obstruction of justice. Police bail cannot include a requirement to reside at a bail hostel or electronic monitoring.

Section 3AA of the *Bail Act* 1976 covers the electronic monitoring of compliance with bail conditions. Electronic monitoring or tagging is available for children and young persons.

This section is amended by the *Criminal Justice Act* 2003, s.19 which provides for further powers in relation to drug users. The court will be able to withold bail from defendants unless they consent to undergo assessments for drugs and participate in follow-up treatment during the period of the remand. The amendments came into force in April 2004 but are dependent on appropriate facilities being available.

Bail may be refused to an offender aged 18 or over who is charged with an imprisonable offence if the following conditions are fulfilled:

a) A drug test taken under s.63B of the *PACE 1984* or s.161 of the Criminal Justice Act 2003 shows the presence in his body of a specified Class A drug.

b) Either the offence is one under s.5(2) or (3)*Misuse of Drugs Act* 1971 (possession or possession with intent to supply) and relates to a specified Class A drug OR the court is satisfied there are substantial grounds for believing that misuse of a specified Class A drug caused or contributed to the offence or the offence was motivated by drug misuse.

c) The offender has refused to undergo assessment and/or follow up treatment offered consequent to the drug tests.

All assessments are carried out by qualified and trained personnel. The Class A drugs are specified by Order by the Secretary of State for the Home Office and listed in Sch.2, Part 1 of the *Misuse of Drugs Act* 1971.

Where the defendant agrees to the assessment and follow up treatment the court may grant bail but a condition must be imposed that the assessment and treatment be undertaken.

Bail Act 1976, s.4

General right to bail of accused persons and others

4.—(1) A person to whom this section applies shall be granted bail except as provided in **5–13** Schedule 1 to this Act.

(2) This section applies to a person who is accused of an offence when—

(a) he appears or is brought before a magistrates' court or the Crown Court in the course of or in connection with proceedings for the offence, or

(b) he applies to a court for bail or for a variation of the conditions of bail in connection with the proceedings.

This subsection does not apply as respects proceedings on or after a person's conviction of the offence or proceedings against a fugitive offender for the offence.

(3) This section also applies to a person who, having been convicted of an offence, appears or is brought before a magistrates' court to be dealt with under Part II of Schedule 3 to the *Powers of Criminal Courts (Sentencing) Act* 2000 (breach of certain community orders).

(4) This section also applies to a person who has been convicted of an offence and whose case is adjourned by the court for the purpose of enabling inquiries or a report to be made to assist the court in dealing with him for the offence.

(5) Schedule 1 to this Act also has effect as respects conditions of bail for a person to whom this section appliesection

(6) In Schedule 1 to this Act "the defendant" means a person to whom this section applies and any reference to a defendant whose case is adjourned for inquiries or a report is a reference to a person to whom this section applies by virtue of subsection (4) above.

(7) This section is subject to section 41 of the *Magistrates' Courts Act* 1980 (restriction of bail by magistrates' court in cases of treason).

(8) This section is subject to section 25 of the *Criminal Justice and Public Order Act* 1994 (exclusion of bail in cases of homicide and rape).

[(9) In taking any decisions required by Part I or II of Schedule 1 to this Act, the considerations to which the court is to have regard include, so far as relevant, any misuse of controlled drugs by the defendant ("controlled drugs" and "misuse" having the same meanings as in the *Misuse of Drugs Act* 1971).

[This section is reprinted as amended by the *Criminal Justice and Court Services Act* 2000, s.58]

5–14   Section 4 of the *Bail Act* 1976 creates a general right to bail for persons charged with an offence. A court must grant bail to any person accused of an offence or brought before a court for breach of a requirement of probation or community service order, if none of the exceptions specified in Sch.1 applies. Where the defendant has previously been remanded in custody by the court, consideration must be given to whether bail should be granted on each occasion that the defendant is brought before the court regardless of whether the defendant makes an application: *Bail Act* 1976, Sch.1, Pt IIA. This ensures that there is the periodic review of detention as required under Art.5 ECHR.

Section 4(1) does not apply once a person has been convicted of an offence. An appellant seeking bail pending the outcome of an appeal has no right to bail under this section. Section 4(1) does not apply to offenders who have been committed to the Crown Court for sentencing following conviction in the magistrates' court. In these situations a magistrate has the power to grant bail but the decision is entirely at the discretion of the court and there is no initial presumption either way. The *Bail Act* 1976 applies to offenders brought before the court in respect of any breach of a requirement of community penalties under the *Criminal Justice Act* 1991, Sch.2, Pt 2. A convicted person has the right to bail if the case is adjourned for the purpose of obtaining reports but under para.7, Sch.1, Pt I of the *Bail Act* 1976 there is an additional exception to the right to bail; the defendant need not be granted bail where it appears to the court that it would be impracticable to complete inquiries or make a report without keeping the defendant in custody.

Section 25 of the *Criminal Justice and Public Order Act* 1994 removes the presumption of bail in the case of persons who have been charged with or convicted of murder, attempted murder, manslaughter, rape or attempted rape. In such circumstances bail shall only be granted if the court or constable is satisfied that there are exceptional circumstances which justify it.

5–15   In *Ilijokov v Bulgaria* [2001] 7 *Archbold News* 1, the European Court of Human Rights held that a provision making pre-trial custody the rule for defendants charged with offences of a specified level of seriousness, except where there was not even a theoretical possibility of absconding, commission of further offences or interference with witnesses violated Art.5(3) of the Convention, because it is for the state to satisfy the court that there are relevant and sufficient reasons for withholding bail. The "exceptional circumstances" referred to in s.25 of the *Criminal Justice and Public Order Act* 1994 preserve a sufficient discretion to ensure that Art.5 is not violated.

Where a drugs test is carried out by the police under s.63B *PACE* 1984, the result of the test is relevant to a bail decision under s.4(9). The misuse of drugs may give rise to a fear of commission of further offences to feed the drug habit or failure to attend if affected by taking drugs.

Bail Act 1976, s.5

Supplementary provisions about decisions on bail

5–16   5.—(1) Subject to subsection (2) below, where—

     (a) a court or constable grants bail in criminal proceedings, or

     (b) a court withholds bail in criminal proceedings from a person to whom section 4 of this act applies, or

(c) a court, officer of a court or constable appoints a time or place or a court or officer of a court appoints a different time or place for a person granted bail in criminal proceedings to surrender to custody, or

(d) a court or constable varies any conditions of bail or imposes conditions in respect of bail in criminal proceedings,

that court, officer or constable shall make a record of the decision in the prescribed manner and containing the prescribed particulars and, if requested to do so by the person in relation to whom the decision was taken, shall cause him to be given a copy of the record of the decision as soon as practicable after the record is made.

(2) Where bail in criminal proceedings is granted by endorsing a warrant of arrest for bail the constable who releases on bail the person arrested shall make the record required by subsection (1) above instead of the judge or justice who issued the warrant.

(2A) Where a magistrates' court or the Crown Court grants bail in criminal proceedings to a person to whom section 4 of this Act applies after hearing representations from the prosecutor in favour of withholding bail, then the court shall give reasons for granting bail.

(2B) A court which is by virtue of subsection (2A) above required to give reasons for its decision shall include a note of those reasons in the record of its decision and, if requested to do so by the prosecutor, shall cause the prosecutor to be given a copy of the record of the decision as soon as practicable after the record is made.

(3) Where a magistrates' court or the Crown Court—

(a) withholds bail in criminal proceedings, or

(b) imposes conditions in granting bail in criminal proceedings, or

(c) varies any conditions of bail or imposes conditions in respect of bail in criminal proceedings,

and does so in relation to a person to whom section 4 of this Act applies, then the court shall, with a view to enabling him to consider making an application in the matter to another court, give reasons for withholding bail or for imposing or varying the conditions.

(4) A court which is by virtue of subsection (3) above required to give reasons for its decision shall include a note of those reasons in the record of its decision and shall (except in a case where, by virtue of subsection (5) below, this need not be done) give a copy of that note to the person in relation to whom the decision was taken.   **5–17**

(5) The Crown Court need not give a copy of the note of the reasons for its decision to the person in relation to whom the decision was taken where that person is represented by counsel or a solicitor unless his counsel or solicitor requests the court to do so.

(6) Where a magistrates' court withholds bail in criminal proceedings from a person who is not represented by counsel or a solicitor, the court shall—

(a) if it is committing him for trial to the Crown Court or if it issues a certificate under subsection (6A) below, inform him that he may apply to the High Court or to the Crown Court to be granted bail;

(b) in any other case, inform him that he may apply to the High Court for that purpose.

(6A) Where in criminal proceedings—

(a) a magistrates' court remands a person in custody under section 11 of the *Powers of Criminal Courts (Sentencing) Act* 2000 (remand for medical examination) or any of the following provisions of the *Magistrates' Courts Act* 1980—

(i) section 5 (adjournment of inquiry into offence);

(ii) section 10 (adjournment of trial); or

(iii) section 18 (initial procedure on information against adult for offence triable either way),

after hearing full argument on an application for bail from him; and

(b) either—

(i) it has not previously heard such argument on an application for bail from him in those proceedings; or

(ii) it has previously heard full argument from him on such an application but it is satisfied that there has been a change in his circumstances or that new considerations have been placed before it,

it shall be the duty of the court to issue a certificate in the prescribed form that they heard full argument on his application for bail before they refused the application.

(6B) Where the court issues a certificate under subsection (6A) above in a case to which paragraph (b)(ii) of that subsection applies, it shall state in the certificate the nature of the change of circumstances or the new considerations which caused it to hear a further fully argued bail application.

(6C) Where a court issues a certificate under subection (6A) above it shall cause the person to whom it refuses bail to be given a copy of the certificate.

5–18   (7) Where a person has given security in pursuance of section 3(5) above and a court is satisfied that he failed to surrender to custody then, unless it appears that he had reasonable cause for his failure, the court may order the forfeiture of the security.

(8) If a court orders the forfeiture of a security under subsection (7) above, the court may declare that the forfeiture extends to such amount less than the full value of the security as it thinks fit to order.

(8A) An order under subsection (7) above shall, unless previously revoked, have effect at the end of twenty-one days beginning with the day on which it is made.

(8B) A court which has ordered the forfeiture of a security under subsection (7) above may, if satisfied on an application made by or on behalf of the person who gave it that he did after all have reasonable cause for his failure to surrender to custody, by order remit the forfeiture or declare that it extends to such amount less than the full value of the security as it thinks fit to order.

(8C) An application under subsection (8B) above may be made before or after the order for forfeiture has taken effect, but shall not be entertained unless the court is satisfied that the prosecution was given reasonable notice of the applicant's intention to make it.

(9) A security which has been ordered to be forfeited by a court under subsection (7) above shall, to the extent of the forfeiture—

     (a) if it consists of money, be accounted for and paid in the same manner as a fine imposed by that court would be;

     (b) if it does not consist of money, be enforced by such magistrates' court as may be specified in the order.

(9A) Where an order is made under subsection (8B) above after the order for forfeiture of the security in question has taken effect, any money which would have fallen to be repaid or paid over to the person who gave the security if the order under subsection (8B) had been made before the order for forfeiture took effect shall be repaid or paid over to him.

(10) In this section "prescribed" means, in relation to the decision of a court or an officer of a court, prescribed by Supreme Court rules, Courts-Martial Appeal rules, Crown Court rules or magistrates' courts rules, as the case requires or, in relation to a decision of a constable, prescribed by direction of the Secretary of State.

(11) This section is subject, in its application to bail granted by a constable, to section 5A of this Act.

[This section is reprinted as amended by the *Criminal Justice and Police Act* 2001, s.129(1)]

5–19   Under this section the court will provide a written bail notice to the defendant It includes details of exceptions found and reasons given for the decision and standard requirements of conditional bail to be deleted or amended as appropriate. There is also a duty on the court under s.5(2A) to give written reasons in cases where bail is granted after the prosecution has objected to bail. The provision of reasons enables the parties affected to consider fully the basis of an appeal.

At the first hearing at which the defendant is a person to whom s.4 applies, the court shall grant the defendant bail unless one of the exceptions under Pt I or II of Sch.1 applies. If the prosecution make representations against the grant of bail the defendant may support the application for bail with any argument in fact or law. The court must consider the question of bail regardless of whether the defendant makes an application for bail and must record reasons if the remand is to be in custody.

If bail is refused at the first hearing, the court is still bound to consider the question of bail at each subsequent hearing. An application for further remand in the absence of the defendant and with his consent under s.128(3A) of the *Magistrates' Courts Act* 1980 is not a hearing for this purpose. Section 4 does not apply in such a case because the defendant does not appear, is not brought before the court and makes no application for bail: *R. v Dover and East Kent Justices Ex p. Dean* [1992] Crim.L.R. 33, DC.

After the first hearing at which the defendant is denied bail the defendant may sup- **5–20** port one more application for bail with any argument in fact or law, whether or not the argument has been raised previously. The purpose of the legislation is to provide for any argument being advanced on two occasions as of right, and at the second hearing the court is obliged to consider the matter *de novo*.

This is not always the effect of the legislation. Sometimes when a defendant faces a serious charge and is brought to court in custody there may be any number of reasons why a bail application is not made on the first appearance. When the defendant next appears before the court, an application for bail may be made and any argument raised as of right. If bail is withheld once more at the second hearing the defendant has no right to raise the same arguments again at later hearings, in effect depriving the defendant of the intended right to have two attempts at contesting the objections to bail made by the prosecution. If no application is made at the first hearing after that at which the court decided not to grant the defendant bail, *Bail Act* 1976, para.2 of Pt IIA, Sch.1 does not apply so as to confer a right to make an application at subsequent hearings based on the same arguments of fact and law. The defendant always has the right to make an application for bail but whether the court is bound to entertain the application is a different question. There must be some material change of circumstance to warrant repeated applications: *R. v Dover and East Kent Justices Ex p. Dean* (above). Pt IIA, para.3 provides that where a person has been remanded in custody then at subsequent hearings the court need not hear arguments as to fact or law which it has heard previously. This implies that it has a discretion to do so. On that basis the court should not hear arguments as to fact or law which it has heard previously unless there has been such a change of circumstances as might justify a different decision. To do so would be to act in an appellate capacity which would be inappropriate: *R. v Slough Justices Ex p. Duncan*, 75 Cr.App.R. 384, DC.

Where the court decides that a defendant should be remanded in custody because it has not been practicable to obtain sufficient information to consider a bail application, this does not amount to a decision to refuse bail within the meaning of para.1 of Pt IIA: *R. v Calder Justices Ex p. Kennedy* [1992] Crim.L.R. 496.

The passage of time may require a court to hear further bail applications to ensure **5–21** that the defendant's rights under Art.5 are reviewed regularly: *Neumeister v Austria (No.1)* (1968) 1 E.H.R.R. 91.

Under s.5(6A) a certificate that a full bail argument has taken place must be issued when the court remands a defendant in custody following the first full bail application. Such a certificate must also be issued if a further full bail application is allowed because of a change in circumstances or the identification of new considerations and the defendant is again remanded in custody. The certificate can be provided immediately and is often incorporated in the printed bail notice given to the defendant. The purpose of the certificate is to form the basis of an appeal against the bail decision to the Crown Court and to confirm that all avenues of argument in the magistrates' court have been exhausted.

A security can be imposed as a condition of bail: s.3. This section provides for the procedure to be followed if the defendant fails to answer his bail. The order of forfeiture only takes effect after 21 days and in the meantime the court may serve a notice of forfeiture on the person who deposited the security whether that be the defendant or someone else on his behalf so they may make representations.

B. BAIL FOLLOWING ADJOURNMENT

Magistrates' Courts Act 1980, s.5

Adjournment of inquiry

5.—(1) A magistrates' court may, before beginning to inquire into an offence as examining **5–22** justices, or at any time during the inquiry, adjourn the hearing, and if it does so shall remand the accused.

(2) The court shall when adjourning fix the time and place at which the hearing is to be resumed; and the time fixed shall be that at which the accused is required to appear or be brought before the court in pursuance of the remand [or would be required to be brought before the court but for section 128(3A) below].

[This section is reprinted as amended by the *Criminal Justice Act* 1982, s.59(1), Sch.9 para.1(a).]

Magistrates' Courts Act 1980, s.6(3), (4)

Discharge or committal for trial

5–23   **6.**—(3) Subject to section 4 of the *Bail Act* 1976 and section 41 below, the court may commit a person for trial—

     (a) in custody, that is to say, by committing him to custody there to be safety kept until delivered in due course of law, or

     (b) on bail in accordance with the *Bail Act* 1976, that is to say, by directing him to appear before the Crown Court for trial;

and where his release on bail is conditional on his providing one or more surety or sureties and, in accordance with section 8(3) of the *Bail Act* 1976, the court fixes the amount in which the surety is to be bound with a view to his entering into his recognizance subsequently in accordance with subsections (4) and (5) or (6) of that section the court shall in the meantime commit the accused to custody in accordance with paragraph (a) of this subsection.

(4) Where the court has committed a person to custody in accordance with paragraph (a) of subsection (3) above, then, if that person is in custody for no other cause, the court may, at any time before his first appearance before the Crown Court, grant him bail in accordance with the *Bail Act* 1976 subject to a duty to appear before the Crown Court for trial.

[This section is reprinted as amended by the *Access to Justice Act* 1999, Sch.13 para.96.]

Crime and Disorder Act 1998, s.52

Provisions supplementing section 51

5–24   **52.**—(1) Subject to section 4 of the *Bail Act* 1976, section 41 of the 1980 Act, regulations under section 22 of the 1985 Act and section 25 of the 1994 Act, the court may send a person for trial under section 51 above—

     (a) in custody, that is to say, by committing him to custody there to be safely kept until delivered in due course of law; or

     (b) on bail in accordance with the *Bail Act* 1976, that is to say, by directing him to appear before the Crown Court for trial.

    (2) Where—

     (a) the person's release on bail under subsection (1)(b) above is conditional on his providing one or more sureties; and

     (b) in accordance with subsection (3) of section 8 of the *Bail Act* 1976, the court fixes the amount in which a surety is to be bound with a view to his entering into his recognisance subsequently in accordance with subsections (4) and (5) or (6) of that section,

the court shall in the meantime make an order such as is mentioned in subsection (1)(a) above.

(3) The court shall treat as an indictable offence for the purposes of section 51 above an offence which is mentioned in the first column of Schedule 2 to the 1980 Act (offences for which the value involved is relevant to the mode of trial) unless it is clear to the court, having regard to any representations made by the prosecutor or the accused, that the value involved does not exceed the relevant sum.

(4) In subsection (3) above "the value involved" and "the relevant sum" have the same meanings as in section 22 of the 1980 Act (certain offences triable either way to be tried summarily if value involved is small).

(5) A magistrates' court may adjourn any proceedings under section 51 above, and if it does so shall remand the accused.

(6) Schedule 3 to this Act (which makes further provision in relation to persons sent to the Crown Court for trial under section 51 above) shall have effect.

Magistrates' Courts Rules 1981, r.93

Variation of arrangements for bail on committal to Crown Court

93. Where a magistrates' court has committed or sent a person on bail to the Crown Court **5–25** for trail or under any of the enactments mentioned in rule 17(1) and subsequently varies any conditions of the bail or imposes any conditions in respect of the bail, the [justices' chief executive for] the court shall send to the appropriate officer of the Crown Court a copy of the record made in pursuance of section 5 of the *Bail Act* 1976 relating to such variation or imposition of conditions.

[This rule is reprinted as amended by the *Magistrates' Courts (Amendment No.2) Rules* 2001, r.3]

Where a magistrates' court commits a person for trial in the Crown Court on bail the bail ceases when the defendant surrenders to the Crown Court. If the Crown Court releases the defendant on bail, it must consider the suitability of any conditions afresh: *R. v Kent Crown Court Ex p. Jodka* (1997) 161 J.P. 638, DC.

Committal for trial is not necessarily a new circumstance which entitles the defendant **5–26** to make a new bail application. In *R. v Slough Justices Ex p. Duncan* [1981] Q.B. 451 it was stated that new arguments in favour of bail may be advanced upon committal for trial because the strength of the prosecution case at the committal hearing may be better assessed.

If after committal for trial but before arraignment at the Crown Court there is an ap- **5–27** plication to vary the conditions of bail, the magistrates' court has concurrent jurisdiction with the Crown Court to hear and determine the application: *R. v Lincoln Magistrates' Court Ex p. Mawer* (1996) 160 J.P. 219.

The magistrates' court also has power to commit a defendant to the Crown Court for sentence under the *Powers of Criminal Courts (Sentencing) Act* 2000, s.3 and s.6 and several other statutory provisions, see Part IV on Sentencing in this work). In each case the court has power to commit either on bail or in custody. Upon committal for sentence the usual practice should be to commit the defendant in custody only if he has been in custody prior to the committal hearing: *R. v Rafferty* [1999] 1 Cr.App.R. 235, CA. In the judgement Thomas J. said —

> "In the usual case where a person who has been on bail pleads guilty at the plea before venue, the usual practice should be to continue bail, even if it is anticipated that a custodial sentence will be imposed by the Crown Court,unless there are good reasons for remanding the defendant in custody".

The encouragement to a defendant to plead guilty at the earliest opportunity is not then affected by a fear of being remanded into custody.

Magistrates' Courts Act 1980, s.10

Adjournment of trial

10.—(1) A magistrates' court may at any time, whether before or after beginning to try an in- **5–28** formation, adjourn the trial, and may do so, notwithstanding anything in this Act, when composed of a single justice.

(2) The court may when adjourning either fix the time and place at which the trial is to be resumed, or, unless it remands the accused, leave the time and place to be determined later by the court; but the trial shall not be resumed at that time and place unless the court is satisfied that the parties have had adequate notice thereof.

(3) A magistrates' court may, for the purpose of enabling inquiries to be made or of determining the most suitable method of dealing with the case, exercise its power to adjourn after convicting the accused and before sentencing him or otherwise dealing with him; but, if it does so, the adjournment shall not be for more than 4 weeks at a time unless the court remands the accused in custody and, where it so remands him, the adjournment shall not be for more than 3 weeks at a time.

(3A) A youth court shall not be required to adjourn any proceedings for an offence at any stage by reason only of the fact—

(a) that the court commits the accused for trial for another offence; or

(b) that the accused is charged with another offence.

(4) On adjourning the trial of an information the court may remand the accused and, where the accused has attained the age of 18 years, shall do so if the offence is triable either way and—

(a) on the occasion on which the accused first appeared, or was brought, before the court to answer to the information he was in custody or, having been released on bail, surrendered to the custody of the court; or

(b) the accused has been remanded at any time in the course of proceedings on the information;

and, where the court remands the accused, the time fixed for the resumption of the trial shall be that at which he is required to appear or be brought before the court in pursuance of the remand or would be required to be brought before the court but for section 128(3A) below.

[This section is reprinted as amended by the *Crime and Disorder Act* 1998, s.47(5).]

Magistrates' Courts Act 1980, s.17C

Intention as to plea adjournment

5–29   **17C.** A magistrates' court proceeding under section 17A or 17B above may adjourn the proceedings at any time, and on doing so on any occasion when the accused is present may remand the accused, and shall remand him if—

(a) on the occasion on which he first appeared, or was brought, before the court to answer to the information he was in custody or, having been released on bail, surrendered to the custody of the court; or

(b) he has been remanded at any time in the course of proceedings on the information;

and where the court remands the accused, the time fixed for the resumption of proceedings shall be that at which he is required to appear or be brought before the court in pursuance of the remand or would be required to be brought before the court but for section 128(3A) below.

Magistrates' Courts Act 1980, s.18(4), (5)

Initial procedure on information against adult for offence triable either way

5–30   **18.**—(4) A magistrates' court proceeding under sections 19 to 23 below may adjourn the proceedings at any time, and on doing so on any occasion when the accused is present may remand the accused, and shall remand him if—

(a) on the occasion on which he first appeared, or was brought, before the court to answer to the information he was in custody or, having been released on bail, surrendered to the custody of the court; or

(b) he has been remanded at any time in the course of proceedings on the information;

and where the court remands the accused, the time fixed for the resumption of the proceedings shall be that at which he is required to appear or be brought before the court in pursuance of the remand or would be required to be brought before the court but for section 128(3A) below.

5–31   (5) The functions of a magistrates' court under sections 19 to 23 below may be discharged by a single justice, but the foregoing provision shall not be taken to authorise the summary trial of an information by a magistrates' court composed of less than two justices.

[This section is reprinted as amended by the *Criminal Procedure and Investigations Act* 1996, s.49(3)]

C. BAIL PENDING AN APPEAL

Magistrates' Courts Act 1980, s.113

Bail on appeal or case stated

5–32   **113.**—(1) Where a person has given notice of appeal to the Crown Court against the decision of a magistrates' court or has applied to a magistrates' court to state a case for the opinion of the

High Court, then, if he is in custody, the magistrates' court may, subject to section 25 of the *Criminal Justice and Public Order Act* 1994 grant him bail.

(2) If a person is granted bail under subsection (1) above, the time and place at which he is to appear (except in the event of the determination in respect of which the case is stated being reversed by the High Court) shall be—

(a) if he has given notice of appeal, the Crown Court at the time appointed for the hearing of the appeal;

(b) if he has applied for the statement of a case, the magistrates' court at such time within 10 days after the judgment of the High Court has been given as may be specified by the magistrates' court;

and any recognizance that may be taken from him or from any surety for him shall be conditioned accordingly.

(3) Subsection (1) above shall not apply where the accused has been committed to the Crown Court for sentence under [section 37] [above or section 3 of the *Powers of Criminal Courts (Sentencing) Act* 2000].

(4) Section 37(6) of the *Criminal Justice Act* 1948 (which relates to the currency of a sentence while a person is released on bail by the High Court) shall apply to a person released on bail by a magistrates' court under this section pending the hearing of a case stated as it applies to a person released on bail by the High Court under section 22 of the *Criminal Justice Act* 1967.

[This is reprinted as amended by the *Powers of Criminal Courts (Sentencing) Act* 2000, Sch.9, para.72.]

5-33 The court may be reluctant to grant the appellant bail pending appeal where a custodial sentence has been imposed following conviction. Bail would only be appropriate in the most exceptional circumstances, *e.g.* if there was a strong likelihood of success of an appeal or that a sentence would have been served by the time the appeal would be heard: *R. v Watton* (1979) 68 Cr.App.R. 293 .

D. Bail on Arrest

Magistrates' Courts Act 1980, s.43

Bail on arrest

5-34 **43.**—(1) Where a person has been granted bail under [Part IV of] the *Police and Criminal Evidence Act* 1984 subject to a duty to appear before a magistrates' court, the court before which he is to appear may appoint a later time as the time at which he is to appear and may enlarge the recognizances of any sureties for him at that time.

(2) The recognizance of any surety for any person granted bail subject to a duty to attend at a police station may be enforced as if it were conditioned for his appearance before a magistrates' court for the petty sessions area in which the police station named in the recognizance is situated.

[This section is reprinted as amended by the *Criminal Justice and Public Order Act* 1994, Sch.10, para.43.]

E. Bail where Appearance before Crown Court Contemplated

Magistrates' Courts Act 1980, s.43A

Functions of magistrates' court where a person in custody is brought before it with a view to his appearance before the Crown Court

5-35 **43A.**—(1) Where a person in custody in pursuance of a warrant issued by the Crown Court with a view to his appearance before the Crown Court is brought before a magistrates' court in pursuance of section 81(5) of the *Supreme Court Act* 1981—

(a) the magistrates' court shall commit him in custody or release him on bail until he can be brought or appear before the Crown Court at the time and place appointed by the Crown Court;

(b) if the warrant is endorsed for bail, but the person in custody is unable to satisfy the conditions endorsed, the magistrates' court may vary those conditions, if satisfied that it is proper to do so.

(2) A magistrates' court shall have jurisdiction under subsection (1) whether or not the offence was committed, or the arrest was made, within the court's area.

[This section is reprinted as amended by the *Supreme Court Act* 1981, s.152(1) and as amended by the *Criminal Justice and Public Order Act* 1994, Sch.3, para.3.]

A person arrested on a Crown Court or 'Bench' warrant may be brought before a magistrates' court usually on a Saturday or other day when the Crown Court is not closed. The case may be adjourned to the next convenient date at the Crown Court with the defendant remanded on bail or in custody.

F. BAIL FOR PERSONS IN CUSTOMS DETENTION

5–36   As from a day to be appointed s.150 of the *Criminal Justice Act* 1988 amends s.114(2) of the *Police and Criminal Evidence Act* 1984 so as to empower the Treasury by order to direct that in relation to customs detention the 1976 Act shall have effect as if references in it to a constable were references to an officer of Customs and Excise of such grade as may be specified in the order.

III. PRINCIPLES FOR GRANTING/DENYING BAIL

(1) Statutory grounds for refusal

5–37   Section 4 of the *Bail Act* 1976 is subject to the First Schedule to the Act, which sets out the reasons why a defendant need not be granted bail. Part 1 applies to imprisonable offences, and Part II to non-imprisonable offences.

Bail Act 1976, Sch.1

SCHEDULE 1

PERSONS ENTITLED TO BAIL: SUPPLEMENTARY PROVISIONS

PART I

Defendants Accused or Convicted of Imprisonable Offences

Defendants to whom Part I applies

5–38   1. Where the offence or one of the offences of which the defendant is accused or convicted in the proceedings is punishable with imprisonment the following provisions of this Part of this Schedule apply.

Exceptions to right to bail

5–39   2. The defendant need not be granted bail if the court is satisfied that there are substantial grounds for believing that the defendant, if released on bail (whether subject to conditions or not) would—

    (a) fail to surrender to custody, or

    (b) commit an offence while on bail, or

    (c) interfere with witnesses or otherwise obstruct the course of justice, whether in relation to himself or any other person.

[2A.—(1) If the defendant falls within this paragraph he may not be granted bail unless the court is satisfied that there is no significant risk of his committing an offence while on bail (whether subject to conditions or not)

(2) The defendant falls within this paragraph if—

    (a) he is aged 18 or over, and

    (b) it appears to the court that he was on bail in criminal proceedings on the date of the offence.]

    3. The defendant need not be granted bail if the court is satisfied that the defendant should be kept in custody for his own protection or, if he is a child or young person, for

his own welfare.

4. The defendant need not be granted bail if he is in custody in pursuance of the **5–40** sentence of a court or of any authority acting under any of the Services Acts.

5. The defendant need not be granted bail where the court is satisfied that it has not been practicable to obtain sufficient information for the purpose of taking the decisions required by this Part of this Schedule for want of time since the institution of the proceedings against him.

[6.—(1) If the defendant falls within this paragraph, he may not be granted bail unless the court is satisfied that there is no significant risk that, if released on bail (whether subject to conditions or not), he would fail to surrender to custody.

(2) Subject to *sub-paragraph (3)* below, the defendant falls within this paragraph if—

   (a) he is aged 18 or over, and
   (b) it appears to the court that, having been released on bail in or on connection with the proceedings for the offence, he failed to surrender to custody.

(3) Where it appears to the court that the defendant has reasonable cause for his failure to surrender to custody, he does not fall within this paragraph unless it also appears to the court that he failed to surrender to custody at the appointed place as soon as reasonably practicable after the appointed time.

(4) For the purposes of *sub-paragraph (3)* above, a failure to give to the defendant a copy of the record of the decision to grant him bail shall not constitute a reasonable cause for his failure to surrender to custody.]

Exception applicable only to defendant whose case is adjourned for inquiries or a report

7. Where his case is adjourned for inquiries or a report, the defendant need not be **5–41** granted bail if it appears to the court that it would be impracticable to complete the inquiries or make the report without keeping the defendant in custody.

Restrictions of conditions of bail

8.—(1) Subject to *sub-paragraph (3)* below, where the defendant is granted bail, no condi- **5–42** tions shall be imposed under subsections (4) to (7) (except subsections (6)(d) or (e)) of section 3 of this Act unless it appears to the court [that it is necessary to do so—

   (a) for then purpose of preventing the occurrence of any of the events mentioned in paragraph 2(1) of this Part of this Schedule or
   (b) for the defendant's own protection or, if he is a child or young person, for his own welfare or in his own interests]

(1A) No condition shall be imposed under section 3(6)(d) of this Act unless it appears to **5–43** be necessary to do so for the purpose of enabling inquiries or a report to be made.

(2) *Sub-paragraphs (1) and (1A)* above also apply on any application to the court to vary the conditions of bail or to impose conditions in respect of bail which has been granted unconditionally.

(3) The restriction imposed by *sub-paragraph (1A)* above shall not apply to the conditions required to be imposed under section 3(6A) of this Act or operate to override the direction in section 11(3) of the *Powers of Criminal Courts (Sentencing) Act* 2000 to a magistrates' court to impose conditions of bail under section 3(6)(d) of this Act of the description specified in the said section 11(3) in the circumstances so specified.

Decisions under paragraph 2

9. In taking the decisions required by paragraph 2 [or 2A] of this Part of this Schedule, **5–44** the court shall have regard to such of the following considerations as appear to it to be relevant, that is to say–

   (a) the nature and seriousness of the offence or default (and the probable method of dealing with the defendant for it),

   (b) the character, antecedents, associations and community ties of the defendant,

   (c) the defendant's record as respects the fulfilment of his obligations under previous grants of bail in criminal proceedings,

   (d) except in the case of a defendant whose case is adjourned for inquiries or a report, the strength of the evidence of his having committed the offence or having defaulted,

as well as to any others which appear to be relevant.

[9AA—(1) This *paragraph* applies if –
  (a) the defendant is under the age of 18, and
  (b) it appears to the court that he was on bail in criminal proceedings on the date of the offence.

(2) In deciding for the purposes of paragraph 2(1) of this Part of this Schedule whether it is satisfied that there are substantial grounds for believing that the defendant, if released on bail (whether subject to conditions or not) would commit an offence while on bail, the court shall give particular weight to the fact that the defendant was on bail in criminal proceedings on the date of the offence.]

[Paragraphs 2A, 6 and 8 are printed as prospectively amended by the *Criminal Justice Act* 2003, ss.13, 14 and 15. Paragraph 9 is reprinted as amended by the *Criminal Justice and Public Order Act* 1994, s.26(b). Paragraph 9AA is inserted by the *Criminal Justice Act* 2003 when in force. Paragraph 9AB will also be inserted by the same Act and it relates to persons under the age of 18.]

5–45   Bail need not be granted if there are substantial grounds for believing that the defendant would fail to surrender to custody, commit an offence whilst on bail or interfere with witnesses or otherwise obstruct the course of justice. The test for withholding bail is more rigorous than the test for imposing conditions on bail. The court need not be satisfied that the consequences in para.2(a)–(c) would actually occur if bail were to be granted. It has to be satisfied that there are substantial grounds for believing that they would occur. However it is not enough for the court to have a subjective belief that there is a risk of one or more of the events in para.2 occurring: *Mansfield Justices Ex p. Sharkey* [1985] Q.B. 613.

Consideration has been given in European case law to the reasons why a person may be refused bail and be deprived of his liberty. Substantial grounds for believing a person may fail to surrender to custody is sufficient grounds but the Court has said that there must be 'a whole set of circumstances .....which give reason to suppose that the consequences and hazards of flight will seem to him to be a lesser evil than continued imprisonment': *Stogmuller v Austria* (1969) 1 E.H.R.R. 155. It has also been indicated that the aspects of the individual case must be taken into account which include,'the character of the person involved, his morals, his home, his occupation, his assets, his family ties and all kinds of links with the country in which he is being prosecuted.': *Neumeister v Austria* (1968) 1 E.H.R.R. 91.

5–46   The severity of the potential sentence alone cannot of itself justify the refusal of bail. There have to exist other grounds that give rise to the belief that the accused may abscond: *Letellier v France* (1992) 14 E.H.R.R. 83; *W v Switzerland* (1993) 17 E.H.R.R. 60; *Mansur v Turkey* 20 E.H.R.R. 535.

In relation to the commission of further offences it has been held that this may amount to 'good and sufficient reason' and detention may be justified to prevent crime: *Matznetter v Austria* (1969) 1 E.H.R.R. 198. Detention may also be justified for the preservation of public order where in offences of particular gravity there are substantial grounds to believe that public disorder may result from the accused's release: *Letellier v France*.

As to the fear of interference with witnesses or the obstruction of justice, the court has indicated that a generalised risk that this might occur is not sufficient. A specific risk must be identifiable and supported by evidence: *Clooth v Belgium* (1991) 14 E.H.R.R. 717. The risk may involve the interference with witnesses, warning suspects or destroying evidence: *Wemhoff v Germany* (1979) 1 E.H.R.R. 55.

5–47   The court must have regard to the four considerations of para.9, Sch.1 as well as others that appear relevant. The desirability of a medical examination of a defendant charged with murder was held to be a relevant consideration which may amount to an exception to bail: *R. v Vernege* [1982] 1 All E.R. 403.

The prosecution, when making representations about bail must ensure that relevant reasons are brought to the attention of the court. Previous convictions are relevant and where the accused has a criminal record, a copy may be handed to the court, but as far as possible detailed oral reference to it should be avoided: *R. v Dyson* 29 Cr.App.R. 104. Sight of the record disqualifies the court from hearing any subsequent trial as the *Magistrates' Courts Act* 1980 provides that a magistrate shall not participate in trying the issue of a defendant's guilt on the summary trial of an information if in the course of the same proceedings, for the purpose of deciding whether the defendant should have bail, he or she has been informed of any previous convictions: *Magistrates' Courts Act* 1980, s.42.

IV. CONDITIONS OF BAIL

Bail Act 1976, Sch.1, para.8

Paragraph 8 gives the power to impose conditions on bail. Section 3 of the *Bail Act* **5–48** 1976 sets out the types of conditions which may be attached to the grant of bail in criminal proceedings. When bail is granted to a person to whom s.4 applies, no condition may be attached unless it is considered necessary for the purpose of preventing absconding, the commission of an offence on bail or interference with witnesses or the obstruction of justice, or for the purpose of obtaining medical or other reports.

The standard conditions are:

Pre-release

1. To provide a security or sureties (for detail see below). The imposition of **5–49** sureties and securities has been considered by the European Court which held that the figure set must take account of the means of the accused who deposits a security or the third person if standing as a surety. The relationship between the accused and the surety should also be considered: *Wemhoff v Germany* (above); *Neumeister v Austria* (above).
2. To surrender a passport to the police. The surrender of a passport or other travel documents and indeed driving documents was held by the European Court to be proportional: *Stogmuller v Austria* (above). It is not appropriate for such documents to be surrendered to the magistrates' court as there is no procedure for the retention or disposal of such items.

Post release

1. A condition of residence to live and sleep each night at a fixed, approved **5–50** address. This may stipulate residence at a bail or other type of hostel. The court should be assured that the address is suitable and in the case of hostels, a place should formally be confirmed by the appropriate authorities. It is also usual for a further condition to be attached when directing residence at a hostel that the rules and regulations of the hostel must be observed. The European Court has approved the proportionality of a condition of residence: *Schmid v Austria* [1985] 44 D.R. 195.
2. A curfew may be imposed ordering the defendant to stay indoors at a specified address during specified hours. The court also has power under s.3(6) to require under a "doorstep" condition that the person bailed present himself at the doorstep of the premises during the hours of curfew if a police officer so demands. Whether any such condition is necessary to protect the public (*i.e.* proportional) is a question of fact for each case. *R. (on the application of CPS) v Chorley Justices* [2002] EWHC 2162.
3. The accused may be directed to report to a police station in person on specific days and at specific times. His attendance will be noted. It is advisable to check that the police station is at a convenient location for the accused and that it is open at the relevant times.
4. A condition of non-contact may be made in relation to specific persons who should be named. This condition is common in charges involving violence where the alleged victim may be named but it may also relate to other witnesses or co-defendants. Direct and indirect contact which may be prohibited includes the use of mobile phones and texting either by the accused or someone else on his behalf.

5. The accused may be prohibited from going to certain specified areas. This could cover a specific address where an offence was said to have occurred or where the alleged victim lives. It could also cover a wider area, such as a shopping centre or the London Tube system where the offence is one that is habitually committed in those places. The area prohibited must be clearly identified and measurements are sometimes used (*e.g.* not to go within 100 metres of ...) and exceptions can be made to the exclusion by permitting appearances at court or solicitors if located within the prohibited area.

6. The accused may be required to attend at all appointments and to co-operate with all directions given for the preparation of reports.

7. A child or young person may be made subject to electronic tagging.

5–52 The court and the police should ensure that the defendant is able to comply with any condition they intend to impose under s.3(6) and that such conditions are clearly expressed, proportional and enforceable. The list above is far from exhaustive and the court and police have a wide discretion to devise and impose such conditions as appear necessary. Any conditions must be designed to address the real risks of failing to surrender, committing further offences, obstructing justice or interfering with witnesses or failing to attend for interviews. The European Court has said that equal care must be taken in fixing appropriate bail conditions as in deciding on continued detention: *Iwanczuk v Poland* (2004) 38 E.H.R.R. 8.

In deciding on conditions the court is entitled to use its knowledge of local events and conditions. In *R. v Mansfield Justices Ex p. Sharkey* [1985] Q.B. 613, Lord Lane said at 625 that:

> The question the justices should ask themselves is a simple one; 'Is this condition necessary for the prevention of the commission of an offence when on bail?' They are not obliged to have substantial grounds. It is enough if they perceive a real and not a fanciful risk of the offence being committed. Thus, section 3(6) and paragraph 8 give the court a wise discretion to inquire whether the condition is necessary.

5–53 The defendants were arrested on suspicion of public order offences allegedly committed during the miners' strike of 1984–85. The court was entitled to impose conditions of bail not to picket except in respect of their own pits. The court was not obliged to have substantial grounds for believing that a repetition of the defendant's conduct would occur. That perception could be based on knowledge of what was happening in the pits in the area.

5–54 Conditions on bail may be imposed in respect of offences which are not punishable by imprisonment. In *R v Bournemouth Magistrates' Court Ex p. Cross* [1989] Crim.L.R. 207, the defendant was in the habit of protesting at fox hunt meets. He was bailed in respect of a public order offence arising from such a protest on the condition that he did not attend another hunt meeting before his next court appearance. The Divisional Court held that the condition had been validly imposed as the magistrates had considered that it was necessary to prevent the commission of further offences.

(1) Sureties

5–55 A person who stands surety enters into a recognisance to pay a fixed sum of money if the defendant fails to attend court.

Bail Act 1976, s.8

Bail with sureties

8.—(1) This section applies where a person is granted bail in criminal proceedings on condition that he provides one or more surety or sureties for the purpose of securing that he surrenders to custody.

(2) In considering the suitability for that purpose of a proposed surety, regard may be had (amongst other things) to—

(a) the surety's financial resources;

(b) his character and any previous convictions of his; and

(c) his proximity (whether in point of kinship, place of residence or otherwise) to the person for whom he is to be surety.

(3) Where a court grants a person bail in criminal proceedings on such a condition but is unable to release him because no surety or no suitable surety is available, the court shall fix the amount in which the surety is to be bound and subsections (4) and (5) below, or in a case where the proposed surety resides in Scotland subsection (6) below, shall apply for the purpose of enabling the recognizance of the surety to be entered into subsequently.

(4) Where this subsection applies the recognizance of the surety may be entered into **5–56** before such of the following persons or descriptions of persons as the court may by order specify or, if it makes no such order, before any of the following persons, that is to say—

(a) where the decision is taken by a magistrates' court, before a justice of the peace, a justices' clerk or a police officer who either is of the rank of inspector or above or is in charge of a police station or, if magistrates' courts rules so provide, by a person of such other description as is specified in the rules;

and—(the provisions here apply only to the Crown Court, High Court and Courts Martial)—magistrates' courts rules may also prescribe the manner in which a recognizance which is to be entered into before such a person is to be entered into and the persons by whom and the manner in which the recognizance may be enforced.

(5) Where a surety seeks to enter into his recognizance before any person in accordance with subsection (4) above but that person declines to take his recognizance because he is not satisfied of the surety's suitability, the surety may apply to—

(a) the court which fixed the amount of the recognizance in which the surety was to be bound, or

(b) a magistrates' court for the petty sessions area in which he resides,

for that court to take his recognizance and that court shall, if satisfied of his suitability, take his recognizance.

(6) Where this subsection applies, the court, if satisfied of the suitability of the proposed surety, may direct that arrangements be made for the recognizance of the surety to be entered into in Scotland before any constable, within the meaning of the *Police (Scotland) Act* 1967, having charge at any police office or station in like manner as the recognizance would be entered into in England or Wales.

(7) Where, in pursuance of subsection (4) or (6) above, a recognizance is entered into otherwise than before the court that fixed the amount of the recognizance, the same consequences shall follow as if it had been entered into before that court.

The obligation of a surety extends only to securing the defendant's attendance at **5–57** court. A surety is not responsible for preventing any other defaults while the defendant is on bail. A surety should only be required where there is a risk that the defendant will fail to surrender to custody.

A surety may be taken in court by the magistrates or out of court by a legal adviser or other person to whom the justices' clerk has delegated the power. A surety may also be taken at a police station by a police officer of the rank of inspector or above or by a prison governor if the accused is in prison: r.86 of the *Magistrates' Courts Rules* 1981. The procedure adopted will depend on the gravity of the charge and the amount of surety fixed by the court. The person taking the surety will investigate the matters listed in s.8(2) and production of bank statements, savings accounts and payslips may be required as evidence of financial resources. The nature of the relationship between the surety and the defendant must also be inquired into so the court may be satisfied of the extent of the influence the surety holds over the defendant. The nature of the responsibility that is being assumed must also be explained to the surety. The surety has a personal duty to ensure that the defendant surrenders to custody at the time and place specified. If the defendant fails to surrender the amount of the recognisance fixed or some of it may be ordered to be paid. If the money is not paid immediately or within a time set, the surety can be committed to prison in default of payment.

The defendant's representative has a particular responsibility to ensure that a surety would be able to meet his or her financial obligations before being tendered to the court: *R. v Birmingham Crown Court Ex p. Rashid Ali* [1999] Crim.L.R. 504.

Bail Act 1976, s.9

Offence of agreeing to indemnify sureties in criminal proceedings

5–58   **9.**—(1) If a person agrees with another to indemnify that other against any liability which that other may incur as a surety to secure the surrender to custody of a person accused or convicted of or under arrest for an offence, he and that other person shall be guilty of an offence.

(2) An offence under subsection (1) above is committed whether the agreement is made before or after the person to be indemnified becomes a surety and whether or not he becomes a surety and whether the agreement contemplates compensation in money or in money's worth.

(3) Where a magistrates' court convicts a person of an offence under subsection (1) above the court may, if it thinks—

     (a) that the circumstances of the offence are such that greater punishment should be inflicted for that offence than the court has power to inflict, or

     (b) in a case where it commits that person for trial to the Crown Court for another offence, that it would be appropriate for him to be dealt with for the offence under subsection (1) above by the court before which he is tried for the other offence,

commit him in custody or on bail to the Crown Court for sentence.

(4) A person guilty of an offence under subsection (1) above shall be liable—

     (a) on summary conviction, to imprisonment for a term not exceeding 3 months or to a fine not exceeding £400 or to both; or

     (b) on conviction on indictment or if sentenced by the Crown Court on committal for sentence under subsection (3) above, to imprisonment for a term not exceeding 12 months or to a fine or to both.

(5) No proceedings for an offence under subsection (1) above shall be instituted except by or with the consent of the Director of Public Prosecutions.

Magistrates' Courts Act 1980, s.119

Postponement of taking recognizance

5–59   **119.**—(1) Where a magistrates' court has power to take any recognizance, the court may, instead of taking it, fix the amount in which the principal and his sureties, if any, are to be bound; and thereafter the recognizance may be taken by any such person as may be prescribed.

(2) Where, in pursuance of this section, a recognizance is entered into otherwise than before the court that fixed the amount of it, the same consequences shall follow as if it had been entered into before that court; and references in this or any other Act to the court before which a recognizance was entered into shall be construed accordingly.

(3) Nothing in this section shall enable a magistrates' court to alter the amount of a recognizance fixed by the High Court [or the Crown Court].

[This section is reprinted as amended by the *Criminal Justice Act* 1982, Sch.14, para.55.]

Magistrates' Courts Rules 1981, r.84

Notice of enlargement of recognizances

5–60   **84.**—(1) If a magistrates' court before which any person is bound by a recognizance to appear enlarges the recognizance to a later time under section 129 of the Act in his absence, it shall give him and his sureties, if any, notice thereof.

(2) If a magistrates' court, under section 129(4) of the Act of 1980, enlarges the recognizance of a surety for a person committed for trial on bail, it shall give the surety notice thereof.

(2) Security

5–61   A person granted bail may be required to give security for his or her surrender to custody: *Bail Act* 1976, s.3(5). In *R. v Truro Magistrates' Court Ex p. Stevens* [2002] 1 W.L.R. 144, DC, the court held that although Parliament had not limited the type of security which might be given under s.3(5) what was envisaged was the lodging of some asset, in cash or in kind, which could be readily forfeited on the defendant's non-appearance. However the security could be given in less simple form if the justice of the case demanded it and it could be readily forfeited in the event of non-appearance without disputes with third parties. While it was permissible for a third party to make an asset available as security for the defendant, where a court failed to make clear the extent to which a third party's interest in registered land belonging to the defendant was the subject of the security, the security was to be interpreted as extending only to the defendant's beneficial interest.

Magistrates' Court Rules 1981, r.85

Directions as to security, etc

5–62

85. Where a magistrates' court, under section 3(5) or (6) of the *Bail Act* 1976, imposes any requirement to be complied with before a person's release on bail, the court may give directions as to the manner in which and the person or persons before whom the requirement may be complied with

Magistrates' Court Rules 1981, r.86

Requirements to be complied with before release

86.—(1) Where a magistrates' court has fixed the amount in which a person (including any surety) is to be bound by a recognizance, the recognizance may be entered into—

   (a) in the case of a surety in connection with bail in criminal proceedings where the accused is in a prison or other place of detention, before the governor or keeper of the prison or place as well as before the persons mentioned in section 8(4)(a) of the *Bail Act* 1976;

   (b) in any other case, before a justice of the peace, a justices' chief executive, a police officer who either is of the rank of inspector or above or is in charge of a police station or, if the person to be bound is in a prison or other place of detention, before the governor or keeper of the prison or place.

   (c) where a person other than a police officer is authorised under section 125A or 125B of the Act of 1980 to execute a warrant of arrest providing for a recognizance to be entered into by the person arrested (but not by any other person), before the person executing the warrant.

(2) The justices' chief executive for a magistrates' court which has fixed the amount in which a person (including any surety) is to be bound by a recognizance or, under section 3(5), (6) or (6A) of the *Bail Act* 1976, imposed any requirement to be complied with before a person's release on bail or any condition of bail shall issue a certificate [...] showing the amount and conditions, if any, of the recognizance, or as the case may be, containing a statement of the requirement or condition of bail; and a person authorised to take the recognizance or do anything in relation to the compliance with such requirement or condition of bail shall not be required to take or do it without production of the certificate as aforesaid.

(3) If any person proposed as a surety for a person committed to custody by a magistrates' court produces to the governor or keeper of the prison or other place of detention in which the person so committed is detained a certificate [...] to the effect that he is acceptable as a surety, signed by any of the justices composing the court or the clerk of the court and signed in the margin by the person proposed as surety, the governor or keeper shall take the recognizance of the person so proposed.

(4) Where the recognizance of any person committed to custody by a magistrates' court or of any surety of such a person is taken by any person other than the court which committed the first-mentioned person to custody, the person taking the recognizance shall send it to the justices' chief executive for that court:

Provided that, in the case of a surety, if the person committed has been committed to the Crown Court for trial or under any of the enactments mentioned in rule 17(1), the person taking the recognizance shall send it to the appropriate officer of the Crown Court.

[This section is reprinted as amended by the *Magistrates' Courts (Miscellaneous Amendments) Rules* 2003, r.35]

(3) Application to vary conditions of bail

Under s.3(8)(a) of the *Bail Act* 1976 where bail has been granted subject to condi-　**5–63**

tions, the magistrates' court may, on application by the person granted bail or the prosecutor or constable vary the conditions of bail or impose conditions in respect of the bail already granted. Notice of the application must be given so that both the defendant and the prosecution can make representations. The defendant is not bound to appear and simple variations can be made in the absence of the defendant. The court is under no duty to notify a surety of any application to vary bail conditions particularly when the surety is expressed to be continuous as the surety should keep himself informed of the bail position. Any ignorance of the variation may be taken into account when the court considers forfeiting the surety: *R. v Wells Street Magistrates' Court Ex p. Albanese* [1982] Q.B. 333. When the defendant has been committed to the Crown Court from the magistrates' court on bail then once he has surrendered to the Crown Court, that court is seised of all bail matters and any application to vary must be made to the Crown Court: *R. v Lincoln Magistrates' Court Ex p. Mawer* (1996) 160 J.P. 219.

V. APPEAL AND RECONSIDERATION

5–64　　The defence and the prosecution have the right to challenge bail decisions made by both the police and the court.

A defendant detained by the police must be produced at a court as soon as is practicable after charge and then application for bail may be made to the court. If a defendant is remanded in custody by the court he has a right of appeal and may apply for bail to the Crown Court.

When the police impose conditions on bail the defendant may appeal to the magistrates' court for the conditions to be removed or varied. Where conditions are imposed by the magistrates' court application may be made to the court to vary them or an appeal against certain conditions may be made to the Crown Court.

The prosecution may appeal to the Crown Court against a decision to grant bail where it was opposed. If fresh information comes to light the prosecution may also apply to the magistrates' court for a decision to grant bail to be reconsidered.

A. Appeal to Magistrates' Court in Respect of Police Bail

Magistrates' Courts Act 1980, s.43B

Power to grant bail where police bail has been granted

5–64.1　　43B.—(1) Where a custody officer—

> (a) grants bail to any person under Part IV of the *Police and Criminal Evidence Act 1984* in criminal proceedings and imposes conditions, or
>
> (b) varies, in relation to any person, conditions of bail in criminal proceedings under section 3(8) of the *Bail Act* 1976

a magistrates' court may, on application by or on behalf of that person, grant bail or vary the conditions.

(2) On an application under subsection (1) the court, if it grants bail and imposes conditions or if it varies the conditions, may impose more onerous conditions.

(3) On determining an application under subsection (1) the court shall remand the applicant, in custody or on bail in accordance with the determination, and, where the court withholds bail or grants bail the grant of bail made by the custody officer shall lapse.

(4) In this section "bail in criminal proceedings" and "vary" have the same meanings as they have in the *Bail Act* 1976.

[This section is reprinted as amended by the *Criminal Justice and Public Order Act* 1994, Sch.3, para.3.]

Magistrates' Courts Rules 1981, r.84A

Procedure on application for bail following grant of conditional police bail

5–65　　84A.—(1) An application under section 43B(1) of the Act of 1980 shall—

> (a) be made in writing;

(b) contain a statement of the grounds upon which it is made;

(c) specify the offence with which the applicant was charged before his release on bail;

(d) specify, or be accompanied by a copy of the note of, the reasons given by the custody officer for imposing or varying the conditions of bail; and

(e) specify the name and address of any surety provided by the applicant before his release on bail to secure his surrender to custody.

(2) Any such application shall be sent to the justices' chief executive for—

(a) the magistrates' court (if any) appointed by the custody officer as the court before which the applicant has a duty to appear; or

(b) if no such court has been appointed, a magistrates' court acting for the petty sessions area in which the police station at which the applicant was granted bail or at which the conditions of his bail were varied, as the case may be, is situated;

and, in either case, a copy shall be sent to a custody officer appointed for that police station.

(3) the justices' chief executive to whom an application is sent under paragraph (2) shall send a notice in writing of the date, time and place fixed for the hearing of the application to—

(a) the applicant;

(b) the prosecutor; and

(c) any surety in connection with bail in criminal proceedings granted to, or the conditions of which were varied by a custody officer in relation to, the applicant.

(4) The time fixed for the hearing shall be not later than 72 hours after receipt of the **5–66** application. In reckoning for the purposes of this paragraph any period of 72 hours, no account shall be taken of Christmas Day, Good Friday, any bank holiday, or any Saturday or Sunday.

(5) Any notice required by this rule to be sent to any person shall either be delivered to him or be sent by post in a letter and, if sent by post to the applicant or a surety of his, shall be addressed to him at his last known or usual place of abode.

(6) If the magistrates' court hearing an application under section 43B(1) of the Act of 1980 discharges or enlarges any recognizance entered into by any surety or increases or reduces the amount in which that person is bound, the [justices' chief executive for] the court shall forthwith give notice thereof to the applicant and to any such surety.

(7) In this rule, "the applicant" means the person making an application under section 43B(1) of the Act of 1980.

[This rule is reprinted as amended by the *Criminal Justice and Public Order Act* 1994, Sch.3, para.3 and the *Magistrates' Courts (Amendment No.2) Rules* 2001, r.3.]

Section 43B effectively allows for an appeal to the magistrates' court against a deci- **5–67** sion of a police officer to grant or vary conditional bail. A person aggrieved by any requirements imposed by the custody officer may apply to the court but the court then has the power to impose more onerous conditions or to remand the applicant in custody as well as to accede to the requested variation. The decision of the court overrides the decision of the officer. The procedure is set down in r.84A which requires the application to be heard within 72 hours with the prosecution and sureties being given notice of the date and time of hearing.

B. Appeal to the High Court

The *Criminal Justice Act* 2003, s.17 abolished the High Court's jurisdiction in re- **5–68** spect of magistrates' court bail where it duplicates that of the Crown Court (as of April 5, 2004).

C. Application to the Crown Court by Defendant

The defendant has a right to apply to the Crown Court for bail, when remanded in **5–69** custody, and against conditions imposed on bail.

Supreme Court Act 1981, s.81(1)(g), (1J)

Bail

81.—(1) The Crown Court may, subject to section 25 of the *Criminal Justice and Public Order Act* 1994, grant bail to any person—

    (g) who has been remanded in custody by a magistrates' court on adjourning a case under section 11 of the *Powers of Criminal Courts (Sentencing) Act* 2000 (remand for medical examination) or—

        (i)   section 5 (adjournment of inquiry into offence);

        (ii)   section 10 (adjournment of trial); or

        (iii)   section 18 (initial procedure on information against adult for offence triable either way);

and the time during which a person is released on bail under any provision of this subsection shall not count as part of any term of imprisonment or detention under his sentence.

(1J) The Crown Court may only grant bail to a person under subsection (1)(g) if the magistrates' court which remanded him in custody has certified under section 5(6A)of the *Bail Act* 1976 that it heard full argument on his application for bail before it refused the application.

[This section is reprinted omitting paras (1)(a)–(f), (1A)–(1I), (2)–(7) and as amended by the *Powers of Criminal Courts (Sentencing) Act* 2000, Sch.9, para.87(c).]

Criminal Justice Act 2003, s.16

Appeal to Crown Court

5–70   **16.**—(1) This section applies where a magistrates' court grants bail to a person ("the person concerned") on adjourning a case under—

    (a) section 10 of the *Magistrates' Courts Act* 1980 (adjournment of trial),

    (b) section 17C of that Act (intention as to plea: adjournment),

    (c) section 18 of that Act (initial procedure on information against adult for offence triable either way),

    (d) section 24C of that Act (intention as to plea by child or young person: adjournment),

    (e) section 52(5) of the *Crime and Disorder Act* 1998 (adjournment of proceedings under section 51 etc), or

    (f) section 11 of the *Powers of Criminal Courts (Sentencing) Act* 2000 (remand for medical examination).

(2) Subject to the following provisions of this section, the person concerned may appeal to the Crown Court against any condition of bail falling within subsection (3).

(3) A condition of bail falls within this subsection if it is a requirement—

    (a) that the person concerned resides away from a particular place or area,

    (b) that the person concerned resides at a particular place other than a bail hostel,

    (c) for the provision of a surety or sureties or the giving of a security,

    (d) that the person concerned remains indoors between certain hours,

    (e) imposed under section 3(6ZAA) of the 1976 Act (requirements with respect to electronic monitoring), or

    (f) the person concerned makes no contact with another person.

(4) An appeal under this section may not be brought unless subsection (5) or (6) applies.

(5) This subsection applies if an application to the magistrates' court under section 3(8)(a) of the 1976 Act (application by or on behalf of person granted bail) was made and determined before the appeal was brought.

(6) This subsection applies if an application to the magistrates' court—

    (a) under section 3(8)(b) of the 1976 Act (application by constable or prosecutor), or

    (b) under section 5B(1) of that Act (application by prosecutor),

was made and determined before the appeal was brought.

(7) On an appeal under this section the Crown Court may vary the conditions of bail.

(8) Where the Crown Court determines an appeal under this section, the person concerned may not bring any further appeal under this section in respect of the conditions of bail unless an application or a further application to the magistrates' court under section 3(8)(a) of the 1976 Act is made and determined after the appeal.

Section 16 of the *Criminal Justice Act* 2003 introduces a power to appeal to the Crown Court against certain conditions of bail relating to residence away from a particular place or area or residence other than at a bail hostel; the provision of a surety or security; a curfew; electronic tagging or non-contact. Such an appeal can only be made where application to vary has already been made to the magistrates' court.

For full certificates of bail see s.5 above.

D. Appeal to the Crown Court by Prosecution

Bail (Amendment) Act 1993, s.1

Prosecution right of appeal

1.—[(1) Where a magistrates' court grants bail to a person who is charged with or convicted **5–71** of an offence punishable by imprisonment, the prosecution may appeal to a judge of the Crown Court against the granting of bail.]

(2) Subsection (1) above applies only where the prosecution is conducted—
  (a) by or on behalf of the Director of Public Prosecutions; or
  (b) by a person who falls within such class or description of person as may be prescribed for the purposes of this section by order made by the Secretary of State.

(3) Such an appeal may be made only if—
  (a) the prosecution made representations that bail should not be granted; and
  (b) the representations were made before it was granted.

(4) In the event of the prosecution wishing to exercise the right of appeal set out in subsection (1) above, oral notice of appeal shall be given to the magistrates' court at the conclusion of the proceedings in which such bail has been granted and before the release from custody of the person concerned.

(5) Written notice of appeal shall thereafter be served on the magistrates' court and the **5–71** person concerned within two hours of the conclusion of such proceedings.

(6) Upon receipt from the prosecution of oral notice of appeal from its decision to grant bail the magistrates' court shall remand in custody the person concerned, until the appeal is determined or otherwise disposed of.

(7) Where the prosecution fails, within the period of two hours mentioned in subsection (5) above, to serve one or both of the notices required by that subsection, the appeal shall be deemed to have been disposed of.

(8) The hearing of an appeal under subsection (1) above against a decision of the magistrates' court to grant bail shall be commenced within forty-eight hours, excluding weekends and any public holiday (that is to say, Christmas Day, Good Friday or a bank holiday), from the date on which oral notice of appeal is given.

(9) At the hearing of any appeal by the prosecution under this section, such appeal shall be by way of re-hearing, and the judge hearing any such appeal may remand the person concerned in custody or may grant bail subject to such conditions (if any) as he thinks fit.

(10) In relation to a child or young person (within the meaning of the *Children and Young Persons Act* 1969)—
  (a) the reference in subsection (1) above to an offence punishable by [a term of]imprisonment is to be read as a reference to an offence which would be so punishable in the case of an adult; and
  (b) the reference in subsection (6) above to remand in custody is to be read subject to the provisions of section 23 of the Act of 1969 (remands to local authority accommodation).

(11) The power to make an order under subsection (2) above shall be exercisable by statutory instrument and any instrument shall be subject to annulment in pursuance of a resolution of either House of Parliament.

[This section is printed as prospectively amended by the *Criminal Justice Act* 2003, s.18. Subsection 1 is substituted and the words in square brackets in subs.(10)(a) are omitted.]

Magistrates' Courts Rules 1981, r.93A

Procedure where prosecution appeals against a decision to grant bail

93A.—(1) Where the prosecution wishes to exercise the right of appeal, under section 1 of **5–73** the *Bail (Amendment) Act* 1993 (hereafter in this rule referred to as "the 1993 Act"), to a judge of the Crown Court against a decision to grant bail, the oral notice of appeal must be given to the clerk of the magistrates' court and to the person concerned, at the conclusion of the proceedings in which such bail was granted and before the release of the person concerned.

(2) When oral notice of appeal is given, the clerk of the magistrates' court shall announce in open court the time at which such notice was given.

(3) A record of the prosecution's decision to appeal and the time the oral notice of appeal was given shall be made in the register and shall contain the particulars set out in the appropriate form prescribed for the purpose.

(4) Where an oral notice of appeal has been given the court shall remand the person concerned in custody by a warrant of commitment.

(5) On receipt of the written notice of appeal required by section 1(5) of the 1993 Act, the court shall remand the person concerned in custody by a warrant of commitment, until the appeal is determined or otherwise disposed of.

(6) A record of the receipt of the written notice of appeal shall be made in the same manner as that of the oral notice of appeal under paragraph (3) above.

(7) If, having given oral notice of appeal, the prosecution fails to serve a written notice of appeal within the two hour period referred to in section 1(5) of the 1993 Act the clerk of the magistrates' court shall, as soon as practicable, by way of written notice (served by the justices' chief executive for the magistrates' court) to the persons in whose custody the person concerned is, direct the release of the person concerned on bail as granted by the magistrates' court and subject to any conditions which it imposed.

5–74   (8) If the prosecution serves notice of abandonment of appeal on the justices' chief executive for the magistrates' court, the clerk shall, forthwith, by way of written notice (served by the justices' chief executive for the magistrates' court) to the Governor of the prison where the person concerned is being held, or the person responsible for any other establishment where such a person is being held, direct his release on bail as granted by the magistrates' court and subject to any conditions which it imposed.

(9) The justices' chief executive for the magistrates' court shall record the prosecution's failure to serve a written notice of appeal, or its service of a notice of abandonment.

(10) Where a written notice of appeal has been served on the justices' chief executive for the magistrates' court, he shall provide as soon as practicable to the appropriate officer of the Crown Court a copy of that written notice, together with—

   (a) the notes of argument made by the justices' chief executive for the court under rule 90Aof these Rules, and

   (b) a note of the date, or dates, when the person concerned is next due to appear in the magistrates' court, whether he is released on bail or remanded in custody by the Crown Court.

(11) Reference in this rule to "the person concerned" are references to such a person within the meaning of section 1 of the 1993 Act.

[This rule is reprinted as amended by the *Magistrates' Courts (Miscellaneous Amendment) Rules* 2003, r.38]

5–75   The prescribed prosecutors under s.1(2)(b) are the Serious Fraud Office, the Trade and Industry Department, Customs and Excise, Secretary of State for Social Security, the Post Office and the Inland Revenue: *Bail (Amendment) Act 1993 (Prescription of Prosecuting Authorities) Order* 1994 (SI 1994/1438).

The prosecution has the right in the specified cases to appeal against a grant of bail when bail was originally opposed. The requirement that the offence carries a minimum sentence of five years imprisonment will be removed by the *Criminal Justice Act* 2003 when in force as s.18 of that Act only requires that the offence be imprisonable. Under s.5(2A), the court has a duty to provide written reasons when bail is granted after the prosecution has objected to bail which assists in the formulation of any subsequent appeal by the prosecution.

The requirement that oral notice of appeal be given to the magistrates' court "at the conclusion of the proceedings" was satisfied where notice was given five minutes after the case had been dealt with when the Legal Adviser was still at court although the magistrates had left the building: *R. v Isleworth Crown Court Ex p. Clark* [1998] 1 Cr.App.R. 257. The hearing must be commenced within 48 hours of the end of the day on which oral notice of appeal is given: *R. v Middlesex Guildhall Crown Court Ex p. Okoli* [2000] 1 Cr.App.R. 1.

Where a defendant who had been granted bail challenged the service of the written **5–76** notice of appeal because it was not served within two hours of the oral notice he claimed that the appeal should be deemed disposed of under s.1(7). The court held, dismissing the appeal, that the prosecutor had used all due diligence to try and serve the notice and the failure to do so was due to circumstances beyond his control. The notice was served only three minutes late and as oral notice had been given the appellant was not prejudiced by this delay: *R. (on the application of Jeffrey) v Crown Court at Warwick* [2002] EWHC 2469.

E. Reconsideration

Bail Act 1976, s.5B

Reconsideration of decisions granting bail

5B.—(1) Where a magistrates' court has granted bail in criminal proceedings in connection **5–77** with an offence, or proceedings for an offence, to which this section applies or a constable has granted bail in criminal proceedings in connection with proceedings for such an offence, that court or the appropriate court in relation to the constable may, on application by the prosecutor for the decision to be reconsidered,—

    (a) vary the conditions of bail,

    (b) impose conditions in respect of bail which has been granted unconditionally, or

    (c) withhold bail.

(2) The offences to which this section applies are offences triable on indictment and offences triable either way.

(3) No application for the reconsideration of a decision under this section shall be made unless it is based on information which was not available to the court or constable when the decision was taken.

(4) Whether or not the person to whom the application relates appears before it, the magistrates' court shall take the decision in accordance with section 4(1) (and Schedule 1) of this Act.

(5) Where the decision of the court on a reconsideration under this section is to with- **5–78** hold bail from the person to whom it was originally granted the court shall—

    (a) if that person is before the court, remand him in custody, and

    (b) if that person is not before the court, order him to surrender himself forthwith into the custody of the court.

(6) Where a person surrenders himself into the custody of the court in compliance with an order under subsection (5) above, the court shall remand him in custody.

(7) A person who has been ordered to surrender to custody under subsection (5) above may be arrested without warrant by a constable if he fails without reasonable cause to surrender to custody in accordance with the order.

(8) A person arrested in pursuance of subsection (7) above shall be brought as soon as practicable, and in any event within 24 hours after his arrest, before a justice of the peace for the petty sessions area in which he was arrested and the justice shall remand him in custody.

In reckoning for the purposes of this subsection any period of 24 hours, no account shall be taken of Christmas Day, Good Friday or any Sunday.

(8A) Where the court, on a reconsideration under this section, refuses to withhold bail from a relevant person after hearing representations from the prosecutor in favour of withholding bail, then the court shall give reasons for refusing to withhold bail.

(8B) In subsection (8A) above, "relevant person" means a person to whom section 4(1) (and Schedule 1) of this Act is applicable in accordance with subsection (4) above.

(8C) A court which is by virtue of subsection (8A) above required to give reasons for its decision shall include a note of those reasons in any record of its decision and, if requested to do so by the prosecutor, shall cause the prosecutor to be given a copy of any such record as soon as practicable after the record is made.

(9) Magistrates' court rules shall include provision—

    (a) requiring notice of an application under this section and of the grounds for it to be given to the person affected, including notice of the powers available to the court under it;

(b) for securing that any representations made by the person affected (whether in writing or orally) are considered by the court before making its decision; and

(c) designating the court which is the appropriate court in relation to the decision of any constable to grant bail.

[This section is reprinted as amended by the *Criminal Justice and Police Act* 2001, s.129(3)]

Magistrates' Courts Rules 1981, r.93B

Procedure on reconsideration of a decision to grant bail

5–79   **93B.**—(1) The appropriate court for the purposes of section 5B of the *Bail Act* 1976 in relation to the decision of a constable to grant bail shall be—

(a) the magistrates' court (if any) appointed by the custody officer as the court before which the person to whom bail was granted has a duty to appear; or

(b) if no such court has been appointed, a magistrates' court acting for the petty sessions area in which the police station at which bail was granted is situated.

(2) An application under section 5B(1) of the *Bail Act* 1976 shall—

(a) be made in writing;

(b) contain a statement of the grounds on which it is made;

(c) specify the offence which the proceedings in which bail was granted were connected with, or for;

(d) specify the decision to be reconsidered (including any conditions of bail which have been imposed and why they have been imposed); and

(e) specify the name and address of any surety provided by the person to whom the application relates to secure his surrender to custody.

(3) Where an application has been made to a magistrates' court under section 5B of the *Bail Act* 1976.

(f) the clerk of that magistrates' court shall fix a date, time and place for the hearing of the application; and

(g) the justices' chief executive shall—

(i) give notice of the application and of the date, time and place so fixed to the person affected; and

(ii) send a copy of the notice to the prosecutor who made the application and to any surety specified in the application.

(4) The time fixed for the hearing shall be not later than 72 hours after receipt of the application. In reckoning for the purpose of this paragraph any period of 72 hours, no account shall be taken of Christmas Day, Good Friday, any bank holiday or any Sunday.

(5) Service of a notice to be given under paragraph(3) to the person affected may be effected by delivering it to him.

(6) At the hearing of an application under section 5B of the *Bail Act* 1976 the court shall consider any representations made by the person affected (whether in writing or orally) before taking any decision under that section with respect to him; and, where the person affected does not appear before the court, the court shall not take such a decision unless it is proved to the satisfaction of the court, on oath or in the manner prescribed by paragraph (1) of rule 67, that the notice required to be given under paragraph (3) was served on him before the hearing.

(7) Where the court proceeds in the absence of the person affected in accordance with paragraph (6)—

(a) if the decision of the court is to vary the conditions of bail or impose conditions in respect of bail which has been granted unconditionally, the justices' chief executive for the court shall notify the person affected;

(b) if the decision of the court is to withhold bail, the order of the court under section 5B(5)(b) of the *Bail Act* 1976 (surrender to custody) shall be signed by the justice issuing it or state his name and be authenticated by the signature of the clerk of the court[...].

(8) Service of any of the documents referred to in paragraph (7) may be effected by delivering it to the person to whom it is directed or by leaving it for him with some person

at his last known or usual place of abode.

[This rule is reprinted as amended by the *Criminal Justice and Public Order Act* 1994, s.30 and the *Magistrates' Courts (Miscellaneous Amendments) Rules* 2003, r.39(2)]

5–80 The prosecutor may apply to the magistrates' court to for bail to be reconsidered when new information comes to light affecting the original bail decision made either by the police or the court. This right does not apply to summary only offences.

It is envisaged that the defendant may be enjoying bail and the prosecutor discovers information not available earlier on the basis of which concerns arise about bail. The application must be heard within 72 hours, with notice being sent to the person affected, the prosecution and any surety. The case can then be dealt with before the scheduled adjourned date.

The court may decide a reconsideration application regardless of whether the accused appears before the court. When the court decides to withhold bail, the defendant may be arrested without a warrant and remanded in custody.

A magistrate is entitled to refuse bail notwithstanding that at the previous hearing unconditional bail had been granted and there had been no subsequent changes in the circumstances, but having sought and obtained further information from the prosecutor at the second hearing which was not sought at the previous hearing: *R. v Tower Bridge Magistrates' Court Ex p. Gilbert* (1988) 152 J.P. 307.

VI. ABSCONDING AND BREACH OF BAIL CONDITIONS

(1) Offence of absconding while on bail

Bail Act 1976, s.6

Offence of absconding by person released on bail

5–81 **6.**—(1) If a person who has been released on bail in criminal proceedings fails without reasonable cause to surrender to custody he shall be guilty of an offence.

(2) If a person who—

(a) has been released on bail in criminal proceedings, and

(b) having reasonable cause therefor, has failed to surrender to custody,

fails to surrender to custody at the appointed place as soon after the appointed time as is reasonably practicable he shall be guilty of an offence.

(3) It shall be for the accused to prove that he had reasonable cause for his failure to surrender to custody.

(4) A failure to give to a person granted bail in criminal proceedings a copy of the record of the decision shall not constitute a reasonable cause for that person's failure to surrender to custody.

(5) An offence under subsection (1) or (2) above shall be punishable either on summary conviction or as if it were a criminal contempt of court.

(6) Where a magistrates' court convicts a person of an offence under subsection (1) or (2) above the court may, if it thinks—

(a) that the circumstances of the offence are such that greater punishment should be inflicted for that offence than the court has power to inflict, or

(b) in a case where it commits that person for trial to the Crown Court for another offence, that it would be appropriate for him to be dealt with for the offence under subsection (1) or (2) above by the court before which he is tried for the other offence,

commit him in custody or on bail to the Crown Court for sentence.

5–82 (7) A person who is convicted summarily of an offence under subsection (1) or (2) above and is not committed to the Crown Court for sentence shall be liable to imprisonment for a term not exceeding 3 months or to a fine not exceeding level 5 on the standard scale or to both and a person who is so committed for sentence or is dealt with as for such a contempt shall be liable to imprisonment for a term not exceeding 12 months or to a fine or to both.

(8) In any proceedings for an offence under subsection (1) or (2) above a document purporting to be a copy of the part of the prescribed record which relates to the time and place appointed for the person specified in the record to surrender to custody and to be duly certified to be a true copy of that part of the record shall be evidence of the time and place appointed for that person to surrender to custody.

(9) For the purposes of subsection (8) above—

    (a) "the prescribed record" means the record of the decision of the court, officer or constable made in pursuance of section 5(1) of this Act;

    (b) the copy of the prescribed record is duly certified if it is certified by the appropriate officer of the court or, as the case may be, by the constable who took the decision or a constable designated for the purpose by the officer in charge of the police station from which the person to whom the record relates was released;

    (c) "the appropriate officer" of the court is—

        (i) in the case of a magistrates' court, the justices' chief executive;

[(10) Section 127 of the *Magistrates' Courts Act* 1980 shall not apply in relation to an offence under subsection (1) or (2) above.

(11) Where a person has been released on bail in criminal proceedings and that bail was granted by a constable, a magistrates' court shall not try that person for an offence under subsection (1) or (2) above in relation to that bail (the "relevant offence") unless either or both of subsection (12) and (13) below applies.

(12) This subsection applies if an information is laid for the relevant offence within 6 months from the time of the commission of the offence.

(13) This subsection applies if an information is laid for the relevant offence no later than 3 months from the time of the occurrence of the first of the events mentioned in subsection (14) below to occur after the commission of the relevant offence.

(14) Those events are—

    (a) the person surrenders to custody at the appointed place;

    (b) the person is arrested, or attends at a police station, in connection with the relevant offence or the offence for which he was granted bail;

    (c) the person appears or is brought before a court in connection with the relevant offence or the offence for which he was granted bail.]

[This section is reprinted as amended by the *Access to Justice Act* 1999, Sch.13, para.89. This section was amended by the *Criminal Justice Act* 2003, s.15(3) which took effect in April 2004. The provisions are printed in square brackets.]

5–83   Under s.3(1) of the *Bail Act* 1976, a person granted bail in criminal proceedings is under a duty to surrender to custody. That duty is enforceable under s.6 of the Act. If a person released on bail fails without reasonable cause to surrender to custody he is guilty of an offence under s.6. Although "surrender to custody" means surrender "at the time and place for the time being appointed for him to do so" the *de minimis* rule should be applied if a defendant is only marginally late. Being seven minutes late was held not to constitute an offence under s.6: *R v Gateshead Justices Ex p. Usher* [1981] Crim.L.R. 491, DC.

The obligation of a person on bail is to comply with the directions of the court. Once a person has reported as instructed to the appropriate court official he has surrendered to custody and is under an implied obligation not to leave without consent. If the defendant leaves he is liable to be arrested under s.7(2) although no offence under s.6 may have been committed: *DPP v Richards* [1988] Q.B. 701.

What amounts to "a reasonable cause" is a matter of fact in each case. A mistake about the date due to an administrative blunder by solicitors did not provide a reasonable excuse but was relevant for mitigation: *Laidlaw v Atkinson, The Times*, August 2, 1986. Whether a mistake by a solicitor, such as giving the defendant the wrong date, amounts to a reasonable excuse is a question of fact to be decided in all the circumstances of the particular case: *R. v Liverpool City JJ Ex p. Santos*, January 23, 1997, DC.

5–84   There are two offences under the section:

1) it is an offence to fail to surrender without reasonable cause; and

2) it is an offence to fail to surrender as soon is as reasonably practicable after having had reasonable cause for failing to surrender initially.

The second limb of the section covers the situation of a defendant who may be too ill to attend as originally expected and so has reasonable cause for not coming to court but then fails to contact the court or surrender himself as soon as he has recovered.

The burden of proving the reasonable cause rests with the defendant to the civil standard of balance of probabilities: *R. v Carr Briant* [1943] K.B. 607.

The court will deal with an absconder as a summary offence. There is no power to commit a bail offence to the Crown Court for trial because it is not an either way offence. The power to commit to the Crown Court only applies after conviction. In *Schiavo v Anderton* [1987] Q.B. 20, DC, the defendant was granted bail in the magistrates' court pending summary trial but failed to answer bail. When he was brought before the court two years later on a warrant, he pleaded guilty to absconding and was committed to the Crown Court for sentence. In the Crown Court he argued that the magistrates' court had had no jurisdiction to try the matter, since no information had been laid within six months of the offences. The Divisional Court held that no information need be laid; the court heard the proceedings of its own motion; and that the matter could be tried only by the court which granted bail.

The *Practice Direction (Consolidated: Criminal) 2002, Amendment No.3* issued on January 22, 2004 gives detailed directions on bail and the failure to surrender in para.I.13.

When a defendant fails to answer his bail, in the absence of any explanation the court will issue a warrant under s.7. When the warrant has been executed and the defendant appears before the court, it will be considered whether an offence under s.6 should be put. If the defendant is on police bail and failed to surrender to custody at his first court appearance the prosecutor will decide whether to initiate proceedings. An information must be laid within six months' of the offence or three months of the surrender to custody, arrest, or court appearance. Usually this is done in court by the prosecutor who may lay an oral information when the warrant is applied for. Where the defendant fails to answer court bail, the court may initiate proceedings by its own motion at any time and the six month time-limit does not apply. The court will be invited to take proceedings by the prosecutor, if proceedings are considered appropriate: see also *Murphy v DPP* [1990] 2 All E.R. 390; *R. v Teeside Magistrates' Court Ex p. Bujnowski* [1997] Crim.L.R. 51.

Whether or not a warrant of arrest has been issued or executed, the question of **5–85** proceedings regarding a possible failure to surrender will be dealt with by the Crown Prosecution Service whose discretion to invite the court to proceed is unfettered: *France v Dewsbury Magistrates' Court* (1987) 152 J.P. 301. The court must give the defendant an opportunity to explain his failure to surrender and also to make submissions before sentence: *R. v Davis (Seaton Roy)* 8 Cr.App.R. 64, CA; *R. v Woods* 11 Cr.App.R. 551, CA. The fact that a defendant has been acquitted of the principal offence does not affect his criminality in relation to any offence under the *Bail Act* 1976: *R. v Clarke* [2000] 1 Cr.App.R. 173.

The court also has the power to commit the defendant to the Crown Court for sentence on a bail offence if they consider their powers of sentencing to be insufficient or if the defendant has other related matters which are being committed for trial.

(2) Liability to arrest

Bail Act 1976, s.7

Liability to arrest for absconding or breaking conditions of bail

7.—(1) If a person who has been released on bail in criminal proceedings and is under a duty **5–86** to surrender into the custody of a court fails to surrender to custody at the time appointed for him to do so the court may issue a warrant for his arrest.

(2) If a person who has been released on bail in criminal proceedings absents himself from the court at any time after he has surrendered into the custody of the court and before the court is ready to begin or to resume the hearing of the proceedings, the court

may issue a warrant for his arrest; but no warrant shall be issued under this subsection where that person is absent in accordance with leave given to him by or on behalf of the court.

(3) A person who has been released on bail in criminal proceedings and is under a duty to surrender into the custody of a court may be arrested without warrant by a constable—

(a) if the constable has reasonable grounds for believing that that person is not likely to surrender to custody;

(b) if the constable has reasonable grounds for believing that that person is likely to break any of the conditions of his bail or has reasonable grounds for suspecting that that person has broken any of those conditions; or

(c) in a case where that person was released on bail with one or more surety or sureties, if a surety notifies a constable in writing that that person is unlikely to surrender to custody and that for that reason the surety wishes to be relieved of his obligations as a surety.

(4) a person arrested in pursuance of subsection (3) above—

(a) shall, except where he was arrested within 24 hours of the time appointed for him to surrender to custody, be brought as soon as practicable and in any event within 24 hours after his arrest before a justice of the peace for the petty sessions area in which he was arrested; and

(b) in the said excepted case shall be brought before the court at which he was to have surrendered to custody.

[In reckoning for the purposes of this subsection any period of 24 hours, no account shall be taken of Christmas Day, Good Friday or any Sunday.]

5–87   (5) A justice of the peace before whom a person is brought under subsection (4) above may, subject to subsection (6) below, if of the opinion that that person—

(a) is not likely to surrender to custody, or

(b) has broken or is likely to break any condition of his bail,

remand him in custody or commit him to custody, as the case may require, or alternatively, grant him bail subject to the same or to different conditions, but if not of that opinion shall grant him bail subject to the same conditions (if any) as were originally imposed.

(6) Where the person so brought before the justice is a child or young person and the justice does not grant him bail, subsection (5) above shall have effect subject to the provisions of section 23 of the *Children and Young Persons Act* 1969 (remands to the care of local authorities).

[This section is reprinted as amended by the *Criminal Law Act* 1977, Sch.12]

Magistrates' Courts Rules 1981, r.92

Notification of bail decision after arrest while on bail

5–88   **92.** Where a person who has been released on bail and is under a duty to surrender into the custody of a court is brought under section 7(4)(a) of the *Bail Act* 1976 before a justice of the peace, the justice shall cause a copy of the record made in pursuance of section 5 of that Act relating to his decision under section 7(5) of that Act in respect of that person to be sent—

(a) in the case of a magistrates' court, to [the justices' chief executive for that court]; or

(b) in the case of any other court, to the appropriate officer thereof.

Provided that this rule shall not apply where the court is a magistrates' court acting for the same petty sessions area as that for which the justice acts.

Where the accused fails to surrender to custody in answer to his or her bail, the court may issue a warrant of arrest. Alternatively the court may adjourn and enlarge the defendant's bail under s.129 of the *Magistrates' Courts Act* 1980 but only if it is satisfied that there is a good reason for the defendant's non-attendance or attendance has been excused by the Court.

Where a suspect is bailed from a police station pursuant to s.37(2) of the *Police and Criminal Evidence Act* 1984 and fails to attend the police station on a prescribed subsequent date he may be arrested without warrant: *Police and Criminal Evidence Act* 1984, s.46A.

A defendant may also be arrested by an officer without a warrant under s.7(3) above. **5–89** The usual reason for arrest is a breach of a bail condition. The arrested person may be brought either before the court to which he should have surrendered or before the court sitting in the area in which he was arrested. The choice of court may be dictated by the time limit which requires the arrested person to be produced at court within 24 hours of his arrest. Where an arrested person is not brought before a court within 24 hours he has an absolute right to be released from custody. Bringing the defendant within the precincts or to the cells of a magistrates' court is not sufficient for this purpose; the defendant must actually appear before the magistrates: *R. v Governor of Glen Parva Young Offenders Institution Ex p. G (a minor)* [1998] 2 Cr.App.R. 349. Once the defendant has been brought before the court, the hearing can then be adjourned to later in the day to be dealt with by a different bench: *R. (on the application of Hussain) v Derby Magistrates' Court* [2001] 1 W.L.R. 2454.

When a person arrested under s.7 is brought before the magistrates' court he must be dealt with according to s.7(5). The magistrate has no power to commit the defendant to the Crown Court for a decision on the breach to be made there even when the original bail was granted by the Crown Court: *R. v Teeside Magistrates' Court Ex p. Ellison* (2001) 165 J.P. 355, DC.

In the case of *R. v Liverpool City Justices Ex p. DPP* (1993) 95 Cr.App.R. 222, DC, detailed consideration was given to the operation of s.7.

— The section contemplates the constable who has arrested the person bailed **5–90** bringing him before the court and stating the grounds for believing that the defendant has broken or is likely to break a condition of his bail; this may well involve the giving of "hearsay" evidence.

— Even where the defendant disputes the ground on which he was arrested, there is no necessity for the giving of evidence on oath or providing an opportunity to the person arrested, or his lawyer to cross-examine, or give evidence himself. Nevertheless the court must give the defendant an opportunity to respond to what the constable alleges.

— The court has no power to adjourn the proceedings, but must consider on the **5–91** material before it whether it is able to form one of the opinions set out in s.7(5) and if it does so, go on to decide whether to remand the defendant in custody or on bail on the same or more stringent conditions.

— If the court feels unable to form one of the opinions set out in s.7(5) it must order the person concerned to be released on bail on the same terms as were originally imposed.

— Proceedings under s.7(5) do not preclude the defendant who has been remanded in custody from making an application for bail to the magistrates' court, Crown Court or to a judge as appropriate. The presumption in favour of granting bail under s.4 of the Act will be subject not only to the exceptions to the right to bail in Pt 1, para.2 of Sch.1 to the Act but also to the exception in para.6 of that Schedule.

Where a person is arrested pursuant to s.7(3) the procedure contained in s.7(5) does **5–92** not involve the determination of a criminal charge within the meaning of Art.6(1) of the European Convention on Human Rights.

In *R. v Havering Magistrates' Court Ex p. DPP* [2001] 1 W.L.R. 805, the DPP applied for judicial review of a decision of justices that proceedings brought against the defendant under the *Bail Act* 1976, s.7(5) should be withdrawn. The justices had found that oral evidence was necessary to show that the defendant had acted in breach of the conditions. The issue before the court related to the compatibility of the procedures under s.7(5) and Sch.1, Pt I, para.6 of the Act with the right to a fair trial and the right to liberty and security guaranteed under the *Human Rights Act* 1998, Sch.1, Pt I, Art.6 and Art.5 respectively. The court held that since s.7 made provision for a means of achieving the purposes for which bail conditions were imposed, liability for detention under s.7 derived from the charge that a defendant faced as a means of securing those purposes and did not equate to the facing of a criminal charge. It followed that Art.6 did not have any direct relevance. The procedures would not breach Art.5 provided that the court evaluated the material presented in the context of the consequences to a defendant and, in particular, took account of the fact that where hearsay evidence was relied on, it had not been subject to cross-examination. A defendant should be given a fair opportunity to comment on the material upon which the proceedings were based. The court is not limited under Art.5 to only considering evidence that was admissible in the strict sense. The facts upon which the decision was based did not need to be proved to the criminal standard of proof. See also *R. v Wirral Borough Magistrates' Court Ex p. McKeown* [2001] 2 Cr.App.R. 2, DC.

In *R. v West London Magistrates' Court Ex p. Vickers* [2004] Crim.L.R. 63, the defendant sought judicial review of the magistrates' decision to remand him in custody following a finding that he had broken conditions of his bail. He argued that the magistrates had been wrong to hold that reasonable excuse was not a defence to an allegation of breaking a bail condition. He submitted that the words "without reasonable cause" should be read into the *Bail Act* 1976, s.7(5) otherwise the provision would be incompatible with the *Human Rights Act* 1998, Sch.1 Pt I, Art.5. The application was refused on the basis that when magistrates were considering whether there had been a breach of a condition of bail under s.7(5), they had a duty to act fairly and give the bailed person the opportunity of responding to the allegation. However, they did not have to consider whether the defendant had a reasonable excuse for breaking the relevant condition. When, having satisfied themselves that a breach of condition had occurred, the magistrates were considering whether to admit the bailed person to bail again or remand him in custody, they should take into account the reasons for the breach, at which point issues relating to reasonable excuse might arise. Provided that the magistrates followed the procedure set out in *R. v Havering Magistrates' Court Ex p. DPP* there would be no breach of Art.5.

(3) Consequences for sureties

Magistrates' Courts Act 1980, s.120

Forfeiture of recognizance

5–93   **120.**—(1) This section applies where—

    (a) a recognizance to keep the peace or to be of good behaviour has been entered into before a magistrates' court; or

    (b) any recognizance is conditioned for the appearance of a person before a magistrates' court, or for his doing any other thing connected with a proceeding before a magistrates' court.

(1A) If, in the case of a recognizance which is conditioned for the appearance of an accused before a magistrates' court, the accused fails to appear in accordance with the condition, the court shall—

    (a) declare the recognizance to be forfeited;

    (b) issue a summons directed to each person bound by the recognizance as surety, requiring him to appear before the court on a date specified in the summons to show cause why he should not be adjudged to pay the sum in which he is bound;

and on that date the court may proceed in the absence of any surety if it is satisfied that he has been served with the summons.

(2) If, in any other case falling within subsection (1) above, the recognizance appears to the magistrates' court to be forfeited, the court may—

    (a) declare the recognizance to be forfeited; and

    (b) adjudge each person bound by it, whether as principal or surety, to pay the sum in which he is bound;

but in a case falling within subsection (1)(a) above, the court shall not declare the recognizance to be forfeited except by order made on complaint.

(3) The court which declares the recognizance to be forfeited may, instead of adjudging any person to pay the whole sum in which he is bound, adjudge him to pay part only of the sum or remit the sum.

(4) Payment of any sum adjudged to be paid under this section, including any costs awarded against the defendant, may be enforced, and any such sum shall be applied, as if it were a fine and as if the adjudication were a summary conviction of an offence not punishable with imprisonment and so much of section 85(1) above as empowers a court to remit fines shall not apply to the sum but so much thereof as relates to remission after a term of imprisonment has been imposed shall so apply; but at any time before the issue of a warrant of commitment to enforce payment of the sum, or before the sale of goods under a warrant of distress to satisfy the sum, the court may remit the whole or any part of the sum either absolutely or on such conditions as the court thinks just.

(5) A recognizance such as is mentioned in this section shall not be enforced otherwise than in accordance with this section, and accordingly shall not be transmitted to the Crown Court nor shall its forfeiture be certified to that Court.

[This section is reprinted as amended by the *Crime and Disorder Act* 1998, s.55.]

5–94 Where a defendant who is on conditional bail with a condition of a surety fails to appear the court must declare the recognisance (the amount of money fixed) forfeit and then issue a summons to the surety requiring appearance before the court to show "just cause" as to why the sum required should not be paid. The court may order that the recognisance be paid in full, or a lesser amount may be ordered reflecting the circumstances of the case. It is also open to the court to remit the recognisance in full and order that nothing be paid. If the recognisance cannot be paid the surety can be given time to pay and a period of imprisonment may be fixed in default of payment.

The power to declare a recognisance to be forfeited is strictly dependant on there being a breach of the condition of the recognisance; a mere breach of a condition of bail by the defendant provides no basis for declaring the recognisance to be forfeited: *R. v Bow Street Magistrates' Court Ex p. Hart* [2002] 1 W.L.R. 1242, DC.

The burden of persuading the court that a recognisance should not be paid is upon the surety. The court must hear such evidence and argument as the surety wishes to put forward. The onus on the surety of showing that the full amount should not be lost is a heavy one: *R. v Uxbridge Justices Ex p. Heward-Mills* [1983] 1 W.L.R. 56. An application to estreat is a civil proceeding and the standard of proof is the ordinary civil standard on the balance of probabilities: *R. v Marlow Justices Ex p. O'Sullivan* [1984] Q.B. 381, DC.

Lack of culpability on the part of the surety is not, of itself, a ground for holding that the recognisance should not be paid: *R. v Crown Court at Warwick Ex p. Smalley* (1987) 84 Cr.App.R. 51. In *R. v Maidstone Crown Court Ex p. Lever and Connell* [1996] 1 Cr.App.R. 524 the Court of Appeal (Criminal Division) reviewed the principles which govern the forfeiture of a recognisance. The applicants provided sureties of £19,000 and £40,000 for the defendant who failed to attend his trial in the Crown Court. When, in breach of his bail, the accused failed to report to the police station one evening, the local police did not inform anyone, not even the police officer in charge of the case. Two days later one surety discovered that the accused had not been at home for two nights and telephoned the other surety and the police. At first instance the judge found that there was no culpability in either surety and that the police were negligent but nonetheless ordered forfeiture of £16,000 and £35,000 respectively. The Divisional Court then refused their application for judicial review. The Court of Appeal said:

5–95 "The general principle is that the purpose of a recognisance is to bring the defendant to court for trial. The basis for estreatment is not as a matter of punishment of the surety, but because he has failed to fulfil the obligation which he undertook. The starting point on the failure to bring a defendant to court is the forfeiture of the full recognisance. The right to estreat is triggered by the non-attendance of the defendant at court. It is for the surety to establish to the satisfaction of the trial court that there are grounds upon which the court may remit for forfeiture part or, wholly exceptionally, the whole recognisance. The presence or absence of culpability is a factor but the absence of culpability, as found in this case by the judge, is not in itself a reason to reduce or set aside the obligation entered into by the surety to pay in the event of a failure to bring the defendant to court. The court may, in the exercise of a wide discretion, decide it would be fair and just to estreat some or all of the recognisance."

Any reduction in the amount of the recognisance should be confined to the really deserving cases and any reduction should be regarded as the exception rather than the rule.

This may be contrasted with the decision in *R. v Southampton Justices Ex p. Green* [1976] Q.B. 11 where it was held that the magistrates had wrongly failed to consider the applicant's culpability. The statement in this case that the recognisance should be remitted in full if the surety used all due diligence and efforts to secure the appearance has been considered in later case law.

5–96   The court's approach was explained again in *R. v Horseferry Stipendiary Magistrate Ex p. Pearson* [1976] 1 W.L.R. 511. The court should approach the question for forfeiture "on the footing that the surety has seriously entered into a serious obligation and ought to pay the amount which he or she has promised unless there are circumstances in the case, relating either to means or culpability, which make it fair and just to pay a smaller sum." In this case the surety made serious efforts to get something done when she feared that the accused would abscond which the court on appeal said had not been taken into account when the recognisance was forfeited.

In a later case it was repeated that it might be proper to remit the recognisance entirely where the surety acted with all due diligence and made every effort to secure the appearance of the accused: *R. v Waltham Forest Justices Ex p. Parfrey* (1980) 2 Cr.App.R.(S.) 208.

The presumption has been said to be that the whole of the recognisance should be estreated in 'normal cases' but the fact that a defendant had attended at all preliminary and committal hearings and had initially arrived at the Crown Court for his trial before absconding in the middle of the day meant that the case was not normal and the blameworthiness of the surety should have been assessed on that basis: *R. v Crown Court at York Ex p. Coleman and How* (1988) 86 Cr.App.R. 151.

5–97   By contrast in another case the court said that the purpose of the surety is to force the defendant to surrender to the court. If the defendant fails to do so, the recognisance should be paid and the surety cannot escape liability by showing he has no means nor that it was not his fault that the defendant did not attend: *R. v Southampton Justices Ex p. Corker* (1976) 120 S.J. 214.

The case law indicates that each case should be dealt with on its merits and there is a wide discretion to remit the recognisance taking into account culpability and means.

Sureties should always be notified when a hearing date was fixed and if no date was fixed, they should be informed of the dates between which the case was likely to be listed. Ignorance of the date would not always be an answer to proceedings for forfeiture: *R. v Reading Crown Court Ex p. Bello* 92 Cr.App.R. 303, CA (Civ. Div). An order for forfeiture was described as 'premature' when the question had been considered in advance of a fixed date for trial. The defendant had gone abroad in breach of his bail conditions. The matter should have been considered once it was known that he would not appear to stand trial: *R. v Inner London Crown Court Ex p. Springhall*, 85 Cr.App.R. 214, DC

5–98   References in the authorities to consideration of means implies that the court should consider the surety's ability to pay and the consequences to the surety of ordering payment in an amount which would inevitably lead to imprisonment for default. There may be cases where the culpability of the surety is so great that an amount may be estreated that he cannot afford thereby making a prison sentence likely: *R. v Crown Court of Wood Green Ex p. Howe*, 93 Cr.App.R. 213, DC

It is relevant for the court in deciding whether to exercise its power under s.120(4) to remit the whole or any part of a sum to consider the potential impact of making payment not just on the surety but others as well: *R v Leicestershire Sipendiary Magistrate Ex p. Kaur* 164 J.P. 127, DC.

When a surety is concerned that the defendant will abscond, he may notify the police in writing of that fact and that he wishes to be relieved of his obligation as a surety under s.7(3)(c). On receipt of such notice the police may then arrest the defendant. A surety is not automatically relieved of his duty by contacting the police to convey his concerns but the court should take into account the efforts made to secure attendance and means of the surety when any forfeiture is considered: *R. v Crown Court at Ipswich Ex p. Reddington* [1981] Crim.L.R. 618. If a surety does wish to withdraw the proper procedure appears to be that an application to vary bail should be made under s.3(8) but as such application can only be made by the prosecution or defence this seems to require that the defendant would need to be before the court when the application was made: *R. v Crown Court at Wood Green Ex p. Howe* [1992] 3 All E.R. 366. When a surety was unrepresented the court should assist by explaining the relevant principles in ordinary language and giving the surety an opportunity to call evidence and advance arguments: *R. v Uxbridge Justices Ex p. Heward-Mills* [1983] 1 W.L.R. 56, DC. Representation by the Criminal Defence Service or the Community Legal Service is not available to an unrepresented surety: *Access to Justice Act* 1999, s.12(2); *R. v The Chief Clerk of Maidstone Crown Court Ex p. Clark* [1995] 2 Cr.App.R. 617, DC.

VII. REMANDS

(1) Introduction

A court may adjourn a case and remand the defendant in custody or bail. Under the **5–99** *Magistrates' Courts Act* 1980, time limits are set on the period of remand. Before conviction when the defendant is remanded in custody the limits are as follows—

1. 3 days in custody to a Police Constable
2. 8 clear days in custody to prison.
3. 28 clear days in custody to prison where the next stage of the proceedings is fixed to occur within that time and the accused at the time of remand is before the court and has previously been remanded in custody by the court in the proceedings.
4. 28 clear days in custody to prison if the defendant is already serving a custodial sentence.
5. 28 clear days in custody to prison where the defendant consents to remands in future in custody in his absence for a maximum of 3 adjournments of 8 clear days. The defendant must be produced in court on the fourth adjournment which will usually be 28 days later.

After conviction a defendant can be remanded into custody for a maximum of three weeks.

Where a defendant is granted bail before conviction the case can be adjourned for any period of time taking into account the interests of justice and the need to ensure a speedy trial. After conviction the time limit on adjournments on bail is four weeks.

Magistrates' Courts Act 1980, s.128

Remand in custody or on bail

128.—(1) Where a magistrates' court has power to remand any person, then, subject to sec- **5–100** tion 4 of the *Bail Act* 1976 and to any other enactment modifying that power, the court may—

(a) remand him in custody, that is to say, commit him to custody to be brought before the court, subject to subsection (3A) below, at the end of the period of remand or at such earlier time as the court may require; or

(b) where it is inquiring into or trying an offence alleged to have been committed by that person or has convicted him of an offence, remand him on bail in accordance with the *Bail Act* 1976, that is to say, by directing him to appear as provided in subsection (4) below; or

(c) except in a case falling within paragraph (b) above, remand him on bail by taking from him a recognizance (with or without sureties) conditioned as provided in that subsection;

and may, in a case falling within paragraph (c) above, instead of taking recognizances in accordance with that paragraph, fix the amount of the recognizances with a view to their being taken subsequently in accordance with section 119 above.

(1A) Where—

    (a) on adjourning a case under section 5, 10(1), 17C, or 18(4) above the court proposes to remand or further remand a person in custody; and

    (b) he is before the court; and

    (d) he is legally represented in that court,

it shall be the duty of the court—

        (i) to explain the effect of subsections (3A) and (3B) below to him in ordinary language; and

        (ii) to inform him in ordinary language that, notwithstanding the procedure for a remand without his being brought before a court, he would be brought before a court for the hearing and determination of at least every fourth application for his remand, and of every application for his remand heard at a time when it appeared to the court that he had no legal representative acting for him in the case.

(1B) For the purposes of subsection (1A) above a person is to be treated as legally represented in a court if, but only if, he has the assistance of a legal representative to represent him in the proceedings in that court.

(1C) After explaining to an accused as provided by subsection (1A) above the court shall ask him whether he consents to hearing and determination of such applications in his absence.

5–101   (2) Where the court fixes the amount of a recognizance under subsection (1) above or section 8(3) of the *Bail Act* 1976 with a view to its being taken subsequently the court shall in the meantime commit the person so remanded to custody in accordance with paragraph (a) of the said subsection (1).

(3) Where a person is brought before the court after remand, the court may further remand him.

(3A) Subject to subsection (3B) below, where a person has been remanded in custody and the remand was not a remand under section 128A below for a period exceeding 8 clear days, the court may further remand him (otherwise than in the exercise of the power conferred by that section) on an adjournment under section 5, 10(1), 17C or 18(4) above without his being brought before it if it is satisfied—

    (a) that he gave his consent, either in response to a question under subsection (1C) above or otherwise, to the hearing and determination in his absence of any application for his remand on an adjournment of the case under any of those provisions; and

    (b) that he has not by virtue of this subsection been remanded without being brought before the court on more than two such applications immediately preceding the application which the court is hearing; and

    (c) that he has not withdrawn his consent to their being so heard and determined.

(3B) The court may not exercise the power conferred by subsection (3A) above if it appears to the court, on an application for a further remand being made to it, that the person to whom the application relates has no legal representative acting for him in the case (whether present in court or not).

(3C) Where—

    (a) a person has been remanded in custody on an adjournment of a case under section 5, 10(1), 17C or 18(4) above; and

    (b) an application is subsequently made for his further remand on such an adjournment; and

    (c) he is not brought before the court which hears and determines the application; and

    (d) that court is not satisfied as mentioned in subsection (3A) above,

the court shall adjourn the case and remand him in custody for the period for which it stands adjourned.

(3D) An adjournment under subsection (3C) above shall be for the shortest period that appears to the court to make it possible for the accused to be brought before it.

(3E) Where—

    (a) on an adjournment of a case under section 5, 10(1), 17C or 18(4) above a person has been remanded in custody without being brought before the court; and

    (b) it subsequently appears—

    (i)   to the court which remanded him in custody; or

    (ii) to an alternate magistrates' court to which he is remanded under section
        130 below,

that he ought not to have been remanded in custody in his absence, the court shall require
him to be brought before it at the earliest time that appears to the court to be possible.

(4) Where a person is remanded on bail under subsection (1) above the court may, **5–102**
where it remands him on bail in accordance with the *Bail Act* 1976 direct him to appear or,
in any other case, direct that his recognizance be conditioned for his appearance—

    (a) before that court at the end of the period of remand; or

    (b) at every time and place to which during the course of the proceedings the hearing
        may be from time to time adjourned;

and, where it remands him on bail conditionally on his providing a surety during an inquiry
into an offence alleged to have been committed by him, may direct that the recognizance of the
surety be conditioned to secure that the person so bailed appears—

    (d) at every time and place to which during the course of the proceedings the hearing
        may be from time to time adjourned and also before the Crown Court in the event of
        the person so bailed being committed for trial there.

(5) Where a person is directed to appear or a recognizance is conditioned for a person's
appearance in accordance with paragraph (b) or (c) of subsection (4) above, the fixing at
any time of the time for him next to appear shall be deemed to be a remand; but nothing
in this subsection or subsection (4) above shall deprive the court of power at any subsequent
hearing to remand him afresh.

(6) Subject to the provisions of sections 128A and 129 below, a magistrates' court shall
not remand a person for a period exceeding 8 clear days, except that—

    (a) if the court remands him on bail, it may remand him for a longer period if he
        and the other party consent;

    (b) where the court adjourns a trial under [section 10(3) above or section 11 of the
        Powers of Criminal Courts (Sentencing) Act 2000], the court may remand him for
        the period of the adjournment;

    (c) where a person is charged with an offence triable either way, then, if it falls to the
        court to try the case summarily but the court is not at the time so constituted, and sit-
        ting in such a place, as will enable it to proceed with the trial, the court may remand
        him until the next occasion on which it will be practicable for the court to be so consti-
        tuted, and to sit in such a place, as aforesaid, notwithstanding that the remand is for a
        period exceeding 8 clear days.

(7) A magistrates' court having power to remand a person in custody may, if the remand **5–103**
is for a period not exceeding 3 clear days, commit him to detention at a police station.

(8) Where a person is committed to detention at a police station under subsection (7)
above—

    (a) he shall not be kept in such detention unless there is a need for him to be so
        detained for the purposes of inquiries into other offences;

    (b) if kept in such detention, he shall be brought back before the magistrates' court
        which committed him as soon as that need ceases;

    (c) he shall be treated as a person in police detention to whom the duties under sec-
        tion 39 of the *Police and Criminal Evidence Act* 1984 (responsibilities in relation to
        persons detained) relate;

    (d) his detention shall be subject to periodic review at the times set out in section 40 of
        that Act (review of police detention).

[This section is reprinted as amended by the *Powers of Criminal Courts (Sentencing) Act* 2000, Sch.9, para.75]

The direction to appear does not put an unconditional duty on a prison governor to **5–104**
produce any prisoner from custody who is on bail for other offences. A formal production order is required under s.29 of the *Criminal Justice Act* 1961 and a request to
produce a prisoner at court must not be unreasonably refused: *R v Governor of Brixton Prison Ex p. Walsh* [1985] A.C. 154. It is usually the responsibility of the Crown
Prosecution Service to arrange for such orders.

A case can be remanded under this section to any petty sessions area within the commission area. There is no requirement that a case must be remanded back to the same court as the jurisdiction of the court extends over the whole commission area: *R. v Avon Magistrates' Courts Committee Ex p. Bath Law Society* [1988] Q.B. 409.

The computation of eight clear days is calculated by counting eight days intervening between the date of appearance and the day when the defendant will be brought before the court again.

When a defendant is remanded on conditional bail with a surety he will only be released once the surety is taken. If no surety is provided, the defendant must be produced from custody after eight days: *Magistrates' Court Rules* 1981, r.23.

5–105   Section 10(3) of the *MCA* 1980 provides that after conviction the court may adjourn a case for inquiries or to determine the most suitable method of dealing with the case either for three weeks if the defendant is in custody or four weeks if he is on bail. Section 11 of the *PCC(S)A* 2000 allows for an adjournment for three weeks in custody or four weeks on bail for medical examination after conviction or when the court is satisfied that a defendant did the act or omission.

A defendant may be remanded in custody for a period exceeding eight clear days where he is legally represented and consents to remands in his absence. The safeguards are that the procedure and the defendant's rights must be clearly explained to him and his consent must be freely given whilst he has the benefit of legal representation and advice. The consent may be given to the maximum of the fourth adjournment after the first appearance and then on that occasion the defendant must be produced. The defendant may withdraw his consent at any time and the case will be re-listed.

Police detention for an adult is for a maximum of three days but for a child or young person it is 24 hours: s.23 of the *Children and Young Persons Act* 1969. Police detention to inquire into 'other offences' is not to be given a restricted meaning but includes other offences that are related to those with which the defendant has already been charged: *R. v Bailey and Smith* (1993) 97 Cr.App.R. 365.

Magistrates' Courts Act 1980, s.128A(2), (3)

Remands in custody for more than eight days

5–106   **128A.**—(2) A magistrates' court may remand the accused in custody for a period exceeding 8 clear days if—

(a) it has previously remanded him in custody for the same offence; and

(b) he is before the court,

but only if, after affording the parties an opportunity to make representations, it has set a date on which it expects that it will be possible for the next stage in the proceedings, other than a hearing relating to a further remand in custody or on bail, to take place, and only—

(i) for a period ending not later than that date; or

(ii) for a period of 28 clear days,

whichever is the less.

(3) Nothing in this section affects the right of the accused to apply for bail during the period of the remand.

[This section is reprinted omitting paras (1) and (4) and as amended by the *Criminal Procedure and Investigations Act* 1996, s.52(2).]

This applies on a second appearance in custody when a remand can then be for up to 28 days in custody if a specific event such as a committal or trial will occur on the next date. It does not apply to interim adjournment dates.

Magistrates' Courts Act 1980, s.129

Further remand

5–107   **129.**—(1) If a magistrates' court is satisfied that any person who has been remanded is unable by reason of illness or accident to appear or be brought before the court at the expiration of the period for which he was remanded, the court may, in his absence, remand him for a further time; and section 128(6) above shall not apply.

(2) Notwithstanding anything in section 128(1) above, the power of a court under subsection (1) above to remand a person on bail for a further time—

(a) where he was granted bail in criminal proceedings, includes power to enlarge the recognizance of any surety for him to a later time;

(b) where he was granted bail otherwise than in criminal proceedings, may be exercised by enlarging his recognizance and those of any sureties for him to a later time.

(3) Where a person remanded on bail is bound to appear before a magistrates' court at any time and the court has no power to remand him under subsection (1) above, the court may in his absence—

(a) where he was granted bail in criminal proceedings, appoint a later time as the time at which he is to appear and enlarge the recognizances of any sureties for him to that time;

(b) where he was granted bail otherwise than in criminal proceedings, enlarge his recognizance and those of any sureties for him to a later time;

and the appointment of the time or the enlargement of his recognizance shall be deemed to be a further remand.

(4) Where a magistrates' court commits a person for trial on bail and the recognizance of any surety for him has been conditioned in accordance with paragraph (a) of subsection (4) of section 128 above the court may, in the absence of the surety, enlarge his recognizance so that he is bound to secure that the person so committed for trial appears also before the Crown Court.

A remand in absence under this section applies equally to defendants in custody or on bail where the defendant does not appear before the court because of illness or accident. The court must have been given solid grounds to found a reliable opinion relating to the illness or accident: *R. v Liverpool City Justices Ex p. Grogan* [1991] 155 J.P. 450.

Magistrates' Courts Act 1980, s.130

Transfer of remand hearings

130.—(1) A magistrates' court adjourning a case under section 5, 10(1), 17C or 18(4) above, **5–108** and remanding the accused in custody, may, if he has attained the age of 17, order that he be brought up for any subsequent remands before an alternate magistrates' court nearer to the prison where he is to be confined while on remand.

(2) The order shall require the accused to be brought before the alternate court at the end of the period of remand or at such earlier time as the alternate court may require.

(3) While the order is in force, the alternate court shall, to the exclusion of the court which made the order, have all the powers in relation to further remand (whether in custody or on bail) and [the grant of a right to representation funded by the Legal Services Commission as part of the Criminal Defence Service] which that court would have had but for the order.

(4) The alternate court may, on remanding the accused in custody, require him to be brought before the court which made the order at the end of the period of remand or at such earlier time as that court may require; and, if the alternate court does so, or the accused is released on bail, the order under subsection (1) above shall cease to be in force.

(4A) Where a magistrates' court is satisfied as mentioned in section 128(3A) above—

(a) subsection (1) above shall have effect as if for the words "he be brought up for any subsequent remands before" there were substituted the words "applications for any subsequent remands be made to";

(b) subsection (2) above shall have effect as if for the words "the accused to be brought before" there were substituted the words "an application for a further remand to be made to" and

(c) subsection (4) above shall have effect as if for the words "him to be brought before" there were substituted the words "an application for a further remand to be made to".

(5) Schedule 5 to this Act shall have effect to supplement this section.

[This section is reprinted as amended by the *Access to Justice Act* 1999, Sch.4, para.18.]

Magistrates' Courts Act 1980, s.131(1), (2)

Remand of accused already in custody

5–109   **131.**—(1) When a magistrates' court remands an accused person in custody and he is already detained under a custodial sentence, the period for which he is remanded may be up to 28 clear days.

(2) But the court shall inquire as to the expected date of his release from that detention; and if it appears that it will be before 28 clear days have expired, he shall not be remanded in custody for more than 8 clear days or (if longer) a period ending with that date.

[This section is reprinted as amended by the *Criminal Justice Act* 1982, s.59(1), Sch.9, para.6 and Sch.16.]

VIII. POLICE BAIL

5–110   The police may bail a defendant pending a return to the police station or an appearance at court. There are no statutory time limits.

Police and Criminal Evidence Act 1984, s.38(1)

Duties of custody officer after charge

38.—(1) Where a person arrested for an offence otherwise than under a warrant endorsed for bail is charged with an offence, the custody officer shall, subject to section 25 of the *Criminal Justice and Public Order Act* 1994, order his release from police detention, either on bail or without bail, unless—

    (a) if the person arrested is not an arrested juvenile—

        (i) his name or address cannot be ascertained or the custody officer has reasonable grounds for doubting whether a name or address furnished by him as his name or address is his real name or address;

        (ii) the custody officer has reasonable grounds for believing that the person arrested will fail to appear in court to answer to bail;

        (iii) in the case of a person arrested for an imprisonable offence, the custody officer has reasonable grounds for believing that the detention of the person arrested is necessary to prevent him from committing an offence;

       (iiia) in the case of a person who has attained the age of 18, the custody officer has reasonable grounds for believing that the detention of the person is necessary to enable a sample to be taken from him under section 63B below,

        (iv) in the case of a person arrested for an offence which is not an imprisonable offence, the custody officer has reasonable grounds for believing that the detention of the person arrested is necessary to prevent him from causing physical injury to any other person or from causing loss of or damage to property;

        (v) the custody officer has reasonable grounds for believing that the detention of the person arrested is necessary to prevent him from interfering with the administration of justice or with the investigation of offences or of a particular offence; or

        (vi) the custody officer has reasonable grounds for believing that the detention of the person arrested is necessary for his own protection;

    (b) if he is an arrested juvenile—

        (i) any of the requirements of paragraph (a) above is satisfied; or

        (ii) the custody officer has reasonable grounds for believing that he ought to be detained in his own interests.

[This section is reprinted as amended by the *Criminal Justice and Court Services Act* 2000, s.57(3)(b).]

Police and Criminal Evidence Act 1984, s.47

Bail after arrest

5–111   **47.**—(1) Subject to subsection (2) below, a release on bail of a person under this Part of this

Act shall be a release on bail granted in accordance with sections 3, 3A, 5 and 5A of the *Bail Act* 1976 as they apply to bail granted by a constable.

(1A) The normal powers to impose conditions of bail shall be available to him where a custody officer releases a person on bail under section 38(1) above (including that subsection as applied by section 40(10) above) but not in any other cases.

In this subsection, "the normal powers to impose conditions of bail" has the meaning given in section 3(6) of the *Bail Act* 1976.

(2) Nothing in the *Bail Act* 1976 shall prevent the re-arrest without warrant of a person released on bail subject to a duty to attend at a police station if new evidence justifying a further arrest has come to light since his release.

(3) Subject to subsections (3A) and (4) below, in this Part of this Act references to "bail" are references to bail subject to a duty—

    (a) to appear before a magistrates' court at such time and such place; or

    (b) to attend at such police station at such time,

as the custody officer may appoint.

(3A) Where a custody officer grants bail to a person subject to a duty to appear before a magistrates' court, he shall appoint for the appearance—

    (a) a date which is not later than the first sitting of the court after the person is charged with the offence; or

    (b) where he is informed by the [justices' chief executive.] for the relevant petty sessions area that the appearance cannot be accommodated until a later date, that later date.

(4) Where a custody officer has granted bail to a person subject to a duty to appear at a police station, the custody officer may give notice in writing to that person that his attendance at the police station is not required.

(6) Where a person who has been granted bail and either has attended at the police station in accordance with the grant of bail or has been arrested under section 46A above is detained at a police station, any time during which he was in police detention prior to being granted bail shall be included as part of any period which falls to be calculated under this Part of this Act.

(7) Where a person who was released on bail subject to a duty to attend at a police station is re-arrested, the provisions of this Part of this Act shall apply to him as they apply to a person arrested for the first time; but this subsection does not apply to a person who is arrested under section 46A above or has attended a police station in accordance with the grant of bail (and who accordingly is deemed by section 34(7) above to have been arrested for an offence).

(8) In the *Magistrates' Courts Act* 1980—   **5–112**

    (a) the following section shall be substituted for section 43—

Bail on arrest

"**43.**—(1) Where a person has been granted bail under the *Police and Criminal Evidence Act* 1984 subject to a duty to appear before a magistrates' court, the court before which he is to appear may appoint a later time as the time at which he is to appear and may enlarge the recognizances of any sureties for him at that time.

(2) The recognizance of any surety for any person granted bail subject to a duty to attend at a police station may be enforced as if it were conditioned for his appearance before a magistrates' court for the petty sessions area in which the police station named in the recognizance is situated."

    ; and

    (b) the following subsection shall be substituted for section 117(3)—

"(3) Where a warrant has been endorsed for bail under subsection (1) above—

    (a) where the person arrested is to be released on bail on his entering into a recognizance without sureties, it shall not be necessary to take him to a police station, but if he is so taken, he shall be released from custody on his entering into the recognizance; and

    (b) where he is to be released on his entering into a recognizance with sureties, he shall be taken to a police station on his arrest, and the custody officer there shall (subject to his approving any surety tendered in compliance with the endorsement) release him from custody as directed in the endorsement.".

[This section is reprinted as amended by the *Access to Justice Act* 1999, Sch.13, para.127.]

Bail Act 1976, s.3A

Conditions of bail in case of police bail

5–113   **3A.**—(1) Section 3 of this Act applies, in relation to bail granted by a custody officer under Part IV of the *Police and Criminal Evidence Act* 1984 in cases where the normal powers to impose conditions of bail are available to him, subject to the following modifications.

(2) Subsection (6) does not authorise the imposition of a requirement to reside in a bail hostel or any requirement under paragraph (d) or (e).

(3) [Subsections (6ZAA), (6ZA), (6A) and (6B)] shall be omitted.

(4) For subsection (8), substitute the following—

"(8) Where a custody officer has granted bail in criminal proceedings he or another custody officer serving at the same police station may, at the request of the person to whom it was granted, vary the conditions of bail; and in doing so he may impose conditions or more onerous conditions.".

(5) Where a constable grants bail to a person no conditions shall be imposed under subsections (4), (5), (6) or (7) of section 3 of this Act unless it appears to the constable that it is necessary to do so

(a) for the purposes of preventing that person from] failing to surrender to custody, or

(b) for the purposes of preventing that person from] committing an offence while on bail, or

(c) for the purposes of preventing that person from] interfering with witnesses or otherwise obstructing the course of justice, whether in relation to himself or any other person or

(d) for that person's own protection or, if he is a child or young person, for his own welfare or in his own interests.

(6) Subsection (5) above also applies on any request to a custody officer under subsection (8) of section 3 of this Act to vary the conditions of bail.

[This section is reprinted as amended by the *Criminal Justice and Police Act* 2001, s.131(4). The amendments of the *Criminal Justice Act* 2003, s.13 came into effect in April 2004.

Bail Act 1976, s.5A

Supplementary provisions in cases of police bail.

5–114   **5A.**—(1) Section 5 of this Act applies, in relation to bail granted by a custody officer under Part IV of the *Police and Criminal Evidence Act* 1984 in cases where the normal powers to impose conditions of bail are available to him, subject to the following modifications.

(1A) Subsections (2A) and (2B) shall be omitted.

(2) For subsection (3) substitute the following—

"(3) Where a custody officer, in relation to any person,—

(a) imposes conditions in granting bail in criminal proceedings, or

(b) varies any conditions of bail or imposes conditions in respect of bail in criminal proceedings,

the custody officer shall, with a view to enabling that person to consider requesting him or another custody officer, or making an application to a magistrates' court, to vary the conditions, give reasons for imposing or varying the conditions.".

(3) For subsection (4) substitute the following—

"(4) A custody officer who is by virtue of subsection (3) above required to give reasons for his decision shall include a note of those reasons in the custody record and shall give a copy of that note to the person in relation to whom the decision was taken.".

(4) Subsections (5) and (6) shall be omitted.

[This section is printed as amended by the *Criminal Justice and Police Act* 2001, s.129(2).]

A custody officer who grants bail subject to conditions including a surety or security or varies the conditions of bail must give reasons and make a record of the decision, but there is no obligation to give reasons for the withholding of bail: *Bail Act* 1976, ss.5 and 5A.

IX. WARRANTS WITH AND WITHOUT BAIL

When a warrant of arrest is issued by the Court, consideration must be given as to **5–115** whether the warrant should be backed for bail or not. The decision will depend on the nature and gravity of the offence charged and the defendant's bail history.

Magistrates' Courts Act 1980, s.117

Warrant endorsed for bail

117.—(1) A justice of the peace on issuing a warrant for the arrest of any person may grant him bail by endorsing the warrant for bail, that is to say, by endorsing the warrant with a direction in accordance with subsection (2) below.

(2) A direction for bail endorsed on a warrant under subsection (1) above shall—

(a) in the case of bail in criminal proceedings, state that the person arrested is to be released on bail subject to a duty to appear before such magistrates' court and at such time as may be specified in the endorsement;

(b) ...(civil proceedings)

and the endorsement shall fix the amounts in which any sureties and, in a case falling within paragraph (b) above, that person is or are to be bound.

(3) Where a warrant has been endorsed for bail under subsection (1) above—

(a) where the person arrested is to be released on bail on his entering into a recognizance without sureties, it shall not be necessary to take him to a police station, but if he is so taken, he shall be released from custody on his entering into the recognizance; and

(b) where he is to be released on his entering into a recognizance with sureties, he shall be taken to a police station on his arrest, and the custody officer there shall (subject to his approving any surety tendered in compliance with the endorsement) release him from custody as directed in the endorsement.

[This section is reprinted as amended by the *Police and Criminal Evidence Act* 1984, ss.47(8)(b), 51, 52.]

X. CUSTODY TIME LIMITS

(1) Introduction

The *Magistrates' Courts Act* 1980 and other enactments provide for limits on the **5–116** periods of time for which a person may be remanded, either in custody or on bail. Custody time limits also apply, which dictate the length of time over which a person may be remanded in custody during the progress of a criminal case. The limits are designed to ensure that where a defendant is in custody, the case will be expedited. If there is any delay the defendant may be released from custody for further adjournments. The custody time limits for cases tried summarily is 56 days from first appearance to trial and for cases going to the Crown Court, the limit is 70 days from first appearance to committal. Application may be made for the limits to be extended in specific circumstances. Time limits do not apply to defendants remanded on bail but time limits do apply in the youth courts to both bail and custody cases, see generally Part V in this work.

Prosecution of Offences Act 1985, s.22

Power of Secretary of State to set time limits in relation to preliminary stages of criminal proceedings

5-117   **22.**—(1) The Secretary of State may by regulations make provision, with respect to any specified preliminary stage of proceedings for an offence, as to the maximum period—

(a) to be allowed to the prosecution to complete that stage;

(b) during which the accused may, while awaiting completion of that stage, be—

(i) in the custody of a magistrates' court; or

(ii) in the custody of the Crown Court;

in relation to that offence.

(2) The regulations may, in particular—

(a) be made so as to apply only in relation to proceedings instituted in specified areas, or proceedings of, or against persons of, specified classes or descriptions;

(b) make different provision with respect to proceedings instituted in different areas, or different provision with respect to proceedings of, or against persons of, different classes or descriptions;

(c) make such provision with respect to the procedure to be followed in criminal proceedings as the Secretary of State considers appropriate in consequence of any other provision of the regulations;

(d) provide for the *Magistrates' Courts Act* 1980 and the *Bail Act* 1976 to apply in relation to cases to which custody or overall time limits apply subject to such modifications as may be specified (being modifications which the Secretary of State considers necessary in consequence of any provision made by the regulations); and

(e) make such transitional provision in relation to proceedings instituted before the commencement of any provision of the regulations as the Secretary of State considers appropriate.

(3) The appropriate court may, at any time before the expiry of a time limit imposed by the regulations, extend, or further extend, that limit; but the court shall not do so unless it is satisfied—

(a) that the need for the extension is due to—

(i) the illness or absence of the accused, a necessary witness, a judge or a magistrate;

(ii) a postponement which is occasioned by the ordering by the court of separate trials in the case of two or more accused or two or more offences; or

(iii) some other good and sufficient cause; and

(b) that the prosecution has acted with all due diligence and expedition.

(4) Where, in relation to any proceedings for an offence, an overall time limit has expired before the completion of the stage of the proceedings to which the limit applies the appropriate court shall stay the proceedings.

5-118   (5) Where—

(a) a person escapes from the custody of a magistrates' court or the Crown Court before the expiry of a custody time limit which applies in his case; or

(b) a person who has been released on bail in consequence of the expiry of a custody time limit—

(i) fails to surrender himself into the custody of the court at the appointed time; or

(ii) is arrested by a constable on a ground mentioned in section 7(3)(b) of the *Bail Act* 1976 (breach, or likely breach, of conditions of bail);

the regulations shall, so far as they provide for any custody time limit in relation to the preliminary stage in question, be disregarded.

(6) Subsection (6A) below applies where—

(a) a person escapes from the custody of a magistrates' court or the Crown Court; or

(b) a person who has been released on bail fails to surrender himself into the custody of the court at the appointed time;

and is accordingly unlawfully at large for any period.

(6A) The following, namely—

(a) the period for which the person is unlawfully at large; and

(b) such additional period (if any) as the appropriate court may direct, having regard to the disruption of the prosecution occasioned by—

(i)   the person's escape or failure to surrender; and

(ii) the length of the period mentioned in paragraph (a) above,

shall be disregarded, so far as the offence in question is concerned, for the purposes of the overall time limit which applies in his case in relation to the stage which the proceedings have reached at the time of the escape or, as the case may be, at the appointed time.

(7) Where a magistrates' court decides to extend, or further extend, a custody or overall time limit or to give a direction under subsection (6A) above, the accused may appeal against the decision to the Crown Court.

(8) Where a magistrates' court refuses to extend, or further extend, a custody or overall time limit, or to give a direction under subsection (6A) above, the prosecution may appeal against the refusal to the Crown Court.

(9) An appeal under subsection (8) above may not be commenced after the expiry of **5–119** the limit in question; but where such an appeal is commenced before the expiry of the limit the limit shall be deemed not to have expired before the determination or abandonment of the appeal.

(10) Where a person is convicted of an offence in any proceedings, the exercise, in relation to any preliminary stage of those proceedings, of the power conferred by subsection (3) above shall not be called into question in any appeal against that conviction.

(11) In this section—

"appropriate court" means—

(a)   where the accused has been committed for trial[, sent for trial under section 51 of the *Crime and Disorder Act* 1998] or indicted for the offence, the Crown Court; and

(b)   in any other case, the magistrates' court specified in the summons or warrant in question or, where the accused has already appeared or been brought before a magistrates' court, a magistrates' court for the same area;

"custody" includes local authority accommodation to which a person is remanded or committed by virtue of section 23 of the *Children and Young Persons Act* 1969, and references to a person being committed to custody shall be construed accordingly;

"custody of the Crown Court" includes custody to which a person is committed in pursuance of—

(a)   section 6 of the *Magistrates' Courts Act* 1980 (magistrates' court committing accused for trial); or

(b)   section 43A of that Act (magistrates' court dealing with a person brought before it following his arrest in pursuance of a warrant issued by the Crown Court); or

(c)   section 5(3)(a) of the *Criminal Justice Act* 1987 (custody after transfer order in fraud case); or

(d)   paragraph 2(1)(a) of Schedule 6 to the *Criminal Justice Act* 1991 (custody after transfer order in certain cases involving children).

"custody of a magistrates' court" means custody to which a person is committed in pursuance of section 128 of the *Magistrates' Courts Act* 1980 (remand);

"custody time limit" means a time limit imposed by regulations made under subsection (1)(b) above or, where any such limit has been extended by a court under subsection (3) above, the limit as so extended;

"preliminary stage", in relation to any proceedings, does not include any stage after the start of the trial (within the meaning given by subsections (11A) and (11B) below);

"overall time limit" means a time limit imposed by regulations made under subsection (1)(a) above or, where any such limit has been extended by a court under subsection (3) above, the limit as so extended; and

"specified" means specified in the regulations.

(11A) For the purposes of this section, the start of a trial on indictment shall be taken to **5–120** occur when a jury is sworn to consider the issue of guilt or fitness to plead or, if the court accepts a plea of guilty before a jury is sworn, when that plea is accepted but this is subject to section 8 of the *Criminal Justice Act* 1987 and section 30 of the *Criminal Procedure and Investigations Act* 1996 (preparatory hearings).

(11ZA) For the purposes of this section, proceedings for an offence shall be taken to begin when the accused is charged with the offence or, as the case may be, an information is laid charging him with the offence.

(11B) For the purposes of this section, the start of a summary trial shall be taken to occur—

(a) when the court begins to hear evidence for the prosecution at the trial or to consider whether to exercise its power under section 37(3) of the *Mental Health Act* 1983 (power to make hospital order without convicting the accused), or

(b) if the court accepts a plea of guilty without proceeding as mentioned above, when that plea is accepted.

(12) For the purposes of the application of any custody time limit in relation to a person who is in the custody of a magistrates' court or the Crown Court—

(a) all periods during which he is in the custody of a magistrates' court in respect of the same offence shall be aggregated and treated as a single continuous period; and

(b) all periods during which he is in the custody of the Crown Court in respect of the same offence shall be aggregated and treated similarly.

(13) For the purposes of section 29(3) of the *Supreme Court Act* 1981 (High Court to have power to make prerogative orders in relation to jurisdiction of Crown Court in matters which do not relate to trial on indictment) the jurisdiction conferred on the Crown Court by this section shall be taken to be part of its jurisdiction in matters other than those relating to trial on indictment.

[This section is reprinted as amended by the *Access to Justice Act* 1999, s.67(3).]

Prosecution of Offence (Custody Time Limits) Regulations 1989, reg.1

5–121   **1.**—(1) These *Regulations* may be cited as the *Prosecution of Offences (Custody Time Limits) (Amendment) Regulations* 1989.

(2) In these *Regulations* "the principal regulations" means the *Prosecution of Offences (Custody Time Limits) Regulations* 1987 and references to a notice of transfer are references to a notice given under section 4 of the *Criminal Justice Act* 1987.

(3) These *Regulations* shall come into force on 1st June 1989, but—

(a) regulations 2 and 4(a) shall not apply in relation to proceedings for an offence instituted before that date except where—

(i) the accused is committed for trial in the Crown Court, or

(ii) notice of transfer is given in respect of the case, or

(iii) a bill of indictment is preferred against the accused under section 2(2)(b) of the *Administration of Justice (Miscellaneous Provisions) Act* 1933, on or after that date; and

(b) regulations 3 and 4(b) shall not apply in relation to proceedings for an offence instituted before that date.

Prosecution of Offence (Custody Time Limits) Regulations 1989, reg.4

Custody time limits in magistrates' courts

5–122   **4.**—(1) The maximum period during which a person accused of an indictable offence other than treason may be in the custody of a magistrates' court in relation to that offence while awaiting completion of any preliminary stage of the proceedings specified in the following provisions of this Regulation shall be as stated in those provisions.

(2) Except as provided in paragraph (3) below, in the case of an offence triable either way the maximum period of custody between the accused's first appearance and the start of summary trial or, as the case may be, the time when the court decides whether or not to commit the accused to the Crown Court for trial shall be 70 days.

(3) In the case of an offence triable either way if, before the expiry of 56 days following the day of the accused's first appearance, the court decides to proceed to summary trial in pursuance of sections 19 to 24 of the 1980 Act the maximum period of custody between the accused's first appearance and the start of the summary trial shall be 56 days.

(4) In the case of an offence triable on indictment exclusively the maximum period of custody between the accused's first appearance and the time when the court decides whether or not to commit the accused to the Crown Court for trial, shall be 70 days.

(4A) In the case of a summary offence, the maximum period of custody beginning with the date of the accused's first appearance and ending with the date of the start of the summary trial shall be 56 days.

(5) The foregoing provisions of this regulation shall have effect as if any reference therein to the time when the court decides whether or not to commit the accused to the Crown Court for trial were a reference—

> (a) where a court proceeds to inquire into an information as examining justices in pursuance of section 6(1) of the 1980 Act, to the time when it begins to hear evidence for the prosecution at the inquiry;

> (b) where a notice has been given under section 4(1)(c) of the *Criminal Justice Act 1987* (in these *Regulations* referred to as a "notice of transfer"), to the date on which notice of transfer was given.

Prosecution of Offence (Custody Time Limits) Regulations 1987, reg.7

Application for extension of custody time limit

7.—(1) An application to a court for the extension or further extension of a custody time limit **5–123** under section 22(3) of the 1985 Act may be made orally or in writing.

(2) Subject to paragraphs (3) and (4) below the prosecution shall—

> (a) not less than 5 days before making such an application in the Crown Court; and

> (b) not less than 2 days before making such an application in a magistrates' court,

give notice in writing to the accused or his representative and to the proper officer of the court stating that it intends to make such an application.

(2A) In paragraph (2) above, "the proper officer of the court" means in relation to an application in the Crown Court the appropriate officer of the court and in relation to an application in a magistrates' court the clerk of the court.

(3) It shall not be necessary for the prosecution to comply with paragraph (2) above if the accused or his representative has informed the prosecution that he does not require such notice.

(4) If the court is satisfied that it is not practicable in all the circumstances for the prosecution to comply with paragraph (2) above, the court may direct that the prosecution need not comply with that paragraph or that the minimum period of notice required by that paragraph to be given shall be such lesser minimum period as the court may specify.

The period of custody begins at the close of the day during which the defendant was **5–124** first remanded and expires at midnight on the relevant day. The relevant day is that prescribed by r.4 of the *Prosecution of Offences (Custody Time Limits) Regulations 1987: R v Governor of Canterbury Prison Ex p. Craig* [1991] 2 Q.B. 195, (1990) 91 Cr.App.R. 7. Once the limit has expired it is the duty of the court and not a prison governor to direct the release on bail of the defendant: *Olutu v Home Office* [1997] 1 All E.R. 385.

The relevant limits are prescribed in r.4 above as 56 days in the case of summary or either wayoffences to be dealt with by way of summary trial and 70 days for either way or indictable offences that are to be committed to the Crown Court for trial. Application may be made to extend the time limits under s.22(3) and r.7. The requirement on the prosecution to give two days notice of an application has been held to be directory only and not mandatory, so the court retains the power to extend the time limit at any time before it expires: *R. v Governor of Canterbury prison Ex p. Craig* [1991] 2 Q.B. 195, (1990) 91 Cr.App.R. 7.

Once a custody time limit has expired and the prosecution have failed to obtain an extension of time the court has no power to extend time and bail must be granted: *R. v Sheffield Justices Ex p. Turner* [1991] 2 W.L.R. 987

Before the court will direct an extension of the time limit it must be satisfied on the balance of probabilities that the two conditions of s.22(3) are met, namely that there is 'good and sufficient cause' for an extension to the time limit and secondly that the prosecution have acted with all 'due diligence and expedition'. Guidance on the approach to be taken by the courts was given in *R. v Crown Court at Manchester Ex p. MacDonald* [1999] 1 All E.R. 805. It is recognised that the there are an infinite number of matters that might amount to "good and sufficient cause". Lack of court time, listing difficulties because of the size and complexity of a case and the unavailability of a senior judge or any judge to hear the case have all been held to amount to 'good and sufficient cause': *Re C* 2000 164 J.P. 693; *R. (on the application of Eliot) v Crown Court at Reading* [2002] 1 Cr.App.R. 3; *R. v Central Criminal Court Ex p. Abu-Wardeh* [1997] 1 All E.R. 159; *R. v Crown Court at Norwich Ex p. Cox* (1993) 97 Cr.App.R. 145 J.P. 80. The seriousness of the offence and shortness of the extension sought do not qualify: *R. v Governor of Winchester Prison Ex p. Roddie* [1991] 2 All E.R. 931.

In *R. (on the application of Bannister) v Crown Court at Guildford*, January 2004, unreported, the court took a more robust view and held that the chronic lack of resources which led to an inability to list an "utterly routine" case did not amount to 'good and sufficient cause'. The court said that positive judicial intervention at listing stage was to be encouraged to ensure that the time limits were observed.

In assessing 'good and sufficient cause' considerations relating to bail are not relevant and extending the limit for the protection of the public could not of itself amount to 'good and sufficient cause': *R. v Sheffield Crown Court Ex p. Headley* [2000] 2 Cr.App.R. 1; *R. (on the application of Eliot) v Crown Court at Reading*. But see *R. v Crown Court at Luton Ex p. Neaves* [1993] 157 J.P. 80 where it was held that an extension for the protection of an individual member of the public from violence was justified.

5–125	With regard to the second condition of 'due diligence and expedition', the court will require such diligence and expedition as would be expected from a competent prosecutor who is alert to his duty. It is an objective test: *R. v Crown Court at Manchester Ex p. MacDonald* (above); *R. v Governor of Winchester prison Ex p. Roddie* (above). When assessing whether due diligence has been used the limits set are to be seen not as a target but a maximum period of time and the prosecution must ensure that the evidence and papers are served on the defence within a reasonable time to permit them to be properly considered by the time of committal: *R. v Crown Court at Norwich Ex p. Parker* (1993) 96 Cr.App.R. 68. The prosecution also had to expedite the case to allow for a contested rather than uncontested committal within the 70 day limit: *R. v Leeds Crown Court Ex p. Briggs* [1998] 2 Cr.App.R. 424. Once the prosecution judge that a piece of evidence is likely to be important, it had a duty to ensure that the evidence reached the defence swiftly. A case had to be advanced as to why there was a delay in delivering evidence: *R. v Central Criminal Court Ex p. Behbehani* [1994] Crim.L.R. 352; *R. (on the application of Smith) v Woolwich Crown Court* [2002] Crim.L.R. 915.

In *R. (on the application of Gibson and Gibson) v Winchester Crown Court* [2004] 1 W.L.R. 1623, it was held by the court that if 'good and sufficient cause' were found, the fact that the prosecution had failed to act with due diligence may be irrelevant as the need for the extension may not be directly referable to their failure. The Court also commented that availability of resources could not be ignored but all relevant considerations must be taken into account when deciding on an extension.

When extending the time limits it is important that the defendant should understand without a doubt why his liberty is being restricted. The application must be clear and understandable and the defendant must be given an opportunity to object and make representations. The order of the court must be clear, detailed and properly recorded: *Re Ward, Ward and Bond* [1991] Crim.L.R. 558.

5–126	The procedure in such applications is informal and Art.6 is not engaged because it does not involve the trial of a criminal charge. Formal rules of evidence do not apply but the defendant must be allowed to question any areas of the application as he wishes: *Wildman v DPP* [2001] Crim.L.R. 565. Where a defendant is charged with various offences at different times, each offence attracts its own custody time limit: *R. v Wirral District Magistrates' Court Ex p. Meikle* [1990] 154 J.P. 1035. A new custody time limit then runs from the date of the new charge but it could amount to an abuse of process by the prosecution if the new charges were preferred solely for the purpose of defeating the custody time limits: *R. v Waltham Forest Magistrates Ex p. Lee and Lee* (1993) 97 Cr.App.R. 287; *R. v Wolverhampton Magistrates Ex p. Uppal* [1995] 159 J.P. 86.

The commencement of a new custody time limit with every new charge does not infringe the right to liberty under Art.5 ECHR. In *R. v Crown Court at Leeds Ex p. Wardle* [2001] 2 Cr.App.R. 20, the defendant was charged originally with murder but the CPS substituted a charge of manslaughter at a later date. It was argued by the defence that new custody time limits did not attach to the new charge which was expressly or impliedly included in the original murder charge. It was also claimed that the detention was therefore in breach of Art.5 ECHR. It was held that a requirement on the magistrates' court to enquire into whether a new charge also constituted one of the potential offences for which a defendant might be convicted on the original charge would place an undue burden on the examining justices. Accordingly, each fresh and different offence charged did give rise to a new custody limit. No breach of Art.5 was found in view of the fact that the proceedings were both lawful and the consequences of the restriction imposed sufficiently accessible. Whilst there was always a risk that the custody time limit might be extended as a result of an arbitrary decision by the prosecution, that risk was subject to judicial control by the court.

More than one application can be made to extend time limits provided the application is made during the currency of the initial time limit or the time limit as extended by the court. This was confirmed in *R. (Haque) v Central Criminal Court* [2003] EWHC 2457, [2003] 10 *Archbold News* 1, QBD. The court also said that the "root and principal cause"of the need for the extension must be looked at rather than whether the prosecution had contributed to that need.

I. OBLIGATIONS TO DISCLOSE EVIDENCE PRE-TRIAL

A. INTRODUCTION

Historically there has been no obligation on the defence to give the court or the pros- **6–1**
ecution advance warning of any evidence that it may seek to adduce at the trial; this absence of obligation being a natural consequence of the rule that it is for the prosecution to prove the case against the accused. There has also been little legal requirement for the prosecution to give notice of its evidence pre-trial, although disclosure of witness statements to the defence has always been regarded as good practise. Since 1985 the obligation on the prosecutor has become more formalised and the law has reached a position where it imposes limited and varying obligations on both sides to reveal its case to the other before the trial.

The disclosure provisions contained in *Criminal Justice Act* 2003 (Pt 5) are not in force at the time of writing but likely to be in force from May 2005. The new regime alters the prosecutor's duty of primary disclosure (to become known as "initial duty"). There are new provisions concerned with the contents of defence case statements, provision for the service of defendant statements upon co-accused, obligations on the defence to give notice of intention to call defence witnesses and to give the prosecution notification of the name and address of any expert who has been instructed by the defence whether or not that expert is to be relied upon. There will also be new sanctions arising from failures on the part of the defence to comply with its obligation to disclose pre-trial.

B. OBLIGATIONS COMMON TO BOTH PARTIES

(1) Obligation to disclose evidence to be adduced in writing

The effect of the *CJA* 1967, s.9, is to require any party proposing to tender a *written* **6–2** *statement* from a witness in evidence to serve to statement upon the other side at least seven days before the evidence is adduced. After the statement has been served the other party can prevent the evidence being adduced in written form by giving notice, within seven days of receipt of the statement, to the party that served the statement. The statement is only admissible if it complies with the requirements particularised in s.9 and therefore it is good practise for all witness statements to be drawn up in the approved form, so that the written document may be used in evidence if the need should arise. Provided no party objects, any statement which complies with the formalities of s.9 may be read in evidence even though less than seven days notice has been given.

Criminal Justice Act 1967 s.9

Proof by written statement

6–3   **9.**—(1) In any criminal proceedings, other than committal proceedings, a written statement by any person shall, if such of the conditions mentioned in the next following subsection as are applicable are satisfied, be admissible as evidence to the like extent as oral evidence to the like effect by that person.

(2) The said conditions are—

(a) the statement purports to be signed by the person who made it;

(b) the statement contains a declaration by that person to the effect that it is true to the best of his knowledge and belief and that he made the statement knowing that, if it were tendered in evidence, he would be liable to prosecution if he wilfully stated in it anything which he knew to be false or did not believe to be true;

(c) before the hearing at which the statement is tendered in evidence, a copy of the statement is served, by or on behalf of the party proposing to tender it, on each of the other parties to the proceedings; and

(d) none of the other parties or their solicitors, within seven days from the service of the copy of the statement, serves a notice on the party so proposing objecting to the statement being tendered in evidence under this section:

Provided that the conditions mentioned in paragraphs (c) and (d) of this subsection shall not apply if the parties agree before or during the hearing that the statement shall be so tendered.

6–4   (3) The following provisions shall also have effect in relation to any written statement tendered in evidence under this section, that is to say—

(a) if the statement is made by a person under the age of eighteen, it shall give his age;

(b) if it is made by a person who cannot read it, it shall be read to him before he signs it and shall be accompanied by a declaration by the person who so read the statement to the effect that it was so read; and

(c) if it refers to any other document as an exhibit, the copy served on any other party to the proceedings under paragraph (c) of the last foregoing subsection shall be accompanied by a copy of that document or by such information as may be necessary in order to enable the party on whom it is served to inspect that document or a copy thereof.

(4) Notwithstanding that a written statement made by any person may be admissible as evidence by virtue of this section—

(a) the party by whom or on whose behalf a copy of the statement was served may call that person to give evidence; and

(b) the court may, of its own motion or on the application of any party to the proceedings, require that person to attend before the court and give evidence.

(5) An application under paragraph (b) of the last foregoing subsection to a court other than a magistrates' court may be made before the hearing and on any such application the powers of the court shall be exercisable by a puisne judge of the High Court, a Circuit judge or Recorder sitting alone.

(6) So much of any statement as is admitted in evidence by virtue of this section shall, unless the court otherwise directs, be read aloud at the hearing and where the court so directs an account shall be given orally of so much of any statement as is not read aloud.

6–5   (7) Any document or object referred to as an exhibit and identified in a written statement tendered in evidence under this section shall be treated as if it had been produced as an exhibit and identified in court by the maker of the statement.

(8) A document required by this section to be served on any person may be served—

   (a) by delivering it to him or to his solicitor; or

   (b) by addressing it to him and leaving it at his usual or last known place of abode or place of business or by addressing it to his solicitor and leaving it at his office; or

   (c) by sending it in a registered letter or by the recorded delivery service or by first class post addressed to him at his usual or last known place of abode or place of business or addressed to his solicitor at his office; or

   (d) in the case of a body corporate, by delivering it to the secretary or clerk of the body at its registered or principal office or sending it in a registered letter or by the recorded delivery service or by first class post addressed to the Secretary or clerk of that body at that office[; and in paragraph (d) of this subsection references to the secretary, in relation to a limited liability partnership, are to any designated member of the limited liability partnership].

(2) Obligation to disclose expert evidence

These Rules provide for mutual disclosure of expert evidence between parties to **6–6** proceedings for the summary trial of an offence where the person charged with the offence pleads not guilty. By virtue of r.2, these rules have effect in relation to proceedings for an offence into which no criminal investigation has begun before April 1, 1997.

Rule 3 requires a party to disclose any expert evidence which he proposes to adduce as soon as practicable after the plea is taken, r.3(1)(b) enables a party to examine the basis of any findings or opinions proposed to be adduced by way of expert evidence by another party. Rule 4 provides for a party to withhold any matter where he has reasonable grounds for suspecting that its disclosure might lead to intimidation or the course of justice being interfered with. In such a case the party is required to give to the other party notice in writing, which must include the grounds on which disclosure is being withheld. By r.5 a party who fails to comply with r.3 in respect of any evidence may not adduce that evidence without the leave of the court.

Magistrates' Courts (Advance Notice of Expert Evidence) Rules SI 1997/705, rr.3–5

3.—(1) Where a magistrates' court proceeds to summary trial in respect of an alleged offence **6–7** and the person charged with that offence pleads not guilty in respect of it, if any party to the proceedings proposes to adduce expert evidence (whether of fact or opinion) in the proceedings (otherwise than in relation to sentence) he shall as soon as practicable after the person charged has so pleaded, unless in relation to the evidence in question he has already done so—

   (a) furnish the other party or parties with a statement in writing of any finding or opinion which he proposes to adduce by way of such evidence; and

   (b) where a request in writing is made to him in that behalf by any other party, provide that party also with a copy of (or if it appears to the party proposing to adduce the evidence to be more practicable, a reasonable opportunity to examine) the record of any observation, test, calculation or other procedure on which such finding or opinion is based and any document or other thing or substance in respect of which any such procedure has been carried out.

(2) A party may by notice in writing waive his right to be furnished with any of the matters mentioned in paragraph (1) above and, in particular, may agree that the statement mentioned in sub-paragraph (a) thereof may be furnished to him orally and not in writing.

(3) In paragraph (1) above, "document" means anything in which information of any description is recorded.

4.—(1) If a party has reasonable grounds for believing that the disclosure of any evidence in **6–8** compliance with the requirements imposed by rule 3 above might lead to the intimidation, or attempted intimidation, of any person on whose evidence he intends to rely in the proceedings, or otherwise to the course of justice being interfered with, he shall not be obliged to comply with those requirements in relation to that evidence.

(2) Where, in accordance with paragraph (1) above, a party considers that he is not obliged to comply with the requirements imposed by rule 3 above with regard to any evidence in relation to any other party, he shall give notice in writing to that party to the effect that the evidence is being withheld and the grounds therefore.

6–9   **5.** A party who seeks to adduce expert evidence in any proceedings and who fails to comply with r.3 above shall not adduce that evidence in those proceedings without the leave of the court.

There is no specific time limit for service of the expert evidence, other than that service should be as soon as practicable after the entering of the plea and only then once the party 'proposes to adduce' it. In some cases it may be that the party is in possession of the evidence for sometime before deciding to rely upon it, which could in appropriate cases justify a delay in serving the report until late in the proceedings. Whether such delay would be justifiable will depend upon the circumstances of each case, but any unreasonable delay may lead to the court refusing leave to allow the evidence to be adduced. Delay in service may also cause the other side to obtain an adjournment, which might lead to a costs order against the delaying party. A time table for the service of experts reports may be set by directions given at a pre-trial review.

C. Obligations on the Defence

6–10   Other than the obligations to give advance notice of evidence to be adduced by written statements (*CJA* 1967, s.9, above) and to disclose expert evidence, above, there is no obligation to disclose evidence pre-trial. Regardless, the defence has the option to provide the court with a defence case statement after the prosecution has provided primary disclosure of unused material, see §§ 6–27 *et seq.* below.

D. Obligations on the Prosecution

(1) Summary offences

6–11   The *Advance Information Rules* 1985 only apply to offences which are triable either way. There is no requirement for advance disclosure of witness statements in summary proceedings: *R. v Kingston upon Hull Justices Ex p. McCann* (1991) 155 J.P. 569. In the interest of ensuring a fair trial the prosecutor should consider disclosure of the evidence pre-trial. Whilst Art.6 of the European Convention on Human Rights does not require that prosecution witness statements be supplied to the accused before trial (*R. v Stratford JJ Ex p. Imbert* [1999] 2 Cr.App.R. 276, DC), Art.6(1) guarantees that everyone charged with a criminal offence has the minimum right to have adequate time and facilities to prepare a defence; therefore if the defence is taken by surprise by evidence adduced during the trial an application for an adjournment, to prepare a response to the evidence, may be justified. The *Attorney-General's Guidelines on Disclosure* (issued November 11, 2000), para.43, (*Archbold Crown Supplement*, §§ A–242 *et seq.*) provide that the prosecutor should provide to the defence all evidence on which the Crown propose to rely in a summary trial so as to allow the accused or their legal advisers sufficient time properly to consider the evidence before it is called; subject to exceptional circumstances in which statements need to be withheld for the protection of witnesses or to avoid interference with the course of justice. *R. v Kingston-Upon-Hull Justices Ex p. McCann* (1991) 155 J.P. 569 suggests that prosecutors inform defendants of their case in summary proceedings unless there are reasons for not doing so, such as the possibility of the defendant intimidating witnesses.

(2) Offences triable either way

6–12   In all either way cases the defence are entitled to be provided with advance disclosure of the prosecution case but this right only applies before the court determines mode of trial. If the parties agree to deal with mode of trial before the prosecution are able to provide advance disclosure then the parties may wish also to agree between themselves that the disclosure will be made voluntarily after mode of trial has been decided.

Criminal Law Act 1977, s.48

Power to make rules as to furnishing of information by prosecutor in criminal proceedings
6–13   **48.**—(1) The power to make rules conferred by [section 144 of the *Magistrates' Courts Act*

1980] shall, without prejudice to the generality of subsection (1) of that section, include power to make, with respect to proceedings against any person for a prescribed offence or an offence of any prescribed class, provision—

> (a) for requiring the prosecutor to do such things as may be prescribed for the purpose of securing that the accused or a person representing him is furnished with, or can obtain, advance information concerning all, or any prescribed class of, the facts and matters of which the prosecutor proposes to adduce evidence; and
>
> (b) for requiring a magistrates' court, if satisfied that any requirement imposed by virtue of paragraph (a) above has not been complied with, to adjourn the proceedings pending compliance with that requirement unless the court is satisfied that the conduct of the case for the accused will not be substantially prejudiced by non-compliance with the requirement.

(2) Rules made by virtue of subsection (1)(a) above—   **6–14**

> (a) may require the prosecutor to do as provided in the rules either—
>> (i)   in all cases; or
>> (ii) only if so requested by or on behalf of the accused;
>
> (b) may exempt facts and matters of any prescribed description from any requirement imposed by the rules, and may make the opinion of the prosecutor material for the purposes of any such exemption; and
>
> (c) may make different provision with respect to different offences or offences of different classes.

(3) It shall not open to person convicted of an offence to appeal against the conviction on the ground that a requirement imposed by virtue of subsection (1) above was not complied with by the prosecutor.

[This section is reprinted as amended by the *Magistrates' Courts Act* 1980, Sch.7, para.151.]

Magistrates' Courts (Advance Information) Rules 1985, rr.3–7

3. As soon as practicable after a person has been charged with an offence in proceedings in   **6–15**
respect of which these Rules apply or a summons has been served on a person in connection with such an offence, the prosecutor shall provide him with a notice in writing explaining the effect of Rule 4 below and setting out the address at which a request under that Rule may be made.

4.—(1) If, in any proceedings in respect of which these Rules apply, either before the magis-   **6–16**
trates' court considers whether the offence appears to be more suitable for summary trial or trial on indictment or, where the accused has not attained the age of [18] years when he appears or is brought before a magistrates' court, before he is asked whether he pleads guilty or not guilty, the accused or a person representing the accused requests the prosecutor to furnish him with advance information, the prosecutor shall, subject to Rule 5 below, furnish him as soon as practicable with either—

> (a) a copy of those parts of every written statement which contain information as to the facts and matters of which the prosecutor proposes to adduce evidence in the proceedings, or
>
> (b) a summary of the facts and matters of which the prosecutor proposes to adduce evidence in the proceedings.

(2) In paragraph (1) above, "written statement" means a statement made by a person on whose evidence the prosecutor proposes to rely in the proceedings and, where such a person has made more than one written statement one of which contains information as to all the facts and matters in relation to which the prosecutor proposes to rely on the evidence of that person, only that statement is a written statement for purposes of paragraph (1) above.

(3) Where in any part of a written statement or in a summary furnished under paragraph (1) above reference is made to a document on which the prosecutor proposes to rely, the prosecutor shall, subject to Rule 5 below, when furnishing the part of the written statement or the summary, also furnish either a copy of the document or such information as may be necessary to enable the person making the request under paragraph (1) above to inspect the document or a copy thereof.

[This rule is reprinted as amended by the *Magistrates' Courts (Criminal Justice Act 1991) (Miscellaneous Amendments) Rules* 1992, r.4(a).]

6–17   **5.**—(1) If the prosecutor is of the opinion that the disclosure of any particular fact or matter in compliance with the requirements imposed by Rule 4 above might lead to any person on whose evidence he proposes to rely in the proceedings being intimidated, to an attempt to intimidate him being made or otherwise to the course of justice being interfered with, he shall not be obliged to comply with those requirements in relation to that fact or matter.

(2) Where, in accordance with paragraph (1) above, the prosecutor considers that he is not obliged to comply with the requirements imposed by Rule 4 in relation to any particular fact or matter, he shall give notice in writing to the person who made the request under that Rule to the effect that certain advance information is being withheld by virtue of that paragraph.

6–18   **6.**—(1) Subject to paragraph (2) below, where an accused appears or is brought before a magistrates' court in proceedings in respect of which these Rules apply, the court shall, before it considers whether the offence appears to be more suitable for summary trial or trial on indictment, satisfy itself that the accused is aware of the requirements which may be imposed on the prosecutor under Rule 4 above.

(2) Where the accused has not attained the age of [18] years when he appears or is brought before a magistrates' court in proceedings in respect of which these Rules apply, the court shall, before the accused is asked whether he pleads guilty or not guilty, satisfy itself that the accused is aware of the requirements which may be imposed on the prosecutor under Rule 4 above.

[This rule is reprinted as amended by the *Magistrates' Courts (Criminal Justice Act 1991) (Miscellaneous Amendments) Rules* 1992, r.4(b).]

6–19   **7.**—(1) If, in any proceedings in respect of which these Rules apply, the court is satisfied that, a request under Rule 4 of these Rules having been made to the prosecutor by or on behalf of the accused, a requirement imposed on the prosecutor by that Rule has not been complied with, the court shall adjourn the proceedings pending compliance with the requirement unless the court is satisfied that the conduct of the case for the accused will not be substantially prejudiced by non-compliance with the requirement.

(2) Where, in the circumstances set out in paragraph (1) above, the court decides not to adjourn the proceedings, a record of that decision and of the reasons why the court was satisfied that the conduct of the case for the accused would not be substantially prejudiced by non-compliance with the requirement shall be entered in the register kept under Rule 66 of the *Magistrates' Courts Rules* 1981.

[This rule is reprinted as amended by SI 1983/523.]

6–20   The purpose of the *Advance Information Rules* 1985 is to enable the defendant and his or her advisers decide on mode of trial or plea. It is not disclosure for the purposes of subsequent committal proceedings or summary trial. Magistrates have no power to direct that advance information be served. The court should adjourn the proceedings under r.7 to allow the prosecution to comply with the advance information rules: *R. v Dunmow Justices Ex p. Nash* (1993) 157 J.P. 1153.

Failure to provide the defendant with advance information is not of itself an abuse of process although continuing default might become an abuse of process: *R. v Willesden Magistrates' Court Ex p. Clemmings* (1988) 152 J.P.N. 46. Nor does such a failure provide grounds for an information to be dismissed: *King v Kucharz* (1989) 153 J.P. 336.

Rule 4 requires the prosecution to supply a written statement containing the facts and matters on which the prosecutor proposes to adduce evidence in the proceedings, or a summary of the facts and matters of which the prosecutor proposes to adduce evidence in the proceedings. A document includes a video for these purposes: *R. v Calderdale Magistrates' Court Ex p. Donahue and Cutler* [2001] Crim.L.R. 141, DC. Where a summary of facts and matters upon which the prosecution intends to rely supplied in accordance with rule 4 contains a reference to DNA profiles that is not a reference to a document on which the prosecutor proposes to rely within the meaning of r.4(3): *R v Croydon Magistrates' Court* [2001] Crim.L.R. 980, DC.

6–21   The prosecution, including local authorities, should reveal the identity of a complainant at an early stage before advance disclosure: *Daventry District Council v Olins* [1990] C.O.D. 244, DC.

II. DISCLOSURE OF MATERIAL WHICH IS NOT RELIED UPON AS EVIDENCE

A. GENERAL

With regard to offences into which a criminal investigation was commenced on or af- **6–22** ter April 1, 1997 the duties and responsibilities of parties with regard to disclosure are contained in Pts I and II of the *Criminal Procedure and Investigations Act* 1996. Part I created an initial staged approach to disclosure. Part II provides for the creation of a code of practice for regulating the conduct of the police in recording and retaining material obtained in the course of a criminal investigation and providing it to the prosecution who then decides on disclosure. The Attorney-General has also issued guidelines on the disclosure of information.

In *R. v Norfolk Stipendiary Magistrate Ex p. Keable* [1998] Crim.L.R. 510 the defendant had been the subject of police surveillance before the appointed day. By virtue of s.1(3) of the Act, Pt I only applied to alleged offences into which no criminal investigation had started prior to the appointed day. The Divisional Court rejected his argument that "alleged offence" has a broader meaning than an offence for which an accused had been charged and included suspected offences which had not been the subject of any charge on the basis that "alleged offences" was intended to mean offences in respect of which an accused had been charged. A criminal investigation begun before the alleged commission of an offence could not properly be described as an investigation into that offence. Where an alleged offence was committed after the appointed day, the duties of the prosecutor under Pt I arose regardless of any prior investigations into related offences which were suspected rather than charged.

B. THE HUMAN RIGHTS ACT 1998

The right to fair trial means that the prosecution should disclose to the defence all **6–23** material evidence in their possession for and against the defendant. Only such measures restricting the right of the defence to disclosure which are strictly necessary are permissible: *Rowe and Davies v UK* (2000) 30 E.H.R.R. 1.

In *R. v B* December 21, 2000, unreported, CA (Crim Div), the court held that the correct approach had been taken to disclosure by balancing the public interest in the need to protect children against the interest of the defendant when determining whether documents bearing on the reliability of the complainants should have been disclosed to the defendant. The balancing approach was compatible with Art.6 which recognised the need to limit the right to disclosure where the public interest so required.

C. DISCLOSURE AT COMMON LAW

Criminal Procedure and Investigations Act 1996, s.21

Common law rules as to disclosure

21.—(1) Where this Part applies as regards things falling to be done after the relevant time in **6–24** relation to an alleged offence, the rules of common law which—

    (a) were effective immediately before the appointed day, and

    (b) relate to the disclosure of material by the prosecutor,

do not apply as regards things falling to be done after that time in relation to the alleged offence.

    (2) Subsection (1) does not affect the rules of common law as to whether disclosure is in the public interest.

    (3) References in subsection (1) to the relevant time are to the time when—

    (a) the accused pleads not guilty (where this Part applies by virtue of section 1(1)),

    (b) the accused is committed for trial (where this Part applies by virtue of section 1(2)(a))

(c) the proceedings are transferred (where this Part applies by virtue of section 1(2)(b) or (c),

(d) the count is included in the indictment (where this Part applies by virtue of section 1(2)(d), or

(e) the bill of indictment is preferred (where this Part applies by virtue of section 1(2)(e)).

(4) The reference in subsection (1) to the appointed day is to the day appointed under section 1(5).

6–25   The common law rules on the disclosure of material by the prosecution to the defence continue to apply notwithstanding the Act to cases where the investigation began before April 1, 1997.

The Act does not alter the common law rules as to whether disclosure is in the public interest, although it does regulate the procedure for making an application to the court for permission to withhold material for which public interest immunity is claimed: see below.

The Act does not abolish the common law obligations relating to the disclosure of information by the prosecution prior to committal for trial in the Crown Court. However, the provisions of the Act are such as to require that those obligations be radically recast: *R. v DPP Ex p. Lee* [1999] 2 Cr.App.R. 304, DC. In particular, the insertion of ss.5A to 5F of the *Magistrates' Courts Act* 1980 reduced the ability of the defendant to participate actively in the committal hearing. Consequently the need for disclosure prior to committal is correspondingly reduced. The disclosure requirements under the Act are intended to be less extensive that would have been required at common law. Although some disclosure may have been required prior to committal, it would undermine the statutory provisions if the defence's right to discovery pre-committal were to exceed the discovery obtainable after committal pursuant to the statute.

6–26   The prosecution's obligation of disclosure at common law is sufficient to require disclosure even where proceedings were instituted by summons for a speeding offence: *R. v Stratford Magistrates' Court Ex p. Johnson* [2003] EWHC 353. The applicant argued the magistrate was incorrect in construing s.1 of the *Criminal Procedure and Investigations Act* 1996 as meaning that it did not apply to proceedings instituted by way of summons. The Divisional Court considered that it was unnecessary to determine the scope of s.1 of the 1996 Act because the prosecution's obligation of disclosure at common law was sufficient to require disclosure in the case.

D. PROSECUTION PRIMARY DISCLOSURE

Criminal Procedure and Investigations Act 1996, s.1

Application of this Part

6–27   **1.**—(1) This Part applies where—

(a) a person is charged with a summary offence in respect of which a court proceeds to summary trial and in respect of which he pleads not guilty,

(b) a person who has attained the age of 18 is charged with an offence which is triable either way, in respect of which a court proceeds to summary trial and in respect of which he pleads not guilty, or

(c) a person under the age of 18 is charged with an indictable offence in respect of which a court proceeds to summary trial and in respect of which he pleads not guilty.

(2) This Part also applies where—

(a) a person is charged with an indictable offence and he is committed for trial for the offence concerned,

(b) a person is charged with an indictable offence and proceedings for the trial of the person on the charge concerned are transferred to the Crown Court by virtue of a notice of transfer given under section 4 of the *Criminal Justice Act* 1987 (serious or complex fraud),

(c) a person is charged with an indictable offence and proceedings for the trial of the person on the charge concerned are transferred to the Crown Court by virtue of a notice of transfer served on a magistrates' court under section 53 of the *Criminal Justice Act* 1991 (certain cases involving children),

 (cc) a person is charged with an offence for which he is sent for trial under section 51 (no committal proceedings for indictable-only offences) of the *Crime and Disorder Act* 1998,

[or

  (f) a bill of indictment charging a person with an indictable offence is preferred under section 22B(3)(a) of the *Prosecution of Offences Act* 1985.]

 (d) a count charging a person with a summary offence is included in an indictment under the authority of section 40 of the *Criminal Justice Act* 1988 (common assault etc.), or

 (e) a bill of indictment charging a person with an indictable offence is preferred under the authority of section 2(2)(b) of the *Administration of Justice (Miscellaneous Provisions) Act* 1933 (bill preferred by direction of Court of Appeal, or by direction or with consent of a judge).

(3) This Part applies in relation to alleged offences into which no criminal investigation has begun before the appointed day.

(4) For the purposes of this section a criminal investigation is an investigation which police officers or other persons have a duty to conduct with a view to it being ascertained—

 (a) whether a person should be charged with an offence, or

 (b) whether a person charged with an offence is guilty of it.

(5) The reference in subsection (3) to the appointed day is to such day as is appointed for the purposes of this Part by the Secretary of State by order.

[This section is reprinted as amended by the *Crime and Disorder Act* 1998, Sch.8, para.125(b).]

The prosecutor's duty of primary disclosure applies when the accused pleads not **6–28** guilty and the court proceeds to summary trial. The disclosure obligations on the prosecution in s.3 only apply if the accused has pleaded not guilty: s.1. The defence is not entitled to disclosure where the accused has pleaded guilty or where the accused has been committed for sentence to the Crown Court following a plea in the magistrates' court. It is only in respect of summary trials that the prosecution is obliged to make primary disclosure. The prosecution's disclosure obligations do not apply to the pre-committal stage. As regards disclosure at this stage the common law rules on disclosure apply: s.21(3)(b), see above.

In *R. v DPP Ex p. Lee* [1999] 2 Cr.App.R. 304, CA (Crim Div), the court considered the timing and extent of the prosecution's disclosure obligations. The disclosure provisions of the *Criminal Procedure and Investigations Act* 1996 commence when the court proceeds to summary trial or in the case of an offence triable on indictment upon committal for trial. Receiving disclosure at this stage ordinarily would not undermine the defendant's right to a fair trial. The prosecution should be aware of the need for advance disclosure of material which he or she recognises should be disclosed at that stage in the interests of justice and fairness. Four examples were considered: (a) prior convictions of a complainant or a deceased which might assist the defendant in a bail application; (b) material which might assist in applying for a stay of proceedings as an abuse of process; (c) material which might support a submission that the defendant should be committed on a lesser charge, or not at all, and (d) material which would allow preparation for trial in a significantly more effective manner than if disclosure were delayed, for example the names of witnesses the prosecution did not intend to call, it was clear that early disclosure in all cases would not normally exceed primary disclosure under s.3, being disclosure of material thought to undermine the prosecution's case. To the extent that a defendant revealed material normally disclosed in the defence statement, secondary disclosure, triggered in response to a defence statement, should be made in advance in respect of examples (a), (b) and (c), but disclosure of material of type (d) would depend on what the defendant revealed.

Criminal Procedure and Investigations Act 1996, ss.3–4

Primary disclosure by prosecutor

6–29   **3.**—(1) The prosecutor must—

(a) disclose to the accused any prosecution material which has not previously been disclosed to the accused and which in the prosecutor's opinion might undermine the case for the prosecution against the accused, or

(b) give to the accused a written statement that there is no material of a description mentioned in paragraph (a)

(2) For the purposes of this section prosecution material is material—

(a) which is in the prosecutor's possession, and came into his possession in connection with the case for the prosecution against the accused, or

(b) which, in pursuance of a code operative under Part II, he has inspected in connection with the case for the prosecution against the accused.

(3) Where material consists of information which has been recorded in any form the prosecutor discloses it for the purposes of this section—

(a) by securing that a copy is made of it and that the copy is given to the accused, or

(b) if in the prosecutor's opinion that is not practicable or not desirable, by allowing the accused to inspect it at a reasonable time and a reasonable place or by taking steps to secure that he is allowed to do so;

and a copy may be in such form as the prosecutor thinks fit and need not be in the same form as that in which the information has already been recorded.

(4) Where material consists of information which has not been recorded the prosecutor discloses it for the purposes of this section by securing that it is recorded in such form as he thinks fit and—

(a) by securing that a copy is made of it and that the copy is given to the accused, or

(b) if in the prosecutor's opinion that is not practicable or not desirable, by allowing the accused to inspect it at a reasonable time and a reasonable place or by taking steps to secure that he is allowed to do so.

(5) Where material does not consist of information the prosecutor discloses it for the purposes of this section by allowing the accused to inspect it at a reasonable time and a reasonable place or by taking steps to secure that he is allowed to do so.

(6) Material must not be disclosed under this section to the extent that the court, on an application by the prosecutor, concludes it is not in the public interest to disclose it and orders accordingly.

(7) Material must not be disclosed under this section to the extent that [it is material the disclosure of which is prohibited by section 17 of the *Regulation of Investigatory Powers Act* 2000.]

[...]

(8) The prosecutor must act under this section during the period which, by virtue of section 12, is the relevant period for this section.

[This section is reprinted as amended by the *Regulation of Investigatory Powers Act* 2000, Sch.4, para.7(1).]

Primary disclosure: further provisions

6–30   **4.**—(1) This section applies where—

(a) the prosecutor acts under section 3, and

(b) before so doing he was given a document in pursuance of provision included, by virtue of section 24(3), in a code operative under Part II.

(2) In such a case the prosecutor must give the document to the accused at the same time as the prosecutor acts under section 3.

The prosecution is obliged to disclose previously undisclosed material to the accused if in the prosecutor's opinion, it might undermine the prosecution's case. If there is no such material then the defence must be given written notice to that effect.

The decision as to whether primary disclosure should be made is for the prosecution: *R. v B* [2000] Crim.L.R. 50. The assistance of a judge should only be sought if he or she can properly decide the question, such as when there is an issue of public interest immunity: see below. The defendant's conviction was quashed because the prosecution had asked the judge to read documents and consider whether they should be disclosed to the defence as undermining the prosecution case thereby transferring the responsibility for judging the weight and impact of the material.

It is a denial of natural justice for a prosecutor to fail to disclose witnesses' statements **6–31** favourable to the defence or to call witnesses: *R. v Leyland Justices Ex p. Hawthorn* [1979] 1 Q.B. 283. The defendant was convicted of driving without due care and attention contrary to the *Road Traffic Act* 1972, s.3. In issue at the trial was whether his car had been either partly or wholly over the centre line of the road. After the trial the police notified the defendant's solicitors of the existence of two further witnesses whose evidence might have been helpful to him. The police had not called these witnesses nor disclosed the existence of statements from these witnesses before. The conviction was quashed.

Where pivotal prosecution evidence comes from a witness with a known prison record it is incumbent upon the prosecution to acquire the prison records. Where disclosure is late, or does not occur, of material relating to a super grass, the test is: had disclosure occurred earlier, or at all, would the information have given rise to cross examination which would or might have materially affected the witnesses' credibility? See *R. v McCartney, Hamlett* [2003] 6 *Archbold News* 2, CA. Non-disclosure of an important witness' previous convictions will not inevitably lead to a conviction being quashed. Convictions will be upheld where the Court of Appeal concludes that the jury would have convicted in any event: *R. v Underwood* (2003) 147 S.J.L.B. 657, CA. Where materials are withheld from the court at first instance and the Court of Appeal, a violation of the right to a fair trial under Article 6 will have occurred: *Dowsett v UK*, *The Times*, July 12, 2003, ECHR. Failure to disclose a previous witness statement that may have undermined a witness's credibility where the evidence determined a guilty verdict will render a conviction unsafe: *R. v Kelly (deceased)*; *R. v Connolly (deceased)* [2003] EWCA Crim 2957.

In *R. v Vasiliou* [2000] Crim.L.R. 845 the Court of Appeal held that the defendant's **6–32** conviction had been rendered unsafe because he could not challenge prosecution witnesses as to their character as the prosecution had not disclosed their previous convictions. Likewise in *R. v Eccleston* unreported, July 1, 2001, CA (Crim Div) the court said that where there has been a failure to disclose the convictions of a prosecution witness, the question was how relevant the missing information was likely to be to the defence, with that view varying according to whether the witness was the complainant or a third party witness whose evidence was not central to the issue. However in both of these cases the court did not consider what triggers the duty of the prosecution to make such disclosure.

In *R. v Mills and Poole* [1998] A.C. 382, the House of Lords considered whether the prosecution has a duty to disclose the name and address of a witness who had given a statement but whom the prosecution had decided not to call because they regarded the witness as unreliable. The defence argued that the rule in *R. v Bryant*, 31 Cr.App.R. 146, which distinguished between disclosing the statement of a credible witness to the defence and informing the defence about a witness considered to be untruthful, could no longer be sustained, as it conflicted with Court of Appeal decisions emphasising the importance of full prosecution disclosure. The House of Lords held that in some circumstances *Bryant* could result in an injustice and should not be retained unless there was strong argument to do so. The risk that disclosure could help the defence to tailor its evidence was outweighed by the risk of injustice and the rule did not conform with the principles of disclosure enunciated since 1990. Therefore, the rule should no longer be applied and the failure to disclose the statement represented a material irregularity in the course of the trial.

The identity of persons who might have witnessed an incident giving rise to criminal **6–33** charges is material capable of undermining the prosecution case or supporting the defence case. Those who dial 999 to report such an incident fall into that category so the duty of disclosure extends to the telephone numbers of the makers of such calls. A general principle of non-disclosure of the identity of persons making 999 calls could not be justified there being no basis in the ordinary course of events for any expectation of confidentiality. However it may be possible to argue otherwise in an individual case: *R. v Heggart* [2001] 1 *Archbold News* 2, CA.

The prosecution may be obliged to disclose the statements of co-defendants: *R. v Cairns* [2003] 1 Cr.App.R. 38. At trial the defendant had requested disclosure of the witness statements of her co-defendants but had been refused on the basis that the *Criminal Procedure and Investigations Act* 1996, s.5(5) limited such disclosure to the prosecution and to the court. The Court of Appeal (Crim Div) held that the statements of both co-defendants should have been disclosed because the prosecution was obliged to disclose a defence statement to a co-defendant if there was a chance that it would assist that co-defendant in his or her own defence.

The prosecution are not entitled to withhold information even if they consider that the defendant is unlikely to use the information during the trial: *R. v Hilton* [2003] EWCA Crim 761. The defendant contended that the prosecution should have disclosed material that resulted from the search of a witness's house, who the prosecution argued the defendant had asked to obtain fake Rolex watches. The Crown argued that even if the material had been disclosed it was unlikely that he would have used it. The Court of Appeal (Crim Div) allowed the appeal on the basis that it was unlikely that the defendant would not have used the undisclosed material in his defence.

6–34   A failure by the prosecution to make proper primary disclosure may result in a defence application to stay proceedings as an abuse of process.

E. Defence Disclosure

6–35   In cases to be tried summarily, the accused is under no obligation to provide a defence case statement or notice of alibi. Compulsory disclosure by the accused only arises where the case is to be tried on indictment and even then does not have to be undertaken until the case has been committed, sent or transferred for trial.

Criminal Procedure and Investigations Act 1996, s.5

Compulsory disclosure by accused

     5.—(1) Subject to subsections (2) to (4), this section applies where—

     (a) this Part applies by virtue of section 1(2), and

     (b) the prosecutor complies with section 3 or purports to comply with it.

     (2) Where this Part applies by virtue of section 1(2)(b), this section does not apply unless—

     (a) a copy of the notice of transfer, and

     (b) copies of the documents containing the evidence.

have been given to the accused under regulations made under section 5(9) of the *Criminal Justice Act* 1987.

     (3) Where this Part applies by virtue of section 1(2)(c), this section does not apply unless—

     (a) a copy of the notice of transfer, and

     (b) copies of the documents containing the evidence.

have been given to the accused under regulations made under paragraph 4 of Schedule 6 to the *Criminal Justice Act* 1991.

     [(3A) Where this Part applies by virtue of section 1(2)(cc), this section does not apply unless—

     (a) copies of the documents containing the evidence have been served on the accused under regulations made under paragraph 1 of Schedule 3 to the *Crime and Disorder Act* 1998; and

     (b) a copy of the notice under subsection (7) of section 51 of that Act has been served on him under that subsection.]

     (4) Where this Part applies by virtue of section 1(2)(e), this section does not apply unless the prosecutor has served on the accused a copy of the indictment and a copy of the set of documents containing the evidence which is the basis of the charge.

(5) Where this section applies, the accused must give a defence statement to the court and the prosecutor.

(6) For the purposes of this section a defence statement is a written statement—

(a) setting out in general terms the nature of the accused's defence,

(b) indicating the matters on which he takes issue with the prosecution, and

(c) setting out, in the case of each such matter, the reason why he takes issue with the prosecution.

(7) If the defence statement discloses an alibi the accused must give particulars of the alibi in the statement, including—

(a) the name and address of any witness the accused believes is able to give evidence in support of the alibi, if the name and address are known to the accused when the statement is given;

(b) any information in the accused's possession which might be of material assistance in finding any such witness, if his name or address is not known to the accused when the statement is given.

(8) For the purposes of this section evidence in support of an alibi is evidence tending to show that by reason of the presence of the accused at a particular place or in a particular area at a particular time he was not, or was unlikely to have been, at the place where the offence is alleged to have been committed at the time of its alleged commission.

(9) The accused must give a defence statement under this section during the period which, by virtue of section 12 is the relevant period for this section.

[This section is reprinted as amended by the *Crime and Disorder Act* 1998, s.119 and Sch.8, para.126.]

Once primary prosecution disclosure has occurred and the case is committed to trial **6–36** in the Crown Court, the defendant must give a defence statement to the prosecution.

Criminal Procedure and Investigations Act 1996 (Defence Disclosure Time Limits) Regulations 1997, regs.2, 3

2. Subject to regulations 3, 4 and 5, the relevant period for sections 5 and 6 of the Act **6–37** (disclosure by the accused) is a period beginning with the day on which the prosecutor complies, or purports to comply, with section 3 of that Act and ending with the expiration of 14 days from that day.

3.—(1) The period referred to in regulation 2 shall, if the court so orders, be extended by so **6–38** many days as the court specifies.

(2) The court may only make such an order if an application which complies with paragraph (3) below is made by the accused before the expiration of the period referred to in regulation 2.

(3) An application under paragraph (2) above shall—

(a) state that the accused believes, on reasonable grounds, that it is not possible for him to give a defence statement under section 5 or, as the case may be, 6 of the Act during the period referred to in regulation 2;

(b) specify the grounds for so believing; and

(c) specify the number of days by which the accused wishes that period to be extended.

(4) The court shall not make an order under paragraph (1) above unless it is satisfied that the accused cannot reasonably give or, as the case may be, could not reasonably have given a defence statement under section 5 or, as the case may be, 6 of the Act during the period referred to in regulation 2.

(5) The number of days by which the period referred to in regulation 2 may be extended shall be entirely at the court's discretion.

The defendant has 14 days within which to give his or her defence statement to the **6–39** prosecution. On application by the defendant made within 14 days the court may extend the time for submission of the defence statement.

Voluntary disclosure by accused

Criminal Procedure and Investigations Act 1996, s.6

6.—(1) This section applies where—   **6–40**

(a) this Part applies by virtue of section 1(1), and

(b) the prosecutor complies with section 3 or purports to comply with it.

(2) The accused—

(a) may give a defence statement to the prosecutor, and

(b) if he does so, must also give such a statement to the court.

(3) Subsection (6) to (8) of section 5 apply for the purposes of this section as they apply for the purposes of that.

(4) If the accused gives a defence statement under this section he must give it during the period which, by virtue of section 12 is the relevant period for this section.

Where the defendant will be tried summarily he or she may give a defence statement to the prosecution following the making of primary disclosure by the prosecution.. Although no adverse inference can be drawn against a defendant who fails to provide a statement, the prosecution have no obligation to provide secondary disclosure unless a defence case statement is served.

A defence statement is a convenient expression used to include the nature of the defence, the matters on which issue is taken and the reasons for taking issue. It is not to be restricted to the general legal description of the defence: *R. v Tibbs* [2000] 2 Cr.App.R. 309, CA. In that case the Court of Appeal (Crim Div) held that giving the word "defence" a limited legal meaning would frustrate the purpose of the Act. Its aim was to ensure both parties had the opportunity to investigate matters relied on by the opposite side and to prevent miscarriages of justice. It would be difficult to compare a restrictive defence statement with the defence given at trial. The defence statement was defined generally as the nature of the defence, the matters on which issue was taken, and the reasons why issue was being taken.

6–41   Where the defendant, upon being confronted with a contradiction between the evidence and the defence statement, asserts that the latter contains a mistake, a judge ought to raise the matter with counsel: *R. v Wheeler* [2001] 1 Cr.App.R. 10, CA. If an defendant volunteers a defence statement in a summary trial, there is the risk that an adverse inference may be drawn if the defence statement is inconsistent with the defence advanced at trial. Section 11 does not disallow or require leave for cross-examination of a defendant on differences between the defence at trial and the defence statement. It was unnecessary under s.11(3) to apply for leave to cross-examine the defendant on differences in the defence and the defence statement: *R. v Tibbs* above.

It is good practice for the defence statement to be signed by the defendant: *R. v Wheeler* above. However a judge has no power to issue a practice direction to the effect that the defendant must sign the defence statement. Where a defence statement is unsigned a judge may require the defendant to satisfy him or her that the defendant has complied with the obligations under the Act be confirming that the document is his or her statement: *R. v Maidstone Crown Court Ex p. Sullivan* [2002] EWHC 967.

If the defence is one of alibi then the defence statement must contain the name and address of the proposed alibi witness or where that information is not available, any information which might be of assistance in locating the witness.

6–42   The Professional Conduct and Complaints Committee of the Bar Council has issued guidance as to the duties of counsel in relation to the preparation of defence statements. There is nothing unprofessional about counsel drafting a defence case statement. Counsel has no obligation to do so if requested to do so for no fee; in publicly funded cases there is no provision for a fee to be payable for this task, unless counsel is assigned under the Representation Order which is most unlikely in a case to be tried summarily. The guidance reminds counsel of the importance of the need to have all the relevant evidence and statements from other material witnesses, as well as the importance of obtaining informed approval from the client before drafting the statement. The guidance is reproduced in full in *Archbold Crown*, § 12–99a.

F. SECONDARY PROSECUTION DISCLOSURE

Criminal Procedure and Investigations Act 1996, s.7

Secondary disclosure by prosecutor

7.—(1) This section applies where the accused gives a defence statement under section 5 or 6. **6–43**

(2) The prosecutor must—

(a) disclose to the accused any prosecution material which has not previously been disclosed to the accused and which might be reasonably expected to assist the accused's defence as disclosed by the defence statement given under section 5 or 6, or

(b) give to the accused a written statement that there is no material of a description mentioned in paragraph (a).

(3) For the purposes of this section prosecution material is material—

(a) which is in the prosecutor's possession and came into his possession in connection with the case for the prosecution against the accused, or

(b) which, in pursuance of a code operative under Part II, he has inspected in connection with the case for the prosecution against the accused.

(4) Subsections (3) to (5) of section 3 (method by which prosecutor discloses) apply for the purposes of this section as they apply for the purposes of that.

(5) Material must not be disclosed under this section to the extent that the court, on an application by the prosecutor, concludes it is not in the public interest to disclose it and orders accordingly.

(6) Material must not be disclosed under this section to the extent that [it is material the disclosure of which is prohibited by section 17 of the *Regulation of Investigatory Powers Act* 2000.]

[...]

(7) The prosecutor must act under this section during the period which, by virtue of section 12 is the relevant period for this section.

[This section is reprinted as amended by the *Regulation of Investigatory Powers Act* 2000, Sch.4, para.7(1).]

If there has been voluntary defence disclosure of a defence statement, the prosecu- **6–44** tion must comply with its secondary disclosure obligations under s.7.

The definition of "prosecution material" in s.7(3) is the same definition as that provided in respect of primary disclosure in s.3(2) of the Act: *R. v Cairns* in § 6–33 above.

G. TIME LIMITS

Criminal Procedure and Investigations Act 1996, s.10

Prosecutor's failure to observe time limits

10.—(1) This section applies if the prosecutor— **6–45**

(a) purports to act under section 3 after the end of the period which, by virtue of section 12, is the relevant period for section 3, or

(b) purports to act under section 7 after the end of the period which, by virtue of section 12, is the relevant period for section 7.

(2) Subject to subsection (3) the failure to act during the period concerned does not on its own constitute grounds for staying the proceedings for abuse of process.

(3) Subsection (2) does not prevent the failure constituting such grounds if it involves such delay by the prosecutor that the accused is denied a fair trial.

Criminal Procedure and Investigations Act 1996, s.12

Time limits

12.—(1) This section has effect for the purpose of determining the relevant period for sec- **6–46** tions 3, 5, 6 and 7.

(2) Subject to subsection (3), the relevant period is a period beginning and ending with such days as the Secretary of State prescribes by regulations for the purposes of the section concerned.

(3) The regulations may do one or more of the following—

(a) provide that the relevant period for any section shall if the court so orders be extended (or further extended) by so many days as the court specifies;

(b) provide that the court may only make such an order if an application is made by a prescribed person and if any other prescribed conditions are fulfilled;

(c) provide that an application may only be made if prescribed conditions are fulfilled;

(d) provide that the number of days by which a period may be extended shall be entirely at the court's discretion;

(e) provide that the number of days by which a period may be extended shall not exceed a prescribed number;

(f) provide that there shall be no limit on the number of applications that may be made to extend a period;

(g) provide that no more than a prescribed number of applications may be made to extend a period;

and references to the relevant period for a section shall be construed accordingly.

(4) Conditions mentioned in subsection (3) may be framed by reference to such factors as the Secretary of State thinks fit.

(5) Without prejudice to the generality of subsection (4), so far as the relevant period for section 3 or 7 is concerned—

(a) conditions may be framed by reference to the nature or volume of the material concerned;

(b) the nature of material may be defined by reference to the prosecutor's belief that the question of non-disclosure on grounds of public interest may arise.

(6) In subsection (3) "prescribed" means prescribed by regulations under this section.

H. Prosecution's Continuing Duty to Review Disclosure

Criminal Procedure and Investigations Act 1996, s.9

Continuing duty of prosecutor to disclose

6–47   **9.**—(1) Subsection (2) applies at all times—

(a) after the prosecutor complies with section 3 or purports to comply with it, and

(b) before the accused is acquitted or convicted or the prosecutor decides not to proceed with the case concerned.

(2) The prosecutor must keep under review the question whether at any given time there is prosecution material which—

(a) in his opinion might undermine the case for the prosecution against the accused, and

(b) has not been disclosed to the accused;

and if there is such material at any time the prosecutor must disclose it to the accused as soon as is reasonably practicable.

(3) In applying subsection (2) by reference to any given time the state of affairs at that time (including the case for the prosecution as it stands at that time) must be taken into account.

(4) Subsection (5) applies at all times—

(a) after the prosecutor complies with section 7 or purports to comply with it, and

(b) before the accused is acquitted or convicted or the prosecutor decides not to proceed with the case concerned.

(5) The prosecutor must keep under review the question whether at any given time there is prosecution material which—

(a) might be reasonably expected to assist the accused's defence as disclosed by the defence statement given under section 5 or 6, and

(b) has not been disclosed to the accused;

and if there is such material at any time the prosecutor must disclose it to the accused as soon as is reasonably practicable.

(6) For the purposes of this section prosecution material is material— **6–48**

(a) which is in the prosecutor's possession and came into his possession in connection with the case for the prosecution against the accused, or

(b) which, in pursuance of a code operative under Part II, he has inspected in connection with the case for the prosecution against the accused.

(7) Subsections (3) to (5) of section 3 (method by which prosecutor discloses) apply for the purposes of this section as they apply for the purposes of that.

(8) Material must not be disclosed under this section to the extent that the court, on an application by the prosecutor, concludes it is not in the public interest to disclose it and orders accordingly.

(9) Material must not be disclosed under this section to the extent that [it is material the disclosure of which is prohibited by section 17 of the *Regulation of Investigatory Powers Act* 2000.]

[…]

[This section is reprinted as amended by the *Regulation of Investigatory Powers Act* 2000, Sch.4, para.7(1).]

I. APPLICATION FOR DISCLOSURE

Criminal Procedure and Investigations Act 1996, s.8

Application by accused for disclosure

8.—(1) This section applies where the accused gives a defence statement under section 5 or 6 **6–49** and the prosecutor complies with section 7 or purports to comply with it or fails to comply with it.

(2) If the accused has at any time reasonable cause to believe that—

(a) there is prosecution material which might be reasonably expected to assist the accused's defence as disclosed by the defence statement given under section 5 or 6 and

(b) the material has not been disclosed to the accused,

the accused may apply to the court for an order requiring the prosecutor to disclose such material to the accused.

(3) For the purposes of this section prosecution material is material—

(a) which is in the prosecutor's possession and came into his possession in connection with the case for the prosecution against the accused.

(b) which, in pursuance of a code operative under Part II, he has inspected in connection with the case for the prosecution against the accused, or

(c) which falls within subsection (4).

(4) Material falls within this subsection if in pursuance of a code operative under Part II the prosecutor must, if he asks for the material, be given a copy of it or be allowed to inspect it in connection with the case for the prosecution against the accused.

(5) Material must not be disclosed under this section to the extent that the court, on an application by the prosecutor, concludes it is not in the public interest to disclose it and orders accordingly.

(6) Material must not be disclosed under this section to the extent that [it is material the disclosure of which is prohibited by section 17 of the *Regulation of Investigatory Powers Act* 2000.]

[This section is reprinted as amended by the *Regulation of Investigatory Powers Act* 2000, Sch.4, para.7(1).]

If a defence statement has been served and the accused or his or her legal advisors **6–50** have reasonable cause to believe that the prosecution possesses material which might assist the accused's case, the accused may apply to the court for an order requiring the material to be disclosed.

Magistrates' Courts (Criminal Procedure and Investigations Act 1996) Disclosure Rules 1997, r.7

Disclosure: application by accused and order of court

6–51   **7.**—(1) This rule applies to an application by the accused under section 8(2).

(2) An application to which this rule applies shall be made by notice in writing to the [justices' chief executive for] the court and shall specify—

   (a) the material to which the application relates;

   (b) that the material has not been disclosed to the accused;

   (c) the reason why the material might be expected to assist the applicant's defence as disclosed by the defence statement given under section 6; and

   (d) the date of service of a copy of the notice on the prosecutor in accordance with paragraph (3) below.

(3) A copy of the notice referred to in paragraph (2) above shall be served on the prosecutor at the same time as it is sent to the [justices' chief executive for] the court.

(4) The prosecutor shall give notice in writing to the [justices' chief executive for] the court within 14 days of service of a notice under paragraph (3) above that—

   (a) he wishes to make representations to the court concerning the material to which the application relates; or

   (b) if he does not so wish, that he is willing to disclose that material;

and a notice under sub-paragraph (a) above shall specify the substance of the representations he wishes to make.

6–52   (5) Subject to paragraphs (6) and (7) below—

   (a) the [justices' chief executive for] the court shall give notice in writing to the prosecutor and the applicant of the date and time when and the place where the hearing will take place;

   (b) the hearing shall be inter partes; and

   (c) the prosecutor and the applicant shall be entitled to make representations to the court.

(6) The court may determine the application without hearing representations from the applicant or the prosecutor unless—

   (a) the prosecutor has given notice under paragraph (4)(a) above and the court considers that the representations should be made at a hearing; or

   (b) the court considers it necessary to hear representations from the applicant or the prosecutor in the interests of justice for the purposes of determining the application.

(7) Where the prosecutor applies to the court for leave to make representations in the absence of the accused, the court may for that purpose sit in the absence of the accused and any legal representative of his.

J. CODE OF PRACTICE

Criminal Procedure and Investigations Act 1996, ss.23–27

Code of practice

6–53   **23.**—(1) The Secretary of State shall prepare a code of practice containing provisions designed to secure—

   (a) that where a criminal investigation is conducted all reasonable steps are taken for the purposes of the investigation and, in particular, all reasonable lines of inquiry are pursued;

   (b) that information which is obtained in the course of a criminal investigation and may be relevant to the investigation is recorded;

   (c) that any record of such information is retained;

   (d) that any other material which is obtained in the course of a criminal investigation and may be relevant to the investigation is retained;

   (e) that information falling within paragraph (b) and material falling within paragraph (d) is revealed to a person who is involved in the prosecution of criminal proceedings arising out of or relating to the investigation and who is identified in accordance with prescribed provisions;

   (f) that where such a person inspects information or other material in pursuance of a requirement that it be revealed to him, and he requests that it be disclosed to the accused, the accused is allowed to inspect it or is given a copy of it;

   (g) that where such a person is given a document indicating the nature of information or other material in pursuance of a requirement that it be revealed to him, and he requests that it be disclosed to the accused, the accused is allowed to inspect it or is given a copy of it;

   (h) that the person who is to allow the accused to inspect information or other material or to give him a copy of it shall decide which of those (inspecting or giving a copy) is appropriate;

   (i) that where the accused is allowed to inspect material as mentioned in paragraph (f) or (g) and he requests a copy, he is given one unless the person allowing the inspection is of opinion that it is not practicable or not desirable to give him one;

   (j) that a person mentioned in paragraph (e) is given a written statement that prescribed activities which the code requires have been carried out.

  (2) The code may include provision—

   (a) that a police officer identified in accordance with prescribed provisions must carry out a prescribed activity which the code requires;

   (b) that a police officer so identified must take steps to secure the carrying out by a person (whether or not a police officer) of a prescribed activity which the code requires;

   (c) that a duty must be discharged by different people in succession in prescribed circumstances (as where a person dies or retires).

  (3) The code may include provision about the form in which information is to be recorded.

  (4) The code may include provision about the manner in which and the period for **6–54** which—

   (a) a record of information is to be retained, and

   (b) any other material is to be retained;

and if a person is charged with an offence the period may extend beyond a conviction or an acquittal.

  (5) The code may include provision about the time when, the form in which, the way in which, and the extent to which, information or any other material is to be revealed to the person mentioned in subsection (1)(c).

  (6) The code must be so framed that it does not apply to material intercepted in obedience to a warrant issued under section 2 of the *Interception of Communications Act* 1985 [or under the authority of an interception warrant under section 5 of the *Regulation of Investigatory Powers Act* 2000.]

  (7) The code may—

   (a) make different provision in relation to different cases or descriptions of case;

   (b) contain exceptions as regards prescribed cases or descriptions of case.

  (8) In this section "prescribed" means prescribed by the code.

[This section is reprinted as amended by the *Regulation of Investigatory Powers Act* 2000, Sch.4, para.7(2).]

Examples of disclosure provisions

  24.—(1) This section gives examples of the kinds of provision that may be included in the **6–55** code by virtue of section 23(5).

  (2) The code may provide that if the person required to reveal material has possession of material which he believes is sensitive he must give a document which—

   (a) indicates the nature of that material, and

   (b) states that he so believes.

  (3) The code may provide that if the person required to reveal material has possession of material which is of a description prescribed under this subsection and which he does not believe is sensitive he must give a document which—

   (a) indicates the nature of that material, and

   (b) states that he does not so believe.

  (4) The code may provide that if—

(a) a document is given in pursuance of provision contained in the code by virtue of subsection (2), and

(b) a person identified in accordance with prescribed provisions asks for any of the material,

the person giving the document must give a copy of the material asked for to the person asking for it or (depending on the circumstances) must allow him to inspect it.

6–56   (5) The code may provide that if—

(a) a document is given in pursuance of provision contained in the code by virtue of subsection (3),

(b) all or any of the material is of a description prescribed under this subsection, and

(c) a person is identified in accordance with prescribed provisions as entitled to material of that description,

the person giving the document must give a copy of the material of that description to the person so identified or (depending on the circumstances) must allow him to inspect it.

(6) The code may provide that if—

(a) a document is given in pursuance of provision contained in the code by virtue of subsection (3),

(b) all or any of the material is not of a description prescribed under subsection (5), and

(c) a person identified in accordance with prescribed provisions asks for any of the material not of that description,

the person giving the document must give a copy of the material asked for to the person asking for it or (depending on the circumstances) must allow him to inspect it.

(7) The code may provide that if the person required to reveal material has possession of material which he believes is sensitive and of such a nature that provision contained in the code by virtue of subsection (2) should not apply with regard to it—

(a) that provision shall not apply with regard to the material,

(b) he must notify a person identified in accordance with prescribed provisions of the existence of the material, and

(c) he must allow the person so notified to inspect the material.

(8) For the purposes of this section material is sensitive to the extent that its disclosure under Part I would be contrary to the public interest.

(9) In this section "prescribed" means prescribed by the code.

Operation and revision of code

6–57   **25.**—(1) When the Secretary of State has prepared a code under section 23—

(a) he shall publish it in the form of a draft,

(b) he shall consider any representations made to him about the draft, and

(c) he may modify the draft accordingly.

(2) When the Secretary of State has acted under subsection (1) he shall lay the code before each House of Parliament, and when he has done so he may bring it into operation on such day as he may appoint by order.

(3) A code brought into operation under this section shall apply in relation to suspected or alleged offences into which no criminal investigation has begun before the day so appointed.

(4) The Secretary of State may from time to time revise a code previously brought into operation under this section; and the preceding provisions of this section shall apply to a revised code as they apply to the code as first prepared.

Effect of code

6–58   **26.**—(1) A person other than a police officer who is charged with the duty of conducting an investigation with a view to it being ascertained—

(a) whether a person should be charged with an offence, or

(b) whether a person charged with an offence is guilty of it,

shall in discharging that duty have regard to any relevant provision of a code which would apply if the investigation were conducted by police officers.

(2) A failure—

(a) by a police officer to comply with any provision of a code for the time being in operation by virtue of an order under section 25, or

(b) by a person to comply with subsection (1),
shall not in itself render him liable to any criminal or civil proceedings.

(3) In all criminal and civil proceedings a code in operation at any time by virtue of an order under section 25 shall be admissible in evidence.

(4) If it appears to a court or tribunal conducting criminal or civil proceedings that—

(a) any provision of a code in operation at any time by virtue of an order under section 25, or

(b) any failure mentioned in subsection (2)(a) or (b),

is relevant to any question arising in the proceedings, the provision or failure shall be taken into account in deciding the question.

Common law rules as to criminal investigations

27.—(1) Where a code prepared under section 23 and brought into operation under section **6–59**
25 applies in relation to a suspected or alleged offence, the rules of common law which—

(a) were effective immediately before the appointed day, and

(b) relate to the matter mentioned in subsection (2),

shall not apply in relation to the suspected or alleged offence.

(2) The matter is the revealing of material—

(a) by a police officer or other person charged with the duty of conducting an investigation with a view to it being ascertained whether a person should be charged with an offence or whether a person charged with an offence is guilty of it;

(b) to a person involved in the prosecution of criminal proceedings.

(3) In subsection (1) "the appointed day" means the day appointed under section 25 with regard to the code as first prepared.

The Code, which came into force on April 1, 1997 (SI 1997/1033) is reproduced in **6–60**
Archbold Supplement, §§ A–232 *et seq.* It applies to police officers and other persons who under the CPIA 1996 are charged with the duty of conducting investigations. It prescribes the duties and functions of investigators and specifies the procedures to be followed in recording information, retaining material, preparing material for the prosecutor and disclosure of material to the accused. It also instructs the police in relation to the handling of sensitive material.

K. ATTORNEY-GENERAL'S GUIDELINES

On November 29, 2000 the Attorney-General issued new guidelines on disclosure of **6–61**
information in criminal proceedings. They were adopted with immediate effect in relation to all cases submitted after that date to the prosecuting authorities in receipt of the guidelines. They were also adopted with regard to cases already submitted to which the *Criminal Procedure and Investigations Act* 1996 applied, so far as they related to stages in the proceedings that had not yet been reached. The guidelines acknowledge that "fair disclosure to an accused is an inseparable part of a fair trial [under Article 6]" (para.1). Whereas the Code issued under the CPIA 1996 is concerned with the responsibilities of investigators the Attorney-General's guidelines are directed at lawyers, particularly prosecutors, as well as disclosure officers. Their scope is not confined to regime governed by the CPIA 1996: there is guidance on the prosecutor's duty to disclose to the defence material significant information that might affect a bail decision (para.34) and material relevant to sentence (para.44). The guidelines also describe the circumstances in which an investigator, disclosure officer or prosecutor should take reasonable steps to obtain material which is in the possession of government departments, other Crown bodies and other agencies (paras 29–30).

L. JOINT OPERATIONAL INSTRUCTIONS

In June 2003 the Crown Prosecution Service issued revised Joint Operational Instruc- **6–62**
tions For the Disclosure of Unused Material (JOPI) (*www.cps.gov.uk/legal/section20/ chapter_k.html*). JOPI is designed to assist CPS and police practitioners to perform

their disclosure duties consistently and effectively. They are designed to provide a practical guide to disclosure principles and procedures, building on the framework of CPIA 1996, the Code and the Attorney-General's guidelines.

M. THIRD PARTY DISCLOSURE

6–63 Where material is sought from a third party, upon whom there is no duty to disclose, the appropriate procedure is to obtain a summons under the *Criminal Procedure (Attendance of Witnesses) Act* 1965. Note however wasted costs orders below.

In some cases the material in question will be in the possession of the police or the prosecution and so will fall within the disclosure regime: Code of Practice.

Documents in the possession of the Home Office are not in the possession of the prosecution for the purposes of the *Criminal Procedure and Investigations Act* 1996: *R. v Stratford Magistrates' court Ex p. Johnson* above. In that case the DPP argued that the Home Office and ACPO were not part of the prosecution process so that a third party disclosure request was necessary. The Divisional Court held that the Home Office approval and conditions for use of the device and the ACPO guidelines could not be said to be in the possession of the prosecution for the purposes of disclosure.

N. PROTECTED MATERIAL

(1) Public interest immunity

6–64 The common law rules as to public interest immunity survived the enactment of the *Criminal Procedure and Investigations Act* 1996: s.21(1). Material must not be disclosed to the extent that the court, on an application by the prosecutor, concludes it is not in the public interest to disclose it and orders accordingly: *Criminal Procedure and Investigations Act* 1996, ss.7(5), 8(5), 9(8). The court is the final arbiter of whether the prosecution was entitled to avoid disclosure on the basis of public interest immunity. The prosecution cannot withhold material without notifying the defendant: *R. v Ward* [1993] 1 W.L.R. 619.

In *R. v Davis, Johnson and Rowe*, 97 Cr.App.R. 110, CA (Crim Div), the court set out guidance on the procedure which should be followed when the prosecution claims public interest immunity:

6–65 1. It is the prosecutor's duty to make disclosure voluntarily, and in accordance with para.2 of the Attorney-General's guidelines.

2. If the prosecution wish to rely on public interest immunity or sensitivity to justify non-disclosure, then, whenever possible, which will be in most cases they must notify the defence that they are applying for a ruling from the court and indicate to the defence at least the category of material which they hold. The defence must then have the opportunity of making representations to the court.

3. Where disclosure of the category of material would be to reveal that which the prosecution contend it would not be in the public interest to reveal, a different procedure would apply. The prosecution should notify the defence of the application, but it need not specify the category of material and the application will be *ex parte*. If the court on hearing the application considers that the normal procedure should apply it will so order. Otherwise it will rule on the *ex parte* application.

4. In exceptional cases the prosecution might consider that to reveal even the fact that an *ex parte* application has been made could "let the cat out of the bag" so as to stultify the application. If so then the prosecution should apply to the court *ex parte* without notice. If the court considered that notice should have been given, or that the normal *inter partes* hearing should have been adopted it can so order.

6–66 The court emphasised that open justice requires maximum disclosure and the opportunity for the defendant to make representations on the basis of the fullest information. If the judge considers that the defendant should have had notice of the application, or of the nature of the material, or that the application should have been made *inter partes*, he or she should so direct.

In *Rowe and Davis v UK* (above) the European Court of Human Rights considered that:

1. The right to a fair trial means that the prosecution should disclose to the defence all material evidence in their possession for and against the defendant.
2. The duty of disclosure is not absolute and in any criminal proceedings there may be competing interests, such as national security or the need to protect witnesses.
3. Only such measures restricting the right of the defence to disclosure as are strictly necessary are permitted under article 6(1).
4. Any difficulties caused to the defence by limiting its rights to disclosure must be sufficiently counterbalanced by the procedure followed by the court.
5. The pre-*Ward* procedure whereby the prosecution could choose to withhold relevant information violated article 6(1).
6. The procedure adopted by the Court of Appeal did not remedy the unfair procedure adopted at trial.

In *Jasper v UK*, 30 E.H.R.R. 441, and *Fitt v UK*, 30 E.H.R.R. 480, the European **6–67** Court of Human Rights also found no violation of art.6(1). The court recognised the need for any difficulties caused by limitations on defence rights to be counterbalanced by the procedures followed by the judicial authorities. The factors which influenced the majority were that the defence had been notified that *ex parte* applications were to be made and, in *Fitt*, had been informed of the category of the material which it was sought to withhold. The defence had been able to outline the defence case to the trial judge, whose decision it was that it was permissible for the prosecution not to disclose the material. The judge had kept the need for disclosure under assessment throughout the trial.

Jasper was distinguished in *Edwards and Lewis v UK* [2003] 15 BHRC 189: the failure to disclose otherwise disclosable material on Pt II grounds following an *ex parte* application rendered a trial unfair where the defendant wished to make an abuse of procedure application and/or apply for the exclusion of prosecution evidence, particularly in cases where a defence allegation of entrapment will be supported by non-disclosed material.

Edwards and Lewis established that the trail judge may invite the Attorney-General to appoint special counsel to assist the court in deciding Pt II applications where preliminary issues of fact are concerned. But in *R. v H and C* [2004] UKHL 3, the House ruled that *Edwards and Lewis* should not be taken as laying down a mandatory procedure but rather only guiding principles: The defence cannot compel disclosure by making general and unspecified allegations and material neutral or damaging to the defence need not be disclosed. Appointment of special counsel must be the last not the first resort (*R. v H and C, ibid*) and the appointment of special counsel is yet to occur and hard to envisage, in the magistrates' court.

The principle of "equality of arms" requires that each party should be afforded a rea- **6–68** sonable opportunity to present his case under conditions which do not place him a substantial disadvantage vis-à-vis his or her opponents. Each party should have the opportunity to know of and comment on the observations filed or evidence adduced by the other party: *Bulut v Austria*, 24 E.H.R.R. 84, *Werner v Austria*; *Szucs v Austria*, 26 E.H.R.R. 310; *JJ v Netherlands*, 28 E.H.R.R. 168.

In *Atlan v UK* (2002) 34 E.H.R.R. 33, it was held that the prosecution's false denials of the existence of undisclosed material and their failure to inform the judge of the true position had violated art.6.

In *R. v Keane* (1994) 99 Cr. App. R. 1, the Court of Appeal held that considered that:

(1) *Ex parte* applications were contrary to the general principle of open justice in

criminal trials and such a procedure should only be adopted on the application of the prosecution for the specific purpose of enabling the court to test a claim that public interest immunity or sensitivity justified non-disclosure of material in the prosecution's possession.

(2) Where the prosecution wished to withhold relevant documents or information from the defence, they should place only relevant documents and information before the court. The judge should carry out a balancing exercise, having regard to the weight of the public interest in non-disclosure and to the importance of the documents to the defence, and if the disputed material might prove a defendant's innocence or avoid a miscarriage of justice, the balance would come down resoundingly in favour of disclosure; but

(3) since here there was a public interest in not disclosing the material withheld and it would not, in any event, have assisted the defence, the balance was clearly in favour of non-disclosure.

6–69 The prosecution should ensure that he or she has sight of all material in respect of which public interest immunity is claimed before the trial begins so that he application can be made at the most convenient time: *R. v Menga and Marshalleck* [1998] Crim.L.R. 58, CA. It is crucial that the prosecution is scrupulously accurate in the information provided in *ex parte* public interest immunity hearings: *R. v Jackson* [2000] Crim.L.R. 377.

Since the court is the final arbiter of whether public interest immunity can be claimed, it should examine for itself the evidence so that it is aware of the facts contained in the material. The court is then able to balance the competing interests of public interest immunity and fairness to the party seeking disclosure: *R. v K(TD)* 97 Cr.App.R. 342. The defendant had applied for production of a videotape of a therapeutic family interview at a children's hospital. Without viewing the tape the judge accepted the hospital's objection to disclosure on the ground of public interest immunity. On appeal, the defendant argued that the tape might have shown the unreliability of the complainant's evidence and that the judge's ruling without seeing the tape amounted to a material irregularity. The Court of Appeal considered that where there was a claim for public interest immunity, the court must balance the competing interests of the hospital's concern about confidentiality and fairness to the defendant, whose liberty was at stake and for whom disclosure could be important. The judge should have examined the evidence himself to test its relevance before ruling on whether the tape should be disclosed. After seeing the video, the Court of Appeal concluded that it would not have been appropriate to order disclosure.

In deciding the question of public interest immunity the judge is not restricted to considering evidence admissible in a court of law. He or she is entitled to view additional material, even if it amounts to hearsay evidence: *R. v Law, The Times*, August 15, 1999, CA.

6–70 When considering the question of public interest immunity the inquiry should focus on whether there is a legal objection to disclosure grounded in the preservation of the public interest as balanced against the interests of the accused: *R. v Brown* [1994] 1 W.L.R. 1599.

In *R. v Governor of Pentonville Prison Ex p. Osman (No.4)* [1991] 1 W.L.R. 281 the defendant had sought and been granted discovery of nine documents relating to his extradition from the Hong Kong government, the Malaysian High Commission and the Foreign Office. The Foreign Secretary wished to prevent references to the documents, which he claimed were subject to public interest immunity. The court considered that in criminal proceedings the public interest in non-disclosure had to be balanced against the interests of justice, the latter being more pressing when a person's liberty was at stake. It held that public interest immunity took precedence because the purpose of revealing the substance of the documents (to show the Hong Kong government's bad faith) was not material to the proceedings. The effectiveness of public interest immunity had not been reduced in the earlier disclosure, as the documents had not been read out in court.

In *R. v Abbott* [2003] EWCA Crim 350 the defendant sought disclosure of the social services files relating to the complainants. He submitted that disclosure should have been ordered because (1) his expert, a behavioural psychologist, had needed to see the files; (2) he should have had the same right of access to the files as the police had had; (3) he would have had access to the files during his employment, and (4) the relevant events having occurred some 20 years previously, the public interest reasons for not disclosing all the files had diminished over time. The Court of Appeal rejected his appeal on the basis that (1) an expert had been present in court to assist the defendant who had been able to see the extensive material provided to the defence and assess the witnesses while they were testifying; (2) the defence had not been entitled to access to everything that the police had seen; they had only been entitled to equal access to everything that had been or might have been relevant to the preparation of the defence; (3) the files were the property of the local authorities concerned. The defendant had no continuing right of access to them by virtue of his past employment, and (4) there was no justification for saying that material that had been highly confidential at the time of the relevant events had become any less confidential. Indeed, it was arguable that the passage of time made it more important to retain confidentiality.

The Code of Practice on Disclosure gives categories of sensitive material. These categories are wider than the types of material which the courts might be prepared to protect via public interest immunity.   **6–71**

Criminal Procedure and Investigations Act 1996, ss.14–16

Public interest: review for summary trials

14.—(1) This section applies where this Part applies by virtue of section 1(1),   **6–72**
(2) At any time—
   (a) after a court makes an order under section 3(6), 7(5), 8(5) or 9(8), and
   (b) before the accused is acquitted or convicted or the prosecutor decides not to proceed with the case concerned,
the accused may apply to the court for a review of the question whether it is still not in the public interest to disclose material affected by its order.
(3) In such a case the court must review that question, and if it concludes that it is in the public interest to disclose material to any extent—
   (a) it shall so order, and
   (b) it shall take such steps as are reasonable to inform the prosecutor of its order.
(4) Where the prosecutor is informed of an order made under subsection (3) he must act accordingly having regard to the provisions of this Part (unless he decides not to proceed with the case concerned).

Public interest: review in other cases

15.—(1) This section applies where this Part applies by virtue of section 1(2).   **6–73**
(2) This section applies at all times—
   (a) after a court makes an order under section 3(6), 7(5), 8(5) or 9(8), and
   (b) before the accused is acquitted or convicted or the prosecutor decides not to proceed with the case concerned.
(3) The court must keep under review the question whether at any given time it is still not in the public interest to disclose material affected by its order.
(4) The court must keep the question mentioned in subsection (3) under review without the need for an application; but the accused may apply to the court for a review of that question.
(5) If the court at any time concludes that it is in the public interest to disclose material to any extent—
   (a) it shall so order, and
   (b) it shall take such steps as are reasonable to inform the prosecutor of its order.
(6) Where the prosecutor is informed of an order made under subsection (5) he must act accordingly having regard to the provisions of this Part (unless he decides not to proceed with the case concerned).

Applications: opportunity to be heard

6–74   **16.** Where—

(a) an application is made under section 3(6), 7(5), 8(5), 9(8), 14(2) or 15(4),

(b) a person claiming to have an interest in the material applies to be heard by the court, and

(c) he shows that he was involved (whether alone or with others and whether directly or indirectly) in the prosecutor's attention being brought to the material,

the court must not make an order under section 3(6), 7(5), 8(5), 9(8), 14(3) or 15(5) (as the case may be) unless the person applying under paragraph (b) has been given an opportunity to be heard.

Magistrates' Courts (Criminal Procedure and Investigations Act 1996) (Disclosure) Rules 1997, rr.2–5

Public interest: application by prosecutor

6–75   **2.**—(1) This rule applies to the making of an application by the prosecutor under section 3(6), 7(5), 8(5) or 9(8) where Part I applies by virtue of section 1(1) (summary trial).

(2) Notice of an application to which this rule applies shall be served on the [justices' chief executive for] the magistrates' court trying the offence referred to in section 1(1) and shall specify the nature of the material to which the application relates.

(3) Subject to paragraphs (4) and (5) below, a copy of the notice of application shall be served on the accused by the prosecutor.

(4) Where the prosecutor has reason to believe that to reveal to the accused the nature of the material to which the application relates would have the effect of disclosing that which the prosecutor contends should not in the public interest be disclosed, paragraph (3) above shall not apply but the prosecutor shall notify the accused that an application to which this rule applies has been made.

(5) Where the prosecutor has reason to believe that to reveal to the accused the fact that an application is being made would have the effect of disclosing that which the prosecutor contends should not in the public interest be disclosed, paragraph (3) above shall not apply.

[This rule is reprinted as amended by the *Magistrates' Courts (Transfer of Justice's Clerk's Functions) (Miscellaneous Amendments) Rules* 2001, Sch.1, para.133.]

Public interest: hearing of application by prosecutor

6–76   **3.**—(1) This rule applies to the hearing of an application by the prosecutor under section 3(6), 7(5), 8(5) or 9(8) where Part I applies by virtue of section 1(1).

(2) Subject to paragraph (3) below and to rule 6(4), where a copy of the notice of application has been served on the accused in accordance with rule 2(3)—

(a) the [justices' chief executive for] the court shall give notice to—

   (i) the prosecutor;

   (ii) the accused; and

   (iii) any person claiming to have an interest in the material to which the application relates who has applied under section 16(b) to be heard by the court,

of the date and time when and the place where the hearing will take place and, unless the court orders otherwise, such notice shall be given in writing;

(b) the hearing shall be inter partes; and

(c) the prosecutor and the accused shall be entitled to make representations to the court.

(3) Where the prosecutor applies to the court for leave to make representations in the absence of the accused, the court may for that purpose sit in the absence of the accused and any legal representative of his.

(4) Subject to rule 6(4), where a copy of the notice of application has not been served on the accused in accordance with rule 2(3)—

(a) the hearing shall be ex parte;

(b) only the prosecutor shall be entitled to make representations to the court; and

(c) the accused shall not be given notice as specified in paragraph (2) above.

[This rule is reprinted as amended by the *Magistrates' Courts (Transfer of Justice's Clerk's Functions) (Miscellaneous Amendments) Rules* 2001, Sch.1, para.133.]

Public interest: non-disclosure order
4.—(1) This rule applies to an order under section 3(6), 7(5), 8(5) or 9(8). **6–77**

(2) On making an order to which this rule applies, the court shall state its reasons for doing so.

(3) In a case where such an order is a made following—
  (a) an application to which rule 2(4) applies, or
  (b) an application notice of which has been served on the accused in accordance with rule 2(3) but the accused has not appeared or been represented at the hearing of that application,
the [justices' chief executive for] the court shall notify the accused that an order has been made.

[This rule is reprinted as amended by the *Magistrates' Courts (Transfer of Justice's Clerk's Functions) (Miscellaneous Amendments) Rules* 2001, Sch.1, para.133.]

Review of non-disclosure order: application by accused
5.—(1) This rule applies to an application by the accused under section 14(2). **6–78**

(2) An application to which this rule applies shall be made by notice in writing to the [justices' chief executive for] the magistrates' court trying the offence referred to in section 1(1) and shall specify the reason why the accused believes the court should review the question mentioned in section 14(2).

(3) A copy of the notice referred to in paragraph (2) above shall be served on the prosecutor at the same time as it is sent to the [justices' chief executive for] the court.

(4) On receipt of an application to which this rule applies the [justices' chief executive for] the court shall take such steps as he thinks fit to ensure that the court determining the application has before it any document or other material which was available to the court which made the order mentioned in section 14(2).

(5) Subject to paragraphs (6) to (8) below and to rule 6(4), the hearing of an application to which this rule applies shall be inter partes and the accused and the prosecutor shall be entitled to make representations to the court.

(6) Where the court considers that there are no grounds on which it might conclude that it is in the public interest to disclose material to any extent it may determine the application without hearing representations from the accused, the prosecutor or any person claiming to have an interest in the material to which the application relates.

(7) Where after hearing the accused's representations the prosecutor applies to the court for leave to make representations in the absence of the accused, the court may for that purpose sit in the absence of the accused and any legal representative of his.

(8) Subject to rule 6(4), where the order to which the application relates was made following an application of which the accused was not notified under rule 2(3) or (4), the hearing shall be *ex parte* and only the prosecutor shall be entitled to make representations to the court.

(9) The [justices' chief executive for] the court shall give notice in writing to—
  (a) the prosecutor;
  (b) except where a hearing takes place in accordance with paragraph (8) above, the accused; and
  (c) any person claiming to have an interest in the material to which the application relates who has applied under section 16(b) to be heard by the court,
of the date and time when and the place where the hearing of an application to which this rule applies will take place and of any order which is made by the court following its determination of the application.

[This rule is reprinted as amended by the *Magistrates' Courts (Transfer of Justice's Clerk's Functions) (Miscellaneous Amendments) Rules* 2001, Sch.1, para.133.]

The problem with the magistrates' courts and public interest immunity is in their **6–79** dual role as triers of law and of fact. When magistrates review documents for which immunity is claimed, it may prejudice their role as triers of fact. A new bench may need to be constituted to try the case after the old bench rules against disclosure. If that new bench were under a continuing duty of review, it would mean that it would be impossible to constitute a bench that was free from appearing prejudiced which would result from looking at the material in question.

However in *R. v Stipendiary Magistrate of Norfolk Ex p. Taylor* (1997) 161 J.P. 773 the Divisional Court considered that the normal practice applicable in the Crown Court should also apply to summary trial. Only in exceptional cases of highly prejudicial material being revealed should a bench disqualify itself from conducting the trial.

(2) Confidentiality

Criminal Procedure and Investigations Act 1996, s.17–18

Confidentiality of disclosed information

6–80   **17.**—(1) If the accused is given or allowed to inspect a document or other object under—

      (a) section 3, 4, 7, 9, 14 or 15, or

      (b) an order under section 8,

then, subject to subsections (2) to (4), he must not use or disclose it or any information recorded in it.

    (2) The accused may use or disclose the object or information—

      (a) in connection with the proceedings for whose purposes he was given the object or allowed to inspect it,

      (b) with a view to the taking of further criminal proceedings (for instance, by way of appeal) with regard to the matter giving rise to the proceedings mentioned in paragraph (a), or

      (c) in connection with the proceedings first mentioned in paragraph (b).

    (3) The accused may use or disclose—

      (a) the object to the extent that it has been displayed to the public in open court, or

      (b) the information to the extent that it has been communicated to the public in open court;

but the preceding provisions of this subsection do not apply if the object is displayed or the information is communicated in proceedings to deal with a contempt of court under section 18.

    (4) If—

      (a) the accused applies to the court for an order granting permission to use or disclose the object or information, and

      (b) the court makes such an order,

the accused may use or disclose the object or information for the purpose and to the extent specified by the court.

6–81   (5) An application under subsection (4) may be made and dealt with at any time, and in particular after the accused has been acquitted or convicted or the prosecutor has decided not to proceed with the case concerned: but this is subject to rules made by virtue of section 19(2).

    (6) Where—

      (a) an application is made under subsection (4), and

      (b) the prosecutor or a person claiming to have an interest in the object or information applies to be heard by the court,

the court must not make an order granting permission unless the person applying under paragraph (b) has been given an opportunity to be heard.

    (7) References in this section to the court are to—

      (a) a magistrates' court, where this Part applies by virtue of section 1(1);

      (b) the Crown Court, where this Part applies by virtue of section 1(2).

    (8) Nothing in this section affects any other restriction or prohibition on the use or disclosure of an object or information, whether the restriction or prohibition arises under an enactment (whenever passed) or otherwise.

Confidentiality: contravention

6–82   **18.**—(1) It is a contempt of court for a person knowingly to use or disclose an object or information recorded in it if the use or disclosure is in contravention of section 17.

(2) The following courts have jurisdiction to deal with a person who is guilty of a contempt under this section—

(a) a magistrates' court, where this Part applies by virtue of section 1(1),

(b) the Crown Court, where this Part applies by virtue of section 1(2).

(3) A person who is guilty of a contempt under this section may be dealt with as follows—

(a) a magistrates' court may commit him to custody for a specified period not exceeding six months or impose on him a fine not exceeding £5,000 or both;

(b) the Crown Court may commit him to custody for a specified period not exceeding two years or impose a fine on him or both.

(4) If—

(a) a person is guilty of a contempt under this section, and

(b) the object concerned is in his possession,

the court finding him guilty may order that the object shall be forfeited and dealt with in such manner as the court may order.

(5) The power of the court under subsection (4) includes power to order the object to be destroyed or to be given to the prosecutor or to be placed in his custody for such period as the court may specify.

(6) If—

(a) the court proposes to make an order under subsection (4), and

(b) the person found guilty, or any other person claiming to have an interest in the object, applies to be heard by the court,

the court must not make the order unless the applicant has been given an opportunity to be heard.

(7) If—   **6–83**

(a) a person is guilty of a contempt under this section and

(b) a copy of the object concerned is in his possession,

the court finding him guilty may order that the copy shall be forfeited and dealt with in such manner as the court may order.

(8) Subsections (5) and (6) apply for the purposes of subsection (7) as they apply for the purposes of subsection (4), but as if references to the object were references to the copy.

(9) An object or information shall be inadmissible as evidence in civil proceedings if to adduce it would in the opinion of the court be likely to constitute a contempt under this section and "the court" here means the court before which the civil proceedings are being taken.

(10) The powers of a magistrates' court under this section may be exercised either of the court's own motion or by order on complaint.

(3) Sexual Offences (Protected Material) Act 1997

The *Sexual Offences (Protected Material) Act* 1997 makes provision for regulating **6–84** access by defendants and others to certain categories of information disclosed by the prosecution or the Criminal Cases Review Commission in connection with proceedings relating to certain sexual and other offences. Nothing in the Act applies to any proceedings for a sexual offence where the defendant was charged with the offence before the commencement of the Act. It comes into force on such day as the Secretary of State may appoint. At the time of writing the Act is still not in force and no date has been appointed for its commencement.

Disclosure and the Criminal Justice Act 2003

Part V of the *CJA* 2003 (due for implementation June, 2005) amends CPIA 1996 **6–85** and will significantly change the obligations of both the prosecution and defence in relation to disclosure. Defendants will be required to provide the prosecution with more detailed written case statements and advance notice of the names and address of witnesses to be called for the defence. The defence will also be required to disclose the identity of any expert witness consulted for the purpose of an opinion, regardless of whether that witness is to be relied upon at trial. This will be the first time that the defence is obliged to disclose its 'unused material'. The amendments to CPIA 1996 will replace the two stage process for disclosure of unused prosecution material with a single, objective test which requires the prosecutor to disclose material which might reasonably be considered capable of undermining the prosecution case, or of assisting the case for the accused.

CHAPTER 7

PRE-TRIAL PROCEDURE

I. PRE-TRIAL HEARING

A. EARLY ADMINISTRATIVE HEARINGS

Some cases heard at the magistrates' court are concluded at the first listing but others **7–1** require more time for preparation and so will be adjourned. Cases are treated differently according to the plea to be tendered. When a not guilty plea is expected then preliminary steps will be taken at the first court appearance to prepare for trial. Pre-trial proceedings consist of considering legal representation, taking a plea and giving directions relating to trial issues and disclosure etc. For guilty pleas, the expectation is that the case will be dealt with on first appearance.

Crime and Disorder Act 1998, s.50

Early administrative hearings
    50.—(1) Where a person ("the accused") has been charged with an offence at a police station, the magistrates' court before whom he appears or is brought for the first time in relation to the charge may, unless the accused falls to be dealt with under section 51 below, consist of a single justice.
    (2) At a hearing conducted by a single justice under this section the accused shall be asked whether he wishes to be granted a right to representation funded by the Legal Services Commission as part of the Criminal Defence Service and, if he does, the justice shall decide whether or not to grant him such a right.
    (3) At such a hearing the single justice—
        (a) may exercise, subject to subsection (2) above, such of his powers as a single justice as he thinks fit; and
        (b) on adjourning the hearing, may remand the accused in custody or on bail.
    (4) This section applies in relation to a justices' clerk as it applies in relation to a single justice; but nothing in subsection (3)(b) above authorises such a clerk to remand the accused in custody or, without the consent of the prosecutor and the accused, to remand the accused on bail on conditions other than those (if any) previously imposed.

[This section is reprinted as amended by the *Access to Justice Act* 1999, Sch.15, para.1]

Police and Criminal Evidence Act 1984, s.47A

Early administrative hearings conducted by justices' clerks
    47A. Where a person has been charged with an offence at a police station, any requirement **7–2**

imposed under this Part for the person to appear or be brought before a magistrates' court shall be taken to be satisfied if the person appears or is brought before the clerk to the justices for a petty sessions area in order for the clerk to conduct a hearing under section 50 of the *Crime and Disorder Act* 1998 (early administrative hearings).

[This section is reprinted as amended by the *Crime and Disorder Act* 1998, Sch.8, para.62]

7–3   Where a defendant is charged at a police station the custody officer may grant him bail to appear at a magistrates' court: s.47 of the *Police and Criminal Evidence Act* 1984. The police and local court will have in place an arrangement for the listing of such cases and the intention is for them to be dealt with expeditiously and certainly within a matter of days: s.46 of the *Crime and Disorder Act* 1998. The prosecutor will attend at the police station the day before the cases are due to be heard to review the files and to assess whether there is likely to be a guilty or not guilty plea. If the offence is admitted on the police files, an early first hearing will take place at court in anticipation of a guilty plea. These cases may be prosecuted by a designated case worker (DCW) from the Crown Prosecution Service and must be heard before a bench of magistrates or a district judge. The DCW has limited rights of audience and cannot deal with contested trials or bail applications. In all other cases, the matter will be listed as an early administrative hearing. These cases can be dealt with by a magistrate sitting alone or by the justices' clerk or a member of the court staff to whom the justices' clerk has delegated the relevant powers. Usually the delegation will be to legal advisers. The powers of the justices' clerk in early administrative hearings are limited by s.50(4).

The powers of a single magistrate exercisable at an early administrative hearing are listed in s.49 of the *Crime and Disorder Act* 1998. This section also lists further limitations on the powers of a justices' clerk who, although he may conduct an early administrative hearing, has no authority to give an indication of seriousness for the purposes of a pre-sentence report. There is power for a justices' clerk to remand a case on bail if the parties agree but he may not remand a defendant in custody for any purposes. There are also restrictions preventing the justices' clerk from giving directions about publicity and ordering separate trials for co-defendants or multiple charges. A case may be transferred before a fully constituted bench if during an early administrative hearing the defendant indicates a wish to plead guilty.

B. Pre-Trial Hearing by Video Link

Crime and Disorder Act 1998, s.57

Use of live television links at preliminary hearings

7–4   **57.**—(1) In any proceedings for an offence, a court may, after hearing representations from the parties, direct that the accused shall be treated as being present in the court for any particular hearing before the start of the trial if, during that hearing—

(a) he is held in custody in a prison or other institution; and

(b) whether by means of a live television link or otherwise, he is able to see and hear the court and to be seen and heard by it.

(2) A court shall not give a direction under subsection (1) above unless—

(a) it has been notified by the Secretary of State that facilities are available for enabling persons held in custody in the institution in which the accused is or is to be so held to see and hear the court and to be seen and heard by it; and

(b) the notice has not been withdrawn.

(3) If in a case where it has power to do so a magistrates' court decides not to give a direction under subsection (1) above, it shall give its reasons for not doing so.

(4) In this section "the start of the trial" has the meaning given by subsection (11A) or (11B) of section 22 of the 1985 Act.

7–5   Many courts now have facilities to deal with a case with the defendant in custody not being physically produced at court but appearing over a live television link from prison or a remand centre.

The link can be used for preliminary hearings only. Trials and sentencing cannot take place over the link. The trial starts when the court begins to hear evidence for the prosecution or when the court accepts a plea of guilty: s.22 of the *Prosecution of Offences Act* 1985. On remanding into custody after the first appearance in person, the court may direct that the next hearing should be by video link. The court must state its reasons if such a direction is not made in a case where it could be. There are facilities at court for legal representatives to take instructions from their clients in confidence over a live television link in interview rooms.

C. Adjournments

Powers of adjournment are conferred on the court by ss.5, 6, 10, 17C, and 18 of the **7–6** *Magistrates' Courts Act* 1980, see §§ 5–27—5–31.

Not all cases will be concluded at first hearing and requests for adjournment will be made to the court, which has a discretion whether to grant an adjournment or not. The party applying for the adjournment should explain the reasons why the case cannot proceed and the issues that need to be addressed with further time. Both parties may require an adjournment in the early stages of a case but the court must always consider the reasons for putting a case off and must make its decision taking into account the interests of justice. The court may require to know the history of the case and whether adjournments have been granted before and the reasons for them. These details should be available from the court file and will be recounted in open court by the legal adviser. The court should also make clear its expectations for progress at the next hearing.

Article 6(3)(b) of the ECHR requires that a defendant should have 'adequate time and facilities' to prepare his defence. The time that is adequate will vary depending on the circumstances but some guidance can be extrapolated from various cases. Seventeen days and 10 days were both held to be a sufficient length of time to enable defence lawyers to prepare for trial: *X v Austria* (1979) 15 D.R. 160 and *Perez Mahia v Spain* (1987) 9 E.H.R.R. 91. The situation may well be different if there is a change of lawyers at a late stage and if instructions are only taken on the day of trial an adjournment may be required: *Goddi v Italy* (1984) 6 E.H.R.R. 457.

In considering adjournment requests the court must continually balance the compet- **7–7** ing interests of time needed for preparation and the right to have a speedy trial.

In *R. v Jisl and Tekin* [2004] EWCA Crim 696, the court confirmed the important role that the judge has to play in case management. It was said that with resources being limited it followed that the proper use of court time required judicial management and control. The court must be fair to all parties and potential problems as well as strategies for saving time needed to be fully canvassed in court. It was held that when a judge went through this process and then gave directions and set a timetable, he would be supported on appeal. Criticism was more likely to be directed at those who chose to ignore the directions.

There are numerous reasons why adjournments may be necessary and some principles can be identified from domestic cases. On the first hearing a defendant may request an adjournment in order to obtain legal representation. The court may inquire into the action taken prior to the appearance but a defendant must be allowed a reasonable time to instruct solicitors and prepare his case. Where a summons was served and listed for hearing on the same day it was held to be a denial of natural justice to refuse an adjournment as the defendant's solicitors, instructed only on the day, did not have enough time to prepare the case: *R. v Thames Magistrates' Court Ex p. Polemis* [1974] 1 W.L.R. 1371.

A defendant who wished to seek his own expert evidence when the prosecution had **7–8** already supplied an independent expert's report was held to have been refused an adjournment without sufficient reason: *R. v Sunderland Justices Ex p. Dryden, The Times*, May 18, 1994.

By the same token a request for an adjournment by the prosecution must not be unreasonably refused. The court has a duty to ascertain the real reasons why the case cannot proceed and should be cautious to accept information at face value. The interests of victims and public confidence in the system of justice must be taken into account.

A complainant in a charge of indecent assault failed to attend at trial and the defence suggested she did not wish to pursue the charge. On appeal it was held that the refusal to adjourn was wrong. It was a serious charge and the witness had not been aware of the trial date: *R. v Neath and Port Talbot Justices Ex p. DPP* [2000] 1 W.L.R. 1376.

A complainant in an assault charge failed to attend at trial because she had been the victim of another unrelated serious attack just prior to the hearing. The prosecution requested an adjournment on the grounds that the witness was too ill to attend but did not disclose the full details of why this was so. On appeal the court held that the reason for failing to attend in this case was of secondary importance. Once it was accepted that a complainant through an unexpected event that was no fault of her own was not fit to attend, there was an extremely powerful argument for an adjournment and as there was no history of delay in the case, the argument for an adjournment became unanswerable: *DPP v Birmingham Magistrates' Court* [2003] EWHC 2352.

The fact that a court may direct that a case should proceed on the next occasion is not binding on a subsequent court. The court dealing with the adjourned case must consider the situation as it is on the day when the matter is presented before it.

7–9   A court refused to grant an adjournment to the defence when it had previously been observed that the case should proceed. Two essential defence witnesses failed to attend on the day fixed for trial. The refusal was held to be contrary to natural justice: *R. v Bristol Magistrates' Court Ex p. Rowles* (1994) R.T.R. 40.

There was a duty on the court to hear the case advanced for the defence in support of an adjournment despite the fact that there was a fixed expectation that the case would proceed: *R. v Bradford Justices Ex p. Wilkinson* [1990] 1 W.L.R. 692.

The provisions of s.10 allow for a court to adjourn a case for a re-trial before a different bench: *R. v Ripon Liberty Justices Ex p. Bugg* (1991) 155 J.P. 213; *R. (on the application of Kendall) v Selby* [2003] EWHC 2909, November 13, 2003.

D. FAILURE TO APPEAR

(1) The accused

7–10   Statute provides for different courses of action when any party to the proceedings fails to attend at court.

Magistrates' Courts Act 1980, s.11

Non-appearance of accused: general provisions

11.—(1) Subject to the provisions of this Act, where at the time and place appointed for the trial or adjourned trial of an information the prosecutor appears but the accused does not, the court may proceed in his absence.

(2) Where a summons has been issued, the court shall not begin to try the information in the absence of the accused unless either it is proved to the satisfaction of the court, on oath or in such other manner as may be prescribed, that the summons was served on the accused within what appears to the court to be a reasonable time before the trial or adjourned trial or the accused has appeared on a previous occasion to answer to the information.

(3) A magistrates' court shall not in a person's absence sentence him to imprisonment or detention in a detention centre or make a detention and training order or an order under [section 119 of the *Powers of Criminal Courts (Sentencing) Act* 2000] that a suspended sentence passed on him shall take effect.

(4) A magistrates' court shall not in a person's absence impose any disqualification on him, except on resumption of the hearing after an adjournment under section 10(3) above; and where a trial is adjourned in pursuance of this subsection the notice required by section 10(2) above shall include notice of the reason for the adjournment.

[This section is reprinted as amended by the *Powers of Criminal Courts (Sentencing) Act* 2000, Sch.9, para.61.]

When a defendant fails to appear the court may proceed in his absence or it may ad- **7–11**
journ the case or it may issue a warrant of arrest: s.13 of the *Magistrates' Courts Act*
1980, see above § 4–4. A defendant represented by his lawyer is deemed not to be
absent (s.122 of the *Magistrates' Courts Act* 1980) so the case may proceed as if he
were there unless provisions of statute expressly require the presence of the accused as
they do in s.11(3) and (4). Disqualifications that may be imposed include disqualification
from driving and also various disqualifications relating to the keeping of animals. A
disqualification cannot be imposed in absence unless the case has been adjourned on at
least one occasion to give the defendant the opportunity to attend and show cause why
a disqualification should not be imposed. Should the defendant fail to attend on the
adjourned hearing the court may lawfully disqualify in absence but this may have
repercussions if a defendant is later charged with driving whilst disqualified and claims
that he was not aware of the conviction or disqualification order.

Article 6 of the ECHR guarantees the right to a fair trial which incorporates the
principle of effective participation in the proceedings. It is in the interests of justice that
a defendant be present at his trial: *Ekbetani v Sweden* (1991) 13 E.H.R.R. 504. The
right to be present at trial is not absolute and it has been recognised that there may be
circumstances in which Art. 6 will not be violated when a case proceeds in the absence of
the accused. For example when the defendant absents himself by his own conduct by
absconding or making himself so ill he is unfit to attend court. In such circumstances
the court must balance the competing claims of giving the defence the opportunity to
present their case and ensuring a trial is heard within a reasonable time.

It would be important to ensure that the defendant is not denied the right to representation in his absence and also the right to a re-hearing on the merits: *Ensslin v Germany* (1978) 14 D.R. 64.

The defendant may also waive his right to be present at trial but this requires an unequivocal waiver. The state is obliged to show that adequate measures have been taken
to trace the defendant and that he has been notified and is aware of the proceedings:
Colozza v Italy (1985) 7 E.H.R.R. 516.

Domestic case law confirms that the approach to trials in absence must comply with **7–12**
Article 6. The law was reviewed in great detail by the Court of Appeal and the House of
Lords in *R. v Hayward, R. v Jones, R. v Purvis* [2001] Q.B. 862 and *R. v Jones*
(2003) 1 A.C. 1. The House of Lords approved the Court of Appeal's judgement which
identified a list of matters relevant to the court's exercise of its discretion to conduct a
trial in the of absence of the defendant. It was recognised that the defendant has a general right to be present at his trial and to be legally represented. The defendant can
waive these rights either wholly or in part. They may be waived wholly if the defendant
deliberately or voluntarily absents himself from the court and they may be waived
partially if he behaves in such a way during the proceedings as to obstruct their proper
course. His rights may also be waived if he withdraws his instructions from those
representing him at any time during the proceedings. The court retains the discretion
to hear a trial in absence, which must be exercised with great care, and it is only in rare
and exceptional cases that a trial should continue in the absence of a defendant,
particularly when he is not represented. Fairness to the defence is of prime importance
but fairness to the prosecution must not be disregarded. The court should have regard
to all the circumstances including:

1. The nature and circumstances of the defendant's behaviour in absenting him or
   herself from the trial or disrupting it, and in particular whether the behaviour
   was voluntary and so plainly waived the right to be present;
2. Whether an adjournment would resolve the matter;
3. The likely length of such an adjournment;
4. Whether the defendant, though absent, wished to be represented or had waived
   his or her right to representation;
5. Whether the defendant's representatives were able to receive instructions from
   him or her and the extent to which they could present the defence;

6. The extent of the disadvantage to the defendant in not being able to present his or her account of events;

7. The risk of the jury reaching an improper conclusion about the absence of the defendant;

8. The general public interest that a trial should take place within a reasonable time;

9. The effect of the delay on the memories of the witnesses;

10. Where there was more than one defendant, and not all had absconded, the undesirability of having separate trials.

In reviewing and approving this judgement Lord Bingham in the House of Lords added in *R. v Jones* that the overriding concern is that the trial, if conducted in absence was as fair as the circumstances could permit and led to a just outcome. Those objects were equally important whether the offence was serious or relatively minor. Also, it was generally desirable that the defendant be represented even if he had voluntarily absconded.

7–13   See also *Practice Direction (Criminal Proceedings: Consolidation) 2002 (Bail: Failure to Surrender and Trials in Absence)* Amendment No.3, issued on January 24, 2004.

These cases related to proceedings in the Crown Court but the principles apply equally to trials in the magistrates' court. In summary proceedings the fact that there can be an appeal that is a complete rehearing and the power to re-open a case under s.142 of the *Magistrates' Courts Act* 1980 are also relevant. Minor offences, particularly road traffic cases are often dealt with in absence. The court needs to be satisfied that the defendant has been given notice of the hearing date which is proved by proper service of the summons or adjournment notice. The documents must be served in accordance with the *Magistrates' Courts Rules* 1981, r.67 (proof of service) and r.99 (method of service). Summonses must be endorsed for service which is effected by delivering it to the person concerned; leaving it with some person at his last known or usual place of abode or sending it by post. The endorsement will indicate how and when the document was served. When the case proceeds in absence the prosecution will either call witnesses or it may apply to proceed on the basis of written statements prepared in accordance with s.9 of the *Criminal Justice Act* 1967. The court will need to be satisfied that these statements have also been served on the defendant and then they can be read out as the prosecution case. The trial must be conducted in accordance with the usual procedure and rules of evidence and the prosecution retains the criminal burden of proof. This does not mean that the court can dismiss a charge against an absent defendant in reliance on a denial made of the offence recorded in the prosecution statement. In *DPP v Gokceli* (1989) 153 J.P. 109, the defendant was summonsed for driving the wrong way down a one way street. When questioned by the officer he denied that he was the driver. The court dismissed the charge on the basis of this evidence. The court held that this was wrong and said that if doubts were raised whilst the prosecution evidence was only in written form then the case should be adjourned so the prosecution may call oral evidence and the defendant should be informed again of his right to be present to challenge the prosecution evidence.

Minor offences which are often heard in absence include television licence offences, vehicle excise licence offences and fare evasion offences on public transport.

The court may be invited to proceed in absence in cases involving more serious charges and then the guidance of *R. v Jones* should be referred to in detail.

It has been held that arrest and detention by the police preventing a defendant from attending his trial is not voluntary absence and the court was criticised for proceeding in absence in those circumstances: *R. (R) v Thames Youth Court* (2002) 166 J.P. 613.

It is a well established principle that the court must be satisfied that the summons was served a reasonable time before the hearing in order to allow a proper opportunity to attend or that the defendant had previously appeared in answer to the summons and so is aware of the proceedings. It is incumbent on the court to be satisfied that not only has the notice of adjournment been sent but also that it has been received. Where a defendant complained that neither he nor his solicitor had received a notice of the adjourned hearing date the trial in absence was held to be a nullity because of the court's failure to investigate fully the reason for the non-attendance: *R. v Seisdon Justices Ex p. Dougan* [1983] 1 All E.R. 6.

The reason why the defendant is absent is a crucial factor in the decision to proceed in absence. The court must inquire and check whether any explanation has been provided for the failure to appear. The court always has a duty to exercise its discretion judicially, giving a fair opportunity to the defendant to be present and to call witnesses and/or give evidence. Where the defendant's failure to attend results from a medical condition, in most cases a medical certificate or letter from a doctor would suffice. If the court suspects the grounds to be spurious or inadequate, it should ordinarily express its doubts, giving the defendant an opportunity to seek to resolve them. The court may call for better evidence, require further enquiries to be made or adopt any further fair expedient. A claim of illness with apparently responsible professional support should not be rejected without the court satisfying itself that it is proper to reject it and that no unfairness would result: *R. v Bolton Magistrates' Court Ex p. Merna* [1991] 2 W.L.R. 239.

7–14 A defendant's right to a fair trial does not encompass the unlimited right to be present on their own terms. A defendant charged with harassment had his trial adjourned on several occasions because of his medical condition, proof of which was provided through certificates and other evidence. The court initially heard the case in absence but allowed a re-hearing. The court then refused an adjournment of the re-hearing applied for again on medical grounds.It was held on appeal that the court exercised its discretion properly and had been entitled to proceed in absence: *R. v Ealing Magistrates' Court Ex p. Burgess* (2001) 165 J.P. 82.

A vital factor affecting the court's discretion to proceed in absence is the provision for the absent defendant to apply for a re-hearing. This may be done under s.14 of the *Magistrates' Courts Act* 1980 whereby proceedings can be declared invalid where the defendant did not know of them, see §§ 4–65—4–67, above. The defendant may also appeal against a conviction and or sentence to the Crown Court, §§ 22–6—22–24, below. The defendant may also apply for the case to be re-opened under s.142 of the *Magistrates' Courts Act* 1980 and the conviction can be deleted and the trial commenced again.

The court may also deal with a case in the absence of the defendant under the provisions of s.12 of the *Magistrates' Courts Act* 1980 which provides for written pleas of guilty to be submitted if certain conditions are fulfilled, see §§ 5–11—5–12 and §§ 5–48—5–63.

(2) The prosecution

Magistrates' Courts Act 1980, s.15

Non-appearance of prosecutor

7–15 15.—(1) Where at the time and place appointed for the trial or adjourned trial of an information the accused appears or is brought before the court and the prosecutor does not appear, the court may dismiss the information or, if evidence has been received on a previous occasion, proceed in the absence of the prosecutor.

(2) Where, instead of dismissing the information or proceeding in the absence of the prosecutor, the court adjourns the trial, it shall not remand the accused in custody unless he has been brought from custody or cannot be remanded on bail by reason of his failure to find sureties.

A prosecutor is not absent if he is represented by counsel or solicitor: s.122 of the *Magistrates' Courts Act* 1980. The prosecutor may be absent if he is physically not present in court or if, although present he is not able to prosecute the case because he does not have the file.

It is apparent from case law that the appeal courts frown upon the use of the power in this section as a punitive measure. In *R. v Shuttleworth* (2002) 166 J.P. 417, a defendant indicated she would plead guilty but the prosecutor could not proceed with the case because he did not have the file. The court purported to dismiss the charge. It was held on appeal that there was a want of prosecution because the file was not available but the purpose of the hearing was for plea and not for trial. The choice for the court in view of the guilty plea was to adjourn the case or proceed without the information from the file. The dismissal of the case was a punitive measure against the CPS which was not a proper exercise of the courts discretion. Costs penalties were available for that and the court failed to have regard to public interests including those of the defendant and victim.

7–16   It is not reasonable to use this power to punish a prosecutor for late attendance without taking into account all the circumstances. Where the CPS were told by the court that a trial was not in the court list and that the court was not sitting the court acted unreasonably in dismissing the charge since the reason for the non-attendance was because the CPS had been misinformed. On discovering the mistake, a prosecutor contacted the court to say he was on his way. The court did not wait for him to arrive but dismissed the charge apparently as a means of punishing the prosecutor for perceived inefficiency which was held to be an improper exercise of its power: *R. v Hendon Justices Ex p. DPP* (1993) 1 All E.R. 411; and see *R. (on the application of the CPS) v Portsmouth Crown Court* [2003] EWHC 1079.

Another device resorted to occasionally by the court is to direct a change of plea from guilty to not guilty so that a charge may be dismissed in the absence of the prosecutor.

The mere fact that a case could be dismissed for want of prosecution is not a good reason to allow a change of plea: *R. v Uxbridge Justices Ex p. Smith* (1977) R.T.R. 93. Allowing a change of plea in order to exercise the discretion to dismiss was held to be in breach of natural justice as the discretion should not be exercised in order to discipline the prosecution: *R. v Sutton Justices Ex p. DPP* (1992) 2 All E.R. 129.

(3) Non-appearance of both parties

Magistrates' Courts Act 1980, s.16

Non-appearance of both parties
7–17   **16.** Subject to section 11(3) and (4) and to section 12 above, where at the time and place appointed for the trial or adjourned trial of an information neither the prosecutor nor the accused appears, the court may dismiss the information or, if evidence has been received on a previous occasion, proceed in their absence.

The circumstances in which the court would proceed in the absence of both the prosecutor and defendant are very limited. It may not do so when the presence of the defendant is required for the imposition of custodial sentences and for disqualification in certain circumstances under s.11, see § 7–11.

The prosecutor and defendant may not be present when a case is dealt with under s.12 which provides for cases to be heard in absence when a written plea of guilty has been received by the court.

(4) Death of the defendant

7–18   The court may receive information that the defendant has died. In such circumstances in the magistrates' court there is no legal requirement for strict proof of this fact. The court may require that a death certificate be produced or the case may be adjourned for the prosecution to investigate the veracity of the report. The prosecution will then make the appropriate application to withdraw the proceedings or offer no evidence with the court register being marked that the defendant is "deceased".

II. MODE OF TRIAL

A. INTRODUCTION

When a person is charged or summonsed to appear at the magistrates' court the **7–19** details of the charge will be recorded on the charge sheet or the summons. The classification of the offence must then be ascertained so that the defendant can be advised of the correct procedure that applies in his case. For summary only matters that can only be tried by the magistrates' court, it will be expected that a plea of guilty or not guilty will be entered at the earliest opportunity: s.9 of the *Magistrates' Courts Act* 1980. As an encouragement to promptness, an early plea of guilty attracts a discount on sentence: s.152 of the *Powers of Criminal Courts (Sentencing) Act* 2000. For indictable only matters that can only be tried at the Crown Court, the case will be sent for trial at the Crown Court at the first hearing unless there is good reason to adjourn: s.51 of the *Crime and Disorder Act* 1998. In respect of offences that can be tried either way, *i.e.* either at the Crown Court or the magistrates' court a procedure is provided for decisions to be made relating to the 'mode of trial' in order to determine at which court the case should be tried. This is found in ss.17A–22 of the *Magistrates' Courts Act* 1980.

The *Criminal Justice Act* 2003, s.41 and Sch.3 which is not yet in force provides for amendments to the mode of trial procedure. The new procedure is described as "allocation" of cases. A decision will still be made as to whether the case is more suitable for summary trial or trial on indictment and "allocation guidelines" will be issued under the Act. Various other amendments are also made to the procedure which are contained in detail in Sch.3.

(1) General

Sections 17A–C provides for the 'plea before venue' procedure. A defendant facing **7–20** an either way offence will be asked by the court at the earliest opportunity if he is prepared to give an indication of his plea. The indication will be that he will plead guilty or not guilty, or he has a right to give no indication of plea. If there is an indication of a guilty plea the court may then proceed as if he had been convicted of the offence and consider sentence. The court may also commit the defendant to the Crown Court for sentence if it is of the opinion that the powers of sentencing in the magistrates' court are not sufficient. If a not guilty plea is indicated or no indication of plea is given then the court must adopt the 'mode of trial' procedure to decide where the case shall be tried. Sections 18–23 of the *MCA* 1980 set out the procedure to be followed. The prosecution is first invited to make representations as to where it considers it is most suitable for the matter to be tried. The defence will then be asked if it has any representations to make as to whether the magistrates' court or Crown Court would be a more suitable venue. Having heard the representations the court will then decide whether the charge is more suitable for summary trial or trial on indictment. In making this decision the court will take into account the powers of sentencing available in the magistrates' court and will consider whether, were there to be a conviction on the charge those powers would be sufficient. In making this decision the court is aided by the Mode of Trial Guidelines. If the court is of the opinion that on conviction of the offence a greater sentence might have to be imposed than it has power to inflict then the court will decline jurisdiction and direct that the case be dealt with at the Crown Court. The defendant is bound by this decision.

If the court is of the opinion that the case is suitable for summary trial because the powers of the magistrate' court would be sufficient then the defendant is asked whether he would consent to summary trial. If he does not consent to summary trial he will be tried at the Crown Court by judge and jury. He may then consent to summary trial or elect to be tried at the Crown Court by a jury. The right to jury trial cannot be denied to a defendant.

Section 17 defines the offences that are triable either way and they are listed in Sch.1 to the Act. Under s.22, some offences that are triable either way according to the Schedule must be tried summarily if the value involved in the offence is small. The procedure for mode of trial may be adapted to cater for this.

Section 25 allows for a change of election so that a summary trial may be changed into a committal for trial or vice versa.

7–21   These provisions apply only to adults aged 18 and over. For the powers of the magistrates' court in relation to youth co-defendants see the commencement of proceedings chapter. The mode of trial procedure in the youth court is dealt with in s.24 of the *Magistrates' Courts Act* 1980, see § 34–119 below.

(2) Procedure

Magistrates' Courts Act 1980, s.17A

Initial procedure: accused to indicate intention as to plea

7–22   17A—(1) This section shall have effect where a person who has attained the age of 18 years appears or is brought before a magistrates' court on an information charging him with an offence triable either way.

(2) Everything that the court is required to do under the following provisions of this section must be done with the accused present in court.

(3) The court shall cause the charge to be written down, if this has not already been done, and to be read to the accused.

(4) The court shall then explain to the accused in ordinary language that he may indicate whether (if the offence were to proceed to trial) he would plead guilty or not guilty, and that if he indicates that he would plead guilty—

    (a) the court must proceed as mentioned in subsection (6) below; and

    (b) he may be committed for sentence to the Crown Court under [section 3 of the *Powers of Criminal Courts (Sentencing) Act* 2000] below if the court is of such opinion as is mentioned in subsection (2) of that section.

(5) The court shall then ask the accused whether (if the offence were to proceed to trial) he would plead guilty or not guilty.

(6) If the accused indicates that he would plead guilty the court shall proceed as if—

    (a) the proceedings constituted from the beginning the summary trial of the information; and

    (b) section 9(1) above was complied with and he pleaded guilty under it.

(7) If the accused indicates that he would plead not guilty section 18(1) below shall apply.

(8) If the accused in fact fails to indicate how he would plead, for the purposes of this section and section 18(1) below he shall be taken to indicate that he would plead not guilty.

(9) Subject to subsection (6) above, the following shall not for any purpose be taken to constitute the taking of a plea—

    (a) asking the accused under this section whether (if the offence were to proceed to trial) he would plead guilty or not guilty;

    (b) an indication by the accused under this section of how he would plead.

[This section is reprinted as amended by the *Powers of Criminal Courts (Sentencing) Act* 2000, Sch.9, para.62.]

7–23   This section applies to a defendant who is 18 years of age or more. An offence triable either way is one that is triable either at the Crown Court on indictment or summarily at the magistrates' court: *Interpretation Act* 1978, Sch.I; s.17 of the *Magistrates' Courts Act* 1980 and Sch.I list offences which are triable either way. The legal adviser in court will explain the procedure for plea before venue to the defendant after identifying that the charge is triable either way. The charge should be read to the defendant and then a recommended form of words has been suggested as follows:—

> "For this charge you may be tried either in the magistrates' court or by a jury in the Crown Court. First however this court must ask you whether, if the case proceeds to trial, you would plead guilty or not guilty. Before you answer that I want to explain what will happen then. If you say that you would plead guilty, the court will hear the prosecution case against you, listen to your mitigation and formally find you guilty. The court will then decide what

sentence it thinks you should receive. Do you understand? (*If yes, say*) If the court believes that you deserve greater punishment than this court can give (or if you have to be sent to the Crown Court to be tried on a related charge) it will send you to the Crown Court to be sentenced. Otherwise you will be sentenced here. If you do not indicate a guilty plea the court will decide whether to send you to the Crown Court for trial Do you understand that or do you want anything to be explained further? (*Unless repeated or further explanation is required say*) Then if the charge against you was to go to trial, would you plead guilty or not guilty."

This pronouncement was devised by the Judicial Studies Board and approved in *R.* **7–24** *v Southampton Magistrates' Court Ex p. Sansome* [1999] 1 Cr.App.R. 112. The form of words is not obligatory and many legal advisers will adopt their own favoured explanation which will include the right to give no indication of plea. This procedure was reviewed and explained in the case of *R. v Warley Magistrates' Court Ex p. DPP* [1998] 2 Cr.App.R. 307. The purpose of s.17A is to give the defendant the opportunity to enter a plea of guilty as soon as possible, to enable him to claim additional credit compared with a plea entered in the Crown Court and to ensure that cases which could properly be dealt with in the magistrates' court remained there. The court had the power to commit for sentence to the Crown Court but having received a plea of guilty and heard from the defence as well as the prosecution it could be fully informed before determining whether to commit for sentence. A plea of guilty before venue in the magistrates' court entitles the defendant who is committed for sentence to the Crown Court to a greater discount than if he had elected trial by jury but changed his plea to guilty only when he appeared at the Crown Court: *R. v Rafferty* [1999] 1 Cr.App.R. 235. For detailed commentary on committal for sentence see Sentencing, Pt IV in this work.

In order to secure the maximum benefit of an early plea the court will expect the plea before venue procedure to take place as soon as possible but the defendant is entitled to receive the relevant information from the prosecution that will affect his plea and the mode of trial decision. If a request for advanced disclosure under the provisions of the *Magistrates' Courts (Advance Information) Rules*) 1985 has not been complied with the court should adjourn the case unless it is satisfied that the failure to disclose does not prejudice the defendant: *R. v Calderdale Magistrates' Courts Ex p. Donahue and Cutler* [2001] Crim.L.R. 141, DC.

Magistrates' Courts Act 1980, ss.17B–18

Intention as to plea: absence of accused

17B.—(1) This section shall have effect where—   **7–25**

   (a) a person who has attained the age of 18 years appears or is brought before a magistrates' court on an information charging him with an offence triable either way.

   (b) the accused is represented by a legal representative,

   (c) the court considers that by reason of the accused's disorderly conduct before the court it is not practicable for proceedings under section 17A above to be conducted in his presence, and

   (d) the court considers that it should proceed in the absence of the accused.

  (2) In such a case—

   (a) the court shall cause the charge to be written down, if this has not already been done, and to be read to the representative;

   (b) the court shall ask the representative whether (if the offence were to proceed to trial) the accused would plead guilty or not guilty;

   (c) if the representative indicates that the accused would plead guilty the court shall proceed as if the proceedings constituted from the beginning the summary trial of the information, and as if section 9(1) above was complied with and the accused pleaded guilty under it;

   (d) if the representative indicates that the accused would plead not guilty section 18(1) below shall apply.

  (3) If the representative in fact fails to indicate how the accused would plead, for the purposes of this section and section 18(1) below he shall be taken to indicate that the accused would plead not guilty.

(4) Subject to subsection (2)(c) above, the following shall not for any purpose be taken to constitute the taking of a plea—

    (a) asking the representative under this section whether (if the offence were to proceed to trial) the accused would plead guilty or not guilty;

    (b) an indication by the representative under this section of how the accused would plead.

Intention as to plea adjournment

7–26   **17C.** A magistrates' court proceeding under section 17A or 17B above may adjourn the proceedings at any time, and on doing so on any occasion when the accused is present may remand the accused, and shall remand him if—

    (a) on the occasion on which he first appeared, or was brought, before the court to answer to the information he was in custody or, having been released on bail, surrendered to the custody of the court; or

    (b) he has been remanded at any time in the course of proceedings on the information;

and where the court remands the accused, the time fixed for the resumption of proceedings shall be that at which he is required to appear or be brought before the court in pursuance of the remand or would be required to be brought before the court but for section 128(3A) below.

[Sections 17B and 17C are reprinted as amended by the *Criminal Procedure and Investigations Act* 1996, s.49(2).]

Initial procedure on information against adult for offence triable either way

7–27   **18.**—(1) Sections 19 to 23 below shall have effect where a person who has attained the age of 18 years appears or is brought before a magistrates' court on an information charging him with an offence triable either way and—

    (a) he indicates under section 17A above that (if the offence were to proceed to trial) he would plead not guilty, or

    (b) his representative indicates under section 17B above that (if the offence were to proceed to trial) he would plead not guilty.

(2) Without prejudice to section 11(1) above, everything that the court is required to do under sections 19 to 22 below must be done before any evidence is called and, subject to subsection (3) below and section 23 below, with the accused present in court.

(3) The court may proceed in the absence of the accused in accordance with such of the provisions of sections 19 to 22 below as are applicable in the circumstances if the court considers that by reason of his disorderly conduct before the court it is not practicable for the proceedings to be conducted in his presence; and subsections (3) to (5) of section 23 below, so far as applicable, shall have effect in relation to proceedings conducted in the absence of the accused by virtue of this subsection (references in those subsections to the person representing the accused being for this purpose read as references to the person, if any, representing him).

(4) A magistrates' court proceeding under sections 19 to 23 below may adjourn the proceedings at any time, and on doing so on any occasion when the accused is present may remand the accused, and shall remand him if—

    (a) on the occasion on which he first appeared, or was brought, before the court to answer to the information he was in custody or, having been released on bail, surrendered to the custody of the court; or

    (b) he has been remanded at any time in the course of proceedings on the information;

and where the court remands the accused, the time fixed for the resumption of the proceedings shall be that at which he is required to appear or be brought before the court in pursuance of the remand or would be required to be brought before the court but for section 128(3A) below.

(5) The functions of a magistrates' court under subsections 19 to 23 below may be discharged by a single justice, but the foregoing provision shall not be taken to authorise the summary trial of an information by a magistrates' court composed of less than two justices.

[This section is reprinted as amended by the *Criminal Procedure and Investigations Act* 1996, section 49(3).]

The mode of trial procedure applies to defendants who are aged 18 or over. Whether **7–28**
the right to elect jury trial under these provisions is engaged for a person who is under
the age of 18 at the time when the offence was committed depends on the actual date
when the defendant appears and the court decides to proceed to determine mode of
trial. If a defendant has attained the age of 18 by the time the mode of trial decision falls
to be made then he has the right to elect jury trial. It is irrelevant that the offence may
have been committed or he may have been charged with the offence when he was
under that age: *R. v Islington North Juvenile Court Ex p. Daley* [1983] 1 A.C. 347,
HL. The fact that a defendant reaches the age of 18 after the mode of trial has been
decided in the youth court but before the trial has commenced does not confer the
right to elect jury trial: *R. v Nottingham Justices Ex p. Taylor* [1992] 1 Q.B. 557, DC.
The taking of a plea in the youth court from a defendant who is under the age of 18
amounts to a decision as to the mode of trial: *R. v West London Justices Ex p. Silely-
Winditt* [2000] Crim.L.R. 926, DC.

These provisions are mandatory. Where the court proceeded to try an either way offence without adopting the procedure for determining mode of trial the defendant
could not be said to have consented to summary trial and the proceedings were held to
be a nullity: *R. v Tottenham Justices Ex p. Arthurs Transport Services* [1981]
Crim.L.R. 180.

Once the decision has been made to try a case summarily and in the case of an adult
there is consent to being so tried, it is too late to serve a notice of transfer: *R. v Fare-
ham Youth Court and Morey Ex p. CPS* (1999) 163 J.P. 812, DC.

Magistrates' Courts Act 1980, s.19

Court to begin by considering which mode of trial appears more suitable
　　19.—(1) The court shall consider whether, having regard to the matters mentioned in **7–29**
subsection (3) below and any representations made by the prosecutor or the accused, the offence
appears to the court more suitable for summary trial or for trial on indictment.
　　(2) Before so considering, the court—
　　　　(a) [...]
　　　　(b) shall afford first the prosecutor and then the accused an opportunity to make
　　　　　　representations as to which mode of trial would be more suitable.
　　(3) The matters to which the court is to have regard under subsection (1) above are the
nature of the case; whether the circumstances make the offence one of serious character;
whether the punishment which a magistrates' court would have power to inflict for it
would be adequate; and any other circumstances which appear to the court to make it
more suitable for the offence to be tried in one way rather than the other.
　　(4) If the prosecution is being carried on by the Attorney General, the Solicitor General
or the Director of Public Prosecutions and he applies for the offence to be tried on indictment, the preceding provisions of this section and sections 20 and 21 below shall not apply,
and the court shall proceed to inquire into the information as examining justices.
　　(5) The power of the Director of Public Prosecutions under subsection (4) above to apply for an offence to be tried on indictment shall not be exercised except with the consent
of the Attorney General.

　　[This section is reprinted as amended by the *Criminal Procedure and Investigations
Act* 1996, s.49(4).]
　　This section will be amended under s.41 and Sch.3 of the *Criminal Justice Act* 2003.
A new s.19 will be substituted which provides for the allocation of case either to sum-
mary trial or trial on indictment.

　　The mode of trial procedure allows for either the court or the defendant to decide **7–30**
that trial at the Crown Court would be most suitable. In the majority of cases the court
will hear representations from the prosecution and the defence and then the court will
decide on suitability. An exception to this procedure is where the prosecution can
dictate that the case be tried at the Crown Court. Only if the prosecution is being
conducted by one of the Chief Law Officers referred to in the section or the DPP with
the consent of the Attorney General can the prosecution application for jury trial over-
ride any decision of the court or the defendant.

The court must have regard to the matters mentioned in subs.(3). The decision is made on the basis of the facts of the case as outlined by the prosecution and the nature and seriousness of the offence must be made out. The court must consider whether its powers of sentencing would be sufficient in view of the information that it has received from the prosecution. Regard may also be had to other circumstances affecting the suitability of the case to be tried one way or the other. The question of plea or the strength of the evidence is not relevant in defence representations because at this stage the court is only concerned with trying to ensure that serious cases are dealt with by the Crown Court. The gravity of the offence will be assessed not on the basis of evidence but on the assertions made by the prosecution. The previous convictions or good character of the defendant are irrelevant to this decision and the court should neither hear nor take into account any information as to the defendant's previous record: *R. v Colchester Justices Ex p. North East Essex Building Co Ltd* [1977] 1 W.L.R. 1109, DC. The defendant's criminal record only becomes relevant after conviction, not at mode of trial stage: *R. v Hammersmith Juvenile Court Ex p. O*, 86 Cr.App.R. 343, DC.

7–31 Under the *Criminal Justice Act* 2003, s.41 and Sch.3 the court will be entitled to hear about the previous convictions of the defendant before making a decision on allocation. This provision is not yet in force.

The *Practice Direction (Criminal Proceedings: Consolidation)* [2002] 1 W.L.R. 2870 contains the most recent version of the National Mode of Trial Guidelines. The object of the guidelines is to provide guidance on the matters to be considered when determining mode of trial. They are not directive. The magistrates retain a duty to consider each case individually and on its own particular facts: *R. v Derby Justices Ex p. DPP, The Times*, August 17, 1999.

The Guidelines indicate that offences triable either way should be tried summarily unless one of the stated special features is present and the magistrates' sentencing powers are inadequate. The magistrates' courts' powers of sentence are limited to a maximum fine of £5,000 or imprisonment of up to six months on a single offence. The factors identified are aggravating features that could make the offence more serious and so might attract a more severe sentence.

Cases in which the decision of the court on mode of trial have been reviewed involve instances of the court retaining jurisdiction for offences which should more properly have been dealt with at the Crown Court.

7–32 Jurisdiction was accepted in the magistrates' court for a defendant charged with a VAT fraud case concerning nearly £200,000. It was held that if there was a conviction the Crown Court was likely to have imposed a heavier sentence. The decision on mode of trial was unreasonable and was quashed: *R. v Northamptonshire Magistrates' Court Ex p. Commissioners of Customs and Excise* [1994] Crim.L.R. 598, DC. In another case of VAT fraud when jurisdiction was accepted the decision was quashed because it was held that the court had failed to apply its mind to the provisions of s.19(3). The court had not considered whether its powers of punishment were sufficient: *R. v Flax Bourton Magistrates' Court Ex p. Commissioners of Customs and Excise* (1996) 160 J.P. 481. In another case the charge was one of possession of Class A drugs (114 ecstasy tablets) with intent to supply, an offence that would normally attract a prison sentence of between two to five years. It was held that the decision to retain summary jurisdiction was perverse. It was reiterated that close regard must be had to the Guidelines in conjunction with s.19(3) when considering jurisdiction: *R. v Horseferry Road Magistrates' Court Ex p. DPP* (1997) C.O.D. 89, DC. Interpretation of the Guidelines was considered when it was held that an assault committed by banging the victim's head against a wall did not involve the "use of a weapon" within the meaning of the Guidelines and so summary jurisdiction could be retained: *R. v Derby Justices Ex p. DPP, The Times*, August 17, 1999.

When the *Criminal Justice Act* 2003 comes into force, allocation guidelines will be issued under s.170 of the Act to which the court will have regard when making decisions as to allocation of cases under the new procedure.

7–33 Any other circumstances may be taken into account when deciding on mode of trial.

The fact that it may be more "convenient and expeditious" to deal with serious offences summarily is not a relevant 'other circumstance' and cannot amount to a reason for accepting jurisdiction. Summary trial is only appropriate where the sentencing powers of the court will be sufficient: *R. v Coe*, 53 Cr.App.R. 66, CA.

The complexity and sensitivity of a case may be taken into account but this will generally contribute to the seriousness of the case in any event. Issues about disclosure cannot of themselves make a case more suitable for trial at the Crown Court. Where a defendant was charged with possession of a pitbull terrier in contravention of the *Dangerous Dogs Act* 1991 disclosure was sought from the prosecution of expert reports prepared for previous cases relating to the identification of dogs as pitbull terriers. The court declined jurisdiction on the basis that it had no power to order disclosure of the reports. It was held that the magistrates' court had power to order disclosure and summary jurisdiction could have been accepted: *R. v Bromley Justices Ex p. Smith and Wilkins, R. v Wells Street Stipendiary Magistrate Ex p. King* [1995] 2 Cr.App.R. 285, DC.

Once a court has made a decision on mode of trial it is not open to a subsequent court to change that decision, thereby acting as a court of appeal. Where a court declined summary jurisdiction, another bench cannot later hear representations and agree to summary trial: *R. v Liverpool Justices Ex p. Crown Prosecution Service* 90 Cr.App.R. 261. There is provision for the mode of trial to be changed but only after the trial or committal has begun, see s.25 at § 7–49 below.)

Magistrates' Courts Act 1980, s.20

Procedure where summary trial appears more suitable

20.—(1) If, where the court has considered as required by section 19(1) above, it appears to **7–34** the court that the offence is more suitable for summary trial, the following provisions of this section shall apply (unless excluded by section 23 below).

(2) The court shall explain to the accused in ordinary language—

    (a) that it appears to the court more suitable for him to be tried summarily for the offence, and that he can either consent to be so tried or, if he wishes, be tried by a jury; and

    (b) that if he is tried summarily and is convicted by the court, he may be committed for sentence to the Crown Court under [section 3 of the *Powers of Criminal Courts (Sentencing) Act* 2000] if the convicting court, is of such opinion as is mentioned in subsection (2) of that section.

(3) After explaining to the accused as provided by subsection (2) above the court shall ask him whether he consents to be tried summarily or wishes to be tried by a jury, and—

    (a) if he consents to be tried summarily, shall proceed to the summary trial of the information;

    (b) if he does not so consent, shall proceed to inquire into the information as examining justices.

[This section is reprinted as amended by the *Powers of Criminal Courts (Sentencing) Act* 2000, Sch.9, para.63.]

This section will be amended by the *Criminal Justice Act* 2003, s.41 and Sch.3 when **7–35** in force. A new s.20 will be substituted providing for the procedure on allocation when summary trial appears more suitable. Under the present s.20, after considering the representations of the prosecution and defence, the court may decide that the case is suitable for summary trial on the basis that if there were to be a conviction the powers of sentencing in the magistrates' court would be sufficient. The defendant must then be asked if he consents to summary trial. He is not bound to do so and there is a right to jury trial. The legal adviser will put the election to the defendant and will explain the procedure and his rights. The recommended form of words is as follows;—

    "It appears to this court more suitable for you to be tried here. You may now consent to be tried by this court, but if you wish, you may choose to be tried by a jury instead. If you are tried by this court and are found guilty, this court may still send you to the Crown Court for sentence if it is of the opinion that greater punishment should be inflicted for the offence than it has power to impose. Do you wish to be tried by this court or do you wish to be tried by a jury?"

This pronouncement was approved in *R. v Southampton Magistrates' Court Ex p. Sansome* [1999] 1 Cr.App.R. 112. The defendant may then consent to be tried at the magistrates' court and the case will proceed as a summary trial, or he may elect trial at the Crown Court and a committal will then ensue.

7–36   The procedure of s.20 must be followed. A summary trial which led to the acquittal of a defendant who had not been put to his election was declared a nullity: *R. v Cardiff Magistrates' Court Ex p. Cardiff City Council, The Times,* February 24, 1987. The court has a discretion to allow a change of election but an application to have the election put again will only be granted if there is some doubt over whether the defendant understood or fully appreciated the procedure and the effect of his choice. In *R. v Birmingham Justices Ex p. Hodgson* [1985] Q.B. 1131, an unrepresented defendant consented to summary trial and in his plea of guilty disclosed a possible defence to the charge he faced. Later, he appeared represented and application was made to have the election put again. It was held that the election on mode of trial was final and binding only when the nature and significance of the choice being made was understood and the court was wrong to refuse to allow the election to be put again.

The fact that the court may feel itself able to deal adequately with the complexities of a case is no ground for refusing to vary an election. A defendant who was unrepresented and had not appreciated the importance and implications of his choice of summary trial was entitled to change his election: *R. v Highbury Corner Metropolitan Stipendiary Magistrates Ex p. Weekes* [1985] Q.B. 1147. The defendant must prove that he lacked the necessary comprehension but if the relevant evidence is not put before the court a proper determination cannot be made. It is incumbent upon the court to ensure that the defence put forward proper reasons which can be duly considered before refusing a request to change an election: *R. v Forest Magistrates Ex p. Spicer* (1989) 153 J.P. 81

7–37   That the defendant was unrepresented when the original election was made does not of itself compel the court to allow the election to be withdrawn: *R. v Lambeth Stipendiary Magistrate Ex p. Wright* [1974] Crim.L.R. 444. The court has an unfettered discretion whether to allow an application to change the election. If satisfied the defendant understood the difference between the two modes of trial, the court was entitled to refuse the application. The fact that a not guilty plea had been entered and the prosecution witnesses were ready to give evidence and the trial would be delayed further are not relevant to the understanding of the applicant: *R. v Bourne Justices Ex p. Cope* [1989] C.O.D. 304, DC.

The defendant has a right to receive a summary of the prosecution case and/or copies of the statements of the proposed prosecution witnesses in advanced disclosure: *Magistrates' Courts (Advance Information) Rules* 1985, see §§ 6–27—6–33 above. Sight of these may be required so that the defendant can make an informed choice between summary trial and trial on indictment.

The right to consent to summary trial or to elect for trial at the Crown Court is given to each defendant individually. Where there are co-defendants, each person must be asked at which court they wish to be tried and different elections must be accepted. The fact that one defendant elects jury trial does not require that all defendants should go to the Crown Court: *R. v Brentwood Justices Ex p. Nicholls* [1992] 1 A.C. 1.

7–38   The decision on mode of trial should not be based on an indication given by defendants that they would elect jury trial. In *R. v Ipswich Magistrates' Court Ex p. Callaghan* (1995) 159 J.P. 748, the legal adviser during the mode of trial procedure asked three defendants whether they were going to elect jury trial. Two defendants indicated that they would and so the court decided to direct Crown Court trial in respect of all three defendants. It was held on appeal that the preliminary inquiry by the legal adviser was incorrect and the court had to decide whether an offence was more suitable for summary or Crown Court trial. This decision cannot be based on a wish to avoid separate trials. Each defendant has an individual right of election which is exercised after the court has decided which mode of trial is more suitable. Once the court has indicated that a case is suitable for summary trial that decision cannot be changed at the request of the prosecutor for the purposes of ensuring that co-defendants, one of whom elected trial by jury, should all be committed to the Crown Court: *R. v Wigan Magistrates' Court Ex p. Layland* [1995] Crim.L.R. 892.

The defendant's right to jury trial does not oblige the prosecution to proceed on the most serious charges disclosed by the facts. Where alternative summary only charges were preferred by the prosecution and no evidence offered on either way offences it was held that no consent was required from the court for the prosecution to conduct the case that way and the defendant had not wrongfully been deprived of a right to elect trial at the Crown Court: *R. v Canterbury and St Augustine Justices Ex p. Klisiak* [1982] Q.B. 398. By the same token the prosecution may upgrade the offences. The addition or substitution of charges by the prosecution so that an offence becomes either way is not a ground for refusing the issue of a summons provided that such process could properly be issued in the light of the facts as presented by the prosecution: *R. v Redbridge Justices and Fox Ex p. Whitehouse* [1992] 94 Cr.App.R. 332 .

Under the *Criminal Justice Act* 2003, s.41 and Sch.3, a new s.20 will be substituted and the defendant will be able to request the court to give an indication as to sentence before deciding whether to consent to summary trial. The court will have a discretion to indicate whether a custodial or non-custodial sentence would be more likely to be imposed if the defendant were to plead guilty. After hearing any such indication of sentence that the court may give the defendant may then re-consider his plea of not guilty. If no such indication of sentence is requested or the court does not agree to give one then the defendant will decide if he consents to summary trial.

Magistrates' Courts Act 1980, s.21

Procedure where trial on indictment appears more suitable

7–39   **21.** If, where the court has considered as required by section 19(1) above, it appears to the court that the offence is more suitable for trial on indictment, the court shall tell the accused that the court has decided that it is more suitable for him to be tried for the offence by a jury, and shall proceed to inquire into the information as examining justices.

7–40   Once the court has declined jurisdiction the defendant has no right to be put to his election. The decision of the court overrides any wish he may have to consent to summary trial and committal to the Crown Court will take place. In some cases a defendant will indicate a guilty plea to a serious charge which, had it been contested would have been considered more suitable to be tried at the Crown Court at the mode of trial stage. On an early guilty plea the court may not decline jurisdiction but the court may still send the defendant to the Crown Court for sentence if the magistrates' courts powers of sentencing are not sufficient. The defendant meanwhile will benefit at the Crown Court from a greater reduction in his sentence to give credit for his pleading guilty at the earliest opportunity.

If an earlier court has declined summary jurisdiction a later court cannot hear representations and agree to summary trial: *R. v Liverpool Justices Ex p. Crown Prosecution Service*, 90 Cr.App.R. 261.

Special procedure for criminal damage charges

Magistrates' Courts Act 1980, s.22

Certain offences triable either way to be tried summarily if value involved is small

7–41   **22.**—(1) If the offence charged by the information is one of those mentioned in the first column of Schedule 2 to this Act (in this section referred to as "scheduled offences") then, the court shall, before proceeding in accordance with section 19 above, consider whether, having regard to any representations made by the prosecutor or the accused, the value involved (as defined in subsection (10) below) appears to the court to exceed the relevant sum.

For the purposes of this section the relevant sum is £5,000.

(2) If, where subsection (1) above applies, it appears to the court clear that, for the offence charged, the value involved does not exceed the relevant sum, the court shall proceed as if the offence were triable only summarily, and sections 19 to 21 above shall not apply.

(3) If, where subsection (1) above applies, it appears to the court clear that, for the offence charged, the value involved exceeds the relevant sum, the court shall thereupon proceed in accordance with section 19 above in the ordinary way without further regard to the provisions of this section.

(4) If, where subsection (1) above applies, it appears to the court for any reason not clear whether, for the offence charged, the value involved does or does not exceed the relevant sum, the provisions of subsections (5) and (6) below shall apply.

(5) The court shall cause the charge to be written down, if this has not already been done, and read to the accused, and shall explain to him in ordinary language—

    (a) that he can, if he wishes, consent to be tried summarily for the offence and that if he consents to be so tried, he will definitely be tried in that way; and

    (b) that if he is tried summarily and is convicted by the court, his liability to imprisonment or a fine will be limited as provided in section 33 below.

(6) After explaining to the accused as provided by subsection (5) above the court shall ask him whether he consents to be tried summarily and—

    (a) if he so consents, shall proceed in accordance with subsection (2) above as if that subsection applied;

    (b) if he does not so consent, shall proceed in accordance with subsection (3) above as if that subsection applied.

(7) [...]

(8) Where a person is convicted by a magistrates' court of a scheduled offence, it shall not be open to him to appeal to the Crown Court against the conviction on the ground that the convicting court's decision as to the value involved was mistaken.

(9) If, where subsection (1) above applies, the offence charged is one with which the accused is charged jointly with a person who has not attained the age of 17, the reference in that subsection to any representations made by the accused shall be read as including any representations made by the person under 18.

(10) In this section "the value involved", in relation to any scheduled offence, means the value indicated in the second column of Schedule 2 to this Act, measured as indicated in the third column of that Schedule; and in that Schedule "the material time" means the time of the alleged offence.

(11) Where—

    (a) the accused is charged on the same occasion with two or more scheduled offences and it appears to the court that they constitute or form part of a series of two or more offences of the same or a similar character; or

    (b) the offence charged consists in incitement to commit two or more scheduled offences,

this section shall have effect as if any reference in it to the value involved were a reference to the aggregate of the values involved.

(12) Subsection (8) of section 12A of the *Theft Act* 1968 (which determines when a vehicle is recovered) shall apply for the purposes of paragraph 3 of Schedule 2 to this Act as it applies for the purposes of that section.

[This section is reprinted as amended by the *Criminal Justice and Public Order Act* 1994, s.46(1).]

7–42   The offences listed in Schedule 2 are—

    1. Offences under s.1 of the *Criminal Damage Act* 1971 (destroying or damaging property), excluding any offence committed by destroying or damaging property by fire.

    2. ...aiding, abetting, counselling or procuring the commission of any such offence; attempting or inciting such offence

    3. Offences under s.12A of the *Theft Act* 1968 (aggravated vehicle taking) where no allegation is made under subs.(1)(b) other than of damage, whether to the vehicle or other property or both.

The Schedule also states that the value involved is the value of the property destroyed or if it is damaged the value of the damage done. It also gives details as to how the value is to be measured according to how much the property would have cost to buy or repair on the open market at the relevant time when the destruction or damage was caused.

The provisions of the Schedule which relate to the offence of criminal damage under s.1 of the *Criminal Damage Act* 1971 are to be treated as only applying to offences under subs.(1) of that section and do not cover offences under subs.(2) and (3) of criminal damage with intent to endanger life, *etc.* or arson: *R. v Burt* (1997) 161 J.P. 77. The offence of aggravated vehicle taking may become summary only when the vehicle is taken without consent and driven and between the time the vehicle was taken and before it was recovered, damage was caused. If injury was also caused then the offence remains triable either way.

7–43 This section reduces offences of criminal damage and aggravated vehicle taking where the value of the damage caused is small to offences that can only be tried summarily. The seriousness of the offence is reflected by the fact that the defendant is thereby deprived of the right to elect trial at the Crown Court unless a series of small value offences has been committed and the aggregate value takes them over the monetary threshold. The relevant amount was fixed at £5,000 by an amendment to this section under s.46 of the *Criminal Justice and Public Order Act* 1994.

Section 33 of the *Magistrates' Courts Act* 1980 provides that the maximum penalty for an offence of criminal damage tried summarily is three months imprisonment or a fine not exceeding level 4 (£2,500). The maximum sentence for aggravated vehicle taking on summary trial is six months imprisonment or a fine on level 5 (£5,000): s.32 of the *Magistrates' Courts Act* 1980.

When the defendant has been charged with a "scheduled offence" he may lose the right to elect trial at the Crown Court even though the offence is initially classified as triable either way. The procedure in ss.17A–21 of the *Magistrates' Courts Act* 1980 must be preceded by consideration of the value of the damage in question.

7–44 Section 18(1) provides that the mode of trial procedure (including s.22) has effect after a not guilty indication in plea before venue but there is no reference in s.17A as to when and if s.22 comes into operation. The situation was resolved in a case where a defendant was charged with aggravated vehicle taking and the value of the damage caused was below £5,000. The court treated the offence as either way from the outset and plea before venue was dealt with under s.17A. The defendant indicated a guilty plea and the court committed him to the Crown Court for sentence. It was held that s.22 specifically provides that if the value of the damage is below £5,000, the offence should be dealt with summarily. This imposes an absolute obligation on the court and takes precedence over the plea before venue procedure. The offence was not triable either way and the court was held to have no power to commit for sentence: *R. v Kelly* [2001] R.T.R. 5, CA. The procedure provided for in s.22 of the *Magistrates' Courts Act* 1980 is taken to prevail over that in s.17A.

Section 22(10) defines "the value involved" by reference to Sch.2 to the 1980 Act. Where the property is beyond repair, the value of the damage is measured as the amount that the property would probably have cost to buy in the open market at the material time, which is the time of the alleged offence. Where the property is capable of repair then the value is the amount that it would cost to repair the damage or the amount to replace the property on the open market, whichever is the less.

Schedule 2 is directed solely to the actual value of the damage caused to the property itself and is not concerned with any consequential damage. Where the actual damage to a GM maize crop was £750 but the consequential damage to research was put at over £5,000 it was held that under Sch.2 if the property was beyond repair, the value of the damage was the market value at the material time so it was limited to £750: *R. v Colchester Magistrates' Court Ex p. Abbott* (2001) 165 J.P. 386.

7–45 A different approach was taken in another case involving damage to an experimental crop of genetically modified maize. The court heard representations that the maize was grown as a development measure with significant investment costs and to treat it as ordinary maize was artificial. The crop was grown for research rather than for sale and was not marketed so it was not easy to assess the value of damage caused. In the circumstances, the value of the crop was uncertain and could well exceed £5,000. It was held that the value was not clear and so the court was entitled to take the view that the charge remained triable either way and the defendants had the right to choose the mode of trial: *R. v Prestatyn Magistrates' Court Ex p. DPP* [2002] EWCA 1177.

The court must consider whether, when the defendant is charged with two or more of the scheduled offences this constitutes or forms part of a series of offences of the same or similar character in which case the aggregate of the values is relevant to deciding whether the charges are triable either way or not: subs.11.

If the offences are committed at different places and involve different types of property they may be too remote to form a series: *R. v Braden* (1988) 152 J.P. 92. The offences do not have to arise out of the same circumstances but they must be of the same or similar character.

7–46   It is not necessary for the court to hear evidence as to the value of the property in question unless they wish to do so. Representations as to the value could comprise submissions, assertions of fact and the production of documents: *R. v Canterbury and St Augustine Justices Ex p. Klisiak* [1982] Q.B. 398. Where the case involved 30 defendants all of whom had driven into a bean field to destroy a crop valued at £5,8000, the prosecution calculated the individual defendant as having caused £100 of the total damage. It was held that the prosecution did not have to charge as a joint enterprise and their approach to calculating the damage was justifiable even if it resulted in the charge becoming summary only: *R. v Salisbury Magistrates Ex p. Mastin* (1987) 84 Cr.App.R. 248. In *R. v Brentwood Justices Ex p. Nicholls* above the House of Lords said (obiter) that it was apparent that the procedure in s.22(4)–(6) refers to accused persons individually and not to accused persons collectively.

Magistrates' Courts Act 1980, s.23

Power of court, with consent of legally represented accused, to proceed in his absence

7–47   **23.**—(1) Where—

    (a) the accused is represented by a legal representative who in his absence signifies to the court the accused's consent to the proceedings for determining how he is to be tried for the offence being conducted in his absence; and

    (b) the court is satisfied that there is good reason for proceeding in the absence of the accused,

the following provisions of this section shall apply.

(2) Subject to the following provisions of this section, the court may proceed in the absence of the accused in accordance with such of the provisions of sections 19 to 22 above as are applicable in the circumstances.

(3) If, in a case where subsection (1) of section 22 above applies, it appears to the court as mentioned in subsection (4) of that section, subsections (5) and (6) of that section shall not apply and the court—

    (a) if the accused's consent to be tried summarily has been or is signified by the person representing him, shall proceed in accordance with subsection (2) of that section as if that subsection applied; or

    (b) if that consent has not been and is not so signified, shall proceed in accordance with subsection (3) of that section as if that subsection applied.

(4) If, where the court has considered as required by section 19(1) above, it appears to the court that the offence is more suitable for summary trial then—

    (a) if the accused's consent to be tried summarily has been or is signified by the person representing him, section 20 above shall not apply, and the court shall proceed to the summary trial of the information; or

    (b) if that consent has not been and is not so signified, section 20 above shall not apply and the court shall proceed to inquire into the information as examining justices and may adjourn the hearing without remanding the accused.

(5) If, where the court has considered as required by section 19(1) above, it appears to the court that the offence is more suitable for trial on indictment, section 21 above shall not apply, and the court shall proceed to inquire into the information as examining justices

and may adjourn the hearing without remanding the accused.

Mode of trial can be dealt with in the absence of the defendant if he is represented **7–48.1**
and his representative signifies the defendant's consent for the procedure of this section
to be adopted.

Magistrates' Courts Act 1980, s.24

This section deals with mode of trial decisions for persons under the age of 18. For **7–48**
the full text of this section, see below Pt V. The adult court only has jurisdiction in relation to mode of trial for young people under the age of 18 when they appear as co-
defendants jointly charged with an adult: s.24(1)(b). The youth may be committed to
the Crown Court when the court considers that it is in the interests of justice that all co-
defendants be committed for trial. The court may also commit the youth for trial on any
other indictable offence with which he is charged at the same time even though they are
not joint charges with the adult: s.24(2).

Reverting and re-electing

Magistrates' Courts Act 1980, s.25

Power to change from summary trial to committal proceedings, and vice versa
    25.—(1) Subsections (2) to (4) below shall have effect where a person who has attained the **7–49**
age of 18 years appears or is brought before a magistrates' court on an information charging
him with an offence triable either way.
    (2) Where the court has (otherwise than in pursuance of section 22(2) above) begun to
try the information summarily, the court may, at any time before the conclusion of the evidence for the prosecution, discontinue the summary trial and proceed to inquire into the
information as examining justices and, on doing so, shall adjourn the hearing.
    (3) Where the court has begun to inquire into the information as examining justices,
then, if at any time during the inquiry it appears to the court, having regard to any
representations made in the presence of the accused by the prosecutor, or made by the accused, and to the nature of the case, that the offence is after all more suitable for summary
trial, the court may, after doing as provided in subsection (4) below, ask the accused
whether he consents to be tried summarily and, if he so consents, may subject to subsection
(3A) below proceed to try the information summarily;
    (3A) Where the prosecution is being carried on by the Attorney General or the Solicitor
General, the court shall not exercise the power conferred by subsection (3) above without
his consent and, where the prosecution is being carried on by the Director of Public
Prosecutions, shall not exercise that power if the Attorney General directs that it should not
be exercised.
    (4) Before asking the accused under subsection (3) above whether he consents to be
tried summarily, the court shall in ordinary language—
        (a) explain to him that it appears to the court more suitable for him to be tried sum-
            marily for the offence, but that this can only be done if he consents to be so tried;
            and
        (b) unless it has already done so, explain to him, as provided in section 20(2)(b)
            above, about the court's power to commit to the Crown Court for sentence.
    (5) Where a person under the age of 18 years appears or is brought before a magis-
trates' court on an information charging him with an indictable offence other than homicide, and the court—
        (a) has begun to try the information summarily on the footing that the case does not
            fall within paragraph (a) or (b) of section 24(1) above and must therefore be tried
            summarily, as required by the said section 24(1); or
        (b) has begun to inquire into the case as examining justices on the footing that the
            case does so fall,
subsection (6) or (7) below, as the case may be, shall have effect.
    (6) If, in a case falling within subsection (5)(a) above, it appears to the court at any time
before the conclusion of the evidence for the prosecution that the case is after all one which

under the said section 24(1) ought not to be tried summarily, the court may discontinue the summary trial and proceed to inquire into the information as examining justices and, on doing so, shall adjourn the hearing.

(7) If, in a case falling within subsection (5)(b) above, it appears to the court at any time during the inquiry that the case is after all one which under the said section 24(1) ought to be tried summarily, the court may proceed to try the information summarily.

(8) If the court adjourns the hearing under subsection (2) or (6) above it may (if it thinks fit) do so without remanding the accused.

[This section is reprinted as amended by the *Criminal Procedure and Investigations Act* 1996, Sch.1(1), para.5(3).]

7–50　After the court has begun a summary trial or a committal it may change the procedure and switch from hearing a summary trial to inquiring into the offence as examining magistrates or it may discontinue a committal and with the defendant's consent, proceed to hear a summary trial of the charge. The decision will be made subject to the evidence that has been called, representations made and the nature of the case. These factors may mean that a less serious case becomes more serious or a case first believed to be serious enough to warrant committal is shown to be less serious. The intention is that the court should keep the mode of trial under continuous review

The power to change the proceedings can only be exercised when the court has begun the trial or committal. When exactly this happens has been the subject of several appeals and attempts to clarify the crucial moment.

The trial must actually have started and the court must have heard some evidence during the summary trial before changing to a committal: *R. v Southend Justices Ex p. Wood* (1988) 152 J.P. 97. The fact that further indictable matters had been brought against the defendant and the court wished to commit on all charges did not affect the requirement to start to hear the evidence on the summary trial before changing to committal: *R. v St Helen's Magistrates Ex p. Critchley* (1988) 152 J.P. 102. Neither did the fact that it was evident that jurisdiction should not have been accepted on a serious charge. Where the court indicated that summary trial was suitable for an offence of possessing cannabis with intent to supply and a later bench indicated that it would use the powers of s.25 to ensure that the case went to the Crown Court, the summary trial was held not to have begun when the court took a deposition from one prosecution witness and did not allow any cross examination. The summary trial had not begun and s.25 did not apply: *R. v Birmingham Stipendiary Magistrate Ex p. Webb* (1992) 157 J.P. 89.

7–51　As to when the case has concluded after trial, it was held that when magistrates disagree on a verdict and adjourn for a rehearing, the prosecution case had not been concluded: *R. v Coventry Justices Ex p. Wilson* [1981] Crim.L.R. 787.

The words 'try' and 'trial' are to be construed narrowly to mean the process of determining guilt or innocence. Although simply entering a not guilty plea does not start a trial, there may be circumstances where the trial process begins after the plea but before any evidence is called. Where the court had accepted jurisdiction in the case of a defendant who was later recommended for committal to the Crown Court for the purposes of a restriction order under the *Mental Health Act* 1983, it was held that the summary trial had started. Although no evidence had been called, the court had heard preliminary submissions regarding the trial process and issues of mental capability. The procedure under s.25 could be adopted and the case was properly committed to the Crown Court: *R. v Horseferry Road Magistrates' Court Ex p. K* [1996] 3 W.L.R. 68.

Section 25 does not apply to summary cases where a plea of guilty has been accepted. No trial then takes place. A defendant consented to summary trial and pleaded guilty to an offence of causing actual bodily harm. His co-defendant elected trial by jury. The court at the next hearing purported to discontinue the trial against the defendant and committed him for trial with his co-defendant. It was held that the power under s.25 was only exercisable during a trial when evidence was tendered to prove guilt. It did not apply after a guilty plea. The defendant could only have been committed to the

Crown Court for sentence: *R. v Dudley Justices Ex p. Gillard* [1986] A.C. 442. This principle remains the same even where the basis of the guilty plea is disputed. It was held inappropriate for a court to direct a not guilty plea be entered and to decline jurisdiction to effect a committal to the Crown Court where the proper course would have been to conduct a Newton hearing and if need be commit for sentence: *R. v Telford Magistrates' Court Ex p. Darlington* (1988) 152 J.P. 215.

Whilst the magistrates' court has a discretion to discontinue a summary trial and then **7–52** commit the defendant to trial in the Crown Court, it is unreasonable to use that procedure to circumvent the principle of individual right of election as expressed in the Brentwood Justices case (above). Three defendants had been jointly charged with theft. Two of the defendants elected jury trial and the third defendant, who had been absent when the co-defendants elected trial, later consented to summary trial. After calling some evidence the prosecution asked the court to discontinue the summary trial pursuant to s.25(2) of the *Magistrates' Courts Act* 1980 and to commit the defendant to the Crown Court for trial with his co-defendants. This was held to be an inappropriate use of s.25: *R. v West Norfolk Justices Ex p. McMullen* (1993) 157 J.P. 461 and see *R. v Bradford Magistrates' Court Ex p. Grant* [1999] Crim.L.R. 324.

Indictable only offences

Indictable only offences cannot be dealt with at the magistrates' court. Such offences **7–53** are sent to the Crown Court for trial.

Crime and Disorder Act 1998, s.51

No committal proceedings for indictable-only offence

51.—(1) Where an adult appears or is brought before a magistrates' court ("the court") **7–54** charged with an offence triable only on indictment ("the indictable-only offence"), the court shall send him forthwith to the Crown Court for trial—

(a) for that offence, and

(b) for any either-way or summary offence with which he is charged which fulfils the requisite conditions (as set out in subsection (11) below).

(2) Where an adult who has been sent for trial under subsection (1) above subsequently appears or is brought before a magistrates' court charged with an either-way or summary offence which fulfils the requisite conditions, the court may send him forthwith to the Crown Court for trial for the either-way or summary offence.

(3) Where—

(a) the court sends an adult for trial under subsection (1) above;

(b) another adult appears or is brought before the court on the same or a subsequent occasion charged jointly with him with an either-way offence; and

(c) that offence appears to the court to be related to the indictable-only offence,

the court shall where it is the same occasion, and may where it is a subsequent occasion, send the other adult forthwith to the Crown Court for trial for the either-way offence.

(4) Where a court sends an adult for trial under subsection (3) above, it shall at the same time send him to the Crown Court for trial for any either-way or summary offence with which he is charged which fulfils the requisite conditions.

(5) Where—

(a) the court sends an adult for trial under subsection (1) or (3) above; and

(b) a child or young person appears or is brought before the court on the same or a subsequent occasion charged jointly with the adult with an indictable offence for which the adult is sent for trial,

the court shall, if it considers it necessary in the interests of justice to do so, send the child or young person forthwith to the Crown Court for trial for the indictable offence.

(6) Where a court sends a child or young person for trial under subsection (5) above, it may at the same time send him to the Crown Court for trial for any either-way or summary offence with which he is charged which fulfils the requisite conditions.

(7) The court shall specify in a notice the offence or offences for which a person is sent for trial under this section and the place at which he is to be tried; and a copy of the notice shall be served on the accused and given to the Crown Court sitting at that place.

(8) In a case where there is more than one indictable-only offence and the court includes an either-way or a summary offence in the notice under subsection (7) above, the court shall specify in that notice the indictable-only offence to which the either-way offence or, as the case may be, the summary offence appears to the court to be related.

(9) The trial of the information charging any summary offence for which a person is sent for trial under this section shall be treated as if the court had adjourned it under section 10 of the 1980 Act and had not fixed the time and place for its resumption.

(10) In selecting the place of trial for the purpose of subsection (7) above, the court shall have regard to—

(a) the convenience of the defence, the prosecution and the witnesses;

(b) the desirability of expediting the trial; and

(c) any direction given by or on behalf of the Lord Chief Justice with the concurrence of the Lord Chancellor under section 75(1) of the *Supreme Court Act* 1981.

(11) An offence fulfils the requisite conditions if—

(a) if appears to the court to be related to the indictable-only offence; and

(b) in the case of a summary offence, it is punishable with imprisonment or involves obligatory or discretionary disqualification from driving.

(12) For the purposes of this section—

(a) "adult" means a person aged 18 or over, and references to an adult include references to a corporation;

(b) "either-way offence" means an offence which, if committed by an adult, is triable either on indictment or summarily;

(c) an either-way offence is related to an indictable-only offence if the charge for the either-way offence could be joined in the same indictment as the charge for the indictable-only offence;

(d) a summary offence is related to an indictable-only offence if it arises out of circumstances which are the same as or connected with those giving rise to the indictable-only offence.

7–55   Where a defendant appears on an indictable only offence, the expectation is that the case will be sent "forthwith" to the Crown Court at the first hearing. The case may be adjourned if the prosecution wish to review the charges and indicate that either way offences may be substituted Related either way offences and summary offences if they are imprisonable or carry disqualification can be sent to the Crown Court with the indictable only charge. If the defendant has been sent to the Crown Court and then appears later at the magistrates' court charged with such related offences they may still be sent to the Crown Court.

The word "charged" does not just mean offences charged at the police station or by the laying of an information but includes charges preferred at or after the first court appearance: *R. (on the application of Salubi) v Bow Street Magistrates' Court* [2002] 1 W.L.R. 3073. Also in this case consideration was given to the question of whether the magistrates' court should deal with an abuse of process argument in s.51 proceedings. It was held that there may be rare cases where the magistrates could decide that a case was brought in bad faith or there was serious misconduct by the prosecution or police which warranted a stay of proceedings at this stage but that usually novel or complex points should be left to the Crown Court or High Court.

Summary trial of an offence that is triable on indictment only is a nullity. The case must be dealt with at the Crown Court: *R. v West* (1964) 1 Q.B. 15.

Transfer of cases to the Crown Court

7–56   Cases of serious fraud or offences involving children may be transferred to the Crown Court to prevent unnecessary delay.

Criminal Justice Act 1987, ss.4, 5

Notices of transfer and designated authorities
    4.—(1) If—

(a) a person has been charged with an indictable offence; and

(b) in the opinion of an authority designated by subsection (2) below or of one of such an authority's officers acting on the authority's behalf the evidence of the offence charged—

    (i) would be sufficient for the person charged to be committed for trial; and

    (ii) reveals a case of fraud of such seriousness or complexity that it is appropriate that the management of the case should without delay be taken over by the Crown Court; and

(c) before the magistrates' court in whose jurisdiction the offence has been charged begins to inquire into the case as examining justices the authority or one of the authority's officers acting on the authority's behalf gives the court a notice (in this Act referred to as a "notice of transfer") certifying that opinion.

the functions of the magistrates' court shall cease in relation to the case, except as provided by section 5(3), (7A) and (8) below and by [paragraph 2 of Schedule 3 to the *Access to Justice Act* 1999].

(2) The authorities mentioned in subsection (1) above (in this Act referred to as "designated authorities") are—

(a) the Director of Public Prosecutions;

(b) the Director of the Serious Fraud Office;

(c) the Commissioners of Inland Revenue;

(d) the Commissioners of Customs and Excise; and

(e) the Secretary of State.

(3) A designated authority's decision to give notice of transfer shall not be subject to appeal or liable to be questioned in any court.

(4) This section and sections 5 and 6 below shall not apply in any case in which section 51 of the *Crime and Disorder Act* 1998 (no committal proceedings for indictable-only offences) applies.

Notices of transfer—procedure

5.—(1) A notice of transfer shall specify the proposed place of trial and in selecting that place **7–57** the designated authority shall have regard to the considerations to which section 7 of the *Magistrates' Courts Act* 1980 requires a magistrates' court committing a person for trial to have regard when selecting the place at which he is to be tried.

(2) A notice of transfer shall specify the charge or charges to which it relates and include or be accompanied by such additional matter as regulations under subsection (9) below may require.

(3) If a magistrates' court has remanded a person to whom a notice of transfer relates in custody, it shall have power, subject to section 4 of the *Bail Act* 1976 and regulations under section 22 of the *Prosecution of Offences Act* 1985—

(a) to order that he shall be safely kept in custody until delivered in due course of law; or

(b) to release him on bail in accordance with the *Bail Act* 1976, that is to say, by directing him to appear before the Crown Court for trial;

and where his release on bail is conditional on his providing one or more surety or sureties and, in accordance with section 8(3) of the *Bail Act* 1976, the court fixes the amount in which the surety is to be bound with a view to his entering into his recognizance subsequently in accordance with subsections (4) and (5) or (6) of that section, the court shall in the meantime make an order such as is mentioned in paragraph (a) of this subsection.

(4) If the conditions specified in subsection (5) below are satisfied, a court may exercise the powers conferred by subsection (3) above in relation to a person charged without his being brought before it in any case in which by virtue of section 128(3A) of the *Magistrates' Courts Act* 1980 it would have power further to remand him on an adjournment such as is mentioned in that subsection.

(5) The conditions mentioned in subsection (4) above are—

(a) that the person in question has given his written consent to the powers conferred by subsection (3) above being exercised without his being brought before the court; and

(b) that the court is satisfied that, when he gave his consent, he knew that the notice of transfer had been issued.

(6) Where notice of transfer is given after a person to whom it relates has been

remanded on bail to appear before a magistrates' court on an appointed day, the requirement that he shall so appear shall cease on the giving of the notice, unless the notice states that it is to continue.

7–58   (7) Where the requirement that a person to whom the notice of transfer relates shall appear before a magistrates' court ceases by virtue of subsection (6) above, it shall be his duty to appear before the Crown Court at the place specified by the notice of transfer as the proposed place of trial or at any place substituted for it by a direction under section 76 of the *Supreme Court Act* 1981.

(7A) If the notice states that the requirement is to continue, when a person to whom the notice relates appears before the magistrates' court, the court shall have—

(a) the powers and duty conferred on a magistrates' court by subsection (3) above, but subject as there provided; and

(b) power to enlarge, in the surety's absence, a recognizance conditioned in accordance with section 128(4)(a) of the *Magistrates' Courts Act* 1980 so that the surety is bound to secure that the person charged appears also before the Crown Court.

(8) For the purposes of the *Criminal Procedure (Attendance of Witnesses) Act* 1965—

(a) any magistrates' court for the petty sessions area for which the court from which a case was transferred sits shall be treated as examining magistrates; and

(b) a person indicated in the notice of transfer as a proposed witness; shall be treated as a person who has been examined by the court.

(9) The Attorney General—

(a) shall by regulations make provision requiring the giving of a copy of a notice of transfer, together with copies of the documents containing the evidence (including oral evidence) on which any charge to which it relates is based—

    (i) to any person to whom the notice of transfer relates; and

    (ii) to the Crown Court sitting at the place specified by the notice of transfer as the proposed place of trial; and

(b) may by regulations make such further provision in relation to notices of transfer, including provision as to the duties of a designated authority in relation to such notices, as appears to him to be appropriate.

(9A) Regulations under subsection (9)(a) above may provide that there shall be no requirement for copies of documents to accompany the copy of the notice of transfer if they are referred to, in documents sent with the notice of transfer, as having already been supplied.

(10) The power to make regulations conferred by subsection (9) above shall be exercisable by statutory instrument subject to annulment in pursuance of a resolution of either House of Parliament.

(11) Any such regulations may make different provision with respect to different cases or classes of case.

Criminal Justice Act 1991, s.53

Notices of transfer in certain cases involving children

7–59   **53.**—(1) If a person has been charged with an offence to which section 32(2) of the 1988 Act applies (sexual offences and offences involving violence or cruelty) and the Director of Public Prosecutions is of the opinion—

(a) that the evidence of the offence would be sufficient for the person charged to be committed for trial;

(b) that a child who is alleged—

    (i) to be a person against whom the offence was committed; or

    (ii) to have witnessed the commission of the offence,

    will be called as a witness at the trial; and

(c) that, for the purpose of avoiding any prejudice to the welfare of the child, the case should be taken over and proceeded with without delay by the Crown Court,

a notice ("notice of transfer") certifying that opinion may be given by or on behalf of the Director to the magistrates' court in whose jurisdiction the offence has been charged.

(2) A notice of transfer shall be given before the magistrates' court begins to inquire into the case as examining justices.

(3) On the giving of a notice of transfer the functions of the magistrates' court shall cease in relation to the case except as provided by paragraphs 2 and 3 of Schedule 6 to this Act or by [paragraph 2 of Schedule 3 to the *Access to Justice Act* 1999].

(4) The decision to give a notice of transfer shall not be subject to appeal or liable to be questioned in any court.

(5) Schedule 6 to this Act (which makes further provision in relation to notices of transfer) shall have effect.

(6) In this section "child" means a person who—

(a) in the case of an offence falling within section 32(2)(a) or (b) of the 1988 Act, is under fourteen years of age or, if he was under that age when any such video recording as is mentioned in section 32A(2) of that Act was made in respect of him, is under fifteen years of age; or

(b) in the case of an offence falling within section 32(2)(c) of that Act, is under seventeen years of age or, if he was under that age when any such video recording was made in respect of him, is under eighteen years of age.

(7) Any reference in subsection (6) above to an offence falling within paragraph (a), (b) or (c) of section 32(2) of that Act includes a reference to an offence which consists of attempting or conspiring to commit, or of aiding, abetting, counselling, procuring or inciting the commission of, an offence falling within that paragraph.

(8) This section shall not apply in any case in which section 51 of the *Crime and Disorder Act* 1998 (no committal proceedings for indictable-only offences) applies.

A notice of transfer may be given specifying the place of trial and the charges and all **7–60** other matters as are required under the *Magistrates' Courts (Notices of Transfer) Rules* 1988 (SI 1988/1701). There will be no need for committal proceedings and the case will be transferred early on in the proceedings. The defendant may apply to the Crown Court for the charge to be dismissed on the grounds that the evidence disclosed would not be sufficient for any jury to convict him on it.

Committal of Summary Offences

Normally summary only offences will be tried by the magistrates' court and the ques- **7–61** tion of mode of trial does not arise. The *Criminal Justice Act* 1988 does make provision for certain summary offences to be dealt with at the Crown Court but only if there is some evident connection between the either way offence that is being committed and the summary offence which justifies the offences being dealt with together. The powers are included in ss.40 and 41.

Criminal Justice Act 1988, s.40

Power to join in indictment count for common assault etc.

40.—(1) A count charging a person with a summary offence to which this section applies may **7–62** be included in an indictment if the charge—

(a) is founded on the same facts or evidence as a count charging an indictable offence; or

(b) is part of a series of offences of the same or similar character as an indictable offence which is also charged,

but only if (in either case) the facts or evidence relating to the offence were disclosed to a magistrates' court inquiring into the offence as examining justices[or are disclosed by material which, in pursuance of regulations made under paragraph 1 of Schedule 3 to the *Crime and Disorder Act* 1998 (procedure where person sent for trial under section 51), has been served on the person charged].

(2) Where a count charging an offence to which this section applies is included in an indictment, the offence shall be tried in the same manner as if it were an indictable offence; but the Crown Court may only deal with the offender in respect of it in a manner in which a magistrates' court could have dealt with him.

(3) The offences to which this section applies are—

(a) common assault;

(aa) an offence under section 90(1) of the *Criminal Justice Act* 1991 (assaulting a prisoner custody officer);

(ab) an offence under section 13(1) of the *Criminal Justice and Public Order Act* 1994 (assaulting a secure training centre custody officer);

(b) an offence under section 12(1) of the *Theft Act* 1968 (taking motor vehicle or other conveyance without authority etc.);

(c) an offence under section 103(1)(b) of the *Road Traffic Act* 1988 (driving a motor vehicle while disqualified);

(d) an offence mentioned in the first column of Schedule 2 to the *Magistrates' Courts Act* 1980 (criminal damage etc.) which would otherwise be triable only summarily by virtue of section 22(2) of that Act; and

(e) any summary offence specified under subsection (4) below.

(4) The Secretary of State may by order made by statutory instrument specify for the purposes of this section any summary offence which is punishable with imprisonment or involves obligatory or discretionary disqualification from driving.

(5) A statutory instrument containing an order under this section shall be subject to annulment in pursuance of a resolution of either House of Parliament.

[This section is reprinted as amended by the *Crime and Disorder Act* 1998, Sch.8, para.66.]

7–63   Section 40 applies when the magistrates' court is dealing with a committal for trial under s.6 or sending a case for trial under s.51 of the *Crime and Disorder Act* 1998. The section does not extend to cases which involve children that are being transferred to the Crown Court under s.53 of the *Criminal Justice Act* 1991: *R. v T and K* [2001] 1 Cr.App.R. 446. The prosecution may prepare the indictment in advance and will list the offences to be tried at the Crown Court. Certain specific offences may be included in the indictment which are would usually be tried summarily. The prerequisite is that the offence must be founded on the same facts or evidence as the indictable charge or be part of a series of offences of the same or similar character. The evidence supporting this connection must be disclosed to the court at the time of the committal or served on the defence where the case is sent. The Crown Court may then deal with the summary matter but its powers will be restricted to those of the magistrates' court.

The specific offences are listed in subs.(3) and include various types of assault, taking a conveyance without authority, driving whilst disqualified and summary only criminal damage. No other offence has been added under subs.(4). The offence of battery was held to be included in the term 'common assault' under this section: *R. v Lynsey* [1995] 3 All E.R. 654.

The offence of driving whilst disqualified was held to be founded on the same facts and evidence as an indictable offence of possessing an offensive weapon when the defendant was driving along with the weapon in his possession in the car: *R. v Bird* [1996] R.T.R. 22. The summary offence must be connected to an indictable offence of the same or similar character and not to another summary offence. Although taking a conveyance was similar to theft of vehicles, driving whilst disqualified was not and could not be said to be founded on the same facts: *R. v Callaghan* (1991) 155 J.P. 965.

7–63.1   The way in which the Crown Court should deal with summary offences added to the indictment has been clarified to some extent particularly with regard to criminal damage offences where the interaction of s.22 and s.33 of the *Magistrates' Courts Act* 1980 and this section has given rise to difficulties. The principle that s.22 determined mode of trial procedure but did not change the classification of the offence as triable either way was first confirmed in *R. v Fennell* (2000) 164 J.P. 386.

The reasoning was examined further in a case where a defendant had an offence of criminal damage added on to the indictment and it was argued that the powers of the Crown Court were limited to those mentioned in s.33, *i.e.* three months imprisonment and/or a fine of £2,500. It was held that s.22 did not apply to where the offence is added to the indictment under s.40 because the required determination of s.22 was not made. As the court had not categorised the offence as being one attracting the reduced penalties the Crown Court retained the sentencing powers of six months and/or a level 5 fine. The value of the damage would be relevant to sentence: *R. v Alden* [2002] 2 Cr.App.R. 326.

Criminal Justice Act 1988, s.41

Power of Crown Court to deal with summary offence where person committed for either way offence

41.—(1) Where a magistrates' court commits a person to the Crown Court for trial on indict- **7–64** ment for an offence triable either way or a number of such offences, it may also commit him for trial for any summary offence with which he is charged and which—

(a) is punishable with imprisonment or involves obligatory or discretionary disqualification from driving; and

(b) arises out of circumstances which appear to the court to be the same as or connected with those giving rise to the offence, or one of the offences, triable either way,

whether or not evidence relating to that summary offence appears on the depositions or written statements in the case; and the trial of the information charging the summary offence shall then be treated as if the magistrates' court had adjourned it under section 10 of the *Magistrates' Courts Act* 1980 and had not fixed the time and place for its resumption.

(2) Where a magistrates' court commits a person to the Crown Court for trial on indictment for a number of offences triable either way and exercises the power conferred by subsection (1) above in respect of a summary offence, the magistrates' court shall give the Crown Court and the person who is committed for trial a notice stating which of the offences triable either way appears to the court to arise out of circumstances which are the same as or connected with those giving rise to the summary offence.

(3) A magistrates' court's decision to exercise the power conferred by subsection (1) above shall not be subject to appeal or liable to be questioned in any court.

(4) The committal of a person under this section in respect of an offence to which section 40 above applies shall not preclude the exercise in relation to the offence of the power conferred by that section; but where he is tried on indictment for such an offence, the functions of the Crown Court under this section in relation to the offence shall cease.

(5) If he is convicted on the indictment, the Crown Court shall consider whether the **7–65** conditions specified in subsection (1) above were satisfied.

(6) If it considers that they were satisfied, it shall state to him the substance of the summary offence and ask him whether he pleads guilty or not guilty.

(7) If he pleads guilty, the Crown Court shall convict him, but may deal with him in respect of that offence only in a manner in which a magistrates' court could have dealt with him.

(8) If he does not plead guilty, the powers of the Crown Court shall cease in respect of the offence except as provided by subsection (9) below.

(9) If the prosecution inform the Court that they would not desire to submit evidence on the charge relating to the summary offence, the Court shall dismiss it.

(10) The Crown Court shall inform the justices' chief executive for the magistrates' court of the outcome of any proceedings under this section.

(11) Where the Court of Appeal allows an appeal against conviction of an offence triable either way which arose out of circumstances which were the same as or connected with those giving rise to a summary offence of which the appellant was convicted under this section—

(a) it shall set aside his conviction of the summary offence and give the justices' chief executive for the magistrates' court notice that it has done so; and

(b) it may direct that no further proceedings in relation to the offence are to be undertaken;

and the proceedings before the Crown Court in relation to the offence shall thereafter be disregarded for all purposes.

(12) A notice under subsection (11) above shall include particulars of any direction given under paragraph (b) of that subsection in relation to the offence.

[This section is reprinted as amended by the *Access to Justice Act* 1999, Sch.15, Pt V(7).]

Section 41 provides for the magistrates' court which commits a person to the Crown **7–66** Court for trial on an either way matter under s.6 of the *Magistrates' Courts Act* 1980 to also commit for trial certain summary offences for which he is charged. The summary offence must be punishable with imprisonment or carry a disqualification from driving. It must also arise out of the same circumstances as the indictable offence.

The summary offence must be charged from the outset rather than added to the indictment as under s.40 but evidence relating to it does not need to have been disclosed in the committal papers. The court will adjourn the summary offence 'sine die' (without a date being fixed) and await the outcome of the Crown Court proceedings. A notice must be served on the Crown Court and defence identifying the either way offence to which the summary offence is linked.

The section does not apply to cases sent under s.51 of the *Crime and Disorder Act* 1998 or cases transferred under the Criminal Justice Acts 1987 and 1991.

7–67 The Crown Court can only deal with a summary offence under this section when there is a conviction on an indictable offence and a guilty plea to the summary offence. On conviction, the sentences available are those of the magistrates' court and the observations about s.22 and the categorisation of criminal damage offences apply equally under this section as they do under s.40. If the defendant is acquitted of the linked indictable offence or pleads not guilty to the summary offence the powers of the Crown Court cease. The Crown Court may then dismiss the case under s.41(9) or send the case back to the magistrates' court for trial.

In *R. v Foote* (1992) 156 J.P. 99, a defendant was committed to the Crown Court for trial on a charge of reckless driving and was also committed under s.41 for on a charge of careless driving. At the Crown Court his plea of guilty to the lesser charge was accepted by the prosecution and the Crown Court proceeded to sentence him. It was held that the conviction and sentence at the Crown Court was a nullity. The case should have been remitted to the magistrates' court where it was deemed to have been adjourned and it should be dealt with there. The provisions of s.41 relating to the conviction of a summary charge on the indictment also applies to charges properly included on the indictment under s.40. Where a defendant pleaded guilty at the Crown Court to an offence of driving whilst disqualified which was a summary only offence which had been included on the indictment under s.40 with a charge of possessing an offensive weapon it was held that the Crown Court could impose a sentence even though the indictable offence was not proceeded with because there was a conviction on the indictment: *R. v Bird*, above.

III. COMMITTAL FOR TRIAL TO THE CROWN COURT

A. INTRODUCTION—CLASSIFICATION OF OFFENCES

7–68 Criminal offences are categorised into three types according to the seriousness of the offence. The gravity of the offence is marked by the length of sentence that can be imposed. The powers of the magistrates' courts are limited to six months' imprisonment or a fine of £5,000 for as single offence. Where there are two or more either way offences the total sentencing powers of the court are increased to 12 months' imprisonment as a maximum. Less serious offences are classified as summary only. The most serious offences are triable on indictment only and must be dealt with at the Crown Court. In between are the either way offences which can be tried at the magistrates' court or the Crown Court. These are offences that cover a wide range of criminal conduct and aggravating features could affect the seriousness of the offence so that Crown Court trial is more suitable with the added sentencing powers of that court.

Summary offences must normally be dealt with in the magistrates' court (but see ss.40 and 41 of the *Criminal Justice Act* 1988). Either way offences may be tried either at the magistrates' court or the Crown Court. The mode of trial procedure is described above: ss.17A–25. Where the case is to be dealt with at the Crown Court it must be committed under ss.6(1) or 6(2) of the *Magistrates' Courts Act* 1980. Indictable only charges cannot be dealt with at the magistrates' court and are sent to the Crown Court under s.51 of the *Crime and Disorder Act* 1998.

A case can also be brought before the Crown Court by applying for a voluntary bill of indictment which is done directly to the Crown Court: s.2 of the *Administration of Justice (Miscellaneous Provisions) Act* 1933.

General

The court, when committing a case for trial is referred to in statute as 'examining **7–69** justices'. Its role is to inquire into the charge and decide whether there is sufficient evidence to put the defendant on trial before a jury. If there is, the case is committed. If not, the case is discharged. The prosecution will prepare the committal documents which will consist of written statements from witnesses, depositions, documents and exhibits. Prior to the committal, a copy of all the papers must be served on the defence who will then review the evidence and decide whether to seek a committal without consideration of the evidence (s.6(2)) or request a contested committal on the basis that there is no case to answer that could be put before a jury: s.6(1).

Standard guidelines are applied locally for the preparation of committal bundles, usually six weeks for cases in custody and eight weeks for those on bail. The original papers will be served on the court to be forwarded to the Crown Court on committal.

Magistrates' Courts Act 1980, s.4

General nature of committal proceedings
    4.—(1) The functions of examining justices may be discharged by a single justice.   **7–70**
    (2) Examining justices shall sit in open court except where any enactment contains an express provision to the contrary and except where it appears to them as respects the whole or any part of committal proceedings that the ends of justice would not be served by their sitting in open court.
    (3) Subject to subsection (4) below, evidence tendered before examining justices shall be tendered in the presence of the accused.
    (4) Examining justices may allow evidence to be tendered before them in the absence of the accused if—
        (a) they consider that by reason of his disorderly conduct before them it is not practicable for the evidence to be tendered in his presence, or
        (b) he cannot be present for reasons of health but is represented by a legal representative and has consented to the evidence being tendered in his absence.

[This section is reprinted as amended by the *Criminal Procedure and Investigations Act* 1996, Sch.1, Pt 1, para.2(3).]

A committal can be heard by a single magistrate. The rule is for the committal to take **7–70.1** place in open court. An exception to this is when a defendant is charged under the *Official Secrets Act* 1920. The presence of the accused at committal may be excused if he is behaving in a disorderly manner or if he is unwell he may then be represented through his lawyer. This section relates only to the process of the committal when the evidence is considered by the court and not to the actual act of committal itself. The evidence must comply with the requirements of ss.5A–F of the *Magistrates' Courts Act* 1980.

Evidence

Magistrates' Courts Act 1980, ss.5A, 5B

Evidence which is admissible
    5A.—(1) Evidence falling within subsection (2) below, and only that evidence, shall be admis- **7–71** sible by a magistrates' court inquiring into an offence as examining justices.
    (2) Evidence falls within this subsection if it—
        (a) is tendered by or on behalf of the prosecutor, and
        (b) falls within subsection (3) below.

(3) The following evidence falls within this subsection—

    (a) written statements complying with section 5B below;

    (b) the documents or other exhibits (if any) referred to in such statements;

    (c) depositions complying with section 5C below;

    (d) the documents or other exhibits (if any) referred to in such depositions;

    (e) statements complying with section 5D below;

    (f) documents falling within section 5E below.

(4) In this section "document" means anything in which information of any description is recorded.

Written statements

7–72   **5B.**—(1) For the purposes of section 5A above a written statement complies with this section if—

    (a) the conditions falling within subsection (2) below are met, and

    (b) such of the conditions falling within subsection (3) below as apply are met.

(2) The conditions falling within this subsection are that—

    (a) the statement purports to be signed by the person who made it;

    (b) the statement contains a declaration by that person to the effect that it is true to the best of his knowledge and belief and that he made the statement knowing that, if it were tendered in evidence, he would be liable to prosecution if he wilfully stated in it anything which he knew to be false or did not believe to be true;

    (c) before the statement is tendered in evidence a copy of the statement is given, by or on behalf of the prosecutor, to each of the other parties to the proceedings.

(3) The conditions falling within this subsection are that—

    (a) if the statement is made by a person under 18 years old, it gives his age;

    (b) if it is made by a person who cannot read it, it is read to him before he signs it and is accompanied by a declaration by the person who so read the statement to the effect that it was so read;

    (c) if it refers to any other document as an exhibit, the copy given to any other party to the proceedings under subsection (2)(c) above is accompanied by a copy of that document or by such information as may be necessary to enable the party to whom it is given to inspect that document or a copy of it.

(4) So much of any statement as is admitted in evidence by virtue of this section shall, unless the court commits the accused for trial by virtue of section 6(2) below or the court otherwise directs, be read aloud at the hearing; and where the court so directs an account shall be given orally of so much of any statement as is not read aloud.

(5) Any document or other object referred to as an exhibit and identified in a statement admitted in evidence by virtue of this section shall be treated as if it had been produced as an exhibit and identified in court by the maker of the statement.

(6) In this section "document" means anything in which information of any description is recorded.

[Sections 5A and 5B are reprinted as amended by the *Criminal Procedure and Investigations Act* 1996, Sch.1, Pt I, para.3.]

7–73   Any statement must be that of the witness. If the witness does not speak English his statement must be recorded in the language in which it was made and signed by him and not written in English by an interpreter. The correct procedure is for the interpreter to provide a written translation of the statement which is then produced as an exhibit: *R. v Raynor* (2001) 165 J.P. 149.

Magistrates' Courts Act 1980, s.5C

Depositions

7–74   **5C.**—(1) For the purposes of section 5A above a deposition complies with this section if—

    (a) a copy of it is sent to the prosecutor under section 97A(9) below,

    (b) the condition falling within subsection (2) below is met, and

    (c) the condition falling within subsection (3) below is met, in a case where it applies.

(2) The condition falling within this subsection is that before the magistrates' court begins to inquire into the offence concerned as examining justices a copy of the deposition is given, by or on behalf of the prosecutor, to each of the other parties to the proceedings.

(3) The condition falling within this subsection is that, if the deposition refers to any other document as an exhibit, the copy given to any other party to the proceedings under subsection (2) above is accompanied by a copy of that document or by such information as may be necessary to enable the party to whom it is given to inspect that document or a copy of it.

(4) So much of any deposition as is admitted in evidence by virtue of this section shall, unless the court commits the accused for trial by virtue of section 6(2) below or the court otherwise directs, be read aloud at the hearing; and where the court so directs an account shall be given orally of so much of any deposition as is not read aloud.

(5) Any document or other object referred to as an exhibit and identified in a deposition admitted in evidence by virtue of this section shall be treated as if it had been produced as an exhibit and identified in court by the person whose evidence is taken as the deposition.

(6) In this section "document" means anything in which information of any description is recorded.

[This section is reprinted as amended by the *Criminal Procedure and Investigations Act* 1996, Sch.1(1), para.3.]

Depositions cover situations where a witness will not provide a statement voluntarily **7–75** under s.5B. The witness may be summonsed or brought before the court by warrant and then the evidence will be taken before the court in the form of a deposition: s.97A of the *Magistrates' Courts Act* 1980.

Magistrates' Courts Act 1980, s.5D

Statements

5D.—(1) For the purposes of section 5A above a statement complies with this section if the **7–76** conditions falling within subsections (2) to (4) below are met.

(2) The condition falling within this subsection is that, before the committal proceedings begin, the prosecutor notifies the magistrates' court and each of the other parties to the proceedings that he believes—

    (a) that the statement might by virtue of section 23 or 24 of the *Criminal Justice Act* 1988 (statements in certain documents) be admissible as evidence if the case came to trial, and

    (b) that the statement would not be admissible as evidence otherwise than by virtue of section 23 or 24of that Act if the case came to trial.

(3) The condition falling within this subsection is that—

    (a) the prosecutor's belief is based on information available to him at the time he makes the notification,

    (b) he has reasonable grounds for his belief, and

    (c) he gives the reasons for his belief when he makes the notification.

(4) The condition falling within this subsection is that when the court or a party is notified as mentioned in subsection (2) above a copy of the statement is given, by or on behalf of the prosecutor, to the court or the party concerned.

(5) So much of any statement as is in writing and is admitted in evidence by virtue of this section shall, unless the court commits the accused for trial by virtue of section 6(2) below or the court otherwise directs, be read aloud at the hearing; and where the court so directs an account shall be given orally of so much of any statement as is not read aloud.

[This section is reprinted as amended by the *Criminal Procedure and Investigations Act* 1996, Sch.1(1), para.3.]

These statements are those to which ss.23 and 24 *Criminal Justice Act* 1988 apply.

Magistratesí Courts Act 1980, s.5E, 5F

Other documents

5E.—(1) The following documents fall within this section—   **7–77**

    (a) any document which by virtue of any enactment is evidence in proceedings before a magistrates' court inquiring into an offence as examining justices;

(b) any document which by virtue of any enactment is admissible, or may be used, or is to be admitted or received, in or as evidence in such proceedings;

(c) any document which by virtue of any enactment may be considered in such proceedings;

(d) any document whose production constitutes proof in such proceedings by virtue of any enactment;

(e) any document by the production of which evidence may be given in such proceedings by virtue of any enactment.

(2) In subsection (1) above—

(a) references to evidence include references to prima facie evidence;

(b) references to any enactment include references to any provision of this Act.

(3) So much of any document as is admitted in evidence by virtue of this section shall, unless the court commits the accused for trial by virtue of section 6(2) below or the court otherwise directs, be read aloud at the hearing; and where the court so directs an account shall be given orally of so much of any document as is not read aloud.

(4) In this section "document" means anything in which information of any description is recorded.

Proof by production of copy

7–78   **5F.**—(1) Where a statement, deposition or document is admissible in evidence by virtue of section 5B, 5C, 5D or 5E above it may be proved by the production of—

(a) the statement, deposition or document, or

(b) a copy of it or the material part of it.

(2) Subsection (1)(b) above applies whether or not the statement, deposition or document is still in existence.

(3) It is immaterial for the purposes of this section how many removes there are between a copy and the original.

(4) In this section "copy", in relation to a statement, deposition or document, means anything onto which information recorded in the statement, deposition or document has been copied, by whatever means and whether directly or indirectly."

[This section is reprinted as amended by the *Criminal Procedure and Investigations Act* 1996, Sch.1 Pt 1, para.3.]

Discharge or committal

Magistrates' Courts Act 1980, s.6

Discharge or committal for trial

7–79   **6.**—(1) A magistrates' court inquiring into an offence as examining justices shall on consideration of the evidence—

(a) commit the accused for trial if it is of opinion that there is sufficient evidence to put him on trial by jury for any indictable offence;

(b) discharge him if it is not of that opinion and he is in custody for no other cause than the offence under inquiry;

but the preceding provisions of this subsection have effect subject to the provisions of this and any other Act relating to the summary trial of indictable offences.

(2) If a magistrates' court inquiring into an offence as examining justices is satisfied that all the evidence tendered by or on behalf of the prosecutor falls within section 5A(3) above, it may commit the accused for trial for the offence without consideration of the contents of any statements, depositions or other documents, and without consideration of any exhibits which are not documents, unless—

(a) the accused or one of the accused has no legal representative acting for him in the case, or

(b) a legal representative for the accused or one of the accused, as the case may be, has requested the court to consider a submission that there is insufficient evidence to put that accused on trial by jury for the offence;

and subsection (1) above shall not apply to a committal for trial under this subsection.

(3) Subject to section 4 of the *Bail Act* 1976 and section 41 below, the court may commit a person for trial—

(a) in custody, that is to say, by committing him to custody there to be safety kept until delivered in due course of law, or

(b) on bail in accordance with the *Bail Act* 1976, that is to say, by directing him to appear before the Crown Court for trial;

and where his release on bail is conditional on his providing one or more surety or sureties and, in accordance with section 8(3) of the *Bail Act* 1976, the court fixes the amount in which the surety is to be bound with a view to his entering into his recognizance subsequently in accordance with subsections (4) and (5) or (6) of that section the court shall in the meantime commit the accused to custody in accordance with paragraph (a) of this subsection.

(4) Where the court has committed a person to custody in accordance with paragraph **7–80** (a) of subsection (3) above, then, if that person is in custody for no other cause, the court may, at any time before his first appearance before the Crown Court, grant him bail in accordance with the *Bail Act* 1976 subject to a duty to appear before the Crown Court for trial.

(5) Where a magistrates' court acting as examining justices commits any person for trial or determines to discharge him, the [justices' chief executive for] the court shall, on the day on which the committal proceedings are concluded or the next day, cause to be displayed in a part of the court house to which the public have access a notice—

(a) in either case giving that person's name, address, and age (if known);

(b) in a case where the court so commits him, stating the charge or charges on which he is committed and the court to which he is committed;

(c) in a case where the court determines to discharge him, describing the offence charged and stating that it has so determined;

but this subsection shall have effect subject to section 4 of the *Sexual Offences (Amendment) Act* 1976 (anonymity of complainant in rape etc. cases).

(6) A notice displayed in pursuance of subsection (5) above shall not contain the name or address of any person under the age of 18 years unless the justices in question have stated that in their opinion he would be mentioned in the notice apart from the preceding provisions of this subsection and should be mentioned in it for the purpose of avoiding injustice to him.

[This section is reprinted as amended by the *Access to Justice Act* 1999, Sch.13, para.96.]

Only an either way offence can be committed to the Crown Court for trial under this **7–81** section. The court does not sit as 'examining justices' when it is dealing with a summary only matter. The committal of such an offence is a nullity: *Bannister v Clarke* [1920] 3 K.B. 598. But see ss.40 and 41 *Criminal Justice Act* 1988 above.

There are two types of committal. Under subs.(2) the court need not consider the evidence contained in the prosecution statements, etc. if it is satisfied that all such documentation complies with the admissibility requirements of s.5A. Under subs.2(a) and (b), the court has to consider the evidence if the defendant is unrepresented or if he wishes to make a submission that there is not sufficient evidence in the prosecution case to put him on trial before a jury. The procedure in the two different committals is set out in rr.6 and 7 of the *Magistrates' Courts Rules* 1981. A contested committal takes place on the basis of the written statements and no live witnesses will be called.

In the committal without consideration of the evidence the defence admits that there is sufficient evidence on the face of the statements for the case to go to trial. If no admission is forthcoming the evidence will be read out to the court and the committal will only take place if the court is of the opinion that there is sufficient evidence to put the defendant on trial.

The function of committal proceedings is to ensure that no person should stand trial unless a 'prima facie' case is made out. The onus of making out the case is on the prosecution: *R. v Epping and Harlow Justices Ex p. Massaro* [1973] Q.B. 433.

The test to be applied is whether there is any evidence that the crime alleged has been committed by the defendant and if there is, whether that evidence is such that a jury, properly directed could convict on it: *R. v Galbraith* [1981] 1 W.L.R. 1039.

The prosecution has a discretion as to which witnesses to rely on and need only bring **7–82** evidence of a prima facie case, not one beyond reasonable doubt. Failure to include the statement of any specific witness is not a breach of natural justice but the prosecution is subject to a duty to be fair and not to mislead the court: *Wilkinson v DPP* (1998) 162 J.P. 591.

The court must be satisfied that the evidence tendered is admissible. Where the committal was based on transcripts of police interviews of co-defendants who implicated the defendant this was held to be inadmissible as it did not comply with s.5A. This was a procedural defect that could not be remedied and the committal was quashed: *R. v Bedwelty Justices Ex p. Williams* [1997] A.C. 225.

But it is not the role of the court to assess the weight of evidence and rule on its admissibility. Where the evidence is legally admissible the case should be committed as the discretion to reject the evidence rests with the trial judge: *R. v Horsham Justices Ex p. Bukhari* (1982) 74 Cr.App.R. 291.

7–83 The court may commit on any indictable offence that is made out in the evidence. It is not restricted to finding sufficient evidence for the offence formally charged. If the court contemplates committing on a lesser charge, it should allow legal representatives to address them and it is bad practice for the prosecution to invite the court to commit on charges made out after the substantive matter has been discharged; *R. v Gloucester Magistrates' Court Ex p. Chung* (1989) 153 J.P. 75.

If the court is not of the opinion that there is sufficient evidence it will discharge the defendant. The prosecution may later charge the defendant again if more evidence comes to light and seek committal once more. There is no question of 'autrefois acquit' arising as the case has not been tried on its merits. The court may entertain charges which have been discharged before but repeated use of the committal procedure may be vexatious or amount to an abuse of process: *R. v Manchester City Justices Ex p. Snelson* [1977] 1 W.L.R. 911.

Section 4 allows for the committal proceedings to take place in the absence of the accused in certain circumstances. Section 6 provides for the court to commit the accused for trial and the *Rules* require that the charge be read to the accused. There is no reference to procedure in the absence of the defendant. It has been held that this does not preclude the court from committing a person in absence. Where the defendant was absent through ill health, but was represented the appeal court said that the provisions of s.4(4) of the *Magistrates' Courts Act* 1980 and s.122 (representation through lawyer) allowed the court to proceed in the absence of the accused as there were no statutory provisions to the contrary: *R. v Liverpool Street Magistrates' Court Ex p. Quantrell* [1999] 2 Cr.App.R. 24, DC. See also *R. v Bow Street Magistrates' Court Ex p. government of Germany* [1998] Q.B. 556.

7–84 In some committals there is a good deal of paperwork to be considered by the court. It is acceptable for the documents in the case to be lodged with the court in advance so that there may be an opportunity to read and digest the evidence. That this is done with out the defence consenting is immaterial. Copies of the statements have to be served on the court in any event under r.70(2) of the *Magistrates' Courts Rules* 1981; *R. v Colchester Stipendiary Magistrate Ex p. Beck* [1979] Q.B. 674, 69 Cr.App.R. 128.

Discharge or committal without consideration of evidence

Magistrates' Courts Rules 1981, r.6

Committal for trial without consideration of evidence

7–85 **6.**—(1) This rule applies to committal proceedings where the accused has a solicitor acting for him in the case and where the court has been informed that all the evidence falls within section 5A(2) of the Act of 1980.

(2) A magistrates' court inquiring into an offence in committal proceedings to which this rule applies shall cause the charge to be written down, if this has not already been done, and read to the accused and shall then ascertain whether he wishes to submit that there is, insufficient evidence to put him on trial by jury for the offence with which he is charged.

(3) If the court is satisfied that the accused or, as the case may be, each of the accused

does not wish to make such a submission as is referred to in paragraph (2) it shall, after receiving any written evidence falling within section 5A(3) of the Act of 1980, determine whether or not to commit the accused for trial without consideration of the evidence, and where it determines not to so commit the accused it shall proceed in accordance with rule 7.

[This rule is reprinted as amended by the *Magistrates' Courts (Amendment) Rules* 1997, r.5(1)(d).]

Magistrates' Courts Rules 1981, r.7

Consideration of evidence at committal proceedings

7.—(1) This rule does not apply to committal proceedings where under section 6(2) of the **7–86** Act of 1980 a magistrates' court commits a person for trial without consideration of the evidence.

(2) A magistrates' court inquiring into an offence as examining justices, having ascertained—

    (a) that the accused has no legal representative acting for him in the case; or

    (b) that the accused's legal representative has requested the court to consider a submission that there is insufficient evidence to put the accused on trial by jury for the offence with which he is charged, as the case may be,

shall permit the prosecutor to make an opening address to the court, if he so wishes, before any evidence is tendered.

(3) After such opening address, if any, the court shall cause evidence to be tendered in accordance with section 5B(4), 5C(4), 5D(5) and 5E(3) of the Act of 1980, that is to say by being read out aloud, except where the court otherwise directs or to the extent that it directs that an oral account be given of any of the evidence.

(4) The court may view any exhibits produced before the court and may take possession of them.

(5) After the evidence has been tendered the court shall hear any submission which the accused may wish to make as to whether there is sufficient evidence to put him on trial by jury for any indictable offence.

(6) The court shall permit the prosecutor to make a submission—

    (a) in reply to any submission made by the accused in pursuance of paragraph (5); or

    (b) where the accused has not made any such submission but the court is nevertheless minded not to commit him for trial.

(7) After hearing any submission made in pursuance of paragraph (5) or (6) the court shall, unless it decides not to commit the accused for trial, cause the charge to be written down, if this has not already been done, and, if the accused is not represented by counsel or a solicitor, shall read the charge to him and explain it in ordinary language.

[This rule is reprinted as amended by the *Magistrates' Courts (Amendment) Rules* 1997, r.7(1).]

Reminder to defendant

On committal the defendant must be advised that live witnesses will not be called at **7–87** the Crown Court trial unless he requests that they attend.

Magistrates' Courts Rules 1981, r.8

Court's reminder to a defendant: right to object to written evidence being read at trial without further proof

8. A magistrates' court which commits a person for trial shall forthwith remind him of his right to object, by written notification to the prosecutor and the Crown Court within 14 days of being committed unless that court in its discretion permits such an objection to be made outside that period, to a statement or deposition being read as evidence at the trial without oral evidence being given by the person who made the statement or deposition, and without the opportunity to cross-examine that person.

[This rule is reprinted as amended by the *Magistrates' Courts (Amendment) Rules* 1997, r.8]

7–87.1   Where a defendant is charged with an offence involving a death the court has a duty to inform the coroner of the charge and proceedings. The coroner is responsible for an inquest: s.17 of the *Coroner's Act* 1988.

Place of trial

Magistrates' Courts Act 1980, s.7

Place of trial on indictment

7–88   **7.** A magistrates' court committing a person for trial shall specify the place at which he is to be tried, and in selecting that place shall have regard to—

(a) the convenience of the defence, the prosecution and the witnesses,

(b) the expediting of the trial, and

(c) any direction given by or on behalf of the Lord Chief Justice with the concurrence of the Lord Chancellor under section 4(5) of the *Courts Act* 1971.

The court will select the appropriate Crown Court according to its location and the directions in the *Practice Direction (Criminal Proceedings: Consolidation)* 2002 which allocate types of cases to different tiers of the Crown Court based on the seriousness of the offence. The case will be adjourned to a fixed date where a Plea and Directions Hearing will take place. The Crown Court provides the appropriate dates. The Crown Court may change the venue once the case has been committed.

Reporting restrictions

Magistrates' Courts Act 1980, s.8

Restrictions on reports of committal proceedings

7–89   **8.**—(1) Except as provided by subsections (2), (3) and (8) below, it shall not be lawful to publish in Great Britain a written report, or to include in a relevant programme for reception in Great Britain a report, of any committal proceedings in England and Wales containing any matter other than that permitted by subsection (4) below.

(2) Subject to subsection (2A) below a magistrates' court shall, on an application for the purpose made with reference to any committal proceedings by the accused or one of the accused, as the case may be, order that subsection (1) above shall not apply to reports of those proceedings.

(2A) Where in the case of two or more accused one of them objects to the making on an order under subsection (2) above, the court shall make the order if, and only if, it is satisfied, after hearing the representations of the accused, that it is in the interests of justice to do so.

(2B) An order under subsection (2) above shall not apply to reports of proceedings under subsection (2A) above, but any decisions of the court to make or not to make such an order may be contained in reports published or included in a relevant programme before the time authorised by subsection (3) below.

(3) It shall not be unlawful under this section to publish or include in a relevant programme a report of committal proceedings containing any matter other than that permitted by subsection (4) below—

(a) where the magistrates' court determines not to commit the accused, or determines to commit none of the accused, for trial, after it so determines;

(b) where the court commits the accused or any of the accused for trial, after the conclusion of his trial or, as the case may be, the trial of the last to be tried;

and where at any time during the inquiry the court proceeds to try summarily the case of one or more of the accused under section 25(3) or (7) below, while committing the other accused or one or more of the other accused for trial, it shall not be unlawful under this section to publish or include in a relevant programme as part of a report of the summary trial, after the court determines to proceed as aforesaid, a report of so much of the committal proceedings containing any such matter as takes place before the determination.

(4) The following matters may be contained in a report of committal proceedings published or included in a relevant programme without an order under subsection (2) above before the time authorised by subsection (3) above, that is to say—

(a) the identity of the court and the names of the examining justices;

(b) the names, addresses and occupations of the parties and witnesses and the ages of the accused and witnesses;

(c) the offence or offences, or a summary of them, with which the accused is or are charged;

(d) the names of the legal representatives engaged in the proceedings;

(e) any decision of the court to commit the accused or any of the accused for trial, and any decision of the court on the disposal of the case of any accused not committed;

(f) where the court commits the accused or any of the accused for trial, the charge or charges, or a summary of them, on which he is committed and the court to which he is committed;

(g) where the committal proceedings are adjourned, the date and place to which they are adjourned;

(h) any arrangements as to bail on committal or adjournment;

(i) whether a right to representation funded by the Legal Services Commission as part of the Criminal Defence Service was granted to the accused or any of the accused.

(5) If a report is published or included in a relevant programme in contravention of this **7–90** section, the following persons, that is to say—

(a) in the case of a publication of a written report as part of a newspaper or periodical, any proprietor, editor or publisher of the newspaper or periodical;

(b) in the case of a publication of a written report otherwise than as part of a newspaper or periodical, the person who publishes it;

(c) in the case of the inclusion of a report in a relevant programme, any body corporate which provides the service in which the programme is included and any person having functions in relation to the programme corresponding to those of an editor of a newspaper,

shall be liable on summary conviction to a fine not exceeding level 5 on the standard scale.

(6) Proceedings for an offence under this section shall not, in England and Wales, be instituted otherwise than by or with the consent of the Attorney-General.

(7) Subsection (1) above shall be in addition to, and not in derogation from, the provisions of any other enactment with respect to the publication of reports and proceedings of magistrates' and other courts.

(8) For the purposes of this section committal proceedings shall, in relation to an information charging an indictable offence, be deemed to include any proceedings in the magistrates' court before the court proceeds to inquire into the information as examining justices; but where a magistrates' court which has begun to try an information summarily discontinues the summary trial in pursuance of section 25(2) or (6) below and proceeds to inquire into the information as examining justices, that circumstance shall not make it unlawful under this section for a report of any proceedings on the information which was published or included in a relevant programme before the court determined to proceed as aforesaid to have been so published or included in a relevant programme.

(10) In this section—

"publish", in relation to a report, means publish the report, either by itself or as part of a newspaper or periodical, for distribution to the public.

"relevant programme" means a programme included in a programme service (within the meaning of the *Broadcasting Act* 1990).

[This section is reprinted as amended by the *Access to Justice Act* 1999, Sch.4, para.16.]

Magistrates' Courts Rules 1981, r.5

Restrictions on reports of committal proceedings

5.—(1) Except in a case where evidence is, with the consent of the accused, to be tendered in **7–91** his absence under section 4(4)(b) of the Act of 1980 (absence caused by ill health), a magistrates' court acting as examining justices shall before admitting any evidence explain to the accused the restrictions on reports of committal proceedings imposed by section 8 of the Act of 1980 and inform him of his right to apply to the court for an order removing those restrictions.

(2) Where a magistrates' court has made an order under section 8(2) of the Act of 1980 removing restrictions on the reports of committal proceedings, such order shall be entered in the register.

(3) Where the court adjourns any such proceedings to another day, the court shall, at the beginning of any adjourned hearing, state that the order has been made.

[This rule is reprinted as amended by the *Magistrates' Courts (Amendment) Rules* 1997, r.4.]

7–92　　Although committal proceedings must normally take place in open court (s.4) reporting restrictions automatically apply under s.8 and the effect of this must be explained to the defendant personally if he is present: r.5.

Application can be made for the restrictions to be lifted. If there is only one defendant the court shall lift the restrictions but if there are two or more defendants and not all of them wish to have the restrictions lifted then the court has to exercise its discretion in the interests of justice.

Subsection (4) lists the information that is not covered by the restrictions and basic details of this nature may be included in a report. Breach of the restrictions is a summary offence under subs.(5).

Before the court makes an order for the lifting of reporting restrictions at committal all the defendants must be present and be given an opportunity to make representations. The lifting of restrictions in a case of murder without hearing submissions from all the defendants was held to be in breach of natural justice: *R. v Wirral District Magistrates' Court Ex p. Meikle* [1991] C.O.D. 2, DC.

Only where a very strong case is made out should the court lift restrictions when not all the accused wish to have them lifted. The interests of justice test was not met when one defendant wanted to lift the restrictions to publicise 'sharp practice' by the police.: *R. v Leeds Justices Ex p. Sykes*, 76 Cr.App.R. 129, DC.

7–93　　Application can be made at any time in the proceedings and before the committal begins. Where a defendant faced several charges and there were several defendants, an application to lift the restrictions was dealt with at the preliminary stage. The case then led to several different sets of committal proceedings. The order made at the start of the initial committal was held to apply to all the committals in which the defendant was later involved. The appeal court did advise that the court should be precise about the extent and effect of the order: *Magistrates' Courts Act* 1980, s.8(8); *R. v Bow Street Magistrates Ex p. Kray* [1969] 1 Q.B. 473.

Section 4(2) of the *Contempt of Court Act* 1981 also applies to committals. The restrictions are imposed in different situations and for different purposes; that is where the publication of committal proceedings was prejudicial to the defendant's interests and where publication of proceedings, whether or not prejudicial to the defendant would be a contempt. A defendant applied for reporting restrictions to be lifted but later on in the committal the court made an order under s.4 of the *Contempt of Court Act* 1981 and re-imposed reporting restrictions. A journalist challenged this decision and the court held that the words "any other proceedings pending or imminent" in s.4(2) included potential proceedings in the Crown Court and so did apply: *R. v Horsham Justices Ex p. Farquharson* [1982] Q.B. 762.

Committal of corporation

Magistrates' Courts Act 1980, Sch.3, paras 1–3(1)

7–94　　1.—(1) A magistrates' court may commit a corporation for trial by an order in writing empowering the prosecutor to prefer a bill of indictment in respect of the offence named in the order.

(2) An order under this paragraph shall not prohibit the inclusion in the bill of indict-

ment of counts that under section 2 of the *Administration of Justice (Miscellaneous Provisions) Act* 1933 may be included in the bill in substitution for, or in addition to, counts charging the offence named in the order.

 2. A representative may on behalf of a corporation—

  (a) make before examining justices such representations as could be made by an accused who is not a corporation;

  (b) consent to the corporation being tried summarily;

  (c) enter a plea of guilty or not guilty on the trial by a magistrates' court of an information.

 3.—(1) Where a representative appears, any requirement of this Act that anything shall be done in the presence of the accused, or shall be read or said to the accused, shall be construed as a requirement that that thing shall be done in the presence of the representative or read or said to the representative.

IV. SEPARATE TRIALS OF INFORMATIONS

A defendant appearing before the magistrates' court may be charged with several of- **7–95** fences arising from one incident or may face further charges concerning unrelated matters. The court must then decide whether to try the cases together or whether separate trials are required. Similarly there may be several co-accused charged with joint offences who may wish to be tried separately. The main issue for the court is to consider the interests of justice and whether a trial will be fair in compliance with Art.6 of the ECHR. Different charges being tried together may result in prejudice being caused to the defence.

In the case of *Chief Constable of Norfolk v Clayton* [1983] 2 A.C. 473, the circumstances in which the court may hear and determine separate informations were reviewed. If in each case the facts are connected, then if the court thinks fit they can be heard together. Before embarking on a joint trial, the court should seek the consent of both the prosecution and the defence. If consent is not forthcoming the court should consider submissions and rule as they think fit in the interests of justice. The fact that the defence does not consent to joint trials is an important factor but does not deprive the court of its discretion to order joint trials.

When the prosecution and defence agree to separate trials, the court may still order joint trial but the court should be slow to reach such a conclusion: *R. v Highbury Corner Magistrates' Court Ex p. McGinley* (1986) 150 J.P. 257. Where a defendant applies for a separate trial because an essential part of his defence consists of an attack on his co-defendant it remained a matter for the discretion of the court whether to allow separate trials: *R. v Grondkowski* [1946] K.B. 369. Separate representation may be granted which would protect the interests of the defendant.

Defendants jointly charged will appear in the dock together and may be jointly or **7–96** separately represented. The practice of putting in the dock defendants who are not jointly charged and who have been arrested at different times and places is discouraged as it gives the impression of 'group justice': *R. v Mansfield Justices Ex p. Sharkey* [1985] Q.B. 613; [1985] 1 All E.R. 193.

It was held that under no circumstances may a court order that a summons and cross-summons should be heard together. Although in many cases joint trials were appropriate the court identified added difficulties with the conduct of such a case which made joint trial inappropriate: *R. v Epsom Justices Ex p. Gibbons* [1984] Q.B. 574.

If the informations are to be tried separately the question that then arises is whether the same bench should hear all the cases. It is a matter of discretion for the bench to decide whether it should try all the charges or whether they should be adjourned to different days before different benches. The court must apply its mind judicially to ensure there is no likelihood of bias. Where a court decided to proceed with hearing six sets of offences against a defendant no bias was apparent because the exercise of the discretion was plainly reviewed after hearing each batch of charges: *R. v Sandwich Justices Ex p. Berry* [1982] Crim.L.R. 121

7–97   Joint trials either of co-defendants or of several charges may give rise to an appearance of bias. The test to be applied is whether a reasonable and fair-minded person, knowing all the facts, would have a reasonable suspicion that a fair trial would not be possible. That some unrelated charges are all included on the same charge sheet was held not to be improper and did not give rise to bias: *R. v Weston-super-mare Justices Ex p. Shaw* [1987] Q.B. 640. But disclosing on the register sheets all charges pending against a defendant could give rise to the appearance of bias and was wrong in law as it did not comply with r.66 of the *Magistrates' Courts Rules* 1981: *R. v Liverpool City Justices Ex p. Topping* [1983] 1 W.L.R. 119

Alternative charges

7–98   The magistrates' court has no inherent power to convict on a lesser offence rather than the one charged in a summary trial. The proper procedure is for the prosecution to charge offences in the alternative. This can be done either right from the start at charge or an alternative offence can be preferred during the course of the proceedings.

      When an alternative charge is brought the defence has a right to an adjournment to consider it. It is a matter for the prosecution which charge to prefer. Where a defendant was charged with assault occasioning actual bodily harm the prosecution preferred an alternative charge of common assault. The defendant said this was an abuse of process because the prosecution wanted to deprive him of his right to jury trial. The motive for choosing a particular charge was held irrelevant in the absence of bad faith: *R. v Sheffield Justices Ex p. DPP* [1993] Crim.L.R. 136; *R. v Canterbury and St Augustine Justices Ex p. Klisiak* [1982] Q.B. 398.

Prosecution not proceeding

7–99   After the defendant has been charged the prosecution may decide that it will not proceed. The case may then be dealt with in one of three ways; withdrawal, no evidence offered, or discontinuance.

Withdrawal of summons

7–100   The court has power to grant an application to withdraw a summons without an adjudication being made. There is no requirement for the matter to be put and a plea to be entered: *R. v Redbridge Justices Ex p. Sainty* [1981] R.T.R. 13.

      The withdrawal of a summons is not the equivalent to an acquittal and so will not act as a bar on the issue of a further summons in respect of the same charge where there has been no adjudication on the merits of the case: *R. v Grays Justices Ex p. Low* [1990] 1 Q.B. 54.

Offering no evidence

7–101   Once the accused has entered a plea of not guilty to the information, it is no longer possible for the prosecution to ask for the matter to be withdrawn. The prosecution may offer no evidence and the case will be dismissed under s.9 of the *Magistrates' Courts Act* 1980. The charge cannot then be revived.

      Where an accused has been lawfully acquitted by a magistrates' court of competent jurisdiction acting within its jurisdiction, he cannot be prosecuted again for the same offence, even if the acquittal resulted from the prosecution not offering any evidence: *R. v Pressick* [1978] Crim.L.R. 377; *R. v Swansea Justices Ex p. Purvis* (1981) 145 J.P. 252.

Statutory discontinuance

Prosecution of Offences Act 1985, s.23

Discontinuance of proceedings in magistrates' courts

7–102   23—(1) Where the Director of Public Prosecutions has the conduct of proceedings for an offence, this section applies in relation to the preliminary stages of those proceedings.

(2) In this section, "preliminary stage" in relation to proceedings for an offence does not include—

    (a) in the case of a summary offence, any stage of the proceedings after the court has begun to hear evidence for the prosecution at the trial;

    (b) in the case of an indictable offence, any stage of the proceedings after—

        (i) the accused has been committed for trial; or

        (ii) the court has begun to hear evidence for the prosecution at a summary trial of the offence

    (c) in the case of any offence, any stage of the proceedings after the accused has been sent for trial under section 51 of the *Crime and Disorder Act* 1998 (no committal proceedings for indictable-only and related offences).

(3) Where, at any time during the preliminary stages of the proceedings, the Director gives notice under this section to the justices' chief executive for the court that he does not want the proceedings to continue, they shall be discontinued with effect from the giving of that notice but may be revived by notice given by the accused under subsection (7) below.

(4) Where, in the case of a person charged with an offence after being taken into custody without a warrant, the Director gives him notice, at a time when no magistrates' court has been informed of the charge, that the proceedings against him are discontinued, they shall be discontinued with effect from the giving of that notice.

(5) The Director shall, in any notice given under subsection (3) above, give reasons for not wanting the proceedings to continue.

(6) On giving any notice under subsection (3) above the Director shall inform the accused of the notice and of the accused's right to require the proceedings to be continued; but the Director shall not be obliged to give the accused any indication of his reasons for not wanting the proceedings to continue.

(7) Where the Director has given notice under subsection (3) above, the accused shall, if he wants the proceedings to continue, give notice to that effect to the justices' chief executive for the court within the prescribed period; and where notice is so given the proceedings shall continue as if no notice had been given by the Director under subsection (3) above.

(8) Where the justices' chief executive forthe court has been so notified by the accused he shall inform the Director.

(9) The discontinuance of any proceedings by virtue of this section shall not prevent the institution of fresh proceedings in respect of the same offence.

(10) In this section "prescribed" means prescribed by rules made under section 144 of the *Magistrates' Courts Act* 1980.

A notice of discontinuance may be served by the prosecution on the court and the **7–103** defence during the preliminary stages of a case. The preliminary stages are defined in subs.(2). A case cannot be discontinued after a case has begun with prosecution evidence being heard in a summary trial or after an indictable case has been committed or sent to the Crown Court.

The defendant may require the proceedings to continue. He is also entitled to apply for costs after a discontinuance.

The prosecution may recharge the offence after a discontinuance.

This power does not affect the right of the prosecution to withdraw or offer no evidence in a case: *Cooke v DPP and Brent Justices* (1992) 156 J.P. 497.

Part II:

Specific Offences

GENERAL PRINCIPLES

I. ACTUS REUS

The *actus reus* consists of the prohibited conduct which forms the basis of the rele- **8–1** vant offence. In the majority of cases, this conduct must be voluntary. It is possible to commit an offence through involuntary conduct, such as where the prohibited act consists of a state of affairs, as was the case in *Winzar v Chief Constable of Kent, The Times*, March 28, 1983, where the relevant offence was "being found drunk on a highway" contrary to the *Licensing Act* 1872, s.12. It was held that the defendant fell within s.12 of the *Licensing Act* 1872 if he was on the highway and was "perceived to be drunk", notwithstanding that his presence there was momentary and not of his own volition.

There is no liability for a failure to do something, unless the law imposes some specific duty upon the individual to act. Specific statutory duties are imposed in the context of many regulatory offences, such as the *Companies Act* 1985, which imposes a positive duty on a company to keep accounting records, or the *Water Resources Act* 1991 which makes it an offence to cause or knowingly permit any poisonous, noxious or polluting matter or any solid waste matter to enter any controlled waters. Other statutes make it a criminal offence to fail to disclose certain information. The *Terrorism Act* 2000, s.19 makes it an offence to fail to disclose a belief or suspicion that another person has committed an offence connected with terrorism and ss.330, 331 and 332 of the *Proceeds of Crime Act* 2002 create offences of failing to disclose possible money launder-ing activities.

Liability for omissions may also stem from the existence of a special relationship be-tween the victim and the accused, which creates a duty to act on the part of the accused. There exist various situations where such a duty of care will arise:

277

(1) Duty arising from the assumption of care or control of children

8–2　The *Children and Young Persons Act* 1933, s.1 creates the offence of wilful neglect and imposes a duty on parents and those who are legally responsible for children to provide or obtain adequate food, clothing and medical care for the child.

(2) Duty arising from the assumption of care for another

8–3　A person who voluntarily assumes the care and responsibility for another person, that other being incapable of caring for himself, may incur a duty to discharge that undertaking. In *Stone v Dobinson* [1977] Q.B. 354, CA, the accused's sister came to live with him and his mistress. The sister was suffering from anorexia, and became unable to care for herself. The accused did not call for medical assistance and left her to die from atoxemia spreading from infected bed scores, prolonged immobilisation and lack of food. Both the accused and his mistress were convicted of manslaughter. The Court of Appeal upheld their convictions, holding that as they had taken the sister into their home, they had assumed a duty of care towards her and had been grossly negligent in the performance of that duty.

(3) Duty arising from contract

8–4　A duty to act may arise from the existence of a contract requiring some conduct from the defendant. In *R. v Pittwood* [1902] 19 T.L.R. 37, the accused was employed to operate a level crossing on a railway. He failed to close the crossing gates when a train was signalled, causing a cart which was crossing when the train came through to be struck leading to the death of one of the carters. The accused was convicted of gross negligent manslaughter, his duty to act arising from the contract with his employers, which required him to discharge his duty as a level crossing operator appropriately.

(4) Duty arising from the fact that the accused creates the relevant danger

8–5　In *R. v Miller* [1983] 2 A.C. 161, HL, Lord Diplock stated (at 176):

> "I see no rational ground for excluding from conduct capable of giving rise to criminal liability, conduct which consists of failing to take measures that lie within one's power to counteract a danger that one has oneself created, if at the time of such conduct one's state of mind is such as constitutes a necessary ingredient of the offence."

(5) Duty arising from the doctor patient/relationship

8–6　If a doctor or medical staff refuse to treat a patient who has withheld his consent to treatment, they will not be guilty of failing to discharge their duty to provide medical care for their patients: *Re C (Adult: Refusal of Treatment)* [1994] 1 W.L.R. 290.

The doctor's duty towards his patient does not however require him to keep the patient alive at all costs. In *Airedale NHS Trust v Bland* [1993] A.C. 789, HL, a patient in a persistent vegetative state was able to breathe normally, but was only sustained by the administration of food being fed through tubes. The House of Lords held that this treatment could be withdrawn, as a large body of informed and responsible medical opinion was of the view that existence in the persistent vegetative state was not a benefit to the patient. Hence the principle of the sanctity of life, which is not absolute, was not violated by ceasing to give medical treatment and care involving invasive manipulation of the patient's body, to which he had not consented and which conferred no benefit upon him. Lord Goff made a vital distinction between acts and omissions in this context, stating that:

> "...the law draws a crucial distinction between cases in which a doctor decides not to provide, or to continue to provide, for his patient treatment or care which could or might prolong his life, and those in which he decides, for example by administering a lethal drug, actively to bring his patient's life to an end. As I have already indicated, the former may be lawful, either

because the doctor is giving effect to his patient's wishes by withholding the treatment or care, or even in certain circumstances in which [on principles which I shall describe] the patient is incapacitated from stating whether or not he gives his consent. But it is not lawful for a doctor to administer a drug to his patient to bring about his death, even though that course is prompted by a humanitarian desire to end his suffering, however great that suffering may be...So to act is to cross the Rubicon which runs between on the one hand the care of the living patient and on the other hand euthanasia—actively causing his death to avoid or to end his suffering." (at 865)

Certain offences cannot be based on omissions. In *R. v Ahmad* [1987] 84 Cr.App.R. **8–7** 64, CA, it was held that the words "does acts" in the *Protection from Eviction Act* 1977 mean that the offence may not be committed by omission. However, the offence of committing acts of gross indecency with a child may be committed by omission: in *R. v Speck* (1977) 65 Cr.App.R. 161, an eight-year-old girl had placed her hand on the accused's trousers over his penis. The accused failed to move her hand, and was convicted of committing acts of gross indecency, his liability hinging on his failure to remove her hand. This would seem to be inconsistent with the view that references to acts exclude omissions, though Ashworth (*Principles of Criminal Law*, 4th ed., 2003) suggests that the case may also be viewed as involving an invitation on the part of the accused (constituted by his inactivity in failing to remove the girl's hand) which can be characterised as an act for the purposes of the offence.

II. CAUSATION

Causation is relevant to the commission of result crimes (those crimes which require a **8–8** specific consequence to flow from the prohibited act (*e.g.* theft)). These crimes are distinguished from what are termed "conduct" crimes, whose *actus reus* consists in the doing of the prohibited act, rather than in the consequences flowing from the commission of this act (*e.g.* rape). For a defendant to be guilty of a result crime, a factual link must first be established between the defendant's conduct and the result he is alleged to have caused.

Once this factual link has been established, the prosecution must then prove that the defendant's conduct was a legal cause of the result alleged to be a consequence of the defendant's actions. For a factual cause to also be a legal cause it must be an "operating and substantial" cause of the consequence in issue: *R. v Smith* [1959] 2 Q.B. 35, CA. The following principles are relevant to the determination of legal causation. They are largely distilled from principles developed in homicide cases, though it may be worth considering the rather different application of the rules of causation in relation to crimes of strict liability or negligence, where considerations of the defendant's culpability in bringing about the prescribed result are less potent. For example, in *Empress Car Co (Abertillery) Ltd v National Rivers Authority* [1999] 2 A.C. 22, HL, the defendant company maintained a diesel tank in a yard. This tank was tampered with by an unknown person, causing the contents of the tank to pass into a nearby river. The House of Lords held that if a necessary additional condition of the actual escape was the act of a third party or a natural event, the justices should consider whether that act or event should be regarded as a matter of ordinary occurrence, which would not negative the effect of the defendant's act, or something extraordinary, leaving open a finding that the defendant did not cause the pollution. Only if the escape could be regarded as something extraordinary would the defendant company escape liability. The issue of culpability was treated as irrelevant to determination of the issue of causation. This approach is in stark contrast to consideration of causation in homicide cases, where the distinction between "but for" and legal causation is used to avoid the conviction of the "morally innocent". Such considerations may be less prevalent in the context of statutory offences, and a different approach may be taken.

(1) The defendant's act must be more than a minimal cause of the result

In *R. v Cato* [1976] 62 Cr.App.R. 41, CA, Lord Widgery C.J., looking at the **8–9** ingredients of the offence of manslaughter stated that:

> "As a matter of law, it was sufficient if the prosecution could establish that it (the defendant's act) was *a* cause, provided it was a cause outside the *de minimis* range, and effectively bearing upon the acceleration of the moment of the victim's death."

In *R. v Notman* [1994] Crim.L.R. 518, CA, it was held that the expression 'a substantial cause' was convenient to indicate that the cause must have been more than just de minimis and avoids the necessity to go into the details of legal causation and remoteness. This approach was also applied in the context of road traffic offences in *R. v Hennigan* [1971] 3 All E.R. 133, CA, where the defendant's conviction for death caused by dangerous driving was upheld, the Court holding that there was nothing in s.1 of the *Road Traffic Act* 1960 which required the manner of the driving to be a substantial or major cause of death. So long as the dangerous driving was a cause and something more than *de minimis*, the statute would operate.

However, indirect causes of the proscribed result may constitute legal causation. In *R. v McKechnie* [1992] 94 Cr.App.R. 51, CA, the defendants attacked the victim, causing serious head injuries. The victim also had a duodenal ulcer, which could not be operated on due to the head injuries inflicted by the defendants. The victim then died when this ulcer burst. The Court of Appeal upheld the manslaughter conviction, despite the fact that the injuries inflicted were not in themselves the cause of the victim's death. In *R. v Miller* [1992] 95 Cr.App.R. 421 it was held that to establish that property has been obtained by deception it is not necessary to isolate the moment when the money or other property is handed over to see whether at that time the lies told operated to deceive the victim. If on the evidence as a whole it can legitimately be said that the various deceptions alleged in the indictment were the cause of the money being handed over it is, or may be, irrelevant that at the final moment the victim suspected or even believed that he or she had been swindled.

(2) The "eggshell skull" rule

8–10   In *R. v Blaue* [1975] 1 W.L.R. 1411, CA, Lawton L.J. stated that:

> "It has long been the policy of the law that those who use violence on other people must take their victims as they find them. This in our judgment means the whole man, not just the physical man."

Hence a defendant who stabbed a woman, who then refused to have a blood transfusion due to her faith, was properly convicted of manslaughter, despite the fact that a blood transfusion would have saved the victim's life.

(3) Novus actus interveniens

8–11   An intervening act will absolve the defendant from any kind of responsibility for the result caused. The intervening act may be the act of a third party, and act of the victim or an unforeseeable natural event (sometimes called "act of God").

(4) Acts of third parties

Unforeseeable acts

8–12   The intervention of a third party may break the chain of causation if the intervention is free, deliberate and informed: *R. v Pagett* [1983] 76 Cr.App.R. 279, CA. In *Pagett*, the defendant shot at police officers who were attempting to arrest him. He had with him his girlfriend, and against her will used her body to shield him from any retaliation by the officers. The officers returned the appellant's fire and as a result the girl was killed. The Court upheld the defendant's manslaughter conviction, holding that the police's actions had not broken the chain of causation between the defendant's act and the victim's death because their action had been a reasonable act performed for the purpose of self-preservation, as well as in the execution of their legal duty to arrest the defendant.

(5) Medical intervention

Negligent medical treatment will only break the chain of causation where it was so in- **8–13** dependent of the defendant's acts and in itself so potent in causing death that they regarded the contribution made by the defendants acts as insignificant: *R. v Cheshire* [1991] 93 Cr.App.R. 251, CA, (medical complications following from the treatment for gunshot wounds leading to the death of the victim.). In *Cheshire*, above, Beldham L.J. concluded that:

> "...when the victim of a criminal attack is treated for wounds or injuries by doctors or other medical staff attempting to repair the harm done, it will only be in the most extraordinary and unusual case that such treatment can be said to be so independent of the acts of the accused that it could be regarded in law as the cause of the victim's death to the exclusion of the accused's acts." (at 257)
>
> "In a case in which the jury have to consider whether negligence in the treatment of injuries inflicted by the accused was the cause of death we think it is sufficient for the judge to tell the jury that they must be satisfied that the Crown have proved that the acts of the accused caused the death of the deceased adding that the accused's acts need not be the sole cause or even the main cause of death it being sufficient that his acts contributed significantly to that result. Even though negligence in the treatment of the victim was the immediate cause of his death, the jury should not regard it as excluding the responsibility of the accused unless the negligent treatment was so independent of his acts, and in itself so potent in causing death, that they regard the contribution made by his acts as insignificant." (at 258)

(6) Acts of the victim

The victim's own act can be said to break the chain of causation between the **8–14** defendant's act and the result caused. In *R. v Roberts* (1972) 56 Cr.App.R. 95, CA, the victim had jumped from a moving car because the defendant had assaulted and threatened her. The appellant was convicted of assault occasioning actual bodily harm. Stephenson L.J. stated:

> "The test is: Was it the natural result of what the alleged assailant said and did, in the sense that it was something that could reasonably have been foreseen as the consequences of what he was saying or doing? As it was put in one of the old cases, it had got to be shown to be his act, and if of course the victim does something so 'daft,' in the words of the appellant in this case, or so unexpected, not that this particular assailant did not actually foresee it but that no reasonable man could be expected to foresee it, then it is only in a very remote and unreal sense a consequence of his assault, it is really occasioned by a voluntary act on the part of the victim which could not reasonably be foreseen and which breaks the chain of causation between the assault and the harm or injury." (at 102)

In *R. v Williams* [1992] 1 W.L.R. 380, CA, the victim had been killed when he jumped from a car driven by the defendants after they had threatened him. The Court of Appeal quashed the defendants' conviction for manslaughter, stating that the defendants would only be guilty if the victim's response was proportionate to the threat issued, in that it was within the ambit of reasonableness and not so daft as to amount to his own voluntary act which would constitute a *novus actus interveniens*. When considering whether the victim acted reasonably, the judge/jury must consider "any particular characteristics of the victim and the fact that in the agony of the moment he may act without thought or deliberation."

The question of what could reasonably be foreseen by the defendant provides an **8–15** objective test: *R. v Marjoram* [2000] Crim.L.R. 372, CA. The defendant, aged 16, was among a group of people who broke into the victim's hostel room, whereupon she fell or jumped into the street and was seriously injured. The defendant appealed against his conviction for grievous bodily harm, contending that in directing the jury on foreseeability, the judge had failed properly to direct the jury that they should consider it in terms of a person of the same age and sex as M involved in similar circumstances. The

Court dismissed his appeal holding that the test of causation was objective. The "reasonable man" would have foreseen the victim's conduct as a natural result of the defendant's actions.

(7) Unforeseeable natural events

8–16 In *Southern Water Authority v Pegrum* [1989] Crim.L.R. 442, it was held that when deciding whether an intervening cause constitutes a defence, the question is whether the intervening cause was of so powerful a nature that the conduct of the defendant was not a cause at all, but was merely part of the surrounding circumstances.

III. MENS REA

8–17 Once the prosecution have established that the defendant committed the *actus reus* of the relevant offence, it must then be proved that the defendant did so with the relevant *mens rea*, *i.e.* that he had the guilty mind necessary for the commission of the offence. Different offences require different mental elements. A fault element may also be applied differently in relation to different offences, hence whilst the most commonly found mental elements can be here outlined for the sake of exposition, it is necessary to bear in mind that their application will vary.

(1) Specific requirements as to state of mind

(a) *"With intent to"*

8–18 The leading cases on intention arise out of convictions for murder; however the relevant principles are of general application: *per* Lord Bridge in *R. v Moloney* [1985] A.C. 905, HL. The relevant cases are *R. v Maloney* (above); *R. v Hancock and Shankland* [1986] A.C. 455, HL; *R. v Nedrick* 83 Cr.App.R. 267, CA, and *R. v Woolin* [1999] 1 A.C. 82, HL.

In *R. v Nedrick* (1986), above, Lord Lane C.J. stated:

> "When determining whether the defendant had the necessary intent, it may therefore be helpful for a jury to ask themselves two questions: [1] How probable was the consequence which resulted from the defendant's voluntary act? [2] Did he foresee that consequence?
>
> If he did not appreciate that death or really serious harm was likely to result from his act, he cannot have intended to bring it about. If he did, but thought that the risk to which he was exposing the person killed was only slight, then it may be easy for the jury to conclude that he did not intend to bring about that result. On the other hand, if the jury are satisfied that at the material time the defendant recognised that death or serious harm would be virtually certain (barring some unforeseen intervention) to result from his voluntary act, then that is a fact from which they may find it easy to infer that he intended to kill or do serious bodily harm, even though he may not have had any desire to achieve that result." (at 270)

8–19 *R. v Woollin*, above, concerned the death of a three-month old baby, as a result of his being thrown against a wall. The House of Lords held that, where the charge is murder, in the rare cases where the simple direction is not enough, the jury should be directed that they are not entitled to infer the necessary intention, unless they feel sure that death or serious bodily harm was a virtual certainty (barring some unforeseen intervention) as a result of the defendant's actions, and the defendant appreciated that such was the case. The decision was one for the jury to reach upon a consideration of all the evidence. The use of the phrase "virtual certainty" was not confined to cases where the evidence of intent was limited to actions of the accused and the consequences of those actions. If the principles gleaned from these murder cases can be extrapolated to all offences, then it seems appropriate to conclude that, ordinarily, the issue of intention is one to be left to common sense.

(b) *"Unlawfully"*

8–20 This means without lawful justification or excuse such as self-defence.

(c) "Maliciously"

This mental requirement appears in the *Offences Against the Person Act* 1861. It is **8–21** established that malice in the sense of ill-will is not required, rather the word requires either actual intention to cause the relevant harm or foresight of the risk of causing that particular kind of harm: *R. v Cunningham* [1957] 2 Q.B. 296, CCA. This decision was upheld in *R. v Savage, R. v Parmenter* [1992] 1 A.C. 699, HL.

(d) "Wilfully"

In *R. v Sheppard* [1981] A.C. 394, HL, Lord Diplock stated that the proper direc- **8–22** tion to be given to a jury on a charge of wilful neglect of a child under s.1 of the *Children and Young Persons Act* 1933 by failing to provide adequate medical aid is that the jury must be satisfied (1) that the child did in fact need medical aid at the time at which the parent is charged with failing to provide it, the *actus reus*, and (2) either that the parent was aware at that time that the child's health might be at risk if it was not provided with medical aid or that the parent's unawareness of this fact was due to his not caring whether his child's health was at risk or not.

(e) "Knowingly"

This requires the prosecution to prove that the defendant knew of all the material **8–23** circumstances of the offence. In *R. v Dunne* (1998) 162 J.P. 399, CA, the offender was convicted of being knowingly concerned in the fraudulent evasion of a prohibition on the importation of goods contrary to s.170(2) of the *Customs and Excise Management Act* 1979 after being arrested on his arrival in the UK by customs officers who suspected that videos in his possession, which the defendant referred to as "blue movies", were obscene. He appealed against conviction, contending that a person could not "know" whether an article he was importing was such as would tend to deprave and corrupt within the meaning of the *Obscene Publications Act* 1959, s.1(1) until a jury had found that it was. The Court dismissed his appeal, holding that "knowingly", in the offence of being knowingly concerned in the fraudulent evasion of a prohibition on the importation of an obscene article, was to be construed as emphasising the requirement of *mens rea*. Whilst a defendant who believed that the obscene videos he was importing were actually videos of sporting events should not be convicted, a defendant who was aware of the true nature of the goods would be liable to conviction if the jury determined that the material fell within the 1959 Act, s.1(1). As the defendant was aware of the nature of the videos and had conceded that they were obscene, there was no basis upon which the defendant could claim that his conviction was unsafe.

(f) "Recklessly"

Prior to the decision in *G* [2003] 3 W.L.R. 1060, HL, the concept of recklessness in **8–24** the criminal law was variable according to the substantive offence charged. The decisions in *R. v Caldwell* [1982] A.C 341 (criminal damage) and *R. v Lawrence* [1982] A.C. 510 (causing death by reckless driving) introduced the concept of objective recklessness, departing from the prior view expressed in *R. v Cunningham* [1957] 2 Q.B. 396, CCA, that recklessness necessarily imparted some degree of subjective fault on the part of the defendant.

In *R. v Cunningham*, above, it was held that a person is reckless as to the consequences of his conduct if he has foreseen that the particular kind of harm might be done and has yet gone on to take the risk of it. In *R. v Caldwell*, above, the decision in *Cunningham* was approved but distinguished; Lord Diplock stated that the concept of recklessness as enshrined in *Cunningham* was relevant and necessary to explain the meaning of the adverb "maliciously" when used in relation to an offence under the *Malicious Damage Act* 1861, but was not relevant and had no bearing upon the meaning of the adjective "reckless" in s.1 of the *Criminal Damage Act* 1971. Lord Diplock went on to state in *R. v Lawrence*, above, that the majority in *R. v Caldwell* had concluded that the adjective "reckless" when used in a criminal statute had not acquired a special meaning as a term of legal art, but bore its popular or dictionary meaning of careless, regardless or heedless of the possible harmful consequences of one's acts.

Even prior to the decision in *R. v G*, the decision in *R. v Caldwell* had been subject to significant modifications. First, the offence which the House was concerned with in *R. v Lawrence* (causing death by reckless driving) was abolished (as was the associated offence of reckless driving). The Court of Appeal had also sought to limit the scope of *Caldwell* to cases concerning reckless driving or criminal damage. However, following *G*, *R. v Caldwell* has no application.

8–25   In *R. v G* [2003] 3 W.L.R. 1060 two children, one aged 11 and the other 12, set fire to newspapers with a lighter and threw some of the papers under a large plastic wheelie-bin, which was in the yard behind a shop. They then left, and the resulting fire caused approximately £1 million worth of damage. It was accepted that neither boy appreciated that there was any risk of the fire spreading in the way that it did. They were convicted of arson, contrary to s.1 of the *Criminal Damage Act* 1971, the judge having ruled that he was bound to direct the jury in accordance with *Caldwell*, above. The House of Lords quashed their convictions, and overruled the majority decision of the House of Lords in *R. v Caldwell*. Lord Bingham first looked to the legislative background of the *Criminal Damage Act* 1971, and stated that:

> "[T]he starting point is to ascertain what Parliament meant by 'reckless' in 1971...s.1 as enacted followed, subject to an immaterial addition, the draft proposed by the Law Commission. It cannot be supposed that by 'reckless' Parliament meant anything different from the Law Commission. The Law Commission's meaning was made plain both in its report [Law Com No. 29] and in Working Paper No 23 which preceded it. These materials [not, it would seem, placed before the House in *R v Caldwell*] reveal a very plain intention to replace the old-fashioned and misleading expression 'maliciously' by the more familiar expression 'reckless' but to give the latter expression the meaning which *R v Cunningham* [1957] 2 All E.R. 412, [1957] 2 Q.B. 396 and Professor Kenny had given to the former. In treating this authority as irrelevant to the construction of 'reckless' the majority fell into understandable but clearly demonstrable error. No relevant change in the mens rea necessary for proof of the offence was intended, and in holding otherwise the majority misconstrued s.1 of the Act." (at para.29)

8–26   He then went on to examine reasons justifying a departure from the decision established in *R. v Caldwell*:

> "First, it is a salutary principle that conviction of serious crime should depend on proof not simply that the defendant caused [by act or omission] an injurious result to another but that his state of mind when so acting was culpable...But it is not clearly blameworthy to do something involving a risk of injury to another if [for reasons other than self-induced intoxication [see *DPP v Majewski* [1976] 2 All E.R. 142, [1977] A.C. 443] one genuinely does not perceive the risk. Such a person may fairly be accused of stupidity or lack of imagination, but neither of those failings should expose him to conviction of serious crime or the risk of punishment." (at para.32)
>
> "Secondly...the model direction formulated by Lord Diplock is capable of leading to obvious unfairness...It is neither moral nor just to convict a defendant [least of all a child] on the strength of what someone else would have apprehended if the defendant himself had no such apprehension. Nor, the defendant having been convicted, is the problem cured by imposition of a nominal penalty." (at para.33)
>
> "Thirdly, I do not think the criticism of *R v Caldwell* expressed by academics, judges and practitioners should be ignored. A decision is not, of course, to be overruled or departed from simply because it meets with disfavour in the learned journals. But a decision which attracts reasoned and outspoken criticism by the leading scholars of the day, respected as authorities in the field, must command attention..." (at para.34)
>
> "Fourthly, the majority's interpretation of 'reckless' in s 1 of the 1971 Act was, as already shown, a misinterpretation. If it were a misinterpretation that offended no principle and gave rise to no injustice there would be strong grounds for adhering to the misinterpretation and leaving Parliament to correct it if it chose. But this misinterpretation is offensive to principle and is apt to cause injustice. That being so, the need to correct the misinterpretation is compelling." (at para.35)

The reasoning of Lord Bingham was accepted by the majority of the House, and the **8–27** concept of recklessness is now restored to the situation before *R. v Caldwell*. The defendant will now be judged to have acted recklessly with respect to (i) a circumstance when he was aware of a risk that it existed or would exist; (ii) a result when he was aware of a risk that it would occur; and it was, in the circumstances known to him, unreasonable to take the risk. This is the definition recommended by the Law Commission in the Draft Criminal Code of 1989 (Law Com No.177).

(g) *"Dishonesty"*

See exposition in relation to the offence of theft at § 11–3.　　　　　　　**8–28**

(h) *"Causes"*

The general rule applicable to a statutory offence of causing another person to do a **8–29** prohibited act is that the offence is only committed if the accused contemplated or desired that the act would ensue and was done on his express or implied authority or as a result of him exercising control or influence over the other person: *Att.-Gen of Hong Kong v Tse Hung-Lit* [1986] A.C. 876, PC.

Where a statute prohibits the causing of a particular result, the word "causes" is to be given a common sense meaning, and does not imply either knowledge or negligence: *Alphacell v Woodward* [1972] A.C. 824, HL. In *Environmental Agency v Empress Car Co (Abertillery) Ltd* [1999] 2 A.C. 22, HL, it was held that on a prosecution for causing pollution under s.85(1) of the *Water Resources Act* 1991 it was necessary to identify what the defendant was alleged to have done to cause the pollution. The prosecution need not prove that the defendant did something which was the immediate cause of the pollution and when the prosecution had identified some act done by the defendant the justices had to decide whether it caused the pollution. If a necessary additional condition of the actual escape was the act of a third party or a natural event, the justices should consider whether that act or event should be regarded as a matter of ordinary occurrence, which would not negative the effect of the defendant's act, or something extraordinary, leaving open a finding that the defendant did not cause the pollution; that the distinction between ordinary and extraordinary was one of fact and degree to which the justices had to apply their common sense and knowledge of what occurred in the locality [but see also § 8–8 above on causation].

(i) *"Negligently"*

An example of negligence being the relevant mental state for the commission of an **8–30** offence can be found in s.3 of the *Road Traffic Act* 1988, which creates the offence of driving without due care and attention. Negligence imports an objective standard for behaviour, which does not vary according to the characteristics of the individual offender.

Certain statutes provide a defence of mistaken belief on reasonable grounds. Thus, s.1 of the *Protection from Eviction Act* 1977 makes it an offence for any person to unlawfully deprive a residential occupier of his occupation of the premises or any part thereof, unless he proves that he believed, and had reasonable cause to believe, that the residential occupier had ceased to reside in the premises. In *R. v Phekoo* [1981] 1 W.L.R. 1117, CA, it was held that there must be a reasonable basis for the asserted belief on behalf of a person charged with an offence under s.1 of the *Protection from Eviction Act* 1977 that the persons he attempts to evict are not residential occupiers of the premises in question. In *R. v King* [1964] 1 Q.B. 285, CA, it was held that an honest belief on reasonable grounds as to the invalidity of a previous marriage, just as an honest belief on reasonable grounds that the spouse is dead, were good defences to a charge of bigamy.

The reasonableness of the defendant's belief will not always be relevant. Where the relevant statute does not indicate that a belief held by a defendant has to be reasonable, the court is to assume that Parliament did not intend to impart any requirement of reasonableness into the belief providing the basis for a defence. In *B v DPP* [2000] 2 W.L.R. 452, HL, the defendant, aged 15, had repeatedly asked a girl, aged 13, who was sitting next to him on a bus to perform oral sex with him. He was charged with inciting a girl under the age of 14 to commit an act of gross indecency with him, contrary to s.1(1) of the *Indecency with Children Act* 1960. It was accepted that he had honestly believed that the girl was over the age of 14, and the justices were asked to rule whether his state of mind could constitute a defence to the charge. The justices ruled that it could not, and he changed his plea to guilty. No finding was made as to whether he had had reasonable grounds for his belief. His conviction was quashed by the House of Lords: *mens rea* was an essential element of every criminal offence unless Parliament expressly or by necessary implication provided to the contrary and, on a true construction of s.1(1) of the Act of 1960 in its statutory context, Parliament had not so provided in respect of the age ingredient of the offence. It was therefore necessary for the prosecution to prove the absence of a genuine belief on the part of the defendant, for which he did not have to have had reasonable grounds, that the victim had been 14 or over.

(j) *Strict liability*

8–31   Offences of strict liability do not require any *mens rea* as to one or more elements of the *actus reus*. All offences of strict liability are statutory offences. Thus in *Pharmaceutical Society of Great Britain v Storkwain Ltd* (1986) 83 Cr.App.R. 359, HL, where the appellants, retail chemists, supplied prescription-only drugs in accordance with a forged prescription and without fault on their part, they were afforded no defence to a charge under s.58(2)(a) of the *Medicines Act* 1968, which prohibits the selling of goods on the basis of a forged prescription 1968 Act, for the prosecution did not have to prove *mens rea*. However, in *Sweet v Parsley* [1970] A.C. 32, HL, they held that for the purposes of the offence of being concerned in the management of premises used for the purpose of smoking cannabis resin contrary to s.5(b) of the *Dangerous Drugs Act* 1965, *mens rea* as to the circumstances of the offence was required. A defendant who was the tenant of a farm, and who sub-let rooms there for short periods was not guilty of the offence under s.5 where she was living elsewhere at the time of the alleged offence and where she visited the farm only occasionally.

It may be thus difficult to determine when the courts will uphold strict liability in respect of a particular statutory offence: the approach in *B v DPP*, above, may be useful.

(k) *Transferred Malice*

8–32   If a person by mistake, or, *e.g.* bad aim causes injury to a person or property other than the person or property which he intended to attack, he is guilty of a crime to the same degree as if he had achieved his object: *R. v Latimer* [1886] 17 Q.B.D. 359. The harm caused must be of the same kind as the harm intended: *R. v Pembliton* [1874] L.R. C.C.R. 119.

IV. ACCESSORIAL LIABILITY

(1) Legislation

Magistrates Courts Act 1980, s.44

Aiders and abettors

8–33   **44.**—(1) A person who aids, abets, counsels or procures the commission by another person of a summary offence shall be guilty of the like offence and may be tried [whether or not he is charged as a principal] either by a court having jurisdiction to try that other person or by a court having by virtue of his own offence jurisdiction to try him.

(2) Any offence consisting in aiding, abetting, counselling or procuring the commission of an offence triable either way [other than an offence listed in Schedule 1 to this Act] shall

by virtue of this subsection be triable either way.

The words 'aids, abets, counsels or procures' should be given their ordinary meaning. The use of four words suggests that there is a difference between the words for if there were none, Parliament would be wasting time in using four words where two or three would do: *Att.-Gen.'s Reference (No.1 of 1975)* [1975] Q.B. 773, CA.

(a) *Aiders and Abettors*

The words 'aiding and abetting' can include acts committed before the commission of **8–34** the *actus reus* of the offence. In *Blakely v DPP* [1991] R.T.R. 405, DC, McCullough J. said, at 411, that there are many accessories before the fact of whose activity none of the words 'counselling, procuring and commanding' would seem to be apt; whilst the words aiding and abetting would seem more appropriate to describe such activity. In *National Coal Board v Gamble* [1959] 1 Q.B. 11; 42 Cr.App.R. 240, DC, the defendant's conviction for aiding and abetting the driving of an overweight lorry was upheld; the servant had loaded coal onto the lorry of the principal knowing that that this load had rendered the lorry overweight and that the driver intended to take it onto the highway and completed the sale of the coal, thus facilitating the commission of the offence.

To establish aiding and abetting, it must be proved that the defendant intended to encourage, and *wilfully* encouraged the crime committed. Mere continued voluntary presence at the scene of the commission of a crime does not of itself necessarily amount to encouragement; but the fact that a person was voluntarily and purposely present witnessing the commission of a crime, and offered no opposition to it, though he might reasonably be expected to prevent and had the power so to do, or at least to express his dissent, might in some circumstances afford cogent evidence upon which to justify finding that he wilfully encouraged, and so aided and abetted; but this is a question of fact: *R. v Clarkson*, 55 Cr.App.R. 445, Ct-MAC. Knowledge of the principal's offence, plus an ability to control his actions, coupled with a deliberate decision not to exercise such control may constitute aiding and abetting: *R. v J.F. Alford Transport Ltd* [1997] 2 Cr.App.R. 326, CA.

A person may be an aider and abettor even though his age or sex renders him incapable of being a principal: *R. v Eldershaw* [1828] 3 C & P 396. A person protected by the offence in question cannot be convicted for aiding and abetting the person who committed the offence against them: *R. v Tyrell* [1894] 1 Q.B. 710, CCR (unlawful sexual intercourse with a girl under 16); *R. v Whitehouse* [1977] Q.B. 868; 65 Cr.App.R. 33, CA (girl under 16 cannot aid and abet incest by her father).

(b) *Joint enterprise*

Where two of more persons embark on a joint enterprise, each is responsible for acts **8–35** done within the scope of that joint enterprise. This shared liability ends when a party to the joint enterprise goes beyond what was agreed as part of the common enterprise. It is for the tribunal of fact to decide whether what was done could be construed as being within the joint enterprise or whether it exceeded it: *R. v Anderson and Morris* [1966] 1 Q.B. 110, CCA; *R. v Lovesey and Peterson* [1970] 1 Q.B. 352, CA; *R. v Powell, R. v English* [1999] 1 A.C. 1, HL.

Where the principal does an act which was within the joint enterprise yet with an intent which was outside the contemplation of the other participants to the joint enterprise, the accessory will not escape all liability, and may be found guilty of the degree of offence appropriate to the intention with which he acted: *R. v Gilmour* [2000] 2 Cr.App.R. 407 (an appellant who foresaw that the principals would carry out the act of throwing a petrol bomb into a house, but did not realise that in doing so they intended to kill or do grievous bodily harm to the occupants would be guilty of manslaughter).

(c) *Counsellors and Procurers*

The word "counsel" does not imply any causal connection with the offence; the es- **8–36** sential elements are that there should be counselling, and the principal offence should be committed by the person counselled acting within the scope of his authority and not by accident: *R. v Calhaem* [1985] Q.B. 808, CA.

As regards procurement, in *Att.-Gen.'s Reference (No.1 of 1975)* [1975] Q.B. 773, CA, it was held that:

> "To procure means to produce by endeavour. You procure a thing by setting out to see that it happens and taking the appropriate steps to produce that happening. We think that there are plenty of instances in which a person may be said to procure the commission of a crime by another even though there is no sort of conspiracy between the two, even though there is no attempt at agreement or discussion as to the form which the offence should take." (at 779).

8–37   With procurement, there must be a causal link between what the accessory did and the commission of the offence. In *Att.-Gen.'s Reference (No.1 of 1975)* [1975] Q.B. 773, CA, the defendant had surreptitiously laced the drinks of a motorist who she knew was about to drive home with sprits. This led to the motorist driving home while the alcohol concentration in his blood was above the prescribed limit contrary to s.6(1) of the *Road Traffic Act* 1972 and, following the motorist's conviction of this offence, the defendant was convicted as having procured the commission of the motorists' offence due to the fact that there was a causal link between the defendant's act and the offence by the motorist who would not have committed it otherwise.

(d) *Agents Provocateurs*

8–38   Whilst the defendant who would not have committed an offence but for the activity of an agent provocateur will have no defence, the question here is whether the agent provocateur may himself be prosecuted. The following principles may be deduced from the relevant authorities: it is unlawful for a police officer to counsel or procure the commission of an offence which would otherwise not take place, but it may be proper for a police officer to take part in, or to encourage an informer to take part in, an offence which is already 'laid on' solely for the purpose of apprehending the offenders: *R. v Birtles*, 53 Cr.App.R. 469, CA; *R. v McCann*, 56 Cr.App.R. 359, CA; *R. v Clarke (D.G.)* 80 Cr.App.R. 344, CA.

(e) *Countermand and withdrawal*

8–39   A secondary party may be able to escape liability for aiding, abetting, counselling or procuring an offence if he makes an effective withdrawal before the offence is actually committed. In *R. v Whitefield*, 79 Cr.App.R. 36, CA it was held that if a person has counselled another to commit a crime, he may escape liability by withdrawal before the crime is committed, but it is not sufficient that he should merely repent or change his mind. If his participation is confined to advice or encouragement, he must at least communicate his change of mind to the other, and the communication must be such as will serve unequivocal notice upon the other party to the common unlawful cause that if he proceeds upon it he does so without the aid and assistance of those who withdraw. In *R. v Robinson* [2000] 5 *Archbold News* 2, CA, it was said that only exceptionally can a person withdraw from a crime he has initiated. To do so, he must communicate his withdrawal in order to give the principal[s] the opportunity to desist rather than complete the crime. This communication is even necessary in the context of spontaneous violence, where the accessory will only be excused from not giving such an opportunity to desist if it is not practicable or reasonable so to communicate, an example of such circumstances being found in *R. v Mitchell and King*, 163 J.P. 75, CA, where the accused had thrown down his weapon and moved away before the final and fatal blows were struck.

(f) *Acquittal of principal*

8–40   A secondary party may be convicted of an offence where the actual perpetrator of the *actus reus* of the substantive offence is either acquitted or convicted of a lesser offence. The secondary party may be convicted of the offence for which the principal is acquitted where there is evidence against the secondary party that may not be admitted against the principal: *R. v Humphreys and Turner* [1965] 3 All E.R. 689, or where there is insufficient evidence that the person charged as a principal was in fact involved in the offence: *R. v Davis* [1977] Crim.L.R. 542, CA.

The secondary party may also be convicted where the principal has some defence that does not benefit the secondary party: *R. v Bourne*, 36 Cr.App.R. 125, CCA; *R. v Cogan and Leek* [1976] 1 Q.B. 217, CA; *DPP v K and B* [1997] 1 Cr.App.R. 36, DC. In *R. v Pickford* [1995] 1 Cr.App.R. 420, CA, it was said, *obiter* that the decisions in *R. v Bourne* and *R. v Cogan and Leek* do not support the proposition that where the principal offender lacks all legal capacity to commit the crime in question another may nevertheless be guilty of aiding and abetting him. They were rather cases in which the person who had committed the acts said to constitute the principal offence was fully capable in law of committing that offence but had a complete defence on the facts.

(2) Mental element of accessories

As regards the intention to aid, abet, counsel or procure, no additional mental ele- **8–41** ment beyond that required for the principal is necessary to make a person guilty as an accessory: *Lynch v DPP for Northern Ireland* [1975] A.C. 653, HL. In *R. v Powell, R. v English* [1999] 1 A.C. 1, HL, it was held that a secondary party is guilty of murder if he participates in a joint venture, realising (but without agreeing thereto) that in the course thereof the principal might use force with intent to kill or cause grievous bodily harm, and the principal does so. The secondary party has lent himself to the enterprise and by doing so, has given assistance and encouragement to the principal in carrying out an enterprise which the secondary party realises may involve murder.

It is submitted that this approach should be adopted in relation to all charges against defendants accused of aiding and abetting the commission of a crime, whatever the crime alleged. Where the defendant is alleged to have counselled or procured the commission of the relevant offence it seems that it is necessary to prove that the defendant intended that the offence or an offence of the same type should be committed: *Ferguson v Weaving* [1951] 1 K.B. 814, at 819; *Att.-Gen.'s Reference (No.1 of 1975)* [1975] Q.B. 773, CA and *Blakely v DPP* [1991] R.T.R. 405, DC.

The secondary party must also know of the essential matters that constitute the offence before he may be convicted of aiding and abetting the commission of an offence: *per* Lord Goddard C.J. in *Johnson v Youden* [1950] 1 K.B. 544, at 546. This is so even where the principal's offence is one of strict liability; in *Smith v Mellors* [1987] 84 Cr.App.R. 279, DC, both defendants were charged under s.6(1) of the *Road Traffic Act* 1972, for driving with excess alcohol (now s.5(1)(a) of the *RTA* 1988). As it could not be determined who was the driver and who was the passenger, it was held that there was no case to answer, as for the purposes of the strict liability offence under s.6(1), for the secondary party to be convicted, it would be necessary to prove that he knew that the principal was driving with excess alcohol. As it could not be determined who was the driver and who the passenger, the question of knowledge could not be addressed.

V. ASSISTING OFFENDERS

(1) Legislation

Criminal Law Act 1967, s.4

Penalties for assisting offenders

4.—(1) Where a person has committed an arrestable offence, any other person who, knowing **8–42** or believing him to be guilty of the offence or of some other arrestable offence, does without lawful authority or reasonable excuse any act with intent to impede his apprehension or prosecution shall be guilty of an offence.

(1A) In this section and section 5 below "arrestable offence" has the meaning assigned to it by section 24 of the *Police and Criminal Evidence Act* 1984.

(2) If on the trial of an indictment for an arrestable offence the jury are satisfied that the offence charged [or some other offence of which the accused might on that charge be found guilty] was committed, but find the accused not guilty of it, they may find him guilty of any offence under subsection (1) above of which they are satisfied that he is guilty in relation to the offence charged [or that other offence].

(3) A person committing an offence under subsection (1) above with intent to impede another person's apprehension or prosecution shall on conviction on indictment be liable to imprisonment according to the gravity of the other person's offence, as follows—

   (a) if that offence is one for which the sentence is fixed by law, he shall be liable to imprisonment for not more than ten years;

   (b) if it is one for which a person [not previously convicted] may be sentenced to imprisonment for a term of fourteen years, he shall be liable to imprisonment for not more than seven years;

   (c) if it is not one included above but is one for which a person [not previously convicted] may be sentenced to imprisonment for a term of ten years, he shall be liable to imprisonment for not more than five years;

   (d) in any other case, he shall be liable to imprisonment for not more than three years.

(4) No proceedings shall be instituted for an offence under subsection (1) above except by or with the consent of the Director of Public Prosecutions:

[This section is printed and amended by the *PACE Act* 1984, s.119(1) and Sch.6, Pt I, para.17; and as repealed in part by the *Theft Act* 1968, s.33(3) and Sch.3, Pt III; the *Criminal Jurisdiction Act* 1975, Sch.6, Pt I; the *CLA* 1977, Sch.13; and the *Extradition Act* 1989, Sch.2.]

8–43   An arrestable offence must have been committed by the person assisted before a defendant can be convicted under this section and proof of that person's guilt is essential to proof of the commission of this offence. However, it is not necessary that the principal offender has been convicted of this arrestable offence: *R. v Donald and Donald*, 83 Cr.App.R. 49, CA. There can be no charge of attempting to commit an offence under s.4 of the *CLA* 1967: *Criminal Attempts Act* 1981, s.1(4).

As *Archbold Crown* notes (at § 18–37) the policy of this section is that those who assist offenders do so at their peril, the punishment being directly related to the nature of the principal offence rather than the knowledge of the defendant. The defendant must however know or positively believe in the guilt of the person convicted, and mere suspicion as to guilt will be insufficient. The statute does not however require that the defendant knew of the particular offence that the assisted person had committed, though the defendant's state of mind may be a relevant factor in mitigation: *R. v Morgan (M M)* [1972] 1 Q.B. 436, CA. The defendant does not have to be proved to have known the identity of the principal offender: *R. v Brindley and Long* [1971] 2 Q.B. 300, CA.

VI. INCHOATE OFFENCES

A. STATUTORY CONSPIRACY

8–44   The *Criminal Law Act* 1977 replaced common law conspiracy with a statutory offence, preserving only common law conspiracy to defraud, and conspiracy to do acts tending to corrupt public morals or outrage public decency. Conspiracy is triable only on indictment and is hence outside the scope of this work: see *Archbold Crown*, §§ 34–1 to 34–70.

B. ATTEMPT

(1) Legislation

Criminal Attempts Act 1981, ss.1, 1A

Attempting to commit an offence

1.—(1) If, with intent to commit an offence to which this section applies, a person does an act **8–45** which is more than merely preparatory to the commission of the offence, he is guilty of attempting to commit the offence.

(1A) Subject to section 8 of the *Computer Misuse Act* 1990 [relevance of external law], if this subsection applies to an act, what the person doing it had in view shall be treated as an offence to which this section applies.

(1B) Subsection (1A) above applies to an act if—

 (a) it is done in England and Wales; and

 (b) it would fall within subsection (1) above as more than merely preparatory to the commission of an offence under section 3 of the *Computer Misuse Act* 1990 but for the fact that the offence, if completed, would not be an offence triable in England and Wales.

(2) A person may be guilty of attempting to commit an offence to which this section applies even though the facts are such that the commission of the offence is impossible.

(3) In any case where—

 (a) apart from this subsection a person's intention would not be regarded as having amounted to an intent to commit an offence; but

 (b) if the facts of the case had been as he believed them to be, his intention would be so regarded,

then, for the purposes of subsection (1) above, he shall be regarded as having had an intent to commit that offence.

(4) This section applies to any offence which, if it were completed, would be triable in England and Wales as an indictable offence, other than—

 (a) conspiracy [at common law or under section 1 of the *Criminal Law Act* 1977 or any other enactment];

 (b) aiding, abetting, counselling, procuring or suborning the commission of an offence;

 (c) offences under section 4(1) [assisting offenders] or 5(1) [accepting or agreeing to accept consideration for not disclosing information about an arrestable offence] of the *Criminal Law Act* 1967.

Extended jurisdiction in relation to certain attempts

1A.—(1) If this section applies to an act, what the person doing the act had in view shall be **8–46** treated as an offence to which section 1(1) above applies.

(2) This section applies to an act if—

 (a) it is done in England and Wales, and

 (b) it would fall within section 1(1) above as more than merely preparatory to the commission of a Group A offence but for the fact that that offence, if completed, would not be an offence triable in England and Wales.

(3) In this section "Group A offence" has the same meaning as in Part 1 of the *Criminal Justice Act* 1993.

(4) Subsection (1) above is subject to the provisions of section 6 of the Act of 1993 [relevance of external law].

(5) Where a person does any act to which this section applies, the offence which he commits shall for all purposes be treated as the offence of attempting to commit the relevant Group A offence.

[Subss.1(1A) and (1B) were inserted by the *Computer Misuse Act* 1990, s.7(3). This section was inserted by the *CJA* 1993, s.5(2) and came into force on June 1, 1999: SI 1999/1189. It is not retrospective: s.7(8) of the 1993 Act.]

For the meaning of 'Group A offence' see s.1(1) and (3) of the 1993 Act.

Criminal Attempts Act 1981, ss.2–4

Application of procedural and other provisions to offences under s.1

8–47   **2.**—(1) Any provision to which this section applies shall have effect with respect to an offence under section 1 above of attempting to commit an offence as it has effect with respect to the offence attempted.

(2) This section applies to provisions of any of the following descriptions made by or under any enactment (whenever passed)—

    (a) provisions whereby proceedings may not be instituted or carried on otherwise than by, or on behalf or with the consent of, any person (including any provisions which also make other exceptions to the prohibition);

    (b) provisions conferring power to institute proceedings;

    (c) provisions as to the venue of proceedings;

    (d) provisions whereby proceedings may not be instituted after the expiration of a time limit;

    (e) provisions conferring a power of arrest or search;

    (f) provisions conferring a power of seizure and detention of property;

    (g) provisions whereby a person may not be convicted [or committed for trial] on the uncorroborated evidence of one witness (including any provision requiring the evidence of not less than two credible witnesses);

    (h) provisions conferring a power of forfeiture, including any power to deal with anything liable to be forfeited;

    (i) provisions whereby, if an offence committed by a body corporate is proved to have been committed with the consent or connivance of another person, that person also is guilty of the offence.

Offences of attempt under other enactments

8–47.1   **3.**—(1) Subsections (2) to (5) below shall have effect, subject to subsection (6) below and to any inconsistent provision in any other enactment, for the purpose of determining whether a person is guilty of an attempt under a special statutory provision.

(2) For the purposes of this Act an attempt under a special statutory provision is an offence which—

    (a) is created by an enactment other than section 1 above, including an enactment passed after this Act; and

    (b) is expressed as an offence of attempting to commit another offence (in this section referred to as "the relevant full offence").

(3) A person is guilty of an attempt under a special statutory provision if, with intent to commit the relevant full offence, he does an act which is more than merely preparatory to the commission of that offence.

(4) A person may be guilty of an attempt under a special statutory provision even though the facts are such that the commission of the relevant full offence is impossible.

(5) In any case where—

    (a) apart from this subsection a person's intention would not be regarded as having amounted to an intent to commit the relevant full offence; but

    (b) if the facts of the case had been as he believed them to be, his intention would be so regarded,

then, for the purposes of subsection (3) above, he shall be regarded as having had an intent to commit that offence.

(6) Subsections (2) to (5) above shall not have effect in relation to an act done before the commencement of this Act.

Trial and penalties

8–48   **4.**—(1) A person guilty by virtue of section 1 above of attempting to commit an offence shall—

    (a) if the offence attempted is murder or any other offence the sentence for which is fixed by law, be liable on conviction on indictment to imprisonment for life; and

    (b) if the offence attempted is indictable but does not fall within paragraph (a) above, be liable on conviction on indictment to any penalty to which he would have been liable on conviction on indictment of that offence; and

> (c) if the offence attempted is triable either way, be liable on summary conviction to any penalty to which he would have been liable on summary conviction of that offence.
>
> (2) In any case in which a court may proceed to summary trial of an information charging a person with an offence and an information charging him with an offence under section 1 above of attempting to commit it or an attempt under a special statutory provision, the court may, without his consent, try the informations together.
>
> (3) Where, in proceedings against a person for an offence under section 1 above, there is evidence sufficient in law to support a finding that he did an act falling within subsection (1) of that section, the question whether or not his act fell within that subsection is a question of fact.
>
> (4) Where, in proceedings against a person for an attempt under a special statutory provision, there is evidence sufficient in law to support a finding that he did an act falling within subsection (3) of section 3 above, the question whether or not his act fell within that subsection is a question of fact.
>
> (5) Subsection (1) above shall have effect—
>
> > (a) subject to section 37 of and Schedule 2 to the *Sexual Offences Act* 1956 [mode of trial of and penalties for attempts to commit certain offences under that Act]; and
> >
> > (b) notwithstanding anything—
> >
> > > (i) in section 32(1) [no limit to fine on conviction on indictment] of the *Criminal Law Act* 1977; or
> > >
> > > (ii) in section 78(1) and (2) [maximum of six months' imprisonment on summary conviction unless express provision made to the contrary] of the *Powers of Criminal Courts (Sentencing) Act* 2000.

[This section is printed as amended by the *PCC(S)A* 2000, s.165(1) and Sch.9, para.82.]

8–49 An offence which is triable only summarily may not be the subject of a criminal attempt under s.1 of the 1981 Act, however, provisions creating summary offences will sometimes create corresponding offences of attempt. Such offences are within the scope of s.3 of the 1981 Act which provides that attempts created by special statutory provision shall be governed by the same rules as those contained in subss.1(1) to (3) of the 1981 Act.

C. INGREDIENTS OF THE OFFENCE

"More than merely preparatory"

8–50 The words should be given their natural and ordinary meaning: *R. v Jones*, 91 Cr.App.R. 351, CA. In *R. v Geddes* [1996] Crim.L.R. 894, CA, it was held that there was no clear delineation between acts amounting to an attempt and those which were merely preparatory and each case depends upon its facts. For an offence to be committed under s.1 the defendant must have moved from the stage of planning and preparation to implementing his intention. In *R. v Qadir and Khan* [1998] Crim.L.R. 828, CA, the court stated that "attempt begins at the moment when the defendant embarks upon the crime proper, as opposed to taking steps rightly regarded as merely preparatory."

"With intent to commit an offence"

8–51 In *R. v Mohan* (1974) 60 Cr.App.R. 272, CA, in relation to the necessary mental element for criminal attempts at common law, James L.J. stated that:

> "The bounds are presently set requiring proof of specific intent, a decision to bring about, in so far as it lies within the accused's power, the commission of the offence which it is alleged the accused attempted to commit, no matter whether the accused desired that consequence of his act or not." (at page 278)

This was approved in *R. v Pearman* (1985) 80 Cr.App.R. 259, CA. Hence it must ordinarily be proved that the defendant acted with a specific intent to commit the particular crime attempted, even if the necessary *mens rea* for the particular crime falls below this high threshold.

8–52   However, whilst intent is required as to the consequences of the prohibited act, the Court of Appeal has held that something less may be sufficient in terms of the circumstances surrounding the offence. In *Att.-Gen.'s Reference (No.3 of 1992)*, 98 Cr.App.R. 383, CA, the defendant had thrown a petrol bomb, which smashed into a wall at the victim. The Court of Appeal considered whether he could be convicted of attempting to commit aggravated criminal damage, contrary to s.1(2) of the *Criminal Damage Act* 1971. The Court of Appeal held that the substantive offence would be committed if the defendant had a specific intent to cause damage by fire to property and was mentally reckless whether the life of another would thus be endangered. Hence it was possible to convict of attempt if the prosecution proved that the respondents, in that state of mind, intended to damage the car by throwing a bomb at it.

Attempting the impossible

8–53   Following the decision in *R. v Shivpuri* [1987] A.C. 1, HL, a defendant may be guilty of an attempt, notwithstanding that the commission of the actual offence was impossible. In *Shivpuri*, applying the language of s.1 of the *Criminal Attempts Act* 1981 to the facts of the case (attempted drugs importation) Lord Bridge stated:

> "[T]he first question to be asked is whether the appellant intended to commit the offences of being knowingly concerned in dealing with and harbouring drugs of Class A or Class B with intent to evade the prohibition on their importation. Translated into more homely language the question may be rephrased, without in any way altering its legal significance, in the following terms: did the appellant intend to receive and store (harbour) and in due course pass on to third parties (deal with) packages of heroin or cannabis which he knew had been smuggled into England from India? The answer is plainly yes, he did. Next, did he in relation to each offence, do an act which was more than merely preparatory to the commission of the offence? (at 19)
>
> ... Here then is the nub of the matter. Does the "act which is more than merely preparatory to the commission of the offence" in section 1 (1) of the Act of 1981 (the *actus reus* of the statutory offence of attempt) require any more than an act which is more than merely preparatory to the commission of the offence which the defendant intended to commit? Section 1 (2) must surely indicate a negative answer; if it were otherwise, whenever the facts were such that the commission of the actual offence was impossible, it would be impossible to prove an act more than merely preparatory to the commission of that offence and subsections (1) and (2) would contradict each other." (at 20)

8–54   A defendant who is not mistaken as to the facts, but who erroneously believes that his actions amount to a criminal office may not be convicted of a criminal attempt. Section 1(2) does not apply in relation to such cases.

Jurisdiction

8–55   The general rule is that if the completed offence would be triable in England and Wales, and attempt to commit it will be so triable: see s.1(1) and (4) of the 1981 Act.

Incitement

8–56   Incitement involves soliciting, encouraging or pressurising another person to commit an offence. It is primarily a common law offence, although there are also certain statutory offences of incitement. Where the offence incited is triable summarily only, incitement to commit that offence will be triable summarily only, and where the offence incited is triable either way, incitement to commit that offence will be triable either way: *Magistrates Courts Act* 1980, s.45 and Sch.1, para.35.

In *Invicta Plastics Ltd v Clare* [1976] R.T.R. 251, DC, it was held that a company which advertised a device that could detect police radar traps was properly convicted at common law for inciting people to use unlicensed apparatus for wireless telegraphy in contravention of s.1(1) of the *Wireless Telegraphy Act* 1949. In *Race Relations Board v Applin* [1973] 1 Q.B. 815, Lord Denning M.R. stated that "a person may incite another to do an act by threatening or by pressure, as well as persuasion."

D. Mens Rea

The defendant must intend that the offence incited will be committed, though as **8–57** with attempts, it may sometimes be the case that recklessness as to the circumstances of the offence will suffice. It is not necessary for the person incited to have the necessary *mens rea* to commit the offence, nor is it necessary that he actually go on to commit the offence incited: *DPP v Armstrong* [2000] Crim.L.R. 379.

In *DPP v Shaw* [1994] Crim.L.R. 365, CA, the appellant was charged with incitement to obtain property by deception by dishonestly inciting a fellow employee to obtain cheques from their employers by falsely accepting bogus invoices, supplied by the appellant, as real invoices for work done. He argued that he was not dishonest, as his intention was to expose the lax nature of the company's security arrangements. The Court of Appeal accepted that if true, this would be a valid defence. For a criticism of this decision, and the view that the appellant was guilty even if his evidence was believed, see the commentary at [1994] Crim.L.R. 365. However, as *Archbold Crown* notes (§ 34–72) it appears from the case transcript (p.7F) that the prosecution conducted its case on the basis that they were alleging (and had to prove) that the inciter was dishonest. *Archbold Crown* submits that this may have been unnecessary, but may go someway towards explaining the decision.

E. Miscellaneous Statutory Provisions

See the *Perjury Act* 1911, s.7(2), 'inciting to commit perjury'; and the *Official Secrets* **8–58** *Act* 1920, s.7, 'inciting, counselling or attempting to procure another to commit an offence against the *Official Secrets Act*s 1911 and 1920'.

(1) Jurisdiction

The common law jurisdiction in respect of incitement is the same as that for conspir- **8–59** acy; see *Archbold Crown* §§ 34–18 *et seq.*

(2) Extended jurisdiction

(a) *Fraud and related offences*

Part I of the *Criminal Justice Act* 1993 gives the courts in England and Wales juris- **8–60** diction to try certain cases of fraud and related offences where there is a significant foreign element in their perpetration and where the jurisdictional rules might prevent them from being so tried.

Incitement to commit a 'Group A' offence (see s.1(1) of the 1993 Act) is a 'Group B' offence within Pt I. For detailed analysis of these provisions see *Archbold Crown*, § 2–46.

(b) *Sexual Offences*

Sexual Offences (Conspiracy and Incitement) Act 1996, ss.2, 3

Incitement to commit certain sexual acts outside the United Kingdom
    2.—(1) This section applies where— **8–61**
        (a) any act done by a person in England and Wales would amount to the offence of incitement to commit a listed sexual offence but for the fact that what he had in view would not be an offence triable in England and Wales,

(b) the whole or part of what he had in view was intended to take place in a country or territory outside the United Kingdom, and

(c) what he had in view would involve the commission of an offence under the law in force in that country or territory.

(2) Where this section applies—

(a) what he had in view is to be treated as that listed sexual offence for the purposes of any charge of incitement brought in respect of that act, and

(b) any such charge is accordingly triable in England and Wales.

(3) Any act of incitement by means of a message [however communicated] is to be treated as done in England and Wales if the message is sent or received in England and Wales.

[This Act came into force on October 1, 1996: s.7(2) and the *Sexual Offences (Conspiracy and Incitement) Act 1996 (Commencement) Order* 1996 (SI 1996/2262). Nothing in s.2 applies to any act or other event occurring before the coming into force of that section: s.7(3).]

Sections 1 and 2: supplementary

8–62   3.—(1) Conduct punishable under the law in force in any country or territory is an offence under that law for the purposes of section 2 however it is described in that law.

(2) Subject to subsection (3), a condition in section 2(1)(c) is to be taken to be satisfied unless, not later than rules of court may provide, the defence serve on the prosecution a notice—

(a) stating that, on the facts as alleged with respect to what the accused had in view, the condition is not in their opinion satisfied,

(b) showing their grounds for that opinion, and

(c) requiring the prosecution to show that it is satisfied.

(3) [...]

(4) The court, if it thinks fit, may permit the defence to require the prosecution to show that the condition is satisfied without the prior service of a notice under subsection (2).

(5) In the Crown Court the question whether the condition is satisfied is to be decided by the judge alone.

(6) In any proceedings in respect of any offence triable by virtue of section 2 it is immaterial to guilt whether or not the accused was a British citizen at the time of any act or other event proof of which is required for conviction of the offence.

(7) [...]

(8) References to an offence of incitement to commit a listed sexual offence include an offence triable in England and Wales as such an incitement by virtue of section 2 [without prejudice to subsection (2) of that section].

(9) Subsection (8) applies to references in any enactment, instrument or document [except those in section 2 of this Act and in Part I of the *Criminal Law Act* 1977].

[This section is printed as amended and repealed in part by the *Criminal Justice (Terrorism and Conspiracy) Act* 1998, s.9(1) and Sch.1, para.9 (effective September 4, 1998).]

Sexual Offences (Conspiracy and Incitement) Act 1996, Sch.

Section 5   SCHEDULE

LISTED SEXUAL OFFENCES

England and Wales

8–63   1.—(1) In relation to England and Wales, the following are listed sexual offences:

(a) offences under the following provisions of the *Sexual Offences Act* 1956—

     (i)   section 1 [rape],

     (ii)   section 5 [intercourse with girl under the age of thirteen],

     (iii)   section 6 [intercourse with girl under the age of sixteen],

     (iv)   section 12 [buggery],

    (v)   section 14 [indecent assault on a girl], and

    (vi) section 15 [indecent assault on a boy],

  (b) an offence under section 1 of the *Indecency with Children Act* 1960 [indecent conduct towards young child].

  (2) In sub-paragraph (1)(a), sub-paragraphs (i), (iv), (v) and (vi) do not apply where the victim of the offence has attained the age of sixteen years.

F. PARTICULAR OFFENCES

Section 5(7) of the *Criminal Law Act* 1977 abolished the offence of incitement to **8–64** conspire. As regards incitements to attempt to commit a crime, as *Archbold Crown* points out, by logic, it would seem that an incitement to attempt to commit an offence must necessarily be an incitement to commit that offence: ss.34–78. It has also been held that where a letter is sent soliciting and inciting the addressee to commit a crime, but is not proved to have reached the intended recipient, the sender may be properly convicted of an attempt to incite the commission of the crime: *R. v Banks* [1873] 12 Cox. 393; *R. v Krause*, 66 J.P. 121; *R. v Cope*, 16 Cr.App.R. 77. It was also held in *R. v Goldman* [2001] Crim.L.R. 822, CA, that a defendant attempted to incite the addressee of his letter to distribute indecent photographs of children even where he was responding to an offer made by the addressee to supply such photographs.

G. INCITING THE IMPOSSIBLE

At common law, incitement to commit an offence could not be committed where it **8–65** was impossible to commit the offence alleged to have been incited. It is necessary to analyse the evidence in order to decide precisely what the defendant is alleged to have incited and whether it was possible to commit that offence: *R. v Fitzmaurice* [1983] Q.B. 1083, CA.

VII. GENERAL DEFENCES

A. INTRODUCTION

Defences can be loosely categorised as those that involve a denial of the necessary **8–66** *mens rea*, and those that do not deny any of the components of the offence, but which claim that there was some legitimate reason for the defendant's conduct that will operate to justify or excuse his offending behaviour.

B. DEFENCES DENYING MENS REA

(1) Infancy

Crime and Disorder Act 1998, s.34

Abolition of rebuttable presumption that a child is doli incapax

  34. The rebuttable presumption of criminal law that a child aged 10 or over is incapable of **8–67** committing an offence is hereby abolished.

Following enactment of this section (30th September 1998) the law relating to the culpability of juveniles can be summarised as follows:

Children aged under 10 are not responsible in criminal law.

Children aged 10–14 are no longer presumed to be incapable of criminal responsibility. The child's age may however be a relevant factor in determining the reasonableness of his actions (where such a factor is relevant.)

(2) Insanity and automatism

Insanity is dealt with in Chapter 35 (and see *Archbold Crown* §§ 17–74—17–102).   **8–68**

Involuntary acts will not attract the sanction of the criminal law, hence a defendant who committed the prohibited act in a state of automatism will have a defence. The relationship between insanity and automatism has been considered in numerous cases:

R. v Quick [1973] Q.B. 910, CA (automatism: hypoglycaemia)

8–68.1 The accused was diabetic and raised the defence of automatism due to an imbalance of insulin, which he was taking on prescription. The Court of Appeal held that as the defendant's mental condition stemmed from the use of insulin, rather than his diabetes, his condition stemmed from an external factor, rather than a bodily disorder, hence the defence of automatism should have been available.

R. v Bailey, 77 Cr.App.R. 76, CA (automatism: hypoglycaemia)

8–68.2 The defendant had assaulted his victim during a period of loss of consciousness caused by hypoglaecemia because of his failure to take sufficient food following his last dose of insulin. The Court of Appeal held that self-induced automatism, other than that due to intoxication from alcohol or drugs, may provide a defence to crimes of basic intent. The question in each case will be whether the prosecution have proved the necessary element of recklessness. For example in cases of assault, if the accused knows that his actions or inaction are likely to make him aggressive, unpredictable or uncontrolled with the result that he may cause some injury to others and he persists in the action or takes no remedial action when he knows it is required, it will then be open to the jury to find that he was reckless.

R. v Hennessy, 89 Cr.App.R. 10, CA. (automatism: hyperglycaemia)

8–69 The defendant was an insulin dependent diabetic and the offences with which he was charged were committed at a time when he had not taken insulin or eaten for several days and was in a hyperglycaemic state. The relevant question was whether the defendant's state was caused by disease or by some external factor. Hyperglycaemia caused by an inherent defect and not corrected by insulin was a disease and any malfunction of the mind thus caused might fall within the *M'Naghten Rules*. However, the stress, anxiety and depression suffered by the appellant could be the result of the operation of external factors; but not in themselves separately or together external factors of the kind capable in law of causing or contributing to a state of automatism. They constituted a state of mind which was prone to recur, lacked the feature of novelty or accident hence the defence of automatism should not have been available to the defendant.

R. v Roach [2002] 3 Archbold News 1, CA

8–69.1 The legal definition of automatism allows that if external factors (taking of prescription drugs and drink) are operative on an underlying condition ('mixed personality disorder') which would not otherwise produce a state of automatism, then the defence should be left to the jury.

R. v Burgess, 93 Cr.App.R. 41, CA (sleepwalking)

8–69.2 The defendant was sleepwalking at the time of commission of the charged offence and alleged non-insane automatism as his defence. The Court of Appeal held that on the question of automatism the judge had to decide, first, whether a proper evidential foundation for the defence of automatism had been laid; and, secondly, whether the evidence showed the case to be one of insane automatism falling within the *M'Naghten Rules*, or one of non-insane automatism. The Court held that sleepwalking was an abnormality or disorder, albeit transitory, due to an internal factor, whether functional or organic. It was a disorder or abnormality which might recur, though the possibility of it recurring in the form of serious violence was unlikely. It therefore amounted to a disease of the mind and the trial judge was correct in ruling that the medical evidence adduced amounted to evidence of insanity within the *M'Naghten Rules*.

See further, *Archbold Crown* § 17–99.

(3) Intoxication

(a) *Introduction*

Different rules apply depending on whether the intoxication is voluntary or **8–70** involuntary. The intoxication will be classed as voluntary where the defendant knowingly takes alcohol or other intoxicating drugs (except when he acts under medical supervision or direction.) A defendant who drinks a spiked drink will be treated as being involuntarily intoxicated. A defendant who forms the *mens rea* required for the crime will not be able to rely on his intoxication as a defence, be that intoxication voluntary or involuntary: *R. v Kingston* (1994) 99 Cr.App.R. 286, HL.

As regards intoxicating drugs, in *R. v Bailey* (1983) 77 Cr.App.R. 76, CA, the Court of Appeal stated that for crimes of basic intent, intoxication due to voluntary consumption of dangerous drugs could not amount to a defence as recklessness will suffice for the *mens rea* of the offence, and such recklessness can be found in the decision to consume dangerous drugs. However, in the context of non-dangerous drugs, such as insulin taken by a diabetic, such recklessness cannot be so easily found as whilst 'It is common knowledge that those who take alcohol to excess or certain sorts of drugs may become aggressive or do dangerous or unpredictable things ... the same cannot be said without more of a man who fails to take food after an insulin injection. If he does appreciate the risk that such a failure may lead to aggressive, unpredictable and uncontrollable conduct and he nevertheless deliberately runs the risk or otherwise disregards it, this will amount to recklessness'; *per* Griffiths L.J. (at 80). In *R. v Hardie* 80 Cr.App.R. 157, CA, the defendant, charged with an offence under the *Criminal Damage Act* 1971, had taken a number of valium tablets (prescribed for someone else). The Court of Appeal held that this did not necessarily amount to voluntary intoxication, Parker L.J stating that:

> "...if the effect of a drug is merely soporific or sedative the taking of it, even in some excessive quantity, cannot in the ordinary way raise a *conclusive* presumption against the admission of proof of intoxication for the purpose of disproving *mens rea* in ordinary crimes, such as would be the case with alcoholic intoxication or incapacity or automatism resulting from the self-administration of dangerous drugs." (at 160)

The relevant question was whether the taking of the drug itself was reckless, which **8–71** would provide the necessary *mens rea* of the offence.

(b) *Voluntary intoxication*

Voluntary intoxication may negate the *mens rea* requirements of crimes of specific **8–72** intent. The exact meaning of this phrase, and whether the lines between crimes of specific and crimes of basic intent are clearly made out is not beyond dispute. However, broadly speaking, crimes of specific intent are those for which only intention will suffice as the necessary mental element. In *R. v Sheehan and Moore*, 60 Cr.App.R. 308, Geoffrey Lane L.J. stated:

> "in cases where drunkenness and its possible effect upon the defendant's *mens rea* is an issue, we think that the proper direction to a jury is, first, to warn them that the mere fact that the defendant's mind was affected by drink so that he acted in a way in which he would not have done had he been sober does not assist him at all, provided that the necessary intention was there. A drunken intent is nevertheless an intent.
>
> Secondly, and subject to this, the jury should merely be instructed to have regard to all the evidence, including that relating to drink, to draw such inferences as they think proper from the evidence, and on that basis to ask themselves whether they feel sure that at the material

time the defendant had the requisite intent." (at 312)

In *R. v Alden and Jones* [2001] 5 *Archbold News* 3, Ct-MAC, the court said that so far as the question of alcohol and specific intent was concerned, the crucial question where there is evidence of the consumption by the defendant of a substantial quantity of drink is whether there is an issue as to the defendant's formation of specific intent by reason of the alcohol which he has taken and that the necessary pre-requisite to a direction of the kind identified in *Sheehan v Moore*, above, is that there must be an issue as to the effect of drunkenness upon the defendant's state of mind.

8–73   Where the prosecution has to prove recklessness, *R. v G* [2004] 1 Cr.App.R. 21, HL, preserves the position whereby the voluntarily intoxicated defendant cannot rely on his intoxication to assert that he did not appreciate the consequences of his actions. Although the House of Lords overruled *Caldwell* as regards the definition of recklessness for the purposes of s.1 of the *Criminal Damage Act* 1971, holding that 'a person acts recklessly within the meaning of s.1 of the 1971 Act with respect to (i) a circumstance when he is aware of a risk that it exists or will exist; (ii) a result when he is aware of a risk that it will occur; and it is, in the circumstances known to him, unreasonable to take the risk', the House held that it was not blameworthy to do something involving a risk of injury to another if (for reasons other than self-induced intoxication) one genuinely did not perceive the risk. The subjective view of recklessness is also adopted in cases involving malicious wounding and assault. In such cases, the fact that the accused was unaware of the relevant risk due to the effect of alcohol will not avail him, provided that the risk is one he would have been aware of had he been sober: *R. v Aitken*, 95 Cr.App.R. 304, Ct-MAC; *R. v Richardson and Irwin* [1999] 1 Cr.App.R. 392, CA.

When the question of drunkenness arises, it is not a question of the capacity of the defendant to form the particular intent which is in issue; what is in issue is simply whether he did form such an intent: *R. v Garlick*, 72 Cr.App.R. 291, CA.

In *DPP v Majewski* (1977) A.C. 443, HL, the appellant had been convicted of assaults occasioning actual bodily harm and assaults on police officers in the execution of their duty. His defence was that by reason of drugs voluntarily taken he did not know what he was doing. The House of Lords held that as regards crimes of basic intent, where the necessary mental element is recklessness, or in the context of assault, foresight that the accused actions would cause another person to have apprehension of immediate and unlawful violence, or would possibly have such a consequence, a voluntarily intoxicated defendant will not be able to assert that due to the intoxication he was senseless and therefore had neither recklessness nor intent as regards the *actus reus* of the offence. Lord Elwyn-Jones L.C. stated:

8–74   "If a man of his own volition takes a substance which causes him to cast off the restraints of reason and conscience, no wrong is done to him by holding him answerable criminally for any injury he may do while in that condition. His course of conduct in reducing himself by drugs and drink to that condition in my view supplies the evidence of *mens rea*, of guilty mind certainly sufficient for crimes of basic intent. It is a reckless course of conduct and recklessness is enough to constitute the necessary *mens rea* in assault cases ... The drunkenness is itself an intrinsic, an integral part of the crime, the other part being the evidence of the unlawful use of force against the victim. Together they add up to criminal recklessness. On this I adopt the conclusion of Stroud in (1920) 36 L.Q.R. at p. 273 ... By allowing himself to get drunk and thereby putting himself in such a condition as to be no longer amenable to the law's commands, a man shows such regardlessness as amounts to *mens rea* for the purpose of all ordinary crimes." (at 464–475)

And at 475:

"My noble and learned friends and I think it may be helpful if we give the following indication of the general lines on which in our view the jury should be directed as to the effect upon the criminal responsibility of the accused of drink or drugs or both, whenever death or physical injury to another person results from something done by the accused for which there is no legal justification and the offence with which the accused is charged is manslaughter or assault at common law or the statutory offence of unlawful wounding under section 20, or of assault occasioning actual bodily harm under section 47 of the *Offences against the Person Act* 1861.

In the case of these offences it is no excuse in law that, because of drink or drugs which the accused himself had taken knowingly and willingly, he had deprived himself of the ability to exercise self-control, to realise the possible consequences of what he was doing, or even to be conscious that he was doing it. As in the instant case, the jury may be properly instructed that they "can ignore the subject of drink or drugs as being in any way a defence" to charges of this character."

Thus for crimes where recklessness is the sufficient *mens rea*, voluntary intoxication **8–75** will not afford an defence. These crimes would seem to include (for the purposes of the magistrates courts; common assault, assault occasioning actual bodily harm, assault on a police officer in the execution of his duty, both offences against s.20 of the *Offences Against the Person Act* 1861, taking a conveyance without the owner's authority contrary to s.12(1) of the *Theft Act* 1968, arson or criminal damage contrary to s.1(1) of the *Criminal Damage Act* 1971 if recklessness is charged, arson or criminal damage contrary to s.1(2) of the *Criminal Damage Act* 1971 if recklessness is alleged.

DPP v Majewski was approved in *R. v G*, above. See also *Archbold Crown*, §§ 17–102—17–117.

(4) Mistake of fact

Since the decision in *R. v Tolson* (1889) L.R. 23 Q.B.D. 168 it has been an accepted **8–76** principle that mistake of fact, in the sense of a belief in circumstances which, if true would make the defendant's conduct innocent, is a defence to some, but not all criminal charges. The QBD (Crown Cases Reserved) in *Tolson* held that it was a good defence to a charge of bigamy that the accused believed on reasonable grounds, that the first spouse was dead.

Mistake negativing ingredient of offence

In *R. v Williams (G.)*, 78 Cr.App.R. 276, CA, the decision in *Morgan* [1976] A.C. **8–77** 182, HL, was applied to a case of assault occasioning actual bodily harm. One of the elements of this offence is that the accused was acting unlawfully, *i.e.* not acting in self-defence, in the defence of others or for the prevention of crime. The prosecution must establish that the accused was aware of the unlawful nature of his actions. Hence if the accused establishes that he believed in facts which would, were they true, have rendered his conduct lawful, the prosecution have failed to prove their case. The reasonableness of the defendant's belief was only relevant to the question of determining whether he did in fact hold that belief. *Williams* was applied in the cases of *R. v Jones (Terence)*, 83 Cr.App.R. 375, CA and *Blackburn v Bowering* (1994) 1 W.L.R. 1324, CA (Civ. Div.) Note the presumptions in the *Sexual Offences Act* 2003 with the effect that *Morgan* no longer applies to sexual offences: see Ch.10.

Mistake not negativing ingredient of offence

In *R. v Tolson*, above, where the defendant was charged with bigamy, her belief that **8–78** her first spouse was dead provided her with a defence as it was found to be based on reasonable grounds. *Tolson* was applied in *Albert v Lavin* (1981) 72 Cr.App.R. 178, DC to a charge of assaulting a police constable in the execution of his duty. It was held that a mistaken belief that the victim was not a police constable would not avail the defendant if there were no reasonable grounds for such a belief. In *R. v Phekoo*, 73 Cr.App.R. 107, it was held that the offence under s.1(3) of the *Protection from Eviction Act* 1977 was not an absolute offence, and that it had to be proved that the defendant intended to harass someone he knew or believed to be a residential occupier, rather than a squatter. The defendant would be entitled to be acquitted if his belief that the person was not a residential occupier was based on reasonable grounds.

As noted in *Archbold Crown*, § 17–13, the distinction between mistakes which negative and element of the offence and those that do not has been blurred by the decision of the House of Lords in *B (A minor) v DPP* [2000] 2 A.C. 428. The defendant was charged with an offence contrary to s.1 of the *Indecency with Children Act* 1960, which provided that a person 'who commits an act of gross indecency with or towards a child under the age of fourteen (subsequently amended to 16) is guilty of an offence.' The House of Lords held that if the defendant honestly believed that the child was 14 or over, he would not be guilty of the offence. The reasonableness of that belief was not relevant. See further *Archbold Crown*, §§ 17–13—17–14.

Mistake is not an available defence as regards offences of strict liability, which carry no requirement of *mens rea*. In *R. v Howells* [1977] Q.B. 614, 65 Cr.App.R. 86, CA, it was held that an honest and reasonable belief that a firearm was an antique, and therefore exempt from the *Firearms Act* 1968 was no defence.

Mistake of law

8–79   An honest and reasonable belief that an action is not criminal is no defence, though it may afford considerable mitigation: *Johnson v Youden* [1950] 1 K.B. 544 at 546.

A mistake as to the civil law may have the effect of negativing *mens rea*. For example, s.2(1)(a) of the *Theft Act* 1968 provides that a person's conduct will not be regarded as dishonest if he appropriates the property in the belief that he has in law the right to deprive the other of it, on behalf of himself or of a third person. In *R. v Smith* [1974] Q.B. 354; 58 Cr.App.R. 320, CA it was held that mistaken belief as to ownership of property is a defence to a charge of criminal damage. As regards alleged contravention of a statutory instrument, s.3(2) of the *Statutory Instruments Act* 1946 provides:

> "In any proceedings against any person for an offence consisting of a contravention of any such statutory instrument, it shall be a defence to prove that the instrument had not been issued by or under the authority of His Majesty's Stationery Office at the date of the alleged contravention unless it is proved that at that date reasonable steps had been taken for the purpose of bringing the purport of the instrument to the notice of the public, or of persons likely to be affected by it, or of the person charged."

See further, *Archbold Crown*, § 17–23.

C. DEFENCES CLAIMING CONDUCT WAS EXCUSABLE

(1) Duress

8–80   In *Lynch v DPP for Northern Ireland* [1975] A.C. 653, HL, Lord Simon stated that "Where so little is clear, this at least seems to be established: that the type of threat which affords a defence must be one of human physical harm (including, possibly, imprisonment), so that threat of injury to property is not enough" (at 686). The threat may relate to a person for whose safety the defendant would have reasonably regarded himself as responsible: *R. v Wright* [2000] Crim.L.R. 510, CA. In *R. v Howe* [1987] A.C. 417, HL, it was held that the relevant test whether a person when charged with a criminal offence was acting under duress is an objective, not subjective, one. This test could be stated as; was the threat was so grave as to cause a person of reasonable firmness, sharing the characteristics of the defendant, to act as he did?

The question of what are the relevant characteristics to which the court should have regard was considered in *R. v Bowen* [1996] 2 Cr.App.R. 157, CA. Stewart-Smith L.J. stated that the following principles apply:

> "(1) The mere fact that the accused is more pliable, vulnerable, timid or susceptible to threats than a normal person are not characteristics with which it is legitimate to invest the reasonable/ordinary person for the purpose of considering the objective test.
> (2) The defendant may be in a category of persons who the jury may think less able to resist pressure than people not within that category. Obvious examples are age, where a young person may well not be so robust as a mature one; possibly sex, though many woman would doubtless consider they had as much moral courage to resist pressure as men; pregnancy, where there is added fear for the unborn child; serious physical disability, which may inhibit

self protection; recognised mental illness or psychiatric condition, such as post traumatic stress disorder leading to learned helplessness.

(3) Characteristics which may be relevant in considering provocation, because they relate to the nature of the provocation, itself will not necessarily be relevant in cases of duress. Thus homosexuality may be relevant to provocation if the provocative words or conduct are related to this characteristic; it cannot be relevant in duress, since there is no reason to think that homosexuals are less robust in resisting threats of the kind that are relevant in duress cases.

(4) Characteristics due to self-induced abuse, such as alcohol, drugs or glue-sniffing, cannot be relevant.

(5) Psychiatric evidence may be admissible to show that the accused is suffering from some mental illness, mental impairment or recognised psychiatric condition provided persons generally suffering from such condition may be more susceptible to pressure and threats and thus to assist the jury in deciding whether a reasonable person suffering from such a condition might have been impelled to act as the defendant did. It is not admissible simply to show that in the doctor's opinion an accused, who is not suffering from such illness or condition, is especially timid, suggestible or vulnerable to pressure and threats. Nor is medical opinion admissible to bolster or support the credibility of the accused." (at 166–167)

The threat must have been effective when the crime was committed, but it is not fatal **8–81** to the defence if the threat is not of immediate injury in the event of non-compliance: *R. v Hudson and Taylor* [1971] 2 Q.B. 202, CA. In *R. v Abdul-Hussain* [1999] Crim.L.R. 570, CA, Rose L.J. examined the necessity of an immediate threat and stated that whilst there should be a close nexus between the threat and the criminal act, this does not require a virtually spontaneous reaction. He went on to state that the judge should have asked whether there was evidence of such fear operating on the minds of the defendants at the time of the offence as to impel them to act as they did and whether, if so, there was evidence that the danger they feared objectively existed and that the offence was a reasonable and proportionate response to it. *R. v Abdul-Hussain* was approved by the Court of Appeal in *R. v Anthony True* [2003] EWCA Crim 2255, CA, where Rix L.J. stated:

"Once evidence of duress is properly raised it should be left to the jury. It should only be removed from the jury if there is no evidence upon which a jury properly directed might think that it was reasonable for the defendant, according to the standards of a reasonable man, to fail to avail himself of opportunities of escape, such as going to the police. That question itself depends on all the circumstances of the case, including the cogency of the threats on the one hand, and the seriousness of the crime which the defendant says he is being coerced into carrying out on the other." (See also *Safi* [2004] 1 Cr.App.R. 14.)

The defendant must avail himself of an opportunity which was reasonably open to him to render the threat ineffective. If he does not, the threat will no longer operate as a defence. In *R. v Baker and Ward* [1999] 2 Cr.App.R. 355, CA, the appellants pleaded guilty to offences for an armed robbery of a superstore. They asserted that they had acted under duress, claiming that because they had failed to pay for one batch of cannabis, they and their families had been threatened with violence and that one of the appellants had been attacked. One of the men involved in the threats and the attack visited them the night before the robbery and told them to rob the store.

The Court held that there were two limitations to the defence of duress; a man **8–82** should not voluntarily put himself in a position where he was likely to be subjected to such compulsion and if a person could avoid the effects of duress by escaping from the duress, without damage to himself or his immediate family, he should do so. As regards the first element a defendant had to be aware of the risk that the group might try to coerce him into committing criminal offences of the type for which he was being tried. Only if a defendant had no reason to anticipate such pressure, would he be entitled to rely on duress.

The Court also held that once it had been established that the defendant had acted due to the threats described and that a man of reasonable firmness would have yielded to such compulsion, the defence of duress would be available subject to two further questions. First, had the prosecution proved that the appellants could have neutralised the threats by going to the police? Secondly, had the prosecution proven that the appellants had voluntarily put themselves in a position, by dealing in cannabis on the scale that they were doing and by incurring debts to their supplier, where they were likely to be subjected to compulsion of the necessary kind to commit offences to obtain money. If the jury answered either question yes then the defence would be unavailable. See also *Z* (2003) Cr.App.R. 173; [2003] Crim.L.R. 627.

A secondary party is liable to conviction of the full offence, although the principal has the defence of duress: *R. v Bourne*, 36 Cr.App.R. 125, CA.

See further *Archbold Crown*, §§ 17–125, 17–126.

(2) Necessity/Duress of Circumstances

8–83   In *R. v Shayler* [2001] 1 W.L.R. 2206, CA, Lord Woolf C.J. stated that 'the distinction between duress of circumstances and necessity has, correctly, been by and large ignored or blurred by the courts...the law has tended to treat duress of circumstances and necessity as one and the same.' (at para.55) He then approved the statement in *Archbold Crown* at § 17–124 that:

> "There has in recent years developed the expression 'duress of circumstances'. The use of the word 'duress' in this contest is misleading. Duress, whether in criminal law or civil law, suggests pressure being brought to bear by one person on another person to persuade that other person to do something which he is unwilling to do. 'Duress of circumstances' has nothing to do with one person being told to commit a crime 'or else': it relates to a situation where a person is driven to commit a crime by force of circumstances. Accordingly, duress of circumstances is more conveniently dealt with under the heading of 'necessity' ... Indeed, it may be that duress, strictly so called, should itself be regarded as a form of the defence of necessity: see *per* Lord Hailsham L.C. in *R. v Howe* and others..."

Stephen, *Digest of the Criminal Law*, p.9 stated that an act which would otherwise be a crime may in some cases be excused if the defendant can show that:

(a) it was done only to avoid consequences which could not otherwise be avoided and which if they had followed, would have inflicted upon him, or upon others whom he was bound to protect, inevitable and irreparable evil;

(b) that no more was done than was reasonably necessary for that purpose; and

(c) that the evil inflicted by it was not disproportionate to the evil avoided.

This statement was approved by Brooke L.J. in *A (Children) (Conjoined Twins: Surgical Separation), Re* [2001] Fam 147, HL, where he concluded that the separation of conjoined twins to save the life of one twin, whilst entailing death for the other would satisfy Stephen's three criteria, and was hence appropriate (at p.204). Each of the three judges in *Re A* stressed the unique nature of the case, and, as *Archbold Crown* notes at § 17–128, it would seem that the defence would only succeed where the inevitable consequence of taking no action would have been the death of two individuals, whereas the consequence of the defendant taking action was to save the life of one of those individuals, albeit at the cost of accelerating the death of the other. As Ward L.J. stated (at p.204):

> "[I]t is important to restate the unique circumstances for which this case is authority. They are that it must be impossible to preserve the life of X without bringing about the death of Y, that Y by his or her very continued existence will inevitably bring about the death of X within a short period of time, and that X is capable of living an independent life but Y is incapable under any circumstances, including all forms of medical intervention, of viable independent existence. As I said at the beginning of this judgment, this is a very unique case."

8–84   In *R. v Safi*, above, it was held that a defendant would have a defence where he reasonably believed that he faced death or serious injury, and a reasonable person in the same circumstances would have acted in the same way. See also *R. v Cairns* [1999] 2 Cr.App.R. 137, CA.

In *R. v Conway* (1989) Q.B. 290, the Court of Appeal concluded that:

> "necessity can only be a defence to a charge of reckless driving where the facts establish

"duress of circumstances," ...i.e., where the defendant was constrained by circumstances to drive as he did to avoid death or serious bodily harm to himself or some other person... Whether "duress of circumstances" is called "duress" or "necessity" does not matter" [at p.164]

Conway was applied in *R. v Martin* (1989) 88 Cr.App.R. 343, CA where Simon **8–85** Brown J. stated:

"The principles may be summarised thus: first, English law does, in extreme circumstances, recognise a defence of necessity. Most commonly this defence arises as duress, that is, pressure on the accused's will from the wrongful threats or violence of another. Equally however it can arise from other objective dangers threatening the accused or others. Arising thus it is conveniently called 'duress of circumstances'.

Second, the defence is available only if, from an objective standpoint, the accused can be said to be acting reasonably and proportionately in order to avoid a threat of death or serious injury.

Third, assuming the defence to be open to the accused on his account of the facts, the issue should be left to the jury, who should be directed to determine these two questions: first, was the accused, or may he have been, impelled to act as he did because as a result of what he reasonably believed to be the situation he had good cause to fear that otherwise death or serious physical injury would result second, if so, would a sober person of reasonable firmness, sharing the characteristics of the accused, have responded to that situation by acting as the accused acted? If the answer to both those questions was Yes, then the jury would acquit the defence of necessity would have been established." [at pp.345–346]

In *DPP v Bell* (1992) R.T.R. 335, DC, the defendant was charged with driving after consuming alcohol in excess of the prescribed limit. He had been out drinking with friends, and it had always been the plan that he would drive home. However, the Crown Court had found as a fact that the defendant was at the time of driving in terror of being caused serious personal injury. They had hence upheld the defendant's plea of duress and quashed the conviction imposed by the justices. The question for the opinion of the High Court was whether, given the defendant's intention to drive anyway, the Crown Court was correct to accept that the defence of duress of circumstance applied to the defendant's driving away from the car park on account of the threatened violence. The DC held that as the Crown Court had accepted that the defendant drove off in terror, the question of the relevance of the fact that the duress may not have been the sine qua non of the defendant's conduct was not a question forming part of the case stated.

The applicability of necessity as a defence to a charges under ss.1 and 4 of the *Official* **8–86** *Secrets Act* 1989 was examined in *R. v Shayler* [2001] 1 W.L.R. 2206, CA. The Court of Appeal held that the defence of necessity was available to such charges, though in the instant case there were a number of difficulties relating to the establishment of the defence. The appellant could not identify the action by some external agency which is going to create the imminent (if not immediate) threats to the life and limb of members of the general public as a result of the security services alleged abuses and blunders. Hence it was impossible to test whether there was sufficient urgency to justify the otherwise unlawful intervention. The appellant's actions could also not be tested against the requirement of proportionality. The appellant's justification for what he did also lacked the required degree of precision as there was no close nexus between his disclosure and the possible injury to members of the public. The Court concluded that there was no necessity or duress as those words are ordinarily understood.

See further, *Archbold Crown*, §§ 17–127—17–132.

(3) Self-defence/protection of private porperty

In *Beckford v The Queen* [1988] A.C. 130, Lord Griffiths stated: **8–87**

"The common law recognises that there are many circumstances in which one person may inflict violence upon another without committing a crime, as for instance, in sporting contests, surgical operations or in the most extreme example judicial execution. The common law has always recognised as one of these circumstances the right of a person to protect himself from attack and to act in the defence of others and if necessary to inflict violence on another in so doing. If no more force is used than is reasonable to repel the attack such force is not unlawful and no crime is committed. Furthermore a man about to be attacked does not have to wait for his assailant to strike the first blow or fire the first shot; circumstances may justify a pre-emptive strike." (at page 144)

He then referred to the speech of Lord Lane C.J. in *R. v Williams (Gladstone)*, (1984) 78 Cr.App.R. 276, which he stated a giving the correct definition of the English law of self-defence: Lord Lane said:

"In a case of self-defence, where self-defence or the prevention of crime is concerned, if the jury came to the conclusion that the defendant believed, or may have believed, that he was being attacked or that a crime was being committed, and that force was necessary to protect himself or to prevent the crime, then the prosecution have not proved their case. If however the defendant's alleged belief was mistaken and if the mistake was an unreasonable one, that may be a powerful reason for coming to the conclusion that the belief was not honestly held and should be rejected. Even if the jury come to the conclusion that the mistake was an unreasonable one, if the defendant may genuinely have been labouring under it, he is entitled to rely upon it." (at page 281)

8–88   An accused who misjudges the degree of force required and who uses force that is seen as excessive will be deprived of the defence: *Palmer v The Queen* [1971] A.C. 814. An accused who mistakenly believes that he is being attacked may still be able to rely on the defence of self-defence. In *R. v Williams* (1984) 78 Cr.App.R. 276, the Court held that the accused's mistake in believing that he was being attacked does not need to be a reasonable one. This subjective approach to mistake will not pertain where the defendant's mistake is due to his own voluntary intoxication: *R. v O'Grady* [1987] Q.B. 995, CA. *O'Grady* was followed in *O'Connor* [1991] Crim.L.R. 135.

Where the accused's mistake is that he believed there were no circumstances warranting the use of force in self defence when in fact there were, the defence of self defence will be unavailable: *Dadson* (1850) 2 Den CC 35.

In *R. v Clegg* [1995] 1 A.C. 482, it was held that that there was no distinction to be drawn between the use of excessive force in self-defence and the use of excessive force in the prevention of crime or in arresting an offender. In *Beckford*, above, Lord Griffiths also held that the test of self-defence involves looking at the use of force to defence the accused or another.

8–89   It is a principle of common law that a person may use such force to defend his property or the property of others from attack or the threat of imminent attack. The court should ask whether

(i) the use of force was reasonable to defend property from actual or imminent damage which constituted or could constitute an unlawful or criminal act.

(ii) on the facts as the defendant considered them to be, whether objectively the force used was no more than reasonable in all the circumstances, given the beliefs.

See *DPP v Bayer* [2003] EWHC 2567, (2004) 168 J.P.N. 15 (sowing of genetically modified maize not unlawful so defence of defence of property not available to those charged with aggravated trespass contrary to s.68 of the *Criminal Justice and Public Order Act* 1994.

See also *Criminal Law Act* 1967, s.3(1):

A person may use such force as is reasonable in the circumstances in the prevention of crime, or in effecting or assisting in the lawful arrest of offenders or suspected offenders or of persons unlawfully at large.

(4) Marital coercion

Criminal Justice Act 1925, s.47

Abolition of presumption of coercion of married woman by husband

8–90   **47.** Any presumption of law that an offence committed by a wife in the presence of her husband is committed under the coercion of the husband is hereby abolished, but on a charged against a wife for any offence other than treason or murder it shall be a good defence to prove that the offence was committed in the presence of, and under the coercion of, the husband.

Coercion was defined in *DPP for Northern Ireland v Lynch* [1975] A.C. 653 as an **8–91** external force which cannot be resisted and which impels its subject to act otherwise than he would wish, per Lord Simon.

In *R. v Shortland* [1996] 1 Cr.App.R. 116, CA it was held to establish the defence of marital coercion under s.47 of the *Criminal Justice Act* 1925 a jury had to be satisfied, on the balance of probabilities, that the will of the defendant wife was so overborne by the wishes of her husband that she had been forced to participate unwillingly. That defence did not necessarily require proof of physical force or the threat of physical force. To succeed, the woman has to prove, on the balance of probabilities that her will was so overborne by the wishes of her husband that she had been forced to participate in the unlawful conduct unwillingly.

CHAPTER 9

OFFENCES OF VIOLENCE

I. COMMON ASSAULT AND BATTERY

A. ASSAULT AND BATTERY

(a) Definition

An assault occurs when the defendant intentionally or recklessly causes another to ap- **9–1** prehend immediate unlawful violence: *R. v Burstow* [1998] A.C. 147, HL. Therefore it is the causing of another to apprehend violence, regardless of whether any violence is used, which defines an assault. A battery is committed when a person intentionally or recklessly applies unlawful force to the complainant. A single information which includes both assault and battery is bad for duplicity and where the allegation is that the defendant intentionally or recklessly applied unlawful force to the complainant then the information should allege "assault by beating": *R. v Norman* [1994] Crim.L.R. 518.

Criminal Justice Act 1988, s.39

Common assault and battery to be summary offences
39. Common assault and battery shall be summary offences and a person guilty of either of them shall be liable to a fine not exceeding level 5 on the standard scale, to imprisonment for a term not exceeding six months, or to both.

(b) Procedure

Common assault and battery are triable summarily. The *Crime and Disorder Act* **9–2** 1998 (see below) created an aggravated form of this offence, committed when an attack is motivated by racial or religious hostility, which is triable either way.

(c) Sentence

The maximum sentence for either offence is a fine not exceeding level 5 on the stan- **9–3** dard scale, imprisonment for a term not exceeding six months, or both. For sentencing provisions relating to the aggravated form of the offence, see s.8(4) below.

The *Magistrates' Court Sentencing Guidelines* (2004) state:

Aggravating factors include on hospital/medical premises, group action, offender in position of authority, premeditated, injury, weapon, victim particularly vulnerable, victim serving the public, offence committed on bail, relevant previous convictions and any failure to respond to previous sentences.

Mitigating factors include impulsive action, minor injury, provocation and single blow.

Guideline: Is it serious enough for a community penalty?

9–4   Racial or religious aggravation cannot be used as an aggravating factor by the sentencer when sentencing for the basic offence of common assault. Where there is evidence that the offence was racially or religiously motivated, the aggravated form of the offence should be charged. See § 9–15, below.

Violence between motorists will in the vast majority of cases lead to custodial sentences: *R. v Fenton* (1994) 15. Cr.App.R.(S.) 682. In the course of a dispute with another motorist, the offender pushed the other motorist in the chest. His sentence of fourteen days imprisonment was reduced to seven.

Where the racially aggravated form of the offence is tried summarily, it will often be committed for sentence. Where it is sentenced by the Magistrates, the approach in *R. v Greenwood* [2003] EWCA Crim 1937 is correct in that the sentence for the offence itself ought to be considered and then the additional penalty for the racial aggravation added.

For general defences to charges of assault and battery see *Archbold Crown* §§ 19–180—19–189.

B. ASSAULT OCCASIONING ACTUAL BODILY HARM

(a) *Definition*

9–5   There must be an assault or battery (see § 9–1, above) which causes some bodily harm. The harm caused may be a direct or indirect consequence of the assault or battery. The harm caused must be something which the defendant could reasonably have foreseen as the consequence of what he was saying or doing towards the complainant: *R. v Roberts*, 56 Cr.App.R. 95, CA.

Offences against the Person Act 1861, s.47

Assault occasioning bodily harm. Common assault

9–5.1   **47.** Whosoever shall be convicted upon an indictment of any assault occasioning actual bodily harm shall be liable ... to imprisonment for not more than five years.

As regards the racially or religiously aggravated form of this offence created by the *Crime and Disorder Act* 1998, s.29, see below s.8(4)(c).

(b) *Procedure*

9–6   The offence is triable either way: *Magistrates' Court Act* 1980, s.17 and Sch.1. The *Practice Direction (Mode of Trial: Guidelines)*(1995) state that cases should be tried summarily unless the court considers that one or more of the following features is present and its sentencing powers are insufficient.

The use of a weapon of a kind likely to cause serious injury
A weapon is used and serious injury is caused.
More than minor injury is caused by kicking, head butting or similar forms of assault.
Serious violence is caused to those whose work has to be done in contact with the public or who are likely to face violence in the course of their work.
Violence to vulnerable people, *i.e.* the elderly or infirm.

Due to the fact that the seriousness of this offence can differ depending on the circumstances, it is of particular importance that the Magistrates hear the facts before making a decision as to whether to accept jurisdiction.

(c) Sentence

When tried summarily, the maximum penalty for the offence is six months imprison- **9–7** ment, a fine not exceeding level five on the standard scale or both.

The *Magistrates' Court Sentencing Guidelines* (2004) state:

> Aggravating factors include deliberate kicking or biting, extensive injuries (may be psychiat- ric) head butting, group action, offender in position of authority, on hospital/medical premises, premeditated, victim particularly vulnerable, victim serving public, weapon, offence committed on bail, relevant previous convictions and any failures to respond to previous sen- tences, abuse of trust (domestic setting).
>
> Mitigating factors include minor injury, provocation and single blow.
>
> **Guideline**: Is it so serious that only custody is appropriate? Are Magistrates' sentencing pow- ers appropriate?

It is usual for racially aggravated forms of the offence to be committed to the Crown Court for sentence.

In *R. v Porter* [2002] EWCA Crim 2124, the offender became involved in a scuffle in **9–8** a public house, during which he threw a glass bottle at a barman's head, causing much blood loss and the need for three stitches. The appellant had drunk about twelve pints of beer prior to the incident. Sentencing him to eight months imprisonment, the judge emphasised the common nature of such offences, committed by men of otherwise good character, and the obligation of the courts to discourage such behaviour. See also *R. v Audit* (1994) 15 Cr.App.R.(S.) 36

A sentence of four months' imprisonment was appropriate for an offender who had fractured someone's nose in the course of an altercation in a taxi queue: *R. v Marples* (1998) 1 Cr.App.R.(S.) 335

Custodial sentences will almost always be appropriate where the assault on a police constable causes actual bodily harm: *R. v Roughsedge (Att.-Gen.'s Reference (No. 7 of 1993))* [1994] R.T.R. 322. Persons in positions of authority may also expect the protec- tion of the courts, hence violence towards public transport employees will be met by im- mediate prison sentences: *R. v Tremlett* (1983) 5 Cr.App.R.(S.) 199, as will violence towards traffic wardens: *R. v Charlton* (1995) 16 Cr.App.R.(S.) 703. A sentence of nine months imprisonment was imposed on an offender convicted of assaulting a schoolteacher: *R. v Byrne* [2000] 1 Cr.App.R.(S.) 282. Heavier sentences will also be passed when the victim of the assault is a hospital worker: *R. v Eastwood* [2002] 2 Cr.App.R.(S.) 72 (offender who assaulted a nurse sentenced to 15 months imprison- ment, Mitchell J. saying that 'if drunks assault staff in hospitals, leniency is the last thing they should expect.')

Equally, prisoners are entitled to the protection of the courts, and prison officers who assault inmates can expect heavy sentences. In *Fryer* [2002] EWCA Crim 825, three prison officers who brutally assaulted an inmate were sentenced to either three or four years' imprisonment. Newman J. described such conduct as going beyond a breach of trust in respect of the individual prisoner concerned, but being rather a breach of trust to society generally.

(d) Elements of the offence

The *mens rea* for the offence of ABH is the same as for common assault and battery. **9–9** To prove the offence contrary to s.47 the prosecution must prove that some hurt or injury calculated to interfere with the health or comfort of the victim was inflicted. The injury need not be permanent, but must be more than merely transient or trifling; *R. v Donovan* [1934] 2 K.B. 498. The actual bodily harm may consist of psychiatric injury but emotional distress or panic are insufficient. If the prosecution allege that the actual bodily harm was psychiatric injury then it should be proved by expert evidence: *R. v Chan-Fook*, 99 Cr.App.R. 147, CA.

C. Wounding or Inflicting Grievous Bodily Harm

(a) *Definition*

Offences against the Person Act 1861, s.20

Inflicting bodily injury, with or without weapon

9–10   **20.** Whosoever shall unlawfully and maliciously wound or inflict any grievous bodily harm upon any other person, either with or without any weapon or instrument, shall be guilty of an offence, and being convicted thereof shall be liable to imprisonment for not more than five years

As to the racially aggravated version of this offence created by the *Crime and Disorder Act* 1998, s.20, see s.4 below.

(b) *Procedure*

9–11   Both the basic and the religiously or racially aggravated form of the offence are triable either way. The *Practice Direction (Mode of Trial: Guidelines)* (1995) states the following as regards determining mode of trial for the basic form of the offence:

Cases should be tried summarily unless one or more of the following features is present in the case and the court considers its sentencing powers to be insufficient.

1. The use of weapon of a kind likely to cause serious injury
2. A weapon is used and serious injury is caused
3. More than minor injury is caused by kicking, head-butting or similar forms of assault
4. Serious violence is caused to those whose work has to be done in contact with the public or who are likely to face violence in the course of their work
5. Violence to vulnerable people.

(c) *Sentence*

9–12   When tried summarily, the maximum penalty for both offences is six months' imprisonment, a fine not exceeding level six on the standard scale or both: *Magistrates' Court Act* 1980, s.32(1) and *Crime and Disorder Act* 1998, s.29(2).

As regards the basic offence, when dealt with summarily, the *Magistrates' Court Sentencing Guidelines* (2004) state:

Aggravating factors include deliberate kicking/biting, extensive injuries, group action, offender in position of authority, on hospital/medical premises, premeditated, victim particularly vulnerable, victim serving public, weapon, offence committed on bail, relevant previous convictions and any failures to respond to previous sentences, abuse of trust (domestic setting).

Mitigating factors include single blow, minor wound and provocation.

Guideline: Is it so serious that only custody is appropriate? Are magistrates' sentencing powers appropriate?

9–13   In *R. v Rogers* (1993) 15 Cr.App.R.(S.) 393, the offender head-butted an opponent during a football match, causing a fracture. Given the defendant's good character and likely effect of a long custodial sentence, the CA reduced his original sentence of nine months imprisonment to four. See also *R. v Moss* [2000] 1 Cr.App.R.(S.) 307 for injuries inflicted in the course of a rugby match.

9–14   In *R. v Clare* [2002] 2 Cr.App.R.(S.) 97, Aikens J. issued guidelines on the correct sentencing approach when the attack involves a single blow leading to injury to the victim. The first relevant factor is the strength of the blow that has been imposed. The second relevant factor is the consequence to the victim. In *Clare*, the blow was described as obviously hard as the victim lost consciousness, with the consequence of two injuries and the need for at least one operation to treat the injuries. A sentence of eighteen months' imprisonment was imposed.

The use of a weapon is likely to necessitate a custodial sentence beyond the sentencing powers of the Magistrates. In *R. v Roberston* [1998] 1 Cr.App.R.(S.) 21, the offender attacked a man in a public house by thrusting a beer glass into his face. His sentence of two and a half years' imprisonment was reduced to two years on appeal. In *R. v Simpson* [1998] 1 Cr.App.R.(S.) 197 an unprovoked attack with a chisel resulted in four years' imprisonment.

(d) *Elements of the offence*

"Grievous bodily harm" has its ordinary and natural meaning of really serious bodily **9–14.1** harm. The harm need not be permanent; *R. v Ashman* [1858] 1 F. & F. 88. The prosecution must prove that the defendant intended to do the particular kind of harm that was done or had been reckless as to whether such harm should occur; the word "aliciously" adds no meaning over and above the requirement for recklessness: *R. v Mowatt* [1968] 1 Q.B. 421, CA. For harm to amount to a "wound" the continuity of the skin must be broken: *R. v Wood* 1 Mood. 278.

D. Racially or Religiously Aggravated Offences

(a) *Definition*

Crime and Disorder Act, 1998, s.29

Racially or religiously aggravated assaults

29.—(1) A person is guilty of an offence under this section if he commits—   **9–15**

    (a) an offence under section 20 of the *Offences Against the Person Act* 1861 (malicious wounding or grievous bodily harm);

    (b) an offence under section 47 of that Act (actual bodily harm); or

    (c) common assault, which is racially or religiously aggravated for the purposes of this section.

  (2) A person guilty of an offence falling within subsection (1)(a) or (b) above shall be liable

    (a) on summary conviction, to imprisonment for a term not exceeding six months or to a fine not exceeding the statutory maximum, or to both;

    (b) on conviction on indictment, to imprisonment for a term not exceeding seven years or to a fine, or to both.

  (3) A person guilty of an offence falling within subsection (1)(c) above shall be liable—

    (a) on summary conviction, to imprisonment for a term not exceeding six months or to a fine not exceeding the statutory maximum, or to both;

    (b) on conviction on indictment, to imprisonment for a term not exceeding two years or to a fine, or to both.

[The words 'or religiously' were inserted by the *Anti-Terrorism, Crime and Security Act* 2001, s.39(5) and (6)(a). This amendment has no effect in relation to anything done before it came into effect, December 14, 2001: s.42.]

(b) *Procedure*

Offences contrary to s.29 are triable either way.   **9–16**

(c) *Sentence*

When tried summarily, the maximum penalty for these offences is six months' **9–17** imprisonment, a fine not exceeding the statutory maximum or both: s.29(2), (3).

The *Magistrates' Court Sentencing Guidelines* (2004) provides a higher guideline for the racially aggravated form of assault, the guideline being 'is the offence so serious that only custody is justified?' For assault occasioning actually bodily harm, the guideline is the same as for the basic form of the offence, though the court is directed to treat the level of racial aggravation as relevant when determining the seriousness of the offence.

Guidance as to the correct sentencing approach was given in *R. v Saunders* [2000] 2 Cr.App.R.(S.) 71, where the Court of Appeal advised the sentencing court to first consider the appropriate sentence for the offence in the absence of racial aggravation, and then add a further term for the racial element, so the total term reflects the overall criminality. Even if the basic offence would not have crossed the custody threshold, the element of racial aggravation may well result in the custody threshold being passed. Relevant factors when determining sentence would be the nature of the hostile demonstration, whether by language, gestures or weapons, its length, whether isolated repeated or persistent, its location, whether public or private the number both of those demonstrating and those demonstrated against and the presence or absence of other features. A discount will be appropriate for, amongst other things, genuine remorse, a plea of guilty and previous good character.

9–18   In *R. v Kelly and Donnelly* [2001] 2 Cr.App.R.(S.) 73, factors seriously aggravating the racial element of the offence in terms of the offender's intention were identified as planning by the offender, the offence being part of a pattern of racist offending by the offender, membership of a group promoting racist activities and the deliberate setting up of the victim for the purpose of humiliating him or being offensive towards him.

Factors aggravating the offence in terms of its impact on the victim include the offence taking place at the victims home, the victim being particularly vulnerable or providing a service to the public, the timing and location of the offence being such as to maximise the harm or distress it caused, the expressions of racial hostility being repeated or prolonged, fear and distress being caused throughout a particular community and particular distress being caused to the victim or the victim's family.

In *R. v Beglin* [2003] 1 Cr.App.R.(S.) 21 the approach in *Saunders* and *Kelly and Donnelly* of demarcating the sentence appropriate for the basic form of the offence and then indicating the addition for the racially aggravated element was affirmed. In the case of a racially aggravated common assault, a sentence of four months' imprisonment was held to be sufficient for the basic form of the offence, hence a sentence of twelve months imprisonment in total was too long. A sentence of eight months imprisonment was substituted, with four months being the appropriate sentence for both the basic part of the offence and the addition for the racial element.

E. Assault with Intent to Resist or Prevent Arrest

(a) *Definition*

Offences against the Person Act 1861, s.38

Assault with intent to commit felony, or on peace officers &c.

9–19   **38.** Whosoever [...] shall assault any person with intent to resist or prevent the lawful apprehension or detainer of himself or of any other person for any offence, shall be guilty of a misdemeanour, and being convicted thereof shall be liable, at the discretion of the court, to be imprisoned for any term not exceeding two years, [...]

[This section is printed as amended by the *Police Act* 1964, Sch.10, Pt I, the *Criminal Law Act* 1967, Sch.3 Pt III and the *Criminal Justice Act* 1948, s.1(2).]

(b) *Procedure*

9–19.1   This offence is triable either way.

(c) *Sentence*

9–20   When tried summarily, the maximum penalty for this offence is six months' imprisonment, a fine not exceeding the statutory maximum, or both.

Sentencing considerations for this offence are largely similar to those for assault upon a police officer occasioning actual bodily harm, see s.2 above.

(d) Elements of the offence

The prosecution must prove: **9–20.1**
- an assault, see § 9–1 above;
- that the person assaulted had the right t apprehend or detain the defendant: see *Self* 95 Cr.App.R. 42;
- an intention to resist or prevent the lawful apprehension or detainer of the defendant or another person.

See *Archbold Crown* §§ 19–256—19–261.

F. ASSAULT ON CONSTABLE IN EXECUTION OF DUTY

(a) Definition

Police Act 1996, s.89(1), (3)–(6)

Assaults on constables

89.—(1) Any person who assaults a constable in the execution of his duty, or a person assist- **9–21** ing a constable in the execution of his duty, shall be guilty of an offence and liable on summary conviction to imprisonment for a term not exceeding six months or to a fine not exceeding level 5 on the standard scale, or to both.

(3) This section also applies to a constable who is a member of a police force maintained in Scotland or Northern Ireland when he is executing a warrant or otherwise acting in England or Wales, by virtue of any enactment conferring powers on him in England and Wales.

(4) In this section references to a person assisting a constable in the execution of his duty include references to any person who is neither a constable nor in the company of a constable but who—

(a) is a member of an international joint investigation team that is led by a member of a police force or by a member of the National Criminal Intelligence Service or of the National Crime Squad; and

(b) is carrying out his functions as a member of that team.

(5) In this section 'international joint investigation team' means any investigation team formed in accordance with—

(a) any framework decision on joint investigation teams adopted under Article 34 of the Treaty on European Union;

(b) the Convention on Mutual Assistance in Criminal Matters between the Member States of the European Union, and the Protocol to that Convention, established in accordance with that Article of that Treaty; or

(c) any international agreement to which the United Kingdom is a party and which is specified for the purposes of this section in an order made by the Secretary of State.

(6) A statutory instrument containing an order under subsection (5) shall be subject to annulment in pursuance of a resolution of either House of Parliament.

(b) Procedure

This offence is triable summarily: *Police Act* 1996, s.89(1). **9–21.1**

(c) Sentence

The maximum penalties for this offence are six months' imprisonment, a fine not **9–22** exceeding level five on the standard scale or both: *Police Act* 1996, s.89(1), (2).

The *Magistrates' Court Sentencing Guidelines* (2004) state:

Aggravating factors include any injuries caused, gross disregard for public authority, group action, premeditated, racial aggravation, religious aggravation, offence committed whilst on bail, relevant previous convictions and any failures to respond to previous sentences.

Mitigating factors include impulsive action and being unaware that the victim was a police officer.

Guideline: Is it so serious that only custody is appropriate?
Sentencing considerations for assault causing actual bodily harm when the victim is a police officer will also be relevant here: see s.2 above.

(d) *Elements of the offence*

9–22.1   The prosecution must prove:
- an assault, see § 9–1 above;
- of a constable;
- in the execution of his duty.

It is not necessary for the prosecution to prove that the defendant knew that the person assaulted was a police constable or in the execution of his duty, though a mistake of fact (a belief that the person was not a constable) may be a defence.
See *Archbold Crown* §§ 19–265—19–276.

G. RESISTING OR WILFULLY OBSTRUCTING CONSTABLE

(a) *Definition*

Police Act 1996, s.89(2)

Assaults on constables

9–23   **89.**—(2) Any person who resists or wilfully obstructs a constable in the execution of his duty, or a person assisting a constable in the execution of his duty, shall be guilty of an offence and liable on summary conviction to imprisonment for a term not exceeding one month or to a fine not exceeding level 3 on the standard scale, or to both.

(b) *Procedure*

9–23.1   This offence is triable summarily: *Police Act* 1996, s.89(2).

(c) *Sentence*

9–24   The maximum penalties are one months' imprisonment, a fine not exceeding level three on the standard scale, or both: *Police Act* 1996, s.89(2)
The *Magistrates' Court Sentencing Guidelines* (2004) state:

> Aggravating factors include racial aggravation, group action, premeditated, offence committed on bail, relevant previous convictions and any failures to respond to previous sentences, religious aggravation.
> Mitigating factors include genuine misjudgement, impulsive action and minor obstruction.
> **Guideline**: Is discharge or fine appropriate?

(d) *Elements of the offence*

9–25   Obstruction is defined as making it more difficult for a police officer to carry out his duty: *Hinchcliffe v Sheldon* [1955] 1 W.L.R. 1207.
Consequently, resisting an unlawful arrest will not amount to obstruction: *Edwards v DPP* (1993) 97 Cr.App.R 301. In *Redmond-Bate v DPP* (1999) 163 J.P. 789, the appellant was one of a group of women preachers who had been arrested on the steps of a cathedral by a constable fearing a breach of the peace following the reaction of some members of the crowd who had gathered to listen. As the actions of the police officer in arresting the appellant were not reasonable, there being no reason to suspect a breach of the peace, the Court of Appeal held that the constable was acting unlawfully when he attempted to arrest her, and she could not be said to be obstructing him in the execution of his duty when she resisted arrest.
In *Green v Moore* [1982] Q.B. 1044 it was held that it is an obstruction of a constable in the execution of his duty, to warn someone so that he may postpone the commission of a crime. Although the net result was the prevention of a crime, liability hinged on the

defendant's *mens rea* and the question of whether the defendant's intention was to assist the potential criminals or to assist the police.

If a constable is acting unlawfully then he is not acting in the course of his duty and the person who obstructs a constable not acting in accordance with his duty cannot be guilty of an offence: *Edwards v DPP* (1993) 97 Cr.App.R. 301.

The obstruction must also be wilful. Hence making the police officers task more dif- **9–26** ficult by genuinely trying to offer assistance will not found a charge under this section: *Wilmott v Atack* [1977] Q.B. 498

A solicitor who attempts to interview witnesses for the purpose of preparing the defence of his client in criminal proceedings and in so doing acts against the instruction of a police officer, is not thereby guilty of obstructing the officer: *Connolly v Dale* [1996] 1 Cr.App.R. 200.

II. OFFENCES INVOLVING CHILDREN

A. Abandonment of Children under Two

(a) *Definition*

Offences Against the Person Act 1861, s.27

Exposing children whereby life is endangered
    27. Whosoever shall unlawfully abandon or expose any child, being under the age of two **9–27** years, whereby the life of such child shall be endangered, or the health of such child shall have been or shall be likely to be permanently injured, shall be guilty of a misdemeanor, and being convicted thereof shall be liable to imprisonment for a term not exceeding five years.

(b) *Procedure*

This offence is triable either way.	**9–27.1**

(c) *Sentence*

When tried summarily, the maximum penalty is six months imprisonment, a fine not **9–27.2** exceeding the statutory maximum or both.

(d) *Elements of the offence*

The prosecution must prove that:	**9–27.3**
    – the defendant wilfully abandoned or exposed the child;
    – that the child was then under two;
    – that its life was thereby endangered or its health was likely to be permanently injured.
See *Archbold Crown*, § 19–290.

B. Child Cruelty

(a) *Definition*

Children and Young Persons Act 1933, s.1

Cruelty to persons under sixteen
    1.—(1) If any person who has attained the age of sixteen years and has has responsibility for **9–28** any child or young person under that age, wilfully assaults, ill-treated, neglects, abandons, or exposes him, or causes or procures him to be assaulted, ill-treated, neglected, abandoned, or exposed, in a manner likely to cause him unnecessary suffering or injury to health (including injury to or loss of sight, or hearing, or limb, or organ of the body, and any mental derangement), that person shall be guilty of a misdemeanour, and shall be liable—

(a) on conviction on indictment, to a fine or alternatively, or in addition thereto, to imprisonment for any term not exceeding ten years;

(b) on summary conviction, to a fine not exceeding £400 pounds, or alternatively,, or in addition thereto, to imprisonment for any term not exceeding six months.

(2) For the purposes of this section—

(a) a parent or other person legally liable to maintain a child or young person, or the legal guardian of a child or young person, shall be deemed to have neglected him in a manner likely to cause injury to his health if he has failed to provide adequate food, clothing, medical aid or lodging for him, or if, having been unable otherwise to provide such food, clothing, medical aid or lodging, he has failed to take steps to procure it to be provided under the enactments applicable in that behalf;

(b) where it is proved that the death of an infant under three years of age was caused by suffocation (not being suffocation caused by disease or the presence of any foreign body in the throat or air passages of the infant) while the infant was in bed with some other person who has attained the age of sixteen years, that other person shall, if he was, when he went to bed, under the influence of drink, be deemed to have neglected the infant in a manner likely to cause injury to its health.

9–29 (3) A person may be convicted of an offence under this section—

(a) notwithstanding that actual suffering or injury to health, or the likelihood of actual suffering or injury to health, was obviated by the action of another person;

(b) notwithstanding the death of the child or young person in question.

(7) Nothing in this section shall be construed as affecting the right of any parent, or (subject to section 548 of the *Education Act* 1996) any other person, having the lawful control or charge of a child or young person to administer punishment to him.

(b) *Procedure*

9–30 This offence is triable either way, when tried summarily, the *Children and Young Persons Act* 1933, s.14 has effect.

It is usual, unless one of the following factors is present, to try this offence summarily:

— neglect over a long period of time, even where the injury may not be substantial;
— injuries that exhibit a sadistic nature;
— where substantial injury is caused.

Children and Young Persons Act 1933, s.14

Mode of charging offences and limitation of time
9–30.1 **14.**—(1) Where a person is charged with committing any of the offences mentioned in the First Schedule to this Act in respect of two or more children or young persons, the same information or summons may charge the offence in respect of all or any of them, but the person charged shall not, if he is summarily convicted, be liable to a separate penalty in respect of each child or young person except upon separate information.

(2) The same information or summons may charge him with the offences of assault, ill-treatment, neglect, abandonment, or exposure, together or separately, and may charge him with committing all or any of those offences in a manner likely to cause unnecessary suffering or injury to health, alternatively or together, but when those offences are charged together the person charged shall not, if he is summarily convicted, be liable to a separate penalty for each.

(4) When any offence mentioned in the First Schedule to this Act charged against any person is a continuous offence, it shall not be necessary to specify in the information, summons, or indictment, the date of the acts constituting the offence.

(c) *Sentence*

9–31 When tried summarily, the maximum penalty is six months imprisonment, a fine not exceeding the statutory maximum or both.

In the case of *R. v Weaver* [1998] 2 Cr.App.R.(S.) 56, a sentence of six years' imprisonment for neglect of a child by its mother which resulted in the death of the child was reduced to three years' imprisonment, and a sentence of three years imprisonment for neglect of a child causing death by its father was reduced to two years' imprisonment. The mother pleaded guilty on the basis that she had failed to ensure that the child was adequately nourished, that she had failed to get medical attention when the child required it, that she had failed to keep the flat where they lived sufficiently clean, and that she had assaulted the child by slapping his thigh. The father pleaded guilty on the basis that he had failed to notice the child's declining condition and to ensure that something was done about it.

In *R. v Harvey* [1987] 9 Cr.App.R.(S.) 524 a mother was convicted of four counts of cruelty to her children. The offender was frequently drunk and smoking cannabis; the family's living accommodation was not kept clean, pornographic material was left about, and the children were told about the appellant's sexual activities; the children were not kept clean and in some cases were denied affection. In one case the appellant failed to arrange medical attention when it was necessary. A sentence of nine months' imprisonment was upheld.

9–32 The act of failing to seek medical assistance can amount to neglect for the purposes of a charge under this section. In *R. v S* [1999] 1 Cr.App.R.(S.) 67, the offence was made out by the failure to seek medical help, and a sentence of four months imprisonment was imposed. In *R. v Laut* [2002] 2 Cr.App.R.(S.) 7, the offender's child fell whilst holding the door of the washing machine closed on his mother's instructions. The offender had been warned on a previous occasion that such conduct was likely to result in injury to the child. The Court stated that its normal practice was not to impose a custodial sentence for a single, albeit wilful act of neglect. However, given the prior warning, the offender's conduct could be classed as a case of serious neglect and hence a sentence of imprisonment was justified. Her original sentence of four months' imprisonment was however reduced to 12 weeks.

(d) *Elements of the offence*

9–32.1 The prosecution must prove that:
  – the defendant is 16 or over;
  – he had responsibility for the child (under16);
  – he acts wilfully: see *Shepherd* [1981] A.C. 394;
  – he assaults, ill-treats, neglects, etc. in a manner likely to cause unnecessary or injury to health.

See *Archbold Crown* §§ 19–297—19–307.

C. Child Abduction

(a) *Definition*

Child Abduction Act 1984, ss.1, 2

Offence of abduction of child by parent, etc.

9–33 **1.**—(1) Subject to subsections (5) and (8) below, a person connected with a child under the age of sixteen commits an offence if he takes or sends the child out of the United Kingdom without the appropriate consent.

  (2) A person is connected with a child for the purposes of this section if—
    (a) he is a parent of the child; or
    (b) in the case of a child whose parents were not married to each other at the time of his birth, there are reasonable grounds for believing that he is the father of the child; or
    (c) he is a guardian of the child; or
    (d) he is a person in whose favour a residence order is in force with respect to the child; or
    (e) he has custody of the child.

(3) In this section 'the appropriate consent', in relation to a child, means—

    (a) the consent of each of the following—

        (i) the child's mother;

        (ii) the child's father, if he has parental responsibility for him;

        (iii) any guardian of the child;

        (iv) any person in whose favour a residence order is in force with respect to the child;

        (v) any person who has custody of the child; or

    (b) the leave of the court granted under or by virtue of any provision of Part II of the *Children Act* 1989; or

    (c) if any person has custody of the child, the leave of the court which awarded custody to him.

(4) A person does not commit an offence under this section by taking or sending a child out of the United Kingdom without obtaining the appropriate consent if—

    (a) he is a person in whose favour there is a residence order in force with respect to the child, and

    (b) he takes or sends him out of the United Kingdom for a period of less than one month.

9–34   (4A) Subsection (4) above does not apply if the person taking or sending the child out of the United Kingdom does so in breach of an order under Part II of the *Children Act* 1989.

(5) A person does not commit an offence under this section by doing anything without the consent of another person whose consent is required under the foregoing provisions if—

    (a) he does it in the belief that the other person—

        (i) has consented; or

        (ii) would consent if he was aware of all the relevant circumstances; or

    (b) he has taken all reasonable steps to communicate with the other person but has been unable to communicate with him; or

    (c) the other person has unreasonably refused to consent,

(5A) Subsection (5)(c) above does not apply if—

    (a) the person who refused to consent is a person—

        (i) in whose favour there is a residence order in force with respect to the child; or

        (ii) who has custody of the child; or

    (b) the person taking or sending the child out of the United Kingdom is, by so acting, in breach of an order made by a court in the United Kingdom.

(6) Where, in proceedings for an offence under this section, there is sufficient evidence to raise an issue as to the application of subsection (5) above, it shall be for the prosecution to prove that that subsection does not apply.

(7) For the purposes of this section—

    (a) 'guardian of a child', 'residence order' and 'parental responsibility' have the same meaning as in the *Children Act* 1989; and

    (b) a person shall be treated as having custody of a child if there is in force an order of a court in the United Kingdom awarding him (whether solely or jointly with another person) custody, legal custody or care and control of the child.

(8) This section shall have effect subject to the provisions of the Schedule to this Act in relation to a child who is in the care of a local authority detained in a place of safety, remanded to a local authority accommodation or the subject of proceedings or an order relating to adoption.

Offence of abduction of child by other persons

9–35   **2.**—(1) Subject to subsection (3) below, a person, other than one mentioned in subsection (2) below. commits an offence if, without lawful authority or reasonable excuse, he takes or detains a child under the age of sixteen—

    (a) so as to remove him from the lawful control of any person having lawful control of the child; or

    (b) so as to keep him out of the lawful control of any person entitled to lawful control of the child.

[(2) The persons are—
  (a) where the father and mother of the child in question were married to each other at the time of his birth, the child's father and mother;
  (b) where the father and mother of the child in question were not married to each other at the time of his birth, the child's mother; and
  (c) any other person mentioned in section 1(2)(c) to (e) above.

(3) In proceedings against any person for an offence under this section, it shall be a defence for that person to prove—
  (a) where the father and mother of the child in question were not married to each other at the time of his birth—
      (i) that he is the child's father; or
      (ii) that, at the time of the alleged offence, he believed, on reasonable grounds, that he was the child's father; or
  (b) that, at the time of the alleged offence, he believed that the child had attained the age of sixteen.

(b) *Procedure*

The offence under s.1 is triable either way. The consent of the DPP is required before **9–36** a prosecution under s.1 of the Act can be brought: *Child Abduction Act* 1984, s.(4)(1)

The offence under s.2 is also triable either way, though there is no need to obtain the DPP's consent before a prosecution can proceed.

(c) *Sentence*

When tried summarily, the maximum penalty is six months' imprisonment, a fine **9–36.1** not exceeding level five on the standard scale or both.

(d) *Elements of the offence*

The prosecution must prove that: **9–36.2**
  – the defendant caused the child to accompany him;
  – the child was thus removed from the control of his lawful guardian;
  – that the child is under 16;
  – the defendant intended to keep the child.

See *Archbold Crown* § 19–314 and §§ 19–317—19–331.

III. HARASSMENT OFFENCES

A. PUTTING PEOPLE IN FEAR OF VIOLENCE

(a) *Definition*

Protection from Harassment Act 1997, s.4

Putting people in fear of violence

4.—(1) A person whose course of conduct causes another to fear, on at least two occasions, **9–37** that violence will be used against him is guilty of an offence if he knows or ought to know that his course of conduct will cause the other so to fear on each of those occasions.

(2) For the purposes of this section, the person whose course of conduct is in question ought to know that it will cause another to fear that violence will be used against him on any occasion if a reasonable person in possession of the same information would think the course of conduct would cause the other so to fear on that occasion.

(3) It is a defence for a person charged with an offence under this section to show that—
  (a) his course of conduct was pursued for the purpose of preventing or detecting crime,
  (b) his course of conduct was pursued under any enactment or rule of law or to

comply with any condition or requirement imposed by any person under any enactment, or

(c) the pursuit of his course of conduct was reasonable for the protection of himself or another or for the protection of his or another's property.

(4) A person guilty of an offence under this section is liable—

(a) on conviction on indictment, to imprisonment for a term not exceeding five years, or a fine, or both, or

(b) on summary conviction, to imprisonment for a term not exceeding six months, or a fine not exceeding the statutory maximum, or both.

(5) If on the trial on indictment of a person charged with an offence under this section the jury find him not guilty of the offence charged, they may find him guilty of an offence under section 2

(6) The Crown Court has the same powers and duties in relation to a person who is by virtue of subsection (5) convicted before it of an offence under section 2 as a magistrates' court would have on convicting him of the offence.

Crime and Disorder Act 1998, s.32

Racially or religiously aggravated harassment etc.

9–38   **32.**—(1) A person is guilty of an offence under this section if he commits—

(a) an offence under section 2 of the *Protection from Harassment Act* 1997 (offence of harassment); or

(b) an offence under section 4 of that Act (putting people in fear of violence), which is racially or religiously aggravated for the purposes of this section.

(3) A person guilty of an offence falling within subsection (1)(a) above shall be liable—

(a) on summary conviction, to imprisonment for a term not exceeding six months or to a fine not exceeding the statutory maximum, or to both;

(b) on conviction on indictment, to imprisonment for a term not exceeding two years or to a fine, or to both.

(4) A person guilty of an offence falling within subsection (1)(b) above shall be liable—

(a) on summary conviction, to imprisonment for a term not exceeding six months or to a fine not exceeding the statutory maximum, or to both;

(b) on conviction on indictment, to imprisonment for a term not exceeding seven years or to a fine, or to both.

(b) *Procedure*

9–39   Both forms of the offence are triable either way: *Protection from Harassment Act* 1997, s.4(4) and *Crime and Disorder Act* 1998, s.32(4).

In general, summary trial is appropriate except where one or more of the following factors is present:

— racial motivation

— a course of conduct over a long period of time

— where the victim was particularly vulnerable

(c) *Sentence*

9–40   As regards the basic offence, when tried summarily, the maximum penalty is six months imprisonment, a fine not exceeding the statutory maximum or both. The court may also impose a restriction order upon an offender convicted of an offence under s.4: *Protection from Harassment Act* 1997, s.5.

The *Magistrates' Court Sentencing Guidelines* (2004) state:

Aggravating factors include disregard of warning, excessive persistence, interference with employment/business, invasion of victims home, involvement of others, threat to use weapons or substance (including realistic imitations), use of violence or grossly offensive material, where photographs or images of a personal nature are involved, offence committed on bail, relevant previous convictions and any failures to respond to previous sentences.

Mitigating factors include initial provocation and short duration.

Guideline: Is it so series that only custody is appropriate?

As regards the racially or religiously aggravated form of the offence, when tried sum- **9–41**
marily, the maximum penalty is six months' imprisonment, a fine not exceeding the
statutory maximum or both. The *Magistrates Courts' Sentencing Guidelines* provide
the same guideline as for the basic form of the offence.

Where the offender has previously breached a court order or has been convicted for
the same offence previously, it is usual for the Magistrates to commit for sentence: *R. v
Liddle* [2000] 1 Cr.App.R.(S.) 131.

A restraining order may be granted in respect of a conviction under this section
subject to the usual requirements for an order of this type. Breach of a restraining order
without reasonable excuse is an offence punishable by imprisonment: s.5.

(d) *Elements of the Offence*

The prosecution must prove: **9–41.1**

– a course of conduct which causes another to fear, on at least two occasions,
  violence against him;
– that the defendant knew or ought to have known that his course of conduct
  would have caused fear or each occasion.

See *Archbold Crown* §§ 19–277b—19–277k.

B. Harassment

(a) *Definition*

Protection from Harassment Act 1997, ss.1, 2

Prohibition of harassment

1.—(1) A person must not pursue a course of conduct— **9–42**
 (a) which amounts to harassment of another, and
 (b) which he knows or ought to know amounts to harassment of the other.

(2) For the purposes of this section, the person whose course of conduct is in question
ought to know that it amounts to harassment of another if a reasonable person in possession of the same information would think the course of conduct amounted to harassment
of the other.

(3) Subsection (1) does not apply to a course of conduct if the person who pursued it
shows—
 (a) that it was pursued for the purpose of preventing or detecting crime,
 (b) that it was pursued under any enactment or rule of law or to comply with any
   condition or requirement imposed by any person under any enactment, or
 (c) that in the particular circumstances the pursuit of the course of conduct was
   reasonable.

Offence of harassment

2.—(1) A person who pursues a course of conduct in breach of section 1 is guilty of an **9–43**
offence.

(2) A person guilty of an offence under this section is liable on summary conviction to
imprisonment for a term not exceeding six months, or a fine not exceeding level 5 on the
standard scale, or both.

For the racially or religiously aggravated from of this offence see *Crime and Disorder
Act* 1998, s.32 (s.9 above).

(b) *Procedure*

The basic form of the offence is triable summarily only: s.2(2). The racially or **9–44**
religiously aggravated form of the offence is triable either way.

(c) *Sentence*

As regards the basic offence, the maximum penalty is six months' imprisonment, a **9–45** fine not exceeding level five on the standard scale or both: s.2(2). The court also has power to issue a restriction order pursuant to s.5 of the 1997 Act. The *Magistrates' Court Sentencing Guidelines* (2000) provide that the same considerations apply as for an offence under s.4 of the 1997 Act, though the guidelines differs, being to consider whether the offence is serious enough for a community penalty.

As regard the racially or religiously aggravated form of the offence, when tried summarily, the maximum penalty is six months' imprisonment, a fine not exceeding the statutory maximum, or both: *Crime and Disorder Act* 1998, s.32(3). The court may also make a restraining order: s.32(7).

(d) *Elements of the offence*

Protection from Harassment Act 1997, s.7

Interpretation of this group of sections

9–46   **7.**—(1) This section applies for the interpretation of sections 1 to 5

(2) References to harassing a person include alarming the person or causing the person distress.

(3) A "course of conduct" must involve conduct on at least two occasions.

(3A) A person's conduct on any occasion shall be taken, if aided, abetted, counselled or procured by another—

  (a) to be conduct on that occasion of the other (as well as conduct of the person whose conduct it is); and

  (b) to be conduct in relation to which the other's knowledge and purpose, and what he ought to have known, are the same as they were in relation to what was contemplated or reasonably foreseeable at the time of the aiding, abetting, counselling or procuring.

(4) "Conduct" includes speech.

9–47   Proof of two incidents can establish the offence, yet the fewer the occasions and the wider they are spread the less likely they are to result in a finding of harassment: *Lau v DPP* (2000) 1 F.L.R. 799. The stalking type of behaviour at which this Act was intended was 'miles away' from a prosecution based on two incidents six months apart between two people who were partners and lived together: *R. v Hills* [2001] 1 F.L.R. 580, CA.

Three threatening and abusive telephone calls made consecutively can amount to a course of conduct, even though the victim listened to all three messages together, and was hence only distressed on one occasion: *Kelly v DPP* (2002) 166 J.P. 621.

When addressing the question of lawful conduct as a defence to charges under s.2 of the 1997 Act, it has been established that conduct in contravention of an injunction designed to prevent it cannot be reasonable: *DPP v Selvanayagam, The Times*, June 23, 1999, DC.

I. SEXUAL OFFENCES

Introduction–the old and new law

The *Sexual Offences Act* 2003 substantially reformed the law relating to sexual **10–1** offences. It came into force on May 1, 2004 and created many new offences. The new offences are dealt with in §§ 10–42 *et seq*. Whilst the 2003 Act did not repeal all earlier legislation in this area, most of the old legislation was either repealed or amended. As the old offences may still be the subject of proceedings in the courts, they are dealt with in this chapter but readers are urged to bear in mind that many 'old' offences were repealed on May 1, 2004 and therefore can only be used to prosecute offences committed before that date.

A. Offences under the Sexual Offences Act 1956

(1) Sexual intercourse with a girl under sixteen

(a) *Definition*

Sexual Offences Act 1956, s.6

Intercourse with girl between thirteen and sixteen

6.—(1) It is an offence, subject to the exceptions mentioned in this section, for a man to have **10–2** unlawful sexual intercourse with a girl under the age of sixteen.

(2) Where a marriage is invalid under section two of the *Marriage Act* 1949, or section one of the *Age of Marriage Act* 1929 (the wife being a girl under the age of sixteen), the invalidity does not make the husband guilty of an offence under this section because he has sexual intercourse with her, if he believes her to be his wife and has reasonable cause for the belief.

(3) A main is not guilty of an offence under this section because he has unlawful sexual intercourse with a girl under the age of sixteen, if he is under the age of twenty-four and has not previously been charged with a like offence, and he believes her to be of the age of sixteen or over and has reasonable cause for the belief.

In this subsection, "a like offence" means an offence under this section or an attempt to commit one, or an offence under paragraph (1) of section five of the *Criminal Law Amendment Act* 1885 (the provision replaced for England and Wales by this Section).

[This section is printed as amended by the *CLA* 1967, s.10(1) and Sch.2, para.14. It was repealed by the *Sexual Offences Act* 2003, Sch.7, para.1 on May 1, 2004.]

(b) *Procedure*

This offence is triable either way. The *Practice Note (Mode of Trial: Guidelines)* **10–3**

(1995) provides that cases of unlawful sexual intercourse should be tried summarily unless the court considers that one or more of the following features are present and that its sentencing powers are insufficient:

    (a) Wide disparity of age
    (b) Breach of position of trust
    (c) The victim is particularly vulnerable.

(c) *Sentence*

10–4   When tried summarily, the maximum penalty for this offence is six months' imprisonment, a fine not exceeding the statutory maximum or both: *Sexual Offences Act* 1956, s.37 and Sch.2; *Magistrates' Courts Act* 1980, s.32.

In *R. v Taylor*, 64 Cr.App.R 182, CA the Court laid down guidelines for sentencing people convicted of this offence. Lawton L.J. referred to the wide spectrum of guilt covered by the offence known as having unlawful sexual intercourse with a girl under the age of sixteen. He distinguished cases of 'virtuous friendship' between two people of a similar age and the case where the man in a supervisory capacity sets out deliberately to seduce a girl under the age of 16 who is in his charge. In the first type of case it would be inappropriate to pass sentences of a punitive nature. As regards the second a sentence near the maximum allowed by law would be appropriate. In between there are many degrees of guilt. Lawton L.J. gave the example of a common type of offender being the youth who picks up a girl of loose morals at a dance, takes her out into the local park and, behind the bushes, has sexual intercourse with her. That is the kind of offence that would normally be dealt with by a fine.

In *Att.-Gen.'s Reference (No.80 of 2000)* [2001] 2 Cr.App.R.(S.) 12, the Attorney General sought leave to refer a sentence of 100 hours' community service imposed for one offence of indecent assault and four offences of unlawful sexual intercourse on account of it being unduly lenient. The victim was 13 years old when they began a consensual sexual relationship. The sentence was held to be too lenient and a period of imprisonment of at least 12 months' should have been imposed.

In *R. v Reeves* [2002] 1 Cr.App.R.(S.) 15 the Court of Appeal held that a sentence of two years' imprisonment imposed for indecently assaulting a 15-year old girl should be reduced to 18 months to provide the offender with a discount for his plea of guilty.

A case at the bottom end of the scale was *R. v Cooke* (1979) 1 Cr.App.R.(S.) 325. The offender pleaded guilty to one act of unlawful sexual intercourse with a girl aged 14 years and 10 months who was sexually experienced and looked older than her true age. A sentence of six months imprisonment was substituted for the original sentence of nine months' imprisonment. In *R. v Wood* (1990) 12 Cr.App.R.(S.) 129, the offender admitted unlawful sexual intercourse with the 15 year old daughter of the woman he had been living with for a number of years. He was sentenced to nine months' imprisonment. In *R. v Wong* [2001] All E.R. (D.) 162 (May) the offender pleaded guilty on the basis that the girl instigated the offence and he admitted being reckless as to whether the girl was 15 or 16. He was sentenced to three months imprisonment.

See also *R. v O'Grady* (1978) 66 Cr.App.R.(S.) 279 and *R. v Harding* (1979) 1 Cr.App.R.(S.) 160

(2) Gross Indecency

(a) *Definition*

Sexual Offences Act 1956, s.13

Indecency between men

10–5   **13.** It is an offence for a man to commit an act of gross indecency with another man otherwise than in the circumstances described below, whether in public or private, or to be a party to the commission by a man of an act of gross indecency with another man, or to procedure the commission by a man of an act of gross indecency with another man.

The circumstances referred to above are that the man is under the age of sixteen and the other man has attained that age.

[This section is printed as amended by the *Sexual Offences (Amendment) Act* 2000, s.2(2)(a) and (b) and is repealed by the *Sexual Offences Act* 2003, Sch.7, para.1 on May 1, 2004.]

Gross Indecency is no longer an offence when committed in private by two consenting persons over the age of sixteen: *Sexual Offences Act* 1967, ss.1 and 4(3).

(b) *Procedure*

This offence is triable either way. Proceedings may not be instituted after the expira- **10–6** tion of 12 months since the commission of the offence: *Sexual Offences Act* 1967, s.7. Where either man was under 16 years of age at the time of the offence, proceedings may not be instituted without the consent of the DPP: *SOA* 1967, s.8

(c) *Sentence*

When tried summarily, the maximum penalty for this offence is six months imprison- **10–7** ment, a fine not exceeding the statutory maximum or both: *SOA* 1956, Sch.2

The guideline judgment for this offence is *R. v Morgan and Dockerty* (CSP B4–92001) where Lawton L.J. stated that in general, first time offenders using public lavatories and behaving in this sort of way in them do not get sent to prison. They are generally fined. The offenders' sentences of three months' and six weeks' imprisonment were varied to fines of £100 and £50 respectively.

In *R. v Clayton* (1981) 3 Cr.App.R.(S.) 67 the offenders were sentenced to four months' imprisonment, recommended in one case for deportation. These sentences were replaced with fines of £50 on appeal, Eastham J. describing the original sentences as excessive, and stating that the appropriate penalty for men of hitherto good character should be a financial penalty.

(d) *Elements of the offence*

There is no need for physical contact between the men, but both must participate. **10–7.1** See *Archbold Crown*, §§ 20–138—20–143.

(3) Permitting girls to use premises for unlawful sexual intercourse

(a) *Definition*

Sexual Offences Act 1956, s.26

Permitting girl between thirteen and sixteen to use premises for intercourse
26. It is an offence for a person who is the owner or occupier of any premises, or who has, or **10–8** acts or assists in, the management or control of any premises, to induce or knowingly suffer a girl under the age of sixteen, to resort to or be on those premises for the purposes of having unlawful sexual intercourse with men or with a particular man.

[Repealed by the *Sexual Offences Act* 2003, Sch.7, para.1 on May 1, 2004.]

(b) *Procedure*

This offence is triable either way. **10–8.1**

(c) *Sentence*

When tried summarily, the maximum penalty for this offence is six months imprison- **10–8.2** ment, a fine not exceeding the statutory maximum or both: *SOA* 1956, s.37 and Sch.2 and *MCA* 1980, s.32.

(d) *Elements of the offence*

10–8.3   See *Archbold Crown*, §§ 20–220—20–222.

(4) Indecent Assault

(a) *Definition*

Sexual Offences Act 1956, ss.14, 15

Indecent assault on a woman

10–9   **14.**—(1) It is an offence, subject to the exception mentioned in subsection (3) of this section, for a person to make an indecent assault on a woman.

(2) A girl under the age of sixteen cannot in law give any consent which would prevent an act being an assault for the purposes of this section.

(3) Where a marriage is invalid under section two of the *Marriage Act* 1949, or section one of the *Age of Marriage Act* 1929 (the wife being a girl under the age of sixteen), the invalidity does not make the husband guilty of any offence under this section by reason of her incapacity to consent while under that age, if he believes her to be his wife and has reasonable cause for the belief.

(4) A woman who is a defective cannot in law give any consent which would prevent an act being an assault for the purposes of this section, but a person is only to be treated as guilty of an indecent assault on a defective by reasons of that incapacity to consent, if that person knew or had reason to suspect her to be a defective.

Indecent assault on a man

10–10   **15.**—(1) It is an offence for a person to make an indecent assault on a man.

(2) A boy under the age of sixteen cannot in law give any consent which would Prevent an act being an assault for the purposes of this section.

(3) A man who is a defective cannot in law give any consent which would prevent an act being an assault for the purposes of this section, but a persons is only to be treated as guilty of an indecent assault on a defective by reason of that incapacity to consent, if that person knew or had reason to suspect him to be a defective

[Sections 14 and 15 were repealed by the *Sexual Offences Act* 2003, Sch.7, para.1 on May 1, 2004.]

(b) *Procedure*

10–11   This offence is triable either way. The *Practice Note (Mode of Trial: Guidelines)* (1995) state that indecent assault should be tried summarily unless the court considers that one or more of the following features is present and that its sentencing powers are insufficient:

     (a) Substantial disparity in age between victim and defendant, and the assault is more than trivial

     (b) Violence or threats of violence

     (c) Relationship of trust and responsibility between defendant and victim

     (d) Several similar offences and the assault more than trivial

     (e) The victim is particularly vulnerable

     (f) Serious nature of the assault.

Cases that have been held suitable for summary disposal include *R. v Tanyildiz* [1998] 1 Cr.App.R.(S.) 362 and *R. v Yazbek* [1998] 1 Cr.App.R.(S.) 406 (both concerning indecent assaults on underground trains).

(c) *Sentence*

10–12   When tried summarily, an offence under ss.14 or 15 carries a maximum penalty of six months' imprisonment, a fine not exceeding the statutory maximum or both: *SOA* 1956, s.37 and Sch.2.

The Magistrates' Association advises that if the victim is a young girl the case ought to go to the Crown Court if the indecency is serious. Any suggestion of attempted penetration or use of force also indicates that the matter should be sent to the Crown Court for sentence. If there is any suggestion that the defendant is not of full adult capacity, it may be appropriate for sentence at summary level. Where the victim is an adolescent girl who 'consents', consideration should be given to sending the matter to the Crown Court for sentence where there are features such as digital interference or oral sex: *R. v Pickup* (1992) 14 Cr.App.R.(S.) 271, CA.

In *R. v Tanyildz* (1998) 1 Cr.App.R.(S.) 362, the offender assaulted a woman on an underground train by pushing his erect penis against her on three occasions. He was sentenced to three months' imprisonment. See also *R. v Townsend* (1994) 16 Cr.App.R.(S.) 553, CA, three months' imprisonment where offender indecently assaulted female passenger on underground train.

The fact that the assault constitutes a breach of trust may result in a higher penalty. **10–13** In *Att.-Gen.'s Reference (No.25 of 1997) (Williams)* [1998] 1 Cr.App.R.(S.) 310, CA, the offender was a shop keeper who indecently assaulted a 15 year-old girl working at his shop on a work placement. His sentence of fines totalling £500 was varied to eight months' imprisonment by the Court of Appeal, the Court stating that this was a campaign of sexual harassment towards a girl in relation to whom he was in a position of trust. In *R. v Owen* [2001] All E.R.(D) 96 (Aug) the offender pleaded guilty to indecently assaulting three girls aged 12 or 14 who stayed overnight with his daughter at parties at which he supplied alcohol. He was sentenced to four months' imprisonment in respect of each offence, to be served consecutively; the Court emphasising that the offences were sordid, and involved some deliberation as the offender had engineered the parties and excessive drinking. He had also acted in breach of trust.

(d) *Elements of the offence*

For a full analysis of the offences of indecent assault, see *Court* [1989] A.C. 28, HL **10–13.1** (which will not apply to offences under the *SOA* 2003).

See also *Archbold Crown*, §§ 20–148—20–155 for s.14 and §§ 20–169—20–167 for s.15.

(5) **Living on the earnings of prostitution**

(a) *Definition*

Sexual Offences Act 1956, s.30

Man living on earnings of prostitution
   30.—(1) It is an offence for a man knowingly to live wholly or in part on the earnings of **10–14** prostitution.
   (2) For the purposes of this section a man who lives with or is habitually in the company of a prostitute, or who exercises control, direction or influence over a prostitute's movements in a way which shows he is aiding, abetting or compelling her prostitution with others, shall be presumed to be knowingly living on the earnings of prostitutions, unless he proves the contrary.

[Repealed by the *Sexual Offences Act* 2003, Sch.7, para.1 on May 1, 2004.]

(b) *Procedure*

This offence is triable either way: *SOA* 1956, s.37(2). **10–14.1**

(c) *Sentence*

When tried summarily, the maximum penalty for this offence is six months' imprison- **10–15** ment, a fine not exceeding the statutory maximum or both: *SOA* 1956, s.37 and Sch.2.

Sentencing guidance is given in *R. v Farrugia* (1979) 69 Cr.App.R 108, Lawton L.J. seeing the presence or absence of coercion as a crucial factor in the sentencing decision. In the absence of any evidence of coercion, whether physical or mental, or of corruption, the old maximum of two years' imprisonment was described as adequate. Anything exceeding two years should be reserved for a case where there is an element of coercion or there is some strong evidence of corruption. Where the offender is running a business of encouraging prostitution, and the circumstances are such that he can be said to be living wholly or in part on the earnings of prostitution, the Court should keep in mind the desirability of taking the profit out of such a way of life.

In *R. v Powell* [2001] 1 Cr.App.R.(S.) 76 the offender's sentence of five years' imprisonment following his conviction for living on the earnings of prostitution was upheld. The victim had been ordered to work as a prostitute by the offender and she agreed because she was scared of him. It was held that five years' imprisonment was not inappropriate where coercion and corruption was evidenced.

Where the prostitute is carrying on her own business without coercion or corruption by the offender a more lenient approach will be taken: *R. v Charlery* (1988) 10 Cr.App.R.(S.) 53, a sentence of four months' imprisonment plus fine of £1500 imposed.

(d) *Elements of the offence*

10–16   The presumptions raised in s.30(2) are raised on proof that
- the accused was living with the prostitute;
- he was habitually at the material time in her company;
- he exercised control, direction or influence over her movements in a way which showed him to be aiding or abetting her prostitution.

It is then presumed that he is living on immoral earnings and that he is doing so knowingly. See *Archbold Crown*, §§ 20–232—20–238.

(6) Woman exercising control over prostitute

(a) *Definition*

Sexual Offences Act 1956, s.31

Woman exercising control over prostitute

10–17   **31.** It is an offence for a woman for purposes of gain to exercise control, direction or influence over a prostitute's movements in a way which shows she is aiding, abetting or compelling her prostitution.

[Repealed by the *Sexual Offences Act* 2003, Sch.7, para.1 on May 1, 2004.]

(b) *Procedure*

10–17.1   This offence is triable either way: *SOA* 1956, s.37(2) and Sch.2, para.1

(c) *Sentence*

10–17.2   When tried summarily, the maximum penalty for this offence is six months' imprisonment, a fine not exceeding the statutory maximum or both: *SOA* 1956, s.37 and Sch.2

(7) Solicitation for immoral purposes

(a) *Definition*

Sexual Offences Act 1956, s.32

Solicitation by men

10–18   **32.** It is an offence for a man persistently to solicit or importune in a public place for immoral purposes.

[Repealed by the *Sexual Offences Act* 2003, Sch.7, para.1 on May 1, 2004.]

(b) *Procedure*

This offence is triable either way.   **10–18.1**

(c) *Sentence*

When tried summarily, the maximum penalty for this offence is six months' imprison- **10–18.2**
ment, a fine not exceeding the statutory maximum or both: *SOA* 1956, s.37(3) and
Sch.2, para.32 and *MCA* 1980, ss.32 34(3)(a).

(d) *Elements of the offence*

Two separate acts of importuning in the period constitute 'persistently'. An immoral **10–18.3**
purpose has to be some kind of sexual activity. See *Archbold Crown*, §§ 20–245—20–
250.

(8) **Keeping a Brothel**

(a) *Definition*

Those offences contained in ss.33–36 of the 1956 Act were not repealed by the 2003   **10–19**
Act. Section 36 was amended so as to make no distinction between male and female
prostitution.

Sexual Offences Act 1956, ss.33–36

Keeping a brothel
33. It is an offence for a person to keep a brothel, or to manage, or act or assist in the   **10–20**
management of, a brothel.

Keeping a brothel used for prostitution
33A.—(1) It is an offence for a person to keep, or to manage, or act or assist in the management of, a brothel to which people resort for practices involving prostitution (whether or not
also for other practices).
(2) In this section "prostitution" has the meaning given by section 51(2) of the *Sexual
Offences Act* 2003.

Landlord letting premises for use as brothel
34. It is an offence for the lessor or landlord of any premises or his agent to let the whole or
part of the premises with the knowledge that it is to be used, in whole or in part, as a brothel, or,
where the whole or part of the premises is used as a brothel, to be wilfully a party to that use
continuing.

Tenant permitting premises to be used as brothel
35.—(1) It is an offence for the tenant or occupier, or person in charge, of any premises
knowingly to permit the whole or part of the premises to be used as a brothel.
(2) Where the tenant or occupier of any premises is convicted (whether under this section or, for an offence committed before the commencement of this Act, under section
thirteen of the *Criminal Law Amendment Act* 1885) of knowingly permitting the whole or
part of the premises to be used as a brothel, the First Schedule to this Act shall apply to enlarge
the rights of the lessor or landlord with respect to the assignment or determination of the lease
or other contract under which the premises are held by the person convicted.
(3) Where the tenant or occupier of any premises is so convicted, or was so convicted
under the said section thirteen before the commencement of this Act, and either—
(a) the lessor or landlord, after having the conviction brought to his notice, fails or
failed to exercise his statutory rights in relation to the lease or contract under
which the premises are or were held by the person convicted; or

(b) The lessor or landlord, after exercising his statutory rights so as to determine that lease or contract, grants or granted a new lease or enters or entered into a new contract of tenancy of the premises to, with or for the benefit of the same person, without having all reasonable provisions to prevent the recurrence of the offence inserted in the new lease or contract;

then, if subsequently an offence under this section is committed in respect of the premises during the subsistence of the lease or contract referred to in paragraph (a) of this subsection or (where paragraph (b) applies) during the subsistence of the new lease or contract, the lessor or landlord shall be deemed to be a party to that offence unless he shows that he took all reasonable steps to prevent the recurrence of the offence.

References in this subsection to the statutory rights of a lessor or landlord refer to his rights under the First Schedule to this Act or under subsection (1) of section five of the *Criminal Law Amendment Act* 1912 (the provision replaced for England and Wales by that Schedule).

Tenant permitting premises to be used for prostitution

36. It is an offence for the tenant or occupier of any premises knowingly to permit the whole or part of the premises to be used for the purposes of habitual prostitution (whether any prostitute involved is male or female).

[These sections are printed as amended by *Sexual Offences Act* 2003. Section 33A was added by the *SOA* 2003, s.55.]

(b) *Procedure*

10–20.1   These offences are triable summarily only: *SOA* 1956, s.37 and Sch.2.

(c) *Sentence*

10–20.2   For each section, the first commission of the offence carries a maximum penalty of three months imprisonment, a fine not exceeding level three on the standard scale or both. For each section, for every offence committed after the first offence, the maximum penalty is six months' imprisonment, a fine not exceeding level four on the standard scale or both: *SOA* 1956, s.37 and Sch.2.

(d) *Elements of the offence*

10–20.3   A brothel is a place where people of opposite sexes are allowed to resort for sexual intercourse, whether the women are common prostitutes or not: *Winter v Woolfe* [1931] 1 K.B. 549. A place which is used by one woman for the purposes of her own prostitution is not a brothel: *Stevens v Christy* (1987) 85 Cr.App.R. 249.

It is not necessary to prove that normal sexual intercourse was offered on the premises to succeed in classifying a premises as a brothel, it will suffice to prove that more than one woman offered herself as a participant in physical acts of indecency for the gratification of men: *Kelly v Purvis* [1983] Q.B. 663.

It is not necessary that a person charged with assisting the management of a brothel exercises control over the management of the brothel. That would be acting in the management of a brothel. The question of assisting in the management of a brothel is a question of fact: *Jones v DPP* (1992) 96 Cr.App.R. 130.

See *Archbold Crown*, §§ 20–286—20–290 for the related offence of keeping a disorderly house.

B. OFFENCES RELATING TO SOLICITING

10–21   See s.7 above for the offence of soliciting for immoral purposes under *Sexual Offences Act* 1956, s.32.

(1) Solicitation of a woman for the purposes of prostitution

(a) *Definition*

Sexual Offences Act 1985, ss.1, 2

Kerb-crawling

1.—(1) A man commits an offence if he solicits a woman (or different women) for the purpose **10–22** of prostitution—

    (a) from a motor vehicle while it is in a street or public place; or

    (b) in a street or public place while in the immediate vicinity of a motor vehicle that he has just got out of or off,

persistently or, in such manner or in such circumstances as to be likely to cause annoyance to the woman (or any of the women) solicited, or nuisance to other persons in the neighbourhood.

(2) A person guilty of an offence under this section shall be liable on summary conviction to a fine not exceeding level 3 on the standard scale

(3) In this section "motor vehicle" has the meaning as in the *Road Traffic Act* 1972.

Persistent soliciting of women for the purpose of prostitution

2.—(1) A man commits an offence if in a street or public place he persistently solicits a woman **10–23** (or different women) for the purpose of prostitution.

(2) A person guilty of an offence under this section shall be liable on summary conviction to a fine not exceeding level 3 on the standard scale.

[Sections 1 and 2 were repealed by the *Sexual Offences Act* 2003, Sch.7, para.1 on May 1, 2004.]

(b) *Procedure*

These offences are triable summarily: s.1(2) and 2(2). **10–23.1**

(c) *Sentence*

Both offences carry a maximum penalty of a fine not exceeding level three on the **10–23.2** standard scale: s.1(2) and 2(2).

(d) *Elements of the offence*

Sexual Offences Act 1985, s.4

Interpretation

4.—(1) References in this Act to a man soliciting a woman for the purpose of prostitution are **10–24** references to his soliciting her for the purpose of obtaining her services as a prostitute.

(2) The use in any provision of this Act of the word "man" without the addition of the word "boy" shall not prevent the provision applying to any person to whom it would have applied if both words had been used, and similarly with the words "woman" and "girl".

(3) Paragraphs (a) and (b) of section 6 of the *Interpretation Act* 1978 (words importing the masculine gender to include the feminine, and vice versa) do not apply to this Act.

(4) For the purposes of this Act "street" includes any bridge, road, lane, footway, subway, square, court, alley or passage, whether a thoroughfare or not, which is for the time being open to the public; and the doorways and entrances of premises abutting on a street (as hereinbefore defined), and any ground adjoining and open to a street, shall be treated as forming part of the street.

(2) Loitering or soliciting for the purpose of prostitution

(a) *Definition*

This offence was not repealed by the 2003 Act but amended so as to make no distinc- **10–25** tion between male and female prostitutes.

Street Offences Act 1959, s.1

Loitering or soliciting for purposes of prostitution

1.—(1) It shall be an offence for a common prostitute whether male or female to loiter or solicit in a street or public place for the purpose of prostitution.

(2) A person guilty of an offence under this section shall be liable on summary conviction to a fine of an amount not exceeding level 2 on the standard scale, or, for an offence committed after a previous conviction, to a fine of an amount not exceeding level 3 on that scale.

(3) A constable may arrest without warrant anyone he finds in a street or public place and suspects, with reasonable cause, to be committing an offence under this section.

(4) For the purposes of this section "street" includes any bridge, road, lane, footway, subway, square, court, alley or passage, whether a thoroughfare or not, which is for the time being open to the public; and the doorways and entrances of premises abutting on a street (as hereinbefore defined), and any ground adjoining and open to a street, shall be treated as forming part of the street.

[This section is printed as amended by the *Sexual Offences Act* 2003, Sch.1, para.2.]

(b) *Procedure*

10–25.1   This offence is triable summarily: *Street Offences Act* 1959, s.1(2).

(c) *Sentence*

10–26   The first offence under this section carries a maximum penalty of a fine not exceeding level two on the standard scale. Each offence thereafter carries a maximum penalty of a fine not exceeding level three on the standard scale: *Street Offences Act* 1959, s.1(2).

(d) *Elements of the offence*

10–26.1   Section 1(1) of the *Street Offences Act* 1959 is confined to women hence solicitation consists of any conduct by a woman that invites or importunes another to engage in an act of prostitution: *DPP v Bull* [1995] Q.B. 88.

The woman does not have to be present in the public place to which she is projecting her solicitous efforts, yet she must be physically present to solicit. An advertisement displaying her services will not suffice: *Weisz v Monahan* [1962] 1 W.L.R. 262.

'Public place' is not defined in s.1 and is a question of fact for the magistrates.

C. Offences Relating to Children

(1) Indecency with children

(a) *Definition*

Indecency with Children Act 1960, s.1

Indecent conduct towards young child

10–27   **1.**—(1) Any person who commits an act of gross indecency with or towards a child under the age of sixteen or who incites a child under that age to such an act with him or another, shall be liable on conviction on indictment to imprisonment for a term not exceeding ten years, or on summary conviction to imprisonment for a term not exceeding six months, to a fine not exceeding the prescribed sum, or to both.

(2) *[...]*

(3) References in the *Children and Young Persons Act* 1933 to the offences mentioned in the First Schedule to that Act shall include offences under this section.

(4) Offences under this section shall be deemed to be offences against the person for the purpose of section three of the *Visiting Forces Act* 1952 (which restricts the trial by United

Kingdom courts of offenders connected with visiting forces).

[Subsection (1) is printed as amended by the *C(S)A* 1997, s.52 (substitutuion of 'ten' for 'two') and the *CJCSA* 2000, s.39 (substitution of 'sixteen' for 'fourteen'). The first of these amendments took effect on October 1, 1997, but does not apply to offences committed before that date: *Crime (Sentences) Act (Commencement No.2 and Transitional Provisions) Order* 1997 (SI 1997/2200). The second amendment took effect on January 11, 2001: *Criminal Justice and Court Services Act* 2000 (Commencement No.1) Order 2000 (SI 2000/3302). Subsection (2) was repealed by the *Police and Criminal Evidence Act* 1984, Sch.7. This section is repealed by the *Sexual Offences Act* 2003, Sch.7, para.1 on May 1, 2004.]

(b) *Procedure*

This offence is triable either way: s.1(1).　　　　　　　　　　　　　**10–27.1**

(c) *Sentence*

When tried summarily, the maximum penalty for this offence is imprisonment for a **10–27.2** term not exceeding six months, a fine not exceeding £400 or both: s.1(1).

(d) *Elements of the offence*

There must be an act, but allowing a child to continue an activity may constitute an **10–27.3** act. See *Archbold Crown*, § 20–277.

D. Miscellaneous Offences

(1) Outraging public decency: indecent exposure

(a) *Definition*

The *Sexual Offences Act* 2003 did not repeal the offences arising under the *Vagrancy* **10–28** and *Town Police Clauses* Acts. The 2003 Act made minor amendments which are reflected below.

Vagrancy Act 1824, s.4

Persons committing certain offences to be deemed rogues and vagabonds
　　4. Every person committing any of the offences herein-before mentioned, after having been **10–29** convicted as an idle and disorderly person; every person wandering abroad and lodging in any barn or outhouse, or in any deserted or unoccupied building, or in the open air, or under a tent, or in any cart or wagon, and not giving a good account of himself or herself; every person wilfully openly, lewdly, and obscenely exposing his person with intent to insult any female; every person wandering abroad, and endeavouring by the exposure of wounds or deformities to obtain or gather alms; every person going about as a gatherer or collector of alms, or endeavouring to procure charitable contributions of any nature or kind, under any false or fraudulent pretence; every person being found in or upon any dwelling house, warehouse, coach-house, stable, or outhouse, or in any inclosed yard, garden, or area, for any unlawful purpose; every suspected person or reputed thief, frequenting any river, canal, or navigable stream, dock, or basin, or any quay, wharf, or warehouse near or adjoining thereto, or any street, highway, or avenue leading thereto, or any place of public resort, or any avenue leading thereto, or any street, with intent to commit an arrestable offence; and every person apprehended as an idle and disorderly person, and violently resisting any constable, or other peace officer so apprehending him or her, and being subsequently convicted of the offence for which he or she shall have been so apprehended; shall be deemed a rogue and vagabond, within the true intent and meaning of this Act; and, subject to section 70 of the *Criminal Justice Act* 1982, it shall be lawful for any justice of the peace to commit such offender (being thereof convicted before him by the confession of such offender, or by the evidence on oath of one or more credible witness or witnesses,) to the house of correction, for any time not exceeding three calendar months.

Town Police Clauses Act 1847, s.28

Penalty on persons committing any of the offences herein named

10–29.1   **28.** Every person who in any street, to the obstruction, annoyance, or danger of the residents or passengers, commits any of the following offences, shall be liable to a penalty not exceeding level 3 on the standard scale for each offence, or, in the discretion of the justice before whom he is convicted, may be committed to prison, there to remain for a period not exceeding fourteen days, and any officer appointed by virtue of this or the special Act or any constable shall take into custody, without warrant, and forthwith convey before a justice, any person who within his view commits any such offence; (that is to say,)

.... Every person who wilfully and indecently exposes his person.

(b) *Procedure*

10–29.2   Both offences are triable summarily.

(c) *Sentence*

10–30   The maximum penalty for the offence under the *Vagrancy Act* 1824 is three months imprisonment, a fine not exceeding level three on the standard scale or both. On a second conviction and committal to the Crown Court, the maximum penalty is imprisonment for 12 months.

The maximum penalty for an offence under the *Town Police Clauses Act* 1847 is imprisonment for a period not exceeding fourteen days, a fine not exceeding level three on the standard scale.

(2) Abuse of a position of trust

(a) *Definition*

Sexual Offences (Amendment) Act 2000, s.3

Abuse of position of trust

10–31   **3.**—(1) Subject to subsections (2) and (3) below, it shall be an offence for a person aged 18 or over—

> (a) to have sexual intercourse (whether vaginal or anal) with a person under that age; or
>
> (b) to engage in any other sexual activity with or directed towards such a person,

if (in either case) he is in a position of trust in relation to that person.

(2) Where a person ("A") is charged with an offence under this section of having sexual intercourse with, or engaging in any other sexual activity with or directed towards, another person ("B"), it shall be a defence for A to prove that, at the time of the intercourse or activity—

> (a) he did not know, and could not reasonably have been expected to know, that B was under 18;
>
> (b) he did not know, and could not reasonably have been expected to know, that B was a person in relation to whom he was in a position of trust; or
>
> (c) he was lawfully married to B.

(3) It shall not be an offence under this section for a person ("A") to have sexual intercourse with, or engage in any other sexual activity with or directed towards, another person ("B") if immediately before the commencement of this Act—

> (a) A was in a position of trust in relation to B; and
>
> (b) a sexual relationship existed between them.

(4) A person guilty of an offence under this section shall be liable—

> (a) on summary conviction, to imprisonment for a term not exceeding six months, or to a fine not exceeding the statutory maximum, or to both;
>
> (b) on conviction on indictment, to imprisonment for a term not exceeding five years, or to a fine, or to both.

[Repealed by the *Sexual Offences Act* 2003, Sch.7 on May 1, 2004.]

(b) *Procedure*

This offence is triable either way: s.3(4).   **10–31.1**

(c) *Sentence*

When tried summarily, the maximum penalty for this offence is six months' imprison- **10–31.2**
ment, a fine not exceeding the statutory maximum or both: s.3(4).

(d) *Elements of the offence*

Sexual Offences (Amendment) Act 2000, ss.3(5), 4

3.—(5) In this section, "sexual activity"—   **10–32**
- (a) does not include any activity which a reasonable person would regard as sexual only with knowledge of the intentions, motives or feelings of the parties; but
- (b) subject to that, means any activity which such a person would regard as sexual in all the circumstances.

Meaning of "position of trust"

4.—(1) For the purposes of section 3 above, a person aged 18 or over ("A") is in a position of **10–32.1**
trust in relation to a person under that age ("B") if any of the four conditions set out below, or
any condition specified in an order made by the Secretary of State by statutory instrument, is
fulfilled.

(2) The first condition is that A looks after persons under 18 who are detained in an
institution by virtue of an order of a court or under an enactment, and B is so detained in
that institution.

(3) The second condition is that A looks after persons under 18 who are resident in a
home or other place in which—
- (a) accommodation and maintenance are provided by an authority under section 23(2) of the *Children Act* 1989 or Article 27(2) of the *Children (Northern Ireland) Order* 1995;
- (b) accommodation is provided by a voluntary organisation under section 59(1) of that Act or Article 75(1) of that *Order*; or
- (c) accommodation is provided by an authority under section 26(1) of the *Children (Scotland) Act* 1995,

and B is resident, and is so provided with accommodation and maintenance or accommodation,
in that place.

(4) The third condition is that A looks after persons under 18 who are accommodated
and cared for in an institution which is—
- (a) a hospital;
- (b) a residential care home, nursing home, mental nursing home or private hospital;
- (c) a community home, voluntary home, children's home or residential establishment; or
- (d) a home provided under section 82(5) of the *Children Act* 1989,

and B is accommodated and cared for in that institution.

(5) The fourth condition is that A looks after persons under 18 who are receiving full-
time education at an educational institution, and B is receiving such education at that
institution.

(6) No order shall be made under subsection (1) above unless a draft of the order has
been laid before and approved by a resolution of each House of Parliament.

(7) A person looks after persons under 18 for the purposes of this section if he is
regularly involved in caring for, training, supervising or being in sole charge of such
persons.

(8) For the purposes of this section a person receives full-time education at an
educational institution if—
- (a) he is registered or otherwise enrolled as a full-time pupil or student at the institution; or
- (b) he receives education at the institution under arrangements with another educational institution at which he is so registered or otherwise enrolled.

10–33

(9) In this section, except where the context otherwise requires—

"authority" means

(a) in relation to Great Britain, a local authority; and

(b) in relation to Northern Ireland, an authority within the meaning given by Article 2(2) of the *Children (Northern Ireland) Order* 1995;

"children's home" has—

(a) in relation to England and Wales, the meaning which would be given by subsection (3) of section 63 of the *Children Act* 1989 if the reference in paragraph (a) of that subsection to more than three children were a reference to one or more children; and

(b) in relation to Northern Ireland, the meaning which would be given by Article 90(1) of the *Children (Northern Ireland) Order* 1995 if, in Article 91(2) of that *Order*, paragraphs (f) and (g) and the words after paragraph (h) were omitted;

"community home" has the meaning given by section 53(1) of the *Children Act* 1989;

"hospital" has—

(a) in relation to England and Wales, the meaning given by section 128(1) of the *National Health Service Act* 1977;

(b) in relation to Scotland, the meaning given by section 108(1) of the *National Health Service (Scotland) Act* 1978; and

(c) in relation to Northern Ireland, the meaning given by Article 2(2) of the *Health and Personal Social Services (Northern Ireland) Order* 1972;

"mental nursing home" has, in relation to England and Wales, the meaning given by section 22(1) of the *Registered Homes Act* 1984;

"nursing home" —

(a) in relation to England and Wales, has the meaning given by section 21(1) of the *Registered Homes Act* 1984;

(b) in relation to Scotland, means a nursing home registered under section 1 of the *Nursing Homes Registration (Scotland) Act* 1938; and

(c) in relation to Northern Ireland, has the meaning given by Article 16(1) of the *Registered Homes (Northern Ireland) Order* 1992;

"private hospital" has—

(a) in relation to Scotland, the meaning given by section 12(2) of the *Mental Health (Scotland) Act* 1984; and

(b) in relation to Northern Ireland, the meaning given by Article 90(2) of the *Mental Health (Northern Ireland) Order* 1986;

"residential care home" —

(a) in relation to England and Wales, has the meaning given by section 1(2) of the *Registered Homes Act* 1984;

(b) in relation to Scotland, means an establishment in respect of which a person is registered under section 62 or 63 of the *Social Work (Scotland) Act* 1968; and

(c) in relation to Northern Ireland, has the meaning given by Article 3(1) of the *Registered Homes (Northern Ireland) Order* 1992;

"residential establishment" has the meaning given by section 93(1) of the *Children (Scotland) Act* 1995 as the meaning of that expression in relation to a place in Scotland;

"voluntary home" has—

(a) in relation to England and Wales, the meaning given by section 60(3) of the *Children Act* 1989; and

(b) in relation to Northern Ireland, the meaning given by Article 74(1) of the *Children (Northern Ireland) Order* 1995.

(3) Indecent Photographs of Children

(a) *Definition*

10–34   The 1978 legislation was not repealed but was amended by the 2003 Act.

Protection of Children Act 1978, ss.1–1B

Indecent photographs of children

1.—(1) [Subject to sections 1A and 1B] it is an offence for a person—

(a) to take, or permit to be taken or to make, any indecent photograph or pseudo-photograph of a child; or
(b) to distribute or show such indecent photographs or pseudo-photographs; or
(c) to have in his possession such indecent photographs or pseudo- photographs, with a view to their being distributed or shown by himself or others; or
(d) to publish or cause to be published any advertisement likely to be understood as conveying that the advertiser distributes or shows such indecent photographs or pseudo-photographs, or intends to do so.

(2) For purposes of this Act, a person is to be regarded as distributing an indecent photograph or pseudo-photographs if he parts with possession of it to, or exposes or offers it for acquisition by, another person.

(3) Proceedings for an offence under this Act shall not be instituted except by or with the consent of the Director of Public Prosecutions.

(4) Where a person is charged with an offence under subsection (1)(b) or (c), it shall be a defence for him to prove—
(a) that he had a legitimate reason for distributing or showing the photographs or pseudo-photographs or (as the case may be) having them in his possession; or
(b) that he had not himself seen the photographs or pseudo-photographs and did not know, nor had any cause to suspect, them to be indecent.

(5) References in the *Children and Young Persons Act* 1933 (except in sections 15 and 99) to the offences mentioned in Schedule 1 to that Act shall include an offence under subsection (1)(a) above.

Marriage and other relationships

1A.—(1) This section applies where, in proceedings for an offence under section 1(1)(a) of **10–34.1** taking or making an indecent photograph of a child, or for an offence under section 1(1)(b) or (c) relating to an indecent photograph of a child, the defendant proves that the photograph was of the child aged 16 or over, and that at the time of the offence charged the child and he—
(a) were married, or
(b) lived together as partners in an enduring family relationship.

(2) Subsections (5) and (6) also apply where, in proceedings for an offence under section 1(1)(b) or (c) relating to an indecent photograph of a child, the defendant proves that the photograph was of the child aged 16 or over, and that at the time when he obtained it the child and he–
(a) were married, or
(b) lived together as partners in an enduring family relationship.

(3) This section applies whether the photograph showed the child alone or with the defendant, but not if it showed any other person.

(4) In the case of an offence under section 1(1)(a), if sufficient evidence is adduced to raise an issue as to whether the child consented to the photograph being taken or made, or as to whether the defendant reasonably believed that the child so consented, the defendant is not guilty of the offence unless it is proved that the child did not so consent and that the defendant did not reasonably believe that the child so consented.

(5) In the case of an offence under section 1(1)(b), the defendant is not guilty of the offence unless it is proved that the showing or distributing was to a person other than the child.

(6) In the case of an offence under section 1(1)(c), if sufficient evidence is adduced to raise an issue both–
(a) as to whether the child consented to the photograph being in the defendant's possession, or as to whether the defendant reasonably believed that the child so consented, and
(b) as to whether the defendant had the photograph in his possession with a view to its being distributed or shown to anyone other than the child,
the defendant is not guilty of the offence unless it is proved either that the child did not so consent and that the defendant did not reasonably believe that the child so consented, or that the defendant had the photograph in his possession with a view to its being distributed or shown to a person other than the child.

Exception for criminal proceedings, investigations etc.

1B.—(1) In proceedings for an offence under section 1(1)(a) of making an indecent **10–34.2**

photograph or pseudo-photograph of a child, the defendant is not guilty of the offence if he proves that—

    (a) it was necessary for him to make the photograph or pseudo-photograph for the purposes of the prevention, detection or investigation of crime, or for the purposes of criminal proceedings, in any part of the world,

    (b) at the time of the offence charged he was a member of the Security Service, and it was necessary for him to make the photograph or pseudo-photograph for the exercise of any of the functions of the Service, or

    (c) at the time of the offence charged he was a member of GCHQ, and it was necessary for him to make the photograph or pseudo-photograph for the exercise of any of the functions of GCHQ.

(2) In this section "GCHQ" has the same meaning as in the *Intelligence Services Act* 1994.

[Section 1 is printed as amended and repealed in part by the *CJPOA* 1994, ss.84(2) and 168(3) and Sch.11.]

(b) *Procedure*

10–34.3   This offence is triable either way: *Protection of Children Act* 1978, s.6(1)

(c) *Sentence*

10–35   When tried summarily, the maximum penalty for this offence is imprisonment for a term not exceeding six months, a fine not exceeding the prescribed sum or both: *Protection of Children Act* 1978, s.6(3)

In *R. v Toomer* [2001] 2 Cr.App.R.(S.) 8, the Court of Appeal issued guidance on sentencing under this section, Kennedy L.J. stating that:

> "First, sentences up to statutory maximum should be imposed where there is a contested case, and there is evidence of commercial or large scale exploitation, and the amount of material is significant, especially if the offender has previous convictions.
> Secondly, non-custodial disposals should normally be reserved for isolated offences where the amount of material is very small, and it is for personal use, or use within a very restricted circle, as for example by passing it to one other recipient, when there is no commercial element and the defendant has pleaded guilty and is a first offender. Thirdly, Where between those two extremes a particular case falls, will depend on the circumstances, and in particular on, first of all, the quality and nature of the material and the quantity thereof, and whether there is any element of exploitation or commercial gain.
> Thirdly, whether the offence is simply one of making; that is to say, in most cases downloading and saving or also involves distribution and, if so, to what extent there has been distribution, whether it has been by e-mail to a single specified recipient, or whether the distribution has been significantly more widespread.
> Fourthly, the character of the defendant is an important factor, and also the effect of the conviction upon the individual.
> Finally, it is of great importance to consider whether there has been a plea of guilty coupled with co-operation from the outset in the investigation."

10–36   In *R. v Jefferson (Peter John)* [2001] EWCA Crim 1278, the offender, 56, was a man of good character who admitted downloading indecent images of children. The images were for his own use and he said he did not know such action was a crime. His appeal against a sentence of three months' imprisonment was allowed, the Court stating that a fine would have been the appropriate penalty, however, as he had served four weeks of his prison sentence he was conditionally discharged. Aggravating factors will include the degree of obscenity involved in the image, the age and number of children involved, whether the children were of one or both sexes and the nature of the conduct to which they were subjected or in which they are depicted as taking part: *R. v Allison* [2001] EWCA Crim 1971 (six months imprisonment where offender pleaded guilty to distributing indecent photographs or pseudo indecent photographs of children).

(d) *Elements of the offence*

10–37   Opening an email attachment of an indecent photograph may constitute 'making'

the photograph or pseudo-photograph: *R. v Smith; R. v Jayson* [2003] 1 Cr.App.R.
13. In deciding whether the photograph is indecent, the test is the recognised standard
of propriety. See *Archbold Crown*, § 31–108.

The magistrates also have power to order searches of premises and powers of forfeiture:

Protection of Children Act 1978, ss.4 and 5

Entry, search and seizure

4.—(1) The following applies where a justice of the peace is satisfied by information on oath, **10–38**
laid by or on behalf of the Director of Public Prosecutions or by a constable, that there is reasonable ground for suspecting that, in any premises in the petty sessions area for which he acts, there are indecent photographs of children and that such photographs—

    (a) are or have been taken there; or

    (b) are or have been shown there, or are kept there with a view to their being
        distributed or shown is an indecent photograph or pseudo-photograph of a child

(2) The justice may issue a warrant under his hand authorising any constable to enter
(if need be by force) and search the premises, and to seize and remove any articles which
he believes (with reasonable cause) to be or include indecent photographs or pseudo-photographs of children .

(3) Articles seized under the authority of the warrant, and not returned to the occupier
of the premises, shall be brought before a justice of the peace acting for the same petty sessions area as the justice who issued the warrant.

(4) This section and section 5 below apply in relation to any stall or vehicle, as they apply in relation to premises, with the necessary modifications of references to premises and
the substitution of references to use for references to occupation.

Forfeiture

5.—(1) The justice before whom any articles are brought in pursuance of section 4 above may **10–39**
issue a summons to the occupier of the premises to appear on a day specified in the summons
before a magistrates' court for that petty sessions area to show cause why they should not be
forfeited.

(2) If the court is satisfied that the articles are in fact indecent photographs or pseudo-photographs of children, the court shall order them to be forfeited; but if the person summoned does not appear, the court shall not make an order unless service of the summons
is proved.

(3) In addition to the persons summoned, any other person being the owner of the
articles brought before the court, or the persons who made them, or any other person
through whose hands they had passed before being seized, shall be entitled to appear
before the court on the day specified in the summons to show cause why they should not
be forfeited.

(4) Where any of the articles are ordered to be forfeited under subsection (2), any
person who appears, or was entitled to appear, to show cause against the making of the order may appeal to the Crown Court.

(5) If as respects any articles brought before it the court does not order forfeiture, the
court may if it thinks fit order the person on whose information the warrant for their
seizure was issued to pay such costs as the court thinks reasonable to any person who
has appeared before it to show cause why the photographs or pseudo-photographs should not
be forfeited; and costs ordered to be paid under this subsection shall be recoverable as a
civil debt.

(6) Where indecent photographs or pseudo-photographs of children are seized under
section 4 above, and a person is convicted under section 1(1) or section 160 of the *Criminal
Justice Act* 1988 of offences in respect of those photographs or pseudo-photographs, the court
shall order them to be forfeited.

(7) An order made under subsection (2) or (6) above (including an order made on appeal) shall not take effect until the expiration of the ordinary time within which an appeal
may be instituted or, where such an appeal is duly instituted, until the appeal is finally
decided or abandoned; and for this purpose—

    (a) an application for a case to be stated or for leave to appeal shall be treated as the
        institution of an appeal; and

(b) where a decision on appeal is subject to a further appeal, the appeal is not finally decided until the expiration of the ordinary time within which a further appeal may be instituted or, where a further appeal is duly instituted, until the further appeal is finally decided or abandoned.

[Sections 4 and 5 are printed as amended and repealed in part by the *CJA* 1988, s.170(1) and Sch.15, paras 61 and 62; and the *CJPOA* 1994, s.168(1), (2) and Schs 9, para.23, and 10, para.37.]

(4) Possession of indecent photographs of children

(a) *Definition*

Criminal Justice Act 1988, s.160

Possession of indecent photograph of child

10–40   **160.**—(1) It is an offence for a person to have any indecent photograph or pseudo-photograph of a child in his possession.

(2) Where a person is charged with an offence under subsection (1) above, it shall be a defence for him to prove—

    (a) that he had a legitimate reason for having the photograph or pseudo-photograph in his possession; or

    (b) that he had not himself seen the photograph or pseudo-photograph and did not know, nor had any cause to suspect, it to be indecent; or

    (c) that the photograph or pseudo-photograph was sent to him without any prior request made by him or on his behalf and that he did not keep it for an unreasonable time.

(2A) A person shall be liable on conviction on indictment of an offence under this section to imprisonment for a term not exceeding five years or a fine, or both

(3) A person shall be liable on summary conviction of an offence under this section to imprisonment for a term not exceeding six months or a fine not exceeding level 5 on the standard scale, or both.

(4) Sections 1(3), 2(3), 3 and 7 of the *Protection of Children Act* 1978 shall have effect as if any reference in them to that Act included a reference to this section.

[This section is printed as amended and repealed in part by the *CJPOA* 1994, ss.84(4)(a) and (b), 86(1) and 168(3) and Sch.11; and the *CJCSA* 2000, s.41(3) (insertion of subs.(2A)). The amendment effected by the 2000 Act came into force on January 11, 2001: *Criminal Justice and Court Services Act* 2000 (Commencement No.1) Order 2000 (SI 2000/3302). There is no transitional provision in the statute or the commencement order. The combined effect of s.3 of the *Human Rights Act* 1988 and Art.7 of the European Convention will, however, be such as to require that the increase in penalty should apply only to offences committed on or after the commencement date.]

(b) *Procedure*

10–41   This offence is triable either way: s.160(2A) and (3).

(c) *Sentence*

10–41.1   When tried summarily, the maximum penalty for this offence is imprisonment for a term not exceeding six months, a fine not exceeding level five on the standard scale, or both: s.160(3).

(d) *Elements of the offence*

10–41.2   The offence of possession is not committed unless the defendant knows he has the photographs in his possession: *Atkins v DPP* [2000] 2 All E.R. 425, DC.

E. OFFENCES UNDER THE SEXUAL OFFENCES ACT 2003

10–42   The new *Sexual Offences Act* 2003 came into force on May 1, 2004.

The Act re-codifies many existing offences and creates a number of new ones. The case law that follows emanates from offences charged under the previous legislation but remains valid nonetheless. All of the offences created in the 2003 Act are either triable either way or only on indictment, save for the single exception of the new offence of sexual activity in a public lavatory, which is triable only in the Magistrates' Court (see 10–152, below). Regarding sentence, there are no Magistrates' Association Guidelines in existence for the new offences created by the 2003 Act. The Sentencing Advisory Panel is preparing advice to the Sentencing Guidelines Council for consideration but no guidelines exist at the time of publication. Information on the preparation of the guidelines is available from *www.sentencing-guidelines.gov.uk.*

(1) Consent—ss.74 to 76

The new legislation brings with it statutory provisions regarding consent contained in **10–43** ss.74–76. The redefinition of consent is one of the most radical innovations in the 2003 Act. The decision in *DPP v Morgan* [1976] A.C. 162 is replaced by the statutory definition. Under the new law the prosecution must prove that B did not consent and that A did not reasonably believe that B was consenting. An honest but unreasonable belief as to the consent of the complainant will no longer entitle the defendant to an acquittal. In determining whether the defendant's belief in consent is reasonable to the court to all the circumstances, including any steps that the defendant has taken to ascertain whether the complainant consents (statute introduces "conclusive presumptions about consent", s.76), § 10–43.3, below.

Sexual Offences Act 2003, ss.74–76

"Consent"

74. For the purposes of this Part, a person consents if he agrees by choice, and has the **10–43.1** freedom and capacity to make that choice.

Evidential presumptions about consent

75.—(1) If in proceedings for an offence to which this section applies it is proved— **10–43.2**

    (a) that the defendant did the relevant act,

    (b) that any of the circumstances specified in subsection (2) existed, and

    (c) that the defendant knew that those circumstances existed,

the complainant is to be taken not to have consented to the relevant act unless sufficient evidence is adduced to raise an issue as to whether he consented, and the defendant is to be taken not to have reasonably believed that the complainant consented unless sufficient evidence is adduced to raise an issue as to whether he reasonably believed it.

    (2) The circumstances are that—

    (a) any person was, at the time of the relevant act or immediately before it began, using violence against the complainant or causing the complainant to fear that immediate violence would be used against him;

    (b) any person was, at the time of the relevant act or immediately before it began, causing the complainant to fear that violence was being used, or that immediate violence would be used, against another person;

    (c) the complainant was, and the defendant was not, unlawfully detained at the time of the relevant act;

    (d) the complainant was asleep or otherwise unconscious at the time of the relevant act;

    (e) because of the complainant's physical disability, the complainant would not have been able at the time of the relevant act to communicate to the defendant whether the complainant consented;

    (f) any person had administered to or caused to be taken by the complainant, without the complainant's consent, a substance which, having regard to when it was administered or taken, was capable of causing or enabling the complainant to be stupefied or overpowered at the time of the relevant act.

    (3) In subsection (2)(a) and (b), the reference to the time immediately before the relevant act began is, in the case of an act which is one of a continuous series of sexual activi-

ties, a reference to the time immediately before the first sexual activity began.

Conclusive presumptions about consent

10–44   **76.**—(1) If in proceedings for an offence to which this section applies it is proved that the defendant did the relevant act and that any of the circumstances specified in subsection (2) existed, it is to be conclusively presumed—

(a) that the complainant did not consent to the relevant act, and

(b) that the defendant did not believe that the complainant consented to the relevant act.

(2) The circumstances are that—

(a) the defendant intentionally deceived the complainant as to the nature or purpose of the relevant act;

(b) the defendant intentionally induced the complainant to consent to the relevant act by impersonating a person known personally to the complainant.

(2) Sexual Assault

(a) *Definition*

Sexual Offences Act 2003, s.3

Sexual assault

10–45   **3.**—(1) A person (A) commits an offence if—

(a) he intentionally touches another person (B),

(b) the touching is sexual,

(c) B does not consent to the touching, and

(d) A does not reasonably believe that B consents.

(2) Whether a belief is reasonable is to be determined having regard to all the circumstances, including any steps A has taken to ascertain whether B consents.

(3) Sections 75 and 76 apply to an offence under this section.

See § 10–43 above, regarding ss.75 and 76.

(3) Touching

(a) *Definition*

10–46   Touching is defined in s.79(8) of the act as:

(a) with any part of the body,

(b) with anything else,

(c) through anything,

Where the victim is under 13, the offence is contained in s.7 and is identical to s.3 above save for the need for the victim to be under 13.

(b) *Venue and Sentence*

10–46.1   This offence is triable either way with a maximum sentence of six months imprisonment, if tried summarily on summary conviction.

(4) Causing a person to engage in sexual activity without consent

(a) *Definition*

Sexual Offences Act 2003, s.4

Causing a person to engage in sexual activity without consent

10–47   **4.**—(1) A person (A) commits an offence if—

(a) he intentionally causes another person (B) to engage in an activity,

(b) the activity is sexual,

(c) B does not consent to engaging in the activity, and

(d) A does not reasonably believe that B consents.

(2) Whether a belief is reasonable is to be determined having regard to all the circumstances, including any steps A has taken to ascertain whether B consents.

(3) Sections 75 and 76 apply to an offence under this section.

See § 10–43 above, regarding ss.75 and 76.

(b) *Venue and Sentence*

This offence is triable either way with a maximum sentence of six months imprison- **10–48** ment, if tried summarily and/or a fine. If however, one or more of the following factors is present, the offence *must* be tried on indictment:

(a) penetration of B's anus or vagina

(b) penetration of B's mouth with a person's penis

(c) penetration of a person's anus or vagina with a part of B's body or by B with anything else

(d) penetration of a person's mouth with B's penis.

Note that s.8 of the act creates a separate offence where a child under 13 is the victim, this must always be tried on indictment regardless of the facts.

F. Child Sex Offences

(1) Child Sex Offences

Child sex offences are those in which the complainant is under the age of 16. There **10–49** are now statutory provisions with respect to the relevance of the complainant's age.

(a) *Relevant Age Provisions*

Complainant is under 13   **10–49.1**

The offence becomes one of strict liability and no issue arises as to the defendant's belief as to the complainant's age.

Complainant is between 13 and 15

It is for the prosecution to prove that the defendant did not believe that the complainant was over 16. The defendant's belief must be reasonable.

The defendant will have an evidential burden to establish that he reasonably believed that the complainant was over 16. If discharged, it then falls to the prosecution to prove the absence of such belief.

(2) Sexual Activity with a child

(a) *Definition*

Sexual Offences Act 2003, s.9

Sexual activity with a child

  9.—(1) A person aged 18 or over (A) commits an offence if—   **10–50**

(a) he intentionally touches another person (B),

(b) the touching is sexual, and

(c) either—

(i) B is under 16 and A does not reasonably believe that B is 16 or over, or

(ii) B is under 13.

Touching is defined in s.79(8) of the act as:

(a) with any part of the body,

    (b) with anything else,

    (c) through anything,

(b) *Venue and Sentence*

10–51   The offence is triable either way with a maximum sentence of 6 months and/or a fine except in the following circumstances where it *must* be tried on indictment:

    Where the defendant is over 18 years of age and one or more of the following occurred:

    (a) penetration of B's anus or vagina

    (b) penetration of B's mouth with a person's penis

    (c) penetration of a person's anus or vagina with a part of B's body or by B with anything else

    (d) penetration of a person's mouth with B's penis.

(3) Causing or inciting a child to engage in sexual activity

(a) *Definition*

Sexual Offences Act 2003, s.10

Causing or inciting a child to engage in sexual activity

10–52   **10.**—(1) A person aged 18 or over (A) commits an offence if—

    (a) he intentionally causes or incites another person (B) to engage in an activity,

    (b) the activity is sexual, and

    (c) either

        (i) B is under 16 and A does not reasonably believe that B is 16 or over, or

        (ii) B is under 13.

(b) *Venue and Sentence*

10–52.2   The offence is triable either way with a maximum sentence of six months and/or a fine except in the following circumstances where it *must* be tried on indictment:

    Where the defendant is over 18 years of age and one or more of the following occurred:

    (e) penetration of B's anus or vagina

    (f) penetration of B's mouth with a person's penis

    (g) penetration of a person's anus or vagina with a part of B's body or by B with anything else

    (h) penetration of a person's mouth with B's penis.

(4) Engaging in sexual activity in the presence of a child

(a) *Definition*

Sexual Offences Act 2003, s.11

Engaging in sexual activity in the presence of a child

10–53   **11.**—(1) A person aged 18 or over (A) commits an offence if—

    (a) he intentionally engages in an activity,

    (b) the activity is sexual,

    (c) for the purpose of obtaining sexual gratification, he engages in it—

        (i) when another person (B) is present or is in a place from which A can be observed, and

        (ii) knowing or believing that B is aware, or intending that B should be aware, that he is engaging in it,

    (d) either

(i) B is under 16 and A does not reasonably believe that B is 16 or over, or

(ii) is under 13.

(b) *Venue and Sentence*

This offence is triable either way with a maximum sentence of six months imprison- **10–53.1**
ment, if tried summarily.

(5) Causing a child to watch a sexual act

(a) *Definition*

Sexual Offences Act 2003, s.12

Causing a child to watch a sexual act

12.—(1) A person aged 18 or over (A) commits an offence if—   **10–54**

(a) for the purpose of obtaining sexual gratification, he intentionally causes another person (B) to watch a third person engaging in an activity, or to look at an image of any person engaging in an activity,

(b) the activity is sexual, and

(c) either

(i) B is under 16 and A does not reasonably believe that B is 16 or over, or

(ii) is under 13.

(b) *Venue and Sentence*

This offence is triable either way with a maximum sentence of six months imprison- **10–54.1**
ment, if tried summarily.

(6) Arranging or facilitating a child sex offence

(a) *Definition*

Sexual Offences Act 2003, s.14

Arranging or facilitating commission of a child sex offence

14.—(1) A person commits an offence if—   **10–55**

(a) he intentionally arranges or facilitates something that he intends to do, intends another person to do, or believes that another person will do, in any part of the world, and

(b) doing it will involve the commission of an offence under any of sections 9 to 13.

(2) A person does not commit an offence under this section if—

(a) he arranges or facilitates something that he believes another person will do, but that he does not intend to do or intend another person to do, and

(b) any offence within subsection (1)(b) would be an offence against a child for whose protection he acts.

(3) For the purposes of subsection (2)facilitating, a person acts for the protection of a child if he acts for the purpose of—

(a) protecting the child from sexually transmitted infection,

(b) protecting the physical safety of the child,

(c) preventing the child from becoming pregnant, or

(d) promoting the child's emotional well-being by the giving of advice,

and not for the purpose of obtaining sexual gratification or for the purpose of causing or encouraging the activity constituting the offence within subsection (1)(b) or the child's participation in it.

(b) *Defence*

There is a specific defence to this offence so as not to criminalise the behaviour of a **10–55.1**
person who provides a child contraception or family planning advice.

(c) *Venue and Sentence*

10–56   This offence is triable either way with a maximum sentence of six months imprisonment, if tried summarily.

(7) **Meeting a child following sexual grooming**

(a) *Definition*

Sexual Offences Act 2003, s.15

Meeting a child following sexual grooming etc.

10–57   **15.**—(1) A person aged 18 or over (A) commits an offence if—
- (a) having met or communicated with another person (B) on at least two earlier occasions, he—
  - (i) intentionally meets B, or
  - (ii) travels with the intention of meeting B in any part of the world,
- (b) at the time, he intends to do anything to or in respect of B, during or after the meeting and in any part of the world, which if done will involve the commission by A of a relevant offence,
- (c) B is under 16, and
- (d) A does not reasonably believe that B is 16 or over.

(2) In subsection (1)—
- (a) the reference to A having met or communicated with B is a reference to A having met B in any part of the world or having communicated with B by any means from, to or in any part of the world;
- (b) "relevant offence" means—
  - (i) an offence under this Part,
  - (ii) an offence within any of paragraphs 61 to 92 of Schedule 3, or
  - (iii) anything done outside England and Wales and Northern Ireland which is not an offence within sub-paragraph (i) or (ii) but would be an offence within sub-paragraph (i) if done in England and Wales.

Note that this offence enables charges to be brought before any other substantive offence takes place.

(b) *Venue and Sentence*

10–57.1   This offence is triable either way with a maximum sentence of six months imprisonment, if tried summarily.

(8) **Abuse of a Position of Trust**

10–58   These offences are identical to the child sex acts above (ss.9 to 12):
- (a) sexual activity with a child (s.16)
- (b) causing or inciting a child to engage in a sexual activity (s.17)
- (c) sexual activity in the presence of a child (s.18)
- (d) causing a child to watch a sex act (s.19)

The complainant must be under 18 for the offences above to be properly charged.

Sexual Offences Act 2003, ss.16–19

Abuse of position of trust: sexual activity with a child

10–59   **16.**—(1) A person aged 18 or over (A) commits an offence if—
- (a) he intentionally touches another person (B),
- (b) the touching is sexual,
- (c) A is in a position of trust in relation to B,
- (d) where subsection (2) applies, A knows or could reasonably be expected to know of the circumstances by virtue of which he is in a position of trust in relation to B, and

(e) either—
  (i) B is under 18 and A does not reasonably believe that B is 18 or over, or
  (ii) B is under 13.
(2) This subsection applies where A—
  (a) is in a position of trust in relation to B by virtue of circumstances within section 21(2), (3), (4) or (5), and
  (b) is not in such a position of trust by virtue of other circumstances.
(3) Where in proceedings for an offence under this section it is proved that the other person was under 18, the defendant is to be taken not to have reasonably believed that that person was 18 or over unless sufficient evidence is adduced to raise an issue as to whether he reasonably believed it.
(4) Where in proceedings for an offence under this section—
  (a) it is proved that the defendant was in a position of trust in relation to the other person by virtue of circumstances within section 21(2), (3), (4) or (5), and
  (b) it is not proved that he was in such a position of trust by virtue of other circumstances,
it is to be taken that the defendant knew or could reasonably have been expected to know of the circumstances by virtue of which he was in such a position of trust unless sufficient evidence is adduced to raise an issue as to whether he knew or could reasonably have been expected to know of those circumstances.

Abuse of position of trust: causing or inciting a child to engage in sexual activity
17.—(1) A person aged 18 or over (A) commits an offence if—   **10–60**
  (a) he intentionally causes or incites another person (B) to engage in an activity,
  (b) the activity is sexual,
  (c) A is in a position of trust in relation to B,
  (d) where subsection (2) applies, A knows or could reasonably be expected to know of the circumstances by virtue of which he is in a position of trust in relation to B, and
  (e) either—
    (i) B is under 18 and A does not reasonably believe that B is 18 or over, or
    (ii) B is under 13.
(2) This subsection applies where A—
  (a) is in a position of trust in relation to B by virtue of circumstances within section 21(2), (3), (4) or (5), and
  (b) is not in such a position of trust by virtue of other circumstances.
(3) Where in proceedings for an offence under this section it is proved that the other person was under 18, the defendant is to be taken not to have reasonably believed that that person was 18 or over unless sufficient evidence is adduced to raise an issue as to whether he reasonably believed it.
(4) Where in proceedings for an offence under this section—
  (a) it is proved that the defendant was in a position of trust in relation to the other person by virtue of circumstances within section 21(2), (3), (4) or (5), and
  (b) it is not proved that he was in such a position of trust by virtue of other circumstances,
it is to be taken that the defendant knew or could reasonably have been expected to know of the circumstances by virtue of which he was in such a position of trust unless sufficient evidence is adduced to raise an issue as to whether he knew or could reasonably have been expected to know of those circumstances.

Abuse of position of trust: sexual activity in the presence of a child
18.—(1) A person aged 18 or over (A) commits an offence if—   **10–61**
  (a) he intentionally engages in an activity,
  (b) the activity is sexual,
  (c) for the purpose of obtaining sexual gratification, he engages in it—
    (i) when another person (B) is present or is in a place from which A can be observed, and
    (ii) knowing or believing that B is aware, or intending that B should be aware, that he is engaging in it,

(d) A is in a position of trust in relation to B,

(e) where subsection (2) applies, A knows or could reasonably be expected to know of the circumstances by virtue of which he is in a position of trust in relation to B, and

(f) either—

    (i) B is under 18 and A does not reasonably believe that B is 18 or over, or

    (ii) B is under 13.

(2) This subsection applies where A—

(a) is in a position of trust in relation to B by virtue of circumstances within section 21(2), (3), (4) or (5), and

(b) is not in such a position of trust by virtue of other circumstances.

(3) Where in proceedings for an offence under this section it is proved that the other person was under 18, the defendant is to be taken not to have reasonably believed that that person was 18 or over unless sufficient evidence is adduced to raise an issue as to whether he reasonably believed it.

(4) Where in proceedings for an offence under this section—

(a) it is proved that the defendant was in a position of trust in relation to the other person by virtue of circumstances within section 21(2), (3), (4) or (5), and

(b) it is not proved that he was in such a position of trust by virtue of other circumstances,

it is to be taken that the defendant knew or could reasonably have been expected to know of the circumstances by virtue of which he was in such a position of trust unless sufficient evidence is adduced to raise an issue as to whether he knew or could reasonably have been expected to know of those circumstances.

Abuse of position of trust: causing a child to watch a sexual act

10–62   **19.**—(1) A person aged 18 or over (A) commits an offence if—

(a) for the purpose of obtaining sexual gratification, he intentionally causes another person (B) to watch a third person engaging in an activity, or to look at an image of any person engaging in an activity,

(b) the activity is sexual,

(c) A is in a position of trust in relation to B,

(d) where subsection (2) applies, A knows or could reasonably be expected to know of the circumstances by virtue of which he is in a position of trust in relation to B, and

(e) either—

    (i) B is under 18 and A does not reasonably believe that B is 18 or over, or

    (ii) B is under 13.

(2) This subsection applies where A—

(a) is in a position of trust in relation to B by virtue of circumstances within section 21(2), (3), (4) or (5), and

(b) is not in such a position of trust by virtue of other circumstances.

(3) Where in proceedings for an offence under this section it is proved that the other person was under 18, the defendant is to be taken not to have reasonably believed that that person was 18 or over unless sufficient evidence is adduced to raise an issue as to whether he reasonably believed it.

(4) Where in proceedings for an offence under this section—

(a) it is proved that the defendant was in a position of trust in relation to the other person by virtue of circumstances within section 21(2), (3), (4) or (5), and

(b) it is not proved that he was in such a position of trust by virtue of other circumstances,

it is to be taken that the defendant knew or could reasonably have been expected to know of the circumstances by virtue of which he was in such a position of trust unless sufficient evidence is adduced to raise an issue as to whether he knew or could reasonably have been expected to know of those circumstances.

(a) *Position of Trust*

Sexual Offences Act 2003, ss.21, 22

Positions of trust

21.—(1) For the purposes of sections 16 to 19, a person (A) is in a position of trust in relation **10–63**
to another person (B) if—

(a) any of the following subsections applies, or

(b) any condition specified in an order made by the Secretary of State is met.

(2) This subsection applies if A looks after persons under 18 who are detained in an
institution by virtue of a court order or under an enactment, and B is so detained in that
institution.

(3) This subsection applies if A looks after persons under 18 who are resident in a home
or other place in which—

(a) accommodation and maintenance are provided by an authority under section
23(2) of the *Children Act* 1989 (c. 41) or Article 27(2) of the *Children (Northern
Ireland) Order* 1995 (S.I. 1995/755 (N.I. 2)), or

(b) accommodation is provided by a voluntary organisation under section 59(1) of
that Act or Article 75(1) of that *Order*,

and B is resident, and is so provided with accommodation and maintenance or accommodation,
in that place.

(4) This subsection applies if A looks after persons under 18 who are accommodated
and cared for in one of the following institutions—

(a) a hospital,

(b) an independent clinic,

(c) a care home, residential care home or private hospital,

(d) a community home, voluntary home or children's home,

(e) a home provided under section 82(5) of the *Children Act* 1989, or

(f) a residential family centre,

and B is accommodated and cared for in that institution.

(5) This subsection applies if A looks after persons under 18 who are receiving education at an educational institution and B is receiving, and A is not receiving, education at
that institution.

(6) This subsection applies if A is appointed to be the guardian of B under Article 159
or 160 of the *Children (Northern Ireland) Order* 1995 (S.I. 1995/755 (N.I. 2)).

(7) This subsection applies if A is engaged in the provision of services under, or pursuant to anything done under—

(a) sections 8 to 10 of the *Employment and Training Act* 1973 (c. 50), or

(b) section 114 of the *Learning and Skills Act* 2000 (c. 21),

and, in that capacity, looks after B on an individual basis.

(8) This subsection applies if A regularly has unsupervised contact with B (whether face **10–64**
to face or by any other means)—

(a) in the exercise of functions of a local authority under section 20 or 21 of the
Children Act 1989 (c. 41), or

(b) in the exercise of functions of an authority under Article 21 or 23 of the *Children
(Northern Ireland) Order* 1995.

(9) This subsection applies if A, as a person who is to report to the court under section 7
of the *Children Act* 1989 or Article 4 of the *Children (Northern Ireland) Order* 1995 on matters relating to the welfare of B, regularly has unsupervised contact with B (whether face to face
or by any other means).

(10) This subsection applies if A is a personal adviser appointed for B under—

(a) section 23B(2) of, or paragraph 19C of Schedule 2 to, the *Children Act* 1989, or

(b) Article 34A(10) or 34C(2) of the *Children (Northern Ireland) Order* 1995,

and, in that capacity, looks after B on an individual basis.

(11) This subsection applies if—

(a) B is subject to a care order, a supervision order or an education supervision order, and

(b) in the exercise of functions conferred by virtue of the order on an authorised person or the authority designated by the order, A looks after B on an individual basis.

(12) This subsection applies if A—

    (a) is an officer of the Service appointed for B under section 41(1) of the *Children Act* 1989,

    (b) is appointed a children's guardian of B under rule 6 or rule 18 of the *Adoption Rules* 1984 (S.I. 1984/265), or

    (c) is appointed to be the guardian ad litem of B under rule 9.5 of the *Family Proceedings Rules* 1991 (S. I. 1991/1247) or under Article 60(1) of the *Children (Northern Ireland) Order* 1995,

and, in that capacity, regularly has unsupervised contact with B (whether face to face or by any other means).

(13) This subsection applies if—

    (a) B is subject to requirements imposed by or under an enactment on his release from detention for a criminal offence, or is subject to requirements imposed by a court order made in criminal proceedings, and

    (b) A looks after B on an individual basis in pursuance of the requirements.

Positions of trust: interpretation

10–65　　**22.**—(1) The following provisions apply for the purposes of section 21.

(2) Subject to subsection (3), a person looks after persons under 18 if he is regularly involved in caring for, training, supervising or being in sole charge of such persons.

(3) A person (A) looks after another person (B) on an individual basis if—

    (a) A is regularly involved in caring for, training or supervising B, and

    (b) in the course of his involvement, A regularly has unsupervised contact with B (whether face to face or by any other means).

(4) A person receives education at an educational institution if—

    (a) he is registered or otherwise enrolled as a pupil or student at the institution, or

    (b) he receives education at the institution under arrangements with another educational institution at which he is so registered or otherwise enrolled.

10–66　　(5) In section 21—

"authority" —

    (a) in relation to England and Wales, means a local authority;

    (b) in relation to Northern Ireland, has the meaning given by Article 2(2) of the *Children (Northern Ireland) Order* 1995 (SI 1995/755 (N.I. 2));

"care home" means an establishment which is a care home for the purposes of the *Care Standards Act* 2000 (c. 14);

"care order" has—

    (a) in relation to England and Wales, the same meaning as in the *Children Act* 1989 (c. 41), and

    (b) in relation to Northern Ireland, the same meaning as in the *Children (Northern Ireland) Order* 1995;

"children's home" has—

    (a) in relation to England and Wales, the meaning given by section 1 of the *Care Standards Act* 2000, and

    (b) in relation to Northern Ireland, the meaning that would be given by Article 9 of the *Health and Personal Social Services (Quality, Improvement and Regulation) (Northern Ireland) Order* 2003 (S.I. 2003/431 (N.I. 9)) ("the 2003 Order") if in paragraph (4) of that Article sub-paragraphs (d), (f) and (g) were omitted;

"community home" has the meaning given by section 53 of the *Children Act* 1989;

"education supervision order" has—

    (a) in relation to England and Wales, the meaning given by section 36 of the *Children Act* 1989, and

    (b) in relation to Northern Ireland, the meaning given by Article 49(1) of the *Children (Northern Ireland) Order* 1995;

"hospital" —

    (a) in relation to England and Wales, means a hospital within the meaning given by section 128(1) of the *National Health Service Act* 1977 (c. 49), or any other establishment which is a hospital within the meaning given by section 2(3) of the *Care Standards Act* 2000 (c. 14);

(b) in relation to Northern Ireland, means a hospital within the meaning given by Article 2(2) of the *Health and Personal Social Services (Northern Ireland) Order* 1972 (S.I. 1972/1265 (N.I. 14)), or any other establishment which is a hospital within the meaning given by Article 2(2) of the 2003 Order;

"independent clinic" has—

(a) in relation to England and Wales, the meaning given by section 2 of the *Care Standards Act* 2000;

(b) in relation to Northern Ireland, the meaning given by Article 2(2) of the 2003 Order;

"private hospital" has the meaning given by Article 90(2) of the *Mental Health (Northern Ireland) Order* 1986 (S.I. 1986/595 (N.I. 4));

"residential care home" means an establishment which is a residential care home for the purposes of the 2003 Order;

"residential family centre" has the meaning given by section 22 of the *Health and Personal Social Services Act (Northern Ireland)* 2001 (c. 3);

"supervision order" has—

(a) in relation to England and Wales, the meaning given by section 31(11) of the *Children Act* 1989 (c. 41), and

(b) in relation to Northern Ireland, the meaning given by Article 49(1) of the *Children (Northern Ireland) Order* 1995 (S.I. 1995/ 755 (N.I. 2));

"voluntary home" has—

(a) in relation to England and Wales, the meaning given by section 60(3) of the *Children Act* 1989, and

(b) in relation to Northern Ireland, the meaning given by Article 74(1) of the *Children (Northern Ireland) Order* 1995.

(b) *Consent*

Sections 16–19 apply regardless of consent between the parties. Importantly **10–67** therefore, the normal age of consent at 16 will not apply to offences under these sections.

(c) *Defences*

There are a number of specific defences to the offences within these sections.   **10–68**

(d) *The age of the complainant*

If the child is between 13 and 18 the prosecution must prove that the defendant did **10–69** not reasonably believe that the child was over 18.

This does not apply where the defendant looks after the complainant in one of the following settings:

(a) where the complainant is detained by virtue of a court order

(b) where the complainant is in a hospital, clinic or care home

(c) where the complainant attends an educational institution

and the defendant looks after the complainant in a caring or training role.

(e) *Knowledge of the position of trust*

Where the defendant could not reasonably be expected to know that a position of **10–70** trust existed, no offence has been committed. If however the defendant looks after the complainant in one of the scenarios above (see age of complainant defence) there will be a presumption that the defendant know of the position of trust unless he can raise significant evidence to the contrary.

(f) *Lawful pre-existing relationships*

Where a lawful marriage exists and the otherwise complainant is over 16 at the time **10–71** of such conduct, no offence will be deemed to having been committed.

(g) *Venue and Sentence*

10–72   In respect of each offence the maximum sentence upon summary conviction is six months imprisonment and/or a fine.

II. FAMILIAL SEXUAL OFFENCES

(1) Definition of a family relationship

10–73   There are three categories of relationship contained in subss.(3), (4) and (5) of s.27 with the presumption differing in each.

Sexual Offences Act 2003, s.27

Family relationships

10–74   **27.**—(1) The relation of one person (A) to another (B) is within this section if—

     (a) it is within any of subsections (2) to (4), or

     (b) it would be within one of those subsections but for section 67 of the *Adoption and Children Act* 2002 (c. 38) (status conferred by adoption).

   (2) The relation of A to B is within this subsection if—

     (a) one of them is the other's parent, grandparent, brother, sister, half-brother, half-sister, aunt or uncle, or

     (b) A is or has been B's foster parent.

   (3) The relation of A to B is within this subsection if A and B live or have lived in the same household, or A is or has been regularly involved in caring for, training, supervising or being in sole charge of B, and—

     (a) one of them is or has been the other's step-parent,

     (b) A and B are cousins,

     (c) one of them is or has been the other's stepbrother or stepsister, or

     (d) the parent or present or former foster parent of one of them is or has been the other's foster parent.

   (4) The relation of A to B is within this subsection if—

     (a) A and B live in the same household, and

     (b) A is regularly involved in caring for, training, supervising or being in sole charge of B.

10–75   (5) For the purposes of this section—

     (a) "aunt" means the sister or half-sister of a person's parent, and "uncle" has a corresponding meaning;

     (b) "cousin" means the child of an aunt or uncle;

     (c) a person is a child's foster parent if—

       (i) he is a person with whom the child has been placed under section 23(2)(a) or 59(1)(a) of the *Children Act* 1989 (c. 41) (fostering for local authority or voluntary organisation), or

       (ii) he fosters the child privately, within the meaning given by section 66(1)(b) of that Act;

     (d) a person is another's partner (whether they are of different sexes or the same sex) if they live together as partners in an enduring family relationship;

     (e) "step-parent" includes a parent's partner and "stepbrother" and "stepsister" include the child of a parent's partner.

(2) Relevance of age

10–76   Where the complainant is under 13, the offences are ones of strict liability. If the complainant is between 13 and 18, the defendant will have the evidential burden of showing that they reasonably believed that the complainant was over 18.

(3) Defences

(a) *Marriage exception*

Where a lawful marriage exists and the otherwise complainant is over 16 at the time **10–77** of such conduct, no offence will be deemed to having been committed.

(b) *Knowledge of the family relationship*

It is for the defendant to raise evidence of a lack of knowledge of a relationship if he **10–78** asserts this to be the case. An example would be conduct with a person and followed by finding out a family relationship between the parties.

(4) Sexual activity with a family member

(a) *Definition*

Sexual Offences Act 2003, s.25

Sexual activity with a child family member
   25.—(1) A person (A) commits an offence if— **10–79**
     (a) he intentionally touches another person (B),
     (b) the touching is sexual,
     (c) the relation of A to B is within section 27,
     (d) A knows or could reasonably be expected to know that his relation to B is of a description falling within that section
Touching is defined in s.79(8) of the act as:
     (a) with any part of the body,
     (b) with anything else,
     (c) through anything,

(b) *Venue and Sentence*

This offence is triable either way. Upon summary conviction the maximum sentence **10–79.1** is six months imprisonment

(5) Inciting a child family member to engage in sexual activity

(a) *Definition*

Sexual Offences Act 2003, s.26

Inciting a child family member to engage in sexual activity
   26.—(1) A person (A) commits an offence if— **10–80**
     (a) he intentionally incites another person (B) to touch, or allow himself to be touched by, A,
     (b) the touching is sexual,
     (c) the relation of A to B is within section 27,
     (d) A knows or could reasonably be expected to know that his relation to B is of a description falling within that section,

(b) *Venue and Sentence*

This offence is triable either way with a maximum sentence of six months imprison- **10–81** ment, if tried summarily and/or a fine. If however, one or more of the following factors is present, the offence *must* be tried on indictment:
     (a) penetration of B's anus or vagina
     (b) penetration of B's mouth with a person's penis

(c) penetration of a person's anus or vagina with a part of B's body or by B with anything else

(d) penetration of a person's mouth with B's penis.

Note that section 8 of the act creates a separate offence where a child under 13 is the victim; this must always be tried on indictment regardless of the facts.

(6) Offences against persons with mental disorders

10–82   The act changed significantly from previous legislation in this area that required the victim to be deemed 'defective' and permission from the DPP sought before a prosecution brought.

Sexual activity is defined in s.78 of the legislation:

Sexual Offences Act 2003, s.78

"Sexual"

10–83   **78.** For the purposes of this Part (except section 71), penetration, touching or any other activity is sexual if a reasonable person would consider that—

(a) whatever its circumstances or any person's purpose in relation to it, it is because of its nature sexual, or

(b) because of its nature it may be sexual and because of its circumstances or the purpose of any person in relation to it (or both) it is sexual.

Mental Disorder

10–84   The meaning of 'mental disorder' is contained in s.79(6) of the Act and mirrors s.1 of the *Mental Health Act* 1983 in its meaning.

Mental Health Act 1983, s.1

Application of Act: "mental disorder"

10–84.1   **1.**—(1) The provisions of this Act shall have effect with respect to the reception, care and treatment of mentally disordered patients, the management of their property and other related matters.

(2) In this Act—

"mental disorder" means mental illness, arrested or incomplete development of mind, psychopathic disorder and any other disorder or disability of mind and "mentally disordered" shall be construed accordingly;

"severe mental impairment" means a state of arrested or incomplete development of mind which includes severe impairment of intelligence and social functioning and is associated with abnormally aggressive or seriously irresponsible conduct on the part of the person concerned and "severely mentally impaired" shall be construed accordingly;

"mental impairment" means a state of arrested or incomplete development of mind (not amounting to severe mental impairment) which includes significant impairment of intelligence and social functioning and is associated with abnormally aggressive or seriously irresponsible conduct on the part of the person concerned and "mentally impaired" shall be construed accordingly;

"psychopathic disorder" means a persistent disorder or disability of mind (whether or not including significant impairment of intelligence) which results in abnormally aggressive or seriously irresponsible conduct on the part of the person concerned;

and other expressions shall have the meanings assigned to them in section 145 below.

(3) Nothing in subsection (2) above shall be construed as implying that a person may be dealt with under this Act as suffering from mental disorder, or from any form of mental disorder described in this section, by reason only of promiscuity or other immoral conduct, sexual deviancy or dependence on alcohol or drugs.

Unable to refuse

10–84.2   The act contains provision for situations where the victim can be deemed 'unable to refuse' where a situation is present to them, due to their mental ability or capacity.

This is contained in subs.(2) of ss.30 to 33—and is only relevant to those offences.

B is unable to refuse if—

(a) he lacks the capacity to choose whether to agree to the touching (whether because he lacks sufficient understanding of the nature or reasonably foreseeable consequences of what is being done, or for any other reason), or

(b) he is unable to communicate such a choice to A.

(7) Sexual Activity with a person with a mental disorder impeding choice and causing or inciting a person with a mental disorder impeding choice to engage in sexual activity

D causes X to have sex with him / D causes X to undress for him for sexual gratifica-   **10–85**
tion / D causes X to have sex with D's friend.

Inclusion of "inciting" to cover scenarios where the actual act(s) does not take place—
s.31.

(a) *Definition*

Sexual Offences Act 2003, ss.30(1), 31(1)

Sexual activity with a person with a mental disorder impeding choice
  30.—(1) A person (A) commits an offence if—   **10–86**
    (a) he intentionally touches another person (B),
    (b) the touching is sexual,
    (c) B is unable to refuse because of or for a reason related to a mental disorder, and
    (d) A knows or could reasonably be expected to know that B has a mental disorder and that because of it or for a reason related to it B is likely to be unable to refuse.

Causing or inciting a person, with a mental disorder impeding choice, to engage in sexual activity
  31.—(1) A person (A) commits an offence if—   **10–86.˙**
    (a) he intentionally causes or incites another person (B) to engage in an activity,
    (b) the activity is sexual,
    (c) B is unable to refuse because of or for a reason related to a mental disorder, and
    (d) A knows or could reasonably be expected to know that B has a mental disorder and that because of it or for a reason related to it B is likely to be unable to refuse.

(b) *Venue and Sentence*

This offence is triable either way with a maximum sentence of six months imprison-   **10–87**
ment, if tried summarily. If however, one or more of the following factors is present, the offence *must* be tried on indictment:

(a) penetration of B's anus or vagina

(b) penetration of B's mouth with a person's penis

(c) penetration of a person's anus or vagina with a part of B's body or by B with anything else

(d) penetration of a person's mouth with B's penis.

Engaging in sexual activity in the presence of a person with a mental disorder impeding choice.

This offence occurs where the defendant engages in sexual activity with another in   **10–87.˙**
the presence of the complainant with a mental disorder for the purpose of sexual gratification. The defendant must know or believe that the complainant is aware of the activity or intends them to be aware of it.

(c) *Definition*

Sexual Offences Act 2003, s.32(1)

Engaging in sexual activity in the presence of a person with a mental disorder impeding choice

10–88   **32.**—(1) A person (A) commits an offence if—

    (a) he intentionally engages in an activity,

    (b) the activity is sexual,

    (c) for the purpose of obtaining sexual gratification, he engages in it—

      (i) when another person (B) is present or is in a place from which A can be observed, and

      (ii) knowing or believing that B is aware, or intending that B should be aware, that he is engaging in it,

    (d) B is unable to refuse because of or for a reason related to a mental disorder, and

    (e) A knows or could reasonably be expected to know that B has a mental disorder and that because of it or for a reason related to it B is likely to be unable to refuse.

(d) *Venue and Sentence*

10–89   This offence is triable either way with a maximum sentence of six months imprisonment, if tried summarily.

(8) Causing a person with a mental disorder to watch a sexual act

10–90   Situations where defendant causes complainant to watch a third person engaging in sexual activity or an image such activity.

(a) *Definition*

Sexual Offences Act 2003, s.33(1)

Causing a person, with a mental disorder impeding choice, to watch a sexual act

10–90.1   **33.**—(1) A person (A) commits an offence if—

    (a) for the purpose of obtaining sexual gratification, he intentionally causes another person (B) to watch a third person engaging in an activity, or to look at an image of any person engaging in an activity,

    (b) the activity is sexual,

    (c) B is unable to refuse because of or for a reason related to a mental disorder, and

    (d) A knows or could reasonably be expected to know that B has a mental disorder and that because of it or for a reason related to it B is likely to be unable to refuse.

10–90.2   As to the definition of an image:

Sexual Offences Act 2003, s.79(5)

Part 1: general interpretation

    79.—(5) References to an image of a person include references to an image of an imaginary person.

Note that the defendant must know or be reasonably expected to know that the complainant has a mental disorder and is unable to consent (supra).

(b) *Venue and Sentence*

10–90.3   This offence is triable either way and carries a maximum sentence of six months imprisonment, if tried summarily.

(9) Inducements to a person with a mental disorder

10–91   The Act contains provisions where scenario's where sexual activity takes place as a result of an inducement by the defendant to the complainant or as a result of a threat or deception.

Inducement, threat or deception to procure sexual activity with a person with a mental disorder.

This section deals with scenarios where the defendant induces (the size of the inducement being irrelevant) threatens (e.g. harm to complainant or someone complainant knows) or deceives (*e.g.* complainant will get into trouble by not engaging in this activity) the complainant into taking part in sexual activity.

(a) *Definition*

Sexual Offences Act 2003, s.34(1)

Inducement, threat or deception to procure sexual activity with a person with a mental disorder

34.—(1) A person (A) commits an offence if—   **10–91.1**
    (a) with the agreement of another person (B) he intentionally touches that person,
    (b) the touching is sexual,
    (c) A obtains B's agreement by means of an inducement offered or given, a threat made or a deception practised by A for that purpose,
    (d) B has a mental disorder, and
    (e) A knows or could reasonably be expected to know that B has a mental disorder.

(b) *Venue and Sentence*

This offence is triable either way with a maximum sentence of six months imprison- **10–92** ment, if tried summarily. If however, one or more of the following factors is present, the offence *must* be tried on indictment:
    (a) penetration of B's anus or vagina
    (b) penetration of B's mouth with a person's penis
    (c) penetration of a person's anus or vagina with a part of B's body or by B with anything else
    (d) penetration of a person's mouth with B's penis.

Engaging in sexual activity in the presence, procured by inducement, threat or deception, of a person with a mental disorder.

This offence is committed where the defendant intentionally engages in sexual activ- **10–92.1** ity in the presence of the mentally disordered complainant and their presence is due to and inducement, threat or deception.

The mental disorder must be known or ought reasonably be known to the defendant.

(c) *Definition*

Sexual Offences Act 2003, s.36(1)

Engaging in sexual activity in the presence, procured by inducement, threat or deception, of a person with a mental disorder

36.—(1) A person (A) commits an offence if—   **10–93**
    (a) he intentionally engages in an activity,
    (b) the activity is sexual,
    (c) for the purpose of obtaining sexual gratification, he engages in it—
        (i) when another person (B) is present or is in a place from which A can be observed, and
        (ii) knowing or believing that B is aware, or intending that B should be aware, that he is engaging in it,
    (d) B agrees to be present or in the place referred to in paragraph (c)(i) because of an inducement offered or given, a threat made or a deception practised by A for the purpose of obtaining that agreement,

(e) B has a mental disorder, and

(f) A knows or could reasonably be expected to know that B has a mental disorder.

(d) *Venue and Sentence*

10–93.1   This offence is triable either way with a maximum sentence of six months imprisonment, if tried summarily.

(10) Causing a person with a mental disorder to watch a sexual act by inducement, threat or deception

10–94   This offence encompasses the situation where the defendant causes the mentally disordered complainant to watch a sexual act by inducement, threat or deception for the defendant's sexual gratification.

The mental disorder must be known or ought reasonably be known to the defendant.

(a) *Definition*

Sexual Offences Act 2003, s.37(1)

Causing a person with a mental disorder to watch a sexual act by inducement, threat or deception

10–95   **37.**—(1) A person (A) commits an offence if—

(a) for the purpose of obtaining sexual gratification, he intentionally causes another person (B) to watch a third person engaging in an activity, or to look at an image of any person engaging in an activity,

(b) the activity is sexual,

(c) B agrees to watch or look because of an inducement offered or given, a threat made or a deception practised by A for the purpose of obtaining that agreement,

(d) B has a mental disorder, and

(e) A knows or could reasonably be expected to know that B has a mental disorder.

(b) *Venue and Sentence*

10–95.1   This offence is triable either way with a maximum sentence of six months imprisonment, if tried summarily.

(c) *Care Workers*

10–96   This section of the act creates separate offences than can be committed by the mentally disorder person's care worker. Within this close relationship, the existance of a mental disorder is sufficient in establishing that aspect of the offence and further, it is no defence to say that the complainant consented to the act.

Each offence that falls under this section must be read with reference to the following definitions and defences.

Care Worker Definition

Sexual Offences Act 2003, s.42

Care workers: interpretation

10–97   **42.**—(1) For the purposes of sections 38 to 41, a person (A) is involved in the care of another person (B) in a way that falls within this section if any of subsections (2) to (4) applies.

(2) This subsection applies if—

(a) B is accommodated and cared for in a care home, community home, voluntary home or children's home, and

(b) A has functions to perform in the home in the course of employment which have brought him or are likely to bring him into regular face to face contact with B.

(3) This subsection applies if B is a patient for whom services are provided—
    (a) by a National Health Service body or an independent medical agency, or
    (b) in an independent clinic or an independent hospital,
and A has functions to perform for the body or agency or in the clinic or hospital in the course of employment which have brought him or are likely to bring him into regular face to face contact with B.

(4) This subsection applies if A—
    (a) is, whether or not in the course of employment, a provider of care, assistance or services to B in connection with B's mental disorder, and
    (b) as such, has had or is likely to have regular face to face contact with B.

(5) In this section—   **10–98**
    "care home" means an establishment which is a care home for the purposes of the *Care Standards Act* 2000 (c. 14);
    "children's home" has the meaning given by section 1 of that Act;
    "community home" has the meaning given by section 53 of the *Children Act* 1989 (c. 41);
    "employment" means any employment, whether paid or unpaid and whether under a contract of service or apprenticeship, under a contract for services, or otherwise than under a contract;
    "independent clinic", "independent hospital" and "independent medical agency" have the meaning given by section 2 of the *Care Standards Act* 2000;
    "National Health Service body" means—
        (a) a Health Authority,
        (b) a National Health Service trust,
        (c) a Primary Care Trust, or
        (d) a Special Health Authority;
    "voluntary home" has the meaning given by section 60(3) of the *Children Act* 1989.
Defences to offences under this section

(11) Defence: Awareness of Condition

This creates a rebuttable presumption of fact if the defendant seeks to state that he **10–99** did not know about the mental disorder. If this evidential burden is discharged, it is then for the Prosecution to prove that he could reasonably be expected to know about the condition.

The provisions are repeated in each section at (subs.2) that creates an offence and states:

Sexual Offences Act 2003, ss.38(2), 39(2), 40(2), 41(2)

(2) Where in proceedings for an offence under this section it is proved that the other person had a mental disorder, it is to be taken that the defendant knew or could reasonably have been expected to know that that person had a mental disorder unless sufficient evidence is adduced to raise an issue as to whether he knew or could reasonably have been expected to know it.

(12) Marriage Exception

Sexual Offences Act 2003, s.43

Sections 38 to 41: marriage exception

43.—(1) Conduct by a person (A) which would otherwise be an offence under any of sections **10–100** 38 to 41 against another person (B) is not an offence under that section if at the time—
    (a) B is 16 or over, and
    (b) A and B are lawfully married.

(2) In proceedings for such an offence it is for the defendant to prove that A and B were lawfully married at the time.

(13) Existing sexual relationship

This defence is designed to not criminalise sexual relationships that pre-date the **10–101** legislation.

Sexual Offences Act 2003, s.44

Sections 38 to 41: sexual relationships which pre-date care relationships

44.—(1) Conduct by a person (A) which would otherwise be an offence under any of sections 38 to 41 against another person (B) is not an offence under that section if, immediately before A became involved in B's care in a way that falls within section 42, a sexual relationship existed between A and B.

(2) Subsection (1) does not apply if at that time sexual intercourse between A and B would have been unlawful.

(3) In proceedings for an offence under any of sections 38 to 41 it is for the defendant to prove that such a relationship existed at that time.

(14) Care Workers—Sexual Activity with a person with a mental disorder

10–102   The offence is committed where the care worker intentionally touches the mentally disordered person—touching as defined in s.78 of the Act, above.

(a) *Definition*

Sexual Offences Act 2003, s.38(1)

Care workers: sexual activity with a person with a mental disorder

0–102.1   **38.**—(1) A person (A) commits an offence if—

     (a) he intentionally touches another person (B),

     (b) the touching is sexual,

     (c) B has a mental disorder,

     (d) A knows or could reasonably be expected to know that B has a mental disorder, and

     (e) A is involved in B's care in a way that falls within section 42.

(b) *Venue and Sentence*

0–102.2   This offence is triable either way with a maximum sentence of six months imprisonment, if tried summarily. If however, one or more of the following factors is present, the offence *must* be tried on indictment:

     (a) penetration of B's anus or vagina

     (b) penetration of B's mouth with a person's penis

     (c) penetration of a person's anus or vagina with a part of B's body or by B with anything else

     (d) penetration of a person's mouth with B's penis.

(15) Care Workers—Causing or inciting sexual activity

10–103   This is where sexual activity as defined under s.78 of the Act above takes place, or incitement for such activity to take place, occurs.

(a) *Definition*

Sexual Offences Act 2003, s.39(1)

Care workers: causing or inciting sexual activity

0–103.1   **39.**—(1) A person (A) commits an offence if—

     (a) he intentionally causes or incites another person (B) to engage in an activity,

     (b) the activity is sexual,

     (c) B has a mental disorder,

     (d) A knows or could reasonably be expected to know that B has a mental disorder, and

(e) A is involved in B's care in a way that falls within section 42.

(b) *Venue and Sentence*

This offence is triable either way with a maximum sentence of six months imprison- **10–103.2**
ment, if tried summarily. If however, one or more of the following factors is present, the
offence *must* be tried on indictment:
  (a) penetration of B's anus or vagina
  (b) penetration of B's mouth with a person's penis
  (c) penetration of a person's anus or vagina with a part of B's body or by B with
      anything else
  (d) penetration of a person's mouth with B's penis.

(16) Care Workers—Sexual Activity in the presence of a person with a mental disorder

This offence is committed where a care worker commits a sexual act for his gratifica- **10–104**
tion, with the mentally disordered person present.

(a) *Definition*

Sexual Offences Act 2003, s.40(1)

Care workers: sexual activity in the presence of a person with a mental disorder
  40.—(1) A person (A) commits an offence if—   **10–104.1**
    (a) he intentionally engages in an activity,
    (b) the activity is sexual,
    (c) for the purpose of obtaining sexual gratification, he engages in it—
        (i) when another person (B) is present or is in a place from which A can be
            observed, and
        (ii) knowing or believing that B is aware, or intending that B should be aware,
             that he is engaging in it,
    (d) B has a mental disorder,
    (e) A knows or could reasonably be expected to know that B has a mental disorder,
        and
    (f) A is involved in B's care in a way that falls within section 42.

(b) *Venue and Sentence*

This offence is triable either way with a maximum sentence of six months imprison- **10–104.2**
ment, if tried summarily.

(17) Care Workers—Causing a person with a mental disorder to watch a sexual act

This offence is committed where the defendant causes the mentally disordered person **10–105**
to watch a third person to commit a sexual act, for the defendant's sexual gratification.

(a) *Definition*

Sexual Offences Act 2003, s.41(1)

Care workers: causing a person with a mental disorder to watch a sexual act
  41.—(1) A person (A) commits an offence if—   **10–106**
    (a) for the purpose of obtaining sexual gratification, he intentionally causes another
        person (B) to watch a third person engaging in an activity, or to look at an image
        of any person engaging in an activity,
    (b) the activity is sexual,

(c) B has a mental disorder,

(d) A knows or could reasonably be expected to know that B has a mental disorder, and

(e) A is involved in B's care in a way that falls within section 42.

(b) *Venue and Sentence*

10–106.1   This offence is triable either way with a maximum sentence of six months imprisonment, if tried summarily.

III. PROSTITUTION / PORNOGRAPHY OFFENCES

10–107   The new legislation takes a far more robust view of offences of this type.

(1) Taking or distributing indecent photographs of children

10–107.1   This offence is actually contained in s.1 of the *Protection of Children Act* 1978, but the *Sexual Offences Act* 2003 amends the legislation to make it an offence where the subject is under 18, rather than the previous age of 16.

Protection of Children Act 1978, s.1

Indecent photographs of children

1.—(1) Subject to sections 1A and 1B, it is an offence for a person—

    (a) to take, or permit to be taken or to make, any indecent photograph or pseudo-photograph of a child; or

    (b) to distribute or show such indecent photographs or pseudo-photographs; or

    (c) to have in his possession such indecent photographs or pseudo-photographs, with a view to their being distributed or shown by himself or others; or

    (d) to publish or cause to be published any advertisement likely to be understood as conveying that the advertiser distributes or shows such indecent photographs or pseudo-photographs, or intends to do so.

(2) For purposes of this Act, a person is to be regarded as distributing an indecent photograph or pseudo-photographs if he parts with possession of it to, or exposes or offers it for acquisition by, another person.

(3) Proceedings for an offence under this Act shall not be instituted except by or with the consent of the Director of Public Prosecutions.

(4) Where a person is charged with an offence under subsection (1)(b) or (c), it shall be a defence for him to prove—

    (a) that he had a legitimate reason for distributing or showing the photographs or pseudo-photographs or (as the case may be) having them in his possession; or

    (b) that he had not himself seen the photographs or pseudo-photographs and did not know, nor had any cause to suspect, them to be indecent.

(5) References in the *Children and Young Persons Act* 1933 (except in sections 15 and 99) to the offences mentioned in Schedule 1 to that Act shall include an offence under subsection (1)(a) above.

Sexual Offences Act 2003, s.45

Indecent photographs of persons aged 16 or 17

10–108   45.—(1) The *Protection of Children Act* 1978 (c. 37) (which makes provision about indecent photographs of persons under 16) is amended as follows.

(2) In section 2(3) (evidence) and section 7(6) (meaning of "child"), for "16" substitute "18".

(3) After section 1 insert—

"Marriage and other relationships

10–109   1A.—(1) This section applies where, in proceedings for an offence under section 1(1)(a) of taking or making an indecent photograph of a child, or for an offence under section 1(1)(b) or (c) relating to an indecent photograph of a child, the defendant proves that the photograph was of the child aged 16 or over, and that at the time of the offence charged the child and he—

(a) were married, or

(b) lived together as partners in an enduring family relationship.

(2) Subsections (5) and (6) also apply where, in proceedings for an offence under section 1(1)(b) or (c) relating to an indecent photograph of a child, the defendant proves that the photograph was of the child aged 16 or over, and that at the time when he obtained it the child and he—

(a) were married, or

(b) lived together as partners in an enduring family relationship.

(3) This section applies whether the photograph showed the child alone or with the defendant, but not if it showed any other person.

10–110 —(4) In the case of an offence under section 1(1)(a), if sufficient evidence is adduced to raise an issue as to whether the child consented to the photograph being taken or made, or as to whether the defendant reasonably believed that the child so consented, the defendant is not guilty of the offence unless it is proved that the child did not so consent and that the defendant did not reasonably believe that the child so consented.

(5) In the case of an offence under section 1(1)(b), the defendant is not guilty of the offence unless it is proved that the showing or distributing was to a person other than the child.

(6) In the case of an offence under section 1(1)(c), if sufficient evidence is adduced to raise an issue both—

(a) as to whether the child consented to the photograph being in the defendant's possession, or as to whether the defendant reasonably believed that the child so consented, and

(b) as to whether the defendant had the photograph in his possession with a view to its being distributed or shown to anyone other than the child,

the defendant is not guilty of the offence unless it is proved either that the child did not so consent and that the defendant did not reasonably believe that the child so consented, or that the defendant had the photograph in his possession with a view to its being distributed or shown to a person other than the child."

(4) After section 160 of the *Criminal Justice Act* 1988 (c. 33) (possession of indecent photograph of child) insert—

The legislation also provides for a defence of marriage. If at the time of the charge (note, not the time of the photographs creation), the subject and the defendant are married; the defence of marriage is valid. Further, the photograph must show the subject alone or with the defendant, not any third party.

The act of distribution must be to someone other than the child subject.

In terms of consent, where the charge is one of taking a photo, the evidential burden lies upon the defendant to show that subject consented or they reasonably believe that to be so. It is for the prosecution to rebut that. Where the charge is under s.1(1)(c) the prosecution must prove absence of consent.

(2) Possession of an indecent photograph of a child

10–111 In much the same way that the new legislation amends the *POCA* 1978, above, s.160 the *CJA* 1988 has also been amended to include subjects aged 17 and 18.

Criminal Justice Act 1988, s.160A

Marriage and other relationships

10–112 **160A.**—(1) This section applies where, in proceedings for an offence under section 160 relating to an indecent photograph of a child, the defendant proves that the photograph was of the child aged 16 or over, and that at the time of the offence charged the child and he—

(a) were married, or

(b) lived together as partners in an enduring family relationship.

(2) This section also applies where, in proceedings for an offence under section 160 re-

lating to an indecent photograph of a child, the defendant proves that the photograph was of the child aged 16 or over, and that at the time when he obtained it the child and he—

    (a) were married, or

    (b) lived together as partners in an enduring family relationship.

(3) This section applies whether the photograph showed the child alone or with the defendant, but not if it showed any other person.

(4) If sufficient evidence is adduced to raise an issue as to whether the child consented to the photograph being in the defendant's possession, or as to whether the defendant reasonably believed that the child so consented, the defendant is not guilty of the offence unless it is proved that the child did not so consent and that the defendant did not reasonably believe that the child so consented."

10–113   In terms of defences, the existing one contained in s.160(2) of the Act is retained.

A new defence of marriage is added—If at the time of the charge (note, not the time of the photographs creation), the subject and the defendant are married; the defence of marriage is valid. Further, the photograph must show the subject alone or with the defendant, not any third party.

In terms of consent, where the charge is one of taking a photo, the evidential burden lies upon the defendant to show that subject consented or they reasonably believe that to be so. If the defendant is able to do so, this will act as a defence unless the prosecution are able to rebut the assertion.

(3) Paying for the sexual services of a child

10–114   This offence has been written quite widely to encompass any form of payment (including non-monetary) to procure the services of a child for sex.

(a) *Definition*

Sexual Offences Act 2003, s.47(1)–(2)

Paying for sexual services of a child

10–115   47.—(1) A person (A) commits an offence if—

    (a) he intentionally obtains for himself the sexual services of another person (B),

    (b) before obtaining those services, he has made or promised payment for those services to B or a third person, or knows that another person has made or promised such a payment, and

    (c) either—

       (i) B is under 18, and A does not reasonably believe that B is 18 or over, or

       (ii) B is under 13.

(2) In this section, "payment" means any financial advantage, including the discharge of an obligation to pay or the provision of goods or services (including sexual services) gratuitously or at a discount.

(b) *The Child's Age*

10–116   If the child is aged between 13 and 17 and the defendant raises the issue that they believed that child was over 18, it is for the prosecution to prove that this belief was not reasonably held.

Where a child is under 13, there is no issue as to the defendant's belief; this element of the offence will have been committed.

(c) *Venue and Sentence*

10–117   This offence is triable either way with a maximum sentence of six months imprisonment, if tried summarily. If however, one or more of the following factors is present, the offence *must* be tried on indictment:

    (a) penetration of B's anus or vagina

    (b) penetration of B's mouth with a person's penis

(c) penetration of a person's anus or vagina with a part of B's body or by B with anything else

(d) penetration of a person's mouth with B's penis.

(4) Causing or inciting child prostitution or pornography

This offence has been created to prosecute those who recruit children into pornography or prostitution when they are not currently involved in it.   **10–118**

(a) *Definition*

Sexual Offences Act 2003, s.48(1)

Causing or inciting child prostitution or pornography

48.—(1) A person (A) commits an offence if—   **10–119**

    (a) he intentionally causes or incites another person (B) to become a prostitute, or to be involved in pornography, in any part of the world, and

    (b) either—

        (i) B is under 18, and A does not reasonably believe that B is 18 or over, or

        (ii) B is under 13.

Pornography is defined at s.51(1) as: **10–119.1**

Sexual Offences Act 2003, s.51(1)

Sections 48 to 50: interpretation

51.—(1) For the purposes of sections 48 to 50, a person is involved in pornography if an indecent image of that person is recorded; and similar expressions, and "pornography", are to be interpreted accordingly.

Prostitute is defined at s.51(2) as: **10–119.2**

Sexual Offences Act 2003, s.51(2)

Sections 48 to 50: interpretation

51.—(2) In those sections "prostitute" means a person (A) who, on at least one occasion and whether or not compelled to do so, offers or provides sexual services to another person in return for payment or a promise of payment to A or a third person; and "prostitution" is to be interpreted accordingly.

(b) *The Child's Age*

If the child is aged between 13 and 17 and the defendant raises the issue that they believed that child was over 18, it is for the prosecution to prove that this belief was not reasonably held.   **10–120**

Where a child is under 13, there is no issue as to the defendant's belief; this element of the offence will have been committed.

(c) *Venue and Sentence*

This offence is triable either way with a maximum sentence of six months imprisonment, if tried summarily.   **10–120.1**

(5) Causing or inciting prostitution for gain

This offence is committed where the defendant intentionally causes or incites another into prostitution for his or a third parties gain, where gain is widely defined.   **10–121**

(a) *Definition*

Sexual Offences Act 2003, s.52(1)

Causing or inciting prostitution for gain

52.—(1) A person commits an offence if—   **10–122**

    (a) he intentionally causes or incites another person to become a prostitute in any part of the world, and

    (b) he does so for or in the expectation of gain for himself or a third person.

10–123   Gain is defined as:

Sexual Offences Act 2003, s.54

Sections 52 and 53: interpretation

    54.—(1) In sections 52 and 53, "gain" means—

        (a) any financial advantage, including the discharge of an obligation to pay or the provision of goods or services (including sexual services) gratuitously or at a discount; or

        (b) the goodwill of any person which is or appears likely, in time, to bring financial advantage.

    (2) In those sections "prostitute" and "prostitution" have the meaning given by section 51(2).

(b) *Venue and Sentence*

10–123.1   This offence is triable either way with a maximum sentence of six months imprisonment, if tried summarily.

(6) Controlling a child prostitute or a child involved in pornography

10–124   This offence relates to a person controlling the activities of a child under 18. It has been drawn widely to encompass any activity of this sort, even if the child is under the control of others.

(a) *Definition*

Sexual Offences Act 2003, s.49(1)

Controlling a child prostitute or a child involved in pornography

10–125   **49.**—(1) A person (A) commits an offence if—

    (a) he intentionally controls any of the activities of another person (B) relating to B's prostitution or involvement in pornography in any part of the world, and

    (b) either—

        (i) B is under 18, and A does not reasonably believe that B is 18 or over, or

        (ii) B is under 13.

(b) *The Child's Age*

10–125.1   If the child is aged between 13 and 17 and the defendant raises the issue that they believed that child was over 18, it is for the prosecution to prove that this belief was not reasonably held.

    Where a child is under 13, there is no issue as to the defendant's belief; this element of the offence will have been committed.

(c) *Venue and Sentence*

10–125.2   This offence is triable either way with a maximum sentence of six months imprisonment, if tried summarily.

(7) Arranging or facilitating child prostitution or pornography

10–126   This offence is committed where a person is involved in any way with child prostitution or pornography. The offence has been drawn widely to cover any activity within this area.

(a) *Definition*

Sexual Offences Act 2003, s.50(1)

Arranging or facilitating child prostitution or pornography

50.—(1) A person (A) commits an offence if—   **10–127**
    (a) he intentionally arranges or facilitates the prostitution or involvement in pornography in any part of the world of another person (B), and
    (b) either—
        (i) B is under 18, and A does not reasonably believe that B is 18 or over, or
        (ii) B is under 13.

(b) *The Child's Age*

If the child is aged between 13 and 17 and the defendant raises the issue that they **10–128** believed that child was over 18, it is for the prosecution to prove that this belief was not reasonably held.

Where a child is under 13, there is no issue as to the defendant's belief; this element of the offence will have been committed.

(c) *Venue and Sentence*

This offence is triable either way with a maximum sentence of six months imprison- **10–129** ment, if tried summarily.

(8) Controlling Prostitution for a gain

This offence is where the control leads to a gain.   **10–130**

(a) *Definition*

Sexual Offences Act 2003, ss.53(1), 54

Controlling prostitution for gain

53.—(1) A person commits an offence if—   **10–131**
    (a) he intentionally controls any of the activities of another person relating to that person's prostitution in any part of the world, and
    (b) he does so for or in the expectation of gain for himself or a third person.

Gain is defined as: **10–132**

Sections 52 and 53: interpretation

54.—(1) In sections 52 and 53, "gain" means—
    (a) any financial advantage, including the discharge of an obligation to pay or the provision of goods or services (including sexual services) gratuitously or at a discount; or
    (b) the goodwill of any person which is or appears likely, in time, to bring financial advantage.

(2) In those sections "prostitute" and "prostitution" have the meaning given by section 51(2).

(9) Keeping a brothel used for prostitution

Amends s.33 to add s.33A of the *Sexual Offences Act* 1956.   **10–133**
Adds the meaning of prostitute at s.51(2) of the *SOA* 2003.

(10) Trafficking into, within and out of the UK for sexual exploitation

Three separate sections create offences of trafficking into (s.57), within (s.58) and out **10–134** of (s.59) the UK.

(a) Definition

Sexual Offences Act 2003, ss.57(1), 58(1), 59(1)

Trafficking into the UK for sexual exploitation

10–135   **57.**—(1) A person commits an offence if he intentionally arranges or facilitates the arrival in the United Kingdom of another person (B) and eithe—

     (a) he intends to do anything to or in respect of B, after B's arrival but in any part of the world, which if done will involve the commission of a relevant offence, or

     (b) he believes that another person is likely to do something to or in respect of B, after B's arrival but in any part of the world, which if done will involve the commission of a relevant offence.

Trafficking within the UK for sexual exploitation

10–136   **58.**—(1) A person commits an offence if he intentionally arranges or facilitates travel within the United Kingdom by another person (B) and either—

     (a) he intends to do anything to or in respect of B, during or after the journey and in any part of the world, which if done will involve the commission of a relevant offence, or

     (b) he believes that another person is likely to do something to or in respect of B, during or after the journey and in any part of the world, which if done will involve the commission of a relevant offence.

Trafficking out of the UK for sexual exploitation

10–137   **59.**—(1) A person commits an offence if he intentionally arranges or facilitates the departure from the United Kingdom of another person (B) and either—

     (a) he intends to do anything to or in respect of B, after B's departure but in any part of the world, which if done will involve the commission of a relevant offence, or

     (b) he believes that another person is likely to do something to or in respect of B, after B's departure but in any part of the world, which if done will involve the commission of a relevant offence.

(11) Relevant Offence and Jurisdiction

10–138   The provisions as to what a relevant offence is are set out at s.60(1) of the act. Section 60 further considers issues of jurisdiction.

Sexual Offences Act 2003, s.60

Sections 57 to 59: interpretation and jurisdiction

10–139   **60.**—(1) In sections 57 to 59, "relevant offence" means—

     (a) an offence under this Part,

     (b) an offence under section 1(1)(a) of the *Protection of Children Act* 1978 (c. 37),

     (c) an offence listed in Schedule 1 to the *Criminal Justice (Children) (Northern Ireland) Order* 1998 (S.I. 1998/1504 (N.I. 9)),

     (d) an offence under Article 3(1)(a) of the *Protection of Children (Northern Ireland) Order* 1978 (S.I. 1978/1047 (N.I. 17)), or

     (e) anything done outside England and Wales and Northern Ireland which is not an offence within any of paragraphs (a) to (d) but would be if done in England and Wales or Northern Ireland.

     (2) Sections 57 to 59 apply to anything done—

     (a) in the United Kingdom, or

     (b) outside the United Kingdom, by a body incorporated under the law of a part of the United Kingdom or by an individual to whom subsection (3) applies.

     (3) This subsection applies to—

     (a) a British citizen,

     (b) a British overseas territories citizen,

     (c) a British National (Overseas),

(d) a British Overseas citizen,

(e) a person who is a British subject under the *British Nationality Act* 1981 (c. 61),

(f) a British protected person within the meaning given by section 50(1) of that Act.

(a) *Venue and Sentence*

This offence is triable either way with a maximum sentence of six months imprison-   **10–140**
ment, a fine, or both; if tried summarily.

(12) Administering a substance with intent

This offence can be charged alongside other offences where a 'date-rape' type drug   **10–141**
or any other substance has been given to the complainant, either directly or indirectly
but at the defendant's behest.

(a) *Definition*

Sexual Offences Act 2003, s.61(1)

Administering a substance with intent

61.—(1) A person commits an offence if he intentionally administers a substance to, or causes   **10–142**
a substance to be taken by, another person (B)—

    (a) knowing that B does not consent, and

    (b) with the intention of stupefying or overpowering B, so as to enable any person to
    engage in a sexual activity that involves B.

(b) *Venue and Sentence*

This offence is triable either way with a maximum sentence of six months imprison-   **10–142.1**
ment or a fine, or both, if tried summarily.

(13) Committing an offence with intent to commit a sexual offence

(a) *Definition*

Sexual Offences Act 2003, s.62(1)–(2)

Committing an offence with intent to commit a sexual offence

62.—(1) A person commits an offence under this section if he commits any offence with the   **10–143**
intention of committing a relevant sexual offence.

(2) In this section, "relevant sexual offence" means any offence under this Part (including an offence of aiding, abetting, counselling or procuring such an offence).

(b) *Venue and Sentence*

This offence is triable either way with a maximum sentence of six months imprison-   **10–143.1**
ment, if tried summarily.

Where the offence is committed by kidnapping or false imprisonment, the matter
must be tried in the Crown Court.

(14) Trespass with intent to commit a sexual offence

(a) *Definition*

Sexual Offences Act 2003, s.63

Trespass with intent to commit a sexual offence

63.—(1) A person commits an offence if—   **10–144**

    (a) he is a trespasser on any premises,

(b) he intends to commit a relevant sexual offence on the premises, and

(c) he knows that, or is reckless as to whether, he is a trespasser.

(2) In this section—

"premises" includes a structure or part of a structure;

"relevant sexual offence" has the same meaning as in s.62;

"structure" includes a tent, vehicle or vessel or other temporary or movable structure.

(b) *Venue and Sentence*

10–144.1   This offence is triable either way with a maximum sentence of six months imprisonment, if tried summarily.

(15) Sex with an adult relative

10–144.2   The act defines two offences, one of penetration and the other of another consenting to the complainant penetrating them.

(a) *Definition*

Sexual Offences Act 2003, ss.64(1)–(4), 65(1)–(4)

Sex with an adult relative: penetration

10–145   **64.**—(1) A person aged 16 or over (A) commits an offence if—

(a) he intentionally penetrates another person's vagina or anus with a part of his body or anything else, or penetrates another person's mouth with his penis,

(b) the penetration is sexual,

(c) the other person (B) is aged 18 or over,

(d) A is related to B in a way mentioned in subsection (2), and

(e) A knows or could reasonably be expected to know that he is related to B in that way.

(2) The ways that A may be related to B are as parent, grandparent, child, grandchild, brother, sister, half-brother, half-sister, uncle, aunt, nephew or niece.

(3) In subsection (2)—

(a) "uncle" means the brother of a person's parent, and "aunt" has a corresponding meaning;

(b) "nephew" means the child of a person's brother or sister, and "niece" has a corresponding meaning.

(4) Where in proceedings for an offence under this section it is proved that the defendant was related to the other person in any of those ways, it is to be taken that the defendant knew or could reasonably have been expected to know that he was related in that way unless sufficient evidence is adduced to raise an issue as to whether he knew or could reasonably have been expected to know that he was.

Sex with an adult relative: consenting to penetration

10–146   **65.**—(1) A person aged 16 or over (A) commits an offence if—

(a) another person (B) penetrates A's vagina or anus with a part of B's body or anything else, or penetrates A's mouth with B's penis,

(b) A consents to the penetration,

(c) the penetration is sexual,

(d) B is aged 18 or over,

(e) A is related to B in a way mentioned in subsection (2), and

(f) A knows or could reasonably be expected to know that he is related to B in that way.

(2) The ways that A may be related to B are as parent, grandparent, child, grandchild, brother, sister, half-brother, half-sister, uncle, aunt, nephew or niece.

(3) In subsection (2)—

(a) "uncle" means the brother of a person's parent, and "aunt" has a corresponding meaning;

(b) "nephew" means the child of a person's brother or sister, and "niece" has a corresponding meaning.

(4) Where in proceedings for an offence under this section it is proved that the defendant was related to the other person in any of those ways, it is to be taken that the defendant knew or could reasonably have been expected to know that he was related in that way unless sufficient evidence is adduced to raise an issue as to whether he knew or could reasonably have been expected to know that he was.

(b) *Venue and Sentence*

Both of these offences are triable either way with a maximum sentence of six months **10–146.1** imprisonment or a fine, if tried summarily.

(16) Exposure

(a) *Definition*

Sexual Offences Act 2003, s.66(1)–(2)

Exposure
 66.—(1) A person commits an offence if—   **10–147**
  (a) he intentionally exposes his genitals, and
  (b) he intends that someone will see them and be caused alarm or distress.
 (2) A person guilty of an offence under this section is liable—

(b) *Venue and Sentence*

This offence is triable either way with a maximum sentence of six months imprison- **10–147.1** ment or a fine, if tried summarily.

(17) Voyeurism

(a) *Definition*

Sexual Offences Act 2003, ss.67(1)–(4), 68

Voyeurism
 67.—(1) A person commits an offence if—   **10–148**
  (a) for the purpose of obtaining sexual gratification, he observes another person doing a private act, and
  (b) he knows that the other person does not consent to being observed for his sexual gratification.
 (2) A person commits an offence if—
  (a) he operates equipment with the intention of enabling another person to observe, for the purpose of obtaining sexual gratification, a third person (B) doing a private act, and
  (b) he knows that B does not consent to his operating equipment with that intention.
 (3) A person commits an offence if—
  (a) he records another person (B) doing a private act,
  (b) he does so with the intention that he or a third person will, for the purpose of obtaining sexual gratification, look at an image of B doing the act, and
  (c) he knows that B does not consent to his recording the act with that intention.
 (4) A person commits an offence if he instals equipment, or constructs or adapts a structure or part of a structure, with the intention of enabling himself or another person to commit an offence under subsection (1).

Voyeurism: interpretation
 68.—(1) For the purposes of section 67, a person is doing a private act if the person is in a **10–149** place which, in the circumstances, would reasonably be expected to provide privacy, and—
  (a) the person's genitals, buttocks or breasts are exposed or covered only with underwear,

(b) the person is using a lavatory, or

(c) the person is doing a sexual act that is not of a kind ordinarily done in public.

(2) In section 67, "structure" includes a tent, vehicle or vessel or other temporary or movable structure.

(b) *Venue and Sentence*

10–149.1　　This offence is triable either way with a maximum sentence of six months imprisonment or a fine, if tried summarily.

(18) Intercourse with an animal

(a) *Definition*

Sexual Offences Act 2003, s.69

Intercourse with an animal

10–150　　69.—(1) A person commits an offence if—

(a) he intentionally performs an act of penetration with his penis,

(b) what is penetrated is the vagina or anus of a living animal, and

(c) he knows that, or is reckless as to whether, that is what is penetrated.

(2) A person (A) commits an offence if—

(a) A intentionally causes, or allows, A's vagina or anus to be penetrated,

(b) the penetration is by the penis of a living animal, and

(c) A knows that, or is reckless as to whether, that is what A is being penetrated by.

(3) A person guilty of an offence under this section is liable—

(a) on summary conviction, to imprisonment for a term not exceeding 6 months or a fine not exceeding the statutory maximum or both;

(b) on conviction on indictment, to imprisonment for a term not exceeding 2 years.

(b) *Venue and Sentence*

10–150.1　　This offence is triable either way with a maximum sentence of six months imprisonment or a fine, if tried summarily.

(19) Sexual penetration of a corpse

(a) *Definition*

Sexual Offences Act 2003, s.70(1)

Sexual penetration of a corpse

10–151　　70.—(1) A person commits an offence if—

(a) he intentionally performs an act of penetration with a part of his body or anything else,

(b) what is penetrated is a part of the body of a dead person,

(c) he knows that, or is reckless as to whether, that is what is penetrated, and

(d) the penetration is sexual.

(b) *Venue and Sentence*

10–151.1　　This offence is triable either way with a maximum sentence of six months imprisonment or a fine, if tried summarily.

(20) Sexual Activity in a pubic lavatory

(a) *Definition*

Sexual Offences Act 2003, s.71(1)–(2)

Sexual activity in a public lavatory

71.—(1) A person commits an offence if— **10–152**
    (a) he is in a lavatory to which the public or a section of the public has or is permitted to have access, whether on payment or otherwise,
    (b) he intentionally engages in an activity, and,
    (c) the activity is sexual.

(2) For the purposes of this section, an activity is sexual if a reasonable person would, in all the circumstances but regardless of any person's purpose, consider it to be sexual.

(b) *Venue and Sentence*

This offence is triable either way with a maximum sentence of six months imprison- **10–153** ment or a fine, if tried summarily.

CHAPTER 11

PROPERTY OFFENCES

I. OFFENCES UNDER THE THEFT ACTS 1968 AND 1978

A. THEFT

(a) *Definition*

Theft Act 1968, s.1

Basic definition of theft

1.—(1) A person is guilty of theft if he dishonestly appropriates property belonging to an- **11–1**

other with the intention of permanently depriving the other of it; and "thief" and "steal" shall be construed accordingly.

(2) It is immaterial whether the appropriation is made with a view to gain, or is made for the thief's own benefit.

(3) The five following sections of this Act shall have effect as regards the interpretation and operation of this section (and, except as otherwise provided by this Act, shall apply only for purposes of this section).

(b) *Procedure*

11–2   Theft is triable either way: *Magistrates' Courts Act* 1980, s.17(1) and Sch.1. The *Practice Direction (Criminal Proceedings: Consolidation)*, Pt V.51 *(Mode of Trial)* states that theft should be tried summarily unless one of the following aggravating features is present and that its sentencing powers are insufficient:

     (a) breach of trust by a person of substantial authority, or in whom a high degree of trust is placed

     (b) theft or fraud which has been committed or disguised in a sophisticated manner

     (c) theft or fraud committed by an organised gang

     (d) the victim is particularly vulnerable to theft or fraud, *e.g.* the elderly and the infirm

     (e) the unrecovered property is of high value (£10,000 or more)

The prosecution must prove that the defendant:

— dishonestly

— appropriated

— property

— belonging to another

— With the intention to permanently deprive the other of that property.

(c) *Elements of the offence*

Dishonestly

Theft Act 1968, s.2

"Dishonestly"

11–3   2.—(1) A person's appropriation of property belonging to another is not to be regarded as dishonest—

     (a) if he appropriates the property in the belief that he has in law the right to deprive the other of it, on behalf of himself or of a third person; or

     (b) if he appropriates the property in the belief that he would have the other's consent if the other knew of the appropriation and the circumstances of it; or

     (c) (except where the property came to him as trustee or personal representative) if he appropriates the property in the belief that the person to whom the property belongs cannot be discovered by taking reasonable steps.

(2) A person's appropriation of property belonging to another may be dishonest notwithstanding that he is willing to pay for the property.

The test of dishonestly is that contained in *R. v Feely* [1973] Q.B. 530 and *R. v Ghosh* [1982] Q.B. 1053, 75 Cr.App.R. 154, CA. The relevant test is to consider the conduct of the defendant by the standards of reasonable and honest people. If the conduct is not found dishonest by these standards then the prosecution will fail. If the conduct is found to be dishonest, the next stage is to consider whether the defendant himself realised that his conduct was dishonest by those standards. If so, then the defendant will be held to have been acting dishonestly. The second question need only be considered when the defendant raises this issue: *R. v Price* (1990) 90 Cr.App.R. 409.

Claim of right

11–4   Section 2(1) offers three occasions when the defendant's appropriation is not to be considered as dishonest. To come within the terms of s.2(1)(a) the defendant must believe that in law he had the right to deprive the other of his property: *R. v Bernard*, 26 Cr.App.R. 137, CCA. It does not matter that there is no basis in law for such a belief: *Bernard*, above, though belief in a moral right is no defence: *Harris v Harrison* [1963] Crim.L.R. 497, DC. See further *Archbold Crown*, §§ 21–24—21–31.

Appropriates

Theft Act 1968, s.3

"Appropriates"

3.—(1) Any assumption by a person of the rights of an owner amounts to an appropriation, **11–5** and this includes, where he has come by the property (innocently or not) without stealing it, any later assumption of a right to it by keeping or dealing with it as owner.

(2) Where property or a right or interest in property is or purports to be transferred for value to a person acting in good faith, no later assumption by him of rights which he believed himself to be acquiring shall, by reason of any defect in the transferor's title, amount to theft of the property.

Appropriation will be established by the assumption of any of the owner's rights in the goods in question. It is not necessary to show assumption of all of the owner's rights: *R. v Morris* [1984] A.C. 320, HL. It is not necessary to show that the appropriation was without the consent of the owner: *Lawrence v Metropolitan Police Comer* [1972] A.C. 626, HL; *R. v Gomez* [1993] A.C. 442, HL; *R. v Hinks* [2001] 2 A.C. 241.

Gifts

Following the majority decision of the House of Lords in *R. v Hinks* (2001) 2 A.C. **11–6** 241, HL, it is now established that where the defence to a charge of theft is that the property is question was given as a gift, the question of the belief in the owner's consent to the giving of the gift is only relevant to the question of dishonesty. Hence the acquisition of indefeasible title to property is capable of amounting to an appropriation of property belonging to another for the purposes of the offence of theft. See further *Archbold Crown*, §§ 21–31—21–47.

Property

Theft Act 1968, s.4

"Property"

4.—(1) "Property" includes money and all other property, real or personal, including things **11–7** in action and other intangible property.

(2) A person cannot steal land, or things forming part of land and severed from it by him or by his directions, except in the following cases, that is to say—

 (a) when he is a trustee or personal representative, or is authorised by power of attorney, or as liquidator of a company, or otherwise, to sell or dispose of land belonging to another, and he appropriates the land or anything forming part of it by dealing with it in breach of the confidence reposed in him; or

 (b) when he is not in possession of the land and appropriates anything forming part of the land by severing it or causing it to be severed, or after it has been severed; or

 (c) when, being in possession of the land under a tenancy, he appropriates the whole or part of any fixture or structure let to be used with the land.

For purposes of this subsection "land" does not include incorporeal hereditaments; "tenancy" means a tenancy for years or any less period and includes an agreement for such a tenancy, but a person who after the end of a tenancy remains in possession as statutory tenant or otherwise is to be treated as having possession under the tenancy, and "let" shall be construed accordingly.

(3) A person who picks mushrooms growing wild on any land, or who picks flowers,

fruit or foliage from a plant growing wild on any land, does not (although not in possession of the land) steal what he picks, unless he does it for reward or for sale or other commercial purpose.

For purposes of this subsection "mushroom" includes any fungus, and "plant" includes any
shrub or tree.

(4) Wild creatures, tamed or untamed, shall be regarded as property; but a person cannot steal a wild creature not tamed nor ordinarily kept in captivity, or the carcase of any
such creature, unless either it has been reduced into possession by or on behalf of another
person and possession of it has not since been lost or abandoned, or another person is in
course of reducing it into possession.

Things or choses in action

11–8   A chose in action is a right over property which can only be claimed or enforced by
action, rather than by taking physical possession. A debt owed by a bank to a customer
is a chose in action and can hence be appropriated. In *R. v Kohn*, 69 Cr.App.R. 395,
CA, the defendant drew cheques on the account of a company of which he was a director for the benefit of various third parties. However the cheques were intended for the
benefit of the defendant, who was charged with theft of the chose in action (being the
debt owed by the bank to the company) and theft of the cheque (being the property of
the company). Where the account was in credit, or within the agreed overdraft limit
(where the bank had an obligation to honour the cheques drawn) it was held that the
defendant had appropriated a chose in action. Where the account was beyond the
agreed overdraft limit (where the bank had no such obligation to honour the cheques
drawn) it was held that there could be no appropriation as there was no chosen action.

Intangible property

11–9   Confidential information per se will not be classed as property for the purposes of
s.4(1): *Oxford v Moss* 68 Cr.App.R. 183, DC. In *Att.-Gen. for Hong Kong v Nai-
Keung* (1987) 1 W.L.R. 1339, PC, export quotas which were transferable for value in a
temporary or permanent basis were property within the meaning of a provision identi-
cally worded to s.4(1) of the 1968 Act. See further *Archbold Crown*, §§ 21–48—21–57.

Belonging to another

Theft Act 1968, s.5

"Belonging to another"

11–10   **5.**—(1) Property shall be regarded as belonging to any person having possession or control of
it, or having in it any proprietary right or interest (not being an equitable interest arising only
from an agreement to transfer or grant an interest).

(2) Where property is subject to a trust, the persons to whom it belongs shall be
regarded as including any person having a right to enforce the trust, and an intention to
defeat the trust shall be regarded accordingly as an intention to deprive of the property
any person having that right.

(3) Where a person receives property from or on account of another, and is under an
obligation to the other to retain and deal with that property or its proceeds in a particular
way, the property or proceeds shall be regarded (as against him) as belonging to the other.

(4) Where a person gets property by another's mistake, and is under an obligation to
make restoration (in whole or in part) of the property or its proceeds or of the value
thereof, then to the extent of that obligation the property or proceeds shall be regarded (as
against him) as belonging to the person entitled to restoration, and an intention not to
make restoration shall be regarded accordingly as an intention to deprive that person of
the property or proceeds.

(5) Property of a corporation sole shall be regarded as belonging to the corporation
notwithstanding a vacancy in the corporation.

11–11   Property will belong to any person who has possession or control of it, or any proprietary right or interest in it, other than an equitable proprietary interest arising from an agreement to transfer or grant an interest. Train tickets purchased from travellers and then sold on will be deemed to remain the property of the train company who issued the tickets, as they retain a proprietary interest in the tickets after their purchase by a customer. Buying and then selling on such tickets will constitute theft: *R. v Marshall* [1998] 2 Cr.App.R. 282, CA.

A company partner, who has a proprietary interest in the shares of the company may steal such shares as the other partner also have a proprietary interest in the shares: *R. v Bonner* (1970) 1 W.L.R. 838.

Things which have been abandoned are not capable of being stolen: *R. v White* 7 Cr.App.R. 266, CCA.

As regards s.5(3) the 'obligation' must be a legal one, as opposed to a social or moral one: *R. v Gilks*, 56 Cr.App.R. 734, CA; *R. v Klineberg and Marsden* [1999] 1 Cr.App.R. 427, CA. The obligation must also be one of which the defendant was aware: *R. v Wills*, 92 Cr.App.R. 297, CA. As regards s.5(4) the obligation to make restoration of another's property got by mistake must be a legal one: *R. v Gilks* (above). See further *Archbold Crown*, §§ 21–58—21–76.

With the intention of permanently depriving the other of it

Theft Act 1968, s.6

"With the intention of permanently depriving the other of it"

6.—(1) A person appropriating property belonging to another without meaning the other   **11–12**
permanently to lose the thing itself is nevertheless to be regarded as having the intention of permanently depriving the other of it if his intention is to treat the thing as his own to dispose of regardless of the other's rights; and a borrowing or lending of it may amount to so treating it if, but only if, the borrowing or lending is for a period and in circumstances making it equivalent to an outright taking or disposal.

(2) Without prejudice to the generality of subsection (1) above, where a person, having possession or control (lawfully or not) of property belonging to another, parts with the property under a condition as to its return which he may not be able to perform, this (if done for purposes of his own and without the other's authority) amounts to treating the property as his own to dispose of regardless of the other's rights.

In *R. v Fernandes* [1996] 1 Cr.App.R. 175, CA, the Court held that s.6 should not   **11–13**
be given a restrictive interpretation, and that the critical notion is whether the 'defendant intended to treat the thing as his own to dispose of regardless of the other's rights' The second limb of subss.(1) and (2) are to be construed as illustrations of this general principle.

A defendant who obtains a cheque dishonestly from another with the intention of presenting the cheque for payment will not be found to have the necessary intention to permanently deprive the owner of the cheque as the cheque form will be returned to the owner via his bank following presentation of the cheque: *R. v Preddy and Slade, R. v Dillon* (1996) A.C. 815, HL. This lacuna has now been filled by s.15A of the *Theft Act* 1968, see § 11–59 below.

A conditional appropriation will not suffice to establish the offence of theft: *R. v Easom* [1971] 2 Q.B. 315, CA. See further *Archbold Crown*, §§ 21–76—21–83.

(d) *Sentence*

When tried summarily the maximum penalty for this offence is imprisonment for a   **11–14**
term not exceeding six months or a fine not exceeding the statutory maximum, or both (*TA* 1968, s.1(7)).

The *Magistrates' Court Sentencing Guidelines on Theft* (2003) state:

Aggravating factors include the high value of goods stolen, planned, sophisticated, adult involving children, organised team, related damage, vulnerable victim, offence committed on bail and previous convictions and failure to respond to previous sentences (if relevant.)

Mitigating factors include impulsive action and the low value of the goods stolen.
Guideline: Is it serious enough to warrant a community penalty?

11–15   The *Magistrates' Court Sentencing Guidelines on Theft in Breach of Trust* (2003) state that:

Aggravating factors include casting suspicion on others, racial aggravation, committed over a period, high value, organised team, planned, senior employee, sophisticated, vulnerable victim, offence committed on bail, relevant previous convictions and any failures to respond to previous sentences.

Mitigating factors include impulsive action, low value of goods taken, previous inconsistent attitude of employer, single item and unsupported junior.

Thieves who steal from shops should be committed to the Crown Court where there is evidence of careful planning and the incident involves removal of goods of some value: *R. v Bailey* (1993) 15 Cr.App.R.(S.) 27. Custodial sentences are generally not thought appropriate for petty thefts, such as shoplifting. In *R. v Bond* (1994) 15 Cr.App.R.(S.) 430, the offender pleaded guilty to theft of goods worth about £3.50 from a shop. The Court of Appeal substituted a probation order of twelve months' duration for the offender's original sentence of three months' imprisonment on the ground that the offence was not so serious that only a custodial sentence could be justified. Custodial sentences for pick pocketing have been upheld by the Court of Appeal when the offender had a record of similar offending (*R. v Mullins* [2000] 2 Cr.App.R. 372 (sentence of three years imprisonment imposed for pick pocketing when offender had 36 previous convictions.) However, isolated actions of pick pocketing committed by one individual should not attract a heavy custodial sentence (*Masagh* (1990-91) 12 Cr.App.R.(S.) 568: sentence of eighteen months' imprisonment reduced to four months' imprisonment).

11–16   In *R. v Flynn and Flynn* (1993) 14 Cr.App.R.(S.) 422 the offenders stole furniture from an elderly couple with a view to persuading them to buy replacements. Their original sentences of six months' and eight months' imprisonment respectively were reduced to three months and four months' imprisonment on appeal, the Court stating that an isolated theft of property worth about £30 (the estimated value of the couple's furniture) would not normally attract a custodial sentence, but this was not a straightforward case of petty dishonesty, as it involved an elderly couple being intimidated in their own home.

Theft from a public telephone box, where the offence is pre-planned and involves a degree of specialist knowledge will warrant a custodial sentence. In *R. v Ulus Arslan* (1994) 15 Cr.App.R.(S.) 90, whilst on bail, the offender had drilled through the back of the cash box in the early hours of the morning and stolen £82. He was sentenced to four months' imprisonment.

Theft of mail and pick-pocketing may warrant a custodial sentence. In *R. v Smith and Read* [1997] 1 Cr.App.R.(S.) 342 the offenders were convicted of attempted theft after having tried to steal from a woman's bag that she was carrying. They each received a sentence of 12 months' imprisonment. In *R. v Muir* (1994) 15 Cr.App.R.(S.) 112, the offender stole a cheque from the mail of another tenant in his house. He then used the cheque to open an account with a false name, and withdrew money from this account. He was sentenced to six months' imprisonment.

11–17   Theft in breach of trust will warrant a more severe penalty, and the *Magistrates' Court Sentencing Guidelines* (2003) advise committal for sentence. In *R. v Clark* [1998] 2 Cr.App.R.(S.) 95 the Court of Appeal suggested guidelines as to appropriate terms of imprisonment. Where the amount stolen is less than £17,500 terms of imprisonment from the very short up to 21 months' will be appropriate. Two to three years' imprisonment would be appropriate for sums between £17,500 and £100,000. Three to four years' imprisonment would be appropriate for sums between £100,000 and £250,000. Five to nine years' imprisonment for sums between £250,000 and £1 million and 10 years' imprisonment or more for sums of £1 million or more, with appropriate discounts where guilty pleas were entered. Consecutive sentences might be justified where sums were stolen on more than one occasion or directed at more than one victim.

In *R. v Pottay* [2001] EWCA Crim 1411, a security guard at a car auction took a car worth £7,000 and two other cars. He was of previous good character, except for the related theft of a tax disc, and he pleaded guilty. His sentence of 12 months' imprisonment concurrent for each theft was reduced to a total of six months imprisonment. In *R. v Hill* [2001] EWCA Crim 2314, CA, the offender was filmed stealing small amounts of money whilst she worked at the Post Office. She pleaded guilty to eighteen charges of theft, the total amount stolen being £210. She was sentenced to three months' imprisonment, the aggravating factor of her theft being in breach of trust being balanced against considerable mitigating circumstances including the recent end of her marriage. In *R. v Ross-Goudling* [1997] 2 Cr.App.R.(S.) 348, the offender was a care assistant employed to look after a person suffering from multiple sclerosis. She stole £8,000 from the patient's building society account by forging her signature, and was sentenced to 15 months' imprisonment. See also *R. v Margaret McCormick* (1995) 16 Cr.App.R.(S.) 134 and *R. v Lazaretti* [2001] All E.R. (D) 244. Note: these are all appeals from the Crown Court to the Court of Appeal.

B. Burglary

(a) *Definition*

Theft Act 1968, s.9

Burglary

9.—(1) A person is guilty of burglary if—   **11–18**

    (a) he enters any building or part of a building as a trespasser and with intent to commit any such offence as is mentioned in subsection (2) below; or

    (b) having entered any building or part of a building as a trespasser he steals or attempts to steal anything in the building or that part of it or inflicts or attempts to inflict on any person therein any grievous bodily harm.

(2) The offences referred to in subsection (1) (a) above are offences of stealing anything in the building or part of a building in question, of inflicting on any person therein any grievous bodily harm or raping any person therein, and of doing unlawful damage to the building or anything therein.

(3) [sentence on indictment]

(4) References in subsections (1) and (2) above to a building, and the reference in subsection (3) above to a building which is a dwelling, shall apply also to an inhabited vehicle or vessel, and shall apply to any such vehicle or vessel at times when the person having a habitation in it is not there as well as at times when he is.

[This section is printed as amended by the *CJA* 1991, s.26(2); and the *CJPOA* 1994, s.168(2) and Sch.10.]

(b) *Procedure*

Burglary is triable either way: *MCA* 1980, s.17 and Sch.1, para.28. Burglary will be   **11–19** triable on indictment only if (i) the burglary comprises the commission of, or an intention to commit an offence which is triable only on indictment: *MCA* 1980, Sch.1, para.28(b) or (ii) if the burglary is in a dwelling house and any person in the dwelling was subjected to violence or the threat of violence, the offence is triable only on indictment: *MCA* 1980, Sch.1, para.28(c).

The *Practice Direction (Criminal Proceedings: Consolidated) Pt V.51* [2002] 1 W.L.R. 2870 *(Mode of Trial)* gives separate guidelines for burglary of a dwelling house and burglary of a non-dwelling. As regards burglary of a dwelling house, the guidelines state that the offence should be tried summarily unless one of the following features are present and the court considers its sentencing powers to be insufficient:

    (a) entry in the daytime when the occupier or another is present

(b) Entry at night of a house which is normally occupied, whether or not the occupier (or another) is present
(c) The offending is alleged to be one of a series of similar offences
(d) When soiling, ransacking, damage or vandalism occurs
(e) The offence has professional hallmarks
(f) The unrecovered property is of high value (£10,000 or more)
(g) The offence is racially motivated.

As regards non-dwellings, the guidelines direct that cases should be tried summarily unless the court considers that one or more of the following factors are present and that its sentencing powers are insufficient:

(a) entry of a pharmacy or doctor's surgery
(b) fear is caused or violence is done to anyone lawfully on the premises (*e.g.* nightwatchman, security guard)
(c) the offence has professional hallmarks
(d) vandalism on a substantial scale
(e) the unrecovered property is of high value (£10,000 or more)
(f) the offence is racially motivated.

11–20   The *Powers of Criminal Courts (Sentencing) Act* 2000 provides that the court must impose a minimum custodial sentence of three years where an offender aged 18 or over is convicted of a third 'domestic burglary' where all of the three domestic burglaries were committed on or after November 30, 1999 and where the circumstances of the offence or the offender do not state that it would be unjust in all the circumstances to impose such a penalty: *PCC(S)A* 2000, s.111. Subsection (4) of s.111 provides that where a person is charged with a domestic burglary which would be triable either way, and the circumstances are such that, if he were convicted of the burglary, he could be sentenced for it under subs.(2) above, the burglary shall be triable only on indictment.

The prosecution must prove that:
— the defendant entered a building or part of a building
— with the intention to steal anything in the building or part of the building in question OR with the intention to inflict on any person in the building grievous bodily harm OR with the intention of raping any person in the building OR of doing unlawful damage to the building or anything therein.
     OR
— the defendant had entered a building as a trespasser and
     he then stole or attempted to steal anything in the building,
     OR,
     he inflicted or attempted to inflict upon any person therein grievous bodily harm.

(c)

(c) *Elements of the offence*

The building

11–21   The word 'building' is to be treated as an ordinary word of the English language and its meaning is a question of fact not law: *Brutus v Cozens* [1973] A.C. 854, HL.

Entry as a trespasser

11–22   The definition of trespass is that used in the law of tort; *i.e.* any intentional, reckless or negligent entry into a building which is in the possession of another person who does not consent to the entry. The defendant must intend, or be reckless as to the facts which make the entry a trespass: *R. v Collins* [1973] Q.B. 100, CA.

The entry

11–23   In *R. v Collins* (above) Lord Edmund-Davies said the entry in question had to be 'effective and substantial.' In *R. v Brown (V.)* [1985] Crim.L.R. 212, CA, the Court held that a man who had both feet on the ground outside a shop 'entered' it when he leant through a broken window with the upper half of his body.

See further *Archbold Crown*, §§ 21–115—21–129.

(d) *Sentence*

The maximum sentence varies depending on whether the burglary is of a dwelling **11–24** or non-dwelling.

(a) **Burglary of a dwelling**

The maximum penalty for burglary of a building or part of a building which is a **11–25** dwelling is 14 years imprisonment on indictment, six months or a fine not exceeding the statutory maximum or both summarily (*TA* 1968, s.9(4))

The *Magistrates' Court Sentencing Guidelines* (2003) state:

> Aggravating factors include force being used or threatened, group enterprise, high value (in economic or sentimental terms property stolen, more than minor trauma caused, professional planning/organisation/execution, racially aggravated, significant damage or vandalism, victim injured, victim present at time, vulnerable victim.
>
> Mitigating factors include first offence of its type and low value property such as electrical items or jewellery stolen and no significant damage or disturbance and no injury or violence, minor part played, theft from attached garage, vacant property.
>
> The Guidelines also state that if the offence is racially or religiously aggravated, or the offender is on bail, this offence is more serious. If the offender has previous convictions their relevance and any failure to respond to previous convictions may increase seriousness.
>
> **Guideline**: Are Magistrates' sentencing powers appropriate?

In *Brewster* [1998] 1 Cr.App.R.(S.) 181, CA, Lord Bingham C.J. stated that not all dwelling house burglars must necessarily receive a custodial sentence. Cases involving impulsive action and goods of little value may be suitable for sentence in the magistrates' court. However, such cases will be comparatively rare, and in general, magistrates should decline from passing sentence for this offence. A custodial sentence was held inappropriate in *R. v Suker* (1990) 12 Cr.App.R.(S.) 290, CA, where the offender, aged 19 with one previous conviction for an offence of a different nature, pleaded guilty to burglary of a dwelling. A householder apprehended S, drunk and climbing through a bathroom window, and held him until the police arrived. S claimed that he was looking for money for a taxi home and would not have harmed anyone or taken any property. A conditional discharge was held to be a more appropriate sentence than detention in a young offenders' institution. In *R. v Finney* [1998] 2 Cr.App.R.(S.) 239, CA, a custodial sentence was held to be inappropriate for an impulsive act committed under the influence of drink, and a sentence of nine months' imprisonment was substituted by probation for two years. In *R. v Fogarty and Mahoney* (1992) 13 Cr.App.R.(S.) 328, the offenders had pleaded guilty to a single count of burglary. They had driven to a rural area and broken into an unoccupied house. They had not stolen anything and were of previous good character. They received sentences of twelve months' imprisonment. A sentence of 18 months' imprisonment was held appropriate for an opportunistic domestic burglary in *R. v Joseph Ashton* [2000] All E.R. (D) 1961 where the offender, who pleaded guilty and had previous convictions, had gained access to a basement flat and was found in possession of property worth £600.

R. v McInerney [2003] Crim.L.R. 209, CA offers guidance on the use of custody as a penalty for domestic burglaries. Cases in which a court would previously have been looking to starting points of up to 18 months' imprisonment may now be dealt with by the imposition of a community sentence. If and only if the court is satisfied that the offender has demonstrated by his or her behaviour that punishment in the community was not practicable should the court resort to a custodial sentence. Where a custodial sentence is necessary, it should be no longer than necessary. Aggravating and mitigating features would alter the appropriate starting point. High level aggravating features included the use or threat of force, injury or especially traumatic effect on the victim, professional planning, vandalism, racially aggravated offences or the deliberate targeting of a vulnerable victim. Medium level aggravating features included the theft of high value goods, burglars working as a group and the victim being at home during the commission of the offence. Mitigating features included the crime being a first offence, nothing or low value property being stolen, the fact that an offender played only a minor part in the offence, the impulsive nature of the crime, the fact that no property was damaged and the entering of an early guilty plea.

(b) Burglary of a non-dwelling

11–26   As regards burglary of a non-dwelling, when tried summarily, the maximum penalty is six months' imprisonment or a fine not exceeding the statutory maximum or both: *TA* 1968, s.9(4).

The *Magistrates' Court Sentencing Guidelines* (2003) state:

> Aggravating factors include forcible entry, group offence, harm to business, night time, occupants frightened, professional operation, repeat victimisation, school premises, soiling, ransacking, damage, racial aggravation, offence committed on bail, relevant previous convictions and any failures to respond to previous sentences.
>
> Mitigating factors include low value of goods stolen, nobody frightened, no damage or disturbance, no forcible entry.
>
> **Guideline**: Is it serious enough for a community penalty?

11–27   A custodial sentence was approved in *R. v Dorries and Dorries* [1993] Crim.L.R. 408, CA where the offenders removed bricks from a wall to gain entry, and were found with a hammer, jemmy and radio scanner in their car. In *R. v Anson* [1999] 1 Cr.App.R.(S.) 331, a sentence of two and a half years imprisonment was upheld for the burglary of a shop, where the offender had disconnected the alarm, forced several doors and stolen goods to the value of £11,913. The courts adopt a more lenient approach in the context of non-residential burglary; in *R. v Carlton* [1993] Crim.L.R. 981, CA it was held that burglary of an unoccupied office late at night involving the theft of a fax machine might not justify a custodial sentence. In *R. v Tetteh* [1993] Crim.L.R. 629, the offender had broken into a YMCA club. Nothing was taken, and the offence was seen as opportunistic and unplanned. The CA held that this case warranted a community sentence.

C. REMOVAL OF ARTICLES FROM PLACES OPEN TO THE PUBLIC

(a) *Definition*

Theft Act 1968, s.11

Removal of articles from places open to the public

11–28   11.—(1) Subject to subsections (2) and (3) below, where the public have access to a building in order to view the building or part of it, or a collection or part of a collection housed in it, any person who without lawful authority removes from the building or its grounds the whole or part of any article displayed or kept for display to the public in the building or that part of it or in its grounds shall be guilty of an offence.

For this purpose "collection" includes a collection got together for a temporary purpose, but references in this section to a collection do not apply to a collection made or exhibited for the purpose of effecting sales or other commercial dealings.

(2) It is immaterial for purposes of subsection (1) above, that the public's access to a building is limited to a particular period or particular occasion; but where anything removed from a building or its grounds is there otherwise than as forming part of, or being on loan for exhibition with, a collection intended for permanent exhibition to the public, the person removing it does not thereby commit an offence under this section unless he removes it on a day when the public have access to the building as mentioned in subsection (1) above.

(3) A person does not commit an offence under this section if he believes that he has

lawful authority for the removal of the thing in question or that he would have it if the person entitled to give it knew of the removal and the circumstances of it.

(b) *Procedure*

11–29 Removal of an article from a place open to the public is triable either way (*MCA* 1980, s.17 and Sch.1, para.28.)

The prosecution must prove that:
— the defendant had access to a building to view it or any part of it, or to view a collection or part of a collection housed there and,
— he removed from the building or its grounds the whole or part of any article displayed or kept in the building for display to the public,
— without lawful authority.

(c) *Elements of the offence*

11–30 The words 'a collection intended for permanent exhibition to the public' mean simply a collection intended to be permanently available for exhibition to the public, for example, a local authority's settled practice of periodically displaying to the public at the gallery the pictures in their permanent collection: *R. v Durkin* [1973] 1 Q.B. 786, CA.

(d) *Defence*

11–31 Where the defendant raises the issue of whether he believed he had lawful authority for the removal of the articles concerned, or that he would have had had the person entitled to authorise the removal had known of the removal and its attendant circumstances the burden is on the prosecution to establish the defendant's bad faith.

(e) *Sentence*

11–32 The maximum penalty when tried on indictment is five years imprisonment (*TA* 1968, s.11(4)). When tried summarily, the maximum penalty is six months' imprisonment and /or a fine not exceeding the statutory maximum.

D. TAKING A CONVEYANCE WITHOUT AUTHORITY

(a) *Definition*

Theft Act 1968, s.12(1)–(4C)

Taking motor vehicle or other conveyance without authority

11–33 **12.**—(1) Subject to subsections (5) and (6) below, a person shall be guilty of an offence if, without having the consent of the owner or other lawful authority, he takes any conveyance for his own or another's use or, knowing that any conveyance has been taken without such authority, drives it or allows himself to be carried in or on it.

(2) A person guilty of an offence under subsection (1) above shall be liable on summary conviction to a fine not exceeding level 5 on the standard scale, to imprisonment for a term not exceeding six months, or to both.

(3) [...]

(4) If on the trial of an indictment for theft the jury are not satisfied that the accused committed theft, but it is proved that the accused committed an offence under subsection (1) above, the jury may find him guilty of the offence under subsection (1).

and if he is found guilty of it, he shall be liable as he would have been liable under subsection (2) above on summary conviction.

(4A) Proceedings for an offence under subsection (1) above (but not proceedings of a kind falling within subsection (4) above) in relation to a mechanically propelled vehicle—
(a) shall not be commenced after the end of the period of three years beginning with the day on which the offence was committed; but
(b) subject to that, may be commenced at any time within the period of six months beginning with the relevant day.

(4B) In subsection (4A)(b) above "the relevant day" means—

    (a) in the case of a prosecution for an offence under subsection (1) above by a public prosecutor, the day on which sufficient evidence to justify the proceedings came to the knowledge of any person responsible for deciding whether to commence any such prosecution;

    (b) in the case of a prosecution for an offence under subsection (1) above which is commenced by a person other than a public prosecutor after the discontinuance of a prosecution falling within paragraph (a) above which relates to the same facts, the day on which sufficient evidence to justify the proceedings came to the knowledge of the person who has decided to commence the prosecution or (if later) the discontinuance of the other prosecution;

    (c) in the case of any other prosecution for an offence under subsection (1) above, the day on which sufficient evidence to justify the proceedings came to the knowledge of the person who has decided to commence the prosecution.

(4C) For the purposes of subsection (4A)(b) above a certificate of a person responsible for deciding whether to commence a prosecution of a kind mentioned in subsection (4B)(a) above as to the date on which such evidence as is mentioned in the certificate came to the knowledge of any person responsible for deciding whether to commence any such prosecution shall be conclusive evidence of that fact.

[This section is printed as amended by the *CJA* 1982, ss.37, 38; the *CJA* 1988, s.37(1); and the *Vehicles (Crime) Act* 2001, s.37(1). Subsection 3 was repealed by *Police and Criminal Evidence Act* 1984, Sch.7. Subsections (4A) to (4C) apply only in relation to offences committed on or after their commencement (October 1, 2001): s.37(2).]

(b) *Procedure*

11–34　　This offence is triable summarily. However, an offence under s.12 may be included in an indictment for another offence in the circumstances set out in the *Criminal Justice Act* 1988, s.40.

The prosecution must prove that:

— the defendant took any conveyance for his own or another's use
— without having the consent of the owner, or lawful authority;
    OR
— the defendant allowed himself to be carried in, or drove himself, any conveyance
— which had, to the defendant's knowledge, been taken without the owner's consent or other lawful authority.

(c) *Elements of the offence*

Theft Act 1968, s.12(5)–(7)

Taking motor vehicle or other conveyance without authority

11–35　　12.—(5) Subsection (1) above shall not apply in relation to pedal cycles; but, subject to subsection (6) below, a person who, without having the consent of the owner or other lawful authority, takes a pedal cycle for his own or another's use, or rides a pedal cycle knowing it to have been taken without such authority, shall on summary conviction be liable to a fine not exceeding level 3 on the standard scale

(6) A person does not commit an offence under this section by anything done in the belief that he has lawful authority to do it or that he would have the owner's consent if the owner knew of his doing it and the circumstances of it.

(7) For purposes of this section—

    (a) "conveyance" means any conveyance constructed or adapted for the carriage of a person or persons whether by land, water or air, except that it does not include a conveyance constructed or adapted for use only under the control of a person not carried in or on it, and "drive" shall be construed accordingly; and

    (b) "owner", in relation to a conveyance which is the subject of a hiring agreement or hire-purchase agreement, means the person in possession of the conveyance under that agreement.

See further *Archbold Crown*, §§ 21–148—21–157.

(d) *Defence*

Where the defendant raises the issue of whether he believed he had lawful authority **11–36** for the taking of the conveyance the burden is on the prosecution to establish the defendant's bad faith.

(e) *Sentence*

The maximum penalty for taking a conveyance without authority is six months' **11–37** imprisonment and/or a fine not exceeding level 5 on the standard scale (s.12(2)). If the offence is committed or attempted in relation to a motor vehicle, there is discretionary disqualification (*Road Traffic Offenders Act* 1988, Sch.2).

The *Magistrates' Court Sentencing Guidelines* (2003) state:

> Aggravating factors shall include group action, premeditated, related damage, professional hallmarks, vulnerable victim, offence committed on bail, relevant previous convictions and any failures to respond to previous sentences.
>
> Mitigating factors shall include the presence of a misunderstanding with the owner, soon returned, vehicle belonging to family or friend.
>
> **Guideline**: is it serious enough for a community penalty?

A custodial sentence may be imposed where the offence forms part of a series of of- **11–38** fences arising out of the same circumstances: in *R. v Jewry* (1986) 8 Cr.App.R.(S.) 491 a sentence of four months' detention was deemed appropriate when the offender stole vehicles, drove them around a city at high speed, eventually colliding head on leaving one car damaged beyond repair. The offender later stated that the cars had been taken for "a bit of fun" and pleaded guilty to two counts of occasioning actual bodily harm, two counts of taking a conveyance, two counts of theft as well as asking two other offences to be taken into consideration. In the view of the Court, these were serious offences involving taking vehicles and deliberately destroying them, and custody was fully merited.

In *R. v Ahmad (Asif)* (1992) 12 Cr.App.R.(S.) 212, CA, the offender pleaded guilty to taking a conveyance without authority, reckless driving and driving while disqualified. A sentence of 200 hours' community service and a compensation order was upheld by the Court of Appeal.

E. Aggravated Vehicle Taking

(a) *Definition*

Theft Act 1968, s.12A(1)–(3)

Aggravated vehicle-taking

12A.—(1) Subject to subsection (3) below, a person is guilty of aggravated taking of a vehicle **11–39** if—

    (a) he commits an offence under section 12(1) above (in this section referred to as a "basic offence") in relation to a mechanically propelled vehicle; and

    (b) it is proved that, at any time after the vehicle was unlawfully taken (whether by him or another) and before it was recovered, the vehicle was driven, or injury or damage was caused, in one or more of the circumstances set out in paragraphs (a) to (d) of subsection (2) below.

  (2) The circumstances referred to in subsection (1)(b) above are—

    (a) that the vehicle was driven dangerously on a road or other public place;

    (b) that, owing to the driving of the vehicle, an accident occurred by which injury was caused to any person;

(c) that, owing to the driving of the vehicle, an accident occurred by which damage was caused to any property, other than the vehicle;

(d) that damage was caused to the vehicle.

(3) A person is not guilty of an offence under this section if he proves that, as regards any such proven driving, injury or damage as is referred to in subsection (1)(b) above, either—

(a) the driving, accident or damage referred to in subsection (2) above occurred before he committed the basic offence; or

(b) he was neither in nor on nor in the immediate vicinity of the vehicle when that driving, accident or damage occurred.

(b) *Procedure*

11–40   This offence is triable either way. However, where the only allegation is of damage to the vehicle or other property or both and the total value of the damage alleged to have been caused is less than the relevant sum, *i.e.* £5,000, the offender has no right to elect trial on indictment: *MCA* 1980, ss.22 and 33 and Sch.2.

If a person charged with the offence under s.12A is found not guilty of that offence, he may still be found guilty of the basic form of the offence: s.12A (5) of the *TA* 1968. This section applies to trial in the magistrates' court as much as to trial in the Crown Court: *R.(H) v Liverpool Youth Court* [2001] Crim.L.R. 487.

The prosecution must prove that:

— the defendant committed an offence under s.12(1) of the *Theft Act* 1968,

— in relation to a mechanically propelled vehicle

— and injury or damage was caused at any time between the taking of the vehicle and its recovery,

— when the vehicle was being driven dangerously on a road or other public place OR

— when an accident occurred which caused injury and was due to the driving of the vehicle OR

— when an accident occurred which caused damage to any property other than the vehicle and was due to the driving of the vehicle OR

— damage was caused to the vehicle.

(c) *Elements of the offence*

Theft Act 1968, s.12A(7), (8)

Aggravated vehicle-taking

11–41   12A.—(7) For the purposes of this section a vehicle is driven dangerously if—

(a) it is driven in a way which falls far below what would be expected of a competent and careful driver; and

(b) it would be obvious to a competent and careful driver that driving the vehicle in that way would be dangerous.

(8) For the purposes of this section a vehicle is recovered when it is restored to its owner or to other lawful possession or custody; and in this subsection "owner" has the same meaning as in section 12 above.

See further *Archbold Crown*, §§ 21–162—21–163a.

(d) *Defence*

11–42   A person will not be guilty of an offence under this section if he proves that, as regards any such proven driving, injury or damage as is referred to in subs.(1)(b) either the driving, accident or damage referred to in subs.(2) above occurred before he committed the basic offence or he was neither in nor on nor in the immediate vicinity of the vehicle when that driving, accident or damage occurred.

(e) *Sentence*

11–43   The maximum penalty on summary conviction is a term of imprisonment not exceeding six months or a fine not exceeding the statutory maximum or both. Section 33(1) of the *Magistrates' Courts Act* 1980 does not apply to the offence of aggravated vehicle taking: s.33(3), *Magistrates' Courts Act* 1980.

This section carries obligatory disqualification and endorsement (3 to 11 points): *Road Traffic Offenders Act* 1988, ss.28, 34, 44, 96 and 97 and Sch.2, Pt.II. The fact that the defendant did not drive the vehicle during the commission of the offence is not a reason to avoid obligatory disqualification (*Road Traffic Offenders Act* 1988, s.34).

The *Magistrates' Court Sentencing Guidelines* (2003) state:

> Aggravating factors include trying to avoid detection or arrest, competitive driving, racing, showing off, disregard of warnings ex. from passengers, group action, police chase, premeditated, serious injury/damage, serious risk, offence committed whilst on bail, relevant previous convictions or any failure to respond to previous sentences.
>
> Mitigating factors include no competitiveness/racing, passenger only, single incident of bad driving, speed not excessive and very minor injury/damage.
>
> **Guideline**: is it so serious that only custody is appropriate?

In *R. v Bird* (1993) 14 Cr.App.R.(S.) 343, CA, Lord Taylor C.J. stated that the aggravating features of this offence will be primarily the overall culpability of the driving; how bad it was and for how long, and to a lesser extent, how much injury or damage, or both was caused. Drink would affect the culpability of the driving, but where it had played a large part it would usually be the subject of another charge. A guilty plea will be a mitigating feature if made with contrition, though the youth of the offender will be less significant in mitigation as the Act is aimed at young offenders.

See also *R. v Timothy* (1995) 16 Cr.App.R.(S.) 1028 and *R. v Frostick* [1998] 1 Cr.App.R.(S.) 257.

F. TAKING OR RIDING A PEDAL CYCLE WITHOUT AUTHORITY

(a) *Definition*

Theft Act 1968, s.12

Taking motor vehicle or other conveyance without authority

11–44 **12.**—(5) Subsection (1) above shall not apply in relation to pedal cycles; but, subject to subsection (6) below, a person who, without having the consent of the owner or other lawful authority, takes a pedal cycle for his own or another's use, or rides a pedal cycle knowing it to have been taken without such authority, shall on summary conviction be liable to a fine not exceeding level 3 on the standard scale

(6) A person does not commit an offence under this section by anything done in the belief that he has lawful authority to do it or that he would have the owner's consent if the owner knew of his doing it and the circumstances of it.

(b) *Procedure*

11–45 This offence is triable summarily only (s.12(6)).

The prosecution must prove that:

— the defendant took a pedal cycle for his own or another's use
— without the consent of the owner or other lawful authority
    OR
— the defendant rode a pedal cycle knowing it to have been taken without the consent of the owner or other lawful authority.

(c) *Elements of the offence*

11–46 The owner of the pedal cycle does not need to be identified; if the offender admits that he did not have the owner's consent, the court is entitled to find that the prosecution had made out a case to answer as it is entitled to infer that the bicycle had an owner: *Sturrock v DPP* (1996) R.T.R. 216.

(d) *Sentence*

11–46.1   The maximum penalty is a fine not exceeding level 3 on the standard scale: *Theft Act* 1968, s.12(5).

G. ABSTRACTING ELECTRICITY

(a) *Definition*

Theft Act 1968, s.13

Abstracting of electricity

11–47   **13.** A person who dishonestly uses without due authority, or dishonestly causes to be wasted or diverted, any electricity shall on conviction on indictment be liable to imprisonment for a term not exceeding five years.

(b) *Procedure*

11–47.1   Abstracting electricity is triable either way: *MCA* 1980, s.17 and Sch.1, para.28).
The prosecution must prove that:
— the defendant dishonestly, or without due authority,
— used any electricity OR
— the defendant dishonestly caused to be wasted or diverted any electricity

(c) *Elements of the offence*

11–48   'Dishonesty' has the same meaning in this context as it does in the context of the offence of theft.
In *R. v McCreadie and Tume*, 96 Cr.App.R. 143, CA, it was held that the offence does not require tampering with the electricity meter. It is sufficient to prove that electricity was used without the authority of the electricity supplier by a person who had no intention of paying for it,

(d) *Sentence*

11–49   When tried summarily, the maximum sentence is six months' imprisonment, a fine not exceeding the statutory maximum or both: *Theft Act* 1968, s.13.
In *R. v Hodkinson* (1980) 2 Cr.App.R.(S.) 331, CA, the offender had fitted a device to the electricity meter at his home, causing the meter to give a false reading. A sentence of one month's imprisonment and a fine of £750 was upheld, the necessity for deterrent sentences being emphasised.
See also *R. v Western* (1987) 9 Cr.App.R.(S.) 6 and *R. v Wright* (1981) 3 Cr.App.R.(S.) 242.

H. OBTAINING BY DECEPTION

(a) *Definition*

Theft Act 1968, s.15(1)

Obtaining property by deception

11–50   **15.**—(1) A person who by any deception dishonestly obtains property belonging to another, with the intention of permanently depriving the other of it, shall on conviction on indictment be liable to imprisonment for a term not exceeding ten years.

(b) *Procedure*

11–51   Obtaining by deception is triable either way (*MCA* 1980, s.17(1)).

The *Practice Direction (Criminal Proceedings: Consolidation)*, Pt V.7 states that fraud should be tried summarily unless the court considers that one or more of the following features is present in the case and that its sentencing powers are insufficient:

(a) Breach of trust by a person in a position of substantial authority, or in whom a high degree of trust is placed.

(b) Fraud which has been committed or disguised in a sophisticated manner

(c) Fraud committed by an organised gang

(d) The victim is particularly vulnerable to fraud, *e.g.* the elderly or infirm,

(e) The unrecovered property is of high value (£10,000 or more)

The *Practice Direction* also states at para V.9 that social security fraud should be **11–52** tried summarily unless the court considers that one or more of the following features is present in the case and that its sentencing powers are insufficient:

(a) Organised frauds on a large scale

(b) The frauds are substantial and carried out over a long period of time.

The prosecution must prove that:

— the defendant dishonestly,

— obtained property belonging to another,

— by deception,

— with the intention of permanently depriving the owner of that property.

(c) *Elements of the offence*

Property

Section 4(1) (§ 11–7 above) applies to s.15. See further *Archbold Crown*, § 21–180.   **11–53**

Deception

'deception' means any deception, (whether deliberate or reckless) by words or **11–54** conduct as to fact or as to law, including a deception as to present intentions of the person using the deception or any other person: *Theft Act* 1968, s.15(4) See further, *Archbold Crown*, §§ 21–181—21–195.

Obtains

The deception must be effective, and must operate on the mind of the person **11–55** deceived: *R. v Laverty* 54 Cr.App.R. 495, CA. Regarding the issue of causation and remoteness, in *R. v Miller* 95 Cr.App.R. 421, CA, it was held that to establish that property has been obtained by deception it is not necessary to isolate the moment when the property was handed over to see if at that moment the lies operated to deceive the victim. If the deception was a cause of the property being handed over, it does not matter that at the final moment the victim suspected or believed that he had been swindled. See further *Archbold Crown*, §§ 21–196—21–204.

Dishonesty

The test of dishonesty for the purposes of this section is that outlined in *R. v Ghosh* **11–56** (above).

(d) *Sentencing*

When tried summarily, the maximum penalty is six months' imprisonment, a fine **11–57** not exceeding the statutory maximum, or both.

The *Magistrates' Court Sentencing Guidelines* (2003) state:

> Aggravating factors include the offence being committed over a long period, large sums or valuable goods, two or more involved, victim particularly vulnerable, offence committed on bail, relevant previous convictions and any failure to respond to previous sentences.
> Mitigating factors include impulsive action, short period and small sum.

Guideline: is it serious enough for a community penalty?

Serious frauds are unlikely to be dealt with in the Magistrates' Court. Examples of fraud that have been tried before the Magistrates include frauds involving breach of trust and social security frauds. Cases of mortgage fraud should normally be sent to the Crown Court for sentence as the values involved are unlikely to be below £10,000. Cases of cheque fraud depend on the value involved. Cases involving sums of above £5,000 should generally be sent to the Crown Court for sentence. Magistrates should consider the offender's record; if there is a record for deception and there are a number of charges with high total value, the matter should be sentenced at the Crown Court. Fraud on the Revenue or Excise also involves examination of the sums of money involved. Cases of £5,000 or above should normally be sent to the Crown Court. The magistrates need to have regard to the period of the fraud; if systematic, the matter should normally be sent to the Crown Court for sentence.

In *R. v Barrick* (1985) 7 Cr.App.R.(S.) 142, the CA offers guidance in relation to frauds involving breach of trust. Upholding a two-year sentence of imprisonment, Lord Lane stated that in the breach of trust cases the court should generally pass a sufficiently substantial term of imprisonment to mark publicly the gravity of the offence. He then listed some of the matters to which the court was to have regard when determining sentence:

   (i) the quality and degree of trust reposed in the offender including his rank

  (ii) the period over which the fraud or the thefts have been perpetrated;

 (iii) the use to which the money or property dishonestly taken was put;

  (iv) the effect upon the victim;

   (v) the impact of the offences on the public and public confidence;

  (vi) the effect on fellow-employees or partners;

 (vii) the effect on the offender himself;

(viii) his own history;

  (ix) those matters of mitigation special to himself such as illness; being placed

under great strain by excessive responsibility or the like; where, as sometimes happens, there has been a long delay, say over two years, between his being confronted with his dishonesty by his professional body or the police and the start of his trial; finally, any help given by him to the police.

11–58   In *R. v Sutton* (1984) 6 Cr.App.R.(S.) 70, CA, the offender was the manageress of a store. She stole a sunbed worth £25 and a sprinkler worth £6. Given her good character and the comparatively trivial breach of trust it was held that a conditional discharge or fine would be an appropriate penalty. In *R. v Aragon* (1995) 16 Cr.App.R.(S.) 930, the offender was convicted of six counts of obtaining by deception; he had claimed for work that he had not performed as a part time immigration appeal adjudicator. He was of previous good character, had claimed about £10,000 and was sentenced to six months' imprisonment.

See also *R. v Mossop* (1985) 7 Cr.App.R.(S.) 283, 930 and *R. v Thomas* (1995) 16 Cr.App.R.(S.) 539 (insurance fraud, sentenced to four months' imprisonment.)

R. v Stewart (1987) 9 Cr.App.R.(S.) 135 is the guideline for cases of benefit fraud. The case indicates that most social security frauds will be appropriately tried before the magistrates' court, with Lord Lane C.J. saying that the run of the mill offences would ordinarily be tried before the magistrates with only the more serious cases coming before the Crown Court. Factors affecting the sentencing decision included i) a guilty plea, ii) the amount of time and the length of time over which the defalcations were persisted in, iii) the circumstances in which the offences began, iv) the use to which the money is put v) previous character vi) matters special to the offender and vii) any voluntary repayment of the amounts overpaid.

R. v Breeze (1994) 15 Cr.App.R.(S.) 94 concerned two counts of obtaining property by deception, the offender having cashed cheques to the value of £264.70 which had been fraudulently obtained from the DSS. A sentence of four months' imprisonment was quashed by the CA which, having regard to the small value of property obtained, and the relatively short period of time between commission of the two offences, concluded that the custody threshold laid down by the *Criminal Justice Act* 1991 had not been crossed. In *R. v Ellison* [1998] 2 Cr.App.R.(S.) 382 a sentence of 10 months' imprisonment was imposed where the offender had pleaded guilty to five counts of obtaining benefit by deception with 88 other offences being taken into consideration. The total overpayment of benefit was £10,948. See also *R. v Tucker* (1994) 15 Cr.App.R.(S.) 349.

I. Obtaining a Money Transfer by Deception

(a) *Definition*

Theft Act 1968, s.15A(1)

Obtaining a money transfer by deception
  15A.—(1) A person is guilty of an offence if by any deception he dishonestly obtains a money   **11–59**
transfer for himself or another.

(b) *Procedure*

Obtaining a money transfer by deception is triable either way (*MCA* 1980, s.17(1)   **11–59.1**
and Sch.1, para.28). For guidance as to when summary trial of fraud cases is appropriate see the *Practice Direction (Criminal Proceedings: Consolidation)*, para.V.51.7, at § 11–51 above.
  The prosecution must prove that:
  — the defendant dishonestly,
  — obtained,
  — a money transfer,
  — by deception.

(c) *Elements of the offence*

Theft Act 1968, ss.15A, 15B

Obtaining a money transfer by deception
  15A.—(1) A person is guilty of an offence if by any deception he dishonestly obtains a money   **11–60**
transfer for himself or another.
  (2) A money transfer occurs when—
      (a) a debit is made to one account,
      (b) a credit is made to another, and
      (c) the credit results from the debit or the debit results from the credit.
  (3) References to a credit and to a debit are to a credit of an amount of money and to a debit of an amount of money.
  (4) It is immaterial (in particular)—
      (a) whether the amount credited is the same as the amount debited;
      (b) whether the money transfer is effected on presentment of a cheque or by another method;
      (c) whether any delay occurs in the process by which the money transfer is effected;
      (d) whether any intermediate credits or debits are made in the course of the money transfer;
      (e) whether either of the accounts is overdrawn before or after the money transfer is effected.
  (5) A person guilty of an offence under this section shall be liable on conviction on indictment to imprisonment for a term not exceeding ten years.

Section 15A: supplementary
  15B.—(1) The following provisions have effect for the interpretation of section 15A of this Act.

(2) "Deception" has the same meaning as in section 15 of this Act.

(3) "Account" means an account kept with—

    (a) a bank; or

    (b) a person carrying on a business which falls within subsection (4) below.

(4) A business falls within this subsection if—

    (a) in the course of the business money received by way of deposit is lent to others; or

    (b) any other activity of the business is financed, wholly or to any material extent, out of the capital of or the interest on money received by way of deposit;

(4A) References in subsection (4) to a deposit must be read with—

    (a) section 22 of the *Financial Services and Markets Act* 2000;

    (b) any relevant order under that section; and

    (c) Schedule 2 to that Act,

but any restriction on the meaning of deposit which arises from the identity of the person making it is to be disregarded.

(5) For the purposes of subsection (4) above—

    (a) all the activities which a person carries on by way of business shall be regarded as a single business carried on by him; and

    (b) "money" includes money expressed in a currency other than sterling or in the European currency unit (as defined in Council Regulation No. 3320/94/EC or any Community instrument replacing it).

[Sections 15A and 15B were inserted by the *Theft (Amendment) Act* 1996, and the provisions have no application to anything done before the day on which the 1996 Act received the Royal Assent. Section 15B is printed as subsequently amended by the *Financial Services and Markets Act 2000 (Consequential Amendments and Repeals) Order* 2001 (SI 2001/3649), art.278.]

(d) *Sentence*

11–61   When tried summarily, the maximum penalty is six months' imprisonment, a fine not exceeding the statutory maximum or both. For sentencing guidelines in s.15 cases generally see s.8(c) above.

In *R. v Roach* [2002] 1 Cr.App.R.(S.) 12, CA, a sentence of eighteen months' imprisonment following guilty pleas to three counts of obtaining a money transfer by deception was upheld in the Court of Appeal. The offender, charged with the care of an elderly lady, would ask her to write blank cheques on which she would add the name of the payee, and hence be able to pay the elderly lady's bills. The offender was in fact completing the cheques in her own favour and obtained £2,875 over a period of 15 months.

J. Obtaining a Pecuniary Advantage by Deception

(a) *Definition*

Theft Act 1968, s.16(1)

Obtaining pecuniary advantage by deception

11–62   16.—(1) A person who by any deception dishonestly obtains for himself or another any pecuniary advantage shall on conviction on indictment be liable to imprisonment for a term not exceeding five years.

(b) *Procedure*

11–63   The offence is triable either way (*MCA* 1980, s.17 and Sch.1, para.28).

The prosecution must prove that:

    — the defendant dishonestly

    — obtained for himself or another person

— any pecuniary advantage
— by deception

(c) *Elements of the offence*

Theft Act 1968, s.16(2)–(3)

Obtaining pecuniary advantage by deception

16.—(2) The cases in which a pecuniary advantage within the meaning of this section is to be **11–64**
regarded as obtained for a person are cases where—

    (a) […]

    (b) he is allowed to borrow by way of overdraft, or to take out any policy of insur-
        ance or annuity contract, or obtains an improvement of the terms on which he is
        allowed to do so; or

    (c) he is given the opportunity to earn remuneration or greater remuneration in an
        office or employment, or to win money by betting.

(3) For purposes of this section "deception" has the same meaning as in section 15 of
this Act.

[Subsection (2)(a) was repealed by *Theft Act* 1978, s.5(5).]

See *Archbold Crown*, §§ 21–219—21–225.

(d) *Sentence*

When tried summarily, the maximum penalty is six months' imprisonment, a fine **11–65**
not exceeding the statutory maximum or both. For sentencing guidelines in fraud cases
generally, see § 11–56 above.

K. FALSE ACCOUNTING

(a) *Definition*

Theft Act 1968, s.17(1)

False accounting

17.—(1) Where a person dishonestly, with a view to gain for himself or another or with **11–66**
intent to cause loss to another,—

    (a) destroys, defaces, conceals or falsifies any account or any record or document
        made or required for any accounting purpose; or

    (b) in furnishing information for any purpose produces or makes use of any ac-
        count, or any such record or document as aforesaid, which to his knowledge is or
        may be misleading, false or deceptive in a material particular;

he shall, on conviction on indictment, be liable to imprisonment for a term not exceeding seven
years.

(b) *Procedure*

The offence is triable either way (*MCA* 1980, s.17 and Sch.1, para.28). For guidance **11–67**
as to when summary trial of fraud cases is appropriate see *Practice Direction (Criminal
Proceedings: Consolidation)*, para.V.51.7 above § 11–51.

The prosecution must prove that;

— The defendant dishonestly,

— With a view to gain for himself or another or with intent to cause loss to another,

— Destroyed, defaced, concealed or falsified any account or any record or document made or required for any accounting purpose; OR

— In furnishing information for any purpose produced or makes use of any account, or any such record or document as aforesaid, which to his knowledge was or may have been misleading, false or deceptive in a material particular.

(c) *Elements of the offence*

Theft Act 1968, s.17(2)

False accounting

11–68   17.—(2) For purposes of this section a person who makes or concurs in making in an account or other document an entry which is or may be misleading, false or deceptive in a material particular, or who omits or concurs in omitting a material particular from an account or other document, is to be treated as falsifying the account or document.

See further *Archbold Crown*, §§ 21-232—21-238.

(c) *Sentence*

11–69   When tried summarily, the maximum penalty is six months' imprisonment, a fine not exceeding the statutory maximum or both.

In *R. v Kefford* [2002] 2 Cr.App.R.(S.) 106, CA, Lord Woolf issued guidance for sentencing in the context of economic crimes, stating that when the offender was of previous good character alternative sentences to imprisonment could be an appropriate punishment. In view of the overcrowded prison system a sentence of imprisonment should only be imposed when necessary and only for as long as necessary. A starting point of eighteen months following guilty pleas for theft and false accounting was held to be excessive, and the sentence was reduced to four months, with twelve months being the appropriate starting point.

In *R. v Spencer* [2002] EWCA Crim 2196, CA (Crim Div) a sentence of 18 months' imprisonment concurrent on each of six counts of false accounting was reduced to a sentence of six months' imprisonment. The appellant was of previous good character, and evidence suggested she had been initially forced to make the fraudulent claims by a violent partner. The CA affirmed the propriety of taking into consideration the Lord Chief Justice's comments in *Kefford* (above) about prison overcrowding.

11–70   See also *R. v Smith* (1994) 15 Cr.App.R.(S.) 145.

L. FALSE STATEMENTS BY OFFICERS OF A COMPANY OR ASSOCIATION

(a) *Definition*

Theft Act 1968, s.19(1)

False statements by company directors, etc.

11–71   19.—(1) Where an officer of a body corporate or unincorporated association (or person purporting to act as such), with intent to deceive members or creditors of the body corporate or association about its affairs, publishes or concurs in publishing a written statement or account which to his knowledge is or may be misleading, false or deceptive in a material particular, he shall on conviction on indictment be liable to imprisonment for a term not exceeding seven years.

(b) *Procedure*

11–72   The offence is triable either way (*MCA* 1980, s.17 and Sch.1, para.28) For guidance as to when summary trial of fraud cases is appropriate see § 11–51 above.

The prosecution must prove that:
— the defendant was the officer of a body corporate or unincorporated association, or was purporting to act as such, and;
— with intent to deceive members or creditors of the body corporate or association about its affairs, he;

— published or concurred in publishing a written statement or account which;
— to his knowledge was or might have been misleading, false or deceptive in a material particular.

(c) *Elements of the offence*

Theft Act 1968, s.19(2)–(3)

False statements by company directors, etc.

11–72.1

19.—(2) For purposes of this section a person who has entered into a security for the benefit of a body corporate or association is to be treated as a creditor of it.

(3) Where the affairs of a body corporate or association are managed by its members, this section shall apply to any statement which a member publishes or concurs in publishing in connection with his functions of management as if he were an officer of the body corporate or association.

See *Archbold Crown*, §§ 30–267—30–269.

(d) *Sentence*

11–73

When tried summarily, the maximum penalty is six months' imprisonment, a fine not exceeding the statutory maximum or both.

For sentencing guidelines in fraud cases generally, see s.8(c) above.

M. SUPPRESSION OF DOCUMENTS

(a) *Definition*

Theft Act 1968, s.20(1)–(2)

Suppression, etc. of documents

11–74

20.—(1) A person who dishonestly, with a view to gain for himself or another or with intent to cause loss to another, destroys, defaces or conceals any valuable security, any will or other testamentary document or any original document of or belonging to, or filed or deposited in, any court of justice or any government department shall on conviction on indictment be liable to imprisonment for a term not exceeding seven years.

(2) A person who dishonestly, with a view to gain for himself or another or with intent to cause loss to another, by any deception procures the execution of a valuable security shall on conviction on indictment be liable to imprisonment for a term not exceeding seven years; and this subsection shall apply in relation to the making, acceptance, indorsement, alteration, cancellation or destruction in whole or in part of a valuable security, and in relation to the signing or sealing of any paper or other material in order that it may be made or converted into, or used or dealt with as, a valuable security, as if that were the execution of a valuable security.

(b) *Procedure*

11–75

This offence is triable either way (*MCA* 1980, s.17 and Sch.1, para.28). For guidance as to when summary trial of fraud cases is appropriate see § 11–51 above.

Section 20 of the *Theft Act* 1968 creates two separate offences. Regarding the offence of destroying a will, the prosecution must prove that:
— the defendant dishonestly
— with a view to gain for himself or another OR with intent to cause loss to another
— destroyed, defaced or concealed,
— any valuable security, any will or other testamentary document or any original document of or belonging to, or filed or deposited in any court of justice or any government department.

11–75.1

As regards the offence of procuring the execution of a valuable security by deception, the prosecution must prove that:

— the defendant dishonestly,
— with a view to gain for himself or another OR with intent to cause loss to another;
— procured the execution of any valuable security
— by deception.

(c) *Elements of the offence*

Theft Act 1968, s.20(3)

Suppression, etc. of documents

11–76   **20.**—(3) For purposes of this section "deception" has the same meaning as in section 15 of this Act, and "valuable security" means any document creating, transferring, surrendering or releasing any right to, in or over property, or authorising the payment of money or delivery of any property, or evidencing the creation, transfer, surrender or release of any such right, or the payment of money or delivery of any property, or the satisfaction of any obligation.

See further, *Archbold Crown*, §§ 21–246—21–255.

(d) *Sentence*

11–77   When tried summarily the maximum penalty for this offence is six months' imprisonment, fine not exceeding statutory maximum or both.

In *R. v Kerr* [1998] 2 Cr.App.R.(S.) 316, CA, the offender was convicted of obtaining the execution of a valuable security by deception. He had forged a deed of gift and a Land Registration form in order to obtain a bungalow. A sentence of three years imprisonment was upheld, the offender had practiced a deception at the land Registry, and hence the sentence could not be considered manifestly excessive. In *R. v Samra* (1992) 13 Cr.App.R.(S.) 168 a sentence of nine months' imprisonment was upheld following pleas of guilty to two counts of procuring the execution of a valuable security by deception. The offender had obtained mortgages on two houses by making false representations about his income, circumstances and intentions. The need for deterrent custodial sentences in the context of mortgage frauds was highlighted in *R. v Evans* (1992) 13 Cr.App.R.(S.) 413. The offender had procured two mortgage advances by the making of false representations in relation to his employment and earnings. His sentence of twelve months imprisonment and order to pay the costs of the prosecution was upheld in the Court of Appeal.

N. HANDLING STOLEN GOODS

(a) *Definition*

Theft Act 1968, s.22

Handling stolen goods

11–78   **22.**—(1) A person handles stolen goods if (otherwise than in the course of the stealing) knowing or believing them to be stolen goods he dishonestly receives the goods, or dishonestly undertakes or assists in their retention, removal, disposal or realisation by or for the benefit of another person, or if he arranges to do so.

(2) A person guilty of handling stolen goods shall on conviction on indictment be liable to imprisonment for a term not exceeding fourteen years.

(b) *Procedure*

11–78.1   This offence is triable either way (*MCA* 1980, s.17 and Sch.1, para.28). The *Practice Direction (Criminal Proceedings: Consolidated)*, para.V.51.8 provides that cases of handling should be tried summarily unless the court considers that one or more of the following features are present and that its sentencing powers are insufficient:

(a) Dishonest handling of stolen property by a receiver who has commissioned the theft
(b) The offence has professional hallmarks
(c) The property is of high value (£10,000 or more)

The prosecution must prove that:

— the defendant dishonestly,
— received OR undertook or assisted in the retention, removal, disposal or realisation by or for the benefit of another person, OR arranged to so undertake or assist, of,
— goods which he knew or believed to be stolen,
— otherwise than in the course of stealing them.

(c) *Elements of the offence*

Stolen goods

The term 'goods' is defined in s.34(2)(b) of the 1968 Act as including money and **11–79** every other description of property except land, and things severed from the land by stealing. The fact that the goods are stolen may be proved by the thief or by circumstantial evidence. See further *Archbold Crown*, §§ 21–294—21–305.

Handling

Handling is proved by establishing that the defendant either received the goods, or **11–80** arranged to do so, or undertook or assisted in their retention, removal, disposal or realisation by or for the benefit of another person, or arranged to do so.

In *R. v Frost* (1964) 48 Cr.App.R. 284, CCA it was held that for a defendant to be convicted of receiving, it must be established that he took possession or control of the property, either jointly or exclusively. The requirement that control is taken of the goods means that proof that the defendant physically handled the goods will not suffice. See further, *Archbold Crown*, §§ 21–304—21–306.

Where a person is charged with undertaking or assisting etc, there is no need to prove possession or control. In *R. v Bloxham* (1983) 1 A.C. 109, HL, the House of Lords examined the ambit of the second limb of the offence established by s.22(1) and concluded that the second limb creates a second offence that can be committed in a number of ways, the activities envisaged by the section being retention, removal, disposal and realisation. Lord Bridge stated:

> 'The offence can be committed in relation to any one of these activities in one or other of two **11–81** ways. First, the offender may himself undertake the activity *for the benefit of* another person. Secondly, the activity may be undertaken by another person and the offender may assist him. Of course, if the thief or an original receiver and his friend act together in, say, removing the stolen goods, the friend may be committing the offence in both ways. But this does not invalidate the analysis and if the analysis holds good, it must follow, I think, that the category of other persons contemplated by the subsection is subject to the same limitations in whichever way the offence is committed.' .

See further, *Archbold Crown*, §§ 21–396—21–307
The words 'or if he arranges to do so' apply to both limbs of s.22(1).

Dishonestly

The relevant test if that established by the case of *R. v Ghosh* (above). See further, **11–82** *Archbold Crown*, § 21–309.

The defendant's knowledge or belief that the goods were stolen at the material time may be established by the direct evidence of the principal offender or circumstantially. This question is subjective, and it is not enough that the goods were handled in circumstances that would put the reasonable man on inquiry. Suspicion that the goods were stolen, even coupled with the fact that the defendant shut his eyes to the circumstances, is not enough, although those matters may be taken into account: *R. v Moys* 79 Cr.App.R. 72, CA. See further *Archbold Crown*, §§ 21–310—21–312.

Proof of guilty knowledge by evidence of the possession of other stolen property of previous conviction

Theft Act 1968, s.27(3), (5)

Evidence and procedure on charge of theft or handling stolen goods

11–83   **27.**—(3) Where a person is being proceeded against for handling stolen goods (but not for any offence other than handling stolen goods), then at any stage of the proceedings, if evidence has been given of his having or arranging to have in his possession the goods the subject of the charge, or of his undertaking or assisting in, or arranging to undertake or assist in, their retention, removal, disposal or realisation, the following evidence shall be admissible for the purpose of proving that he knew or believed the goods to be stolen goods—

     (a) evidence that he has had in his possession, or has undertaken or assisted in the retention, removal, disposal or realisation of, stolen goods from any theft taking place not earlier than twelve months before the offence charged; and

     (b) (provided that seven days' notice in writing has been given to him of the intention to prove the conviction)

evidence that he has within the five years preceding the date of the offence charged been convicted of theft or of handling stolen goods.

     (5) This section is to be construed in accordance with section 24 of this Act; and in subsection (3)(b) above the reference to handling stolen goods shall include any corresponding offence committed before the commencement of this Act.

For further detail and principles of the doctrine of recent possession as evidence of guilty knowledge, see *Archbold Crown*, §§ 21–313—21–310.

(d) *Sentence*

11–84   When tried summarily the maximum penalty for this offence is six months' imprisonment, a fine not exceeding the statutory maximum or both.

The *Magistrates' Court Sentencing Guidelines* (2003) amend the guidelines on handling stolen goods in line with Court of Appeal guidance. They state:

> Aggravating factors include commission of the offence whilst on bail, high level of profit accruing to handler, high value (including sentimental) of goods, provision by handler of regular outlet for stolen goods, proximity of the handler to the primary offence, seriousness of the primary offence, sophistication, the particular facts e.g. the goods handled were the proceeds of a domestic burglary and threats of violence or abuse of power by handler in order to obtain goods.

> Mitigating factors include: Immediate offer of restitution to victim, isolated offence committed by defendant of hitherto good character, little or no benefit accruing to handler and low monetary value of goods.

> **Guideline**: Is it serious enough for a community penalty?

11–85   In *R. v Webbe* [2001] Crim.L.R. 668, the Court of Appeal considered guidelines for sentencing in cases of handling stolen goods proposed by the Sentencing Advisory Panel (see *R. v Webbe* below). The Court agreed with the panel's view that the handler's advance knowledge of the original offence was an important question; where the handler had knowledge of the original offence, the seriousness of the handling was inevitably linked to the seriousness of the original offence. The replacement value of the goods involved a helpful indication of the seriousness of the offence, although not the determining factor. Other factors identified as relevant considerations were the level of sophistication of the handler, the ultimate destination of the goods, the criminal origin of the goods, the impact on the victim, the level of profit made or expected by the handler and the precise role played by the handler. The Court also held that handling cases at or towards the lower end of the scale were characterised by the handler having no connection with the original offence, an absence of sophistication on the part of the handler, the less serious nature of the original offence, the relatively low value of goods and the absence of any significant profit.

Aggravating factors include: closeness of the handler to the primary offence; particular seriousness in the primary offence; high value of goods to the loser, including sentimental value; the fact that the goods were the proceeds of a domestic burglary; sophistication in relation to the handling; a high level of profit made or expected by the handler; the provision by the handler of a regular outlet for the stolen goods. Threats of violence or abuse of power by the handler over others, for example an adult commissioning criminal activity by children or a drug dealer pressurising addicts to steal to pay for their habit. The commission of an offence while on bail was also an aggravating factor.

Mitigating factors included the low monetary value of goods, the fact that the offence was a one-off offence committed by an otherwise honest defendant, the fact that there was little no benefit to the defendant and the fact that voluntary restitution had been made. The Court also agreed that other mitigating factors included personal mitigation, ready co-operation with the police and a timely plea of guilty. Previous convictions were relevant. In *R. v Wilson* (1980) 2 Cr.App.R.(S.) 196, the offender, a man of good character pleaded guilty to handling stolen caravans worth some £4,500.

The CA stated that imprisonment was the only way of dealing with these offences **11–86** since the property was of considerable value. However, for a man in the appellant's position a short immediate sentence of imprisonment, perhaps coupled with a fine, was likely to have all the deterrent effect that it was desired to achieve. The offender was sentenced to two months' imprisonment.

O. Retaining a Wrongful Credit

(a) *Definition*

Theft Act 1968, s.24A(1)

Dishonestly retaining a wrongful credit
　24A.—(1) A person is guilty of an offence if—　　　　　　　　　　　　　　**11–87**
　　(a) a wrongful credit has been made to an account kept by him or in respect of which he has any right or interest;
　　(b) he knows or believes that the credit is wrongful; and
　　(c) he dishonestly fails to take such steps as are reasonable in the circumstances to secure that the credit is cancelled.

[This section was inserted as from December 18, 1996 by the *Theft (Amendment) Act* 1996, s.2(1).]

(b) **Procedure**

This offence is triable either way (*MCA* 1980, s.17 and Sch.1, para.28).　　　**11–87.1**
The prosecution must prove that:
　— a wrongful credit was made to an account kept by the defendant, or to an account in respect of which he had any right or interest and;
　— the defendant knew or believed that the credit was wrongful and;
　— he dishonestly;
　— failed to take such steps as were reasonable in the circumstances to secure that the credit is cancelled.

(c) *Elements of the offence*

Theft Act 1968, s.24A(2)–(9)

Dishonestly retaining a wrongful credit
　24A.—(2) References to a credit are to a credit of an amount of money.　**11–88**

(3) A credit to an account is wrongful if it is the credit side of a money transfer obtained contrary to section 15A of this Act.

(4) A credit to an account is also wrongful to the extent that it derives from—

    (a) theft;

    (b) an offence under section 15A of this Act;

    (c) blackmail; or

    (d) stolen goods.

(5) In determining whether a credit to an account is wrongful, it is immaterial (in particular) whether the account is overdrawn before or after the credit is made.

(6) A person guilty of an offence under this section shall be liable on conviction on indictment to imprisonment for a term not exceeding ten years.

(7) Subsection (8) below applies for purposes of provisions of this Act relating to stolen goods (including subsection (4) above).

(8) References to stolen goods include money which is dishonestly withdrawn from an account to which a wrongful credit has been made, but only to the extent that the money derives from the credit.

(9) In this section "account" and "money" shall be construed in accordance with section 15B of this Act.

See *Archbold Crown*, § 21–323g.

(d) *Sentence*

11–88.1   When tried summarily, the maximum penalty is six months' imprisonment, a fine not exceeding the statutory maximum or both.

P. Advertising Rewards for Return of Goods Stolen or Lost

(a) *Definition*

Theft Act 1968, s.23

Advertising rewards for return of goods stolen or lost

11–89   **23.** Where any public advertisement of a reward for the return of any goods which have been stolen or lost uses any words to the effect that no questions will be asked, or that the person producing the goods will be safe from apprehension or inquiry, or that any money paid for the purchase of the goods or advanced by way of loan on them will be repaid, the person advertising the reward and any person who prints or publishes the advertisement shall on summary conviction be liable to a fine not exceeding level 3 on the standard scale.

(b) *Procedure*

11–89.1   This offence is triable summarily only: *Theft Act* 1968, s.23.

The prosecution must prove that:

— the defendant advertised a reward for the return of any goods stolen or lost, or printed or published such an advertisement and

— the advertisement used words to the effect that no questions will be asked, or that the person producing the goods will be safe from apprehension or inquiry or that any money paid for the purchase of the goods or advanced by way of loan will be repaid.

(c) *Elements of the offence*

11–90   The provision prohibits public advertisements which couple the offer of a reward for information with the caveat that no questions shall be asked. The offence is one of strict liability, publishing an advert for the return of goods for a reward stating that no questions would be asked will establish the offence, mens rea does not need to be proved: *Denham v Scott* (1983) 77 Cr.App.R. 210.

(d) *Sentence*

The maximum penalty for this offence is a fine not exceeding level three on the standard scale: *Theft Act* 1968, s.23.   **11–90.1**

Q. GOING EQUIPPED

(a) *Definition*

Theft Act 1968, s.25(1), (3)–(5)

Going equipped for stealing, etc.
25.—(1) A person shall be guilty of an offence if, when not at his place of abode, he has with   **11–91**
him any article for use in the course of or in connection with any burglary, theft or cheat.

(3) Where a person is charged with an offence under this section, proof that he had
with him any article made or adapted for use in committing a burglary, theft or cheat shall
be evidence that he had it with him for such use.

(4) Any person may arrest without warrant anyone who is, or whom he, with reasonable
cause, suspects to be, committing an offence under this section.

(5) For purposes of this section an offence under section 12(1) of this Act of taking a
conveyance shall be treated as theft, and "cheat" means an offence under section 15 of this
Act.

(b) *Procedure*

This offence is triable either way (*MCA* 1980, s.17 and Sch.1, para.28).   **11–91.1**
The prosecution must prove that:
— the defendant was not at his place of abode and;
— he had with him any article for use in the course of or in connection with any
   burglary, theft or cheat.

(c) *Elements of the offence*

Theft Act 1968, s.25

Going equipped for stealing, etc.
25.—(3) Where a person is charged with an offence under this section, proof that he had   **11–92**
with him any article made or adapted for use in committing a burglary, theft or cheat shall be
evidence that he had it with him for such use.

(4) Any person may arrest without warrant anyone who is, or whom he, with reasonable
cause, suspects to be, committing an offence under this section.

(5) For purposes of this section an offence under section 12(1) of this Act of taking a
conveyance shall be treated as theft, and "cheat" means an offence under section 15 of this
Act.

See *Archbold Crown*, §§ 21-328—21-330.

(d) *Sentence*

When tried summarily, the maximum penalty for this offence is six months' imprison-   **11–93**
ment, a fine not exceeding the statutory maximum or both.

The *Magistrates' Court Sentencing Guidelines* (2003) state:

> Aggravating factors include premeditated, group action, sophisticated, specialised equipment,
> number if items, people put in fear, offence committed on bail, relevant previous convictions
> and any failure to respond to previous sentences.
> No mitigating factors are listed.
> **Guideline**: Is it serious enough for a community penalty? Consider forfeiture of equipment.

In *R. v Ferry and Wynn* [1997] 2 Cr.App.R.(S.) 42 a sentence of twelve months' imprisonment for going equipped to steal from telephone boxes was upheld by the Court of Appeal. The offenders were in possession of a cordless drill and other tools, and a map indicating the location of other telephone boxes. A custodial sentence was held to be justified as the offences involved a sustained enterprise to break into telephone boxes in rural areas, and could not be compared with a single attack on a telephone box in an urban area.

For information on the general provisions of the *Theft Act* 1968, ss.26–34, see *Archbold Crown*, §§ 21-331—21-339.

R. Obtaining Services by Deception

(a) *Definition*

Theft Act 1978, s.1

Obtaining services by deception

11–94   1.—(1) A person who by any deception dishonestly obtains services from another shall be guilty of an offence.

(2) It is an obtaining of services where the other is induced to confer a benefit by doing some act, or causing or permitting some act to be done, on the understanding that the benefit has been or will be paid for.

(3) Without prejudice to the generality of subsection (2) above, it is an obtaining of services where the other is induced to make a loan, or to cause or permit a loan to be made, on the understanding that any payment (whether by way of interest or otherwise) will be or has been made in respect of the loan.

[Subs.(3) was inserted by the *Theft (Amendment) Act* 1996, s.4(1); in relation to things done on or after December 18, 1996.]

(b) *Procedure*

11–94.1   This offence is triable either way (*Theft Act* 1978, s.4(1)). For guidance as to when the offence is appropriately tried summarily, see § 11–51 (above)

The prosecution must prove that;
— The defendant dishonestly
— Obtained services from another.

(c) *Elements of the offence*

11–95   'Deception' has the same meaning as in s.15 of the *Theft Act* 1968 (above).

In *R. v Graham, R. v Kansal, R. v Ali, R. v Marsh* [1997] Cr.App.R. 302, CA, it was held that the meaning of "services" should not be restricted and is wide enough to embrace professional services, commercial services and financial services, the essential conditions being that a service must confer a benefit and be rendered on the understanding that it had been or would be paid for.

See further *Archbold Crown*, § 21–34.

(d) *Sentence*

11–96   When tried summarily, the maximum penalty is six months imprisonment, a fine not exceeding the statutory maximum or both. In *R. v Takyi (Daniel)* [1998] 1 Cr.App.R.(S.) 372, CA, the offender had attempted to board an international flight by presenting a passport belonging to another person and a ticket in that person's name. The Court of Appeal reduced his sentence of nine months' imprisonment to three months' imprisonment, holding that the integrity of the airport system was of such public importance that in normal circumstances a custodial sentence would follow from an offence involving the improper use of a passport.

However, in *R. v Osman* [1999] 1 Cr.App.R.(S.) 230, CA a sentence of nine months' imprisonment for passport fraud (prosecuted under the *Forgery and Counterfeiting Act* 1981, s.3) was upheld, the Court of Appeal stating that the decision in *Takyi* should be confined to its own facts. The courts should try when sentencing to discourage others who may be tempted to abuse the system.

S. EVASION OF LIABILITY BY DECEPTION

(a) Definition

Theft Act 1978, s.2(1)

Evasion of liability by deception

2.—(1) Subject to subsection (2) below, where a person by any deception—   **11–97**
    (a) dishonestly secures the remission of the whole or part of any existing liability to make a payment, whether his own liability or another's; or
    (b) with intent to make permanent default in whole or in part on any existing liability to make a payment, or with intent to let another do so, dishonestly induces the creditor or any person claiming payment on behalf of the creditor to wait for payment (whether or not the due date for payment is deferred) or to forgo payment; or
    (c) dishonestly obtains any exemption from or abatement of liability to make a payment.
he shall be guilty of an offence.

(b) *Procedure*

This offence is triable either way (*Theft Act* 1978, s.4(1)).   **11–98**
The prosecution must prove that either:
— the defendant dishonestly,
— secured the remission of the whole or any part of any existing liability to make a payment, whether his own or another's.
OR
— the defendant dishonestly,
— induced the creditor or any person claiming payment on behalf of the creditor to wait for payment or to forgo payment,
— with intention to make a permanent default in whole or in part on any existing liability to make a payment.
OR
— the defendant dishonestly
— obtained any exemption from or abatement of liability to make a payment.

(3) *Elements of the offence*

Theft Act 1978, s.2(2)–(4)

Evasion of liability by deception

2.—(2) For purposes of this section "liability" means legally enforceable liability; and subsection (1) shall not apply in relation to a liability that has not been accepted or established to pay compensation for a wrongful act or omission.   **11–98.1**

(3) For purposes of subsection (1)(b) a person induced to take in payment a cheque or other security for money by way of conditional satisfaction of a pre-existing liability is to be treated not as being paid but as being induced to wait for payment.

(4) For purposes of subsection (1)(c) "obtains" includes obtaining for another or enabling another to obtain.

See *Archbold Crown*, §§ 21-345—21-349.

(d) *Sentence*

When tried summarily, the maximum penalty is six months imprisonment, a fine not   **11–99** exceeding the statutory maximum or both. For sentencing guidelines on offences of fraud generally, see *Magistrates' Court Sentencing Guidelines* (2003) pertaining to *Theft Act* 1968, s.15, (above).

T. MAKING OFF WITHOUT PAYMENT

(a) *Definition*

Theft Act 1978, s.3

Making off without payment

11–100 **3.**—(1) Subject to subsection (3) below, a person who, knowing that payment on the spot for any goods supplied or service done is required or expected from him, dishonestly makes off without having paid as required or expected and with intent to avoid payment of the amount due shall be guilty of an offence.

(2) For purposes of this section "payment on the spot" includes payment at the time of collecting goods on which work has been done or in respect of which service has been provided.

(3) Subsection (1) above shall not apply where the supply of the goods or the doing of the service is contrary to law, or where the service done is such that payment is not legally enforceable.

(4) Any person may arrest without warrant anyone who is, or whom he, with reasonable cause, suspects to be, committing or attempting to commit an offence under this section.

(b) *Procedure*

11–101 This offence is triable either way (*Theft Act* 1978, s.4(1)). For guidance as to when the offence is appropriately tried summarily, see above.

The prosecution must prove that:

— the defendant knew that payment on the spot for any goods supplied or service done was required or expected of him and

— he dishonestly

— made off without having paid as required or expected,

— with intent to avoid payment of the amount due.

(c) *Elements of the offence*

11–102 'Making off' involves a departure from the spot where payment was required: *R. v Brooks*, 76 Cr.App.R. 66, CA. In *R. v Allen* (1985) A.C. 1029, HL it was held that the following must be proved to secure a conviction under s.3(1) that the defendant in fact made off without making payment on the spot; (2) the following mental elements—(a) knowledge that payment on the spot was required or expected of him; and (b) dishonesty; and (c) intent to avoid payment of the amount due.

See further *Archbold Crown*, §§ 21–352—21–355.

(d) *Sentence*

11–103 When tried summarily, the maximum penalty is six months' imprisonment, a fine not exceeding the statutory maximum or both.

For sentencing guidelines on offences of fraud generally, see *Magistrates' Court Sentencing Guidelines* (2003) pertaining to the *Theft Act* 1968, s.15.

When dealt with summarily, the *Magistrates' Court Sentencing Guidelines* (2003) state:

Aggravating factors include deliberate plan, high value, two or more involved, racial aggravation, victim particularly vulnerable, offence committed on bail, relevant previous convictions and any failures to respond to previous sentences.
Mitigating factors include impulsive action, low value.

Guideline: is it serious enough for a community penalty?

In *R. v Foster* (1994) 15 Cr.App.R.(S.) 340 a sentence of three months' imprison- **11–104** ment was upheld for making off without payment of taxi fares of between £37 and £63. The appellant had previous convictions for conspiracy to burgle and theft, and was subject to a suspended sentence of nine months at the time of the offences. That sentence was activated consecutively, meaning that the total sentence was one of twelve months' imprisonment.

II. OFFENCES OF FORGERY, PERSONATION AND CHEATING

A. FORGERY

(a) *Definition*

Forgery and Counterfeiting Act 1981, s.1

The offence of forgery
1. A person is guilty of forgery if he makes a false instrument, with the intention that he or **11–105** another shall use it to induce somebody to accept it as genuine, and by reason of so accepting it to do or not to do some act to his own or any other person's prejudice.

(b) *Procedure*

This offence is triable either way: *Forgery and Counterfeiting Act* 1981, s.6. **11–105.1** The prosecution must prove that:
— the defendant made a false instrument
— with the intention that he or another should use it to induce somebody to accept it as genuine and to hence,
— do or not do some act to his own or another person's prejudice by reason of that acceptance.

(c) *Elements of the offence*

The intention required for a charge under s.1 is (a) the intention that the false instru- **11–106** ment will be used to induce somebody to accept it as genuine and (b) the intention to induce somebody by reason of so accepting it to do or not do some act to his own or another person's prejudice: *R. v Campbell*, 80 Cr.App.R. 47, CA.

Forgery and Counterfeiting Act 1981, s.8

Meaning of "instrument"
8.—(1) Subject to subsection (2) below, in this Part of this Act "instrument" means— **11–107**
    (a) any document, whether of a formal or informal character;
    (b) any stamp issued or sold by a postal operator;
    (c) any Inland Revenue stamp; and
    (d) any disc, tape, sound track or other device on or in which information is re-
        corded or stored by mechanical, electronic or other means.

(2) A currency note within the meaning of Part II of this Act is not an instrument for the purposes of this Part of this Act.

(3) A mark denoting payment of postage which a postal operator authorises to be used instead of an adhesive stamp is to be treated for the purposes of this Part of this Act as if it were a stamp issued by the postal operator concerned.

(3A) In this section "postal operator" has the same meaning as in the *Postal Services Act* 2000.

(4) In this Part of this Act "Inland Revenue stamp" means a stamp as defined in section 27 of the *Stamp Duties Management Act* 1891.

[This section is printed as amended by the *Postal Services Act 2000 (Consequential Modifications No.1) Order* 2001 (SI 2001/1149), Art.3(1) and Sch.1, para.50.]

Forgery and Counterfeiting Act 1981, s.9

Meaning of "false" and "making"

11–108   **9.**—(1) An instrument is false for the purposes of this Part of this Act—

(a) if it purports to have been made in the form in which it is made by a person who did not in fact make it in that form; or

(b) if it purports to have been made in the form in which it is made on the authority of a person who did not in fact authorise its making in that form; or

(c) if it purports to have been made in the terms in which it is made by a person who did not in fact make it in those terms; or

(d) if it purports to have been made in the terms in which it is made on the authority of a person who did not in fact authorise its making in those terms; or

(e) if it purports to have been altered in any respect by a person who did not in fact alter it in that respect; or

(f) if it purports to have been altered in any respect on the authority of a person who did not in fact authorise the alteration in that respect; or

(g) if it purports to have been made or altered on a date on which, or at a place at which, or otherwise in circumstances in which, it was not in fact made or altered; or

(h) if it purports to have been made or altered by an existing person but he did not in fact exist.

(2) A person is to be treated for the purposes of this Part of this Act as making a false instrument if he alters an instrument so as to make it false in any respect (whether or not it is false in some other respect apart from that alteration).

Forgery and Counterfeiting Act 1981, s.10

Meaning of "prejudice" and "induce"

11–109   **10.**—(1) Subject to subsections (2) and (4) below, for the purposes of this Part of this Act an act or omission intended to be induced is to a person's prejudice if, and only if, it is one which, if it occurs—

(a) will result—

(i) in his temporary or permanent loss of property; or

(ii) in his being deprived of an opportunity to earn remuneration or greater remuneration; or

(iii) in his being deprived of an opportunity to gain a financial advantage otherwise than by way of remuneration; or

(b) will result in somebody being given an opportunity—

(i) to earn remuneration or greater remuneration from him; or

(ii) to gain a financial advantage from him otherwise than by way of remuneration; or

(c) will be the result of his having accepted a false instrument as genuine, or a copy of a false instrument as a copy of a genuine one, in connection with his performance of any duty.

(2) An act which a person has an enforceable duty to do and an omission to do an act which a person is not entitled to do shall be disregarded for the purposes of this Part of this Act.

(3) In this Part of this Act references to inducing somebody to accept a false instrument as genuine, or a copy of a false instrument as a copy of a genuine one, include references to inducing a machine to respond to the instrument or copy as if it were a genuine instrument or, as the case may be, a copy of a genuine one.

(4) Where subsection (3) above applies, the act or omission intended to be induced by the machine responding to the instrument or copy shall be treated as an act or omission to a person's prejudice.

(5) In this section "loss" includes not getting what one might get as well as parting with what one has.

See further *Archbold Crown*, § 22–8—22–25.

(d) *Sentence*

11–110   When tried summarily, the maximum penalty for this offence is six months' imprisonment or a fine not exceeding the statutory maximum or both: *Forgery and Counterfeiting Act* 1981, s.6.

In *R. v Lincoln* (1994) 15 Cr.App.R.(S.) 333, a husband forged his estranged wife's signature on a contract of sale of house and Land Registry transfer. The original sentence of twelve months' imprisonment for this offence was reduced to six months' imprisonment on appeal. It was held that forgery of documents of title to property must be visited by an immediate custodial sentence in all but the most exceptional circumstances yet in view of the mitigating circumstances, the sentence would be reduced to six months.

In *R. v Dover* (1995) 16 Cr.App.R.(S.) 61, the offender pleaded guilty to two counts of forgery, one of procuring the execution of a valuable security by deception and one of theft. The offender had forged an estimate for the repair of the storm-damaged block of flats that he was responsible for managing, and then kept the difference between the actual cost of repair and the insurance companies' payment for himself. He was sentenced to five months' imprisonment, the court stating 'having regard to the breach of trust involved in the offence of theft and the serious nature of the forgeries involving as they do fraud upon an insurance company, five months was, looked at in the round a very lenient sentence.'

B. Copying a False Instrument

(a) *Definition*

Forgery and Counterfeiting Act 1981, s.2

The offence of copying a false instrument
2. It is an offence for a person to make a copy of an instrument which is, and which he knows **11–111**
or believes to be, a false instrument, with the intention that he or another shall use it to induce somebody to accept it as a copy of a genuine instrument, and by reason of so accepting it to do or not to do some act to his own or any other person's prejudice

(b) *Procedure*

This offence is triable either way: *Forgery and Counterfeiting Act* 1981, s.6. The **11–111.1**
prosecution must prove that:
— the defendant made a copy of an instrument which,
— he knew or believed to be a false instrument and
— he intended that he or another should use the copy to induce somebody to accept it as a copy of a genuine instrument and
— to cause that other person to do or not do some act to his or another person's prejudice by reason of so accepting the copy.

(c) *Elements of the offence*

For the definition of 'instrument', see s.8 of the 1981 Act (above); of 'false', s.9 (above) **11–111.2**
and of 'prejudice' or 'induce' see s.10 (above).

(d) *Sentence*

When tried summarily, the maximum penalty is six months imprisonment, a fine not **11–112**
exceeding the statutory maximum or both: *Forgery and Counterfeiting Act* 1981, s.6.

C. Using a False Instrument, Using Copy of a False Instrument

(a) *Definition*

Forgery and Counterfeiting Act 1981, ss.3, 4

The offence of using a false instrument
3. It is an offence for a person to use an instrument which is, and which he knows or believes **11–113**

411

to be, false, with the intention of inducing somebody to accept it as genuine, and by reason of so accepting it to do or not to do some act to his own or any other person's prejudice.

The offence of using a copy of a false instrument

1–113.1   **4.** It is an offence for a person to use a copy of an instrument which is, and which he knows or believes to be, a false instrument, with the intention of inducing somebody to accept it as a copy of a genuine instrument, and by reason of so accepting it to do or not to do some act to his own or any other person's prejudice.

(b) *Procedure*

11–114   This offence is triable either way: *Forgery and Counterfeiting Act* 1981, s.6.

(c) *Elements of the offence*

11–115   The prosecution must prove that either:
— the defendant used an instrument that is, and that he knew or believed to be, false
— with the intention of inducing somebody to accept it as genuine and
— to cause that person to do or not to do some act to his own or any other person's prejudice by reason of so accepting the instrument as genuine.

OR
— the defendant used a copy of an instrument that is, and that he knew or believed to be false
— with the intention of inducing somebody to accept it as a copy of a genuine instrument and,
— to cause that person to do or not to do some act to his own or any other person's prejudice by reason of so accepting the instrument as a copy of a genuine instrument.

See *Archbold Crown*, §§ 22–26—22–30.

(d) *Sentence*

11–115.1   When tried summarily, the maximum penalty is six months imprisonment, a fine not exceeding the statutory maximum or both: *Forgery and Counterfeiting Act* 1981, s.6.

In *R. v Duffy* (1994) 15 Cr.App.R.(S.) 677, the offender pleaded guilty to forgery of a candidate's nomination form in connection with a local election and was sentenced to six months' imprisonment. It was held that the offence was here a technical one. As such, a custodial sentence was unwarranted; a substantial financial penalty would have been appropriate. As D had served a month in custody, an absolute discharge was substituted.

In *R. v Balasubramaniam* [2002] 2 Cr.App.R.(S.) 17, a sentence of twelve months' imprisonment for attempting to use a false passport to travel to Canada to visit the appellant's sick mother reduced to six months. The court found that this was a case where there was a plea of guilty by a person of good character, but it was not an exceptional case where a sentence of less than six months could be justified. There were no aggravating features to justify a sentence in excess of six to nine months. This was not a case of using a false passport for financial gain or to subvert entry requirements or to seek employment in a country that would not otherwise grant admission. The facts placed the particular case at the bottom of the six months to nine months bracket. The Court would substitute a sentence of six months' imprisonment.

In *R. v Daljit Singh* [1999] 1 Cr.App.R.(S.) 490, the offender pleaded guilty before a magistrates' court to using a false passport in order to board a flight to Canada. The Court of Appeal upheld his sentence of eight months' imprisonment. Rose L.J. explaining that for reasons of deterrence 'cases involving the use of false passports will almost always merit a significant period of custody.'

D. CUSTODY OR CONTROL OF CERTAIN FALSE INSTRUMENTS AND MANUFACTURE, CUSTODY OR CONTROL OF EQUIPMENT OR MATERIALS WITH WHICH SUCH INSTRUMENTS MAY BE MADE

(a) *Definition*

Forgery and Counterfeiting Act 1981, s.5(1)–(4)

Offences relating to money orders, share certificates, passports, etc.

5.—(1) It is an offence for a person to have in his custody or under his control an instrument **11–116** to which this section applies which is, and which he knows or believes to be, false, with the intention that he or another shall use it to induce somebody to accept it as genuine, and by reason of so accepting it to do or not to do some act to his own or any other person's prejudice.

(2) It is an offence for a person to have in his custody or under his control, without lawful authority or excuse, an instrument to which this section applies which is, and which he knows or believes to be, false.

(3) It is an offence for a person to make or to have in his custody or under his control a machine or implement, or paper or any other material, which to his knowledge is or has been specially designed or adapted for the making of an instrument to which this section applies, with the intention that he or another shall make an instrument to which this section applies which is false and that he or another shall use the instrument to induce somebody to accept it as genuine, and by reason of so accepting it to do or not to do some act to his own or any other person's prejudice.

(4) It is an offence for a person to make or to have in his custody or under his control any such machine, implement, paper or material, without lawful authority or excuse.

(c) *Procedure*

These offences are triable either way: *Forgery and Counterfeiting Act* 1981, s.6   **11–117**
The prosecution must prove that either:
— the defendant had in his custody or under his control
— an instrument of the kind listed in s.5(3) of the 1981 Act which
— he knows or believes to be false with
— the intention that he or another shall induce somebody to accept it as genuine and
— cause that person to do or not do some act to his own or another person's prejudice by reason of him accepting the instrument as genuine.
OR
— the defendant had in his custody or under his control
— an instrument of the kind listed in s.5(3) of the 1981 Act which
— is, and which he knows to be false
— without lawful authority or excuse.
OR
— the defendant had in his custody or under his control
— a machine or implement, or paper or any other material which
— to his knowledge is or has been designed or adapted for the making of an instrument of the kind listed in s.5(3) of the 1981 Act.
— with the intention that he or another shall make an instrument of the kind listed in s.5(3) of the 1981 Act which is false and
— that he or another shall use the instruments to induce somebody to accept it as genuine and
— cause that person to do or not do some act to his own or another person's prejudice by reason of him accepting the instrument as genuine.
OR
— the defendant had in his custody or under his control
— any such machine, implement, paper or material as described in s.5(3)

413

— without lawful authority or excuse.

(c) *Elements of the offence*

Forgery and Counterfeiting Act 1981, s.5(5), (6)

Offences relating to money orders, share certificates, passports, etc.

11–118   **5.**—(5) The instruments to which this section applies are—
(a) money orders;
(b) postal orders;
(c) United Kingdom postage stamps;
(d) Inland Revenue stamps;
(e) share certificates;
(f) passports and documents which can be used instead of passports;
(g) cheques;
(h) travellers' cheques;
(j) cheque cards;
(k) credit cards;
(l) certified copies relating to an entry in a register of births, adoptions, marriages or deaths and issued by the Registrar General, the Registrar General for Northern Ireland, a registration officer or a person lawfully authorised to register marriages; and
(m) certificates relating to entries in such registers.

(6) In subsection (5)(e) above "share certificate" means an instrument entitling or evidencing the title of a person to a share or interest—
(a) in any public stock, annuity, fund or debt of any government or state, including a state which forms part of another state; or
(b) in any stock, fund or debt of a body (whether corporate or unincorporated) established in the United Kingdom or elsewhere.

See further *Archbold Crown*, §§ 22–32—22–36.

(d) *Sentence*

11–119   When tried summarily, the maximum penalty is six months imprisonment, a fine not exceeding the statutory maximum or both: *Forgery and Counterfeiting Act* 1981, s.6.

In *R. v Siliavski* [2000] 1 Cr.App.R.(S.) 23, the offender pleaded guilty to possessing forged passports after four forged Greek passports were found concealed in his trousers at Heathrow Airport. He was sentenced to twelve months imprisonment and recommended for deportation. This sentence was reduced to six months on appeal, the Garland J. drawing a distinction between cases involving use of a false passport and cases involving mere carrying. This distinction was disapproved in *R. v Cheema* [2002] 2 Cr.App.R.(S.) 79, CA. A sentence of three years imprisonment was substituted for a sentence of four years imprisonment where the offender had been convicted of having custody or control of twelve false passports. Pill L.J. disapproved of lenient treatment in the context of carrying in of false passports and advocated the use of deterrent sentences to stop others 'taking part as couriers in a lucrative but obnoxious trade.'

E. Counterfeiting Notes or Coins

(a) *Definition*

Forgery and Counterfeiting Act 1981, s.14

Offences of counterfeiting notes and coins

11–120   **14.**—(1) It is an offence for a person to make a counterfeit of a currency note or of a protected coin, intending that he or another shall pass or tender it as genuine.

(2) It is an offence for a person to make a counterfeit of a currency note or of a protected

coin without lawful authority or excuse.

(b) *Procedure*

These offences are triable either way: *Forgery and Counterfeiting Act* 1981, s.22.   **11–121**
The prosecution must prove either that;
— The defendant made a counterfeit of a currency note or a protected coin
— With the intention that he or another should pass or tender it as genuine
OR
— The defendant made a counterfeit of a currency note or a protected coin
— Without lawful authority or excuse.

(c) *Elements of the offence*

Forgery and Counterfeiting Act 1981, s.27

Meaning of "currency note" and "protected coin"
    27.—(1) In this Part of this Act—   **11–122**
        "currency note" means—
            (a) any note which—
                (i)   has been lawfully issued in England and Wales, Scotland, Northern
                      Ireland, any of the Channel Islands, the Isle of Man or the Republic
                      of Ireland; and
                (ii) is or has been customarily used as money in the country where it was
                      issued; and
                (iii) is payable on demand; or
            (b) any note which—
                (i)   has been lawfully issued in some country other than those mentioned
                      in paragraph (a)(i) above; and
                (ii) is customarily used as money in that country; and
        "protected coin" means any coin which—
            (a) is customarily used as money in any country; or
            (b) is specified in an order made by the Treasury for the purposes of this
                Part of this Act.
    (2) The power to make an order conferred on the Treasury by subsection (1) above
shall be exercisable by statutory instrument.
    (3) A statutory instrument containing such an order shall be laid before Parliament after
being made.

The *Forgery and Counterfeiting (Protected Coins) Order* 1981 (SI 1981/1505) **11–123**
specifies the following coins for the purposes of Pt II of the Act:
    Sovereign:
    Half Sovereign:
    Krugerrand:
    Any coin denominated as a fraction of a Kruggerand
    Maria-Theresa thaler bearing the date of 1780.
The *Forgery and Counterfeiting (Protected Coins) Order* (1999) (SI 1999/2095)
specifies any euro coin produced in accordance with Council Regulation No 975/98/EC
by or at the instance of a member state which has adopted the single currency, for the
purposes of Pt II of the 1981 Act.

Forgery and Counterfeiting Act 1981, s.28

Meaning of "counterfeit"
    28.—(1) For the purposes of this Part of this Act a thing is a counterfeit of a currency note or **11–124**
of a protected coin—
        (a) if it is not a currency note or a protected coin but resembles a currency note or

protected coin (whether on one side only or on both) to such an extent that it is reasonably capable of passing for a currency note or protected coin of that description; or

(b) if it is a currency note or protected coin which has been so altered that it is reasonably capable of passing for a currency note or protected coin of some other description.

(2) For the purposes of this Part of this Act—

(a) a thing consisting of one side only of a currency note, with or without the addition of other material, is a counterfeit of such a note;

(b) a thing consisting—

(i) of parts of two or more currency notes; or

(ii) of parts of a currency note, or of parts of two or more currency notes, with the addition of other material,

is capable of being a counterfeit of a currency note.

(3) References in this Part of this Act to passing or tendering a counterfeit of a currency note or a protected coin are not to be construed as confined to passing or tendering it as legal tender.

See further *Archbold Crown*, §§ 25–241—25–245.

(d) *Sentence*

11–125   When tried summarily, offences under both s.14(1) and (2) are punishable by a maximum sentence of six months' imprisonment, a fine not exceeding the statutory maximum or both.

In *R. v Howard* (1986) 82 Cr.App.R. 262, CA it was said that where a defendant is convicted of passing counterfeit notes, the issue of which undermines the whole economy of the country, in nearly every case this requires a custodial sentence to punish the wrongdoer and deter him from committing the same sort of offence in the future and to act as a deterrent to others. The offender pleaded guilty to having custody of counterfeit currency (£20 notes) and tendering one such counterfeit note, and was sentenced to concurrent terms of two years' imprisonment. *Howard* was followed in *R. v Luxford* [1996] 1 Cr.App.R.(S.) 186, CA, where the offender pleaded guilty to having custody of a counterfeit currency note and was sentenced to nine months' imprisonment. He appealed against sentence, submitting that the judge gave insufficient credit for a plea of guilty, good character and the pre-sentence report. The court held that whilst the sentence imposed was excessive, a custodial sentence would be an inevitable punishment for this offence. A sentence of four months' imprisonment was substituted. See also *Crick* (1981) 3 Cr.App.R.(S.) 275.

F. PASSING COUNTERFEIT NOTES AND COINS

(a) *Definition*

Forgery and Counterfeiting Act 1981, s.15

Offences of passing etc. counterfeit notes and coins

11–126   **15.**—(1) It is an offence for a person—

(a) to pass or tender as genuine any thing which is, and which he knows or believes to be, a counterfeit of a currency note or of a protected coin; or

(b) to deliver to another any thing which is, and which he knows or believes to be, such a counterfeit, intending that the person to whom it is delivered or another shall pass or tender it as genuine.

(2) It is an offence for a person to deliver to another, without lawful authority or excuse, any thing which is, and which he knows or believes to be, a counterfeit of a currency note or of a protected coin.

(b) *Procedure*

11–126.1   These offences are triable either way: *Forgery and Counterfeiting Act* 1981, s.22.

The prosecution must prove that either:
— the defendant passed or tendered, OR delivered to another
— any thing which is, and which he knows to be a counterfeit of a currency note or a protected coin
— intending that the person to whom it is delivered shall pass or tender it as genuine.

OR
— the defendant delivered to another
— without lawful authority or excuse
— any thing which is, and which he knows to be a counterfeit of a currency note or a protected coin.

(c) Elements of the offence

For the meaning of 'currency note' 'protected coin' and 'counterfeit' see ss.27 and 28 **11–127** of the 1981 Act (above).

(d) Sentence

When tried summarily, offences under both s.14(1) and (2) are punishable by a **11–128** maximum sentence of six months' imprisonment, a fine not exceeding the statutory maximum or both.

In *R. v Derbyshire* (1992) 13 Cr.App.R.(S.) 126 the offender pleaded guilty to three counts of delivering counterfeit goods with intent, having bought nine forged notes which he then sold on to three other men. He was sentenced to twelve months' imprisonment. On appeal, it was held that the offences were at or near the bottom of the scale for offences of their type and the appropriate sentence was six months' imprisonment. In *R. v Shah* (1987) 9 Cr.App.R.(S.) 167 the offender was convicted of tendering a counterfeit note. He had attempted to buy a record offering a forged £50 note. The offender claimed he had picked up the note without realising what it was, and there was no other evidence of dealing with counterfeit notes. The Court of Appeal upheld his sentence of twelve months' imprisonment, to be suspended for two years, with a supervision order, Steyn J. stating that in the absence of exceptional circumstances an immediate custodial sentence is necessary in all cases involving the tendering or passing of forged banknotes. A case lying towards the less serious end of the spectrum is *R. v Dickens* (1993) 14 Cr.App.R.(S.) 76. The offender had tendered a counterfeit £20 note in a shop. He admitted that he knew the note was counterfeit, but claimed that he had received it innocently in change for a £50 note, and decided to pass it on. He was sentenced to 12 months' imprisonment. On appeal, the propriety of an immediate custodial sentence was approved, yet 12 months was manifestly excessive, and a sentence of six months was substituted.

In *R. v Wake* (1992) 13 Cr.App.R.(S.) 422, the offender was convicted of two counts of passing a counterfeit note. The Court of Appeal held that although an immediate custodial sentence was entirely appropriate, a sentence of 12 months' imprisonment for this offence was manifestly excessive and a sentence of three months' imprisonment was appropriate. A sentence of four months' imprisonment was imposed where the offender had been in possession of 47 counterfeit £5 notes for 20 minutes after the driver of the car in which he was a passenger gave him them to conceal from the police: *R. v Luxford* [1996] 1 Cr.App.R.(S.) 186, CA.

G. Custody or Control of Counterfeits

(a) Definition

Forgery and Counterfeiting Act 1981, s.16

Offences involving the custody or control of counterfeit notes and coins
    16.—(1) It is an offence for a person to have in his custody or under his control any thing **11–129**

which is; and which he knows or believes to be, a counterfeit of a currency note or of a protected coin, intending either to pass or tender it as genuine or to deliver it to another with the intention that he or another shall pass or tender it as genuine.

(2) It is an offence for a person to have in his custody or under his control, without lawful authority or excuse, any thing which is, and which he knows or believes to be, a counterfeit of a currency note or of a protected coin.

(3) It is immaterial for the purposes of subsections (1) and (2) above that a coin or note is not in a fit state to be passed or tendered or that the making or counterfeiting of a coin or note has not been finished or perfected.

(b) *Procedure*

11-129.1   These offences are triable either way: *Forgery and Counterfeiting Act* 1981, s.22. The prosecution must prove that:
— the defendant had in his custody or under his control
— any thing which was and which he knew or believed to be
— a counterfeit of a currency note or protected coin
— intending either to pass or tender it as genuine or to deliver it to another with the intention that he or another shall pass or tender it as genuine
OR
— the defendant had in his custody or under his control
— any thing which was and which he knew or believed to be
— a counterfeit of a currency note or protected coin.

(c) *Elements of the offence*

11-130   For the meaning of 'currency note' 'protected coin' and 'counterfeit' see ss.27 and 28 of the 1981 Act, above. See further *Archbold Crown*, §§ 25-247—25-249.

(d) *Sentence*

11-130.1   When tried summarily, offences under both s.14(1) and (2) are punishable by a maximum sentence of six months' imprisonment, a fine not exceeding the statutory maximum or both.

In *R. v Torry* (1983) 5 Cr.App.R.(S.) 326, CA, the offender pleaded guilty to one count of handling stolen goods and one of having custody or control of a counterfeit currency note. 46 counterfeit £20 had been found at his house, and he received a sentence of eighteen months' imprisonment for possession of the counterfeit notes. This was substituted for a sentence of 12 months on appeal due to the mitigating circumstances of the offender. See also *R. v Carter* (1983) 5 Cr.App.R.(S.) 256.

H. MAKING, CUSTODY OR CONTROL OF COUNTERFEITING MATERIALS AND IMPLEMENTS

(a) *Definition*

Forgery and Counterfeiting Act, s.17

Offences involving the making or custody or control of counterfeiting materials and implements

11-131   17.—(1) It is an offence for a person to make, or to have in his custody or under his control, any thing which he intends to use, or to permit any other person to use, for the purpose of making a counterfeit of a currency note or of a protected coin with the intention that it be passed or tendered as genuine.

(2) It is an offence for a person without lawful authority or excuse—
(a) to make; or
(b) to have in his custody or under his control,

any thing which, to his knowledge, is or has been specially designed or adapted for the making of a counterfeit of a currency note.

(3) Subject to subsection (4) below, it is an offence for a person to make, or to have in his custody or under his control, any implement which, to his knowledge, is capable of imparting to any thing a resemblance—

(a) to the whole or part of either side of a protected coin; or
(b) to the whole or part of the reverse of the image on either side of a protected coin.

(4) It shall be a defence for a person charged with an offence under subsection (3) above to show—

(a) that he made the implement or, as the case may be, had it in his custody or under his control, with the written consent of the Treasury; or
(b) that he had lawful authority otherwise than by virtue of paragraph (a) above, or a lawful excuse, for making it or having it in his custody or under his control.

(b) *Procedure*

These offences are triable either way: *Forgery and Counterfeiting Act* 1981, s.22. **11–132**
The prosecution must prove that:

— the defendant made, or had in his custody or under his control,
— any thing which he intends to use, or to permit any other person to use, for the purpose of making a counterfeit of a currency note or of a protected coin with
— with the intention that it be passed or tendered as genuine.

OR

— the defendant made, or had in his custody or under his control,
— any thing which, to his knowledge, had been specially designed or adapted for the making of a counterfeit of a currency note,
— without lawful authority or excuse.

OR

— the defendant made, or had in his custody or control
— any implement which, to his knowledge was capable of imparting to any thing a resemblance either to the whole or part of a protected coin, or to the whole or part of the reverse of the image on either side of a protected coin, and,
— the defendant did not make the implement or, have it in his custody or under his control with the written consent of the Treasury; or with lawful authority otherwise than by virtue of permission of the Treasury, or lawful excuse.

(c) *Elements of the offence*

For the meaning of 'currency note' 'protected coin' and 'counterfeit' see ss.27 and 28 **11–133**
of the 1981 Act, above. See also *Archbold Crown*, §§ 25-250—25-252.

(d) *Sentence*

When tried summarily, offences under both s.14(1) and (2) are punishable by a **11–133.**
maximum sentence of six months' imprisonment, a fine not exceeding the statutory maximum or both.

I. Reproducing British Currency

(a) *Definition*

Forgery and Counterfeiting Act 1981 ss.18(1), 19(1)

The offence of reproducing British currency notes
   18.—(1) It is an offence for any person, unless the relevant authority has previously consented **11–134**
in writing, to reproduce on any substance whatsoever, and whether or not on the correct scale,

any British currency note or any part of a British currency note.

Offences of making etc. imitation British coins

11–134.1   **19.**—(1) It is an offence for a person—

(a) to make an imitation British coin in connection with a scheme intended to promote the sale of any product or the making of contracts for the supply of any service; or

(b) to sell or distribute imitation British coins in connection with any such scheme, or to have imitation British coins in his custody or under his control with a view to such sale or distribution,

unless the Treasury have previously consented in writing to the sale or distribution of such imitation British coins in connection with that scheme.

(b) *Procedure*

11–135   These offences are triable either way: *Forgery and Counterfeiting Act* 1981, s.22

The prosecution must prove that:

— the defendant produced, on any substance, or to any scale whatsoever,

— any British currency note or any part of a British currency note

— without the written consent of the relevant consenting authority.

OR

— the defendant made an imitation British coin,

— in connection with a scheme intended to promote the sale of any product or the making of contracts for the supply of any service.

OR

— the defendant sold or distributed imitation British coins,

— in connection with a scheme intended to promote the sale of any product or the making of contracts for the supply of any service.

OR

— the defendant had imitation British coins in his custody or control,

— with a view to their sale or distribution,

— without the written consent of the Treasury to such sale or distribution of imitation British coins.

(c) *Elements of the offence*

Forgery and Counterfeiting Act 1981, ss.18(2) and 19(2)

The offence of reproducing British currency notes

11–136   **18.**—(2) In this section—

"British currency note" means any note which—

(a) has been lawfully issued in England and Wales, Scotland or Northern Ireland; and

(b) is or has been customarily used as money in the country where it was issued; and

(c) is payable on demand; and

"the relevant authority", in relation to a British currency note of any particular description, means the authority empowered by law to issue notes of that description.

See *Archbold Crown*, §§ 25–252—25–254.

Offences of making etc. imitation British coins

11–136.1   **19.**—(2) In this section—

"British coin" means any coin which is legal tender in any part of the United Kingdom; and

"imitation British coin" means any thing which resembles a British coin in shape, size and the substance of which it is made.

(d) *Sentence*

When tried summarily, offences under both s.14(1) and (2) are punishable by a **11–136** maximum sentence of six months' imprisonment, a fine not exceeding the statutory maximum or both.

J. Prohibition of Importation and Exportation on Counterfeits

(a) *Definition*

Forgery and Counterfeiting Act 1981, ss.20, 21

Prohibition of importation of counterfeit notes and coins
   20. The importation, landing or unloading of a counterfeit of a currency note or of a **11–137** protected coin without the consent of the Treasury is hereby prohibited.

Prohibition of exportation of counterfeit notes and coins
   21.—(1) The exportation of a counterfeit of a currency note or of a protected coin without **11–137** the consent of the Treasury is hereby prohibited.
   (2) A counterfeit of a currency note or of a protected coin which is removed to the Isle of Man from the United Kingdom shall be deemed to be exported from the United Kingdom—
      (a) for the purposes of this section; and
      (b) for the purposes of the customs and excise Acts, in their application to the prohibition imposed by this section.
   (3) [Amends *Isle of Man Act* 1979 (c. 58), s.9(1)]

(b) *Procedure*

Sections 20 and 21 do not create offences, rather they impose prohibitions. The rele- **11–138** vant offences are those committed under the *Customs and Excise Management Act* 1979, ss.50 and 68.

III. MISCELLANEOUS OFFENCES

A. Interference with Vehicles

(a) *Definition*

Criminal Attempts Act 1981 s.9

Interference with vehicles
   9.—(1) A person is guilty of the offence of vehicle interference if he interferes with a motor **11–139** vehicle or trailer or with anything carried in or on a motor vehicle or trailer with the intention that an offence specified in subsection (2) below shall be committed by himself or some other person.
   (2) The offences mentioned in subsection (1) above are—
      (a) theft of the motor vehicle or trailer or part of it;
      (b) theft of anything carried in or on the motor vehicle or trailer; and
      (c) an offence under section 12(1) of the *Theft Act* 1968 (taking and driving away without consent);
and, if it is shown that a person offender of an offence under this section intended that one of those offences should be committed, it is immaterial that it cannot be shown which it was.

[This section is printed as amended by the *CJA* 1982, s.46, the *Police and Criminal Evidence Act* 1984, Sch.7 and the *Road Traffic (Consequential Provisions) Act* 1988, Sch.3.]

(b) *Procedure*

The offence is triable summarily: *Criminal Attempts Act* 1981, s.9(3).   **11–140**

The prosecution must prove that:
— the defendant interfered,
— with a motor vehicle or trailer or with anything carried in or on a motor vehicle or trailer
— with the intention that one of the following offences should be committed by himself or some other person; theft of the motor vehicle or trailer or part of it; theft of anything carried in or on the motor vehicle or trailer; taking or diving a vehicle away without consent (offence created by s.12(1) of the *Theft Act* 1968).

(c) *Elements of the offence*

11–141   "Motor vehicle" and "trailer" have the meanings assigned to them by s.185(1) of the *Road Traffic Act* 1988 (s.9(5)). Interference is not defined within the Act. In *Reynolds and Warren v Metropolitan Police* [1982] Crim.L.R. 831 it was held that more than looking into vehicles and touching them was necessary to establish interference.

(d) *Sentence*

11–142   The maximum penalty for this offence is imprisonment for a term not exceeding three months or a fine not exceeding level four on the standard scale or both: *Criminal Attempts Act* 1981, s.9(3).

The *Magistrates' Court Sentencing Guidelines* (2003) state:

> Aggravating factors include disabled passenger vehicle, emergency service vehicle, racial aggravation, group action, planned, related damage, offence committed on bail, relevant previous convictions and any failures to respond to previous sentences.
>
> Mitigating factors shall include impulsive action.
>
> **Guideline**: Is it serious enough for a community penalty?

B. FRAUDULENT USE OF TELECOMMUNICATION SYSTEMS

(a) *Definition*

Telecommunications Act 1984 ss.42, 42A

Fraudulent use of telecommunication system

11–143   **42.**—(1) A person who dishonestly obtains a service to which this subsection applies with intent to avoid payment of any charge applicable to the provision of that service shall be guilty of an offence and liable—

     (a) on summary conviction, to imprisonment for a term not exceeding six months or to a fine not exceeding the statutory maximum or to both;

     (b) on conviction on indictment, to imprisonment for a term not exceeding [five years] or to a fine or to both.

(2) Subsection (1) above applies to any service (other than a service such as is mentioned in section 297(1) of the *Copyright, Designs and Patents Act* 1988) which is provided by means of a telecommunication system the running of which is authorised by a licence granted under section 7 above.

Possession or supply of anything for fraudulent purpose in connection with use of telecommunication system

11–144   **42A.**—(1) Subsection (2) below applies if a person has in his custody or under his control anything (other than an unauthorised decoder as defined in section 297A(4) of the *Copyright, Designs and Patents Act* 1988) which may be used for the purpose of obtaining, or for a purpose connected with the obtaining of, a service to which section 42(1) above applies.

(2) If the person intends—

     (a) to use the thing—

         (i) to obtain such a service dishonestly, or

         (ii) for a purpose connected with the dishonest obtaining of such a service,

     (b) dishonestly to allow the thing to be used to obtain such a service, or

(c) to allow the thing to be used for a purpose connected with the dishonest obtaining of such a service,

he shall be guilty of an offence.

(3) Subsection (4) below applies if a person supplies or offers to supply anything[(other than an unauthorised decoder as defined in section 297A(4) of the *Copyright, Designs and Patents Act* 1988)] which may be used for the purpose of obtaining, or for a purpose connected with the obtaining of, a service to which section 42(1) above applies.

(4) If the person supplying or offering to supply the thing knows or believes that the person to whom it is supplied or offered intends or intends if it is supplied to him—

(a) to use it—
(i) to obtain such a service dishonestly, or
(ii) for a purpose connected with the dishonest obtaining of such a service,
(b) dishonestly to allow it to be used to obtain such a service, or
(c) to allow it to be used for a purpose connected with the dishonest obtaining of such a service,

he shall be guilty of an offence.

(5) A person guilty of an offence under this section shall be liable—

(a) on summary conviction, to imprisonment for a term not exceeding six months or to a fine not exceeding the statutory maximum or to both, and
(b) on conviction on indictment, to imprisonment for a term not exceeding five years or to a fine or to both.

(6) In this section, references to use of a thing include, in the case of a thing which is used to record any data, use of any of the data.

(b) *Procedure*

These offences are triable either way. As regards the offence under s.42 of the 1984 **11–145** Act the prosecution must prove that:

— the defendant dishonestly obtained,
— a service which is provided by means of a telecommunication system the running of which is authorised by a licence,
— with the intention to permanently avoid payment of any charge applicable to the provision of that service.

As regards the offence under s.42A of the 1984 Act, the prosecution must prove that:

— the defendant had in his custody or under his control anything (other than an unauthorised decoder as defined in s.297A(4) of the *Copyright, Designs and Patents Act* 1988) which may be used for the purpose of obtaining, or for a purpose connected with the obtaining of,
— a service which is provided by means of a telecommunication system the running of which is authorised by a licence, and
— the defendant intended to use the thing to obtain such a service dishonestly, or for a purpose connected with the dishonest obtaining of such a service OR the defendant intended dishonestly to allow the thing to be used to obtain such a service, OR the defendant intended to allow the thing to be used for a purpose connected with the dishonest obtaining of such a service.

OR

— the defendant supplied or offered to supply anything (other than an unautho- **11–146** rised decoder as defined in s.297A(4) of the *Copyright, Designs and Patents Act* 1988) which may be used for the purpose of obtaining, or for a purpose connected with the obtaining of,
— a service which is provided by means of a telecommunication system the running of which is authorised by a licence, and
— the defendant knew or believed that the person to whom it is supplied or offered intended or intended if it was supplied to him to use it to obtain such a service dishonestly, or for a purpose connected with the dishonest obtaining of such a service OR the defendant intended dishonestly to allow it to be used to obtain such a service,

OR

— the defendant to allow it to be used for a purpose connected with the dishonest obtaining of such a service.

(c) Sentence

11–147   When tried summarily, the maximum penalty for these offences is imprisonment for a term not exceeding six months, a fine not exceeding the statutory maximum or both: s.41(1)(a) and s.42A(5)).

In *R. v Nadig* (1993) 14 Cr.App.R.(S.) 49, the offenders were seen using a telephone in a public telephone box to make an international call whilst one of the offenders was using a tone-dialling device. Their original sentences of two months' imprisonment, suspended, and a fine of £1,000 each was varied to a conditional discharge on appeal, the fact that they were first time offenders and that this was an isolated offence being significant.

In *R. v Stephens* [2002] 2 Cr.App.R.(S.) 67, the offender pleaded guilty before a magistrates' court to an offence under s.42A, and was committed to the Crown Court for sentence. His activity concerned modifying mobile telephones to enable calls to be made for free. His original sentence of 18 months imprisonment was reduced to twelve months' imprisonment on appeal. Whilst the offence was held to definitely pass the custody threshold, an appropriate discount for the guilty plea had to be given.

C. FRAUDULENT RECEIPT OF PROGRAMMES

(a) Definition

Copyright, Designs and Patents Act 1988, s.297

Offence of fraudulently receiving programmes

11–148   **297.**—(1) A person who dishonestly receives a programme included in a broadcasting or cable programme service provided from a place in the United Kingdom with intent to avoid payment of any charge applicable to the reception of the programme commits an offence and is liable on summary conviction to a fine not exceeding level 5 on the standard scale.

(2) Where an offence under this section committed by a body corporate is proved to have been committed with the consent or connivance of a director, manager, secretary or other similar officer of the body, or a person purporting to act in any such capacity, he as well as the body corporate is guilty of the offence and liable to be proceeded against and punished accordingly.

In relation to a body corporate whose affairs are managed by its members "director" means a member of the body corporate.

(b) Procedure

11–149   This offence is triable summarily only (s.297(1)).

The prosecution must prove that:

— the defendant dishonestly,
— received a programme included in a broadcasting of a cable programme service provided from a place in the UK,
— with intent to avoid payment of any charge applicable to the reception of the programme.

(c) Sentence

1–149.1   The maximum penalty for this offence is a fine not exceeding level 5 on the standard scale: s.297(1).

D. Harassment of Debtors

(a) *Definition*

Administration of Justice Act 1970, s.40

Punishment for unlawful harassment of debtors

40.—(1) A person commits an offence if, with the object of coercing another person to pay **11–150** money claimed from the other as a debt due under a contract, he—

    (a) harasses the other with demands for payment which, in respect of their frequency or the manner or occasion of making any such demand, or of any threat or publicity by which any demand is accompanied, are calculated to subject him or members of his family or household to alarm, distress or humiliation;

    (b) falsely represents, in relation to the money claimed, that criminal proceedings lie for failure to pay it;

    (c) falsely represents himself to be authorised in some official capacity to claim or enforce payment; or

    (d) utters a document falsely represented by him to have some official character or purporting to have some official character which he knows it has not.

(2) A person may be guilty of an offence by virtue of subsection (1)(a) above if he concerts with others in the taking of such action as is described in that paragraph, notwithstanding that his own course of conduct does not by itself amount to harassment.

(3) Subsection (1)(a) above does not apply to anything done by a person which is reasonable (and otherwise permissible in law) for the purpose—

    (a) of securing the discharge of an obligation due, or believed by him to be due, to himself or to persons for whom he acts, or protecting himself or them from future loss; or

    (b) of the enforcement of any liability by legal process.

(4) A person guilty of an offence under this section shall be liable on summary conviction to a fine of not more than £100, and on a second or subsequent conviction to a fine of not more than £400.

[This section is printed as amended by the *CJA* 1982, ss.35, 38 and 46.]

(b) *Procedure*

This offence is triable summarily only (s.40(4)). The prosecution must prove that the **11–151** defendant:

    — harassed one of his debtors with demands for payment which, in respect of their frequency or the manner or occasion of making any such demand, or of any threat or publicity by which any demand is accompanied, were calculated to subject him or members of his family or household to alarm, distress or humiliation or,

    — falsely represented, in relation to the money claimed, that criminal proceedings lay for failure to pay it, or

    — falsely represented himself to be authorised in some official capacity to claim or enforce payment; or

    — uttered a document falsely represented by him to have some official character or purporting to have some official character which he knows it has not, with

    — the object of coercing the debtor to pay money claimed from as a debt due under a contract.

(c) *Elements of the offence*

An agreement for the supply of electricity between a tariff customer and a public **11–152** electricity supplier under the *Electricity Act* 1989 is not a contract, as the rights and liabilities under this arrangement are governed by statute: *Norweb plc v Dixon* [1995] 3 All E.R. 952.

The phrase "calculated to subject" in s.40(1) means 'likely to subject' and not 'intending to subject': *Norweb plc v Dixon* (above).

(d) *Sentence*

11–153   The maximum penalty for the first commission of this offence is a fine of not more than £100, and on a second or subsequent conviction, a fine of not more than £400: s.40(4).

CHAPTER 12

PUBLIC ORDER OFFENCES

I. OFFENCES UNDER THE PUBLIC ORDER ACT 1936

A. PROHIBITION OF UNIFORMS IN CONNECTION WITH POLITICAL OBJECTS

(a) Definition

Public Order Act 1936, s.1(1)

Prohibition of uniforms in connection with political objects

12–1   1.—(1) Subject as hereinafter provided, any person who in any public place or at any public meeting wears uniform signifying his association with any political organisation or with the promotion of any political object shall be guilty of an offence: .

Provided that, if the chief officer of police is satisfied that the wearing of any such uniform as aforesaid on any ceremonial, anniversary, or other special occasion will not be likely to involve risk of public disorder, he may, with the consent of a Secretary of State, by order permit the wearing of such uniform on that occasion either absolutely or subject to such conditions as may be specified in the order.

12–1.1   The prosecution must prove that:

— the defendant wore a uniform signifying his association with any political organisation or promotion of any political object,

— in a public place or at a public meeting and,

— the chief officer of police had not, with the consent of the Secretary of State, made an order permitting the wearing of such a uniform.

(b) Procedure

12–2   This offence is triable summarily. Section 1(2) provides that proceedings may not be instituted without the consent of the Attorney General.

(c) Elements of the offence

12–3   Any item worn to show mutual association can amount to a "uniform" without proof of its previous use as such. In *O'Moran v DPP* [1975] Q.B. 864, the Court of Appeal took the view that the wearer's association with a political organisation may be proved either by showing that the uniform has in the past been associated with a political organisation or by proving that the conduct of the wearer on the occasion complained of indicates activity of a political character. The prosecution does not have to specify the particular political organisation.

The terms 'meeting', 'public meeting' and 'public place' are defined in s.9 of the 1936 Act:

Public Order Act 1936, s.9(1)

Interpretation, &c.

9.—(1) In this Act the following expressions have the meanings hereby respectively assigned **12–3.1**
to them, that is to say—

"Meeting" means a meeting held for the purpose of the discussion of matters of public
interest or for the purpose of the expression of views on such matters;

"Public meeting" includes any meeting in a public place and any meeting which the public
or any section thereof are permitted to attend, whether on payment or otherwise.

"Public place" includes any highway, or in Scotland any road within the meaning of the
Roads (Scotland) Act 1984 and any other premises or place to which at the material
time the public have or are permitted to have access, whether on payment or otherwise.

In *Marsh v Arscott* (1982) 75 Cr.App.R. 211, DC, McCullough J. stated that 'it is **12–4**
important to have regard to the words 'at the material time' in the definition of 'public
place." The Court held that a shop car park could not amount to a public place at
11.30p.m. on a Saturday night when the shop was closed. Where the public do have access to a given place at the material time, it will be classed as a public place, despite the
fact that entry can be refused to certain people: in *Lawrenson v Oxford* [1982]
Crim.L.R. 185, a public house with open doors inviting the public to enter was held to
be a public place. A place will still be classed as a public place even where the public are
denied access to certain parts, hence in *Cawley v Frost* (1977) 64 Cr.App.R. 20, a
football ground was classed as a public place, with Lord Widgery C.J. stating that
'*Prima facie* the whole establishment should be considered and the court should not be
deterred ... merely by finding that access to certain portions of the establishment had
been denied to the public.' Premises such as a front garden will not be classed as a public place, as people are only entitled to enter on an individual basis as visitors: *R. v Edwards* (1978) 67 Cr.App.R. 228.

(d) *Sentence*

The maximum penalty is three months or a fine not exceeding level four on the stan- **12–5**
dard scale: *Public Order Act* 1936, s.7(2).

B. Prohibition of Quasi-Military Organisations

(a) *Definition*

Public Order Act 1936, s.2

2.—(1) If the members or adherents of any association of persons, whether incorporated or **12–6**
not, are—

(a) organised or trained or equipped for the purposes of enabling them to be
employed in usurping the functions of the police or of the armed forces of the
Crown; or

(b) organised and trained or organised and equipped either for the purpose of enabling them to be employed for the use or display of physical force in promoting
any political object, or in such manner as to arouse reasonable apprehension that
they are organised and either trained or equipped for that purpose;

then any person who takes part in the control or management of the association, or in so organising or training as aforesaid any members or adherents thereof, shall be guilty of an offence
under this section

Provided that in any proceedings against a person charged with the offence of taking part in
the control or management of such an association as aforesaid it shall be a defence to that charge
to prove that he neither consented to nor connived at the organisation, training, or equipment
of members or adherents of the association in contravention of the provisions of this section.

(2) No prosecution shall be instituted under this section without the consent of the
Attorney-General.

(3) [powers of the High Court]

(4) In any criminal or civil proceedings under this section proof of things done or of

words written, spoken or published (whether or not in the presence of any party to the proceedings) by any person taking part in the control or management of an association or in organising, training or equipping members or adherents of an association shall be admissible as evidence of the purposes for which, or the manner in which, members or adherents of the association (whether those persons or others) were organised, or trained, or equipped.

(5) [powers of the High Court]

(6) Nothing in this section shall be construed as prohibiting the employment of a reasonable number of persons as stewards to assist in the preservation of order at any public meeting held upon private premises, or the making of arrangements for that purpose or the instruction of the persons to be so employed in their lawful duties as such stewards, or their being furnished with badges or other distinguishing signs.

12–7   The prosecution need to prove that:
— the defendant has managed or controlled an association, or has organised or taken part in the organisation or training of an association whose members are,
— organised or trained or equipped for the purposes of enabling them to be employed in usurping the functions of the police or of the armed forces of the Crown, OR
— organised and trained or organised and equipped either for the purpose of enabling them to be employed for the use or display of physical force in promoting any political object, OR
— arouse reasonable apprehension that they are organised and either trained or equipped for that purpose.

(b) *Procedure*

12–8   This offence is triable either way: *Public Order Act* 1936, s.7(1). Section 2(2) of the 1936 Act establishes that no prosecution shall take place without the consent of the Attorney General.

(c) *Elements of the offence*

12–9   The fact that there was no evidence of actual attacks or plans for attacks on opponents will not necessarily remove the grounds for 'reasonable apprehension' that the association is organised and equipped for the purpose of enabling them to be employed for use or display of physical force in promoting a political object: *R. v Jordan and Tyndall* [1963] Crim.L.R. 124, CCA.

(d) *Specific Defences*

12–9.1   A specific defence to proceedings brought under this section is established in s.2 of the 1936 Act:

Public Order Act 1936, s.2(1)

12–10   'Provided that in any proceedings against a person charged with the offence of taking part in the control or management of such an association as aforesaid it shall be a defence to that charge to prove that he neither consented to nor connived at the organisation, training, or equipment of members or adherents of the association in contravention of the provisions of this section.'

12–10.1   Furthermore;

Public Order Act 1936, s.2(6)

Prohibition of quasimilitary organisations

2.—(6) Nothing in this section shall be construed as prohibiting the employment of a reasonable number of persons as stewards to assist in the preservation of order at any public meeting held upon private premises, or the making of arrangements for that purpose or the instruction of the persons to be so employed in their lawful duties as such stewards, or their being furnished with badges or other distinguishing signs.

(e) *Sentence*

When tried summarily, the maximum penalty for this offence is six months imprison- **12–10.2** ment or a fine not exceeding the prescribed sum or both: *Public Order Act* 1936, s.7(1)).

II. OFFENCES UNDER THE PUBLIC ORDER ACT 1986

A. VIOLENT DISORDER

(a) *Definition*

Public Order Act 1986, s.2

Violent disorder

2.—(1) Where 3 or more persons who are present together use or threaten unlawful violence **12–11** and the conduct of them (taken together) is such as would cause a person of reasonable firmness present at the scene to fear for his personal safety, each of the persons using or threatening unlawful violence is guilty of violent disorder.

(2) It is immaterial whether or not the 3 or more use or threaten unlawful violence simultaneously.

(3) No person of reasonable firmness need actually be, or be likely to be, present at the scene.

(4) Violent disorder may be committed in private as well as in public places.

(5) A person guilty of violent disorder is liable on conviction on indictment to imprisonment for a term not exceeding 5 years or a fine or both, or on summary conviction to imprisonment for a term not exceeding 6 months or a fine not exceeding the statutory maximum or both.

The prosecution need to prove that: **12–11.1**
— three or more persons who were present together,
— used or threatened unlawful violence and,
— the conduct of them taken together is such as would cause a person of reasonable firmness present at the scene to fear for his personal safety.

(b) *Procedure*

Violent disorder is triable either way, though the *Practice Direction (Criminal* **12–12** *Proceedings: Consolidation), para.V.51.11* provides that 'cases of violent disorder should normally be committed for trial'.

(d) *Elements of the offence*

'3 or more persons'

As to the requirement that there be three of more persons present together using or **12–13** threatening unlawful violence before there can be a conviction of anyone, see *R. v Fleming* (1989) 153 J.P. 517, and *R. v Worton* (1989) 154 J.P. 201. See also *R. v Mahroof* (1988) 88 Cr.App.R. 371. If one of more of the named defendants is acquitted due to a lack of *mens rea*, the remaining defendants may be found guilty, even if there are only two of them: *Public Order Act* 1986, s.6(7).

'Use or threaten'

Being part of a group of people following a man for three-quarters of a mile along a **12–14** footpath in the middle of the night will amount to violent disorder: *R. v Brodie* [2000]

Crim.L.R. 775, CA. The Court held that such conduct would involve a considerable implicit menace, amounting to a threat and that a person of reasonable firmness present during and throughout such action would have been put in fear for his or her personal safety.

'Unlawful violence'

12–15   The defences of self-defence and reasonable defence of others are preserved by the use of the phrase 'unlawful violence.' Actions no more than necessary to restore the peace are also permissible: *R. v Rothwell and Barton* [1993] Crim.L.R. 626, CA. See also *Archbold Crown*, §§ 29–15—29–16.

(d) *Sentence*

12–16   When tried summarily the maximum penalty is six months' imprisonment, a fine not exceeding the statutory maximum or both: s.2(5).

The *Magistrates' Court Sentencing Guidelines* (2003) provide that aggravating factors include racial aggravation, busy public place, fighting between rival groups, large group, people actually put in fear, planned, vulnerable victims, weapon, offence committed on bail, relevant previous convictions and failure to respond to previous sentences.

Mitigating factors include impulsive action, nobody afraid and provocation. The guideline question is 'is it so serious that only custody is appropriate? Are magistrates' sentencing powers appropriate?'

In *Tomlinson* (1993) 157 J.P. 695, it was held that the essence of the offence of violent disorder lies in the using of violence in circumstances where so many people were present as to cause or inspire fear in the general public. The offenders' participation in a demonstration against poll tax culminated in fighting and shouting that caused fear amongst the general public. D1 was sentenced to four months' imprisonment, and D2 and D3 were sentenced to six months imprisonment and youth custody respectively.

12–17   In *Shanoor* (1998) 162 J.P. 731, the involvement of the offender in a brawl outside a nightclub was characterised as spontaneous, with no weapon being used and no injury caused. A sentence of six months imprisonment imposed by the Crown Court was substituted by a short Community Service order at the Court of Appeal. In *R. v Pickard* (2000) the defendant was sentenced to eighteen months' detention in a young offenders' institution following a guilty plea to violent disorder. His co-defendants (all younger) received non-custodial sentences, however a distinction was drawn in his case due to his age and history of violent offending. As he had engaged in a racially motivated confrontation and had previously failed to respond to community sentences, custody was inevitable, however his sentence was reduced to twelve months on appeal.

B. Affray

(a) *Definition*

Public Order Act 1986 s.3

Affray

12–18   **3.**—(1) A person is guilty of affray if he uses or threatens unlawful violence towards another and his conduct is such as would cause a person of reasonable firmness present at the scene to fear for his personal safety.

(2) Where 2 or more persons use or threaten the unlawful violence, it is the conduct of them taken together that must be considered for the purposes of subsection (1).

(3) For the purposes of this section a threat cannot be made by the use of words alone.

(4) No person of reasonable firmness need actually be, or be likely to be, present at the scene.

(5) Affray may be committed in private as well as in public places.

(6) A constable may arrest without warrant anyone he reasonably suspects is committing affray.

(7) A person guilty of affray is liable on conviction on indictment to imprisonment for a term not exceeding 3 years or a fine or both, or on summary conviction to imprisonment for a term not exceeding 6 months or a fine not exceeding the statutory maximum or both.

The prosecution must prove that: **12–18.1**
— the defendant has used or threatened unlawful violence towards another, or two or more persons, their conduct being considered together, have used or threatened unlawful violence, and,
— this conduct is such as would cause a person of reasonable firmness present at the scene to fear for his personal safety.

(b) *Procedure*

Affray is triable either way. The *Practice Direction (Criminal Proceedings: Consoli-*   **12–19**
dation), para.V.51.11 provides that cases of affray should be tried summarily unless the court consider that one or more of the following features is present in the case and that their sentencing powers are insufficient:
(a) Organised violence or use of weapons
(b) Significant injury or substantial damage
(c) The offence has clear racial motivation
(d) An attack upon police officers, ambulance staff, fire-fighters and the like.

(c) *Elements of the offence*

In *R. v Thind* [1999] Crim.L.R. 842, CA, the Court stated that 'for an affray to take   **12–20**
place there needs to be: (a) the use or threat of violence by the defendant; (b) to another person; which (c), would cause a third person to fear for his or her own safety.' What amounts to a threat depends on the facts of each case. In *I v DPP, M v DPP, H v DPP* [2002] 1 A.C. 285, HL, it was held that whilst the mere possession of petrol bombs which were neither brandished nor waved might constitute a threat of unlawful violence for the purposes of an affray under the 1986 Act, the offence required a threat to be directed towards another person present at the scene; where only police officers were present at the scene, no such threat would be made. Making a threat in an aggressive tone of voice is not enough: *R. v Robinson* [1993] Crim.L.R. 581, CA.

The conduct is judged by the standard of the hypothetical person of reasonable firmness, this person does not necessarily have to be at the scene of the offence: *R. v Davison* [1992] Crim.L.R. 31, CA. It is this hypothetical reasonable bystander that has to be put in fear of his safety, not the victim himself: *R. v Sanchez* [1996] Crim.L.R. 572, CA.

The use of the word 'unlawful' means that the defences of self defence, acting in the defence of others etc are all available: see *R. v Rothwell and Barton*, above.

See also *Archbold Crown*, §§ 29–22—29–25.

(d) *Sentence*

When tried summarily, the maximum penalty is six months' imprisonment, a fine   **12–21**
not exceeding the statutory maximum or both: s.3(7).

The *Magistrates' Court Sentencing Guidelines* (2003) state that aggravating factors include racial aggravation, busy public place, group action, injuries caused, people actually put in fear, vulnerable victim, offence committed on bail, relevant previous convictions and any failures to respond to previous sentences. If the offence is football related, this will be treated as an aggravating factor. Mitigating factors include offender acting alone, provocation, did not start the trouble, stopped as soon as the police arrived. The guideline asks 'is it so serious that only custody is appropriate? Are Magistrates' sentencing powers appropriate?'

An unprovoked attack in a public place with a racial motive will warrant a deterrent sentence: *R. v M (Paul Simon) (A Juvenile)*. [1998] 2 Cr.App.R.(S.) 398. In *R. v Fox*

[1999] 1 Cr.App.R.(S.) 332 the Court of Appeal reduced a sentence of nine months' imprisonment to four months. The offender pleaded guilty to affray, having intervened during the arrest of a friend. A custodial sentence was held to be necessary, though one of four months was appropriate.

12–22   In *R. v Charles & Jones* (1989) 11 Cr.App.R.(S.) 125, CA, the offenders, both of previous good character had a fight in a restaurant, following offensive remarks made by a party at another table. The fight involved chairs being broken and used as weapons and some members of the other party were slightly injured. The CA considered a sentence of three months' imprisonment appropriate. In *R. v Grzybowski and Grzybowski* (1994) 15 Cr.App.R.(S.) 139, CA, a gang of youths went to the home of another late at night armed with a piece of wood. One offender broke a window and later put his fist through the window. The householder then squirted the second offender with ammonia, who then ran away. A sentence of 12 months' detention in a young offender institution and 18 months' imprisonment for the older offender was upheld by the CA, who emphasised that 'the gravamen of this type of offence was its effect on law-abiding members of the public.'

See also *Holmes* [1999] 2 Cr.App.R.(S.) 100 and *Oliver* [1999] 1 Cr.App.R.(S.) 394.

C. Fear or Provocation of Violence

(a) *Definition*

Public Order Act 1986, s.4

Fear or provocation of violence
12–23   **4.**—(1) A person is guilty of an offence if he—
     (a) uses towards another person threatening, abusive or insulting words or behaviour, or
     (b) distributes or displays to another person any writing, sign or ostensible representation which is threatening, abusive or insulting,
     (c) with intent to cause that person to believe that immediate unlawful violence will be used against him or another by any person, or to provoke the immediate use of unlawful violence by that person or another,
     (d) or whereby that person is likely to believe that such violence will be used or it is likely that such violence will be provoked.

(2) An offence under this section may be committed in a public or a private place, except that no offence is committed where the words or behaviour are used, or the writing, sign or ostensible representation is distributed or displayed, by a person inside a dwelling and the other person is also inside that or another dwelling.

(3) A constable may arrest without warrant anyone he reasonably suspects is committing an offence under this section.

(4) A person guilty of an offence under this section is liable on summary conviction to imprisonment for a term not exceeding 6 months or a fine not exceeding level 5 on the standard scale or both.

Racially or Religiously Aggravated Offences

Crime and Disorder Act 1998, s.31

Racially or religiously aggravated public order offences
12–24   **31.**—(1) A person is guilty of an offence under this section if he commits—
     (a) an offence under section 4 of the *Public Order Act* 1986 (fear or provocation of violence);
     (b) an offence under section 4A of that Act (intentional harassment, alarm or distress); or
     (c) an offence under section 5 of that Act (harassment, alarm or distress),
   [hich is racially [or religiously] aggravated for the purposes of this section.

(2) A constable may arrest without warrant anyone whom he reasonably suspects to be committing an offence falling within subsection (1)(a) or (b) above.

(3) A constable may arrest a person without warrant if—

(a) he engages in conduct which a constable reasonably suspects to constitute an offence falling within subsection (1)(c) above;

(b) he is warned by that constable to stop; and

(c) he engages in further such conduct immediately or shortly after the warning.

The conduct mentioned in paragraph (a) above and the further conduct need not be of the same nature.

(4) A person guilty of an offence falling within subsection (1)(a) or (b) above shall be liable—

(a) on summary conviction, to imprisonment for a term not exceeding six months or to a fine not exceeding the statutory maximum, or to both;

(b) on conviction on indictment, to imprisonment for a term not exceeding two years or to a fine, or to both.

(5) A person guilty of an offence falling within subsection (1)(c) above shall be liable on summary conviction to a fine not exceeding level 4 on the standard scale.

(6) If, on the trial on indictment of a person charged with an offence falling within subsection (1)(a) or (b) above, the jury find him not guilty of the offence charged, they may find him guilty of the basic offence mentioned in that provision.

(7) For the purposes of subsection (1)(c) above, section 28(1)(a) above shall have effect as if the person likely to be caused harassment, alarm or distress were the victim of the offence.

This section came into force on September 30, 1998: *Crime and Disorder Act* 1998 **12–25** (Commencement No.2 and Transitional Provisions Order 1998 (SI 1998/2327). The words 'or religiously' were added as from December 14, 2001, with no retrospective effect: *Anti-Terrorism, Crime and Security Act* 2001, ss.39(5), (6), 42.

Crime and Disorder Act, s.28

Meaning of "racially or religiously aggravated"

28.—(1) An offence is racially or religiously aggravated for the purposes of sections 29 to 32 **12–26** below if—

(a) at the time of committing the offence, or immediately before or after doing so, the offender demonstrates towards the victim of the offence hostility based on the victim's membership (or presumed membership) of a racial or religious group; or

(b) the offence is motivated (wholly or partly) by hostility towards members of a racial or religious group based on their membership of that group.

(2) In subsection (1)(a) above—

"membership", in relation to a racial or religious group, includes association with members of that group;

"presumed" means presumed by the offender.

(3) It is immaterial for the purposes of paragraph (a) or (b) of subsection (1) above whether or not the offender's hostility is also based, to any extent, on any other factor not mentioned in that paragraph.

(4) In this section "racial group" means a group of persons defined by reference to race, colour, nationality (including citizenship) or ethnic or national origins.

[(5) In this section "religious group" means a group of persons defined by reference to religious belief or lack of religious belief.]

The language of the statute should be given a broad and non-technical meaning: *R.* **12–27** *v White (Anthony)* [2001] 1 W.L.R. 1352, CA.

As regards the basic form of the offence, the prosecution must prove that:

— the defendant used threatening, abusive or insulting words or behaviour towards another person OR

— the defendant distributed or displayed to another person any writing, sign or other visible representation which is threatening or abusive or insulting AND

— the defendant intended to cause that person to believe that immediate unlawful violence would be used against him or another by any other person OR

— the defendant intended to provoke the immediate use of unlawful violence by that person or another OR

— the person is likely to believe that unlawful violence will be used or it is likely that such violence will be provoked.

12–28   As regards the racially or religiously aggravated form of this offence, the prosecution must prove:

— The defendant committed an offence under s.4 of the *Public Order Act* 1986 and

— The offence was racially or religiously aggravated; *i.e.* that at the time of committing the offence or immediately before or after doing so the offender demonstrated towards the victim hostility based on the victim's membership (or perceived membership) of a racial or religious group OR the offence was motivated, wholly or partly, by hostility towards members of a racial group based on their membership of that racial group.

(b) *Procedure*

12–29   The basic form of this offence is triable summarily only: s.4(4).

The racially aggravated form of the offence is triable either way: *Crime and Disorder Act* 1998, s.31(4).

(c) *Elements of the offence*

'Threatening, abusive or insulting'

12–30   'Insulting' is to be given its ordinary meaning and the question whether words or behaviour are insulting is a question of fact': *Brutus v Cozens* (1973) A.C. 854. In *Vigon v DPP* (1998) 162 J.P. 115 it was held that that installing a partially hidden video camera in a changing area, so that customers trying on swimwear would be filmed amounted to insulting behaviour, the wording of s.5 not being limited to 'rowdy behaviour.'

'likely to'

12–31   It is the state of mind of the victim which is crucial, rather than the statistical risk of violence occurring within a short space of time: *DPP v Ramos* [2000] Crim.L.R. 768, DC. (See further *Archbold Crown*, § 29–29). In *Valentine v DPP* (1997) COD 339, DC, it was held that the defendant's threats caused a woman to fear immediate unlawful violence the next time she went to work, but only because she may have gone to work the same evening that the threat was made.

'uses towards'

12–32   The words "used towards" in s.4(1)(a) connote present physical presence, so that the person against whom the words were used must perceive with his own senses the threatening words and behaviour: *Atkin v DPP* (1989) 89 Cr.App.R. 199, DC. It was not necessary for the victim to give evidence in court to prove that he did perceive the words or behaviour: *Swanston v DPP*, 161 J.P. 203, DC.

'immediate unlawful violence'

12–33   The word "immediate" does not mean "instantaneous," but only a relatively short time interval may elapse between the act which is threatening, abusive or insulting and the unlawful violence. "Immediate" connotes proximity in time and proximity in causation; that it is likely that violence will result within a relatively short period of time and without any other intervening occurrence: *R. v Horseferry Road Magistrates Court Ex p. Siadatan* [1991] 1 Q.B. 280, DC.

(d) *Sentence*

The maximum penalty for the basic form of the offence is six months imprisonment, **12–34** a fine not exceeding level 5 on the standard scale or both: s.4(4).

The *Magistrates' Court Sentencing Guidelines* (2003) state:

> Aggravating factors include group action, people put in fear, vulnerable victims, on hospital/medical premises, victim serving the public, offence committed on bail, relevant previous convictions and any failure to respond to previous sentences.
>
> Mitigating factors include minor matter, short duration.
>
> **Guideline**: is it serious enough for a community penalty?

When tried summarily, the maximum penalty for the aggravated form of the offence **12–35** is six months imprisonment, a fine not exceeding the statutory maximum or both: *Crime and Disorder Act* 1998, s.31(4). The *Magistrates' Court Sentencing Guidelines* also provide a higher guideline for sentencing the aggravated form of the offence, stating: is the offence so serious that only custody is appropriate?

In *R. v Saunders* [2000] 2 Cr.App.R.(S.) 71, CA, Rose L.J. issued guidance in relation to racially aggravated assaults and racially aggravated offences more generally. He stated that those who indulge in racially aggravated violence must expect to be punished severely, in order to discourage the repetition of that behaviour by them or others. Relevant factors for the purposes of determining the increase in sentence to reflect the racially or religiously aggravated element of the offence will include the nature of the hostile demonstration, whether by language, gestures or weapons; its length, whether isolated, repeated, or persistent; its location, whether public or private; the number both of those demonstrating and those demonstrated against; and the presence or absence of other features. A discount in the overall sentence will be appropriate in accordance with general sentencing principles for, among other things, genuine remorse, a plea of guilty and previous good character.

In *R. v Miller* [1999] 2 Cr.App.R.(S.) 392, CA the offender was sentenced to 18 months' imprisonment for racially aggravated threatening words and behaviour and to travelling on a railway without a ticket. Although M pleaded guilty, the evidence against him was overwhelming and he had a record of many previous convictions, some of them serious. The sentence was recognised as severe, yet upheld as it needed to be, to reflect public concern about conduct which damaged good racial relations within the community.

D. Intentionally Causing Harassment, Alarm or Distress

(a) *Definition*

Public Order Act 1986, s.4A

Intentional harassment, alarm or distress

4A.—(1) A person is guilty of an offence if, with intent to cause a person harassment, alarm **12–36** or distress, he—

    (a) uses threatening, abusive or insulting words or behaviour, or disorderly behaviour, or

    (b) displays any writing, sign or ostensible representation which is threatening, abusive or insulting,

thereby causing that or another person harassment, alarm or distress.

    (2) An offence under this section may be committed in a public or a private place, except that no offence is committed where the words or behaviour are used, or the writing, sign or ostensible representation is displayed, by a person inside a dwelling and the person who is harassed, alarmed or distressed is also inside that or another dwelling.

(3) It is a defence for the accused to prove—

　(a) that he was inside a dwelling and had no reason to believe that the words or behaviour used, or the writing, sign or ostensible representation displayed, would
be heard or seen by a person outside that or any other dwelling, or

　(b) that his conduct was reasonable.

[This section was inserted by the *CJPOA* 1994, s.152.]

12–37　For definition of the racially or religiously aggravated form of this offence see *Crime
and Disorder Act* 1998, s.31 (subs.5 above).

As regards the basic form of the offence the prosecution need to prove that:

— the defendant used threatening, abusive or insulting words or behaviour or
displayed any writing, sign or ostensible representation which was threatening,
abusive or insulting,

— the defendant so behaved with the intention to cause a person harassment,
alarm or distress, and,

— the defendant thereby caused that or another person alarm or distress.

12–37.1　As regards the racially aggravated form of the offence the prosecution need to prove
that:

— the defendant committed an offence under s.4A of the *Public Order Act* 1986
and

— the offence was racially or religiously aggravated; *i.e.* that at the time of committing the offence or immediately before or after doing so the offender demonstrated towards the victim hostility based on the victim's membership (or
perceived membership) of a racial or religious group OR the offence was
motivated, wholly or partly, by hostility towards members of a racial group
based on their membership of that racial group

(b) *Procedure*

12–38　The basic form of this offence is triable summarily only: s.4A(5). The racially aggravated form of the offence is triable either way: *Crime and Disorder Act* 1998,
s.31(4). The *Magistrates' Court Sentencing Guidelines* recommend committal for
sentence.

(c) *Elements of the offence*

12–39　An intention to cause harassment alarm or distress must be established: *DPP v
Weeks Independent*, July 17, 2000. Harassment, alarm and distress are to be treated as
ordinary words of the English language, the approach of the Court in *Brutus v Cozens*
(1973) A.C. 854, being adopted in this context.

(d) *Specific Defence*

12–40　Section 4A(3) establishes that the accused will have a defence if he can prove that he
had no reason to believe that there was any person within hearing or sight who was
likely to be caused harassment, alarm or distress, or that he was inside a dwelling and
had no reason to believe that the words or behaviour used, or the writing, sign or
ostensible representation displayed, would be heard or seen by a person outside that or
any other dwelling, or that his conduct was reasonable.

(e) *Sentence*

12–41　The maximum penalty for the basic form of the offence is six months' imprisonment,
a fine not exceeding level five on the standard scale or both: s.4A(5).

The *Magistrates' Court Sentencing Guidelines* (2003) state:

Aggravating factors include football hooliganism, group action, victims specially targeted high
degree of planning, night-time offence, weapon, offence committed on bail, relevant previous
convictions and any failures to respond to previous sentences.

Mitigating factors include short duration of offence.

Guideline: is it serious enough for a community penalty?

When tried summarily, the maximum penalty for the aggravated form of the offence **12–41.1** is six months' imprisonment, a fine not exceeding the statutory maximum or both: *Crime and Disorder Act* 1998, s.31(4).

The *Magistrates' Court Sentencing Guidelines* (2003) provide a higher guideline **12–42** for the aggravated form of the offence, the guideline being whether the offence is so serious that only a custodial sentence is appropriate.

E. HARASSMENT, ALARM OR DISTRESS.

(a) *Definition*

Public Order Act 1986, s.5(1), (2)

Harassment, alarm or distress

5.—(1) A person is guilty of an offence if he—   **12–43**
  (a) uses threatening, abusive or insulting words or behaviour, or disorderly behaviour, or
  (b) displays any writing, sign or ostensible representation which is threatening, abusive or insulting,
within the hearing or sight of a person likely to be caused harassment, alarm or distress thereby.

(2) An offence under this section may be committed in a public or a private place, except that no offence is committed where the words or behaviour are used, or the writing, sign or ostensible representation is displayed, by a person inside a dwelling and the other person is also inside that or another dwelling.

For definition of the racially or religiously aggravated form of this offence see the **12–43.1** *Crime and Disorder Act* 1998, s.31 (subs.5 above).

As regards the basic form of this offence, the prosecution need to prove that:
  — the defendant used threatening, abusive or insulting words or behaviour, or **12–44** disorderly behaviour OR
  — the defendant displayed any writing sign or ostensible representation which is threatening, abusive or insulting and
  — such conduct took place within the hearing or sight of a person likely to be caused harassment, alarm or distress thereby.

As regards the racially or religiously aggravated form of the offence, the prosecution **12–45** must prove that:
  — the defendant committed an offence under s.4A of the *Public Order Act* 1986 and
  — the offence was racially or religiously aggravated; *i.e.* that at the time of committing the offence or immediately before or after doing so the offender demonstrated towards the victim hostility based on the victim's membership (or perceived membership) of a racial or religious group OR the offence was motivated, wholly or partly, by hostility towards members of a racial group based on their membership of that racial group.

(b) *Procedure*

Both the basic and the aggravated forms of this offence are triable summarily only.   **12–46**

(c) *Elements of the offence*

'Harassment, alarm or distress'

Whether a person is likely to be caused harassment, alarm or distress is a matter of **12–47** fact to be determined by the magistrates; it is not necessary that the victim's alarm is due to fears for his own personal safety, he could be concerned about the safety of some third party: *Lodge v DPP, The Times*, October 26, 1998.

'Display'

12–48   In *Chappell v DPP* (1988) 89 Cr.App.R. 82, it was held that dropping letters through a letter box was not an offence under s.5 because the writing of words which were then concealed in an envelope was not a "display" within s.5(1)(b). Where the letter was opened in the absence of the sender it could not be said that the sender "uses...words or behaviour...within the hearing or sight of that person" within s.5(1)(a).

Mens rea

12–49   The accused must intend his words, behaviour, representation or sign to be threatening, abusive or insulting, or be aware that they may be threatening, abusive or insulting, or he must intend his behaviour to be, or be aware that it could be disorderly: *Public Order Act* 1986, s.6(4).

(d) *Specific Defence*

Public Order Act 1986, s.5(3)

Harassment, alarm or distress

12–50   5.—(3) It is a defence for the accused to prove—

(a) that he had no reason to believe that there was any person within hearing or sight who was likely to be caused harassment, alarm or distress, or

(b) that he was inside a dwelling and had no reason to believe that the words or behaviour used, or the writing, sign or other visible representation displayed, would be heard or seen by a person outside that or any other dwelling, or

(c) that his conduct was reasonable.

12–50.1   The defence of reasonable conduct is to be proved objectively: *DPP v Clarke* (1992) 94 Cr.App.R. 359; (1991) 156 J.P. 267. In *Percy v DPP* (2002) 166 J.P. 93 the offender had defaced an American flag, and while outside an American airbase she put the flag on the road and trod upon it. The court was asked to consider whether the offender's protest fell within her right to freedom of expression under the *Human Rights Act* 1998. It was held that whilst it had been open to the district judge to find a pressing social need to prevent the denigration of objects of veneration and cultural importance, the next issue to consider was whether the restriction on the offender's freedom of expression through the imposition of a criminal penalty was proportionate. The fact that she could have demonstrated her message by some other means other than defacing the flag was a factor to be taken into account but was only one of a number of factors. Other relevant considerations included whether the accused's behaviour had gone beyond legitimate protest, whether the behaviour had not been part of an open expression on an issue of public interest but had been disproportionate and unreasonable, the knowledge of the accused of the likely effect of his or her conduct upon those who witnessed it and whether the use of a flag had no relevance to the conveying of the message of protest and had been used as a gratuitous and calculated insult.

(e) *Sentence*

12–51   The maximum penalty for the basic form of the offence is a fine not exceeding level three on the standard scale: *Public Order Act* 1986, s.5(6).

The *Magistrates' Court Sentencing Guidelines* (2003) state:

> Aggravating factors include group action, vulnerable victim, offence committed on bail, relevant previous convictions and any failure to respond to previous sentences.
> Mitigating factors include stopping as soon as police arrived and trivial incident.

Guideline: Is discharge or fine appropriate?

The maximum penalty for the aggravated form of the offence is a fine not exceeding **12–51.1**
level four on the standard scale: *Crime and Disorder Act* 1998, s.31(5). The *Magis-trates' Court Sentencing Guidelines* (2003) provide a higher guideline for the aggravated form of the offence, being whether the offence is serious enough for a com-
munity sentence.

F. Control of Processions, Assemblies and Meetings

(1) Notice and conditions relating to public processions

Public Order Act 1986, ss.11, 12

Advance notice of public processions

11.—(1) Written notice shall be given in accordance with this section of any proposal to hold **12–52**
a public procession intended—
  (a) to demonstrate support for or opposition to the views or actions of any person or
    body of persons,
  (b) to publicise a cause or campaign, or
  (c) to mark or commemorate an event,
unless it is not reasonably practicable to give any advance notice of the procession.

  (2) Subsection (1) does not apply where the procession is one commonly or customarily
held in the police area (or areas) in which it is proposed to be held or is a funeral procession organised by a funeral director acting in the normal course of his business.

  (3) The notice must specify the date when it is intended to hold the procession, the time
when it is intended to start it, its proposed route, and the name and address of the person
(or of one of the persons) proposing to organise it.

  (4) Notice must be delivered to a police station—
  (a) in the police area in which it is proposed the procession will start, or
  (b) where it is proposed the procession will start in Scotland and cross into England,
    in the first police area in England on the proposed route.

  (5) If delivered not less than 6 clear days before the date when the procession is intended
to be held, the notice may be delivered by post by the recorded delivery service; but section 7 of the *Interpretation Act* 1978 (under which a document sent by post is deemed to have
been served when posted and to have been delivered in the ordinary course of post) does not
apply.

  (6) If not delivered in accordance with subsection (5), the notice must be delivered by
hand not less than 6 clear days before the date when the procession is intended to be held
or, if that is not reasonably practicable, as soon as delivery is reasonably practicable.

  (7) Where a public procession is held, each of the persons organising it is guilty of an offence if—
  (a) the requirements of this section as to notice have not been satisfied, or
  (b) the date when it is held, the time when it starts, or its route, differs from the date,
    time or route specified in the notice.

  (8) It is a defence for the accused to prove that he did not know of, and neither
suspected nor had reason to suspect, the failure to satisfy the requirements or (as the case
may be) the difference of date, time or route.

  (9) To the extent that an alleged offence turns on a difference of date, time or route, it
is a defence for the accused to prove that the difference arose from circumstances beyond
his control or from something done with the agreement of a police officer or by his
direction.

  (10) A person guilty of an offence under subsection (7) is liable on summary conviction
to a fine not exceeding level 3 on the standard scale.

Imposing conditions on public processions

12.—(1) If the senior police officer, having regard to the time or place at which and the cir- **12–53**
cumstances in which any public procession is being held or is intended to be held and to its
route or proposed route, reasonably believes that—

441

(a) it may result in serious public disorder, serious damage to property or serious disruption to the life of the community, or

(b) the purpose of the persons organising it is the intimidation of others with a view to compelling them not to do an act they have a right to do, or to do an act they have a right not to do,

he may give directions imposing on the persons organising or taking part in the procession such conditions as appear to him necessary to prevent such disorder, damage, disruption or intimidation,including conditions as to the route of the procession or prohibiting it from entering any public place specified in the directions.

(2) In subsection (1) "the senior police officer" means—

(a) in relation to a procession being held, or to a procession intended to be held in a case where persons are assembling with a view to taking part in it, the most senior in rank of the police officers present at the scene, and

(b) in relation to a procession intended to be held in a case where paragraph does not apply, the chief officer of police.

(3) A direction given by a chief officer of police by virtue of subsection (2) shall be given in writing.

(4) A person who organises a public procession and knowingly fails to comply with a condition imposed under this section is guilty of an offence, but it is a defence for him to prove that the failure arose from circumstances beyond his control.

(5) A person who takes part in a public procession and knowingly fails to comply with a condition imposed under this section is guilty of an offence, but it is a defence for him to prove that the failure arose from circumstances beyond his control.

(6) A person who incites another to commit an offence under subsection (5) is guilty of an offence.

(7) A constable in uniform may arrest without warrant anyone he reasonably suspects is committing an offence under subsection (4), (5) or (6).

(8) A person guilty of an offence under subsection (4) is liable on summary conviction to imprisonment for a term not exceeding 3 months or a fine not exceeding level 4 on the standard scale or both.

(9) A person guilty of an offence under subsection (5) is liable on summary conviction to a fine not exceeding level 3 on the standard scale.

(10) A person guilty of an offence under subsection (6) is liable on summary conviction to imprisonment for a term not exceeding 3 months or a fine not exceeding level 4 on the standard scale or both, notwithstanding section 45(3) of the *Magistrates' Courts Act* 1980 (inciter liable to same penalty as incited).

(11) In Scotland this section applies only in relation to a procession being held, and to a procession intended to be held in a case where persons are assembling with a view to taking part in it.

12–54   Regarding the offence of failing to give notice of a public procession, the prosecution must prove that:

— the organiser of a public procession (it not being one to which s.11(2) of the 1986 Act applies) failed to give notice to a police station in the area in which the procession started OR

— notice having been given to the relevant police station, the date when the procession was held, the time when it started, or its route, differed from the date, time or route specified in the notice.

Regarding the offence of failing to comply with conditions imposed on public processions, the prosecution must prove that:

— an organiser of a public procession knowingly failed to comply with conditions imposed under s.12 of the *Public Order Act* 1986 OR

— a participant in a public procession knowingly failed to comply with conditions imposed under s.12 of the *Public Order Act* 1986 OR

— a person incited another to commit an offence under s.12(5) of the *Public Order Act* 1986.

(b) *Procedure*

12–55   Both of these offences are triable summarily only.

(c) *Specific Defence*

A defendant will have a defence to a charge under s.11 if he can prove that he did **12–56** not know of, and neither suspected nor had reason to suspect, the failure to satisfy the requirements or (as the case may be) the difference of date, time or route: *Public Order Act* 1986, s.11(8).

A defendant will have a defence to a charge under s.12 if he can prove that the failure to comply with a condition imposed was due to circumstances beyond the defendant's control: *Public Order Act* 1986, s.12(5)

(d) *Sentence*

The maximum penalty for both these offences is a fine not exceeding level three on **12–57** the standard scale.

(2) Contravention of prohibition on a public procession

Public Order Act 1986, s.13

Prohibiting public processions

13.—(1) If at any time the chief officer of police reasonably believes that, because of particular **12–58** circumstances existing in any district or part of a district, the powers under section 12 will not be sufficient to prevent the holding of public processions in that district or part from resulting in serious public disorder, he shall apply to the council of the district for an order prohibiting for such period not exceeding 3 months as may be specified in the application the holding of all public processions (or of any class of public procession so specified) in the district or part concerned.

(2) On receiving such an application, a council may with the consent of the Secretary of State make an order either in the terms of the application or with such modifications as may be approved by the Secretary of State.

(3) Subsection (1) does not apply in the City of London or the metropolitan police district.

(4) If at any time the Commissioner of Police for the City of London or the Commissioner of Police of the Metropolis reasonably believes that, because of particular circumstances existing in his police area or part of it, the powers under section 12will not be sufficient to prevent the holding of public processions in that area or part from resulting in serious public disorder, he may with the consent of the Secretary of State make an order prohibiting for such period not exceeding 3 months as may be specified in the order the holding of all public processions (or of any class of public procession so specified) in the area or part concerned.

(5) An order made under this section may be revoked varied by a subsequent order **12–59** made in the same way, that is, in accordance with subsections (1) and (2) or subsection (4), as the case may be.

(6) Any order under this section shall, if not made in writing, be recorded in writing as soon as practicable after being made.

(7) A person who organises a public procession the holding of which he knows is prohibited by virtue of an order under this section is guilty of an offence.

(8) A person who takes part in a public procession the holding of which he knows is prohibited by virtue of an order under this section is guilty of an offence.

(9) A person who incites another to commit an offence under subsection (8) is guilty of an offence.

(10) A constable in uniform may arrest without warrant anyone he reasonably suspects is committing an offence under subsection (7), (8) or (9).

(11) A person guilty of an offence under subsection (7) is liable on summary conviction to imprisonment for a term not exceeding 3 months or a fine not exceeding level 4 on the standard scale or both.

(12) A person guilty of an offence under subsection (8) is liable on summary conviction to a fine not exceeding level 3 on the standard scale.

(13) A person guilty of an offence under subsection (9) is liable on summary conviction

to imprisonment for a term not exceeding 3 months or a fine not exceeding level 4 on the standard scale or both, notwithstanding section 45(3) of the *Magistrates' Courts Act* 1980.

12–60   The prosecution must prove that:
— a person organised a public procession the holding of which he knows to be prohibited under s.13 of the *Public Order Act* 1986 OR
— a person took part in a public procession the holding of which he knows to be prohibited under s.13 of the *Public Order Act* 1986 OR
— a person incited another to commit an offence under s.13(8) of the *Public Order Act* 1986.

(b) *Procedure*

12–61   An offence under this section is triable summarily only.

(c) *Sentence*

12–62   The maximum penalty for the offence of organising, or inciting the commission of an offence by another is imprisonment for a term not exceeding three months, or a fine not exceeding level four on the standard scale or both. The maximum penalty for the offence of participating in the prohibited procession is a fine not exceeding level three on the standard scale.

(3) Contravening prohibition on trespassory assemblies

(a) *Definition*

Public Order Act 1986, s.14A–14C

Prohibiting trespassory assemblies

12–63   **14A.**—(1) If at any time the chief officer of police reasonably believes that an assembly is intended to be held in any district at a place on land to which the public has no right of access or only a limited right of access and that the assembly—
(a) is likely to be held without the permission of the occupier of the land or to conduct itself in such a way as to exceed the limits of any permission of his or the limits of the public's right of access, and
(b) may result—
   (i) in serious disruption to the life of the community, or
   (ii) where the land, or a building or monument on it, is of historical, architectural, archaeological or scientific importance, in significant damage to the land, building or monument,
he may apply to the council of the district for an order prohibiting for a specified, period the holding of all trespassory assemblies in the district or a part of it, as specified.

(2) On receiving such an application, a council may—
(a) in England and Wales, with the consent of the Secretary of State make an order either in the terms of the application or with such modifications as may be approved by the Secretary of State; or
(b) in Scotland, make an order in the terms of the application.

(3) Subsection (1) does not apply in the City of London or the metropolitan police district.

12–64   (4) If at any time the Commissioner of Police for the City of London or the Commissioner of Police of the Metropolis reasonably believes that an assembly is intended to be held at a place on land to which the public has no right of access or only a limited right of access in his police area and that the assembly—
(a) is likely to be held without the permission of the occupier of the land or to conduct itself in such a way as to exceed the limits of any permission of his or the limits of the public's right of access, and
(b) may result—
   (i) in serious disruption to the life of the community, or

(ii)   where the land, or a building or monument on it, is of historical, architectural, archaeological or scientific importance, in significant damage to the land, building or monument,

he may with the consent of the Secretary of State make an order prohibiting for a specified period the holding of all trespassory assemblies in the area or a part of it, as specified.

(5) An order prohibiting the holding of trespassory assemblies operates to prohibit any assembly which—

(a)   is held on land to which the public has no right of access or only a limited right of access, and

(b)   takes place in the prohibited circumstances, that is to say, without the permission of the occupier of the land or so as to exceed the limits of any permission of his or the limits of the public's right of access.

(6) No order under this section shall prohibit the holding of assemblies for a period exceeding 4 days or in an area exceeding an area represented by a circle with a radius of 5 miles from a specified centre.

(7) An order made under this section may be revoked varied by a subsequent order made in the same way, that is, in accordance with subsection (1) and (2) or subsection (4), as the case may be.

(8) Any order under this section shall, if not made in writing, be recorded in writing as soon as practicable after being made.

(9) In this section and sections 14B and 14C—

"assembly" means an assembly of 20 or more persons;

"land" means land in the open air;

"limited", in relation to a right of access by the public to land, means that their use of it is restricted to use for a particular purpose (as in the case of a highway or road) or is subject to other restrictions;

"occupier" means—

(a)   in England and Wales, the person entitled to possession of the land by virtue of an estate or interest held by him; or

(b)   in Scotland, the person lawfully entitled to natural possession of the land, and in subsections (1) and (4) includes the person reasonably believed by the authority applying for or making the order to be the occupier;

"public" includes a section of the public; and

"specified" means specified in an order under this section.

(10) In relation to Scotland, the references in subsection (1) above to a district and to the council of the district shall be construed—

(a)   as respects applications before 1st April 1996, as references to the area of a regional or islands authority and to the authority in question; and

(b)   as respects applications on and after that date, as references to a local government area and to the council for that area.

(11) In relation to Wales, the references in subsection (1) above to a district and to the council of the district shall be construed, as respects applications on and after 1st April 1996, as references to a county or county borough and to the council for that county or county borough.

Offences in connection with trespassory assemblies and arrest therefor

14B.—(1) A person who organises an assembly the holding of which he knows is prohibited **12–65** by an order under section 14A is guilty of an offence.

(2) A person who takes part in an assembly which he knows is prohibited by an order under section 14A is guilty of an offence.

(3) In England and Wales, a person who incites another to commit an offence under subsection (2) is guilty of an offence.

(4) A constable in uniform may arrest without a warrant anyone he reasonably suspects to be committing an offence under this section.

(5) A person guilty of an offence under subsection (1) is liable on summary conviction to imprisonment for a term not exceeding 3 months or a fine not exceeding level 4 on the standard scale or both.

(6) A person guilty of an offence under subsection (2) is liable on summary conviction to a fine not exceeding level 3 on the standard scale.

(7) A person guilty of an offence under subsection (3) is liable on summary conviction to imprisonment for a term not exceeding 3 months or a fine not exceeding level 4 on the standard scale or both, notwithstanding section 45(3) of the *Magistrates' Courts Act* 1980.

(8) Subsection (3) above is without prejudice to the application of any principle of Scots Law as respects art and part guilt to such incitement as is mentioned in that subsection.

Stopping persons from proceeding to trespassory assemblies

12–66   **14C.**—(1) If a constable in uniform reasonably believes that a person is on his way to an assembly within the area to which an order under section 14A applies which the constable reasonably believes is likely to be an assembly which is prohibited by that order, he may, subject to subsection (2) below—

     (a)   stop that person, and

     (b)   direct him not to proceed in the direction of the assembly.

(2) The power conferred by subsection (1) may only be exercised within the area to which the order applies.

(3) A person who fails to comply with a direction under subsection (1) which he knows has been given to him is guilty of an offence.

(4) A constable in uniform may arrest without a warrant anyone he reasonably suspects to be committing an offence under this section.

(5) A person guilty of an offence under subsection (3) is liable on summary conviction to a fine not exceeding level 3 on the standard scale.

12–66.1   The prosecution must prove that:

— a person organised an assembly which he knew was prohibited by an order made under s.14A of the *Public Order Act* 1986 OR

— a person participated in an assembly which he knew to be prohibited under s.14A of the *Public Order Act* 1986 OR

— a person participated in an assembly which he knew to be prohibited under s.14A of the *Public Order Act* 1986 OR

— a person incited another to commit an offence under s.14B(2) of the *Public Order Act* 1986.

(b) *Procedure*

12–67   The offences under this section are triable summarily only.

(c) *Defences*

12–68   In *Jones v DPP* (1999) 2 A.C. 240, the HL (allowing the appeal by a majority) held that there was a public right of peaceful assembly on a public highway and provided those activities are reasonable, they should not constitute a trespass, it being a question of fact and degree for the court of trial to in each case to decide whether the user was reasonable, this right being subject to the requirement that the activity in question does not amount to a public or private nuisance and does not obstruct the highway by unreasonably impeding the primary right of the general public to pass and repass. Although the matter was essentially one to be judged in the light of the particular case, a peaceful assembly which did not obstruct the highway did not necessarily constitute a trespassory assembly so as to constitute the circumstances for an offence within s.14B(2) of the 1986 Act, where an order under s.14A was in force, *per* Lord Hutton.

(d) *Sentence*

12–69   The maximum penalty for the offence of organising a trespassory assembly, or inciting another to commit an offence under s.14B is imprisonment for a term not exceeding three months or a fine not exceeding level 4 on the standard scale or both. The maximum penalty for the offence of participating in a trespassory assembly is a fine not exceeding level three on the standard scale.

(4) Interpretation

Public Order Act 1986, s.16

Interpretation

16. In this Part—   **12–70**

"the City of London" means the City as defined for the purposes of the Acts relating to the City of London police;

"the metropolitan police district" means that district as defined in section 76 of the *London Government Act* 1963;

"public assembly" means an assembly of 20 or more persons in a public place which is wholly or partly open to the air;

"public place" means—

(a) any highway, or in Scotland any road within the meaning of the *Roads (Scotland) Act* 1984, and

(b) any place to which at the material time the public or any section of the public has access, on payment or otherwise, as of right or by virtue of express or implied permission;

"public procession" means a procession in a public place.

G. Acts Intended or Likely to stir up Racial Hatred

(a) *Definition*

Public Order Act 1986, s.18

Use of words or behaviour or display of written material

18.—(1) A person who uses threatening, abusive or insulting words or behaviour, or displays **12–71**
any written material which is threatening, abusive or insulting, is guilty of an offence if—

(a) he intends thereby to stir up racial hatred, or

(b) having regard to all the circumstances racial hatred is likely to be stirred up thereby.

(2) An offence under this section may be committed in a public or a private place, except that no offence is committed where the words or behaviour are used, or the written material is displayed, by a person inside a dwelling and are not heard or seen except by other persons in that or another dwelling.

(3) A constable may arrest without warrant anyone he reasonably suspects is committing an offence under this section.

(4) In proceedings for an offence under this section it is a defence for the accused to prove that he was inside a dwelling and had no reason to believe that the words or behaviour used, or the written material displayed, would be heard or seen by a person outside that or any other dwelling.

(5) A person who is not shown to have intended to stir up racial hatred is not guilty of an offence under this section if he did not intend his words or behaviour, or the written material, to be, and was not aware that it might be, threatening, abusive or insulting.

(6) This section does not apply to words or behaviour used, or written material displayed, solely for the purpose of being included in a programme included in a programme service.

[This section is printed as amended by the *Broadcasting Act* 1990, s.164(1), (2).]
The prosecution must prove that: **12–72**

— the defendant used threatening, abusive or insulting words or behaviour, or displayed any written material which is threatening, abusive or insulting AND

— he intended to stir up racial hatred by so doing OR

— having regard to all the circumstances, racial hatred was likely to be stirred up by his actions.

(b) *Procedure*

This offence is triable either way. No proceedings may be instituted without the **12–73**
consent of the Attorney General: *Public Order Act* 1986, s.27(3).

(c) Elements of the offence

Public Order Act 1986, ss.17, 26, 29

Meaning of "racial hatred"

12–74   **17.** In this Part "racial hatred" means hatred against a group of persons defined by reference to colour, race, nationality (including citizenship) or ethnic or national origins.

Savings for reports of parliamentary or judicial proceedings

12–74.1   **26.**—(1) Nothing in this Part applies to a fair and accurate report of proceedings in Parliament or in the Scottish Parliament.

(2) Nothing in this Part applies to a fair and accurate report of proceedings publicly heard before a court or tribunal exercising judicial authority where the report is published contemporaneously with the proceedings or, if it is not reasonably practicable or would be unlawful to publish a report of them contemporaneously, as soon as publication is reasonably practicable and lawful.

Interpretation

12–75   **29.** In this Part—

"distribute", and related expressions, shall be construed in accordance with section 19(3) (written material) and section 21(2) (recordings);

"dwelling" means any structure or part of a structure occupied as a person's home or other living accommodation (whether the occupation is separate or shared with others) but does not include any part not so occupied, and for this purpose "structure" includes a tent, caravan, vehicle, vessel or other temporary or movable structure;

"programme" means any item which is included in a programme service

"programme service" has the same meaning as in the *Broadcasting Act* 1990;

"publish", and related expressions, in relation to written material, shall be construed in accordance with section 19(3)

"racial hatred" has the meaning given by section 17

"recording" has the meaning given by section 21(2) and "play" and "show", and related expressions, in relation to a recording, shall be construed in accordance with that provision;

"written material" includes any sign or ostensible representation.

For the meaning of 'threatening, abusive or insulting' see the materials on s.4 of the *Public Order Act* 1986 (§ 12–30 above).

(d) Defences

12–76   Section 19(2) establishes a defence for a defendant who did not intend to stir up racial hatred if he can prove that he was not aware of the content of the material and did not suspect, and had no reason to suspect that it was threatening, abusive or insulting. The burden of proof of establishing this defence lies on the accused.

The defence in s.26 of the *Public Order Act* 1986 relating to exceptions for reports of Parliamentary and judicial proceedings applies to s.19.

(e) Sentence

12–77   When tried summarily, the maximum penalty is six months' imprisonment, a fine not exceeding the statutory maximum or both. The court also has power to order forfeiture when the offence consists of displaying written material.

When tried summarily, the maximum penalty is six months' imprisonment, a fine not exceeding the statutory maximum or both. The court also has power under s.25 of the 1986 Act to order forfeiture when the offence consists of displaying written material.

Possession of threatening, abusive or insulting material with a view to publication led to a 12 month custodial sentence in *Gray* [1999] 1 Cr.App.R.(S.) 50, Judge Peter Crawford Q.C. emphasising the grave social damage done by offences and remarks of a racist nature.

H. Publishing or Distributing Written Material Stirring up Racial Hatred

(a) *Definition*

Public Order Act 1986, s.19

Publishing or distributing written material

19.—(1) A person who publishes or distributes written material which is threatening, abusive **12–78** or insulting is guilty of an offence if—
- (a) he intends thereby to stir up racial hatred, or
- (b) having regard to all the circumstances racial hatred is likely to be stirred up thereby.

(2) In proceedings for an offence under this section it is a defence for an accused who is not shown to have intended to stir up racial hatred to prove that he was not aware of the content of the material and did not suspect, and had no reason to suspect, that it was threatening, abusive or insulting.

(3) References in this Part to the publication or distribution of written material are to its publication or distribution to the public or a section of the public.

The prosecution must prove that: **12–78.1**
- the defendant published or distributed written material which is threatening, abusive or insulting, and,
- he intended to stir up racial hatred OR
- having regard to all the circumstances, racial hatred was likely to be stirred up by such publication or distribution

(b) *Procedure*

This offence is triable either way. No proceedings may be instituted without the **12–79** consent of the Att-Gen: *Public Order Act* 1986, s.27(3).

(c) *Elements of the offence*

For the meaning of 'Racial Hatred' see s.17 of the 1986 Act, above. For the meaning **12–80** of 'threatening, abusive or insulting', see § 12–30 and *Brutus v Cozens* (1973) A.C. 854, above. For the meaning of 'written material' see s.29 of the 1986 Act, above.

(d) *Defences*

The defence established by s.26 of the 1986 Act applies to proceedings instituted **12–81** under this section.

I. Public Performance, Distribution, Broadcasting and Possession of Materials Stirring up Racial Hatred

(1) Public performance of a play stirring up racial hatred

(a) *Definition*

Public Order Act 1986, s.20(1), (5), (6)

Public performance of play

20.—(1) If a public performance of a play is given which involves the use of threatening, **12–82** abusive or insulting words or behaviour, any person who presents or directs the performance is guilty of an offence if—
- (a) he intends thereby to stir up racial hatred, or
- (b) having regard to all the circumstances (and, in particular, taking the performance as a whole) racial hatred is likely to be stirred up thereby.

(5) In this section "play" and "public performance" have the same meaning as in the *Theatres Act* 1968.

(6) The following provisions of the *Theatres Act* 1968 apply in relation to an offence under this section as they apply to an offence under section 2 of that Act—

> section 9 (script as evidence of what was performed),
>
> section 10(power to make copies of script),
>
> section 15 (powers of entry and inspection).

[This section is printed as amended by the *Broadcasting Act* 1990, s.164(1), (2).]

12–82.1   The prosecution must prove that:

— the defendant was the director or presenter of a play involving the use of threatening, abusive or insulting words or behaviour and,

— the play was performed for the public and,

— the defendant intended thereby to stir up racial hatred OR

— having regard to all the circumstances, racial hatred was likely to be stirred up by the performance of the play.

(b) *Procedure*

12–83   This offence is triable either way. Proceedings may not be instituted without the consent of the Attorney-General: *Public Order Act* 1986, s.27.

(c) *Elements of the offence*

12–84   For the meaning of racial hatred, see s.17 of the 1986 Act, above.

The words 'play' and 'public performance' have the same meaning as in the *Theatres Act* 1968:

Theatres Act 1968, s.18(1)

Interpretation

12–85   **18.**—(1) In this Act—

"play" means—

(a) any dramatic piece, whether involving improvisation or not, which is given wholly or in part by one or more persons actually present and performing and in which the whole or a major proportion of what is done by the person or persons performing, whether by way of speech, singing or action, involves the playing of a role; and

(b) any ballet given wholly or in part by one or more persons actually present and performing, whether or not it falls within paragraph (a) of this definition;

"public performance" includes any performance in a public place within the meaning of the *Public Order Act* 1936 and any performance which the public or any section thereof are permitted to attend, whether on payment or otherwise;

(d) *Defences*

Public Order Act 1986, s.20(2)–(4)

Public performance of play

12–86   **20.**—(2) If a person presenting or directing the performance is not shown to have intended to stir up racial hatred, it is a defence for him to prove—

(a) that he did not know and had no reason to suspect that the performance would involve the use of the offending words or behaviour, or

(b) that he did not know and had no reason to suspect that the offending words or behaviour were threatening, abusive or insulting, or

(c) that he did not know and had no reason to suspect that the circumstances in which the performance would be given would be such that racial hatred would be likely to be stirred up.

(3) This section does not apply to a performance given solely or primarily for one or more of the following purposes—

(a) rehearsal,

(b) making a recording of the performance, or

(c) enabling the performance to be included in a programme service;

but if it is proved that the performance was attended by persons other than those directly connected with the giving of the performance or the doing in relation to it of the things mentioned in paragraph (b) or (c), the performance shall, unless the contrary is shown, be taken not to have been given solely or primarily for the purposes mentioned above.

(4) For the purposes of this section—

(a) a person shall not be treated as presenting a performance of a play by reason only of his taking part in it as a performer,

(b) a person taking part as a performer in a performance directed by another shall be treated as a person who directed the performance if without reasonable excuse he performs otherwise than in accordance with that person's direction, and

(c) a person shall be taken to have directed a performance of a play given under his direction notwithstanding that he was not present during the performance;

and a person shall not be treated as aiding or abetting the commission of an offence under this section by reason only of his taking part in a performance as a performer.

(e) *Sentence*

When tried summarily, the maximum penalty for an offence under this section is six **12–87** months' imprisonment, a fine not exceeding the statutory maximum or both: *POA* 1986, s.27(3).

(2) Distributing, Showing or Playing a Recording Stirring up Racial Hatred

(a) *Definition*

Public Order Act 1986, s.21

Distributing, showing or playing a recording

21.—(1) A person who distributes, or shows or plays, a recording of visual images or sounds **12–88** which are threatening, abusive or insulting is guilty of an offence if—

(a) he intends thereby to stir up racial hatred, or

(b) having regard to all the circumstances racial hatred is likely to be stirred up thereby.

(2) In this Part "recording" means any record from which visual images or sounds may, by any means, be reproduced; and references to the distribution, showing or playing of a recording are to its distribution, showing or playing to the public or a section of the public.

(3) In proceedings for an offence under this section it is a defence for an accused who is not shown to have intended to stir up racial hatred to prove that he was not aware of the content of the recording and did not suspect, and had no reason to suspect, that it was threatening, abusive or insulting.

(4) This section does not apply to the showing or playing of a recording solely for the purpose of enabling the recording to be included in a programme service.

[This section is printed as amended by the *Broadcasting Act* 1990, s.164(1), (2).]

The prosecution must prove that: **12–89**

— the defendant distributed, showed or played a recording or visual images or sounds and,

— these visual images or sounds were threatening, abusive or insulting and,

— he so acted with the intention to stir up racial hatred OR

— having regard to all the circumstances, racial hatred was likely to be stirred up by such actions.

(b) *Procedure*

12–90   This offence is triable either way. Proceedings may not be instituted without the consent of the Attorney General: *POA* 1986, s.27(1).

(c) *Elements of the offence*

12–91   For the meaning of 'racial hatred' see s.18 of the 1986 Act, above. For the meaning of 'threatening, abusive or insulting, see *Brutus v Cozens*, above.

(d) *Defence*

12–92   A person who is not shown to have intended to stir up racial hatred will have a defence if he can prove that he was not aware of the contents of the recording and he did not suspect, or have any reason to suspect that the recording was threatening, abusive or insulting: *POA* 1986, s.21(2).

The defence applying to fair and accurate reports of parliamentary or judicial proceedings is also available: *POA* 1986, s.26.

(e) *Sentence*

12–93   When tried summarily, the maximum penalty for this offence is six months imprisonment, a fine not exceeding the statutory maximum, or both: *POA* 1986, s.27(3).

(3) Broadcasting a Programme Stirring up Racial Hatred

(a) *Definition*

Public Order Act 1986, s.22

Broadcasting or including programme in cable programme service

12–94   **22.**—(1) If a programme involving threatening, abusive or insulting visual images or sounds is included in a programme service, each of the persons mentioned in subsection (2) is guilty of an offence if—

  (a) he intends thereby to stir up racial hatred, or

  (b) having regard to all the circumstances racial hatred is likely to be stirred up thereby.

(2) The persons are—

  (a) the person providing the programme service,

  (b) any person by whom the programme is produced or directed, and

  (c) any person by whom offending words or behaviour are used.

(3) If the person providing the service, or a person by whom the programme was produced or directed, is not shown to have intended to stir up racial hatred, it is a defence for him to prove that—

  (a) he did not know and had not reason to suspect that the programme would involve the offending material, and

  (b) having regard to the circumstances in which the programme was included in a programme service, it was not reasonably practicable for him to secure the removal of the material.

(4) It is a defence for a person by whom the programme was produced or directed who is not shown to have intended to stir up racial hatred to prove that he did not know and had not reason to suspect—

  (a) that the programme would be included in a programme service, or

  (b) that the circumstances in which the programme would be so included would be such that racial hatred would be likely to be stirred up.

(5) It is a defence for a person by whom offending words or behaviour were used and who is not shown to have intended to stir up racial hatred to prove that he did not know and had no reason to suspect—

  (a) that a programme involving the use of the offending material would be included in a programme service, or

(b) that the circumstances in which a programme involving the use of the offending material would be so included, or in which a programme so included would involve the use of the offending material, would be such that racial hatred would be likely to be stirred up.

(6) A person who is not shown to have intended to stir up racial hatred is not guilty of an offence under this section if he did not know, and had no reason to suspect, that the offending material was threatening, abusive or insulting.

[This section is printed as amended by the *Broadcasting Act* 1990, s.164(3).] The prosecution must prove that: **12–95**
— a programme involving threatening, abusive or insulting visual images or sounds was included in a programme service and
— the defendant was either the person providing the programme service, a person by whom the programme is produced or directed or a person by whom offending words and behaviour are used and
— he intended to stir up racial hatred OR
— having regard to all the circumstances racial hatred is likely to be stirred up by such actions.

(b) *Procedure*

This offence is triable either way. Proceedings may not be instituted without the **12–96** consent of the Attorney General: *POA* 1986, s.27(1).

(c) *Elements of the offence*

For the meaning of 'racial hatred' see s.18 of the 1986 Act, above. For the meaning of **12–97** 'threatening, abusive or insulting, see *Brutus v Cozens*, above.

(d) *Defence*

A person providing the service, or directing or producing the programme who is not **12–98** shown to have intended to stir up racial hatred will have a defence if it can be shown that he did not know and had no reason to suspect that the programme would involve the offending material and having regard to all the circumstances in which the programme was included in the programme service, it was not reasonably practicable for him to secure the removal of the programme from the programme service: *POA* 1986, s.22(3).

A person directing or producing the programme who is shown not to intend to stir up racial hatred will have a defence if it can be shown that he did not know and had no reason to suspect that the programme would be included in the programme service or that the circumstances of the programme's inclusion in the programme service would be such as to stir up racial hatred: *POA* 1986, s.22(4). A person who used offending words or behaviour in the programme who is not shown to have intended to stir up racial hatred will have a defence if he can prove he did not know and had no reason to suspect that the programme involving the offending conduct would be included in the service programme or that the circumstances involving the use of the programme in the service programme would involve the use of the offending material, or that the circumstances in which a programme so included would involve the use of the offending material would be such as to involve the stirring up of racial hatred: *POA* 1986, s.22(5).

A person who is not shown to have intended to stir up racial hatred will not be guilty of an offence if he did not know and had no reason to suspect that the offending material was abusive, threatening or insulting: s.22(6).

(e) *Sentence*

When tried summarily, the maximum penalty for this offence is six months imprison- **12–99** ment, a fine not exceeding the statutory maximum, or both: *POA* 1986, s.27(3).

(4) Possession of Racially Inflammatory Material

(a) *Definition*

Public Order Act 1986, s.23

Possession of racially inflammatory material

12–100   **23.**—(1) A person who has in his possession written material which is threatening, abusive or insulting, or a recording of visual images or sounds which are threatening, abusive or insulting, with a view to—

     (a) in the case of written material, its being displayed, published, distributed, or included in a cable programme service, whether by himself or another, or

     (b) in the case of a recording, its being distributed, shown, played, or included in a cable programme service, whether by himself or another,

is guilty of an offence if he intends racial hatred to be stirred up thereby or, having regard to all the circumstances, racial hatred is likely to be stirred up thereby.

(2) For this purpose regard shall be had to such display, publication, distribution, showing, playing, or inclusion in a programme service as he has, or it may reasonably be inferred that he has, in view.

(3) In proceedings for an offence under this section it is a defence for an accused who is not shown to have intended to stir up racial hatred to prove that he was not aware of the content of the written material or recording and did not suspect, and had no reason to suspect, that it was threatening, abusive or insulting.

[This section is printed as amended by the *Broadcasting Act* 1990, s.164(4).]

(b) *Procedure*

12–101   This offence is triable either way and requires the consent of the Attorney-General before proceedings can be instituted: *POA* 1986, s.27(1).

(c) *Elements of the offence*

12–102   For the meaning of 'racial hatred' see s.18 of the 1986 Act, above. For the meaning of 'threatening, abusive or insulting, see *Brutus v Cozens*, above. 'Written material' means any sign or other visible representation: *POA* 1986, s.29.

(d) *Defence*

12–103   A person who is not shown to have intended to stir up racial hatred will have a defence if he can prove that he was not aware of the content of the written material or recording, and did not suspect and had no reason to suspect that it was threatening, abusive or insulting: *POA* 1986, s.23(3).

(e) *Sentence*

12–104   When tried summarily this offence carries a maximum penalty of six months imprisonment, a fine not exceeding the statutory maximum or both: *POA* 1986, s.27(3).

J. CONTAMINATION OF OR INTERFERENCE WITH GOODS

(a) *Definition*

Public Order Act 1986, s.38(1)–(3)

Contamination of or interference with goods with intention of causing public alarm or anxiety, etc.

12–105   **38.**—(1) It is an offence for a person, with the intention—

     (a) of causing public alarm or anxiety, or

     (b) of causing injury to members of the public consuming or using the goods, or

(c) of causing economic loss to any person by reason of the goods being shunned by members of the public, or

(d) of causing economic loss to any person by reason of steps taken to avoid any such alarm or anxiety, injury or loss,

to contaminate or interfere with goods, or make it appear that goods have been contaminated or interfered with, or to place goods which have been contaminated or interfered with, or which appear to have been contaminated or interfered with, in a place where goods of that description are consumed, used, sold or otherwise supplied.

(2) It is also an offence for a person, with any such intention as is mentioned in paragraph (a), (c) or (d) of subsection (1), to threaten that he or another will do, or to claim that he or another has done, any of the acts mentioned in that subsection.

(3) It is an offence for a person to be in possession of any of the following articles with a view to the commission of an offence under subsection (1)—

(a) materials to be used for contaminating or interfering with goods or making it appear that goods have been contaminated or interfered with, or

(b) goods which have been contaminated or interfered with, or which appear to have been contaminated or interfered with.

The prosecution must prove that: **12–106**

— the defendant had the intention of causing public alarm or anxiety OR causing injury to members of the public consuming or using the goods OR causing economic loss to any person by reason of the goods being shunned by members of the public OR causing economic loss to any person by reason of steps taken to avoid such anxiety and,

— he contaminated or interfered with goods OR made it appear that goods had been contaminated OR placed goods which had been or appeared to be contaminated or interfered with in a place where goods of that description are sold, used or otherwise supplied OR

— he threatened that he or another would do, or claimed that he or another had done, any of the acts mentioned above OR

— the defendant was in possession of materials to be used for the contamination of or interference with goods or materials used for making it appear that goods have been contaminated or interfered with or the defendant was in possession of goods which have been contaminated or interfered with, or which appear to have been contaminated or interfered with.

(b) *Procedure*

These offences are triable either way: *POA* **1986, s.38(4).**   **12–106**

(c) *Elements of the offence*

Public Order Act 1986, s.38(5), (6)

Contamination of or interference with goods with intention of causing public alarm or anxiety, etc.

38.—(5) In this section "goods" includes substances whether natural or manufactured and   **12–107**
whether or not incorporated in or mixed with other goods.

(6) The reference in subsection (2) to a person claiming that certain acts have been committed does not include a person who in good faith reports or warns that such acts have been, or appear to have been, committed.

(d) *Sentence*

When tried summarily, the maximum penalty is six months' imprisonment, a fine   **12–108**
not exceeding the statutory maximum or both.

III. OFFENCES IN CONNECTION WITH SPORTING ACTIVITY

A. Football Offences

(a) *Definition*

Football (Offences) Act 1991, ss.2–4

Throwing of missiles

12–109   **2.** It is an offence for a person at a designated football match to throw anything at or towards—

    (a) the playing area, or any area adjacent to the playing area to which spectators are not generally admitted, or

    (b) any area in which spectators or other persons are or may be present,

without lawful authority or lawful excuse (which shall be for him to prove).

Indecent or racialist chanting

    3.—(1) It is an offence to engage or take part in chanting of an indecent or racialist nature at a designated football match.

    (2) For this purpose—

    (a) "chanting" means the repeated uttering of any words or sounds (whether alone or in concert with one or more others); and

    (b) "of a racialist nature" means consisting of or including matter which is threatening, abusive or insulting to a person by reason of his colour, race, nationality (including citizenship) or ethnic or national origins.

Going onto the playing area

12–110   **4.** It is an offence for a person at a designated football match to go onto the playing area, or any area adjacent to the playing area to which spectators are not generally admitted, without lawful authority or lawful excuse (which shall be for him to prove).

12–111   To establish the offence of throwing of missiles, the prosecution must prove that:

    — the defendant was at a designated football match and,

    — he threw something at or towards the playing area, or any area adjacent to the playing area to which spectators are not normally admitted OR

    — he threw something at or towards any area in which spectators or other persons are or may be present without lawful authority or lawful excuse.

12–112   To establish the offence of indecent or racialist chanting, the prosecution must prove that:

    — the defendant was at a designated football match and,

    — he engaged in indecent or racialist chanting.

To establish the offence of going on to the playing area, the prosecution must prove that:

    — the defendant was at a designated football match and,

    — he went onto the playing area, or onto any area adjacent to the playing area to which spectators are not generally admitted, without lawful authority or lawful excuse.

(b) *Procedure*

12–113   These offences are all triable summarily: *Football (Offences) Act* 1991, s.5(2).

(c) *Elements of the offence*

Football (Offences) Act 1991, s.1

Designated football matches

12–114   **1.**—(1) In this Act a "designated football match" means an association football match designated, or of a description designated, for the purposes of this Act by order of the Secretary of State.

Any such order shall be made by statutory instrument which shall be subject to annulment in pursuance of a resolution of either House of Parliament.

(2) References in this Act to things done at a designated football match include anything done at the ground—

(a) within the period beginning two hours before the start of the match or (if earlier) two hours before the time at which it is advertised to start and ending one hour after the end of the match; or

(b) where the match is advertised to start at a particular time on a particular day but does not take place on that day, within the period beginning two hours before and ending one hour after the advertised starting time.

(d) *Sentence*

The maximum penalty for these offences is a fine not exceeding level three on the **12–115** standard scale: *Football (Offences) Act* 1991, s.5(2).

B. OFFENCES UNDER THE FOOTBALL SPECTATORS ACT 1989

(1) **Unauthorised Attendance**

(a) *Definition*

The Football Spectators Act 1989, s.2

Offences relating to unauthorised attendance at designated football matches

2.—(1) If a person who is not, in relation to the match, an authorised spectator enters or **12–116** remains on premises as a spectator during a period relevant to a designated football match that person commits an offence and so does a person who attempts to commit an offence under this subsection of entering premises.

(2) Where a person is charged under subsection(1) above with an offence of entering or remaining on premises, and was at the time of the alleged offence not disqualified from being a member of the national football membership scheme, it shall be a defence to prove that he was allowed to enter the premises as a spectator by a person reasonably appearing to him to have lawful authority to do so.

(3) A person guilty of an offence under subsection (1) above shall be liable on summary conviction to imprisonment for a term not exceeding one month or a fine not exceeding level 3 on the standard scale or to both.

(4) A constable who reasonably suspects that a person has committed an offence under subsection (1) above may arrest him without a warrant.

The prosecution must prove that: **12–117**
— the defendant was not an authorised spectator and
— he entered or remained on premises as a spectator during a designated football match OR
— he attempted to do so.

(b) *Procedure*

This offence is triable summarily.   **12–118**

(c) *Elements of the offence*

The *Football Spectators (Prescription) Order* 2000 (SI 2000/2126) designates **12–119** matches for the purposes of this Act.

(d) *Defence*

Where a person was not disqualified from being a member of the national football **12–120** membership scheme at the time of the alleged offence he shall have a defence if he can prove that he was allowed to enter the premises as a spectator by a person reasonably appearing to him to have lawful authority to do so: *Football Spectators Act* 1989, s.2(3).

(2) Admitting Spectators to Unlicensed Premises

(a) *Definition*

Football Spectators Act 1989, s.9

Offence of admitting spectators to unlicensed premises

12–121   **9.**—1) Subject to subsection (2) below, if persons are admitted as spectators to, or permitted to remain as spectators on, any premises during a period relevant to a designated football match without a licence to admit spectators being in force, any responsible person commits an offence.

(2) Where a person is charged with an offence under this section it shall be a defence to prove either that the spectators were admitted in an emergency or—

     (a) that the spectators were admitted without his consent; and

     (b) that he took all reasonable precautions and exercised all due diligence to avoid the commission of such an offence.

(3) A person guilty of an offence under this section shall be liable—

     (a) on summary conviction, to a fine not exceeding the statutory maximum; or

     (b) on conviction on indictment, to a fine or to imprisonment for a term not exceeding two years, or to both.

12–122   The prosecution has to prove that:

— persons were admitted as spectators, or allowed to remain as spectators to any premises during a period relevant to a designated football match and,

— there was no license to admit spectators in force and,

— the defendant was responsible.

(b) *Procedure*

12–123   This offence is triable summarily only.

(c) *Elements of the offence*

12–124   The *Football Spectators (Prescription) Order* 2000 (SI 2000/2126) designates matches for the purposes of this Act. The relevant licenses are issued by the Football Licensing Authority under the *Football Spectators (Seating) Order* 1994 (SI 1994/1666). Section 10(13) of the 1989 Act also creates a summary offence of failing to observe any term or condition of a licence granted to admit spectators to any premises for the purpose of watching any designated football match played there. A defendant accused of such an offence will have a defence if he can prove that the contravention took place without his consent and that he took all precautions and exercised due diligence to avoid the commission of such an offence.

(d) *Defences*

12–125   The defendant will have a defence if he can establish that he admitted the spectators in an emergency that he took all reasonable precautions and exercised all due diligence to avoid the commission of such an offence: *Football Spectators Act* 1989, s.9(2).

(e) *Sentence*

12–126   When tried summarily, the offence under s.9 carries a maximum penalty of a fine not exceeding the statutory maximum.

C. Breach of Banning Orders

(a) *Definition*

Football Spectators Act 1989, ss.14J, 19

Offences

14J.—(1) A person subject to a banning order who fails to comply with—   **12–127**
    (a) any requirement imposed by the order, or
    (b) any requirement imposed under section 19(2B) or (2C) below,
is guilty of an offence.

(2) A person guilty of an offence under this section is liable on summary conviction to imprisonment for a term not exceeding six months, or a fine not exceeding level 5 on the standard scale, or both.

Functions of enforcing authority and local police

19.—(1) The enforcing authority and the officer responsible for the police station at which he   **12–128** reports initially shall have the following functions as respects any person subject to a banning order.

(2) On a person reporting initially at the police station, the officer responsible for the station may make such requirements of that person as are determined by the enforcing authority to be necessary or expedient for giving effect to the banning order, so far as relating to regulated football matches outside England and Wales.

(2A) If, in connection with any regulated football match outside England and Wales, the enforcing authority is of the opinion that requiring any person subject to a banning order to report is necessary or expedient in order to reduce the likelihood of violence or disorder at or in connection with the match, the authority must give him a notice in writing under subsection (2B) below.

(2B) The notice must require that person—
    (a) to report at a police station specified in the notice at the time, or between the times, specified in the notice,
    (b) if the match is outside the United Kingdom and the order imposes a requirement as to the surrender by him of his passport, to surrender his passport at a police station specified in the notice at the time, or between the times, specified in the notice,
and may require him to comply with any additional requirements of the order in the manner specified in the notice.

(2C) In the case of any regulated football match, the enforcing authority may by notice in writing require any person subject to a banning order to comply with any additional requirements of the order in the manner specified in the notice.

(2D) The enforcing authority may establish criteria for determining whether any requirement under subsection (2B) or (2C) above ought to be imposed on any person or any class of person.

(2E) A notice under this section—
    (a) may not require the person subject to the order to report except in the control period in relation to a regulated football match outside England and Wales or an external tournament,
    (b) may not require him to surrender his passport except in the control period in relation to a regulated football match outside the United Kingdom or an external tournament which includes such matches.

(2F) Where a notice under this section requires the person subject to the order to surrender his passport, the passport must be returned to him as soon as reasonably practicable after the end of the control period in question.

(5) The enforcing authority, in exercising their functions under this section, shall have   **12–129** regard to any guidance issued by the Secretary of State under section 21 below.

(6) A person who, without reasonable excuse, fails to comply with any requirement imposed on him under subsection (2) above shall be guilty of an offence.

(7) A person guilty of an offence under subsection (6) above shall be liable on summary conviction to a fine not exceeding level 2 on the standard scale.

(b) *Procedure*

12–130 Breach of any requirement of a Banning Order imposed under s.19(2B) or (2C) is a summary offence: s.14J.

Breach of any requirement of a Banning Order imposed under s.19(2) is a summary offence: s.19(6).

(c) *Elements of the offence*

Football Spectators Act 1989, s.14

Main definitions

12–131 **14.**—(1) This section applies for the purposes of this Part.

(2) "Regulated football match" means an association football match (whether in England and Wales or elsewhere) which is a prescribed match or a match of a prescribed description.

(3) "External tournament" means a football competition which includes regulated football matches outside England and Wales.

(4) "Banning order" means an order made by the court under this Part which—

    (a) in relation to regulated football matches in England and Wales, prohibits the person who is subject to the order from entering any premises for the purpose of attending such matches, and

    (b) in relation to regulated football matches outside England and Wales, requires that person to report at a police station in accordance with this Part.

(5) "Control period", in relation to a regulated football match outside England and Wales, means the period—

    (a) beginning five days before the day of the match, and

    (b) ending when the match is finished or cancelled.

(6) "Control period", in relation to an external tournament, means any period described in an order made by the Secretary of State—

    (a) beginning five days before the day of the first football match outside England and Wales which is included in the tournament, and

    (b) ending when the last football match outside England and Wales which is included in the tournament is finished or cancelled, but, for the purposes of paragraph (a), any football match included in the qualifying or pre-qualifying stages of the tournament is to be left out of account.

(7) References to football matches are to football matches played or intended to be played.

(8) "Relevant offence" means an offence to which Schedule 1 to this Act applies.

(d) *Sentence*

12–132 The offence under s.14J carries a maximum penalty of imprisonment for a term not exceeding six months, or a fine not exceeding level 5 on the standard scale, or both.

The offence under s.19(6) carries a maximum penalty of a fine not exceeding level two on the standard scale.

D. Ticket Touts

(a) *Definition*

Criminal Justice and Public Order Act 1994, s.166(1)

Sale of tickets by unauthorised persons

12–133 **166.**—(1) It is an offence for an unauthorised person to sell, or offer or expose for sale, a ticket for a designated football match in any public place or place to which the public has access or, in the course of a trade or business, in any other place.

12–134 The prosecution must prove that:

    — the defendant sold, or offered, or exposed for sale,

— a ticket for a designated football match,
— in any public place or place to which the public have access, or any other place in the course of trade or business.

(b) *Procedure*

This offence is triable summarily: *CJPO 1998*, s.166(3). **12–135**

(c) *Elements of the offence*

Criminal Justice and Public Order Act 1994, s.166(2)

Sale of tickets by unauthorised persons
166.—(2) For this purpose— **12–136**
    (a) a person is "unauthorised" unless he is authorised in writing to sell tickets for the match by the home club or by the organisers of the match;
    (b) a "ticket" means anything which purports to be a ticket; and
    (c) a "designated football match" means a football match of a description, or a particular football match, for the time being designated for the purposes of Part I of the *Football Spectators Act* 1989 or which is a regulated football match for the purposes of Part II of that Act.

(d) *Sentence*

The maximum penalty is a fine not exceeding level five on the standard scale: *CJPO* **12–136.1**
1998, s.166(5).

E. Offences in connection with Alcohol on Coaches and Trains

(a) *Definition*

Sporting Events (Control of Alcohol etc.) Act 1985, s.1(1)–(4)

Offences in connection with alcohol on coaches and trains
1.—(1) This section applies to a vehicle which— **12–137**
    (a) is a public service vehicle or railway passenger vehicle, and
    (b) is being used for the principal purpose of carrying passengers for the whole or part of a journey to or from a designated sporting event.
(2) A person who knowingly causes or permits intoxicating liquor to be carried on a vehicle to which this section applies is guilty of an offence—
    (a) if the vehicle is a public service vehicle and he is the operator of the vehicle or the servant or agent of the operator, or
    (b) if the vehicle is a hired vehicle and he is the person to whom it is hired or the servant or agent of that person.
(3) A person who has intoxicating liquor in his possession while on a vehicle to which this section applies is guilty of an offence.
(4) A person who is drunk on a vehicle to which this section applies is guilty of an offence.

The prosecution must prove that: **12–138**
— the defendant was the operator, or servant or agent of the operator of a public service vehicle or the defendant was the person to whom, or a servant or agent of the person to whom a hired vehicle was hired and,
— the vehicle was being used to carry passengers to of from a designated sporting event and
— the defendant knowingly caused or permitted intoxicating liquor to be carried on to the vehicle OR
— the defendant was a passenger on such a vehicle and he had intoxicating liquor in his possession during a journey to or from a designated sporting event OR

— the defendant was a passenger on such a vehicle and he was drunk during a journey to or from a designated sporting event.

(b) Procedure

12–138.1   These offences are triable summarily only: *Sporting Events (Control of Alcohol etc.) Act* 1985, s.8.

(c) Elements of the offence

Sporting Events (Control of Alcohol etc.) Act 1985, s.9(3)

Interpretation

12–139   **9.**—(3) "Designated sporting event"—

(a) means a sporting event or proposed sporting event for the time being designated, or of a class designated, by order made by the Secretary of State, and

(b) includes a designated sporting event within the meaning of Part V of the *Criminal Justice (Scotland) Act* 1980;

and an order under this subsection may apply to events or proposed events outside Great Britain as well as those in England and Wales.

(d) Sentence

Sporting Events (Control of Alcohol etc.)Act 1985, s.8(a)–(c)

Penalties for offences

12–140   **8.** A person guilty of an offence under this Act shall be liable on summary conviction—

(a) in the case of an offence under section 1(2) to a fine not exceeding level 4 on the standard scale,

(b) in the case of an offence under section 1(3)...to a fine not exceeding level 3 on the standard scale or to imprisonment for a term not exceeding three months or both,

(c) in the case of an offence under section 1(4)...to a fine not exceeding level 2 on the standard scale.

F. Offences connected with Alcohol, Containers etc. at Sports Grounds

(a) Definition

Sporting Events (Control of Alcohol etc.) Act 1985, s.2(1)

Offences in connection with alcohol, containers etc. at sports grounds

12–141   **2.**—(1) A person who has intoxicating liquor or an article to which this section applies in his possession—

(a) at any time during the period of a designated sporting event when he is in any area of a designated sports ground from which the event may be directly viewed, or

(b) while entering or trying to enter a designated sports ground at any time during the period of a designated sporting event at that ground,

is guilty of an offence.

12–142   The prosecution must prove that:

— the defendant was, during the period of a designated sporting event, in any area of a designated sports ground from which this event could be viewed, OR

— the defendant was entering or trying to enter a designated sports ground at any time during the period of a designated sporting event at the ground AND

— he had in his possession intoxicating liquor OR

— he had in his possession a bottle, can or other portable container (including such an article when crushed or broken) which is for holding any drink, and is of a kind which, when empty, is normally discarded or returned to, or left to be recovered by, the supplier, or forms part of such an article. (n.b. Bottles/articles used for holding any medicinal product do not fall under this section.)

(b) *Procedure*

This offence is triable summarily: *Sporting Events (Control of Alcohol etc.) Act* **12–143** 1985, s.8.

(c) *Elements of the offence*

Sporting Events (Control of Alcohol etc.) Act 1985, s.2(3), 9(1)–(4)

2.—(3) This section applies to any article capable of causing injury to a person struck by it, **12–144** being—

    (a) a bottle, can or other portable container (including such an article when crushed or broken) which—

        (i) is for holding any drink, and

        (ii) is of a kind which, when empty, is normally discarded or returned to, or left to be recovered by, the supplier, or

    (b) part of an article falling within paragraph (a) above;

but does not apply to anything that is for holding any medicinal product (within the meaning of the *Medicines Act* 1968).

Interpretation

9.—(1) The following provisions shall have effect for the interpretation of this Act.   **12–145**

(2) "Designated sports ground" means any place—

    (a) used (wholly or partly) for sporting events where accommodation is provided for spectators, and

    (b) for the time being designated, or of a class designated, by order made by the Secretary of State; and an order under this subsection may include provision for determining for the purposes of this Act the outer limit of any designated sports ground.

(3) "Designated sporting event" —

    (a) means a sporting event or proposed sporting event for the time being designated, or of a class designated, by order made by the Secretary of State, and

    (b) includes a designated sporting event within the meaning of Part V of the *Criminal Justice (Scotland) Act* 1980;

    and an order under this subsection may apply to events or proposed events outside Great Britain as well as those in England and Wales.

(4) The period of a designated sporting event is the period beginning two hours before **12–146** the start of the event or (if earlier) two hours before the time at which it is advertised to start and ending one hour after the end of the event, but—

    (a) where an event advertised to start at a particular time on a particular day is postponed to a later day, the period includes the period in the day on which it is advertised to take place beginning two hours before and ending one hour after that time, and

    (b) where an event advertised to start at a particular time on a particular day does not take place, the period is the period referred to in paragraph (a) above.

(d) *Sentence*

In the case of an offence under s.2(1) the maximum penalty is a fine not exceeding **12–147** level three on the standard scale or to imprisonment for a term not exceeding three months or both: *Sporting Events (Control of Alcohol etc.) Act* 1985, s.8(b).

In the case of an offence under s.2(2) the maximum penalty is a fine not exceeding level two on the standard scale: *Sporting Events (Control of Alcohol etc.) Act* 1985, s.8(c).

IV. OFFENCES CONNECTED WITH OFFENSIVE WEAPONS

A. Offences relating to Firearms Certificates

12–148   For offences under the *Firearms Act* 1968, see *Archbold Crown*, §§ 24–1—24–90.

B. Offences connected with Possession of Offensive Weapons

(a) *Definition*

Prevention of Crime Act 1953, s.1

Prohibition of the carrying of offensive weapons without lawful authority or reasonable excuse

12–149   **1.**—(1) Any person who without lawful authority or reasonable excuse, the proof whereof shall lie on him, has with him in any public place any offensive weapon shall be guilty of an offence, and shall be liable—

     (a) on summary conviction, to imprisonment for a term not exceeding six months or a fine not exceeding the prescribed sum or both;

     (b) on conviction on indictment, to imprisonment for a term not exceeding two years or a fine, or both.

(2) Where any person is convicted of an offence under subsection (1) of this section the court may make an order for the forfeiture or disposal of any weapon in respect of which the offence was committed.

(3) [...]

(4) In this section "public place" includes any highway and any other premises or place to which at the material time the public have or are permitted to have access, whether on payment or otherwise; and "offensive weapon" means any article made or adapted for use for causing injury to the person, or intended by the person having it with him for such use by him.

[This section is printed as amended by the *Public Order Act* 1986, s.40(2) and Sch.2, the *CJA* 1988, s.46(1); the *Offensive Weapons Act* 1996, s.2(1); and as repealed in part by the *CLA* 1977, s.32(1), and the *PACE Act* 1984, ss.26(1), 119(2) and Sch.7. The reference to 'the prescribed sum' is substituted by virtue of the *MCA* 1980, s.32(2).]

12–150   The prosecution must prove that:

— the defendant had an offensive weapon,

— in his possession,

— in a public place,

— without lawful authority or reasonable excuse.

(b) *Procedure*

12–151   This offence is triable either way.

(c) *Elements of the offence*

'Has with him'

12–152   The words 'has with him in a public place' mean 'knowingly has with him in any public place' it being for the prosecution to prove knowledge: *R. v Cugullere*, 45 Cr.App.R. 108, CCA. Once a person has something knowingly, he continues to have it until he does something to rid himself of it: *R. v McCalla*, 87 Cr.App.R. 372, CA. In *R. v Glidewell*, 163 J.P. 557, CA, it was held that forgetfulness could be a reasonable excuse; the defendant being a taxi driver who had not placed the relevant items in his car and who had intended to clear them out. The words 'has with him' also denote something more than mere possession of the article: *McCalla* (above) and *R. v Daubney*, (2000) 164 J.P. 519, CA.

Where a person uses an article offensively in a public place, the offensive use of the article is not conclusive of the question whether he had it with him as an offensive weapon within s.1(1): *R. v Jura* [1954] 1 Q.B. 503, CA; *R. v Veasley* [1999] Crim.L.R. 158, CA, (motorist assaulting horsewoman with Krooklock not necessarily guilty under s.1(1)); *C v DPP* [2002] Crim.L.R. 322, QBD (dog lead not an offensive weapon where its use on police officers was immediately preceded by detaching the lead from the dog.) See further *Archbold Crown*, §§ 24–110—24–113.

'Public place'

The definition in s.1(4) is the same as that in the *Firearms Act* 1968, the *Public Order Act* 1936 and the *Criminal Law Act* 1967. In *Knox v Anderton* (1983) 76 Cr.App.R. 156, QBD the Divisional Court held that the justices were entitled to find that premises where there are no barriers or notices restricting access, such as the upper landing of a block of flats which could be entered by members of the public without hindrance, were a public place. Where access to the landing of a block of flats is restricted and can only be gained through the use of a key, security code, tenants intercom or caretaker, the landing will not be classified as a public place, access being dependant on the consent of the occupiers of the flats: *Williams v DPP* (1992) 95 Cr.App.R. 415. See further *Archbold Crown*, §§ 24–113—24–114. **12–153**

'Offensive weapon'

In *R. v Simpson (C)*, 78 Cr.App.R. 115, CA, the Court identified three categories of offensive weapon: **12–154**
   a) those made for use for causing injury to the person, *i.e.* offensive *per se* those adapted for such a purpose
   b) those not so made or adapted, but carried with the intention of causing injury to the person.

In the first two categories, the prosecution do not have to establish that the defendant had the weapon with him for the purpose of inflicting injury.

Offensive per se

In *R. v Simpson* (above) Lord Lane C.J. gave as instances of weapons offensive *per se* a bayonet, a stiletto or a handgun. Weapons which are manufactured for an innocent purpose are not offensive *per se*: *R. v Petrie* (1961) 45 Cr.App.R. 72, CA (razor). Where there is doubt as to whether a weapon is an offensive weapon *per se*, the deciders of fact must have their attention drawn to the statutory definition, but determining whether any weapon is an offensive weapon is a matter of fact: *R. v Williamson* (1978) 67 Cr.App.R. 35, CA. **12–155**

'adapted for use'

Whether an article falls into this category is a question of fact for the justices. Examples of weapons adapted for use include a bottle deliberately broken to attack the victim: *Simpson* (above) and a potato with a razor blade inserted into it: *Williamson* (above). **12–155.1**

'intended for use for causing injury'

Intention to use the weapon to cause injury must be proved for such an article to be categorised as an offensive weapon. It is for the prosecution to prove the element of **12–156** intention: *R. v Petrie* (1961) 1 W.L.R. 358. In *Patterson v Block* (1984) 81 L.S.Gaz 2458, DC, the Court held that justices were entitled to find the requisite intention where the defendant had with him a lock knife for the purposes of self defence. See further *Archbold Crown*, §§ 24–119—24–121.

'without lawful authority or reasonable excuse'

12–157   The burden of establishing lawful authority or reasonable excuse rests on the defendant. In *Bryan v Mott* (1975) 62 Cr.App.R. 71, the Divisional Court held that the reference to lawful authority applies to those people from time to time carry an offensive weapon as a matter of duty, for example a soldier with his rifle and a police officer with his truncheon.

The application of the excuse of self defence was explained by Lord Widgery C.J. in *Evans v Hughes*, 56 Cr.App.R. 813, DC where he said:

> 'It may be a reasonable excuse for the carrying of an offensive weapon that the carrier is in anticipation of imminent attack and is carrying it for his own personal defence, but what is abundantly clear to my mind is that this Act never intended to sanction the permanent or constant carriage of an offensive weapon merely because of some constant or enduring supposed or actual threat or danger to the carrier'

For further examples of reasonable excuse see *Archbold Crown*, §§ 24–122—24–124.

(d) *Sentence*

12–158   When tried summarily, the maximum penalty for this offence is a term of imprisonment not exceeding six months, a fine not exceeding the prescribed sum or both.

The *Magistrates' Court Sentencing Guidelines* (2003) state:

> Aggravating factors include location of offence, group action or joint possession, racial aggravation, people put in fear/weapon brandished, planned use, very dangerous weapon, offence committed on bail, relevant previous convictions and any failure to respond to previous sentences.
>
> Mitigating factors include acting out of genuine fear, no attempt to use, not premeditated.
>
> **Guideline**: Is it so serious that only custody is appropriate?

12–159   A sentence of six months' imprisonment was held appropriate where the offender was convicted of possessing an offensive weapon (vegetable knife) and held two previous convictions for the same offence: *R. v Shorter* (1988) 10 Cr.App.R.(S.) 4. In *R. v Simpson* (1992) 13 Cr.App.R.(S.) 665, the offender was found in possession of an unopened flick knife with a three inch blade. He was sentenced to nine months' imprisonment.

C. Having a Bladed Article in a Public Place

(a) *Definition*

Criminal Justice Act 1988, s.139

Offence of having article with blade or point in public place

12–160   **139.**—(1) Subject to subsections (4) and (5) below, any person who has an article to which this section applies with him in a public place shall be guilty of an offence.

(2) Subject to subsection (3) below, this section applies to any article which has a blade or is sharply pointed except a folding pocketknife.

(3) This section applies to a folding pocketknife if the cutting edge of its blade exceeds 3 inches.

(4) It shall be a defence for a person charged with an offence under this section to prove that he had good reason or lawful authority for having the article with him in a public place.

(5) Without prejudice to the generality of subsection (4) above, it shall be a defence for a person charged with an offence under this section to prove that he had the article with him—

(a) for use at work;

(b) for religious reasons; or

(c) as part of any national costume.

(6) A person guilty of an offence under subsection (1) above shall be liable

(a) on summary conviction, to imprisonment for a term not exceeding six months, or a fine not exceeding the statutory maximum, or both;

(b) on conviction on indictment, to imprisonment for a term not exceeding two years, or a fine, or both.

(7) In this section "public place" includes any place to which at the material time the public have or are permitted access, whether on payment or otherwise.

(8) This section shall not have effect in relation to anything done before it comes into force.

The prosecution must prove that: **12–161**

— the defendant had in his possession, in a public place,

— a bladed article, or article that was sharply pointed (folding pocketknifes being an exception under this section).

(b) *Procedure*

This offence is triable either way.   **12–162**

(c) *Elements of the offence*

For the meaning of 'has with him' see § 12–152, above.   **12–163**

A lock-knife will not be classified a as folding pocketknife because it is not immediately foldable at all times: *R. v Deegan* [1998] 2 Cr.App.R. 121, CA.

The meaning of the phrases 'good reason' and 'for use are work' is to be determined by the jury, or justices when the offence is tried summarily: *R. v Manning* [1998] Crim.L.R. 198. See further *Archbold Crown*, § 24–128.

(d) *Defence*

It shall be a defence for the accused to prove that he had the article with him for use   **12–164** at work, for religious reasons or as part of any national costume: *Criminal Justice Act* 1988, s.139(4) and (5).

(e) *Sentence*

When tried summarily, the maximum penalty for this offence is imprisonment for a   **12–165** term not exceeding six months, a fine of the prescribed sum or both: s.139(6)(a).

D. HAVING AN ARTICLE WITH A BLADE OR POINT (OR OFFENSIVE WEAPON) ON SCHOOL PREMISES

(a) *Definition*

Criminal Justice Act 1988, s.139A

Offence of having article with blade or point (or offensive weapon) on school premises

139A.—(1) Any person who has an article to which section 139 of this Act applies with him   **12–166** on school premises shall be guilty of an offence.

(2) Any person who has an offensive weapon within the meaning of section 1 of the *Prevention of Crime Act* 1953 with him on school premises shall be guilty of an offence.

(3) It shall be a defence for a person charged with an offence under subsection (1) or (2) above to prove that he had good reason or lawful authority for having the article or weapon with him on the premises in question.

(4) Without prejudice to the generality of subsection (3) above, it shall be a defence for a person charged with an offence under subsection (1) or (2) above to prove that he had the article or weapon in question with him—

    (a) for use at work,
    (b) for educational purposes,
    (c) for religious reasons, or
    (d) as part of any national costume.

12–167   (5) A person guilty of an offence—
    (a) under subsection (1) above shall be liable—
      (i) on summary conviction to imprisonment for a term not exceeding six months, or a fine not exceeding the statutory maximum, or both;
      (ii) on conviction on indictment, to imprisonment for a term not exceeding two years, or a fine, or both;
    (b) under subsection (2) above shall be liable—
      (i) on summary conviction, to imprisonment for a term not exceeding six months, or a fine not exceeding the statutory maximum, or both;
      (ii) on conviction on indictment, to imprisonment for a term not exceeding four years, or a fine, or both.

(6) In this section and section 139B, "school premises" means land used for the purposes of a school excluding any land occupied solely as a dwelling by a person employed at the school; and "school" has the meaning given by section 4 of the *Education Act* 1996

(7) [*Northern Ireland*]

[This section was inserted by the *Offensive Weapons Act* 1996, s.4(4). It is printed as amended by the *Education Act* 1996, s.582(1) and Sch.37, para.69.]

12–168   The prosecution must prove:
— the defendant had an article to which s.139 of the *CJA* 1988 applies with him on school premises OR
— the defendant had an offensive weapon within the meaning of s.1 of the *Prevention of Crime Act 1953* with him on school premises.

(b) *Procedure*

12–169   This offence is triable either way.

(c) *Elements of the offence*

12–170   For the meaning of 'has with him' see § 12–152, above. For the meaning of 'for good reason' and 'for use at work', see § 12–163, above.

(d) *Defence*

12–171   The defendant will have a defence if he can prove that he was carrying the article in question on the relevant premises for use at work, for educational purposes, for religious reasons or as part of any national costume: *CJA* 1988, s.139A(4).

(e) *Sentence*

12–172   When tried summarily, the offences carry a maximum punishment of six months imprisonment, a fine not exceeding the statutory maximum or both: *CJA* 1988, s.139A(5).

V. OFFENCES UNDER THE KNIVES ACT 1997

A. UNLAWFUL MARKETING OF KNIVES

(a) *Definition*

Knives Act 1997, ss.1, 2

Unlawful marketing of knives

12–173   **1.**—(1) A person is guilty of an offence if he markets a knife in a way which—

(a) indicates, or suggests, that it is suitable for combat; or
(b) is otherwise likely to stimulate or encourage violent behaviour involving the use of the knife as a weapon.

(2) "Suitable for combat" and "violent behaviour" are defined in section 10.

(3) For the purposes of this Act, an indication or suggestion that a knife is suitable for combat may, in particular, be given or made by a name or description—
(a) applied to the knife;
(b) on the knife or on any packaging in which it is contained; or
(c) included in any advertisement which, expressly or by implication, relates to the knife.

(4) For the purposes of this Act, a person markets a knife if—
(a) he sells or hires it;
(b) he offers, or exposes, it for sale or hire; or
(c) he has it in his possession for the purpose of sale or hire.

(5) A person who is guilty of an offence under this section is liable—
(a) on summary conviction to imprisonment for a term not exceeding six months or to a fine not exceeding the statutory maximum, or to both;
(b) on conviction on indictment to imprisonment for a term not exceeding two years or to a fine, or to both.

Publications

2.—(1) A person is guilty of an offence if he publishes any written, pictorial or other material **12–174** in connection with the marketing of any knife and that material—
(a) indicates, or suggests, that the knife is suitable for combat; or
(b) is otherwise likely to stimulate or encourage violent behaviour involving the use of the knife as a weapon.

(2) A person who is guilty of an offence under this section is liable—
(a) on summary conviction to imprisonment for a term not exceeding six months or to a fine not exceeding the statutory maximum, or to both;
(b) on conviction on indictment to imprisonment for a term not exceeding two years or to a fine, or to both.

Regarding the offence of unlawful marketing of knives, the prosecution must estab- **12–175** lish that:
— the defendant sold or hired, offered or exposed for sale or hire or had in his possession for the purpose of sale or hire a knife and,
— the manner in which he so marketed the knife indicates, or suggests that it is suitable for combat OR,
— is otherwise likely to stimulate or encourage violent behaviour involving the use of the knife as a weapon.

Regarding the offence of unlawful publication of materials in connection with the **12–176** marketing of knives, the prosecution must prove that:
— the defendant published any written, pictorial or other material in connection with the marketing of any knife and
— that material suggests that the knife is suitable for combat OR
— is likely to stimulate or encourage violent behaviour involving the use of the knife as a weapon.

(b) *Procedure*

These offences are triable either way.   **12–177**

(c) *Elements of the offence*

Knives Act 1997, s.10

Interpretation
10. In this Act—   **12–178**

"the court" means—
- (a) in relation to England and Wales or Northern Ireland, the Crown Court or a magistrate's court;
- (b) in relation to Scotland, the sheriff;

"knife" means an instrument which has a blade or is sharply pointed;

"marketing" and related expressions are to be read with section 1(4);

"publication" includes a publication in electronic form and, in the case of a publication which is, or may be, produced from electronic data, any medium on which the data are stored;

"suitable for combat" means suitable for use as a weapon for inflicting injury on a person or causing a person to fear injury;

"violent behaviour" means an unlawful act inflicting injury on a person or causing a person to fear injury.

(d) Defences

Knives Act 1997, ss.3, 4

Exempt trades

12–179   **3.**—(1) It is a defence for a person charged with an offence under section 1 to prove that—
- (a) the knife was marketed—
    - (i) for use by the armed forces of any country;
    - (ii) as an antique or curio; or
    - (iii) as falling within such other category (if any) as may be prescribed;
- (b) it was reasonable for the knife to be marketed in that way; and
- (c) there were no reasonable grounds for suspecting that a person into whose possession the knife might come in consequence of the way in which it was marketed would use it for an unlawful purpose.

(2) It is a defence for a person charged with an offence under section 2 to prove that
- (a) the material was published in connection with marketing a knife—
    - (i) for use by the armed forces of any country;
    - (ii) as an antique or curio; or
    - (iii) as falling within such other category (if any) as may be prescribed;
- (b) it was reasonable for the knife to be marketed in that way; and
- (c) there were no reasonable grounds for suspecting that a person into whose possession the knife might come in consequence of the publishing of the material would use it for an unlawful purpose.

(3) In this section "prescribed" means prescribed by regulations made by the Secretary of State.

Other defences

12–180   **4.**—(1) It is a defence for a person charged with an offence under section 1 to prove that he did not know or suspect, and had no reasonable grounds for suspecting, that the way in which the knife was marketed—
- (a) amounted to an indication or suggestion that the knife was suitable for combat; or
- (b) was likely to stimulate or encourage violent behaviour involving the use of the knife as a weapon.

(2) It is a defence for a person charged with an offence under section 2 to prove that he did not know or suspect, and had no reasonable grounds for suspecting, that the material—
- (a) amounted to an indication or suggestion that the knife was suitable for combat; or
- (b) was likely to stimulate or encourage violent behaviour involving the use of the knife as a weapon.

(3) It is a defence for a person charged with an offence under section 1 or 2 to prove that he took all reasonable precautions and exercised all due diligence to avoid committing the offence

(e) Sentence

When tried summarily, the maximum penalty is six months' imprisonment, a fine **12–181**
not exceeding the prescribed sum, or both: s.1(5)(a) and s.2(2)(a).

B. Sale of Knives to persons under 16

(a) Definition

Criminal Justice Act 1988, s.141A

Sale of knives and certain articles with blade or point to persons under sixteen
  141A.—(1) Any person who sells to a person under the age of sixteen years an article to **12–182**
which this section applies shall be guilty of an offence and liable on summary conviction to
imprisonment for a term not exceeding six months, or a fine not exceeding level 5 on the standard scale, or both.
  (2) Subject to subsection (3) below, this section applies to—
    (a) any knife, knife blade or razor blade,
    (b) any axe, and
    (c) any other article which has a blade or which is sharply pointed and which is
        made or adapted for use for causing injury to the person.
  (3) This section does not apply to any article described in—
    (a) section 1 of the *Restriction of Offensive Weapons Act* 1959.
    (b) an order made under section 141(2) of this Act, or
    (c) an order made by the Secretary of State under this section.
  (4) It shall be a defence for a person charged with an offence under subsection (1)
above to prove that he took all reasonable precautions and exercised all due diligence to
avoid the commission of the offence.
  (5) The power to make an order under this section shall be exercisable by statutory
instrument which shall be subject to annulment in pursuance of a resolution of either
House of Parliament.

The prosecution must prove that: **12–183**
— the defendant sold a person under the age of 16,
— any knife, knife blade or razor blade, any axe or any other article which has a
  blade or which is sharply pointed and which is made or adapted for use for
  causing injury to the person.

(b) Procedure

This offence is triable summarily.   **12–184**

(c) Elements of the offence

Regarding what constitutes an article made or adapted to cause injury, see section **12–185**
above.

(d) Defence

It will be a defence for the accused to establish that he took all reasonable precautions **12–186**
and exercised all due diligence to avoid the commission of the offence.

(e) Sentence

The maximum penalty for this offence is imprisonment for a term not exceeding six **12–187**
months, a fine not exceeding the level five on the standard scale or both.

C. Offences Relating to the Manufacture of Offensive Weapons

The following four offences are all triable summarily only. They concern the **12–188** manufacture, sale or hire of dangerous weapons, the manufacture, sale and hire of offensive weapons, the sale and letting of a crossbow to a person under 17, and the purchase and hiring of a crossbow by a person under 17.

(a) *Legislation*

Restriction of Offensive Weapons Act 1959, s.1

Penalties for offences in connection with dangerous weapons

12–189   **1.**—(1) Any person who manufactures, sells or hires or offers for sale or hire, or exposes or has in his possession for the purpose of sale or hire or lends to gives to any other person—

(a) any knife which has a blade which opens automatically by hand pressure applied to a button, spring or other device in or attached to the handle of the knife, sometimes known as a "flick knife" or "flick gun"; or

(b) any knife which has a blade which is released from the handle or sheath thereof by the force of gravity or the application of centrifugal force and which, when released, is locked in place by means of a button, spring, lever, or other device, sometimes known as a "gravity knife",

shall be guilty of an offence and shall be liable on summary conviction in the case of a first offence to imprisonment for a term not exceeding three months or to a fine not exceeding fifty pounds or to both such imprisonment and fine, and in the case of a second or subsequent offence to imprisonment for a term not exceeding six months or to a fine not exceeding two hundred pounds or to both such imprisonment and fine.

(2) The importation of any such knife as is described in the foregoing subsection is hereby prohibited.

Criminal Justice Act 1988, s.141(1)

Offensive weapons

12–190   **141.**—(1) Any person who manufactures, sells or hires or offers for sale or hire, exposes or has in his possession for the purpose of sale or hire, or lends or gives to any other person, a weapon to which this section applies shall be guilty of an offence and liable on summary conviction to imprisonment for a term not exceeding six months or to a fine not exceeding level 5 on the standard scale or both.

This section applies to weapons listed by the Secretary of State in an order, and must not include any weapon subject to the *Firearms Act* 1968, or crossbows. The order currently in force is the *Criminal Justice Act 1998 (Offensive Weapons) Order 198* (SI 1988/2019).

Crossbows Act 1987, ss.1, 2

Sale and letting on hire

12–191   **1.** A person who sells or lets on hire a crossbow or a part of a crossbow to a person under the age of seventeen is guilty of an offence, unless he believes him to be seventeen years of age or older and has reasonable ground for the belief.

Purchase and hiring

12–192   **2.** A person under the age of seventeen who buys or hires a crossbow or a part of a crossbow is guilty of an offence.

(b) *Sentence*

12–192.1   A person guilty of an offence under s.1 of the *Crossbows Act* 1987 is liable to imprisonment for a term not exceeding six months, to a fine not exceeding level five on the standard scale, or to both. The court may also make a forfeiture order regarding any crossbow or part of a crossbow in respect of which the offence was committed: s.6(1) and (3). A person guilty of an offence under s.2 is liable to a fine not exceeding level three on the standard scale. The court may also make a forfeiture order regarding any crossbow or part of a crossbow in respect of which the offence was committed: s.6(2) and (3).

VI. OFFENCES AFFECTING THE ENJOYMENT OF PROPERTY

A. Unlawful Eviction and Harassment of Occupier

(a) *Definition*

Protection from Eviction Act 1977, s.1

Unlawful eviction and harassment of occupier

1.—(1) In this section "residential occupier", in relation to any premises, means a person oc- **12–193**
cupying the premises as a residence, whether under a contract or by virtue of any enactment or
rule of law giving him the right to remain in occupation or restricting the right of any other
person to recover possession of the premises.

(2) If any person unlawfully deprives the residential occupier of any premises of his occupation of the premises or any part thereof, or attempts to do so, he shall be guilty of an
offence unless he proves that he believed, and had reasonable cause to believe, that the residential occupier had ceased to reside in the premises.

(3) If any person with intent to cause the residential occupier of any premises—
  (a) to give up the occupation of the premises or any part thereof; or
  (b) to refrain from exercising any right or pursuing any remedy in respect of the
      premises or part thereof;
does acts likely to interfere with the peace or comfort of the residential occupier or members of
his household, or persistently withdraws or withholds services reasonably required for the occupation of the premises as a residence, he shall be guilty of an offence.

(3A) Subject to subsection (3B) below, the landlord of a residential occupier or an agent
of the landlord shall be guilty of an offence if—
  (a) he does acts likely to interfere with the peace or comfort of the residential oc-
      cupier or members of his household, or
  (b) he persistently withdraws or withholds services reasonably required for the oc-
      cupation of the premises in question as a residence,
and (in either case) he knows, or has reasonable cause to believe, that that conduct is likely to
cause the residential occupier to give up the occupation of the whole or part of the premises or
to refrain from exercising any right or pursuing any remedy in respect of the whole or part of
the premises.

(3B) A person shall not be guilty of an offence under subsection (3A) above if he proves
that he had reasonable grounds for doing the acts or withdrawing or withholding the services in question.

(3C) In subsection (3A) above "landlord", in relation to a residential occupier of any
premises, means the person who, but for—
  (a) the residential occupier's right to remain in occupation of the premises, or
  (b) a restriction on the person's right to recover possession of the premises,
      would be entitled to occupation of the premises and any superior landlord under
      whom that person derives title.

(4) A person guilty of an offence under this section shall be liable—
  (a) on summary conviction, to a fine not exceeding £400 or to imprisonment for a
      term not exceeding 6 months or to both;
  (b) on conviction on indictment, to a fine or to imprisonment for a term not exceed-
      ing 2 years or to both.

(5) Nothing in this section shall be taken to prejudice any liability or remedy to which a **12–194**
person guilty of an offence thereunder may be subject in civil proceedings.

(6) Where an offence under this section committed by a body corporate is proved to
have been committed with the consent or connivance of, or to be attributable to any neglect on the part of, any director, manager or secretary or other similar officer of the body
corporate or any person who was purporting to act in any such capacity, he as well as the
body corporate shall be guilty of that offence and shall be liable to be proceeded against
and punished accordingly.

[This section is printed as amended by the *Housing Act* 1988, s.29(1), (2).]

This section creates three offences. As regards the offence of unlawfully depriving the **12–195**
residential occupier of his occupation of the premises, the prosecution must prove that:

— the defendant unlawfully deprived, or attempted to unlawfully deprive, the residential occupier (defined in s.1(1)) of his occupation of the premises and

— he did not believe, or have reasonable cause to believe that the residential occupier had ceased to reside in the premises.

12–196   As regards the offence of doing acts likely to interfere with the peace or comfort of the residential occupier, the prosecution must prove that:

— the defendant intended to cause the residential occupier of any premises to give up his occupation of the premises or to refrain from exercising any right or pursuing any remedy in respect of the premises or part thereof and

— he did acts likely to interfere with the peace or comfort of the residential occupier or members of his household OR

— he persistently withdrew or withheld services reasonably required for the occupation of the premises as a residence.

12–197   As regards the offence of the landlord or agent of the landlord doings acts likely to interfere with the peace or comfort of the residential occupier, or withholding services, the prosecution must prove that:

— the defendant was the landlord, or agent of the landlord of the premises in question and,

— he did acts likely to interfere with the peace or comfort of the residential occupier or members of his household or persistently withdrew or withheld services reasonably required for the occupation of the premises in question as a residence and

— he knew, or had reasonable cause to believe that such conduct is likely to cause the residential occupier to give up the occupation of the whole or part of the premises or to refrain from exercising any right or remedy in respect of the whole or part of the premises.

(b) *Procedure*

12–198   These offences are triable either way.

(c) *Elements of the offence*

12–199   Whether the defendant believes, or has reasonable cause to believe that the residential occupier had ceased to reside in the premises are questions of fact for the jury (or justices when the offence is tried summarily): *R. v Davidson-Acres* [1980] Crim.L.R. 50, CA.

In *R. v Yuthiwattana*, 80 Cr.App.R. 55, CA, the Court held that s.1(2) of the 1977 Act is concerned with eviction. The necessary eviction does not need to be permanent, but cases which would more accurately be described as 'locking out' cases, where a person was shut out of premises for a short period of time but was allowed to remain in occupation of the premises would more accurately fall under subs.(3). See further *Archbold Crown*, § 29–64.

The offence under subs.(3) requires the necessary intention to cause the owner or occupier to give up occupation of the premises or to refrain from exercising any right or pursuing any remedy in respect of the premises. In *R. v AMK (Property Management) Ltd* [1985] Crim.L.R. 600, CA, an appeal was successful because the trial judge had failed to make it clear that intent to cause the occupiers to leave was different from the consequences of building works being carried out being that the occupiers would have to leave. In *Schon v Camden London Borough Council* (1986) 84 L.G.R. 830, it was held that whilst an intention to persuade the occupier to leave for a limited period of time would not establish an intention to cause her to leave the premises. It would however establish the intent required under the second limb of s.1(3) as it would be an intention to cause the occupier to refrain from exercising her right to live in and be physically present at the premises.

12–200   For examples of acts found to be likely to interfere with the peace and comfort of the occupier see *R. v Yuthiwattana*, above, (failure to provide a front door key as well as entering the occupier's room without permission, removing his record player and records and shouting at him).

(d) *Defences*

Section 1(2) of the 1977 Act makes it a defence to any eviction offence for the accused **12–201** to prove that he believed, and had reasonable cause to believe that the residential occupier had ceased to reside in the premises. Section 1(3)(B) also provides a defence to a charge under subs.(3)(B) if the accused can prove that had reasonable grounds for doing the acts or withdrawing or withholding the services in question.

(e) *Sentence*

When tried summarily, the maximum punishment is a fine not exceeding the **12–202** prescribed sum, imprisonment for a term not exceeding six months or both: *Protection From Eviction Act* 1977, s.1(4).

In *Pittard* (1994) 15 Cr.App.R.(S.) 108 the accused was convicted of unlawful eviction and interference with the peace and comfort of a residential occupier. He had let a house to a lady as a sole occupier. While she was away, he broke into the house, moved in, changed the locks and upon her return indicated his intention to stay in the house. His original sentence of a £600 in respect of each count and an order to pay £2000 towards the cost of the prosecution was reduced to a fine of £100, the costs order being upheld.

B. Use or Threat of Violence for the Purposes of Securing Entry to Premises

(a) *Definition*

Criminal Law Act 1977, s.6(1)–(4)

Violence for securing entry

6.—(1) Subject to the following provisions of this section, any person who, without lawful **12–203** authority, uses or threatens violence for the purpose of securing entry into any premises for himself or for any other person is guilty of an offence, provided that—

(a) there is someone present on those premises at the time who is opposed to the entry which the violence is intended to secure; and

(b) the person using or threatening the violence knows that that is the case.

(1A) Subsection (1) above does not apply to a person who is a displaced residential occupier or a protected intending occupier of the premises in question or who is acting on behalf of such an occupier; and if the accused adduces sufficient evidence that he was, or was acting on behalf of, such an occupier he shall be presumed to be, or to be acting on behalf of, such an occupier unless the contrary is proved by the prosecution.

(2) Subject to subsection (1A) above, The fact that a person has any interest in or right to possession or occupation of any premises shall not for the purposes of subsection (1) above constitute lawful authority for the use or threat of violence by him or anyone else for the purpose of securing his entry into those premises.

(4) It is immaterial for the purposes of this section—

(a) whether the violence in question is directed against the person or against property; and

(b) whether the entry which the violence is intended to secure is for the purpose of acquiring possession of the premises in question or for any other purpose.

The prosecution must establish that: **12–204**

— the defendant, without lawful authority, used or threatened violence for the purpose of securing entry into any premises and,

— there is someone present on those premises at the time who is opposed to the entry which the violence is intended to secure and

— the defendant knew that this was the case.

(b) *Procedure*

12–205   This is offence is triable summarily only: s.6(5).

(c) *Elements of the offence*

12–206   It is immaterial whether the violence in question is directed against the person or against property: (s.6(4)(a). Likewise, it is immaterial whether the entry which the violence is intended to secure is for the purpose of acquiring possession of the premises in question or for any other purpose (s.6(4)(b)).

Key terms are defined in ss.12 and 12A of the 1977 Act.

Criminal Law Act 1977, ss.12, 12A(1)–(7)

Supplementary positions

12–207   **12.**—(1) In this Part of this Act—

     (a) "premises" means any building, any part of a building under separate occupation, any land ancillary to a building, the site comprising any building or buildings together with any land ancillary thereto, and (for the purposes only of sections 10 and 11 above) any other place; and

     (b) "access" means, in relation to any premises, any part of any site or building within which those premises are situated which constitutes an ordinary means of access to those premises (whether or not that is its sole or primary use).

(2) References in this section to a building shall apply also to any structure other than a movable one, and to any movable structure, vehicle or vessel designed or adapted for use for residential purposes; and for the purposes of subsection (1) above—

     (a) part of a building is under separate occupation if anyone is in occupation or entitled to occupation of that part as distinct from the whole; and

     (b) land is ancillary to a building if it is adjacent to it and used (or intended for use) in connection with the occupation of that building or any part of it.

(3) Subject to subsection (4) below, any person who was occupying any premises as a residence immediately before being excluded from occupation by anyone who entered those premises, or any access to those premises, as a trespasser is a displaced residential occupier of the premises for the purposes of this Part of this Act so long as he continues to be excluded from occupation of the premises by the original trespasser or by any subsequent trespasser.

(4) A person who was himself occupying the premises in question as a trespasser immediately before being excluded from occupation shall not by virtue of subsection (3) above be a displaced residential occupier of the premises for the purposes of this Part of this Act.

12–208   (5) A person who by virtue of subsection (3) above is a displaced residential occupier of any premises shall be regarded for the purposes of this Part of this Act as a displaced residential occupier also of any access to those premises.

(6) Anyone who enters or is on or in occupation of any premises by virtue of—

     (a) any title derived from a trespasser; or

     (b) any licence or consent given by a trespasser or by a person deriving title from a trespasser,

shall himself be treated as a trespasser for the purposes of this Part of this Act (without prejudice to whether or not he would be a trespasser apart from this provision); and references in this Part of this Act to a person's entering or being on or occupying any premises as a trespasser shall be construed accordingly.

(7) Anyone who is on any premises as a trespasser shall not cease to be a trespasser for the purposes of this Part of this Act by virtue of being allowed time to leave the premises, nor shall anyone cease to be a displaced residential occupier of any premises by virtue of any such allowance of time to a trespasser.

(7A) Subsection (6) also applies to the Secretary of State if the tenancy or licence is granted by him under Part III of the *Housing Associations Act* 1985.

(8) No rule of law ousting the jurisdiction of magistrates' courts to try offences where a dispute of title to property is involved shall preclude magistrates' courts from trying offences under this Part of this Act.

Protected intending occupiers: supplementary provisions

12A.—(1) For the purposes of this Part of this Act an individual is a protected intending oc-   **12–209** cupier of any premises at any time if at that time he falls within subsection (2), (4) or (6) below.

(2) An individual is a protected intending occupier of any premises if—

(a) he has in those premises a freehold interest or a leasehold interest with not less than two years still to run;

(b) he requires the premises for his own occupation as a residence;

(c) he is excluded from occupation of the premises by a person who entered them, or any access to them, as a trespasser; and

(d) he or a person acting on his behalf holds a written statement—

(i) which specifies his interest in the premises;

(ii) which states that he requires the premises for occupation as a residence for himself; and

(iii) with respect to which the requirements in subsection (3) below are fulfilled.

(3) The requirements referred to in subsection (2)(d)(iii) above are—

(a) that the statement is signed by the person whose interest is specified in it in the presence of a justice of the peace or commissioner for oaths; and

(b) that the justice of the peace or commissioner for oaths has subscribed his name as a witness to the signature.

(4) An individual is also a protected intending occupier of any premises if—

(a) he has a tenancy of those premises (other than a tenancy falling within subsection (2)(a) above or (6)(a) below) or a licence to occupy those premises granted by a person with a freehold interest or a leasehold interest with not less than two years still to run in the premises;

(b) he requires the premises for his own occupation as a residence;

(c) he is excluded from occupation of the premises by a person who entered them, or any access to them, as a trespasser; and

(d) he or a person acting on his behalf holds a written statement—

(i) which states that he has been granted a tenancy of those premises or a licence to occupy those premises;

(ii) which specifies the interest in the premises of the person who granted that tenancy or licence to occupy ("the landlord");

(iii) which states that he requires the premises for occupation as a residence for himself; and

(iv) with respect to which the requirements in subsection (5) below are fulfilled.

(5) The requirements referred to in subsection (4)(d)(iv) above are—

(a) that the statement is signed by the landlord and by the tenant or licensee in the presence of a justice of the peace or commissioner for oaths;

(b) that the justice of the peace or commissioner for oaths has subscribed his name as a witness to the signatures.

(6) An individual is also a protected intending occupier of any premises if—   **12–210**

(a) he has a tenancy of those premises (other than a tenancy falling within subsection (2)(a) or (4)(a) above) or a licence to occupy those premises granted by an authority to which this subsection applies;

(b) he requires the premises for his own occupation as a residence;

(c) he is excluded from occupation of the premises by a person who entered the premises, or any access to them, as a trespasser; and

(d) there has been issued to him by or on behalf of the authority referred to in paragraph (a) above a certificate stating that—

(i) he has been granted a tenancy of those premises or a licence to occupy those premises as a residence by the authority; and

(ii) the authority which granted that tenancy or licence to occupy is one to which this subsection applies, being of a description specified in the certificate.

(7) Subsection (6) above applies to the following authorities—

    (a) any body mentioned in section 14 of the *Rent Act* 1977 (landlord's interest belonging to local authority etc.);

    (b) the Housing Corporation;

    (c) Housing for Wales and;

    (d) a registered social landlord within the meaning of the *Housing Act* 1985

(d) *Sentence*

12–211   The maximum penalty for this offence is imprisonment for a term not exceeding six months, a fine not exceeding level five on the standard scale or both: *Criminal Law Act* 1977, s.6(5).

C. ADVERSE OCCUPATION OF RESIDENTIAL PREMISES

(a) *Definition*

Criminal Law Act 1977, s.7(1)–(5), (7)

Adverse occupation of residential premises

12–212   **7.**—(1) Subject to the following provisions of this section and to section 12A(9) below, any person who is on any premises as a trespasser after having entered as such is guilty of an offence if he fails to leave those premises on being required to do so by or on behalf of—

    (a) a displaced residential occupier of the premises; or

    (b) an individual who is a protected intending occupier of the premises.

(2) In any proceedings for an offence under this section it shall be a defence for the accused to prove that he believed that the person requiring him to leave the premises was not a displaced residential occupier or protected intending occupier of the premises or a person acting on behalf of a displaced residential occupier or protected intending occupier.

(3) In any proceedings for an offence under this section it shall be a defence for the accused to prove—

    (a) that the premises in question are or form part of premises used mainly for non-residential purposes; and

    (b) that he was not on any part of the premises used wholly or mainly for residential purposes.

12–213   (4) Any reference in the preceding provisions of this section to any premises includes a reference to any access to them, whether or not any such access itself constitutes premises, within the meaning of this Part of this Act.

(5) A person guilty of an offence under this section shall be liable on summary conviction to imprisonment for a term not exceeding six months or to a fine not exceeding level 5 on the standard scale or to both.

(7) Section 12 below contains provisions which apply for determining when any person is to be regarded for the purposes of this Part of this Act as a displaced residential occupier of any premises or of any access to any premises and section 12A below contains provisions which apply for determining when any person is to be regarded for the purposes of this Part of this Act as a protected intending occupier of any premises or of any access to any premises.

12–214   The prosecution must prove that:

— the defendant entered the premises as a trespasser and

— he was asked to leave the premises by a displaced residential occupier of the premises or by an individual who is a protected intending occupier of the premises and

— he refused to leave.

(b) *Procedure*

12–215   This offence is triable summarily: s.7(5).

(c) *Elements of the offence*

For the meaning of 'displaced residential occupier' and 'protected intending oc- **12–216** cupier' see ss.12, 12A of the 1977 Act, above.

(d) *Sentence*

The maximum penalty is imprisonment for a term not exceeding six months, or a **12–217** fine not exceeding level five on the standard scale or both: s.7(5).

D. TRESPASSING DURING THE CURRENCY OF AN INTERIM POSSESSION ORDER

(a) *Definition*

Criminal Justice and Public Order Act 1994, s.76

Interim possession orders: trespassing during currency of order

76.—(1) This section applies where an interim possession order has been made in respect of **12–218** any premises and served in accordance with rules of court; and references to "the order" and "the premises" shall be construed accordingly.

(2) Subject to subsection (3), a person who is present on the premises as a trespasser at any time during the currency of the order commits an offence.

(3) No offence under subsection (2) is committed by a person if—

(a) he leaves the premises within 24 hours of the time of service of the order and does not return; or

(b) a copy of the order was not fixed to the premises in accordance with rules of court.

(4) A person who was in occupation of the premises at the time of service of the order **12–219** but leaves them commits an offence if he re-enters the premises as a trespasser or attempts to do so after the expiry of the order but within the period of one year beginning with the day on which it was served.

(5) A person guilty of an offence under this section shall be liable on summary conviction to imprisonment for a term not exceeding six months or a fine not exceeding level 5 on the standard scale or both.

(6) A person who is in occupation of the premises at the time of service of the order shall be treated for the purposes of this section as being present as a trespasser.

(7) A constable in uniform may arrest without a warrant anyone who is, or whom he reasonably suspects to be, guilty of an offence under this section.

(8) In this section—

"interim possession order" has the same meaning as in section 75 above and "rules of court" is to be construed accordingly; and

"premises" has the same meaning as in that section that is to say the same meaning as in Part II of the *Criminal Law Act* 1977 (offences relating to entering and remaining on property).

Regarding the offence of trespass, the prosecution must prove that: **12–220**
— the defendant was present on the premises as a trespasser,
— during the currency of an interim possession order.

Regarding the offence of re-entering premises as a trespasser, the prosecution must prove that:

— the defendant was in occupation of the premises at the time of service of the interim possession order and,

— he then left the premises, and re-entered as a trespasser or attempted to re-enter the premises,

— after the expiry of the order, but within one year of the date on which the order was served.

(b) *Procedure*

This offence is triable summarily only: s.76(5), *CJPOA* 1994.   **12–221**

(c) Elements of the offence

12–222   "interim possession order" has the same meaning as in s.75(4) of the 1994 Act namely 'an interim possession order made under rules of court for the bringing of summary proceedings for possession of premises which are occupied by trespassers.'

By s.75(4) of the 1994 Act 'premises' has the same meaning as in Pt II of the *Criminal Law Act* 1977 (offences relating to entering and remaining on property) and 'statement' in relation to an interim possession order means any statement, in writing or oral and whether as to fact or belief, made in or for the purpose of the proceedings.'

(d) Defence

12–223   The accused will have a defence if he can establish that he left the premises within 24 hours of the time of service of the order and does not return, or a copy of the order was not fixed to the premises in accordance with the rules of court: s.76(3).

(e) Sentence

12–223.1   The maximum penalty is a term of imprisonment not exceeding six months, a fine not exceeding level 5 on the standard scale or both: s.76(5) of the *CJPOA* 1994.

E. INTERIM POSSESSION ORDERS; FALSE OR MISLEADING STATEMENTS

(a) Definition

Criminal Justice and Public Order Act 1994, s.75

Interim possession orders: false or misleading statements

12–224   **75.**—(1) A person commits an offence if, for the purpose of obtaining an interim possession order, he—

(a) makes a statement which he knows to be false or misleading in a material particular; or

(b) recklessly makes a statement which is false or misleading in a material particular.

(2) A person commits an offence if, for the purpose of resisting the making of an interim possession order, he—

(a) makes a statement which he knows to be false or misleading in a material particular; or

(b) recklessly makes a statement which is false or misleading in a material particular.

(3) A person guilty of an offence under this section shall be liable—

(a) on conviction on indictment, to imprisonment for a term not exceeding two years or a fine or both;

(b) on summary conviction, to imprisonment for a term not exceeding six months or a fine not exceeding the statutory maximum or both.

(4) In this section—

"interim possession order" means an interim possession order (so entitled) made under rules of court for the bringing of summary proceedings for possession of premises which are occupied by trespassers;

"premises" has the same meaning as in Part II of the *Criminal Law Act* 1977 (offences relating to entering and remaining on property); and

"statement", in relation to an interim possession order, means any statement, in writing or oral and whether as to fact or belief, made in or for the purposes of the proceedings.

12–224.1   The prosecution must prove that:

— the defendant knowingly or recklessly made a false or misleading statement,

— for the purpose of obtaining an interim possession order or

— for the purpose of resisting the making of an interim possession order.

(b) Procedure

12–225   This offence is triable either way: s.75(3) of the *CJPOA* 1994.

(c) *Elements of the offence*

Criminal Justice and Public Order Act, s.75(4)

See § 12–224, above.   **12–226**

(d) *Sentence*

When tried summarily, the maximum penalty is imprisonment for a term not exceed-   **12–227**
ing six months or a fine not exceeding the statutory maximum or both: *CJPOA* 1994,
s.75(3).

F. AGGRAVATED TRESPASS

(a) *Definition*

Criminal Justice and Public Order Act 1994, s.68(1)–(3), (5)

Offence of aggravated trespass
   68.—(1) A person commits the offence of aggravated trespass if he trespasses on land in the   **12–228**
open air and, in relation to any lawful activity which persons are engaging in or are about to
engage in on that or adjoining land in the open air, does there anything which is intended by
him to have the effect—
   (a) of intimidating those persons or any of them so as to deter them or any of them
        from engaging in that activity,
   (b) of obstructing that activity, or
   (c) of disrupting that activity.
   (2) Activity on any occasion on the part of a person or persons on land is "lawful" for
the purposes of this section if he or they may engage in the activity on the land on that occasion without committing an offence or trespassing on the land.
   (3) A person guilty of an offence under this section is liable on summary conviction to
imprisonment for a term not exceeding three months or a fine not exceeding level 4 on
the standard scale, or both.
   (5) In this section "land" does not include—
   (a) the highways and roads excluded from the application of section 61 by
        paragraph (b) of the definition of land in subsection (9) of that section; or
   (b) a road within the meaning of the *Roads (Northern Ireland) Order* 1993.

The prosecution must prove that: **12–229**
   — the defendant trespasses on land in the open air and,
   — does something which is intended to intimidate, obstruct or disrupt,
   — the lawful activities of people on the land.

(b) *Procedure*

The offence is triable summarily: s.68(3) of the *CJPOA* 1994.   **12–230**

(c) *Elements of the offence*

'Lawful activity'

By s.68(2) an activity is lawful if the persons engaged in it may do so without commit-   **12–231**
ting an offence or trespassing on the land. The persons engaged in the lawful activity
must be physically present on the land: *Tilly v DPP* [2002] Crim.L.R. 128.

Disruption

Where the charge is under s.68(1)(c) an intention to disrupt the lawful activity must   **12–232**
be proved, yet actual disruption need not be established. In *Winde v DPP* (1996) 160

J.P. 713 when trespassers ran towards a hunt without actually disrupting it, the requisite intention to disrupt was found to be present and a charge under s.68(1)(c) could proceed.

(d) Sentence

12–233   The maximum penalty is a term of imprisonment not exceeding three months or a fine not exceeding level four on the standard scale or both: s.68(3) of the *CJPOA* 1994.

G. Failure to Leave or Re-Entry to Land After Police Direction to Leave

(a) Definition

Criminal Justice and Public Order Act 1994, s.61(4)

Power to remove trespassers on land
12–234   **61.**—(4) If a person knowing that a direction under subsection (1) above has been given which applies to him—
     (a) fails to leave the land as soon as reasonably practicable, or
     (b) having left again enters the land as a trespasser within the period of three months beginning with the day on which the direction was given,
he commits an offence and is liable on summary conviction to imprisonment for a term not exceeding three months or a fine not exceeding level 4 on the standard scale, or both.

The prosecution must prove that:
— the defendant knew that a police direction to leave had been given to him,
— he then failed to leave the land as soon as was practicable or
— he left the land, and then re-entered as a trespasser within a period of three months from the date on which the direction to leave was given.

(b) Procedure

12–235   This offence is triable summarily: s.61(4) of the *CJPOA* 1994.

(c) Elements of the offence

12–236   A direction to leave must be given before the offence under s.61 can be committed:

Criminal Justice and Public Order Act 1994, s.61(1)

Power to remove trespassers on land
     61.—(1) If the senior police officer present at the scene reasonably believes that two or more persons are trespassing on land and are present there with the common purpose of residing there for any period, that reasonable steps have been taken by or on behalf of the occupier to ask them to leave and—
     (a) that any of those persons has caused damage to the land or to property on the land or used threatening, abusive or insulting words or behaviour towards the occupier, a member of his family or an employee or agent of his, or
     (b) that those persons have between them six or more vehicles on the land,
he may direct those persons, or any of them, to leave the land and to remove any vehicles or other property they have with them on the land.

12–236.1   A direction under s.61 cannot be issued until the trespassers have failed to comply with steps taken by the occupier to ask them to leave. *R. (on the application of Fuller) v Chief Constable of Dorset* [2003] Q.B. 480 held that a s.61 direction was invalid when given at the same time as instructions to leave the premises. The purported s.61 notice was also held to be invalid as it required vacation in two days time, a s.61 notice can only direct immediate vacation of a site.

Key terms are defined in s.61(9) of the 1994 Act.

Criminal Justice and Public Order Act 1994, s.61(9), (1)

Power to remove trespassers on land
61.—(9) In this section—   **12–237**
"common land" means common land as defined in section 22 of the *Commons Registration Act* 1965;
"commoner" means a person with rights of common as defined in section 22 of the *Commons Registration Act* 1965;
"land" does not include—

    (a) buildings other than—

        (i) agricultural buildings within the meaning of, in England and Wales, paragraphs 3 to 8 of Schedule 5 to the *Local Government Finance Act* 1988 or, in Scotland, section 7(2) of the *Valuation and Rating (Scotland) Act* 1956, or

        (ii) scheduled monuments within the meaning of the *Ancient Monuments and Archaeological Areas Act* 1979;

    (b) land forming part of—

        (i) a highway unless it falls within the classifications in section 54 of the *Wildlife and Countryside Act* 1981 (footpath, bridleway or byway open to all traffic or road used as a public path) or is a cycle track under the *Highways Act* 1980 or the *Cycle Tracks Act* 1984; or

        (ii) a road within the meaning of the *Roads (Scotland) Act* 1984 unless it falls within the definitions in section 151(2)(a)(ii) or (b) (footpaths and cycle tracks) of that Act or is a bridleway within the meaning of section 47 of the *Countryside (Scotland) Act* 1967;

"the local authority", in relation to common land, means any local authority which has powers in relation to the land under section 9 of the *Commons Registration Act* 1965;
"occupier" (and in subsection (8) "the other occupier") means—

    (a) in England and Wales, the person entitled to possession of the land by virtue of an estate or interest held by him; and

    (b) in Scotland, the person lawfully entitled to natural possession of the land;

"property", in relation to damage to property on land, means—

    (a) in England and Wales, property within the meaning of section 10(1) of the *Criminal Damage Act* 1971; and

    (b) in Scotland, either—

        (i) heritable property other than land; or

        (ii) corporeal movable property, and

"damage" includes the deposit of any substance capable of polluting the land;
"trespass" means, in the application of this section—

    (a) in England and Wales, subject to the extensions effected by subsection (7) above, trespass as against the occupier of the land;

    (b) in Scotland, entering, or as the case may be remaining on, land without lawful authority and without the occupier's consent; and

"trespassing" and "trespasser" shall be construed accordingly;
"vehicle" includes—

    (a) any vehicle, whether or not it is in a fit state for use on roads, and includes any chassis or body, with or without wheels, appearing to have formed part of such a vehicle, and any load carried by, and anything attached to, such a vehicle; and

    (b) a caravan as defined in section 29(1) of the *Caravan Sites and Control of Development Act* 1960;

and a person may be regarded for the purposes of this section as having a purpose of residing in a place notwithstanding that he has a home elsewhere.

Power to remove trespassers on land
    61.—(1) If the senior police officer present at the scene reasonably believes that two or more **12–238** persons are trespassing on land and are present there with the common purpose of residing

there for any period, that reasonable steps have been taken by or on behalf of the occupier to ask them to leave and—

    (a) that any of those persons has caused damage to the land or to property on the land or used threatening, abusive or insulting words or behaviour towards the occupier, a member of his family or an employee or agent of his, or

    (b) that those persons have between them six or more vehicles on the land,

he may direct those persons, or any of them, to leave the land and to remove any vehicles or other property they have with them on the land.

(d) Defence

12–239   The accused will have a defence if he can show that he was not trespassing on the land, or that he had a reasonable excuse for failing to leave the land as soon as reasonably practicable or, as the case may be, for again entering the land as a trespasser: s.61(6) of the *CJPOA* 1994.

(e) Sentence

12–240   The maximum penalty is imprisonment for a term not exceeding three months or a fine not exceeding level 4 on the standard scale or both: s.61(4).

H. FAILURE TO LEAVE LAND OR RE-ENTRY TO LAND: RAVES

(a) Definition

Criminal Justice and Public Order Act 1994, s.63

Powers to remove persons attending or preparing for a rave

12–241   **63.**—(1) This section applies to a gathering on land in the open air of 100 or more persons (whether or not trespassers) at which amplified music is played during the night (with or without intermissions) and is such as, by reason of its loudness and duration and the time at which it is played, is likely to cause serious distress to the inhabitants of the locality; and for this purpose—

    (a) such a gathering continues during intermissions in the music and, where the gathering extends over several days, throughout the period during which amplified music is played at night (with or without intermissions); and

    (b) "music" includes sounds wholly or predominantly characterised by the emission of a succession of repetitive beats.

(2) If, as respects any land [in the open air], a police officer of at least the rank of superintendent reasonably believes that—

    (a) two or more persons are making preparations for the holding there of a gathering to which this section applies,

    (b) ten or more persons are waiting for such a gathering to begin there, or

    (c) ten or more persons are attending such a gathering which is in progress,

he may give a direction that those persons and any other persons who come to prepare or wait for or to attend the gathering are to leave the land and remove any vehicles or other property which they have with them on the land.

(3) A direction under subsection (2) above, if not communicated to the persons referred to in subsection (2) by the police officer giving the direction, may be communicated to them by any constable at the scene.

(4) Persons shall be treated as having had a direction under subsection (2) above communicated to them if reasonable steps have been taken to bring it to their attention.

12–242   (5) A direction under subsection (2) above does not apply to an exempt person.

(6) If a person knowing that a direction has been given which applies to him—

    (a) fails to leave the land as soon as reasonably practicable, or

    (b) having left again enters the land within the period of 7 days beginning with the day on which the direction was given,

he commits an offence and is liable on summary conviction to imprisonment for a term not exceeding three months or a fine not exceeding level 4 on the standard scale, or both.

(7) In proceedings for an offence under this section it is a defence for the accused to

show that he had a reasonable excuse for failing to leave the land as soon as reasonably practicable or, as the case may be, for again entering the land.

(8) A constable in uniform who reasonably suspects that a person is committing an offence under this section may arrest him without a warrant.

(9) This section does not apply—   **12–243**
    (a) in England and Wales, to a gathering licensed by an entertainment licence; or
    (b) [Scotland]
(10) In this section—
    "entertainment licence" means a licence granted by a local authority under—
        (a) Schedule 12 to the *London Government Act* 1963;
        (b) section 3 of the *Private Places of Entertainment (Licensing) Act* 1967; or
        (c) Schedule 1 to the *Local Government (Miscellaneous Provisions) Act* 1982;
    "exempt person", in relation to land (or any gathering on land), means the occupier, any member of his family and any employee or agent of his and any person whose home is situated on the land;
    "land in the open air" includes a place partly open to the air;
    "local authority" means—
        (a) in Greater London, a London borough council or the Common Council of the City of London;
        (b) in England outside Greater London, a district council or the council of the Isles of Scilly;
        (c) in Wales, a county council or county borough council; and
    "occupier", "trespasser" and "vehicle" have the same meaning as in section 61.

(11) Until 1st April 1996, in this section "local authority" means, in Wales, a district council.

The prosecution must prove that: **12–244**
  — the relevant gathering is one to which s.63(1) applies,
  — the defendant knew that a police direction to leave had been issued to him and
  — he failed to leave the land as soon as was reasonably practicable or,
  — he left the land, and then re-entered as a trespasser within a period of seven days from the date on which the direction to leave was given.

(b) *Procedure*

This offence is triable summarily: s.63(6) of the *CJPOA* 1994.   **12–245**

(c) *Elements of the offence*

A direction under s.63(2) may be communicated by any constable at the scene (s.63(3)) **12–246**
and persons shall be treated as having had a direction under subs.(2) above communicated to them if reasonable steps have been taken to bring it to their attention (s.63(4)).

Section 63(5) establishes that a direction given under subs.(2) will not apply to an 'exempt person'. Such a person is defined by s.63(10) as 'the occupier, any member of his family and any employee or agent of his and any person whose home is situated on the land.' By s.63(9) the section does not apply to a gathering licensed by an entertainment licence.

(d) *Defence*

A person will also have a defence if he can establish that he had a reasonable excuse **12–247**
for failing to leave the land as soon as reasonably practicable or, as the case may be, for again entering the land (s.63(7)).

(e) *Sentence*

The maximum penalty is imprisonment for a term not exceeding three months or a   **12–248**
fine not exceeding level four on the standard scale or both: s.63(6) of the *CJPOA* 1994.

A forfeiture order may be imposed under s.66(1) of the 1994 Act where a person has been convicted of this offence and the court is satisfied that sound equipment which has been seized from him under s.64(4) or which was in his possession or under his control at the relevant time, has been used at the gathering.

I. Unauthorised Campers: Failure to Leave or Returning to the Land

(a) *Definition*

Criminal Justice and Public Order Act 1994, s.77

Power of local authority to direct unauthorised campers to leave land

12–249   **77.**—(1) If it appears to a local authority that persons are for the time being residing in a vehicle or vehicles within that authority's area—

     (a) on any land forming part of a highway;

     (b) on any other unoccupied land; or

     (c) on any occupied land without the consent of the occupier,

the authority may give a direction that those persons and any others with them are to leave the land and remove the vehicle or vehicles and any other property they have with them on the land.

(2) Notice of a direction under subsection (1) must be served on the persons to whom the direction applies, but it shall be sufficient for this purpose for the direction to specify the land and (except where the direction applies to only one person) to be addressed to all occupants of the vehicles on the land, without naming them.

(3) If a person knowing that a direction under subsection (1) above has been given which applies to him—

     (a) fails, as soon as practicable, to leave the land or remove from the land any vehicle or other property which is the subject of the direction, or

     (b) having removed any such vehicle or property again enters the land with a vehicle within the period of three months beginning with the day on which the direction was given,

he commits an offence and is liable on summary conviction to a fine not exceeding level 3 on the standard scale.

(4) A direction under subsection (1) operates to require persons who re-enter the land within the said period with vehicles or other property to leave and remove the vehicles or other property as it operates in relation to the persons and vehicles or other property on the land when the direction was given.

12–250   (5) In proceedings for an offence under this section it is a defence for the accused to show that his failure to leave or to remove the vehicle or other property as soon as practicable or his re-entry with a vehicle was due to illness, mechanical breakdown or other immediate emergency.

(6) In this section—

"land" means land in the open air;

"local authority" means—

     (a) in Greater London, a London borough or the Common Council of the City of London;

     (b) in England outside Greater London, a county council, a district council or the Council of the Isles of Scilly;

     (c) in Wales, a county council or a county borough council;

"occupier" means the person entitled to possession of the land by virtue of an estate or interest held by him;

"vehicle" includes—

     (a) any vehicle, whether or not it is in a fit state for use on roads, and includes any body, with or without wheels, appearing to have formed part of such a vehicle, and any load carried by, and anything attached to, such a vehicle; and

     (b) a caravan as defined in section 29(1) of the *Caravan Sites and Control of Development Act* 1960;

and a person may be regarded for the purposes of this section as residing on any land notwithstanding that he has a home elsewhere.

(7) Until 1st April 1996, in this section "local authority" means, in Wales, a county council or a district council.

The prosecution must prove that: **12–251**
— the local council issued a direction to leave the land to the defendant and
— the defendant failed to leave the land, or remove any vehicle from the land that formed the subject matter of the local council's direction as soon as was reasonably practicable or,
— the defendant had removed any relevant vehicle or property and then re-entered the land within a period of three months beginning at the date at which the direction was given.

(b) *Procedure*

This offence is triable summarily only: s.77(3) of the *CJPOA* 1994.   **12–252**

(c) *Elements of the offence*

A direction to leave the land must be given before the offence can be committed: **12–252** s.77(1) of the *CJPOA* 1994.

(d) *Defence*

The accused will have a defence if he can establish that his failure to leave or to **12–253** remove the vehicle or other property as soon as practicable or his re-entry with a vehicle was due to illness, mechanical breakdown or other immediate emergency: s.77(5).

(e) *Sentence*

The maximum penalty is a fine not exceeding level three on the standard scale: **12–253** s.77(3) of the *CJPOA* 1994.

J. Trespassing with Firearm in Building or on Land

(a) *Definition*

Firearms Act 1968, s.20(1), (2)

Trespassing with firearm
20.—(1) A person commits an offence if, while he has a firearm or imitation firearm with **12–254** him, he enters or is in any building or part of a building as a trespasser and without reasonable excuse (the proof whereof lies on him).
(2) A person commits an offence if, while he has a firearm with him, he enters or is on any land as a trespasser and without reasonable excuse (the proof whereof lies on him).

[This section is printed as amended by the *Firearms (Amendment) Act* 1994, s.2.]
The prosecution must prove that: **12–254**
— the defendant entered any building, part of a building or land as a trespasser and without reasonable excuse and
— was carrying a firearm or imitation forearm with him.

(b) *Procedure*

The offence of trespassing with a firearm in a building is triable either way, unless the **12–255** weapon concerned is an air weapon or an imitation firearm, in which case the offence is summary only. The mode of trial for trespassing on any land with a firearm is summary only.

(c) *Elements of the offence*

The term 'firearm' is defined in s.57 of the *Firearms Act* 1968 as a lethal barrelled **12–256** weapon of any description from which any shot, bullet or other missile can be discharged, and includes:

    (a) any prohibited weapon, whether it is such a lethal weapon as aforesaid or not; and

    (b) any component part of such a lethal or prohibited weapon; and

    (c) any accessory to any such weapon designed or adapted to diminish the noise or flash caused by firing the weapon.'

12–257   The *Firearms Act* 1968, s.20(3) defines 'land' as including land covered by water. The offender must be proved to have the firearm with him, which denotes more than mere possession, and involves a very close physical link and a degree of immediate control over the weapon by the man alleged to have the firearm with him: *R. v Kelt* [1977] 3 All E.R. 1099, CA.

(d) *Sentence*

12–258   When tried summarily, the offence of trespassing in a building with a firearm is punishable by a term of imprisonment not exceeding six months or a fine not exceeding the prescribed sum or both. The offence of trespassing with a firearm on any land is punishable with a term of imprisonment not exceeding three months and a fine not exceeding level four on the standard scale.

K. TRESPASSING WITH WEAPONS OF OFFENCE

(a) *Definition*

Criminal Law Act 1977, s.8(1)

Trespassing with a weapon of offence

12–259   **8.**—(1) A person who is on any premises as a trespasser, after having entered as such, is guilty of an offence if, without lawful authority or reasonable excuse, he has with him on the premises any weapon of offence.

The prosecution must prove that:

— the defendant entered and was present on any premises as a trespasser and

— without any lawful authority or reasonable excuse, he had with him on the premises any weapon of offence.

(b) *Procedure*

12–260   This offence is triable summarily: s.8(3) of the *CLA* 1977.

(c) *Elements of the offence*

12–261   The term 'premises' bears the same meaning as it does in s.12 of the *Criminal Law Act* 1977.

    Section 8(2) defines 'weapon of offence' as any article made or adapted for causing injury to or incapacitating a person, or intended by the person having it with him for such use.

(d) *Sentence*

12–262   The maximum penalty for this offence is six months imprisonment, a fine not exceeding level 5 on the standard scale or both: s.8(3) of the *CLA* 1977.

L. Obstruction of Court Officers Executing Process Against Unauthorised Occupiers

(a) *Definition*

Criminal Law Act 1977, s.10(1)–(3)

Obstruction of enforcement officers and court officers executing High Court or county court process

10.—(1) Without prejudice to section 8(2) of the *Sheriffs Act* 1887 but subject to the follow-   **12–263** ing provisions of this section, a person is guilty of an offence if he resists or intentionally obstructs any person who is in fact an officer of a court engaged in executing any process issued by the High Court or by any county court for the purpose of enforcing any judgment or order for the recovery of any premises or for the delivery of possession of any premises.

(2) Subsection (1) above does not apply unless the judgment or order in question was given or made in proceedings brought under any provisions of rules of court applicable only in circumstances where the person claiming possession of any premises alleges that the premises in question are occupied solely by a person or persons (not being a tenant or tenants holding over after the termination of the tenancy) who entered into or remained in occupation of the premises without the licence or consent of the person claiming possession or any predecessor in title of his.

(3) In any proceedings for an offence under this section it shall be a defence for the accused to prove that he believed that the person he was resisting or obstructing was not an officer of a court.

[This section is printed as amended by the *CJA* 1982, s.46.]

The prosecution must prove that: **12–264**
— the defendant resisted, or intentionally obstructed any officer of the court who,
— was executing any process for the purpose of enforcing any judgement or order for the recovery of premises or the delivery of possession of any premises.

(b) *Procedure*

This offence is triable summarily: s.10(4) of the *CLA* 1977.   **12–264.1**

(c) *Elements of the offence*

An 'officer of the court' is defined as any sheriff, under sheriff, deputy sheriff, bailiff   **12–265** or officer of a sheriff and any bailiff or other person who is an officer of a county court within the meaning of the *County Courts Act* 1959, s.10(6).

For the definition of 'premises' see *Criminal Law Act* 1977, s.12.

(d) *Defence*

The accused will have a defence if he can prove that he believed that the person he   **12–266** was restricting or obstructing was not an officer of the court: s.10(3).

(e) *Sentence*

The maximum penalty for this offence is imprisonment for a term not exceeding six   **12–267** months, a fine not exceeding level five on the standard scale, or both: s.10(4) of the *CLA* 1977.

VII. MISCELLANEOUS OFFENCES

A. Drunk and Disorderly

(a) Definition

Criminal Justice Act 1967, s.91(1)

Drunkenness in a public place

12–268   **91.**—(1) Any person who in any public place is guilty, while drunk, of disorderly behaviour may be arrested without warrant by any person and shall be liable on summary conviction to a fine not exceeding level 3 on the standard scale.

12–269   [This section is printed as amended by the *CLA* 1977, Sch.13 and the *CJA* 1982, ss.38 and 46.]

2–269.1   The prosecution must prove that:
— the defendant was found in a public place whilst drunk and,
— behaving in a disorderly fashion.

(b) *Procedure*

12–270   This offence is triable summarily: s.91(1).

(c) *Elements of the offence*

'Drunk'

12–271   "drunk" means the taking of intoxicating liquor to an extent which affects steady self-control. It does not apply to a person who is disorderly as a result of sniffing glue: *Neale v RMJE (a minor)* (1985) 80 Cr.App.R. 20.

'Disorderly'

12–272   The meaning of the word 'disorderly' has not been the subject of any reported decision and should bear its natural and ordinary meaning.

'Public Place'

12–273   'public place' includes any highway and any other premises or place which at the material time the public have or are permitted to have access, whether on payment or otherwise: s.91(4). The common parts of a block of flats, access to which is controlled so as to restrict entry to residents, their visitors and tradesmen and others who were there in a private capacity, not as members of the general public, will not be a public place: *Williams v DPP* (1992) 156 J.P. 804.

(d) *Sentence*

12–274   The maximum penalty is a fine not exceeding level three on standard scale: s.91(1). The *Magistrates' Court Sentencing Guidelines* state:

> Aggravating factors include offensive language or behaviour, with group, on hospital/medical premises, offence committed on bail, relevant previous convictions and any failure to respond to previous sentences.
> Mitigating factors include being induced by others, no significant disturbance and not threatening.
> **Guideline**: Is discharge or fine appropriate?

B. Bomb Hoaxes

(a) *Definition*

Criminal Law Act 1977, s.51

Bomb hoaxes

51.—(1) A person who—   **12–275**

 (a) places any article in any place whatever; or

 (b) dispatches any article by post, rail or any other means whatever of sending things
   from one place to another,

with the intention (in either case) of inducing in some other person a belief that it is likely to
explode or ignite and thereby cause personal injury or damage to property is guilty of an
offence.

In this subsection "article" includes substance.

(2) A person who communicates any information which he knows or believes to be false
to another person with the intention of inducing in him or any other person a false belief
that a bomb or other thing liable to explode or ignite is present in any place or location
whatever is guilty of an offence.

(3) For a person to be guilty of an offence under subsection (1) or (2) above it is not necessary for him to have any particular person in mind as the person in whom he intends to
induce the belief mentioned in that subsection.

(4) A person guilty of an offence under this section shall be liable—

 (a) on summary conviction, to imprisonment for a term not exceeding six months or
   to a fine not exceeding £1,000, or both;

 (b) on conviction on indictment, to imprisonment for a term not exceeding seven
   years.

[Section 51(4) is printed as amended by the *CJA* 1991, s.26(4).]

The prosecution must prove that: **12–276**

 — the defendant placed any article in any place, or dispatched any article by post,
   rail or other means of sending things from one place to another and

 — he intended to induce a belief in some person that such thing is likely to explode
   or ignite, thereby causing personal injury or damage to property OR

 — the defendant communicated any information that he knows or believes to be
   false to another person and

 — he intended to induce in that, or any other person, a false belief that a bomb or
   other thing liable to explode or ignite is present in any place or location.

(b) *Procedure*

This offence is triable either way.   **12–277**

(c) *Elements of the offence*

The words 'There is a bomb' said to the operator on a 999 call were sufficient to give **12–278**
rise to an offence under s.51(2), a person communicating the false information does not
need to specify a 'place or location': *R. v Webb*, *The Times*, June 19, 1995, CA.

(d) *Sentence*

When tried summarily, the maximum penalty for this offence is imprisonment for a **12–279**
term not exceeding six months, or a fine not exceeding £1000 or both: s.51(4)(a).

C. Use of Noxious Substance or Things to cause Harm and Intimimidate

(a) Definition

Anti-Terrorism, Crime and Security Act 2001, s.113

Use of noxious substances or things to cause harm and intimidate

12–279.1   **113.**—(1) A person who takes any action which—

(a) involves the use of a noxious substance or other noxious thing;

(b) has or is likely to have an effect falling within subsection (2); and

(c) is designed to influence the government or to intimidate the public or a section of the public,

is guilty of an offence.

(2) Action has an effect falling within this subsection if it—

(a) causes serious violence against a person anywhere in the world;

(b) causes serious damage to real or personal property anywhere in the world;

(c) endangers human life or creates a serious risk to the health or safety of the public or a section of the public; or

(d) induces in members of the public the fear that the action is likely to endanger their lives or create a serious risk to their health or safety;

but any effect on the person taking the action is to be disregarded.

(3) A person who—

(a) makes a threat that he or another will take any action which constitutes an offence under subsection (1); and

(b) intends thereby to induce in a person anywhere in the world the fear that the threat is likely to be carried out,

is guilty of an offence.

(4) A person guilty of an offence under this section is liable—

(a) on summary conviction, to imprisonment for a term not exceeding six months or a fine not exceeding the statutory maximum (or both); and

(b) on conviction on indictment, to imprisonment for a term not exceeding fourteen years or a fine (or both).

(5) In this section—

"the government" means the government of the United Kingdom, of a part of the United Kingdom or of a country other than the United Kingdom; and

"the public" includes the public of a country other than the United Kingdom.

(b) Procedure

12–280   This offence is triable either way.

(c) Elements of the offence

12–281   Substance includes any biological agent and any other natural or artificial substance (whatever its form, origin or method of production): see s.115(1).

For a person to be guilty of this offence, it is not necessary for him to have any particular person in mind as the person in whom he intends to induce the belief in question: s.115(2).

(d) Sentence

12–282   When tried summarily, the maximum penalty for this offence is imprisonment for a term not exceeding six months, or a fine not exceeding £1000 or both: s.113(4).

D. Hoaxes involving Noxious Substances or things

(a) *Definition*

Anti-Terrorism, Crime and Security Act 2001, s.114

Hoaxes involving noxious substances or things

114.—(1) A person is guilty of an offence if he—   **12–283**
- (a) places any substance or other thing in any place; or
- (b) sends any substance or other thing from one place to another (by post, rail or any other means whatever);

with the intention of inducing in a person anywhere in the world a belief that it is likely to be (or contain) a noxious substance or other noxious thing and thereby endanger human life or create a serious risk to human health.

(2) A person is guilty of an offence if he communicates any information which he knows or believes to be false with the intention of inducing in a person anywhere in the world a belief that a noxious substance or other noxious thing is likely to be present (whether at the time the information is communicated or later) in any place and thereby endanger human life or create a serious risk to human health.

(3) A person guilty of an offence under this section is liable—
- (a) on summary conviction, to imprisonment for a term not exceeding six months or a fine not exceeding the statutory maximum (or both); and
- (b) on conviction on indictment, to imprisonment for a term not exceeding seven years or a fine (or both).

(b) *Procedure*

This offence is triable either way.   **12–284**

(c) *Elements of the offence*

'Substance includes any biological agent and any other natural or artificial substance **12–285** (whatever its form, origin or method of production): see s.115(1).

For a person to be guilty of this offence, it is not necessary for him to have any particular person in mind as the person in whom he intends to induce the belief in question: s.115(2).

(d) *Sentence*

When tried summarily, the maximum penalty for this offence is imprisonment for a **12–286** term not exceeding six months, or a fine not exceeding £1000 or both: s.114(3).

E. Information about Acts of Terrorism

(a) *Definition*

Terrorism Act 2000, s.38B

Information about acts of terrorism

38B.—(1) This section applies where a person has information which he knows or believes **12–287** might be of material assistance—
- (a) in preventing the commission by another person of an act of terrorism, or
- (b) in securing the apprehension, prosecution or conviction of another person, in the United Kingdom, for an offence involving the commission, preparation or instigation of an act of terrorism.

(2) The person commits an offence if he does not disclose the information as soon as reasonably practicable in accordance with subsection (3).

(3) Disclosure is in accordance with this subsection if it is made—
- (a) in England and Wales, to a constable,

    (b) in Scotland, to a constable, or

    (c) in Northern Ireland, to a constable or a member of Her Majesty's forces.

    (4) It is a defence for a person charged with an offence under subsection (2) to prove that he had a reasonable excuse for not making the disclosure.

    (5) A person guilty of an offence under this section shall be liable—

    (a) on conviction on indictment, to imprisonment for a term not exceeding five years, or to a fine or to both, or

    (b) on summary conviction, to imprisonment for a term not exceeding six months, or to a fine not exceeding the statutory maximum or to both.

    (6) Proceedings for an offence under this section may be taken, and the offence may for the purposes of those proceedings be treated as having been committed, in any place where the person to be charged is or has at any time been since he first knew or believed that the information might be of material assistance as mentioned in subsection (1).

(b) *Procedure*

12–288   This offence is triable either way.

(c) *Sentence*

12–289   When tried summarily, the maximum penalty for this offence is imprisonment for a term not exceeding six months, or a fine not exceeding £1000 or both: s.38B(5).

F. INTIMIDATION OR ANNOYANCE BY VIOLENCE OR OTHERWISE

(a) *Definition*

Trade Union and Labour Relations (Consolidation) Act 1992, s.241

Intimidation or annoyance by violence or otherwise

12–290   **241.**—(1) A person commits an offence who, with a view to compelling another person to abstain from doing or to do any act which that person has a legal right to do or abstain from doing, wrongfully and without legal authority—

    (a) uses violence to or intimidates that person or his wife or children, or injures his property,

    (b) persistently follows that person about from place to place,

    (c) hides any tools, clothes or other property owned or used by that person, or deprives him of or hinders him in the use thereof,

    (d) watches or besets the house or other place where that person resides, works, carries on business or happens to be, or the approach to any such house or place, or

    (e) follows that person with two or more other persons in a disorderly manner in or through any street or road.

    (2) A person guilty of an offence under this section is liable on summary conviction to imprisonment for a term not exceeding six months or a fine not exceeding level 5 on the standard scale, or both.

    (3) A constable may arrest without warrant anyone he reasonably suspects is committing an offence under this section.

12–291   The prosecution must prove that:

— the defendant used violence towards, or intimidated, another person, that person's wife or that person's children or the defendant injured that person's property, or,

— the defendant wrongfully and without legal authority, persistently followed another person about from place to place, or,

— the defendant wrongfully and without legal authority, hid any tools, clothes or other property owned or used by another person or deprived him or hindered him in the use of such items, or

— the defendant wrongfully and without legal authority, watched or beset the house or other place where another person resides, works, carries on business or happens to be, or watched or beset the approach of any such house or place or,

— the defendant wrongfully and without legal authority, followed another person with two or more persons in a disorderly manner in or through any street or road, with,

— a view to compelling that other person to abstain from doing or to do any act which that person has a legal right to do or abstain from doing.

(b) *Procedure*

This offence is triable summarily: s.241(2).   **12–292**

(c) *Elements of the offence*

Application to peaceful picketing: **12–293**

Trade Union and Labour Relations (Consolidation) Act 1992, s.220

Peaceful picketing
220.—(1) It is lawful for a person in contemplation or furtherance of a trade dispute to attend—

    (a) at or near his own place of work, or

    (b) if he is an official of a trade union, at or near the place of work of a member of
the union whom he is accompanying and whom he represents,

for the purpose only of peacefully obtaining or communicating information, or peacefully
persuading any person to work or abstain from working.

    (2) If a person works or normally works—

    (a) otherwise than at any one place, or

    (b) at a place the location of which is such that attendance there for a purpose
mentioned in subsection (1) is impracticable,

his place of work for the purposes of that subsection shall be any premises of his employer from
which he works or from which his work is administered.

    (3) In the case of a worker not in employment where—

    (a) his last employment was terminated in connection with a trade dispute, or

    (b) the termination of his employment was one of the circumstances giving rise to a
trade dispute,

in relation to that dispute his former place of work shall be treated for the purposes of subsection (1) as being his place of work.

    (4) A person who is an official of a trade union by virtue only of having been elected or
appointed to be a representative of some of the members of the union shall be regarded
for the purposes of subsection (1) as representing only those members; but otherwise an
official of a union shall be regarded for those purposes as representing all its members.

Section 241 may also be applied to the actions of an anti-roads protester: *Todd v*   **12–293.1**
DPP [1996] Crim.L.R. 344.

(d) *Sentence*

The maximum penalty is six months' imprisonment, a fine not exceeding level five   **12–293.2**
on the standard scale or both: s.241(2).

G. PUBLIC NUISANCE

Public nuisance is an offence at common law, triable either way. When tried sum-   **12–294**
marily, the statutory maxima apply as regards sentencing: see *Magistrates' Courts Act*
1980, s.17(1) and Sch.1.

A person is guilty of a public nuisance when he (a) does an act not warranted by law,
or (b) omits to discharge a legal duty, if the effect of the act or omission is to endanger
the life, health, property, morals or comfort of the public, or to obstruct the public in

the exercise or enjoyment of rights common to all Her Majesty's subjects: *Stephen's Digest of the Criminal Law* (9th ed., 1900), p.184, definition approved in *R. v Shorrock* [1994] Q.B. 279. See further *Archbold Crown*, §§ 31–40—31–42.

The question of how widely spread a nuisance must be for it to qualify as a public nuisance was addressed in *Att.-Gen. v P.Y.A Quarries Ltd* [1957] 2 Q.B. 169, CA where it was held that the question whether the local community within the sphere of a neighbourhood comprised a sufficient number of persons to constitute a class of the public was a question of fact in every case. See further *Archbold Crown*, § 31–42.

12–295   The mens rea of the offence will be established if the prosecution can show that the defendant knew or ought to have known that as a result of his action, a public nuisance would be committed: *R. v Shorrock* [1994] Q.B. 279, 98 Cr.App.R. 67, CA.

See further *Archbold Crown*, §§ 31–50—31–58.

H. Breach of the Peace and Powers to bind over

Public Order Act 1986, s.40(4)

Amendments, repeals and savings

12–296   **40.**—(4) Nothing in this Act affects the common law powers in England and Wales to deal with or prevent a breach of the peace.

12–296.1   In *R. v Howell* [1982] Q.B. 416 it was held that there is a breach of the peace whenever harm is actually done or is likely to be done to a person or in his presence to his property or a person is in fear of being so harmed through an assault, an affray, a riot, unlawful assembly or other disturbance.

Binding over to keep the peace

12–297   The Magistrates may bind over a person to keep the peace following a complaint (*MCA* 1980, s.115) or by the court's own motion under common law and statutory powers, notably the *Justices of the Peace Act* 1361.

When the court is acting of its own motion, it may make a binding over order at any time before the conclusion of criminal proceedings, on withdrawal of the case by the prosecution, on a decision by the prosecution to offer no evidence, on an adjournment, or upon acquittal of the defendant, where the magistrate considers that there might be a breach of the peace in the future.

The person bound over is required to enter into a recognizance in an amount which will be forfeited if he fails to keep the peace for a specified period.

If the person fails, or refuses to enter into a recognisance the magistrates' may order imprisonment. This may be for a maximum of six months or until the person complies with the order: *MCA* 1980, s.115(3). The *PCC(S)A* 2000, s.89 provides that imprisonment cannot be imposed on a person under the age of 21. A person between 18 and 20 who refuses to consent to be bound over may be detained under s.108 of the *PCC(S)A* 2000. A person under the age of 18 may be detained at an attendance centre.

The *PCC(S)A* 2000, s.139(1) establishes the relevant penalties for non-compliance with the terms of the binding over order. The court may forfeit the whole or part of the recognisance in its discretion, allow payment, direct time for payment, direct payment by instalments or reduce or discharge the recognisance. It is not allowed to impose a prison term.

In the magistrates' court, a recognisance can only be declared to be forfeit following an order on complaint: *MCA* 1980, s.20, by virtue of whichever power the bind over was originally imposed.

See also Part IV on Sentencing, in this work.

I. Contempt of Court

12–298   See § 18–57, below.

CHAPTER 13

ROAD TRAFFIC OFFENCES

Throughout road traffic law, there are a number of words or phrases that recur and **13–1** which have developed a specialist meaning. The key words that relate to offences covered by this work are set out below and the key principles that apply to the interpretation is described. For further information, reference should be made to *Wilkinson's Road Traffic Offences*, Ch.1.

I. DEFINITIONS

A. ACCIDENT

There is no statutory definition of this term in relation to road traffic offences. Al- **13–2** though some judicial suggestions have been made, it is recognised that the word is one in common use and, when faced with the issue, a court should ask itself "Would an ordinary man in the circumstances of the case say there had been an accident?": *Chief Constable of West Midlands Police v Billingham* [1979] R.T.R. 446.

It is clear that it can be the result of a deliberate act. In *Chief Constable of Staffordshire v Lees* [1981] R.T.R. 506, a defendant deliberately drove at a gate and smashed it. This was a breath test case and the powers of the police constable depended on there having been an accident. The court considered that it would be wrong for those powers to be exercisable where something happened as a result of a careless act but not where there had been a deliberate act. In the civil case of *Charlton v Fisher* [2001] EWCA Civ 112; [2001] R.T.R. 33, a car was deliberately driven into the rear of another stationary car and a person in that car was injured. In order to be able to claim successfully against the driver's insurance, the injured person had to show there had been an accident and the Court of Appeal considered that there had been.

It is also clear that there does not need to be any contact between vehicles. In the Scottish case of *Bremner v Westwater* (1993) 1994 S.L.T. 707, the issue arose in the context of whether a notice of intended prosecution, see § 13–13 below, was needed. The defendant had driven erratically at night without lights. In overtaking another vehicle, he had caused an oncoming vehicle to brake sharply and drive onto the verge in order to avoid a collision and the overtaken vehicle also had to brake sharply. It was held that this could properly be described as an accident.

B. IN CHARGE OF

13–3   There is no statutory definition of this phrase which is very much a question of fact and degree. The leading case is *DPP v Watkins* [1989] 2 W.L.R. 966 which identified two classes of cases which could be identified—those cases where the defendant was the owner or otherwise in lawful possession of the vehicle or had recently driven it and those cases where none of those descriptions applied. In the first situation, there would usually be an assumption that he was in charge unless he had given the charge of the vehicle to another person. However, if the defendant adduces sufficient evidence to show that there was no likelihood of him driving the vehicle whilst unfit, the prosecution must also prove that there was a real risk of him driving: *Road Traffic Act* 1988, ss.4(3) or 5(2) in the light of the decision in *DPP v Sheldrake* [2003] EWHC 273.

Where the defendant was not the owner or in lawful possession or had not recently driven the vehicle but was nonetheless sitting in the vehicle or otherwise involved in some way with it, the court will look to see if he was, in practice, voluntarily in control or in such a position that he might be expected to take control imminently—where the defendant was, what he was doing and what his intentions were would all be relevant.

In either class of case the court will need to consider where the defendant was in relation to the vehicle (and, if he was inside, where he was), what he was doing, whether he had a key that fitted the ignition, any evidence showing that the defendant intended to demonstrate his control of the vehicle (whether by driving or in some other way) and, finally, whether anyone else was in or near the vehicle and, if so, for what reason. An unusual application of this principle was seen in *DPP v Janman* [2004] EWHC Admin 101. A person was supervising a provisional licence holder. He had consumed sufficient alcohol to be over the limit and was prosecuted for being "in charge". Although there may be exceptional cases where a supervisor could demonstrate that there was no likelihood of driving the vehicle, that will be a very difficult task for the supervisor. It is of the essence of the role of a supervisor of a provisional licence holder that they must be prepared to intervene when necessary.

C. DRIVE/DRIVER

13–4   Almost inevitably, the plain meaning of these words has been stretched to ensure that culpable behaviour is properly brought within the remit of the various offences. That has been less necessary where an alternative of being "in charge" of a vehicle has been available.

The essence of driving is having control over the movement of the vehicle. Key elements can be drawn from the decisions in *R. v MacDonagh* [1974] R.T.R. 372 and

Burgoyne v Phillips [1983] R.T.R. 49. This is a question of fact, needing to accord with the ordinary meaning of "driving". It will involve substantial control over the movement and direction of the vehicle. It will probably require the presence of the driver inside the vehicle, at least to some extent so standing outside pushing the vehicle has not generally been found to be "driving". It may however be "using" or "attempting to drive".

Issues have also arisen as to when driving stops as there will be times when a person is clearly driving a vehicle even though it is not in motion. Key principles were summarised in *Edkins v Knowles* [1973] Q.B. 748. There will be interludes in a journey when the vehicle will stop and the questions to be asked will be concerning the purpose and length of the stop and whether the driver left the vehicle. If the journey is continuing and the stop of short duration or because of traffic congestion, then the driving will continue. If the journey has ended then, allowing for a short while to switch the engine off etc. the driving is likely to have come to an end. This may be particularly significant in prosecutions for using a hand held mobile telephone whilst driving. Whilst the purpose of creating the offence is one of road safety, there is no limitation of the definition of "drive" for that offence. However, it can be expected that prosecution will not follow where, although the driving continues, none the less there is no possible adverse effect on road safety, such as when a car is stationary at the roadside or stuck in traffic with no prospect of moving immediately.

More than one person may be driving the same vehicle. In *Tyler v Whatmore* [1976] **13–5** R.T.R. 83, a passenger was leaning across the person in the driving seat with both hands on the wheel and obstructing the view of the person in the driving seat who continued to control the propulsion of the vehicle but could not steer it. Both were driving. However, a passenger who grabbed the steering wheel causing the car to leave the road was not driving: *Jones v Pratt* [1983] R.T.R. 54.

D. Mechanically Propelled Vehicle

There are a variety of terms defined in the *Road Traffic Act* 1988 and elsewhere to **13–6** cover vehicles used on roads. In s.185 of the 1988 Act, a motor vehicle is defined as a "mechanically propelled vehicle intended or adapted for use on roads". There are further definitions of "motor car", "invalid carriage", "motor cycle" etc. which all use the phrase mechanically propelled vehicle.

This is a term which has been judicially considered on many occasions, often turning on whether a vehicle which undoubtedly has been a mechanically propelled vehicle continues to come within that definition even though it is no longer able to be driven. In connection with offences under the *Vehicle Excise and Registration Act* 1994, liability is being extended to vehicles that not only are mechanically propelled vehicles but also to ones that have at some stage been a mechanically propelled vehicle: Sch.5 to the *Finance Act* 2002.

The test to be applied is set out in *Binks v Department of the Environment* [1975] R.T.R. 318. as "whether the vehicle has reached such a stage that it can be said that there is no reasonable prospect of the vehicle ever being made mobile again".

E. Road or other Public Place

There are a range of definitions of "road" for various purposes and it will be a ques- **13–7** tion of fact and degree whether something is a road or other public place in the circumstances of any alleged offence.

In essence, a "road" is a highway and any other road to which the public has access: *Road Traffic Act* 1988, s.192(1). It is a definable way for passage between two points: *Oxford v Austin* [1981] R.T.R. 416. It will have the physical character of a defined or definable route or way, with ascertained or ascertainable edges, leading from one point to another with the function of serving as a means of access enabling travellers to move from one point to another along that route: *Cutter v Eagle Star Insurance Co. Ltd* [1998] 4 All E.R. 417. A public road is a road repairable at public expense.

A road to which the public have access is one on which the public generally can be found without having to overcome a physical obstruction or to defy an express or implied prohibition: *Harrison v Hill* 1932 J.C. 13. Connotations of public expense in maintaining it should not be imported: *DPP v Cargo Handling Ltd* [1992] R.T.R. 318.

13–8   The extent of the definition of "other public place" has often arisen in the context of car parks. Provided the public generally could be expected to use the area (even if only for purposes that not every member of the public would choose to avail themselves of) then it is likely to be a public place. Thus, courts have brought within the definition a hospital car park: *DPP v Greenwood* [1997] C.O.D. 278, an "airside" road at Heathrow Airport: *DPP v Neville* (1996) 160 J.P. 758, a lane leading from a cross-Channel ferry through the immigration terminal: *DPP v Coulman* [1993] R.T.R. 230 and a caravan park : *DPP v Vivier* [1991] 4 All E.R. 18.

F. USING, CAUSING AND PERMITTING

13–9   These terms are commonly used in relation to road traffic offences and their meaning has been developed in attempts to ensure that the purposes of the legislation are achieved.

Certain statutory provisions impose absolute liability on the user; for instance, if a vehicle is used and the use is not covered by insurance, the user is generally liable whether or not aware of the absence of insurance cover. The user will be the driver but will also often include a person whose vehicle was being used by another person for his purposes and under his control—often the employer/employee relationship. However, "use" is defined more restrictively where there are alternatives such as "causing" or "permitting" which could be used.

"Causing" unlawful use requires proof of knowledge of the facts making the use unlawful where there is an alternative offence of "using". Where that alternative is not provided, "causing", though it requires a positive act, will not necessarily require knowledge.

13–10   "Permitting" unlawful use is less precise than "causing" it. The extent to which knowledge is required will vary depending on the offence. For instance, permitting use without insurance will require proof that the use was permitted but not that it was known that the use was uninsured.

For a further exploration of these terms, see *Wilkinson's Road Traffic Offences* Ch.1.

G. VEHICLE

13–11   This can have a very wide meaning. In most instances for road traffic offences it is used with some other limiting factors, such as "motor vehicle" or "mechanically propelled vehicle" but it will sometimes be used on its own. In those circumstances, the dictionary definition of "a thing used for transporting people or goods on land" becomes relevant.

A bicycle is a vehicle as are trams, trolley buses and horse-drawn carts. In some circumstances, it may include a pram or a pushchair. For instance, one of the occasions in which the obligation to stop after an accident arises is where damage is caused to a vehicle and it is likely that a pram would be a vehicle for those purposes at least.

II. BAD DRIVING

13–12   There are two main offences dealt with in Magistrates' Courts where the issue is whether the standard of driving fell below an acceptable standard. These offences are dangerous driving: *Road Traffic Act* 1988, s.2 and driving without due care and attention or without reasonable consideration for other road users: *Road Traffic Act* 1988, s.3. As well as issues surrounding the assessment of a particular piece of driving, there will be difficult decisions needing to be made on sentencing since the consequences of bad driving do not always correlate with the badness of the driving.

A. WARNING OF PROSECUTION

In order to secure a conviction under either s.2 or 3, the prosecution must have **13–13** complied with the requirements to give notice of intended prosecution: *Road Traffic Offenders Act* 1988, s.1. Unless an accident has occurred of which the driver was aware (*Road Traffic Offenders Act* 1988, s.2(1)), the driver must receive warning of prosecution within 14 days of the offence. This warning may be given at the time of the offence, by service of the summons (or copy of a charge sheet) within 14 days of the offence or by the prosecutor sending notice to the driver or the registered keeper of the vehicle within 14 days. Where the notice is by service of the summons, that must take place within the 14 days. Where the notification is by notice, it is only necessary for that to be sent within the 14 days. For further information, refer to *Wilkinson's Road Traffic Offences*, Ch.2.

B. DANGEROUS DRIVING

Road Traffic Act 1988, s.2

Dangerous driving
    2. A person who drives a mechanically propelled vehicle dangerously on a road or other pub- **13–14** lic place is guilty of an offence.

(a) *What must the prosecution prove?*

The elements of this offence that the prosecution must prove are that: **13–15**
— the defendant was the driver
— the vehicle was being driven
— the vehicle was a mechanically propelled vehicle
— the vehicle was being driven dangerously
— the vehicle was being driven on a road or other public place.

A defendant who is acquitted of dangerous driving may be found guilty of driving **13–16** without due care and attention or without reasonable consideration even though no charge has been preferred—see Alternative Verdict below at § 13–22.

For issues of identification, see § 21–83 in this work.

For issues surrounding the meaning of "drive", see § 13–4.

The phrase "mechanically propelled vehicle" is wider than "vehicle"; again this is more fully explored in § 13–11 above.

The phrase "road or other public place" has been subject to detailed consideration; this also is explored more fully in a general paragraph above.

(b) *Mode of trial*

Dangerous driving is an either way offence and particular care needs to be taken in **13–17** assessing mode of trial. Latest statistical information (2001) shows that 27 per cent of cases were committed for trial or for sentence to be dealt with in the Crown Court. Of those sentenced in the Crown Court in 2001 (1,123), 77 per cent received a custodial sentence (average length 10 months). In respect of those sentenced with in a magistrates' court in 2001 (2,617), 30 per cent received a custodial sentence (average length 4 months), 50 per cent received a community penalty and 17 per cent were fined.

The *Mode of Trial Guidelines (Consolidated Criminal Practice Direction)*, para.51.17, state that cases of dangerous driving should be tried summarily unless the court considers that one or more of the following features is present in the case *and* that its sentencing powers are insufficient. These features are:
    (a) Alcohol or drugs contributing to the dangerous driving;

(b) Grossly excessive speed;
(c) Racing;
(d) Prolonged course of dangerous driving;
(e) Other related offences;
(f) Significant injury or damage sustained.

(c) Meaning of "dangerous driving"

13–18   The definition is set out in statute in *Road Traffic Act* 1988, s.2A.

Road Traffic Act 1988, s.2A

Meaning of dangerous driving

2A.—(1) For the purposes of sections 1 and 2 above a person is to be regarded as driving dangerously if (and, subject to subsection (2) below, only if)—

     (a) the way he drives falls far below what would be expected of a competent and careful driver, and

     (b) it would be obvious to a competent and careful driver that driving in that way would be dangerous.

(2) A person is also to be regarded as driving dangerously for the purposes of sections 1 and 2 above if it would be obvious to a competent and careful driver that driving the vehicle in its current state would be dangerous.

(3) In subsections (1) and (2) above "dangerous" refers to danger either of injury to any person or of serious damage to property; and in determining for the purposes of those subsections what would be expected of, or obvious to, a competent and careful driver in a particular case, regard shall be had not only to the circumstances of which he could be expected to be aware but also to any circumstances shown to have been within the knowledge of the accused.

(4) In determining for the purposes of subsection (2) above the state of a vehicle, regard may be had to anything attached to or carried on or in it and to the manner in which it is attached or carried.

13–19   There are, therefore, two routes by which the offence is committed, one related to the way of driving (s.2A(1)), one related to the decision to drive the vehicle at all: s.2A(2). The first (and more common) route test has two main parts both of which relate to a "competent and careful driver" and both of which must be proved.

The first part requires that the manner of driving falls "far below" that of a competent and careful driver: s.2A(1)(a). (For the lesser offence under s.3 of careless driving, the test is "below the standard of a reasonable, prudent and competent driver".) This is an objective test and the authorities indicate that the court should not add in an element that imports to the "competent and careful driver" of the test any of the characteristics of the defendant concerned or what the offender believed the situation to be: *R. v Collins* [1997] R.T.R. 439.

The second part (s.2A(1)(b)) requires proof that it would have been obvious to a competent and careful driver that driving in the way the defendant drove would be dangerous. Again an objective test and again two main elements, what is meant by "obvious" and what is meant by "dangerous".

13–20   In relation to "obvious", a dictionary definition of "seen or realised at first glance, evident" has been used in relation to offences under s.2A(2) and would be equally applicable here. Would it be obvious to the careful and competent driver that driving in this way would be dangerous? In addition, s.2A(3) requires a court to take account not only of what would be obvious to the careful and competent driver but also what was actually known to the defendant. Therefore, if something was known to the driver that would not have been obvious, the standard of driving has to be assessed in the light of that additional knowledge.

In relation to "dangerous", s.2A(3) is defined as meaning danger of injury to any person or of serious damage to property. The injury may be to any person, including the driver, and there is no limitation on the nature of the injury. However, it is suggested that that injury should be physical injury (as proposed in the Road Traffic Law Review (the North Report) that led to the creation of this offence) but there is no requirement that injury should have occurred, just that there was a danger of such injury occurring. In relation to property, there is again no further definition but there is the qualification that the damage must be "serious". Again, it would appear to be quite acceptable for that property to be the mechanically propelled vehicle being driven by the defendant as well as any other property.

The second route by which the offence is committed is by driving a mechanically propelled vehicle when it was obvious that to do so in its current state would be dangerous: s.2A(2). The state of the vehicle includes anything attached to it or carried on it or in it and the manner in which it is attached or carried: s.2A(4). Again the determinant of what is obvious is the careful and competent driver. The test is whether there is evidence that it would be obvious (that is, capable of being seen or realised at first glance, evident) that it would be dangerous (that is, liable to cause injury or serious damage to property) to drive the vehicle in that state. In addition, anything of which the driver was actually aware should be taken into account even where that would not have been obvious to a careful and competent driver: s.2A(3).

A difficult issue was considered in *R. v Marchant* [2003] EWCA Crim 2099; [2003] **13–21** Crim.L.R. 806. An agricultural vehicle had (as part of its construction) a grab with spikes attached to its front. It was authorised by the Secretary of State for use on public roads. The grab was in the recommended position for use on the roads. Whilst the vehicle was waiting to turn off the road, a motor cyclist ran into it and was killed. The driver was prosecuted for causing death by dangerous driving relying on s.2A(2). Allowing the driver's appeal against conviction, the Court of Appeal (Criminal Division) stated that, whilst there will be cases where it will be appropriate to prosecute those responsible for vehicles in a dangerous condition even where they had been authorised by the Secretary of State, that would be where the driver had manoeuvred the vehicle in a dangerous fashion. Where, as here, the danger was in the design, it is unlikely to be appropriate to prosecute the user at all.

Despite this route being limited in the statute to the defective state of the vehicle, it appears to have been extended to circumstances where it was the "defective" state of the driver that caused the danger. In *R. v Marison* [1997] R.T.R. 457, the driver suffered from diabetes and was aware that there was a real risk that he would suffer a sudden hypoglycaemic attack which would cause him to lose control of the vehicle. He did suffer such an attack resulting in the car crashing into an oncoming vehicle and killing the driver. The Judge drew an analogy with s.2A(2) and this was supported by the Court of Appeal.

Alternative verdict

A court faced with an offence of dangerous driving and finding the defendant not **13–22** guilty can instead find the defendant guilty of driving without due care and attention even though no charge has been preferred and even though it would not be possible to lay an information because too much time had elapsed from the date of the offence: *Road Traffic Offenders Act* 1988, s.24.

(d) *Penalty*

The maximum sentence at present is two years imprisonment on indictment and/or **13–23** an unlimited fine; on summary trial, six months imprisonment and/or a fine up to level 5. Proposals to increase the maximum period of imprisonment on indictment are under consideration by the Government subject to the conclusion of a Review of Road Traffic Offences causing death or serious injury. A significant issue is the gap between the maximum custodial sentence for this offence and for causing death by dangerous driving which is 14 years imprisonment. The same standard of driving may result in death, in very serious injury or in no injury at all and it is these issues that are under consideration in the Review and must be grappled with by those having to pass sentence.

Mandatory disqualification and endorsement follows (including an obligation to be re-tested). In the absence of "special reasons", see below at § 13–181, the minimum period of disqualification is 12 months. For more information on disqualification and endorsement generally, see §§ 13–155 et seq. below.

See also the power to deprive the offender of the vehicle contained in s.143(1), (6) and (7) of the *Powers of Criminal Courts (Sentencing) Act* 2000, see §§ 13–185 and 26–161, below.

(e) Sentence

13–24   There are commonly agreed aggravating and mitigating factors. Closely following recent guidance from the Court of Appeal (Criminal Division) in relation to the related offence of causing death by dangerous driving, the *Magistrates' Court Sentencing Guidelines* (2003) state that aggravating factors include seeking to avoid detection or apprehension, engagement in competitive driving including racing or showing off, disregard of warnings, perhaps from passengers or others in vicinity, evidence of alcohol or drugs, excessive speed, prolonged, persistent bad driving, serious risk and using a hand held mobile telephone. Mitigating circumstances include driving in an emergency and speed that was not excessive.

In *R. v Cooksley; R. v Stride; R. v Cook (Att.-Gen.'s Reference (No.152 of 2002))* [2003] 2 Cr.App.R. 18, the Court of Appeal issued a new guideline judgment for sentencing for the offence of causing death by dangerous driving, incorporating the advice of the Sentencing Advisory Panel. Although considering offences with the additional element of causing death and with a much higher maximum penalty, nonetheless the occurrence of death or serious injury may not depend on the nature of the driving and so the principles that relate to the quality of driving are likely to be equally applicable. The court identified factors indicating a highly culpable standard of driving at the time of the offence. In addition to those included in the *Magistrates' Court Sentencing Guidelines* (2003), these included aggressive driving, driving while the driver's attention was distracted, *e.g.* by reading or using a mobile phone, driving when knowingly suffering from a medical condition, driving when knowingly deprived of adequate sleep or rest, driving a poorly maintained or dangerously loaded vehicle, especially when motivated by commercial concerns, other offences committed at the same time, previous convictions for motoring offences, particularly offences involving bad driving or the consumption of alcohol before driving, irresponsible behaviour at the time of the offence, *e.g.* failing to stop, claiming one of the victims was responsible for the crash, and where the offence was committed on bail. Additional mitigating factors included a good driving record and the fact the offender had been seriously injured as a result of the dangerous driving.

In the course of the judgment, the Court emphasised that, although the offence is one which does not require an intention to drive dangerously [or an intention to injure], since the driving has to fall "far below" the standard of driving that would be expected of a competent and careful driver and the driving must be such that it would be obvious to the same competent and careful driver that driving in that way would be dangerous, it will usually be obvious to the offender that the driving was dangerous and he therefore deserves to be punished accordingly.

13–25   The courts have demonstrated a readiness to protect people who are particularly vulnerable to the commission of this offence. In *R. v Joseph* [2002] 1 Cr.App.R.(S.) 20, the defendant had deliberately driven at a traffic warden and driven off with him on the bonnet of the vehicle, trying to shake him off. The Court of Appeal endorsed the observations of the sentencing judge that it was the duty of the courts to give protection to traffic wardens and other public servants who were carrying out public duties, and emphasised the propriety of a deterrent custodial sentence. The defendant was sentenced to ten months' imprisonment. Leveson J. stated:

> "Parking attendants, in particular, are subject to vilification and abuse if not worse. It is a very
> real reflection on the hazards of the job that this particular parking attendant felt it appropri-

ate to carry a tape recorder with him to record what happened when confronted by angry motorists. The fact that others have complained about this particular attendant does not take this appellant's position or the character of his driving any further. An immediate custodial sentence, in the form of a deterrent sentence, which inevitably pays less attention to the individual circumstances of the offender was both proper and, in our judgment, inevitable" (at p.75–76)

For "road rage" cases of dangerous driving, where no accident or injury results and there was no consumption of alcohol, but there is evidence to suggest furious driving in temper with an intent of causing fear and possible injury, the appropriate sentencing bracket lies between six and 12 months: *R. v Howells* [2003] 1 Cr.App.R.(S.) 61, CA.

See also *R. v Arthur* [2001] 2 Cr.App.R.(S.) 67; *R. v Smith* [2002] 2 Cr.App.R.(S.) 28.

C. Careless or Inconsiderate Driving

Road Traffic Act 1988, s.3

Careless, and inconsiderate, driving
3. If a person drives a mechanically propelled vehicle on a road or other public place without **13–26** due care and attention, or without reasonable consideration for other persons using the road or place, he is guilty of an offence.

(a) *What must the prosecution prove?*

The elements of this offence that the prosecution must prove are that: **13–27**
— the defendant was the driver
— the vehicle was being driven
— the vehicle was a mechanically propelled vehicle
— the vehicle was being driven on a road or other public place
— the vehicle was being driven without due care and attention *or*
— the vehicle was being driven without reasonable consideration for other persons using the road or place.

For issues of identification, see § 21–83 in this work.
For issues surrounding the meaning of "drive", see § 13–4 above.   **13–27.1**
The phrase "mechanically propelled vehicle" is wider than "vehicle"; again this is more fully explored in § 13–11 above.
The phrase "road or other public place" has been subject to detailed consideration; this also is explored more fully in §§ 13–7 and 13–8 above.

(b) *Mode of trial*

These offences are summary only.   **13–28**

(c) *Standard of driving*

Statute does not assist in defining the standard of driving for the offences contained **13–29** in s.3. That standard is widely accepted as being that of a reasonable, prudent and competent driver in all the circumstances of the case. The standard has an element that is to be judged objectively (the reasonable etc. driver) and one that is subjective (the circumstances of the case). The most commonly prosecuted part of this section is the allegation of driving without due care and attention which is more widely drawn than the other limb of s.3.

Driving without reasonable consideration is almost always going to be capable of falling within the offence of driving without due care and attention since no reasonable, prudent and competent driver would drive without reasonable consideration for other road users. However, that does not work in reverse since, for the second limb, there must be other persons using the road or other public place whereas that is not necessary for the first limb. It may be that there are now fewer reasons why the second limb should be prosecuted at all.

The cause of the failure to drive at the acceptable standard is not, therefore, relevant to conviction (though it may be to sentence) but how the reasonable, etc. driver would be expected to conduct himself or herself is to be judged on the basis of the circumstances as they actually were. There can be some fine judgements as to whether the reasonable driver of the test would have avoided getting into the situation altogether or whether accepting that the situation occurred, the actions of the driver have to be tested against this standard. Thus, the fact that the driver is a learner driver or otherwise inexperienced does not affect the assessment of what the standard of driving should be whereas the standard may well vary with the time of day, type of road, or weather conditions. There is no need for anyone to be adversely affected.

13–30   It is not unusual for any accident to be observed by no one other than the driver. In those circumstances, the court is entitled to draw inferences from the nature of the circumstances in which the accident occurred to justify finding the offence proved providing the facts are strong enough to enable the court to be satisfied beyond reasonable doubt that the standard of driving was below that required: *Scott v Warren* [1974] R.T.R. 104. If an explanation (other than a fanciful one) is put forward by the defendant, it is for the prosecution to disprove it: *R. v Spurge* [1961] 2 All E.R. 688.

The Highway Code can be used to assist in understanding what is expected in any given situation. Failure to observe the Code does not of itself prove the case but it will tend to show that the standard of driving was unacceptable.

Once it is proved that the driving fell below the acceptable standard, there are a limited number of defences that have been created—mechanical defect, sudden loss of visibility or sudden illness. The underlying principle is that the driver has been deprived of control of the vehicle by something of which he was not aware. If the driver, without fault, can show that he was deprived of control because of a mechanical defect of which he was unaware and which he could not have discovered by the exercise of reasonable prudence then he ought to be acquitted. Similarly, if he finds himself unexpectedly blinded by headlights or by the sun and an accident occurs before he can stop, that can be a defence. In such circumstances, the reasonable and prudent driver will quickly reduce speed or stop his vehicle but there will be a very short time in which it is accepted that the defence would arise. Finally, sudden illness may again raise a defence providing it could not be anticipated and the reactions of the driver when he became aware of the illness were those of a reasonable and prudent driver. Falling asleep is not sufficient since that could have been anticipated: *Henderson v Jones* (1955) 119 J.P. 305.

(d) Penalty

13–31   The maximum penalty is a fine of level 4 (£2,500). It is an endorsable offence within the range of 3–9 penalty points and so disqualification may be imposed.

(e) Sentence

13–32   The *Magistrates' Court Sentencing Guidelines* (2003) provide that aggravating factors include driving at excessive speed, high degree of carelessness, serious risk and using a hand held mobile telephone. Mitigating factors include minor risk, momentary lapse of concentration, negligible/parking damage, sudden change in weather conditions. The guidelines also provide that death, serious injury or damage is capable of counting as an aggravating factor.

The most likely penalty is a fine with penalty points. However, disqualification should be considered where there is a risk of further poor driving. This may be until a further test is passed which will be particularly appropriate where there are concerns about the overall driving ability of the defendant.

A court will have to face situations where the seriousness of the result of the bad driving is greatly out of proportion to how bad the driving was—a relatively minor lapse can result in death. For may years, courts have based sentence for this offence primarily on the degree of fault. In *R. v Krawec* (1984) 6 Cr.App.R.(S.) 367, the appellant was convicted of driving without due care and attention on an indictment for causing death by reckless driving. Reducing the fine, Lord Lane C.J. stated that:

> the unforeseen and unexpected results of the carelessness are not in themselves relevant to penalty. The primary considerations are the quality of the driving, the extent to which the appellant on the particular occasion fell below the standard of the reasonably competent driver; in other words, the degree of carelessness and culpability. The unforeseen consequences may sometimes be relevant to those considerations. In the present case the fact that the appellant failed to see the pedestrian until it was too late and therefore collided with him was plainly a relevant factor. We do not think that the fact that the unfortunate man died was relevant on this charge.

However, that approach has been steadily changing and the different approach was evident in *R. v Johnson* [1998] 2 Cr.App.R.(S.) 453, where the CA held that the consequences of the driver's carelessness were relevant to determination of his culpability.

In *R. v King* [2001] 2 Cr.App.R.(S.) 114, CA, the Court of Appeal again approached the situation where driving without due care and attention results in tragic consequences. The appellant was convicted of three offences of driving without due care and attention having been acquitted of three counts of causing death by dangerous driving. He was fined £2,250 and disqualified for a period of three years. Holding that this sentence was too high, the Court of Appeal substituted a fine of £1,500 and disqualification for two years. While culpability or criminality remained the primary consideration in sentencing for driving without due care and attention where death had resulted, the sentencing judge was entitled to bear in mind that he was dealing with an offence that had led to death. Mackay J. reviewed the authorities on sentencing in this difficult situation, and stated:

> "The sentencer must still, therefore, make it his primary task to assess culpability, but should **13–33** not close his eyes to the fact that death has resulted, especially multiple death, where, as here, that was all too readily foreseeable as the consequence of the admitted lack of care in this case."

However, the maximum penalty remains a fine and that should be capable of being **13–33.1** paid within one year.

D. FAILING TO STOP AFTER AN ACCIDENT, FAILING TO REPORT AN ACCIDENT

Road Traffic Act 1988, s.170

Duty of driver to stop, report accident and give information or documents

170.—(1) This section applies in a case where, owing to the presence of a mechanically **13–34** propelled vehicle on a road or other public place, an accident occurs by which—

    (a) personal injury is caused to a person other than the driver of that mechanically propelled vehicle, or

    (b) damage is caused—

        (i) to a vehicle other than that mechanically propelled vehicle or a trailer drawn by that mechanically propelled vehicle, or

        (ii) to an animal other than an animal in or on that mechanically propelled vehicle or a trailer drawn by that mechanically propelled vehicle, or

        (iii) to any other property constructed on, fixed to, growing in or otherwise forming part of the land on which the road or place in question is situated or land adjacent to such land.

(2) The driver of the mechanically propelled vehicle must stop and, if required to do so by any person having reasonable grounds for so requiring, give his name and address and also the name and address of the owner and the identification marks of the vehicle.

(3) If for any reason the driver of the mechanically propelled vehicle does not give his name and address under subsection (2) above, he must report the accident.

(4) A person who fails to comply with subsection (2) or (3) above is guilty of an offence.

(5) If, in a case where this section applies by virtue of subsection (1)(a) above, the driver of a motor vehicle does not at the time of the accident produce such a certificate of insurance or security, or other evidence, as is mentioned in section 165(2)(a) of this Act—

(a) to a constable, or

(b) to some person who, having reasonable grounds for so doing, has required him to produce it,

the driver must report the accident and produce such a certificate or other evidence.

This subsection does not apply to the driver of an invalid carriage.

13–35 (6) To comply with a duty under this section to report an accident or to produce such a certificate of insurance or security, or other evidence, as is mentioned in section 165(2)(a) of this Act, the driver—

(a) must do so at a police station or to a constable, and

(b) must do so as soon as is reasonably practicable and, in any case, within twenty-four hours of the occurrence of the accident.

(7) A person who fails to comply with a duty under subsection (5) above is guilty of an offence, but he shall not be convicted by reason only of a failure to produce a certificate or other evidence if, within seven days after the occurrence of the accident, the certificate or other evidence is produced at a police station that was specified by him at the time when the accident was reported.

(8) In this section "animal" means horse, cattle, ass, mule, sheep, pig, goat or dog.

(a) *What must the prosecution prove?*

13–36 The elements of this offence that the prosecution must prove are that:
— an accident occurs
— the accident was due to the presence of a mechanically propelled vehicle on a road or other public place
— personal injury or damage was caused
— that the driver of the mechanically propelled vehicle failed to fulfil the obligation placed on him to stop and report.

For the meaning of "accident", "mechanically propelled vehicle" and "road or other public place" see §§ 13–4 *et seq.* above.

13–37 The obligation on the driver arises regardless of the responsibility for the accident. Once an accident has occurred as a result of the presence of a mechanically propelled vehicle on a road or other public place and there has been the qualifying injury or damage, then the obligation is on the driver of that vehicle to stop, to give the requisite details on request and, in certain circumstances, to report the accident to the police.

A driver can avoid this responsibility where he proves that he did not know that an accident had occurred. Once the prosecution has proved that an accident has occurred where the obligation arose to stop, in order to avoid responsibility, the defendant must prove (on the balance of probabilities) that he was unaware of the accident: *Harding v Price* [1948] 1 All E.R. 283. The more obvious the accident (noise of impact or damage to defendant's vehicle may be relevant) the more difficult it will be for the defendant to discharge the onus of proof.

(b) *Mode of trial*

13–38 These offences are summary only.

(c) *Driver*

13–39 The accident must arise from the presence of a mechanically propelled vehicle on a road or other public place. The obligations arising under this section fall on the driver of that vehicle. This is a potentially wide definition and there is no requirement to prove that the driver of the vehicle in question caused the accident. However, there must be a direct causal connection between the vehicle and the accident occurring. In *Quelch v Phipps* [1955] 2 All E.R. 302, an accident occurred when a passenger got off a bus which he thought was slowing down for traffic lights. In fact, those lights had changed to green by the time the bus would have halted and so the driver continued. The driver was unaware of the accident until informed by the conductor at the next stop. Having not exchanged the necessary particulars with the passenger, the driver should have reported the accident. Since the accident happened through the passenger getting out of a motor vehicle on a road, it occurred "owing to the presence of a motor vehicle on a road" and came within the meaning of the section. Since the driver knew of the accident, albeit after the event, he was under an obligation to report it. The obligation to stop and report is designed to ensure that those who suffer as a result of bad driving have enough information to pursue any claims for compensation. A stationary vehicle may lead to liability if parked badly and the bad parking was such as to lead to the accident whereas a properly parked vehicle is unlikely to lead to liability.

(d) *Qualifying injury or damage*

13–40　For the obligations to arise, there must have been injury or damage. If injury is the basis, the injury must be to a person other than the driver of the mechanically propelled vehicle. So, if *A* and *B* are involved in an accident and *B* is injured but there is no other damage, the obligations to stop and report fall on *A* but not on *B*. This applies equally whether *B* is in the same vehicle as *A* or in a different vehicle.

A must stop and must give the specified details (s.170(2)) and, because personal injury has been caused to someone else, unless he produces proof of insurance, he must produce that proof to the police: s.170(5).

If damage is the basis, then that damage may be to another vehicle (or trailer), to an animal in that other vehicle or trailer or to property on or close to the road. The types of animal are described in s.170(8) which limits them to any horse, cattle, ass, mule, sheep, pig, goat or dog.

13–41　The property has to be constructed on, fixed to, growing in or otherwise forming part of the land in question. It therefore has to have some degree of permanence—something placed temporarily on the land will not be sufficient.

(e) *Obligation imposed*

13–42　Where the obligation exists, the driver must stop. He must also give certain details. If he fails to give those details he must provide them to the police within the time specified in the section.

It is an absolute obligation to stop. This means to stop and to remain at the scene long enough to allow someone who has the right to do so to require the driver to provide the information that the section obliges him to give: *Lee v Knapp* [1966] 3 All. E.R. 961. This does not have to be an indefinite time, simply something sufficient in the circumstances prevailing at the time. There is no obligation on a driver to go and look for somebody who may be entitled to the information: *Mutton v Bates (No.1)* [1984] R.T.R. 256. The stopping must be at the scene. Driving on for 80 yards before stopping and returning has been held to be insufficient compliance: *McDermott v DPP* [1997] R.T.R. 474.

Any person having reasonable grounds for so doing, may require the driver to give his name and address and also the name and address of the owner and the identification marks of the vehicle. The purpose of this is to ensure that anyone who may have a claim against the driver has sufficient information to pursue it. It may be acceptable, therefore, for the address to be one through which the driver can be reached even if not the place where he is currently residing: *DPP v McCarthy* [1999] R.T.R. 323.

13–43　Where personal injury has occurred to another person, if the driver does not produce proof of insurance at the scene to the police or to another person having reasonable grounds for requiring it, he must report the accident and produce the proof: s.170(5). Alternatively, if the proof of insurance is not produced when the accident is reported, that proof must be produced at a Police Station which must be a station specified by the driver when he reported the accident.

If a driver does not give his name and address to anyone (for whatever reason) or produce the insurance certificate where that is required, he must report the accident to the police. He must do this by reporting it to a police station or to a constable as soon as reasonably practicable. Even where it is not reasonably practicable, that time must be within 24 hours of the accident.

The reporting must be done personally since the requirement is to report "at" a police station or "to" a constable: *Wisdom v Macdonald* [1983] R.T.R. 186.

(f) *Penalties*

13–44   The maximum penalty for an offence under this section is a fine of level 5 (£5000) and/or six months imprisonment. All offences are endorsable with a range of 5–10 points. Disqualification can be imposed.

See also the power to deprive the offender of the vehicle contained in subss.143(1), (6) and (7) of the *Powers of Criminal Courts (Sentencing) Act* 2000 (see §§ 13–185 and 26–161 *et seq.*).

(g) *Sentence*

13–45   This section contains a range of sentence with differing levels of seriousness. A court passing sentence will do so against the background of the purpose of the section and the reason why the defendant failed to fulfil his obligation.

The purpose of the offences stems from the recognition that causing an accident will, at the very least, lead to issues of compensating those who have suffered loss as a result and may lead to criminal proceedings. The motivation of the defendant may range from panic or fear for personal safety through to a deliberate attempt to avoid responsibility for a more serious offence, perhaps because the driver suspected that his alcohol level was such that he would be liable for compulsory disqualification.

A defendant may commit an offence in the following ways:

13–46	s.170(2)	Failing to stop (but still reporting the accident)
		Stopping but not giving details (but reporting the accident)
		Stopping but not giving details (and not reporting the accident)
		Stopping, giving details but not producing proof of insurance even though personal injury caused to another person
	s.170(3)	Not reporting the accident at all
		Reporting the accident but later than permitted
	s.170(7)	Failing to produce proof of insurance when required—if it was not produced at the scene of the accident, it should be produced when reporting the accident or within 7 days of reporting it

13–47   The *Magistrates' Court Sentencing Guidelines* (2003) draw attention to the possibility that there could be evidence of driving after drinking alcohol or that there had been a serious injury or damage both of which would make the offence more serious. However, a belief that his identity was known or a decision to leave because of fear for his safety would mitigate the seriousness. Other mitigating factors include the defendant having later reported the incident despite his initial failure to stop, negligible damage being caused and the fact that there was no-one at the scene and the defendant failed to report, or that the defendant stayed at the scene but failed to give or left before leaving full particulars.

Given the purposes behind the offence, the most serious offences are where a driver both fails to stop and to report the accident, the least serious where sufficient information for practical purposes was given voluntarily although not complying with the requirements of the section.

Although the offences are imprisonable, it is suggested that this power should be used only rarely. Use may be appropriate where the Court considers that the defendant was deliberately trying to evade responsibility for a more serious offence for which he would have received a custodial sentence or where serious injury was caused which could have been better treated if the defendant had stopped.

Those committing these offences are most likely to receive a financial penalty. **13–48** Disqualification should be considered for the more serious offences though short periods are likely to be sufficient to emphasise the importance of the responsibility place on drivers. If the offence was accompanied by driving below an acceptable standard, there is likely to be a separate offence.

In terms of penalty points, the top end should be reserved for circumstances where there is a failure both to stop and to report.

III. ALCOHOL/DRUGS RELATED OFFENCES

This is a highly complex (and much litigated) area of the criminal law. This work sets **13–49** outs the key areas and the key issues. For a more detailed examination, reference should be made to *Wilkinson's Road Traffic Offences*. There are two main offences (those under ss.4 and 5) and then other offences arising from the two stages for producing evidence to assess the amount of alcohol or drugs involved.

A. Driving etc. whilst Unfit through Alcohol or Drugs

Road Traffic Act 1988, s.4

Driving, or being in charge, when under influence of drink or drugs
   4.—(1) A person who, when driving or attempting to drive a mechanically propelled vehicle **13–50** on a road or other public place, is unfit to drive through drink or drugs is guilty of an offence.

   (2) Without prejudice to subsection (1) above, a person who, when in charge of a mechanically propelled vehicle which is on a road or other public place, is unfit to drive through drink or drugs is guilty of an offence.

   (3) For the purposes of subsection (2) above, a person shall be deemed not to have been in charge of a mechanically propelled vehicle if he proves that at the material time the circumstances were such that there was no likelihood of his driving it so long as he remained unfit to drive through drink or drugs.

   (4) The court may, in determining whether there was such a likelihood as is mentioned in subsection (3) above, disregard any injury to him and any damage to the vehicle.

   (5) For the purposes of this section, a person shall be taken to be unfit to drive if his ability to drive properly is for the time being impaired.

   (6) A constable may arrest a person without warrant if he has reasonable cause to suspect that that person is or has been committing an offence under this section.

   (7) For the purpose of arresting a person under the power conferred by subsection (6) above, a constable may enter (if need be by force) any place where that person is or where the constable, with reasonable cause, suspects him to be.

   (8) Subsection (7) above does not extend to Scotland, and nothing in that subsection affects any rule of law in Scotland concerning the right of a constable to enter any premises for any purpose.

(a) *Mode of trial*

These offences are summary only.   **13–51**

(b) *What must the prosecution prove?*

The prosecution must prove that: **13–52**
— the defendant
— drove *or* attempted to drive *or* was in charge of
— a mechanically propelled vehicle

511

— on a road or other public place

— whilst unfit through drink or drugs.

For issues of identification, see § 21–83 in this work.

For issues surrounding the meaning of "drive", see § 13–4 above.

The phrase "mechanically propelled vehicle" is wider than "vehicle"; again this is more fully explored in § 13–6 above.

The phrase "road or other public place" has been subject to detailed consideration; this also is explored more fully in § 13–7 above.

In order to prove an offence under this section, the prosecution must prove that the defendant was unfit to drive and that that was due to drink or to drugs. To that extent, it is more widely drawn than s.5 which is restricted to alcohol and sets a standard that is capable of precise measurement. Since evidence available to support a charge under s.5 is also admissible under s.4, it is likely that charges under s.4 are more likely to be used where the presence of *alcohol* is not the cause of the unfitness.

A person is unfit to drive if "his ability to drive properly is for the time being impaired": s.4(5). It is the ability to drive *properly* that is impaired not the ability to drive at all. This may be evidenced by the way the vehicle was being driven, or by involvement in an accident where there was nothing that would normally cause such an accident or it may be evidenced by the condition of the defendant. Where alcohol is alleged to be the cause of the unfitness, a certificate of analysis obtained under s.7 of the 1988 Act (see § 13–72 below) is admissible and must be taken into account: s.15(2) and (3) of the *Road Traffic Offenders Act* 1988.

13–53   Where drugs are alleged to be the cause of the unfitness, s.11 of the *Road Traffic Act* 1988 defines "drug" as meaning any intoxicant other than alcohol. According to the Oxford Concise Dictionary, "intoxicate" can have three variants—it can mean to cause someone to lose control of their faculties; it can also mean to poison or to excite or exhilarate—presumably it is the first variant that is intended! It is possible that the effect of alcohol could be increased when taken in conjunction with certain drugs and a conviction under s.4 would be appropriate in such circumstances where the combined effect impaired the defendant's ability to drive properly whereas the amount of alcohol on its own may have caused the level in the body to be below the legal limit. Under s.7 of the 1988 Act, the police may require a person to provide samples of breath, blood or urine for analysis in the course of an investigation concerning a possible offence under s.4. A breath test will not disclose useful information about drugs. Where a medical practitioner advises the police officer that the defendant's condition might be due to drugs (and there must be a clear oral statement to that effect by the medical practitioner), the police officer can require the defendant to provide a specimen of blood or urine even if a specimen of breath has already been provided: s.7(3)(c). A certificate of analysis must be taken into account (ss.15 and 16 of the *Road Traffic Offenders Act* 1988) but, in contrast to a certificate relating to alcohol, there is no statutory assumption that the proportion of drug in a specimen is not less than at the time the offence was committed. Since the Act does not provide a level that must be exceeded for an offence under s.4 (as it does for an offence under s.5), it will be for the court to assess whether the defendant was unfit and whether this was due to the presence of the drugs identified in the certificate.

If the defendant wishes to allege that the level in the analysis was caused by consumption of alcohol or drugs after the driving, etc. had ceased but before the sample was provided, then the onus is on the defendant to satisfy the court on the balance of probabilities not only that that happened but also that the amount was sufficient to render the reading invalid as proof that the defendant was unfit at the time of the offence or, in the case of alcohol, above the prescribed limit, s.15(3) of the *Road Traffic Offenders Act* 1988.

(c) *Penalties*

13–54   The maximum penalty for **driving or attempting to drive** is a fine of level 5 (currently £5000) and/or six months imprisonment. There is a mandatory requirement to disqualify from driving (in the absence of special reasons) for one year (though see § 13–178 for the circumstances where that minimum is increased). On endorsement only, there will be penalty points of between 3 and 11.

The maximum penalty for **being in charge** is a fine of level 4 (currently £2500) and/or three months imprisonment. There is a discretionary requirement to disqualify from driving. On endorsement, there will be penalty points of 10.

See also the power to deprive the offender of the vehicle contained in s.143(1), (6) and (7) of the *Powers of Criminal Courts (Sentencing) Act* 2000 (see §§ 13–185 and 26–161 below).

(d) Sentence

The primary factor for the court in determining sentence will be the extent of the **13–55** intoxication. Lower penalties are generally imposed for being in charge than for driving.

Normally, financial penalties are considered sufficient together with the disqualification which is mandatory in the case of driving offences and discretionary for in charge offences.

Aggravating features set out in the *Magistrates' Court Sentencing Guidelines* (2003) include the extent to which driving was actually shown to be impaired and the type of vehicle being driven; for instance, whether it was carrying passengers for reward or driving a large goods vehicle.

A community penalty should certainly be considered for the higher readings or for a **13–56** second offence. Particularly appropriate may be the orders which require unpaid work and those which impose a curfew. Whilst imprisonment is possible, given that this is not an offence of violence, imprisonment should be used only rarely and only when an offender has demonstrated that they intend to continue to drive in an intoxicated state.

Regarding the offences arising from being "in charge", given that it is open to the defendant to show that there was no likelihood that he/she would drive (which would be a defence), it is likely that the overall penalty will be similar to that for the driving offences albeit on a slightly lower scale. The higher maximum penalty for the driving offence reflects the potential for the most serious offences to be in that category.

B. DRIVING ETC. WITH EXCESS ALCOHOL IN THE BODY

Road Traffic Act 1988, s.5

Driving or being in charge of a motor vehicle with alcohol concentration above prescribed limit

5.—(1) If a person—   **13–57**
    (a) drives or attempts to drive a motor vehicle on a road or other public place, or
    (b) is in charge of a motor vehicle on a road or other public place,
after consuming so much alcohol that the proportion of it in his breath, blood or urine exceeds the prescribed limit he is guilty of an offence.

    (2) It is a defence for a person charged with an offence under subsection (1)(b) above to prove that at the time he is alleged to have committed the offence the circumstances were such that there was no likelihood of his driving the vehicle whilst the proportion of alcohol in his breath, blood or urine remained likely to exceed the prescribed limit.

    (3) The court may, in determining whether there was such a likelihood as is mentioned in subsection (2) above, disregard any injury to him and any damage to the vehicle.

(a) Mode of trial

These offences are summary only.   **13–58**

(b) What must the prosecution prove?

The prosecution must prove that: **13–59**

— the defendant
— drove *or* attempted to drive *or* was in charge of
— a mechanically propelled vehicle
— on a road or other public place
— after consuming so much alcohol
— that the proportion in his breath, blood or urine
— exceeded the prescribed limit.

13–59.1   For issues of identification, see § 21–83 in this work.

For issues surrounding the meaning of "drive", see § 13–4 above.

The phrase "mechanically propelled vehicle" is wider than "vehicle"; again this is more fully explored in § 13–6 above. The phrase "road or other public place" has been subject to detailed consideration; this also is explored more fully in § 13–7 above.

"Consuming" has been defined more widely than just "drinking"; entry into the body by other means can also be included: *DPP v Johnson (David)* [1995] R.T.R. 9.

The proportion of alcohol can be assessed through an analysis of breath or of blood or of urine. This is provided for by s.7—see § 13–72 below.

13–60   The prescribed limit is set out in s.11(2) of the *Road Traffic Act* 1988.

in breath, the limit is 35 microgrammes of alcohol in 100 millilitres of breath

in blood, the limit is 80 milligrammes of alcohol in 100 millilitres of blood

in urine, the limit is 107 milligrammes of alcohol in 100 millilitres of urine

This limit must be exceeded before a prosecution can be commenced, *e.g.* the analysis must be at least 81mg in blood, 80 is not sufficient. In practice, the police will normally allow for a margin of error and not prosecute unless the reading is 40/92/123 or more.

If a defendant wishes to allege that the analysis showed an excess as a result of alcohol consumed after the driving, etc. had ceased but before the sample was taken, then the defendant must prove (on the balance of probabilities) both that alcohol had been consumed in those circumstances and that the amount would have been sufficient to take the reading over the limit: s.15(3) of the *Road Traffic Offenders Act* 1988. Unless the effect of the alcohol would have been obvious, expert evidence must be adduced.

(c) *Penalties*

13–61   The maximum penalty for **driving or attempting to drive** is a fine of level 5 (currently £5000) and/or six months imprisonment. There is a mandatory requirement to disqualify from driving (in the absence of special reasons) for one year (though see see § 13–178 for circumstances where that minimum is increased). On endorsement only, there will be penalty points of between 3 and 11.

The maximum penalty for **being in charge** is a fine of level 4 (currently £2500) and/or three months imprisonment. There is a discretionary requirement to disqualify from driving. On endorsement, there will be penalty points of 10.

See also the power to deprive the offender of the vehicle contained in subss.143(1), (6) and (7) of the *Powers of Criminal Courts (Sentencing) Act* 2000 (see § 13–185 below).

(d) *Sentence*

13–62   The *Magistrates' Court Sentencing Guidelines* (2003) provide that aggravating circumstances include the defendant's ability to drive being seriously impaired, causing injury, fear or damage, the occurrence of a police chase, evidence of the nature of the driving. The type of vehicle is also relevant as a possible aggravating factor, for example if the defendant was carrying passengers for reward or was driving a large goods vehicle. The fact that the defendant gave a high reading when breathalysed will also be an aggravating factor. Mitigating factors include driving in an emergency, moving a vehicle a very short distance and the fact that the level of intoxication was due to drinks being spiked.

In *R. v Shoult* [1996] 2 Cr.App.R.(S.) 234, the Court of Appeal approved the guidelines as to penalties set out by the Magistrates' Association in the equivalent of the *Magistrates' Court Sentencing Guidelines* notwithstanding the fact that each case must be judged on its won merits. However, since 1996, there has been a greater recognition that prison should be reserved for violent offences and there has also been a considerable change in the range of community sentence that are available. A community penalty should certainly be considered for the higher readings or for a second offence. Particularly appropriate may be the orders which require unpaid work and those which impose a curfew. Whilst imprisonment is possible, given that this is not an offence of violence, imprisonment should be used only rarely and only when an offender has demonstrated that they intend to continue to drive in an intoxicated state.

C. Failure to Supply a Preliminary Specimen of Breath

Road Traffic Act 1988, s.6

6.—(1) Where a constable in uniform has reasonable cause to suspect—   **13–63**

(a) that a person driving or attempting to drive or in charge of a motor vehicle on a road or other public place has alcohol in his body or has committed a traffic offence whilst the vehicle was in motion, or

(b) that a person has been driving or attempting to drive or been in charge of a motor vehicle on a road or other public place with alcohol in his body and that that person still has alcohol in his body, or

(c) that a person has been driving or attempting to drive or been in charge of a motor vehicle on a road or other public place and has committed a traffic offence whilst the vehicle was in motion,

he may, subject to section 9 of this Act, require him to provide a specimen of breath for a breath test.

(2) If an accident occurs owing to the presence of a motor vehicle on a road or other public place, a constable may, subject to section 9 of this Act, require any person who he has reasonable cause to believe was driving or attempting to drive or in charge of the vehicle at the time of the accident to provide a specimen of breath for a breath test.

(3) A person may be required under subsection (1) or subsection (2) above to provide a   **13–64** specimen either at or near the place where the requirement is made or, if the requirement is made under subsection (2) above and the constable making the requirement thinks fit, at a police station specified by the constable.

(4) A person who, without reasonable excuse, fails to provide a specimen of breath when required to do so in pursuance of this section is guilty of an offence.

(5) A constable may arrest a person without warrant if—

(a) as a result of a breath test he has reasonable cause to suspect that the proportion of alcohol in that person's breath or blood exceeds the prescribed limit, or

(b) that person has failed to provide a specimen of breath for a breath test when required to do so in pursuance of this section and the constable has reasonable cause to suspect that he has alcohol in his body,

but a person shall not be arrested by virtue of this subsection when he is at a hospital as a patient.

(6) A constable may, for the purpose of requiring a person to provide a specimen of breath under subsection (2) above in a case where he has reasonable cause to suspect that the accident involved injury to another person or of arresting him in such a case under subsection (5) above, enter (if need be by force) any place where that person is or where the constable, with reasonable cause, suspects him to be.

(7) Subsection (6) above does not extend to Scotland, and nothing in that subsection shall affect any rule of law in Scotland concerning the right of a constable to enter any premises for any purpose.

(8) In this section "traffic offence" means an offence under—

(a) any provision of Part II of the *Public Passenger Vehicles Act* 1981,

(b) any provision of the *Road Traffic Regulation Act* 1984,

(c) any provision of the *Road Traffic Offenders Act* 1988 except Part III, or

(d) any provision of this Act except Part V.

(a) *Mode of trial*

13–65   These offences are triable summarily only.

(b) *What must the prosecution prove?*

13–66   The prosecution must prove that:
— the defendant
— having been required to provide a breath specimen under this section
— failed to do so
— [without reasonable excuse].

For issues of identification, see § 21–83 in this work.

13–66.1   A person commits an offence by failing to provide this preliminary specimen of breath without reasonable excuse. The purpose of the test is to obtain an indication whether the proportion of alcohol is likely to exceed the prescribed limit.

The prosecution must prove that the test was lawfully required but was not provided. It is for the defendant to initiate the "reasonable excuse" but, once that is done, it is for the prosecution to negative that defence.

There are a number of elements that must exist before a requirement is lawfully made under this section.

1) The test must be required by a *constable in uniform* where the reason for the requirement is that:
— the constable has reasonable cause to **suspect** that
— a person who is driving/attempting to drive/in charge of
— a motor vehicle (*note: not a "mechanically propelled vehicle"*)
— on a road or other place
— either
— has alcohol in his body (s.6(2)) or
— has committed a traffic offence whilst the vehicle was in motion (s.6(4)).

Similarly where the constable in uniform has reasonable cause to suspect that the person *has been* driving/attempting to drive/in charge of a motor vehicle with adjustments to reflect the fact that the driving, etc. has ceased: s.6(3).

2) The test may be required by a *constable* where the reason for the requirement is that:
— an accident has occurred
— owing to the presence of a motor vehicle on a road or other public place
— and the constable has reasonable cause to **believe**
— that the person was driving/in charge at the time of the accident (s.6(5)).

13–67   The test must be taken at or near the place where the requirement is made save that, where the requirement arises from an accident as in 2) above, the constable may require it to be taken at a police station if he thinks fit: s.6A(3). If a person is at a hospital as a patient, the requirement for a breath test may only be made after notice has been given to the medical practitioner in charge of the case. The medical practitioner may object on the grounds that either requiring or taking the test would be prejudicial to the proper care and treatment of the patient; in those circumstances, the requirement may not be made. If a requirement is made, it must be for the taking of this preliminary breath test at the hospital: s.9(1). "Hospital" is defined in s.11(2).

13–68   A "constable" is any police officer of whatever rank. The purpose of the requirement that the constable be in uniform is to ensure that he is easily identifiable as a police constable. Accordingly, not wearing a helmet but otherwise being in uniform was sufficient: *Wallwork v Giles* (1969) 114 S.J. 36.

In relation to most circumstances, the constable must have reasonable cause to "suspect" that the qualifying circumstances exist. In relation to the power following an accident, the constable must have reasonable cause to "believe" that a person was the driver etc. The distinction is a matter of degree. It is for the prosecution to prove that the officer had reasonable cause to suspect or believe.

One of the grounds for requiring a test is where there is suspicion that the person has committed a traffic offence whilst the vehicle was in motion. "Traffic offence" is defined in s.6(8) and covers a wide variety of offences.

The breath test must be taken by means of a device of a type approved by the Secre- **13–69** tary of State. A number of Breath Test (Type Approval) Orders have been made, the most recent approving the Alcosensor IV UK (1999) and the Alcolmeter SL-400B (2000). Each device will operate in different ways. In the absence of bad faith, it is not necessary to comply fully with the manufacturer's instructions (see *DPP v Carey* [1969] 3 All E.R. 1662)—the specimen must be sufficient to enable the test to be carried out and for the objective of the test to be achieved: s.1(3).

Refusal to take a test is a failure to take the test for the purposes of an offence under s.6 (see s.11(2)). Refusal can be inferred from the actions of the person concerned, such as an attempt to abscond. If a person fails to take the test in a way that complies with s.11(3), he may be arrested if the constable has reasonable cause to suspect that the person has alcohol in his body: s.6D(2). If a person takes the test and the device indicates that the level of alcohol is higher than permitted then that person also will be arrested: s.6(5)(a). A person who is at hospital as a patient may not be arrested under s.6: s.6D(3).

The range of reasonable excuses for failing to provide this specimen of breath is limited and largely restricted to circumstances where the person is physically unable to provide sufficient breath in a way that allows the test to be completed. It is not sufficient to assert that no alcohol had been consumed or that the person had not been driving, etc.

(c) *Penalty*

The maximum penalty is a fine of up to level 3 (currently £1000). It is endorsable **13–70** with 4 penalty points and disqualification is discretionary.

(d) *Sentence*

The *Magistrates' Court Sentencing Guidelines* recommend a starting point at level **13–71** A (50 per cent of weekly income). The penalty will reflect the fact that refusal to supply this sample does not of itself prevent the gathering of evidence to show whether the principal offence has been committed.

D. FAILURE TO SUPPLY A SPECIMEN FOR ANALYSIS

The requirement to provide for analysis a specimen of breath, blood or urine is the **13–71.'** key element in the gaining of evidence to support charges of driving etc. whilst under the influence of alcohol. This includes the offence of causing death by careless driving under the influence of drugs or alcohol.

If the specimen is provided, it will show the level of alcohol; if the person fails to provide a specimen without reasonable excuse, an offence is committed under s.7(6) and the maximum penalty is the same as for the substantive offence of which the person would have been liable to have been convicted if the specimen had been provided and the level of alcohol shown to be above the limit.

Road Traffic Act 1988, ss.7–11

Provision of specimen for analysis

7.—(1) In the course of an investigation into whether a person has committed an offence **13–72** under section 3A, 4 or 5 of this Act a constable may, subject to the following provisions of this section and section 9 of this Act, require him—

    (a) to provide two specimens of breath for analysis by means of a device of a type approved by the Secretary of State, or

(b) to provide a specimen of blood or urine for a laboratory test

13–73   (2) A requirement under this section to provide specimens of breath can only be made at a police station.

(3) A requirement under this section to provide a specimen of blood or urine can only be made at a police station or at a hospital; and it cannot be made at a police station unless—

> (a) the constable making the requirement has reasonable cause to believe that for medical reasons a specimen of breath cannot be provided or should not be required, or
>
> (b) at the time the requirement is made a device or a reliable device of the type mentioned in subsection (1)(a) above is not available at the police station or it is then for any other reason not practicable to use such a device there, or
>
> (bb) a device of the type mentioned in subsection (1)(a) above has been used at the police station but the constable who required the specimens of breath has reasonable cause to believe that the device has not produced a reliable indication of the proportion of alcohol in the breath of the person concerned, or
>
> (c) the suspected offence is one under section 3A or 4 of this Act and the constable making the requirement has been advised by a medical practitioner that the condition of the person required to provide the specimen might be due to some drug;

but may then be made notwithstanding that the person required to provide the specimen has already provided or been required to provide two specimens of breath.

13–74   (4) If the provision of a specimen other than a specimen of breath may be required in pursuance of this section the question whether it is to be a specimen of blood or a specimen of urine and, in the case of a specimen of blood, the question who is to be asked to take it shall be decided (subject to subsection (4A)) by the constable making the requirement.

(4A) Where a constable decides for the purposes of subsection (4) to require the provision of a specimen of blood, there shall be no requirement to provide such a specimen if—

> (a) the medical practitioner who is asked to take the specimen is of the opinion that, for medical reasons, it cannot or should not be taken; or
>
> (b) the registered health care professional who is asked to take it is of that opinion and there is no contrary opinion from a medical practitioner;

and, where by virtue of this subsection there can be no requirement to provide a specimen of blood, the constable may require a specimen of urine instead.

(5) A specimen of urine shall be provided within one hour of the requirement for its provision being made and after the provision of a previous specimen of urine.

(6) A person who, without reasonable excuse, fails to provide a specimen when required to do so in pursuance of this section is guilty of an offence.

(7) A constable must, on requiring any person to provide a specimen in pursuance of this section, warn him that a failure to provide it may render him liable to prosecution.

Specimens of blood taken from persons incapable of consenting

13–75   **7A.**—(1) A constable may make a request to a medical practitioner for him to take a specimen of blood from a person ('the person concerned') irrespective of whether that person consents if—

> (a) that person is a person from whom the constable would (in the absence of any incapacity of that person and of any objection under section 9) be entitled under section 7 to require the provision of a specimen of blood for a laboratory test;
>
> (b) it appears to that constable that that person has been involved in an accident that constitutes or is comprised in the matter that is under investigation or the circumstances of that matter;
>
> (c) it appears to that constable that that person is or may be incapable (whether or not he has purported to do so) of giving a valid consent to the taking of a specimen of blood; and
>
> (d) it appears to that constable that that person's incapacity is attributable to medical reasons.

13–76   (2) A request under this section—

> (a) shall not be made to a medical practitioner who for the time being has any

responsibility (apart from the request) for the clinical care of the person concerned; and

(b) shall not be made to a medical practitioner other than a police medical practitioner unless—

    (i) it is not reasonably practicable for the request to made to a police medical practitioner; or

    (ii) it is not reasonably practicable for such a medical practitioner (assuming him to be willing to do so) to take the specimen.

(3) It shall be lawful for a medical practitioner to whom a request is made under this section, if he thinks fit—

(a) to take a specimen of blood from the person concerned irrespective of whether that person consents; and

(b) to provide the sample to a constable.

(4) If a specimen is taken in pursuance of a request under this section, the specimen **13–77** shall not be subjected to a laboratory test unless the person from whom it was taken—

(a) has been informed that it was taken; and

(b) has been required by a constable to give his permission for a laboratory test of the specimen; and

(c) has given his permission.

(5) A constable must, on requiring a person to give his permission for the purposes of this section for a laboratory test of a specimen, warn that person that a failure to give the permission may render him liable to prosecution.

(6) A person who, without reasonable excuse, fails to give his permission for a laboratory test of a specimen of blood taken from him under this section is guilty of an offence.

(7) In this section 'police medical practitioner' means a medical practitioner who is engaged under any agreement to provide medical services for purposes connected with the activities of a police force.

Choice of specimens of breath

8.—(1) Subject to subsection (2) below, of any two specimens of breath provided by any **13–78** person in pursuance of section 7 of this Act that with the lower proportion of alcohol in the breath shall be used and the other shall be disregarded.

(2) If the specimen with the lower proportion of alcohol contains no more than 50 microgrammes of alcohol in 100 millilitres of breath, the person who provided it may claim that it should be replaced by such specimen as may be required under section 7(4) of this Act and, if he then provides such a specimen, neither specimen of breath shall be used.

(3) The Secretary of State may by regulations substitute another proportion of alcohol in the breath for that specified in subsection (2) above.

Protection for hospital patients

9.—(1) While a person is at a hospital as a patient he shall not be required to provide a speci- **13–79** men of breath for a breath test or to provide a specimen for a laboratory test unless the medical practitioner in immediate charge of his case has been notified of the proposal to make the requirement; and—

(a) if the requirement is then made, it shall be for the provision of a specimen at the hospital, but

(b) if the medical practitioner objects on the ground specified in subsection (2) below, the requirement shall not be made.

(1A) While a person is at a hospital as a patient, no specimen of blood shall be taken from him under section 7A of this Act and he shall not be required to give his permission for a laboratory test of a specimen taken under that section unless the medical practitioner in immediate charge of his case—

(a) has been notified of the proposal to take the specimen or to make the requirement; and

(b) has not objected on the ground specified in subsection (2).

(2) The ground on which the medical practitioner may object is—

(a) in a case falling within subsection (1), that the requirement or the provision of the specimen or (if one is required) the warning required by section 7(7) of this Act would be prejudicial to the proper care and treatment of the patient; and

(b) in a case falling within subsection (1A), that the taking of the specimen, the requirement or the warning required by section 7A(5) of this Act would be so prejudicial.

Detention of persons affected by alcohol or a drug

13–80   **10.**—(1) Subject to subsections (2) and (3) below, a person required to provide a specimen of breath, blood or urine may afterwards be detained at a police station until it appears to the constable that, were that person then driving or attempting to drive a mechanically propelled vehicle on a road, he would not be committing an offence under section 4 or 5 of this Act.

(2) A person shall not be detained in pursuance of this section if it appears to a constable that there is no likelihood of his driving or attempting to drive a mechanically propelled vehicle whilst his ability to drive properly is impaired or whilst the proportion of alcohol in his breath, blood or urine exceeds the prescribed limit.

(3) A constable must consult a medical practitioner on any question arising under this section whether a person's ability to drive properly is or might be impaired through drugs and must act on the medical practitioner's advice.

Interpretation

13–81   **11.**—(1) The following provisions apply for the interpretation of sections 3A to 10 of this Act.

(2) In those sections—

"breath test" means a preliminary test for the purpose of obtaining, by means of a device of a type approved by the Secretary of State, an indication whether the proportion of alcohol in a person's breath or blood is likely to exceed the prescribed limit,

"drug" includes any intoxicant other than alcohol,

"fail" includes refuse,

"hospital" means an institution which provides medical or surgical treatment for in-patients or out-patients,

"the prescribed limit" means, as the case may require—

     (a)   35 microgrammes of alcohol in 100 millilitres of breath,

     (b)   80 milligrammes of alcohol in 100 millilitres of blood, or

     (c)   107 milligrammes of alcohol in 100 millilitres of urine, or such other proportion as may be prescribed by regulations made by the Secretary of State.

"registered health care professional" means a person (other than a medical practitioner) who is—

     (a)   a registered nurse; or

     (b)   a registered member of a health care profession which is designated for the purposes of this paragraph by an order made by the Secretary of State.

13–82   (2A) A health care profession is any profession mentioned in section 60(2) of the *Health Act* 1999 (c. 8) other than the profession of practising medicine and the profession of nursing.

(2B) An order under subsection (2) shall be made by statutory instrument; and any such statutory instrument shall be subject to annulment in pursuance of a resolution of either House of Parliament.

(3) A person does not provide a specimen of breath for a breath test or for analysis unless the specimen—

     (a)   is sufficient to enable the test or the analysis to be carried out, and

     (b)   is provided in such a way as to enable the objective of the test or analysis to be satisfactorily achieved.

(4) A person provides a specimen of blood if and only if—

     (a)   he consents to the taking of such a specimen from him; and

     (b)   the specimen is taken from him by a medical practitioner or, if it is taken in a police station, either by a medical practitioner or by a registered health care professional.

(a) *Mode of trial*

13–83   These offences are triable summarily only.

(b) What must the prosecution prove?

The prosecution must prove that: **13–84**
— the defendant
— failed to provide a specimen
— [without reasonable excuse]
— when required to do so pursuant to s.7.
For issues of identification, see § 21–83.

"Fail" includes "refuse": s.11(2). A specimen of breath must be sufficient to enable the analysis to be carried out and the objective of the analysis to be satisfactorily achieved: s.11(3).

Once the possibility of a reasonable excuse is raised by the defence, it is for the pros-   **13–85**
ecution to satisfy the court beyond reasonable doubt that there was no reasonable excuse. Although it is a question of fact whether a defendant has a reasonable excuse, nonetheless it is a question of law as to whether particular circumstances can be a reasonable excuse for failing to provide a specimen. The category has been very narrowly drawn and little can justify failing or refusing to provide a specimen unless it arises out of a physical or mental inability to provide a specimen or a substantial risk to health in its provision: *R. v Lennard* [1973] R.T.R. 252.

The majority of the circumstances have arisen in connection with specimens of blood. In relation to the provision of specimens of breath, most normal people could do what is required without effort. It will, therefore, require powerful evidence to justify finding a reasonable excuse and courts have been warned not to be gullible: *DPP v Eddowes* [1991] R.T.R. 35. Most commonly, issues are likely to be raised in the context of the driver suffering from asthma. The statement of the Court of Appeal in *Lennard* that "No excuse can be adjudged a reasonable one unless a person from whom the specimen is required is physically or mentally unable to provide it or the provision of the specimen would entail a substantial risk to his health" has been re-iterated in the context of asthma sufferers in both *Eddowes* and *DPP v Curtis* [1993] R.T.R. 72. For a situation where a reasonable excuse was found, see *DPP v Falzarano* [2001] R.T.R. 14 where evidence was given by her doctor that the driver was subject to panic attacks in stressful situations. A sufficient causative link was found on the facts between the condition and the failure to provide the specimen.

In relation to specimens of urine, the obligation is to provide two specimens, the second (which is to be used for analysis) within an hour of the first. A genuine physical inability to provide the second specimen can amount to a reasonable excuse but is likely to be followed by the police utilising the power to require a specimen of blood.

Inability to understand the statutory warning that a person is liable for prosecution   **13–86**
for failing to provide a specimen for analysis may amount to a reasonable excuse where that is due to the person's limited command of English. Where it cannot be understood by the defendant because of self induced intoxication, then that cannot be a reasonable excuse.

There is no entitlement to delay the taking of a specimen to any significant extent in order to enable the suspect to receive legal advice: *Campbell v DPP* [2004] R.T.R. 5; *Kennedy v DPP* [2004] R.T.R. 6.

(c) "Required pursuant to s.7"

There needs to be an investigation into whether a person has committed an offence   **13–87**
under s.3A (causing death by careless driving under the influence of drink or drugs), s.4 (driving etc. whilst unfit through drink or drugs) or s.5 (driving etc. with excess alcohol in the body). If there is, a constable may require that person to provide a specimen for analysis. That specimen may consist of two specimens of breath (which will be analysed by a device approved by the Secretary of State) or a specimen of blood or a specimen of urine: s.7(1). The constable requiring the specimen must warn that a failure to provide the specimen may lead to prosecution: s.(7).

Specimens of *breath* can only be required at a police station: s.7(2).

Specimens of *blood* or *urine* can only be required at a police station or a hospital: s.7(3). Such a specimen can only be required at a police station in circumstances set out in s.7(3) but, if any of these circumstances exist, the request can be made even if the person has already provided (or been required to provide) two specimens of breath.

13–88 Once it is possible to require a specimen of blood or urine, it is for the constable to choose which: s.7(4). It is also for the constable to choose who is to be asked to take a sample of blood which may be a medical practitioner or a registered health care professional (as defined in s.11(2)). The person must consent to the taking of blood: s.11(4). The medical practitioner or registered health care professional may form the opinion that the specimen of blood cannot or should not be taken. In those circumstances, the requirement may not be made: s.7(4A). This still leaves the option of breath or urine. If the opinion is that of a registered health care professional, it can be overridden by a medical practitioner: s.7(4A)(b). If the person subject to the requirement is in hospital as a patient, the medical practitioner in immediate charge of the case must be notified. If he objects on the ground that either giving the statutory warning or taking the specimen would be prejudicial to the proper care and treatment of the patient, then the requirement must not be made. If it is made, the specimen must be provided at the hospital and will then be of blood or urine: s.9.

As stated above, s.11(4) requires a person to consent to the taking of a specimen of blood. Section 7A, however, provides an additional procedure where a constable considers that the subject of the requirement is incapable (for medical reasons) of giving valid consent. This procedure arises where the subject has been involved in an accident that is part of the matter under investigation and is a person from whom a specimen would normally be requested (subject to the possibility of objection under s.9—prejudicial to the proper care and treatment of the patient). In such circumstances, a constable may request a medical practitioner to take a specimen from the subject. That medical practitioner will not be a medical practitioner who has current responsibility for the clinical care of the subject and will normally be a police medical practitioner (as defined in s.7A(7)) unless it is not reasonably practicable to ask a police medical practitioner or for such a medical practitioner to take the specimen: s.7A(2). A specimen taken in this way may not be sent for analysis until the subject has been told it has been taken and has given his permission for it to be sent for analysis. He must be warned that failure to give permission may render him liable for prosecution. It is an offence to fail to give permission without reasonable excuse.

Where specimens of breath are given, the one with the lower reading is to be used: s.8(1). If that reading is 50 microgrammes or below, the person providing it may claim that it be replaced by such a specimen as may be required under s.7(4) (blood or urine—at the choice of the constable). If that alternative specimen is provided, neither breath specimens may be used: s.8(2).

(d) *Penalty (s.7 or s.7A)*

13–89 The maximum penalty for **driving or attempting to drive** is a fine of level 5 (currently £5000) and/or six months imprisonment. There is a mandatory requirement to disqualify from driving (in the absence of special reasons) for one year (though see § 13–178 for the circumstances where that minimum is increased). On endorsement only, there will be penalty points of between 3 and 11.

The maximum penalty for **being in charge** is a fine of level 4 (currently £2500) and/or three months imprisonment. There is a discretionary requirement to disqualify from driving. On endorsement, there will be penalty points of 10.

(e) *Sentence*

13–90 The *Magistrates' Court Sentencing Guidelines* (2003) provide that aggravating factors include the occurrence of a police chase, the causing of injury, fear or damage, the type of vehicle driven, any evidence of the nature of the driving and the defendant's ability to drive being seriously impaired. Mitigating factors include the defendant not being the driver of the vehicle.

See also the power to deprive the offender of the vehicle contained in s.143(1), (6) and (7) of the *Powers of Criminal Courts (Sentencing) Act* 2000 (see §§ 13–185 and 26–161 below).

E. Driving whilst Disqualified; Obtaining a Licence whilst Disqualified

A person may be disqualified from driving in a number of different ways, see § 13– **13–91** 178 below. Once disqualified *by a court*, it is an offence either to obtain a licence or to drive a vehicle. Where the disqualification is until a relevant test is passed, see § 13–180 below, the disqualified person can drive as a learner driver pending passing that test.

A person who is disqualified from holding a particular licence because of their age (s.102, *Road Traffic Act* 1988)—*e.g.* under 16 for a moped, under 17 for a motor bicycle or car)—but nonetheless drives a vehicle of the type in question, is liable to be prosecuted for the offence of driving without holding an appropriate licence: s.87, *Road Traffic Act* 1988, see below § 13–119.

The offence under s.103(1)(b) of driving whilst disqualified is an arrestable offence where a police constable has reasonable cause to suspect that a person is driving who is disqualified.

F. Obtaining Licence, or Driving, while Disqualified

Road Traffic Act 1988, s.103

Obtaining licence, or driving, while disqualified

103.—(1) A person is guilty of an offence if, while disqualified for holding or obtaining a **13–92** licence, he—
    (a) obtains a licence, or
    (b) drives a motor vehicle on a road.

(2) A licence obtained by a person who is disqualified is of no effect (or, where the disqualification relates only to vehicles of a particular class, is of no effect in relation to vehicles of that class)."

(3) A constable in uniform may arrest without warrant any person driving a motor vehicle on a road whom he has reasonable cause to suspect of being disqualified.

(4) Subsections (1) and (3) above do not apply in relation to disqualification by virtue of section 101 of this Act.

(5) Subsections (1)(b) and (3) above do not apply in relation to disqualification by virtue of section 102 of this Act.

(6) In the application of subsections (1) and (3) above to a person whose disqualification is limited to the driving of motor vehicles of a particular class by virtue of—
    (a) section 102, 117 or 117A of this Act, or
    (b) subsection (9) of section 36 of the *Road Traffic Offenders Act* 1988 (disqualification until test is passed),
the references to disqualification for holding or obtaining a licence and driving motor vehicles are references to disqualification for holding or obtaining a licence to drive and driving motor vehicles of that class."

G. Disqualification of Persons Under Age

Road Traffic Act 1988, s.101

Disqualification of persons under age

101.—(1) A person is disqualified for holding or obtaining a licence to drive a motor vehicle **13–93** of a class specified in the following Table if he is under the age specified in relation to it in the second column of the Table.

TABLE

Class of motor vehicle	Age (in years)
1. Invalid carriage	16
2. Moped	16
3. Motor bicycle	17
4. Agricultural or forestry tractor	17
5. Small vehicle	17
6. Medium-sized goods vehicle	18
7. Other motor vehicle	21

In relation to certain classes of vehicles and in certain circumstances, different ages apply (see reg.9 of the *Motor Vehicles (Driving Licence) Regulations* 1999 (SI 1999/2864). These variants are shown in the Table below against the classes as numbered in the table above.

TABLE

Class of motor vehicle	Age (in years)
3. Certain large motor bicycles	21
4. Certain agricultural or forestry tractors	16
5. Small vehicles driven by certain people	16
6. Heavier medium-sized goods vehicle	21
7. Various other motor vehicles	18

H. DISQUALIFICATION TO PREVENT DUPLICATION OF LICENCES

Road Traffic Act 1988, s.102

Disqualification to prevent duplication of licences

13–94   102. A person is disqualified for obtaining a licence authorising him to drive a motor vehicle of any class so long as he is the holder of another licence authorising him to drive a motor vehicle of that class, whether the licence is suspended or not.

(a) *What must the prosecution prove?*

Obtaining a licence whilst disqualified

13–95   — the defendant was disqualified (other than by age)
— the defendant obtained a licence

Since it is possible to obtain licences in advance of the commencement date, this offence is committed where a licence is obtained that purports to give authority to drive covering a period while the person to whom it is issued is disqualified.

Driving while disqualified

13–96   The prosecution must prove that:
— the defendant was the driver
— defendant was disqualified (other than by age)
— the vehicle was being driven
— the vehicle was a motor vehicle
— the vehicle was being driven on a road.

For issues concerning identification, see see § 13–178 below.

For drive, motor vehicle and road, see §§ 13–4 *et seq.* above. Note that this is an offence committed on a road and not on a road or other public place.

13–96.1 The obligation is on the prosecution to prove that the defendant was disqualified. There has to be cogent evidence linking the person who drove the vehicle with the person who had been disqualified. There are many ways in which evidence can be brought to prove this link. In *R. v Derwentside JJ Ex p. Heaviside* [1996] R.T.R. 384, three methods of proof were given—formal admission by the defendant, fingerprints, and then the evidence of the person in court when the defendant was disqualified. This is not an exhaustive list and the court will need to act on any cogent evidence. In *DPP v Mooney* [1997] R.T.R. 434 the defendant had made admissions to the police (but not the formal admission listed above) and this was held sufficient to support the certificate of conviction recording the order of disqualification. In *Moran v CPS* (2000) 164 J.P 562 an admission to the police and confirmation that that admission had been made by the defendant whilst giving evidence in court was held to be sufficient even without a certificate of conviction.

13–97 Once it is proved that the defendant was the driver of the motor vehicle on a road at a time when he was disqualified, then it is no defence that the defendant was unaware either of his disqualification or that the disqualification was still in force. This has meant a defendant being convicted even though his driving licence had been returned to him by the licensing authority by mistake: *R. v Bowsher* [1973] R.T.R. 202. Similarly, a defendant was convicted even where he mistakenly believed he was not driving on a "road": *R. v Miller* [1973] R.T.R. 479. Even where a disqualification is subsequently quashed on appeal, a person who drives whilst the disqualification is in force commits the offence under s.103: *R. v Thames Magistrates' Court Ex p. Levy* [1997] T.L.R. 394. A court may suspend a disqualification pending appeal, but, in the absence of such an order, the disqualification applies regardless of the outcome of the appeal.

A person from outside Great Britain can be disqualified by a court and will commit an offence under s.103(1) by driving a motor vehicle on a road while disqualified even though a licence or permit issued by another state is held. Similarly, a person disqualified elsewhere is not necessarily disqualified from driving in this country though he may be committing the offence of driving otherwise than in accordance with a licence; it will depend on the effect of the disqualification as provided for in the law of the country in which it was imposed.

(b) *Mode of Trial*

13–98 These offences are summary only.

(c) *Penalties*

13–99 For **driving while disqualified**, the maximum penalty is a fine at level 5 and/or six months imprisonment or both. It is an endorsable offence requiring 6 penalty points. Disqualification is discretionary.

For **obtaining a licence while disqualified**, the maximum penalty is a fine of level 3. The offence is not endorsable.

(d) *Sentence*

13–100 Aggravating and mitigating factors for driving whilst disqualified are set out in the *Magistrates' Court Sentencing Guidelines* (2003). They emphasise driving for remuneration, efforts being made to avoid detection, taking a long distance drive, planned, long term evasion, previous disqualified driving and recent disqualification as aggravating factors. Mitigating factors include driving in an emergency, the situation where the full period of disqualification had expired but the test had not been retaken and driving for a short distance.

There are different views on the appropriate level of sentence. There are many who consider that this offence is often a flagrant disregard for an order of the court and that imprisonment should be the starting point. Others point to the fact that people committing this offence have not committed a violent offence and, in the absence of any other offences, have not caused damage to other people or to property; accordingly, a non-custodial sentence should usually be appropriate.

Sentencing practice indicates that, during 2002, approximately 49 per cent of those convicted received a custodial sentence. Almost half of the adults sentenced to custody received a sentence of three months or less. However, from January 1, 2004, the revised *Magistrates' Court Sentencing Guidelines* changed the entry point for this offence from custody to a community sentence. Given the emphasis on a custodial sentence being reserved for dangerous, violent or seriously persistent offenders, it is likely that greater use will be made of community sentences, particularly those containing an element of punishment such as unpaid work and curfew orders.

IV. REGULATORY OFFENCES

A. Using a Motor Vehicle without Insurance

Road Traffic Act 1988, ss.143–150

13–101   The requirement for insurance to be obtained to cover some of the adverse consequences of the use of a motor vehicle reflects the need to ensure that the damage caused by a motor vehicle can be financially compensated. In addition, vehicle owners or users can choose to insure against damage to their own vehicle, however caused. Where damage is caused as a result of the use of a motor vehicle and the user is not insured, it may be possible for compensation to be obtained through the Motor Insurers Bureau (MIB): see *Wilkinson's Road Traffic Offences*, Ch.10.

Road Traffic Act 1988, ss.143–145, 147–150

Users of motor vehicles to be insured or secured against third-party risks

13–102   **143.**—(1) Subject to the provisions of this Part of this Act—

    (a) a person must not use a motor vehicle on a road or other public place unless there is in force in relation to the use of the vehicle by that person such a policy of insurance or such a security in respect of third party risks as complies with the requirements of this Part of this Act, and

    (b) a person must not cause or permit any other person to use a motor vehicle on a road [or other public place] unless there is in force in relation to the use of the vehicle by that other person such a policy of insurance or such a security in respect of third party risks as complies with the requirements of this Part of this Act.

(2) If a person acts in contravention of subsection (1) above he is guilty of an offence.

(3) A person charged with using a motor vehicle in contravention of this section shall not be convicted if he proves—

    (a) that the vehicle did not belong to him and was not in his possession under a contract of hiring or of loan,

    (b) that he was using the vehicle in the course of his employment, and

    (c) that he neither knew nor had reason to believe that there was not in force in relation to the vehicle such a policy of insurance or security as is mentioned in subsection (1) above.

(4) This Part of this Act does not apply to invalid carriages.

Exceptions from requirement of third-party insurance or security

13–103   **144.**—(1) Section 143 of this Act does not apply to a vehicle owned by a person who has deposited and keeps deposited with the Accountant General of the Supreme Court the sum of £500, 000, at a time when the vehicle is being driven under the owner's control.

    (1A) ...

(1B) ...
(2) Section 143 does not apply—
  (a) to a vehicle owned—
      (i) by the council of a county or county district in England and Wales the
          Broads Authority, the Common Council of the City of London, the council
          of a London borough, a National Park authority, the Inner London Educa-
          tion Authority, the London Fire and Emergency Planning Authority, or a
          joint authority (other than a police authority) established by Part IV of the
          Local Government Act 1985,
      (ii) ... or
      (iii) by a joint board or committee in England or Wales, or joint committee in
          Scotland, which is so constituted as to include among its members
          representatives of any such council,
          at a time when the vehicle is being driven under the owner's control,
  (b) to a vehicle owned by a police authority, at a time when it is being driven under the **13–104**
      owner's control, or to a vehicle at a time when it is being driven for police purposes by
      or under the direction of a constable, or by a person employed by a police authority,
      or
  (ba) to a vehicle owned by the Service Authority for the National Criminal Intelligence
      Service or the Service Authority for the National Crime Squad, at a time when it is be-
      ing driven under the owner's control, or to a vehicle at a time when it is being driven
      for the purposes of the body maintained by such an Authority by or under the Direc-
      tion of a constable, or by a person employed by such an Authority;
  (c) to a vehicle at a time when it is being driven on a journey to or from any place under-
      taken for salvage purposes pursuant to Part IX of the *Merchant Shipping Act* 1995,
  (d) to the use of a vehicle for the purpose of its being provided in pursuance of a direc-
      tion under section 166(2)(b) of the *Army Act* 1955 or under the corresponding provi-
      sion of the *Air Force Act* 1955,
  (da) to a vehicle owned by a health service body, as defined in section 60(7) of the *National
      Health Service and Community Care Act* 1990 by a Primary Care Trust established
      under section 16A of the *National Health Service Act* 1977[, by a Local Health
      Board established under section 16BA of that Act or by the Commission for Health
      Improvement, at a time when the vehicle is being driven under the owner's control].
  (db) to an ambulance owned by a National Health Service trust established under Part I of
      the *National Health Service and Community Care Act* 1990 or the *National
      Health Service (Scotland) Act* 1978, at a time when a vehicle is being driven under
      the owner's control
  (e) to a vehicle which is made available by the Secretary of State to any person, body or
      local authority in pursuance of section 23 or 26 of the *National Health Service Act*
      1977 at a time when it is being used in accordance with the terms on which it is so
      made available,
  (f) to a vehicle which is made available by the Secretary of State to any local authority,
      education authority or voluntary organisation in Scotland in pursuance of section 15
      or 16 of the *National Health Service (Scotland) Act* 1978 at a time when it is being
      used in accordance with the terms on which it is so made available.

Requirements in respect of policies of insurance
145.—(1) In order to comply with the requirements of this Part of this Act, a policy of insur- **13–105**
ance must satisfy the following conditions.
(2) The policy must be issued by an authorised insurer.
(3) Subject to subsection (4) below, the policy—
  (a) must insure such person, persons or classes of persons as may be specified in the
      policy in respect of any liability which may be incurred by him or them in respect
      of the death of or bodily injury to any person or damage to property caused by,
      or arising out of, the use of the vehicle on a road or other public place in Great
      Britain, and
  (aa) must, in the case of a vehicle normally based in the territory of another member
      State, insure him or them in respect of any civil liability which may be incurred
      by him or them as a result of an event related to the use of the vehicle in Great
      Britain if,—

     (i) according to the law of that territory, he or they would be required to be insured in respect of a civil liability which would arise under that law as a result of that event if the place where the vehicle was used when the event occurred were in that territory, and

    (ii) the cover required by that law would be higher than that required by paragraph (a) above, and

  (b) must, in the case of a vehicle normally based in Great Britain, insure him or them in respect of any liability which may be incurred by him or them in respect of the use of the vehicle and of any trailer, whether or not coupled, in the territory other than Great Britain and Gibraltar of each of the member States of the Communities according to—

     (i) the law on compulsory insurance against civil liability in respect of the use of vehicles of the State in whose territory the event giving rise to the liability occurred; or

    (ii) if it would give higher cover, the law which would be applicable under this Part of this Act if the place where the vehicle was used when that event occurred were in Great Britain; and

  (c) must also insure him or them in respect of any liability which may be incurred by him or them under the provisions of this Part of this Act relating to payment for emergency treatment.

13–106   (4) The policy shall not, by virtue of subsection (3)(a) above, be required—

  (a) to cover liability in respect of the death, arising out of and in the course of his employment, of a person in the employment of a person insured by the policy or of bodily injury sustained by such a person arising out of and in the course of his employment, or

  (b) to provide insurance of more than £250,000 in respect of all such liabilities as may be incurred in respect of damage to property caused by, or arising out of, any one accident involving the vehicle, or

  (c) to cover liability in respect of damage to the vehicle, or

  (d) to cover liability in respect of damage to goods carried for hire or reward in or on the vehicle or in or on any trailer (whether or not coupled) drawn by the vehicle, or

  (e) to cover any liability of a person in respect of damage to property in his custody or under his control, or

  (f) to cover any contractual liability.

    (4A) In the case of a person—

  (a) carried in or upon a vehicle, or

  (b) entering or getting on to, or alighting from, a vehicle,

the provisions of paragraph (a) of subsection (4) above do not apply unless cover in respect of the liability referred to in that paragraph is in fact provided pursuant to a requirement of the *Employers' Liability (Compulsory Insurance) Act* 1969.

    (5) "Authorised insurer" has the same meaning as in section 95.

    (6) If any person or body of persons ceases to be a member of the Motor Insurers' Bureau, that person or body shall not by virtue of that cease to be treated as an authorised insurer for the purposes of this Part of this Act or the *Road Traffic (NHS Charges) Act* 1999—

  (a) in relation to any policy issued by the insurer before ceasing to be such a member, or

  (b) in relation to any obligation (whether arising before or after the insurer ceased to be such a member) which the insurer may be called upon to meet under or in consequence of any such policy or under section 157 of this Act or section 1 of the Act of 1999 by virtue of making a payment in pursuance of such an obligation.

Issue and surrender of certificates of insurance and of security

13–107   **147.**—(1) A policy of insurance shall be of no effect for the purposes of this Part of this Act unless and until there is delivered by the insurer to the person by whom the policy is effected a certificate (in this Part of this Act referred to as a "certificate of insurance") in the prescribed form and containing such particulars of any conditions subject to which the policy is issued and of any other matters as may be prescribed.

    (2) A security shall be of no effect for the purposes of this Part of this Act unless and

until there is delivered by the person giving the security to the person to whom it is given a certificate (in this Part of this Act referred to as a "certificate of security") in the prescribed form and containing such particulars of any conditions subject to which the security is issued and of any other matters as may be prescribed.

(3) Different forms and different particulars may be prescribed for the purposes of subsection (1) or (2) above in relation to different cases or circumstances.

(4) Where a certificate has been delivered under this section and the policy or security to which it relates is cancelled by mutual consent or by virtue of any provision in the policy or security, the person to whom the certificate was delivered must, within seven days from the taking effect of the cancellation—

    (a) surrender the certificate to the person by whom the policy was issued or the security was given, or

    (b) if the certificate has been lost or destroyed, make a statutory declaration to that effect.

(5) A person who fails to comply with subsection (4) above is guilty of an offence.

Avoidance of certain exceptions to policies or securities

148.—(1) Where a certificate of insurance or certificate of security has been delivered under **13–108** section 147 of this Act to the person by whom a policy has been effected or to whom a security has been given, so much of the policy or security as purports to restrict—

    (a) the insurance of the persons insured by the policy, or

    (b) the operation of the security,

(as the case may be) by reference to any of the matters mentioned in subsection (2) below shall, as respects such liabilities as are required to be covered by a policy under section 145 of this Act, be of no effect.

(2) Those matters are—

    (a) the age or physical or mental condition of persons driving the vehicle,

    (b) the condition of the vehicle,

    (c) the number of persons that the vehicle carries,

    (d) the weight or physical characteristics of the goods that the vehicle carries,

    (e) the time at which or the areas within which the vehicle is used,

    (f) the horsepower or cylinder capacity or value of the vehicle,

    (g) the carrying on the vehicle of any particular apparatus, or

    (h) the carrying on the vehicle of any particular means of identification other than any means of identification required to be carried by or under the [*Vehicle Excise and Registration Act* 1994].

(3) Nothing in subsection (1) above requires an insurer or the giver of a security to pay any sum in respect of the liability of any person otherwise than in or towards the discharge of that liability.

(4) Any sum paid by an insurer or the giver of a security in or towards the discharge of **13–109** any liability of any person which is covered by the policy or security by virtue only of subsection (1) above is recoverable by the insurer or giver of the security from that person.

(5) A condition in a policy or security issued or given for the purposes of this Part of this Act providing—

    (a) that no liability shall arise under the policy or security, or

    (b) that any liability so arising shall cease,

in the event of some specified thing being done or omitted to be done after the happening of the event giving rise to a claim under the policy or security, shall be of no effect in connection with such liabilities as are required to be covered by a policy under section 145 of this Act.

(6) Nothing in subsection (5) above shall be taken to render void any provision in a policy or security requiring the person insured or secured to pay to the insurer or the giver of the security any sums which the latter may have become liable to pay under the policy or security and which have been applied to the satisfaction of the claims of third parties.

(7) Notwithstanding anything in any enactment, a person issuing a policy of insurance under section 145 of this Act shall be liable to indemnify the persons or classes of persons specified in the policy in respect of any liability which the policy purports to cover in the case of those persons or classes of persons.

Avoidance of certain agreements as to liability towards passengers

13–110   **149.**—(1) This section applies where a person uses a motor vehicle in circumstances such that under section 143 of this Act there is required to be in force in relation to his use of it such a policy of insurance or such a security in respect of third-party risks as complies with the requirements of this Part of this Act.

(2) If any other person is carried in or upon the vehicle while the user is so using it, any antecedent agreement or understanding between them (whether intended to be legally binding or not) shall be of no effect so far as it purports or might be held—

(a) to negative or restrict any such liability of the user in respect of persons carried in or upon the vehicle as is required by section 145 of this Act to be covered by a policy of insurance, or

(b) to impose any conditions with respect to the enforcement of any such liability of the user.

(3) The fact that a person so carried has willingly accepted as his the risk of negligence on the part of the user shall not be treated as negativing any such liability of the user.

(4) For the purposes of this section—

(a) references to a person being carried in or upon a vehicle include references to a person entering or getting on to, or alighting from, the vehicle, and

(b) the reference to an antecedent agreement is to one made at any time before the liability arose.

Insurance or security in respect of private use of vehicle to cover use under car-sharing arrangements

13–111   **150.**—(1) To the extent that a policy or security issued or given for the purposes of this Part of this Act—

(a) restricts the insurance of the persons insured by the policy or the operation of the security (as the case may be) to use of the vehicle for specified purposes (for example, social, domestic and pleasure purposes) of a non-commercial character, or

(b) excludes from that insurance or the operation of the security (as the case may be)—

(i) use of the vehicle for hire or reward, or

(ii) business or commercial use of the vehicle, or

(iii) use of the vehicle for specified purposes of a business or commercial character,

then, for the purposes of that policy or security so far as it relates to such liabilities as are required to be covered by a policy under section 145 of this Act, the use of a vehicle on a journey in the course of which one or more passengers are carried at separate fares shall, if the conditions specified in subsection (2) below are satisfied, be treated as falling within that restriction or as not falling within that exclusion (as the case may be).

(2) The conditions referred to in subsection (1) above are—

(a) the vehicle is not adapted to carry more than eight passengers and is not a motor cycle,

(b) the fare or aggregate of the fares paid in respect of the journey does not exceed the amount of the running costs of the vehicle for the journey (which for the purposes of this paragraph shall be taken to include an appropriate amount in respect of depreciation and general wear), and

(c) the arrangements for the payment of fares by the passenger or passengers carried at separate fares were made before the journey began.

(3) Subsections (1) and (2) above apply however the restrictions or exclusions described in subsection (1) are framed or worded.

(4) In subsections (1) and (2) above "fare" and "separate fares" have the same meaning as in section 1(4) of the *Public Passenger Vehicles Act* 1981.

(a) *What must the prosecution prove?*

13–112   The prosecution must prove that the defendant used (or caused or permitted another person to use) a vehicle on a road or other public place. Having done that, it is for the defence to prove (on the balance of probabilities) that the use was covered by insurance or a relevant security.

For identification, see § 21–83 above.
For use and for causing or permitting use, see §§ 13–9 and 13–10 above.
For vehicle, see § 13–11 above (note the exemption for invalid carriages: s.143(4)).
For road or other public place, see § 13–7 above.

(b) Mode of trial

This offence is summary only. Proceedings for an offence must be commenced within **13–113** six months of the offence coming to the knowledge of the prosecutor providing that is no more than three years from the date the offence was committed.

(c) Insurance

The obligation is to be insured against third party risks. The insurance in force may **13–114** be limited so as to restrict the circumstances in which the vehicle is used; this may be by reference to the purposes for which the vehicle is being used or the person who is using it. It is not possible for the insurance to exclude certain things—see ss.145, 148 and 150.

Certain vehicles can be used without insurance, generally vehicles owned and being used for the purposes of specified national or local government functions: s.144. Crown vehicles are also exempt. The situations most commonly encountered are vehicles owned by a County Council at a time when the vehicle is being driven under the control of the owner (s.144(2)(a)) and vehicles owned by a police authority and driven under the control of the authority or any vehicle when it is being driven for police purposes by or under the direction of a constable or employee of a police authority: s.144(2)(b).

To satisfy the provisions of s.143, an insurance policy does not become effective until a certificate is delivered to the person taking out the cover. The certificate must be in the prescribed form. Those issuing the certificate must keep a record and, on request, must give details without charge to the Secretary of State or to any Chief Officer of Police. If a defendant who has lost his copy of the certificate is facing difficulties obtaining a duplicate, a formal police request will need to be complied with by the insurance company.

(d) Defence

A special defence is provided for those using in the course of their employment **13–115** vehicles they do not own whilst unaware of the lack of cover: s.143(3).

It is for the defendant to prove (on the balance of probabilities) that:
— the vehicle did not belong to him
— that he was using the vehicle in the course of his employment
— he did not know (and had no reason to believe) that the vehicle was not insured.

(e) Penalty

The maximum penalty is a fine up to a maximum of level 5 (£5000). It is an endors- **13–116** able offence with a range of 6–8 penalty points. Disqualification is discretionary.

(f) Sentence

The offence can be committed in a very wide range of circumstances from the consci- **13–117** entious individual who (after years of proper insurance) overlooked the need to renew or believed on reasonable (but mistaken) grounds that the use was covered to the individual who deliberately chooses not to insure, probably because he perceives the cost of insurance to be so high and the risk of detection so low that it is a risk worth taking.

The dilemma for a court is that the financial penalty it could legitimately impose on the relatively feckless offender is probably substantially below the cost of insurance. However, this is a regulatory offence; the consequence for any victim can be great but it is not in itself an offence that is dangerous or violent.

The *Magistrates' Court Sentencing Guidelines* identify as aggravating factors deliberate driving without insurance, giving false details, the type of vehicle (use of a LGV, HGV, PCV, PSV or taxi or private hire vehicle warranting a higher penalty) and no reference to insurance ever having been held. Mitigating factors include an accidental oversight, a genuine mistake, responsibility for insurance resting with another (*e.g.* the parent, owner, lender, hirer) and the type of vehicle (smaller vehicles, *e.g.* moped, warranting less severe penalties). The starting point for consideration is whether discharge or a fine is appropriate. It is most likely to be a financial penalty. It should be noted that the user may have been offered a fixed penalty and that will in the sum of £200.

13–118   In addition to a financial penalty, a court may impose a period of disqualification, perhaps for a relatively short period depending on the circumstances. However, the recurring dilemma for courts is that the cost of insurance can outweigh any financial penalty that can realistically be paid within one year. In those circumstances, the court may wish to consider a community penalty containing a punishment element such as unpaid work or a curfew order.

B. Using a Vehicle without Holding a Driving Licence

Road Traffic Act 1988, s.87

Drivers of motor vehicles to have driving licences

13–119   **87.**—(1) It is an offence for a person to drive on a road a motor vehicle of any class otherwise than in accordance with a licence authorising him to drive a motor vehicle of that class.

(2) It is an offence for a person to cause or permit another person to drive on a road a motor vehicle of any class otherwise than in accordance with a licence authorising that other person to drive a motor vehicle of that class.

(a) *Mode of Trial*

13–120   This offence is triable summarily only.

(b) *What must the prosecution prove?*

13–121   — the defendant
— drove
— on a road
— a motor vehicle

The **defence** must then show (on the balance of probabilities) that that driving was in accordance with a licence granted to the defendant.

For issues of identification, see § 21–83 in this work.

For issues surrounding the meaning of "drive", see § 13–4.

The phrase "mechanically propelled vehicle" is wider than "vehicle"; see § 13–6.

The phrase "road or other public place" has been subject to detailed consideration; see § 13–7, above.

13–122   The offence is committed by driving a motor vehicle whilst not holding a licence authorising the use of that type of vehicle. Licences may be restricted by virtue of the type of vehicle able to be used or by the age of the person entitled to use a particular type of vehicle. A full licence will only be issued following the passing of an appropriate test (both theory and practical); in most circumstances, a provisional licence can be issued enabling a person to use a vehicle in controlled circumstances (usually involving supervision by a full licence holder aged over 21).

Different tests are administered for different vehicles; for instance, a person holding a full driving licence authorising the use of a motor car and small goods vehicles will need to pass a separate test before being authorised to drive medium sized goods vehicles or small buses.

All licences have an age restriction; a moped can be used by a person 16 or over, a motor car or motor bicycle by a person aged 17 or over, most HGV licences require the driver to be aged at least 21 (see § 13–93 above for further detail). Full licences are granted until the age of 70 (except where the presence of disease or disability requires a shorter period). Thereafter, they may be renewed for three year periods. If the licence is issued as a photocard, then that photocard must be surrendered at least every 10 years in order that a more recent photograph can be incorporated.

A person who drives a motor vehicle whilst under the age at which a licence could be **13–123** granted (*e.g.* 15 year old driving a car) commits an offence under this section rather than that of driving whilst disqualified under s.103. Although a person below the set age is disqualified from holding or obtaining a licence: s.101. Section.103(4) provides that they do not commit an offence under that section by driving, see § 13–91 above.

The most complex conditions apply to provisional licence holders. In respect of motorcycles, there are limits on the size of the engine in the vehicle which can be used (generally "learner motor cycles") and "L" plates must be displayed. Passengers may not be carried. A person who fails to comply with those obligations commits an offence under this section. In respect of other vehicles, there is a general requirement that provisional licence holders be supervised by a "qualified driver" present in the vehicle. Generally, this will be a full licence holder for that class of vehicle who is over 21 years of age and has held that type of licence for at least three years. Whilst any "qualified driver" can supervise or teach a provisional licence holder, in relation to motor cars, instruction for money or money's worth can only be given by a person registered or licensed under Pt V of the *Road Traffic Act* 1988.

There are further extensive provisions governing the entitlement of drivers from abroad—see *Wilkinson's Road Traffic Offences*, Ch.11.

(c) *Sentence*

The maximum penalty is a fine of level 3 (£1000). The *Magistrates' Court Sentenc-* **13–124** *ing Guidelines* (2003) provide that the starting point for this offence is guideline fine A (50 per cent of the defendant's weekly income).

It is endorsable (and thus disqualifiable) in some circumstances with a range of 3–6 penalty points.

The offence is endorsable where the driving did not accord with any licence that could have been granted to the driver. Thus, a full licence holder whose licence had expired but who would have been entitled to have it renewed and who drove a vehicle authorised by that licence would not be subject to endorsement or disqualification. However, a provisional licence holder who fails to display "L" plates or to be properly supervised would be liable to endorsement. Similarly, a person who drives a vehicle for which a licence could not have been issued (*e.g.* a 15 year old driving a car) is subject to endorsement. Some full licences give provisional entitlement for other classes of vehicle. A person driving a vehicle in circumstances which are only covered by the provisional entitlement who fails to comply with the conditions of the provisional licence will be liable to endorsement.

C. FORGERY OF DOCUMENTS

With the increased emphasis on safety which affects both the testing of vehicles and **13–125** the licensing of their users, there will be a risk that some will seek to avoid the law by fraudulent means. These sections provide a series of offences designed to penalise those who make misrepresentations (whether or not in documentary form) and those who create documents that are false.

Road Traffic Act 1988, ss.173–174, 176

Forgery of documents, etc

173.—(1) A person who, with intent to deceive—　　　　　　　　　　　　　　**13–126**
　　　(a) forges, alters or uses a document or other thing to which this section applies, or

(b) lends to, or allows to be used by, any other person a document or other thing to which this section applies, or

(c) makes or has in his possession any document or other thing so closely resembling a document or other thing to which this section applies as to be calculated to deceive,

is guilty of an offence.

13–127   (2) This section applies to the following documents and other things—

(a) any licence under any Part of this Act or, in the case of a licence to drive, any counterpart of such a licence,

(aa) any counterpart of a Community licence,

(b) any test certificate, goods vehicle test certificate, plating certificate, certificate of conformity or Minister's approval certificate (within the meaning of Part II of this Act),

(c) any certificate required as a condition of any exception prescribed under section 14 of this Act,

(cc) any seal required by regulations made under section 41 of this Act with respect to speed limiters,.

(d) any plate containing particulars required to be marked on a vehicle by regulations under section 41 of this Act or containing other particulars required to be marked on a goods vehicle by sections 54 to 58 of this Act or regulations under those sections,

(dd) any document evidencing the appointment of an examiner under section 66A of this Act,

(e) any records required to be kept by virtue of section 74 of this Act,

(f) any document which, in pursuance of section 89(3) of this Act, is issued as evidence of the result of a test of competence to drive,

(ff) any certificate provided for by regulations under section 97(3A) of this Act relating to the completion of a training course for motor cyclists,

(g) any certificate under section 133A or any badge or certificate prescribed by regulations made by virtue of section 135 of this Act,

(h) any certificate of insurance or certificate of security under Part VI of this Act,

(j) any document produced as evidence of insurance in pursuance of Regulation 6 of the *Motor Vehicles (Compulsory Insurance) (No. 2) Regulations* 1973,

(k) any document issued under regulations made by the Secretary of State in pursuance of his power under section 165(2)(a) of this Act to prescribe evidence which may be produced in lieu of a certificate of insurance or a certificate of security,

(l) any international road haulage permit, and

(m) a certificate of the kind referred to in section 34B(1) of the *Road Traffic Offenders Act* 1988."

(3) In the application of this section to England and Wales "forges" means makes a false document or other thing in order that it may be used as genuine.

(4) In this section "counterpart" and "Community licence" have the same meanings as in Part III of this Act.

False statements and withholding material information

13–128   174.—(1) A person who knowingly makes a false statement for the purpose—

(a) of obtaining the grant of a licence under any Part of this Act to himself or any other person, or

(b) of preventing the grant of any such licence, or

(c) of procuring the imposition of a condition or limitation in relation to any such licence, or

(d) of securing the entry or retention of the name of any person in the register of approved instructors maintained under Part V of this Act, or

(dd) of obtaining the grant to any person of a certificate under section 133A of this Act, or

(e) of obtaining the grant of an international road haulage permit to himself or any other person,

is guilty of an offence.

(2) A person who, in supplying information or producing documents for the purposes

either of sections 53 to 60 and 63 of this Act or of regulations made under sections 49 to 51, 61, 62 and 66(3) of this Act—

(a) makes a statement which he knows to be false in a material particular or recklessly makes a statement which is false in a material particular, or

(b) produces, provides, sends or otherwise makes use of a document which he knows to be false in a material particular or recklessly produces, provides, sends or otherwise makes use of a document which is false in a material particular,

is guilty of an offence.

(3) A person who—　　　　　　　　　　　　　　　　　　　　　　　　　**13–129**

(a) knowingly produces false evidence for the purposes of regulations under section 66(1) of this Act, or

(b) knowingly makes a false statement in a declaration required to be made by the regulations,

is guilty of an offence.

(4) A person who—

(a) wilfully makes a false entry in any record required to be made or kept by regulations under section 74 of this Act, or

(b) with intent to deceive, makes use of any such entry which he knows to be false,

is guilty of an offence.

(5) A person who makes a false statement or withholds any material information for the purpose of obtaining the issue—

(a) of a certificate of insurance or certificate of security under Part VI of this Act, or

(b) of any document issued under regulations made by the Secretary of State in pursuance of his power under section 165(2)(a) of this Act to prescribe evidence which may be produced in lieu of a certificate of insurance or a certificate of security,

is guilty of an offence.

Power to seize articles in respect of which offences under sections 173 to 175 may have been committed

176.—(1) If a constable has reasonable cause to believe that a document produced to him—　**13–130**

(a) in pursuance of section 137 of this Act, or

(b) in pursuance of any of the preceding provisions of this Part of this Act,

is a document in relation to which an offence has been committed under section 173, 174 or 175 of this Act or under section 115 of the *Road Traffic Regulation Act* 1984, he may seize the document.

(1A) Where a licence to drive or a counterpart of any such licence or of any Community licence may be seized by a constable under subsection (1) above, he may also seize the counterpart, the licence to drive or the Community licence (as the case may be) produced with it.

(2) When a document is seized under subsection (1) above, the person from whom it was taken shall, unless—

(a) the document has been previously returned to him, or

(b) he has been previously charged with an offence under any of those sections,

be summoned before a magistrates' court or, in Scotland, the sheriff to account for his possession of the document.

(3) The court or sheriff must make such order respecting the disposal of the document and award such costs as the justice of the case may require.

(3A) An order under subsection (3) above respecting the disposal of any such licence or Community licence to drive or a counterpart of any such licence or Community licence may include an order respecting the disposal of any document seized under subsection (1A) above.

(4) If a constable, an examiner appointed under section 66A of this Act has reasonable cause to believe that a document or plate carried on a motor vehicle or by the driver of the vehicle is a document or plate to which this subsection applies, he may seize it.

For the purposes of this subsection the power to seize includes power to detach from a vehicle.

(5) Subsection (4) above applies to a document or plate in relation to which an offence　**13–131** has been committed under sections 173, 174 or 175 of this Act in so far as they apply—

(a) to documents evidencing the appointment of examiners under section 66A of this Act, or

(b) to goods vehicle test certificates, plating certificates, certificates of conformity or Minister's approval certificates (within the meaning of Part II of this Act), or

(c) to plates containing plated particulars (within the meaning of that Part) or containing other particulars required to be marked on goods vehicles by sections 54 to 58 of this Act or regulations made under them, or

(d) to records required to be kept by virtue of section 74 of this Act, or

(e) to international road haulage permits.

(6) When a document or plate is seized under subsection (4) above, either the driver or owner of the vehicle shall, if the document or plate is still detained and neither of them has previously been charged with an offence in relation to the document or plate under section 173, 174 or 175 of this Act, be summoned before a magistrates' court or, in Scotland, the sheriff to account for his possession of, or the presence on the vehicle of, the document or plate.

(7) The court or sheriff must make such order respecting the disposal of the document or plate and award such costs as the justice of the case may require.

(8) In this section "counterpart" and "Community licence" have the same meanings as in Part III of this Act.

(a) *Mode of trial*

13–132   These offences are triable either way. General mode of trial considerations are listed in the *Practice Direction (Criminal Proceedings: Consolidation)*. In relation to offences of fraud, there is a presumption towards summary trial. Factors that might suggest trial on indictment include breach of trust by a person in a position of *substantial* authority or in whom a high degree of trust is placed, conducting (or disguising) the fraud in a sophisticated manner, organised gang and victim particularly vulnerable.

(b) *What must the prosecution prove?*

13–133   There are a range of elements: in each case there must be an intent to deceive and the offences must be committed in relation to a document or similar to which the section applies—these are listed in s.173(2). Perhaps the most common subjects of the offence are test and insurance certificates but a wide range of other documents are included.

If the document is one to which the section applies and if there is an intent to deceive, an offence is committed either by creating a document intended to deceive or using such a document in one way or another.

(c) *Creating a document or other thing*

13–134   This can be by forgery, by altering or by creating something that so closely resembles the real thing (without actually copying the real thing) as to be calculated to deceive. "Forges" is defined in s.173(3) as meaning "making ... in order that it may be used as genuine".

(d) *Using a document etc*

13–135   This can be straightforward use but also includes lending a document or thing to another person (or at least allowing them to use it) or having in your possession a document so closely resembling the real things as to be calculated to deceive.

For an offence of "using" under s.173(1)(a), the use must be of one of the specified documents. If it is a forgery or an altered document, it may be that the prosecution would need to be under s.173(1)(c): see *Holloway v Brown* [1978] R.T.R. 537. However, that strict interpretation may be less likely now.

(e) *Making false statements or withholding material information*

13–136   It is an offence to make false statements in order to secure one of four effects set out

in s.175(1) or in the circumstances set out in s.175(2) or (3) or (5). The prosecution must prove that:
— the defendant
— knowingly (or, in relation to s.174(2), recklessly)
— made a false statement
— for one of the specified purposes.
For issues of identification, see § 21–83 in this work.

(f) Issuing false documents

It is also an offence to issue a document of certain specified types in the knowledge **13–137** that it is false in a material particular.

(g) Penalties

Forgery, etc. of documents (under s.173(1)) are either way offences. At the Crown **13–138** Court, they are punishable by up to two years imprisonment and/or an unlimited fine. In a magistrates' court, the maximum punishment is a fine of level 5. The offences are not endorsable.

The making of false statements under s.174 and the issue of false documents under s.175 are punishable only in a magistrates' court with a maximum fine of level 4 (currently £2,500).

(h) Sentencing

These offences are punishable by imprisonment only in the Crown Court. In most **13–139** instances, a financial penalty will result but, for the more serious offences, a community penalty would be appropriate particularly one containing a significant punishment element. Since these are not violent offences, a custodial sentence would only be appropriate where there has been a sophisticated and substantial organisation or a very substantial breach of trust.

D. Traffic Signs

Road Traffic Act 1988, s.36

It is an offence to fail to comply with traffic signs properly placed. This section states **13–140** the law generally and then deals specifically with the four signs that, on conviction, are endorsable.

Road Traffic Act 1988, s.36

Drivers to comply with traffic signs
 36.—(1) Where a traffic sign, being a sign— **13–140.1**
   (a) of the prescribed size, colour and type, or
   (b) of another character authorised by the Secretary of State under the provisions in that behalf of the *Road Traffic Regulation Act* 1984,
has been lawfully placed on or near a road, a person driving or propelling a vehicle who fails to comply with the indication given by the sign is guilty of an offence.
   (2) A traffic sign shall not be treated for the purposes of this section as having been lawfully placed unless either—
   (a) the indication given by the sign is an indication of a statutory prohibition, restriction or requirement, or
   (b) it is expressly provided by or under any provision of the Traffic Acts that this section shall apply to the sign or to signs of a type of which the sign is one;
and, where the indication mentioned in paragraph (a) of this subsection is of the general nature only of the prohibition, restriction or requirement to which the sign relates, a person shall not be convicted of failure to comply with the indication unless he has failed to comply with the prohibition, restriction or requirement to which the sign relates.

(3) For the purposes of this section a traffic sign placed on or near a road shall be deemed—

    (a) to be of the prescribed size, colour and type, or of another character authorised by the Secretary of State under the provisions in that behalf of the *Road Traffic Regulation Act* 1984, and

    (b) (subject to subsection (2) above) to have been lawfully so placed,

unless the contrary is proved.

(4) Where a traffic survey of any description is being carried out on or in the vicinity of a road, this section applies to a traffic sign by which a direction is given—

    (a) to stop a vehicle,

    (b) to make it proceed in, or keep to, a particular line of traffic, or

    (c) to proceed to a particular point on or near the road on which the vehicle is being driven or propelled,

being a direction given for the purposes of the survey (but not a direction requiring any person to provide any information for the purposes of the survey).

(5) Regulations made by the Secretary of State for the Environment, Transport and the Regions, the Secretary of State for Wales and the Secretary of State for Scotland acting jointly may specify any traffic sign for the purposes of column 5 of the entry in Schedule 2 to the *Road Traffic Offenders Act* 1988 relating to offences under this section (offences committed by failing to comply with certain signs involve discretionary disqualification).

(a) *What the prosecution must prove*

13–141   The prosecution must prove that:

— the defendant

— drove or propelled

— a vehicle

— failed to comply with a sign.

Although a sign has to be lawfully placed and to be of a prescribed size etc., there is a presumption that that is the case unless the contrary is proved: s.36(3). Thus it is for the defence to prove (on the balance of probabilities) that a sign was not lawfully placed or was not of the prescribed size, colour, type or character (for more detail, see *Wilkinson*, Pt 2, s.B83).

(b) *Mode of trial*

13–142   This offence is summary only.

(c) *Sentencing*

13–142.1   Contravention of most traffic signs is punishable by a fine only—up to level 3 (£1000). However, in respect of a small number of signs, it is endorsable with three penalty points and thus subject to discretionary disqualification. The relevant signs are traffic lights, pedestrian crossings, double white lines, stop signs.

E. SPEEDING

Road Traffic Regulation Act 1984, ss.81, 82, 84–87, 89

General speed limit for restricted roads

13–143   81.—(1) It shall not be lawful for a person to drive a motor vehicle on a restricted road at a speed exceeding 30 miles per hour.

(2) The Ministers acting jointly may by order made by statutory instrument and approved by a resolution of each House of Parliament increase or reduce the rate of speed fixed by subsection (1) above, either as originally enacted or as varied under this subsection.

What roads are restricted roads

13–143.1   82.—(1) Subject to the provisions of this section and of section 84(3) of this Act, a road is a restricted road for the purposes of section 81 of this Act if—

(a) in England and Wales, there is provided on it a system of street lighting furnished by means of lamps placed not more than 200 yards apart;

(b) in Scotland, there is provided on it a system of carriageway lighting furnished by means of lamps placed not more than 185 metres apart and the road is of a classification or type specified for the purposes of this subsection in regulations made by the Secretary of State.

(2) The traffic authority for a road may direct—

(a) that the road which is a restricted road for the purposes of section 81 of this Act shall cease to be a restricted road for those purposes, or

(b) that the road which is not a restricted road for those purposes shall become a restricted road for those purposes.

(3) A special road is not a restricted road for the purposes of section 81 on or after the date declared by the traffic authority, by notice published in the prescribed manner, to be the date on which the special road, or the relevant part of the special road, is open for use as a special road.

Speed limits on roads other than restricted roads

84.—(1) An order made under this subsection as respects any road may prohibit—   **13–144**

(a) the driving of motor vehicles on that road at a speed exceeding that specified in the order,

(b) the driving of motor vehicles on that road at a speed exceeding that specified in the order during periods specified in the order, or

(c) the driving of motor vehicles on that road at a speed exceeding the speed for the time being indicated by traffic signs in accordance with the order.

(1A) An order made by virtue of subsection (1)(c) above may—

(a) make provision restricting the speeds that may be indicated by traffic signs or the periods during which the indications may be given, and

(b) provide for the indications to be given only in such circumstances as may be determined by or under the order;

but any such order must comply with regulations made under subsection (1B) below, except where the Secretary of State authorises otherwise in a particular case.

(1B) The Secretary of State may make regulations governing the provision which may be made by orders of local authorities under subsection (1)(c) above, and any such regulations may in particular—

(a) prescribe the circumstances in which speed limits may have effect by virtue of an order,

(b) prescribe the speed limits which may be specified in an order, and

(c) make transitional provision and different provision for different cases.

(2) The power to make an order under subsection (1) is exercisable by the traffic authority, who shall before exercising it in any case give public notice of their intention to do so.

(3) While an order made by virtue of subsection (1)(a) above is in force as respects a road, that road shall not be a restricted road for the purposes of section 81 of this Act.

(4) This section does not apply to any part of a special road which is open for use as a special road.

(5) Section 68(1)(c) of this Act shall apply to any order made under subsection (1) above.

(6) Any reference in a local Act to roads subject to a speed limit shall, unless the contrary intention appears, be treated as not including a reference to roads subject to a speed limit imposed only by virtue of subsection (1)(b) or (c) above.

Traffic signs for indicating speed restrictions

85.—(1) For the purpose of securing that adequate guidance is given to drivers of motor   **13–145**
vehicles as to whether any, and if so what, limit of speed is to be observed on any road, it shall be the duty of the Secretary of State, in the case of a road for which he is the traffic authority, to erect and maintain traffic signs in such positions as may be requisite for that purpose.

(2) In the case of any other road, it is the duty of the local traffic authority—

(a) to erect and maintain traffic signs in such positions as may be requisite in order to give effect to general or other directions given by the Secretary of State for the purpose mentioned in subsection (1) above, and

(b) to alter or remove traffic signs as may be requisite in order to give effect to such directions, either in consequence of the making of an order by the Secretary of State or otherwise.

(3) If a local traffic authority makes default in executing any works required for the performance of the duty imposed on them by subsection (2) above, the Secretary of State may himself execute the works; and the expense incurred by him in doing so shall be recoverable by him from the local traffic authority and, in England or Wales, shall be so recoverable summarily as a civil debt.

(4) Where no such system of street or carriageway lighting as is mentioned in section 82(1) is provided on a road, but a limit of speed is to be observed on the road, a person shall not be convicted of driving a motor vehicle on the road at a speed exceeding the limit unless the limit is indicated by means of such traffic signs as are mentioned in subsection (1) or subsection (2) above.

13–146   (5) In any proceedings for a contravention of section 81 of this Act, where the proceedings relate to driving on a road provided with such a system of street or carriageway lighting, evidence of the absence of traffic signs displayed in pursuance of this section to indicate that the road is not a restricted road for the purposes of that section shall be evidence that the road is a restricted road for those purposes.

(6) Where by regulations made under section 17(2) of this Act a limit of speed is to be observed, then, if it is to be observed—

    (a) on all special roads, or

    (b) on all special roads provided for the use of particular classes of traffic, or

    (c) on all special roads other than special roads of such description as may be specified in the regulations, or

    (d) as mentioned in paragraph (a), (b) or (c) above except for such lengths of special road as may be so specified,

this section shall not apply in relation to that limit (but without prejudice to its application in relation to any lower limit of maximum speed or, as the case may be, any higher limit of minimum speed, required by any such regulations to be observed on any specified length of any specified special road).

(7) The power to give general directions under subsection (2) above shall be exercisable by statutory instrument

Speed limits for particular classes of vehicles

13–147   **86.**—(1) It shall not be lawful for a person to drive a motor vehicle of any class on a road at a speed greater than the speed specified in Schedule 6 to this Act as the maximum speed in relation to a vehicle of that class.

(2) Subject to subsections (4) and (5) below, the Secretary of State may by regulations vary, subject to such conditions as may be specified in the regulations, the provisions of that Schedule.

(3) Regulations under this section may make different provision as respects the same class of vehicles in different circumstances.

(5) The Secretary of State shall not have power under this section to vary the speed limit imposed by section 81 of this Act.

(6) The Secretary of State shall not have power under this section to impose a speed limit, as respects driving on roads which are not restricted roads for the purposes of section 81 of this Act, on a vehicle which—

    (a) is constructed solely for the carriage of passengers and their effects;

    (b) is not adapted to carry more than 8 passengers exclusive of the driver;

    (c) is neither a heavy motor car nor an invalid carriage;

    (d) is not drawing a trailer; and

    (e) is fitted with pneumatic tyres on all its wheels.

Exemption of fire brigade, ambulance and police vehicles from speed limits

13–148   **87.** No statutory provision imposing a speed limit on motor vehicles shall apply to any vehicle on an occasion when it is being used for fire brigade, ambulance or police purposes, if the observance of that provision would be likely to hinder the use of the vehicle for the purpose for which it is being used on that occasion.

Speeding offences generally

13–149   **89.**—(1) A person who drives a motor vehicle on a road at a speed exceeding a limit imposed by or under any enactment to which this section applies shall be guilty of an offence.

(2) A person prosecuted for such an offence shall not be liable to be convicted solely on the evidence of one witness to the effect that, in the opinion of the witness, the person prosecuted was driving the vehicle at a speed exceeding a specified limit.

(3) The enactments to which this section applies are—
   (a) any enactment contained in this Act except section 17(2);
   (b) section 2 of the *Parks Regulation (Amendment) Act* 1926; and
   (c) any enactment not contained in this Act, but passed after 1st September 1960, whether before or after the passing of this Act.

(4) If a person who employs other persons to drive motor vehicles on roads publishes or issues any time-table or schedule, or gives any directions, under which any journey, or any stage or part of any journey, is to be completed within some specified time, and it is not practicable in the circumstances of the case for that journey (or that stage or part of it) to be completed in the specified time without the commission of such an offence as is mentioned in subsection (1) above, the publication or issue of the time-table or schedule, or the giving of the directions, may be produced as prima facie evidence that the employer procured or (as the case may be) incited the persons employed by him to drive the vehicles to commit such an offence.

(a) *What must the prosecution prove?*

— the defendant   **13–150**
— drove
— a motor vehicle
— on a road (note only "road" not "other public place")
— at a speed
— exceeding a limit imposed by or under an enactment to which this section applies

(b) *Mode of Trial*

This offence is summary only.   **13–151**
A prosecution must be initiated within six months.

(c) *Warning of intended prosecution*

By virtue of Sch.1 to the *Road Traffic Offenders Act* 1988, the prosecution must   **13–152** have complied with the requirements to give notice of intended prosecution: *Road Traffic Offenders Act* 1988, s.1. Unless an accident has occurred of which the driver was aware (*Road Traffic Offenders Act* 1988, s.2(1)), the driver must receive warning of prosecution within 14 days of the offence. This warning may be given at the time of the offence, by service of the summons (or copy of a charge sheet) within 14 days of the offence or by the prosecutor sending notice to the driver or the registered keeper of the vehicle within 14 days. Where the notice is by service of the summons, that must take place within the 14 days. Where the notification is by notice, it is only necessary for that to be sent within the 14 days. However, by virtue of s.2(3) of the Act, failure to comply with these requirements is not to be a bar to conviction where the name and address of the driver or the registered keeper could not have been ascertained by the exercise of reasonable diligence in time to comply with the requirements of the section. Similarly where the accused contributed to the failure by his own conduct—perhaps by leaving the scene or not registering the vehicle correctly.

For further information, refer to *Wilkinson's Road Traffic Offences*, Ch.2.

(d) *Limits and exceptions*

Limits can apply to roads or to different types of vehicle and care must be taken   **13–153** regarding both factors. Although, by s.89(2), the evidence of one witness is not sufficient for the defendant to be convicted, a wide range of devices have been developed for producing supporting evidence ranging from the humble speedometer to sophisticated radar and camera devices.

The principle exemption is contained in s.87 and exempts vehicles used for "fire brigade, ambulance or police purposes" where adherence to the speed limit would be "likely to hinder" the use of the vehicle on that occasion. The vehicle does not have to be an ambulance or a fire engine, etc. but it both must be being used for the purposes specified and adherence to the speed limit must hinder the use of the vehicle on that occasion. Thus, bringing a human organ from one part of the country to another for use in a transplant operation where speed is of the essence is likely to meet the criteria. The exemption is only from speed limits—there is still the obligation to drive with due care and attention etc.

(e) *Penalty*

13–154   Exceeding the speed limit is generally subject to a maximum fine of level 3; the exception is where the speed limit exceeded is the overall maximum on a motorway when it becomes level 4 (currently £2,500). The level of financial penalty (and the number of penalty points) will generally vary by reference to the speed and the proportion by which it exceeded the limit. Thus, exceeding a 30 mph limit by 15 mph will be more serious than exceeding a 60 mph limit by the same amount. Also relevant as aggravating factors will be the type of vehicle (LGV, HGV, PCV or taxi/private hire vehicle), the location, time of day and visibility at the time of the offence, serious risk taken and the fact that the defendant was towing a caravan or trailer at the time of the offence. Mitigating factors include driving in an emergency. The starting point is generally a fine.

Many offences are dealt with by a fixed penalty and, in that case, three penalty points will be endorsed on the licence. If the offender is convicted by a court, there is a range of 3–6 points; again the point in the range will depend mainly on the proportion by which the actual speed exceeded the limit. If a fixed penalty would have been offered but for some reason it was not, the court is often inclined to stay with both the financial penalty and the number of penalty points.

Disqualification for relatively short periods will be appropriate where the risks were greater, and is usually considered seriously in any case once a speed limit is exceeded by 30 mph.

V. EFFECT OF PENALTIES

13–155   Many road traffic offences lead, on conviction, to a requirement that details of the offender be endorsed onto the offender's driving record and/or to the possibility of disqualification from driving. In most cases, disqualification is at the discretion of the court but, in some cases, the court is obliged to disqualify the offender unless there are "special reasons" (see below) for not doing so. Similarly, where endorsement is required, it is always mandatory in the absence of "special reasons". There is also the consequential power to deprive an offender of the vehicle used in certain circumstances.

A. ENDORSEMENT

Road Traffic Offenders Act 1988, ss.44–48, 28(1)–(6)

Endorsement of licences

13–156   **44.**—(1) Where a person is convicted of an offence involving obligatory endorsement, the court must order there to be endorsed on the counterpart of any licence held by him particulars of the conviction and also—

(a) if the court orders him to be disqualified, particulars of the disqualification, or

(b) if the court does not order him to be disqualified—

(i) particulars of the offence, including the date when it was committed, and

(ii) the penalty points to be attributed to the offence.

(2) Where the court does not order the person convicted to be disqualified, it need not make an order under subsection (1) above if for special reasons it thinks fit not to do so.

(3) In relation to Scotland, references in this section to the court include the district court.

(4) This section is subject to section 48 of this Act.

Effect of endorsement

45.—(1) An order that any particulars or penalty points are to be endorsed on [the counter-part of] any licence held by the person convicted shall, whether he is at the time the holder of a licence or not, operate as an order that the counterpart of any licence he may then hold or may subsequently obtain is to be so endorsed until he becomes entitled under subsection (4) below to have a licence issued to him [with its counterpart] free from the particulars or penalty points.   **13–157**

(2) On the issue of a new licence to a person, any particulars or penalty points ordered to be endorsed on the [counterpart of] any licence held by him shall be entered on [the counterpart] of the licence unless he has become entitled under subsection (4) below to have a licence issued to him [with its counterpart] free from those particulars or penalty points.

(3) [...]

(4) A person [the counterpart of] whose licence has been ordered to be endorsed is entitled to have a new licence issued to him free from the endorsement if, after the end of the period for which the endorsement remains effective, [issued to him with effect from the end of the period for which the endorsement remains effective a new licence with a coun-terpart free from the endorsement if] he applies for a new licence in pursuance of section 97(1) of the *Road Traffic Act* 1988, surrenders any subsisting licence[and its counterpart], pays the fee prescribed by regulations under Part III of that Act and satisfies the other requirements of section 97(1).

(5) An endorsement ordered on a person's conviction of an offence remains effective (subject to subsections (6) and (7) below)—

(a) if an order is made for the disqualification of the offender, until four years have elapsed since the conviction, and

(b) if no such order is made, until either—

(i) four years have elapsed since the commission of the offence, or

(ii) an order is made for the disqualification of the offender under section 35 of this Act.

(6) Where the offence was one under section 1 of that Act (causing death by dangerous driving and dangerous driving), the endorsement remains in any case effective until four years have elapsed since the conviction.

(7) Where the offence was one—

(a) section 3A, 4(1) or 5(1)(a) of that Act (driving offences connected with drink or drugs), or

(b) under section 7(6) of that Act (failing to provide specimen) involving obligatory disqualification,

the endorsement remains effective until eleven years have elapsed since the conviction.

Combination of disqualification and endorsement with probation orders and orders for discharge

46.—(1) Notwithstanding anything in section 14(3) of the *Powers of Criminal Courts (Sentencing) Act* 2000(conviction of offender discharged to be disregarded for the purposes of enactments relating to disqualification), a court in England and Wales which on convicting a person of an offence involving obligatory or discretionary disqualification makes—   **13–158**

(a) a probation order, or

(b) an order discharging him absolutely or conditionally,

may on that occasion also exercise any power conferred, and must also discharge any duty imposed, on the court by sections 34, 35, 36 or 44 of this Act.

(2) A conviction—

(a) in respect of which a court in England and Wales has ordered a person to be dis-qualified, or

(b) of which particulars have been endorsed [on the counterpart of] any licence held by him,

is to be taken into account, notwithstanding anything in section 14(1) of the *Powers of Criminal Courts (Sentencing) Act* 2000 (conviction of offender discharged to be disregarded for the purpose of subsequent proceedings), in determining his liability to punishment or disqualifica-tion for any offence involving obligatory or discretionary disqualification committed subsequently.

(3) Where—

(a) a person is charged in Scotland with an offence involving obligatory or discretionary disqualification, and

(b) the court makes an order in respect of the offence under section 228(probation) or 246(2) or (3) (absolute discharge) of the *Criminal Procedure (Scotland) Act* 1995,

then, for the purposes of sections 34, 35, 36, 44 and 45 of this Act, he shall be treated as if he had been convicted of an offence of the kind in question and section 247 of that Act shall not apply.

Supplementary provisions as to disqualifications and endorsements

13–159   **47.**—(1) In any case where a court exercises its power under section 34, 35 or 44 of this Act not to order any disqualification or endorsement or to order disqualification for a shorter period than would otherwise be required, it must state the grounds for doing so in open court and, if it is a magistrates' court or, in Scotland, a court of summary jurisdiction, must cause them to be entered in the register (in Scotland, record) of its proceedings.

(2) Where a court orders the endorsement of [the counterpart of] any licence held by a person it may, and where a court orders the holder of a licence to be disqualified for a period of 56 days or more it must, send the licence, on its licence [and its counterpart], on its [their] being produced to the court, to the Secretary of State; and if the court orders the endorsement but does not send the licence [and its counterpart] to the Secretary of State it must send him notice of the endorsement.

(2A) Subsection (2) above is subject to section 2(2) of and paragraph 7(2) of Schedule 1 *Road Traffic (New Drivers) Act* 1995 (obligation of court to send licence and its counterpart to the Secretary of State).

(3) Where on an appeal against an order for the endorsement of a licence or the disqualification of a person the appeal is allowed, the court by which the appeal is allowed must send notice of that fact to the Secretary of State.

(4) A notice sent by a court to the Secretary of State in pursuance of this section must be sent in such manner and to such address and contain such particulars as the Secretary of State may determine, and a licence [and the counterpart] of a licence so sent in pursuance of this section must be sent to such address as the Secretary of State may determine.

Exemption from disqualification and endorsement for certain construction and use offences

13–160   **48.**—(1) Where a person is convicted of an offence under section 40A of the *Road Traffic Act* 1988 (using vehicle in dangerous condition etc) the court must not—

(a) order him to be disqualified, or

(b) order any particulars or penalty points to be endorsed on the counterpart of any licence held by him,

if he proves that he did not know, and had no reasonable cause to suspect, that the use of the vehicle involved a danger of injury to any person.

(2) Where a person is convicted of an offence under section 41A of the *Road Traffic Act* 1988 (breach of requirement as to brakes, steering-gear or tyres) the court must not—

(a) order him to be disqualified, or

(b) order any particulars or penalty points to be endorsed on the counterpart of any licence held by him,

if he proves that he did not know, and had no reasonable cause to suspect, that the facts of the case were such that the offence would be committed.

(3) In relation to licences which came into force before 1st June 1990, the references in subsections (1) and (2) above to the counterpart of a licence shall be construed as references to the licence itself.

Penalty points to be attributed to an offence

31–161   **28.**—(1) Where a person is convicted of an offence involving obligatory endorsement, then, subject to the following provisions of this section, the number of penalty points to be attributed to the offence is—

(a) the number shown in relation to the offence in the last column of Part I or Part II of Schedule 2 to this Act, or

(b) where a range of numbers is shown, a number within that range.

(2) Where a person is convicted of an offence committed by aiding, abetting, counselling

or procuring, or inciting to the commission of, an offence involving obligatory disqualification, then, subject to the following provisions of this section, the number of penalty points to be attributed to the offence is ten.

(3) Where both a range of numbers and a number followed by the words "(fixed penalty)" is shown in the last column of Part I of Schedule 2 to this Act in relation to an offence, that number is the number of penalty points to be attributed to the offence for the purposes of sections 57(5) and 77(5) of this Act; and, where only a range of numbers is shown there, the lowest number in the range is the number of penalty points to be attributed to the offence for those purposes.

(4) Where a person is convicted (whether on the same occasion or not) of two or more offences committed on the same occasion and involving obligatory endorsement, the total number of penalty points to be attributed to them is the number or highest number that would be attributed on a conviction of one of them (so that if the convictions are on different occasions the number of penalty points to be attributed to the offences on the later occasion or occasions shall be restricted accordingly).

(5) In a case where (apart from this subsection) subsection (4) above would apply to two or more offences, the court may if it thinks fit determine that that subsection shall not apply to the offences (or, where three or more offences are concerned, to any one or more of them).

(6) Where a court makes such a determination it shall state its reasons in open court and, if it is a magistrates' court, or in Scotland a court of summary jurisdiction, shall cause them to be entered in the register (in Scotland, record) of its proceedings.

The offences involving obligatory endorsement are set out in Sch.2 to the *Road* **13–162** *Traffic Offenders Act* 1988. Where endorsement is required, it will contain particulars of the conviction, any disqualification or, if no disqualification is imposed, particulars of the offence and the penalty points attributed to the offence. Codes have been allocated to all endorsable offences and to all sentences that could be imposed.

The number of penalty points may be fixed by statute or a range may be given (for example, careless driving has a range of 3–9 points) which allows the court to reflect the varying levels of seriousness. When the number of points reaches a particular level (see below), the court must disqualify the offender in the absence of "mitigating circumstances" (see below).

The requirement is to endorse "any licence held by" the offender. The order must be made whether or not the offender actually holds a licence: see s.45 of the *Road Traffic Offenders Act* 1988. The licence referred to is one issued under Pt III of the *Road Traffic Act* 1988 (s.108 of the *Road Traffic Act* 1988) and does not include, *e.g.* international driving permits, foreign driving licences or heavy goods vehicles licences. However, the details need to be notified to the Secretary of State and a record kept. An accumulation of points will still lead to disqualification even though no licence issued under Pt III is ever held.

Where an offender is convicted of more than one offence committed on the same oc- **13–163** casion, the court will generally attribute just the highest number of points to be allocated to any one of the offences: s.28(4) of the *Road Traffic Offenders Act* 1988. Thus, where an offender is convicted of careless driving and of using a vehicle without insurance and the court decides to impose 4 penalty points for the careless driving and 7 penalty points for the no insurance, it will be the 7 points alone that will be endorsed on then licence. However, the court retains the discretion to endorse more than one set of points where it thinks fit (s.28(5)) but must then give its reasons for so doing (s.28(6)). If that was applied to the example above, the offender would then have 11 points endorsed. Where the court disqualifies the offender, no further penalty points are endorsed either for the offence on which the disqualification is ordered or any other offence of which he is convicted on the same occasion: *Martin v DPP* [2000] R.T.R. 188. This is also the case where the disqualification is obligatory: s.44(1) of the *Road Traffic Offenders Act* 1988.

In considering what level of points to attribute where a range is prescribed, the court will be primarily concerned with the gravity of the offence—the more serious the offence within its class, the higher the number of points. However, this decision will also be taken within the context of the overall purpose of sentencing in criminal cases which will encompass the need to impose a punishment proportionate to the offence and the need to reduce the likelihood of the offender committing further offences. Since the court will always have the power to disqualify wherever it is required to endorse, there will be no need to increase the penalty points beyond what the offence justifies. However, a court may legitimately take the view that the goal of reducing crime justifies fixing the level of points in a way that leaves the offender in no doubt that a further conviction will lead to disqualification.

B. DISQUALIFICATION

Road Traffic Offenders Act 1988, ss.34, 34A, 35–39, 42, 43, 29, 26

Disqualification for certain offences

13–164   **34.**—(1) Where a person is convicted of an offence involving obligatory disqualification, the court must order him to be disqualified for such period not less than twelve months as the court thinks fit unless the court for special reasons thinks fit to order him to be disqualified for a shorter period or not to order him to be disqualified.

(1A) Where a person is convicted of an offence under section 12A of the *Theft Act* 1968 (aggravated vehicle-taking), the fact that he did not drive the vehicle in question at any particular time or at all shall not be regarded as a special reason for the purposes of subsection (1) above.

(2) Where a person is convicted of an offence involving discretionary disqualification, and either—

    (a) the penalty points to be taken into account on that occasion number fewer than twelve, or

    (b) the offence is not one involving obligatory endorsement,

the court may order him to be disqualified for such period as the court thinks fit.

(3) Where a person convicted of an offence under any of the following provisions of the *Road Traffic Act* 1988, that is—

    (aa) section 3A (causing death by careless driving when under the influence of drink or drugs),

    (a) section 4(1) (driving or attempting to drive while unfit),

    (b) section 5(1)(a) (driving or attempting to drive with excess alcohol),

    (c) section 7(6) (failing to provide a specimen) where that is an offence involving obligatory disqualification,

    (d) section 7A(6) (failing to allow a specimen to be subjected to laboratory test) where that is an offence involving obligatory disqualification;

has within the ten years immediately preceding the commission of the offence been convicted of any such offence, subsection (1) above shall apply in relation to him as if the reference to twelve months were a reference to three years.

(4) Subject to subsection (3) above, subsection (1) above shall apply as if the reference to twelve months were a reference to two years—

    (a) in relation to a person convicted of—

        (i) manslaughter, or in Scotland culpable homicide, or

        (ii) an offence under section 1 of the *Road Traffic Act* 1988 (causing death by dangerous driving), or

        (iii) an offence under section 3A of that Act (causing death by careless driving while under the influence of drink or drugs), and

    (b) in relation to a person on whom more than one disqualification for a fixed period of 56 days or more has been imposed within the three years immediately preceding the commission of the offence.

(4A) For the purposes of subsection (4)(b) above there shall be disregarded any disqualification imposed under section 26 of this Act or section 147 of the *Powers of Criminal Courts (Sentencing) Act* 2000 or section 223A or 436A of the *Criminal Procedure (Scotland) Act* 1975 (offences committed by using vehicles) and any disqualification imposed in respect of an offence of stealing a motor vehicle, an offence under section 12 or 25 of the *Theft Act* 1968, an offence under section 178 of the *Road Traffic Act* 1988, or an attempt to commit such an offence.

(5) The preceding provisions of this section shall apply in relation to a conviction of an

offence committed by aiding, abetting, counselling or procuring, or inciting to the commission of, an offence involving obligatory disqualification as if the offence were an offence involving discretionary disqualification.

(6) This section is subject to section 48 of this Act.

Reduced disqualification period for attendance on courses

34A.—(1) This section applies where—   **13–165**

(a) a person is convicted of an offence under section 3A (causing death by careless driving when under influence of drink or drugs), 4 (driving or being in charge when under influence of drink or drugs), 5 (driving or being in charge with excess alcohol) or 7 (failing to provide a specimen) of the *Road Traffic Act* 1988, and

(b) the court makes an order under section 34 of this Act disqualifying him for a period of not less than twelve months.

(2) Where this section applies, the court may make an order that the period of disqualification imposed under section 34 shall be reduced if, by a date specified in the order under this section, the offender satisfactorily completes a course approved by the Secretary of State for the purposes of this section and specified in the order.

(3) The reduction made by an order under this section in a period of disqualification imposed under section 34 shall be a period specified in the order of not less than three months and not more than one quarter of the unreduced period (and accordingly where the period imposed under section 34 is twelve months, the reduced period shall be nine months).

(4) The court shall not make an order under this section unless—

(a) it is satisfied that a place on the course specified in the order will be available for the offender,

(b) the offender appears to the court to be of or over the age of 17,

(c) the court has explained the effect of the order to the offender in ordinary language, and has informed him of the amount of the fees for the course and of the requirement that he must pay them before beginning the course, and

(d) the offender has agreed that the order should be made.

(5) The date specified in an order under this section as the latest date for completion of a course must be at least two months before the last day of the period of disqualification as reduced by the order.

(6) An order under this section shall name the petty sessions area (or in Scotland the sheriff court district or, where an order has been made under this section by a stipendiary magistrate, the commission area) in which the offender resides or will reside.

Disqualification for repeated offences

35.—(1) Where—   **13–166**

(a) a person is convicted of an offence to which this subsection applies, and

(b) the penalty points to be taken into account on that occasion number twelve or more,

the court must order him to be disqualified for not less than the minimum period unless the court is satisfied, having regard to all the circumstances, that there are grounds for mitigating the normal consequences of the conviction and thinks fit to order him to be disqualified for a shorter period or not to order him to be disqualified.

(1A) Subsection (1) above applies to—

(a) an offence involving discretionary disqualification and obligatory endorsement, and

(b) an offence involving obligatory disqualification in respect of which no order is made under section 34 of this Act.

(2) The minimum period referred to in subsection (1) above is—

(a) six months if no previous disqualification imposed on the offender is to be taken into account, and

(b) one year if one, and two years if more than one, such disqualification is to be taken into account;

and a previous disqualification imposed on an offender is to be taken into account if it was for a fixed period of 56 days or more and was imposed within the three years immediately preceding the commission of the latest offence in respect of which penalty points are taken into account under section 29 of this Act.

(3) Where an offender is convicted on the same occasion of more than one offence to which subsection (1) above applies—

(a) not more than one disqualification shall be imposed on him under subsection (1) above,

(b) in determining the period of the disqualification the court must take into account all the offences, and

(c) for the purposes of any appeal any disqualification imposed under subsection (1) above shall be treated as an order made on the conviction of each of the offences.

(4) No account is to be taken under subsection (1) above of any of the following circumstances—

(a) any circumstances that are alleged to make the offence or any of the offences not a serious one,

(b) hardship, other than exceptional hardship, or

(c) any circumstances which, within the three years immediately preceding the conviction, have been taken into account under that subsection in ordering the offender to be disqualified for a shorter period or not ordering him to be disqualified.

(5) References in this section to disqualification do not include a disqualification imposed under section 26 of this Act or section 147 of the *Powers of Criminal Courts (Sentencing) Act* 2000 or section 223A or 436A of the *Criminal Procedure (Scotland) Act* 1975 (offences committed by using vehicles) or a disqualification imposed in respect of an offence of stealing a motor vehicle, an offence under section 12 or 25 of the *Theft Act* 1968, an offence under section 178 of the *Road Traffic Act* 1988, or an attempt to commit such an offence.

(5A) The preceding provisions of this section shall apply in relation to a conviction of an offence committed by aiding, abetting, counselling, procuring, or inciting to the commission of, an offence involving obligatory disqualification as if the offence were an offence involving discretionary disqualification.

(6) In relation to Scotland, references in this section to the court include the district court.

(7) This section is subject to section 48 of this Act.

Disqualification until test is passed

13–167   **36.**—(1) Where this subsection applies to a person the court must order him to be disqualified until he passes the appropriate driving test.

(2) Subsection (1) above applies to a person who is disqualified under section 34 of this Act on conviction of—

(a) manslaughter, or in Scotland culpable homicide, by the driver of a motor vehicle, or

(b) an offence under section 1 (causing death by dangerous driving) or section 2 (dangerous driving) of the *Road Traffic Act* 1988.

(3) Subsection (1) above also applies—

(a) to a person who is disqualified under section 34 or 35 of this Act in such circumstances or for such period as the Secretary of State may by order prescribe, or

(b) to such other persons convicted of such offences involving obligatory endorsement as may be so prescribed.

(4) Where a person to whom subsection (1) above does not apply is convicted of an offence involving obligatory endorsement, the court may order him to be disqualified until he passes the appropriate driving test (whether or not he has previously passed any test).

(5) In this section—

"appropriate driving test" *means*—

(a) an extended driving test, where a person is convicted of an offence involving obligatory disqualification or is disqualified under section 35 of this Act,

(b) a test of competence to drive, other than an extended driving test, in any other case,

"extended driving test" means a test of competence to drive prescribed for the purposes of this section, and

"test of competence to drive" means a test prescribed by virtue of section 89(3) of the *Road Traffic Act* 1988.

(6) In determining whether to make an order under subsection (4) above, the court shall have regard to the safety of road users.

(7) Where a person is disqualified until he passes the extended driving test—

(a) any earlier order under this section shall cease to have effect, and

(b) a court shall not make a further order under this section while he is so disqualified.

(8) Subject to subsection (9) below, a disqualification by virtue of an order under this **13–168** section shall be deemed to have expired on production to the Secretary of State of evidence, in such form as may be prescribed by regulations under section 105 of the *Road Traffic Act* 1988, that the person disqualified has passed the test in question since the order was made.

(9) A disqualification shall be deemed to have expired only in relation to vehicles of such classes as may be prescribed in relation to the test passed by regulations under that section.

(10) Where there is issued to a person a licence on the counterpart of which are endorsed particulars of a disqualification under this section, there shall also be endorsed the particulars of any test of competence to drive that he has passed since the order of disqualification was made.

(11) For the purposes of an order under this section, a person shall be treated as having passed a test of competence to drive other than an extended driving test if he passes a corresponding test conducted—

(a) under the law of Northern Ireland, the Isle of Man, any of the Channel Islands, another EEA State, Gibraltar or a designated country or territory, or

(b) for the purposes of obtaining a British Forces licence (as defined by section 88(8) of the *Road Traffic Act* 1988);

and accordingly subsections (8) to (10) above shall apply in relation to such a test as they apply in relation to a test prescribed by virtue of section 89(3) of that Act.

(11A) For the purposes of subsection (11) above, "designated country or territory" means a country or territory designated by order under section 108(2) of the *Road Traffic Act* 1988 but a test conducted under the law of such a country or territory shall not be regarded as a corresponding test unless a person passing such a test would be entitled to an exchangeable licence as defined in section 108(1) of that Act.

(12) This section is subject to section 48 of this Act.

(13) The power to make an order under subsection (3) above shall be exercisable by statutory instrument; and no such order shall be made unless a draft of it has been laid before and approved by resolution of each House of Parliament.

(14) The Secretary of State shall not make an order under subsection (3) above after the end of 2001 if he has not previously made such an order.

Effect of order of disqualification

37.—(1) Where the holder of a licence is disqualified by an order of a court, the licence shall **13–169** be treated as being revoked with effect from the beginning of the period of disqualification.

(1A) Where—

(a) the disqualification is for a fixed period shorter than 56 days in respect of an offence involving obligatory endorsement, or

(b) the order is made under section 26 of this Act,

subsection (1) above shall not prevent the licence from again having effect at the end of the period of disqualification.

(2) Where the holder of the licence appeals against the order and the disqualification is suspended under section 39 of this Act, the period of disqualification shall be treated for the purpose of subsection (1) above as beginning on the day on which the disqualification ceases to be suspended.

(3) Notwithstanding anything in Part III of the *Road Traffic Act* 1988, a person disqualified by an order of a court under section 36 of this Act is (unless he is also disqualified otherwise than by virtue of such an order) entitled to obtain and to hold a provisional licence and to drive a motor vehicle in accordance with the conditions subject to which the provisional licence is granted.

Appeal against disqualification

38.—(1) A person disqualified by an order of a magistrates' court under section 34 or 35 of **13–170** this Act may appeal against the order in the same manner as against a conviction.

(2) A person disqualified by an order of a court in Scotland may appeal against the order in the same manner as against a sentence.

Suspension of disqualification pending appeal

13–171 **39.**—(1) Any court in England and Wales (whether a magistrates' court or another) which makes an order disqualifying a person may, if it thinks fit, suspend the disqualification pending an appeal against the order.

(2) The court by or before which a person disqualified by an order of a court in Scotland was convicted may, if it thinks fit, suspend the disqualification pending an appeal against the order.

(3) Where a court exercises its power under subsection (1) or (2) above, it must send notice of the suspension to the Secretary of State.

(4) The notice must be sent in such manner and to such address and must contain such particulars as the Secretary of State may determine.

Removal of disqualification

13–172 **42.**—(1) Subject to the provisions of this section, a person who by an order of a court is disqualified may apply to the court by which the order was made to remove the disqualification.

(2) On any such application the court may, as it thinks proper having regard to—

(a) the character of the person disqualified and his conduct subsequent to the order,

(b) the nature of the offence, and

(c) any other circumstances of the case,

either by order remove the disqualification as from such date as may be specified in the order or refuse the application.

(3) No application shall be made under subsection (1) above for the removal of a disqualification before the expiration of whichever is relevant of the following periods from the date of the order by which the disqualification was imposed, that is—

(a) two years, if the disqualification is for less than four years,

(b) one half of the period of disqualification, if it is for less than ten years but not less than four years,

(c) five years in any other case;

and in determining the expiration of the period after which under this subsection a person may apply for the removal of a disqualification, any time after the conviction during which the disqualification was suspended or he was not disqualified shall be disregarded.

13–173 (4) Where an application under subsection (1) above is refused, a further application under that subsection shall not be entertained if made within three months after the date of the refusal.

(5) If under this section a court orders a disqualification to be removed, the court—

(a) must cause particulars of the order to be endorsed on the counterpart of the licence, if any, previously held by the applicant, and

(b) may in any case order the applicant to pay the whole or any part of the costs of the application.

(5A) Subsection (5)(a) above shall apply only where the disqualification was imposed in respect of an offence involving obligatory endorsement; and in any other case the court must send notice of the order made under this section to the Secretary of State.

(5B) A notice under subsection (5A) above must be sent in such manner and to such address, and must contain such particulars, as the Secretary of State may determine.

(6) The preceding provisions of this section shall not apply where the disqualification was imposed by order under section 36(1) of this Act.

Rule for determining end of period of disqualification

13–174 **43.** In determining the expiration of the period for which a person is disqualified by an order of a court made in consequence of a conviction, any time after the conviction during which the disqualification was suspended or he was not disqualified shall be disregarded.

Interim disqualification

13–175 **26.**—(1) Where a magistrates' court—

(a) commits an offender to the Crown Court under section 6 of the *Powers of Criminal Courts (Sentencing) Act* 2000 or any enactment mentioned in subsection (4) of that section applies, or

(b) remits an offender to another magistrates' court under section 10 of that Act,
to be dealt with for an offence involving obligatory or discretionary disqualification, it may order
him to be disqualified until he has been dealt with in respect of the offence.

(2) Where a court in England and Wales—
    (a) defers passing sentence on an offender under section 1 of that Act in respect of
an offence involving obligatory or discretionary disqualification, or
    (b) adjourns after convicting an offender of such an offence but before dealing with
him for the offence,
it may order the offender to be disqualified until he has been dealt with in respect of the offence.

(3) Where a court in Scotland—
    (a) adjourns a case under section 179 or section 380 of the *Criminal Procedure
(Scotland) Act* 1975 (for inquiries to be made or to determine the most suitable
method of dealing with the offender);
    (b) remands a person in custody or on bail under section 180 or section 381 of the
Criminal Procedure (Scotland) Act 1975 (to enable a medical examination and
report to be made);
    (c) defers sentence under section 219 or section 432 of the *Criminal Procedure
(Scotland) Act* 1975;
    (d) remits a convicted person to the High Court for sentence under section 104 of
the *Criminal Procedure (Scotland) Act* 1975,
in respect of an offence involving obligatory or discretionary disqualification, it may order the accused to be disqualified until he has been dealt with in respect of the offence.

(4) Subject to subsection (5) below, an order under this section shall cease to have effect
at the end of the period of six months beginning with the day on which it is made, if it has
not ceased to have effect before that time.

(5) In Scotland, where a person is disqualified under this section where section 219 or
section 432 of the *Criminal Procedure (Scotland) Act* 1975 (deferred sentence) applies and
the period of deferral exceeds 6 months, subsection (4) above shall not prevent the imposition
under this section of any period of disqualification which does not exceed the period of deferral.

(6) Where a court orders a person to be disqualified under this section ("the first order"), no court shall make a further order under this section in respect of the same offence
or any offence in respect of which an order could have been made under this section at the
time the first order was made.

(7) Where a court makes an order under this section in respect of any person it must—
    (a) require him to produce to the court any licence held by him and its counterpart,
and
    (b) retain the licence and counterpart until it deals with him or (as the case may be)
cause them to be sent to the proper officer of the court which is to deal with him.

(2) In subsection (7) above "proper officer" means—
    (a) in relation to a magistrates' court in England and Wales, the justices' chief
executive for the court, and
    (b) in relation to any other court, the clerk of the court.

(8) If the holder of the licence has not caused it and its counterpart to be delivered, or **13–176**
has not posted them, in accordance with section 7 of this Act and does not produce the
licence and counterpart as required under subsection (7) above, then he is guilty of an
offence.

(9) Subsection (8) above does not apply to a person who—
    (a) satisfies the court that he has applied for a new licence and has not received it, or
    (b) surrenders to the court a current receipt for his licence and its counterpart is-
sued under section 56 of this Act, and produces the licence and counterpart to
the court immediately on their return.

(10) Where a court makes an order under this section in respect of any person, sections
44(1), 47(2) and 91A(5) of this Act and section 109(3) of the *Road Traffic Act* 1988 (Northern
Ireland drivers' licences) shall not apply in relation to the order, but—
    (a) the court must send notice of the order to the Secretary of State, and
    (b) if the court which deals with the offender determines not to order him to be disquali-
fied under section 34 or 35 of this Act, it must send notice of the determination to the
Secretary of State.

(11) A notice sent by a court to the Secretary of State in pursuance of subsection (10)

above must be sent in such manner and to such address and contain such particulars as the Secretary of State may determine.

(12) Where on any occasion a court deals with an offender—

(a) for an offence in respect of which an order was made under this section, or

(b) for two or more offences in respect of any of which such an order was made,

any period of disqualification which is on that occasion imposed under section 34 or 35 of this Act shall be treated as reduced by any period during which he was disqualified by reason only of an order made under this section in respect of any of those offences.

(13) Any reference in this or any other Act (including any Act passed after this Act) to the length of a period of disqualification shall, unless the context otherwise requires, be construed as a reference to its length before any reduction under this section.

(14) In relation to licences which came into force before 1st June 1990, the references in this section to counterparts of licences shall be disregarded.

Penalty points to be taken into account on conviction

13–177　　　**29.**—(1) Where a person is convicted of an offence involving obligatory endorsement, the penalty points to be taken into account on that occasion are (subject to subsection (2) below)—

(a) any that are to be attributed to the offence or offences of which he is convicted, disregarding any offence in respect of which an order under section 34 of this Act is made, and

(b) any that were on a previous occasion ordered to be endorsed on the counterpart of any licence held by him, unless the offender has since that occasion and before the conviction been disqualified under section 35 of this Act.

(2) If any of the offences was committed more than three years before another, the penalty points in respect of that offence shall not be added to those in respect of the other.

(3) In relation to licences which came into force before 1st June 1990, the reference in subsection (1) above to the counterpart of a licence shall be construed as a reference to the licence itself.

13–178　　Wherever a court is obliged to endorse details of a conviction on a licence, it may also disqualify the offender from holding or obtaining a licence. It is an offence (punishable by a fine of level 5 and/or six months imprisonment) to drive a motor vehicle whilst disqualified by an order of a court, see § 13–91 above.

A disqualification is generally for a prescribed period during which the offender may not lawfully drive any vehicle on a road. The period starts from the moment it is imposed. However, a disqualification may also (or instead) be until the offender has passed a relevant driving test. In those circumstances, the offender may drive as if a provisional licence holder pending the successful taking of the test (though if this order is combined with a disqualification for a fixed period, that period must first expire before the offender can commence to drive as a provisional licence holder): s.37(3) of the *Road Traffic Offenders Act* 1988.

Orders of disqualification may be mandatory or discretionary. Mandatory disqualification follows conviction of "an offence involving obligatory disqualification". In these circumstances, the minimum period of disqualification is 12 months: s.34(1) of the *Road Traffic Offenders Act* 1988. This minimum is extended to two years where the offender has had at least two disqualifications of at least 56 days imposed on him within the three years that preceded the *commission of the offence* currently before the court: s.34(4)(b). The minimum is extended to three years in relation to the obligatorily disqualifiable offences relating to alcohol/drug influenced driving where the offender has been convicted of one of those offences within the 10 years preceding the *commission* of the current offence: s.34(3). The only discretion to not impose this disqualification either at all or for a lesser period arises where the court finds "special reasons" (see below). Where the disqualification is for at least 12 months and arises from certain alcohol/drug influenced offences, the court may authorise the period to be reduced if the offender satisfactorily completes a suitable course. The court will specify the extent of the reduction—at least three months but no more than one quarter of the total period: s.34A of the *Road Traffic Offenders Act* 1988.

A further circumstance where a court is obliged to disqualify is where the total number of penalty points to be taken into account amounts to at least 12. The court must disqualify for at least six months unless it finds "mitigating circumstances" (see below). This period of six months is increased to one year or two years if there are previous disqualifications of at least 56 days imposed in the three years prior to the *commission* of the current offence. The increase to one year follows one such disqualification; the increase to two years follows two or more previous disqualifications. Certain disqualifications do not count for these purposes: s.35(5).

Points on a licence are taken into account and added to those imposed for the current offence. The points on a licence must be in respect of an offence committed within three years (before or after) of the current offence: s.29(2). However, those points will be disregarded if there has been a disqualification under s.35 (totting-up) between the earlier imposition of the points and the commission of the current offence: s.29(1)(b). Other disqualifications (*e.g.* obligatory disqualifications under s.34) do not have the same effect. **13–179**

A different, more stringent, power applies where offences are committed within the first two years after a person first passes a driving test. If 6 points are acquired for offences committed prior to the end of that two year period, the licence is automatically revoked: *Road Traffic (New Drivers) Act* 1995. This is not a disqualification. A person whose licence is revoked who drives subsequently will not be driving whilst disqualified but may be driving other than in accordance with a licence. They will be able to apply for a further provisional licence and must comply with the conditions until an appropriate test is passed.

Discretionary disqualification can follow commission of an endorsable offence. It may also be imposed on commission of certain other offences that are not endorsable. In those circumstances, there is no minimum period.

Different procedures regarding the retention of the licence by the court apply depending on whether the period of the disqualification is 56 days or more: s.47 of the *Road Traffic Offenders Act* 1988. Where the period is less than 56 days (or is an interim disqualification under s.29), the licence automatically has effect again at the end of the period: s.37(1A). Otherwise, the licence will be retained by the court and sent to the Secretary of State; the driver will need to apply for its return before the end of the period of disqualification to ensure that it is in his possession when he is entitled to drive again.

As well as a disqualification for a fixed period (after which the offender can drive as before) the court may impose a disqualification until the offender passes a driving test. This driving test will normally be the usual test of competence to drive but, where the offender is also disqualified under s.35 (totting-up) the test will be an extended one: s.36(4), (5).

Interim disqualification

A court which adjourns a case for sentence after conviction or which defers sentence or remits an offender to another court for sentence may impose an interim disqualification in respect of any endorsable offence. This disqualification may not last longer than six months. Any period will be attributed to a disqualification imposed as a sentence. **13—180**

Obligatory disqualification or endorsement can only be avoided where a court finds "special reasons" for doing so. Special reasons may reduce a period of disqualification below the minimum set by statute but may not reduce the penalty points below the lower limit fixed—in relation to points, finding special reasons will enable the court to avoid endorsing any points at all. Disqualification under s.35 (totting-up) may only be avoided where a court finds "mitigating circumstances". Even where either is found to exist, the court retains its discretion and may still disqualify or endorse if it thinks fit. Both these terms have been subject to extensive case law. For a full examination of the authorities, see *Wilkinson's Road Traffic Offences*, Ch.21. This is one of the inevitable consequences of courts being subject to mandatory orders—whilst this promotes consistency and reinforces the seriousness of the offences, it also requires an elaborate system to be created to avoid injustice in the small number of unusual cases that inevitably arise.

Special reasons

13–181   A special reason must be "special to the facts that constitute the offence". It must be one relevant to the offence and not the offender and it must be something that a court ought properly to take into account when passing sentence: *R. v Crossen* [1939] 1 N.I. 106; *Whittal v Kirby* [1946] 2 All E.R. 552. In *R. v Wickens* (1958) 42 Cr.App.R. 236 the court set out four criteria which have to be satisfied before special reasons can be found to exist. The circumstance put forward must be a mitigating or extenuating circumstance; it must not amount in law to a defence to the charge; it must be something which is directly connected with the offence and it must be something which is proper for the court to take into accountwhen imposing sentence. Courts are generally difficult to persuade that special reasons exist.

Given that Parliament has prescribed these orders as part of the penalty for the offences, it seems that the reason has to be outside of the mischief at which the offence is aimed: see *Nicholson v Brown* [1974] R.T.R. 177.

13–182   Thus special reasons have been found where the defendant was coping with a true emergency (though the courts have been very careful about what constitutes such an emergency and examine closely alternative courses of action in the circumstances) or where the driving was for a very short distance. However, courts have been very cautious over accepting the shortness of the distance driven as sufficient by itself for alcohol or drug related offences. In *Chatters v Burke* [1986] 3 All E.R. 168 seven relevant factors were set out. As well as the distance driven, the court will consider the manner in which it was driven, the state of the vehicle, whether the driver intended to drive further, the road and traffic conditions at the time and the reason for the car being driven. The most important factor will be the extent to which it was possible that danger would be caused through contact with either other road users or with pedestrians.

It is for the defendant to satisfy the court that the special reason exists.

Mitigating Circumstances

13–183   The obligation to disqualify a person who collects at least 12 penalty points is capable of being avoided only if the court is satisfied, having regard to all the circumstances, that there are grounds for mitigating the normal consequences of the conviction: s.35(1). The narrowness of this is emphasised in s.35(4). This precludes a court from taking into account any of the circumstances that are said to make the offence not serious, of hardship unless it is exceptional and states that nothing may be used to support the finding if it has been taken into account in the three years preceding conviction of the current offence in order to avoid or reduce a disqualification to which a defendant would otherwise have been liable under s.35.

It is for the defendant to satisfy the court that the grounds exist. It is not open to the defendant to argue that any of the offences are not serious; disqualification in these circumstances is designed for situations where a driver repeatedly commits offences that do not in themselves warrant disqualification. The wording of s.34(4)(a) seems clearly to encompass not only the latest offence but also any others that are taken into account. If the defendant wishes to rely on hardship then the court will need to be satisfied that that hardship is exceptional. The hardship may be experienced by someone other than the defendant but it must be more than the ordinary hardship that is likely to be experienced when a person is disqualified from driving. This is a question of fact and degree and no precise guidance is possible save that courts are generally difficult to persuade. If mitigating circumstances are found and the court is prepared to allow them to influence the disqualification, that may lead to a reduction in the minimum period or no disqualification at all. In the absence of mitigating circumstances, a court has no alternative but to disqualify for the minimum period provided by statute in the circumstances of the case.

C. Deprivation of Motor Vehicle

Powers of Criminal Courts (Sentencing) Act 2000, s.143

Powers to deprive offender of property used etc. for purposes of crime

143.—(1) Where a person is convicted of an offence and the court by or before which he is **13–184**
convicted is satisfied that any property which has been lawfully seized from him, or which was in
his possession or under his control at the time when he was apprehended for the offence or
when a summons in respect of it was issued—

    (a) has been used for the purpose of committing, or facilitating the commission of,
        any offence, or

    (b) was intended by him to be used for that purpose,

the court may (subject to subsection (5) below) make an order under this section in respect of
that property.

(2) Where a person is convicted of an offence and the offence, or an offence which the
court has taken into consideration in determining his sentence, consists of unlawful possession of property which—

    (a) has been lawfully seized from him, or

    (b) was in his possession or under his control at the time when he was apprehended
        for the offence of which he has been convicted or when a summons in respect of
        that offence was issued,

the court may (subject to subsection (5) below) make an order under this section in respect of
that property.

(3) An order under this section shall operate to deprive the offender of his rights, if any,
in the property to which it relates, and the property shall (if not already in their possession) be taken into the possession of the police.

(4) Any power conferred on a court by subsection (1) or (2) above may be exercised—

    (a) whether or not the court also deals with the offender in any other way in respect
        of the offence of which he has been convicted; and

    (b) without regard to any restrictions on forfeiture in any enactment contained in an
        Act passed before 29th July 1988.

(5) In considering whether to make an order under this section in respect of any property, a court shall have regard—

    (a) to the value of the property; and

    (b) to the likely financial and other effects on the offender of the making of the order
        (taken together with any other order that the court contemplates making).

(6) Where a person commits an offence to which this subsection applies by—

    (a) driving, attempting to drive, or being in charge of a vehicle, or

    (b) failing to comply with a requirement made under section 7 or 7A of the *Road
        Traffic Act* 1988 (failure to provide specimen for analysis or laboratory test (or to give
        permission for such a test) in the course of an investigation into whether the offender
        had committed an offence while driving, attempting to drive or being in charge of a
        vehicle, or

    (c) failing, as the driver of a vehicle, to comply with subsection (2) or (3) of section 17
        of the *Road Traffic Act* 1988 (duty to stop and give information or report accident),

the vehicle shall be regarded for the purposes of subsection (1) above (and section 144(1)(b)
below) as used for the purpose of committing the offence (and for the purpose of committing
any offence of aiding, abetting, counselling or procuring the commission of the offence).

(7) Subsection (6) above applies to—

    (a) an offence under the *Road Traffic Act* 1988 which is punishable with imprisonment;

    (b) an offence of manslaughter; and

    (c) an offence under section 35 of the *Offences Against the Person Act* 1861 (wanton
        and furious driving).

(8) Facilitating the commission of an offence shall be taken for the purposes of subsection (1) above to include the taking of any steps after it has been committed for the purpose
of disposing of any property to which it relates or of avoiding apprehension or detection.

An additional sanction available to a court for some road traffic offences is the power **13–185**
to deprive the offender of the vehicle used while committing the offence. The effect of

the order must be proportionate to the offence (s.143(5)) but it is a sanction which may have considerable impact. A motor vehicle used in connection with offences described in this chapter would not automatically fall within the remit of this section since it would not have been used for the purposes set out in s.143(1) nor would it come within s.143(2) which requires the offence to be one of unlawful possession. However, that remit is extended by subss.(6) and (7) to include offences punishable under the *Road Traffic Act* 1988 by imprisonment which consist of driving, attempting to drive or being in charge of the vehicle, failure to provide a specimen for analysis and failing to stop and report an accident. See also § 26–161 below.

CHAPTER 14

OFFENCES INVOLVING DRUGS

For general introduction and definitions, see *Archbold Crown* §§ 26–1—26–25. Of **14–1** particular note is the reclassification of four substances, namely cannabis, cannabis resin (both previously Class B) cannabinol and cannabinol derivatives (both previously Class C). All four are now Class C (*Misuse of Drugs Act 1971 (Modification) (No.2) Order* 2003 (SI 2003/3201). But note that possession of cannabis and cannabis resin continue to be arrestable offences; s.3 of the *Criminal Justice Act* 2003 (SI 2004/81).

I. OFFENCES UNDER THE MISUSE OF DRUGS ACT 1971

A. PROHIBITION ON IMPORTATION AND EXPORTATION OF CONTROLLED DRUGS

(a) *Definition*

Misuse of Drugs Act 1971, s.3

Restriction of importation and exportation of controlled drugs
3.—(1) Subject to subsection (2) below—   **14–2**
   (a) the importation of a controlled drug; and
   (b) the exportation of a controlled drug,
are hereby prohibited.
   (2) Subsection (1) above does not apply—
   (a) to the importation or exportation of a controlled drug which is for the time being
       excepted from paragraph (a) or, as the case may be, paragraph (b) of subsection
       (1) above by regulations under section 7 of this Act; or
   (b) to the importation or exportation of a controlled drug under and in accordance
       with the terms of a licence issued by the Secretary of State and in compliance
       with any conditions attached thereto.

14–2.1   Section 3 does not create an offence: the offence of evading the prohibitions imposed thereby arises from the combined effect of s.3 and s.170 of the *Customs and Excise Management Act* 1979.

B. Restriction of Production and Supply of Controlled Drugs

(a) *Definition*

Misuse of Drugs Act 1971, s.4

Restriction of production and supply of controlled drugs

14–3   **4.**—(1) Subject to any regulations under section 7 of this Act for the time being in force, it shall not be lawful for a person—

     (a) to produce a controlled drug; or

     (b) to supply or offer to supply a controlled drug to another.

(2) Subject to section 28 of this Act, it is an offence for a person—

     (a) to produce a controlled drug in contravention of subsection (1) above; or

     (b) to be concerned in the production of such a drug in contravention of that subsection by another.

(3) Subject to section 28 of this Act, it is an offence for a person—

     (a) to supply or offer to supply a controlled drug to another in contravention of subsection (1) above; or

     (b) to be concerned in the supplying of such a drug to another in contravention of that subsection; or

     (c) to be concerned in the making to another in contravention of that subsection of an offer to supply such a drug.

(b) *Procedure*

14–4   This offence is triable either way. The *Practice Note (Mode of Trial: Guidelines)* (1995) provide that cases of supplying Class A drugs should be committed for trial; cases of supplying Class B drugs should be committed for trial unless there is only small-scale supply for no payment. No guidelines are given in relation to Class C drugs.

Section 25(4) of the 1971 Act also provides that a magistrates' court in England and Wales may try an information for an offence under the 1971 Act if the information was laid at any time within twelve months from the commission of the offence.

(c) *Sentence*

14–5   It is necessary to draw a distinction between the three different classifications of drugs. When tried summarily, an offence under s.4(2) committed in relation to a Class A or B drug carries a maximum penalty of six months imprisonment, a fine not exceeding the prescribed sum, or both. Commission involving a Class C drug carries a maximum penalty of three months' imprisonment, a fine not exceeding £2,500 or both. An offence under s.4(3), when tried summarily, carries the same maximum penalties as regards each classification of drug.

When cases of production and supply of Class A drugs are dealt with summarily, the *Magistrates' Court Sentencing Guidelines* (2004) state:

> Aggravating factors include commercial production, large amount, deliberate adulteration, quantity, venue, *e.g.* prisons, educational establishments, sophisticated operation, supply to children, offence committed on bail, relevant previous convictions and any failure to respond to previous sentences.
>
> Mitigating factors include: small amount of drug involved.
>
> **Guideline**: Are the magistrates' sentencing powers sufficient?

14–6   However, in the guideline judgment of *Aramah* (1982) 4 Cr.App.R.(S.) 407 Lord Lane C.J. indicated that it would rarely be appropriate for offences involving Class A drugs to be tried summarily, stating:

'Class A drugs and particularly heroin and morphine: It is common knowledge that these are the most dangerous of all the addictive drugs…consequently, anything which the courts of this country can do by way of deterrent sentences on those found guilty of crimes involving those Class A drugs should be done.'

When cases of production and supply of Class B drugs are dealt with summarily, the *Magistrates' Court Sentencing Guidelines* (2004) state:

Aggravating factors include commercial production, large amount, venue, e.g. prison, educational establishments, deliberate adulteration, offence committed on bail, relevant previous convictions and failures to respond to previous sentences.
Mitigating factors include no commercial motive, small amount.
In all cases forfeiture of all drugs and equipment should be considered.

The CA decision in *Ronchetti* [1998] 2 Cr.App.R.(S.) 100 gives guidance concerning **14–7** appropriate penalties for particular quantities of drugs. Lord Justice Rose stated:

'…we have been invited by the Crown to give some indication for the guidance of judges of first instance, in relation to the sort of level of sentence which is appropriate for importations of the order of 100 kg. In conformity with, but by way of addendum to, *Aramah*, we would suggest that, following a trial, the importation of 100 kg by persons playing more than a subordinate role, should attract a sentence of seven to eight years. In our judgment, 10 years is the appropriate starting point, following a trial, for importations of 500 kg or more, by such persons. Larger importations will, as the authorities show, attract a higher starting point. That starting point should, in our judgment, rise according to the roles played, the weight involved, and all the other circumstances of the case, up to the statutory maximum of 14 years provided by Parliament. The fact that, in a particular case of massive importation, an even greater quantity of the drug might one day have to be dealt with by the courts, is not in itself, in our judgment, a reason for not imposing the maximum sentence where those at the top of an organisation are before the court.'

In *Wijs* [1998] 2 Cr.App.R. 436, a case concerning the importation and possession of amphetamine with intent to supply the CA stated that following conviction for importing amphetamine after a contested trial a custodial sentence will almost invariably be called for, save in exceptional circumstances or where the quantity of the drug is so small as to be compatible only with personal consumption by the importer. The ordinary level of sentence on conviction following a contested trial (and on quantities calculated on the basis of 100 per cent pure amphetamine base) should be:

(1) Up to 500 grammes: up to two years' imprisonment.
(2) More than 500 grammes but less than 2.5 kilos: two-four years' imprisonment.
(3) More than 2.5 kilos but less than 10 kilos: four-seven years' imprisonment.
(4) More than 10 kilos but less than 15 kilos: seven-10 years' imprisonment. (5) More than 15 kilos: upwards of 10 years' imprisonment, subject to the statutory maximum of 14 years' imprisonment.

For general sentencing guidelines, see *Archbold Crown*, §§ 26–107—26–117.

(d) *Elements of the offence*

"Supply" includes distributing (s.37(1)) but the term is not further elaborated by the **14–8** statute. The word "supply" has to be given its ordinary everyday meaning: *Holmes v Chief Constable of Merseyside* [1976] Crim.L.R. 125, DC. In *R. v McGinnis* [1987] A.C. 303, HL, the majority opinion drew a distinction between a "custodier" who has the necessary intent to supply when he returns controlled drugs to a person who had deposited them with him and a "depositor" who places the drugs in the temporary possession of the "custodier" without an intention of enabling the "custodier" to use the drugs for his own purposes.

Misuse of Drugs Act 1971, s.28

Proof of lack of knowledge etc. to be a defence in proceedings for certain offences
    28.—(1) This section applies to offences under any of the following provisions of this Act, that **14—8.1** is to say section 4(2) and (3), section 5(2) and (3), section 6(2) and section 9.

(2) Subject to subsection (3) below, in any proceedings for an offence to which this section applies it shall be a defence for the accused to prove that he neither knew of nor suspected nor had reason to suspect the existence of some fact alleged by the prosecution which it is necessary for the prosecution to prove if he is to be convicted of the offence charged.

(3) Where in any proceedings for an offence to which this section applies it is necessary, if the accused is to be convicted of the offence charged, for the prosecution to prove that some substance or product involved in the alleged offence was the controlled drug which the prosecution alleges it to have been, and it is proved that the substance or product in question was that controlled drug, the accused—

    (a) shall not be acquitted of the offence charged by reason only of proving that he neither knew nor suspected nor had reason to suspect that the substance or product in question was the particular controlled drug alleged; but

    (b) shall be acquitted thereof—

        (i) if he proves that he neither believed nor suspected nor had reasons to suspect that the substance or product in question was a controlled drug; or

        (ii) if he proves that he believed the substance or product in question to be a controlled drug, or a controlled drug of a description, such that, if it had in fact been that controlled drug or a controlled drug of that description, he would not at the material time have been committing any offence to which this section applies.

(4) Nothing in this section shall prejudice any defence which it is open to a person charged with an offence to which this section applies to raise apart from this section.

See further *Archbold Crown* §§ 26-32—26-49a.

C. Restriction of Possession of Controlled Drugs

Misuse of Drugs Act 1971, s.5

Restriction of possession of controlled drugs

14-9   **5.**—(1) Subject to any regulations under section 7 of this Act for the time being in force, it shall not be lawful for a person to have a controlled drug in his possession.

(2) Subject to section 28 of this Act and to subsection (4) below, it is an offence for a person to have a controlled drug in his possession in contravention of subsection (1) above.

(3) Subject to section 28 of this Act, it is an offence for a person to have a controlled drug in his possession, whether lawfully or not, with intent to supply it to another in contravention of section 4(1) of this Act.

(4) In any proceedings for an offence under subsection (2) above in which it is proved that the accused had a controlled drug in his possession, it shall be a defence for him to prove—

    (a) that, knowing or suspecting it to be a controlled drug, he took possession of it for the purpose of preventing another from committing or continuing to commit an offence in connection with that drug and that as soon as possible after taking possession of it he took all such steps as were reasonably open to him to destroy the drug or to deliver it into the custody of a person lawfully entitled to take custody of it; or

    (b) that, knowing or suspecting it to be a controlled drug, he took possession of it for the purpose of delivering it into the custody of a person lawfully entitled to take custody of it and that as soon as possible after taking possession of it he took all such steps as were reasonably open to him to deliver it into the custody of such a person.

(5) Subsection (4) above shall apply in the case of proceedings for an offence under section 19(1) of this Act consisting of an attempt to commit an offence under subsection (2) above as it applies in the case of proceedings for an offence under subsection (2), subject to the following modifications, that is to say—

    (a) for the references to the accused having in his possession, and to his taking possession of, a controlled drug there shall be substituted respectively references to his attempting to get, and to his attempting to take, possession of such a drug; and

(b) in paragraphs (a) and (b) the words from "and that as soon as possible" onwards shall be omitted.

(6) Nothing in subsection (4) or (5) above shall prejudice any defence which it is open to a person charged with an offence under this section to raise apart from that subsection.

(b) *Procedure*

This offence is triable either way: s.25 and Sch.4 to the Act.   **14–10**

The *Practice Note (Mode of Trial: Guidelines)* (1995) cases of possession of Class A drugs should be committed for trial unless the amount is small and consistent with only personal use; cases of class B drugs should be committed for trial when the quantity is substantial. No guideline is given in relation to Class C drugs.

Section 25(4) of the 1971 Act also provides that a magistrates' court in England and Wales may try an information for an offence under the 1971 Act if the information was laid at any time within twelve months from the commission of the offence.

(c) *Sentence*

It is necessary to draw a distinction between the three different classifications of **14–11** drugs. When tried summarily, the maximum penalty for an offence under s.5(2) as regards a Class A is six months imprisonment, a fine not exceeding the prescribed sum, or both. As regards a Class B drug, the maximum penalty is three months imprisonment, a fine of not more than £3,000 or both, and as regards a Class C drug, six months' imprisonment, a fine of not more than £2,500 or both: *Misuse of Drugs Act* 1971, s.25 and Sch.4.

When cases of simple possession of class A drugs are dealt with summarily, the *Magistrates' Court Sentencing Guidelines* (2004) state:

> Aggravating factors include there being an amount other than a very small quantity, the offence is committed whilst on bail, relevant previous convictions and failure to respond to previous sentences.
> Mitigating factors include there being a very small quantity of the drug.
> **Guideline**: Is it serious enough for a community penalty?

However following the guideline judgement of *Aramah* (1982) 4 Cr.App.R.(S.) 407 **14–12** offences involving Class A drugs will rarely be tried summarily.

In *R. v Busby* [2000] 1 Cr.App.R.(S.) 279, the offender pleaded guilty to possessing a Class A substance (Ecstasy) and a Class B drug (amphetamine) in each case with intent to supply. He possessed fourteen Ecstasy tablets and four Amphetamine tablets. He admitted that he intended to share the drugs with two friends and was sentenced to six months' imprisonment by the CA. The short custodial sentence was explained by the fact that imprisonment sends out a clear message to others who need to hear the consequences of this kind of offence. In *Att.-Gen.'s Reference (No.20 of 2002)* [2003] 1 Cr.App.R.(S.) 58 the offender pleaded guilty to possessing Ecstasy with intent to supply. He was found with 24 tablets in his car, and 760 tablets in his bedroom. He admitted he had been selling drugs for a year. He was sentenced to a community punishment and rehabilitation order and ordered to pay £200 prosecution costs. The CA agreed with the Attorney-General that this sentence was unduly lenient and given that the offender had already completed his community punishment, substituted a sentence of two years imprisonment, emphasising the need for custodial sentences in such cases. In *R. v Campbell* (1992) 13 Cr.App.R.(S.) 630, the appellant was convicted of possessing a class A drug, having been found in possession of 106 capsules each containing amphetamine sulphate and a strip of card impregnated with LSD. He was sentenced to 12 months' imprisonment.

When cases of simple possession of Class B drugs are dealt with summarily, the *Mag-* **14–13** *istrates Court Sentencing Guidelines* (2004) state:

> Aggravating factors include large amount, offence committed on bail, relevant previous convictions and any failures to respond to previous sentences

Mitigating factors include small amount of the drug.

Guideline: Is discharge or fine appropriate?

14–14 The guideline fine is starting point B and in all cases forfeiture of all drugs and equipment should be considered.

The *Aramah* guidelines indicate that in cases of simple possession of small amounts of cannabis for personal use, a fine will often be the appropriate penalty, unless the history shows a 'persistent flouting of the law', which may render a custodial sentence appropriate.

In *R. v Gregory* (1993) 14 Cr.App.R.(S.) 403 the offender pleaded guilty to possessing a class A drug with intent to supply, possessing a class A drug, possessing a class B drug, and permitting premises to be used for smoking opium. G was sentenced to six months' imprisonment for possessing heroin with intent to supply, three months for possessing a class A drug, three months for possessing a class B drug, all concurrent, and 15 months' consecutive for allowing premises to be used for smoking opium.

14–15 The CA held that in relation to class B drugs, it might be appropriate to pass a non-custodial sentence in respect of an offence of this kind, but any criminal conduct which facilitated the use of a class A drug must be regarded as serious, even without a commercial motive. It was submitted that G had not corrupted those who used his flat, or profited from them but he had provided the venue in which they could take class A drugs in comparative safety. However, the sentence of 15 months was considered too long and a sentence of six months was substituted, consecutive to the other sentences.

In *R. v Doyle* [1996] 1 Cr.App.R.(S.) 449, the offender pleaded guilty to possession of cannabis with intent to supply and simple possession of cannabis. On a search of his premises the police had found a pot containing five grams of cannabis and a further 380 grams hidden in his garden. He was sentenced to six months' imprisonment. In *R. v Busuttill* [2001] EWCA Crim 627, the defendant pleaded guilty to possession of forty packages of cannabis resin with intent to supply, stating that he was storing them for an associate without payment. He was sentenced to six months' imprisonment.

Supplying drugs to a serving prisoner may result in a more severe penalty. In *R. v Doyle* [1998] 1 Cr.App.R.(S.) 79, CA, the defendant smuggled cannabis to her boyfriend who was serving a prisoner sentence. She was sentenced to twelve months' imprisonment, the Court stating that in view of the pressing nature of the issue of drug culture in prisons, 'six months is no longer the tariff for passing drugs to a prisoner.'

For general sentencing guidelines, see *Archbold Crown* §§ 26–107—26–117.

(d) *Elements of the offence*

14–16 The specific defence provided by s.28 of the 1971 Act is also available to a charge under this section (see above).

"Possession" is not defined by the statute, save that "things which a person has in his possession shall be taken to include anything subject to his control which is the custody of another(s), s.13(3). Possession requires physical custody of the drug and the intention to possess it: *Warner v MPC* [1969] 2 A.C. 256. A person does not have possession of something which has been put into his pocket or house without his knowledge. But a mistake as to the precise quality of the substance under the defendant's control does not itself prevent him from being in possession (*e.g.* possession of heroin believing it to be cannabis or aspirin): *Searl v Randolph* [1972] Crim.L.R. 779, DC. If the drugs are contained inside a package or box then the defendant was in possession of the contents; but the defendant was not in possession if the contents were quite different in kind from what he believed them to be: *R. v McNamaa*, 87 Cr.App.R. 246, CA. Provided physical custody and knowledge can be proved, the quantity of the drug is not relevant to the issue of possession: *R. v Boyesen* [1982] A.C. 768, HL; *DPP v Brooks* [1974] A.C. 862.

See further *Archbold Crown* §§ 26–54—26–78.

D. RESTRICTION OF CULTIVATION OF THE CANNABIS PLANT

(a) *Definition*

Misuse of Drugs Act 1971, s.6

Restriction of cultivation of cannabis plant
6.—(1) Subject to any regulations under section 7 of this Act for the time being in force, it **14–17** shall not be lawful for a person to cultivate any plant of the genus Cannabis.
(2) Subject to section 28 of this Act, it is an offence to cultivate any such plant in contravention of subsection (1) above.

(b) *Procedure*

This offence is triable either way. Section 25(4) of the 1971 Act also provides that a **14–18** magistrates' court in England and Wales may try an information for an offence under the 1971 Act if the information was laid at any time within twelve months from the commission of the offence.

(c) *Sentence*

When tried summarily, the maximum penalty for this offence is six months' imprison- **14–19** ment, a fine not exceeding the prescribed sum, or both: s.25 and Sch.4.

When dealt with summarily, the *Magistrates' Court Sentencing Guidelines* (2000) state:

> Aggravating factors include commercial cultivation, large quantity, offence committed on bail, relevant previous convictions and any failure to respond to previous sentences.
> Mitigating factors include not for personal use, not commercial, not responsible for planting, small-scale cultivation.
> **Guideline**: Is discharge or fine appropriate?

The guideline fine is starting point B. In all cases forfeiture of all drugs and equipment should be considered.

In *R. v Marsland* (1994) 15 Cr.App.R.(S.) 665 the offender pleaded guilty to pro- **14–20** ducing cannabis. Police officers searching the appellant's premises were shown a room in which 22 mature cannabis plants were growing; the room had been adapted for the purpose. A further 55 cannabis plants in various stages of growth were found in other parts of the house. The appellant claimed that he was producing cannabis solely for his own use, and he was sentenced to nine months' imprisonment.

(d) *Elements of the offence*

The specific defence provided by s.28 of the 1971 Act is also available to a charge **14–21** under this section, above. See *Archbold Crown*, § 26–80.

Authorisation Of Activities Otherwise Unlawful Under ss.3 to 6

Misuse of Drugs Act 1971, s.7

Authorisation of activities otherwise unlawful under foregoing provisions
7.—(1) The Secretary of State may by regulations—   **14–22**
    (a) except from section 3(1)(a) or (b), 4(1)(a) or (b) or 5(1) of this Act such controlled drugs as may be specified in the regulations; and
    (b) make such other provision as he thinks fit for the purpose of making it lawful for persons to do things which under any of the following provisions of this Act, that is to say sections 4(1), 5(1) and 6(1), it would otherwise be unlawful for them to do.
(2) Without prejudice to the generality of paragraph (b) of subsection (1) above, regula-

tions under that subsection authorising the doing of any such thing as is mentioned in that paragraph may in particular provide for the doing of that thing to be lawful—

(a) if it is done under and in accordance with the terms of a licence or other authority issued by the Secretary of State and in compliance with any conditions attached thereto; or

(b) if it is done in compliance with such conditions as may be prescribed.

(3) Subject to subsection (4) below, the Secretary of State shall so exercise his power to make regulations under subsection (1) above as to secure—

(a) that it is not unlawful under section 4(1) of this Act for a doctor, dentist, veterinary practitioner or veterinary surgeon, acting in his capacity as such, to prescribe, administer, manufacture, compound or supply a controlled drug, or for a pharmacist or a person lawfully conducting a retail pharmacy business, acting in either case in his capacity as such, to manufacture, compound or supply a controlled drug; and

(b) that it is not unlawful under section 5(1) of this Act for a doctor, dentist, veterinary practitioner, veterinary surgeon, pharmacist or person lawfully conducting a retail pharmacy business to have a controlled drug in his possession for the purpose of acting in his capacity as such.

(4) If in the case of any controlled drug the Secretary of State is of the opinion that it is in the public interest—

(a) for production, supply and possession of that drug to be either wholly unlawful or unlawful except for purposes of research or other special purposes; or

(b) for it to be unlawful for practitioners, pharmacists and persons lawfully conducting retail pharmacy businesses to do in relation to that drug any of the things mentioned in subsection (3) above except under a licence or other authority issued by the Secretary of State,

he may by order designate that drug as a drug to which this subsection applies; and while there is in force an order under this subsection designating a controlled drug as one to which this subsection applies, subsection (3) above shall not apply as regards that drug.

(5) Any order under subsection (4) above may be varied or revoked by a subsequent order thereunder.

(6) The power to make orders under subsection (4) above shall be exercisable by statutory instrument, which shall be subject to annulment in pursuance of a resolution of either House of Parliament.

(7) The Secretary of State shall not make any order under subsection (4) above except after consultation with or on the recommendation of the Advisory Council.

(8) References in this section to a person's "doing" things include references to his having things in his possession.

(9) In its application to Northern Ireland this section shall have effect as if for references to the Secretary of State there were substituted references to the Ministry of Home Affairs for Northern Ireland and as if for subsection (6) there were substituted—

"(6) Any order made under subsection (4) above by the Ministry of Home Affairs for Northern Ireland shall be subject to negative resolution within the meaning of section 41(6) of the *Interpretation Act (Northern Ireland)* 1954 as if it were a statutory instrument within the meaning of that Act."

For *Misuse of Drugs Regulations* 2001, see *Archbold Crown*, §§ 26–131—26–170e.

Misuse of Drugs (Amendment) Regulations 2003, regs 1–2

14–24   **1.** These *Regulations* may be cited as the *Misuse of Drugs (Amendment) Regulations* 2003 and shall come into force on 1st July 2003.

2.—(1) The *Misuse of Drugs Regulations* 2001, shall be amended as follows.

(2) In paragraph 1 of Schedule 2 there shall be inserted—

(a) after "Dihydrocodeinone O-carboxymethyloxime", "Dihydroetorphine"; and

(b) after "Racemorphan", "Remifentanil".

(3) In paragraph 1, Part 1 of Schedule 4 there shall be inserted—

(a) after "Haloxazolam", "4-Hydroxy-n-butyric acid"; and

(b) after "N-Ethylamphetamine", "Zolpidem".

(4) In paragraph 1, Part II of Schedule 4 there shall be inserted—

(a) before "Atamestane", "4-Androstene-3, 17-dione" and "5-Androstene-3, 17 diol"; and

(b) after "Nandrolone", "19-Nor-4-Androstene-3, 17-dione" and "19-Nor-5-Androstene-3, 17 diol".

E. Offences Committed by Occupiers of Premises

(a) Definition

Misuse of Drugs Act 1971, s.8

Occupiers etc. of premises to be punishable for permitting certain activities to take place there

8. A person commits an offence if, being the occupier or concerned in the management of **14–25** any premises, he knowingly permits or suffers any of the following activities to take place on those premises, that is to say—

(a) producing or attempting to produce a controlled drug in contravention of section 4(1) of this Act;

(b) supplying or attempting to supply a controlled drug to another in contravention of section 4(1) of this Act, or offering to supply a controlled drug to another in contravention of section 4(1);

(c) preparing opium for smoking;

(d) smoking cannabis, cannabis resin or prepared opium

(b) Procedure

This offence is triable either way.   **14–26**

Section 25(4) of the 1971 Act also provides that a magistrates' court in England and Wales may try an information for an offence under the 1971 Act if the information was laid at any time within twelve months from the commission of the offence.

(c) Sentence

When tried summarily, and the offence concerns a Class A or B drug, the maximum **14–27** penalty is six months' imprisonment, a fine not exceeding the prescribed sum, or both. When the offence concerns a Class C drug, the maximum penalty is three months' imprisonment, a fine not exceeding £2,500 or both: s.25 and Sch.4.

In *R. v Coulson* [2001] 1 Cr.App.R.(S.) 121, a sentence of 30 months' imprisonment was upheld in the case of an offender who had allowed his premises to be used for supplying heroin. See also *R. v Setchall* [2002] 1 Cr.App.R.(S.) 76.

(d) Elements of the offence

The word 'occupier' includes those with the requisite degree of control to be able to **14–28** exclude those who might otherwise use the premises for the forbidden purposes. 'Permits' involves an unwillingness to prevent the activity which may be inferred from failure to take reasonable steps (judged objectively) to prevent it. See *Archbold Crown*, §§ 26–86—26–88.

F. Opium: Prohibited Activities

(a) Definition

Misuse of Drugs Act 1971, s.9

Prohibition of certain activities etc. relating to opium

9. Subject to section 28 of this Act, it is an offence for a person—   **14–29**

(a) to smoke or otherwise use prepared opium; or

(b) to frequent a place used for the purpose of opium smoking; or

(c) to have in his possession—

    (i) any pipes or other utensils made or adapted for use in connection with the smoking of opium, being pipes or utensils which have been used by him or with his knowledge and permission in that connection or which he intends to use or permit others to use in that connection; or

    (ii) any utensils which have been used by him or with his knowledge and permission in connection with the preparation of opium for smoking.

(b) *Procedure*

14–30　　This offence is triable either way.

(c) *Sentence*

14–31　　When tried summarily, the maximum penalty for this offence is six months' imprisonment, a fine not exceeding the prescribed sum, or both: s.25 and Sch.4.

(d) *Elements of the Offence*

14–32　　'prepared opium' means opium prepared for smoking and includes dross and any other residues remaining after opium has been smoked: *Misuse of Drugs Act* 1971, s.37(1).

G. INCITEMENT

Misuse of Drugs Act 1971, s.19

Attempts etc. to commit offences

14–33　　**19.** It is an offence for a person to attempt to commit an offence under any other provision of this Act or to incite or attempt to incite another to commit such an offence.

14–34　　By s.25(3) of, and Sch.4 to the 1971 Act, the offence of incitement is triable and punishable in the same way as the substantive offence cited.

H. PARTICIPATION IN OFFENCES OUTSIDE THE UNITED KINGDOM

(a) *Definition*

Misuse of Drugs Act 1971, s.20

Assisting in or inducing commission outside United Kingdom of offence punishable under a corresponding law

14–35　　**20.** A person commits an offence if in the United Kingdom he assists in or induces the commission in any place outside the United Kingdom of an offence punishable under the provisions of a corresponding law in force in that place.

(b) *Procedure*

14–36　　This offence is triable either way.

Section 25(4) of the 1971 Act also provides that a magistrates' court in England and Wales may try an information for an offence under the 1971 Act if the information was laid at any time within twelve months from the commission of the offence.

(c) *Sentence*

14–37　　When tried summarily, the maximum penalty for this offence is six months' imprisonment, a fine not exceeding the prescribed sum, or both: s.25 and Sch.4.

This is also a drug trafficking offence: *Drug Trafficking Act* 1994, s.1(3)(b). A minimum custodial sentence of seven years applies to the third Class A drug trafficking offence. A forfeiture order or a confiscation order may also be imposed for a drug trafficking offence.

(d) *Elements of the Offence*

'Assisting' is to be construed as an ordinary English word: *Vickers* (1975) 1 W.L.R. **14–38** 811.

'Corresponding law' is defined in s.36 of the 1971 Act:

Misuse of Drugs Act 1971, s.36

Meaning of "corresponding law", and evidence of certain matters by certificate
36.—(1) In this Act the expression "corresponding law" means a law stated in a certificate   **14–38.1** purporting to be issued by or on behalf of the government of a country outside the United Kingdom to be a law providing for the control and regulation in that country of the production, supply, use, export and import of drugs and other substances in accordance with the provisions of the Single Convention on Narcotic Drugs signed at New York on 30th March 1961 or a law providing for the control and regulation in that country of the production, supply, use, export and import of dangerous or otherwise harmful drugs in pursuance of any treaty, convention or other agreement or arrangement to which the government of that country and Her Majesty's Government in the United Kingdom are for the time being parties.

(2) A statement in any such certificate as aforesaid to the effect that any facts constitute an offence against the law mentioned in the certificate shall be evidence, and in Scotland sufficient evidence, of the matters stated.

I. Power to Direct Special Precautions at Certain Premises

(a) *Definition*

Misuse of Drugs Act 1971, s.11

Power to direct special precautions for safe custody of controlled drugs to be taken at certain premises
11.—(1) Without prejudice to any requirement imposed by regulations made in pursuance   **14–39** of section 10(2)(a) of this Act, the Secretary of State may by notice in writing served on the occupier of any premises on which controlled drugs are or are proposed to be kept give directions as to the taking of precautions or further precautions for the safe custody of any controlled drugs of a description specified in the notice which are kept on those premises.

(2) It is an offence to contravene any directions given under subsection (1) above.

(b) *Procedure*

This offence is triable either way.   **14–40**

Section 25(4) of the 1971 Act also provides that a magistrates' court in England and Wales may try an information for an offence under the 1971 Act if the information was laid at any time within twelve months from the commission of the offence

(c) *Sentence*

When tried summarily, the maximum penalty is six months' imprisonment, a fine   **14–41** not exceeding the prescribed sum, or both.

J. Direction Relating to Prescribing by Practitioners

For offences under ss.12 and 13 of the 1971 Act, see *Archbold Crown*, § 26–93.   **14–42**

K. Failure to Comply with Notice Requiring Information Relating to Prescribing Supply etc of Drugs

(a) *Definition*

Misuse of Drugs Act 1971, s.17

Power to obtain information from doctors, pharmacists etc. in certain circumstances

14–43   **17.**—(1) If it appears to the Secretary of State that there exists in any area in Great Britain a social problem caused by the extensive misuse of dangerous or otherwise harmful drugs in that area, he may by notice in writing served on any doctor or pharmacist practising in or in the vicinity of that area, or on any person carrying on a retail pharmacy business within the meaning of the *Medicines Act* 1968 at any premises situated in or in the vicinity of that area, require him to furnish to the Secretary of State, with respect to any such drugs specified in the notice and as regards any period so specified, such particulars as may be so specified relating to the quantities in which and the number and frequency of the occasions on which those drugs—

     (a) in the case of a doctor, were prescribed, administered or supplied by him;

     (b) in the case of a pharmacist, were supplied by him; or

     (c) in the case of a person carrying on a retail pharmacy business, were supplied in the course of that business at any premises so situated which may be specified in the notice.

(2) A notice under this section may require any such particulars to be furnished in such manner and within such time as may be specified in the notice and, if served on a pharmacist or person carrying on a retail pharmacy business, may require him to furnish the names and addresses of doctors on whose prescriptions any dangerous or otherwise harmful drugs to which the notice relates were supplied, but shall not require any person to furnish any particulars relating to the identity of any person for or to whom any such drug has been prescribed, administered or supplied.

(3) A person commits an offence if without reasonable excuse (proof of which shall lie on him) he fails to comply with any requirement to which he is subject by virtue of subsection (1) above.

(4) A person commits an offence if in purported compliance with a requirement imposed under this section he gives any information which he knows to be false in a material particular or recklessly gives any information which is so false.

(5) In its application to Northern Ireland this section shall have effect as if for the references to Great Britain and the Secretary of State there were substituted respectively references to Northern Ireland and the Ministry of Home Affairs for Northern Ireland.

(b) *Procedure*

14–44   The offence under s.17(3) is triable summarily, the offence under s.17(4) is triable either way: s.25 and Sch.4.

(c) *Sentence*

14–45   The maximum penalty for the offence under s.17(3) is a fine not exceeding level three on the standard scale: s.25 and Sch.4. When tried summarily, the maximum sentence for an offence committed under s.17(4) is six months imprisonment, a fine not exceeding the prescribed sum, or both:

L. Miscellaneous Offences

Misuse of Drugs Act 1971, s.18

Miscellaneous offences

14–46—14–64   **18.**—(1) It is an offence for a person to contravene any regulations made under this Act other than regulations made in pursuance of section 10(2)(h) or (i).

(2) It is an offence for a person to contravene a condition or other term of a licence issued under section 3 of this Act or of a licence or other authority issued under regulations

made under this Act, not being a licence issued under regulations made in pursuance of section 10(2)(i).

(3) A person commits an offence if, in purported compliance with any obligation to give information to which he is subject under or by virtue of regulations made under this Act, he gives any information which he knows to be false in a material particular or recklessly gives any information which is so false.

(4) A person commits an offence if, for the purpose of obtaining, whether for himself or another, the issue or renewal of a licence or other authority under this Act or under any regulations made under this Act, he—

(a) makes any statement or gives any information which he knows to be false in a material particular or recklessly gives any information which is so false; or

(b) produces or otherwise makes use of any book, record or other document which to his knowledge contains any statement or information which he knows to be false in a material particular.

For the Regulations which may be contravened under s.18(1), see *Archbold Crown*, § 26–94.

II. MISCELLANEOUS OFFENCES

A. INTOXICATING SUBSTANCES

(a) *Definition*

Intoxicating Substances (Supply) Act 1985, s.1

Offence of supply of intoxicating substance

1.—(1) It is an offence for a person to supply or offer to supply a substance other than a con- **14–65** trolled drug—

(a) to a person under the age of eighteen whom he knows, or has reasonable cause to believe, to be under that age; or

(b) to a person—

    (i) who is acting on behalf of a person under that age; and

    (ii) whom he knows, or has reasonable cause to believe, to be so acting,

if he knows or has reasonable cause to believe that the substance is, or its fumes are, likely to be inhaled by the person under the age of eighteen for the purpose of causing intoxication.

(2) In proceedings against any person for an offence under subsection (1) above it is a defence for him to show that at the time he made the supply or offer he was under the age of eighteen and was acting otherwise than in the course or furtherance of a business.

(3) A person guilty of an offence under this section shall be liable on summary conviction to imprisonment for a term not exceeding six months or to a fine not exceeding level 5 on the standard scale, or to both.

(4) In this section "controlled drug" has the same meaning as in the *Misuse of Drugs Act* 1971.

(b) *Procedure*

This offence is triable summarily only: s.1(3).   **14–66**

(c) *Sentence*

The maximum penalty for this offence is six months imprisonment of a fine not **14–67** exceeding level five on the standard scale or both: s.1(3).

B. MANUFACTURE OR SUPPLY OF SCHEDULED SUBSTANCES

(a) *Definition*

Criminal Justice (International Co-operation) Act 1990, s.12

Manufacture and supply of scheduled substances

14–68   **12.**—(1) It is an offence for a person—

(a) to manufacture a scheduled substance; or

(b) to supply such a substance to another person,

knowing or suspecting that the substance is to be used in or for the unlawful production of a controlled drug.

(1A) A person does not commit an offence under subsection (1) above if he manufactures or, as the case may be, supplies the scheduled substance with the express consent of a constable.

(2) A person guilty of an offence under subsection (1) above is liable—

(a) on summary conviction, to imprisonment for a term not exceeding six months or a fine not exceeding the statutory maximum or both;

(b) on conviction on indictment, to imprisonment for a term not exceeding fourteen years or a fine or both.

(3) In this section "a controlled drug" has the same meaning as in the *Misuse of Drugs Act* 1971 and "unlawful production of a controlled drug" means the production of such a drug which is unlawful by virtue of section 4(1)(a) of that Act.

(4) In this section and elsewhere in this Part of this Act "a scheduled substance" means a substance for the time being specified in Schedule 2 to this Act.

(5) Her Majesty may by Order in Council amend that Schedule (whether by addition, deletion or transfer from one Table to the other) but—

(a) no such Order shall add any substance to the Schedule unless—

(i) it appears to Her Majesty to be frequently used in or for the unlawful production of a controlled drug; or

(ii) it has been added to the Annex to the Vienna Convention under Article 12 of that Convention; and

(b) no such Order shall be made unless a draft of it has been laid before and approved by a resolution of each House of Parliament.

(b) *Procedure*

14–69   This offence is triable either way, though no proceedings may be instituted without the consent of the DPP or the Commissioners of Customs and Excise: *Criminal Justice (International Co-operation) Act* 1990, s.21(2)(a).

(c) *Sentence*

14–70   When tried summarily, the maximum sentence is six months imprisonment, a fine not exceeding the statutory maximum or both: s.12(2). The offence is classed as a drug trafficking offence (*Drug Trafficking Act* 1994, s.1(3)(d), hence a minimum custodial sentence of seven years must be imposed for the third commission of the third Class A drug trafficking offence. A forfeiture or confiscation order may also be imposed.

(d) *Elements of the Offence*

14–71   Schedule 2 to the 1990 Act specifies what shall be classed as a 'scheduled substance'.

Criminal Justice (International Co-operation) Act 1990, Sch.2

SCHEDULE 2

SUBSTANCES USEFUL FOR MANUFACTURING CONTROLLED DRUGS

TABLE I

N-Acetylanthranilic Acid   **14–71.1**
Ephedrine
Ergometrine
Ergotamine
Isosafrole
Lysergic Acid
3, 4-Methylene-Dioxyphenyl-2-Propanone
Norephedrine
1-Phenyl-2-Propanone
Piperonal
Pseudoephedrine
Safrole

The salts of the substances listed in this Table whenever the existence of such salts is possible.

TABLE II

Acetic Anhydride
Acetone
Anthranilic Acid
Ethyl Ether
Hydrochloric Acid
Methyl Ethyl Ketone (also referred to as 2-Butanone or M.E.K.)
Phenylacetic Acid
Piperidine
Potassium Permanganate
Sulphuric Acid
Toluene

The salts of the substances listed in this Table except hydrochloric acid and sulphuric acid whenever the existence of such salts is possible.

C. Failure to comply with Regulations made under Criminal Justice (International Co-operation) Act 1990

(a) *Definition*

Criminal Justice (International Co-operation) Act 1990, s.13

Regulations about scheduled substances
   13.—(1) The Secretary of State may by regulations make provision—   **14–72**
      (a) imposing requirements as to the documentation of transactions involving scheduled substances;
      (b) requiring the keeping of records and the furnishing of information with respect to such substances;
      (c) for the inspection of records kept pursuant to the regulations;
      (d) for the labelling of consignments of scheduled substances.
   (2) Regulations made by virtue of subsection (1)(b) may, in particular, require—
      (a) the notification of the proposed exportation of substances specified in Table I in

Schedule 2 to this Act to such countries as may be specified in the regulations; and

(b) the production, in such circumstances as may be so specified, of evidence that the required notification has been given;

and for the purposes of section 68 of the *Customs and Excise Management Act* 1979 (offences relating to exportation of prohibited or restricted goods) any such substance shall be deemed to be exported contrary to a restriction for the time being in force with respect to it under this Act if it is exported without the requisite notification having been given.

(3) Regulations under this section may make different provision in relation to the substances specified in Table I and Table II in Schedule 2 to this Act respectively and in relation to different cases or circumstances.

(4) The power to make regulations under this section shall be exercisable by statutory instrument subject to annulment in pursuance of a resolution of either House of Parliament.

(5) Any person who fails to comply with any requirement imposed by the regulations or, in purported compliance with any such requirement, furnishes information which he knows to be false in a material particular or recklessly furnishes information which is false in a material particular is guilty of an offence and liable—

(a) on summary conviction, to imprisonment for a term not exceeding six months or a fine not exceeding the statutory maximum or both;

(b) on conviction on indictment, to imprisonment for a term not exceeding two years or a fine or both.

(6) No information obtained pursuant to the regulations shall be disclosed except for the purposes of criminal proceedings or of proceedings under the provisions of relating to the confiscation of the proceeds of drug trafficking or corresponding provisions in force in Northern Ireland [or of proceedings under Part 2, 3 or 4 of the *Proceeds of Crime Act* 2002.

(b) *Procedure*

14–73   This offence is triable either way: s.13(5).

(c) *Sentence*

14–74   When tried summarily, the maximum penalty for this offence is six months' imprisonment, a fine not exceeding the statutory maximum or both: s.13(5).

(d) *Elements of the offence*

14–75   The *Controlled Drugs (Substances Useful for Manufacture) Regulations* 1991 (SI 1991/1285) have been made in accordance with s.13.

Controlled Drugs (Substances Useful for Manufacture) Regulations 1991, regs 1–7

1.—(1) These Regulations may be cited as the *Controlled Drugs (Substances Useful for Manufacture) Regulations* 1991 and shall come into force on 1st July 1991.

(2) These Regulations are made under section 2(2) of the 1972 Act and section 13 of the 1990 Act, subject to the following exceptions:

(a) regulations 3 to 6 are made under section 2(2) of the 1972 Act alone; and

(b) regulation 7 is made under section 13 of the 1990 Act alone.

2. In these Regulations:

"the 1972 Act" means the *European Communities Act* 1972;

"the 1979 Act" means the *Customs and Excise Management Act* 1979;

"the 1990 Act" means the *Criminal Justice (International Co-operation) Act* 1990;

"the Community Regulation" means Council Regulation (EEC) No. 3677/90, and "operator" has the same meaning as in that Regulation.

3. Subject to regulations 4 and 6 below:

(a) the obligations imposed on operators by Articles 2(2) and (3), 4 and 5 of the Community Regulation and by virtue of regulation 5 below shall be treated as if they were requirements imposed on them by regulations made under section

13(1) of the 1990 Act;

4. In Article 4 of the Community Regulation: **14–75.1**
(a) the words "the competent authorities of the Member State" shall be taken as a
reference to the Secretary of State;

5.—(1) An operator who is concerned in an export, import or transit operation involving a   **14–75.2**
scheduled substance shall ensure that he has the documentation required by Article 2(1) of the
Community Regulation.

In this paragraph, "export", "import", "scheduled substance" and "transit" have the same
meanings as in the Community Regulation.

(2) The obligations imposed by Article 2(4) of the Community Regulation shall be
complied with by the operator mentioned in paragraph (1) of this regulation, and in that
Article the words "the competent authorities" shall be taken as a reference to the Secretary
of State.

5A.—(1) An operator who is concerned in an export operation involving a scheduled
substance in Category 1 of the Annex to the Community Regulation shall ensure that he has the
authorisation required by Article 4 of that Regulation.

(2) An operator who is concerned in an export operation involving a scheduled
substance in Category 2 of the Annex to the Community Regulation shall ensure that he
has such authorisation as is required by Article 5 of that Regulation.

(3) An operator who is concerned in an export operation involving a scheduled
substance in Category 3 of the Annex to the Community Regulation shall ensure that he
has such authorisation, if any, as is required by Article 5a of that Regulation.

(4) For the purposes of section 68 of the 1979 Act (offences relating to exportation of
prohibited or restricted goods) any scheduled substance shall be deemed to be exported
contrary to a restriction for the time being in force with respect to it under these Regulations if it is exported without the requisite authorisation having been obtained.

(5) In this regulation, "export" (except where it occurs in paragraph (4) above) and
"scheduled substance" have the same meanings as in the Community Regulation, and in
Articles 4, 5 and 5a of the Community Regulation the words "the competent authorities"
shall be taken as a reference to the Secretary of State.

5B. An operator who fails to comply with any of the requirements imposed by Article 2a of
the Community Regulation is guilty of an offence and liable:
(a) on summary conviction, to imprisonment for a term not exceeding 3 months or
a fine not exceeding the statutory maximum or both;
(b) on conviction on indictment, to imprisonment for a term not exceeding two
years or a fine or both.

5C.—(1) An operator who fails to comply with any of the requirements imposed by virtue of
regulation 5A above is guilty of an offence and liable to the same penalties as an operator who is
guilty of an offence under regulation 5B above.

(2) The powers conferred by subsection (1) of section 23 of the *Misuse of Drugs Act*
1971 shall be exercisable also for the purposes of the execution of Articles 4, 5 and 5a of the
Community Regulation and subsection (3) of that section (excluding paragraph (a)) shall apply
also to the offence under paragraph (1) above, taking references in those subsections to controlled drugs as references to scheduled substances within the meaning of the Community
Regulation.

5D. Any reference in regulations 5B and 5C above to an operator who fails to comply with
the requirements mentioned in those regulations shall include an operator who, in purported
compliance with any such requirement:
(a) furnishes information which he knows to be false in a material particular; or
(b) recklessly furnishes information which is false in a material particular.

6. Where a person is convicted of an offence contrary to section 68 of the 1979 Act [as a result   **14–75.4**
of the application of regulation 5A above,]or section 13(5) of the 1990 Act as a result of the application of regulation 3 above:
(a) section 68(1) of the 1979 Act shall have effect as if after the words "greater" there
were added the words "but not exceeding the statutory maximum";
(b) section 68(3)(a) of the 1979 Act shall have effect as if after the words "greater"
there were added the words "but not exceeding the statutory maximum", and
for the words "6 months" there were substituted the words "3 months";

(c) section 68(3)(b) of the 1979 Act shall have effect as if for the words "7 years" there were substituted the words "2 years";

(d) section 13(5)(a) of the 1990 Act shall have effect as if for the words "6 months" there were substituted the words "3 months".

14–75.5　　7. A person who produces or supplies a scheduled substance specified in Table 1 in Schedule 2 to the 1990 Act shall:

(a) make a record of each quantity of such scheduled substance produced or supplied by him, as the case may be; and

(b) preserve all records made under this regulation for a period of not less than two years from the end of the calendar year in which the production or supply, as the case may be, took place.

In this regulation, "produce" and "supply" have the same meanings as in the *Misuse of Drugs Act* 1971.

[Regulations 3, 4, 5–5D and 6 are reprinted as amended by the *Controlled Drugs (Substances Useful for Manufacture) (Amendment) Regulations* (SI 1992/2914), regs 3(b), 4, 5 and 6 respectively.]

D. Ships used for Illicit Traffic

(a) *Definition*

Criminal Justice (International Co-operation) Act 1990, s.19

Ships used for illicit traffic

14–76　　**19.**—(1) This section applies to a British ship, a ship registered in a state other than the United Kingdom which is a party to the Vienna Convention (a "Convention state") and a ship not registered in any country or territory.

(2) A person is guilty of an offence if on a ship to which this sections applies, wherever it may be, he—

(a) has a controlled drug in his possession; or

(b) is in any way knowingly concerned in the carrying or concealing of a controlled drug on the ship,

knowing or having reasonable grounds to suspect that the drug is intended to be imported or has been exported contrary to section 3(1) of the *Misuse of Drugs Act* 1971 or the law of any state other than the United Kingdom.

(3) A certificate purporting to be issued by or on behalf of the government of any state to the effect that the importation or export of a controlled drug is prohibited by the law of that state shall be evidence, and in Scotland sufficient evidence, of the matters stated.

(4) A person guilty of an offence under this section is liable—

(a) in a case where the controlled drug is a Class A drug—

(i) on summary conviction, to imprisonment for a term not exceeding six months or a fine not exceeding the statutory maximum or both;

(ii) on conviction on indictment, to imprisonment for life or a fine or both;

(b) in a case where the controlled drug is a Class B drug—

(i) on summary conviction, to imprisonment for a term not exceeding six months or a fine not exceeding the statutory maximum or both;

(ii) on conviction on indictment, to imprisonment for a term not exceeding fourteen years or a fine or both;

(c) in a case where the controlled drug is a Class C drug—

(i) on summary conviction, to imprisonment for a term not exceeding three months or a fine not exceeding the statutory maximum or both;

(ii) on conviction on indictment, to imprisonment for a term not exceeding five years or a fine or both.

(5) In this section "a controlled drug" and the references to controlled drugs of a specified Class have the same meaning as in the said Act of 1971; and an offence under this section shall be included in the offences to which section 28 of that Act (defences) applies.

(b) *Procedure*

14–77　　Each offence is triable either way, though the consent of the DPP or the Commissioners of Customs and Excise: *Criminal Justice (International Co-operation) Act* 1990, s.21(2)(a). The consent of the Secretary of State of the powers conferred by Sch.3 is required to institute proceedings when the offence is alleged to have been committed outside the landward limits of the territorial sea of the UK on a ship registered in a state which is party to the Vienna Convention. The *Territorial Waters Jurisdiction Act* 1878, s.3 does not apply to these proceedings: *Criminal Justice (International Co-operation) Act* 1990, s.21(3).

(c) *Sentence*

Where the offence committed involves a Class A drug, when tried summarily, the **14–78** maximum penalty is six months imprisonment, a fine not exceeding the statutory maximum or both: s.19(4)(a).

Where the offence committed involves a Class B drug, when tried summarily, the maximum penalty is six months imprisonment, a fine not exceeding the statutory maximum or both: s.19(4)(b).

Where the offence committed involves a Class C drug, when tried summarily, the maximum penalty is three months imprisonment, a fine not exceeding the statutory maximum or both: s.19(4)(c).

(d) *Elements of the offence*

Criminal Justice (International Co-operation) Act 1990, s.24

Interpretation of Part II

24.—(1) In this Part of this Act—   **14–79**

"British ship" means a ship registered in the United Kingdom or a colony;

" Convention state" has the meaning given in section 19(1) above;

"scheduled substance" has the meaning given in section 12(4) above;

"ship" includes any vessel used in navigation;

"the territorial sea of the United Kingdom" includes the territorial sea adjacent to any of the Channel Islands, the Isle of Man or any colony;

"the Vienna Convention" means the United Nations Convention against Illicit Traffic in Narcotic Drugs and Psychotropic Substances which was signed in Vienna on 20th December 1988.

(2) Any expression used in this Part of this Act which is also used in the *Drug Trafficking Act* 1994 has the same meaning as in that Act and, in section 22(1), "drug trafficking offences" includes drug trafficking offences within the meaning of the *Criminal Justice (Confiscation) (Northern Ireland) Order* 1990.

(3) In relation to Scotland, any expression used in this Part of this Act which is also used in the *Criminal Justice (Scotland) Act* 1987 has the same meaning as in that Act and "drug trafficking offence" means an offence to which section 1 of that Act relates.

(4) If in any proceedings under this Part of this Act any question arises whether any country or territory is a state or is a party to the Vienna Convention, a certificate issued by or under the authority of the Secretary of State shall be conclusive evidence on that question.

The defence established by s.28 of the *Misuse of Drugs Act* 1971 applies to this section: s.19(5).

E. FAILURE TO PROVIDE A SAMPLE AT A POLICE STATION FOR TESTING

(a) *Definition*

Police and Criminal Evidence Act 1984, ss.63B, 63C

Testing for presence of Class A drugs

63B.—(1) A sample of urine or a non-intimate sample may be taken from a person in police **14–80**

detention for the purpose of ascertaining whether he has any specified Class A drug in his body if the following conditions are met.

(2) The first condition is—

(a) that the person concerned has been charged with a trigger offence; or

(b) that the person concerned has been charged with an offence and a police officer of at least the rank of inspector, who has reasonable grounds for suspecting that the misuse by that person of any specified Class A drug caused or contributed to the offence, has authorised the sample to be taken.

(3) The second condition is that the person concerned has attained the age of 18.

(4) The third condition is that a police officer has requested the person concerned to give the sample.

(5) Before requesting the person concerned to give a sample, an officer must—

(a) warn him that if, when so requested, he fails without good cause to do so he may be liable to prosecution, and

(b) in a case within subsection (2)(b) above, inform him of the giving of the authorisation and of the grounds in question.

(6) A sample may be taken under this section only by a person prescribed by regulations made by the Secretary of State by statutory instrument.

No regulations shall be made under this subsection unless a draft has been laid before, and approved by resolution of, each House of Parliament.

(7) Information obtained from a sample taken under this section may be disclosed—

(a) for the purpose of informing any decision about granting bail in criminal proceedings (within the meaning of the *Bail Act* 1976) to the person concerned;

(b) where the person concerned is in police detention or is remanded in or committed to custody by an order of a court or has been granted such bail, for the purpose of informing any decision about his supervision;

(c) where the person concerned is convicted of an offence, for the purpose of informing any decision about the appropriate sentence to be passed by a court and any decision about his supervision or release;

(d) for the purpose of ensuring that appropriate advice and treatment is made available to the person concerned.

(8) A person who fails without good cause to give any sample which may be taken from him under this section shall be guilty of an offence.

Testing for presence of Class A drugs: supplementary

14–81   **63C.**—(1) A person guilty of an offence under section 63B above shall be liable on summary conviction to imprisonment for a term not exceeding three months, or to a fine not exceeding level 4 on the standard scale, or to both.

(2) A police officer may give an authorisation under section 63B above orally or in writing but, if he gives it orally, he shall confirm it in writing as soon as is practicable.

(3) If a sample is taken under section 63B above by virtue of an authorisation, the authorisation and the grounds for the suspicion shall be recorded as soon as is practicable after the sample is taken.

(4) If the sample is taken from a person detained at a police station, the matters required to be recorded by subsection (3) above shall be recorded in his custody record.

(5) Subsections (11) and (12) of section 62 above apply for the purposes of section 63B above as they do for the purposes of that section; and section 63B above does not prejudice the generality of sections 62 and 63 above.

(6) In section 63B above—

"Class A drug" and "misuse" have the same meanings as in the *Misuse of Drugs Act* 1971;

"specified" (in relation to a Class A drug) and "trigger offence" have the same meanings as in Part III of the *Criminal Justice and Court Services Act* 2000.

(b) *Procedure*

14–82   This offence is triable summarily. It was introduced as an amendment to *PACE* 1984 by s.57 of the *Criminal Justice and Court Services Act* 2000.

(c) *Sentence*

Maximum penalty is three months imprisonment, or to fine not exceeding level 4 on **14–83** the standard scale, or both.

(d) *Elements of the offence*

See ss.63B and 63C above. The conditions for testing are as follows: **14–84**

1. Person charged with a trigger offence OR that the person concerned has been charged with an offence and a police officer of at least the rank of inspector, who has reasonable grounds for suspecting that the misuse by that person of any specified Class A drug caused or contributed to the offence, has authorised the sample to be taken
2. That the detainee has reached the age of 18
3. That the Police Officer has requested the detainee to give the sample

Trigger offences are set out in Sch.6 to the *CJCSA* 2000 and include: theft, robbery, burglary, aggravated burglary, TDA, aggravated, obtaining property by deception, going equipped, production and supply of controlled drugs, possession of drugs, possession with intent to supply.

Before a sample has been given, a police officer must warn the detainee that if when so requested he fails without good cause to do so, he may be liable to prosecution (three months or level 4 fine s.63B(8)), and where inspector authorised the sample (latter part of condition 1) must inform him of the authorisation and grounds.

At the time of writing, the Home Office had announced its intention to expand the category of persons and offences to which mandatory drug testing will apply.

CHAPTER 15

CUSTOMS AND EXCISE OFFENCES

I. INTRODUCTION

A. CUSTOMS AND EXCISE MANAGEMENT ACT 1979

(1) Definitions and Applications

Customs and Excise Management Act 1979, s.1

Interpretation

1.—(1) In this Act, unless the context otherwise requires— **15–1**
"aerodrome" means any area of land or water designed, equipped, set apart of commonly used for affording facilities for the landing and departure of aircraft;
"approved wharf" has the meaning given by section 20A below;
"armed forces" means the Royal Navy, the Royal Marines, the regular army and the regular air force, and any reserve or auxiliary force of any of those services which has been called out on permanent service, or embodied;
"assigned matter" means any matter in relation to which the Commissioners are for the time being required in pursuance of any enactment to perform any duties;
"boarding station" means a boarding station for the time being appointed under section 19 below;
"boundary" means the land boundary of Northern Ireland;
"British ship" means a British ship within the meaning of the *Merchant Shipping Act* 1995;
"claimant", in relation to proceedings for the condemnation of any thing as being forfeited, means a person claiming that the thing is not liable to forfeiture;
"coasting ship" has the meaning given by section 69 below;
"commander", in relation to an aircraft, includes any person having or taking the charge or command of the aircraft;
"the Commissioners" means the Commissioners of Customs and Excise;
"Community transit goods" —
  (a) in relation to imported goods, means—
    (i) goods which have been imported under the internal or external

Community transit procedure for transit through the United Kingdom with a view to exportation where the importation was and the transit and exportation are to be part of one Community transit operation; or

(ii) goods which have, at the port or airport at which they were imported, been placed under the internal or external Community transit procedure for transit through the United Kingdom with a view to exportation where the transit and exportation are to be part of one Community transit operation;

(b) in relation to goods for exportation, means—

(i) goods which have been imported as mentioned in paragraph (a)(i) of this definition and are to be exported as part of the Community transit operation in the course of which they were imported; or

(ii) goods which have, under the internal or external Community transit procedure, transited the United Kingdom from the port or airport at which they were imported and are to be exported as part of the Community transit operation which commenced at that port or airport and for the purposes of paragraph (a)(i) above the Isle of Man shall be treated as if it were part of the United Kingdom;

"container" includes any bundle or package and any box, cask or other receptacle whatsoever;

"the customs and excise Acts" means the Customs and Excise Acts 1979 and any other enactment for the time being in force relating to customs or excise;

"the Customs and Excise Acts 1979" means—

this Act,

the *Customs and Excise Duties (General Reliefs) Act* 1979,

the *Alcoholic Liquor Duties Act* 1979,

the *Hydrocarbon Oil Duties Act* 1979, and

the *Tobacco Products Duty Act* 1979;

"customs and excise airport" has the meaning given by section 21(7) below;

"customs and excise station" has the meaning given by section 26 below;

"designation order" has the meaning given by section 100A(5);

"drawback goods" means goods in the case of which a claim for drawback has been or is to be made;

"dutiable goods", except in the expression "dutiable or restricted goods", means goods of a class or description subject to any duty of customs or excise, whether or not those goods are in fact chargeable with that duty, and whether or not that duty has been paid thereon;

"dutiable or restricted goods" has the meaning given by section 52 below;

"examination station" has the meaning given by section 22A below;

"excise duty point" has the meaning given by section 1 of the *Finance (No. 2) Act* 1992;

"excise licence trade" means, subject to subsection (5) below, a trade or business for the carrying on of which an excise licence is required;

"excise warehouse" means a place of security approved by the Commissioners under subsection (1) (whether or not it is also approved under subsection (2)) of section 92 below, and, except in that section, also includes a distiller's warehouse;

"exporter", in relation to goods for exportation or for use as stores, includes the shipper of the goods and any person performing in relation to an aircraft functions corresponding with those of a shipper;

"free zone" has the meaning given by section 100A(2);

"free zone goods" are goods which are within a free zone;

"goods" includes stores and baggage;

15–2

"holiday", in relation to any part of the United Kingdom, means any day that is a bank holiday in that part of the United Kingdom under the *Banking and Financial Dealings Act* 1971, Christmas Day, Good Friday and the day appointed for the purposes of customs and excise for the celebration of Her Majesty's birthday;

"hovercraft" means a hovercraft within the meaning of the *Hovercraft Act* 1968;

"importer", in relation to any goods at any time between their importation and the time when they are delivered out of charge, includes any owner or other person for the time being possessed of or beneficially interested in the goods and, in relation to goods imported by means of a pipe-line, includes the owner of the pipe-line;

"justice" and "justice of the peace" in Scotland includes a sheriff and in Northern Ireland, in relation to any powers and duties which can under any enactment for the time being in force be exercised and performed only by a resident magistrate, means a resident magistrate;

"land" and "landing", in relation to aircraft, include alighting on water;

"law officer of the Crown" means the Attorney General or for the purpose of criminal proceedings in Scotland, the Lord Advocate or, for the purpose of civil proceedings in Scotland, the appropriate Law Officer within the meaning of section 4A of the *Crown Suits (Scotland) Act* 1857 or in Northern Ireland the Attorney General for Northern Ireland;

"licence year", in relation to an excise licence issuable annually, means the period of 12 months ending on the date on which that licence expires in any year;

"master", in relation to a ship, includes any person having or taking the charge or command of the ship;

"night" means the period between 11 pm and 5 am;

"occupier", in relation to any bonded premises, includes any person who has given security to the Crown in respect of those premises;

"officer" means, subject to section 8(2) below, a person commissioned by the Commissioners; **15–3**

"owner", in relation to an aircraft, includes the operator of the aircraft; "owner", in relation to a pipe-line, means (except in the case of a pipe-line vested in the Crown which in pursuance of arrangements in that behalf is operated by another) the person in whom the line is vested and, in the said excepted case, means the person operating the line;

"perfect entry" means an entry made in accordance with regulation 5 of the *Customs Controls on Importation of Goods Regulations* 1991 or warehousing regulations as the case may require;

"pipe-line" has the meaning given by section 65 of the *Pipe-lines Act* 1962 (that Act being taken, for the purposes of this definition, to extend to Northern Ireland);

"port" means a port appointed by the Commissioners under section 19 below;

"prescribed area" means such an area in Northern Ireland adjoining the boundary as the Commissioners may by regulations prescribe;

"prescribed sum", in relation to the penalty provided for an offence, has the meaning given by section 171(2) below;

"prohibited or restricted goods" means goods of a class or description of which the importation, exportation or carriage coastwise is for the time being prohibited or restricted under or by virtue of any enactment;

"proper", in relation to the person by, with or to whom, or the place at which, anything is to be done, means the person or place appointed or authorised in that behalf by the Commissioners;

"proprietor", in relation to any goods, includes any owner, importer, exporter, shipping or other person for the time being possessed of or beneficially interested in those goods; **15–4**

"Queen's warehouse" means any place provided by the Crown or appointed by the Commissioners for the deposit of goods for security thereof and of the duties chargeable thereon;

"registered excise dealer and shipper" means a revenue trader approved and registered by the Commissioners under section 100G below;

"registered excise dealers and shippers regulations" means regulations under section 100G below;

"representative", in relation to any person from whom the Commissioners assess an amount as being excise duty due, means his personal representative, trustee in bankruptcy or interim or permanent trustee, any receiver or liquidator appointed in relation to him or any of his property or any other person acting in a representative capacity in relation to him; **15–5**

"the revenue trade provisions of the customs and excise Acts" means—

   (a) the provisions of the customs and excise Acts relating to the protection, security, collection or management of the revenues derived from the duties of excise on goods produced or manufactured in the United Kingdom;

(b) the provisions of the customs and excise Acts relating to any activity or facility for the carrying on or provision of which an excise licence is required;

(c) the provisions of the *Betting and Gaming Duties Act* 1972 (so far as not included in paragraph (b) above);

(d) the provisions of Chapter II of Part I of the *Finance Act* 1993;

(e) the provisions of sections 10 to 15 of, and Schedule 1 to, the *Finance Act* 1997;

"revenue trader" means—

(a) any person carrying on a trade or business subject to any of the revenue trade provisions of the customs and excise Acts, or which consists of or includes—

(i) the buying, selling, importation, exportation, dealing in or handling of any goods of a class or description which is subject to a duty of excise (whether or not duty is chargeable on the goods);

(ia) the buying, selling, importation, exportation, dealing in or handling of tickets or chances on the taking of which lottery duty is or will be chargeable;

(ib) being (within the meaning of sections 10 to 15 of the *Finance Act* 1997 the provider of any premises for gaming;

(ic) the organisation, management or promotion of any gaming (within the meaning of the *Gaming Act* 1968 or the *Betting, Gaming, Lotteries and Amusements (Northern Ireland) Order* 1985), or

(ii) the financing or facilitation of any such transactions or activities as are mentioned in sub-paragraph (i), (ia), (ib) or (ic) above, whether or not that trade or business is an excise licence trade, and;

(b) any person who is a wholesaler or an occupier of an excise warehouse (so far as not included in paragraph (a) above), and includes a registered club;

15–6

"ship" and "vessel" include any boat or other vessel whatsoever (and, to the extent provided in section 2 below, any hovercraft);

"shipment" includes loading into an aircraft, and "shipped" and cognate expressions shall be construed accordingly;

"stores" means, subject to subsection (4) below, goods for use in a ship or aircraft and includes fuel and spare parts and other articles of equipment, whether or not for immediate fitting;

"tons register" means the tons of a ship's net tonnage as ascertained and registered according to the tonnage regulations of the *Merchant Shipping Act* 1995 or, in the case of a ship which is not registered under that Act, ascertained in like manner as if it were to be so registered;

"transit goods", except in the expression "Community transit goods", means imported goods entered on importation for transit or transhipment;

"transit or transhipment", in relation to the entry of goods, means transit through the United Kingdom or transhipment with a view to the re-exportation of the goods in question or transhipment of those goods for use as stores;

15–7

"transit shed" has the meaning given by section 25A below;

"United Kingdom waters" means any waters (including inland waters) within the seaward limits of the territorial sea of the United Kingdom;

"vehicle" includes a railway vehicle;

"victualling warehouse" means a place of security approved by the Commissioners under subsection (2) (whether or not it is also a place approved under subsection (1) of section 92 below).

"warehouse", except in the expressions "Queen's warehouse" and "distiller's warehouse", means a place of security approved by the Commissioners under subsection (1) or (2) or subsections (1) and (2) of section 92 below and, except in that section, also includes a distiller's warehouse; and "warehoused" and cognate expressions shall, subject to subsection (4) of that section and any regulations made by virtue of section 93(2)(da)(i) or (ee) or (4) below, be construed accordingly;

"warehousing regulations" means regulations under section 93 below.

(2) This Act and the other Acts included in the Customs and Excise Acts 1979 shall be **15–8** construed as one Act but where a provision of this Act refers to this Act that reference is not to be construed as including a reference to any of the others.

(3) Any expression used in this Act or in any instrument made under this Act to which a meaning is given by any other Act included in the Customs and Excise Acts 1979 has, except where the context otherwise requires, the same meaning in this Act or any such instrument as in that Act; and for ease of reference the Table below indicates the expressions used in this Act to which a meaning is given by any other such Act—

Alcoholic Liquor Duties Act 1979
"beer"
"brewer" and "registered brewer"
"cider"
"compounder"
"distiller"
"distiller's warehouse"
"dutiable alcoholic liquor"
"licensed", in relation to producers of wine or made-wine
"made-wine"
"producer of made-wine"
"producer of wine"
"proof"
"rectifier"
"registered club"
"spirits"
"wholesaler"
"wine"
Hydrocarbon Oil Duties Act 1979
"rebate"
"refinery"
Tobacco Products Duty Act 1979
"tobacco products"

(4) Goods for use in a ship or aircraft as merchandise for sale to persons carried in the **15–9** ship or aircraft shall be treated for the purposes of the customs and excise Acts as stores if, and only if—
(a) the goods are to be sold by retail either—
(i)   in the course of a relevant journey, or
(ii) for consumption on board;
and
(b) the goods are not treated as exported by virtue of regulations under section 12 of the *Customs and Excise Duties (General Reliefs) Act* 1979 (goods for use in naval ships or establishments).

(4A) For the purposes of subsection (4) above a relevant journey is any journey begin- **15–10** ning in the United Kingdom and having an immediate destination outside the member States.

(4B) In relation to goods treated as stores by virtue of subsection (4) above, any reference in the customs and excise Acts to the consumption of stores shall be construed as referring to the sale of the goods as mentioned in paragraph (a) of that subsection.

(5) A person who deals in or sells tobacco products in the course of a trade or business carried on by him shall be deemed for the purposes of this Act to be carrying on an excise licence trade (and to be a revenue trader) notwithstanding that no excise licence is required for carrying on that trade or business.

(6) In computing for the purposes of this Act any period expressed therein as a period of clear days no account shall be taken of the day of the event from which the period is computed or of any Sunday or holiday.

(7) The provisions of this Act in so far as they relate to customs duties apply, notwithstanding that any duties are imposed for the benefit of the Communities, as if the

revenue from duties so imposed remained part of the revenues of the Crown.

[This section is printed as amended by the *Isle of Man Act* 1979, s.13 and Sch.1; the *Betting and Gaming Duties Act* 1981, s.34(1) and Sch.5, para.5(a); the *Finance Act* 1981, s.11(1) and Sch.8, Pt I, para.1(1), (2); the *Finance Act* 1984, s.8 and Sch.4, Pt II, para.1; the *Finance (No.2) Act* 1987, s.103(3); the *Territorial Sea Act* 1987, s.3(1), (4), Sch.1, para.4(1) and Sch.2; the *Finance Act* 1991, s.11(1), (2); the *Customs Controls on Importation of Goods Regulations* 1991 (SI 1991/2724), reg. 6(1) and (2); the *Finance (No.2) Act* 1992, s.3 and Sch.2; the *Finance Act* 1993, s.30; and the *Merchant Shipping Act* 1995, Sch.13. Immaterial definitions in subs.(1) have been omitted.]

Customs and Excise Management Act 1979, s.5

Time of importation, exportation, etc.

15–12   5.—(1) The provisions of this section shall have effect for the purposes of the customs and excise Acts.

(2) Subject to subsections (3) and (6) below, the time of importation of any goods shall be deemed to be—

    (a) where the goods are brought by sea, the time when the ship carrying them comes within the limits of a port;

    (b) where the goods are brought by air, the time when the aircraft carrying them lands in the United Kingdom or the time when the goods are unloaded in the United Kingdom, whichever is the earlier;

    (c) where the goods are brought by land, the time when the goods are brought across the boundary into Northern Ireland.

(3) In the case of goods brought by sea of which entry is not required under regulation 5 of the *Customs Controls on Importation of Goods Regulations* 1991, the time of importation shall be deemed to be the time when the ship carrying them came within the limits of the port at which the goods are discharged.

(4) Subject to subsections (5) and (7) below, the time of exportation of any goods from the United Kingdom shall be deemed to be—

    (a) where the goods are exported by sea or air, the time when the goods are shipped for exportation;

    (b) where the goods are exported by land, the time when they are cleared by the proper officer at the last customs and excise station on their way to the boundary.

(5) In the case of goods of a class or description with respect to the exportation of which any prohibition or restriction is for the time being in force under or by virtue of any enactment which are exported by sea or air, the time of exportation shall be deemed to be the time when the exporting ship or aircraft departs from the last port or customs and excise airport at which it is cleared before departing for a destination outside the United Kingdom.

(6) Goods imported by means of a pipe-line shall be treated as imported at the time when they are brought within the limits of a port or brought across the boundary into Northern Ireland.

(7) Goods exported by means of a pipe-line shall be treated as exported at the time when they are charged into that pipe-line for exportation.

(8) A ship shall be deemed to have arrived at or departed from a port at the time when the ship comes within or, as the case may be, leaves the limits of that port.

[This section is printed as amended by the *Customs and Excise (Single Market etc.) Regulations* 1992 (SI 1992/3095), reg.10(1), Sch.1, para.3.]

(2) Proceedings in the Magistrates' Court

15–13   No proceedings for an offence under this Act shall be instituted except by order of the Commissioners and proceedings shall be in the name of an officer: s.145. Any officer authorised for that purpose may conduct proceedings in the magistrates' court: s.155. Proceedings may not be commenced for an indictable offence after twenty years have elapsed since the day the offence was committed and for a summary offence after three years but subject to that a summary offence may be commenced within six months from the date upon which sufficient evidence to warrant the proceedings came to the knowledge of the prosecuting authority: s.146A. A certificate of the latter fact is sufficient. Proceedings may be commenced in any court having jurisdiction in the place where the person charged with the offence resides or is found, where anything was seized or detained in connection with the charge or where the offence was committed: s.148.

Where two or more persons are liable for an offence they may be proceeded against jointly or severally and shall each be liable for the full amount of any pecuniary penalty although the court may mitigate that penalty: s.150.

Proceedings take place in the normal way save that: **15–14**

— the court may not change from committal proceedings to a summary trial without the consent of the Commissioners or, where the proceedings were brought in the name of the Attorney-General, his consent.

— the prosecutor may appeal to the Crown Court: s.147.

II. OFFENCES IN CONNECTION WITH COMMISSIONERS, OFFICERS, ETC.

A. Impersonating a Customs Officer

(a) *Definition*

Customs and Excise Management Act 1979, s.13

Unlawful assumption of character of officer, etc.

13. If, for the purpose of obtaining admission to any house or other place, or of doing or **15–15** procuring to be done any act which he would not be entitled to do or procure to be done of his own authority, or for any other unlawful purpose, any person falsely assumes the name, designation or character of a Commissioner or officer or of a person appointed by the Commissioners he may be detained and shall, in addition to any other punishment to which he may have rendered himself liable, be liable—

(a) on summary conviction, to a penalty of the prescribed sum, or to imprisonment for a term not exceeding 3 months, or to both; or

(b) on conviction on indictment, to a penalty of any amount, or to imprisonment for a term not exceeding 2 years, or to both.

[This section is printed as amended by the *PACE Act* 1984, s.114(1).]

(b) *Procedure*

This offence is triable either way.   **15–16**

(c) *Elements of the offence*

The prosecution must prove that the defendant either: **15–17**

— committed an act or gained admission to a house or other place
— acted unlawfully or outside his authority
— was impersonating an officer at the time.

(d) *Sentence*

The maximum penalty is three months' imprisonment, a £5000 fine or both: *Customs* **15–18** *and Excise Management Act* 1979, s.171.

B. Bribery and Collusion

(a) Definition

Customs and Excise Act 1979, s.15

Bribery and collusion

15–19   **15.**—(1) If any Commissioner or officer or any person appointed or authorised by the Commissioners to discharge any duty relating to an assigned matter—

(a) directly or indirectly asks for or takes in connection with any of his duties any payment or other reward whatsoever, whether pecuniary or other, or any promise or security for any such payment or reward, not being a payment or reward which he is lawfully entitled to claim or receive; or

(b) enters into or acquiesces in any agreement to do, abstain from doing, permit, conceal or connive at any act or thing whereby Her Majesty is or may be defrauded or which is otherwise unlawful, being an act or thing relating to an assigned matter,

he shall be guilty of an offence under this section.

(2) If any person—

(a) directly or indirectly offers or gives to any Commissioner or officer or to any person appointed or authorised by the Commissioners as aforesaid any payment or other reward whatsoever, whether pecuniary or other, or any promise or security for any such payment or reward; or

(b) proposes or enters into any agreement with any Commissioner, officer or person appointed or authorised as aforesaid,

in order to induce him to do, abstain from doing, permit, conceal or connive at any act or thing whereby Her Majesty is or may be defrauded or which is otherwise unlawful, being an act or thing relating to an assigned matter, or otherwise to take any course contrary to his duty, he shall be guilty of an offence under this section.

(3) Any person committing an offence under this section shall be liable on summary conviction to a penalty of level 5 on the standard scale and may be detained.

(b) Procedure

15–20   This offence is triable summarily.

(c) Elements of the offence

15–21   In the case of an officer (s.15(1)) the prosecution must prove:

— he has asked for or has taken money or other reward to which he is not entitled

— he has agreed to perform an act or omission as a result

— the act or omission will deprive the government of excise duty or is otherwise unlawful.

In the case of any person (s.15(2)) the prosecution must prove:

— he has given or offered money or a reward directly or indirectly to a customs officer or has made an agreement or proposed to a customs officer

— that offer, gift, agreement or proposal is intended to make the officer perform an act or omission or allow or conceal something

— the act *etc.* may or has deprived the government of excise duty.

(d) Sentence

15–22   The maximum penalty is a fine of £5000.

C. Obstruction

(a) *Definition*

Customs and Excise Management Act 1979, s.16

Obstruction of officers, etc.

16.—(1) Any person who—   **15–23**

(a) obstructs, hinders, molests or assaults any person duly engaged in the performance of any duty or the exercise of any power imposed or conferred on him by or under any enactment relating to an assigned matter, or any person acting in his aid; or

(b) does anything which impedes or is calculated to impede the carrying out of any search for any thing liable to forfeiture under any such enactment or the detention, seizure or removal of any such thing; or

(c) rescues, damages or destroys any thing so liable to forfeiture or does anything calculated to prevent the procuring or giving of evidence as to whether or not any thing is so liable to forfeiture; or

(d) prevents the detention of any person by a person duly engaged or acting as aforesaid or rescues any person so detained.

or who attempts to do any of the aforementioned things, shall be guilty of an offence under this section.

(2) A person guilty of an offence under this section shall be liable—

(a) on summary conviction, to a penalty of the prescribed sum, or to imprisonment for a term not exceeding 3 months, or to both; or

(b) on conviction on indictment, to a penalty of any amount, or to imprisonment for a term not exceeding 2 years, or to both.

(3) Any person committing an offence under this section and any person aiding or abetting the commission of such an offence may be detained.

[This section is printed as amended by the *PACE Act* 1984, s.114(1).]

(b) *Procedure*

This offence is triable either way.   **15–24**

(c) *Elements of the offence*

The prosecution must prove that the defendant has: **15–25**

— obstructed or assaulted someone acting in the course of his duty or assisting someone who is so acting or

— impeded a search, detention or forfeiture or

— rescued, damaged, destroyed an item liable to forfeiture or evidence or

— prevented the detention of a person by an officer

It should be noted that this is a much wider section than that of obstructing a police officer in the execution of his duty and includes both obstruction and assault.

In *George and Davies* [1981] Crim.L.R.185 the giving of a false name was held to be obstruction.

(d) *Sentence*

The maximum penalty is three months' imprisonment or a fine of £5000 or both.   **15–26**

There is no Magistrates' Courts Sentencing Guideline for this offence but the guideline for assaulting a police officer is custody and the guideline for obstruction is a discharge or fine.

III. OFFENCES OF ILLEGAL IMPORTATION AND EXPORTATION

A. Illegal Importation

(a) Definition

Customs and Excise Management Act 1979, s.50

Penalty for improper importation of goods

15–27   **50.**—(1) Subsection (2) below applies to goods of the following descriptions, that is to say—

(a) goods chargeable with a duty which has not been paid; and

(b) goods the importation, landing or unloading of which is for the time being prohibited or restricted by or under any enactment.

(2) If any person with intent to defraud Her Majesty of any such duty or to evade any such prohibition or restriction as is mentioned in subsection (1) above—

(a) unships or lands in any port or unloads from any aircraft in the United Kingdom or from any vehicle in Northern Ireland any goods to which this subsection applies, or assists or is otherwise concerned in such unshipping, landing or unloading; or

(b) removes from their place of importation or from any approved wharf, examination station, transit shed or customs and excise station any goods to which this subsection applies or assists or is otherwise concerned in such removal,

he shall be guilty of an offence under this subsection and may be detained.

(3) If any person imports or is concerned in importing any goods contrary to any prohibition or restriction for the time being in force under or by virtue of any enactment with respect to those goods, whether or not the goods are unloaded, and does so with intent to evade the prohibition or restriction, he shall be guilty of an offence under this subsection and may be detained.

(4) Subject to subsection (5), (5A) or (5B) below, a person guilty of an offence under subsection (2) or (3) above shall be liable—

(a) on summary conviction, to a penalty of the prescribed sum or of three times the value of the goods, whichever is the greater, or to imprisonment for a term not exceeding 6 months, or to both; or

(b) on conviction on indictment, to a penalty of any amount, or to imprisonment for a term not exceeding 7 years, or to both.

15–28   (5) In the case of an offence under subsection (2) or (3) above in connection with a prohibition or restriction on importation having effect by virtue of section 3 of the *Misuse of Drugs Act* 1971, subsection (4) above shall have effect subject to the modifications specified in Schedule 1 to this Act.

(5A) In the case of an offence under subsection (2) or (3) above in connection with the prohibition contained in section 20 of the *Forgery and Counterfeiting Act* 1981, subsection (4)(b) above shall have effect as if for the words "2 years" there were substituted the words "10 years".

(5B) In the case of an offence under subsection (2) or (3) above in connection with the prohibition contained in regulation 2 of the *Import of Seal Skins Regulations* 1996, subsection (4) above shall have effect as if—

(a) for paragraph (a) there were substituted the following—

"(a) on summary conviction, to a fine not exceeding the statutory maximum or to imprisonment for a term not exceeding three months, or to both"

and

(b) in paragraph (b) for the words "7 years" there were substituted the words "2 years".

(6) If any person—

(a) imports or causes to be imported any goods concealed in a container holding goods of a different description; or

(b) directly or indirectly imports or causes to be imported or entered any goods found, whether before or after delivery, not to correspond with the entry made thereof,

he shall be liable on summary conviction to a penalty of three times the value of the goods or level 3 on the standard scale, whichever is the greater.

(7) In any case where a person would, apart from this subsection, be guilty of—   **15–29**
   (a) an offence under this section in connection with the importation of goods contrary to a prohibition or restriction; and
   (b) a corresponding offence under the enactment or other instrument imposing the prohibition or restriction, being an offence for which a fine or other penalty is expressly provided by that enactment or other instrument,
he shall not be guilty of the offence mentioned in paragraph (a) of this subsection.

[This section is printed as amended by the *Forgery and Counterfeiting Act* 1981, s.23(1) (insertion of subs.(5A)); the *CJA* 1982, ss.37, 46; the *PACE Act* 1984, s.114(1); the *Finance Act* 1988, s.12(1)(a), (6) (substitution of "7 years" for "2 years" in subs.(4)(b)); and the *Import of Seal Skins Regulations* 1996 (SI 1996/2686).]

(b) *Procedure*

This offence is triable either way.   **15–30**

(c) *Elements of the offence*

The prosecution must prove (s.50(2)):   **15–31**
— the goods are taxable or prohibited or restricted
— the defendant has either landed or assisted in the landing of the goods or has removed or assisted in the removal of the goods from an approved area
— the defendant either does not intend to pay the duty or intends to evade the prohibition or restriction.
The prosecutor must prove (s.50(3)) that the defendant:
— has imported prohibited or restricted goods
— intended to evade the prohibition or restriction
According to s.154 once importation has been proved it is presumed to be unlawful unless, the defence can prove otherwise. For time of importation see s.5 above. An intention to evade is necessary: *Frailey v Charlton* [1920] 1 K.B. 147. In *R. v Smith (Donald)* [1973] Q.B. 924, CA it was held that there can be no goods which are merely "unloaded" or "landed" and not imported. In *R. v Hurford-Jones*, 65 Cr.App.R. 263, CA it was held that evade does not have the same connotation as fraud or dishonesty in the revenue laws.

(d) *Sentence*

The maximum penalty is a fine of £5000 or a penalty of three times the value of the   **15–32**
goods, whichever is the greater or imprisonment for a term not exceeding six months, or both.
There are enhanced penalties under s.50(5) and Sch.1 for certain types of goods. In the case of drugs, where the drug concerned is a Class A or B drug, on summary conviction, the penalty is six months imprisonment, a fine of £5000 or three times the value of the goods, whichever is the greater. If the drug is a Class C drug, on summary conviction, the maximum penalty is three months' imprisonment, a fine not exceeding £500 or three times the value of the goods, whichever is the greater.

B. IMPROPER UNLOADING OF GOODS LOADED ETC. FOR EXPORTATION

(a) *Definition*

Customs and Excise Management Act 1979, s.67

Offences in relation to exportation of goods
   67.—(1) If any goods which have been loaded or retained on board any ship or aircraft for   **15–33**

exportation are not exported to and discharged at a place outside the United Kingdom but are unloaded in the United Kingdom, then, unless—

    (a) the unloading was authorised by the proper officer; and

    (b) except where that officer otherwise permits, any duty chargeable and unpaid on the goods is paid and any drawback or allowance paid in respect thereof is repaid,

the master of the ship or the commander of the aircraft and any person concerned in the unshipping, relanding, landing, unloading or carrying of the goods from the ship or aircraft without such authority, payment or repayment shall each be guilty of an offence under this section.

(2) The Commissioners may impose such conditions as they see fit with respect to any goods loaded or retained as mentioned in subsection (1) above which are permitted to be unloaded in the United Kingdom.

(3) If any person contravenes or fails to comply with, or is concerned in any contravention of or failure to comply with, any condition imposed under subsection (2) above he shall be guilty of an offence under this section.

(4) Where any goods loaded or retained as mentioned in subsection (1) above or brought to a customs and excise station for exportation by land are—

    (a) goods from warehouse, other than goods which have been kept, without being warehoused, in a warehouse by virtue of section 92(4) below;

    (b) transit goods;

    (c) other goods chargeable with a duty which has not been paid;

    (d) drawback goods,

then if any container in which the goods are held is without the authority of the proper officer opened, or any mark, letter or device on any such container or on any lot of the goods is without that authority cancelled, obliterated or altered, every person concerned in the opening, cancellation, obliteration or alteration shall be guilty of an offence under this section.

(5) Any goods in respect of which an offence under this section is committed shall be liable to forfeiture and any person guilty of an offence under this section shall be liable on summary conviction to a penalty of three times the value of the goods or level 3 on the standard scale, whichever is the greater.

(b) *Procedure*

15–34   This offence is triable summarily.

(c) *Elements of the offence*

15–35   The prosecution must prove that:

— the goods are intended for export

— the goods have been loaded on a vessel or aircraft

— the goods have been unloaded without authorisation

— the duty has not been paid.

(d) *Sentence*

15–36   The maximum penalty is forfeiture of goods and a fine of three times the value of the goods or a fine not exceeding level three, *i.e.* £1000, whichever is the greater.

C. Illegal Exportation

(a) *Definition*

Customs and Excise Management Act 1979, s.68

Offences in relation to exportation of prohibited or restricted goods

15–37   **68.**—(1) If any goods are—

    (a) exported or shipped as stores; or

    (b) brought to any place in the United Kingdom for the purpose of being exported or shipped as stores, and the exportation or shipment is or would be contrary to any prohibition or restriction for the time being in force with respect to those goods under or by virtue of any enactment, the goods shall be liable to forfeiture and the exporter or intending exporter of the goods and any agent of his concerned in the exportation or shipment or intended exportation or shipment shall each be liable on summary conviction to a penalty of three times the value of the goods or level 3 on the standard scale, whichever is the greater.

(2) Any person knowingly concerned in the exportation or shipment as stores, or in the attempted exportation or shipment as stores, of any goods with intent to evade any such prohibition or restriction as is mentioned in subsection (1) above shall be guilty of an offence under this subsection and may be detained.

(3) Subject to subsection (4) or (4A)below, a person guilty of an offence under subsection (2) above shall be liable—

    (a) on summary conviction, to a penalty of the prescribed sum or of three times the value of the goods, whichever is the greater, or to imprisonment for a term not exceeding 6 months, or to both; or

    (b) on conviction on indictment, to a penalty of any amount, or to imprisonment for a term not exceeding 7 years, or to both.

(4) In the case of an offence under subsection (2) above in connection with a prohibition **15–38** or restriction on exportation having effect by virtue of section 3 of the *Misuse of Drugs Act* 1971, subsection (3) above shall have effect subject to the modifications specified in Schedule 1 to this Act.

(4A) In the case of an offence under subsection (2) above in connection with the prohibition contained in section 21 of the *Forgery and Counterfeiting Act* 1981, subsection (3)(b) above shall have effect as if for the words "2 years" there were substituted the words "10 years".

(5) If by virtue of any such restriction as is mentioned in subsection (1) above any goods may be exported only when consigned to a particular place or person and any goods so consigned are delivered to some other place or person, the ship, aircraft or vehicle in which they were exported shall be liable to forfeiture unless it is proved to the satisfaction of the Commissioners that both the owner of the ship, aircraft or vehicle and the master of the ship, commander of the aircraft or person in charge of the vehicle—

    (a) took all reasonable steps to secure that the goods were delivered to the particular place to which or person to whom they were consigned; and

    (b) did not connive at or, except under duress, consent to the delivery of the goods to that other place or person.

(6) In any case where a person would, apart from this subsection, be guilty of—

    (a) an offence under subsection (1) or (2) above; and

    (b) a corresponding offence under the enactment or instrument imposing the prohibition or restriction in question, being an offence for which a fine or other penalty is expressly provided by that enactment or other instrument,

he shall not be guilty of the offence mentioned in paragraph (a) of this subsection.

(b) *Procedure*

This offence is triable either way. **15–39**

(c) *Elements of the offence*

The prosecution must prove: **15–40**

— the goods are prohibited from being exported

— the goods have either been brought to a place to be exported or have been exported

— the defendant knew of the plan to export the goods and intended to evade the prohibition.

There is a statutory defence. In *Garrett v Arthur Churchill (Glass) Ltd* [1970] 1 Q.B. 92 it was said that the question whether a defendant was knowingly concerned in the exportation of goods with intent to evade the prohibition should be treated as one question. In *R. v Uxbridge Justices Ex p. Sofaer* (1987) 85 Cr.App.R. 367, it was held that destruction of the goods will not necessarily prejudice the defendant or breach natural justice where secondary evidence in the form of photographs can be put before the court.

(d) *Sentence*

15–41   The maximum penalty is a fine of £5000, or three times the value of the goods, whichever is the greater, or imprisonment for a term not exceeding six months or both. The enhanced penalties provided for drug exportation are the same as those provided under s.67, and are provided by Sch.1 to the Act and ss.(4) and (4A) of s.68.

D. CONTROL OF PERSONS ENTERING OR LEAVING THE UK

(a) *Definition*

Customs and Excise Management Act 1979, s.78

Customs and excise control of persons entering or leaving the United Kingdom

15–42   78.—(1) Any person entering the United Kingdom shall, at such place and in such manner as the Commissioners may direct, declare any thing contained in his baggage or carried with him which—

(a) he has obtained outside the United Kingdom; or

(b) being dutiable goods or chargeable goods, he has obtained in the United Kingdom without payment of duty or tax,

and in respect of which he is not entitled to exemption from duty and tax by virtue of any order under section 13 of the *Customs and Excise Duties (General Reliefs) Act* 1979 (personal reliefs).

In this subsection "chargeable goods" means goods on the importation of which value added tax is chargeable or goods obtained in the United Kingdom before 1st April 1973 which are chargeable goods within the meaning of the *Purchase Tax Act* 1963; and "tax" means value added tax or purchase tax.

(1A) Subsection (1) above does not apply to a person entering the United Kingdom from the Isle of Man as respects anything obtained by him in the Island unless it is chargeable there with duty or value added tax and he has obtained it without payment of the duty or tax.

(1B) Subsection (1) above does not apply to a person entering the United Kingdom from another member State, except—

(a) where he arrives at a customs and excise airport in an aircraft in which he began his journey in a place outside the member States; or

(b) as respects such of his baggage as—

(i) is carried in the hold of the aircraft in which he arrives at a customs and excise airport, and

(ii) notwithstanding that it was transferred on one or more occasions from aircraft to aircraft at an airport in a member State, began its journey by air from a place outside the member States.

15–43   (2) Any person entering or leaving the United Kingdom shall answer such questions as the proper officer may put to him with respect to his baggage and any thing contained therein or carried with him, and shall, if required by the proper officer, produce that baggage and any such thing for examination at such place as the Commissioners may direct.

(2A) Subject to subsection (1A) above, where the journey of a person arriving by air in the United Kingdom is continued or resumed by air to a destination in the United Kingdom which is not the place where he is regarded for the purposes of this section as entering the United Kingdom, subsections (1) and (2) above shall apply in relation to that person on his arrival at that destination as they apply in relation to a person entering the United Kingdom.

(3) Any person failing to declare any thing or to produce any baggage or thing as required by this section shall be liable on summary conviction to a penalty of three times the value of the thing not declared or of the baggage or thing not produced, as the case may be, or level 3 on the standard scale, whichever is the greater.

(4) Any thing chargeable with any duty or tax which is found concealed, or is not declared, and any thing which is being taken into or out of the United Kingdom contrary to any prohibition or restriction for the time being in force with respect thereto under or by virtue of any enactment, shall be liable to forfeiture.

[This section is printed as amended by the *Isle of Man Act* 1979, s.13, Sch.1; the *CJA* 1982, s.38, 46; the *Finance (No.2) Act* 1992, s.5; and the *Customs and Excise (Single Market etc.) Regulations* 1992 (SI 1992/3095), reg.3(10).]

(b) *Procedure*

This offence is triable summarily: s.78(3).   **15–44**

(c) *Elements of the offence*

The prosecution must prove: **15–45**
— the goods are dutiable
— they were bought outside the UK
— they were not declared or produced.

It is an absolute offence: *R. v Customs and Excise Commissioners Ex p. Claus* (1988) 86 Cr.App.R. 189. It applies only to persons entering or leaving the United Kingdom, and no reasonable grounds to suspect that the person entering or leaving is carrying a prohibited or restricted article or a dutiable article on which duty has not been paid need exist. This distinction is however, qualified by the *Finance Act (No.2)* 1992, s.4. A thing carried with him may be the shoes that he wears: *R. v Lucien* [1995] Crim.L.R. 807, CA.

(d) *Sentence*

The maximum penalty is a fine of three times the value of the goods or a fine not   **15–46**
exceeding level three, *i.e.* £1000, whichever is the greater.

Finance Act 1992, s.4

Enforcement powers

4.—(1) Except in a case falling within subsection (2) below, the powers to which this section   **15–47**
applies shall not be exercisable in relation to any person or thing entering or leaving the United Kingdom so as to prevent, restrict or delay the movement of that person or thing between different member States.

(2) The cases in which a power to which this section applies may be exercised as mentioned in subsection (1) above are those where it appears to the person on whom the power is conferred that there are reasonable grounds for believing that the movement in question is not in fact between different member States or that it is necessary to exercise the power for purposes connected with—

    (a) securing the collection of any Community customs duty or giving effect to any Community legislation relating to any such duty;

    (b) the enforcement of any prohibition or restriction for the time being in force by virtue of any Community legislation with respect to the movement of goods into or out of the member States; or

    (c) the enforcement of any prohibition or restriction for the time being in force by virtue of any enactment with respect to the importation or exportation of goods into or out of the United Kingdom.

(3) Subject to subsection (4) below, this section applies to any power which is conferred on the Commissioners of Customs and Excise or any officer or constable under any of the following provisions of the *Customs and Excise Management Act* 1979, that is to say—

    (a) section 21 (control of movement of aircraft into and out of the United Kingdom);

    (b) section 26(power to regulate movement by land into and out of Northern Ireland);

    (c) section 27 (officers' powers of boarding);

    (d) section 28 (officers' powers of access);

    (e) section 29 (officers' powers to detain ships);

    (f) section 34 (power to prevent flight of aircraft);

    (g) section 78 (questions as to baggage of person entering or leaving the United Kingdom);

(h) section 164 (powers of search).

15–48   (4) The Treasury may by order made by statutory instrument add any power conferred by any enactment contained in the customs and excise Acts to the powers to which this section applies; and a statutory instrument containing an order under this subsection shall be subject to annulment in pursuance of a resolution of either House of Parliament.

(5) In this section—

"Community customs duty" includes any agricultural levy of the Economic Community; and

"the customs and excise Acts" and "goods" have the same meanings as in the *Customs and Excise Management Act* 1979;

and for the purposes of this section a power shall be taken to be exercised otherwise than in relation to a person or thing entering or leaving the United Kingdom in any case where the power is exercisable irrespective of whether the person or thing in question is entering or leaving the United Kingdom.

(6) This section shall come into force on 1st January 1993.

15–49   Section 78 does not provide a basis for permitting customs officers to conduct rub-down, strip or intimate searches. This power is only exercisable by virtue of s.164 of the 1979 Act: *R. v Lucien*, above.

15–50   The *Channel Tunnel (Customs and Excise) Order* 1990 (SI 1990/2167), Sch., para.17B (inserted by the *Channel Tunnel (International Arrangements) Order* 1993 (SI 1993/1813) Sch.5, para.27) as amended by the *Channel Tunnel (Miscellaneous Provisions) Order* 1994 (SI 1994/1405) provides that for the purposes of s.78 of the 1979 Act:

(a) a person intending to travel to the United Kingdom through the tunnel who has entered a control zone in France or Belgium shall be treated as being a person entering the United Kingdom,

(b) a person who has travelled from the United Kingdom through the tunnel and is in such a control zone shall be treated as still being a person leaving the United Kingdom, and

(c) concealment shall be taken to include concealment in such a control zone.

E. Smuggling

(a) *Definition*

Customs and Excise Management Act 1979, s.85(1)

Penalty for interfering with revenue vessels, etc.

15–51   **85.**—(1) Any person who save for just and sufficient cause interferes in any way with any ship, aircraft, vehicle, buoy, anchor, chain, rope or mark which is being used for the purposes of any functions of the Commissioners under Parts III to VII of this Act shall be liable on summary conviction to a penalty of level 1 on the standard scale.

(b) *Procedure*

15–52   This offence is triable summarily.

(c) *Elements of the offence*

15–53   The prosecution must prove that the defendant:
— interfered with a customs vessel/vehicle/aircraft *etc.*
— had no just cause.

(d) *Sentence*

15–54   The maximum penalty is a level one fine, *i.e.* £200.

F. UNTRUE DECLARATIONS

(a) *Definition*

Customs and Excise Management Act 1979, s.167

Untrue declarations, etc.

167.—(1) If any person either knowingly or recklessly—   **15–55**
   (a) makes or signs, or causes to be made or signed, or delivers or causes to be
delivered to the Commissioners or an officer, any declaration, notice, certificate
or other document whatsoever; or
   (b) makes any statement in answer to any question put to him by an officer which he
is required by or under any enactment to answer,
being a document or statement produced or made for any purpose of any assigned matter,
which is untrue in any material particular, he shall be guilty of an offence under this subsection
and may be detained; and any goods in relation to which the document or statement was made
shall be liable to forfeiture.

(2) Without prejudice to subsection (4) below, a person who commits an offence under
subsection (1) above shall be liable—
   (a) on summary conviction, to a penalty of the prescribed sum, or to imprisonment
for a term not exceeding 6 months, or to both; or
   (b) on conviction on indictment, to penalty of any amount, or to imprisonment for a
term not exceeding 2 years, or to both.

(3) If any person—
   (a) makes or signs, or causes to be made or signed, or delivers or causes to be
delivered to the Commissioners or an officer, any declaration, notice, certificate
or other document whatsoever; or
   (b) makes any statement in answer to any question put to him by an officer which he
is required by or under any enactment to answer.
being a document or statement produced or made for any purpose of any assigned matter,
which is untrue in any material particular, then, without prejudice to subsection (4) below, he
shall be liable on summary conviction to a penalty of level 4 on the standard scale.

(4) Where by reason of any such document or statement as is mentioned in subsection
(1) or (3) above the full amount of any duty payable is not paid or any overpayment is
made in respect of any drawback, allowance, rebate or repayment of duty, the amount of
the duty unpaid or of the overpayment shall be recoverable as a debt due to the Crown or
may be summarily recovered as a civil debt.

(5) An amount of excise duty, or the amount of an overpayment in respect of any
drawback, allowance, rebate or repayment of any excise duty, shall not be recoverable as
mentioned in subsection (4) above unless the Commissioners have assessed the amount of
the duty or of the overpayment as being excise duty due from the person mentioned in
subsection (1) or (3) above and notified him or his representative accordingly.

[Subsections.(1)–(3) are printed as amended by the *CJA* 1982, ss.38 and 46; and the
PACE Act 1984, s.114(1). Subsection (5) was inserted by the *Finance Act* 1997, s.50
and Sch.6, para.5.]

(b) *Procedure*

This offence is triable either way.   **15–56**

(c) *Elements of the offence*

The prosecution must prove that the defendant: **15–57**
— made a certificate or statement which was untrue
— knew or was reckless as to whether it was untrue.

(d) *Sentence*

The maximum penalty is six months imprisonment and/or a fine not exceeding   **15–58**
£5000. The duty may also be reclaimed.

G. Counterfeiting Documents

(a) *Definition*

Customs and Excise Management Act 1979, s.168

Counterfeiting documents, etc.

15–59   **168.**—(1) If any person—

(a) counterfeits or falsifies any document which is required by or under any enactment relating to an assigned matter or which is used in the transaction of any business relating to an assigned matter; or

(b) knowingly accepts, receives or uses any such document so counterfeited or falsified; or

(c) alters any such document after it is officially issued; or

(d) counterfeits any seal, signature, initials or other mark of, or used by, any officer for the verification of such a document or for the security of goods or for any other purpose relating to an assigned matter,

he shall be guilty of an offence under this section and may be detained.

(2) A person guilty of an offence under this section shall be liable—

(a) on summary conviction, to a penalty of the prescribed sum, or to imprisonment for a term not exceeding 6 months, or to both; or

(b) on conviction on indictment, to a penalty of any amount, or to imprisonment for a term not exceeding 2 years, or to both.

[This section is printed as amended by the *PACE Act* 1984, s.114(1).]

(b) *Procedure*

15–60   This offence is triable either way.

(c) *Elements of the offence*

15–61   The prosecution must prove that the defendant either:

— forged or falsified a document

— accepted or used such a document

— altered an official document

— forged a seal etc.

(d) *Sentence*

15–62   When tried summarily, the maximum penalty is six months' imprisonment, a fine not exceeding the prescribed sum, or both: s.168(2)(b).

H. Fraudulent Evasion of Duty

(a) *Definition*

Customs and Excise Management Act 1979, s.170

Penalty for fraudulent evasion of duty, etc.

15–63   **170.**—(1) Without prejudice to any other provision of the Customs and Excise Acts 1979, if any person—

(a) knowingly acquires possession of any of the following goods, that is to say—

(i) goods which have been unlawfully removed from a warehouse or Queen's warehouse;

(ii) goods which are chargeable with a duty which has not been paid; or

(iii) goods with respect to the importation or exportation of which any prohibition or restriction is for the time being in force under or by virtue of any enactment; or

(b) is in any way knowingly concerned in carrying, removing, depositing, harbouring, keeping or concealing or in any manner dealing with any such goods,

and does so with intent to defraud Her Majesty of any duty payable on the goods or to evade any such prohibition or restriction with respect to the goods he shall be guilty of an offence under this section and may be detained.

(2) Without prejudice to any other provision of the Customs and Excise Acts 1979, if any person is, in relation to any goods, in any way knowingly concerned in any fraudulent evasion or attempt at evasion—

(a) of any duty chargeable on the goods;

(b) of any prohibition or restriction for the time being in force with respect to the goods under or by virtue of any enactment; or

(c) of any provision of the Customs and Excise Acts 1979 applicable to the goods,

he shall be guilty of an offence under this section and may be detained.

(3) Subject to subsection (4), (4A) or (4B) below, a person guilty of an offence under this **15–64** section shall be liable—

(a) on summary conviction, to a penalty of the prescribed sum or of three times the value of the goods, whichever is the greater, or to imprisonment for a term not exceeding 6 months, or to both; or

(b) on conviction on indictment, to a penalty of any amount, or to imprisonment for a term not exceeding 7 years, or to both.

(4) In the case of an offence under this section in connection with prohibition or restriction on importation or exportation having effect by virtue of section 3 of the *Misuse of Drugs Act* 1971, subsection (3) above shall have effect subject to the modifications specified in Schedule 1 to this Act.

(4A) In the case of an offence under this section in connection with the prohibitions contained in sections 20 and 21 of the *Forgery and Counterfeiting Act* 1981, subsection (3)(b) above shall have effect as if for the words "2 years" there were substituted the words "10 years".

(4B) In the case of an offence under subsection (1) or (2) above in connection with the prohibition contained in regulation 2 of the *Import of Seal Skins Regulations* 1996, subsection (3) above shall have effect as if—

(a) for paragraph (a) there were substituted the following—

"(a) on summary conviction, to a fine not exceeding the statutory maximum or to imprisonment for a term not exceeding three months, or to both"

; and

(b) in paragraph (b) for the words "7 years" there were substituted the words "2 years".

(5) In any case where a person would, apart from this subsection, be guilty of—   **15–65**

(a) an offence under this section in connection with a prohibition or restriction; and

(b) a corresponding offence under the enactment or other instrument imposing the prohibition or restriction, being an offence for which a fine or other penalty is expressly provided by that enactment or other instrument,

he shall not be guilty of the offence mentioned in paragraph (a) of this subsection.

(6) Where any person is guilty of an offence under this section, the goods in respect of which the offence was committed shall be liable to forfeiture.

[This section is printed as amended by the *Forgery and Counterfeiting Act* 1981, s.23(3) (insertion of subs.(4A); the *PACE Act* 1984, s.144(1); the *Finance Act* 1988, s.12(1)(a) (substitution of "7 years" for "2 years" in subs.3(b))); the *Finance (No.2) Act* 1992, s.3, Sch.2, para.7; and the *Import of Seal Skins Regulations* 1996 (SI 1996/2686).]

(b) *Procedure*

This offence is triable either way.   **15–66**

(c) *Elements of the Offence*

The prosecution must prove: **15–67**

— the goods fall within the categories listed in s.170(1)(a)

— possession or knowledge of the removal, keeping or hiding of goods subject to a prohibition or restriction

— an intention not to pay the duty or to evade a prohibition or restriction.

The prosecution must prove that there has been an importation and must establish a link between the offence and the prohibited importation: *R. v Watts and Stack* [1980] Crim.L.R. 38. Further, the prosecution must prove that the defendant knows that the goods are subject to a prohibition or restriction and that the operation he is concerned with is an operation designed to get around that prohibition or restriction but it does not have to prove that the defendant knows the precise category of goods involved: *R. v Hussain* [1969] 2 Q.B. 567; *R. v Shivpuri* [1987] A.C. 1; *R. v Forbes* [2001] 4 All E.R. 97. In *R. v Taaffe* [1984] A.C. 539 it was held that the accused was to be judged on the facts as he believed them to be; see also *R. v Ellis* [1987] Crim.L.R. 44. In *R. v Cohen* [1951] 1 K.B. 505 it was held that possession raises a presumption that goods are knowingly in the defendant's possession.

Trans-shipment within Heathrow airport customs area from one aircraft coming from one country to another aircraft going to another country falls within the section: *R. v Smith* [1973] 2 All E.R. 1161. Steps taken abroad leading to fraudulent evasion in this country can lead to a charge in this country: *R. v Wall* [1974] 2 All E.R. 245. A person prepared to look after a parcel sent from abroad for a friend, knowing that the parcel was likely to contain drugs having been promised some for himself, can be charged with fraudulent evasion: *Att.-Gen.'s Reference (No.1 of 1998)* (1999) 163 J.P. 390 . If an undercover customs officer undertook the importation the organiser could still be convicted (in this case of an attempt): *R. v Latif* [1996] 1 All E.R. 353. The offence is a continuing one: *R. v Green* [1975] 3 All E.R. 1011. The burden of proof is on the defendant to show that the duty has been paid: s.154. See *Archbold Crown*, §§ 25–454—25–478.

(d) *Sentence*

15–68   The maximum sentence is a fine of £5000 or three times the value of the goods concerned, whichever is the greater, and/or imprisonment for a term not exceeding six months.

The *Magistrates' Court Sentencing Guidelines* (2003) state:

> Aggravating factors of the offence include being an organiser, more than one journey, commercial operation, sophisticated operation, imports two or more dutiable goods, offence committed on bail, relevant previous convictions and any failures to respond to previous sentences.
>
> Mitigating factors of the offence include supply to a restricted group, small quantity of goods.
>
> **Guideline**: Is it so serious that only custody is appropriate? Are the court's sentencing powers appropriate?

15–69   In *R. v Dosanjh* [1999] 1 Cr.App.R. 371 the CA laid down guidelines for cases of evading import duty. Emphasising the need for deterrent sentences in this context, the Court said that cases involving less than £10,000 will frequently be dealt with by the magistrates' court. When the amount evaded is thousands of pounds, custody will generally be called for and on a plea of guilty, sentences of up to six months will generally be appropriate.

This guidance was modified in *R. v Czyzewski* [2003] EWCA Crim 2139 in relation to duty evasion on alcohol and tobacco following proposals from the Sentencing Advisory Panel. Following a trial, for a defendant with no previous convictions and disregarding any personal mitigation, the following starting points are appropriate; (i) where the duty evaded is less than £1,000 and the level of personal profit is small, a moderate fine. If there is particularly strong mitigation and provided there has been no earlier warning, a conditional discharge may be appropriate; (ii) where the duty evaded by a first time offender is not more than £10,000 (approx. 65,000 cigarettes) or the defendant's offending is at a low level, either within an organisation or persistently as an individual, a community sentence, or curfew order enforced by tagging, or higher level of fine. The custody threshold is likely to be passed if any of the aggravating factors below are present;(iii) where the duty evaded is between £10,000 and £100,000, whether the defendant is operating individually or at a low level within an organisation, up to nine months custody. Some of these cases can appropriately be dealt with by magistrates but others, particularly if marked by any of the aggravating features, should be dealt with by the Crown Court; (iv) when the duty evaded is in excess of £100,000, the length of the custodial sentence will be determined principally by the degree of professionalism of the defendant and the presence or absence of other aggravating factors. Subject to this, the duty evaded will indicate starting points as follows: (i) £100,000–£500,000, nine months to three years; (ii) £500,000–£1 million, three to five years; (iii) in excess of £1 million five to seven years.

The aggravating features mentioned are if a defendant: (i) played an organisational role; (ii) made repeated importations, particularly in the face of a warning from the authorities; (iii) was a professional smuggler; (iv) used a legitimate business as a front; (v) abused a position of privilege; (vi) used children or vulnerable adults; (vii) dealt in goods with an additional health risk because of possible contamination; or (viii) disposed of goods to under aged purchasers.

I. TAKING STEPS TO EVADE EXCISE DUTY

(a) Definition

Customs and Excise Management Act 1979, s.170B

Offence of taking preparatory steps for evasion of excise duty
170B. Offence of taking preparatory steps for evasion of excise duty.   **15–70**
(1) If any person is knowingly concerned in the taking of any steps with a view to the fraudulent evasion, whether by himself or another, of any duty of excise on any goods, he shall be liable—

  (a) on summary conviction, to a penalty of the prescribed sum or of three times the amount of the duty, whichever is the greater, or to imprisonment for a term not exceeding six months or to both; and

  (b) on conviction on indictment, to a penalty of any amount or to imprisonment for a term not exceeding seven years or to both.

(2) Where any person is guilty of an offence under this section, the goods in respect of which the offence was committed shall be liable to forfeiture.

[This section was inserted by the *Finance (No.2) Act* 1992, s.3 and Sch.2, para.8.]

(b) Procedure

This offence is triable either way: s.170B(1)   **15–71**

(c) Elements of the Offence

The prosecution must prove that: **15–72**
— steps have been taken to evade duty
— the defendant knew what he was doing.
Under legislation relating to value added tax, taking steps has been held to include omissions: *R. v McCarthy* [1981] S.T.C. 298, CA.

(d) Sentence

The maximum sentence is imprisonment for a term not exceeding six months or a   **15–73**
£5000 fine or three times the value of the goods, or both.

CHAPTER 16

REGULATORY OFFENCES

I. AEROPLANES AND AIRPORTS

A. TRESPASSING ON LICENSED AERODROMES

(a) Definition

Civil Aviation Act 1982, s.39

Trespassing on licensed aerodromes

16–1   **39.**—(1) Subject to subsection (2) below, if any person trespasses on any land forming part of an aerodrome licensed in pursuance of an *Air Navigation Order*, he shall be liable on summary conviction to a fine not exceeding level 3 on the standard scale

(2) No person shall be liable under this section unless it is proved that, at the material time, notices warning trespassers of their liability under this section were posted so as to be readily seen and read by members of the public, in such positions on or near the boundary of the aerodrome as appear to the court to be proper.

[This section is printed as amended by the *Criminal Justice Act* 1982, ss.38 and 36 and the *Anti-Terrorism, Crime and Security Act* 2001, s.83(1).]

(b) Procedure

16–2   This offence is triable summarily.

(c) Sentence

16–3   The maximum penalty for this offence is a fine not exceeding level three on the standard scale.

B. DANGEROUS FLYING

(a) Definition

Civil Aviation Act 1982, s.81

Dangerous flying

16–4   **81.**—(1) Where an aircraft is flown in such a manner as to be the cause of unnecessary danger to any person or property on land or water, the pilot or the person in charge of the aircraft, and also the owner thereof, unless he proves to the satisfaction of the court that the aircraft was so flown without his actual fault or privity, shall be liable on summary conviction to a fine nor exceeding level 4 on the standard scale or to imprisonment for a term not exceeding six months or to both.

(2) In this section the expression "owner" in relation to an aircraft includes any person to whom the aircraft is hired at the time of the offence.

(3) The provisions of this section shall be in addition to and not in derogation of the powers conferred on Her Majesty in Council by section 60 above.

[This section is printed as amended by the *CJA* 1982, ss.38 and 46.]

(b) *Procedure*

This offence is triable summarily. **16–5**

(c) *Sentence*

The maximum penalty for this offence is a fine not exceeding level four on the stan- **16–6** dard scale, imprisonment for a term not exceeding six months or both.

C. PROHIBITION OF AERIAL ADVERTISING

(a) *Definition*

Civil Aviation Act 1982, s.82

Prohibition of aerial advertising and propaganda

82.—(1) Save in such circumstances as may be prescribed, no aircraft while in the air over **16–7** any part of the United Kingdom shall be used, whether wholly or partly for emitting or display- ing any advertisement or other communication in such a way that the advertisement or com- munication is audible or visible from the ground.

(2) Any person who uses an aircraft, or knowingly causes or permits an aircraft to be used, in contravention of subsection (1) above shall be guilty of an offence and liable on summary conviction—

    (a) in the case of a first conviction of an offence under this section, to a fine not exceeding level 4 on the standard scale

    (b) in any other case, to a fine not exceeding level 4 on the standard scale or to imprisonment for a term not exceeding three months or to both;

but (without prejudice to section 105(3) below) a previous conviction of an offence under section 7 of the *Civil Aviation (Licensing) Act* 1960 shall be treated as a conviction of an offence under this section for the purposes of determining whether a conviction of an offence under this section is a first such conviction.

[This section has been printed as amended by the *Criminal Justice Act* 1982, ss.35, 38 and 46.]

(b) *Procedure*

This offence is triable summarily. **16–8**

(c) *Sentence*

Upon first conviction, the maximum penalty for this offence is a fine not exceeding **16–9** level four on the standard scale. In any other case, the maximum penalty is a fine not exceeding level four on the standard scale, imprisonment for a term not exceeding three months or both.

For guidance as to circumstances in which aerial advertising may be permitted, see the *Civil Aviation (Aerial Advertising) Regulations* 1995 (SI 1995/2943). Regulation 4 provides that:

Civil Aviation (Aerial Advertising) Regulations 1995, reg.4

Prescribed circumstances

4. For the purposes of section 82 of the *Civil Aviation Act* 1982 (which prohibits aerial **16–10**

advertising and propaganda, save in such circumstances as may be prescribed), the following circumstances are prescribed—

    (a) the use of any aircraft for the emission or display of any communication for one or more of the following purposes—

        (i) complying with the law of the United Kingdom or any other country, being law in force in relation to the aircraft;

        (ii) securing the safety of the aircraft or any person or property therein;

        (iii) the furtherance, by or on behalf of a Government department, by a person acting under any public duty or by a person providing ambulance or rescue facilities by air, of measures in connection with circumstances, existing or imminent at the time the aircraft is used, which may cause danger to persons or property;

        (iv) civil defence, military or police purposes;

    (b) save as provided in paragraph (c) below, the use of any aircraft, other than a captive balloon, for the display of any mark or inscription (other than an illuminated sign) on the body of the aircraft;

    (c) the use of any captive balloon which at all stages of its flight—

        (i) is not more than seven metres in any linear dimension; or

        (ii) does not have a total capacity of more than 20 cubic metres;
        for the display of any mark or inscription on the body of the balloon;

    (d) the use of any aeroplane for the display of any mark or inscription on a banner towed behind the aeroplane;

    (e) the use of any kite or captive balloon, other than a controllable balloon, for the display of any mark or inscription on a banner or pennant attached to its mooring cables;

    (f) the use of any airship for communicating information by means of an illuminated sign attached to the airship;

    (g) the use of any helicopter for communicating information by means of an illuminated or non-illuminated sign attached to but not towed behind the helicopter;

    (h) the use of any balloon in free controlled flight which displays any identifying mark or inscription on any basket, car or other equipment attached thereto.

16–11   Regulation 3 defines key terms used in the regulations:

Civil Aviation (Aerial Advertising) Regulations 1995, reg.3

Interpretation

16–11.1   **3.** In these Regulations, unless the context otherwise requires—

    (a) "captive balloon", "controllable balloon", "flight" and "free controlled flight" shall have the meanings assigned to them by article 118(1) of the *Air Navigation (No. 2) Order* 1995; and

    (b) "aircraft", "aeroplane", "airship", "balloon", "helicopter" and "kite" shall be construed in accordance with article 118(5) of the *Air Navigation (No. 2) Order* 1995.

D. HIJACKING

(a) *Definition*

Aviation Security Act 1982, s.1

Hijacking

16–12   **1.**—(1) A person on board an aircraft in flight who unlawfully, by the use of force or by threats of any kind, seizes the aircraft or exercises control of it commits the offence of hijacking, whatever his nationality, whatever the State in which the aircraft is registered and whether the aircraft is in the United Kingdom or elsewhere, but subject to subsection (2) below.

    (2) If—

    (a) the aircraft is used in military, customs or police service, or

(b) both the place of take-off and the place of landing are in the territory of the State in which the aircraft is registered,
subsection (1) above shall not apply unless—
  (i)   the person seizing or exercising control of the aircraft is a United Kingdom national; or
  (ii) his act is committed in the United Kingdom; or
  (iii) the aircraft is registered in the United Kingdom or is used in the military or customs service of the United Kingdom or in the service of any police force in the United Kingdom.

(3) A person who commits the offence of hijacking shall be liable, on conviction on indictment, to imprisonment for life.

(4) If the Secretary of State by order made by statutory instrument declares—
  (a) that any two or more States named in the order have established an organisation or agency which operates aircraft; and
  (b) that one of those States has been designated as exercising, for aircraft so operated, the powers of the State of registration,
the State declared under paragraph (b) of this subsection shall be deemed for the purposes of this section to be the State in which any aircraft so operated is registered; but in relation to such an aircraft subsection (2)(b) above shall have effect as if it referred to the territory of any one of the States named in the order.

(5) For the purposes of this section the territorial waters of any State shall be treated as part of its territory.

(b) *Procedure*

This offence is triable on indictment only.   **16–13**

E. Destroying, Damaging or Endangering Safety of Aircraft

(a) *Definition*

Aviation Security Act 1982, s.2

Destroying, damaging or endangering safety of aircraft
2.—(1) It shall, subject to subsection (4) below, be an offence for any person unlawfully and **16–14** intentionally—
  (a) to destroy an aircraft in service or so to damage such an aircraft as to render it incapable of flight or as to be likely to endanger its safety in flight; or
  (b) to commit on board an aircraft in flight any act of violence which is likely to endanger the safety of the aircraft.

(2) It shall also, subject to subsection (4) below, be an offence for any person unlawfully and intentionally to place, or cause to be placed, on an aircraft in service any device or substance which is likely to destroy the aircraft, or is likely so to damage it as to render it incapable of flight or as to be likely to endanger its safety in flight; but nothing in this subsection shall be construed as limiting the circumstances in which the commission of any act—
  (a) may constitute an offence under subsection (1) above, or
  (b) may constitute attempting or conspiring to commit, or aiding, abetting, counselling or procuring, or being art and part in, the commission of such an offence.

(3) Except as provided by subsection (4) below, subsections (1) and (2) above shall apply whether any such act as is therein mentioned is committed in the United Kingdom or elsewhere, whatever the nationality of the person committing the act and whatever the State in which the aircraft is registered.

(4) Subsections (1) and (2) above shall not apply to any act committed in relation to an aircraft used in military, customs or police service unless—
  (a) the act is committed in the United Kingdom, or
  (b) where the act is committed outside the United Kingdom, the person committing it is a United Kingdom national.

(5) A person who commits an offence under this section shall be liable, on conviction on indictment, to imprisonment for life.

(6) In this section "unlawfully"—

    (a) in relation to the commission of an act in the United Kingdom, means so as (apart from this Act) to constitute an offence under the law of the part of the United Kingdom in which the act is committed, and

    (b) in relation to the commission of an act outside the United Kingdom, means so that the commission of the act would (apart from this Act) have been an offence under the law of England and Wales if it had been committed in England and Wales or of Scotland if it had been committed in Scotland.

(7) In this section "act of violence" means—

    (a) any act done in the United Kingdom which constitutes the offence of murder, attempted murder, manslaughter, culpable homicide or assault or an offence under section 18, 20, 21, 22, 23, 24, 28 or 29 of the *Offences against the Person Act* 1861 or under section 2 of the *Explosive Substances Act* 1883, and

    (b) any act done outside the United Kingdom which, if done in the United Kingdom, would constitute such an offence as is mentioned in paragraph (a) above.

(b) *Procedure*

16–15   This offence is triable only on indictment.

F. OTHER ACTS ENDANGERING OR LIKELY TO ENDANGER THE SAFETY OF AIRCRAFT

(a) *Definition*

Aviation Security Act 1982, s.3

Other acts endangering or likely to endanger safety of aircraft

16–16   **3.**—(1) It shall, subject to subsections (5) and (6) below, be an offence for any person unlawfully and intentionally to destroy or damage any property to which this subsection applies, or to interfere with the operation of any such property, where the destruction, damage or interference is likely to endanger the safety of aircraft in flight.

(2) Subsection (1) above applies to any property used for the provision of air navigation facilities, including any land, building or ship so used, and including any apparatus or equipment so used, whether it is on board an aircraft or elsewhere.

(3) It shall also, subject to subsections (4) and (5) below, be an offence for any person intentionally to communicate any information which is false, misleading or deceptive in a material particular, where the communication of the information endangers the safety of an aircraft in flight or is likely to endanger the safety of aircraft in flight.

(4) It shall be a defence for a person charged with an offence under subsection (3) above to prove—

    (a) that he believed, and had reasonable grounds for believing, that the information was true; or

    (b) that, when he communicated the information, he was lawfully employed to perform duties which consisted of or included the communication of information and that he communicated the information in good faith in the performance of those duties.

(5) Subsections (1) and (3) above shall not apply to the commission of any act unless either the act is committed in the United Kingdom, or, where it is committed outside the United Kingdom—

    (a) the person committing it is a United Kingdom national; or

    (b) the commission of the act endangers or is likely to endanger the safety in flight of a civil aircraft registered in the United Kingdom or chartered by demise to a lessee whose principal place of business, or (if he has no place of business) whose permanent residence, is in the United Kingdom; or

    (c) the act is committed on board a civil aircraft which is so registered or so chartered; or

    (d) the act is committed on board a civil aircraft which lands in the United Kingdom with the person who committed the act still on board.

(6) Subsection (1) above shall also not apply to any act committed outside the United Kingdom and so committed in relation to property which is situated outside the United Kingdom and is not used for the provision of air navigation facilities in connection with international air navigation, unless the person committing the act is a United Kingdom national.

(7) A person who commits an offence under this section shall be liable, on conviction on indictment, to imprisonment for life.

(8) In this section "civil aircraft" means any aircraft other than an aircraft used in military, customs or police service and "unlawfully" has the same meaning as in section 2 of this Act.

(b) *Procedure*

This offence is triable only on indictment.   **16–17**

G. OFFENCES IN RELATION TO CERTAIN DANGEROUS ARTICLES

(a) *Definition*

Aviation Security Act 1982, s.4

Offences in relation to certain dangerous articles

4.—(1) It shall be an offence for any person without lawful authority or reasonable excuse **16–18** (the proof of which shall lie on him) to have with him—

(a) in any aircraft registered in the United Kingdom, whether at a time when the aircraft is in the United Kingdom or not, or

(b) in any other aircraft at a time when it is in, or in flight over, the United Kingdom, or

(c) in any part of an aerodrome in the United Kingdom, or

(d) in any air navigation installation in the United Kingdom which does not form part of an aerodrome,

any article to which this section applies.

(2) This section applies to the following articles, that is to say—

(a) any firearm, or any article having the appearance of being a firearm, whether capable of being discharged or not;

(b) any explosive, any article manufactured or adapted (whether in the form of a bomb, grenade or otherwise) so as to have the appearance of being an explosive, whether it is capable of producing a practical effect by explosion or not, or any article marked or labelled so as to indicate that it is or contains an explosive; and

(c) any article (not falling within either of the preceding paragraphs) made or adapted for use for causing injury to or incapacitating a person or for destroying or damaging property, or intended by the person having it with him for such use, whether by him or by any other person.

(3) For the purposes of this section a person who is for the time being in an aircraft, or **16–19** in part of an aerodrome, shall be treated as having with him in the aircraft, or in that part of the aerodrome, as the case may be, an article to which this section applies if—

(a) where he is in an aircraft, the article, or an article in which it is contained, is in the aircraft and has been caused (whether by him or by any other person) to be brought there as being, or as forming part of, his baggage on a flight in the aircraft or has been caused by him to be brought there as being, or as forming part of, any other property to be carried on such a flight, or

(b) where he is in part of an aerodrome (otherwise than in an aircraft), the article, or an article in which it is contained, is in that or any other part of the aero-drome and has been caused (whether by him or by any other person) to be brought into the aerodrome as being, or as forming part of, his baggage on a flight from that aerodrome or has been caused by him to be brought there as be-ing, or as forming part of, any other property to be carried on such a flight on which he is also to be carried.

notwithstanding that the circumstances may be such that (apart from this subsection) he would not be regarded as having the article with him in the aircraft or in a part of the aerodrome, as the case may be.

(4) A person guilty of an offence under this section shall be liable—

(a) on summary conviction, to a fine not exceeding the statutory maximum or to imprisonment for a term not exceeding three months or to both;

(b) on conviction on indictment, to a fine or to imprisonment for a term not exceeding five years or to both.

(5) Nothing in subsection (3) above shall be construed as limiting the circumstances in which a person would, apart from that subsection, be regarded as having an article with him as mentioned in subsection (1) above.

(b) *Procedure*

16–20   This offence is triable either way: s.(4).

(c) *Sentence*

16–21   When tried summarily, the maximum penalty for this offence is a fine not exceeding the statutory maximum, imprisonment for a term not exceeding three months or both.

Aviation Security Act 1982, s.8

Prosecution of offences and proceedings

16–22   **8.**—(1) Proceedings for an offence under any of the preceding provisions of this Part of this Act (other than sections 4 and 7) shall not be instituted—

(a) in England and Wales, except by, or with the consent of, the Attorney General; and

(b) in Northern Ireland, except by, or with the consent of, the Attorney General for Northern Ireland.

(2) As respects Scotland, for the purpose of conferring on the sheriff jurisdiction to entertain proceedings for an offence under or by virtue of section 2, 3 or 6(2)(b) or (c) of this Act, any such offence shall, without prejudice to any jurisdiction exercisable apart from this subsection, be deemed to have been committed in any place in Scotland where the offender may for the time being be.

H. Airport Byelaws

Airports Act 1986, ss.63, 64

Airport byelaws

16–23   **63.**—(1) Where an airport is either—

(a) designated for the purposes of this section by an order made by the Secretary of State, or

(b) managed by the Secretary of State,

the airport operator (whether the Secretary of State or some other person) may make byelaws for regulating the use and operation of the airport and the conduct of all persons while within the airport.

(2) Any such byelaws may, in particular, include byelaws—

(a) for securing the safety of aircraft, vehicles and persons using the airport and preventing danger to the public arising from the use and operation of the airport;

(b) for controlling the operation of aircraft within, or directly above, the airport for the purpose of limiting or mitigating the effect of noise, vibration and atmospheric pollution caused by aircraft using the airport;

(c) for preventing obstruction within the airport;

(d) for regulating vehicular traffic anywhere within the airport, except on roads within the airport to which the road traffic enactments apply, and in particular (with that exception) for imposing speed limits on vehicles within the airport and for restricting or regulating the parking of vehicles or their use for any purpose or in any manner specified in the byelaws;

(e) for prohibiting waiting by hackney carriages except at standings appointed by such person as may be specified in the byelaws;

(f) for prohibiting or restricting access to any part of the airport;

(g) for preserving order within the airport and preventing damage to property within it;

(h) for regulating or restricting advertising within the airport;

(i) for requiring any person, if so requested by a constable or airport official, to leave the airport or any particular part of it, or to state his name and address and the purpose of his being within the airport;

(j) for securing the safe custody and redelivery of any property which, while not in proper custody, is found within the airport or in an aircraft within the airport, and in particular—

    (i) for requiring charges to be paid in respect of any such property before it is redelivered; and

    (ii) for authorising the disposal of any such property if it is not redelivered before the end of such period as may be specified in the byelaws;

(k) for restricting the area which is to be taken as constituting the airport for the purposes of the byelaws.

(3) In paragraph (d) of subsection (2) "the road traffic enactments" means the enactments (whether passed before or after this Act) relating to road traffic, including the lighting and parking of vehicles, and any order or other instrument having effect by virtue of any such enactment.

(4) In paragraph (i) of subsection (2) "airport official" means a person authorised by the airport operator; and any such official shall not exercise any power under a byelaw made by virtue of that paragraph without producing written evidence of his authority if required to do so.

(5) Byelaws made under this section by a person other than the Secretary of State shall not have effect until they are confirmed by the Secretary of State, and the provisions of Schedule 3 shall apply to any such byelaws.

(6) Before any byelaws are made by the Secretary of State under this section, he shall take such steps as appear to him to be appropriate for giving public notice of the proposed byelaws and for affording an opportunity for representations to be made with respect to them; and the Secretary of State shall have regard to any such representations and may then make the byelaws in the form proposed or in that form with such modifications as he thinks fit.

(7) Any byelaws made by the Secretary of State under this section shall be made by statutory instrument.

(8) Section 236(9) of the *Local Government Act* 1972 and section 202(13) of the *Local Government (Scotland) Act* 1973 (notice of byelaws made by one local authority to be given to another) and section 237 of the Act of 1972 and section 203 of the Act of 1973 (penalties) shall not apply to any byelaws made by a local authority under this section.

Byelaws: penalties and power to revoke in certain cases

64.—(1) Any person contravening any byelaws made under section 63 shall be liable on summary conviction to a fine not exceeding such amount as, subject to subsection (2) of this section, may be specified by the byelaws in relation to the contravention.   **16–24**

(2) The maximum fines that byelaws may specify by virtue of subsection (1) are fines of an amount at the fourth level on the standard scale or of a lower amount.

(3) Where any person other than the Secretary of State has made any byelaw in relation to any airport by virtue of section 63(2)(b), the Secretary of State may, after consulting that person, by order—

(a) revoke or vary that byelaw if the Secretary of State considers it appropriate to do so by reason of his having designated the airport for the purposes of section 78 of the 1982 Act (regulation of noise and vibration from aircraft); or

(b) revoke or vary that byelaw to the extent that it appears to the Secretary of State to be inconsistent with the safety of persons or vehicles using the airport, of aircraft or of the general public or to be inconsistent with any international obligation of the United Kingdom.

The following airports in England and Wales have been designated: **16–25**
Biggin Hill, Birmingham, Blackpool, Bournemouth (Hurn), Bristol, Cardiff-Wales, Coventry, East Midlands, Exeter, Humberside, Leeds/Bradford, Liverpool, London-

Gatwick, London-Heathrow, London-Stanstead, Luton, Manchester, Newcastle, Norwich, Southampton, Southend, Tees-side: *Airport Byelaws (Designation) Order* 1987, (SI 1987/380) and Bainbridge, Carlisle, Gloucester/Cheltenham, Redhill and Swansea: *Airport Byelaws (Designation) (No.2) Order 1987* (SI 1987/2246).

II. ANIMALS

A. CRUELTY TO ANIMALS

(a) Definition

Protection of Animals Act 1911, s.1

Offences of cruelty

16–26
1.—(1) If any person—
(a) shall cruelly beat, kick, ill-treat, over-ride, over-drive, over-load, torture, infuriate, or terrify any animal, or shall cause or procure, or, being the owner, permit any animal to be so used, or shall, by wantonly or unreasonably doing or omitting to do any act, or causing or procuring the commission or omission of any act, cause any unnecessary suffering, or, being the owner, permit any unnecessary suffering to be so caused to any animal; or
(b) shall convey or carry, or cause or procure, or, being the owner, permit to be conveyed or carried, any animal in such manner or position as to cause that animal any unnecessary suffering; or
(c) shall cause, procure, or assist at the fighting or baiting of any animal; or shall keep, use, manage, or act or assist in the management of, any premises or place for the purpose, or partly for the purpose of fighting or baiting any animal, or shall permit any premises or place to be so kept, managed, or used, or shall receive, or cause or procure any person to receive, money for the admission of any person to such premises or place; or
(d) shall wilfully, without any reasonable cause or excuse, administer, or cause or procure, or being the owner permit, such administration of, any poisonous or injurious drug or substance to any animal, or shall wilfully, without any reasonable cause or excuse, cause any such substance to be taken by any animal; or
(e) shall subject, or cause to procure, or being the owner permit, to be subjected, any animal to any operation which is performed without due care and humanity; or
(f) shall tether any horse, ass or mule under such conditions or in such manner as to cause that animal unnecessary suffering;
such person shall be guilty of an offence of cruelty within the meaning of this Act, and shall be liable on summary conviction to imprisonment for a term not exceeding six months, a fine not exceeding level five on the standard scale, or both.

16–27
(2) For the purposes of this section, an owner shall be deemed to have permitted cruelty within the meaning of this Act if he shall have failed to exercise reasonable care and supervision in respect of the protection of the animal therefrom:

Provided that, where an owner is convicted of permitting cruelty within the meaning of this Act by reason only of his having failed to exercise such care and supervision, he shall not be liable to imprisonment without the option of a fine.

(3) Nothing in this section shall render illegal any act lawfully done under [the *Animals (Scientific Procedures) Act* 1986 or shall apply—
(a) to the commission or omission of any act in the course of the destruction, or the preparation for destruction, of any animal as food for mankind, unless such destruction or such preparation was accompanied by the infliction of unnecessary suffering; or
(b) to the coursing or hunting of any captive animal, unless such animal is liberated in an injured, mutilated, or exhausted condition; but a captive animal shall not, for the purposes of this section, be deemed to be coursed or hunted before it is liberated for the purpose of being coursed or hunted, or after it has been recaptured, or if it is under control and a captive animal shall not be deemed to be coursed or hunted within the meaning of this subsection if it is coursed or hunted in an enclosed space from which it has no reasonable chance of escape.

[This section is printed as amended by the *Protection of Animals Act (1911)* **16–28**
Amendment Act 1912, s.1, the *Protection of Animal (1911) Amendment Act* 1921, s.1,
the *Criminal Law Act* 1977, Sch.617, the *CJA* 1987, s.1 and the *Protection Against
Cruel Tethering Act* 1988, s.1.]

(b) *Procedure*

This offence is triable summarily: s.1(1).   **16–29**

(c) *Elements of the offence*

Cruelty is defined as 'unnecessary suffering'; whether the suffering caused was unnec- **16–30**
essary, and whether the animal's suffering was caused by a human are questions of fact
for the magistrates. The higher the risk of injury to the animal the more likely the court
is to find that the human's conduct caused the animal's suffering. Where the defendant
set his dog down holes to flush out badgers or foxes and the dog was injured after a
confrontation with a wild animal, it was held that unnecessary suffering was caused:
Bandiera v RSPCA (2000) 164 J.P. 307, DC. The question to be considered is whether
the action taken was necessary so that the shooting of a stray dog that has trespassed
onto farm land may be held to cause unnecessary suffering if no other means were first
tried to drive the animal away or prevent the mischief it was doing: *Barnard v Evans*
[1925] 2 K.B. 794.

The suffering becomes unnecessary when it is not inevitable, in that it can be
terminated or alleviated by some reasonably practicable measure. The test to be applied
is an objective one. A dog owner who failed to take her pet to the vet for over 10 years
because she feared that it might have to be put down was held to have caused unnecessary suffering to the animal: *RSPCA v Issacs* [1994] Crim.L.R. 517.

The offence under s.1(1)(c) of procuring animal fights was held not to apply to a defendant who sent his dog into a badger sett. The court said that the section was aimed at
exhibitions of fighting between domestic animals and that the description 'animal' in the
Act meant a domestic and not a captive animal: *Crown Prosecution Service v Barry*
(1989) 153 J.P. 557.

(d) *Sentence*

The maximum sentence for this offence is six months imprisonment, a fine not **16–31**
exceeding level five on the standard scale or both.

Protection of Animals Act 1911, s.2

Power for court to order destruction of animal
    2. Where the owner of an animal is convicted of an offence of cruelty within the meaning of **16–32**
this Act, it shall be lawful for the court, if the court is satisfied that it would be cruel to keep the
animal alive, to direct that the animal be destroyed, and to assign the animal to any suitable
person for that purpose; and the person to whom such animal is so assigned shall, as soon as
possible, destroy such animal, or cause or procure such animal to be destroyed, in his presence
without unnecessary suffering. Any reasonable expenses incurred in destroying the animal may
be ordered by the court to be paid by the owner, and thereupon shall be recoverable summarily
as a civil debt:
    Provided that, unless the owner assent, no order shall be made under this section except
upon the evidence of a duly registered veterinary surgeon.

There is no right of appeal to the Crown Court against a Destruction Order: s.14 of
the *Protection of Animals Act* 1911.

Protection of Animals Act 1911, s.3

Power for court to deprive person convicted of cruelty of ownership of animal
    3. If the owner of any animal shall be guilty of cruelty within the meaning of this Act to the **16–33**

animal, the court, upon his conviction thereof, may, if they think fit, in addition to any other punishment, deprive such person of the ownership of the animal, and may make such order as to the disposal of the animal as they think fit under the circumstances:

Provided that no order shall be made under this section, unless it is shown by evidence as to a previous conviction, or as to the character of the owner, or otherwise, that the animal, if left with the owner, is likely to be exposed to further cruelty.

Protection of Animals (Amendment) Act 1954, s.1

Power to disqualify persons convicted of cruelty to animals

16–34   **1.**—(1) Where a person has been convicted under the *Protection of Animals Act* 1911 or the *Protection of Animals (Scotland) Act* 1912 of an offence of cruelty to any animal the court by which he is convicted may, if it thinks fit, in addition to or in substitution for any other punishment, order him to be disqualified, for such period as it thinks fit, for having custody of any animal or any animal of a kind specified in the order.

(2) A court which has ordered the disqualification of a person in pursuance of this section may, if it thinks fit, suspend the operation of the order—

(a) for such period as the court thinks necessary for enabling arrangements to be made for the custody of any animal or animals to which the disqualification relates; or

(b) pending an appeal.

(3) A person who is disqualified by virtue of an order under this section may, at any time after the expiration of twelve months from the date of the order, and from time to time apply to the court by which the order was made to remove the disqualification, and on any such application the court may, as it thinks proper, having regard to the character of the applicant and his conduct subsequent to the order, the nature of the offence of which he was convicted, and any other circumstances of the case, either—

(a) direct that, as from such date as may be specified in the direction, the disqualification be removed or the order be so varied as to apply only to animals of a kind specified in the direction; or

(b) refuse the application:

Provided that where on an application under this section the court directs the variation of the order or refuses the application, a further application thereunder shall not be entertained if made within twelve months after the date of the direction or, as the case may be, the refusal.

[As amended by the *Protection of Animals (Amendment) Act* 1988, s.1.]

Protection of Animals Amendment Act 1954 s.2

Breach of disqualification order

16–35   **2.** If a person has custody of any animal in contravention of an order made under this Act, he shall be liable on summary conviction to a fine not exceeding level 3 on the standard scale or to imprisonment for a term not exceeding three months or to both such fine and imprisonment.

16–35.1   The question of whether a defendant has custody of an animal in a particular case is a question of fact for the magistrates. The essence of custody is control or the power to control. Thus a person with sole physical control of an animal, even for a short time, had custody of that animal. Physical control could be shared between two or more people, in which case, those people would have joint custody. If one person, however, had actual physical control subject to direction, supervision or control by another, the one with actual physical control might or might not have custody, depending upon the degree and effectiveness of the direction, supervision and control which was exercised by the other person. Where a defendant had been disqualified for 10 years from having custody of horses after a conviction for cruelty to horses she gave the animals to her niece. She was observed feeding and watering the horses subsequently. It was held that as she had made arrangements for the grazing of the horses and had also fed and watered them she had custody and was in breach of her disqualification: *Taylor and Taylor v RSPCA* (2001) 2 Cr.App.R. 24. A defendant who was disqualified from having custody of dogs held the lead of a dog for over an hour when under the supervision of the owner of the dog. The court held that he did not in those circumstances have custody of the animal so that he would be in breach of his disqualification: *R. v Miller* [1994] Crim.L.R. 516.

B. DOGS FOULING LAND

(a) *Definition*

Dogs (Fouling of Land) Act 1996, s.3

Offence

3.—(1) If a dog defecates at any time on designated land and a person who is in charge of **16–36** the dog at that time fails to remove the faeces from the land forthwith, that person shall be guilty of an offence unless—

(a) he has a reasonable excuse for failing to do so; or

(b) the owner, occupier or other person or authority having control of the land has consented (generally or specifically) to his failing to do so.

(2) A person who is guilty of an offence under this section shall be liable on summary conviction to a fine not exceeding level 3 on the standard scale.

(3) Nothing in this section applies to a person registered as a blind person in a register compiled under section 29 of the *National Assistance Act* 1948.

(4) For the purposes of this section—

(a) a person who habitually has a dog in his possession shall be taken to be in charge of the dog at any time unless at that time some other person is in charge of the dog;

(b) placing the faeces in a receptacle on the land which is provided for the purpose, or for the disposal of waste, shall be a sufficient removal from the land; and

(c) being unaware of the defecation (whether by reason of not being in the vicinity or otherwise), or not having a device for or other suitable means of removing the faeces, shall not be a reasonable excuse for failing to remove the faeces.

(b) *Procedure*

This offence is triable summarily only: s.3(2).   **16–37**

(c) *Elements of the offence*

The Act applies to land which is open to the air and to which the public have access. **16–38** The land may be designated for the purposes of this Act by the local authority: s.1.

(d) *Defence*

Section 3(1) provides that an accused will have a defence if he can establish that he **16–39** had a reasonable excuse for failing to remove the dog's faeces or that the owner, occupier or other person or authority having control of the land has consented (generally or specifically) to his failing to do so. Being unaware of the defecation dose not amount to a reasonable excuse: s.3(4)(c).

(e) *Sentence*

The maximum penalty for this offence is a fine not exceeding level three on the stan- **16–40** dard scale. The offence may be dealt with by a fixed penalty notice.

C. DANGEROUS DOGS

Dogs Act 1871, s.2

Dangerous dogs may be destroyed

2. Any court of summary jurisdiction may take cognizance of a complaint that a dog is **16–41** dangerous, and not kept under proper control, and if it appears to the court having cognizance of such complaint that such dog is dangerous, the court may make an order in a summary way directing the dog to be kept by the owner under proper control or destroyed

[This section is printed as amended by the *Dangerous Dogs Act* 1989, s.2(3)(a) (4).]

A complaint may be made by a police officer: *Smith v Baker*, 125 J.P. 53.

16–42   The court has jurisdiction to hear a complaint under this section even if the conduct complained of occurred outside of the commission area. Jurisdiction is founded on the location of the animal at the time when the summons is applied for and the complaint relates to the dangerousness of the animal which should be kept under proper control no matter where it might be: *Shufflebottom v Chief Constable of Greater Manchester* (2003) 167 J.P. 153.

The term 'dangerous' is to be given its ordinary, every day meaning and the question of whether it is kept under 'proper control' is a question of fact for the court. The dog does not have to be dangerous only to human beings or livestock. The fact that it is dangerous to other dogs is sufficient: *Briscoe v Shattock* (1998) 163 J.P. 201. But the fact that a dog killed two pet rabbits on one occasion was held not to make it dangerous because it was in the nature of dogs to hunt and kill other small animals: *Sansom v Chief Constable of Kent* [1981] Crim.L.R. 617.

The court may order destruction of the animal and further powers are contained in s.1 of the *Dangerous Dogs Act* 1989, below.

Costs may be ordered under s.64 of the *Magistrates Courts Act* 1980.

Dangerous Dogs Act 1989, s.1

Additional powers of court on complaint about dangerous dog

16–43   **1.**—(1) Where a magistrates' court makes an order under section 2 of the *Dogs Act* 1871 directing a dog to be destroyed it may also—

     (a) appoint a person to undertake its destruction and require any person having custody of the dog to deliver it up for that purpose; and

     (b) if it thinks fit, make an order disqualifying the owner for having custody of a dog for such period as is specified in the order.

(2) An appeal shall lie to the Crown Court against any order under section 2 of that Act or under subsection (1) above; and, unless the owner of a dog which is ordered to be delivered up and destroyed gives notice to the court that made the order that he does not intend to appeal against it, the dog shall not be destroyed pursuant to the order—

     (a) until the end of the period within which notice of appeal to the Crown Court against the order can be given; and

     (b) if notice of appeal is given within that period, until the appeal is determined or withdrawn.

(3) Any person who fails to comply with an order under section 2 of the said Act of 1871 to keep a dog under proper control or to deliver a dog up for destruction as required by an order under subsection (1)(a) above is guilty of an offence and liable on summary conviction to a fine not exceeding level 3 on the standard scale and the court may, in addition, make an order disqualifying him for having custody of a dog for such period as is specified in the order.

(4) A person who is disqualified for having custody of a dog by virtue of an order made under subsection (1)(b) or (3) above may, at any time after the end of the period of one year beginning with the date of the order, apply to the court that made it (or any magistrates' court acting for the same petty sessions area as that court) for a direction terminating the disqualification.

16–44   (5) On an application under subsection (4) above the court may—

     (a) having regard to the applicant's character, his conduct since the disqualification was imposed and any other circumstances of the case, grant or refuse the application; and

     (b) order the applicant to pay all or any part of the costs of the application;

and where an application in respect of an order is refused no further application in respect of that order shall be entertained if made before the end of the period of one year beginning with the date of the refusal.

(6) Any person who has custody of a dog in contravention of an order made under subsection (1)(b) or (3) above is guilty of an offence and liable on summary conviction to a fine not exceeding level 5 on the standard scale.

(7) This section shall apply to Scotland subject to the following adaptations—

    (a) in subsection (1) for the words "magistrates' court" there shall be substituted the words "court of summary jurisdiction";

    (b) in subsection (2)—

        (i) for the words "shall lie to the Crown Court" there shall be substituted the words "may be made to the High Court within a period of 7 days commencing with the date of the order";

        (ii) for paragraph (a) there shall be substituted—

"(a) until the end of the said period of 7 days;and ";

    (c) in subsection (4) the words "(or any magistrates' court acting for the same petty sessions area as that court)" shall be omitted.

(a) *Definition*

Dangerous Dogs Act 1991, s.1

Dogs bred for fighting

1.—(1) This section applies to—   **16–45**

    (a) any dog of the type known as the pit bull terrier;

    (b) any dog of the type known as the Japanese tosa; and

    (c) any dog of any type designated for the purposes of this section by an order of the Secretary of State, being a type appearing to him to be bred for fighting or to have the characteristics of a type bred for that purpose.

(2) No person shall—

    (a) breed, or breed from, a dog to which this section applies;

    (b) sell or exchange such a dog or offer, advertise or expose such a dog for sale or exchange;

    (c) make or offer to make a gift of such a dog or advertise or expose such a dog as a gift;

    (d) allow such a dog of which he is the owner or of which he is for the time being in charge to be in a public place without being muzzled and kept on a lead; or

    (e) abandon such a dog of which he is the owner or, being the owner or for the time being in charge of such a dog, allow it to stray.

(3) After such day as the Secretary of State may by order appoint for the purposes of this subsection no person shall have any dog to which this section applies in his possession or custody except—

    (a) in pursuance of the power of seizure conferred by the subsequent provisions of this Act; or

    (b) in accordance with an order for its destruction made under those provisions;

but the Secretary of State shall by order make a scheme for the payment to the owners of such dogs who arrange for them to be destroyed before that day of sums specified in or determined under the scheme in respect of those dogs and the cost of their destruction.

(4) Subsection (2)(b) and (c) above shall not make unlawful anything done with a view to   **16–46** the dog in question being removed from the United Kingdom before the day appointed under subsection (3) above.

(5) The Secretary of State may by order provide that the prohibition in subsection (3) above shall not apply in such cases and subject to compliance with such conditions as are specified in the order and any such provision may take the form of a scheme of exemption containing such arrangements (including provision for the payment of charges or fees) as he thinks appropriate.

(6) A scheme under subsection (3) or (5) above may provide for specified functions under the scheme to be discharged by such persons or bodies as the Secretary of State thinks appropriate.

(7) Any person who contravenes this section is guilty of an offence and liable on summary conviction to imprisonment for a term not exceeding six months or a fine not exceed-

ing level 5 on the standard scale or both except that a person who publishes an advertisement in contravention of subsection (2)(b) or (c)—

    (a) shall not on being convicted be liable to imprisonment if he shows that he published the advertisement to the order of someone else and did not himself devise it; and

    (b) shall not be convicted if, in addition, he shows that he did not know and had no reasonable cause to suspect that it related to a dog to which this section applies.

(8) An order under subsection (1)(c) above adding dogs of any type to those to which this section applies may provide that subsections (3) and (4) above shall apply in relation to those dogs with the substitution for the day appointed under subsection (3) of a later day specified in the order.

(9) The power to make orders under this section shall be exercisable by statutory instrument which, in the case of an order under subsection (1) or (5) or an order containing a scheme under subsection (3), shall be subject to annulment in pursuance of a resolution of either House of Parliament.

(b) Procedure

16–47   This offence is triable summarily.

(c) Elements

16–48   This section applies specifically to dogs bred for fighting. The appointed day referred to in s.1(3) was November 30, 1991 (SI 1991/1742). The word 'type' has wider and different meaning from the description 'breed'. It was held to include any dog which had a substantial amount or most of the physical characteristics of the breed of dog in question, *e.g.* a pitbull terrier: *R. v Crown Court at Knightsbridge Ex p. Dunne* [1993] 4 All E.R. 491. An offence is committed if the dog is in a car, when the car itself is in a public place: *Bates v DPP* (1993) 157 J.P. 1004.

This is an absolute offence and it is no defence to a charge of allowing a dog to be off the lead and unmuzzled for the owner to say he was intoxicated at the time: *DPP v Kellet* (1994) 158 J.P. 1138. Nor is it a defence for the owner to say that the dog was not muzzled or kept on a lead as a necessity to avoid serious harm to the dog itself: *Cichon v DPP* [1994] Crim.L.R.

(d) Sentence

16–48.1   The sentence is a maximum of six months imprisonment or a fine not exceeding level 5 or both.

The court also has power to make destruction and disqualification orders under ss.4 and 4A (see below).

(a) Definition

Dangerous Dogs Act 1991, s.3

Keeping dogs under proper control

16–49   **3.**—(1) If a dog is dangerously out of control in a public place—

    (a) the owner; and

    (b) if different, the person for the time being in charge of the dog,

is guilty of an offence, or, if the dog while so out of control injures any person, an aggravated offence, under this subsection.

(2) In proceedings for an offence under subsection (1) above against a person who is the owner of a dog but was not at the material time in charge of it, it shall be a defence for the accused to prove that the dog was at the material time in the charge of a person whom he reasonably believed to be a fit and proper person to be in charge of it.

(3) If the owner or, if different, the person for the time being in charge of a dog allows it to enter a place which is not a public place but where it is not permitted to be and while it is there—

(a) it injures any person; or

(b) there are grounds for reasonable apprehension that it will do so,

he is guilty of an offence, or, if the dog injures any person, an aggravated offence, under this subsection.

(4) A person guilty of an offence under subsection (1) or (3) above other than an aggravated offence is liable on summary conviction to imprisonment for a term not exceeding six months or a fine not exceeding level 5 on the standard scale or both; and a person guilty of an aggravated offence under either of those subsections is liable—

(a) on summary conviction, to imprisonment for a term not exceeding six months or a fine not exceeding the statutory maximum or both;

(b) on conviction on indictment, to imprisonment for a term not exceeding two years or a fine or both.

(5) It is hereby declared for the avoidance of doubt that an order under section 2 of the *Dogs Act* 1871 (order on complaint that dog is dangerous and not kept under proper control)—

(a) may be made whether or not the dog is shown to have injured any person; and

(b) may specify the measures to be taken for keeping the dog under proper control, whether by muzzling, keeping on a lead, excluding it from specified places or otherwise.

(6) If it appears to a court on a complaint under section 2 of the said Act of 1871 that the dog to which the complaint relates is a male and would be less dangerous if neutered the court may under that section make an order requiring it to be neutered.

(7) The reference in section 1(3) of the *Dangerous Dogs Act* 1989 (penalties) to failing to comply with an order under section 2 of the said Act of 1871 to keep a dog under proper control shall include a reference to failing to comply with any other order made under that section; but no order shall be made under that section by virtue of subsection (6) above where the matters complained of arose before the coming into force of that subsection.

(b) *Procedure*

This offence is triable summarily only unless it is an aggravated offence in which case **16–50** it is triable either way. An offence is aggravated under s.3(1) if, while the dog is out of control, it injures any person.

(c) *Elements*

This section applies to any kind of dog. A dog is defined as being dangerously out of **16–51** control 'on any occasion on which there are grounds for reasonable apprehension that it will injure any person, whether or not it actually does so, but references to a dog injuring a person or there being grounds for reasonable apprehension that it will do so do not include references to any case in which the dog is being used for a lawful purpose by a constable or a person in the service of the Crown.': s.10(3) of the Act. This is an objective test.

A public place is 'any street, road or other place, (whether or not enclosed) to which the public have or are permitted to have access whether for payment or otherwise and includes the common parts of a building containing two or more separate dwellings.': s.10(2) of the Act.

An offence may be committed in a public place if the dog is dangerously out of control. An offence may also be committed in a place which is not a public place and where the dog is not permitted to be but only if the dog injures any person or there is a reasonable apprehension that it will do so: s.3(3). This offence is aggravated if a person is injured.

(d) *Defence*

This is an absolute offence. It is no defence for the owner to say that they never re- **16–52** alised that the dog would behave in a dangerous manner: *R. v Bezzina* 158 J.P. 671.

The offence may be committed by the owner of the dog or any person for the time being in charge of the dog. The defence under s.3(2) requires clear and plain evidence that the owner has placed the dog in the charge of another identifiable person: *R. v Huddart* [1999] Crim.L.R. 568.

(e) *Sentence*

16–53　　For a summary offence the sentence is a maximum term of imprisonment of six months or a fine not exceeding level 5 or both.

On conviction on indictment the sentence is a maximum term of imprisonment of two years and a fine or both. The court also has power to make destruction and disqualification orders under ss.4 and 4A, below.

When imposing sentence the courts should look at the consequences of the offence. The nature and extent of the obligations of dog owners had to be marked by a custodial sentence when there was a seriously aggravated offence. In a case where a pack of five dogs attacked and seriously injured a boy of seven in a public park, a sentence of three months imprisonment was held to be appropriate for a defendant of good character who entered a plea of guilty: *R. v Cox, The Times*, February 20, 2004.

(f) *Other penalties*

Dangerous Dogs Act 1991, ss.4, 4A, 4B

Destruction and disqualification orders

16–54　　**4.**—(1) Where a person is convicted of an offence under section 1 or 3(1) or (3) above or of an offence under an order made under section 2 above the court—

(a) may order the destruction of any dog in respect of which the offence was committed and, subject to subsection (1A) below, shall do so in the case of an offence under section 1 or an aggravated offence under section 3(1) or (3) above; and

(b) may order the offender to be disqualified, for such period as the court thinks fit, for having custody of a dog.

(1A) Nothing in subsection (1)(a) above shall require the court to order the destruction of a dog if the court is satisfied—

(a) that the dog would not constitute a danger to public safety; and

(b) where the dog was born before 30th November 1991 and is subject to the prohibition in section 1 (3) above, that there is a good reason why the dog has not been exempted from that prohibition.

(2) Where a court makes an order under subsection (1)(a) above for the destruction of a dog owned by a person other than the offender, the owner may appeal to the Crown Court against the order.

(3) A dog shall not be destroyed pursuant to an order under subsection (1)(a) above—

(a) until the end of the period for giving notice of appeal against the conviction or against the order; and

(b) if notice of appeal is given within that period, until the appeal is determined or withdrawn,

unless the offender and, in a case to which subsection (2) above applies, the owner of the dog give notice to the court that made the order that there is to be no appeal.

(4) Where a court makes an order under subsection (1)(a) above it may—

(a) appoint a person to undertake the destruction of the dog and require any person having custody of it to deliver it up for that purpose; and

(b) order the offender to pay such sum as the court may determine to be the reasonable expenses of destroying the dog and of keeping it pending its destruction.

(5) Any sum ordered to be paid under subsection (4)(b) above shall be treated for the purposes of enforcement as if it were a fine imposed on conviction.

(6) Any person who is disqualified for having custody of a dog by virtue of an order under subsection (1)(b) above may, at any time after the end of the period of one year beginning with the date of the order, apply to the court that made it (or a magistrates' court acting for the same petty sessions area as that court) for a direction terminating the disqualification.

16–55　　(7) On an application under subsection (6) above the court may—

(a) having regard to the applicant's character, his conduct since the disqualification was imposed and any other circumstances of the case, grant or refuse the application; and

(b) order the applicant to pay all or any part of the costs of the application;
and where an application in respect of an order is refused no further application in respect
of that order shall be entertained if made before the end of the period of one year beginning with the date of the refusal.

(8) Any person who—

(a) has custody of a dog in contravention of an order under subsection (1)(b) above;
or

(b) fails to comply with a requirement imposed on him under subsection (4)(a)
above,

is guilty of an offence and liable on summary conviction to a fine not exceeding level 5 on
the standard scale.

(9) In the application of this section to Scotland—

(a) in subsection (2) for the words "Crown Court against the order" there shall be
substituted the words "High Court of Justiciary against the order within the period of seven days beginning with the date of the order";

(b) for subsection (3)(a) there shall be substituted—

"(a) until the end of the period of seven days beginning with the date of the order";

(c) for subsection (5) there shall be substituted—

"(5) section 221 of the *Criminal Procedure (Scotland) Act* 1995 shall apply in relation to
the recovery of sums ordered to be paid under subsection (4)(b) above as it applies to fines
ordered to be recovered by civil diligence in pursuance of Part XI of that Act."

; and

(d) in subsection (6) the words "(or a magistrates' court acting for the same petty sessions
area as that court)" shall be omitted.

Contingent destruction orders

4A.—(1) Where—   **16–56**

(a) a person is convicted of an offence under section 1 above or an aggravated offence under section 3(1) or (3) above;

(b) the court does not order the destruction of the dog under section 4(1)(a) above;
and

(c) in the case of an offence under section 1 above, the dog is subject to the prohibition in section 1(3) above.

the court shall order that, unless the dog is exempted from that prohibition within the requisite
period, the dog shall be destroyed.

(2) Where an order is made under subsection (1) above in respect of a dog, and the dog
is not exempted from the prohibition in section 1(3) above within the requisite period, the
court may extend that period.

(3) Subject to subsection (2) above, the requisite period for the purposes of such an order is the period of two months beginning with the date of the order.

(4) Where a person is convicted of an offence under section 3(1) or (3) above, the court
may order that, unless the owner of the dog keeps it under proper control, the dog shall
be destroyed.

(5) An order under subsection (4) above—

(a) may specify the measures to be taken for keeping the dog under proper control,
whether by muzzling, keeping on a lead, excluding it from specified places or
otherwise; and

(b) if it appears to the court that the dog is a male and would be less dangerous if
neutered, may require it to be neutered.

(6) Subsections (2) to (4) of section 4 above shall apply in relation to an order under
subsection (1) or (4) above as they apply in relation to an order under subsection (1)(a) of
that section.

Destruction orders otherwise than on a conviction

4B.—(1) Where a dog is seized under section 5(1) or (2) below and it appears to a justice of   **16–57**
the peace, or in Scotland a justice of the peace or sheriff—

(a) that no person has been or is to be prosecuted for an offence under this Act or an
order under section 2 above in respect of that dog (whether because the owner
cannot be found or for any other reason); or

(b) that the dog cannot be released into the custody or possession of its owner without the owner contravening the prohibition in section 1(3) above,

he may order the destruction of the dog and, subject to subsection (2) below, shall do so if it is one to which section 1 above applies.

(2) Nothing in subsection (1)(b) above shall require the justice or sheriff to order the destruction of a dog if he is satisfied—

(a) that the dog would not constitute a danger to public safety; and

(b) where the dog was born before 30th November 1991 and is subject to the prohibition in section 1(3) above, that there is a good reason why the dog has not been exempted from that prohibition.

(3) Where in a case falling within subsection (1)(b) above the justice or sheriff does not order the destruction of the dog, he shall order that, unless the dog is exempted from the prohibition in section 1(3) above within the requisite period, the dog shall be destroyed.

(4) Subsections (2) to (4) of section 4 above shall apply in relation to an order under subsection (1)(b) or (3) above as they apply in relation to an order under subsection (1)(a) of that section.

(5) Subsections (2) and (3) of section 4A above shall apply in relation to an order under subsection (3) above as they apply in relation to an order under subsection (1) of that section, except that the reference to the court in subsection (2) of that section shall be construed as a reference to the justice or sheriff.

[These sections are printed as amended by the *Dangerous Dogs (Amendment) Act 1997*, s.1(4), s.2 and s.3(1).]

16–58   Before an order of destruction is made the rules of natural justice require that the owner, if he has not already been notified, should be advised of the hearing and be given the opportunity to attend court and make representations: *R. v Trafford Magistrates Court Ex p. Riley* (1996) 160 J.P. 418.

The power under s.4B may not be exercised where a prosecution has been discontinued but if there is a further new incident involving the dog then fresh proceedings may be instituted after seizure and this will not be an abuse of the courts powers: *R. v Walton Street Justices Ex p. Crothers* (1996) 160 J.P. 427.

In *R. v Holland* [2003] 1 Cr.App.R.(S.) 60, CA, a disqualification order disqualifying the appellant for 10 years from keeping a dog, and an order for the destruction of the dog, was upheld in a case where a bull terrier attacked a child.

Whilst the destruction order was mandatory under s.4(1)(a) and s.4(1A) of the 1991 Act unless the judge was satisfied that the dog did not constitute a danger to public safety, the order disqualifying the appellant from having the custody of the dog was discretionary. The disqualification order had been made to protect the victim child from anxiety when she visited her grandparents who lived next to the owner of the bull terrier. The Court stated that in cases of this kind a balance should be struck between the sensitivities of the victim on the one hand and restriction on the freedom of the custodian on the other. The disqualification order prohibited the appellant from keeping any dog at all. The statute made provision for a disqualified person to apply to a court for a direction terminating the disqualification and it would be open to the appellant to make such an application in due course.

Dangerous Dogs Act 1991, s.5

Seizure, entry of premises and evidence.

16–59   **5.**—(1) A constable or an officer of a local authority authorised by it to exercise the powers conferred by this subsection may seize—

(a) any dog which appears to him to be a dog to which section 1 above applies and which is in a public place—

(i) after the time when possession or custody of it has become unlawful by virtue of that section; or

(ii) before that time, without being muzzled and kept on a lead;

(b) any dog in a public place which appears to him to be a dog to which an order under section 2 above applies and in respect of which an offence against the order has been or is being committed; and

(c) any dog in a public place (whether or not one to which that section or such an order applies) which appears to him to be dangerously out of control.

(2) If a justice of the peace is satisfied by information on oath, or in Scotland a justice of the peace or sheriff is satisfied by evidence on oath, that there are reasonable grounds for believing—

(a) that an offence under any provision of this Act or of an order under section 2 above is being or has been committed; or

(b) that evidence of the commission of any such offence is to be found,

on any premises he may issue a warrant authorising a constable to enter those premises (using such force as is reasonably necessary) and to search them and seize any dog or other thing found there which is evidence of the commission of such an offence.

(3) A warrant issued under this section in Scotland shall be authority for opening lock-fast places and may authorise persons named in the warrant to accompany a constable who is executing it.

(5) If in any proceedings it is alleged by the prosecution that a dog is one to which section 1 or an order under section 2 above applies it shall be presumed that it is such a dog unless the contrary is shown by the accused by such evidence as the court considers sufficient; and the accused shall not be permitted to adduce such evidence unless he has given the prosecution notice of his intention to do so not later than the fourteenth day before that on which the evidence is to be adduced.

[This section is printed as amended by the *Dangerous Dogs (Amendment) Act* 1997, s.3(2).]

Dangerous Dogs Act 1991, s.6

Dogs owned by young persons

6. Where a dog is owned by a person who is less than sixteen years old any reference to its **16–60** owner in section 1(2)(d) or (e) or 3 above shall include a reference to the head of the household, if any, of which that person is a member or, in Scotland, to the person who has his actual care and control.

III. COMPANIES

There are many offences under the *Companies Act* 1985 which are not included in **16–61** this publication. For the powers of the court in relation to disqualification of company **—16–69** officers as an ancillary order on sentencing, see the *Company Directors Disqualification Act* 1986, ss.1, 5, §§ 27–26—27–29.

A. INSIDER DEALING

(a) *Definition*

Criminal Justice Act 1993, ss.52, 53

The offence

52.—(1) An individual who has information as an insider is guilty of insider dealing if, in the **16–70** circumstances mentioned in subsection (3), he deals in securities that are price-affected securities in relation to the information.

(2) An individual who has information as an insider is also guilty of insider dealing if—

(a) he encourages another person to deal in securities that are (whether or not that other knows it) price-affected securities in relation to the information, knowing or having reasonable cause to believe that the dealing would take place in the circumstances mentioned in subsection (3); or

(b) he discloses the information, otherwise than in the proper performance of the functions of his employment, office or profession, to another person.

(3) The circumstances referred to above are that the acquisition or disposal in question occurs on a regulated market, or that the person dealing relies on a professional intermediary or is himself acting as a professional intermediary.

(4) This section has effect subject to section 53.

Defences

16–71   **53.**—(1) An individual is not guilty of insider dealing by virtue of dealing in securities if he shows—

    (a) that he did not at the time expect the dealing to result in a profit attributable to the fact that the information in question was price-sensitive information in relation to the securities, or

    (b) that at the time he believed on reasonable grounds that the information had been disclosed widely enough to ensure that none of those taking part in the dealing would be prejudiced by not having the information, or

    (c) that he would have done what he did even if he had not had the information.

(2) An individual is not guilty of insider dealing by virtue of encouraging another person to deal in securities if he shows—

    (a) that he did not at the time expect the dealing to result in a profit attributable to the fact that the information in question was price-sensitive information in relation to the securities, or

    (b) that at the time he believed on reasonable grounds that the information had been or would be disclosed widely enough to ensure that none of those taking part in the dealing would be prejudiced by not having the information, or

    (c) that he would have done what he did even if he had not had the information.

(3) An individual is not guilty of insider dealing by virtue of a disclosure of information if he shows—

    (a) that he did not at the time expect any person, because of the disclosure, to deal in securities in the circumstances mentioned in subsection (3) of section 52; or

    (b) that, although he had such an expectation at the time, he did not expect the dealing to result in a profit attributable to the fact that the information was price-sensitive information in relation to the securities.

(4) Schedule 1 (special defences) shall have effect.

(5) The Treasury may by order amend Schedule 1.

(6) In this section references to a profit include references to the avoidance of a loss.

(b) *Procedure*

16–72   This offence is triable either way: *CJA* 1993, s.61.

(c) *Elements of the offence*

Criminal Justice Act 1993, s.54

Securities to which Part V applies

16–73   **54.**—(1) This Part applies to any security which—

    (a) falls within any paragraph of Schedule 2; and

    (b) satisfies any conditions applying to it under an order made by the Treasury for the purposes of this subsection;

and in the provisions of this Part (other than that Schedule) any reference to a security is a reference to a security to which this Part applies.

(2) The Treasury may by order amend Schedule 2.

See the *Insider Dealing (Securities and Regulated Markets) Order* 1994 (SI 1994/187).

The special defences referred to in Sch.1 relate to market makers, market information and the price stabilisation rules.

(d) *Sentence*

Criminal Justice Act 1993, s.61

Penalties and prosecution

16–74   **61.**—(1) An individual guilty of insider dealing shall be liable—

(a) on summary conviction, to a fine not exceeding the statutory maximum or imprisonment for a term not exceeding six months or to both; or

(b) on conviction on indictment, to a fine or imprisonment for a term not exceeding seven years or to both.

(2) Proceedings for offences under this Part shall not be instituted in England and Wales except by or with the consent of—

(a) the Secretary of State; or

(b) the Director of Public Prosecutions.

(3) In relation to proceedings in Northern Ireland for offences under this Part, subsection (2) shall have effect as if the reference to the Director of Public Prosecutions were a reference to the Director of Public Prosecutions for Northern Ireland.

IV. CONSUMER PROTECTION

A. Prohibition of False Trade Descriptions

(a) *Definition*

Trade Descriptions Act 1968, ss.1–6

Prohibition of false trade descriptions

1.—(1) Any person who, in the course of a trade or business,—   **16–75**

(a) applies a false trade description to any goods; or

(b) supplies or offers to supply any goods to which a false trade description is applied;

shall, subject to the provisions of this Act, be guilty of an offence.

(2) Sections 2 to 6 of this Act shall have effect for the purposes of this section and for the interpretation of expressions used in this section, wherever they occur in this Act.

Trade description

2.—(1) A trade description is an indication, direct or indirect, and by whatever means given, **16–76** of any of the following matters with respect to any goods or parts of goods, that is to say—

(a) quantity, size or gauge;

(b) method of manufacture, production, processing or reconditioning;

(c) composition;

(d) fitness for purpose, strength, performance, behaviour or accuracy;

(e) any physical characteristics not included in the preceding paragraphs;

(f) testing by any person and results thereof;

(g) approval by any person or conformity with a type approved by any person;

(h) place or date of manufacture, production, processing or reconditioning;

(i) person by whom manufactured, produced, processed or reconditioned;

(j) other history, including previous ownership or use.

(2) The matters specified in subsection (1) of this section shall be taken—   **16–77**

(a) in relation to any animal, to include sex, breed or cross, fertility and soundness;

(b) in relation to any semen, to include the identity and characteristics of the animal from which it was taken and measure of dilution.

(3) In this sections "quantity" includes length, width, height, area, volume, capacity, weight and number.

(4) Notwithstanding anything in the preceding provisions of this section, the following shall be deemed not to be trade descriptions, that is to say, any description or mark applied in pursuance of—

(b) section 2 of the *Agricultural Produce (Grading and Marking) Act* 1928 (as amended by the *Agricultural Produce (Grading and Marking) Amendment Act* 1931) or any corresponding enactment of the Parliament of Northern Ireland;

(c) the *Plant Varieties and Seeds Act* 1964;

(d) the *Agriculture and Horticulture Act* 1964 or any Community grading rules within the meaning of Part III of that Act;

(e) the *Seeds Act (Northern Ireland) 1965*;

(f) the *Horticulture Act (Northern Ireland)* 1966;

any statement made in respect of, or mark applied to, any material in pursuance of Part IV of the *Agriculture Act* 1970, any name or expression to which a meaning has been assigned under section 70 of that Act when applied to any material in the circumstances specified in that section any mark prescribed by a system of classification compiled under section 5 of the *Agriculture Act* 1967 and any designation, mark or description applied in pursuance of a scheme brought into force under section 6(1) or an order made under section 25(1) of the *Agriculture Act* 1970.

(g) the *Consumer Protection Act* 1987;

(h) the *Plant Varieties Act* 1997.

16–78　　　(5) Notwithstanding anything in the preceding provisions of this section, (a) where provision is made under the *Food Act* 1984, the *Food and Drugs (Scotland) Act* 1956 the *Food Safety Act* 1990 or the *Food and Drugs Act (Northern Ireland)* 1958 or the *Consumer Protection Act* 1987 prohibiting the application of a description except to goods in the case of which the requirements specified in that provision are complied with, that description, when applied to such goods, shall be deemed not to be a trade description.

(b) where by virtue of any provision made under Part V of the *Medicines Act* 1968 (or made under any provisions of the said Part V as applied by an order made under section 104 or section 105 of that Act) anything which, in accordance with this Act, constitutes the application of a trade description to goods is subject to any requirements or restrictions imposed by that provision, any particular description specified in that provision, when applied to goods in circumstances to which those requirements or restrictions are applicable, shall be deemed not to be a trade description

False trade description

16–79　　　**3.**—(1) A false trade description is a trade description which is false to a material degree.

(2) A trade description which, though not false, is misleading, that is to say, likely to be taken for such an indication of any of the matters specified in section 2 of this Act as would be false to a material degree, shall be deemed to be a false trade description.

(3) Anything which, though not a trade description, is likely to be taken for an indication of any of those matters and, as such an indication, would be false to a material degree, shall be deemed to be a false trade description.

(4) A false indication, or anything likely to be taken as an indication which would be false, that any goods comply with a standard specified or recognised by any person or implied by the approval of any person shall be deemed to be a false trade description, if there is no such person or no standard so specified, recognised or implied.

Applying a trade description to goods

16–80　　　**4.**—(1) A person applies a trade description to goods if he—

(a) affixes or annexes it to or in any manner marks it on or incorporates it with—

(i) the goods themselves, or

(ii) anything in, on or with which the goods are supplied; or

(b) places the goods in, on or with anything which the trade description has been affixed or annexed to, marked on or incorporated with, or places any such thing with the goods; or

(c) uses the trade description in any manner likely to be taken as referring to the goods.

(2) An oral statement may amount to the use of a trade description.

(3) Where goods are supplied in pursuance of a request in which a trade description is used and the circumstances are such as to make it reasonable to infer that the goods are supplied as goods corresponding to that trade description, the person supplying the goods shall be deemed to have applied that trade description to the goods.

Trade descriptions used in advertisements

16–81　　　**5.**—(1) The following provisions of this section shall have effect where in an advertisement a trade description is used in relation to any class of goods.

(2) The trade description shall be taken as referring to all goods of the class, whether or not in existence at the time the advertisement is published—

(a) for the purpose of determining whether an offence has been committed under paragraph (a) of section 1(1) of this Act; and

(b) where goods of the class are supplied or offered to be supplied by a person publishing or displaying the advertisement, also for the purpose of determining whether an offence has been committed under paragraph (b) of the said section 1(1).

(3) In determining for the purposes of this section whether any goods are of a class to which a trade description used in an advertisement relates regard shall be had not only to the form and content of the advertisement but also to the time, place, manner and frequency of its publication and all other matters making it likely or unlikely that a person to whom the goods are supplied would think of the goods as belonging to the class in relation to which the trade description is used in the advertisement.

Offer to supply
6. A person exposing goods for supply or having goods in his possession for supply shall be deemed to offer to supply them. **16–82**

(b) *Procedure*

This offence is triable either way: *Trade Descriptions Act* 1968, s.18. **16–83**

(c) *Elements of the offence*

'In the course of a trade or business'
Professionals are not excluded from the scope of the Act; the term 'trade or business' **16–84** applies to them as well: *Roberts v Leonard* (1995) 159 J.P. 711. A person engaging in a hobby of repairing and selling cars in his spare time was held not to be subject to the act as his activities could not be termed a 'trade or business' for the purposes of s.1: *Blakemore v Bellamy* (1982) 147 J.P. 89.

There needs to be some degree of regularity in the transactions for them to form part of the normal practice of a business, however this does not necessarily mean that a one-off venture in the nature of trade carried out with a view to profit would not fall under the scope of s.1(1): *Davies v Sumner* [1984] 3 All E.R. 831.

The Act does not apply to an expert who gives an opinion in respect of the condition of goods: *Wycombe Marsh Garages Ltd v Fowler* [1972] 3 All E.R. 248.

Trade description
The particular words complained of must be looked at as a whole: *Evans v British* **16–85** *Doughnut Co Ltd* [1944] 1 K.B. 102. Where functional goods are supplied with instructions for their use the goods must be fit for use in accordance with those instructions as understood by the reasonable purchaser: *Janbo Trading Ltd. v Dudley MBC* (1993) 157 J.P. 1056.

This is a strict liability offence and the prosecution do not have to prove dishonesty: **16–86** *Alec Norman Garages Ltd v Phillips* (1984) 148 J.P. 741.

False trade descriptions are sometimes used in the second-hand car market. The Act provides for the offence of applying a false description, which might be done by an unscrupulous trader and also the offence of supplying goods to which a false trade description has been applied, which might be an offence committed by the less than careful trader. Whether an advertising slogan used to encourage buyers amounts to a false trade description is a matter of fact in each case but there is no requirement to prove that the buyer has actually been deceived. Where a car was described as being in 'excellent condition throughout' it was no defence to say that the car was in as good a condition as could be expected for a car of its age and mileage and in an unrepaired state. It was held that a false trade description had been applied as there were 17 defects in the car: *Chidwick v Beer* [1974] R.T.R. 415. To say a car is in 'showroom condition throughout' cannot be described as a mere puff but it was held to be a false trade description as the car had defects requiring repair. The term referred to the interior, exterior and mechanical condition of the car and not just it's appearance: *Hawkins v Smith* [1978] Crim.L.R. 578.

When the mileage on a car is altered the false reading on the odometer is capable of amounting to a false trade description: *Hammerton Cars Ltd v London Borough of Redbridge* [1976] 3 All E.R. 758. A trader who alters the reading himself cannot hide behind any disclaimer that may be attached to the vehicle but where the car is supplied or offered for supply a disclaimer may neutralise any trade description attached if it is 'bold, precise and compelling': *Norman v Bennett* [1974] R.T.R. 441. *R v Southwood* [1987] 3 All E.R. 556.

(d) *Sentence*

16–87   When tried summarily the maximum penalty for this offence is a fine not exceeding the statutory maximum: *Trade Descriptions Act* 1968, s.18. On conviction on indictment, the penalty is a fine or a term of imprisonment not exceeding two years or both.

Trade Descriptions Act 1968, s.20

Offences by corporations

16–88   **20.**—(1) Where an offence under this Act which has been committed by a body corporate is proved to have been committed with the consent and connivance of, or to be attributable to any neglect on the part of, any director, manager, secretary or other similar officer of the body corporate, or any person who was purporting to act in any such capacity, he as well as the body corporate shall be guilty of that offence and shall be liable to be proceeded against and punished accordingly.

(2) In this section "director", in relation to any body corporate established by or under any enactment for the purpose of carrying on under national ownership any industry or part of an industry or undertaking, being a body corporate whose affairs are managed by the members thereof, means a member of that body corporate.

16–89   There must be evidence of conduct that amounts to neglect. In *Lewin v Bland* (1984) 148 J.P. 69 the defendant was the managing director of a garage that dealt in cars and he instructed his service manager to complete a service book in respect of a second hand car that had been sold. The book was completed inaccurately by his employee and the director was prosecuted for applying a false trade description. It was held that there was no evidence of neglect and the defendant was entitled to expect that his employee would follow his instructions properly without the need to check his work. The conviction was quashed.

Trade Descriptions Act 1968, s.19

Time limit for prosecutions

16–90   **19.**—(1) No prosecution for an offence under this Act shall be commenced after the expiration of three years from the commission of the offence or one year from its discovery by the prosecutor, whichever is the earlier.

(2) Notwithstanding anything in section 127(1) of the *Magistrates' Courts Act* 1980, a magistrates' court may try an information for an offence under this Act if the information was laid at any time within twelve months from the commission of the offence.

(3) Notwithstanding anything in section 23 of the *Summary Jurisdiction (Scotland) Act* 1954 (limitation of time for proceedings in statutory offences) summary proceedings in Scotland for an offence under this section may be commenced at any time within twelve months from the time when the offence was committed, and subsection (2) of the said section 23 shall apply for the purposes of this subsection as it applies for the purposes of that section.

(4) Subsections (2) and (3) of this section do not apply where—

    (a) the offence was committed by the making of an oral statement; or

    (b) the offence was one of supplying goods to which a false trade description is applied, and the trade description was applied by an oral statement; or

    (c) the offence was one where a false trade description is deemed to have been applied to goods by virtue of section 4(3) of this Act and the goods were supplied in pursuance of an oral request.

16–91   An offence is discovered when all the relevant facts necessary to found a charge are disclosed to the prosecution: *Newham London Borough v Co-operative Retail Services Ltd* (1985) 149 J.P. 421.

The time limit for these either way offences is three years (s.19(1)).

(e) *Defences*

Trade Descriptions Act 1968, ss.24, 25

Defence of mistake, accident, etc.

16–92

24.—(1) In any proceedings for an offence under this Act it shall, subject to subsection (2) of this section, be a defence for the person charged to prove—

(a) that the commission of the offence was due to a mistake or to reliance on information supplied to him or to the act or default of another person, an accident or some other cause beyond his control; and

(b) that he took all reasonable precautions and exercised all due diligence to avoid the commission of such an offence by himself or any person under his control.

(2) If in any case the defence provided by the last foregoing subsection involves the allegation that the commission of the offence was due to the act or default of another person or to reliance on information supplied by another person, the person charged shall not, without leave of the court, be entitled to rely on that defence unless, within a period ending seven clear days before the hearing, he has served on the prosecutor a notice in writing giving such information identifying or assisting in the identification of that other person as was then in his possession.

(3) In any proceedings for an offence under this Act of supplying or offering to supply goods to which a false trade description is applied it shall be a defence for the person charged to prove that he did not know, and could not with reasonable diligence have ascertained, that the goods did not conform to the description or that the description had been applied to the goods.

Innocent publication of advertisement

16–93

25. In proceedings for an offence under this Act committed by the publication of an advertisement it shall be a defence for the person charged to prove that he is a person whose business it is to publish or arrange for the publication of advertisements and that he received the advertisement for publication in the ordinary course of business and did not know and had no reason to suspect that its publication would amount to an offence under this Act.

The defence under s.24(1) is available to those charged with applying a false trade **16–94** description and those charged with supplying or offering to supply goods to which a false trade description has been applied. The defendant must prove on a balance of probabilities that he has done all that could be reasonably expected of him to investigate the person whom he says was responsible for the default: *McGuire v Sittingbourne Co-op Society Ltd* [1976] Crim.L.R. 268. Notice of the details of the third party must be served on the prosecution s.24(2).

The defence under subs.(3) is only available to those charged with supplying or offering to supply goods with a false trade description. The test of 'reasonable diligence' is whether, in view of all the circumstances and the defendant's position as a trader, he used all diligence to ascertain whether the goods conformed to their description. A car salesman should be put on inquiry by an abnormally low odometer reading for a vehicle and although he may not be under a duty to trace the entire history of the car he should have made some inquiries and carefully examined the vehicle: *Simmons v Ravenhill* (1983) 148 J.P. 109.

B. CRIMINAL LIABILITY FOR MAKING OR DEALING WITH INFRINGING ARTICLES ETC.

(a) *Definition*

Copyright, Design and Patents Act 1988, s.107

Criminal liability for making or dealing with infringing articles, &c.

107.—(1) A person commits an offence who, without the licence of the copyright owner— **16–95**

    (a) makes for sale or hire, or

    (b) imports into the United Kingdom otherwise than for his private and domestic use, or

    (c) possesses in the course of a business with a view to committing any act infringing the copyright, or

    (d) in the course of a business—

      (i) sells or lets for hire, or

      (ii) offers or exposes for sale or hire, or

      (iii) exhibits in public, or

      (iv) distributes, or

    (e) distributes otherwise than in the course of a business to such an extent as to affect prejudicially the owner of the copyright,

an article which is, and which he knows or has reason to believe is, an infringing copy of a copyright work.

(2) A person commits an offence who—

    (a) makes an article specifically designed or adapted for making copies of a particular copyright work, or

    (b) has such an article in his possession,

knowing or having reason to believe that it is to be used to make infringing copies for sale or hire or for use in the course of a business.

(2A) A person who infringes copyright in a work by communicating the work to the public—

    (a) in the course of a business, or

    (b) otherwise than in the course of a business to such an extent as to affect prejudicially the owner of the copyright,

commits an offence if he knows or has reason to believe that, by doing so, he is infringing copyright in that work.

16–96   (3) Where copyright is infringed (otherwise than by reception of a communication to the public)—

    (a) by the public performance of a literary, dramatic or musical work, or

    (b) by the playing or showing in public of a sound recording or film,

any person who caused the work to be so performed, played or shown is guilty of an offence if he knew or had reason to believe that copyright would be infringed.

(4) A person guilty of an offence under subsection (1)(a), (b), (d)(iv) or (e) is liable—

    (a) on summary conviction to imprisonment for a term not exceeding six months or a fine not exceeding the statutory maximum, or both;

    (b) on conviction on indictment to a fine or imprisonment for a term not exceeding ten years, or both.

(4A) A person guilty of an offence under subsection (2A) is liable—

    (a) on summary conviction to imprisonment for a term not exceeding three months or a fine not exceeding the statutory maximum, or both;

    (b) on conviction on indictment to a fine or imprisonment for a term not exceeding two years, or both.

(5) A person guilty of any other offence under this section is liable on summary conviction to imprisonment for a term not exceeding six months or a fine not exceeding level 5 on the standard scale, or both.

(6) Sections 104 to 106 (presumptions as to various matters connected with copyright) do not apply to proceedings for an offence under this section; but without prejudice to their application in proceedings for an order under section 108 below.

[This section is printed as amended by the *Copyright etc. and Trade Marks (Offences and Enforcement) Act* 2002, s.1.]

(b) *Procedure*

16–97   This offence is triable either way: *Copyright, Design and Patents Act* 1988, s.107(4).

Copyright, Designs and Patents Act 1988, s.110

Offence by body corporate: liability of officers

16–98   110.—(1) Where an offence under section 107 committed by a body corporate is proved to have been committed with the consent or connivance of a director, manager, secretary or other similar officer of the body, or a person purporting to act in any such capacity, he as well as the body corporate is guilty of the offence and liable to be proceeded against and punished accordingly.

(2) In relation to a body corporate whose affairs are managed by its members "director" means a member of the body corporate.

(c) *Sentence*

When tried summarily, the maximum sentence for this offence is imprisonment for a **16–99** period not exceeding six months, a fine not exceeding the statutory maximum or both: *Copyright, Design and Patents Act* 1988, s.107(4). As regards offences concerning publication rights, the maximum punishment on summary conviction is imprisonment for a term not exceeding three months, or a fine not exceeding level five on the standard scale or both: *Copyright and Related Rights Regulations* 1996, (SI 1996/2967).

In *R. v Carter* (1992) 13 Cr.App.R.(S.) 576, CA, a suspended sentence of nine- **16–100** months imprisonment imposed for making and hiring pirate video tapes was upheld by the Court of Appeal, Jowitt J. stating that 'counterfeiting of video films is a serious offence. In effect to make and distribute pirate copies of films is to steal from the true owner of the copyright, the property for which he has to expend money in order to possess it. It is an offence really of dishonesty.'

C. Unauthorised Use of Trade Mark

(a) *Definition*

Trade Marks Act 1994, s.92

Unauthorised use of trade mark, &c. in relation to goods

92.—(1) A person commits an offence who with a view to gain for himself or another, or with **16–101** intent to cause loss to another, and without the consent of the proprietor—

(a) applies to goods or their packaging a sign identical to, or likely to be mistaken for, a registered trade mark, or

(b) sells or lets for hire, offers or exposes for sale or hire or distributes goods which bear, or the packaging of which bears, such a sign, or

(c) has in his possession, custody or control in the course of a business any such goods with a view to the doing of anything, by himself or another, which would be an offence under paragraph (b).

(2) A person commits an offence who with a view to gain for himself or another, or with intent to cause loss to another, and without the consent of the proprietor—

(a) applies a sign identical to, or likely to be mistaken for, a registered trade mark to material intended to be used—

(i) for labelling or packaging goods,

(ii) as a business paper in relation to goods, or

(iii) for advertising goods, or

(b) uses in the course of a business material bearing such a sign for labelling or packaging goods, as a business paper in relation to goods, or for advertising goods, or

(c) has in his possession, custody or control in the course of a business any such material with a view to the doing of anything, by himself or another, which would be an offence under paragraph (b).

(3) A person commits an offence who with a view to gain for himself or another, or with intent to cause loss to another, and without the consent of the proprietor—

(a) makes an article specifically designed or adapted for making copies of a sign identical to, or likely to be mistaken for, a registered trade mark, or

(b) has such an article in his possession, custody or control in the course of a business,

knowing or having reason to believe that it has been, or is to be, used to produce goods, or material for labelling or packaging goods, as a business paper in relation to goods, or for advertising goods.

(4) A person does not commit an offence under this section unless—

(a) the goods are goods in respect of which the trade mark is registered, or

(b) the trade mark has a reputation in the United Kingdom and the use of the sign takes or would take unfair advantage of, or is or would be detrimental to, the distinctive character or the repute of the trade mark.

(5) It is a defence for a person charged with an offence under this section to show that he believed on reasonable grounds that the use of the sign in the manner in which it was used, or was to be used, was not an infringement of the registered trade mark.

(6) A person guilty of an offence under this section is liable—

(a) on summary conviction to imprisonment for a term not exceeding six months or a fine not exceeding the statutory maximum, or both;

(b) on conviction on indictment to a fine or imprisonment for a term not exceeding ten years, or both.

(b) *Procedure*

16–102   This offence is triable either way: *Trade Marks Act* 1994, s.92(6).

Offences by partnerships and bodies corporate

16–103   **101.**—(1) Proceedings for an offence under this Act alleged to have been committed by a partnership shall be brought against the partnership in the name of the firm and not in that of the partners; but without prejudice to any liability of the partners under subsection (4) below.

(2) The following provisions apply for the purposes of such proceedings as in relation to a body corporate—

(a) any rules of court relating to the service of documents,

(b) in England and Wales or Northern Ireland, Schedule 3 to the *Magistrates' Courts Act* 1980 or Schedule 4 to the *Magistrates' Courts (Northern Ireland) Order* 1981 (procedure on charge of offence).

(3) A fine imposed on a partnership on its conviction in such proceedings shall be paid out of the partnership assets.

(4) Where a partnership is guilty of an offence under this Act, every partner, other than a partner who is proved to have been ignorant of or to have attempted to prevent the commission of the offence, is also guilty of the offence and liable to be proceeded against and punished accordingly.

(5) Where an offence under this Act committed by a body corporate is proved to have been committed with the consent or connivance of a director, manager, secretary or other similar officer of the body, or a person purporting to act in any such capacity, he as well as the body corporate is guilty of the offence and liable to be proceeded against and punished accordingly.

(c) *Elements of the offence*

16–104   In *R. v Johnstone* [2003] 2 Cr.App.R 33, CA, the defendant was involved in activities relating to bootleg recordings on CDs of performances of well known bands all of whom had registered their names as trade marks. He claimed that the use of the names of the bands on the CD covers was not an indication of 'trade origin' under the terms of s.11 of the Act but simply described the performer whose music was on the CD. It was held by the House of Lords that the inclusion of the artists' names did not amount to an offence against s.92 as the names were not an indication of 'trade origin'. Whether it was such an indication was a question of fact in each case and the onus of proof was on the prosecution; the test was how the use of the sign would be perceived by the average consumer of the type of goods in question. The defendant was held to be not guilty of the offence.

(d) *Defences*

16–105   Section 92(5) of the 1994 Act provides that a person will have a defence to a charge under the section if he can prove he believed on reasonable grounds that the use of the sign in the manner in which it was used, or was to be used, was not an infringement of the registered trade mark.

In *Torbay Council v Singh* [1999] 2 Cr.App.R. 451, DC, the defendant sold children's clothes bearing the identical logo to that of the registered trade mark of the 'Teletubbies'. He was assured by his supplier that the goods were not counterfeit and did not infringe any trade mark. He pleaded not guilty on the basis of the defence afforded by s.92(5) and that he believed on reasonable grounds that his use of the sign in the manner in which it was used was not an infringement of the registered trade mark. As he was ignorant of the existence of the registered trade mark it was argued that there had been no infringement. The court on appeal held that the subsection did not speak of a reasonable belief in the absence of a registration. It spoke of a reasonable belief that the "manner" of use of the sign did not infringe "the registered trade mark" which presupposed an awareness by a defendant of the existence of the registration against which he could match his manner of use of the allegedly offending sign. The trader could not rely on his ignorance as a defence to a charge under s.92. This case was overruled by the *Johnstone* case (above) where the House of Lords said that it made no sense to confine the defence of s.92(5) to cases where the defendant is aware of the existence of the trade mark but to exclude those where he is not. It was held that the defence did apply when the defendant was unaware of the registration.

However, subs.92(5) does afford a defence for the trader who honestly and reason- **16–106** ably believes that his goods are genuine. In *R. v Rhodes* [2002] EWCA Crim 1390, it was held that s.92(5) of the *Trade Marks Act* 1994 provides a broad general defence albeit subject to the limitation that a person will be deemed to know about any registered trade mark so that he could not, relying on that subsection, assert a defence that he was ignorant of it. The defendant with an honest and reasonable belief in the authenticity of the goods will be able to rely on the defence in s.92(5).

(e) *Sentence*

When tried summarily, the maximum penalty for this offence is imprisonment for a **16–107** period not exceeding six months, a fine not exceeding the statutory maximum or both: *Trade Marks Act* 1994, s.92(6).

D. SELLING FOOD NOT OF THE NATURE, SUBSTANCE OR QUALITY DEMANDED

(a) *Definition*

Food Safety Act 1990, s.14

Selling food not of the nature or substance or quality demanded
  14.—(1) Any person who sells to the purchaser's prejudice any food which is not of the **16–108** nature or substance or quality demanded by the purchaser shall be guilty of an offence.
  (2) In subsection (1) above the reference to sale shall be construed as a reference to sale for human consumption; and in proceedings under that subsection it shall not be a defence that the purchaser was not prejudiced because he bought for analysis or examination.

(b) *Procedure*

This offence is triable either way: *Food Safety Act* 1990, s.35.   **16–109**

The person may be a limited company: *R. v ICR Haulage Ltd* [1944] K.B. 551.

Vicarious liability applies so that a servant who sells on behalf of his master may be convicted: *Goodfellow v Johnson* [1966] 1 Q.B. 83, and a master can be liable for the sale by his servant who has authority to sell: *United Dairies (London) Ltd v Beckenham Corporation* [1963] 1 Q.B. 434.

Food Safety Act 1990, s.36

Offences by bodies corporate
  36.—(1) Where an offence under this Act which has been committed by a body corporate is **16–110**

proved to have been committed with the consent or connivance of, or to be attributable to any neglect on the part of—

(a) any director, manager, secretary or other similar officer of the body corporate; or

(b) any person who was purporting to act in any such capacity,

he as well as the body corporate shall be deemed to be guilty of that offence and shall be liable to be proceeded against and punished accordingly.

(2) In subsection (1) above "director", in relation to any body corporate established by or under any enactment for the purpose of carrying on under national ownership any industry or part of an industry or undertaking, being a body corporate whose affairs are managed by its members, means a member of that body corporate.

(c) *Elements of the offence*

Food Safety Act 1990, s.1

Meaning of "food" and other basic expressions

16–111   **1.**—(1) In this Act "food" includes—

(a) drink;

(b) articles and substances of no nutritional value which are used for human consumption;

(c) chewing gum and other products of a like nature and use; and

(d) articles and substances used as ingredients in the preparation of food or anything falling within this subsection.

(2) In this Act "food" does not include—

(a) live animals or birds, or live fish which are not used for human consumption while they are alive;

(b) fodder or feeding stuffs for animals, birds or fish;

(c) controlled drugs within the meaning of the *Misuse of Drugs Act* 1971; or

(d) subject to such exceptions as may be specified in an order made by the Secretary of State—

(i) medicinal products within the meaning of the *Medicines Act* 1968 in respect of which product licences within the meaning of that Act are for the time being in force; or

(ii) other articles or substances in respect of which such licences are for the time being in force in pursuance of orders under section 104 or 105 of that Act (application of Act to other articles and substances).

(3) In this Act, unless the context otherwise requires—

"business" includes the undertaking of a canteen, club, school, hospital or institution, whether carried on for profit or not, and any undertaking or activity carried on by a public or local authority;

"commercial operation", in relation to any food or contact material, means any of the following, namely—

(a) selling, possessing for sale and offering, exposing or advertising for sale;

(b) consigning, delivering or serving by way of sale;

(c) preparing for sale or presenting, labelling or wrapping for the purpose of sale;

(d) storing or transporting for the purpose of sale;

(e) importing and exporting; and, in relation to any food source, means deriving food from it for the purpose of sale or for purposes connected with sale;

"contact material" means any article or substance which is intended to come into contact with food;

"food business" means any business in the course of which commercial operations with respect to food or food sources are carried out;

"food premises" means any premises used for the purposes of a food business;

"food source" means any growing crop or live animal, bird or fish from which food is intended to be derived (whether by harvesting, slaughtering, milking, collecting eggs or otherwise);

"premises" includes any place, any vehicle, stall or moveable structure and, for such purposes as may be specified in an order made by the Secretary of State, any ship or aircraft of a description so specified.

(4) The reference in subsection (3) above to preparing for sale shall be construed, in relation to any contact material, as a reference to manufacturing or producing for the purpose of sale.

[This section is printed as amended by Medicines for Human Use (Marketing Authorisations Etc.) Regulations 1994 (SI 1994/3144) and the *Food Standards Act* 1999, Sch.5, para.8.]

A sale will not be prejudicial to the purchaser where it is brought to his notice that **16–112** the article offered to him is not of the same nature or quality as the article he has asked for: *Sandys v Jackson* (1905) 69 J.P. 171. The fact that the goods are sold below the market price is not *prima facie* evidence of their quality deficiency: *Heywood v Whitehead* (1897) 76 L.T. 781.

In the absence of a prescribed minimum standard for the product in question, where there is sufficient evidence for the justices to decide what is a proper standard for that product and that the product in question was below it, the justices will be entitled to find that the retailers are guilty of selling an article which was not the article demanded: *Tonkin v Victor Value and Piper Products* [1962] 1 W.L.R. 339, DC.

(d) *Defences*

Food Safety Act 1990, s.21

Defence of due diligence

21.—(1) In any proceedings for an offence under any of the preceding provisions of this Part **16–113** (in this section referred to as "the relevant provision"), it shall, subject to subsection (5) below, be a defence for the person charged to prove that he took all reasonable precautions and exercised all due diligence to avoid the commission of the offence by himself or by a person under his control.

(2) Without prejudice to the generality of subsection (1) above, a person charged with an offence under section 8, 14 or 15 above who neither—

(a) prepared the food in respect of which the offence is alleged to have been committed; nor

(b) imported it into Great Britain,

shall be taken to have established the defence provided by thatsubsection if he satisfies the requirements of subsection (3) or (4) below.

(3) A person satisfies the requirements of this subsection if he proves—

(a) that the commission of the offence was due to an act or default of another person who was not under his control, or to reliance on information supplied by such a person;

(b) that he carried out all such checks of the food in question as were reasonable in all the circumstances, or that it was reasonable in all the circumstances for him to rely on checks carried out by the person who supplied the food to him; and

(c) that he did not know and had no reason to suspect at the time of the commission of the alleged offence that his act or omission would amount to an offence under the relevant provision.

(4) A person satisfies the requirements of this subsection if he proves—

(a) that the commission of the offence was due to an act or default of another person who was not under his control, or to reliance on information supplied by such a person;

(b) that the sale or intended sale of which the alleged offence consisted was not a sale or intended sale under his name or mark; and

(c) that he did not know, and could not reasonably have been expected to know, at the time of the commission of the alleged offence that his act or omission would amount to an offence under the relevant provision.

(5) If in any case the defence provided by subsection (1) above involves the allegation that the commission of the offence was due to an act or default of another person, or to reliance on information supplied by another person, the person charged shall not, without leave of the court, be entitled to rely on that defence unless—

(a) at least seven clear days before the hearing; and

(b) where he has previously appeared before a court in connection with the alleged offence, within one month of his first such appearance,

he has served on the prosecutor a notice in writing giving such information identifying or assisting in the identification of that other person as was then in his possession.

(6) In subsection (5) above any reference to appearing before a court shall be construed as including a reference to being brought before a court.

16–114   In *Carrick DC v Taunton Vale Meat Traders' Ltd* (1994) 158 J.P. 347, DC, it was held that an error of judgement by a meat inspector is a valid defence to the charge of supplying meat unfit for human consumption under the *Food Safety Act* 1990. No further precautions were deemed necessary to determine the fitness of the meat for human use. The defendant had had the meat examined by a meat inspector, and was therefore not liable for the inspector's error of judgement.

(e) *Sentence*

16–115   When tried summarily, the maximum penalty for this offence is six months' imprisonment or a fine not exceeding £20,000 or both: *Food Safety Act* 1990, s.35 (see § 16–127).

E. FALSELY DESCRIBING OR PRESENTING FOOD

(a) *Definition*

Food Safety Act 1990 s.15

Falsely describing or presenting food

16–116   **15.**—(1) Any person who gives with any food sold by him, or displays with any food offered or exposed by him for sale or in his possession for the purpose of sale, a label, whether or not attached to or printed on the wrapper or container, which—

(a) falsely describes the food; or

(b) is likely to mislead as to the nature or substance or quality of the food,

shall be guilty of an offence.

(2) Any person who publishes, or is a party to the publication of, an advertisement (not being such a label given or displayed by him as mentioned in subsection (1) above) which—

(a) falsely describes any food; or

(b) is likely to mislead as to the nature or substance or quality of any food,

shall be guilty of an offence.

(3) Any person who sells, or offers or exposes for sale, or has in his possession for the purpose of sale, any food the presentation of which is likely to mislead as to the nature or substance or quality of the food shall be guilty of an offence.

(4) In proceedings for an offence under subsection (1) or (2) above, the fact that a label or advertisement in respect of which the offence is alleged to have been committed contained an accurate statement of the composition of the food shall not preclude the court from finding that the offence was committed.

(5) In this section references to sale shall be construed as references to sale for human consumption.

(b) *Procedure*

16–117   The offences created under this section are triable either way: *Food Safety Act* 1990, s.35. The section creates distinct offences and the summons must be clear as to which of the offences is being alleged: *Ward v Barking and Dagenham LBC* [2000] E.H.L.R. 263, QBD.

(c) *Defences*

16–118   In addition to the defence available under s.21 of the 1990 Act, see § 16–113 above, the defendant may be able to rely on the defence relating to publication in the course of business established by s.22.

Food Safety Act 1990, s.22

Defence of publication in the course of business

22. In proceedings for an offence under any of the preceding provisions of this Part consist- **16–119** ing of the advertisement for sale of any food, it shall be a defence for the person charged to prove—

(a) that he is a person whose business it is to publish or arrange for the publication of advertisements; and

(b) that he received the advertisement in the ordinary course of business and did not know and had no reason to suspect that its publication would amount to an offence under that provision.

(d) *Sentence*

When tried summarily, the maximum penalty for this offence is six months' imprison- **16–120** ment or a fine not exceeding the statutory maximum or both: *Food Safety Act* 1990, s.35, see § 16–127.

F. FOOD SAFETY AND CONSUMER PROTECTION

(a) *Regulations*

Food Safety Act 1990, s.16

Food safety and consumer protection

16.—(1) The Secretary of State may by regulations make— **16–121**

(a) provision for requiring, prohibiting or regulating the presence in food or food sources of any specified substance, or any substance of any specified class, and generally for regulating the composition of food;

(b) provision for securing that food is fit for human consumption and meets such microbiological standards (whether going to the fitness of the food or otherwise) as may be specified by or under the regulations;

(c) provision for requiring, prohibiting or regulating the use of any process or treatment in the preparation of food;

(d) provision for securing the observance of hygienic conditions and practices in connection with the carrying out of commercial operations with respect to food or food sources;

(e) provision for imposing requirements or prohibitions as to, or otherwise regulating, the labelling, marking, presenting or advertising of food, and the descriptions which may be applied to food; and

(f) such other provision with respect to food or food sources, including in particular provision for prohibiting or regulating the carrying out of commercial operations with respect to food or food sources, as appears to them to be necessary or expedient—

(i) for the purpose of securing that food complies with food safety requirements or in the interests of the public health; or

(ii) for the purpose of protecting or promoting the interests of consumers.

(2) The Secretary of State may also by regulations make provision—

(a) for securing the observance of hygienic conditions and practices in connection with the carrying out of commercial operations with respect to contact materials which are intended to come into contact with food intended for human consumption;

(b) for imposing requirements or prohibitions as to, or otherwise regulating, the labelling, marking or advertising of such materials, and the descriptions which may be applied to them; and

(c) otherwise for prohibiting or regulating the carrying out of commercial operations with respect to such materials.

(3) Without prejudice to the generality of subsection (1) above, regulations under that subsection may make any such provision as is mentioned in Schedule 1 to this Act.

(4) In making regulations under subsection (1) above, the Secretary of State shall have regard to the desirability of restricting, so far as practicable, the use of substances of no nutritional value as foods or as ingredients of foods.

(5) In subsection (1) above and Schedule 1 to this Act, unless the context otherwise requires—

    (a) references to food shall be construed as references to food intended for sale for human consumption; and

    (b) references to food sources shall be construed as references to food sources from which such food is intended to be derived.

(b) *Elements*

16–122   A multitude of regulations have been made applying to various specific foodstuffs.

The *Food Safety (General Food Hygiene) Regulations* 1995 (SI 1995/1763) as amended apply to proprietors of food businesses. The regulations impose a duty on proprietors to ensure that the preparation, processing, manufacturing, packaging storing, transportation, distribution, handling and offering for sale or supply of food are carried out hygienically: reg.4. Schedule 1 to the regulations sets out the rules of hygiene that must be complied with. Offences against s.16 should state separately each specific requirement that it is alleged has been breached.

(c) *Sentence*

16–123   When tried summarily, the maximum penalty for failure to comply with regulations made under this section is six months' imprisonment or a fine not exceeding the statutory maximum or both: *Food Safety Act* 1990, s.35, see § 16–127.

Food Safety Act 1990, ss.20, 34

Offences due to fault of another person

16–124   **20.** Where the commission by any person of an offence under any of the preceding provisions of this Part is due to an act or default of some other person, that other person shall be guilty of the offence; and a person may be charged with and convicted of the offence by virtue of this section whether or not proceedings are taken against the first-mentioned person.

Time limit for prosecutions

16–125   **34.** No prosecution for an offence under this Act which is punishable under section 35(2) below shall be begun after the expiry of—

    (a) three years from the commission of the offence; or

    (b) one year from its discovery by the prosecutor,

whichever is the earlier.

16–126   In the case of a continuing offence discovery may occur on any day that the offence continues to be committed: *R. v Thames Metropolitan Stipendiary Magistrate Ex p. London Borough of Hackney* (1994) 158 J.P. 305.

Food Safety Act 1990, s.35

Punishment of offences

16–127   **35.**—(1) A person guilty of an offence under section 33(1) above shall be liable on summary conviction to a fine not exceeding level 5 on the standard scale or to imprisonment for a term not exceeding three months or to both.

(2) A person guilty of any other offence under this Act shall be liable—

    (a) on conviction on indictment, to a fine or to imprisonment for a term not exceeding two years or to both;

    (b) on summary conviction, to a fine not exceeding the relevant amount or to imprisonment for a term not exceeding six months or to both.

(3) In subsection (2) above "the relevant amount" means —
    (a) in the case of an offence under section 7, 8 or 14 above, £ 20,000;
    (b) in any other case, the statutory maximum.
(4) If a person who is—
    (a) licensed under section 1 of the *Slaughterhouses Act* 1974 to keep a knacker's yard;
    (b) registered under section 4 of the *Slaughter of Animals (Scotland) Act* 1980 in respect of any premises for use as a slaughterhouse; or
    (c) licensed under section 6 of the *Slaughter of Animals (Scotland) Act* 1980 to use any premises as a knacker's yard,
is convicted of an offence under Part II of this Act, the court may, in addition to any other punishment, cancel his licence or registration.

Section 33(1) referred to in this section is the offence of obstructing officers acting under their powers in the Act. Section 7 is the offence of rendering food injurious to health and s.8 is the offence of selling food not in compliance with food safety requirements.

V. HIGHWAYS

A. OFFENCES UNDER THE HIGHWAYS ACT 1980

Interpretation

Highways Act 1980, s.328

Meaning of "highway"
328.—(1) In this Act, except where the context otherwise requires, "highway" means the **16–128** whole or a part of a highway other than a ferry or waterway.
(2) Where a highway passes over a bridge or through a tunnel, that bridge or tunnel is to be taken for the purposes of this Act to be a part of the highway.
(3) In this Act, "highway maintainable at the public expense" and any other expression defined by reference to a highway is to be construed in accordance with the foregoing provisions of this section.

Section 329 includes further lengthy provisions on interpretation.

Highways Act 1980, s.312

Restriction on institution of proceedings
312.—(1) Subject to subsection (3) below, proceedings for an offence under any provision of **16–129** this Act to which this section applies or under byelaws made under any such provision shall not, without the written consent of the Attorney General, be taken by any person other than the person aggrieved, or a highway authority or council having an interest in the enforcement of the provision or byelaws in question.
(2) This section applies to sections 167 and 177 above and to the provisions of this Act specified in Schedule 22 to this Act.
(3) A constable may take proceedings—
    (a) for an offence under paragraph (b) of section 171(6) above; or
    (b) for an offence under paragraph (c) of that subsection consisting of failure to perform a duty imposed by section 171(5)(a) above; or
    (c) for an offence under section 174 above,
without the consent of the Attorney General.

The offences referred to in this section are as follows: s.171(6) is one of failing without reasonable excuse to comply with directions relating to placing traffic signs in connection with a deposit or excavation; s.171(5) imposes a duty of signposting, fencing and lighting of obstructions and excavations on the highway; s.174 details the precautions to be taken by persons executing works in the street. The police may prosecute these offences.

Highways Act 1980, Sch.22

SCHEDULE 22

PROVISIONS OF THIS ACT TO WHICH SECTIONS 288, 294, 312, 338, 339 AND 341 OF THIS ACT APPLY

Provisions contained in Part IV

16–130   1. Section 36(6) and (7) and section 38.

Provisions contained in Part V

2. Section 66(2) to (8), sections 73 and 77 and section 96(4) and (5).

Provisions contained in Part IX

3. Sections 133, and 151 to 153, section 154(1), and 154(4) so far as relating to a notice under 154(1), sections 163 and 165, sections 171 to 174, 176, 178 and 179, section 180 other than subsection (2) and subsection (4) so far as relating to subsection (2), and section 185.

Provisions contained in Part X

4. Sections 186 to 188, 190 to 107, 200 and 201.

Provisions contained in Part XI

5. The private street works code, sections 226 and 228, section 230(1) to (6), and sections 231, 233, 236 and 237.

Provisions contained in Part XII

6. Section 239(6) and section 241.

Provisions contained in Part XIV

7. Sections 286, 295, 297, 303, 304, and 305.

Highways Act 1980, s.314

Offences by body corporate

16–131   **314.**—(1) Where an offence under any provision of this Act to which this section applies is committed by a body corporate and it is proved to have been committed with the consent or connivance of, or to be attributable to any neglect on the part of, any director, manager, secretary or other similar officer of the body corporate or any person who was purporting to act in any such capacity, he as well as the body corporate is guilty of that offence and liable to be proceeded against and punished accordingly.

(2) Where the affairs of a body corporate are managed by its members, subsection (1) above applies in relation to the acts and defaults of a member in connection with his functions of management as if he were a director of the body corporate.

(3) This section applies to sections 139, 140, 167, 168, 177 and 181 above.

[This section is printed as amended by the *New Roads and Street Works Act* 1991, Sch.8.]

16–131.1   The offences referred to in this section are: s.139 relates to the control of builders' skips; s.140 covers the removal of builders' skips; s.167 provides for powers relating to retaining walls near streets; s.168 relates to building operations affecting public safety; and s.177 imposes a restriction on the construction of buildings over highways.

Highways Act 1980, s.319

Judges and justices not to be disqualified by liability to rates

16–132   **319.** The judge of any court or a justice of the peace is not disqualified for acting in cases arising under this Act by reason only of his being as one of several ratepayers, or as one of any other class of persons, liable in common with the others to contribute to, or to be benefited by, any rate or fund out of which any expenses of a council are to be defrayed.

B. Damage to Highway

(a) *Definition*

Highways Act 1980, s.131

Penalty for damaging highway etc.

131.—(1) If a person, without lawful authority or excuse—   **16–133**

    (a) makes a ditch or excavation in a highway which consists of or comprises a carriageway, or

    (b) removes any soil or turf from any part of a highway, except for the purpose of improving the highway and with the consent of the highway authority for the highway, or

    (c) deposits anything whatsoever on a highway so as to damage the highway, or

    (d) lights any fire, or discharges any firearm or firework, within 50 feet from the centre of a highway which consists of or comprises a carriageway, and in consequence thereof the highway is damaged,

he is guilty of an offence.

(2) If a person without lawful authority or excuse pulls down or obliterates a traffic sign placed on or over a highway, or a milestone or direction post (not being a traffic sign) so placed, he is guilty of an offence; but it is a defence in any proceedings under this subsection to show that the traffic sign, milestone or post was not lawfully so placed.

(3) A person guilty of an offence under this section is liable to a fine not exceeding level three on the standard scale.

[This section is printed as amended by the *Criminal Justice Act* 1982, ss.35, 38 and 46.]

(b) *Procedure*

This offence is triable summarily: *Highways Act* 1980, s.310.   **16–134**

(c) *Sentence*

The maximum penalty for the offences under this section is a fine not exceeding level **16–135** three on the standard scale.

C. Wilful Obstruction

(a) *Definition*

Highways Act 1980, s.137

Penalty for wilful obstruction

137.—(1) If a person, without lawful authority or excuse, in any way wilfully obstructs the **16–136** free passage along a highway he is guilty of an offence and liable to a fine not exceeding level 3 on the standard scale.

(2) [...]

[This section is printed as amended by the *Criminal Justice Act* 1982, ss.38 and 46 and partially repealed by the *Police and Criminal Evidence Act* 1984, Sch.7.]

(b) *Procedure*

This offence is triable summarily: *Highways Act* 1980, s.310.   **16–137**

(c) *Elements of the offence*

Lawful authority is given by permits and licences granted to market and street trad- **16–138** ers and those collecting for charitable causes. A lawful excuse may be found if the activities engaged in are lawful in themselves and they may or may not be reasonable.

The test of whether a particular use of a highway by a vehicle, such as a van selling hot-dogs, constitutes an obstruction is whether the use is unreasonable having regard to all the circumstances including its duration, position and purpose and whether it causes an actual, rather than a potential obstruction: *Nagy v Weston* [1965] 1 All E.R. 78. It is sufficient to constitute the offence that the accused, without lawful authority or excuse, by exercise of his free will does something or omits to do something, which causes an obstruction or the continuance of an obstruction: *Arrowsmith v Jenkins* [1963] 2 Q.B. 561. In *Waltham Forest LBC v Mills* [1980] R.T.R. 201, QBD, the defendant conducted a business of serving tea and snacks to the public from a mobile snack bar which he stationed on a part of the highway which had been designated as a layby. People who stopped to buy snacks parked their motorcycles and cars in the layby and, on some occasions when the layby entrance was blocked by motorcycles, on the side of the carriageway itself. It was held that this constituted an unreasonable obstruction of the highway and that selling refreshments on the highway was of itself an unreasonable user. In *Hertfordshire County Council v Bolden* (1987) 151 J.P. 252, the defendant owned premises adjoining a public highway. He sometimes used part of the highway verge bordering his premises for the display and sale of garden produce. It was held that such activities could form unreasonable obstructions for the purpose of the offence under s.137, that such obstructions could not be said to be *de minimis* and hence outside the scope of s.137 and that the fact that they did not cause inconvenience to anyone did not mean that they were insufficient to constitute offences.

16–139   As regards peaceful picketing under s.134 of the *Industrial Relations Act* 1971 (now the *Trade Union and Labour Relations Act (Consolidation) Act* 1992, s.220), in *Broome v DPP* [1974] 1 All E.R. 314, it was held that s.134 made lawful the attendance of pickets only for the purposes specified therein and did not require the person whom it was sought to persuade to submit to any constraint or restriction of his right to personal freedom. Hence whilst driver can be invited to stop and listen to the protest, they cannot be compelled to stop by a blockade on the highway. Where the highway is obstructed by a peaceful protest the question of whether the use of the highway is reasonable or not must be considered: *Hirst v Chief Constable of West Yorkshire* (1987) 85 Cr.App.R. 143.

The onus is on the prosecution to prove that the defendant was obstructing the highway without lawful authority or excuse. A defendant does not acquire a license to perform an unlawful act through the fact that the police or other prosecuting authority have refrained from prosecuting in respect of the alleged obstruction for a number of years: *Redbridge London Borough v Jacques* (1971) 1 All E.R. 260.

16–140   In *Westminster City Council v Haw* (2002) EWHC 2073, it was held that the Art.10 right to freedom of expression contained in the ECHR is not a trump card to authorise any protest, but rather is a significant consideration to take into account when considering the reasonableness of the obstruction of the highway. In this case the court held that there was a wilful obstruction as protest placards encroached onto the pavement but the defendant's activities were neither unlawful nor unreasonable.

(d) *Sentence*

16–141   The maximum penalty for this offence is a fine not exceeding level three on the standard scale.

D. BUILDERS' SKIPS

(a) *Definition*

Highways Act 1980, s.139

Control of builders' skips

16–142   **139.**—(1) A builders' skip shall not be deposited on a highway without the permission of the highway authority for the highway.

(2) A permission under this section shall be a permission for a person to whom it is granted to deposit, or cause to be deposited, a skip on the highway specified in the permission, and a highway authority may grant such permission either unconditionally or subject to such conditions as may be specified in the permission including, in particular, conditions relating to—

(a) the siting of the skip;

(b) its dimensions;

(c) the manner in which it is to be coated with paint and other material for the purpose of making it immediately visible to oncoming traffic;

(d) the care and disposal of its contents;

(e) the manner in which it is to be lighted or guarded;

(f) its removal at the end of the period of permission.

(3) If a builder's skip is deposited on a highway without a permission granted under this section, the owner of the skip is, subject to subsection (6) below, guilty of an offence and liable to a fine not exceeding level 3 on the standard scale.

(4) Where a builder's skip has been deposited on a highway in accordance with a **16–143** permission granted under this section, the owner of the skip shall secure—

(a) that the skip is properly lighted during the hours of darkness and, where regulations made by the Secretary of State under this section require it to be marked in accordance with the regulations (whether with reflecting or fluorescent material or otherwise), that it is so marked;

(b) that the skip is clearly and indelibly marked with the owner's name and with his telephone number or address;

(c) that the skip is removed as soon as practicable after it has been filled;

(d) that each of the conditions subject to which that permission was granted is complied with;

and, if he fails to do so, he is, subject to subsection (6) below, guilty of an offence and liable to a fine not exceeding level 3 on the standard scale .

(5) Where the commission by any person of an offence under this section is due to the act or default of some other person, that other person is guilty of the offence, and a person may be charged with and convicted of the offence by virtue of this subsection whether or not proceedings are taken against the first-mentioned person.

(6) In any proceedings for an offence under this section it is a defence, subject to subsection (7) below, for the person charged to prove that the commission of the offence was due to the act or default of another person and that he took all reasonable precautions and exercised all due diligence to avoid the commission of such an offence by himself or any person under his control.

(7) A person charged with an offence under this section is not, without leave of the **16–144** court, entitled to rely on the defence provided by subsection (6) above unless, within a period ending 7 clear days before the hearing, he has served on the prosecutor a notice in writing giving such information identifying or assisting in the identification of that other person as was then in his possession.

(8) Where any person is charged with an offence under any other enactment for failing to secure that a builder's skip which has been deposited on a highway in accordance with a permission granted under this section was properly lighted during the hours of darkness, it is a defence for the person charged to prove that the commission of the offence was due to the act or default of another person and that he took all reasonable precautions and exercised all due diligence to avoid the commission of such an offence by himself or any person under his control.

(9) Where a person is charged with obstructing, or interrupting any user of, a highway by depositing a builder's skip on it, it is a defence for the person charged to prove that the skip was deposited on it in accordance with a permission granted under this section and either—

(a) that each of the requirements of subsection (4) above had been complied with; or

(b) that the commission of any offence under that subsection was due to the act or default of another person and that he took all reasonable precautions and exercised all due diligence to avoid the commission of such an offence by himself or any person under his control.

(10) Nothing in this section is to be taken as authorising the creation of a nuisance or of a danger to users of a highway or as imposing on a highway authority by whom a permission has been granted under this section any liability for any injury, damage or loss resulting from the presence on a highway of the skip to which the permission relates.

(11) In this section section 140 and section 140A below—

"builder's skip" means a container designed to be carried on a road vehicle and to be placed on a highway or other land for the storage of builders' materials, or for the removal and disposal of builders' rubble, waste, household and other rubbish or earth; and

"owner", in relation to a builder's skip which is the subject of a hiring agreement, being an agreement for a hiring of not less than one month, or a hire purchase agreement, means the person in possession of the skip under that agreement.

[Printed as amended by the *Criminal Justice Act* 1982, ss.38 and 46, the *Transport Act* 1982, s.65 and the *New Roads and Street Works Act* 1991, Sch.8.]

(b) *Procedure*

16–145   This offence is triable summarily: *Highways Act* 1980, s.310.

(c) *Elements of the offence*

16–146   Depositing means more than just placing, putting down or delivering the skip. The offence applies to incidents of leaving or allowing the skip to remain: *Craddock v Green* [1983] R.T.R. 479.

Permission granted by the local authority must be in writing and specific to the location: *York City Council v Poller* [1976] R.T.R. 479 and *Highways Act* 1980, s.320.

For the purposes of subs.4(a) the relevant regulations are the *Builders' Skips (Markings) Regulations* 1984 (SI 1984/1933).

It is a defence under subs.6 to prove that the commission of the offence was due to the act or default of a person other than the person charged and that due diligence was exercised to avoid the commission of the offence. The other person does not have to be identified: *PGM Building Co Ltd v Kensington and Chelsea (Royal) LBC* [1982] R.T.R. 107. See also *York City Council v Poller* [1976] R.T.R. 37. Note the requirements contained in subs.(7) concerning the requirement that a defendant seeking to rely on the defence established by subs.(6) must serve on the prosecutor a notice in writing giving information identifying or assisting in the identification of that other person as was then in his possession within a period ending seven clear days before the hearing,

(d) *Sentence*

16–147   The maximum penalty for the offences under this section is fine not exceeding level 3 on the standard scale.

E. REMOVAL OF BUILDERS' SKIPS

(a) *Definition*

Highways Act 1980, s.140

Removal of builders' skips

16–148   140.—(1) The following provisions of this section have effect in relation to a builder's skip deposited on a highway notwithstanding that it was deposited on it in accordance with a permission granted under section 139 above.

(2) The highway authority for the highway or a constable in uniform may require the owner of the skip to remove or reposition it or cause it to be removed or repositioned.

(3) A person required to remove or reposition, or cause to be removed or repositioned, a skip under a requirement made by virtue of subsection (2) above shall comply with the

requirement as soon as practicable, and if he fails to do so he is guilty of an offence and liable to a fine not exceeding level 3 on the standard scale.

(4) The highway authority for the highway or a constable in uniform may themselves remove or reposition the skip or cause it to be removed or repositioned.

(5) Where a skip is removed under subsection (4) above, the highway authority or, as the case may be, the chief officer of police shall, where practicable, notify the owner of its removal, but if the owner cannot be traced, or if after a reasonable period of time after being so notified he has not recovered the skip, the highway authority or chief officer of police may dispose of the skip and its contents.

(6) Any expenses reasonably incurred by a highway authority or chief officer of police in the removal or repositioning of a skip under subsection (4) above or the disposal of a skip under subsection (5) above may be recovered from the owner of the skip in any court of competent jurisdiction or summarily as a civil debt.

(7) Any proceeds of the disposal of a skip under subsection (5) above shall be used in the first place to meet the expenses reasonably incurred in the removal and disposal of the skip and thereafter any surplus shall be given to the person entitled to it if he can be traced and if not may be retained by the highway authority or the chief officer of police, as the case may be; and any surplus so retained by a chief officer of police shall be paid into the police fund.

(8) References in this section to expenses incurred in the removal of a skip include references to expenses incurred in storing the skip until it is recovered by the owner or, as the case may be, disposed of.

(9) The owner of a skip is not guilty of an offence under section 139(4) above of failing to secure that a condition relating to the siting of the skip was complied with if the failure resulted from the repositioning of the skip under subsection (3) or (4) above.

[This section is printed as amended by the *Criminal Justice Act* 1982, ss.38 and 46.]

(b) *Procedure*

This offence is triable summarily: *Highways Act* 1980, s.310.   **16–148.**

(c) *Elements of the offence*

A requirement that a skip be removed must be communicated to a potential offender **16–149** by a constable in uniform going to that person and telling him of the requirement: *R. v Worthing Justices Ex p. Waste Management Ltd* (1988) 152 J.P. 362.

(d) *Sentence*

The maximum penalty for the offence under this section is a fine not exceeding level **16–150** three on the standard scale.

VI. IMMIGRATION

A. Illegal Entry and Similar Offences

(a) *Definition*

Immigration Act 1971, s.24

Illegal entry and similar offences
    24.—(1) A person who is not a British citizen shall be guilty of an offence punishable on sum- **16–151** mary conviction with a fine of not more than level 5 on the standard scale or with imprisonment for not more than six months, or with both, in any of the following cases—
    (a) if contrary to this Act he knowingly enters the United Kingdom in breach of a deportation order or without leave;
    (b) if, having only a limited leave to enter or remain in the United Kingdom, he knowingly either—
        (i) remains beyond the time limited by the leave; or

    (ii) fails to observe a condition of the leave;

  (c) if, having lawfully entered the United Kingdom without leave by virtue of section 8(1) above, he remains without leave beyond the time allowed by section 8(1);

  (d) if, without reasonable excuse, he fails to comply with any requirement imposed on him under Schedule 2 to this Act to report to a medical officer of health or to attend, or submit to a test or examination, as required by such an officer;

  (e) if, without reasonable excuse, he fails to observe any restriction imposed on him under Schedule 2 or 3 to this Act as to residence, as to his employment or occupation or as to reporting to the police, to an immigration officer or to the Secretary of State;

  (f) if he leaves a train in the United Kingdom after being placed on board under Schedule 2 or 3 to this Act with a view to his removal from the United Kingdom;

  (g) if he leaves or seeks to leave the United Kingdom through the tunnel system in contravention of a restriction imposed by or under an Order in Council under section 3(7) of this Act.

(1A) A person commits an offence under subsection (1)(b)(i) above on the day when he first knows that the time limited by his leave has expired and continues to commit it throughout any period during which he is in the United Kingdom thereafter; but a person shall not be prosecuted under that provision more than once in respect of the same limited leave.

(3) The extended time limit for prosecutions which is provided for by section 28 below shall apply to offences under subsection (1)(a) and (c) above.

(4) In proceedings for an offence against subsection (1)(a) above of entering the United Kingdom without leave,—

  (a) any stamp purporting to have been imprinted on a passport or other travel document by an immigration officer on a particular date for the purpose of giving leave shall be presumed to have been duly so imprinted, unless the contrary is proved;

  (b) proof that a person had leave to enter the United Kingdom shall lie on the defence if, but only if, he is shown to have entered within six months before the date when the proceedings were commenced.

[This section is printed as amended by the *British Nationality Act* 1981, Sch.4; the *Criminal Justice Act* 1982, ss.38 and 46; the *Immigration Act* 1988, s.6 and Sch.1; the *Asylum and Immigration Act* 1996, ss.4 and 6; and the *Immigration and Asylum Act* 1999, Schs 14 and 16.]

(b) *Procedure*

16–152   This offence is triable summarily: *Immigration Act* 1971, s.24.

(c) *Elements of the offence*

16–153   Section 8 allows for seamen and aircraft crew who arrive in the UK to enter without leave and remain in the country until their vessel leaves again.

The power to give or refuse leave to enter or remain in the UK is only exercisable in writing: s.4(1). To prosecute under s.24 there must be evidence of a written notice. A defective stamp in a passport which omitted to note that leave was limited did not amount to sufficient notice although verbal information had been given: *Lamptey v Owen* [1982] Crim.L.R. 42.

These are continuing offences which may be prosecuted at any time whilst the limited leave or conditions on leave apply: *Manickavasagar v Metropolitan Police Commissioner* [1987] Crim.L.R. 50.

Immigration Act 1971, s.28

Proceedings

16–154   **28.**—(1) Where the offence is one to which, under section 24 or 26 above, an extended time limit for prosecutions is to apply, then—

  (a) an information relating to the offence may in England and Wales be tried by a magistrates' court if it is laid within six months after the commission of the offence, or if it is laid within three years after the commission of the offence and not more than two months after the date certified by an officer of police above the rank of chief superintendent to be the date on which evidence sufficient to justify proceedings came to the notice of an officer of the police force to which he belongs; and

(b) summary proceedings for the offence may in Scotland be commenced within six months after the commission of the offence, or within three years after the commission of the offence and not more than two months after the date on which evidence sufficient in the opinion of the Lord Advocate to justify proceedings came to his knowledge; and

(c) a complaint charging the commission of the offence may in Northern Ireland be heard and determined by a magistrates' court if it is made within six months after the commission of the offence, or if it is made within three years after the commission of the offence and not more than two months after the date certified by an officer of police not below the rank of assistant chief constable to be the date on which evidence sufficient to justify the proceedings came to the notice of the police in Northern Ireland.

(2) For purposes of subsection (1)(b) above proceedings shall be deemed to be commenced on the date on which a warrant to apprehend or to cite the accused is granted, if such warrant is executed without undue delay; and a certificate of the Lord Advocate as to the date on which such evidence as is mentioned in subsection (1)(b) came to his knowledge shall be conclusive evidence.

(3) For the purposes of the trial of a person for an offence under this Part of this Act, the offence shall be deemed to have been committed either at the place at which it actually was committed or at any place at which he may be.

(4) Any powers exercisable under this Act in the case of any person may be exercised notwithstanding that proceedings for an offence under this Part of this Act have been taken against him.

[This section is printed as amended by the *Immigration Act* 1988, Sch.1 and the *Immigration and Asylum Act* 1999, Sch.14.]

The certificate of awareness of sufficient evidence may be signed after a not guilty **16–155**
plea is entered but before the trial begins. The court does not start to try the case until evidence is called: *Quazi v DPP* (1988) 152 J.P. 385.

(d) *Sentence*

The maximum penalty for this offence is a fine of not more than level 5 on the stan- **16–156**
dard scale, imprisonment for a period of not more than six months or both: *Immigration Act* 1971, s.24(1).

A recommendation for deportation can be made by a court on convicting a person who is over 18 and not a British citizen of an imprisonable offence—see Sentencing, Part IV in this work.

B. Deception

(a) *Definition*

Immigration Act 1971, s.24A

Deception
24A.—(1) A person who is not a British citizen is guilty of an offence if, by means which **16–157**
include deception by him—

(a) he obtains or seeks to obtain leave to enter or remain in the United Kingdom; or

(b) he secures or seeks to secure the avoidance, postponement or revocation of enforcement action against him.

(2) "Enforcement action", in relation to a person, means—

(a) the giving of directions for his removal from the United Kingdom ("directions") under Schedule 2 to this Act or section 10 of the *Immigration and Asylum Act* 1999;

   (b) the making of a deportation order against him under section 5 of this Act; or
   (c) his removal from the United Kingdom in consequence of directions or a deportation order.

(3) A person guilty of an offence under this section is liable—

   (a) on summary conviction, to imprisonment for a term not exceeding six months or to a fine not exceeding the statutory maximum, or to both; or
   (b) on conviction on indictment, to imprisonment for a term not exceeding two years or to a fine, or to both.

[This section was inserted by the *Asylum and Immigration Act* 1996, s.28.]

(b) *Procedure*

16–158   This offence is triable either way: s.24A(3). The extended time limit for prosecutions provided under s.28 applies to this section: s.24A(4).

(c) *Sentence*

16–159   The maximum penalty for an offence under this section is imprisonment for a term not exceeding six months, a fine not exceeding the statutory maximum or both: s.24(3). A recommendation for deportation can be made by a court on convicting a person over 18 who is not a British citizen of an imprisonable offence—see Sentencing, Part IV in this work.

C. ASSISTING ILLEGAL ENTRY AND HARBOURING

(a) *Definition*

Immigration Act 1971, s.25

Assisting unlawful immigration to member State

16–160   25.—(1) A person commits an offence if he—

   (a) does an act which facilitates the commission of a breach of immigration law by an individual who is not a citizen of the European Union,
   (b) knows or has reasonable cause for believing that the act facilitates the commission of a breach of immigration law by the individual, and
   (c) knows or has reasonable cause for believing that the individual is not a citizen of the European Union.

(2) In subsection (1) "immigration law" means a law which has effect in a member State and which controls, in respect of some or all persons who are not nationals of the State, entitlement to—

   (a) enter the State,
   (b) transit across the State, or
   (c) be in the State.

(3) A document issued by the government of a member State certifying a matter of law in that State—

   (a) shall be admissible in proceedings for an offence under this section, and
   (b) shall be conclusive as to the matter certified.

(4) Subsection (1) applies to anything done—

   (a) in the United Kingdom,
   (b) outside the United Kingdom by an individual to whom subsection (5) applies, or
   (c) outside the United Kingdom by a body incorporated under the law of a part of the United Kingdom.

(5) This subsection applies to—

   (a) a British citizen,
   (b) a British overseas territories citizen,
   (c) a British National (Overseas),

(d) a British Overseas citizen,

(e) a person who is a British subject under the *British Nationality Act* 1981, and

(f) a British protected person within the meaning of that Act.

(6) A person guilty of an offence under this section shall be liable—

(a) on conviction on indictment, to imprisonment for a term not exceeding 14 years, to a fine or to both, or

(b) on summary conviction, to imprisonment for a term not exceeding six months, to a fine not exceeding the statutory maximum or to both.

[This section is printed as amended by the *Criminal Law Act* 1977, s.28, the *MCA* **16–161** 1980, s.32(2), the *British Nationality Act* 1981, Sch.4, the *Criminal Justice Act* 1982, ss.38 and 46, the *Asylum and Immigration Act* 1996, s.5 and the *Immigration and Asylum Act* 1999, s.29 and Schs 14 and 16 and the *British Overseas Territories Act* 2002, s.2(3).]

(b) *Procedure*

This offence is triable either way: s.25(1). The extended time limit for prosecutions **16–162** provided under s.28 applies to this section: s.25(4).

(c) *Elements of the offence*

The offence under s.25(1) can relate to the implementation of arrangements for **16–163** facilitating entry which, on usual principles, would be completed by the carrying out of such arrangements, irrespective of whether or not entry has taken place. The charge can properly relate to a would-be or intending illegal entrant, as opposed to someone who had already become an illegal entrant by reason of passing through or attempting to pass through immigration control by concealment or deception: *R v Eyck* [2000] All E.R. 569, CA. In *Eyck* (above) the Court held that it was a matter for the jury to decide whether it had been proved that passengers carried in a car driven by the defendant onto a UK bound ferry intended to enter or seek to enter illegally and whether the defendant was knowingly concerned in carrying out arrangements for facilitating such illegal entry. If they so decided, a conviction under s.25 would be appropriate. The Court also held that an offence under s.25(1)(b) may relate to an intending asylum claimant.

It is a crime to assist illegal immigrants to leave their disembarkation port, even if **16–164** they have already technically entered the United Kingdom. In *R. v Amat Jit Singh* (1973) 1 All E.R. 122, CA, Lawton L.J. stated that s.25 defines the offences which can be committed by those who help illegal entrants. He continued:

'The help may come in two ways: the illegal entrant may be given help to get into the United Kingdom or he may be helped after he has arrived here. Section 25 (1) was intended to deal with the first kind of help; section 25 (2) with the second: but they are not mutually exclusive. The help to get in may be, and often is, continued without any break long after the illegal entry has been effected. There may be no dividing line between helping to effect entry and helping by way of harbouring...Now those who are minded to enter the United Kingdom illegally have no wish to be discovered as soon as they disembark. Effective arrangements for an illegal entry would be likely to include plans for getting the entrant away as quickly as possible from the point of disembarkation. Those who made or carried out such plans would be facilitating entry into the United Kingdom.'

Section 25(2) creates two separate offences of harbouring: the first involves knowl- **16–165** edge that a person is an "illegal entrant" as defined in s.33 and the second, knowledge that the person was an "overstayer" as defined in s.24. The prosecution must state in the information the illegal status relied upon for alleging that the accused knew or believed that status to exist. If the prosecution intends to establish one or other of the offences it must lay separate informations, otherwise it will lay itself open to arguments of duplicity: *Rahman and Qadir v DPP* [1993] Crim.L.R. 874.

VII. POLICE

A. POWER TO MAKE ORDERS IN RESPECT OF PROPERTY IN POSSESSION OF POLICE

Police (Property) Act 1897, s.1

Power to make orders with respect to property in possession of police

16–166   **1.**—(1) Where any property has come into the possession of the police in connexion with their investigation of a suspected offence, a court of summary jurisdiction may, on application, either by an officer of police or by a claimant of the property, make an order for the delivery of the property to the person appearing to the magistrate or court to be the owner thereof, or, if the owner cannot be ascertained, make such order with respect to the property as to the magistrate or court may seem meet.

(2) An order under this section shall not affect the right of any person to take within six months from the date of the order legal proceedings against any person in possession of property delivered by virtue of the order for the recovery of the property, but on the expiration of those six months the right shall cease.

[This section is printed as amended by the *Theft Act* 1968, the *Criminal Justice Act* 1972, s.58 and the *Consumer Credit Act* 1974, Sch.5 and the *Statute Law (Repeals) Act* 1989, Sch.1.]

16–167   The police come into possession of property when investigating offences but if the charge is dropped or the accused acquitted and there is a dispute over ownership it may be necessary for an order to be applied for to allow the police to release the property. If no relevant order is made at the end of the proceedings, the police or a claimant may apply to the magistrates court for an order under the *Police (Property) Act* 1897. The court will decide who appears to be the 'owner' of the property.

An application is made by way of complaint for a summons and costs may be ordered under s.64 of the *Magistrates' Courts Act* 1980: *R. v Uxbridge Justices Ex p. Metropolitan Police Commissioner* [1981] Q.B. 829.

16–168   The court should not make use of this procedure when there are real difficulties in deciding ownership or if questions of legal ownership are in dispute and the word 'owner' should be given its ordinary and popular meaning: *Raymond Lyons & Co v Metropolitan Police Commissioner* [1975] Q.B. 321. The fact that proceedings are pending at the County Court for delivery up of the property does not of itself make the issue complex and beyond the magistrates' jurisdiction: *R. v Maidstone Magistrates' Court Ex p. Knight* (2000) WL 1027029. The fact that the owner of the property may have come by it illegally is irrelevant. The question at issue is who has good or better possessory title: *Costello v Chief Constable of Derbyshire* [2001] 3 All E.R. 150 and *Haley v Chief Constable of Northumbria* (2002) 166 J.P. 719. The morality of the claim is also irrelevant and where a claimant was acquitted of soliciting murder it was held that the nature of the charge was not a good reason for the magistrates declining to return the £10,000 that was paid to a police officer who posed as a hired assassin: *R. (on the application of Carter) v Ipswich Magistrates Court* [2002] EWHC 332.

B. IMPERSONATION OF A POLICE OFFICER

(a) *Definition*

Police Act 1996, s.90

Impersonation, etc.

16–169   **90.**—(1) Any person who with intent to deceive impersonates a member of a police force or special constable, or makes any statement or does any act calculated falsely to suggest that he is such a member or constable, shall be guilty of an offence and liable on summary conviction to imprisonment for a term not exceeding six months or to a fine not exceeding level 5 on the standard scale, or to both.

(2) Any person who, not being a constable, wears any article of police uniform in circumstances where it gives him an appearance so nearly resembling that of a member of a police force as to be calculated to deceive shall be guilty of an offence and liable on summary conviction to a fine not exceeding level 3 on the standard scale.

(3) Any person who, not being a member of a police force or special constable, has in his possession any article of police uniform shall, unless he proves that he obtained possession of that article lawfully and has possession of it for a lawful purpose, be guilty of an offence and liable on summary conviction to a fine not exceeding level 1 on the standard scale.

(4) In this section—
  (a) "article of police uniform" means any article of uniform or any distinctive badge or mark or document of identification usually issued to members of police forces or special constables, or anything having the appearance of such an article, badge, mark or document.
  (aa) "member of a police force" includes a member of the British Transport Police Force, and
  (b) "special constable" means a special constable appointed for a police area.

[This section is printed as amended by the *Anti-Terrorism, Crime and Security Act* 2001, Sch.7.]

(b) *Procedure*

The offences in this section are triable summarily: s.90(1), (2), (3).   **16–170**

(c) *Elements of the offence*

It is an offence to wear uniform which is likely to deceive persons into thinking that   **16–171**
one is a police officer, even if that deception is not intended. In *Turner v Shearer* [1973] 1 All E.R. 397, DC, the defendant was wearing secondhand articles of police uniform, and persons were misled into thinking that he was a police officer. The defendant did not intend to mislead anyone. The Divisional Court held that "calculated" meant "likely," not "intended" and the defendant was convicted.

(d) *Sentence*

The offence under subs.(1) carries a maximum penalty of six months imprisonment,   **16–172**
a fine not exceeding the statutory maximum or both: s.90(1).

The offence under subs.(2) carries a maximum penalty of a fine not exceeding level three on the standard scale: s.90(2).

The offence under subs.(3) carries a maximum penalty of a fine not exceeding level one on the standard scale: s.90(3).

VIII. PRISONS

A. HARBOURING AN ESCAPED PRISONER

(a) *Definition*

Criminal Justice Act 1961, s.22

22.—(1) […]   **16–173**

(2) If any person knowingly harbours a person who has escaped from a prison or other institution to which the said section thirty-nine applies, or who, having been sentenced in any part of the United Kingdom or in any of the Channel Islands or the Isle of Man to imprisonment or detention, is otherwise unlawfully at large, or gives to any such person any assistance with intent to prevent, hinder or interfere with his being taken into custody, he shall be liable—
  (a) on summary conviction, to imprisonment for a term not exceeding six months or to a fine not exceeding one hundred pounds, or to both;

(b) on conviction on indictment, to imprisonment for a term not exceeding ten years, or to a fine, or to both.

(3) In the following enactments (which make provision for the application of sections thirty-nine to forty-two of the *Prison Act* 1952) that is to say, subsection (3) of section one hundred and twenty-two of the *Army Act* 1955, subsection (3) of section one hundred and twenty-two of the *Air Force Act* 1955 and subsection (3) of section eighty-two of the *Naval Discipline Act* 1957, references to the said section thirty-nine shall be construed as including references to subsection (2) of this section.

(4) [...]

[This section is printed as amended by the *Children and Young Persons Act* 1969, s.72 and Sch.6, *Criminal Law Act* 1977, s.28 and the *Prison Security Act* 1992, s.2.]

(b) *Procedure*

16–174　　　This offence is triable either way: s.22(2).

(c) *Elements of the offence*

16–175　　　In *Darch v Weight* (1984) 79 Cr.App.R 40, CA it was held that 'harbour' meant to shelter or provide refuge and that could be done irrespective of any interest in the premises concerned. Merely giving assistance to an escaped prisoner without actually sheltering him would not amount to "harbouring" him. The defendant was a lodger in a house into which the landlady admitted three escaped prisoners. Both she and the landlady were charged and convicted, though the landlady's conviction was later quashed by the Crown Court. On the defendant's appeal, the Divisional Court held that as the defendant had done no positive act to provide shelter, she was not guilty of "harbouring" under s.22(2) of the 1961 Act.

The yard of a police station is not a "prison or other institution" within the meaning of the *Prison Act* 1952, s.39: *Nicoll v Catron* (1985) 81 Cr.App.R 339, DC.

The offence of escaping from custody and being unlawfully at large is a common law offence, triable on indictment only.

(d) *Sentence*

16–176　　　When tried summarily, the maximum penalty for this offence is imprisonment for a term not exceeding six months, a fine not exceeding the statutory maximum or both: *CJA* 1961, s.22(2)(a).

IX. PUBLIC HEALTH

A. PROHIBITION ON UNLICENSED DISPOSAL OF WASTE

(a) *Definition*

Control of Pollution Act 1974, s.3

Prohibition of unlicensed disposal of waste

16–177　　　**3.**—(1) Except in prescribed cases, a person shall not—

　　(a) deposit controlled waste on any land or cause or knowingly permit controlled waste to be deposited on any land; or

　　(b) use any plant or equipment, or cause or knowingly permit any plant or equipment to be used, for the purpose of disposing of controlled waste or of dealing in a prescribed manner with controlled waste,

unless the land on which the waste is deposited or, as the case may be, which forms the site of the plant or equipment is occupied by the holder of a licence issued in pursuance of section 5 of this Act (in this Part of this Act referred to as a "disposal licence") which authorises the deposit or use in question and the deposit or use is in accordance with the conditions, if any, specified in the licence.

(2) Except in a case falling within the following subsection, a person who contravenes any of the provisions of the preceding subsection shall, subject to subsection (4) of this section, be guilty of an offence and liable on summary conviction to a fine of an amount not exceeding £400 or on conviction on indictment to imprisonment for a term not exceeding two years or a fine or both.

(3) A person who contravenes paragraph (a) of subsection (1) of this section in a case where—

(a) the waste in question is of a kind which is poisonous, noxious or polluting; and

(b) its presence on the land is likely to give rise to an environmental hazard; and

(c) it is deposited on the land in such circumstances or for such a period that whoever deposited it there may reasonably be assumed to have abandoned it there or to have brought it there for the purpose of its being disposed of (whether by himself or others) as waste,

shall, subject to the following subsection, be guilty of an offence and liable on summary conviction to imprisonment for a term not exceeding six months or a fine not exceeding £400 or both or, on conviction on indictment, to imprisonment for a term not exceeding five years or a fine or both.

(4) It shall be a defence for a person charged with an offence under this section to prove—

(a) that he—

(i) took care to inform himself, from persons who were in a position to provide the information, as to whether the deposit or use to which the charge relates would be in contravention of subsection (1) of this section, and

(ii) did not know and had no reason to suppose that the information given to him was false or misleading and that the deposit or use might be in contravention of that subsection; or

(b) that he acted under instructions from his employer and neither knew nor had reason to suppose that the deposit or use was in contravention of the said subsection (1); or

(c) in the case of an offence of making, causing or permitting a deposit or use otherwise than in accordance with conditions specified in a disposal licence, that he took all such steps as were reasonably open to him to ensure that the conditions were complied with; or

(d) that the acts specified in the charge were done in an emergency in order to avoid danger to the public and that, as soon as reasonably practicable after they were done, particulars of them were furnished to the disposal authority in whose area the acts were done.

(5) In this section and subsections (5) and (6) of the following section 'land' includes land covered with waters where the land is above the low-water mark of ordinary spring tides and the waters are not inland waters (within the meaning of Chapter I of Part III of the *Water Act* 1989).

[This section will be repealed by the *Environmental Protection Act* 1990, Sch.16, when it comes into force.]

(b) *Procedure*

This offence is triable either way: s.(3)(c).   **16–178**

(c) *Elements of the offence*

The offence of depositing controlled waste is committed when waste is left on land   **16–179** from which it will later be removed, and does not occur only when the waste reaches its final place of deposit: *R. v Metropolitan Stipendiary Magistrate Ex p. London Waste Regulation Authority* [1993] 3 All E.R. 113, QBD. This finding was approved in *R. v Smith (David Brian)* [1999] Env.L.R. 433, CA, the Court emphasising that the purpose of the 1974 Act was to protect the environment from the consequences of dumping waste and it would diminish its efficacy if the meaning of "deposit" under s.3(1) was restricted to "final deposit".

Controlled waste is defined in s.30(1) of the 1974 Act as 'household, industrial and commercial waste or any such waste.' Section 30(5) provides that '(a) household waste consists of waste from a private dwelling or residential home or from premises forming part of a university or school or other educational establishment or forming part of a hospital or nursing home (b) industrial waste consists of waste from any factory within the meaning of the *Factories Act* 1961 and any premises occupied by a body corporate established by or under any enactment for the purpose of carrying on under national ownership any industry or part of an industry or any undertaking, excluding waste from any mine or quarry and (c) commercial waste consists of waste from premises used wholly or mainly for the purposes of a trade or business or the purposes of sport, recreation or entertainment excluding—

(i) household and industrial waste and (ii) waste from any mine or quarry and waste from premises used for agriculture within the meaning of the *Agriculture Act* 1947 or, in Scotland, the *Agriculture (Scotland) Act* 1948, and (iii) waste of any other description prescribed for the purposes of this sub-paragraph.'

(d) *Defences*

16–180   Section 3(4) provides a defence to a charge under this section. In *Durham CC v Peter Connors Industrial Services Ltd* [1993] Env.L.R. 197, QBD, it was held that in order to establish a defence under s.3(4) it had to be shown that the defendant company charged with depositing waste had received information about each specific deposit to which a charge related and then a judgment on whether that deposit might contravene the section could be formed. The defendant company had operated a blanket system of checks whereby drivers were instructed to check, so far as possible, that there were no toxic materials in the waste deposited. There was no reason for the defendant to believe that the information from the drivers was false or misleading but it was not specific enough to provide a defence under s.3(4).

B. Prohibition on Unauthorised or Harmful Deposit Treatment of Waste

(a) *Definition*

Environmental Protection Act 1990, s.33

Prohibition on unauthorised or harmful deposit, treatment or disposal etc. of waste

16–181   **33.**—(1) Subject to subsection (2) and (3) below and, in relation to Scotland, to section 54 below, a person shall not—

     (a) deposit controlled waste, or knowingly cause or knowingly permit controlled waste to be deposited in or on any land unless a waste management licence authorising the deposit is in force and the deposit is in accordance with the licence;

     (b) treat, keep or dispose of controlled waste, or knowingly cause or knowingly permit controlled waste to be treated, kept or disposed of—

         (i) in or on any land, or

         (ii) by means of any mobile plant,

     except under and in accordance with a waste management licence;

     (c) treat, keep or dispose of controlled waste in a manner likely to cause pollution of the environment or harm to human health.

(2) Subsection (1) above does not apply in relation to household waste from a domestic property which is treated, kept or disposed of within the curtilage of the dwelling by or with the permission of the occupier of the dwelling.

(3) Subsection (1)(a), (b) or (c) above do not apply in cases prescribed in regulations made by the Secretary of State and the regulations may make different exceptions for different areas.

(4) The Secretary of State, in exercising his power under subsection (3) above, shall have regard in particular to the expediency of excluding from the controls imposed by waste management licences—

     (a) any deposits which are small enough or of such a temporary nature that they may be so excluded;

(b) any means of treatment or disposal which are innocuous enough to be so excluded;

(c) cases for which adequate controls are provided by another enactment than this section.

(5) Where controlled waste is carried in and deposited from a motor vehicle, the person **16–182** who controls or is in a position to control the use of the vehicle shall, for the purposes of subsection (1)(a) above, be treated as knowingly causing the waste to be deposited whether or not he gave any instructions for this to be done.

(6) A person who contravenes subsection (1) above or any condition of a waste management licence commits an offence.

(7) It shall be a defence for a person charged with an offence under this section to prove—

(a) that he took all reasonable precautions and exercised all due diligence to avoid the commission of the offence; or

(b) that he acted under instructions from his employer and neither knew nor had reason to suppose that the acts done by him constituted a contravention of subsection (1) above; or

(c) that the acts alleged to constitute the contravention were done in an emergency in order to avoid danger to human health in a case where—

   (i) he took all such steps as were reasonably practicable in the circumstances for minimising pollution of the environment and harm to human health; and

   (ii) particulars of the acts were furnished to the waste regulation authority as soon as reasonably practicable after they were done.

(8) Except in a case falling within subsection (9) below, a person who commits an offence under this section shall be liable—

(a) on summary conviction, to imprisonment for a term not exceeding six months or a fine not exceeding £20,000 or both; and

(b) on conviction on indictment, to imprisonment for a term not exceeding two years or a fine or both.

(9) A person who commits an offence under this section in relation to special waste shall be liable—

(a) on summary conviction, to imprisonment for a term not exceeding six months or a fine not exceeding £20,000 or both;

(b) on conviction on indictment, to imprisonment for a term not exceeding five years or a fine or both.

[This section is printed as amended by the *Environment Act* 1995, Sch.22.]

(b) *Procedure*

This offence is triable either way: s.33(8).   **16–183**

(c) *Elements of the offence*

The requirement as to knowledge relates to knowledge that the waste is being **16–184** deposited, rather than knowledge that the deposit breaches the license conditions. In *Shanks & McEwan (Teesside) Ltd v Environment Agency* [1999] Q.B. 333, QBD, it was held that it was sufficient for the prosecution to prove that the company had on the relevant day knowingly operated and held out the site for the reception and deposit of controlled waste, and that the deposit had not been in accordance with a condition of the licence.

The burden of proof that a defendant had deposited or accepted delivery of "special waste" will lie on the prosecution. However, the burden of proving that the deposit of waste was conducted with prior approval will lie on the defendant, the standard of proof being on the balance of probabilities: *Environment Agency v ME Foley Contractors Ltd* [2002] EWHC 258; [2002] 1 W.L.R. 1754, QBD.

(d) *Defence*

Subsection (6) provides a defence of due diligence, acting under employer instruc- **16–185** tions or acting under conditions of emergency.

(e) *Sentence*

16–186   When tried summarily, the maximum penalty for this offence is imprisonment for a term not exceeding six months, a fine not exceeding £20,000 or both.

C. Leaving Litter

(a) *Definition*

Environmental Protection Act 1990, s.87

Offence of leaving litter

16–187   **87.**—(1) If any person throws down, drops or otherwise deposits in, into or from any place to which this section applies, and leaves, any thing whatsoever in such circumstances as to cause, or contribute to, or tend to lead to, the defacement by litter of any place to which this section applies, he shall, subject to subsection (2) below, be guilty of an offence.

(2) No offence is committed under this section where the depositing and leaving of the thing was—

    (a) authorised by law, or

    (b) done with the consent of the owner, occupier or other person or authority having control of the place in or into which that thing was deposited.

(3) This section applies to any public open place and, in so far as the place is not a public open place, also to the following places—

    (a) any relevant highway or relevant road and any trunk road which is a special road;

    (b) any place on relevant land of a principal litter authority;

    (c) any place on relevant Crown land;

    (d) any place on relevant land of any designated statutory undertaker;

    (e) any place on relevant land of any designated educational institution;

    (f) any place on relevant land within a litter control area of a local authority.

(4) In this section "public open place" means a place in the open air to which the public are entitled or permitted to have access without payment; and any covered place open to the air on at least one side and available for public use shall be treated as a public open place.

(5) A person who is guilty of an offence under this section shall be liable on summary conviction to a fine not exceeding level 4 on the standard scale.

(6) A local authority, with a view to promoting the abatement of litter, may take such steps as the authority think appropriate for making the effect of subsection (5) above known to the public in their area.

(7) In any proceedings in Scotland for an offence under this section it shall be lawful to convict the accused on the evidence of one witness.

(b) *Procedure*

16–188   This offence is triable summarily only: s.87(5).

(c) *Elements of the offence*

16–189   A telephone kiosk will not be regarded as a "public open space" or a covered place available for public use as they are not open to air on at least one side, but instead have three fixed sides and one door which was usually closed except for access: *DPP v Felix* [1998] Crim.L.R. 657. The court added that the phrase "otherwise deposits in" was extremely wide and that 'deposits' meant no more than places or puts.

The word "litter" should be given its natural meaning of "miscellaneous rubbish left lying about". This will include commercial waste: *Westminster City Council v Riding* (1996) Env.L.R. 95, QBD.

(d) *Sentence*

16–190   The maximum penalty for this offence is a fine not exceeding level four on the standard scale: s.87(5).

D. Health and Safety Offences

Offences

Health and Safety at Work Act 1974

Sections 2–7 of the Act impose general duties on employers to ensure the health and **16–191** safety and welfare at work of their employees and other persons who may be affected by the employer's undertaking, *e.g.* sub-contractors: s.2. A similar duty is imposed on self-employed persons and their workforce who are not employees: s.3.

Persons concerned with premises have a duty relating to health and safety towards persons other than their employees who use premises as a place of work: s.4.

Manufacturers have a duty as regards articles and substances for use at work: s.6.

Employees also have a general duty to take reasonable care for their own health and safety and that of other people affected by their actions: s.7.

(a) *Definition*

Health and Safety at Work Act 1974, s.33

Offences

33.—(1) It is an offence for a person—   **16–192**

    (a) to fail to discharge a duty to which he is subject by virtue of sections 2 to 7;

    (b) to contravene section 8 or 9;

    (c) to contravene any health and safety regulations or any requirement or prohibition imposed under any such regulations (including any requirement or prohibition to which he is subject by virtue of the terms of or any condition or restriction attached to any licence, approval, exemption or other authority issued, given or granted under the regulations);

    (d) to contravene any requirement imposed by or under regulations under section 14 or intentionally to obstruct any person in the exercise of his powers under that section;

    (e) to contravene any requirement imposed by an inspector under section 20 or 25;

    (f) to prevent or attempt to prevent any other person from appearing before an inspector or from answering any question to which an inspector may by virtue of section 20(2) require an answer;

    (g) to contravene any requirement or prohibition imposed by an improvement notice or a prohibition notice (including any such notice as modified on appeal);

    (h) intentionally to obstruct an inspector in the exercise or performance of his powers or duties or to obstruct a customs officer in the exercise of his powers under section 25A;

    (i) to contravene any requirement imposed by a notice under section 27(1);

    (j) to use or disclose any information in contravention of section 27(4) or 28;

    (k) to make a statement which he knows to be false or recklessly to make a statement which is false where the statement is made—

        (i) in purported compliance with a requirement to furnish any information imposed by or under any of the relevant statutory provisions; or

        (ii) for the purpose of obtaining the issue of a document under any of the relevant statutory provisions to himself or another person;

    (l) intentionally to make a false entry in any register, book, notice or other document required by or under any of the relevant statutory provisions to be kept, served or given or, with intent to deceive, to make use of any such entry which he knows to be false;

    (m) with intent to deceive, to use a document issued or authorised to be issued under any of the relevant statutory provisions or required for any purpose thereunder or to make or have in his possession a document so closely resembling any such document as to be calculated to deceive;

    (n) falsely to pretend to be an inspector;

(o) to fail to comply with an order made by a court under section 42.

(1A) Subject to any provision made by virtue of section 15(6)(d), a person guilty of an offence under subsection (1)(a) above consisting of failing to discharge a duty to which he is subject by virtue of sections 2 to 6 shall be liable—

(a) on summary conviction, to a fine not exceeding £20,000;

(b) on conviction on indictment, to a fine.

(2) A person guilty of an offence under paragraph (d), (f), (h) or (n) of subsection (1) above, or of an offence under paragraph (e) of that subsection consisting of contravening a requirement imposed by an inspector under section 20, shall be liable on summary conviction to a fine not exceeding level 5 on the standard scale

(2A) A person guilty of an offence under subsection (1)(g) or (o) above shall be liable—

(a) on summary conviction, to imprisonment for a term not exceeding six months, or a fine not exceeding £20,000, or both;

(b) on conviction on indictment, to imprisonment for a term not exceeding two years, or a fine, or both.

16–193   (3) Subject to any provision made by virtue of section 15(6)(d) or (e) or by virtue of paragraph 2(2) of Schedule 3, a person guilty of an offence under subsection (1) above not falling within subsection (1A), (2) or (2A) above, or of an offence under subsection (1)(e) above not falling within the preceding subsection, or of an offence under any of the existing statutory provisions, being an offence for which no other penalty is specified, shall be liable—

(a) on summary conviction, to a fine not exceeding £400;

(b) on conviction on indictment—

(i) if the offence is one to which this sub-paragraph applies, to imprisonment for a term not exceeding two years, or a fine, or both;

(ii) if the offence is not one to which the preceding sub-paragraph applies, to a fine.

(4) Subsection (3)(b)(i) above applies to the following offences—

(a) an offence consisting of contravening any of the relevant statutory provisions by doing otherwise than under the authority of a licence issued by the Executive something for the doing of which such a licence is necessary under the relevant statutory provisions;

(b) an offence consisting of contravening a term of or a condition or restriction attached to any such licence as is mentioned in the preceding paragraph;

(c) an offence consisting of acquiring or attempting to acquire, possessing or using an explosive article or substance (within the meaning of any of the relevant statutory provisions) in contravention of any of the relevant statutory provisions;

(d) [...]

(e) an offence under subsection (1)(j) above.

[This section is printed as amended by the *Employment Protection Act* 1975, Sch.15, the *Criminal Law Act* 1977, s.28 and Schs.1 and 6, the *Forgery and Counterfeiting Act* 1981, the *Criminal Justice Act* 1982, s.46, the *Consumer Protection Act* 1987, Sch.3 and the *Offshore Safety Act* 1992, s.4.]

(b) *Procedure*

16–194   All of the offences created by s.33(1) are triable either way, except those created by subss.1(d), (e), (f), (h) and (n) which are triable summarily only.

Health and Safety at Work Act 1974, s.34(1)–(4), 36–38

Extension of time for bringing summary proceedings

16–195   34.—(1) Where—

(a) a special report on any matter to which section 14 of this Act applies is made by virtue of subsection (2)(a) of that section; or

(b) a report is made by the person holding an inquiry into any such matter by virtue of subsection (2)(b) of that section; or

(c) a coroner's inquest is held touching the death of any person whose death may have been caused by an accident which happened while he was at work or by a disease which he contracted or probably contracted at work or by any accident, act or omission which occurred in connection with the work of any person whatsoever; or

(d) a public inquiry into any death that may have been so caused is held under the *Fatal Accidents and Sudden Deaths Inquiry (Scotland) Act* 1976,

and it appears from the report or, in a case falling within paragraph (c) or (d) above, from the proceedings at the inquest or inquiry, that any of the relevant statutory provisions was contravened at a time which is material in relation to the subject-matter of the report, inquest or inquiry, summary proceedings against any person liable to be proceeded against in respect of the contravention may be commenced at any time within three months of the making of the report or, in a case falling within paragraph (c) or (d) above, within three months of the conclusion of the inquest or inquiry.

(2) Where an offence under any of the relevant statutory provisions is committed by reason of a failure to do something at or within a time fixed by or under any of those provisions, the offence shall be deemed to continue until that thing is done.

(3) Summary proceedings for an offence to which this subsection applies may be commenced at any time within six months from the date on which there comes to the knowledge of a responsible enforcing authority evidence sufficient in the opinion of that authority to justify a prosecution for that offence; and for the purposes of this subsection—

(a) a certificate of an enforcing authority stating that such evidence came to its knowledge on a specified date shall be conclusive evidence of that fact; and

(b) a document purporting to be such a certificate and to be signed by or on behalf of the enforcing authority in question shall be presumed to be such a certificate unless the contrary is proved.

(4) The preceding subsection applies to any offence under any of the relevant statutory provisions which a person commits by virtue of any provision or requirement to which he is subject as the designer, manufacturer, importer or supplier of any thing; and in that subsection "responsible enforcing authority" means an enforcing authority within whose field of responsibility the offence in question lies, whether by virtue of section 35 or otherwise.

Offences due to fault of other person

36.—(1) Where the commission by any person of an offence under any of the relevant statutory provisions is due to the act or default of some other person, that other person shall be guilty of the offence, and a person may be charged with and convicted of the offence by virtue of this subsection whether or not proceedings are taken against the first-mentioned person. **16–196**

(2) Where there would be or have been the commission of an offence under section 33 by the Crown but for the circumstance that that section does not bind the Crown, and that fact is due to the act or default of a person other than the Crown, that person shall be guilty of the offence which, but for that circumstance, the Crown would be committing or would have committed, and may be charged with and convicted of that offence accordingly.

(3) The preceding provisions of this section are subject to any provision made by virtue of section 15(6).

Offences by bodies corporate

37.—(1) Where an offence under any of the relevant statutory provisions committed by a body corporate is proved to have been committed with the consent or connivance of, or to have been attributable to any neglect on the part of, any director, manager, secretary or other similar officer of the body corporate or a person who was purporting to act in any such capacity, he as well as the body corporate shall be guilty of that offence and shall be liable to be proceeded against and punished accordingly. **16–197**

(2) Where the affairs of a body corporate are managed by its members, the preceding subsection shall apply in relation to the acts and defaults of a member in connection with his functions of management as if he were a director of the body corporate.

Restriction on institution of proceedings in England and Wales

38. Proceedings for an offence under any of the relevant statutory provisions shall not, in England and Wales, be instituted except by an inspector or the Environment Agency or by or with the consent of the Director of Public Prosecutions. **16–198**

[This section is printed as amended by the *Environment Act* 1995, Sch.22.]

16–199　When tried summarily, the maximum penalty for the offence created by subs.33(1)(a) (failing to discharge a duty to which the defendant is subject by virtue of ss.2 to 6 of the 1974 Act) is a fine not exceeding £20,000: s.33(1A).

When tried summarily, the maximum penalty for an offence under subs.33(1)(g) or (o) is imprisonment for a term not exceeding six months, or a fine not exceeding £20,000 or both: s.33(2A).

The maximum penalty for an offence under subss.33(1)(d), (e), (f), (h) or (n) is a fine not exceeding level five on the standard scale: s.33(2).

All other offences created by this section carry the maximum penalty of a fine: s.33(3).

For guidelines on the level of fine to be imposed and the factors to be taken into account when sentencing companies for offences in breach of health and safety legislation:*R. v Howe and Son (Engineers) Ltd* [1999] 2 All E.R. 249. The court must take into the account the seriousness of the offence and the means of the corporate offender.

X.　PUBLIC TRANSPORT

16–200　Public transport includes trains, underground railways and buses. This section covers the railways but regulations apply to other forms of public transport. For the purposes of this section, the principles explained apply equally to similar offences committed on other modes of transport but they are covered by specific, separate regulations etc.

A.　OBSTRUCTION OF THE OFFICERS OF ANY RAILWAY COMPANY, TRESPASSING UPON ANY RAILWAY

(a) *Definition*

Railway Regulation Act 1840, s.16

For punishment of persons obstructing the officers of any railway company, or trespassing upon any railway

16–201　　**16.** If any person shall wilfully obstruct or impede any officer or agent of any railway company in the execution of his duty upon any railway, or upon or in any of the stations or other works or premises connected therewith, or if any person shall wilfully trespass upon any railway, or any of the stations or other works or premises connected therewith, and shall refuse to quit the same upon request to him made by any officer or agent of the said company, every such person so offending, and all others aiding or assisting therein, shall, upon conviction by a magistrates' court, at the discretion of the court, forfeit to her Majesty any sum not exceeding level 1 on the standard scale level 3 on the standard scale and in default of payment thereof shall or may be imprisoned.

[This section is printed as amended by the *Summary Jurisdiction Act* 1848, s.4, the *Statute Law Revision (No.2) Act* 1888, the *Statute Law Revision Act* 1892, the *Magistrates' Courts Act* 1952, Sch.6, the *British Railways Act* 1965, s.35(1), the *London Transport Act* 1965, s.34(1), the *British Railways Act* 1977, Sch.1, the *CJA* 1982, s.46 and the *Police and Criminal Evidence Act* 1984, Sch.6.]

(b) *Procedure*

16–202　This offence is triable summarily.

(c) *Elements of the offence*

16–203　The word 'railway' extends to all railways constructed under the powers of any Act of Parliament and intended for the conveyance of passengers in or upon carriages drawn or impelled by the power of steam or by any other mechanical power; 'company' includes the proprietors for the time being of any such railway: *Railway Regulation Act* 1840, s.21.

The ambit of s.16 was considered in *R. (On the Application of Mair) v Criminal Injuries Compensation Board* [2002] P.I.Q.R. P4, QBD. The applicant was a railway employee seeking to challenge the refusal of the CICB to award him compensation for post traumatic stress disorder suffered as a result of watching a young boy lose his arm beneath the wheels of a train. The applicant argued that his PTSD was attributable to "an offence of trespass on a railway." The application was dismissed, the court finding that there had been no offence committed at the time of the incident. The section makes it an offence to refuse to leave railway premises when required, but the injured boy had only been required to leave the train and there was no implicit request to leave the track or the platform. Hence a request to leave a train will not found a charge of trespass if the individual chooses to remain on the train platform. Stanley Burnton J. explained the working of s.16 by stating:

> 'It can be seen that there are two parts of that particular statutory provision. The first part is concerned with a person who wilfully obstructs or impedes any officer or agent of a railway company in the execution of his duties. It is not suggested that that provision applied in this case. The second part is concerned with wilful trespass on a railway, and the words are "or if any person shall trespass upon any railway, or any of the stations or any works or premises connected therewith, and shall refuse to quit the same upon request to him made by any officer or agent of the said company".
>
> Pausing there for a moment, the words clearly refer to premises or land or works, works in the sense of an electrical substation. They do not refer to a train as such, and it is not suggested that they do. That is the first point. The second point is that the provision requires a refusal on the part of the offender to quit the same upon a request. If there is no request and a refusal to comply with the request, there is no offence committed under that part of this statute.'

A railway company can exclude anyone not wishing to use the railway, or anyone unwilling to comply with conditions: *Perth General Station Committee v Ross* (1897) A.C. 479.

(c) *Sentence*

The offence under s.16 of the 1840 Act carries a maximum penalty of one month's **16–204** imprisonment or a fine not exceeding level three on the standard scale.

B. PENALTY FOR TRESPASSING ON RAILWAYS

(a) *Definition*

Railway Regulation Act 1868, s.23

23. If any person shall be or pass upon any railway, except for the purpose of crossing the **16–205** same at any authorized crossing, after having once received warning by the company which works such railway, or by any of their agents or servants, not to go or pass thereon, every person so offending shall forfeit and pay any sum not exceeding level 1 on the standard scale for every such offence.

[This section is printed as amended by the *Regulation of Railways Act* 1871, s.14, the *Criminal Law Act* 1977, s.31 and the *CJA* 1982, s.46.]

(b) *Procedure*

This offence is triable summarily.   **16–206**

(c) *Sentence*

This offence is punishable by a fine not exceeding level 1 on the standard scale.   **16–207**

C. Penalty for Avoiding Payment of Fare

(a) *Definition*

Regulation of Railways Act 1889, s.5

16–208　　　**5.**—(1) Every passenger by a railway shall, on request by an officer or servant of a railway company, either produce, and if so requested deliver up, a ticket showing that his fare is paid, or pay his fare from the place whence he started, or give the officer or servant his name and address; and in case of default shall be liable on summary conviction to a fine not exceeding level 2 on the standard scale

(2) If a passenger having failed either to produce, or if requested to deliver up, a ticket showing that his fare is paid, or to pay his fare, refuses or fails on request by an officer or servant of a railway company, to give his name and address, any officer of the company or any constable may detain him until he can be conveniently brought before some justice or otherwise discharged by due course of law.

(3) If any person—

(a) Travels or attempts to travel on a railway without having previously paid his fare, and with intent to avoid payment thereof; or

(b) Having paid his fare for a certain distance, knowingly and wilfully proceeds by train beyond that distance without previously paying the additional fare for the additional distance, and with intent to avoid payment thereof; or

(c) Having failed to pay his fare, gives in reply to a request by an officer of a railway company a false name or address,

he shall be liable on summary conviction to a fine not exceeding level 3 on the standard scale, or, in the discretion of the court to imprisonment for a term not exceeding three months

(4) The liability of an offender to punishment under this section shall not prejudice the recovery of any fare payable by him.

(5) In this section—

(a) "railway company" includes an operator of a train, and

(b) "operator", in relation to a train, means the person having the management of that train for the time being.

[This section is printed as amended by the *Transport Act* 1962, ss.84(2) and 93(1), the *British Railways Act* 1965, s.35(5), the *British Railways Act* 1971, s.18, the *British Railways Act* 1977, Sch.1, the *CJA* 1982, ss.35 and 46, the *Police and Criminal Evidence Act* 1984, Sch.7 and *(SI* 1994/857).]

(b) *Procedure*

16–209　　　This offence is triable summarily: s.5(2)(c).

(c) *Elements of the offence*

16–210　　　The 'fare' means the fare by the train and the class of carriage in which the passenger travels; a person who had purchased a workman's ticket, marked "not transferable," which had been issued by a railway company to another person, from that person, and had travelled on the railway without having purchased a ticket from the railway company, had travelled on the railway "without having previously paid his fare, and with intent to avoid payment thereof" within the meaning of the statute: *Reynolds v Beasley* [1919] 1 K.B. 215. A person travelling in a first class carriage with a second class ticket and fraudulently intending to avoid payment of a first class fare may be convicted for 'without having previously paid his fare': *Gillingham v Walker* (1881) 45 J.P. 470.

Proof of intent to avoid payment is the necessary mental element of the offence, this intent does not have to be to defraud: *Browning v Floyd* (1946). A person is still travelling on a railway for the purpose of *Regulation of Railways Act* 1889, s.5, after he has alighted from his train and before he passes the ticket barrier. If, therefore, he conceives an intention to avoid payment of his fare at that stage he is guilty of an offence against the section: *Bremme v Dubury* [1964] All E.R. 193, DC.

The intention to avoid payment does not have to be permanent. Where a fare was underpaid and the defendant said he intended to pay the excess if he were later tracked down and requested to do so this did not provide a defence: *Corbyn v Saunders* [1978] 2 All E.R. 697.

XI. SCHOOL ATTENDANCE

A. Failing to Secure Regular Attendance at School

(a) *Definition*

Education Act 1996, s.444

Offence: failure to secure regular attendance at school of registered pupil

16–211

444.—(1) If a child of compulsory school age who is a registered pupil at a school fails to attend regularly at the school, his parent is guilty of an offence.

(1A) If in the circumstances mentioned in subsection (1) the parent knows that his child is failing to attend regularly at the school and fails without reasonable justification to cause him to do so, he is guilty of an offence.

(2) Subsections (3) to (6) below apply in proceedings for an offence under this section in respect of a child who is not a boarder at the school at which he is a registered pupil.

(3) The child shall not be taken to have failed to attend regularly at the school by reason of his absence from the school—

(a) with leave,

(b) at any time when he was prevented from attending by reason of sickness or any unavoidable cause, or

(c) on any day exclusively set apart for religious observance by the religious body to which his parent belongs.

(4) The child shall not be taken to have failed to attend regularly at the school if the parent proves—

(a) that the school at which the child is a registered pupil is not within walking distance of the child's home, and

(b) that no suitable arrangements have been made by the local education authority for any of the following—

(i) his transport to and from the school,

(ii) boarding accommodation for him at or near the school, or

(iii) enabling him to become a registered pupil at a school nearer to his home.

(5) In subsection (4) "walking distance"—

(a) in relation to a child who is under the age of eight, means 3.218688 kilometres (two miles), and

(b) in relation to a child who has attained the age of eight, means 4.828032 kilometres (three miles), in each case measured by the nearest available route.

(6) If it is proved that the child has no fixed abode, subsection (4) shall not apply, but the parent shall be acquitted if he proves—

(a) that he is engaged in a trade or business of such a nature as to require him to travel from place to place,

(b) that the child has attended at a school as a registered pupil as regularly as the nature of that trade or business permits, and

(c) if the child has attained the age of six, that he has made at least 200 attendances during the period of 12 months ending with the date on which the proceedings were instituted.

16–212

(7) In proceedings for an offence under this section in respect of a child who is a boarder at the school at which he is a registered pupil, the child shall be taken to have failed to attend regularly at the school if he is absent from it without leave during any part of the school term at a time when he was not prevented from being present by reason of sickness or any unavoidable cause.

(8) A person guilty of an offence under subsection (1) is liable on summary conviction to a fine not exceeding level 3 on the standard scale.

(8A) A person guilty of an offence under subsection (1A) is liable on summary conviction—

    (a) to a fine not exceeding level 4 on the standard scale, or

    (b) to imprisonment for a term not exceeding three months,

or both.

(8B) If, on the trial of an offence under subsection (1A), the court finds the defendant not guilty of that offence but is satisfied that he is guilty of an offence under subsection (1), the court may find him guilty of that offence.

(9) In this section "leave", in relation to a school, means leave granted by any person authorised to do so by the governing body or proprietor of the school.

(b) *Procedure*

16–213   These offences are triable summarily only.

(c) *Elements of the offence*

16–213.1   Under the Act every local education authority has a duty to secure that education is available at primary, secondary and higher level to meet the needs of the population of their area. The Act places a duty on parents to ensure attendance at school of their children. Subsection (1) creates the offence of failing to attend school regularly and subs.(1A) creates the aggravated offence of knowing that a pupil is failing to attend school and failing without reasonable justification to cause the child to attend school. The latter offence requires an element of knowledge and connivance which attracts a more severe sentence on conviction.

Compulsory school age is defined as lasting between the ages of five to 16 years of age: s.8. The presumption that a child is of compulsory school age is rebuttable by the parent; s.445. The definition of parent includes a person with parental responsibility or one who cares for the child: s.576.

16–214   Unavoidable cause in subs.3(b) does not include the chronic illness of a parent or other family duties: *Jenkins v Howells* [1949] 2 K.B. 218. The test of 'unavoidable cause' is higher than that of 'reasonable cause': *Jarman v Mid Glamorgan Education Authority* (1985) LS Gaz.R. 1249.

In *Telford and Wrekin Council v Ashley* [2001] C.L.Y. 1986, MC, a single parent was convicted of failing to secure her son's attendance at school. Over a four-month period, the boy's attendance had been recorded at 14 per cent. There had been five home visits by the Education Welfare Officer, together with two pupil planning meetings and both parents had received oral and written warnings, including a final written warning, and the boy had been excluded from school twice. The mother asserted a defence of duress based on the physical and verbal abuse she had endured from her son following her attempts to make him attend school. The justices held that whilst the defence of duress was applicable to charges under s.444 of the Act, notwithstanding the special defence of "unavoidable cause" provided for in that section, it could not be established that verbal abuse, accompanied by "pushing and shoving away" of the parent by the child, constituted duress so as to afford a parent a defence to a charge under s.444 of the Act.

16–215   In *Bath and North East Somerset District Council v Warman* [1999] E.L.R. 81, [1999] Ed.C.R. 517, QBD, a mother was prosecuted for failing to secure her daughter's attendance at school. The daughter had left home in mid 1997, whilst she was aged 15, and gone to live with her long-term boyfriend. The mother did not discover where she was living until Christmas 1997. The mother had objected to the daughter leaving home but could not stop her. She did not contact the police or social services because she did not think that they would do anything and she did not in any event think that her daughter would be at risk. The Divisional Court held that the circumstances of the case did not give rise to an unavoidable cause for the child's absence from school, and the justices' decision to acquit the mother was wrong. The case was remitted with a direction to convict, with a recommendation that the appropriate penalty would be a conditional discharge, the court questioning the propriety of prosecuting the mother for a criminal offence.

In subs.4(a) the route is not prevented from being available because of fears for the child's safety walking along that route alone. The pupil may need to be accompanied to guard against perceived dangers but the route remains available: *Essex County Council v Rogers* [1987] A.C. 66.

Under subs.4(b)(iii), it is the arrangements that must be suitable and not the choice of school nearer to the pupil's home: *R. v Dyfed County Council Ex p. S* [1995] 1 F.C.R. 113.

(d) Sentence

The maximum penalty for the offence established by subs.(1) is a fine not exceeding **16–216** level 3 on the standard scale. The maximum penalty for the offence established by subs.1A is a fine not exceeding level 4 on the standard scale, imprisonment for a term not exceeding three months or both.

The *Magistrates' Court Sentencing Guidelines* (2003) provide that in relation to the offence under s.444(1A), aggravating factors include the relevant conduct having a harmful effect on other children in the family, the presence of a lack of parental effort to ensure attendance, parental collusion and the use of threats to teachers, pupils and/or officials. Mitigating factors include the absence being due to the physical or mental health of child, the presence of a substantiated history of bullying, drugs etc. The starting point for consideration of sentence is whether the offence is serious enough to warrant a community penalty.

Parenting orders may also be made following the commission of an offence under this section: *Crime and Disorder Act* 1998, s.8.

Crime and Disorder Act 1998, s.8

Parenting orders

8.—(1) This section applies where, in any court proceedings— **16–217**
    (a) a child safety order is made in respect of a child;
    (b) an anti-social behaviour order or sex offender order is made in respect of a child or young person;
    (c) a child or young person is convicted of an offence; or
    (d) a person is convicted of an offence under section 443 (failure to comply with school attendance order) or section 444 (failure to secure regular attendance at school of registered pupil) of the *Education Act* 1996.

(2) Subject to subsection (3) and section 9(1) below and to section 19(5) of, and paragraph 13(5) of Schedule 1 to, the *Powers of Criminal Courts (Sentencing) Act* 2000, if in the proceedings the court is satisfied that the relevant condition is fulfilled, it may make a parenting order in respect of a person who is a parent or guardian of the child or young person or, as the case may be, the person convicted of the offence under section 443 or 444 ("the parent").

(3) A court shall not make a parenting order unless it has been notified by the Secretary of State that arrangements for implementing such orders are available in the are in which it appears to the court that the parent resides or will reside and the notice has not been withdrawn.

(4) A parenting order is an order which requires the parent—
    (a) to comply, for a period not exceeding twelve months, with such requirements as are specified in the order; and
    (b) subject to subsection (5) below, to attend, for a concurrent period not exceeding three months and not more than once in any week, such counselling or guidance sessions as may be specified in directions given by the responsible officer;
and in this subsection "week" means a period of seven days beginning with a Sunday.

(5) A parenting order may, but need not, include such a requirement as is mentioned **16–218** in subsection (4)(b) above in any case where such an order has been made in respect of the parent on a previous occasion.

(6) The relevant condition is that the parenting order would be desirable in the interests of preventing—
> (a) in a case falling within paragraph (a) or (b) of subsection (1) above, any repetition of the kind of behaviour which led to the child safety order, anti-social behaviour order or sex offender order being made;
> (b) in a case falling within paragraph (c) of that subsection, the commission of any further offence by the child or young person;
> (c) in a case falling within paragraph (d) of that subsection, the commission of any further offence under section 443 or 444 of the *Education Act* 1996.

(7) The requirements that may be specified under subsection (4)(a) above are those which the court considers desirable in the interests of preventing any such repetition or, as the case may be, the commission of any such further offence.

(8) In this section and section 9 below "responsible officer", in relation to a parenting order, means one of the following who is specified in the order, namely—
> (a) an officer of a local probation board;
> (b) a social worker of a local authority social services department; and
> (bb) a person nominated by a person appointed as chief education officer under section 532 of the *Education Act* 1996.
> (c) a member of a youth offending team.

[This section is printed as amended by the *Criminal Justice and Court Services Act* 2000, s.73.]

16–219   See also *Bath and North East Somerset District Council v Warman* (above), where the court recommended a conditional discharge as an appropriate penalty in the circumstances of the offence, and Rose L.J. stated 'one can well understand that it is of the highest importance that the parents of children should be persuaded to comply with the statutory obligation which bears upon them in the terms of the section of the Act to ensure that their children do go to school. But, for my part, I have some doubt as to whether, in the particular circumstances of this case, the prosecution of the mother for a criminal offence was a wholly desirable exercise.'

XII. SOCIAL SECURITY

A. DISHONEST REPRESENTATIONS FOR OBTAINING BENEFIT

(a) *Definition*

Social Security Administration Act 1992, s.111A

Dishonest representations for obtaining benefit etc.

16–220   **111A.**—(1) If a person dishonestly—
> (a) makes a false statement or representation; or
> (b) produces or furnishes, or causes or allows to be produced or furnished, any document or information which is false in a material particular;

with a view to obtaining any benefit or other payment or advantage under the relevant social security legislation (whether for himself or for some other person), he shall be guilty of an offence.

(1A) A person shall be guilty of an offence if—
> (a) there has been a change of circumstances affecting any entitlement of his to any benefit or other payment or advantage under any provision of the relevant social security legislation;
> (b) the change is not a change that is excluded by regulations from the changes that are required to be notified;
> (c) he knows that the change affects an entitlement of his to such a benefit or other payment or advantage; and
> (d) he dishonestly fails to give a prompt notification of that change in the prescribed manner to the prescribed person.

16–221   (1B) A person shall be guilty of an offence if—

(a) there has been a change of circumstances affecting any entitlement of another person to any benefit or other payment or advantage under any provision of the relevant social security legislation;

(b) the change is not a change that is excluded by regulations from the changes that are required to be notified;

(c) he knows that the change affects an entitlement of that other person to such a benefit or other payment or advantage; and

(d) he dishonestly causes or allows that other person to fail to give a prompt notification of that change in the prescribed manner to the prescribed person.

(1C) This subsection applies where—

(a) there has been a change of circumstances affecting any entitlement of a person ('the claimant') to any benefit or other payment or advantage under any provision of the relevant social security legislation;

(b) the benefit, payment or advantage is one in respect of which there is another person ('the recipient') who for the time being has a right to receive payments to which the claimant has, or (but for the arrangements under which they are payable to the recipient) would have, an entitlement; and

(c) the change is not a change that is excluded by regulations from the changes that are required to be notified.

(1D) In a case where subsection (1C) above applies, the recipient is guilty of an offence if—

(a) he knows that the change affects an entitlement of the claimant to a benefit or other payment or advantage under a provision of the relevant social security legislation;

(b) the entitlement is one in respect of which he has a right to receive payments to which the claimant has, or (but for the arrangements under which they are payable to the recipient) would have, an entitlement; and

(c) he dishonestly fails to give a prompt notification of that change in the prescribed manner to the prescribed person.

(1E) In a case where that subsection applies, a person other than the recipient is guilty **16–222** of an offence if—

(a) he knows that the change affects an entitlement of the claimant to a benefit or other payment or advantage under a provision of the relevant social security legislation;

(b) the entitlement is one in respect of which the recipient has a right to receive payments to which the claimant has, or (but for the arrangements under which they are payable to the recipient) would have, an entitlement; and

(c) he dishonestly causes or allows the recipient to fail to give a prompt notification of that change in the prescribed manner to the prescribed person.

(1F) In any case where subsection (1C) above applies but the right of the recipient is confined to a right, by reason of his being a person to whom the claimant is required to make payments in respect of a dwelling, to receive payments of housing benefit—

(a) a person shall not be guilty of an offence under subsection (1D) or (1E) above unless the change is one relating to one or both of the following—

(i)   the claimant's occupation of that dwelling;

(ii) the claimant's liability to make payments in respect of that dwelling; but

(b) subsections (1D)(a) and (1E)(a) above shall each have effect as if after "knows" there were inserted "or could reasonably be expected to know".

(1G) For the purposes of subsections (1A) to (1E) above a notification of a change is prompt if, and only if, it is given as soon as reasonably practicable after the change occurs.

(3) A person guilty of an offence under this section shall be liable—

(a) on summary conviction, to imprisonment for a term not exceeding six months, or to a fine not exceeding the statutory maximum, or to both; or

(b) on conviction on indictment, to imprisonment for a term not exceeding seven years, or to a fine, or to both.

(4) In the application of this section to Scotland, in subsections (1) to (1E) for "dishonestly" substitute "knowingly".

[This section was inserted by the *Social Security Administration (Fraud) Act* 1997, s.13 as amended by the *Child Support, Pensions and Social Security Act* 2000, Sch.6 and the *Social Security Fraud Act* 2001, Sch.1.]

(b) *Procedure*

16–223   These offences are triable either way: *Social Security Administration Act* 1992, s.111A(3).

Social Security Administration Act 1992, s.116

Legal Proceedings

16–224   **116.**—(1) Any person authorised by the Secretary of State in that behalf may conduct any proceedings under any provision of this Act other than section 114 or under any provision of the *Jobseekers Act* 1995 before a magistrates' court although not a barrister or solicitor.

(2) Notwithstanding anything in any Act—

(a) proceedings for an offence under this Act other than an offence relating to housing benefit or council tax benefit, or for an offence under the *Jobseekers Act* 1995, may be begun at any time within the period of 3 months from the date on which evidence, sufficient in the opinion of the Secretary of State to justify a prosecution for the offence, comes to his knowledge or within a period of 12 months from the commission of the offence, whichever period last expires; and

(b) proceedings for an offence under this Act relating to housing benefit or council tax benefit may be begun at any time within the period of 3 months from the date on which evidence, sufficient in the opinion of the appropriate authority to justify a prosecution for the offence, comes to the authority's knowledge or within a period of 12 months from the commission of the offence, whichever period last expires.

(2A) Subsection (2) above shall not be taken to impose any restriction on the time when proceedings may be begun for an offence under section 111A above.

(3) For the purposes of subsection (2) above—

(a) a certificate purporting to be signed by or on behalf of the Secretary of State as to the date on which such evidence as is mentioned in paragraph (a) of that subsection came to his knowledge shall be conclusive evidence of that date; and

(b) a certificate of the appropriate authority as to the date on which such evidence as is mentioned in paragraph (b) of that subsection came to the authority's knowledge shall be conclusive evidence of that date.

(4) In subsection (2) and (3) above "the appropriate authority" means, in relation to an offence which relates to housing benefit and concerns any dwelling—

(b) if it relates to a rent rebate, the authority who are the appropriate housing authority by virtue of that subsection; and

(c) if it relates to rent allowance, the authority who are the appropriate local authority by virtue of that subsection.

(5) In subsection (2) and (3) above "the appropriate authority" means, in relation to an offence relating to council tax benefit, such authority as is prescribed in relation to the offence.

16–225   (5A) In relation to proceedings for an offence under section 114 above, the references in subsections (2)(a) and (3)(a) to the Secretary of State shall have effect as references to the Inland Revenue.

(7) In the application of this section to Scotland, the following provisions shall have effect in substitution for subsections (1) to (5A) above—

(a) proceedings for an offence under this Act or the *Jobseekers Act* 1995 may, notwithstanding anything in section 136 of the *Criminal Procedure (Scotland) Act* 1995, be commenced at any time within the period of 3 months from the date on which evidence, sufficient in the opinion of the Lord Advocate to justify proceedings, comes to his knowledge, or within the period of 12 months from the commission of the offence, whichever period last expires;

(aa) this subsection shall not be taken to impose any restriction on the time when proceedings may be commenced for an offence under section 111A above;

(b) for the purposes of this subsection—

(i) a certificate purporting to be signed by or on behalf of the Lord Advocate as to the date on which such evidence as is mentioned above came to his knowledge shall be conclusive evidence of that date; and

(ii) subsection (3) of section 136 of the said *Act of* 1995 (date of commencement of proceedings) shall have effect as it has effect for the purposes of that section.

[This section is printed as amended by the *Local Government Finance Act* 1992, Sch.9, the *Jobseekers Act* 1995, Sch.2, the *Social Security Administration (Fraud) Act* 1997, Sch.1, the *Social Security Contributions (Transfer of Functions etc.) Act* 1999, Sch.1 and the *Welfare Reform and Pensions Act* 1999, Sch.11.]

(c) *Elements of the offence*

This section does not apply to cases where the benefit or other payment or advantage **16–226** is or relates to, or the failure to notify relates to tax credit: *Tax Credit Act* 1999, Sch.2

The prosecution must prove dishonesty.

The right to free legal advice under *PACE* Code C 3.15 will not apply to interviews conducted at the offices of the Benefits Agency: *R. (on the application of Secretary of State for Social Security) v South Central Division Magistrates, Daily Telegraph,* November 28, 2000, QBD.

(d) *Sentence*

When tried summarily, the maximum penalty for this offence is imprisonment for a **16–227** term not exceeding six months, a fine not exceeding the statutory maximum or both.

In *R. v Heath* [2003] EWCA Crim 2607 the defendant was aged 36. She was a mother of four children and was in receipt of income support, housing benefit and council tax benefit. She then obtained work as a cleaner in a cinema at weekends. Initially that was on a part-time basis and did not affect her entitlement to benefits; however, she later began working full-time without informing, as she should have done, the Benefits Agency. She was subsequently charged with three offences of making false statements to obtain benefits, contrary to s.111A of the *Social Security Administration Act* 1992, to which she pleaded guilty. Her original sentence of 12 months imprisonment was reduced on appeal. The Court substituted a sentence of five months imprisonment, given the net loss to the taxpayer, the early plea, the fact that initially her claims were lawful, and that there was no evidence pointing to luxurious living, indeed the reverse and having regard to the fact that she had four children to support.

For additional guidance on sentencing see *R. v Stewart* [1987] 2 All E.R. 383, CA, **16–228** but bearing in mind the warning issued by Mr Justice Mitchell in *Heath* (above) that it has of course to be remembered that £10,000 in 1987 is not worth the same today. In *Stewart*, relevant factors to be taken into account when sentencing for this offence included (1) a guilty plea; (2) the amount involved and the length of time over which the defalcations were persisted in; (3) the circumstances in which the offence began; (4) the use to which the money so obtained was put; (5) previous character; (6) matters special to the offender; and (7) any voluntary payment of the amounts overpaid.

B. FALSE REPRESENTATIONS FOR OBTAINING BENEFIT

(a) *Definition*

Social Security Administration Act 1992, s.112

False representations for obtaining benefit etc.

112.—(1) If a person for the purpose of obtaining any benefit or other payment under the **16–229** relevant social security legislation whether for himself or some other person, or for any other purpose connected with that legislation—

(a) makes a statement or representation which he knows to be false; or

(b) produces or furnishes, or knowingly causes or knowingly allows to be produced or furnished, any document or information which he knows to be false in a material particular, he shall be guilty of an offence.

(1A) A person shall be guilty of an offence if—

(a) there has been a change of circumstances affecting any entitlement of his to any benefit or other payment or advantage under any provision of the relevant social security legislation;

(b) the change is not a change that is excluded by regulations from the changes that are required to be notified;

(c) he knows that the change affects an entitlement of his to such a benefit or other payment or advantage; and

(d) he fails to give a prompt notification of that change in the prescribed manner to the prescribed person.

16–230   (1B) A person is guilty of an offence under this section if—

(a) there has been a change of circumstances affecting any entitlement of another person to any benefit or other payment or advantage under any provision of the relevant social security legislation;

(b) the change is not a change that is excluded by regulations from the changes that are required to be notified;

(c) he knows that the change affects an entitlement of that other person to such a benefit or other payment or advantage; and

(d) he causes or allows that other person to fail to give a prompt notification of that change in the prescribed manner to the prescribed person.

(1C) In a case where subsection (1C) of section 111A above applies, the recipient is guilty of an offence if—

(a) he knows that the change affects an entitlement of the claimant to a benefit or other payment or advantage under a provision of the relevant social security legislation;

(b) the entitlement is one in respect of which he has a right to receive payments to which the claimant has, or (but for the arrangements under which they are payable to the recipient) would have, an entitlement; and

(c) he fails to give a prompt notification of that change in the prescribed manner to the prescribed person.

(1D) In a case where that subsection applies, a person other than the recipient is guilty of an offence if—

(a) he knows that the change affects an entitlement of the claimant to a benefit or other payment or advantage under a provision of the relevant social security legislation;

(b) the entitlement is one in respect of which the recipient has a right to receive payments to which the claimant has, or (but for the arrangements under which they are payable to the recipient) would have, an entitlement; and

(c) he causes or allows the recipient to fail to give a prompt notification of that change in the prescribed manner to the prescribed person.

(1E) Subsection (1F) of section 111A above applies in relation to subsections (1C) and (1D) above as it applies in relation to subsections (1D) and (1E) of that section.

(1F) For the purposes of subsections (1A) to (1D) above a notification of a change is prompt if, and only if, it is given as soon as reasonably practicable after the change occurs.

(2) A person guilty of an offence under this section shall be liable on summary conviction to a fine not exceeding level 5 on the standard scale, or to imprisonment for a term not exceeding 3 months, or to both.

[This section is printed as amended by the *Social Security Administration (Fraud) Act* 1997, s.14 and Sch.1, the *Child Support, Pensions and Social Security Act* 2000, Sch.6 and the *Social Security Fraud Act* 2001, s.16(3).]

(b) *Procedure*

16–231   This offence is triable summarily. For provisions relating to the institution of legal proceedings, see s.116 of the 1992 Act, (above).

(c) *Elements of the offence*

16–232   This section does not apply to cases where the benefit or other payment or advantage is or relates to, or the failure to notify relates to tax credit: *Tax Credit Act* 1999, Sch.2.

It is not necessary to prove that the false statement was made with the intention to defraud the Department of Social Security. The offence is made out when it is proved that the defendant made a statement that he knew to be false: *DSS v Bavi* (1996) C.O.D. 260, QBD.

An applicant for housing benefit will be required to declare whether he was the registered owner of a property other than his main home. In *Fairbank v Lambeth Magistrates' Court* [2002] EWHC 785, QBD, the defendant's failure to do so constituted a false representation under the *Social Security Administration Act* 1992, s.112 notwithstanding his claim that he held the property on trust for another.

(d) *Sentence*

The maximum penalty for this offence is a fine not exceeding level five on the standard scale, imprisonment for a term not exceeding three months or both.   **16–233**

Sentencing guidelines can be found in the cases of *R. v Heath* and *R. v Stewart*, above.

XIII. STREET TRADING

A. Unlicensed Street Trading

(a) *Definition*

London Local Authorities Act 1990, s.38

38.—(1) A person who—   **16–234**
    (a) is not the holder of a street trading licence or a temporary licence and who engages in street trading in a borough; or
    (b) is the holder of a temporary licence and who engages in street trading in a borough on a day or in a place not specified in that temporary licence;
shall be guilty of an offence and shall be liable on summary conviction to a fine not exceeding level 3 on the standard scale.

(2) In any proceedings for an offence under this section or for an offence of aiding, abetting, counselling or procuring the commission of an offence under this section where it is shown that—
    (a) any article or thing was displayed (whether or not in or on any receptacle) in any street; or
    (b) any receptacle or equipment used in the provision of any service was available in any street in such circumstances that a service was being offered;
the article or thing shall be presumed to have been exposed or offered for sale and the receptacle or equipment shall be presumed to have been available for the provision of a service at such time and in such position as it was displayed or available by the person having care or control or appearing to have care and control thereof unless in either case, it is shown to the satisfaction of the court that the article or thing or receptacle or equipment was brought into that street for some purpose other than for the purpose of selling it or exposing or offering it for sale or using it in the course of the provision of the service in a street.

(3) Where an offence under this section committed by a body corporate is proved to have been committed with the consent or connivance of, or to be attributable to any neglect on the part of, any director, manager, secretary or other similar officer of the body corporate, or any person who was purporting to act in any such capacity, he, as well as the body corporate, shall be guilty of the offence and liable to the same maximum penalty as the body corporate.

(4) If an authorised officer or a constable has reasonable grounds for suspecting that a person has committed an offence under this section he may seize any article or thing being offered or exposed for sale or receptacle being used by that person which may be required to be used in evidence in any proceedings in respect of that offence or may be thesubject of forfeiture under subsection (5) below, provided that no article or thing which is of a perishable nature shall be seized under the provisions of this subsection.

(4A)

(a) The following provisions of this subsection shall have effect where any article or thing (including any receptacle) is seized under subsection (4) above and references in those provisions to proceedings are to proceedings in respect of the alleged offence in relation to which the article or thing is seized.

(b) Subject to paragraph (e) below, at the conclusion of the proceedings the article or thing shall be returned to the person from whom it was seized unless the court orders it to be forfeited under subsection (5) below.

(c) Subject to paragraph (d) below, where a receptacle seized under subsection (4) above is a motor vehicle used for ice cream trading, the borough council or the Commissioner of Police of the Metropolis (as the case may be) shall, within three days of the receipt of an application in writing by the owner or registered keeper of the vehicle, permit him to remove it.

(d) Paragraph (c) above shall not apply where—

   (i) the owner or registered keeper of the vehicle has been convicted of an offence under this Part of this Act; or

   (ii) the owner or registered keeper of the vehicle is being prosecuted for a previous alleged offence under this Part of this Act; or

   (iii) the vehicle has been used in the commission of such an offence or previous alleged offence;

if the offence or previous alleged offence was committed or is alleged to have been committed no more than three years before the seizure and (in the case of an alleged offence) the proceedings are continuing.

(e) If no proceedings are instituted before the expiration of a period of 28 days beginning with the date of seizure, or any proceedings instituted within that period are discontinued, at the expiration of that period or, as the case may be, on the discontinuance of the proceedings, the article or thing shall be returned to the person from whom it was seized unless it has not proved possible, after diligent enquiry, to identify that person and ascertain his address.

(f) Where the article or thing is not returned because it has not proved possible to identify the person from whom it was seized and ascertain his address the borough council (whether the article or thing was seized by a constable or by an authorised officer) may apply to a magistrates' court for an order as to the manner in which it should be dealt with.

16–235 (5) Subject to subsection (6) below the court by or before which a person is convicted of an offence under this section or for an offence of aiding, abetting, counselling or procuring the commission of an offence under this section may order anything produced to the court, and shown to the satisfaction of the court to relate to the offence, to be forfeited and dealt with in such manner as the court may order.

(6) The court shall not order anything to be forfeited under subsection (5) above where a person claiming to be the owner of or otherwise interested in it applies to be heard by the court, unless an opportunity has been given to him to show cause why the order should not be made and in considering whether to make such an order a court shall have regard—

   (i) to the value of the property; and

   (ii) to the likely financial and other effects on the offender of the making of the order (taken together with any other order that the court contemplates making).

(7) An authorised officer shall produce his authority if required to do so by the person having care or control of anything seized in pursuance of the powers in subsection (4) above.

16–236 (a) This subsection shall have effect where—

   (i) an article, thing or receptacle is seized under subsection (4) above; and

      (A) not less than six months have passed since the date of the seizure and no information has been laid against any person for an offence under this section in respect of the acts or circumstances which occasioned the seizure; or

      (B) proceedings for such an offence have been brought and either the person charged has been acquitted (whether or not on appeal) and the time for appealing against or challenging the acquittal

(where applicable) has expired without an appeal or challenge being brought, or the proceedings (including any appeal) have been
withdrawn by, or have failed for want of prosecution by, the person
by whom the original proceedings were brought.
  (b) When this subsection has effect a person who has or at the time of seizure had a
       legal interest in the article, thing or receptacle seized may recover compensation
       from the borough council or (where it is seized by a constable) the Commissioner
       of Police of the Metropolis by civil action in the County Court in respect of any
       loss suffered by him as a result of the seizure.
  (c) The court may not make an order for compensation under paragraph (b) above
       unless it is satisfied that seizure was not lawful under subsection (4) above.

[This section is printed as amended by the *London Local Authorities Act* 1994, s.6.]

(b) *Procedure*

This offence is triable summarily only: s.38(1).   **16–237**

(c) *Elements of the offence*

Unlicensed street trading can range from selling small items from a box or tray to   **16–238**
selling food from barbecues or braziers or ice-cream or hot-dogs from vans. Such trading is allowed but only under the control of licences issued by local authorities.
  Items used in illegal street trading can be seized in an effort to prevent further
offending. Perishables cannot be seized but grills and cooking utensils, vans and carts
can be removed and forfeiture proceedings be taken.
  In the case of ice-cream vans, the owner or keeper of the vehicle that has been seized
has a limited right to have the vehicle returned. If there is a history of offending in relation to the owner or the vehicle then forfeiture proceedings may follow. In such applications the owner of any goods subject to possible forfeiture must be given the opportunity
to attend court to show cause why the items should not be forfeited.
  The power to order forfeiture contained in subs.(5) only applies to goods produced
to the court. Goods can be produced to the court either by being brought physically
into the courtroom or by the making of arrangements for the court to view the goods.
Alternatively, in appropriate circumstances a written statement could be made under
the *Criminal Justice Act* 1967, s.9: *R. (on the application of London borough of Islington) v Jordan* (2002) 167 J.P. 1, DC. Where there is a late objection to the non-
production of the goods magistrates have power to adjourn the matter to some later
date to allow the item to be produced or to arrange to view the goods at some convenient occasion on the same or a future date (*ibid.*).

(d) *Sentence*

The maximum penalty for this offence is a fine not exceeding level 3 on the standard   **16–239**
scale: s.38(1).
  The court also has a power to forfeit the relevant goods under s.38(5).

XIV. TELEVISION LICENCES

The *Communications Act* 2003 covers the provision and regulation of electronic   **16–240**
communication networks and broadcasting. It also deals with the 'licensing of TV reception' in Part 4. Television receivers must be authorised for installation or use by a
licence.

(a) *Definition*

Communications Act 2003, ss.363–365

Licence required for use of TV receiver
  363.—(1) A television receiver must not be installed or used unless the installation and use of   **16–241**
the receiver is authorised by a licence under this Part.

(2) A person who installs or uses a television receiver in contravention of subsection (1) is guilty of an offence.

(3) A person with a television receiver in his possession or under his control who—

 (a) intends to install or use it in contravention of subsection (1), or

 (b) knows, or has reasonable grounds for believing, that another person intends to install or use it in contravention of that subsection,

is guilty of an offence.

(4) A person guilty of an offence under this section shall be liable, on summary conviction, to a fine not exceeding level 3 on the standard scale.

(5) Subsection (1) is not contravened by anything done in the course of the business of a dealer in television receivers solely for one or more of the following purposes—

 (a) installing a television receiver on delivery;

 (b) demonstrating, testing or repairing a television receiver.

(6) The Secretary of State may by regulations exempt from the requirement of a licence under subsection (1) the installation or use of television receivers—

 (a) of such descriptions,

 (b) by such persons,

 (c) in such circumstances, and

 (d) for such purposes,

as may be provided for in the regulations.

(7) Regulations under subsection (6) may make any exemption for which such regulations provide subject to compliance with such conditions as may be specified in the regulations.

TV licences

16–242   **364.**—(1) A licence for the purposes of section 363 ("a TV licence")—

 (a) may be issued by the BBC subject to such restrictions and conditions as the BBC think fit; and

 (b) must be issued subject to such restrictions and conditions as the Secretary of State may require by a direction to the BBC.

(2) The matters to which the restrictions and conditions subject to which a TV licence may be issued may relate include, in particular—

 (a) the description of television receivers that may be installed and used under the licence;

 (b) the persons authorised by the licence to install and use a television receiver;

 (c) the places where the installation and use of the television receiver is authorised by the licence;

 (d) the circumstances in which the installation and use of such a receiver is so authorised;

 (e) the purposes for which the installation and use of such a receiver is so authorised;

 (f) the use of such receiver in a manner that causes, or may cause, interference (within the meaning of the *Wireless Telegraphy Act* 1949) with wireless telegraphy.

(3) The restrictions and conditions subject to which a TV licence may be issued do not include—

 (a) a provision conferring a power of entry to any premises; or

 (b) a provision prohibited by a direction to the BBC by the Secretary of State.

(4) A TV licence shall continue in force, unless previously revoked by the BBC, for such period as may be specified in the licence.

(5) The BBC may revoke or modify a TV licence, or the restrictions or conditions of such a licence—

 (a) by a notice to the holder of the licence; or

 (b) by a general notice published in such manner as may be specified in the licence.

(6) It shall be the duty of the BBC to exercise their power under subsection (5) to revoke or modify a TV licence, or any of its restrictions or conditions, if they are directed to do so by the Secretary of State.

(7) A direction by the Secretary of State under this section may be given either generally in relation to all TV licences (or all TV licences of a particular description) or in relation to a particular licence.

(8) A notice under subsection (5)(a) must be given—

(a) in the manner specified in the licence; or

(b) if no manner of service is so specified, in the manner authorised by section 394.

(9) For the purposes of the application, in relation to the giving of such a notice, of—

(a) section 394; and

(b) section 7 of the *Interpretation Act* 1978 (service by post) in its application for the purposes of that section,

a person's proper address is any address where he is authorised by a TV licence to install or use a TV receiver or, if there is no such address, his last known address.

TV licence fees

365.—(1) A person to whom a TV licence is issued shall be liable to pay—   **16–243**

(a) on the issue of the licence (whether initially or by way of renewal), and

(b) in such other circumstances as regulations made by the Secretary of State may provide,

such sum (if any) as may be provided for by any such regulations.

(2) Sums which a person is liable to pay by virtue of regulations under subsection (1) must be paid to the BBC and are to be recoverable by them accordingly.

(3) The BBC are entitled, in such cases as they may determine, to make refunds of sums received by them by virtue of regulations under this section.

(4) Regulations under this section may include provision—

(a) for the means by which an entitlement to a concession must be established; and

(b) for the payment of sums by means of an instalment scheme set out in the regulations.

(5) The reference to a concession in subsection (4) is a reference to any concession under which a person is, on the satisfaction of specified requirements—

(a) exempted from the liability to pay a sum in respect of a TV licence; or

(b) required to pay only a reduced sum in respect of such a licence.

(6) The consent of the Treasury shall be required for the making of any regulations under this section by the Secretary of State.

(7) Subject to subsection (8), sums received by the BBC by virtue of any regulations under this section must be paid into the Consolidated Fund.

(8) The BBC may retain, out of the sums received by them by virtue of regulations under this section, any sums they require for making refunds of sums so received.

(b) *Procedure*

The offence is triable summarily only.   **16–244**

The procedure where the offence is committed by a body corporate is contained in s.404 of the *Communications Act* 2003.

Communications Act 2003, s.404

Criminal liability of company directors etc.

404.—(1) Where an offence under any enactment to which this section applies is committed   **16–245** by a body corporate and is proved to have been committed with the consent or connivance of, or to be attributable to any neglect on the part of—

(a) a director, manager, secretary or other similar officer of the body corporate, or

(b) a person who was purporting to act in any such capacity,

he (as well as the body corporate) is guilty of that offence and shall be liable to be proceeded against and punished accordingly.

(2) Where an offence under any enactment to which this section applies—

(a) is committed by a Scottish firm, and

(b) is proved to have been committed with the consent or connivance of, or to be attributable to any neglect on the part of a partner of the firm,

he (as well as the firm) is guilty of that offence and shall be liable to be proceeded against and punished accordingly.

(3) In this section "director", in relation to a body corporate whose affairs are managed by its members, means a member of the body corporate.

(4) The enactments to which this section applies are every enactment contained in—
(a) this Act;
(b) the *Wireless Telegraphy Act* 1949;
(c) the *Marine, etc.,Broadcasting (Offences) Act* 1967;
(d) the *Wireless Telegraphy Act* 1967; or
(e) the *Telecommunications Act* 1984.

(5) Section 14(2) of the *Wireless Telegraphy Act* 1949 (which is superseded by this section) shall cease to have effect.

(c) *Elements of the offence*

16–246   This Act replaces the provisions of the *Wireless Telegraphy Act* 1949 in so far as it applied to licences for television sets. Relevant regulations came into force on April 1, 2004 in the *Communications (Television Licensing) Regulations* 2004 (SI 2004/692). Interpretation of the various terms used in the statute are found in the Act itself.

Communications Act 2003, ss.367–368

Interpretation of provisions about dealer notification
16–247   **367.**—(1) Section 6 of the *Wireless Telegraphy Act* 1967 (interpretation of provisions requiring notification of sale and hire of television sets) shall be amended as follows.

(2) In subsection (1), for the definitions of "television dealer", "television programme" and "television set" there shall be substituted—

"television dealer" means a person of any description specified in regulations made by the Secretary of State setting out the descriptions of persons who are to be television dealers for the purposes of this Part;
"television set" means any apparatus of a description specified in regulations made by the Secretary of State setting out the descriptions of apparatus that are to be television sets for the purposes of this Part.

(3) After that subsection there shall be inserted—

(1A) Regulations under subsection (1) defining a television set may provide for references to such a set to include references to software used in association with apparatus.

Meanings of "television receiver" and "use"
16–248   **368.**—(1) In this Part "television receiver" means any apparatus of a description specified in regulations made by the Secretary of State setting out the descriptions of apparatus that are to be television receivers for the purposes of this Part.

(2) Regulations under this section defining a television receiver may provide for references to such a receiver to include references to software used in association with apparatus.

(3) References in this Part to using a television receiver are references to using it for receiving television programmes.

(4) The power to make regulations under this section defining a television receiver includes power to modify subsection (3).

16–249   The definition of a television receiver is found in regulation 9.

Communications (Television Licensing) Regulations 2004, reg.9

Meaning of "television receiver"
9.—(1) In Part 4 of the Act (licensing of TV reception), "television receiver" means any apparatus installed or used for the purpose of receiving (whether by means of wireless telegraphy or otherwise) any television programme service, whether or not it is installed or used for any other purpose.

(2) In this regulation, any reference to receiving a television programme service includes a reference to receiving by any means any programme included in that service, where that programme is received at the same time (or virtually the same time) as it is received by members of the public by virtue of its being broadcast or distributed as part of that service.

16–250   A television licence applies to the specified location recorded on the licence and authorises the person living there or anyone else living at the premises or visiting or working there to install and use either black and white or colour television sets at that address. The location may include not only premises but also a vehicle, vessel or caravan. The regulations set the amount of the fees and also provide for concessions in certain circumstances.

The offences are those of using or installing the receiver, or of intending to use or install it or knowing that someone else intends to use or install it. This dispenses with the need for the prosecution to prove that the television receiver was actually being used without a licence but still requires the intention to be proved.

(d) *Defence*

Section 363(5) exempts television dealers from having a licence where the receiver is **16–251** being installed on delivery or the receiver is being demonstrated, tested or repaired.

(e) *Powers to enforce*

Communications Act 2003, s.366

Powers to enforce TV licensing
366.—(1) If a justice of the peace, a sheriff in Scotland or a lay magistrate in Northern **16–252** Ireland is satisfied by information on oath that there are reasonable grounds for believing—
    (a) that an offence under section 363 has been or is being committed,
    (b) that evidence of the commission of the offence is likely to be on premises specified in the information, or in a vehicle so specified, and
    (c) that one or more of the conditions set out in subsection (3) is satisfied,
he may grant a warrant under this section.

    (2) A warrant under this section is a warrant authorising any one or more persons authorised for the purpose by the BBC or by OFCOM—
    (a) to enter the premises or vehicle at any time (either alone or in the company of one or more constables); and
    (b) to search the premises or vehicle and examine and test any television receiver found there.

    (3) Those conditions are—
    (a) that there is no person entitled to grant entry to the premises or vehicle with whom it is practicable to communicate;
    (b) that there is no person entitled to grant access to the evidence with whom it is practicable to communicate;
    (c) that entry to the premises or vehicle will not be granted unless a warrant is produced;
    (d) that the purpose of the search may be frustrated or seriously prejudiced unless the search is carried out by a person who secures entry immediately upon arriving at the premises or vehicle.

    (4) A person is not to enter premises or a vehicle in pursuance of a warrant under this section at any time more than one month after the day on which the warrant was granted.

    (5) The powers conferred by a warrant under this section on a person authorised by OFCOM are exercisable in relation only to a contravention or suspected contravention of a condition of a TV licence relating to interference with wireless telegraphy.

    (6) A person authorised by the BBC, or by OFCOM, to exercise a power conferred by a warrant under this section may (if necessary) use such force as may be reasonable in the exercise of that power.

    (7) Where a person has the power by virtue of a warrant under this section to examine or test any television receiver found on any premises, or in any vehicle, it shall be the duty—
    (a) of a person who is on the premises or in the vehicle, and
    (b) in the case of a vehicle, of a person who has charge of it or is present when it is searched,
to give the person carrying out the examination or test all such assistance as that person may reasonably require for carrying it out.

(8) A person is guilty of an offence if he—
    (a) intentionally obstructs a person in the exercise of any power conferred on that person by virtue of a warrant under this section; or
    (b) without reasonable excuse, fails to give any assistance that he is under a duty to give by virtue of subsection (7).

(9) A person guilty of an offence under subsection (8) shall be liable, on summary conviction, to a fine not exceeding level 5 on the standard scale.

(10) In this section—
"interference", in relation to wireless telegraphy, has the same meaning as in the *Wireless Telegraphy Act* 1949; and
"vehicle" includes vessel, aircraft or hovercraft.

(11) In the application of this section to Scotland, the reference in subsection (1) to information on oath shall have effect as a reference to evidence on oath.

(12) In the application of this section to Northern Ireland, the reference in subsection (1) to a lay magistrate shall have effect, in relation to times before the coming into force of sections 9 and 10 of the *Justice (Northern Ireland) Act* 2002, as a reference to a justice of the peace.

Warrants of entry and search of premises may be granted together with a power to test equipment found there. The conditions of the section must be met and it is an offence intentionally to obstruct or fail to assist any person executing the warrant.

(f) *Sentence*

16–253   The maximum penalty is a fine not exceeding level 3.

XV. VIDEO RECORDINGS

A. Supplying Video Recordings of Unclassified Work

(a) *Definition*

Video Recordings Act 1984, s.9

Supplying video recording of unclassified work

16–254   **9.**—(1) A person who supplies or offers to supply a video recording containing a video work in respect of which no classification certificate has been issued is guilty of an offence unless—
    (a) the supply is, or would if it took place be, an exempted supply, or
    (b) the video work is an exempted work.

(2) It is a defence to a charge of committing an offence under this section to prove that the accused believed on reasonable grounds—
    (a) that the video work concerned or, if the video recording contained more than one work to which the charge relates, each of those works was either an exempted work or a work in respect of which a classification certificate had been issued, or
    (b) that the supply was, or would if it took place be, an exempted supply by virtue of section 3(4) or (5) of this Act.

(3) A person guilty of an offence under this section shall be liable—
    (a) on conviction on indictment, to imprisonment for a term not exceeding two years or a fine or both,
    (b) on summary conviction, to imprisonment for a term not exceeding six months or a fine not exceeding £20,000 or both.

[This section is printed as amended by the *Criminal Justice and Public Order Act* 1994, s.88.]

(b) *Procedure*

16–255   This offence is triable either way: s.9(3).

Video Recordings Act 1984, s.15

Time limit for prosecutions

15.—(1) No prosecution for an offence under this Act shall be brought after the expiry of the **16–256** period of three years beginning with the date of the commission of the offence or one year beginning with the date of its discovery by the prosecutor, whichever is earlier.

(2) In Scotland, the reference in subsection (1) above to the date of discovery by the prosecutor shall be construed as a reference to the date on which evidence sufficient in the opinion of the Lord Advocate to warrant proceedings came to his knowledge.

(3) For the purposes of subsection (2) above—

(a) a certificate signed by the Lord Advocate or on his behalf and stating the date on which evidence came to his knowledge shall be conclusive evidence of that fact;

(b) a certificate purporting to be signed as mentioned in paragraph (a) above shall be presumed to be so signed unless the contrary is proved; and

(c) a prosecution shall be deemed to be brought on the date on which a warrant to apprehend or to cite the accused is granted provided that the warrant is executed without undue delay.

[This section is printed as substituted by the *Criminal Justice and Public Order Act* 1994, Sch.10.]

Video Recordings Act 1984, s.16

Offences by bodies corporate

16.—(1) Where an offence under this Act committed by a body corporate is proved to have **16–257** been committed with the consent or connivance of, or to be attributable to any neglect on the part of, any director, manager, secretary or other similar officer of the body corporate, or any person who was purporting to act in any such capacity, he as well as the body corporate shall be guilty of the offence and shall be liable to be proceeded against and punished accordingly.

(2) Where the affairs of a body corporate are managed by its members, subsection (1) above shall apply in relation to the acts and defaults of a member in connection with his functions of management as if he were a director of the body corporate.

(c) *Defence*

Video Recordings Act 1984, s.14A

14A. Without prejudice to any defence specified in the preceding provisions of this Act in re- **16–258** lation to a particular offence, it is a defence to a charge of committing any offence under this Act to prove—

(a) that the commission of the offence was due to the act or default of a person other than the accused, and

(b) that the accused took all reasonable precautions and exercised all due diligence to avoid the commission of the offence by any person under his control.

In *Bilon v WH Smith Trading Limited* (2001) 165 J.P. 701, QBD, the defendant had supplied a video recording in respect of which no classification certificate had been issued. The recording had been in the form of a CD Rom attached to the cover of a magazine which had been supplied to the defendant by a long standing supplier. The defendant relied on the statutory defence contained in the *Video Recordings Act* 1984, s.14A(b), contending that it had taken all reasonable precautions and had exercised all due diligence. The Court held that they were entitled to rely on the defence of due diligence, despite having taken no positive steps to avoid the commission of the offence. Under s.14A(b) of the 1984 Act, the retailer merely had to show that he had acted without negligence. The defendant had traded with the supplier for 20 years, the supplier was a reputable publisher, and had supplied the defendant with discs previously without any cause for concern. In all the circumstances, it had not been negligent for the defendant to rely on the supplier not to supply a disc and magazine without the defendant having first ensured that the disc had obtained the necessary classification certificate.

(d) *Sentence*

16–259 When tried summarily the maximum penalty for this offence is imprisonment for a term not exceeding six months, a fine not exceeding the £20,000 or both: s.9(3)(b).

Video Recordings Act 1984, s.21

Forfeiture

16–260 21.—(1) Where a person is convicted of any offence under this Act, the court may order any video recording—

(a) produced to the court, and

(b) shown to the satisfaction of the court to relate to the offence,

to be forfeited.

(2) The court shall not order any video recording to be forfeited under subsection (1) above if a person claiming to be the owner of it or otherwise interested in it applies to be heard by the court, unless an opportunity has been given to him to show cause why the order should not be made.

(3) References in this section to a video recording include a reference to any spool, case or other thing on or in which the recording is kept.

(4) An order made under subsection (1) above in any proceedings in England and Wales or Northern Ireland shall not take effect until the expiration of the ordinary time within which an appeal may be instituted or, where such an appeal is duly instituted, until the appeal is finally decided or abandoned; and for this purpose—

(a) an application for a case to be stated or for leave to appeal shall be treated as the institution of an appeal; and

(b) where a decision on appeal is subject to a further appeal, the appeal is not finally decided until the expiration of the ordinary time within which a further appeal may be instituted or, where a further appeal is duly instituted, until the further appeal is finally decided or abandoned.

(5) [*Scotland*]

B. POSSESSION OF VIDEO RECORDINGS OF UNCLASSIFIED WORK FOR THE PURPOSES OF SUPPLY

(a) *Definition*

Video Recordings Act 1984, s.10

Possession of video recording of unclassified work for the purposes of supply

16–261 10.—(1) Where a video recording contains a video work in respect of which no classification certificate has been issued, a person who has the recording in his possession for the purpose of supplying it is guilty of an offence unless—

(a) he has it in his possession for the purpose only of a supply which, if it took place, would be an exempted supply, or

(b) the video work is an exempted work.

(2) It is a defence to a charge of committing an offence under this section to prove—

(a) that the accused believed on reasonable grounds that the video work concerned or, if the video recording contained more than one work to which the charge relates, each of those works was either an exempted work or a work in respect of which a classification certificate had been issued,

(b) that the accused had the video recording in his possession for the purpose only of a supply which he believed on reasonable grounds would, if it took place, be an exempted supply by virtue of section 3(4) or (5) of this Act, or

(c) that the accused did not intend to supply the video recording until a classification certificate had been issued in respect of the video work concerned.

(3) A person guilty of an offence under this section shall be liable—

(a) on conviction on indictment, to imprisonment for a term not exceeding two years or a fine or both,

(b) on summary conviction, to imprisonment for a term not exceeding six months or a fine not exceeding £20,000 or both.

[This section is printed as amended by the *Criminal Justice and Public Order Act 1994*, s.88.]

(b) *Procedure*

This offence is triable either way: s.10(3). The provisions as to time limits for proceed- **16–262** ings and offences by corporations detailed above apply to charges under this section.

(c) *Defences*

The defence established by s.14A of the 1984 Act (above) is applicable to a charge **16–263** under this section.

(d) *Sentence*

When tried summarily the maximum penalty for this offence is imprisonment for a **16–264** term not exceeding six months, a fine not exceeding the £20, 000 or both: s.9(3)(b). The provisions regarding forfeiture detailed above are applicable to a charge under this section.

C. SUPPLYING A VIDEO RECORDING OF CLASSIFIED WORK IN BREACH OF CLASSIFICATION

(a) *Definition*

Video Recordings Act 1984, s.11

Supplying video recording of classified work in breach of classification

11.—(1) Where a classification certificate issued in respect of a video work states that no video **16–265** recording containing that work is to be supplied to any person who has not attained the age specified in the certificate, a person who supplies or offers to supply a video recording contain- ing that work to a person who has not attained the age so specified is guilty of an offence unless the supply is, or would if it took place be, an exempted supply.

(2) It is a defence to a charge of committing an offence under this section to prove—
    (a) that the accused neither knew nor had reasonable grounds to believe that the classification certificate contained the statement concerned,
    (b) that the accused neither knew nor had reasonable grounds to believe that the person concerned had not attained that age, or
    (c) that the accused believed on reasonable grounds that the supply was, or would if it took place be, an exempted supply by virtue of section 3(4) or (5) of this Act.

(3) A person guilty of an offence under this section shall be liable, on summary convic- tion, to imprisonment for a term not exceeding six months or a fine not exceeding level 5 on the standard scale or both.

[This section is printed as amended by the *Criminal Justice and Public Order Act 1994*, s.88.]

(b) *Procedure*

This offence is triable summarily: s.11(3). The provisions as to time limits for proceed- **16–266** ings and offences by corporations detailed above apply to charges under this section.

(c) *Elements of the offence*

The offence consists of supplying a classified video to a person under the specified **16–267** age. A Trading Standards Officer instructed his son, who was under 18 to go and buy a video meant for over 18s for the purposes of an investigation.The defence claimed that the boy's evidence should be inadmissible. The court held that in the absence of any evidence that the witness was acting as an 'agent provocateur' his evidence was admissible: *Ealing London Borough v Woolworths Plc* [1995] Crim.L.R. 58.

(d) *Defences*

16–268   The defence established by s.14A of the 1984 Act, above, is applicable to a charge under this section.

(e) *Sentence*

16–269   The maximum penalty for this offence is imprisonment for a term not exceeding six months, a fine of level five on the standard scale or both: s.11(3). The provisions regarding forfeiture detailed above are applicable to a charge under this section.

CORRUPTION OFFENCES

I. INTRODUCTION

The law in this area is soon to be reformed. Building on the Law Commission report **17–1** *Legislating the Criminal Code: Corruption (Law Com No 248, 1998)* the Government plans to replace the overlapping and occasionally inconsistent provisions on corruption with a single, clear statute. The draft Corruption Bill which was published in 2003 (Cm 5777) would have removed the presumption of corruption contained in s.2 of the *Prevention of Corruption Act* 1916, see below, the subject of a possible incompatibility with the ECHR. The Bill also acted on a recommendation from the Joint Committee on Parliamentary Privilege as regards evidence in corruption cases (HL Paper 43 and HC 214, March 1999, para.167).

The main changes which would have been brought about by the 2003 Bill included **17–2** the creation of three new offences; corruptly conferring an advantage, corruptly obtaining an advantage and performing functions corruptly. The draft Bill also offered a definition of the term 'conferring an advantage' which would have covered both acts and omissions, and a definition of the term 'conferring an advantage corruptly.' The draft Bill also established a statutory definition of 'corruptly' and created exceptions to the new offences which would have precluded a finding of corruption where the relevant reward was conferred by someone acting on behalf of a principal or the public, or where an agent's principal agent's principal knew of all the material circumstances surrounding the conferring of the advantage and gave his consent (the latter not applying where the principal's functions are for the benefit of the public.) Statutory definitions of 'corruptly' in the context of obtaining an advantage, and of 'performing functions as an agent corruptly' were featured in the draft legislation, and the terms 'agent' and 'principal' were put on a statutory basis. The draft Bill would also have provided that evidence could be adduced of Parliamentary proceedings in allegations of corruption, implementing a recommendation made by the Joint Committee on Parliamentary Privilege (HL Paper 43 and HC 214, March 1999, para.167). See Joint Committee on the Draft Corruption Bill (HL Paper 157, HC 705).

However, at the time of publication of this work, a Corruption Bill has yet to be laid before Parliament. The UK signed the UN Convention against Corruption on December 9, 2003.

II. THE CURRENT LAW

A. CORRUPTION IN A PUBLIC OFFICE

(a) *Definition*

Public Bodies Corrupt Practices Act 1889, ss.1, 2

Corruption in office a misdemeanor.

1.—(1) Every person who shall by himself or by or in conjunction with any other person, cor- **17–3**

ruptly solicit or receive, or agree to receive, for himself, or for any other person, any gift, loan, fee, reward, or advantage whatever as an inducement to, or reward for, or otherwise on account of any member, officer, or servant of a public body as in this Act defined, doing or forbearing to do anything in respect of any matter or transaction whatsoever, actual or proposed, in which the said public body is concerned, shall be guilty of a misdemeanour.

(2) Every person who shall by himself or by or in conjunction with any other person corruptly give, promise, or offer any gift, loan, fee, reward, or advantage whatsoever to any person, whether for the benefit of that person or of another person, as an inducement to or reward for or otherwise on account of any member, officer, or servant of any public body as in this Act defined, doing or forbearing to do anything in respect of any matter or transaction whatsoever, actual or proposed, in which such public body as aforesaid is concerned, shall be guilty of a misdemeanour.

Penalty for offences

17–4   **2.** Any person on conviction for offending as aforesaid shall, at the discretion of the court before which he is convicted,

     (a) be liable

         (i)   on summary conviction, to imprisonment for a term not exceeding 6 months or to a fine not exceeding the statutory maximum, or to both; and

         (ii)   on conviction on indictment, to imprisonment for a term not exceeding 7 years or to a fine, or to both; and

     (b) in addition be liable to be ordered to pay to such body, and in such manner as the court directs, the amount or value of any gift, loan, fee, or reward received by him or any part thereof; and

     (c) be liable to be adjudged incapable of being elected or appointed to any public office for five years from the date of his conviction, and to forfeit any such office held by him at the time of his conviction; and

     (d) in the event of a second conviction for a like offence he shall, in addition to the foregoing penalties, be liable to be adjudged to be for ever incapable of holding any public office, and to be incapable for five years of being registered as an elector, or voting at an election either of members to serve in Parliament or of members of any public body, and the enactments for preventing the voting and registration of persons declared by reason of corrupt practices to be incapable of voting shall apply to a person adjudged in pursuance of this section to be incapable of voting; and

     (e) if such person is an officer or servant in the employ of any public body upon such conviction he shall, at the discretion of the court, be liable to forfeit his right and claim to any compensation or pension to which he would otherwise have been entitled.

[This section is printed as amended by the *Representation of the People Act* 1948, ss.52(7) and 80 and the *CJA* 1988, s.47.]

(b) *Procedure*

17–5   This offence is triable either way: s.2(a). No proceedings may be instituted without the consent of the Attorney-General: *Public Bodies Corrupt Practices Act* 1889, s.4.

The prosecution must prove that:

— the defendant, by himself or with any other person;

— corruptly solicited or received, or agreed to receive;

— for himself or any other person;

— any gift, loan, fee, reward or advantage;

— as an inducement to, or reward for or otherwise on account of any member, officer or servant of a public body;

— doing or forbearing from doing anything in respect of any matter or transaction proposed in which the said public body is concerned.

Or, the prosecution must prove that:

— the defendant, by himself or with any other person;

— corruptly gave, promised or offered;

— any gift, loan, fee, reward or advantage whatsoever to any person;
— as an inducement to or reward for or otherwise on account for any member, officer or servant of any public body;
— doing or forbearing to do anything in respect of any matter or transaction proposed in which the said public body is concerned.

(c) *Elements of the offence*

Prevention of Corruption Act 1916, s.7

Interpretation.

7. In this Act—   **17–6**

The expression "public body" means any council of a county or county of a city or town, any council of a municipal borough, also any board, commissioners, select vestry, or other body which has power to act under and for the purposes of any Act relating to local government, or the public health, or to poor law or otherwise to administer money raised by rates in pursuance of any public general Act, [and includes any body which exists in a country or territory outside the United Kingdom and is equivalent to any body described above:

The expression "public office" means any office or employment of a person as a member, officer, or servant of such public body:

The expression "person" includes a body of persons, corporate or unincorporate:

The expression "advantage" includes any office or dignity, and any forbearance to demand any money or money's worth or valuable thing, and includes any aid, vote, consent, or influence, or pretended aid, vote, consent, or influence, and also includes any promise or procurement of or agreement or endeavour to procure, or the holding out of any expectation of any gift, loan, fee, reward, or advantage, as before defined.

[This section is printed as amended by the *Anti-terrorism, Crime and Security Act* 2001, s.108(3).]

'*Corruptly*'

The word "corruptly" as used in the Act denotes that the person making the offer did **17–7** so deliberately and with the intention that the person to whom it was addressed should enter into a corrupt bargain: *R. v Smith* [1960] 2 Q.B. 423, CA.

The *Prevention of Corruption Act* 1916, s.2 creates a presumption of corruption.

Prevention of Corruption Act 1916, s.2

Presumption of corruption in certain cases.

2. Where in any proceedings against a person for an offence under the *Prevention of Cor-* **17–8** *ruption Act* 1906, or the *Public Bodies Corrupt Practices Act* 1889, it is proved that any money, gift, or other consideration has been paid or given to or received by a person in the employment of His Majesty or any Government Department or a public body by or from a person, or agent of a person, holding or seeking to obtain a contract from His Majesty or any Government Department or public body, the money, gift, or consideration shall be deemed to have been paid or given and received corruptly as such inducement or reward as is mentioned in such Act unless the contrary is proved.

This section has no application in relation to anything which would not be an offence apart from ss.108 and 109 of the *Anti-Terrorism, Crime and Security Act* 2001; s.110 of the 2001 Act.

In *R. v Braithwaite* (1983) 77 Cr.App.R. 34, CA, Lord Lane C.J. offered guidance as **17–9** to the operation of the presumption created by s.2:

'when the matters in that section have been fulfilled, the burden of proof is lifted from the shoulders of the prosecution and descends upon the shoulders of the defence. It then becomes necessary for the defendant to show, on a balance of probabilities, that what was going on was not reception corruptly as inducement or reward. In an appropriate case it is the Judge's duty to direct the jury first of all that they must decide whether they are satisfied so as to feel sure that the defendant received money or gift or consideration, and then to go on to direct them that if they are so satisfied, then under section 2 of the 1916 Act the burden of proof shifts.' (at p.38)

17–9.2   In *R. v Mills* (1979) 68 Cr.App.R. 154, CA, it was held that the presumption can be rebutted only by evidence of an innocent explanation, supported by evidence, established on the balance of probabilities.

'Reward'

17–10   The offence under s.1 of the *Public Bodies Corrupt Practices Act* 1889 lies not in showing favour to the application but in accepting a reward for doing so, hence corruption includes the receipt of money for a past favour without any prior agreement, and the words 'doing or forbearing to do' are applicable both to past and future conduct: *R. v Parker* (1986) 82 Cr.App.R. 69, CA; *R. v Andrews Weatherfoil Ltd* [1972] 1 W.L.R. 118, CA.

(d) *Sentence*

17–10.1   When tried summarily, the maximum penalty is six months imprisonment, a fine not exceeding the statutory maximum or both: *Public Bodies Corrupt Practices Act* 1889, s.2.

17–11   In *R. v Bennet and Wilson* [1996] 1 Cr.App.R.(S.) 162 the offenders were convicted respectively of receiving and giving a bribe on two occasions. The first offender was employed in a Government Department responsible for the procurement of publicity material, the second was managing director of a group of companies involved in supplying printing work to the department. Their original sentences of nine months imprisonment each were substituted by sentences of four months' imprisonment by the Court of Appeal, the Court affirming the propriety of a custodial sentence in cases of corruption. A sentence of three months' imprisonment was imposed in *R. v Ozdemir* (1985) 7 Cr.App.R.(S.) 382, CA, where the appellant was convicted of corruption after being stopped whilst in the passenger seat of a car driven by his 14-year-old son. When the police officer indicated that the boy would be reported for driving without a licence, O offered him £50 for a free meal at O's restaurant not to do so. The Court of Appeal were influenced by the fact that the appellant was a man of good character, the bribe involved only a small sum and the offence he was seeking to avoid by offering the bribe related to his son, not directly to him.

17–12   In *R. v Dearnley* [2001] 2 Cr.App.R.(S.) 42, CA, the appellants were convicted of corruption. The first appellant was employed by a Metropolitan council with responsibility for property management. The second appellant's companies provided security services to the council over a period of several years. The second appellant supplied to the first appellant a car valued at £5,445. The first appellant secured a loan from the council to pay for the car, and used the money so obtained to clear debts. Their original sentences of 18 months' imprisonment were reduced to 10 months' imprisonment by the Court of Appeal, Rafferty J. stating that

> "it is seldom a surprise when corrupt individuals prove to be of hitherto good character. Were it otherwise they would, in general, not be in a position from which to behave in a fashion which strikes at the principle of fair competition. Public confidence in people such as these appellants is undermined, irrespective of the amounts pocketed by an individual, by virtue of the evil which is corruption. Custody is inevitable; it is rightly seen as a deterrent to those tempted to depart from their usual scrupulous standards." (at para.H4)

B. Corruption of Agents

(a) *Definition*

Prevention of Corruption Act 1906, s.1

Punishment of corrupt of transactions with agents

17–13   **1.**—(1) If any agent corruptly accepts or obtains, or agrees to accept or attempts to obtain, from any person, for himself or for any other person, any gift or consideration as an inducement or reward for doing or for bearing to do, or for having after the passing of this Act done or forborne to do, any act in relation to his principal's affairs or business, or for showing or forbearing to show favour or disfavour to any person in relation to his principal's affairs or business; or

If any person corruptly gives or agrees to given or offers any gift or consideration to any agent as an inducement or reward for doing or forbearing to do, or for having after the passing of this Act done or forborne to do, any act in relation to this principal's affairs or business, or for showing or forbearing to show favour or disfavour to any person in relation to his principal's affairs or business; or

If any person knowingly gives to any agent, or if any agent knowingly uses with intent to deceive his principal, any receipt, account, or other document in respect of which the principal is interested, and which contains any statement which is false or erroneous or defective in any material particular, and which to his knowledge is intended to mislead the principal:

he shall be guilty of a misdemeanour, and shall be liable—

   (a) on summary conviction, to imprisonment for a term not exceeding 6 months or to a fine not exceeding the statutory maximum, or to both; and

   (b) on conviction on indictment, to imprisonment for a term not exceeding 7 years or to a fine, or to both.

(2) For the purposes of this Act the expression "consideration" includes valuable consideration of any kind; the expression "agent" includes any person employed by or acting for another; and the expression "principal" includes an employer

(3) A person serving under the Crown or under any corporation or any, borough, county, or district council, or any board of guardians, is an agent within the meaning of this Act.

(4) For the purposes of this Act it is immaterial if—

   (a) the principal's affairs or business have no connection with the United Kingdom and are conducted in a country or territory outside the United Kingdom;

   (b) the agent's functions have no connection with the United Kingdom and are carried out in a country or territory outside the United Kingdom

[This section is printed as amended by the *CJA* 1988, s.47 and the *Anti-Terrorism, Crime and Security Act* 2001, s.108(4); and as repealed in part by the *Local Authorities, etc. (Miscellaneous Provisions) (No.2) Order* 1974 (SI 1974/595). The amendment effected by the 2001 Act (insertion of subs.(4)) took effect on February 14, 2002: *Anti terrorism, Crime and Security Act 2001 (Commencement No.3) Order* 2002 (SI 2002/228).]

(b) *Procedure*

This offence is triable either way. No proceedings may be instituted without the **17–14** consent of the Attorney-General: *Prevention of Corruption Act* 1906, s.2.

The prosecution must prove that:

— the defendant corruptly accepted or obtained, or agreed to accept or attempted to obtain.

— from any other person;

— for himself or for any other person;

— any gift or consideration as an inducement or reward;

— for doing or forbearing to do any act in relation to his principal's affairs or business or for showing or forbearing to show favour or disfavour to any person in relation to his principal's affairs or business.

OR　　　　　　　　　　　　　　　　　　　　　　　　　　　　　　　　　**17–14.1**

— the defendant corruptly gave or agreed to give or offered;

— any gift or consideration;

— to any agent;

— as an inducement or reward;

— for doing or forbearing to do any act in relation to his principal's affairs or business or for showing or forbearing to show favour or disfavour to any person in relation to his principal's affairs or business.

OR
- the defendant knowingly gave to any agent, or any agent knowingly uses with intent to deceive his principal;
- any receipt, account or other document in respect of which the principal is interested
- which contains any statement which is false or erroneous or defective in any material particular
- which is, to his knowledge intended to mislead the principal.

(c) Elements of the offence

'Agent'

17–15   Whether someone is 'serving under the Crown' will not be determined by looking to whether he is employed by the Crown, but by looking at whether the duties he performs are on behalf of the Crown, and necessary for the Crown to exercise its functions through some human agency: *R. v Barrett*, 63 Cr.App.R.174, CA.

'Corruptly'

17–16   See generally, above.

'Consideration'

17–17   The word "consideration" has to be given its legal meaning which indicates that there was a contract or bargain of some kind between the parties which has to be contrasted with the word "gift" which envisages no such contract between the parties and therefore no consideration: *R. v Braithwaite* [1983] 2 All E.R. 87, CA.

'In relation to his principal's affairs'

17–18   The words "any act in relation to his principal's affairs" should be widely construed, and it is not necessary that the corrupt consideration should be received as an agent: *Morgan v DPP* [1970] 3 All E.R. 1053, QBD.

Document intended to deceive principal

17–19   The first two paragraphs of s.1(1) refer to dishonest conduct by an employee with a third party affecting the employer. Since the ordinary meaning of "receipt" and "account" in the third paragraph refers to documents inter partes, the words "or other document" on their true construction also refer to documents passing *inter partes*. They does not apply to a internal document which had never been intended to go to a third party and had not come from one: *R. v Tweedie* [1984] Q.B. 729, CA.

Prevention of Corruption Act 1916, s.4

Short title and interpretation.

17–20   **4.**—(1) This Act may be cited as the *Prevention of Corruption Act* 1916, and the *Public Bodies Corrupt Practices Act* 1889, the *Prevention of Corruption Act* 1906, and this Act may be cited together as the Prevention of Corruption Acts 1889 to 1916.

(2) In this Act and in the *Public Bodies Corrupt Practices Act* 1889, the expression "public body" includes, in addition to the bodies mentioned in the last-mentioned Act, local and public authorities of all descriptions (including authorities existing in a country or territory outside the United Kingdom).

(3) A person serving under any such public body is an agent within the meaning of the *Prevention of Corruption Act* 1906, and the expressions "agent" and "consideration" in this Act have the same meaning as in the *Prevention of Corruption Act* 1906, as amended by this Act.

[This section in printed as amended by the *Anti-terrorism, Crime and Security Act* 2001, s.108(4).]

(d) Sentence

17–21   When tried summarily, the maximum penalty for this offence is six months imprisonment, a fine not exceeding the statutory maximum or both: *Prevention of Corruption Act* 1906, s.1(1)(b).

In *R. v Wilcox* (1995) 16. Cr.App.R.(S.) 197 the offender pleaded guilty to conspiring to act corruptly, having received £32,000 in respect of the renewal of contracts by the company for whom he worked with another company. He had not however, used any improper influence to secure the renewal of the contract and had not solicited payment. His sentence of twelve months' imprisonment was substituted for one of six months by the Court of Appeal, although the aggravating effect of the large amounts of money involved was affirmed.

C. ABUSES IN RESPECT OF HONOURS

(a) *Definition*

Honours (Prevention of Abuses) Act 1925, s.1

Punishment of abuses in connection with the grant of honours

1.—(1) If any person accepts or obtains or agrees to accept or attempts to obtain from any **17–22** person, for himself or for any other person, or for any purpose, any gift, money or valuable consideration as an inducement or reward for procuring or assisting or endeavouring to procure the grant of a dignity or title of honour to any person, or otherwise in connection with such a grant, he shall be guilty of a misdemeanour.

(2) If any person gives, or agrees or proposes to give, or offers to any person any gift, money or valuable consideration as an inducement or reward for procuring or assisting or endeavouring to procure the grant of a dignity or title of honour to any person, or otherwise in connection with such a grant, he shall be guilty of a misdemeanour.

(3) Any person guilty of a misdemeanour under this Act shall be liable on conviction on indictment to imprisonment for a term not exceeding two years or to a fine not exceeding five hundred pounds, or to both such imprisonment and such fine, or on summary conviction to imprisonment for a term not exceeding three months or to a fine not exceeding fifty pounds, or to both such imprisonment and such fine, and where the person convicted (whether on indictment or summarily) received any such gift, money, or consideration as aforesaid which is capable of forfeiture, he shall in addition to any other punishment be liable to forfeit the same to His Majesty.

[This section is printed as amended by the *CLA* 1977, s.32(1) and the *MCA* 1980, s.32(2) (substitution of reference to the prescribed sum).]

(b) *Procedure*

This offence is triable either way: s.1(3).   **17–23**

The prosecution must prove that:
— the defendant accepted or obtained, or agreed to accept or obtain from any person;
— for himself or for any other person, or for any purpose;
— any gift, money or valuable consideration as an inducement or reward;
— for procuring or assisting or endeavouring to procure the grant of a dignity or title of honour to any person or otherwise in connection with such a grant.

OR
— the defendant gave, agreed, or proposed to give, or offered;
— to any person;
— any gift, money or valuable consideration as an inducement or reward;
— for procuring or assisting or endeavouring to procure the grant of a dignity or title of honour to any person or otherwise in connection with such a grant.

(c) *Sentence*

17–24   When tried summarily, the maximum penalty for this offence is imprisonment for a term not exceeding three months, or to a fine not exceeding five thousand pounds: s.1(3).

CHAPTER 18

OFFENCES AGAINST PUBLIC MORALS AND POLICY

I. OFFENCES AGAINST PUBLIC MORALS AND POLICY

A. BIGAMY

(a) *Definition*

Offences against the Person Act 1861, s.57

Bigamy. Offence may be dealt with where offender shall be apprehended. Not to extend to second marriages, &c. herein stated

57. Whosoever, being married, shall marry any other person during the life of the former **18–1** husband or wife, whether the second marriage shall have taken place in England or Ireland or elsewhere, shall be guilty of felony, and being convicted thereof shall be liable to be imprisoned for any term not exceeding seven years...

Provided, that nothing in this section contained shall extend to any second marriage contracted elsewhere than in England and Ireland by any other than a subject of Her Majesty, or to any person marrying a second time whose husband or wife shall have been continually absent from such person for the space of seven years then last past, and shall not have been known by such person to be living within that time, or shall extend to any person who, at the time of such second marriage, shall have been divorced from the bond of the first marriage, or to any person whose former marriage shall have been declared void by the sentence of any court of competent jurisdiction.

[This section is printed as amended by the *CJA* 1948, s.1(1); and as repealed in part by the *CJA* 1925, s.49 and Sch.3; and the *CLA* 1967, s.10(2) and Sch.3.]

(b) *Procedure*

This offence is triable either way: *Magistrates' Courts Act* 1980, s.17(1) and Sch.1. **18–2** The prosecution must prove that:

— the defendant was married,
— when he married another person,
— during the life of the former husband or wife.

(c) Elements of the offence

'Being married'

18–3   The time for determining whether a person was "married" within the meaning of s.57 is the time of the alleged bigamous ceremony. As a marriage polygamous at inception could become monogamous by a change in domicile and in the law of the country where the marriage was celebrated, a defendant whose potentially polygamous marriage still subsisted at the date of the second marriage, but which had become monogamous both by operation of a change in the law and the defendant's acquisition of English domicile with monogamy as part of the personal law could properly be convicted of bigamy: *R. v Sagoo* [1975] Q.B. 885, 61 Cr.App.R. 191, CA.

The first marriage must be strictly proved by the production of the certificate of the registrar of marriages: *R. v Lindsay* [1902] 66 J.P. 505. The words 'or elsewhere' in the statute mean that the marriage can have taken place in any other part of the world. A British subject resident in England is liable to be convicted of bigamy although both marriages were solemnised in Scotland: *R. v Topping* (1856) Dears. 647.

'Second marriage'

18–4   Where a person, already bound by an existing marriage, goes through with another person a form of marriage known to and recognised by the law as capable of producing a valid marriage, for the purpose of a pretended and fictitious marriage, such person is guilty of bigamy, notwithstanding any special circumstances which, independently of the bigamous character of the marriage, may constitute a legal disability in the parties, or make the form of marriage resorted to inapplicable to their case. Hence in *R. v Allen* (1865-72) L.R. 1 C.C.R. 367, a defendant who went through a ceremony of marriage with his wife's niece, whilst his wife was still living was properly found guilty of bigamy, despite the fact that the second marriage would be void for reasons of co-sanguinity. The validity of the second marriage is immaterial: *R. v Robinson* [1938] 1 All E.R. 301, 26 Cr.App.R. 129, CCA.

Mens Rea

18–5   An honest belief on reasonable grounds as to the invalidity of a previous marriage, will be a good defence to a charge of bigamy: *R. v King* [1964] 1 Q.B. 285, 48 Cr.App.R. 17, CCA. An honest and reasonable belief at the time of the second marriage that the first marriage had been dissolved will also be a good defence: *R. v Gould* [1968] 2 Q.B. 65, 52 Cr.App.R. 152, CA, as will an honest belief on reasonable grounds that the first husband or wife has died before the second marriage, even though the seven years of continued absence specified in the Act has not expired: *R v Tolson* (1889) 23 Q.B.D. 168, CCR.

The defence of seven years' absence of the lawful husband or wife continues to be available in relation to a third or subsequent marriage: *R. v Taylor* [1950] 2 All E.R. 170.

For provisions relating to evidence, see *Archbold Crown*, §§ 31–11 to 31–30.

(d) Defence

18–6   To establish the defence of seven years' absence provided in the statute, the defendant must not have known at any period during the seven years that the spouse was alive: *R. v Cullen* (1840) 9 C & P. 681.

A belief on reasonable grounds that the first spouse is dead will also provide a defence to a charge of bigamy: *R. v Tolson* (1889) 23 Q.B.D. 168, CCR (defendant believed husband was lost at sea following disappearance of husband and general report that the husband had been lost in a vessel bound for America, which went down with all hands on board. Before the seven years' absence established in the statute had expired, the defendant, supposing herself to be a widow, went through the ceremony of marriage with another man. The circumstances were all known to the second husband, and the ceremony was in no way concealed. Her first husband later returned from America. The defendant was found not guilty of bigamy, the Court holding that a bona fide belief on reasonable grounds in the death of the husband at the time of the second marriage afforded a good defence to the charge).

(e) *Sentence*

When tried summarily, the maximum penalty is six months' imprisonment, a fine **18–7** not exceeding the statutory maximum or both. A custodial sentence should be passed where the innocent party has been deceived and has suffered some injury as a consequence: *R. v Smith (James)* 15 Cr.App.R.(S.) 407, CA.

In *R. v Smith (James)* the offender had been married three times. He was separated, though not divorced from his third wife when he went through a marriage ceremony with another woman. He had produced a statement of divorce from his second marriage and stated there had been no further marriage. The woman discovered they were not married when they separated. Sentenced to six months' imprisonment.

Marriage to evade immigration control will require the imposition of a deterrent sentence and hence a custodial sentence is inevitable and wholly correct in principle: *R. v Cairns* [1997] 1 Cr.App.R.(S.) 118. An offender who married for money to enable the woman to evade immigration control was sentenced to nine months' imprisonment.

II. OBSCENE OR INDECENT PUBLICATIONS AND DISPLAYS ETC.

A. PROHIBITION ON PUBLICATION OF OBSCENE MATTER

(a) *Statute*

Obscene Publications Act 1959, s.2

Prohibition of publication of obscene matter
　　2.—(1) Subject as hereinafter provided, any person who, whether for gain or not, publishes **18–8** an obscene article or who has an obscene article for publication for gain (whether gain to himself or gain to another)shall be liable—

> (a) on summary conviction to a fine not exceeding one hundred pounds or to imprisonment for a term not exceeding six months;
> (b) on conviction on indictment to a fine or to imprisonment for a term not exceeding three years or both.

　　(2) [...]
　　(3) A prosecution [...] for an offence against this section shall not be commenced more than two years after the commission of the offence.

　　(3A) Proceedings for an offence under this section shall not be instituted except by or with the consent of the Director of Public Prosecutions in any case where the article in question is a moving picture film of a width of not less than sixteen millimetres and the relevant publication or the only other publication which followed or could reasonably have been expected to follow from the relevant publication took place or (as the case may be) was to take place in the course of a film exhibition; and in this subsection "the relevant publication" means—

> (a) in the case of any proceedings under this section for publishing an obscene article, the publication in respect of which the defendant would be charged if the proceedings were brought; and
> (b) in the case of any proceedings under this section for having an obscene article for publication for gain, the publication which, if the proceedings

were brought, the defendant would be alleged to have had in contemplation.

18–9 (4) A person publishing an article shall not be proceeded against for an offence at common law consisting of the publication of any matter contained or embodied in the article where it is of the essence of the offence that the matter is obscene.

(4A) Without prejudice to subsection (4) above, a person shall not be proceeded against for an offence at common law—

 (a) in respect of a film exhibition or anything said or done in the course of a film exhibition, where it is of the essence of the common law offence that the exhibition or, as the case may be, what was said or done was obscene, indecent, offensive, disgusting or injurious to morality; or

 (b) in respect of an agreement to give a film exhibition or to cause anything to be said or done in the course of such an exhibition where the common law offence consists of conspiring to corrupt public morals or to do any act contrary to public morals or decency.

(5) A person shall not be convicted of an offence against this section if he proves that he had not examined the article in respect of which he is charged and had no reasonable cause to suspect that it was such that his publication of it would make him liable to be convicted of an offence against this section.

(6) In any proceedings against a person under this section the question whether an article is obscene shall be determined without regard to any publication by another person unless it could reasonably have been expected that the publication by the other person would follow from publication by the person charged.

(7) In this section "film exhibition" has the same meaning as in the *Cinemas Act* 1985.

[This section is printed as amended by the *Obscene Publications Act* 1964, s.1(1); the *CLA* 1977, s.53, the *MCA* 1980, s.32(2) (substitution of reference to 'the prescribed sum') and the *Cinemas Act* 1985, s.24(1) and Sch.2, para.6; and as repealed in part by the *CLA* 1977, s.65(5) and Sch.13.]

Obscene Publications Act 1964, s.1

Obscene articles intended for publication for gain

18–10 **1.**—(1) [...]

(2) For the purpose of any proceedings for an offence against the said section 2 a person shall be deemed to have an article for publication for gain if with a view to such publication he has the article in his ownership, possession or control.

(3) In proceedings brought against a person under the said section 2 for having an obscene article for publication for gain the following provisions shall apply in place of subsections (5) and (6) of that section, that is to say,—

 (a) he shall not be convicted of that offence if he proves that he had not examined the article and had no reasonable cause to suspect that it was such that his having it would make him liable to be convicted of an offence against that section; and

 (b) the question whether the article is obscene shall be determined by reference to such publication for gain of the article as in the circumstances it may reasonably be inferred he had in contemplation and to any further publication that could reasonably be expected to follow from it, but not to any other publication.

18–11 (4) Where articles are seized under section 3 of the *Obscene Publications Act* 1959 (which provides for the seizure and forfeiture of obscene articles kept for publication for gain), and a person is convicted under section 2 of that Act of having them for publication for gain, the court on his conviction shall order the forfeiture of those articles:

Provided that an order made by virtue of this subsection (including an order so made on appeal) shall not take effect until the expiration of the ordinary time within which an appeal in the matter of the proceedings in which the order was made may be instituted or, where such an appeal is duly instituted, until the appeal is finally decided or abandoned; and for this purpose—

 (a) an application for a case to be stated or for leave to appeal shall be treated as the institution of an appeal; and

 (b) where a decision on appeal is subject to a further appeal, the appeal shall not be deemed to be finally decided until the expiration of the ordinary time within which a further appeal may be instituted or, where a further appeal is duly instituted, until the further appeal is finally decided or abandoned.

(5) References in section 3 of the *Obscene Publications Act* 1959 and this section to publication for gain shall apply to any publication with a view to gain, whether the gain is to accrue by way of consideration for the publication or in any other way.

[Subsection 1(1) amends section 2(1) of the 1959 Act.]

Obscene Publications Act 1964, s.2

Negatives, etc. for production of obscene articles
   2.—(1) The *Obscene Publications Act* 1959 (as amended by this Act) shall apply in relation   **18–12**
to anything which is intended to be used, either alone or as one of a set, for the reproduction or manufacture therefrom of articles containing or embodying matter to be read, looked at or listened to, as if it were an article containing or embodying that matter so far as that matter is to be derived from it or from the set.
   (2) For the purposes of the *Obscene Publications Act* 1959 (as so amended) an article shall be deemed to be had or kept for publication if it is had or kept for the reproduction or manufacture therefrom of articles for publication; and the question whether an article so had or kept is obscene shall—
   (a) for purposes of section 2 of the Act be determined in accordance with section 1(3)(b) above as if any reference there to publication of the article were a reference to publication of articles reproduced or manufactured from it; and
   (b) for purposes of section 3 of the Act be determined on the assumption that articles reproduced or manufactured from it would be published in any manner likely having regard to the circumstances in which it was found, but in no other manner.

(b) *Procedure*

This offence is triable either way: *Obscene Publications Act* 1959, s.2(1). The offences   **18–13**
under this section are arrestable offences: *PACE* 1984, s.24 and Sch.1A.
   The consent of the DPP is required to institute proceedings where the relevant article is a moving picture film of width 16mm or more, and the relevant publication is by way of film exhibition as defined in the *Cinemas Act* 1985: *Obscene Publications Act* 1964, s.2(3A).
   A prosecution may not be commenced more than two years after the commission of the offence: *Obscene Publications Act* 1964, s.2(3).
   The prosecution must prove that:
   — the defendant published for gain or otherwise, or had for publication for gain,
   — an obscene article.

(c) *Elements of the offence*

'Obscene'

Obscene Publications Act 1959, s.1(1)

Test of obscenity
   1.—(1) For the purposes of this Act an article shall be deemed to be obscene if its effect or   **18–14**
(where the article comprises two or more distinct items) the effect of any one of its items is, if taken as a whole, such as to tend to deprave and corrupt persons who are likely, having regard to all relevant circumstances, to read, see or hear the matter contained or embodied in it.

   The test of obscenity is whether the effect of the article was such as to tend to deprave   **18–15**
and corrupt persons who were likely to read it, so that obscenity depends on the article and not the author, therefore intention and the defendant's honesty of purpose will be irrelevant: *Shaw v DPP* [1962] A.C. 220, CA. Obscenity and depravity are not confined to sex, and include material that advocates drug taking: *John Calder (Publications) Ltd v Powell* [1965] 1 Q.B. 508, DC. It also includes material that tends to induce violence: *DPP v A. and B.C. Chewing Gum Ltd* [1968] 1 Q.B. 159, DC.

18–16   The sole test of obscenity on a charge under s.1(1) of the *Obscene Publications Act 1959* is whether the article has a tendency to deprave and corrupt. The test for obscenity in an article consisting of individual items is to be applied to the items individually; if the test shows one item to be obscene it is enough to make the whole article obscene: *R. v Anderson* [1972] 1 Q.B. 304, CA.

The meaning of the words 'deprave' and 'corrupt' were articulated by Byrne J. in the Lady Chatterly case:

> 'To deprave means to make morally bad, to pervert, to debase or to corrupt morally. To corrupt means to render morally unsound or rotten, to destroy the moral purity or chastity, to pervert or ruin good quality, to debase, to defile':

R. v Penguin Books Ltd [1961] Crim.L.R. 176 at 177. This definition was approved in *R. v Calder and Boyars Ltd* [1969] 1 Q.B. 151, DC. The words 'deprave and corrupt' in s.1(1) of the Act refer primarily to the effect on the minds, including the emotions, of the persons who read or saw it: *DPP v Whyte* [1972] A.C. 849, HL.

18–17   'Persons' in s.1(1) of the Act of 1959 means 'some persons,' though in a suitable case the *de minimis* principle may be applied. To delimit a main group of customers for the articles with all minor groups eliminated is not a proper application of the subsection: *per* Lord Pearson in *DPP v Whyte* (above) (p.866). In relation to a book, the relevant test is whether the effect of the book was to deprave and corrupt what in the opinion of the justices was a significant proportion of the persons likely to read it: *R. v Calder and Boyars Ltd*, above.

See further *Archbold Crown*, §§ 31–63 to 31–70.

'Article'

Obscene Publications Act 1959, s.1(2)

Test of obscenity
18–18   1.—(2) In this Act "article" means any description of article containing or embodying matter to be read or looked at or both, any sound record, and any film or other record of a picture or pictures.

'Publishes'

Obscene Publications Act 1959, s.1(3)–(6)

Test of obscenity
18–19   1.—(3) For the purposes of this Act a person publishes an article who—
(a) distributes, circulates, sells, lets on hire, gives, or lends it, or who offers it for sale or for letting on hire; or
(b) in the case of an article containing or embodying matter to be looked at or a record, shows, plays or projects it, or, where the matter is data stored electronically, transmits that data.

(4) For the purposes of this Act a person also publishes an article to the extent that any matter recorded on it is included by him in a programme included in a programme service.

(5) Where the inclusion of any matter in a programme so included would, if that matter were recorded matter, constitute the publication of an obscene article for the purposes of this Act by virtue of subsection (4) above, this Act shall have effect in relation to the inclusion of that matter in that programme as if it were recorded matter.

(6) In this section "programme" and "programme service" have the same meaning as in the *Broadcasting Act* 1990.

[This subsection is printed as amended by the *CLA* 1977, s.53; and the *CJPOA* 1994, s.168(1) and Sch.9, para.3; and as repealed in part by the *Broadcasting Act* 1990, ss.162 and 203(3) and Sch.21. Subsections (4) to (6) were inserted by the 1990 Act, s.162(1)(b).]

The forms of publication included in the definition in s.1(3)(a) fall into three distinct groups: in the first group, comprising the words "sells, lets on hire, gives, or lends", publication is to an individual; in the second group, comprising the words "distributes, circulates", publication is on a wider scale involving more than one person; in the third group, a mere offer for sale or letting on hire constitutes publication.

The first issue involves consideration of the article itself and the age and occupation **18–21** of the person to whom the article is published. The fact that the person accused may be wholly unaware of the age or occupation of the individual to whom it is published is irrelevant, the vendor of potentially obscene matter to an unknown recipient takes the risk of the latter being someone whom the article would tend to deprave or corrupt. The second issue involves consideration of the age and occupation of the individual to whom the article is published and evidence that the individual to whom the article was published kept it locked up is a relevant, but not conclusive, factor. The third issue involves similar considerations to those involved in the first issue: *R. v Barker*, 46 Cr.App.R. 227 , CCA.

Uploading or downloading of a webpage will constitute publication: *R. v Perrin* [2002] 4 *Archbold News* 2, CA.

See further *Archbold Crown*, §§ 31–72 to 31–73.

(d) *Defence*

Obscene Publications Act 1959, s.4

Defence of public good

4.—(1) Subject to subsection (1A) of this section a person shall not be convicted of an offence **18–22** against section two of this Act, and an order for forfeiture shall not be made under the foregoing section, if it is proved that publication of the article in question is justified as being for the public good on the ground that it is in the interests of science, literature, art or learning, or of other objects of general concern.

(1A) Subsection (1) of this section shall not apply where the article in question is a moving picture film or soundtrack, but—

    (a) a person shall not be convicted of an offence against section 2 of this Act in relation to any such film or soundtrack, and

    (b) an order for forfeiture of any such film or soundtrack shall not be made under section 3 of this Act,

if it is proved that publication of the film or soundtrack is justified as being for the public good on the ground that it is in the interests of drama, opera, ballet or any other art, or of literature or learning.

(2) It is hereby declared that the opinion of experts as to the literary, artistic, scientific or other merits of an article may be admitted in any proceedings under this Act either to establish or to negative the said ground.

(3) In this section "moving picture soundtrack" means any sound record designed for playing with a moving picture film, whether incorporated with the film or not.

[This section is printed as amended by the *CLA* 1977, subss.53(6), (7).]

DPP v Jordan [1977] A.C. 699, HL, held that consideration of whether the defen- **18–23** dant has succeeded in establishing the defence under s.4(1) only falls to be considered once it has been established that the article in question was obscene and that it was published by the defendant.

The "other objects" and the nature of the "general concern" referred to in s.4(1) fall within the same area as science, literature, art and learning already mentioned, so that expert evidence relating to the alleged beneficial effect of the material on the sexual behaviour and attitudes of some particular persons will not be admissible: *DPP v Jordan*, above.

See further *Archbold Crown*, §§ 31–88 to 31–92.

(e) *Sentence*

When tried summarily, the maximum penalty for this offence is six months imprison- **18–24** ment, a fine not exceeding the statutory maximum or both: *Obscene Publications Act* 1959, s.2(1).

In *R. v Pace* [1998] 1 Cr.App.R.(S.) 121, CA the defendant's conviction of three months' imprisonment for possessing obscene articles for publication for gain was upheld. The defendant had been employed in a shop where pornographic videos were for sale, and his conviction was on the basis of one video tape. The defendant was sentenced on the basis that he was a "front man" working for the operators of the shop, but was aware of the general nature of the stock.

18–25   In *R. v Xenofhontos and Mace* (1992) 13 Cr.App.R.(S.) 580, CA, sentences of twelve months' imprisonment for dealing in obscene video tapes were reduced to six months. The appellants were concerned together in selling obscene video cassettes. A total of 214 cassettes were recovered from them. The appellants admitted that they bought 100 cassettes every weekend with a view to resale. The tapes were not the worst kind of obscene videos, and did not involve children or animals and they were sold to adults only.

Obscene Publications Act 1959, s.3

Powers of search and seizure

18–26   **3.**—(1) If a justice of the peace is satisfied by information on oath that there is reasonable ground for suspecting that, in any premises in the petty sessions area for which he acts, or on any stall or vehicle in that area, being premises or a stall or vehicle specified in the information, obscene articles are, or are from time to time, kept for publication for gain, the justice may issue a warrant under his hand empowering any constable to enter (if need be by force) and search the premises, or to search the stall or vehicle and to seize and remove any articles found therein or thereon which the constable has reason to believe to be obscene articles and to be kept for publication for gain.

(2) A warrant under the foregoing subsection shall, if any obscene articles are seized under the warrant, also empower the seizure and removal of any documents found in the premises or, as the case may be, on the stall or vehicle which relate to a trade or business carried on at the premises or from the stall or vehicle.

(3) Subject to subsection (3A) of this section any articles seized under subsection (1) of this section shall be brought before a justice of the peace acting for the same petty sessions area as the justice who issued the warrant, and the justice before whom the articles are brought may thereupon issue a summons to the occupier of the premises or, as the case may be, the user of the stall or vehicle to appear on a day specified in the summons before a magistrates' court for that petty sessions area to show cause why the articles or any of them should not be forfeited; and if the court is satisfied, as respects any of the articles, that at the time when they were seized they were obscene articles kept for publication for gain, the court shall order those articles to be forfeited:

Provided that if the person summoned does not appear, the court shall not make an order unless service of the summons is proved. Provided also that this subsection does not apply in relation to any article seized under subsection (1) of this section which is returned to the occupier of the premises or, as the case may be, to the user of the stall or vehicle in or on which it was found

(3A) Without prejudice to the duty of a court to make an order for the forfeiture of an article where section 1(4) of the *Obscene Publications Act* 1964 applies (orders made on conviction), in a case where by virtue of subsection (3A) of section 2 of this Act proceedings under the said section 2 for having an article for publication for gain could not be instituted except by or with the consent of the Director of Public Prosecutions, no order for the forfeiture of the article shall be made under this section unless the warrant under which the article was seized was issued on an information laid by or on behalf of the Director of Public Prosecutions

18–27   (4) In addition to the person summoned, any other person being the owner, author or maker of any of the articles brought before the court, or any other person through whose hands they had passed before being seized, shall be entitled to appear before the court on the day specified in the summons to show cause why they should not be forfeited.

(5) Where an order is made under this section for the forfeiture of any articles, any person who appeared, or was entitled to appear, to show cause against the making of the order may appeal to the Crown Court, and no such order shall take effect until the expiration of the period within which notice of appeal to the Crown Court may be given against the order, or, if before the expiration thereof notice of appeal is duly given or application

is made for the statement of a case for the opinion of the High Court, until the final determination or abandonment of the proceedings on the appeal or case.

(6) If as respects any articles brought before it the court does not order forfeiture, the court may if it thinks fit order the person on whose information the warrant for the seizure of the articles was issued to pay such costs as the court thinks reasonable to any person who has appeared before the court to show cause why those articles should not be forfeited; and costs ordered to be paid under this subsection shall be enforceable as a civil debt.

(7) For the purposes of this section the question whether an article is obscene shall be determined on the assumption that copies of it would be published in any manner likely having regard to the circumstances in which it was found, but in no other manner.

[This section is printed as amended by the *Courts Act* 1971, s.56(2), Sch.8, para.37 and Sch.9, Pt I; and the *CLA* 1977, ss.53(5), 65(4) and Sch.12; and as repealed in part by the *PACE Act* 1984, s.119(2) and Sch.7, Pt 1.]

B. Sending Obscene Material through the Post

(a) *Definition*

Postal Services Act 2000, s.85

Prohibition on sending certain articles by post

85.—(1) A person commits an offence if he sends by post a postal packet which encloses any   **18–28** creature, article or thing of any kind which is likely to injure other postal packets in course of their transmission by post or any person engaged in the business of a postal operator.

(2) Subsection (1) does not apply to postal packets which enclose anything permitted (whether generally or specifically) by the postal operator concerned.

(3) A person commits an offence if he sends by post a postal packet which encloses—

(a) any indecent or obscene print, painting, photograph, lithograph, engraving, cinematograph film or other record of a picture or pictures, book, card or written communication, or

(b) any other indecent or obscene article (whether or not of a similar kind to those mentioned in paragraph (a)).

(4) A person commits an offence if he sends by post a postal packet which has on the packet, or on the cover of the packet, any words, marks or designs which are of an indecent or obscene character.

(5) A person who commits an offence under this section shall be liable—

(a) on summary conviction, to a fine not exceeding the statutory maximum,

(b) on conviction on indictment, to a fine or to imprisonment for a term not exceeding twelve months or to both.

(b) *Procedure*

This offence is triable either way. The prosecution must prove that: **18–29**
— the defendant sent by post;
— a packet which encloses any creature, article or thing of any kind;
— which is likely to injure other postal packets in the course of their transmission by post;
OR
— the defendant sent by post;
— any indecent or obscene print, painting, photograph, lithograph, engraving, cinematograph film or other record of a picture or pictures, book, card or written communication or any other indecent or obscene article;
OR
— the defendant sent by post;
— any postal packet which has on the cover of the packet;
— any words, marks or designs which are of an indecent or obscene character.

(c) *Elements of the offence*

The meaning of "obscene" in s.11 of the *Post Office Act* 1953 is the ordinary mean-   **18–30** ing of that word which includes shocking, lewd and indecent matter: *R. v Anderson* [1972] 1 Q.B. 304, CA. The test is objective, and the character of the addressee and the effect on the recipient are immaterial: *R. v Straker* [1965] Crim.L.R. 229, CCA.

See further *Archbold Crown*, § 25–325.

(d) *Sentence*

18–31 When tried summarily, the maximum penalty is a fine not exceeding the statutory maximum: *Postal Services Act* 2000, s.85(5).

Where the offence involves neither direct corruption nor commercial exploitation of pornography, and offender is of previous good character, a custodial sentence need not be imposed: *R. v Littleford* (1984) 6 Cr.App.R.(S.) 272.

C. Publications Harmful to Children and Young Persons

(a) *Definition*

Children and Young Persons (Harmful Publications) Act 1955, s.2

Penalty for printing, publishing, selling, &c., works to which this Act applies

18–32 **2.**—(1) A person who prints, publishes, sells or lets on hire a work to which this Act applies, or has any such work in his possession for the purpose of selling it or letting it on hire, shall be guilty of an offence and liable, on summary conviction, to imprisonment for a term not exceeding four months or to a fine not exceeding one hundred pounds or to both:

Provided that, in any proceedings taken under this subsection against a person in respect of selling or letting on hire or of having it in his possession for the purpose of selling it or letting it on hire, it shall be a defence for him to prove that he had not examined the contents of the work and had no reasonable cause to suspect that it was one to which this Act applies.

(2) A prosecution for an offence under this section shall not, in England or Wales, be instituted except by, or with the consent, of the Attorney General.

(b) *Procedure*

18–33 This offence is triable summarily. Proceedings cannot be instituted without the consent of the Attorney-General: s.(2)(2).

The prosecution must prove that:

— the defendant printed, published, sold or let out on hire;
— a work to which the Act applies (defined in s.1 of the 1955 Act (below)), or had any such work in his possession;
— for the purposes of selling it or letting it on hire.

(c) *Elements of the offence*

Children and Young Persons (Harmful Publications) Act 1955, s.1

Works to which this Act Applies

18–34 **1.** This Act applies to any book, magazine or other like work which is of a kind likely to fall into the hands of children or young persons and consists wholly or mainly of stories told in pictures (with or without the addition of written matter), being stories portraying—

 (a) the commission of crimes; or
 (b) acts of violence or cruelty; or
 (c) incidents of a repulsive or horrible nature;

in such a way that the work as a whole would tend to corrupt a child or young person into whose hands it might fall.

'Child'

Children and Young Persons (Harmful Publications) Act 1955, s.5(2)

Short title, interpretation, extent, commencement and duration

18–35 **5.**—(2) In this Act the expressions "child" and "young person" have the meanings assigned to them respectively by section one hundred and seven of the *Children and Young Persons Act* 1933, or, in Scotland, by section one hundred and ten of the *Children and Young Persons (Scotland) Act* 1937, the expression "plate" (except where it occurs in the expression "photographic plate") includes block, mould, matrix and stencil and the expression "photographic film" includes photographic plate.

Hence 'child' denotes a person under the age of 14 years, 'young person' denotes a person who has attained the age of 14 years but who is under the age of 18 years: *Children and Young Persons Act* 1933, s.107.

(d) *Defence*

Section 2 of the 1955 Act provides that a defendant charged with selling or letting on **18–36** hire a work or of having it in his possession for the purpose of selling it or letting it on hire will have a defence if he can establish that he had not examined the contents of the work and had no reasonable cause to suspect that it was one within the scope of the Act.

(e) *Sentence*

The maximum sentence for this offence is imprisonment for a term not exceeding **18–37** four months, a fine not exceeding one hundred pounds or both.

D. OBSCENE PERFORMANCES OF PLAYS

(a) *Definition*

Theatres Act 1968, s.2

Prohibition of presentation of obscene performances of plays

2.—(1) For the purposes of this section a performance of a play shall be deemed to be **18–38** obscene if, taken as a whole, its effect was such as to tend to deprave and corrupt persons who were likely, having regard to all relevant circumstances, to attend it.

(2) Subject to sections 3 and 7 of this Act, if an obscene performance of a play is given, whether in public or private, any person who (whether for gain or not) presented or directed that performance shall be liable—

(a) on summary conviction, to a fine not exceeding the prescribed sum or to imprisonment for a term not exceeding six months;

(b) on conviction on indictment, to a fine or to imprisonment for a term not exceeding three years, or both.

(3) A prosecution on indictment for an offence under this section shall not be commenced more than two years after the commission of the offence.

(4) No person shall be proceeded against in respect of a performance of a play or anything said or done in the course of such a performance—

(a) for an offence at common law where it is of the essence of the offence that the performance or, as the case may be, what was said or done was obscene, indecent, offensive, disgusting or injurious to morality; or

(b) [...]

(c) [...]

and no person shall be proceeded against for an offence at common law of conspiring to corrupt public morals, or to do any act contrary to public morals or decency, in respect of an agreement to present or give a performance of a play, or to cause anything to be said or done in the course of such a performance.

[This section is printed as amended by the *MCA* 1980, s.32(2) (substitution of reference to the 'prescribed sum'). Subsection (4)(b) was repealed by the *Indecent Displays (Control) Act* 1981 and subs.(4)(c) was repealed by the *Civic Government (Scotland) Act* 1982]

(b) *Procedure*

This offence is triable either way. Proceedings may not be instituted without the **18–39** consent of the Attorney-General: *Theatres Act* 1968, s.8.

The prosecution must prove that:
— The defendant, for gain or otherwise,
— Presented or directed a performance,
— Of a play whose effect was such as to tend to deprave and corrupt persons who were likely, having regard to all relevant circumstances, to attend it.

Theatres Act 1968, s.9

Script as evidence of what was performed

18–40   **9.**—(1) Where a performance of a play was based on a script, then, in any proceedings for an offence under section 2[...] or 6 of this Act alleged to have been committed in respect of that performance—

(a) an actual script on which that performance was based shall be admissible as evidence of what was performed and of the manner in which the performance or any part of it was given; and

(b) if such a script is given in evidence on behalf of any party to the proceedings then, except in so far as the contrary is shown, whether by evidence given on behalf of the same or any other party, the performance shall be taken to have been given in accordance with that script.

(2) In this Act "script", in relation to a performance of a play, means the text of the play (whether expressed in words or in musical or other notation) together with any stage or other directions for its performance, whether contained in a single document or not.

[This section is printed as amended by the *Public Order Act* 1986, s.40(3) and Sch.3.]

Theatres Act 1968, s.10

Power to make copies of scripts

18–41   **10.**—(1) If a police officer of or above the rank of superintendent has reasonable grounds for suspecting—

(a) that an offence under section 2 or 6 of this Act has been committed by any person in respect of a performance of a play; or

(b) that a performance of a play is to be given and that an offence under the said section 2 or 6 is likely to be committed by any person in respect of that, performance,

he may make an order in writing under this section relating to that person and that performance.

(2) Every order made under this section shall be signed by the police officer by whom it is made, shall name the person to whom it relates, and shall describe the performance to which it relates in a manner sufficient to enable that performance to be identified.

(3) Where an order under this section has been made, any police officer, on production if so required of the order—

(a) may require the person named in the order to produce, if such a thing exists, an actual script on which the performance was or, as the case may be, will be based; and

(b) if such a script is produced to him, may require the person so named to afford him an opportunity of causing a copy thereof to be made.

(4) Any person who without reasonable excuse fails to comply with a requirement under subsection (3) above shall be liable on summary conviction to a fine not exceeding level 3 on the standard scale.

(5) Where, in the case of a performance of a play based on a script, a copy of an actual script on which that performance was based has been made by or on behalf of a police officer by virtue of an order under this section relating to that performance, section 9(1) of this Act shall apply in relation to that copy as it applies in relation to an actual script on which the performance was based.

Theatres Act 1968, s.16

Offences by bodies corporate

18–42   **16.** Where any offence under this Act committed by a body corporate is proved to have been committed with the consent or connivance of, or to be attributable to any neglect on the part of, any director, manager, secretary or other similar officer of the body corporate, or any person purporting to act in any such capacity, he as well as the body corporate shall be guilty of that offence and shall be liable to be proceeded against and punished accordingly.

(c) *Elements of the offence*

Theatres Act 1968, s.18

Interpretation

18.—(1) In this Act—   **18–43**
"licensing authority" means—
  (a) as respects premises in a London borough or the City of London, the council of that borough or the Common Council, as the case may be;
  (b) as respect premises in a district in England, the council of that district;
  (bb) as respects premises in a county or county borough in Wales, the council of that area;
  (c) in relation to Scotland, a council constituted under section 2 of the *Local Government etc. (Scotland) Act* 1994;
"play" means—
  (a) any dramatic piece, whether involving improvisation or not, which is given wholly or in part by one or more persons actually present and performing and in which the whole or a major proportion of what is done by the person or persons performing, whether by way of speech, singing or action, involves the playing of a role; and
  (b) any ballet given wholly or in part by one or more persons actually present and performing, whether or not it falls within paragraph (a) of this definition;
"police officer" means a member, or in Scotland a constable, of a police force;
"premises" includes any place;
"public performance" includes any performance in a public place within the meaning of the *Public Order Act* 1936 and any performance which the public or any section thereof are permitted to attend, whether on payment or otherwise;
"script" has the meaning assigned by section 9(2) of this Act.
(2) For the purposes of this Act—
  (a) a person shall not be treated as presenting a performance of a play by reason only of his taking part therein as a performer;
  (b) a person taking part as a performer in a performance of a play directed by another person shall be treated as a person who directed the performance if without reasonable excuse he performs otherwise than in accordance with that person's direction; and
  (c) a person shall be taken to have directed a performance of a play given under his direction notwithstanding that he was not present during the performance;
and a person shall not be treated as aiding or abetting the commission of an offence under section 2 or 6 of this Act in respect of a performance of a play by reason only of his taking part in that performance as a performer.

(d) *Defence*

Theatres Act 1968, ss.3, 7

Defence of public good

3.—(1) A person shall not be convicted of an offence under section 2 of this Act if it is proved **18–44** that the giving of the performance in question was justified as being for the public good on the ground that it was in the interest of drama, opera, ballet or any other art, or of literature or learning.
(2) It is hereby declared that the opinion of experts as to the artistic, literary or other merits of a performance of a play may be admitted in any proceedings for an offence under section 2 of this Act either to establish or negative the said ground.

Exceptions for performances given in certain circumstances

18–45   **7.**—(1) Nothing in sections 2 to 4 of this Act shall apply in relation to a performance of a play given on a domestic occasion in a private dwelling.

(2) Nothing in sections 2 to 6 of this Act shall apply in relation to a performance of a play given solely or primarily for one or more of the following purposes, that is to say—

(a) rehearsal; or

(b) to enable—

(i) a record or cinematograph film to be made from or by means of the performance; or

(ii) the performance to be broadcast; or

(iii) the performance to be included in a programme service (within the meaning of the *Broadcasting Act* 1990) but in any proceedings for an offence under section 2 or 6 of this Act alleged to have been committed in respect of a performance of a play or an offence at common law alleged to have been committed in England and Wales by the publication of defamatory matter in the course of a performance of a play, if it is proved that the performance was attended by persons other than persons directly connected with the giving of the performance or the doing in relation thereto of any of the things mentioned in paragraph (b) above, the performance shall be taken not to have been given solely or primarily for one or more of the said purposes unless the contrary is shown.

(3) In this section—

"broadcast" means broadcast by wireless telegraphy (within the meaning of the *Wireless Telegraphy Act* 1949), whether by way of sound broadcasting or television;

"cinematograph film" means any print, negative, tape or other article on which a performance of a play or any part of such a performance is recorded for the purposes of visual reproduction;

"record" means any record or similar contrivance for reproducing sound, including the sound—track of a cinematograph film;

[This section is printed as amended by the *Cable and Broadcasting Act* 1984, s.57(1) and Sch.5, para.21(2); the *Public Order Act* 1986, Sch.3; and the *Broadcasting Act* 1990, s.203(1), Sch.20, para.13.]

(e) *Sentence*

18–46   When tried summarily, the maximum penalty is six months' imprisonment, a fine not exceeding the prescribed sum or both.

E. PROVOCATION OF BREACH OF THE PEACE BY MEANS OF PUBLIC PERFORMANCE OF A PLAY

(a) *Definition*

Theatres Act 1968, s.6

Provocation of breach of peace by means of public performance of a play

18–47   **6.**—(1) Subject to section 7 of this Act, if there is given a public performance of a play involving the use of threatening, abusive or insulting words or behaviour, any person who (whether for gain or not) presented or directed that performance shall be guilty of an offence under this section if—

(a) he did so with intent to provoke a breach of the peace; or

(b) the performance, taken as a whole, was likely to occasion a breach of the peace.

(2) A person guilty of an offence under this section shall be liable—

on summary conviction to a fine not exceeding level 5 on the standard scale or to imprisonment for a term not exceeding six months or to both.

[This section is printed as amended by the *CLA* 1977, Sch.1 and the *CJA* 1982, s.46.]

(b) *Procedure*

This offence is triable summarily. Proceedings may not be instituted without the **18–48**
consent of the Attorney-General: *Theatres Act* 1968, s.8.

The prosecution must prove that:
— the defendant presented, for gain or otherwise;
— a public performance of a play;
— which involved the use of threatening, abusive or insulting words or behaviour
   and;
— he intended to provoke a breach of the peace by doing so or;
— the performance, taken as a whole was likely to occasion a breach of the peace.

(c) *Elements of the offence*

See s.18 of the 1968 Act (above).   **18–49**

(d) *Defence*

See s.7 of the 1968 Act (above).   **18–50**

(e) *Sentence*

The maximum sentence for this offence is a fine not exceeding level five on the stan- **18–51**
dard scale, six months imprisonment, or both: *Theatres Act*, s.6(2).

F. INDECENT DISPLAYS

(a) *Definition*

Indecent Displays (Control) Act 1981, s.1

Indecent displays
   1.—(1) If any indecent matter is publicly displayed the person making the display and any **18–52**
person causing or permitting the display to be made shall be guilty of an offence.
   (2) Any matter which is displayed in or so as to be visible from any public place shall, for
the purposes of this section, be deemed to be publicly displayed.
   (3) In subsection (2) above, "public place", in relation to the display of any matter,
means any place to which the public have or are permitted to have access (whether on payment or otherwise) while that matter is displayed except—
   (a) a place to which the public are permitted to have access only on payment
        which is or includes payment for that display; or
   (b) a shop or any part of a shop to which the public can only gain access by
        passing beyond an adequate warning notice; but the exclusions contained in
        paragraphs (a) and (b) above shall only apply where persons under the age
        of 18 years are not permitted to enter while the display in question is
        continuing.
   (4) Nothing in this section applies in relation to any matter—
   (a) included by any person in a television broadcasting service or other television
        programme service (within the meaning of Part I of the *Broadcasting Act* 1990);
   (b) included in the display of an art gallery or museum and visible only from within
        the gallery or museum; or
   (c) displayed by or with the authority of, and visible only from within a building oc-
        cupied by, the Crown or any local authority; or
   (d) included in a performance of a play (within the meaning of the *Theatres Act*
        1968); or
   (e) included in a film exhibition as defined in the *Cinemas Act* 1985—
        (i) given in a place which as regards that exhibition is required to be licensed
             under section 1 of that Act or by virtue only of section 5, 7 or 8 of that Act
             is not required to be so licensed; or

    (ii) which is an exhibition to which section 6 of that Act applies given by an exempted organisation as defined in subsection (6) of that section.

(5) In this section "matter" includes anything capable of being displayed, except that it does not include an actual human body or any part thereof; and in determining for the purpose of this section whether any displayed matter is indecent—

    (a) there shall be disregarded any part of that matter which is not exposed to view; and

    (b) account may be taken of the effect of juxtaposing one thing with another.

(6) A warning notice shall not be adequate for the purposes of this section unless it complies with the following requirements—

    (a) The warning notice must contain the following words, and no others—

"WARNING

Persons passing beyond this notice will find material on display which they may consider indecent. No admittance to persons under 18 years of age."

    (b) The word "WARNING" must appear as a heading.

    (c) No pictures or other matter shall appear on the notice.

    (d) The notice must be so situated that no one could reasonably gain access to the shop or part of the shop in question without being aware of the notice and it must be easily legible by any person gaining such access.

[This section is printed as amended by the *Cinemas Act* 1985, s.24(1), Sch.2, para.13 and the *Broadcasting Act* 1990, s.203(1), Sch.20, para.30.]

(b) *Procedure*

18–53   This offence is triable either way: *Indecent Displays (Control) Act* 1981, s.4(1).

Indecent Displays (Control) Act 1981, s.2

Powers of arrest, seizure and entry

18–54   **2.**—(1) [...]

(2) A constable may seize any article which he has reasonable grounds for believing to be or to contain indecent matter and to have been used in the commission of an offence under this Act.

(3) In England and Wales, a justice of the peace if satisfied on information on oath that there are reasonable grounds for suspecting that an offence under this Act has been or is being committed on any premises and, in Scotland, a sheriff or justice of the peace on being so satisfied on evidence on oath, may issue a warrant authorising any constable to enter the premises specified in the information or, as the case may be, evidence (if need be by force) within fourteen days from the date of issue of the warrant to seize any article which the constable has reasonable grounds for believing to be or to contain indecent matter and to have been used in the commission of an offence under this Act.

[This section is printed as amended by *PACE* 1984, s.26(1) and Sch.7.]

Indecent Displays (Control) Act 1981, s.3

Offences by corporations

18–55   **3.**—(1) Where a body corporate is guilty of an offence under this Act and it is proved that the offence occurred with the consent or connivance of, or was attributable to any neglect on the part of, any director, manager, secretary or other officer of the body, or any person who was purporting to act in any such capacity he, as well as the body corporate, shall be deemed to be guilty of that offence and shall be liable to be proceeded against and punished accordingly.

(2) Where the affairs of a body corporate are managed by its members, subsection (1) shall apply in relation to the acts and defaults of a member in connection with his functions of management as if he were a director of the body corporate.

See further *Archbold Crown*, §§ 31–116 to 31–121.

(d) *Sentence*

18–56   When tried summarily, the maximum penalty is a fine not exceeding the statutory maximum: *Indecent Displays (Control) Act* 1981, s.4(1).

III. OFFENCES AGAINST THE ADMINISTRATION OF JUSTICE

A. CONTEMPT OF COURT

The *Contempt of Court Act* 1981 gave statutory powers to magistrates to deal with **18–57** contempt in the face of the court. In addition, magistrates have powers to punish fine defaulters under ss.75 to 96 of the *Magistrates' Courts Act* 1980, and to punish defaults in respect of other orders under s.63 of the *MCA* 1980, which provides that any person disobeying an order of the magistrates' court to do anything other than payment of money may be fined up to a maximum of £50 a day for every day during which he is in default or a sum not exceeding £5000, or the court may commit him to custody until he has remedied his default or for a period not exceeding two months.

(1) Contempt in the face of the court

(a) *Definition*

Contempt of Court Act 1981, s.12

Offences of contempt of magistrates' courts

12.—(1) Section 135 of the *Powers of Criminal Courts (Sentencing) Act* 2000 (limit on **18–58** fines in respect of young persons) and a magistrates' court has jurisdiction under this section to deal with any person who—

   (a) wilfully insults the justice or justices, any witness before or officer of the court or any solicitor or counsel having business in the court, during his or their sitting or attendance in court or in going to or returning from the court; or

   (b) wilfully interrupts the proceedings of the court or otherwise misbehaves in court.

(2) In any such case the court may order any officer of the court, or any constable, to take the offender into custody and detain him until the rising of the court; and the court may, if it thinks fit, commit the offender to custody for a specified period not exceeding one month or impose on him a fine not exceeding £2,500, or both.

(2A) A fine imposed under subsection (2) above shall be deemed, for the purposes of any enactment, to be a sum adjudged to be paid by a conviction..

(4) A magistrates' court may at any time revoke an order of committal made under subsection (2) and, if the offender is in custody, order his discharge.

(5) Section 135 of the *Powers of Criminal Courts (Sentencing) Act* 2000 (limits on fines in respect of young persons) and the following provisions of the *Magistrates' Courts Act* 1980 apply in relation to an order under this section as they apply in relation to a sentence on conviction or finding of guilty of an offence; and those provisions of the *Magistrates' Courts Act* 1980 are sections 75 to 91 (enforcement); section 108 (appeal to Crown Court); section 136 (overnight detention in default of payment); and section 142(1) (power to rectify mistakes).

[This section is printed as amended by the *Powers of Criminal Courts (Sentencing) Act* 2000, Sch.9.]

Magistrates' Courts Act 1980, s.97(4)

Summons to witness and warrant for his arrest

97.—(4) If any person attending or brought before a magistrates' court refuses without just **18–59** excuse to be sworn or give evidence, or to produce any document or thing, the court may commit him to custody until the expiration of such period not exceeding one month as may be specified in the warrant or until he sooner gives evidence or produces the document or thing or impose on him a fine not exceeding £2,500 or both.

For the offence under s.12 of the *Contempt of Court Act* 1981, the prosecution must prove that:

— the defendant wilfully insulted the justice or justices, or any witness before or officer of the court or any solicitor or counsel having business in the court

— during his or their sitting or attendance in court or in going to or returning from the court.

OR

that the defendant wilfully interrupted the proceedings of the court or otherwise misbehaved in court.

Regarding the offence under s.87 of the *MCA* 1980, the prosecution must prove that:

— the defendant was attending or brought before a magistrates' court and they
— refused without just excuse to be sworn or give evidence, or to produce any document or thing.

(b) *Procedure*

18–60   These offences are triable summarily only.

The magistrates' courts possess powers to imprison fine defaulters, as well as those who default in respect of other orders under s.63(3) of the *Magistrates' Courts Act* 1980. They are also able to deal with contempt in the face of the court under s.12 of the *Contempt of Court Act* 1981 and s.97 of the *MCA* 1980.

The *Practice Direction (Criminal Proceedings: Consolidated)*, para.V.54, (Contempt in the face of the magistrates' court) sets out the relevant principles governing the exercise of the magistrates' powers under these sections. The Direction provides:

General

18–61   **54.1** Section 12 of the *Contempt of Court Act* 1981 gives magistrates' courts the power to detain until the court rises, someone, whether a defendant or another person present in court, who wilfully insults anyone specified in section 12 or who interrupts proceedings. In any such case, the court may order any officer of the court, or any constable, to take the offender into custody and detain him until the rising of the court; and the court may, if it thinks fit, commit the offender to custody for a specified period not exceeding one month or impose a fine not exceeding level 4 on the standard scale or both. This power can be used to stop disruption of their proceedings. Detention is until the person can be conveniently dealt with without disruption of the proceedings. Prior to the court using the power the offender should be warned to desist or face the prospect of being detained.

54.2 Magistrates' courts also have the power to commit to custody any person attending or brought before a magistrates' court who refuses without just cause to be sworn or to give evidence under section 97(4) of the *Magistrates' Courts Act* 1980, until the expiration of such period not exceeding one month as may be specified in the warrant or until he sooner gives evidence or produces the document or thing, or impose on him a fine not exceeding £2,500, or both.

54.3 In the exercise of any of these powers, as soon as is practical, and in any event prior to an offender being proceeded against, an offender should be told of the conduct which it is alleged to constitute his offending in clear terms. When making an order under section 12 the justices should state their findings of fact as to the contempt.

54.4 Exceptional situations require exceptional treatment. While this direction deals with the generality of situations, there will be a minority of situations where the application of the direction will not be consistent with achieving justice in the special circumstances of the particular case. Where this is the situation, the compliance with the direction should be modified so far as is necessary so as to accord with the interests of justice.

54.5 The power to bind persons over to be of good behaviour in respect of their conduct in court should cease to be exercised.

Contempt consisting of wilfully insulting anyone specified in section 12 or interrupting proceedings

18–62   **54.6** In the case of someone who wilfully insults anyone specified in section 12 or interrupts proceedings, if an offender expresses a willingness to apologise for his misconduct, he should be brought back before the court at the earliest convenient moment in order to make the apology and to give undertakings to the court to refrain from further misbehaviour.

54.7 In the majority of cases, an apology and a promise as to future conduct should be sufficient for justices to order an offender's release. However, there are likely to be certain cases where the nature and seriousness of the misconduct requires the justices to consider using their powers under section 12(2) of the *Contempt of Court* 1981 Act either to fine or to order the offender's committal to custody.

Where an offender is detained for contempt of court

54.8 Anyone detained under either of these provisions in paragraph 54.1 or 54.2 should be seen by the duty solicitor or another legal representative and be represented in proceedings if they so wish. Public funding should generally be granted to cover representation. The offender must be afforded adequate time and facilities in order to prepare his case. The matter should be resolved the same day if at all possible.

54.9 The offender should be brought back before the court before the justices conclude their daily business. The justices should ensure that he understands the nature of the proceedings, including his opportunity to apologise or give evidence and the alternative of them exercising their powers.

54.10 Having heard from the offender's solicitor, the justices should decide whether to take further action.

Sentencing of an offender who admits being in contempt

54.11 If an offence of contempt is admitted the justices should consider whether they are **18–63** able to proceed on the day or whether to adjourn to allow further reflection. The matter should be dealt with on the same day if at all possible. If the justices are of the view to adjourn they should generally grant the offender bail unless one or more of the exceptions to the right to bail in the *Bail Act* 1976 are made out.

54.12 When they come to sentence the offender where the offence has been admitted, the justices should first ask the offender if he has any objection to them dealing with the matter. If there is any objection to the justices dealing with the matter a differently constituted panel should hear the proceedings. If the offender's conduct was directed to the justices, it will not be appropriate for the same bench to deal with the matter.

54.13 The justices should consider whether an order for the offender's discharge is appropriate, taking into account any time spent on remand, whether the offence was admitted and the seriousness of the contempt. Any period of committal should be for the shortest time commensurate with the interests of preserving good order in the administration of justice.

Trial of the issue where the contempt is not admitted

54.14 Where the contempt is not admitted the justices' powers are limited to making arrangements for a trial to take place. They should not at this stage make findings against the offender.

54.15 In the case of a contested contempt the trial should take place at the earliest opportunity and should be before a bench of justices other than those before whom the alleged contempt took place. If a trial of the issue can take place on the day such arrangements should be made taking into account the offender's rights under Article 6 of the European Convention for the Protection of Human Rights and Fundamental Freedoms (Rome, November 4, 1950; TS 71 (1953); Cmd. 8969). If the trial cannot take place that day the justices should again bail the offender unless there are grounds under the *Bail Act* 1976 to remand him in custody.

54.16 The offender is entitled to call and examine witnesses where evidence is relevant. If the offender is found by the court to have committed contempt the court should again consider first whether an order for his discharge from custody is sufficient to bring proceedings to an end. The justices should also allow the offender a further opportunity to apologise for his contempt or to make representations. If the justices are of the view that they must exercise their powers to commit to custody under section 12(2) of the 1981 Act, they must take into account any time spent on remand and the nature and seriousness of the contempt. Any period of committal should be for the shortest period of time commensurate with the interests of preserving good order in the administration of justice.

Default in respect of orders made by the court

Magistrates' Courts Act 1980, s.63(3)

Orders other than for payment of money

63.—(3) Where any person disobeys and order of a magistrates' court made under an Act **18–64** passed after 31st December 1879 to do anything other than the payment of money or to abstain from doing anything the court may—

> (a) order him to pay a sum not exceeding £50 for every day during which he is in default or a sum not exceeding £5,000; or

(b) commit him to custody until he has remedied his default or for a period not exceeding 2 months;

but a person who is ordered to pay a sum for every day during which he is in default or who is committed to custody until he has remedied his default shall not by virtue of this section be ordered to pay more than £1,000 or be committed for more than 2 months in all for doing or abstaining from doing the same thing contrary to the order (without prejudice to the operation of this section in relation to any subsequent default).

Contempt of Court Act 1981, s.17

Disobedience to certain orders of magistrates' courts

18–65   17.—(1) The powers of a magistrates' court under subsection (3) of section 63 of the *Magistrates' Courts Act* 1980 (punishment by fine or committal for disobeying an order to do anything other than the payment of money or to abstain from doing anything) may be exercised either of the court's own motion or by order on complaint.

(2) In relation to the exercise of those powers the provisions of the *Magistrates' Court Act* 1980 shall apply subject to the modifications set out in Schedule 3 to this Act.

18–65.1   All of the above offences are triable summarily only.

(c) *Elements of the offence*

18–66   As regards contempt in the face of the court under s.12 of the *MCA* 1980, a person 'wilfully' interrupts the proceedings of the court if he commits the acts causing disruption deliberately with the intention that they should interrupt the proceedings of the court or if, knowing that there is a risk that his acts will interrupt the proceedings, he nevertheless goes on deliberately to do those acts: *Bodden v Metropolitan Police Commr.* [1990] 2 W.L.R. 76, CA. Section 12(a) does not apply to the making of threats: *R. v Havant Justices Ex p. Palmer* (1985) 149 J.P. 609, DC, though threats may constitute 'misbehaviour' under s.12(b). A witness at a summary trial, after giving evidence threatened to "get" the defendant and his solicitor who were waiting outside court whilst the magistrates considered their decision. The Divisional Court held that a threat was not an "insult" within the *Contempt of Court Act* 1981, s.12(1)(a) and the magistrates had no power to deal with the defendant.

18–67   In construing the words 'otherwise misbehaves' regard has to be had to the fact that the 1981 Act is a criminal statute and that the other prohibitions in s.12 are qualified by the word 'wilfully'. A court has to find some element of defiance in the contemnor's conduct, the absence of which will result in the court having no power to punish under s.12 of the 1981 Act: *Hooker, Re* [1993] C.O.D. 190. The defendant had been fined £500 for using a tape recorder without permission in court. She was told not to leave court before it was paid. The magistrate said she showed no signs of remorse. The court held that her conduct had not had any effect on the proceedings until the magistrate interrupted them, and her conduct lacked the necessary element of defiance to make punishment under s.12 appropriate.

(d) *Sentence*

18–68   The maximum penalty for the offence under s.12 is imprisonment for a period not exceeding one month, or a fine not exceeding £2,500 or both. The court may also order that the defendant be detained until the rising of the court. The maximum penalty for the offence under s.97 is committal to custody until the defendant gives evidence or produces the relevant document or for a period not exceeding one month or a fine not exceeding £2,500 or both. The offence of defaulting on orders other than fines contained in s.63(3) of the *MCA* 1980 is punishable with a sentence of imprisonment for a period not exceeding two months, or until he has remedied his default, or order him to pay a sum of order him to pay a sum not exceeding £50 for every day during which he is in default or a sum not exceeding £5,000. However the offender cannot be ordered to pay more than £1,000 or be committed for more than two months in all for doing or abstaining from doing the same thing contrary to the order.

B. PERJURY

Although s.1 of the *Perjury Act* 1911 is triable on indictment only, s.89 of the *Criminal Justice Act* 1967, and s.106 of the *Magistrates' Courts Act* 1980 create the offence of making a false statement in criminal proceedings, which is triable either way (both sections are assimilated into the *Perjury Act* 1911, and the *MCA* 1980, s.17 and Sch.1, para.14 makes all offences under the *Perjury Act* 1911 triable either way, except for the offences under ss.1, 3 and 4, ss.3 and 4 of the *Perjury Act* 1911 containing express provisions for summary jurisdiction.) **18–69**

(a) *Legislation*

Criminal Justice Act 1967, s.89

False written statements tendered in evidence

89.—(1) If any person in a written statement tendered in evidence in criminal proceedings by virtue of section 9 of this Act or in proceedings before a court-martial by virtue of the said section 9 as extended by section 12 above or by section 99A of the *Army Act* 1955 or section 99A of the *Air Force Act* 1955 wilfully makes a statement material in those proceedings which he knows to be false or does not believe to be true, he shall be liable on conviction on indictment to imprisonment for a term not exceeding two years or a fine or both. **18–70**

(2) The *Perjury Act* 1911 shall have effect as if this section were contained in that Act.

[This section is printed as amended by the *Magistrates' Courts Act* 1980, Sch.9 and the *Armed Forces Act* 1976, Sch.9, para.15.]

Magistrates' Courts Act 1980, s.106

False written statements tendered in evidence

106.—(1) If any person in a written statement admitted in evidence in criminal proceedings by virtue of section 5B above wilfully makes a statement material in those proceedings which he knows to be false or does not believe to be true, he shall be liable on conviction on indictment to imprisonment for a term not exceeding 2 years or a fine or both. **18–71**

(2) The *Perjury Act* 1911 shall have effect as if this section were contained in that Act.

[This section is printed as amended by the *Criminal Procedure and Investigations Act* 1996, Sch.1(I), para.12.]

(b) *Procedure*

These offences are triable either way (see above). **18–72**
The prosecution must prove that:
— the defendant, in a written statement tendered in evidence in criminal proceedings or in proceedings before a court-martial, or in a written statement admitted in evidence in criminal proceedings
— wilfully made a statement
— material in those proceedings
— which he knows to be false or does not believe to be true.

(c) *Elements of the offence*

Wilfully

The prosecution are required to prove that the statement was made deliberately and not inadvertently or by mistake: *R. v Millward* [1985] Q.B. 519, CA. **18–73**

Materiality

The matter of materiality is an issue to be determined objectively by the judge. The **18–74** defendant's belief on the materiality of the statement is irrelevant: *R. v Millward* [1985] Q.B. 519, CA. See further *Archbold Crown*, §§ 28–160 to 28–162.

Falsity

18–75   The defendant may be convicted where the statement that he believed to be false turns out to be true, as the sections only require the making of a statement which is known or believed to be untrue See further *Archbold Crown*, § 28–163.

Perjury Act 1911, s.13

Corroboration

18–76   **13.** A person shall not be liable to be convicted of any offence against this Act, or of any offence declared by any other Act to be perjury or subornation of perjury, or to be punishable as perjury or subornation of perjury, solely upon the evidence of one witness as to the falsity of any statement alleged to be false.

See further *Archbold Crown*, § 28–165.

(c) *Sentence*

18–77   As these offences are designated as triable either way by s.17 and Sch.1 of the *MCA* 1980, s.32 of the *MCA* 1980 prescribed the maximum penalty for these offences. Section 32(1) provides that on summary conviction of any of the offences triable either way listed in Sch.1 to this Act a person shall be liable to imprisonment for a term not exceeding six months or to a fine not exceeding the prescribed sum or both.

C. FALSE UNSWORN STATEMENTS UNDER EVIDENCE (PROCEEDINGS IN OTHER JURISDICTIONS)

(a) *Definition*

Perjury Act 1911, s.1A

False unsworn statement under Evidence (Proceedings in Other Jurisdictions) Act 1975

18–78   **1A.** If any person, in giving any testimony (either orally or in writing) otherwise than on oath, where required to do so by an order under section 2 of the *Evidence (Proceedings in Other Jurisdictions) Act* 1975, makes a statement—
(a) which he knows to be false in material particular, or
(b) which is false in a material particular and which he does not believe to be true,
he shall be guilty of an offence and shall be liable on conviction on indictment to imprisonment for a term not exceeding two years or a fine or both.

(b) *Procedure*

18–79   This offence is triable either way: *MCA* 1980, s.17 and Sch.1.
The prosecution must prove that:
— the defendant, in giving any testimony, otherwise than on oath
— where required to do so under s.2 of the *Evidence (Proceedings in Other Jurisdictions) Act* 1975
— made a statement which
— he knew to be false in a material particular or
— which was false in a material particular and he did not believe it to be true.

(c) *Sentence*

18–80   See s.32 of the *MCA* 1980, which provides that on summary conviction of any of the offences triable either way listed in Sch.1 to this Act a person shall be liable to imprisonment for a term not exceeding six months or to a fine not exceeding the prescribed sum or both.

D. FALSE STATEMENTS ON OATH NOT IN JUDICIAL PROCEEDING

(a) *Definition*

Perjury Act 1911, s.2

False statements on oath made otherwise than in a judicial proceedings

2. If any person—   **18–81**

(1) being required or authorised by law to make any statement on oath for any purpose, and being lawfully sworn (otherwise than in a judicial proceeding) wilfully makes a statement which is material for that purpose and which he knows to be false or does not believe to be true; or

(2) wilfully uses any false affidavit for the purposes of the *Bills of Sale Act* 1878, as amended by any subsequent enactment,

he shall be guilty of a misdemeanour, and, on conviction thereof on indictment, shall be liable to penal servitude for a term not exceeding seven years or to imprisonment, for a term not exceeding two years, or to a fine or to both such penal servitude or imprisonment and fine.

(b) *Procedure*

This offence is triable either way: *MCA* 1980, s.17 and Sch.1.   **18–82**

The prosecution must prove that:

— the defendant was required or authorised by law to make any statement on oath for any purpose and

— they were lawfully sworn and;

— they wilfully made a statement which is material for that purpose,

— which they knew to be false or did not believe was true or

— wilfully used any false affidavit for the purposes of the *Bills of Sale Act* 1878, as amended by any subsequent enactment.

(c) *Elements of the offence*

For the meaning of 'wilfully', see above.   **18–83**

For the meaning of falsity, see above.

(d) *Sentence*

See s.32 of the *MCA* 1980, which provides that on summary conviction of any of the   **18–84**
offences triable either way listed in Sch.1 to this Act a person shall be liable to imprisonment for a term not exceeding six months or to a fine not exceeding the prescribed sum or both.

E. FALSE STATEMENTS WITH REFERENCE TO MARRIAGE

(a) *Definition*

Perjury Act 1911, s.3

False statements, &c. with reference to marriage

3.—(1) If any person—   **18–85**

(a) for the purpose of procuring a marriage, or a certificate or licence for marriage, knowingly and wilfully makes a false oath, or makes or signs a false declaration, notice or certificate required under any Act of Parliament for the time being in force relating to marriage; or

(b) knowingly and wilfully makes, or knowingly and wilfully causes to be made, for the purposes of being inserted in any register of marriage, a false statement as to any particular required by law to be known and registered relating to any marriage; or

(c) forbids the issue of any certificate or licence for marriage by falsely representing himself to be a person whose consent to the marriage is required by law knowing such representation to be false, or

(d) with respect to a declaration made under section 16(1A) or 27B(2) of the *Marriage Act* 1949—

    (i) enters a caveat under subsection (2) of the said section 16, or

    (ii) makes a statement mentioned in subsection (4) of the said section 27B,

which he knows to be false in a material particular.

he shall be guilty of a misdemeanour, and, on conviction thereof on indictment, shall be liable to penal servitude for a term not exceeding seven years or to imprisonment, for a term not exceeding two years, or to a fine or to both such penal servitude or imprisonment and fine and on summary conviction thereof shall be liable to a penalty not exceeding the statutory maximum

(2) No prosecution for knowingly and wilfully making a false declaration for the purpose of procuring any marriage out of the district in which the parties or one of them dwell shall take place after the expiration of eighteen months from the solemnization of the marriage to which the declaration refers.

18–86   [This section is printed as amended by the *Criminal Justice Act* 1925, s.28(1), the *Criminal Justice Act* 1967, Sch.3, the *Criminal Law Act* 1977, s.28 and the *Marriage (Prohibited Degrees of Relationship) Act* 1986, s.4.]

(b) *Procedure*

18–87   This offence is triable either way: *Perjury Act* 1911, s.3(3)(1).

The prosecution must prove that:

— the defendant for the purpose of procuring a marriage, or a certificate or licence for marriage

— knowingly and wilfully makes a false oath, or makes or signs a false declaration, notice or certificate or;

— knowingly and wilfully makes, or knowingly and wilfully causes to be made, for the purposes of being inserted in any register of marriage, a false statement as to any particular required by law to be known and registered relating to any marriage; or

— forbade the issue of any certificate or licence for marriage by falsely representing himself to be a person whose consent to the marriage is required by law knowing such representation to be false, or

— with respect to a declaration made under ss.16(1A) or 27B(2) of the *Marriage Act* 1949—

    entered a caveat under subs.(2) of the said s.16, or

    made a statement mentioned in subs.(4) of the said s.27B,

— which he knew to be false in a material particular.

(c) *Sentence*

18–88   When tried summarily, the maximum penalty for this offence is a fine not exceeding the statutory maximum.

F. False Statements in Relation to Births and Deaths

(a) *Definition*

Perjury Act 1911, s.4

False statements, &c. as to births or deaths

18–89   **4.**—(1) If any person—

(a) wilfully makes any false answer to any question put to him by any registrar of births or deaths relating to the particulars required to be registered concerning any birth or death, or, wilfully gives to any such registrar any false information concerning any birth or death or the cause of any death; or

(b) wilfully makes any false certificate or declaration under or for the purposes of any Act relating to the registration of births or deaths, or, knowing any such certificate or declaration to be false, uses the same as true or gives or sends the same as true to any person; or

(c) wilfully makes, gives or uses any false statement or declaration as to a child born alive as having been still-born, or as to the body of a deceased person or a still-born child in any coffin, or falsely pretends that any child born alive was still-born; or

(d) makes any false statement with intent to have the same inserted in any register of births or deaths: he shall be guilty of a misdemeanour and shall be liable—

   (i) on conviction thereof on indictment to penal servitude for a term not exceeding seven years, or to imprisonment for a term not exceeding two years, or to a fine instead of either of the said punishments; and

   (ii) on summary conviction thereof, to a penalty not exceeding the statutory maximum

(2) A prosecution on indictment for an offence against this section shall not be commenced more than three years after the commission of the offence.

[This section is printed as amended by the *Criminal Justice Act* 1925, s.28(2), the *Criminal Justice Act* 1967, Sch.3 and the *Criminal Law Act* 1977, s.20.]

(b) *Prosecution*

This offence is triable either way: s.4(d).   **18–90**

(c) *Sentence*

When tried summarily, the maximum penalty for this offence is a fine not exceeding **18–91** the statutory maximum.

G. FALSE STATUTORY DECLARATIONS WITHOUT OATH

(a) *Definition*

Perjury Act 1911, s.5

False statutory declarations and other false statements without oath

5. If any person knowingly and wilfully makes (otherwise than on oath) a statement false in a **18–92** material particular, and the statement is made—

(a) in a statutory declaration; or

(b) in an abstract, account, balance sheet, book, certificate, declaration, entry, estimate, inventory, notice, report, return, or other document which he is authorised or required to make, attest, or verify, by any public general Act of Parliament for the time being in force; or

(c) in any oral declaration or oral answer which he is required to make by, under, or in pursuance of any public general Act of Parliament for the time being in force,

he shall be guilty of a misdemeanour and shall be liable on conviction thereof on indictment to imprisonment, for any term not exceeding two years, or to a fine or to both such imprisonment and fine.

(b) *Procedure*

This offence is triable either way: *MCA* 1980, s.17 and Sch.1.   **18–93**
The prosecution must prove that:
— the defendant knowingly and wilfully made
— otherwise than on oath

713

— a statement false in a material particular and

— the statement was made in an abstract, account, balance sheet, book, certificate, declaration, entry, estimate, inventory, notice, report, return, or other document which he is authorised or required to make, attest, or verify, by any public general Act of Parliament for the time being in force; or

— in any oral declaration or oral answer which he is required to make by, under, or in pursuance of any public general Act of Parliament for the time being in force.

(c) Sentence

18–94   As these offences are designated as triable either way by s.17 and Sch.1 of the *MCA* 1980, s.32 of the *MCA* 1980 prescribed the maximum penalty for these offences. Section 32(1) provides that on summary conviction of any of the offences triable either way listed in Sch.1 to this Act a person shall be liable to imprisonment for a term not exceeding six months or to a fine not exceeding the prescribed sum or both.

H. False Declarations to Obtain Registration

(a) Definition

Perjury Act 1911, s.6

False declarations, &c. to obtain registration, &c. for carrying on a vocation

18–95   **6.** If any person—

(a) procures or attempts to procure himself to be registered on any register or roll kept under or in pursuance of any public general Act of Parliament for the time being in force of persons qualified by law to practice any vocation or calling; or

(b) procures or attempts to procure a certificate of the registration of any person on any such register or roll as aforesaid,

by wilfully making or producing or causing to be made or produced either verbally or in writing, any declaration, certificate, or representation which he knows to be false or fraudulent, he shall be guilty of a misdemeanour and shall be liable on conviction thereof on indictment to imprisonment for any term not exceeding twelve months, or to a fine, or to both such imprisonment and fine.

(b) Procedure

18–96   This offence is triable either way: *MCA* 1980, s.17 and Sch.1.

The prosecution must prove that:

— the defendant procured, or attempted to procure themselves to be registered on any register or roll kept under or in pursuance of any public general Act of Parliament for the time being in force of persons qualified by law to practice any vocation or calling; or

— procured or attempted to procure a certificate of the registration of any person on any such register or roll as aforesaid

— by wilfully making or producing or causing to be made or produced either verbally or in writing, any declaration, certificate, or representation

— which they knew to be false or fraudulent.

(c) Sentence

18–97   As these offences are designated as triable either way by s.17 and Sch.1 of the *MCA* 1980, s.32 of the *MCA* 1980 prescribed the maximum penalty for these offences. Section 32(1) provides that on summary conviction of any of the offences triable either way listed in Sch.1 to this Act a person shall be liable to imprisonment for a term not exceeding six months or to a fine not exceeding the prescribed sum or both.

Part III

Summary Trial

SUMMARY TRIAL

I. HEARING IN OPEN COURT

A. GENERAL PRINCIPLE

In general, criminal proceedings should be heard in open court: *Magistrates' Courts* **19–1**

Act 1980, s.121(4) and European Convention on Human Rights, Art.6(1). It allows public scrutiny, guarantees a fair trial and maintains public confidence: *Pretto v Italy* 6 E.H.R.R. 182 at para.21; *Stefanelli v San Marino* (2001) 33 E.H.R.R. 16. The public and press must be admitted to the courtroom and evidence must be given publicly. If evidence is not given orally but by way of statement this is read aloud either fully or in summary.

19–2   Access by the press is particularly important: *Axen v Germany*, 6 E.H.R.R. 195 at para.25. In *Att.-Gen. v Leveller Magazine Ltd* [1979] A.C. 440 Lord Diplock stated:

> If the way that the courts behave cannot be hidden from the public ear and eye this provides a safeguard against judicial arbitrariness or idiosyncrasy and maintains the public confidence in the administration of justice. The application of this principle of open justice has two aspects: as respects proceedings in the court itself it requires that they should be held in open court to which the press and public are admitted and that, in criminal cases at any rate, all evidence communicated to the court is communicated publicly. As respects the publication to a wider public of fair and accurate reports of proceedings that have taken place in court the principle requires that nothing should be done to discourage this.

> However since the purpose of the general rule is to serve the ends of justice it may be necessary to depart from it where the nature or circumstances of the particular proceeding are such that the application of the general rule in its entirety would frustrate or render impracticable the administration of justice or would damage some other public interest for whose protection Parliament has made some statutory derogation from the rule. Apart from statutory exceptions, however, where a court in the exercise of its inherent power to control the conduct of the proceedings before it departs in any way from the general rule, the departure is justified to the extent and to no more than the extent that the court reasonably believes to be necessary in order to serve the ends of justice.

B. Closed Court in the Interests of Justice

19–3   A magistrates' court has the power to exclude the press and the public, but only when it is necessary for the administration of justice: *R. v Malvern Justices Ex p. Evans*; *R. v Evesham Justices Ex p. McDonogh* [1988] Q.B. 553; *R. v Richards* 163 J.P. 246, CA see Art.6(1), ECHR above.

In *R. v Denbigh Justices Ex p. Williams and Evans* [1974] Q.B. 759, DC the court stated at 765 that:

> The injunction to the presiding judge or magistrate is: do your best to enable the public to come in and see what is happening, having a proper common sense regard for the facilities available and the facility for keeping order, security and the like ... the presence of absence of the press is a vital factor in deciding whether a particular hearing was or was not in open court. I find it difficult to imagine a case which can be said to be held publicly if the press have been actively excluded. On the other hand, the fact that the press is present is not conclusive the other way ...

19–4   In this case the court considered that persons of objectionable character or children of "tender years" could be excluded if it was necessary for the proper conduct of the trial. In *X v Austria* (1963) App.No.1913/63 2 Digest 438, the public was excluded in a trial for sexual offences against children. In *McPherson v McPherson* [1936] A.C. 177, PC, closure of the court was upheld where there was disorder or the anticipation of it.

Generally no distinction should be drawn between exclusion of the press and the public. There may be situations, however, where such a distinction may be necessary to ensure that justice can be done without a completely closed hearing. Where the court is satisfied that an important prosecution witness would refuse to give evidence unless the public were not permitted in court, it is entitled to close the court to the general public but with members of the press remaining: *R. v Richards* (1999) 163 J.P. 246, CA; *R. v Waterfield* (1974) 60 Cr.App.R. 296, CA.

Protection of public decency is not a sufficient reason to justify excluding the public from court: *Scott v Scott* [1913] A.C. 417. In *R. v Waterfield*, above, the court considered that the public had no right to see exhibits, particularly if the exhibit is an obscene film, but it might want to know the type of films involved. If a judge excludes the general public when such films are shown, the press should normally be permitted to remain so that they can provide the public with information upon which to base opinions.

The risk of financial damage, or damage to reputation or goodwill, resulting from **19–5** the institution of proceedings concerning a person's business is not a valid reason for departing from the principle that proceedings should be heard in open court: *R. v Dover Justices Ex p. Dover DC* [1992] Crim.L.R. 371, DC. The "necessity" principle does not justify a private sitting because of the embarrassing nature of the evidence, or to deny or prevent an opportunity to show interest: *R. v Chancellor of Chichester Consistory Court Ex p. News Group Newspapers Ltd* [1992] C.O.D. 48, DC.

It may also be necessary to protect a witness's right to life under Art.2, ECHR: *R. v Lord Saville of Newdigate Ex p. A* [2000] 1 W.L.R. 1855. This case concerned the anonymity of soldiers giving evidence to the "Bloody Sunday" tribunal in Northern Ireland and their fear of reprisal. The court has to balance the conflicting interests of the defendant and any witness.

When a court considers excluding the public it should draw a distinction between matters which should never meet the public eye and matters where the concern is in relation to making matters known before the conclusion of the trial or related proceedings and the risk of prejudice arising therefrom. In the latter situation the risk of prejudice can often be dealt with by an order under s.4(2) of the *Contempt of Court Act* 1981 or the postponing of a press report: *R. v Crook*, 93 Cr.App.R. 17, CA.

Contempt of Court Act 1981 s.4(2)

4.—(2) In any such proceedings the court may, where it appears to be necessary for avoiding **19–6** a substantial risk of prejudice to the administration of justice in those proceedings, or in any other proceedings pending or imminent, order that the publication of any report of the proceedings, or any part of the proceedings, be postponed for such period as the court thinks necessary for that purpose.

These powers should not be used where the court is concerned merely for the welfare of the defendant: *R. v Newtownabbey Magistrates' Court Ex p. Belfast Telegraph Newspapers Ltd, The Times*, August 27, 1997, QBD. Restrictions under the *Contempt of Court Act* 1981 are only allowed where there is a substantial risk of prejudice to the administration of justice.

Even when it is claimed that the safety of the witness is at stake the court should consider whether he can be adequately protected by means which are less drastic than total exclusion of the public, for example, the making of a statement or an order prohibiting the publication of a person's name under s.11 of the *Contempt of Court Act* 1981or by using a letter to designate his name and the use of screens: *R. v Reigate Justices Ex p. Argus Newspapers* (1983) 5 Cr.App.R.(S.) 181; *R v Lord Saville of Newdigate Ex p. A* above. The screening of an accused from a witness in a terrorist trial has been upheld: *X v UK* 15 E.H.R.R. CD 113.

See § 20–26 below.

C. STATUTORY EXCEPTIONS

The general rule that a summary trial must be held in open court is subject to several **19–7** statutory exceptions.

Children and Young Persons Act 1933, ss.36, 37

Prohibition against children being present in court during the trial of other persons

36. No child (other than an infant in arms) shall be permitted to be present in court during **19–8** the trial of any other person charged with an offence, or during any proceedings preliminary thereto, except during such time as his presence is required as a witness or otherwise for the purposes of justice or while the court consents to his presence; and any child present in court when under this section he is not to be permitted to be so shall be ordered to be removed ...

[This section is reprinted as amended by the *Access to Justice Act* 1999, Sch.15, para.1.]

Power to clear court while child or young person is giving evidence in certain cases

19–9   **37.**—(1) Where, in any proceedings in relation to an offence against, or any conduct contrary to, decency or morality, a person who, in the opinion of the court, is a child or young person is called as a witness, the court may direct that all or any persons, not being members or officers of the court or parties to the case, their counsel or solicitors, or persons otherwise directly concerned in the case, be excluded from the court during the taking of the evidence of that witness:

Provided that nothing in this section shall authorise the exclusion of bona fide representatives of a newspaper or news agency.

(2) The powers conferred on a court by this section shall be in addition and without prejudice to any other powers of the court to hear proceedings in camera.

Children under fourteen years of age (other than babies) are generally excluded from court although application may be made to the court to allow such a child to be present. This sometimes happens when a defendant's child cannot be looked after elsewhere. It may also happen when a party of schoolchildren wish to visit the court. Each application will be dealt with on its merits and will, amongst other matters, depend upon the nature of the court proceedings. The court may also clear the court where a child is giving evidence.

Official Secrets Act 1920, s.8(4)

Provisions as to trial and punishment of offences

19–10   **8.**—(4) In addition and without prejudice to any powers which a court may possess to order the exclusion of the public from any proceedings if, in the course of proceedings before a court against any person for an offence under the principal Act or this Act or the proceedings on appeal, or in the course of the trial of a person for felony or misdemeanour under the principal Act or this Act, application is made by the prosecution, on the ground that the publication of any evidence to be given or of any statement to be made in the course of the proceedings would be prejudicial to the national safety, that all or any portion of the public shall be excluded during any part of the hearing, the court may make an order to that effect, but the passing of sentence shall in any case take place in public.

[This section is reprinted excluding paras (1)–(3) and (5) and as amended by the *Criminal Justice Act* 1948, s.(2) and the *Criminal Procedure (Scotland) Act* 1975, s.221(2).]

Although cases under this Act are finalised in the Crown Court there may be instances where, *e.g.*, on a bail application the prosecution will make use of this section.

Youth Justice and Criminal Evidence Act 1999, s.43

Procedure on applications under section 41

19–11   **43.**—(1) An application for leave shall be heard in private and in the absence of the complainant.

In this section "leave" means leave under section 41.

(2) Where such an application has been determined, the court must state in open court (but in the absence of the jury, if there is one)—

    (a) its reasons for giving, or refusing, leave, and

    (b) if it gives leave, the extent to which evidence may be adduced or questions asked in pursuance of the leave,

and, if it is a magistrates' court, must cause those matters to be entered in the register of its proceedings.

    (3) Rules of court may make provision—

    (a) requiring applications for leave to specify, in relation to each item of evidence or question to which they relate, particulars of the grounds on which it is asserted that leave should be given by virtue of subsection (3) or (5) of section 41;

    (b) enabling the court to request a party to the proceedings to provide the court with information which it considers would assist it in determining an application for leave;

(c) for the manner in which confidential or sensitive information is to be treated in connection with such an application, and in particular as to its being disclosed to, or withheld from, parties to the proceedings.

This section provides for a court to sit in private when hearing an application for leave to adduce evidence or to cross-examine on a complainant's sexual history.

D. PUBLICITY

Contempt of Court Act 1981, s.4

Contemporary reports of proceedings

4.—(1) Subject to this section a person is not guilty of contempt of court under the strict li- **19–12** ability rule in respect of a fair and accurate report of legal proceedings held in public, published contemporaneously and in good faith.

(2) In any such proceedings the court may, where it appears to be necessary for avoiding a substantial risk of prejudice to the administration of justice in those proceedings, or in any other proceedings pending or imminent, order that the publication of any report of the proceedings, or any part of the proceedings, be postponed for such period as the court thinks necessary for that purpose.

(3) For the purposes of subsection (1) of this section […] a report of proceedings shall be treated as published contemporaneously—

(a) in the case of a report of which publication is postponed pursuant to an order under subsection (2) of this section, if published as soon as practicable after that order expires;

(b) in the case of a report of committal proceedings of which publication is permitted by virtue only of subsection (3) of section 8 of the *Magistrates' Courts Act* 1980, if published as soon as practicable after publication is so permitted.

[This section is reprinted as amended by the *Defamation Act* 1996, Sch.2, para.1.]

Contempt of Court Act 1981, s.11

Publication of matters exempted from disclosure in court.

11. In any case where a court (having power to do so) allows a name or other matter to be **19–13** withheld from the public in proceedings before the court, the court may give such directions prohibiting the publication of that name or matter in connection with the proceedings as appear to the court to be necessary for the purpose for which it was so withheld.

The press plays an important part in keeping the public informed of court proceedings and it is important that reports are fair and accurate. Adverse publicity may give rise to a breach of Art.6(1) of the European Convention on Human Rights and may constitute grounds for a stay of the proceedings.

In *R. v Bow Street Stipendiary Magistrate Ex p. DPP* (1992) 95 Cr.App.R. 9, DC **19–14** the defendants were police officers who had interviewed suspects who were later charged and convicted of the Guildford and Woolwich pub bombings in 1974. The only evidence against those suspects was confession evidence obtained in an interview in the presence of the defendant police officers. A subsequent police investigation revealed discrepancies between the typed and hand–written notes of the interview made by the defendant police officers. Those who had been convicted of the bombings successfully appealed and were released in October 1989. In December 1990, the police officers were charged with conspiring to pervert the course of justice and in a preliminary application argued abuse of process on the grounds that adverse media coverage of their case was so prejudicial that a fair trial was not possible. The stipendiary magistrate upheld the application but on review the Divisional Court held that the publicity could not affect the fairness of the trial and quashed the magistrate's decision.

The court may postpone the publication of reports under s.4 or restrict the publication of reports under s.11 where it is necessary to avoid a substantial risk to the prejudice of the administration of justice. The *Practice Direction (Criminal Proceedings: Consolidation)* [2002] 1 W.L.R. 2870, para.I.3 directs that a permanent record of such orders is kept and that an order is formulated in precise terms having regard to the decision in *R. v Horsham Justices Ex p. Farquharson* [1982] Q.B. 762.The order must be reduced into writing and must state (a) its precise scope, (b) the time at which it shall cease to have effect, if appropriate, and (c) the specific purpose of making the order. The court will give copies to the parties and display the order in a prominent position in the courthouse.

19–15   Representatives of the press may address the court before an order is made: *R. v Clerkenwell Magistrates' Court Ex p. Telegraph plc* [1993] 2 All E.R. 183. In *Ex p. The Telegraph Group plc* [2001] 1 W.L.R. 1983, it was stated that a court should take a three stage approach. First, the court should consider whether reporting would give rise to a " not insubstantial" risk of prejudice, secondly whether a s.4(2) order would eliminate it or whether it could be overcome by less restrictive measures and thirdly, whether the degree of risk contemplated would be tolerable as the "lesser of two evils".

Before the application is heard the name or other matter must be withheld: *R. v Arundel Justices Ex p. Westminster Press Ltd* [1985] 2 All E.R. 390. In *Tower Bridge Magistrates' Court Ex p. Osborne* [1988] Crim.L.R. 382, it was said that it is generally necessary to hear such an application *in camera*.

The general right of publication in s.4(1) is subject to several statutory restrictions in relation to:

— committal proceedings: see § 7–53.

— youths

— certain adult witnesses

— rape cases

— derogatory assertions made in mitigating statements.

Children and Young Persons Act 1933, s.39

Power to prohibit publication of certain matter in newspapers

19–16   39.—(1) In relation to any proceedings in any court […], the court may direct that—

    (a) no newspaper report of the proceedings shall reveal the name, address or school, or include any particulars calculated to lead to the identification, of any child or young person concerned in the proceedings, either as being the person [by or against] or in respect of whom the proceedings are taken, or as being a witness therein:

    (b) no picture shall be published in any newspaper as being or including a picture of any child or young person so concerned in the proceedings as aforesaid;

except in so far (if at all) as may be permitted by the direction of the court.

(2) Any person who publishes any matter in contravention of any such direction shall on summary conviction be liable in respect of each offence to a fine not exceeding [level 5 on the standard scale].

[This section is reprinted as amended by the *Children and Young Persons Act* 1963, ss.57(1), 64 and Sch.5, and the *Criminal Justice Act* 1982, ss.38, 46.]

19–17   This is a discretionary order which may be made in any court and is generally made of the court's own motion. It is different from the general prohibition in s.49 which applies to Youth courts. An order under s.39 need not be made during the course of the proceedings to which it relates; it may be made at any time: *R. v Harrow Crown Court Ex p. Perkins, R v Cardiff Crown Court Ex p. M (a minor)* (1998) 162 J.P. 527, DC.

19–18   A court has the discretion to hear anybody in support of, or in opposition to, the making of an order under s.39: *R. v Central Criminal Court Ex p. Crook* [1995] 2 Cr.App.R. 212 where the judge heard representations on behalf of the press and the children in question.

Where the alleged victim is a ward of court, it is for the court in the criminal proceedings, not the wardship judge, to make any orders restraining reporting of the criminal trial. The guardian *ad litem* will provide the prosecution with the material necessary to make the application. In *R. (a minor) (Wardship: restriction on publication)*, *Re* [1994] 2 F.L.R. 637, CA (Civ Div) the defendant applied for an order on the basis that he might feel inhibited in presenting his defence as he apprehended that it would lead to publicity harmful to his child and perhaps weaken his position in the wardship proceeding.

Although *R. v Central Criminal Court Ex p. Crook*, above, suggested a formal pro- **19–19** cedure for reducing orders under s.39 to writing by means of a *pro forma*, the normal practice in the magistrates' court is for the order to be written in precise terms in accordance with the section in the court register. Vague restrictions may cause a prosecution for contravening such an order under s.39(2) to founder: *Briffett and Bradshaw v DPP* (2002) 166 J.P. 66, DC.

Permission may be given for the register to be inspected and the justices' clerk will always clarify matters for the press.

There is no power to prohibit the publication of the name of a defendant who is not a child or young person although this may be the unintentional result of such an order. Where this is likely the court may hear representations on the identification of particular details: *R. v Southwark Crown Court Ex p. Goodwin* [1992] Q.B. 190 94 Cr.App.R. 34, CA.

In *R. v Tyne Tees Television Ltd, The Times*, October 20, 1997 the Court of Appeal considered that where there has been an alleged breach of an order under s.39, the better course is to report the matter for consideration as to whether there should be a prosecution for the specific summary offence under s.39 (2) rather than deal with the matter as an alleged contempt of court. The court declined to rule whether contempt proceedings would ever be appropriate in view of the specific statutory offence.

When considering an application under s.39 in respect of a child or young person **19–20** who is the defendant, considerable weight should be given to the actual age of the offender and to the potential damage to any young person of public identification as a criminal before becoming an adult: *R. v Inner London Crown Court Ex p. B* [1996] C.O.D. 17, DC. There must be good reason for making an order. It is not only in rare and exceptional cases that such an order would be made, or once made, would be lifted: *R. v Leicester Crown Court Ex p. S (a minor)* (1992) 94 Cr.App.R. 143, DC. In considering whether to lift an order the welfare of the child must be taken into account but the weight to be given to it changes where there has been a conviction, particularly in a serious case. It must be remembered that the public has a legitimate interest in knowing the outcome of proceedings in court and there is a potential deterrent effect in respect of the conduct of others in the disgrace accompanying the identification of those guilty of serious offences: *R. v Central Criminal Court Ex p. S* [1999] 1 F.L.R. 480, DC.

An appeal against the making of an order is by way of case stated or judicial review.

Youth Justice and Criminal Evidence Act 1999, s.44

Restrictions on reporting alleged offences involving persons under 18

44.—(1) This section applies (subject to subsection (3)) where a criminal investigation has **19–21** begun in respect of—

    (a) an alleged offence against the law of—

        (i)　England and Wales, or

        (ii)　Northern Ireland; or

    (b) an alleged civil offence (other than an offence falling within paragraph (a)) committed (whether or not in the United Kingdom) by a person subject to service law.

    (2) No matter relating to any person involved in the offence shall while he is under the age of 18 be included in any publication if it is likely to lead members of the public to identify him as a person involved in the offence.

    (3) The restrictions imposed by subsection (2) cease to apply once there are proceedings in a court (whether a court in England and Wales, a service court or a court in Northern Ireland) in respect of the offence.

(4) For the purposes of subsection (2) any reference to a person involved in the offence is to—

    (a) a person by whom the offence is alleged to have been committed; or

    (b) if this paragraph applies to the publication in question by virtue of subsection (5)—

        (i) a person against or in respect of whom the offence is alleged to have been committed, or

        (ii) a person who is alleged to have been a witness to the commission of the offence;

    except that paragraph (b)(i) does not include a person in relation to whom section 1 of the *Sexual Offences (Amendment) Act* 1992 (anonymity of victims of certain sexual offences) applies in connection with the offence.

(5) Subsection (4)(b) applies to a publication if—

    (a) where it is a relevant programme, it is transmitted, or

    (b) in the case of any other publication, it is published,

on or after such date as may be specified in an order made by the Secretary of State.

(6) The matters relating to a person in relation to which the restrictions imposed by subsection (2) apply (if their inclusion in any publication is likely to have the result mentioned in that subsection) include in particular—

    (a) his name,

    (b) his address,

    (c) the identity of any school or other educational establishment attended by him,

    (d) the identity of any place of work, and

    (e) any still or moving picture of him.

19–22

(7) Any appropriate criminal court may by order dispense, to any extent specified in the order, with the restrictions imposed by subsection (2) in relation to a person if it is satisfied that it is necessary in the interests of justice to do so.

(8) However, when deciding whether to make such an order dispensing (to any extent) with the restrictions imposed by subsection (2) in relation to a person, the court shall have regard to the welfare of that person.

(9) In subsection (7) "appropriate criminal court" means—

    (a) in a case where this section applies by virtue of subsection (1)(a)(i) or (ii), any court in England and Wales or (as the case may be) in Northern Ireland which has any jurisdiction in, or in relation to, any criminal proceedings (but not a service court unless the offence is alleged to have been committed by a person subject to service law);

    (b) in a case where this section applies by virtue of subsection (1)(b), any court falling within paragraph (a) or a service court.

(10) The power under subsection (7) of a magistrates' court in England and Wales may be exercised by a single justice.

(11) In the case of a decision of a magistrates' court in England and Wales, or a court of summary jurisdiction in Northern Ireland, to make or refuse to make an order under subsection (7), the following persons, namely—

    (a) any person who was a party to the proceedings on the application for the order, and

    (b) with the leave of the Crown Court, any other person,

may, in accordance with rules of court, appeal to the Crown Court against that decision or appear or be represented at the hearing of such an appeal.

(12) On such an appeal the Crown Court—

    (a) may make such order as is necessary to give effect to its determination of the appeal; and

    (b) may also make such incidental or consequential orders as appear to it to be just.

(13) In this section—

    (a) "civil offence" means an act or omission which, if committed in England and Wales, would be an offence against the law of England and Wales;

    (b) any reference to a criminal investigation, in relation to an alleged offence, is to an investigation conducted by police officers, or other persons charged with the duty of investigating offences, with a view to it being ascertained whether a person should be charged with the offence;

(c) any reference to a person subject to service law is to—
  (i) a person subject to military law, air-force law or the *Naval Discipline Act* 1957, or
  (ii) any other person to whom provisions of Part II of the *Army Act* 1955, Part II of the *Air Force Act* 1955 or Parts I and II of the *Naval Discipline Act* 1957 apply (whether with or without any modifications).

When this section comes into force then the reporting of a crime before proceedings **19–23** commence where a person under the age of 18 is a victim or a potential witness or defendant is prohibited where it may lead to his identification. The court may lift the restriction if it satisfied that it is in the interests of justice to do so.

Youth Justice and Criminal Evidence Act 1999, s.45

Power to restrict reporting of criminal proceedings involving persons under 18
  45.—(1) This section applies (subject to subsection (2)) in relation to—   **19–24**
  (a) any criminal proceedings in any court (other than a service court) in England and Wales or Northern Ireland; and
  (b) any proceedings (whether in the United Kingdom or elsewhere) in any service court.

(2) This section does not apply in relation to any proceedings to which section 49 of the *Children and Young Persons Act* 1933 applies.

(3) The court may direct that no matter relating to any person concerned in the proceedings shall while he is under the age of 18 be included in any publication if it is likely to lead members of the public to identify him as a person concerned in the proceedings.

(4) The court or an appellate court may by direction ("an excepting direction") dispense, to any extent specified in the excepting direction, with the restrictions imposed by a direction under subsection (3) if it is satisfied that it is necessary in the interests of justice to do so.

(5) The court or an appellate court may also by direction ("an excepting direction") dispense, to any extent specified in the excepting direction, with the restrictions imposed by a direction under subsection (3) if it is satisfied—
  (a) that their effect is to impose a substantial and unreasonable restriction on the reporting of the proceedings, and
  (b) that it is in the public interest to remove or relax that restriction;
but no excepting direction shall be given under this subsection by reason only of the fact that the proceedings have been determined in any way or have been abandoned.

(6) When deciding whether to make—   **19–25**
  (a) a direction under subsection (3) in relation to a person, or
  (b) an excepting direction under subsection (4) or (5) by virtue of which the restrictions imposed by a direction under subsection (3) would be dispensed with (to any extent) in relation to a person,
the court or (as the case may be) the appellate court shall have regard to the welfare of that person.

(7) For the purposes of subsection (3) any reference to a person concerned in the proceedings is to a person—
  (a) against or in respect of whom the proceedings are taken, or
  (b) who is a witness in the proceedings.

(8) The matters relating to a person in relation to which the restrictions imposed by a direction under subsection (3) apply (if their inclusion in any publication is likely to have the result mentioned in that subsection) include in particular—
  (a) his name,
  (b) his address,
  (c) the identity of any school or other educational establishment attended by him,
  (d) the identity of any place of work, and
  (e) any still or moving picture of him.

(9) A direction under subsection (3) may be revoked by the court or an appellate court.

(10) An excepting direction—

(a) may be given at the time the direction under subsection (3) is given or subsequently; and

(b) may be varied or revoked by the court or an appellate court.

(11) In this section "appellate court", in relation to any proceedings in a court, means a court dealing with an appeal (including an appeal by way of case stated) arising out of the proceedings or with any further appeal.

19–25.1 When this section is in force the court will have power to restrict reporting in relation to a witness or defendant under the age of 18. This section will supersede s.39 of the *Children and Young Persons Act* 1933, above.

Youth Justice and Criminal Evidence Act 1999, s.46

Power to restrict reports about certain adult witness in criminal proceedings

19–26 **46.**—(1) This section applies where—

(a) in any criminal proceedings in any court (other than a service court) in England and Wales or Northern Ireland, or

(b) in any proceedings (whether in the United Kingdom or elsewhere) in any service court,

a party to the proceedings makes an application for the court to give a reporting direction in relation to a witness in the proceedings (other than the accused) who has attained the age of 18.

In this section "reporting direction" has the meaning given by subsection (6).

(2) If the court determines—

(a) that the witness is eligible for protection, and

(b) that giving a reporting direction in relation to the witness is likely to improve—

(i) the quality of evidence given by the witness, or

(ii) the level of co-operation given by the witness to any party to the proceedings in connection with that party's preparation of its case,

the court may give a reporting direction in relation to the witness.

19–27 (3) For the purposes of this section a witness is eligible for protection if the court is satisfied—

(a) that the quality of evidence given by the witness, or

(b) the level of co-operation given by the witness to any party to the proceedings in connection with that party's preparation of its case,

is likely to be diminished by reason of fear or distress on the part of the witness in connection with being identified by members of the public as a witness in the proceedings.

(4) In determining whether a witness is eligible for protection the court must take into account, in particular—

(a) the nature and alleged circumstances of the offence to which the proceedings relate;

(b) the age of the witness;

(c) such of the following matters as appear to the court to be relevant, namely—

(i) the social and cultural background and ethnic origins of the witness,

(ii) the domestic and employment circumstances of the witness, and

(iii) any religious beliefs or political opinions of the witness;

(d) any behaviour towards the witness on the part of—

(i) the accused,

(ii) members of the family or associates of the accused, or

(iii) any other person who is likely to be an accused or a witness in the proceedings.

(5) In determining that question the court must in addition consider any views expressed by the witness.

(6) For the purposes of this section a reporting direction in relation to a witness is a direction that no matter relating to the witness shall during the witness's lifetime be included in any publication if it is likely to lead members of the public to identify him as being a witness in the proceedings.

(7) The matters relating to a witness in relation to which the restrictions imposed by a reporting direction apply (if their inclusion in any publication is likely to have the result mentioned in subsection (6)) include in particular—

(a) the witness's name,
(b) the witness's address,
(c) the identity of any educational establishment attended by the witness,
(d) the identity of any place of work, and
(e) any still or moving picture of the witness.

(8) In determining whether to give a reporting direction the court shall consider—
(a) whether it would be in the interests of justice to do so, and
(b) the public interest in avoiding the imposition of a substantial and unreasonable restriction on the reporting of the proceedings.

(9) The court or an appellate court may by direction ("an excepting direction") dispense, **19–28** to any extent specified in the excepting direction, with the restrictions imposed by a reporting direction if—
(a) it is satisfied that it is necessary in the interests of justice to do so, or
(b) it is satisfied—
  (i) that the effect of those restrictions is to impose a substantial and unreasonable restriction on the reporting of the proceedings, and
  (ii) that it is in the public interest to remove or relax that restriction;
but no excepting direction shall be given under paragraph (b) by reason only of the fact that the proceedings have been determined in any way or have been abandoned.

(10) A reporting direction may be revoked by the court or an appellate court.

(11) An excepting direction—
(a) may be given at the time the reporting direction is given or subsequently; and
(b) may be varied or revoked by the court or an appellate court.

(12) In this section—
(a) "appellate court", in relation to any proceedings in a court, means a court dealing with an appeal (including an appeal by way of case stated) arising out of the proceedings or with any further appeal;
(b) references to the quality of a witness's evidence are to its quality in terms of completeness, coherence and accuracy (and for this purpose "coherence" refers to a witness's ability in giving evidence to give answers which address the questions put to the witness and can be understood both individually and collectively);
(c) references to the preparation of the case of a party to any proceedings include, where the party is the prosecution, the carrying out of investigations into any offence at any time charged in the proceedings.

When this section is in force, the court will have the power to restrict reports about **19–29** an adult witness' evidence if it believes that the witness is afraid or distressed about being identified and as a result the quality of the evidence that the witness would give or the witness' cooperation is likely to be diminished. The court will take into account the nature of the offence, the age, social, cultural background and ethnic origins, domestic and employment circumstances, religious or political beliefs of the witness and any behaviour of the defendant, his family and friends or other witnesses towards the witness. The court will also want to be satisfied that the order is likely to improve the quality of the evidence or the witness' cooperation. The court will take the witness' views into account.

Youth Justice and Criminal Evidence Act 1999, Sch.7, para.6

SCHEDULE 7

6.—(1) Section 44 applies in relation to an alleged offence whether the criminal investiga- **19–30** tion into it is begun before or after the coming into force of that section.

(2) The restrictions imposed by subsection (2) of section 44 do not apply to the inclusion of matter in a publication if—
(a) where the publication is a relevant programme, it is transmitted, or
(b) in the case of any other publication, it is published,
before the coming into force of that section.

(3) Nothing in section 45 or 46 applies in relation to proceedings instituted before the commencement date for that section.

(4) In sub-paragraph (3) the reference to the institution of proceedings shall be construed—

    (a) in the case of proceedings in England in Wales (other than proceedings before a service court), in accordance with paragraph 1(2);

    (b) in the case of proceedings in Northern Ireland (other than proceedings before a service court), in the accordance with sub-paragraph (5);

    (c) in the case of proceedings before a service court (wherever held) in accordance with sub-paragraph (6).

19–31   (5) In the case of proceedings falling within sub-paragraph (4)(b)—

    (a) proceedings other than proceedings on appeal are to be taken to be instituted—

        (i) where a justice of the peace issues a summons under Article 20 of the *Magistrates' Courts (Northern Ireland) Order* 1981, when the complaint for the offence is made;

        (ii) where a justice of the peace issues a warrant for the arrest of any person under that Article, when the complaint for the offence is made;

        (iii) where a person is charged with the offence after being taken into custody without a warrant, when he is informed of the particulars of the charge;

        (iv) where an indictment is presented under the authority of section 2(2)(c), (d), (e) or (f) of the *Grand Jury (Abolition) Act (Northern Ireland)* 1969, when the indictment is presented to the court;

    and where the application of this paragraph would result in there being more than one time for the institution of the proceedings, they shall be taken to have been instituted at the earliest of those times; and

    (b) proceedings on appeal are to be taken to be instituted at the time when the notice of appeal is given or (as the case may be) the reference under section 10 or 12 of the *Criminal Appeal Act* 1995 is made.

(6) In the case of proceedings falling within sub-paragraph (4)(c)—

    (a) proceedings other than proceedings on appeal are to be taken to be instituted when the prosecuting authority prefers a charge in respect of the offence under section 83B(4) of the *Army Act* 1955, section 83B(4) of the *Air Force Act* 1955 or section 52I(4) of the *Naval Discipline Act* 1957; and

    (b) proceedings on appeal are to be taken to be instituted when the application for leave to appeal is lodged in accordance with section 9 of the *Courts-Martial (Appeals) Act* 1968 or (as the case may be) the reference under section 34 of that Act is made.

Youth Justice and Criminal Evidence Act 1999, s.47

Restrictions on reporting directions under Chapter I or II

19–32   47.—(1) Except as provided by this section, no publication shall include a report of a matter falling within subsection (2).

(2) The matters falling within this subsection are—

    (a) a direction under section 19 or 36 or an order discharging, or (in the case of a direction under section 19) varying, such a direction;

    (b) proceedings—

        (i) on an application for such a direction or order, or

        (ii) where the court acts of its own motion to determine whether to give or make any such direction or order.

(3) The court dealing with a matter falling within subsection (2) may order that subsection (1) is not to apply, or is not to apply to a specified extent, to a report of that matter.

(4) Where—

    (a) there is only one accused in the relevant proceedings, and

    (b) he objects to the making of an order under subsection (3),

the court shall make the order if (and only if) satisfied after hearing the representations of the accused that it is in the interests of justice to do so; and if the order is made it shall not apply to the extent that a report deals with any such objections or representations.

19–33   (5) Where—

    (a) there are two or more accused in the relevant proceedings, and

    (b) one or more of them object to the making of an order under subsection (3), the court shall make the order if (and only if) satisfied after hearing the representations of each of the accused that it is in the interests of justice to do so; and if the order is made it shall not apply to the extent that a report deals with any such objections or representations.

(6) Subsection (1) does not apply to the inclusion in a publication of a report of matters after the relevant proceedings are either—

(a) determined (by acquittal, conviction or otherwise), or

(b) abandoned,

in relation to the accused or (if there is more than one) in relation to each of the accused.

(7) In this section "the relevant proceedings" means the proceedings to which any such direction as is mentioned in subsection (2) relates or would relate.

(8) Nothing in this section affects any prohibition or restriction by virtue of any other enactment on the inclusion of matter in a publication.

The reporting of a direction in relation to special measures or prohibiting cross ex- **19–33.1** amination of a particular witness or an order varying or discharging such a direction is prohibited unless the court directs otherwise. If the court is minded to allow publication it shall hear the objections or representations of any defendant and must only make the order if it is in the interests of justice and to the extent that the report deals with the objections or representations.

Youth Justice and Criminal Evidence Act 1999 s.49

Offences under Chapter IV

49.—(1) This section applies if a publication—   **19–34**

(a) includes any matter in contravention of section 44(2) or of a direction under section 45(3) or 46(2); or

(b) includes a report in contravention of section 47.

(2) Where the publication is a newspaper or periodical, any proprietor, any editor and any publisher of the newspaper or periodical is guilty of an offence.

(3) Where the publication is a relevant programme—

(a) any body corporate or Scottish partnership engaged in providing the programme service in which the programme is included, and

(b) any person having functions in relation to the programme corresponding to those of an editor of a newspaper,

is guilty of an offence.

(4) In the case of any other publication, any person publishing it is guilty of an offence.

(5) A person guilty of an offence under this section is liable on summary conviction to a fine not exceeding level 5 on the standard scale.

(6) Proceedings for an offence under this section in respect of a publication falling within subsection (1)(b) may not be instituted—

(a) in England and Wales otherwise than by or with the consent of the Attorney General, or

(b) in Northern Ireland otherwise than by or with the consent of the Attorney General for Northern Ireland.

This section applies to youth courts only—see Chapter 30. It is a mandatory restriction. In *T v DPP*; *North East Press Ltd* [2003] EWHC Admin 2408, the defendant had attained the age of 18 during the course of proceedings against him in the youth court. It was held that the restriction applies only for so long as the person concerned continues to be a child or young person.

Youth Justice and Criminal Evidence Act 1999, s.52

Decisions as to public interest for purposes of Chapter IV

52.—(1) Where for the purposes of any provision of this Chapter it falls to a court to **19–35** determine whether anything is (or, as the case may be, was) in the public interest, the court must have regard, in particular, to the matters referred to in subsection (2) (so far as relevant).

(2) Those matters are—

(a) the interest in each of the following—

    (i)   the open reporting of crime,

    (ii)   the open reporting of matters relating to human health or safety, and

    (iii)   the prevention and exposure of miscarriages of justice;

  (b)   the welfare of any person in relation to whom the relevant restrictions imposed by or under this Chapter apply or would apply (or, as the case may be, applied); and

  (c)   any views expressed—

    (i)   by an appropriate person on behalf of a person within paragraph (b) who is under the age of 16 ("the protected person"), or

    (ii)   by a person within that paragraph who has attained that age.

  (3) In subsection (2) "an appropriate person", in relation to the protected person, has the same meaning as it has for the purposes of section 50.

Where, in the future, a court has to have regard to the public interest when making an order in relation to reporting under the *Youth Justice and Criminal Evidence Act 1999*, it will have regard, in particular, to the public interest in the open reporting of crime, health and safety, the prevention of miscarriages of justice and the welfare of any person to whom the reporting restrictions apply.

Sexual Offences (Amendment) Act 1976, s.4

Anonymity of complainants in rape etc cases

19–36   **4.**—(1) Except as authorised by a direction given in pursuance of this section—

  (a)   after an allegation that a women or man has been the victim of a rape offence has been made by the woman or man or by any other person, neither the name nor the address of the woman or man nor a still or moving picture of her or him shall during that person's lifetime—

    (i)   be published in England and Wales in a written publication available to the public; or

    (ii)   be included in a relevant programme for reception in England and Wales, if that is likely to lead members of the public to identify that person as an alleged victim of such an offence; and

  (b)   after a person is accused of a rape offence, no matter likely to lead members of the public to identify a woman or man as the complainant in relation to that accusation shall during that person's lifetime—

    (i)   be published in England and Wales in a written publication available to the public; or

    (ii)   be included in a relevant programme for reception in England and Wales; but nothing in this subsection prohibits the publication or inclusion in a relevant programme of matter consisting only of a report of criminal proceedings other than proceedings at, or intended to lead to, or on an appeal arising out of, a trial at which the accused is charged with the offence.

  (1A) In subsection (1) above "picture" includes a likeness however produced.

  (2) If, before the commencement of a trial at which a person is charged with a rape offence, he or another person against whom the complainant may be expected to give evidence at the trial applies to a judge of the Crown Court for a direction in pursuance of this subsection and satisfies the judge—

  (a)   that the direction is required for the purpose of inducing persons to come forward who are likely to be needed as witnesses at the trial; and

  (b)   that the conduct of the applicant's defence at the trial is likely to be substantially prejudiced if the direction is not given,

the judge shall direct that the preceding subsection shall not, by virtue of the accusation alleging the offence aforesaid, apply in relation to the complainant.

19–37   (3) If at a trial the judge is satisfied that the effect of subsection (1) of this section is to impose a substantial and unreasonable restriction upon the reporting of proceedings at the trial and that it is in the public interest to remove or relax the restriction, he shall direct that that subsection shall not apply to such matter as is specified in the direction; but a direction shall not be given in pursuance of this subsection by reason only of the outcome of the trial.

(4) If a person who has been convicted of an offence and given notice of appeal to the Court of Appeal against the conviction, or notice of an application for leave so to appeal, applies to the Court of Appeal for a direction in pursuance of this subsection and satisfies the Court—

(a) that the direction is required for the purpose of obtaining evidence in support of the appeal; and

(b) that the applicant is likely to suffer substantial injustice if the direction is not given,

the Court shall direct that subsection (1) of this section shall not, by virtue of an accusation which alleges a rape offence and is specified in the direction, apply in relation to a complainant so specified.

(5) If any matter is published or included in a relevant programme in contravention of subsection (1) of this section, the following persons, namely—

(a) in the case of a publication in a newspaper or periodical, any proprietor, any editor and any publisher of the newspaper or periodical;

(b) in the case of any other publication, the person who publishes it; and

(c) in the case of matter included in a relevant programme, any body corporate which is engaged in providing the service in which the programme is included and any person having functions in relation to the programme corresponding to those of an editor of a newspaper,

shall be guilty of an offence and liable on summary conviction to a fine not exceeding level 5 on the standard scale.

(5A) Where a person is charged with an offence under subsection (5) of this section in **19–38** respect of the publication of any matter or the inclusion of any matter in a relevant programme, it shall be a defence, subject to subsection (5B) below, to prove that the publication or programme in which the matter appeared was one in respect of which the woman or man had given written consent to the appearance of matter of that description.

(5B) Written consent is not a defence if it is proved that any person interfered unreasonably with the peace or comfort of the woman or man with intent to obtain the consent.

(6) For the purposes of this section a person is accused of a rape offence if—

(a) an information is laid alleging that he has committed a rape offence; or

(b) he appears before a court charged with a rape offence; or

(c) a court before which he is appearing commits him for trial on a new charge alleging a rape offence; or

(d) a bill of indictment charging him with a rape offence is preferred before a court in which he may lawfully be indicted for the offence,

and references in this section and section 7(5) of this Act to an accusation alleging a rape offence shall be construed accordingly; and in this section—

"complainant", in relation to a person accused of a rape offence or an accusation alleging a rape offence, means the woman or man against whom the offence is alleged to have been committed; and

"relevant programme" means a programme included in a programme service (within the meaning of the *Broadcasting Act* 1990);

"written publication" includes a film, a sound track and any other record in permanent form but does not include an indictment or other document prepared for use in particular legal proceedings.

(6A) For the purposes of this section, where it is alleged or there is an accusation that an offence of incitement to rape or conspiracy to rape has been committed, the person who is alleged to have been the intended victim of the rape shall be regarded as the alleged victim of the incitement or conspiracy or, in the case of an accusation, as the complainant.

(7) Nothing in this section—

(b) affects any prohibition or restriction imposed by virtue of any other enactment upon a publication or upon matter included in a relevant programme;

and a direction in pursuance of this section does not affect the operation of subsection (1) of this section at any time before the direction is given.

[This section is reprinted as amended by the *Criminal Justice and Public Order Act* 1994, Sch.9, para.13.]

This section prevents the identification of victims in rape cases whether they are male **19–38.1** or female. It will be repealed by Sch.6 of the *Youth Justice and Criminal Evidence Act 1999* when in force.

Criminal Procedure and Investigations Act 1996, ss.58–61

Orders in respect of certain assertions

19–39   **58.**—(1) This section applies where a person has been convicted of an offence and a speech in mitigation is made by him or on his behalf before—

    (a) a court determining what sentence should be passed on him in respect of the offence, or

    (b) a magistrates' court determining whether he should be committed to the Crown Court for sentence.

(2) This section also applies where a sentence has been passed on a person in respect of an offence and a submission relating to the sentence is made by him or on his behalf before—

    (a) a court hearing an appeal against or reviewing the sentence, or

    (b) a court determining whether to grant leave to appeal against the sentence.

(3) Where it appears to the court that there is a real possibility that an order under subsection (8) will be made in relation to the assertion, the court may make an order under subsection (7) in relation to the assertion.

(4) Where there are substantial grounds for believing—

    (a) that an assertion forming part of the speech or submission is derogatory to a person's character (for instance, because it suggests that his conduct is or has been criminal, immoral or improper), and

    (b) that the assertion is false or that the facts asserted are irrelevant to the sentence,

the court may make an order under subsection (8) in relation to the assertion.

19–40   (5) An order under subsection (7) or (8) must not be made in relation to an assertion if it appears to the court that the assertion was previously made—

    (a) at the trial at which the person was convicted of the offence, or

    (b) during any other proceedings relating to the offence.

(6) Section 59 has effect where a court makes an order under subsection (7) or (8).

(7) An order under this subsection—

    (a) may be made at any time before the court has made a determination with regard to sentencing;

    (b) may be revoked at any time by the court;

    (c) subject to paragraph (b), shall cease to have effect when the court makes a determination with regard to sentencing.

(8) An order under this subsection—

    (a) may be made at any time before the court has made a determination with regard to sentencing, but only if it is made as soon as is reasonably practicable after the making of the determination;

    (b) may be revoked at any time by the court;

    (c) subject to paragraph (b), shall cease to have effect at the end of the period of 12 months beginning with the day on which it is made;

    (d) may be made whether or not an order has been made under subsection (7) with regard to the case concerned.

(9) For the purposes of subsection (7) and (8) the court makes a determination with regard to sentencing—

    (a) when it determines what sentence should be passed (where this section applies by virtue of subsection (1)(a);

    (b) when it determines whether the person should be committed to the Crown Court for sentence (where this section applies by virtue of subsection (1)(b));

    (c) when it determines what the sentence should be (where this section applies by virtue of subsection (2)(a));

    (d) when it determines whether to grant leave to appeal (where this section applies by virtue of subsection (2)(b).

Restriction on reporting of assertions

19–41   **59.**—(1) Where a court makes an order under section 58(7) or (8) in relation to any assertion, at any time when the order has effect the assertion must not—

(a) be published in Great Britain in a written publication available to the public, or

(b) be included in a relevant programme for reception in Great Britain.

(2) In this section—

"relevant programme" means a programme included in a programme service, within the meaning of the *Broadcasting Act* 1990;

"written publication" includes a film, a soundtrack and any other record in permanent form but does not include an indictment or other document prepared for use in particular legal proceedings.

(3) For the purposes of this section an assertion is published or included in a programme if the material published or included—

(a) names the person about whom the assertion is made or, without naming him, contains enough to make it likely that members of the public will identify him as the person about whom it is made, and

(b) reproduces the actual wording of the matter asserted or contains its substance.

Reporting of assertions: offences

60.—(1) If an assertion is published or included in a relevant programme in contravention of **19–42** section 59, each of the following persons is guilty of an offence—

(a) in the case of publication in a newspaper or periodical, any proprietor, any editor and any publisher of the newspaper or periodical;

(b) in the case of publication in any other form, the person publishing the assertion;

(c) in the case of an assertion included in a relevant programme, any body corporate engaged in providing the service in which the programme is included and any person having functions in relation to the programme corresponding to those of an editor of a newspaper.

(2) A person guilty of an offence under this section is liable on summary conviction to a fine of an amount not exceeding level 5 on the standard scale.

(3) Where a person is charged with an offence under this section it is a defence to prove that at the time of the alleged offence—

(a) he was not aware, and neither suspected nor had reason to suspect, that an order under section 58(7) or (8) had effect at that time, or

(b) he was not aware, and neither suspected nor had reason to suspect, that the publication or programme in question was of, or (as the case may be) included, the assertion in question.

(4) Where an offence under this section committed by a body corporate is proved to have been committed with the consent or connivance of, or to be attributable to any neglect on the part of—

(a) a director, manager, secretary or other similar officer of the body corporate, or

(b) a person purporting to act in any such capacity,

he as well as the body, corporate is guilty of the offence and liable to be proceeded against and punished accordingly.

(5) In relation to a body corporate whose affairs are managed by its members "director" in subsection (4) means a member of the body corporate.

(6) Subsections (2) and (3) of section 59 apply for the purposes of this section as they apply for the purposes of that.

Reporting of assertions: commencement and supplementary

61.—(1) Section 58 applies where the offence mentioned in subsection (1) or (2) of that sec- **19–43** tion is committed on or after the appointed day.

(2) The reference in subsection (1) to the appointed day is to such day as is appointed for the purposes of this section by the Secretary of State by order.

(3) Nothing in section 58 or 59 affects any prohibition or restriction imposed by virtue of any other enactment on a publication or on matter included in a programme.

(4) Nothing in section 58 or 59 affects section 3 of the *Law of Libel Amendment Act* 1888 (privilege of newspaper reports of court proceedings).

(5) Section 8 of the *Law of Libel Amendment Act* 1888 (order of judge required for prosecution for libel published in a newspaper) does not apply to a prosecution for an offence under section 60.

(6) In section 159 of the *Criminal Justice Act* 1988 (appeal to Court of Appeal against

orders restricting reports etc.) in subsection (1) the following paragraph shall be inserted after paragraph (a)—

"(aa) an order made by the Crown Court under section 58(7) or (8) of the *Criminal Procedure and Investigations Act* 1996 of the *Criminal Procedure and Investigations Act* 1996 in a case where the Court has convicted a person on a trial on indictment;".

19–44   When a plea in mitigation is made to the court the defendant or his representative may try to minimise his offending behaviour by making remarks about the victim's character suggesting that the victim's conduct has been immoral, improper or criminal. If the court finds that there are substantial grounds for believing that the assertion is derogatory and that either it is false or irrelevant to the sentence, it can make a s.58 order. An interim order may be made as soon as the assertion has been made but only if there is a real possibility that a final order will be made. A final order may be made before sentence is passed or afterwards. If it is made after sentence it must be made as soon as is reasonably practicable. The effect of such an order is to bar publication of the assertion which is the subject of the order. An order cannot be made if it appears that the assertion has previously been made at the trial or during any other proceedings in relation to the offence.

An interim order will cease when the defendant is sentenced. A final order continues until it is either revoked by the court or at the end of twelve months beginning on the day on which it is made.

For the purposes of s.61(1) where an offence is committed over a period of more than one day, or at some time during a period of more than one day, it must be taken to be committed on the last of the days in the period: *Criminal Procedure and Investigations Act* 1996 s.75(2), (3).

Reporting of Magistrates' Names

19–45   The names of district judges and magistrates do not routinely appear on court lists. An application may be made for the disclosure of such names to the legal adviser in court or after the hearing to the justices' clerk. Names but not addresses are usually given unless the clerk reasonably believes that the information is wanted for a purely mischievous purpose: *R. v Felixstowe Justices Ex p. Leigh* [1987] Q.B. 582

Photographs

Criminal Justice Act 1925, s.41

Prohibition on taking photographs, &c., in court

19–46   **41.**—(1) No person shall—

(a) take or attempt to take in any court any photograph, or with a view to publication make or attempt to make in any court any portrait or sketch, of any person, being a judge of the court or a juror or a witness in or a party to any proceedings before the court, whether civil or criminal; or

(b) publish any photograph, portrait or sketch taken or made in contravention of the foregoing provisions of this section or any reproduction thereof;

and if any person acts in contravention of this section be shall, on summary conviction, be liable in respect of each offence to a fine not exceeding fifty pounds.

(2) For the purposes of this section—

(a) the expression "court" means any court of justice, including the court of a coroner:

(b) the expression "Judge" includes […], registrar, magistrate, justice and coroner:

(c) a photograph, portrait or sketch shall be deemed to be a photograph, portrait or sketch taken or made in court if it is taken or made in the court-room or in the building or in the precincts of the building in which the court is held, or if it is a photograph, portrait or sketch taken or made of the person while he is entering or leaving the court-room or any such building or precincts as aforesaid.

[This section is reprinted as amended by the *Courts Act* 1971, Sch.11.]

The issue here is one of identification of people. It is intended to ensure a fair trial. It **19–47**
is not a general prohibition on taking photographs of the court building. Neither does it
prevent an artist who has sat in court and observed the proceedings from producing a
sketch thereafter so long as the sketching does not take place within the prohibited
areas.

The precincts of the building could be taken to mean any area surrounding the
courthouse a photograph of which would identify a person as being linked with that
courthouse.

The filming of a defendant in the cell area of a magistrates' court for the purpose of
having the film compared with a picture taken by CCTV of a person committing a robbery was held to be unlawful as being in breach of this prohibition: *R. v Loveridge, Lee
and Loveridge* [2001] 2 Cr.App.R. 29, CA.

Tape Recordings

Contempt of Court Act 1981 s.9

Use of tape recorders

9.—(1) Subject to subsection (4) below, it is a contempt of court—　　　　　**19–48**

(a) to use in court, or bring into court for use, any tape recorder or other instrument
for recording sound, except with the leave of the court;

(b) to publish a recording of legal proceedings made by means of any such instrument, or any recording derived directly or indirectly from it, by playing it in the
hearing of the public or any section of the public, or to dispose of it or any recording so derived, with a view to such publication;

(c) to use any such recording in contravention of any conditions of leave granted
under paragraph (a).

(2) Leave under paragraph (a) of subsection (1) may be granted or refused at the **19–49**
discretion of the court, and if granted may be granted subject to such conditions as the
court thinks proper with respect to the use of any recording made pursuant to the leave;
and where leave has been granted the court may at the like discretion withdraw or amend
it either generally or in relation to any particular part of the proceedings.

(3) Without prejudice to any other power to deal with an act of contempt under
paragraph (a) of subsection (1), the court may order the instrument, or any recording
made with it, or both, to be forfeited; and any object so forfeited shall (unless the court
otherwise determines on application by a person appearing to be the owner) be sold or
otherwise disposed of in such manner as the court may direct.

(4) This section does not apply to the making or use of sound recordings for purposes
of official transcripts of proceedings.

The *Practice Direction (Criminal Proceedings: Consolidation)* (2002) gives guid- **19–50**
ance on the exercise of the court's discretion stating the following factors may be of
relevance:

— reasonable need

— risk of briefing witnesses out of court

— distraction or disturbance by the use of the recorder.

Applications to sit in camera

The term "in camera" covers situations where the court sits in the absence of the **19–51**
press and public. The court may exclude the press and the public during the application itself and will do so if it is intimated that the administration of justice could be
prejudiced by the reasons for the application being stated in open court. Once it is clear
that justice will not be prejudiced the court will open the courtroom again and will sum-
marise what has occurred whilst "in camera". If the court decides to sit "in camera" for
all or part of the hearing itself, it will open the court to announce that fact and give general reasons for so doing: *R. v Tower Bridge JJ Ex.p. Osborne* (1989) 88 Cr.App.R.
28.

Generally a defendant and his advocate must not be excluded from a hearing "in camera" nor should restrictions be placed on an advocate as to what he may disclose to his client or his instructing solicitor if there is one: *R. v Preston* (1994) 2 A.C. 130, HL.

19–52   Where the disclosure of certain matters might be against the public interest because it might compromise state security or the proper functioning of a public service, the prosecutor will claim immunity from disclosure. Difficulties may arise where public interest immunity is sought by the prosecution and an application is made to hear arguments regarding disclosure in the absence of the defendant and his advocate. In most cases the defence will be given notice of an application and may make representations. There will be a few highly sensitive cases, however, where the defendant and his advocate will be excluded. The court, in dealing with such an exceptional application, may consider the appointment of special independent counsel to take part in the proceedings but that is a course of last resort as it presents its own difficulties such as ethical problems with the taking of full instructions and the usual client/counsel relationship. The cardinal and overriding requirement is that of a fair: *R. v H* ; *R. v C* [2004] UKHL 3 [2004] 2 W.L.R. 235 (see Public Interest Immunity, § 19–101 below)

II. LANGUAGE

A. GENERAL

19–53   Court proceedings are ordinarily conducted in English: see *Trepca Mines, Re* [1960] 1 W.L.R. 24.

B. INTERPRETERS

19–54   Interpreters are used for witnesses and defendants where they do not understand English. In accordance with Art.6(3), ECHR above where a defendant does not understand the English language or does not understand it sufficiently to follow court proceedings the evidence at trial should be translated to him. Similarly where the defendant is deaf, mute or both the court must ensure that proper means are taken to communicate to the defendant the case made against him and to enable him to make an answer to it. Sign language may be used or the evidence could be reduced to writing. It has been held that where the indication of the need for an interpreter arose only during the defence case and that there had been no prejudice to the defendant the court's refusal to appoint an interpreter did not render the trial unfair: *Wei Hai Restaurant Ltd v Kingston upon Hull City Council* (2002) 166 J.P. 185, DC.

Where the difficulty in interpretation was such as to make it impossible for a witness's evidence to be tested by cross-examination, the conviction was quashed: *R. v Irmie*, 12 Cr.App.R. 283

It is important that the interpreter is someone who can be expected to interpret impartially: *R. v Mitchell* [1970] Crim.L.R. 153, CA.

19–55   In *R. v West London Youth Court Ex p. N* [2000] 1 W.L.R. 2368, DC, the police interviewed the 11-year-old defendant who spoke only Bosnian Romany. A relative, acting as the appropriate adult, was used for the second limb of a double interpretation process consisting of interpretation from one language into a second language, and then from the second language into a third language. There were no competent or qualified interpreters in Bosnian Romany in the United Kingdom who could act as interpreters in the criminal proceedings and the designated interpreter did not have a high enough level of understanding to meet the needs of the case. The process of double translation was ruled unlawful by the magistrates' court. On review, the Divisional Court held that double interpretation was acceptable and a necessary method of interpretation during both interview and trial on the condition that it had been impossible to find an interpreter who spoke fluently both in English and in a language in which the defendant was fluent. Both interpreters have to be suitably qualified and wholly impartial. It is not sufficient to use an appropriate adult for one limb; they are not impartial as their function is to assist the person questioned. It is important to ensure a proper, mutual understanding between the defendant and the interpreter, between the two interpreters and their common language, and also to ensure that the second interpreter was fluent in the English language.

Evidence from a police officer as to what the defendant had said during an interview, **19–56** as related to the officer by an interpreter, is hearsay; the only valid witness is the interpreter: *R. v Attard* (1959) 43 Cr.App.R. 90.

If the interpreter used at the Police Station is to be called as a prosecution witness, a separate interpreter should be used for the court.

Interpreters are paid fees by the court. The right to free interpretation is unqualified. A convicted person cannot therefore be ordered to pay the costs of an interpreter: *Luedicke, Belkacem and Koc v Germany* (1979–80) 2 E.H.R.R. 149. The fees include travelling time but not travelling expenses. The latter may be claimed separately. See § 37–4 below.

C. Courts in Wales and Monmouthshire

Welsh Language Act 1993, ss.22, 24

Use of Welsh in legal proceedings

22.—(1) In any legal proceedings in Wales the Welsh language may be spoken by any party, **19–57** witness or other person who desires to use it, subject in the case of proceedings in a court other than a magistrates' court to such prior notice as may be required by rules of court; and any necessary provision for interpretation shall be made accordingly.

(2) Any power to make rules of court includes power to make provision as to the use, in proceedings in or having a connection with Wales, of documents in the Welsh language.

Provision of interpreters

24.—(1) The Lord Chancellor may make rules as to the provision and employment of **19–58** interpreters of the Welsh and English languages for the purposes of proceedings before courts in Wales.

(2) The interpreters shall be paid, out of the same fund as the expenses of the court are payable, such remuneration in respect of their services as the Lord Chancellor may determine.

(3) The Lord Chancellor's powers under this section shall be exercised with the consent of the Treasury.

The *Practice Direction (Criminal Proceedings: Consolidation)* (2002), paras III.22 and 23 applies. The purpose of the direction is to give effect to the *Welsh Language Act* 1993 which provides for equal status for Welsh and English in Wales. Legal representatives are under a duty to inform the court where Welsh will be used so that appropriate listing arrangements can be made.

III. REPRESENTATION OF THE DEFENDANT

A. Legal Representation

Magistrates' Courts Act 1980, s.122

Appearance by counsel or solicitor

122.—(1) A party to any proceedings before a magistrates' court may be represented by [a **19–59** legal representative].

(2) Subject to subsection (3) below, an absent party so represented shall be deemed not to be absent.

(3) Appearance of a party by [a legal representative] shall not satisfy any provision of any enactment or any condition of a recognizance expressly requiring his presence.

[This section is reprinted as amended by the *Courts and Legal Services Act* 1990, s.125(3), Sch.18, para.25(3)(b).] As to rights of audience see § 2–30 above.

Art.6(3), ECHR above guarantees the right to legal representation. The provision of legal aid is subject to the means of the defendant and confined to cases where the interests of justice require it: see § 36–21 below.

A defendant is entitled to be represented by a lawyer of his choosing if it is reasonably practicable. It is not an absolute right although his choice should be respected: *Goddi v Italy* (1984) 6 E.H.R.R. 457. The overriding consideration is the requirements of justice, for both prosecution and defence, in the circumstances of the case: *R. v De Oliveira* [1997] Crim.L.R. 600, CA. It will depend not only on the defendant's choice but on the availability of the advocate, a suitably equipped court, witnesses as well as the time scale of the case. Where an advocate withdraws because of professional reasons or is dismissed by his client, the court has a discretion to grant an adjournment so that a new advocate can be instructed. It is not appropriate for the court to seek an explanation for the withdrawal or dismissal. The court is, however, entitled to take into account the likelihood that another advocate would suffer the same fate as the original, the interests of witnesses and of the public. Additional matters to consider are the stage that the trial has reached and the apparent ability of the defendant to conduct his or her own case: *R. v Al-Zubeidi* [1999] Crim.L.R. 906, CA. The defendant is always at liberty to ask the court's permission to conduct his own defence: *R v Lyons* 68 Cr.App.R. 104, CA.

The wrongful denial of the defendant's right to legal representation is likely to result in the quashing of the conviction: *R. v Kingston* (1948) 32 Cr.App.R. 183, CA; *R. v Harris* [1985] Crim.L.R. 244, CA.

B. Right to Conduct Own Defence

19–60 A defendant has the right to conduct his own defence with or without the services of a solicitor: *R. v Woodward* [1944] K.B. 118; *R. v De Courcy*, 48 Cr.App.R. 323, CA. An unrepresented defendant cannot however rely on the disadvantages of lack of representation to support an argument that there was inequality of arms at trial to render the conviction unsafe: *Van Geyseghem v Belgium* (2001) 35 E.H.R.R. 24; *R. v Walton* [2001] 8 *Archbold News* 2, CA.

In magistrates' courts many defendants represent themselves and the legal adviser has a specific duty to assist by putting questions to witnesses on the defendant's behalf.

Magistrates' Courts Rules 1981, r.13A(2)

19–61 13A.—(2) If an accused who is not legally represented instead of asking a witness in support of the charge questions by way of cross-examination, makes assertions, the court shall then put to the witness such questions as it thinks necessary on behalf of the accused and may for this purpose question the accused in order to bring out or clear up any point arising out of such assertions.

The more serious the charge, the more complex the case and the greater the potential for penalty, the more likely it is that representation will be needed to ensure a fair trial: *Hinds v Att.-Gen. of Barbados* [2002] 2 W.L.R. 470, PC. A court may place reasonable restrictions on the right of a defendant to appear without a lawyer in a complex case: *Croissant v Germany* 16 E.H.R.R. 135, *Philis v Greece* (1998) 25 E.H.R.R. 417 . There are also restrictions on the right to cross examine witnesses: s.36 of the *Youth Justice and Criminal Evidence Act* 1999.

C. McKenzie Friends

19–62 Although a defendant may not be represented by someone who has no right of audience he may apply to the court to have with him a "friend" who will assist him by taking notes, prompting and quietly giving advice: *McKenzie v McKenzie* (1970) 3 W.L.R. 472. The case of *R. v Leicester City Justices Ex p. Barrow* [1991] 2 Q.B. 260 confirmed that the right does not go beyond assistance.

D. REPRESENTATION OF A CORPORATE DEFENDANT

Magistrates' Courts Act 1980, Sch.3, paras 2–3

2. A representative may on behalf of a corporation—   **19–63**
   (a) make before examining justices such representations as could be made by an accused who is not a corporation;
   (b) consent to the corporation being tried summarily;
   (c) enter a plea of guilty or not guilty on the trial by a magistrates' court of an information.

3.—(1) Where a representative appears, any requirement of this Act that anything shall be done in the presence of the accused, or shall be read or said to the accused, shall be construed as a requirement that that thing shall be done in the presence of the representative or read or said to the representative.

(2) Where a representative does not appear, any such requirement, and any requirement that the consent of the accused shall be obtained for summary trial, shall not apply.

[This Schedule is reprinted as amended by *Criminal Procedure and Investigations Act* 1996, Sch.1, para.13.]

A company may be represented by an appointed lawyer, a director or the secretary. **19–64** It is advisable for a solicitor to be appointed by the company's representative: *R. v Birmingham and Gloucester Railway Co., TRe LCC and London Tramways Co,* ; *R. v Manchester Corprn* and *R. v Ascanio Puck & Co and Paice* (1912) 76 J.P. 487. It is usual to request the completion of a form in the following words:

> *R. v X Co.*
> *I appoint .... to represent the company in the above case*
> *Signed A.B. Director/Secretary*
> *This also applies to unincorporated bodies: Companies Act* 1985, s.734.

IV. PLEA

A. GENERAL

The first stage in a summary trial is for the court through the legal adviser to read **19–65** the information to the defendant and ask him whether he pleads guilty or not guilty.

Magistrates' Courts Act 1980, s.9

Procedure on trial
   9.—(1) On the summary trial of an information, the court shall, if the accused appears, state **19–66** to him the substance of the information and ask him whether he pleads guilty or not guilty.

(2) The court, after hearing the evidence and the parties, shall convict the accused or dismiss the information.

(3) If the accused pleads guilty, the court may convict him without hearing evidence.

Magistrates' Courts Rules 1981, r.13A(1)

Procedure on information where accused is not legally represented
   13A.—(1) The court shall explain to an accused who is not legally represented the substance **19–67** of the charge in simple language.

[This section is reprinted as amended by the *Magistrates' Courts (Miscellaneous Amendments) Rules* 1993, r.3(b).]

The defendant, unless it is a company, should be asked personally to plead even where he is represented; *R. v Wakefield Justices Ex.p. Butterworth* [1970]1 All E.R. 1181. Where a defendant does not attend court but is represented, he is deemed to be present under s.122 of the *Magistrates' Courts Act* 1980. In those circumstances the court may allow the advocate to enter a plea of guilty on the defendant's behalf.

B. Plea of Guilty

19–68   If the defendant pleads guilty to an information the court may convict the defendant without hearing any evidence. In the absence of a guilty plea, the court is under a duty to hear evidence and either convict the defendant or dismiss the information: *Magistrates' Courts Act* 1980, s.9(2). The prosecution will read out the facts in open court: The *Practice Direction (Criminal Proceedings: Consolidation)*, para.III.26, above. Where the defendant is unrepresented the legal adviser will ensure that he understands the elements of the offence, especially if the facts suggest that he has a defence: *R. v Griffiths*, 23 Cr.App.R. 153, CA; *R. v Blandford Justices Ex p. G (an infant)*, above. A plea of guilty must be unequivocal: *R. v Tottenham Justices Ex p. Rubens* [1970] 1 All E.R. 879.

Where the defendant unequivocally admits the essential ingredients of an offence but disputes various facts, the court should hear evidence on the facts disputed, make findings and proceed to sentence; it should not direct that pleas of not guilty are entered: *R. v Telford Justices Ex p. Darlington* (1988) 87 Cr.App.R. 194. On the other hand, where a court receives facts in mitigation which are inconsistent with a guilty plea that plea must be considered equivocal and a plea of not guilty entered: *R. v Durham Quarter Sessions Ex p. Virgo* [1952] 2 Q.B. 1.

19–69   Pleas which are entered under duress may also be covered by the rule that the plea must be unequivocal: *R. v Huntingdon Crown Court Ex p. Jordan* [1981] Q.B. 857. In that case, the defendant pleaded guilty to theft in the magistrates' court where she was jointly charged with her husband. She appealed against conviction to the Crown Court, on the ground that both the offence and the plea were made under the duress of her husband. The judge ruled that the defendant's plea had been unequivocal and that the court has no jurisdiction to entertain the appeal. On application for judicial review it was held that the Crown Court had jurisdiction to inquire into an allegedly equivocal plea and to remit the matter to the magistrates if satisfied that the plea was equivocal. That jurisdiction extended to cases where an apparently unequivocal plea was entered under duress and was in fact a nullity.

Where the defendant wishes to plead guilty but there is a substantial dispute between the prosecution and defence version of events, the court should conduct a *Newton* hearing: *R. v Newton* (1982) 77 Cr.App.R. 13; *R. v Williams* (1983) 5 Cr.App.R. 134. The procedure will follow that of a trial and the parties will be able to call witnesses. The court will then decide the facts upon which it proposes to sentence. See Chapter 23 below.

Criminal Justice Act 1925, s.33

Procedure on charge of offence against corporation

19–70   **33.**—(1) [repealed]

(2) [repealed]

(3) On arrangement of a corporation, the corporation may enter in writing by its representative a plea of guilty or not guilty, and if either the corporation does not appear by a representative or, though it does so appear, fails to enter as aforesaid any plea, the court shall order a plea of not guilty to be entered and the trial shall proceed as though the corporation had duly entered a plea of not guilty.

(4) Provision may be made by rules under the *Indictments Act* 1915 with respect to the service on any corporation charged with an indictable offence of any documents requiring to be served in connection with the proceedings, except in so far as such provision may be made by rules under section 144 of the *Magistrates' Courts Act* 1980.

(5) [repealed]

(6) In this section the expression "representative" in relation to a corporation means a person duly appointed by the corporation to represent it for the purpose of doing any act or thing which the representative of a corporation is by this section authorized to do, but a person so appointed shall not, by virtue only of being so appointed, be qualified to act on behalf of the corporation before any court for any other purpose.

A representative for the purposes of this section need not be appointed under the seal of the corporation, and a statement in writing purporting to be signed by a managing director of the corporation, or by any person (by whatever name called) having, or being one of the persons having, the management of the affairs of the corporation, to the effect that the person named in the statement has been appointed as the representative of the corporation for the purposes of this section shall be admissible without further proof as prima facie evidence that that person has been so appointed.

[This section is reprinted as amended by the *Magistrates' Courts Act* 1952, s.132, Sch.6, the *Courts Act* 1971, Sch.8, para.19, and the *Magistrates' Courts Act* 1980, Sch.7, para.5.]

Where a company via its representative (see above) fails to appear the court will enter a not guilty plea and will hear the evidence.

C. PLEA OF GUILTY BY POST

Magistrates' Courts Act 1980, s.12

Non-appearance of accused; plea of guilty

12.—(1) This section shall apply where—   **19–71**

(a) a summons has been issued requiring a person to appear before a magistrates' court, other than a youth court, to answer to an information for a summary of-fence, not being—

    (i) an offence for which the accused is liable to be sentenced to be imprisoned for a term exceeding 3 months; or

    (ii) an offence specified in an order made by the Secretary of State by statutory instrument; and

(b) the justices' chief executive for the court is notified by or on behalf of the prosecu-tor that the documents mentioned in subsection (3) below have been served upon the accused with the summons.

(2) The reference in subsection (1)(a) above to the issue of a summons requiring a person to appear before a magistrates' court other than a youth court includes a reference to the issue of a summons requiring a person who has attained the age of 16 at the time when it is issued to appear before a youth court.

(3) The documents referred to in subsection (1)(b) above are—

(a) a notice containing such statement of the effect of this section as may be prescribed;

(b) either of the following, namely—

    (i) a concise statement of such facts relating to the charge as will be placed before the court by the prosecutor if the accused pleads guilty without ap-pearing before the court, or

    (ii) a copy of such written statement or statements complying with subsections (2)(a) and (b) and (3) of section 9 of the *Criminal Justice Act* 1967 (proof by written statement) as will be so placed in those circumstances; and

(c) if any information relating to the accused will or may, in those circumstances, be placed before the court by or on behalf of the prosecutor, a notice containing or describing that information.

(4) Where the justices' chief executive for the court receives a notification in writing purporting to be given by the accused or by a legal representative acting on his behalf that the accused desires to plead guilty without appearing before the court—

(a) the justices' chief executive for the court shall inform the prosecutor of the receipt of the notification; and

(b) the following provisions of this section shall apply:

(5) If at the time and place appointed for the trial or adjourned trial of the informa-tion—

(a) the accused does not appear; and

(b) it is proved to the satisfaction of the court, on oath or in such manner as may be prescribed, that the documents mentioned in subsection (3) above have been served upon the accused with the summons,

the court may, subject to section 11(3) and (4) above and subsections (6) to (8) below, proceed to hear and dispose of the case in the absence of the accused, whether or not the prosecutor is also absent, in like manner as if both parties had appeared and the accused had pleaded guilty.

19–72   (6) If at any time before the hearing the [justices' chief executive for] the court receives an indication in writing purporting to be given by or on behalf of the accused that he wishes to withdraw the notification—

(a) the [justices' chief executive for] the court shall inform the prosecutor of the withdrawal; and

(b) the court shall deal with the information as if the notification had not been given.

(7) Before accepting the plea of guilty and convicting the accused under subsection (5) above, the court shall cause the following to be read out before the court by the clerk of the court, namely—

(a) in a case where a statement of facts as mentioned in subsection (3)(b)(i) above was served on the accused with the summons, that statement;

(aa) in a case where a statement or statements as mentioned in subsection (3)(b)(ii) above was served on the accused with the summons and the court does not otherwise direct, that statement or those statements;

(b) any information contained in a notice so served, and any information described in such a notice and produced by or on behalf of the prosecutor;

(c) the notification under subsection (4) above; and

(d) any submission received with the notification which the accused wishes to be brought to the attention of the court with a view to mitigation of sentence.

(7A) Where the court gives a direction under subsection (7)(aa) above the court shall cause an account to be given orally before the court by the clerk of the court of so much of any statement as is not read aloud.

(7B) Whether or not a direction under paragraph (aa) of subsection (7) above is given in relation to any statement served as mentioned in that paragraph the court need not cause to be read out the declaration required by section 9(2)(b) of the *Criminal Justice Act* 1967.

(8) If the court proceeds under subsection (5) above to hear and dispose of the case in the absence of the accused, the court shall not permit—

(a) any other statement with respect to any facts relating to the offence charged; or

(b) any other information relating to the accused,

to be made or placed before the court by or on behalf of the prosecutor except on a resumption of the trial after an adjournment under section 10(3) above.

19–73   (9) If the court decides not to proceed under subsection (5) above to hear and dispose of the case in the absence of the accused, it shall adjourn or further adjourn the trial for the purpose of dealing with the information as if the notification under subsection (4) above had not been given.

(10) In relation to an adjournment on the occasion of the accused's conviction in his absence under subsection (5) above or to an adjournment required by subsection (9) above, the notice required by section 10(2) above shall include notice of the reason for the adjournment.

(11) No notice shall be required by section 10(2) above in relation to an adjournment—

(a) which is for not more than 4 weeks; and

(b) the purpose of which is to enable the court to proceed under subsection (5) above at a later time.

(12) No order shall be made under subsection (1) above unless a draft of the order has been laid before and approved by resolution of each House of Parliament.

(13) Any such document as is mentioned in subsection (3) above may be served in Scotland with a summons which is so served under the *Summary Jurisdiction (Process) Act* 1881.

19–73.1   [This section is reprinted as amended by the *Access to Justice Act* 1999, Sch.19, para.97.]

Magistrates' Courts Act 1980, Sch.3, para.4

19–74   4.—(1) Notification or intimation for the purposes of subsections (2) and (3) of section 12 above may be given on behalf of a corporation by a director or the secretary of the corporation; and those subsections shall apply in relation to a notification or intimation purporting to be so given as they apply to a notification or intimation purporting to be given by an individual accused.

(2) In this paragraph "director", in relation to a corporation which is established by or under any enactment for the purpose of carrying on under national ownership any industry or part of an industry or undertaking and whose affairs are managed by the members thereof, means a member of that corporation.

The defendant may enter a plea of guilty by post if the conditions in s.12 of the *Magistrates' Courts Act* 1980 are met. Provided that the court receives the defendant's notification of a guilty plea by post before the hearing date, it does not matter that it was received after the return date specified in the summons: *R. v Norham and Islandshire Justices Ex p. Sunter Bros Ltd* [1961] 1 W.L.R. 364. If there are several summonses it is essential that the defendant makes it clear to which one he is pleading guilty: *R. v Burnham Bucks Justices Ex p. Ansorge* [1959] 1 W.L.R. 1041. If the offence is endorsable or disqualifiable the defendant must also send his driving licence and a statement of his date of birth and sex: *Road Traffic Offenders Act* 1988, s.8.

The defendant may withdraw a plea of guilty by post at any time before the hearing **19–75** by giving the court written notice: *Magistrates' Courts Act* 1980, s.12(6). The court has jurisdiction at the hearing to allow a change of plea so that a defendant who has earlier pleaded guilty by post may contest the matter: *R. v Bristol Justices Ex p. Sawyers* [1988] Crim.L.R. 754.

The notification of the guilty plea, the statement of facts served by the prosecution or the written statement under the *Criminal Justice Act* 1967, s.9 and any statements submitted in mitigation must be read out by the legal adviser in open court. Failure to do so will render the proceedings a nullity: *R. v Oldham Justices Ex p. Morrissey* [1959] 1 W.L.R. 58; *R. v Epping and Ongar Justices Ex p. Breach* [1987] R.T.R. 233. Such a defect cannot be remedied by s.142(2) of the *Magistrates' Courts Act* 1980 (see below) because the defendant has not been found guilty but has simply notified his or her intention to plead guilty. The prosecution may serve a fresh summons upon the original information: *R. v Epping and Ongar Justices Ex p. Breachi*, above.

The court has a residual discretion to decide that the case is not suitable to be dealt with by way of a plea of guilty by post. The court may adjourn the matter for the defendant to appear. The notice of adjournment sent to the defendant must specify the reason for the adjournment: *R. v Mason* [1965] 2 All E.R. 308

Magistrates' Courts Act 1980, s.12A

Application of section 12 where accused appears

12A.—(1) Where the clerk of the court has received such a notification as is mentioned in **19–76** subsection (4) of section 12 above but the accused nevertheless appears before the court at the time and place appointed for the trial or adjourned trial, the court may, if he consents, proceed under subsection (5) of that section as if he were absent.

(2) Where the clerk of the court has not received such a notification and the accused appears before the court at that time and place and informs the court that he desires to plead guilty, the court may, if he consents, proceed under section 12(5) above as if he were absent and the clerk had received such a notification.

(3) For the purposes of subsections (1) and (2) above, subsections (6) to (11) of section 12 above shall apply with the modifications mentioned in subsection (4) or, as the case may be, subsection (5) below.

(4) The modifications for the purposes of subsection (1) above are that—

    (a) before accepting the plea of guilty and convicting the accused under subsection (5) of section 12 above, the court shall afford the accused an opportunity to make an oral submission with a view to mitigation of sentence; and

    (b) where he makes such a submission, subsection (7)(d) of that section shall not apply.

(5) The modifications for the purposes of subsection (2) above are that—

    (a) subsection (6) of section 12 above shall apply as if any reference to the notification under subsection (4) of that section were a reference to the consent under subsection (2) above;

(b) subsection (7)(c) and (d) of that section shall not apply; and

(c) before accepting the plea of guilty and convicting the accused under subsection (5) of that section, the court shall afford the accused an opportunity to make an oral submission with a view to mitigation of sentence.

[This section is reprinted as amended by the *Criminal Justice and Public Order Act* 1994, Sch.5, para.2.]

19–77　　Sometimes a defendant will appear in court despite having sent a written plea of guilty by post. In those circumstances, the legal adviser will ask the defendant whether he wishes the guilty plea to stand and, if so, the written plea of guilty procedure will be followed save that the defendant will be offered an opportunity to address the court personally.

D. PLEA OF NOT GUILTY

19–78　　Where the defendant pleads not guilty the court will proceed to trial. The case will generally be adjourned to a date when the witnesses can attend and which, within a reasonable timescale, is convenient to the parties. An estimate of the length of the hearing will be sought and directions for carrying out certain matters may be made.

E. FAILURE TO PLEAD

19–79　　Where the defendant fails to plead to the information then the court will hear the evidence in accordance with s.9(2) of the *Magistrates' Courts Act* 1980 as if there had been a plea of not guilty.

F. CHANGE OF PLEA

19–80　　A magistrates' court may in its discretion allow a defendant to change his plea from guilty to not guilty at any stage before sentence is passed: *S (an infant) v Recorder of Manchester* [1971] A.C. 481. The question is whether the original plea was unequivocal and entered with proper understanding of the charge.

There is no automatic rule that a defendant who was unrepresented when the plea was entered is entitled to change the plea upon subsequently obtaining legal representation in the period before sentencing: *R v South Tameside Magistrates' Court Ex p. Rowland* [1983] 3 All E.R. 689.

Where the defendant is represented and it becomes apparent that the advocate has advised the defendant to plead guilty under a mistaken view of the nature of the charge, the court should consider whether a change of plea should be allowed on the basis of equivocality: *P. Foster (Haulage) Ltd v Roberts* [1978] 2 All E.R. 751.

19–81　　Where a plea of guilty is withdrawn, evidence of that plea as a confession of fact is admissible at the trial. The court should however carefully balance the probative value of such evidence against its prejudicial nature and will not normally admit it: *R. v Rimmer* [1972] 1 W.L.R. 268

Where a defendant changes his plea from not guilty to guilty, it is improper for the court to inquire into the defendant's reasons or motives for the change of plea unless the new plea is equivocal: *R. v Eccles Justices Ex p. Fitzpatrick*, 89 Cr.App.R. 324.

The case of *R. v Bow Street Magistrates' Court Ex p. Welcombe* (1992) 156 J.P. 609 is authority for saying that upon a change of plea, where the offence is triable either way the court should proceed to allow the defendant to consider whether to consent to summary trial. This case was heard before the plea before venue procedure was introduced. It is submitted that the same principles should now apply.

19–82　　Once the court has pronounced sentence it is *functus officio* and the conviction recorded upon the plea of guilty can be challenged only by way of appeal to the Crown Court. Where it is clear that a mistake has arisen, however, the court may consider its powers under s.142(2) of the *Magistrates' Courts Act* 1980, below.

Similarly, if a plea of guilty is unequivocal the court should not make use of s.142 to allow it to be withdrawn in order to substitute a plea of not guilty: *R. v Croydon Youth Court Ex p. DPP* [1997] 2 Cr.App.R. 411.

V. PRELIMINARY ISSUES

A magistrates' court determines its own procedure within statutory restraints: *R. v* **19–83** *Epping and Ongar Justices Ex p. Manby* [1986] Crim.L.R. 555.

At the start of a trial certain preliminary matters may be dealt with, for example, disqualification of magistrates, amendment of charge or summons, fitness to plead, pleas of autrefois acquit or convict, abuse of process and public interest immunity.

The judiciary in magistrates' courts are arbiters of both law and fact and admissibility of evidence should not generally be decided as a separate issue. Sometimes, however, a court will deal with admissibility of evidence as a preliminary point: *ADC (an infant) v Chief Constable of Greater Manchester* [1987] Crim.L.R. 497. In that case, once the question of admissibility is determined there is no need to repeat the evidence later: *F (an infant) v Chief Constable of Kent* [1982] Crim.L.R. 682.

A. FITNESS TO PLEAD

There is no procedure in the magistrates' courts for determining a person's fitness to **19–84** plead. The court may, if the offence is triable either way, commit him to the Crown Court to have the question of fitness determined by a jury.

The usual procedure is that, if the defendant is thought to be suffering from a mental disability, the court or the defence will request psychiatric reports. Many magistrates' courts have an on site facility to produce such reports. The prosecutor may then, in the light of such reports, not proceed with the charge. Alternatively, the court may hear evidence and, having satisfied itself that the defendant did the act or made an omission but without convicting him, make a hospital order under the *Mental Health Act* 1983, s.37(3). In the case of *R. v Lincoln (Kesteven) Justices Ex p. O'Connor* [1983] 1 W.L.R. 335 it was held that in an exceptional case, where the defendant was legally represented the court could conclude that the offence had occurred without hearing evidence. See Mentally Disordered Offenders, Chapter 35, below).

B. AUTREFOIS ACQUIT AND AUTREFOIS CONVICT

A person cannot be tried for an offence if he or she has previously been acquitted or **19–85** convicted of the same, or substantially the same, offence: *Connelly v DPP* [1964] A.C. 1254. A person should not be tried for offences on an ascending scale of seriousness: *R v Beedie* [1998] Q.B. 356. In such circumstances the defendant may also plead *autrefois acquit* or *autrefois convict*.

Strictly speaking a plea of *autrefois acquit* or *autrefois convict* may only be raised in a trial on indictment, however the principles giving rise to such pleas are the same in the magistrates' court: *DPP v Porthouse* (1989) 89 Cr.App.R. 21. There is no special procedure in the magistrates' courts for pleading *autrefois acquit* or *autrefois convict*.

The defendant, however, has the burden of proving on the balance of probabilities that there has been a previous conviction or acquittal on the merits: *R. v Coughlan and Young* (1976) 63 Cr.App.R. 33.

For a plea of *autrefois acquit* to succeed the defendant must have been put in genuine jeopardy at an earlier hearing: *R. v Dabhade* [1993] 2 W.L.R. 129. There must have been a hearing on the merits: *R. v Pressick* [1978] Crim.L.R. 377. A procedural irregularity resulting in an acquittal is not sufficient to put a defendant in jeopardy: *Williams v DPP*, (1991) 93 Cr.App.R. 319, [1991] 1 W.L.R. 1160. Neither is the situation where a defendant has been charged and acquitted of an offence unknown to law: *DPP v Porthouse* (above). The withdrawal of a summons does not equate with an acquittal: *R. v Grays Justices Ex p. Low* [1990] 1 Q.B. 54.

19–86   Where a prosecutor has been properly asked to choose upon which information to proceed the plea of autrefois acquit cannot be raised. If a charge is summarily dismissed because the prosecution recognises the difficulties which exist in prosecuting that charge, and a new charge is substituted, a plea of *autrefois acquit* on the first charge cannot be made: *Broadbent v High* [1985] R.T.R. 359. If there has been an acquittal of a lesser offence which contains the same ingredients of a greater offence the defendant cannot be convicted in a subsequent trial of the greater offence because the conviction would effectively reverse the acquittal for the lesser offence. A defendant could still be found guilty of the full offence, however, if he was acquitted of an attempt to commit that offence: *R. v Velasquez* [1996] 1 Cr.App.R. 155

A plea of *autrefois acquit* may not be raised when the prosecution chooses to offer no evidence on a lesser charge which contains the same ingredients of a more serious charge upon which the prosecution wishes to proceed: *DPP v Khan* [1997] R.T.R. 82. In this case the defendant pleaded not guilty to charges of dangerous driving and driving without reasonable consideration for other road users. The prosecution offered no evidence on the without reasonable consideration and he was acquitted. The prosecution proceeded on the dangerous driving and the defendant was convicted. The Divisional Court, on an appeal from the Crown Court, held that the defendant had not been under a misapprehension that the prosecution intended to proceed with only the more serious charge and, at the time of acquittal on the lesser charge, the justices had not considered the merits of the charge.

19–87   Where the prosecution offers no evidence on an information charging an offence triable either way, and no plea has been taken nor any decision reached as to the mode of trial, a defendant is entitled to consent to summary trial, plead not guilty and have the case dismissed. If fresh informations were then laid charging the same offences, it would be open to the defendant to plead autrefois acquit: *R. v Bradford Magistrates' Court Ex p. Daniel, The Independent,* June 16, 1997 (C.S.).

If the court acquits when acting outside its jurisdiction a plea of *autrefois acquit* cannot be made: *R. v West* [1964] 1 Q.B. 15. In this case the magistrates had purported to dismiss a charge which was triable on indictment only.

C. Abuse of Process

19–88   The court will refuse to allow the prosecution to proceed where it considers that the prosecution amounts to an abuse of the process of the court and is oppressive and vexatious. The question is whether in the circumstances it is possible for the particular defendant to have a fair trial.

In *R. v Willesden Justices Ex p. Clemmings* (1988) 87 Cr.App.R. 280, Bingham L.J. stated that there are two situations where abuse of process could lead to a magistrates' court's stopping a prosecution from going ahead. Either the prosecution has manipulated or misused the process of the court so as to deprive the defendant of a protection provided by law or taken unfair advantage of a technicality or on the balance of probabilities that the defendant has been or would be prejudiced in the preparation or conduct of his or her defence by delay on the part of the prosecution which was unjustifiable. An abuse of process is something so unfair and wrong that the court should not allow the prosecution to proceed: *Connelly v DPP* [1964] A.C. 1254, HL; *DPP v Humphreys* [1977] A.C. 1, HL; *Hui Chi-Ming v R* [1992] 1 A.C. 34.

The power to stay a summary trial or committal proceedings on the ground of abuse of process should be used sparingly: *R. v Oxford City Justices Ex p. Smith* (1982) 75 Cr.App.R. 200; *R. v Horsham Justices Ex p. Reeves* (1982) 75 Cr.App.R. 236; *R. v Telford Justices Ex p. Badhan* [1991] 2 Q.B. 78; *R. v Barry Magistrates Court Ex p. Malpas* [1998] C.O.D. 90. In *R. v Childs, The Times,* November 30, 2002, CA. It was said that abuse of process arguments distort the trial process in cases where they are unwarranted; if such arguments are advanced without justification, courts should make it clear that this is inappropriate conduct and should take appropriate steps where court time has been wasted as a result.

In *R. v Horseferry Road Magistrates' Court Ex p. Bennett* [1994] 1 A.C. **19–89** 42, the House of Lords confirmed that justices have the power to stay criminal proceedings for abuse of process but held that such power should be strictly confined to matters directly affecting the fairness of the trial of the particular defendant with whom they are dealing, such as delay, or unfair manipulation of court procedures. The wider supervisory responsibility for upholding the rule of law is vested in the High Court. Where a question arises as to the deliberate abuse of extradition procedures, the court should exercise its discretion to grant an adjournment to facilitate an application to the High Court. Even in cases concerning complaints directed to the fairness or propriety of the trial process itself it is always open to a magistrates' court to decline jurisdiction and leave the matter to be pursued in the High Court: *R. v Belmarsh Magistrates' Court Ex p. Watts* [1999] 2 Cr.App.R. 188, DC. In *R. v Horseferry Magistrates' Court Ex p. DPP* [1999] C.O.D. 441, DC the court suggested that in the sort of situation under consideration an abuse of process application might be better addressed to the court of trial than to the committal court. An application to the High Court by way of judicial review would seek prohibition of the continuation of the proceedings rather than to quash the decision to institute the proceedings.

In *R. v Leeds Youth Court Ex p. P(A)* (2001) 165 J.P. 684, DC the court considered the extent of the jurisdiction of magistrates in respect of an abuse of process. The court held that whatever the exact limits might be, there is no jurisdiction to stay proceedings on the basis of a failure by the prosecution to comply with the rules requiring the giving of advance information. The proper remedy in such cases is to adjourn the proceedings to enable the information to be provided.

An attempt to prefer fresh charges against a defendant based on similar charges al- **19–90** ready rejected in old-style committal proceedings is vexatious and frivolous and an abuse of process: *R. v Horsham Justices Ex p. Reeves*, above.

The onus is on the accused to show on a balance of probabilities that a fair trial is no longer possible: *R. v Telford Justices Ex p. Badhan*, above; *R. v Great Yarmouth Magistrates Ex p. Thomas* [1992] Crim.L.R. 116. In *Tan v Cameron* [1992] 2 A.C. 205 PC, however, the court considered that the question of whether the proceedings should be stayed is one that should be considered as a whole and nothing is to be gained by introducing shifting burdens of proof.

The court must determine an application to stay proceedings for an abuse of process on the material provided by the prosecution and defence. There is a right to call evidence: *R. v Clerkenwell Magistrates' Court Ex p. Bell* [1991] Crim.L.R. 468.

Delay

In the *Att.-Gen.'s Reference (No.2 of 2001)* [2003] UKHL 68, the House of Lords **19–91** (Lords Hope and Rogers dissenting) stated that, in order for there to be a stay of proceedings on the grounds of delay, the court must be satisfied that either a fair hearing is no longer possible or it is for any compelling reason unfair to try the defendant.

Lord Bingham, delivering the judgement and referring to Art.6, ECHR, stated:

> First, the right of a criminal defendant was to a hearing. The article required that hearing to have certain characteristics. If the hearing was shown not to have been fair, a conviction could be quashed and a retrial ordered if a fair trial could still be held. If the hearing was shown to have been by a tribunal lacking independence or impartiality or legal authority, a conviction could be quashed and a retrial ordered if a fair trial could still be held. If judgement had not been given publicly, judgement could be given publicly. But time, once spent, could not be recovered. If a breach of the reasonable time requirement was shown to have occurred it could not be cured. It would, however, be anomalous if breach of the reasonable time requirement had an effect more far-reaching than breach of the defendant's other article 6(1) rights when, as had to be assumed, the breach did not taint the basic fairness of the hearing at all, and even more anomalous that the right to a hearing should be vindicated by ordering that there should not be a hearing at all.
>
> Second, a rule of automatic termination of proceedings on breach of the reasonable time

requirement could not sensibly be applied in civil proceedings. An unmeritorious defendant might no doubt be very happy to seize on such a breach to escape his liability, but termination of the proceedings would defeat the claimant's right to a hearing altogether and seeking to make good his loss in compensation from the state could well be a very unsatisfactory alternative.

19–92   Third, a rule of automatic termination on proof of a breach of the reasonable time requirement had been shown to have the effect in practice of emasculating the right which the guarantee was designed to protect. It had to be recognised that the Convention was directed not to departures from the ideal but to infringements of basic human rights, and the threshold of proving a breach of the reasonable time requirement was a high one, not easily crossed: see the privy Council decision in *Dyer v Watson* [2002]3 W.L.R. 1488, 1508, paragraph 52). Judges should not be vexed with applications based on lapses of time which, even if they should not have occurred, aroused no serious concern. There was, however, a very real risk that if proof of a breach was held to require automatic termination of the proceedings the judicial response would be to set the threshold unacceptably high since, as Justice La Forest put it in *Rahey v The Queen* (1987) 39 DLR 481, 516): 'Few judges relish the prospect of unleashing dangerous criminals on the public'.

Fourth, the Strasbourg jurisprudence gave no support to the contention that there should be no hearing of a criminal charge once a reasonable time has passed. It was of course true that the European Court of Human Rights examined cases retrospectively, and it could not quash convictions. But it was significant that, in its interpretation and application of the Convention it had never treated the holding of a hearing as a violation or a proper subject of compensation: see *Bunkate v The Netherlands* (1995) 19 E.H.R.R. 477, 484, paragraph 25). If, through the action or inaction of a public authority, a criminal charge was not determined at a hearing within a reasonable time, there was necessarily a breach of the defendant's Convention right under article 6(1). For such breach there had to be afforded such remedy as might be just (s.8(1) of the 1998 Act) and appropriate or, in Convention terms, effective, just and proportionate. The appropriate remedy would depend on the nature of the breach and all the circumstances, including particularly the stage of the proceedings at which the breach was established. If the breach was established before the hearing, the appropriate remedy might be a public acknowledgement of the breach, action to expedite the hearing to the greatest extent practicable and perhaps, if the defendant was in custody, his release on bail. It would not be appropriate to stay or dismiss the proceedings unless (a) there could no longer be a fair hearing or (b) it would otherwise be unfair to try the defendant. The public interest in the final determination of criminal charges required that such a charge should not be stayed or dismissed if any lesser remedy would be just and proportionate in all the circumstances. The prosecutor and the court would not act incompatibly with the defendant's Convention right in continuing to prosecute or entertain proceedings after a breach was established in a case where neither of conditions (a) or (b) was met, since the breach consisted in the delay which had accrued and not in the prospective hearing.

If the breach of the reasonable time requirement was established retrospectively, after there had been a hearing, the appropriate remedy might be a public acknowledgement of the breach, a reduction in the penalty imposed on a convicted defendant or the payment of compensation to an acquitted defendant. Unless (a) the hearing was unfair or (b) it was unfair to try the defendant at all, it would not be appropriate to quash any conviction. Again, in any case where, neither condition (a) nor (b) applied, the prosecutor and the court would not act incompatibly with the defendant's Convention right in prosecuting or entertaining the proceedings but only in failing to procure a hearing within a reasonable time.

There might well be cases where the delay was of such an order…as to make it unfair that the proceedings against a defendant should continue. Such cases would, however, be very exceptional and a stay would never be an appropriate remedy if any lesser remedy would adequately vindicate the defendant's Convention right.

19–93   The House of Lords confirmed that in considering whether a criminal charge has been determined within a reasonable time for the purposes of Art.6, the relevant time will normally start to run from the date when the defendant is charged by the police or served with a summons. Any period prior to a formal charge may be considered if the defendant has during that period been substantially affected by the conduct of the prosecution but time would not ordinarily run until after a suspect had been interviewed under caution. Arrest would not ordinarily mark the beginning of the period but an official indication that a person would be reported with a view to prosecution might do so.

The interviewing of a person for the purposes of a regulatory inquiry would not meet the test: *Fayed v United Kingdom* (1994) 18 E.H.R.R. 393.

In *Dyer v Watson* [2002] 4 All E.R. 1, the Privy Council considered the effect of delay in criminal proceedings. It held that the threshold of proving that a trial has not occurred within a reasonable time is a high one. If the period which has elapsed is one which, on its face, gives rise to real concern, it is necessary to look into the detailed circumstances of the particular case and it must be possible to justify any lapse of time which appears to be excessive. Regard must be had to the complexity of the case, the conduct of the defendant and the manner in which the case has been dealt with by the prosecution and the courts. There is no general obligation on a prosecutor to act with all due expedition and diligence but a marked lack of expedition if unjustified would indicate a breach of the reasonable time requirement.

Where substantial delay has occurred which can be attributed in part to the inefficiency of the prosecutor and in part to the conduct of the defendant, the court must consider to what extent the delay is attributable to the prosecution. If it is substantial and the defendant has been or must have been prejudiced thereby this power must be exercised in the defendant's favour.   **19–94**

The fact that there is a six–month limitation period within which to bring most summary offences is an indication that such cases ought to be disposed of expeditiously. Although the information must be laid within the time limit the date of the summons may be outside that limit. The following cases must now, however, be read in the light of Lord Bingham's judgment in the *Att.-Gen.'s Reference (No.2 of 2001)*, above.

The refusal of the issue of a summons when the information was laid on the last permissible day has been upheld: *R. v Clerk to the Medway Justices Ex p. DHSS* [1986] Crim.L.R. 686, DC.

Where a summons is ambiguous as to which of two inconsistent offences may have been committed, it is an abuse of process for the prosecution not to give particulars of the offence to be proceeded with to the defence, before the expiry of the six month period: *R. v Newcastle-Upon-Tyne Justices Ex p. Hindle* [1984] 1 All E.R. 770. A police officer saw the defendant after a road accident and formed the view he had been drinking. The defendant told the officer he had consumed alcohol since the accident. He was arrested, provided a specimen of blood which was above the limit. He was summoned for an offence under the *Road Traffic Act* 1972, s.6(1), pleaded not guilty and the matter was adjourned to a date outside the six month time limit. The defendant then received a summons for obstruction of a police officer. It was unclear whether the obstruction summons was on the basis that the defendant had lied to the officer about the drink (consistent with the s.6(1) summons) or because he had deliberately consumed alcohol to frustrate the excess alcohol summons (inconsistent with the s.6(1) summons). The prosecution refused to provide particulars. When the matters came before the court a defence submission that the obstruction summons was an abuse of process was rejected. On review it was held that since the obstruction summons was ambiguous and could have applied to inconsistent offences, and the prosecution had refused to give particulars, the summons was prejudicial and an abuse of process since it allowed the prosecution to postpone their decision on which offence to prosecute until after the expiry of the six month period.

The inquiry into an offence does not begin merely by the hearing of submissions as to abuse of process relating to the transfer of proceedings to another court. The inquiry into the offence begins only with the calling of witnesses, the opening of the prosecution case or some other pertinent step: *R. v Worcester Magistrates' Court Ex p. Bell*, 157 J.P. 921, DC.   **19–95**

Manipulation or misuse of the process of court

In *R. v Lincoln Magistrates' Court Ex p. Wickes Building Supplies Ltd, The Times*, August 6, 1993, DC, it was held that the laying of a multiplicity of charges in respect of each Sunday trading breach under s.47 of the *Shops Act* 1950, when the   **19–96** lawfulness of that section was being challenged in the European Court of Justice, was not an abuse of process. It had been argued that the deliberate stacking up of informations by the prosecutor during a time when (a) the law was uncertain (b) there was no possibility of conviction pending clarification of the law and (c) the prosecuting local authority would not risk seeking a civil injunction, was oppressive and vexatious and amounted to a manipulation of the process that would make it unfair to try the accused.

In *R. v Rotherham Justices Ex p. Brough* (1991) C.O.D. 89, DC, the prosecution had deliberately taken steps to ensure that a defendant who was charged with an offence that would be triable only on indictment in the case of an adult did not appear before the court until he had reached the age where the justices ceased to have a discretion whether or not to deal with it themselves. Although the court viewed the procedure as incorrect, it was held not to amount to an abuse of process because, on the facts the conduct of the prosecution showed at most a lack of judgment rather than misconduct or *mala fides*. There was no prejudice to the defendant because the delay involved had been minimal, the justices would probably have committed the case to the Crown Court anyway, and in the event of conviction the judge would undoubtedly take account of the defendant's age at the time of the offence and the circumstances of the committal.

19–97　　Where a summary trial is adjourned part-heard before the conclusion of the case for the prosecution and, at the adjourned hearing, the prosecution proposed to call a witness whom they had not intended to call at the original hearing but of whose existence they had always been aware, any objection based on an assertion that an unfair advantage had been taken should be dealt with by reference to s.78 of the *Police and Criminal Evidence Act* 1984, and not as an abuse of process.

It is an abuse of process for the prosecution, upon realising, after the magistrates had retired to consider sentence, that the charge was punishable only by way of fine, to invite the magistrates back into court, and then invite them to substitute a charge in respect of the same facts which carried the possibility of a custodial sentence: *R. v Harlow Magistrates Court Ex p. O'Farrell* [2000] Crim.L.R. 589, DC.

Where one magistrates' court has refused to issue a summons in respect of an information alleging an offence, it is an abuse of process to apply for a summons to another magistrates' court in respect of an identical information without disclosing the fact of the first court's refusal to issue a summons: *Gleaves v Insall; Bolton v Insall; Gleaves v Insall* [1999] 2 Cr.App.R. 466, DC.

19–98　　The prosecution of a person who, in exchange for his co-operation, has received an undertaking, promise or representation from the police that he would not be charged with an offence, is capable of amounting to an abuse of process. It is not necessary for the applicant to show that the police had the power to make the decision not to prosecute; nor is it necessary for him to show that the case was one of bad faith: *R v Croydon JJ. Ex p. Dean* 98 Cr.App.R. 76, DC.

In *R v Horseferry Road Magistrates' Court Ex p. DPP* (1999) C.O.D. 441, DC a prosecution had been instituted despite an assurance of no prosecution having been given by the police to the defendant's solicitor the court concluded that it would be unfair to try the defendant in such circumstances and stayed the proceedings. The Divisional Court disagreed; breach of an assurance not to prosecute cannot of itself amount to an abuse of process.

An abuse of process exists where a plaintiff in civil proceedings is in effective control of criminal proceedings against the same defendant to the extent that the prosecution is unable to exercise its duties independently: *R. v Leominster Magistrates' Court Ex p. Aston Manor Brewery Co., The Times*, January 8, 1997, DC.

19–99　　Machinations on the part of the prosecutor to prevent potential defence witnesses from giving evidence would be highly likely to amount to an abuse of process: *R v Schlesinger* [1995] Crim.L.R. 137, CA.

In *R. (Ebrahim) v Feltham Magistrates' Court; Mouat v DPP* [2001] 2 Cr.App.R. 23, DC guidance was given as to the approach that should be followed when an application to stay proceedings as an abuse of process is founded on the non-availability of a video recording that would, allegedly, contain relevant material. The first issue in such cases is the nature and extent, in the particular circumstance of the case, of the duty, if any, of the investigating authority and/or of the prosecutor to obtain and/or retain the material in question. In this context, recourse should be had to the code of practice issued under s.25 of the *Criminal Procedure and Investigations Act* 1996 and the Attorney General's Guidance on Disclosure. If, in the circumstances, there was no duty to obtain and /or retain that material before the defence first sought its retention, then there can be no question of the subsequent trial being unfair on that ground. If there has been a breach of the obligation to obtain or retain the relevant material it will be necessary to decide whether the defence have shown, on a balance or probabilities, that owing to the absence of the relevant material the defendant would suffer serious prejudice to the extent that a fair trial could not take place and in ruling on that question the court should also bear in mind that the trial process itself is equipped to deal with the bulk of complaints on which applications for a stay are founded. A stay should also be granted if the behaviour of the prosecution has been so bad that it is not fair that the defendant should be tried, and in this regard a useful test is that there should be either an element of bad faith or at least some serious fault.

This was approved in *R. v Sahdev* [2002] EWCA Crim 1064. Here the defendant **19–100** had been convicted of possession of a bladed article in a public place and two counts of racially aggravated common assault at Hammersmith Tube Station. The area was monitored by British Transport Police cameras. The incident may also have been filmed by other security cameras belonging to shops and unknown to the Police at the time. These cameras were not investigated and it was alleged that the defendant could not thus receive a fair trial. The Court of Appeal held that the failure of the Police to investigate the evidence from the other cameras was not unreasonable and therefore the appellant could receive a fair trial.

Whilst serious failings on the part of the police or the prosecution may make it unfair to try a defendant in a particular case, that will be a rare occurrence in the absence of serious misbehaviour; if it is not such a case, then the only issue is whether it remains possible for the defendant to have a fair trial: *R. v Sadler* (2002) 166 J.P. 481, CA.

D. Public Interest Immunity

This doctrine is normally encountered in the higher courts but may be argued in the **19–101** magistrates' courts particularly in cases where informers are involved. It prevents material from being disclosed by the prosecution to the defence where the public interest in non-disclosure outweighs the public interest that, in the administration of justice, the courts should have the fullest possible access to all relevant material. Where disclosure is ordered the prosecution may often not proceed with the case.

The anonymity of informers has been upheld in several cases, for example: *Savage v Chief Constable of Hampshire* [1997] 2 All E.R. 631. Those who allow premises to be used for police surveillance have been protected: *R. v Johnson (K)*, 88 Cr.App.R. 131. Informations upon which search warrants have been issued as well as reports from the police to the DPP have also been protected through non-disclosure: *Taylor v Anderton, The Times*, October 21, 1986. Information relating to the judicial process is covered as are documents relating to the welfare of children.

In *Rowe and Davis v UK, The Times*, March 1, 2000, the ECHR stated that it is a **19–102** fundamental aspect of the right to a fair trial that criminal proceedings should be adversarial and that there should be equality of arms between the prosecution and defence. The right to an adversarial trial means, in a criminal case, that the prosecution and defence must be given the opportunity to have knowledge of and comment on the observations filed and the evidence adduced by the other party. The court went on to state that courts have to weigh national security and the need to protect witnesses at risk of reprisals and keep secret police methods of investigation of crime against the interest of the accused.

In *R. v H; R. v C* (above) the House of Lords confirmed that in cases where public interest immunity was argued some derogation from the rule of full disclosure might be justified but it had to be the minimum necessary to protect the public interest in question. In giving the judgement Lord Bingham identified three classes of case:

"1. Most cases in which a public interest immunity issue arose.

The prosecution had to notify the defence that they were applying for a court ruling and had to indicate to the defence at least the category of material they held; namely, the broad ground on which immunity was claimed, and the defence had to have the opportunity to make representations to the court. Thus there was an inter partes hearing in open court with reference at least to the category of the material.

2. Cases where the prosecution contended that the public interest would be injured if disclosure were made even of the category of material.

The prosecution still had to notify the defence of the application, but the category of material need not be specified.

The defence would still have an opportunity to address the court on the procedure to be adopted, but the application would be made to the court in the absence of the defendant or his representatives.

If the court considered that the application fell into the first class it would order that procedure to be followed, otherwise it would rule it was a highly exceptional case.

3. Highly exceptional were cases where the public interest would be injured even by disclosure that an ex parte application was to be made.

In such cases the application would be without notice to the defence. But if the court considered that the case should be within class 1 or 2 it would so order."

19–103   He went on to say that the appointment of special counsel was a matter of last resort and gave guidance on the questions a court should ask:

"1. What was the material which the prosecution sought to withhold? That had to be considered by the court in detail.

2. Was the material such as might weaken the prosecution case or strengthen that of the defence? If "No", disclosure should not be ordered. If "Yes" full disclosure should, subject to 3,4 and 5, be ordered.

3. Was there a real risk of serious prejudice to an important public interest (and if so, what) if full disclosure were ordered? If "No", full disclosure should be ordered.

4.If the answer to 2 and 3 was "Yes", could the defendant's interest be protected without disclosure or disclosure be ordered to an extent or in a way which would give adequate protection to the public interest in question and also afford adequate protection to the interest of the defence?

That question required the court to consider, with specific reference to the material which the prosecutor sought to withhold, the facts of the case and the defence as disclosed, whether the prosecution should formally admit what the defence sought to establish or whether disclosure short of full disclosure might be ordered.

That might be done in appropriate cases by the preparation of summaries or extracts of evidence or the provision of documents in an edited or anonymised form, provided the documents supplied were in each instance approved by the judge.

In appropriate cases, the appointment of special counsel might be a necessary step to ensure that the contentions of the prosecution were tested and the interests of the defendant protected.

In cases of exceptional difficulty the court might require the appointment of special counsel to ensure a correct answer to questions 2 and 3 as well as 4.

5.Did the measures proposed in answer to 4 represent the minimum derogation from the golden rule of full disclosure

6.If limited disclosure was ordered under 4 or 5, might the effect be to render the trial process, viewed as a whole, unfair to the defendant?

If "Yes" then fuller disclosure should be ordered even if that led or might lead the prosecution to discontinue the proceedings so as to avoid having to make disclosure.

7.If the answer to 6 when first given as "No", did that remain the correct answer as the trial unfolded, evidence was adduced and the defence advanced?

It was important that the answer to 6 should not be treated as a final, once—for-all answer, but as a provisional answer which the court had to keep under review."

19–104   Lord Bingham gave specific guidance in relation to magistrates' courts:

"The relevant principles had been correctly applied in *R. (DPP) v Acton Youth Court* [2001] 1 W.L.R. 1828). If public interest immunity applications were confined, as they should be, to material undermining the prosecution case or strengthening that of the defence, the bench would not be alerted to material damaging to the defendant.

If it was, the principles governing the court's decision whether to recuse itself were the same as in the case of any other tribunal of fact, but the court's duty of continuing review ordinarily militated in favour of continuing proceedings before the court which determined the immunity application.

If a case raised complex and contentious immunity issues, and the court had discretion to send the case to the crown court for trial, the magistrates court should carefully consider whether those issues were best resolved at the crown court.

The occasions when it would be appropriate to appoint special counsel in the magistrates court would be even rarer than in the crown court."

VI. THE PROSECUTION CASE

A. PROSECUTION OPENING SPEECH

Magistrates' Courts Rules 1981, r.13

Order of evidence and speeches: information

13.—(1) On the summary trial of an information, where the accused does not plead guilty, **19–105** the prosecutor shall call the evidence for the prosecution, and before doing so may address the court.

(2) At the conclusion of the evidence for the prosecution, the accused may address the court, whether or not he afterwards calls evidence.

(3) At the conclusion of the evidence, if any, for the defence, the prosecutor may call evidence to rebut that evidence.

(4) At the conclusion of the evidence for the defence [...] and the evidence, if any, in rebuttal, the accused may address the court if he has not already done so.

(5) Either party may, with the leave of the court, address the court a second time, but where the court grants leave to one party it shall not refuse leave to the other.

(6) Where both parties address the court twice the prosecutor shall address the court for the second time before the accused does so.

[This rule is reprinted as amended by the *Magistrates' Courts (Amendment) Rules* 1983, Sch.1, para.3(b).]

The prosecutor's opening speech sets the parameters of the case. It succinctly outlines **19–106** and sometimes analyses the facts upon which the prosecution relies. It must be borne in mind that the judiciary in the magistrates' courts do not need the same sort of explanations as a jury in the crown court. They will, however, appreciate the scene being set for the evidence to follow. The prosecutor is under no obligation to open its case and in many simple cases chooses not to do so.

Where a case has been adjourned part heard and the court has difficulty in remembering the evidence it may allow the prosecutor to open his case again on the adjourned hearing so that he may remind the court of the evidence given. In those circumstances, the defence advocate should also be allowed to address the court: *L and B v DPP* [1998] 2 Cr.App.R. 69.

B. RULE REQUIRING PROSECUTION TO CALL ALL ITS EVIDENCE BEFORE THE CLOSE OF THE CASE

The prosecution must call all the evidence on which it intends to rely before the close **19–107** of its case: *R v Rice* (1963) 47 Cr.App.R. 79. The court has a discretion, however, to allow the prosecution to call evidence after it has closed its case and before the court considers its decision. The question to be decided is whether it is in the interests of justice that the evidence should be called, and in particular, whether there is any risk of any prejudice whatsoever to the defendant: *Jolly v DPP* [2000] Crim.L.R. 471, DC.

In *James v South Glamorgan County Council* (1994) 99 Cr.App.R. 321 the

Divisional Court held that the unusual circumstances in the case, including a change of court location of which some witnesses had not been informed, meant that the magistrates were entitled to allow the prosecution to call evidence after it had closed its case.

The prosecution may not call evidence after closing its case if the evidence concerns matters of substance: *R v Gainsborough Justices Ex p. Green* 78 Cr.App.R. 9. In that case two informations against the defendant alleged various breaches of a community service order. The probation officer called evidence to support one breach only. It transpired that the defendant had had a reasonable excuse for not attending (which the defendant formally admitted). Instead of acceding to a submission of no case to answer the justices allowed the officer to re-open her case and call evidence of the other alleged breaches. The defendant's appeal against conviction was allowed because a prosecutor should only be allowed to call evidence after close of his or her case in exceptional circumstances.

19–108　　In *Phelan v Back* [1972] 1 All E.R. 901, however, it was said "we must not allow the rules to be our masters, they must remain our servants, and the authorities show a wide range of circumstances in which prosecution witnesses can be called or recalled after the close of the prosecution case."

The court's discretion extends to the admission of some substantive evidence such as evidence which has not been adduced through an oversight: *Piggott v Sims* [1973] R.T.R. 15. In *Matthews v Morris* [1981] Crim.L.R. 495 the Divisional Court held that the magistrates were correct to have allowed the prosecution to reopen its case to tender a statement which by mistake had not been tendered as part of the prosecution case, but which had been served on the defendant under the *Criminal Justice Act* 1967, s.9. No injustice had been caused to the defendant by the admission of the evidence.

The prosecution may be permitted to call purely technical evidence, for example, a statutory instrument: *Hammond v Wilkinson* [2001] Crim.L.R. 323, DC or a statutory notice: *Royal v Prescott-Clark* [1966] 1 W.L.R. 788 or evidence of the functioning of an intoximeter device: *Cook v DPP* [2001] Crim.L.R. 321, DC.

If the evidence was not available for the first time until after the close of the prosecution case the magistrates may admit it as a matter of discretion: *R. v Rice*, above. In *R. v Doran* (1972) 56 Cr.App.R. 429 the judge allowed the prosecution to call two witnesses after the close of its case. The witnesses were members of the public who had been present at the trial and realised during the course of the defence case that they could give evidence. The Court of Appeal held that the question in every case was whether it was right to serve the ends of justice that the evidence should be admitted and that in such a case the court must be vigilant to ensure that no injustice is done to the defendants.

19–109　　If further evidence is to be called the court should ensure that proper notice of it has been given to the defendant. The prosecution should serve the evidence by way of notice and the court should grant an adjournment if necessary: *R. v Dartey* (1987) 84 Cr.App.R. 352.

The prosecution may also call evidence in order to rebut a new matter which the prosecution could not have foreseen: *R. v Owen* [1952] 2 Q.B. 362. Whether a matter is reasonably foreseeable is a matter for the court to determine in the circumstances of the case: *R v Mendy* (1977) 64 Cr.App.R. 4.

C. DUTY OF PROSECUTION IN CALLING WITNESSES

19–110　　Once the prosecution has served witness statements it is those witnesses which it is expected to call. The prosecution has a discretion whether to call witnesses to give evidence in chief or to tender them for cross-examination only.

Generally the prosecution ought to call or offer to call all the witnesses who give direct evidence of the primary facts of the case, unless for good reason, it regards the witnesses' evidence as unworthy of belief. In the case of *R. v Oliva* (1965) 49 Cr.App.R. 298; [1965] 1 W.L.R. 1028, Lord Parker C.J. said at 309–310:

"The prosecution does not, of course, put forward every witness as a witness of truth, but where the witness's evidence is capable of belief, then it is their duty, well recognised, that he should be called, even though the evidence that he is going to give is inconsistent with the case sought to be proved. Their discretion must be exercised in a manner which is calculated to further the interests of justice, and at the same time be fair to the defence. If the prosecution appear to be exercising that discretion improperly, it is open to the judge of trial to interfere and in his discretion in turn to invite the prosecution to call a particular witness, and, if they refuse, there is the ultimate sanction in the judge himself calling that witness."

In *R. v Haringey Justices Ex p. DPP* [1996] 2 W.L.R. 114 the prosecution decided **19–111** not to call a police officer who had been suspended from duty. The defence wished the officer to be present. The court invited the prosecution to call the witness and when the prosecution declined to do so, dismissed the case. It was held that the court could not force the prosecution to call the witness but it could call the witness itself. See also *R. v Baldwin* [1978] Crim.L.R. 104

The prosecution must take all reasonable steps to secure the attendance of each of its witnesses at trial, including the making of an application for a summons or warrant—see below. If, however, despite such steps, it has proved impossible to have the witnesses present the court might in its discretion permit the trial to proceed, provided no injustice would be done: *R. v Cavanagh and Shaw* (1972) 56 Cr.App.R. 407. In that case, the witness was out of the country and there was no information as to when he would be back. The court, in exercising its discretion, would consider the desire of the defence to call the witness if the prosecution did not, the extent to which the evidence would help the defence, the chances of securing the attendance of the witness in a reasonable time and whether delay would result in other witnesses not being available and the willingness of the prosecution to proceed.

In *R. v Wellingborough Justices Ex p. Francois* (1994) 158 J.P. 813 the Divisional Court held that a prosecutor had acted improperly when she did not call two prosecution witnesses or tender them for cross-examination because she was due to prosecute another case in another court later that day. As a result it was open to the justices to invite the prosecution to tender the witness and, if it refused, to call the witnesses itself.

The prosecution has a discretion over the order in which it calls its witnesses. Any witness should remain outside the courtroom until called unless the witness is an expert who may need to hear the evidence because his opinion is based on the facts. This is a rule of practice not law: *R v Bexley Justices Ex p. King*, above; *Moore v Registrar of Lambeth County Court* [1969] 1 W.L.R. 141.

The prosecution must call all its evidence before closing its case except evidence in **19–112** rebuttal (see below) and where it has omitted to call evidence of a mere formality as distinct from a central issue in the case. In *R v Francis* (1990) 154 J.P. 358 evidence of the defendant's identity was allowed to be adduced after the prosecution case had closed because the failure to introduce it as part of the case had arisen out of a misunderstanding over whether the name of the person who had been identified in a parade was in issue.

D. No Case to Answer

At the close of the prosecution case, the court may dismiss the case of its own motion **19–113** or on a submission that there is no evidence which the defendant need answer.

In *R v Galbraith* 73 Cr.App.R. 124, CA the Court of Appeal set out the test to be applied in the Crown Court. Lord Lane C.J. stated at 127 that:

(1)If there is no evidence that the crime alleged has been committed by the defendant there is no difficulty—the judge will stop the case. (2) The difficulty arises where there is some evidence but it is of a tenuous character, for example, because of inherent weakness or vagueness or because it is inconsistent with other evidence. (a) Where the judge concludes that the prosecution evidence, taken at its highest, is such that a jury properly directed could not properly convict on it, it is his duty, on a submission being made, to stop the case. (b) Where however the prosecution evidence is such that its strength or weakness depends on the view to be taken of a witness's reliability, or other matters which are generally speaking within the province of the jury and where on one possible view of the facts there *is* evidence on which the jury could properly come to the conclusion that the defendant is guilty, then the judge should allow the matter to be tried by the jury.

This test is also used in the magistrates courts. The court is entitled to dismiss a case of its own motion. If it proposes to do so, however, it should allow submissions to be made by the party it proposes to decide against: *DPP v Cosier* [2000] C.O.D. 284. Questions of credibility do not normally arise in a finding that there is no case to answer: *Brookes v DPP* [1994] 1 A.C. 568, PC; *R. v Barking and Dagenham Justices Ex p. DPP* (1995) 159 J.P. 373.

19–114   In *R. v Pydar Justices Ex p. Foster* (1996) 160 J.P. 87, evidence of the defendant's intoximeter reading had been handed to the prosecutor by the police officer in court and the case was then closed, but the defendant had submitted there was no case to answer because the reading had not been produced in evidence. His application for review was dismissed because an exhibit was available for the court to examine whenever it wished and, as the justices had jurisdiction over it, it was for the defence to lay the foundations for their submissions through cross-examination or by calling evidence. Defence counsel could not wait to point out the exhibit and then submit that there was no case to answer.

The court could re-open a case despite acceding to a submission of no case to answer, where an error had been identified by the prosecution and agreed by the defence after the court had given its reasons: *Steward v DPP, The Times*, September 25, 2003.

19–115   In *R v Gleeson* [2004] 1 Cr.App.R. 29, Auld L.J. stated that a criminal trial is not a game, its object is to ensure that the guilty are convicted and the innocent acquitted. It is contrary to defence counsel's professional duty and not in the legitimate interests of the defendant to take advantage of procedural errors made by the prosecution in delaying identifying those errors at issue in the case until the last possible moment. It is wrong to wait to make a submission of no case on an unanswerable legal challenge rather than point out a prosecution error earlier. Here the court allowed the indictment to be amended at that late stage.

There is no obligation on the court to give reasons for rejecting a submission of no case to answer: *Moran v DPP* (2002) 166 J.P. 467; *Harrison v Department of Social Security* [1997] C.O.D. 220.

VII. THE DEFENCE CASE

19–116   A defendant may be represented or unrepresented. He or she may choose to give evidence or to remain silent.

A. SEQUENCE OF THE DEFENCE EVIDENCE

19–117   At the conclusion of the prosecution's case, the defendant may address the court regardless of whether or not he calls evidence: *Magistrates' Courts Rules* 1981, r.13(2) above. By making an opening speech however the defence is then deprived of the making a speech at the end of the case, unless leave of the court is obtained: *Magistrates' Courts Rules* 1981, r.13(4) and (5). If leave for a closing speech is given in these circumstances, then the prosecution must also be given the opportunity to address the court again: *Magistrates' Courts Rules* 1981, r.13(5).

The defendant is not obliged to give evidence at trial or to call any witnesses. He may no longer make an unsworn statement from the dock.

Criminal Justice Act 1982, s.72

Abolition of right of accused to make unsworn statement

72.—(1) Subject to subsections (2) and (3) below, in any criminal proceedings the accused shall not be entitled to make a statement without being sworn, and accordingly, if he gives evidence, he shall do so[(subject to sections 55 and 56 of the *Youth Justice and Criminal Evidence Act* 1999)] on oath and be liable to cross-examination; but this section shall not affect the right of the accused, if not represented by counsel or a solicitor, to address the court or jury otherwise than on oath on any matter on which, if he were so represented, counsel or a solicitor could address the court or jury on his behalf.

(2) Nothing in subsection (1) above shall prevent the accused making a statement without being sworn—

(a) if it is one which he is required by law to make personally; or

(b) if he makes it by way of mitigation before the court passes sentence upon him.

(3) Nothing in this section applies—

(a) to a trial; or

(b) to proceedings before a magistrates' court acting as examining justices,

which began before the commencement of this section.

[This section is reprinted as amended by the *Youth Justice and Criminal Evidence Act* 1999, Sch.4, para.10.]

In *R. v Farnham Justices Ex p. Gibson* [1991] R.T.R. 309 the policy requiring a de- **19–118** fendant to give evidence from the dock, not from the witness box, was declared unlawful. At his trial for driving with excess breath-alcohol and for failing to stop after an accident, the defendant was compelled by the justices, as a matter of policy, to give his evidence from the dock, not from the witness box as the other witnesses had done. The defendant argued on review that the policy requiring him to give evidence from the dock was unlawful in the light of the *Criminal Evidence Act* 1898, s.1(g). It was held that the justices, in exceptional circumstances, could deny a person the right to give evidence from the witness box but that right could only be denied by reason of misconduct or some other specific consideration. By being compelled to give evidence from the dock, the defendant was adversely treated compared to the other witnesses and justice was not seen to be done.

If the defendant chooses to testify he must do so on oath and is liable to be cross-examined by both the advocate for the prosecution and for any co-defendants: *R. v Hilton* [1972] 1 Q.B. 421, 55 Cr.App.R. 466.

Criminal Justice and Public Order Act 1994, s.35

Effect of accused's silence at trial

35.—(1) At the trial of any person for an offence, subsections (2) and (3) below apply unless— **19–119**

(a) the accused's guilt is not in issue; or

(b) it appears to the court that the physical or mental condition of the accused makes it undesirable for him to give evidence;

but subsection (2) below does not apply if, at the conclusion of the evidence for the prosecution, his legal representative informs the court that the accused will give evidence or, where he is unrepresented, the court ascertains from him that he will give evidence.

(2) Where this subsection applies, the court shall, at the conclusion of the evidence for the prosecution, satisfy itself (in the case of proceedings on indictment, in the presence of the jury) that the accused is aware that the stage has been reached at which evidence can be given for the defence and that he can, if he wishes, give evidence and that, if he chooses not to give evidence, or having been sworn, without good cause refuses to answer any question, it will be permissible for the court or jury to draw such inferences as appear proper from his failure to give evidence or his refusal, without good cause, to answer any question.

(3) Where this subsection applies, the court or jury, in determining whether the accused is guilty of the offence charged, may draw such inferences as appear proper from the failure of the accused to give evidence or his refusal, without good cause, to answer any question.

(4) This section does not render the accused compellable to give evidence on his own behalf, and he shall accordingly not be guilty of contempt of court by reason of a failure to do so.

(5) For the purposes of this section a person who, having been sworn, refuses to answer any question shall be taken to do so without good cause unless—

(a) he is entitled to refuse to answer the question by virtue of any enactment, whenever passed or made, or on the ground of privilege; or

(b) the court in the exercise of its general discretion excuses him from answering it.

[...]

(7) This section applies—

(a) in relation to proceedings on indictment for an offence, only if the person charged with the offence is arraigned on or after the commencement of this section;

(b) in relation to proceedings in a magistrates' court, only if the time when the court begins to receive evidence in the proceedings falls after the commencement of this section.

[This section is reprinted as amended by the *Crime and Disorder Act* 1998, Sch.10, para.1.]

19–120   The duty to warn the defendant about adverse inferences arises where the defendant is present. Note the *Practice Direction (Criminal Proceedings: Consolidation)*, para.IV.44, although applying to crown courts only, is generally used by magistrates' courts.

Where the defendant is represented, the representative should inform the court as to whether the defendant intends to give evidence. If the defendant intends to give evidence the case should proceed in the normal way. If the representative states that his client does not wish to give evidence, he should be asked whether he has advised his client of the provisions of the section. If he has, then the case should proceed.

Where the defendant is unrepresented the court has a duty under s.35(2) of the Act to "satisfy itself" that the defendant is aware of the provisions. The legal adviser will advise the unrepresented defendant in the terms of the practice direction.

Police and Criminal Evidence Act 1984, s.79

Time for taking accused's evidence

19–121   79. If at the trial of any person for an offence—

(a) the defence intends to call two or more witnesses to the facts of the case; and

(b) those witnesses include the accused,

the accused shall be called before the other witness or witnesses unless the court in its discretion otherwise directs.

Where there are co-defendants it is usual for the first charged or named on the court list to give evidence first.

B. Role of Legal Representatives

19–122   Barristers and solicitors are officers of the court and should not mislead it in any way. They have a duty to draw the court's attention to the law and that includes guideline cases on sentencing: *Att.-Gen.'s Reference (No.52 of 2003)* [2003] EWCA Crim 3731, *The Times*, December 12, 2003. The court, on the other hand, must not ask advocates questions which might compromise them in any way, for example, a court should ask an advocate whether he has seen a list of previous convictions relating to his client not whether he has agreed them. It is the duty of a defence advocate to put his client's case to the court.

The following statement of principles which governs the conduct of defence counsel was made by the Chairman of the Bar following the rejection of complaints about defence counsel's conduct in *R. v McFadden* (1976) 62 Cr.App.R. 187:

It is the duty of counsel when defending an accused on a criminal charge to present to the court, fearlessly and without regard to his personal interests, the defence of that accused. It is not his function to determine the truth or falsity of that defence, nor should he permit his personal opinion of that defence to influence his conduct of it. No counsel may refuse to defence because of his opinion of the character of the accused nor of the crime charged. That is a cardinal rule of the Bar ... Counsel also has a duty to the court and to the public. This duty includes the clear presentation of the issues and the avoidance of waste of time, repetition and prolixity. In the conduct of every case counsel must be mindful of this public responsibility.

The remarks made in *Att.-Gen.'s Ref.(No. 52 of 2003)*, above, also apply.

C. Unrepresented Defendant　　　　　　　19–122.1

Where the defendant is unrepresented the legal adviser has several duties in relation　**19–123** to him.

Magistrates' Courts Rules 1981, r.13A

Procedure on information where accused is not legally represented

13A.—(1) The court shall explain to an accused who is not legally represented the substance　**19–124** of the charge in simple language.

(2) If an accused who is not legally represented instead of asking a witness in support of the charge questions by way of cross-examination, makes assertions, the court shall then put to the witness such questions as it thinks necessary on behalf of the accused and may for this purpose question the accused in order to bring out or clear up any point arising out of such assertions.

[This rule was inserted by the *Magistrates' Courts (Miscellaneous Amendments) Rules* 1993, r.3(b).]

Although the rules refer to the court it is usual for the legal adviser, in accordance　**19–125** with the *Practice Direction (Criminal Proceedings: Consolidation)*, para.V.55, above, to assist an unrepresented defendant. The legal adviser will explain the nature of the charge, the consequences of not giving evidence (s.35 of the *Criminal Justice and Public Order Act* 1994 above), and will assist the defendant in turning the statements he makes about his defence into questions which can be put to witnesses. The legal adviser is also under a duty to ensure that an unrepresented defendant understands evidential issues and that he is not prejudiced by conduct which might put his or her bad character in evidence. If such a course is anticipated by the nature of the questions asked by the defendant in person, the prosecution should ask for an adjournment so that the legal adviser may explain to the defendant the risk of pursuing such a line of questioning: *R. v Weston-Super-Mare Justices Ex p. Townsend* (1968) 132 J.P. 526.

D. Rebuttal of Evidence

At the conclusion of the defence case the prosecution may call rebuttal evidence. This　**19–126** evidence should be confined to a matter which arises unexpectedly in the course of the defence case: *R. v Whelan* (1881) 14 Cox C.C. 595; *Price v Humphries* [1958] 2 Q.B. 353 although the court has a discretion to allow evidence which is not strictly of a rebutting nature. This should also extend to calling evidence to rebut assertions made by a co-defendant.

E. Viewing the Scene of the Crime

The court may be invited to view the scene of an alleged offence. If the court agrees　**19–127** to view the scene, then both prosecution and defence should be present or be given the opportunity to be present. The view should take place before the conclusion of the evidence so that both parties have the opportunity of commenting on it: *Parry v Boyle* (1986) 83 Cr.App.R. 310. The defendant, even when he is legally represented, should be allowed to be present. Failure to allow the defendant to attend a view is contrary to the fairness of the proceedings: *R. v Ely Justices Ex p. Burgess* (1993) 157 J.P. 484.

If a magistrate attends the scene of an alleged offence unofficially during an adjournment it does not necessarily mean that an irregularity has occurred. If the parties allow the trial to continue with the knowledge that an unofficial view has occurred and no prejudice is alleged, then the conviction is unlikely to be quashed on that basis: *Telfer and Telfer v DPP* (1996) 160 J.P. 512.

F. CLOSING SPEECH

19–128   The defence will address the court on both facts and law. The prosecution will have a right to reply to a legal argument. In those circumstances the defence will have a further opportunity to argue its case. It is general practice for the legal adviser to advise magistrates in open court so that the legal representatives know the exact basis of the advice.

VIII. THE DECISION

19–129   Under s.9(2) of the *Magistrates' Courts Act* 1980, above, the court has a statutory duty either to convict or acquit the defendant. A magistrates' court has no power to return a verdict of not guilty as charged in the information but guilty of a lesser offence: *Lawrence v Same* [1968] 2 Q.B. 93. There are two statutory exceptions:

Road Traffic Offenders Act 1988, s.24(1)–(3)

Alternative verdicts: general

19–130   **24.**—(1) Where—

  (a) a person charged with an offence under a provision of the *Road Traffic Act* 1988 specified in the first column of the Table below (where the general nature of the offences is also indicated) is found not guilty of that offence, but

  (b) the allegations in the indictment or information (or in Scotland complaint) amount to or include an allegation of an offence under one or more of the provisions specified in the corresponding entry in the second column,

he may be convicted of that offence or of one or more of those offences.

(2) Where the offence with which a person is charged is an offence under section 3A of the *Road Traffic Act* 1988, subsection (1) above shall not authorise his conviction of any offence of attempting to drive.

(3) Where a person is charged with having committed an offence under section 4(1) or 5(1)(a) of the *Road Traffic Act* 1988 by driving a vehicle, he may be convicted of having committed an offence under the provision in question by attempting to drive.

Offence charged	*Alternative*
Section 1 (causing death by dangerous driving)	Section 2 (dangerous driving) Section 3 (careless, and inconsiderate, driving)
Section 2 (dangerous driving)	Section 3 (careless, and inconsiderate, driving)
Section 3A (causing death by careless driving when under influence of drink or drugs)	Section 3 (careless, and inconsiderate, driving)Section 4(1) (driving when unfit to drive through drink or drugs)Section 5(1)(a) (driving with excess alcohol in breath, blood or urine)Section 7(6) (failing to provide specimen)
Section 4(1) (driving or attempting to drive when unfit to drive through drink or drugs)	Section 4(2) (being in charge of a vehicle when unfit to drive through drink or drugs)
Section 5(1)(a) (driving or attempting to drive with excess alcohol in breath, blood or urine)	Section 5(1)(b) (being in charge of a vehicle with excess alcohol in breath, blood or urine)
Section 28 (dangerous cycling)	Section 29 (careless, and inconsiderate, cycling)

Theft Act 1968, s.12A(5)

Aggravated vehicle-taking

19–131   **12A.**—(5) If a person who is charged with an offence under this section is found not guilty of that offence but it is proved that he committed a basic offence, he may be convicted of the basic offence.

[This section is reprinted as amended by *Aggravated Vehicle-Taking Act* 1992, s.1(1) and omitting paras.(1)–(4) and (6)–(8).]

Where an information charges an attempt but the evidence establishes the full offence, the court may convict the defendant of the attempt: *Webley v Buxton* [1977] Q.B. 481.

Magistrates are under a duty to reach a decision and a mandatory order will be **19–132** granted against them if they do not: *R. v Bridgend Justices Ex p. Randall* [1975] Crim.L.R. 287; *R. v Bromley Justices Ex p. Haymills (Contractors) Ltd* [1984] Crim.L.R. 235. If the magistrates are unable to reach a decision on the issue of guilt then the prosecution has failed to prove its case and the proper decision is one of not guilty.

A bench of magistrates reaches its decisions by majority and that is the reason for securing an odd number of magistrates on the bench: *Barnsley v Marsh* [1947] K.B. 672. There is no casting vote procedure. If magistrates are evenly numbered and equally divided, it will be necessary for the case to be adjourned for rehearing before a differently constituted court of three magistrates: *R v Redbridge Justices Ex p. Ram* [1992] Q.B. 384. Alternatively they may refuse to adjourn and may dismiss the information. The dismissal is a bar to a second information for the same offence: *Kinnis v Graves* (1898) 67 L.J. Q.B. 583.

The court may use its local knowledge when deciding a question of fact however it should inform the prosecution and defence that it is going to do so, so that the parties may comment on the knowledge which the court claims to have: *Bowman v DPP* [1991] R.T.R. 263; *Norbrook Laboratories (GB) Ltd v Health & Safety Executive* [1998] E.H.L.R. 207.

The court is not obliged to give detailed reasons for its decision: *R. v Brent Justices Ex p. McGowan* (2002) 166 J.P. 29. It is unnecessary for reasons to be elaborate or in the form of a judgement reciting the charges, the evidence and the findings of fact. The essence of the exercise is to inform the defendant why he has been found guilty. This can be done in a few simple sentences: see *R. (on the application of H) v Thames Youth Court and the Crown prosecution Service* [2002] EWHC 2046.

WITNESSES

I. SECURING THE ATTENDANCE OF WITNESSES

Magistrates' Courts Act 1980, s.97

Summons to witness and warrant for his arrest

97.—(1) Where a justice of the peace for any commission area is satisfied that any person in **20–1**

761

England or Wales is likely to be able to give material evidence, or produce any document or thing likely to be material evidence, [...] at the summary trial of an information or hearing of a complaint by a magistrates court for that commission area and that that person will not voluntarily attend as a witness or will not voluntarily produce the document or thing, the justice shall issue a summons directed to that person requiring him to attend before the court at the time and place appointed in the summons to give evidence or to produce the document or thing.

(2) If a justice of the peace is satisfied by evidence on oath of the matters mentioned in subsection (1) above, and also that it is probable that a summons under that subsection would not procure the attendance of the person in question, the justice may instead of issuing a summons issue a warrant to arrest that person and bring him before such a court as aforesaid at a time and place specified in the warrant; but a warrant shall not be issued under this subsection where the attendance is required for the hearing of a complaint.

(2A) A summons may also be issued under subsection (1) above if the justice is satisfied that the person in question is outside the British Islands but no warrant shall be issued under subsection (2) above unless the justice is satisfied by evidence on oath that the person in question is in England or Wales.

(2B) A justice may refuse to issue a summons under subsection (1) above in relation to the summary trial of an information if he is not satisfied that an application for the summons was made by a party to the case as soon as reasonably practicable after the accused pleaded not guilty.

(2C) In relation to the summary trial of an information, subsection (2) above shall have effect as if the reference to the matters mentioned in subsection (1) above included a reference to the matter mentioned in subsection (2B) above.

(3) On the failure of any person to attend before a magistrates' court in answer to a summons under this section, if—

    (a) the court is satisfied by evidence on oath that he is likely to be able to give material evidence or produce any document or thing likely to be material evidence in the proceedings; and

    (b) it is proved on oath, or in such other manner as may be prescribed, that he has been duly served with the summons, and that a reasonable sum has been paid or tendered to him for costs and expenses; and

    (c) it appears to the court that there is no just excuse for the failure,

the court may issue a warrant to arrest him and bring him before the court at a time and place specified in the warrant.

(4) If any person attending or brought before a magistrates' court refuses without just excuse to be sworn or give evidence, or to produce any document or thing, the court may commit him to custody until the expiration of such period not exceeding one month as may be specified in the warrant or until he sooner gives evidence or produces the document or thing or impose on him a fine not exceeding £2,500 or both.

(5) A fine imposed under subsection (4) above shall be deemed, for the purposes of any enactment, to be a sum adjudged to be paid by a conviction.

20–2   [This section is reprinted as amended by the *Criminal Procedure and Investigations Act* 1996, Sch.1, para.7(a).]

20–3   The court may issue a summons or a warrant to secure the attendance of a witness. It is important that if the court is to serve the summons "conduct money", *i.e.* sufficient money to enable the witness to attend court is deposited with the court.

II. SWEARING OF A WITNESS

A. GENERAL

20–4   Unless a particular statute allows unsworn evidence, all evidence given before a magistrates' court will be given on oath: *Magistrates' Courts Act* 1980, s.98. A child's evidence will be given unsworn but witnesses aged 14 years or over must give evidence on oath: *R. v Sharman* [1998] 1 Cr.App.R. 406; *Youth Justice and Criminal Evidence Act* 1999, s.55(2)(a).

B. FORM OF OATH

Oaths Act 1978, s.1

Manner of administration of oaths
1.—(1) Any oath may be administered and taken in England, Wales or Northern Ireland in **20–5** the following form and manner—
The person taking the oath shall hold the New Testament, or, in the case of a Jew, the Old Testament, in his uplifted hand, and shall say or repeat after the officer administering the oath the words "I swear by Almighty God that ...", followed by the words of the oath prescribed by law.

(2) The officer shall (unless the person about to take the oath voluntarily objects thereto, or is physically incapable of so taking the oath) administer the oath in the form and manner aforesaid without question.

(3) In the case of a person who is neither a Christian nor a Jew, the oath shall be administered in any lawful manner.

(4) In this section "officer" means any person duly authorised to administer oaths.

Magistrates' courts have facilities to administer the oath in accordance with most religions and will ask a witness outside of court how he wishes to be sworn so that the oath taking in court proceeds in a proper manner.

The purpose of taking an oath is that it should be binding on a witness's conscience. **20–6** The question whether a witness who is neither a Christian nor a Jew has been lawfully sworn depends on whether the oath appears to the court to be binding on the conscience of the witness and whether the witness himself considers his conscience bound. If a Muslim takes the oath using the New Testament he could still be lawfully sworn. The question of whether an oath is lawfully administered does not depend on what may be the considerable intricacies of the particular religion adhered to by the witness: *R. v Kemble* [1990] 1 W.L.R. 1111.

C. AFFIRMATION

Oaths Act 1978, ss.5–6

Making of solemn affirmations
5.—(1) Any person who objects to being sworn shall be permitted to make his solemn affir- **20–7** mation instead of taking an oath.

(2) Subsection (1) above shall apply in relation to a person to whom it is not reasonably practicable without inconvenience or delay to administer an oath in the manner appropriate to his religious belief as it applies in relation to a person objecting to be sworn.

(3) A person who may be permitted under subsection (2) above to make his solemn affirmation may also be required to do so.

(4) A solemn affirmation shall be of the same force and effect as an oath.

It is not usual to ask whether someone objects to taking the oath. A witness is asked **20–8** to choose between the oath and affirmation.

Form of affirmation
6.—(1) Subject to subsection (2) below, every affirmation shall be as follows—

"I... do solemnly, sincerely and truly declare and affirm,"

and then proceed with the words of the oath prescribed by law, omitting any words of imprecation or calling to witness.

(2) Every affirmation in writing shall commence—

"I... do solemnly and sincerely affirm,"

and the form in lieu of jurat shall be "Affirmed at... this ... day of ... 19..., Before me."

D. UNSWORN TESTIMONY

Youth Justice and Criminal Evidence Act 1999, ss.55–57

Determining whether witness to be sworn

20–9　　**55.**—(1) Any question whether a witness in criminal proceedings may be sworn for the purpose of giving evidence on oath, whether raised—

(a) by a party to the proceedings, or

(b) by the court of its own motion,

shall be determined by the court in accordance with this section.

(2) The witness may not be sworn for that purpose unless—

(a) he has attained the age of 14, and

(b) he has a sufficient appreciation of the solemnity of the occasion and of the particular responsibility to tell the truth which is involved in taking an oath.

(3) The witness shall, if he is able to give intelligible testimony, be presumed to have a sufficient appreciation of those matters if no evidence tending to show the contrary is adduced (by any party).

(4) If any such evidence is adduced, it is for the party seeking to have the witness sworn to satisfy the court that, on a balance of probabilities, the witness has attained the age of 14 and has a sufficient appreciation of the matters mentioned in subsection (2)(b).

(5) Any proceedings held for the determination of the question mentioned in subsection (1) shall take place in the absence of the jury (if there is one).

(6) Expert evidence may be received on the question.

(7) Any questioning of the witness (where the court considers that necessary) shall be conducted by the court in the presence of the parties.

(8) For the purposes of this section a person is able to give intelligible testimony if he is able to—

(a) understand questions put to him as a witness, and

(b) give answers to them which can be understood.

Reception of unsworn evidence

20–10　　**56.**—(1) Subsections (2) and (3) apply to a person (of any age) who—

(a) is competent to give evidence in criminal proceedings, but

(b) (by virtue of section 55(2)) is not permitted to be sworn for the purpose of giving evidence on oath in such proceedings.

(2) The evidence in criminal proceedings of a person to whom this subsection applies shall be given unsworn.

(3) A deposition of unsworn evidence given by a person to whom this subsection applies may be taken for the purposes of criminal proceedings as if that evidence had been given on oath.

(4) A court in criminal proceedings shall accordingly receive in evidence any evidence given unsworn in pursuance of subsection (2) or (3).

(5) Where a person ("the witness") who is competent to give evidence in criminal proceedings gives evidence in such proceedings unsworn, no conviction, verdict or finding in those proceedings shall be taken to be unsafe for the purposes of any of sections 2(1), 13(1) and 16(1) of the *Criminal Appeal Act* 1968 (grounds for allowing appeals) by reason only that it appears to the Court of Appeal that the witness was a person falling within section 55(2) (and should accordingly have given his evidence on oath).

Penalty for giving false unsworn evidence

20–11　　**57.**—(1) This section applies where a person gives unsworn evidence in criminal proceedings in pursuance of section 56(2) or (3).

(2) If such a person wilfully gives false evidence in such circumstances that, had the evidence been given on oath, he would have been guilty of perjury, he shall be guilty of an offence and liable on summary conviction to—

(a) imprisonment for a term not exceeding 6 months, or

(b) a fine not exceeding £1,000,

or both.

(3) In relation to a person under the age of 14, subsection (2) shall have effect as if for

the words following "on summary conviction" there were substituted "to a fine not exceeding £250".

A witness may not take the oath unless he is fourteen years old. He must also appreciate the solemnity of the occasion and the responsibility to tell the truth. This may be ascertained from the fact that he is able to give an intelligent explanation of what has happened. It is for the party calling the witness to satisfy the court of those matters on a balance of probabilities and, in certain circumstances, expert evidence may be received. If it is found that he is incapable of giving sworn evidence then his evidence will be taken unsworn.

III. COMPETENCE AND COMPELLABILITY

A. General

A witness is competent if he can lawfully give evidence and compellable if he can be **20–12** lawfully required to give evidence.

Youth Justice and Criminal Evidence Act 1999, s.53

Competence of witnesses to give evidence

53.—(1) At every stage in criminal proceedings all persons are (whatever their age) competent **20–13** to give evidence.

(2) Subsection (1) has effect subject to subsections (3) and (4).

(3) A person is not competent to give evidence in criminal proceedings if it appears to the court that he is not a person who is able to—

(a) understand questions put to him as a witness, and

(b) give answers to them which can be understood.

(4) A person charged in criminal proceedings is not competent to give evidence in the proceedings for the prosecution (whether he is the only person, or is one of two or more persons, charged in the proceedings).

(5) In subsection (4) the reference to a person charged in criminal proceedings does not include a person who is not, or is no longer, liable to be convicted of any offence in the proceedings (whether as a result of pleading guilty or for any other reason).

B. Determining Competency

The general rule that all persons are competent to give evidence at every stage in **20–14** criminal proceedings is subject to a test of competence contained in the *Youth Justice and Criminal Evidence Act* 1999, s.54.

Youth Justice and Criminal Evidence Act 1999, s.54

Determining competence of witnesses

54.—(1) Any question whether a witness in criminal proceedings is competent to give evi- **20–15** dence in the proceedings, whether raised—

(a) by a party to the proceedings, or

(b) by the court of its own motion,

shall be determined by the court in accordance with this section.

(2) It is for the party calling the witness to satisfy the court that, on a balance of probabilities, the witness is competent to give evidence in the proceedings.

(3) In determining the question mentioned in subsection (1) the court shall treat the witness as having the benefit of any directions under section 19 which the court has given, or proposes to give, in relation to the witness.

(5) Expert evidence may be received on the question.

(6) Any questioning of the witness (where the court considers that necessary) shall be conducted by the court in the presence of the parties.

Any objection to a witness's competency must be made before he is sworn or gives ev- **20–16** idence: *R. v Hampshire* [1996] Q.B.1; [1995] 2 Cr.App.R. 319, CA. In *R. v Yacoob* (1981) 72 Cr.App.R. 313, CA, the court said that the beginning of the trial was the appropriate time for determining competence and compellability of prosecution witnesses. If, prior to the hearing, an objection has been raised with the prosecution then the evidence to be given by that witness should not be referred to in the opening speech.

C. Children

20–17   All persons of whatever age are competent to give evidence: s.53(1)(above). The evidence of a child will be received unless it appears to the court that the child is incapable of giving intelligible testimony; that is evidence which is capable of being understood: *R. v Hampshire* [1996] Q.B. 1. The procedure of determining intelligible testimony is the same for children as for adults: s.55. The issue of competence should be dealt with as early as possible, not as an act of "ratification" after the evidence has been given. It is not an issue to be resolved in response to an adversarial examination and cross-examination but is a matter for the court to decide having heard the child in person. The legal adviser will generally talk to the child about why he is there and whether he understands what telling the truth means. In *G v DPP* [1998] Q.B. 919 it was held that the test is within the competence of the court and there is no need for expert evidence unless there are special circumstances, for example, the child is mentally handicapped. The fact that a child under ten years of age cannot be prosecuted for the offence of wilfully giving false evidence contrary to the *Youth Justice and Criminal Evidence Act* 1999, s.57 is not a reason for excluding the unsworn evidence of a competent child: *R. v N* (1992) 95 Cr.App.R. 256.

The *Practice Direction (Criminal Proceedings: Consolidation)* [2002] 1 W.L.R. 2870, para.I.5, above, applies to wards of court.

D. Mentally Disordered Persons

20–18   A witness who is prevented from giving rational testimony by reason of mental illness or drunkenness is not competent. Where a witness appears to be unable to give intelligible testimony by reason of mental illness or intoxication, the court should ascertain whether the witness is capable of understanding the questions put to him or to give answers which can be understood pursuant to the provisions of ss.54–57 of the *Youth Justice and Criminal Evidence Act* 1999. This may be done by calling expert evidence. See *R. v Hill* (1851) 2 Den. 254; *R. v Dunning* [1965] Crim.L.R. 372. The worth of the evidence will ultimately be a matter for the court. In cases of mental illness this will depend on degree. In *R. v Hill*, above, the circumstances were such that the proper course was to reject the evidence.

E. The Accused

Criminal Evidence Act 1898, s.1

Competency of witnesses in criminal cases

20–19   1.—(1)

     (a) A person... charged shall not be called as a witness in the proceedings except upon his own application.

     (e) A person charged and being a witness...may be asked any question in cross-examination notwithstanding that it would tend to incriminate him as to the offence charged

     (2) A person charged in criminal proceedings who is called as a witness in the proceedings may be asked any question in cross-examination notwithstanding that it would tend to criminate him as to any offence with which he is charged in the proceedings.

[This section is reprinted as amended by *Police and Criminal Evidence Act* 1984, Sch.7, the *Criminal Justice and Public Order Act* 1994, Sch.10, para.2 and Sch.11 and the *Youth Justice and Criminal Evidence Act* 1999, s.67(1) and Sch.4, para.1.]

The defendant is not a compellable witness for the prosecution: *R. v Rhodes* [1899]   **20–20**
1 Q.B. 77 and a defendant cannot be compelled to give evidence against a co-defendant:
R. v Payne LR 1 CCR 349; *R. v Grant*, 30 Cr.App.R. 99; *R. v Sharrock* (1948) 32
Cr.App.R. 124.

A defendant who has pleaded guilty is not a "person charged" within the meaning of
s.1 of the 1898 Act because he is not concerned in any issue before the judge of fact. A
defendant who has pleaded guilty is therefore competent and compellable to give evidence for a co-defendant: *R. v Boal* [1965] 1 Q.B. 402. A plea of guilty by a co-
defendant is not evidence against the defendant: *R. v Smith* (1984) 148 J.P. 215.

A co-defendant who has been acquitted is not a "person charged" within the *Criminal Evidence Act* 1898, s.1, and is therefore compellable as a witness: *R. v Conti* (1974)
58 Cr.App.R. 387, CA. Those concerned with the charge should not be called by the
prosecution: *R. v Pipe* (1967) 51 Cr.App.R. 17. The prosecution may, however, call an
accomplice who is to be charged and tried separately: *R. v Palmer* (1994) 99 Cr.App.R.
83.

The defendant is a competent witness for himself. He is not, however, a compellable
witness for the defence: *Criminal Evidence Act* 1898, s.1(1). An acquitted person called
by the defendant may be cross-examined by a co-defendant.

A defendant who gives evidence for a co-defendant is liable to be cross-examined on
the issue of his own guilt: *R. v Rowland* [1910] 1 K.B. 458. If a defendant refuses to
answer questions incriminating other persons, the court is not bound to receive his or
her evidence: *R. v Minihane* 16 Cr.App.R. 38.

F. THE DEFENDANT'S SPOUSE

Police and Criminal Evidence Act 1984, s.80

Competence and compellability of the defendant's spouse
    80.—(2) In any proceedings the wife or husband of a person charged in the proceedings   **20–21**
shall, subject to subsection (4) below, be compellable to give evidence on behalf of that person.

(2A) In any proceedings the wife or husband of a person charged in the proceedings
shall, subject to subsection (4) below, be compellable—

(a) to give evidence on behalf of any other person charged in the proceedings but
only in respect of any specified offence with which that other person is charged;
or

(b) to give evidence for the prosecution but only in respect of any specified offence
with which any person is charged in the proceedings.

(3) In relation to the wife or husband of a person charged in any proceedings, an offence is a specified offence for the purposes of subsection (2A) above if—

(a) it involves an assault on, or injury or a threat of injury to, the wife or husband or
a person who was at the material time under the age of 16;

(b) it is a sexual offence alleged to have been committed in respect of a person who
was at the material time under that age; or

(c) it consists of attempting or conspiring to commit, or of aiding, abetting, counselling, procuring or inciting the commission of, an offence falling within paragraph
(a) or (b) above.

(4) No person who is charged in any proceedings shall be compellable by virtue of
subsection (2) or (2A) above to give evidence in the proceedings.

(4A) References in this section to a person charged in any proceedings do not include a
person who is not, or is no longer, liable to be convicted of any offence in the proceedings
(whether as a result of pleading guilty or for any other reason).

(5) In any proceedings a person who has been but is no longer married to the accused
shall be compellable to give evidence as if that person and the accused had never been
married.

(6) Where in any proceedings the age of any person at any time is material for the
purposes of subsection (3) above, his age at the material time shall for the purposes of that
provision be deemed to be or to have been that which appears to the court to be or to have
been his age at that time.

(7) In subsection (3)(b) above "sexual-offence" means an offence under the *Sexual Offences Act* 1956, the *Indecency with Children Act* 1960, the *Sexual Offences Act* 1967, section 54 of the *Criminal Law Act* 1977 or the *Protection of Children Act* 1978.

(8) [repealed.]

(9) Section 1(d) of the *Criminal Evidence Act* 1898 (communications between husband and wife) and section 43(1) of the *Matrimonial Causes Act* 1965 (evidence as to marital intercourse) shall cease to have effect.

[This section is reprinted as amended by the *Youth Justice and Criminal Evidence Act* 1999, Sch.6, para.1.]

A spouse is competent to give evidence against a defendant but is only compellable in the terms of the statute.

20-22   Section 80 does not apply to the defendant's unmarried partner: *R. v Pearce* [2002] 1 Cr.App.R. 39, CA. Although the compellability of a family member to give evidence against another might conflict with the right to family life under Art.8 of the European Convention on Human Rights the interference may be justified under Art.8(2) as necessary in a democratic society for the prevention of crime.

The position of a wife of a second polygamous marriage is no different from that of a woman who has not gone through a marriage ceremony at all or who has gone through a ceremony which was invalid: *R. v Yacoob* (1981) 72 Cr.App.R. 313, CA; *R. v Khan* (1987) 84 Cr.App.R. 44, CA.

The prosecution has a duty to disclose to the defence that a spouse has informed the prosecutor outside the court that he does not wish to give evidence against his spouse and that the statement given to the police is inaccurate: *R. v Birmingham Justices Ex p. Shields, The Times,* August 3, 1994,, CA. The prosecution must also inform the court so that the spouse can be warned that he need not give evidence. Once a spouse has started to give evidence he must complete it and may be treated as a hostile witness if he shows an unwillingness to continue: *R. v Pitt* [1983] Q.B. 25.

G. Other Witnesses

20-23   The sovereign is a competent but not compellable witness. Foreign heads of state, diplomatic and consular staff, members of the family of a diplomatic agent, members of the administrative and technical staff of a diplomatic mission and members of their families, persons connected with consular posts and members of staff of international organisations enjoy total or partial immunity from compellability to give evidence.

See *Diplomatic Privileges Act* 1964, s.1(1), Sch.1, Arts 1, 30, 37, 38(2) and 39; *State Immunity Act* 1978, s.14; *International Organisations Act* 1968, s.5.

High Court judges and those of inferior courts are not compellable witnesses: *Warren v Warren* [1997] 1 F.C.R. 237, CA. Magistrates and their legal advisers, however, are compellable: *Re McC (a minor)* [1985] A.C. 528.

IV. THE PROTECTION OF WITNESSES

A. General

20-24   Witnesses give their evidence in open court and with their identity disclosed. In special circumstances a witness may be allowed to give evidence anonymously. The decision as to whether a witness may give evidence without being identified is a matter for the court's discretion: *R. v Taylor* [1995] Crim.L.R. 253. The factors for the court to consider when exercising that discretion are:

1. Whether there are real grounds for fear of the consequences if evidence were given and the identity of the witness were revealed;

2. The evidence must be sufficiently relevant and important to make it unfair for the prosecution to proceed without that evidence;

3. The prosecution must satisfy the court that the creditworthiness of the witness has been fully investigated;

4. There must be no undue prejudice to the defendant; and

5. The court must balance the need for protection of the witness against the unfairness or the appearance of unfairness to the defendant.

In *R. v Watford Magistrates' Court Ex p. Lenman* [1993] Crim.L.R. 388 the **20–25** Divisional Court upheld the magistrates' decision to allow witnesses to give evidence anonymously because they were afraid of reprisals. If a court is satisfied that there is a real risk to the administration of justice because witnesses have reasonable grounds to fear for their safety if their identity is disclosed, it is entirely within its powers to take reasonable steps to protect and reassure the witnesses so that they will not be deterred from coming forward. The purpose is to secure justice.

The *Youth Justice and Criminal Evidence Act* 1999 has subsequently been enacted to provide for special measures to be taken for the protection of and assistance for vulnerable witnesses. These include screening witnesses from the defendant, giving evidence by live link, video recorded evidence in chief, video recorded examination and cross-examination, examination of a witness through an intermediary, protection from cross-examination by the defendant in person and restrictions on the type of questions asked.

B. SPECIAL MEASURES

Youth Justice and Criminal Evidence Act 1999, ss.16–23

Witnesses eligible for assistance on grounds of age or incapacity

16.—(1) For the purposes of this Chapter a witness in criminal proceedings (other than the **20–26** accused) is eligible for assistance by virtue of this section—

(a) if under the age of 17 at the time of the hearing; or

(b) if the court considers that the quality of evidence given by the witness is likely to be diminished by reason of any circumstances falling within subsection (2).

(2) The circumstances falling within this subsection are—

(a) that the witness—

(i) suffers from mental disorder within the meaning of the *Mental Health Act* 1983, or

(ii) otherwise has a significant impairment of intelligence and social functioning;

(b) that the witness has a physical disability or is suffering from a physical disorder.

(3) In subsection (1)(a) "the time of the hearing", in relation to a witness, means the time when it falls to the court to make a determination for the purposes of section 19(2) in relation to the witness.

(4) In determining whether a witness falls within subsection (1)(b) the court must consider any views expressed by the witness.

(5) In this Chapter references to the quality of a witness's evidence are to its quality in terms of completeness, coherence and accuracy; and for this purpose "coherence" refers to a witness's ability in giving evidence to give answers which address the questions put to the witness and can be understood both individually and collectively.

A witness under the age of seventeen at the time of the hearing is automatically considered to be vulnerable.

Witnesses eligible for assistance on grounds of fear or distress about testifying

17.—(1) For the purposes of this Chapter a witness in criminal proceedings (other than the **20–27** accused) is eligible for assistance by virtue of this subsection if the court is satisfied that the quality of evidence given by the witness is likely to be diminished by reason of fear or distress on the part of the witness in connection with testifying in the proceedings.

(2) In determining whether a witness falls within subsection (1) the court must take into account, in particular—

(a) the nature and alleged circumstances of the offence to which the proceedings relate;

(b) the age of the witness;

(c) such of the following matters as appear to the court to be relevant, namely—
    (i) the social and cultural background and ethnic origins of the witness,
    (ii) the domestic and employment circumstances of the witness, and
    (iii) any religious beliefs or political opinions of the witness;
(d) any behaviour towards the witness on the part of—
    (i) the accused,
    (ii) members of the family or associates of the accused, or
    (iii) any other person who is likely to be an accused or a witness in the proceedings.

(3) In determining that question the court must in addition consider any views expressed by the witness.

(4) Where the complainant in respect of a sexual offence is a witness in proceedings relating to that offence (or to that offence and any other offences), the witness is eligible for assistance in relation to those proceedings by virtue of this subsection unless the witness has informed the court of the witness' wish not to be so eligible by virtue of this subsection.

Special measures available to eligible witnesses

20–28   **18.**—(1) For the purposes of this Chapter—
(a) the provision which may be made by a special measures direction by virtue of each of sections 23 to 30 is a special measure available in relation to a witness eligible for assistance by virtue of section 16; and
(b) the provision which may be made by such a direction by virtue of each of sections 23 to 28 is a special measure available in relation to a witness eligible for assistance by virtue of section 17;
but this subsection has effect subject to subsection (2).

(2) Where (apart from this subsection) a special measure would, in accordance with subsection (1)(a) or (b), be available in relation to a witness in any proceedings, it shall not be taken by a court to be available in relation to the witness unless—
(a) the court has been notified by the Secretary of State that relevant arrangements may be made available in the area in which it appears to the court that the proceedings will take place, and
(b) the notice has not been withdrawn.

(3) In subsection (2) "relevant arrangements" means arrangements for implementing the measure in question which cover the witness and the proceedings in question.

(4) The withdrawal of a notice under that subsection relating to a special measure shall not affect the availability of that measure in relation to a witness if a special measures direction providing for that measure to apply to the witness's evidence has been made by the court before the notice is withdrawn.

(5) The Secretary of State may by order make such amendments of this Chapter as he considers appropriate for altering the special measures which, in accordance with subsection (1)(a) or (b), are available in relation to a witness eligible for assistance by virtue of section 16 or (as the case may be) section 17, whether—
(a) by modifying the provisions relating to any measure for the time being available in relation to such a witness,
(b) by the addition—
    (i) (with or without modifications) of any measure which is for the time being available in relation to a witness eligible for assistance by virtue of the other of those sections, or
    (ii) of any new measure, or
(c) by the removal of any measure.

Special measures direction relating to eligible witness

20–29   **19.**—(1) This section applies where in any criminal proceedings—
(a) a party to the proceedings makes an application for the court to give a direction under this section in relation to a witness in the proceedings other than the accused, or
(b) the court of its own motion raises the issue whether such a direction should be given.

(2) Where the court determines that the witness is eligible for assistance by virtue of section 16 or 17, the court must then—

    (a) determine whether any of the special measures available in relation to the witness (or any combination of them) would, in its opinion, be likely to improve the quality of evidence given by the witness; and

    (b) if so—

        (i) determine which of those measures (or combination of them) would, in its opinion, be likely to maximise so far as practicable the quality of such evidence; and

        (ii) give a direction under this section providing for the measure or measures so determined to apply to evidence given by the witness.

    (3) In determining for the purposes of this Chapter whether any special measure or measures would or would not be likely to improve, or to maximise so far as practicable, the quality of evidence given by the witness, the court must consider all the circumstances of the case, including in particular—

    (a) any views expressed by the witness; and

    (b) whether the measures or measures must tend to inhibit such evidence being effectively tested by a party to the proceedings.

    (4) A special measures direction must specify particulars of the provision made by the direction in respect of each special measure which is to apply to the witness's evidence.

    (5) In this Chapter "special measures direction" means a direction under this section.

    (6) Nothing in this Chapter is to be regarded as affecting any power of a court to make an order or give leave of any description (in the exercise of its inherent jurisdiction or otherwise)—

    (a) in relation to a witness who is not an eligible witness, or

    (b) in relation to an eligible witness where (as, for example, in a case where a foreign language interpreter is to be provided) the order is made or the leave is given otherwise than by reason of the fact that the witness is an eligible witness.

Further provisions about directions: general

    20.—(1) Subject to subsection (2) and section 21(8), a special measures direction has binding **20–30** effect from the time it is made until the proceedings for the purposes of which it is made are either—

    (a) determined (by acquittal, conviction or otherwise), or

    (b) abandoned,

in relation to the accused or (if there is more than one) in relation to each of the accused.

    (2) The court may discharge or vary (or further vary) a special measures direction if it appears to the court to be in the interests of justice to do so, and may do so either—

    (a) on an application made by a party to the proceedings, if there has been a material change of circumstances since the relevant time, or

    (b) of its own motion.

    (3) In subsection (2) "the relevant time" means —

    (a) the time when the direction was given, or

    (b) if a previous application has been made under that subsection, the time when the application (or last application) was made.

    (4) Nothing in section 24(2) and (3), 27(4) to (7) or 28(4) to (6) is to be regarded as affecting the power of the court to vary or discharge a special measures direction under subsection (2).

    (5) The court must state in open court its reasons for—

    (a) giving or varying,

    (b) refusing an application for, or for the variation or discharge of, or

    (c) discharging,

a special measures direction and, if it is a magistrates' court, must cause them to be entered in the register of its proceedings.

    (6) Rules of court may make provision—

    (a) for uncontested applications to be determined by the court without a hearing;

    (b) for preventing the renewal of an unsuccessful application for a special measures direction except where there has been a material change of circumstances;

    (c) for expert evidence to be given in connection with an application for, or for varying or discharging, such a direction;

    (d) for the manner in which confidential or sensitive information is to be treated in connection with such an application and in particular as to its being disclosed to, or withheld from, a party to the proceedings.

Special provisions relating to child witnesses

20–31 　　21.—(1) For the purposes of this section—

(a) a witness in criminal proceedings is a "child witness" if he is an eligible witness by reason of section 16(1)(a) (whether or not he is an eligible witness by reason of any other provision of section 16 or 17);

(b) a child witness is "in need of special protection" if the offence (or any of the offences) to which the proceedings relate is—

 (i) an offence falling within section 35(3)(a) (sexual offences etc.), or

 (ii) an offence falling within section 35(3)(b), (c) or (d) (kidnapping, assaults etc.); and

(c) a "relevant recording", in relation to a child witness, is a video recording of an interview of the witness made with a view to its admission as evidence in chief of the witness.

(2) Where the court, in making a determination for the purposes of section 19(2), determines that a witness in criminal proceedings is a child witness, the court must—

(a) first have regard to subsections (3) to (7) below; and

(b) then have regard to section 19(2);

and for the purposes of section 19(2), as it then applies to the witness, any special measures required to be applied in relation to him by virtue of this section shall be treated as if they were measures determined by the court, pursuant to section 19(2)(a) and (b)(i), to be ones that (whether on their own or with any other special measures) would be likely to maximise, so far as practicable, the quality of his evidence.

(3) The primary rule in the case of a child witness is that the court must give a special measures direction in relation to the witness which complies with the following requirements—

(a) it must provide for any relevant recording to be admitted under section 27 (video recorded evidence in chief); and

(b) it must provide for any evidence given by the witness in the proceedings which is not given by means of a video recording (whether in chief or otherwise) to be given by means of a live link in accordance with section 24.

(4) The primary rule is subject to the following limitations—

(a) the requirement contained in subsection (3)(a) or (b) has effect subject to the availability (within the meaning of section 18(2)) of the special measure in question in relation to the witness;

(b) the requirement contained in subsection (3)(a) also has effect subject to section 27(2); and

(c) the rule does not apply to the extent that the court is satisfied that compliance with it would not be likely to maximise the quality of the witness's evidence so far as practicable (whether because the application to that evidence of one or more other special measures available in relation to the witness would have that result or for any other reason).

20–32 　　(5) However, subsection (4)(c) does not apply in relation to a child witness in need of special protection.

(6) Where a child witness is in need of special protection by virtue of subsection (1)(b)(i), any special measures direction given by the court which complies with the requirement contained in subsection (3)(a) must in addition provide for the special measure available under section 28 (video recorded cross-examination or re-examination) to apply in relation to—

(a) any cross-examination of the witness otherwise than by the accused in person, and

(b) any subsequent re-examination.

(7) The requirement contained in subsection (6) has effect subject to the following limitations—

(a) it has effect subject to the availability (within the meaning of section 18(2)) of that special measure in relation to the witness; and

(b) it does not apply if the witness has informed the court that he does not want that special measure to apply in relation to him.

(8) Where a special measures direction is given in relation to a child witness who is an eligible witness by reason only of section 16(1)(a), then—

(a) subject to subsection (9) below, and

(b) except where the witness has already begun to give evidence in the proceedings, the direction shall cease to have effect at the time when the witness attains the age of 17.

(9) Where a special measures direction is given in relation to a child witness who is an eligible witness by reason only of section 16(1)(a) and—

(a) the direction provides—

    (i) for any relevant recording to be admitted under section 27 as evidence in chief of the witness, or

    (ii) for the special measure available under section 28 to apply in relation to the witness, and

(b) if it provides for that special measure to so apply, the witness is still under the age of 17 when the video recording is made for the purposes of section 28,

then, so far as it provides as mentioned in paragraph (a)(i) or (ii) above, the direction shall continue to have effect in accordance with section 20(1) even though the witness subsequently attains that age.

In the case of a child witness, the court will normally direct that a video recorded **20–33** interview will be admitted as the child's evidence in chief and any other evidence will be given by live link so long as facilities are available and the quality of the evidence would be improved. Cases are often transferred to adjacent courthouses where facilities exist. Safeguards in relation to video recorded evidence in chief are contained in s.27(2). Where the child witness is in need of special protection under s.21(5) the quality of evidence test does not apply and it is almost automatic that a direction will be given to admit video recorded evidence in chief and any other evidence by live link.

Extension of provisions of section 21 to certain witnesses over 17

22.—(1) For the purposes of this section—   **20–34**

(a) a witness in criminal proceedings (other than the accused) is a "qualifying witness" if he—

    (i) is not an eligible witness at the time of the hearing (as defined by section 16(3)), but

    (ii) was under the age of 17 when a relevant recording was made;

(b) a qualifying witness is "in need of special protection" if the offence (or any of the offences) to which the proceedings relate is—

    (i) an offence falling within section 35(3)(a) (sexual offences etc.), or

    (ii) an offence falling within section 35(3)(b), (c) or (d) (kidnapping, assaults etc.); and

(c) a "relevant recording", in relation to a witness, is a video recording of an interview of the witness made with a view to its admission as evidence in chief of the witness.

(2) Subsections (2) to (7) of section 21 shall apply as follows in relation to a qualifying witness—

(a) subsections (2) to (4), so far as relating to the giving of a direction complying with the requirement contained in subsection (3)(a), shall apply to a qualifying witness in respect of the relevant recording as they apply to a child witness (within the meaning of that section);

(b) subsection (5), so far as relating to the giving of such a direction, shall apply to a qualifying witness in need of special protection as it applies to a child witness in need of special protection (within the meaning of that section); and

(c) subsections (6) and (7) shall apply to a qualifying witness in need of special protection by virtue of subsection (1)(b)(i) above as they apply to such a child witness as is mentioned in subsection (6).

Screening witness from accused

23.—(1) A special measures direction may provide for the witness, while giving testimony or **20–35** being sworn in court, to be prevented by means of a screen or other arrangement from seeing the accused.

(2) But the screen or other arrangement must not prevent the witness from being able to see, and to be seen by—

(a) the judge or justices (or both) and the jury (if there is one);
(b) legal representatives acting in the proceedings; and
(c) any interpreter or other person appointed (in pursuance of the direction or otherwise) to assist the witness.

(3) Where two or more legal representatives are acting for a party to the proceedings, subsection (2)(b) is to be regarded as satisfied in relation to those representatives if the witness is able at all material times to see and be seen by at least one of them.

20–36　　An application for a special measures direction may be made by the parties or the court may give a direction of its own motion. The court must be satisfied that either the witness is a child or the quality of evidence is likely to be impaired without a direction. In the latter case quality may be impaired on the grounds of mental or physical disability, impairment of intelligence, fear or distress.

An application must be made on a prescribed form sent to the court and copied to the other parties within fourteen days of a plea of not guilty or within twenty eight days of a defendant's first appearance if before the youth court. These time limits may be extended upon application with good reason: *Magistrates' Courts (Special Measures Directions) Rules* 2002 (SI 2002/1687). A late application may be entertained at the trial.

An unopposed application may be determined by a single justice. Where the application is opposed there must be a hearing of which all parties must receive notice as they have a right to attend and be heard. The court must give notice of its decision to the parties together with reasons

20–37　　Upon a change of circumstances an application may be renewed, varied, or discharged.

20–38　　In *KL and LK v DPP* (2002) 166 J.P. 369, QBD, the precaution of bringing a screen into court before an application was concluded was confirmed to be a sensible course of action and could not suggest that the magistrates had pre-judged the issue.

In *R. v X* (1990) 91 Cr.App.R. 36, CA where a screen was used and social workers had been permitted to sit alongside the child witnesses when they gave evidence, the Court of Appeal stated that to have anyone sitting alongside a witness was a course of conduct that had to be undertaken with considerable care and the court had to be astute to ensure that nothing improper occurred and no undue encouragement was given to the witness. The *Practice Direction (Criminal Proceedings: Consolidation)*, para.III.29 (above) gives guidance on the use of a witness supporter. It states that the supporter should be independent, have no previous knowledge or personal involvement in the case and should be suitably trained. An usher should be available to assist.

Any special measures direction does not affect common law or statutory rules governing the admissibility of evidence: *R. v Brentford Youth Court* [2003] EWHC Admin. 2409.

Youth Justice and Criminal Evidence Act 1999, ss.24–25

Evidence by live link

20–39　　**24.**—(1) A special measures direction may provide for the witness to give evidence by means of a live link.

(2) Where a direction provides for the witness to give evidence by means of a live link, the witness may not give evidence in any other way without the permission of the court.

(3) The court may give permission for the purposes of subsection (2) if it appears to the court to be in the interests of justice to do so, and may do so either—
(a) on an application by a party to the proceedings, if there has been a material change of circumstances since the relevant time, or
(b) of its own motion.

(4) In subsection (3) "the relevant time" means —
(a) the time when the direction was given, or
(b) if a previous application has been made under that subsection, the time when the application (or last application) was made.

(5) Where in proceedings before a magistrates' court—
    (a) evidence is to be given by means of a live link in accordance with a special measures direction, but
    (b) suitable facilities for receiving such evidence are not available at any petty-sessional court-house in which that court can (apart from this subsection) lawfully sit,
the court may sit for the purposes of the whole or any part of those proceedings at a place where such facilities are available and which has been appointed for the purposes of this subsection by the justices acting for the petty sessions area for which the court acts.

(6) A place appointed under subsection (5) may be outside the petty sessions area for which it is appointed; but (if so) it is to be regarded as being in that area for the purpose of the jurisdiction of the justices acting for that area.

(7) In this section "petty-sessional court-house" has the same meaning as in the *Magistrates' Courts Act* 1980 and "petty sessions area" has the same meaning as in the *Justices of the Peace Act* 1997.

(8) In this Chapter "live link" means a live television link or other arrangement whereby a witness, while absent from the courtroom or other place where the proceedings are being held, is able to see and hear a person there and to be seen and heard by the persons specified in section 23(2)(a) to (c).

Evidence given in private
25.—(1) A special measures direction may provide for the exclusion from the court, during **20–40** the giving of the witness's evidence, of persons of any description specified in the direction.

(2) The persons who may be so excluded do not include—
    (a) the accused,
    (b) legal representatives acting in the proceedings, or
    (c) any interpreter or other person appointed (in pursuance of the direction or otherwise) to assist the witness.

(3) A special measures direction providing for representatives of news gathering or reporting organisations to be so excluded shall be expressed not to apply to one named person who—
    (a) is a representative of such an organisation, and
    (b) has been nominated for the purpose by one or more such organisations,
unless it appears to the court that no such nomination has been made.

(4) A special measures direction may only provide for the exclusion of persons under this section where—
    (a) the proceedings relate to a sexual offence; or
    (b) it appears to the court that there are reasonable grounds for believing that any person other than the accused has sought, or will seek, to intimidate the witness in connection with testifying in the proceedings.

(5) Any proceedings from which persons are excluded under this section (whether or not those persons include representatives of news gathering or reporting organisations) shall nevertheless be taken to be held in public for the purposes of any privilege or exemption from liability available in respect of fair, accurate and contemporaneous reports of legal proceedings held in public.

The provisions have been held to be compatible with the ECHR: *R. v Camberwell* **20–41** *Green Youth Court* [2003] 2 Cr.App.R. 16. The case considered six defendants who were all charged with offences of robbery or assault, and were all aged 16 or under. In applications for judicial review of the decisions to make special measures directions under the 1999 Act, it was submitted that as s.21(5) required the court to give a special measures direction in relation to the evidence of a child witness in need of special protection, the court was deprived of any power to consider whether the restriction on the rights of the defendant was necessary or in the interests of justice and thus the provision was incompatible with Art.6 of the European Convention on Human Rights. The Divisional Court held that s.21(5) of the 1999 Act provided a primary rule requiring a timely special measures direction in relation to child witnesses in need of special protection. That enabled appropriate arrangements to be made, so that such witnesses had the comfort of an assurance from an early stage in the proceedings as to how they would be giving evidence. It was held that the subsection did not breach Art.6 or any part of it as questions of justification, fairness and equality were irrelevant to the statutory task. In addition, the fairness of proceedings challenged by reference to Art.6 could only be judged retrospectively by reference to the trial and any appeal, not prospectively before the trial had taken place. The Court also stated that there was nothing in the fair trial provisions of Art.6, or the entitlement to examine witness in Art.6(3)(d), which prohibited a vulnerable witness from giving evidence in a room apart from the defendant. On the contrary, Strasbourg jurisprudence recognised that vulnerable witnesses, as well as defendants, had rights and might need protection. Neither could a live link, nor a video recording of evidence in chief, infringe the right to examine witnesses provided the defendant's lawyers could see as well as hear the witness and could cross-examine.

V. METHODS OF GIVING ORAL TESTIMONY

A. Video Recording

Youth Justice and Criminal Evidence Act 1999, s.27

Video recorded evidence in chief

20–42   **27.**—(1) A special measures direction may provide for a video recording of an interview of the witness to be admitted as evidence in chief of the witness.

(2) A special measures direction may, however, not provide for a video recording, or a part of such a recording, to be admitted under this section if the court is of the opinion, having regard to all the circumstances of the case, that in the interests of justice the recording, or that part of it, should not be so admitted.

(3) In considering for the purposes of subsection (2) whether any part of a recording should not be admitted under this section, the court must consider whether any prejudice to the accused which might result from that part being so admitted is outweighed by the desirability of showing the whole, or substantially the whole, of the recorded interview.

(4) Where a special measures direction provides for a recording to be admitted under this section, the court may nevertheless subsequently direct that it is not to be so admitted if—

    (a) it appears to the court that—
        (i) the witness will not be available for cross-examination (whether conducted in the ordinary way or in accordance with any such direction), and
        (ii) the parties to the proceedings have not agreed that there is no need for the witness to be so available; or
    (b) any rules of court requiring disclosure of the circumstances in which the recording was made have not been complied with to the satisfaction of the court.

(5) Where a recording is admitted under this section—

    (a) the witness must be called by the party tendering it in evidence, unless—
        (i) a special measures direction provides for the witness's evidence on cross-examination to be given otherwise than by testimony in court, or
        (ii) the parties to the proceedings have agreed as mentioned in subsection (4)(a)(ii); and
    (b) the witness may not give evidence in chief otherwise than by means of the recording—
        (i) as to any matter which, in the opinion of the court, has been dealt with adequately in the witness's recorded testimony, or
        (ii) without the permission of the court, as to any other matter which, in the opinion of the court, is dealt with in that testimony.

(6) Where in accordance with subsection (2) a special measures direction provides for part only of a recording to be admitted under this section, references in subsections (4) and (5) to the recording or to the witness's recorded testimony are references to the part of the recording or testimony which is to be so admitted.

20–43   (7) The court may give permission for the purposes of subsection (5)(b)(ii) if it appears to the court to be in the interests of justice to do so, and may do so either—

(a) on an application by a party to the proceedings, if there has been a material change of circumstances since the relevant time, or

(b) of its own motion.

(8) In subsection (7) "the relevant time" means —

(a) the time when the direction was given, or

(b) if a previous application has been made under that subsection, the time when the application (or last application) was made.

(9) The court may, in giving permission for the purposes of subsection (5)(b)(ii), direct that the evidence in question is to be given by the witness by means of a live link; and, if the court so directs, subsections (5) to (7) of section 24 shall apply in relation to that evidence as they apply in relation to evidence which is to be given in accordance with a special measures direction.

(10) A magistrates' court inquiring into an offence as examining justices under section 6 of the *Magistrates' Courts Act* 1980 may consider any video recording in relation to which it is proposed to apply for a special measures direction providing for it to be admitted at the trial in accordance with this section.

(11) Nothing in this section affects the admissibility of any video recording which would be admissible apart from this section.

See the Home Office *Achieving Best Evidence in Criminal Proceedings: Guidance for Vulnerable or Intimidated Witnesses including Children* (2002).

In *R. v DPP* [1997] 2 Cr.App.R. 78, DC the court held that failure to comply with **20–44** the earlier *Memorandum of Good Practice* was a matter to be taken into account by a court in deciding whether to exercise its discretion to refuse to admit the recording. The decision should not depend so much on the nature and extent of any breaches, as on whether the passages tainted by the breaches are confirmed by other untainted passages or are corroborated by independent evidence.

In *R. v D and S* (2002) 166 J.P. 792, CA it was held that a failure to comply with the Home Office and Dept. of Health Memorandum of Good Practice did not *per se* render the complainant's video evidence inadmissible. In *KL and LK v DPP* (2002) 166 J.P. 369, QBD, the precaution of bringing a screen into court before an application was concluded was confirmed to be a sensible course of action and could not suggest that the magistrates had pre-judged the issue:

Youth Justice and Criminal Evidence Act 1999, ss.28–31, 33

Video recorded cross-examination or re-examination

28.—(1) Where a special measures direction provides for a video recording to be admitted **20–45** under section 27 as evidence in chief of the witness, the direction may also provide—

(a) for any cross-examination of the witness, and any re-examination, to be recorded by means of a video recording; and

(b) for such a recording to be admitted, so far as it relates to any such cross-examination or re-examination, as evidence of the witness under cross-examination or on re-examination, as the case may be.

(2) Such a recording must be made in the presence of such persons as rules of court or the direction may provide and in the absence of the accused, but in circumstances in which—

(a) the judge or justices (or both) and legal representatives acting in the proceedings are able to see and hear the examination of the witness and to communicate with the persons in whose presence the recording is being made, and

(b) the accused is able to see and hear any such examination and to communicate with any legal representative acting for him.

(3) Where two or more legal representatives are acting for a party to the proceedings, subsection (2)(a) and (b) are to be regarded as satisfied in relation to those representatives if at all material times they are satisfied in relation to at least one of them.

(4) Where a special measures direction provides for a recording to be admitted under this section, the court may nevertheless subsequently direct that it is not to be so admitted if any requirement of subsection (2) or rules of court or the direction has not been complied with to the satisfaction of the court.

(5) Where in pursuance of subsection (1) a recording has been made of any examination of the witness, the witness may not be subsequently cross-examined or re-examined in respect of any evidence given by the witness in the proceedings (whether in any recording admissible under section 27 or this section or otherwise than in such a recording) unless the court gives a further special measures direction making such provision as is mentioned in subsection (1)(a) and (b) in relation to any subsequent cross-examination, and re-examination, of the witness.

(6) The court may only give such a further direction if it appears to the court—

(a) that the proposed cross-examination is sought by a party to the proceedings as a result of that party having become aware, since the time when the original recording was made in pursuance of subsection (1), of a matter which that party could not with reasonable diligence have ascertained by then, or

(b) that for any other reason it is in the interests of justice to give the further direction.

(7) Nothing in this section shall be read as applying in relation to any cross-examination of the witness by the accused in person (in a case where the accused is to be able to conduct any such cross-examination).

B. INTERMEDIARY

Examination of witness through intermediary

20–46   **29.**—(1) A special measures direction may provide for any examination of the witness (however and wherever conducted) to be conducted through an interpreter or other person approved by the court for the purposes of this section ("an intermediary").

(2) The function of an intermediary is to communicate—

(a) to the witness, questions put to the witness, and

(b) to any person asking such questions, the answers given by the witness in reply to them,

and to explain such questions or answers so far as necessary to enable them to be understood by the witness or person in question.

(3) Any examination of the witness in pursuance of subsection (1) must take place in the presence of such persons as rules of court or the direction may provide, but in circumstances in which—

(a) the judge or justices (or both) and legal representatives acting in the proceedings are able to see and hear the examination of the witness and to communicate with the intermediary, and

(b) (except in the case of a video recorded examination) the jury (if there is one) are able to see and hear the examination of the witness.

(4) Where two or more legal representatives are acting for a party to the proceedings, subsection (3)(a) is to be regarded as satisfied in relation to those representatives if at all material times it is satisfied in relation to at least one of them.

(5) A person may not act as an intermediary in a particular case except after making a declaration, in such form as may be prescribed by rules of court, that he will faithfully perform his function as intermediary.

(6) Subsection (1) does not apply to an interview of the witness which is recorded by means of a video recording with a view to its admission as evidence in chief of the witness; but a special measures direction may provide for such a recording to be admitted under section 27 if the interview was conducted through an intermediary and—

(a) that person complied with subsection (5) before the interview began, and

(b) the court's approval for the purposes of this section is given before the direction is given.

(7) Section 1 of the *Perjury Act* 1911 (perjury) shall apply in relation to a person acting as an intermediary as it applies in relation to a person lawfully sworn as an interpreter in a judicial proceeding; and for this purpose, where a person acts as an intermediary in any proceeding which is not a judicial proceeding for the purposes of that section, that proceeding shall be taken to be part of the judicial proceeding in which the witness's evidence is given.

20–47   Where provision is made for examination of a witness via a live link to be made through an intermediary the witness shall be accompanied at the link only by the intermediary and such others as may be acceptable to the court: The *Magistrates'*

Courts (Special Measures Directions) Rules 2002 (SI 2002/1687) as amended.

Aids to communication

30. A special measures direction may provide for the witness, while giving evidence (whether **20–48** by testimony in court or otherwise), to be provided with such device as the court considers appropriate with a view to enabling questions or answers to be communicated to or by the witness despite any disability or disorder or other impairment which the witness has or suffers from.

Status of evidence given under Chapter I

31.—(1) Subsections (2) to (4) apply to a statement made by a witness in criminal proceedings **20–49** which, in accordance with a special measures direction, is not made by the witness in direct oral testimony in court but forms part of the witness's evidence in those proceedings.

(2) The statement shall be treated as if made by the witness in direct oral testimony in court; and accordingly—

(a) it is admissible evidence of any fact of which such testimony from the witness would be admissible;

(b) it is not capable of corroborating any other evidence given by the witness.

(3) Subsection (2) applies to a statement admitted under section 27 or 28 which is not made by the witness on oath even though it would have been required to be made on oath if made by the witness in direct oral testimony in court.

(4) In estimating the weight (if any) to be attached to the statement, the court must have regard to all the circumstances from which an inference can reasonably be drawn (as to the accuracy of the statement or otherwise).

(5) Nothing in this Chapter (apart from subsection (3)) affects the operation of any rule of law relating to evidence in criminal proceedings.

(6) Where any statement made by a person on oath in any proceeding which is not a judicial proceeding for the purposes of section 1 of the *Perjury Act* 1911 (perjury) is received in evidence in pursuance of a special measures direction, that proceeding shall be taken for the purposes of that section to be part of the judicial proceeding in which the statement is so received in evidence.

(7) Where in any proceeding which is not a judicial proceeding for the purposes of that Act—

(a) a person wilfully makes a false statement otherwise than on oath which is subsequently received in evidence in pursuance of a special measures direction, and

(b) the statement is made in such circumstances that had it been given on oath in any such judicial proceeding that person would have been guilty of perjury,

he shall be guilty of an offence and liable to any punishment which might be imposed on conviction of an offence under section 57(2) (giving of false unsworn evidence in criminal proceedings).

(8) In this section "statement" includes any representation of fact, whether made in words or otherwise.

Interpretation etc. of Chapter I

33.—(1) In this Chapter—   **20–50**

"eligible witness" means a witness eligible for assistance by virtue of section 16 or 17;

"live link" has the meaning given by section 24(8);

"quality", in relation to the evidence of a witness, shall be construed in accordance with section 16(5);

"special measures direction" means (in accordance with section 19(5)) a direction under section 19.

(2) In this Chapter references to the special measures available in relation to a witness shall be construed in accordance with section 18.

(3) In this Chapter references to a person being able to see or hear, or be seen or heard by, another person are to be read as not applying to the extent that either of them is unable to see or hear by reason of any impairment of eyesight or hearing.

(4) In the case of any proceedings in which there is more than one accused—

(a) any reference to the accused in sections 23 to 28 may be taken by a court, in connection with the giving of a special measures direction, as a reference to all or any of the accused, as the court may determine, and

(b) any such direction may be given on the basis of any such determination.

C. WITNESS OVERSEAS

20–51 Section 32 of the *Criminal Justice Act* 1988 allows witnesses who are overseas to give evidence by video link. It applies to certain offences only and because of this there is no provision for magistrates other than youth courts to hear evidence from witnesses overseas in this manner. See further *Archbold Crown*, § 8–65.

VI. WRITTEN EVIDENCE AT SUMMARY TRIAL

A. STATEMENTS

Criminal Justice Act 1967, s.9

Proof by written statement

20–52 **9.**—(1) In any criminal proceedings, other than committal proceedings, a written statement by any person shall, if such of the conditions mentioned in the next following subsection as are applicable are satisfied, be admissible as evidence to the like extent as oral evidence to the like effect by that person.

(2) The said conditions are—

(a) the statement purports to be signed by the person who made it;

(b) the statement contains a declaration by that person to the effect that it is true to the best of his knowledge and belief and that he made the statement knowing that, if it were tendered in evidence, he would be liable to prosecution if he wilfully stated in it anything which he knew to be false or did not believe to be true;

(c) before the hearing at which the statement is tendered in evidence, a copy of the statement is served, by or on behalf of the party proposing to tender it, on each of the other parties to the proceedings; and

(d) none of the other parties or their solicitors, within seven days from the service of the copy of the statement, serves a notice on the party so proposing objecting to the statement being tendered in evidence under this section:

Provided that the conditions mentioned in paragraphs (c) and (d) of this subsection shall not apply if the parties agree before or during the hearing that the statement shall be so tendered.

(3) The following provisions shall also have effect in relation to any written statement tendered in evidence under this section, that is to say—

(a) if the statement is made by a person under the age of eighteen, it shall give his age;

(b) if it is made by a person who cannot read it, it shall be read to him before he signs it and shall be accompanied by a declaration by the person who so read the statement to the effect that it was so read; and

(c) if it refers to any other document as an exhibit, the copy served on any other party to the proceedings under paragraph (c) of the last foregoing subsection shall be accompanied by a copy of that document or by such information as may be necessary in order to enable the party on whom it is served to inspect that document or a copy thereof.

(4) Notwithstanding that a written statement made by any person may be admissible as evidence by virtue of this section—

(a) the party by whom or on whose behalf a copy of the statement was served may call that person to give evidence; and

(b) the court may, of its own motion or on the application of any party to the proceedings, require that person to attend before the court and give evidence.

20–53 (5) An application under paragraph (b) of the last foregoing subsection to a court other than a magistrates' court may be made before the hearing and on any such application the powers of the court shall be exercisable by a puisne judge of the High Court, a Circuit judge or Recorder sitting alone.

(6) So much of any statement as is admitted in evidence by virtue of this section shall, unless the court otherwise directs, be read aloud at the hearing and where the court so directs an account shall be given orally of so much of any statement as is not read aloud.

(7) Any document or object referred to as an exhibit and identified in a written statement tendered in evidence under this section shall be treated as if it had been produced as an exhibit and identified in court by the maker of the statement.

(8) A document required by this section to be served on any person may be served—

(a) by delivering it to him or to his solicitor; or

(b) by addressing it to him and leaving it at his usual or last known place of abode or place of business or by addressing it to his solicitor and leaving it at his office; or

(c) by sending it in a registered letter or by the recorded delivery service or by first class post addressed to him at his usual or last known place of abode or place of business or addressed to his solicitor at his office; or

(d) in the case of a body corporate, by delivering it to the secretary or clerk of the body at its registered or principal office or sending it in a registered letter or by the recorded delivery service or by first class post addressed to the Secretary or clerk of that body at that office[; and in paragraph (d) of this subsection references to the secretary, in relation to a limited liability partnership, are to any designated member of the limited liability partnership].

[This section is reprinted as amended by the *Limited Liability Partnership Regulations* 2001, Sch.5, para.4.]

There must be strict compliance with the requirements of this section and the *Magistrates' Courts Rules* 1981 otherwise the statement will be inadmissible: *Patterson v DPP* [1990] Crim.L.R. 651. Form 14 of the *Magistrates' Courts (Forms) Rules* 1981 provides a precedent of a notice for the prosecution to send to the defendant when it wants to tender a statement in evidence under s.9. A statement admitted in evidence pursuant to s.9 is not taken to be conclusive evidence. It will be treated as if the maker had given oral evidence and appropriate weight will be given to it. Where the evidence is crucial to the case it is desirable for the witness to be called in person: *Lister v Quaife* (1982) 75 Cr.App.R. 313, [1983] 1 W.L.R. 48.   **20–54**

A statement may be edited where there is irrelevant, inadmissible or prejudicial material or several statements may be reduced to one statement: see *Practice Direction (Criminal Proceedings: Consolidation)* para.III.24.

B. ADMISSION OF FACTS

Criminal Justice Act 1967, s.10

Proof by formal admission

10.—(1) Subject to the provisions of this section, any fact of which oral evidence may be given in any criminal proceedings may be admitted for the purpose of those proceedings by or on behalf of the prosecutor or defendant, and the admission by any party of any such fact under this section shall as against that party be conclusive evidence in those proceedings of the fact admitted.   **20–55**

(2) An admission under this section—

(a) may be made before or at the proceedings;

(b) if made otherwise than in court, shall be in writing;

(c) if made in writing by an individual, shall purport to be signed by the person making it and, if so made by a body corporate, shall purport to be signed by a director or manager, or the secretary or clerk, or some other similar officer of the body corporate;

(d) if made on behalf of a defendant who is an individual, shall be made by his counsel or solicitor;

(e) if made at any state before the trial by a defendant who is an individual, must be approved by his counsel or solicitor (whether at the time it was made or subsequently) before or at the proceedings in question.

(3) An admission under this section for the purpose of proceedings relating to any matter shall be treated as an admission for the purpose of any subsequent criminal proceedings relating to that matter (including any appeal or retrial).

(4) An admission under this section may with the leave of the court be withdrawn in the

proceedings for the purpose of which it is made or any subsequent criminal proceedings relating to the same matter.

[This section is reprinted as amended by the *Summary Appeal Court (Navy) Rules* 2000, Sch.3(II), para.8(b).]

20–56   Where a fact is admitted orally in court by or on behalf of the prosecutor or defendant, the fact admitted will be written down and signed by or on behalf of the party making the admission: *Magistrates' Courts Rules* 1981, r.71. A form is usually available for this purpose.

Leave to withdraw an admission is unlikely to be given under s.10(4) without cogent evidence that the admissions were made by reason of mistake or misunderstanding: *R. v Kolton* [2000] Crim.L.R. 761.

VII. EXAMINATION IN CHIEF

A. GENERAL

20–57   After the witness has been sworn or has affirmed the party who calls the witness, either in person or through a legal representative, will ask him questions to adduce relevant and admissible evidence which is supportive of the party's case.

B. IDENTIFICATION OF THE WITNESS

20–58   The witness will be asked to state his full name. A witness is only asked for his address in exceptional circumstances and if it is relevant to an issue at trial. He may be asked for his occupation and if he is, it is not considered objectionable: *R. v DS* [1999] Crim.L.R. 911, CA.

C. LEADING QUESTIONS

20–59   Witnesses should not be asked leading questions in examination in chief unless they relate to formal or introductory matters or facts which are not in dispute: *R. v Robinson* (1897) 61 J.P. 520. A leading question is one which suggests the desired answer or assumes the existence of a disputed fact. If a person or object is to be identified in court a leading question may be used: *R. v Watson* (1817) 2 Stark 116.

Whereas answers to leading questions are admissible, the weight of the evidence is reduced: *R. v Wilson*, 9 Cr.App.R. 124, CCA; *Moor v Moor* [1954] 1 W.L.R. 927. In certain circumstances the court, in the interests of justice, may use its discretion to allow such questions. In *Ex p. Bottomley* [1909] 2 K.B. 14, a magistrate died in the course of proceedings. When a witness was recalled before a new magistrate a leading question was allowed to elicit whether a deposition represented the evidence already given.

Where a witness gives evidence of a fact and another witness is called in order to contradict him, the latter may be asked directly whether that fact ever took place: *Courteen v Touse* (1807) 1 Camp. 43. Leading questions may also be asked when a witness has been classified as hostile: see below.

D. REFRESHING MEMORY

20–60   The rules will differ according to whether criminal proceedings have commenced before or after April 5, 2004 when the relevant part of the *Criminal Justice Act* 2003 was brought into effect: The *Criminal Justice Act 2003 (Commencement No.3 and Transitional Provisions) Order* 2004 (SI 2004/829 (C35)).

Proceedings commencing before April 5, 2004

A witness may refresh his memory by reading any note made or verified by him when his memory was clear: *Att.-Gen.'s Reference (No.3 of 1979)* (1979) 69 Cr.App.R. 411, CA. The writing must have been made contemporaneously with the events in question. In *R. v Simmonds* (1967) 51 Cr.App.R. 316, CA the court held that customs officers could read at trial their notes of lengthy interviews which they had made at the first convenient opportunity after the interviews. The rule refers to any witness not merely police officers or other "professional" witnesses. It also includes the defendant: *R. v Britton* (1987) 85 Cr.App.R. 14, CA.

Whether a note is made contemporaneously is a matter for fact and degree: *R. v* **20–61** *Simmonds* above. If the note was not written at the first available opportunity it must have been made or checked either at the time of the transaction or shortly after when the facts were still fresh in the witness's mind: *R. v Richardson* [1971] 2 Q.B. 484. The giving of evidence is not a memory test and witnesses may read through their statements outside the courtroom prior to giving evidence so long as the other side is informed. In *R. v Da Silva* (1990) 90 Cr.App.R. 233, CA the court held that it was in the judge's discretion and in the interests of justice to permit a witness who had begun to give evidence to refresh his memory from a statement made around the time of the events even if it did not fit within the definition of contemporaneous. The judge should in these circumstances be satisfied that:

1. The witness indicated that he or she could not now recall the details of events **20–62** because of the lapse of time;
2. The statement was made much nearer the time of the events and the contents of the statement represented the witness's recollection at the time it was made;
3. The witness had not read the statement before coming to court; and
4. The witness wished to have an opportunity to read the statement before continuing to give evidence.

It makes no difference whether the witness leaves the witness box to read the statement or reads it in the witness box, provided that the statement is removed from him when he gives evidence and is not allowed to refer to the document again.

In *R. v South Riddle Magistrates' Court Ex p. Cochrane* [1996] 2 Cr.App.R. 544 **20–63** the Divisional Court held that the Court of Appeal in *R. v Da Silva*, above, had not intended to say that it was only where the four conditions were satisfied could a witness refresh his memory from a non-contemporaneous document. With regard to the third condition the court held that there was no difference between a witness who had not read the statement before coming to court and a witness who had.

A witness may use any form of writing falling within the rule. The court must hear how the document came into being; for example, the witness may give evidence that he made a statement to the police; that it was made on such and such a date; and at the time it was made the matters dealt with were fresh in his mind. The witness may, when answering those questions, refresh his memory from the statement.

The document used may have been written by someone other than the witness provided that the document was made when the facts were fresh in the witness's mind and the witness verified the accuracy of the document at the time: *R. v Kelsey*, (1982) 74 Cr.App.R. 213, CA. This is often the case where a witness statement is taken by the police: *Lau Pak Ngam v R* [1966] Crim.L.R. 443; *R. v Richardson*, above.

The witness need not have any independent recollection of the facts: *R. v Bryant* **20–64** *and Dickinson*, 31 Cr.App.R. 146, CA. A witness who has kept a record as part of his duty is entitled to look at that record and give evidence that he is satisfied that he kept the record accurately and that as a particular event is recorded on a particular day, the event did happen as recorded.

Where the original document no longer exists and the witness has no independent recollection of the facts, a copy may not be used: *R. v Harvey* (1869) 11 Cox 546. If the copy was made or verified by the witness at the time when his memory was still fresh, however, it will be admissible as a duplicate or quasi-original: *Burton v Plummer* (1834) 2 A & E 341. If a copy is not proved to be correct or consists of an imperfect extract made by a witness it cannot be used to refresh memory regardless of whether the original is in existence: *Alcock v Royal Exchange Assurance* (1849) 13 Q.B. 292, *R. v St Martins* (1834) 1 A & E 210.

A witness may refresh his memory from a statement prepared from his original notes, provided that it is substantially the same as the notes, even though it does not contain all the material in the notes, and to that extent is not an exact copy: *R. v Cheng*, 63 Cr.App.R. 20, CA. It would be different if the statement bore little relation to the original notes. Where a Police officer had made his notes from brief jottings of questions and answers in an interview when it was fresh in his mind, he could refresh his memory from his notes even if at that time he could neither decipher the jottings or recollect the interview: *Att.-Gen.'s Reference (No.3 of 1979)* (1979) 69 Cr.App.R. 411.

20–65   In *R. v Bass* [1953] 1 Q.B. 680 police officers had denied collaborating in making the notes in their books, which were identical. The judge refused to exhibit them. It was held on appeal that the credibility and accuracy of the officers was vital and as they had denied collaborating in the making of their notes the jury should have been given the opportunity of examining them.

A witness may refresh his memory from a tape recording: *R. v Mills and Rose*, (1962) 46 Cr.App.R. 336, CA. Where a witness is permitted to refresh his memory from a contemporaneous document it is the oral testimony not the document which is the witness's evidence. The document may be inspected: *Senat v Senat* [1965] P 172. The witness may be cross-examined upon relevant matters contained in the statement and the notes are admissible to rebut any suggestion in cross-examination that the evidence is concocted: *Owen v Edwards* (1993) 77 Cr.App.R. 191, DC; *R. v Sekhon* (1987) 85 Cr.App.R. 19, CA. If, in this way, the document becomes evidence, the document is not evidence of the facts stated in it. The document is only an aide-memoire and cannot amount to corroboration of the witness's evidence, or be evidence in support: *R. v Virgo* (1978) 67 Cr.App.R. 323, CA.

20–66   **Proceedings commencing on or after April 5, 2004**

Criminal Justice Act 2003, s.139

Use of documents to refresh memory

139.—(1) A person giving oral evidence in criminal proceedings about any matter may, at any stage in the course of doing so, refresh his memory of it from a document made or verified by him at an earlier time if—

    (a) he states in his oral evidence that the document records his recollection of the matter at that earlier time, and

    (b) his recollection of the matter is likely to have been significantly better at that time than it is at the time of his oral evidence.

   (2) Where—

    (a) a person giving oral evidence in criminal proceedings about any matter has previously given an oral account, of which a sound recording was made, and he states in that evidence that the account represented his recollection of the matter at that time,

    (b) his recollection of the matter is likely to have been significantly better at the time of the previous account than it is at the time of his oral evidence, and

    (c) a transcript has been made of the sound recording,

he may, at any stage in the course of giving his evidence, refresh his memory of the matter from that transcript.

20–67   A witness may refresh his memory from a document made or checked earlier if he states that it records his recollection at that time and at that time his recollection is likely to have been significantly better than the present. He may also, in similar circumstances, refer to a manuscript of a sound recording.

E. Previous Consistent Statements

20–68   The fact that a witness has remained consistent in his story is not proof that what he says is true. A witness may, therefore, not give evidence of what he said on other occasions as proof of the facts in issue. See further *Archbold Crown*, § 8–102.

A witness's previous consistent statements (often called self serving statements) cannot be admitted to show that the witness has remained consistent: *R. v Roberts*, 28

Cr.App.R. 102; *R. v Larkin* [1943] K.B. 174; *R. v Oyesiku* (1972) 56 Cr.App.R. 240. In *R. v Williams* [1998] Crim.L.R. 495, CA the court held that where there is no suggestion of recent fabrication, a previous statement is inadmissible if the sole purpose of seeking to introduce it is to argue that the statement shows that the maker had knowledge of certain facts at the time it was made thus showing that the witness could not have had such knowledge unless he had been there, thereby making his evidence more credible. This rule is sometimes referred to as the rule against narrative and applies in examination-in-chief, cross-examination and re-examination.

In *R. v Beattie* (1989) 89 Cr.App.R. 302, it was stated that a party calling a witness should only put a previous consistent statement to the witness in the following three circumstances:

(1) Complaints in sexual cases

Complaints in sexual cases may be admitted provided that they are made at the first **20–69** reasonable opportunity and are voluntary. In *R. v Lillyman* [1896] 2 Q.B. 167, a rape case, it was held that the fact that a complaint was made by the victim shortly after the alleged occurrence together with the particulars of the complaint, meant that the evidence could be used, not as evidence of the facts in issue, but as evidence of the consistency of the conduct of the victim with the account told by her in court. Such statements are relevant to the question of whether the complainant was a victim of the alleged conduct: *R. v Churchill* [1999] Crim.L.R. 220. They are not an independent confirmation of the complainant's evidence because they do not come from an independent source: *R. v Wright* (1990) 90 Cr.App.R. 91 at 97; *R. v Islam* [1999] 1 Cr.App.R. 22; *R. v NK* [1999] Crim.L.R. 980. If the particulars of the complaint are not consistent with the complainant's evidence then the introduction of the previous statement serves no purpose: *R. v Wright*, above.

Evidence of a fresh complaint is admissible whether or not non-consent is legally a **20–70** necessary part of the issue or whether it is a collateral issue. The complaint is not admissible in order to show that consent was not given but to show that the complaint was consistent with the sworn evidence of the complainant: *R. v Osbourne* [1905] 1 K.B. 551.

If the complainant does not give evidence, there will be no evidence with which the previous complaint can be consistent and it should not be admitted: *R. v Guttridges* (1840) 9 C & P 471; *R. v Wallwork*, 42 Cr.App.R. 153. If the person to whom the complaint was made does not give evidence, the complainant's evidence of complaint lacks independent confirmation and is of little assistance: *White v R* [1999] A.C. 210.

In *R. v Valentine* [1996] 2 Cr.App.R. 213 the principles for deciding whether a **20–71** complaint was made at the first reasonable opportunity were summarised:

1. To be admissible a complaint had to be recent, although it did not have to be made at the very first opportunity which presented itself;
2. The first reasonable opportunity depended on such circumstances as the character of the complainant, her relationship to the person to whom she made the complaint, and her relationship to a person she had the opportunity to complain to but chose not to;
3. A complaint did not have to be ruled inadmissible if an earlier complaint had been made as long as it was made reasonably soon after the offence.

In *R. v M* [1999] 1 W.L.R. 307 it was stated that communication was not a critical **20–72** element. In that case a daughter had alleged sexual abuse by her father between 1983 and 1987. In 1988 she had typed a letter to Childline complaining about the abuse but had never sent it. The letter was considered admissible.

A complaint must also have been made voluntarily and not as a result of leading or intimidating questions: *R. v Osbourne*, above. The question is whether the statement was spontaneous in that it was an unassisted and unvarnished account of what occurred. The statement may have been made in response to questions but that does not of itself make the complaint inadmissible. Admissibility is within the court's discretion and regard will be had to the character of the questions asked, the relationship between the questioner and the complainant and all other circumstances: *R. v Norcott* [1917] 1 K.B. 347.

(2) Res gestae

20–73　　A statement may be admitted if it forms part of the events in issue, *i.e.* the *res gestae*: *R. v Roberts*, 28 Cr.App.R. 102. A previous statement of a witness which is so closely associated in time, place and circumstance with some act or event in issue that it can be said to form part of the *res gestae* is admissible as evidence of consistency to confirm evidence given by the witness to the same effect.

In *R. v Andrews* [1987] A.C. 281 it was stated that the prosecution should not invoke the *res gestae* doctrine as a device to avoid calling an available witness, thereby depriving the defence of cross-examining him. The issue of whether the doctrine could be used where it was felt that the witness might be untruthful was discussed in *Att.-Gen.'s Reference (No.1 of 2003)* [2003] 2 Cr.App.R. 29. If the witness were available he should be called.

See further *Archbold Crown*, § 11–30.

(3) Statements to rebut suggestion of recent fabrication

20–74　　Statements may also be admitted to rebut a suggestion of recent fabrication. The earlier statement is not evidence of the truth of the facts in issue but shows consistency and rebuts the suggestion of fabrication: *R. v Benjamin*, 8 Cr.App.R. 146. In this case it was alleged that a police officer had fabricated his evidence. The prosecution was allowed to introduce the officer's notebook in which he had recorded observations at the time.

In *R. v Oyesiku* (1972) 56 Cr.App.R. 240, the Court of Appeal approved the following statement:

> If the credit of a witness is impugned as to some material fact to which he deposes upon the ground that his account is a late invention or has been lately devised or reconstructed, even though not with conscious dishonesty, that makes admissible a statement to the same effect as the account he gave as a witness, if it was made by the witness contemporaneously with the event or at a time sufficiently early to be inconsistent with the suggestion that his account is a late invention or reconstruction.

20–75　　A statement may be admitted under this exception though it has been rejected as a recent complaint on the ground that it was not made at the first opportunity that reasonably offered itself: *R. v Tyndale* [1999] Crim.L.R. 320, CA.

In *R. v Ali (Hawar Hussein), The Times*, November 21, 2003, CA Crim Div., it was stated that although there was no general further exception beyond the three categories outlined in *R. v Beattie* (above) there was a residual discretion which permitted questions in re-examination in order to correct an evidential position which would otherwise have been onerous or misleading.

The *Criminal Justice Act* 2003 provides for previous statements of witnesses and when this part of the Act is brought into force account will have to be taken of s.120 below.

Criminal Justice Act 2003, s.120

20–76　　**120.**—(1) This section applies where a person (the witness) is called to give evidence in criminal proceedings.

(2) If a previous statement by the witness is admitted as evidence to rebut a suggestion that his oral evidence has been fabricated, that statement is admissible as evidence of any matter stated of which oral evidence by the witness would be admissible.

(3) A statement made by the witness in a document—

　　(a) which is used by him to refresh his memory while giving evidence,

　　(b) on which he is cross-examined, and

(c) which as a consequence is received in evidence in the proceedings,
is admissible as evidence of any matter stated of which oral evidence by him would be admissible.

(4) A previous statement by the witness is admissible as evidence of any matter stated of which oral evidence by him would be admissible, if—

(a) any of the following three conditions is satisfied, and

(b) while giving evidence the witness indicates that to the best of his belief he made the statement, and that to the best of his belief it states the truth.

(5) The first condition is that the statement identifies or describes a person, object or place.

(6) The second condition is that the statement was made by the witness when the mat- **20–77** ters stated were fresh in his memory but he does not remember them, and cannot reasonably be expected to remember them, well enough to give oral evidence of them in the proceedings.

(7) The third condition is that—

(a) the witness claims to be a person against whom an offence has been committed,

(b) the offence is one to which the proceedings relate,

(c) the statement consists of a complaint made by the witness (whether to a person in authority or not) about conduct which would, if proved, constitute the offence or part of the offence,

(d) the complaint was made as soon as could reasonably be expected after the alleged conduct,

(e) the complaint was not made as a result of a threat or a promise, and

(f) before the statement is adduced the witness gives oral evidence in connection with its subject matter.

(8) For the purposes of subsection (7) the fact that the complaint was elicited (for example, by a leading question) is irrelevant unless a threat or a promise was involved.

(4) Evidence of previous identification

Where there has been considerable delay between the offence and trial so that there **20–78** is the danger that the witness's recollection of the defendant's features will be put in question, it will strengthen the value of the evidence it if can be shown that soon after the commission of the offence the witness saw and recognised the defendant: *R. v Fannon* (1922) 22 SR (NSW) 427. Evidence that a witness identified the defendant out of court may be given by the witness and by any person who witnessed the identification: *R. v Christie* [1914] A.C. 545. A photofit portrait was admitted in *R. v Cook* [1987] Q.B. 417 and a police artist's impression in *R. v Smith* [1976] Crim.L.R. 511.

F. Unfavourable and Hostile Witnesses

If a witness does not come up to proof he is regarded as unfavourable. In such a sit- **20–79** uation the party is only able to call another witness to prove what the unfavourable witness failed to establish: Ewer v Ambrose (1825) 3 B & C 746. Where two equally credible witnesses contradict each other, in *Sumner and Leivesley v John Brown & Co* (1909) 25 T.L.R. 745 it was said that the party calling them is not entitled to accredit one and discredit the other. In *R. v Brent* [1973] Crim.L.R. 295 it was said that that case does not apply to criminal proceedings because the prosecution has a duty to call all relevant evidence.

Criminal Procedure Act 1865, s.3

How far witness may be discredited by the party producing

3. A party producing a witness shall not be allowed to impeach his credit by general evidence **20–80** of bad character; but he may, in case the witness shall in the opinion of the judge prove adverse, contradict him by other evidence, or, by leave of the judge, prove that he has made at other times a statement inconsistent with his present testimony; but before such last-mentioned proof can be given the circumstances of the supposed statement, sufficient to designate the particular occasion, must be mentioned to the witness, and he must be asked whether or not he has made such statement.

20–80.1   A hostile witness is much more than an unfavourable witness. Hostility is defined as an unwillingness to tell the truth of what happened and is determined by the court's considering the witness's demeanour and answers, if any. It is the court's determination and it is within the court's discretion to allow a party to cross-examine its own witness: *R. v Booth* (1982) 74 Cr.App.R. 123, CA. *Rice v Howard* (1886) 26 Q.B.D. 681. *Honeyghon and Sayles* [1999] Crim.L.R. 221, CA. The court should also consider allowing the witness to refresh his memory from a witness statement: *R. v Maw* [1994] Crim.L.R. 841, CA.

20–81   The court must have regard to what is likely to happen if the witness is confronted with a previous statement, and to the possibility of serious prejudice and lack of credibility if a damaging statement is elicited. Where a witness is cross-examined on his previous inconsistent statement, the statement does not become evidence of the facts stated in it: *R. v Dibble*, 1 Cr.App.R. 155; *R. v Newton and Dyer* [1987] Crim.L.R. 687. When a hostile witness admits making an unsworn statement but later states on oath, that the contents are untrue, the statement should not be exhibited and the effect is to render the evidence of the witness negligible: *R. v Harris* [1927] 2 K.B. 587, 20 Cr.App.R. 144. Where a hostile witness admits that he has been threatened and the earlier statement was in fact true the court, if it believes the witness, may take that evidence into account.

A hostile defence witness may be cross-examined on a previous inconsistent statement: *R. v Booth* (1982) 74 Cr.App.R. 123.

A witness may be treated as hostile at any stage of his evidence, including re-examination: *R. v Powell* [1985] Crim.L.R. 592, CA.

VIII. CROSS EXAMINATION

A. General

20–82   A sworn witness is liable to be cross-examined by the other party or anyone else having a legitimate interest: *R. v Bingham and Cooke* [1999] 1 W.L.R. 598. It is not necessary for the witness to have been examined-in-chief before being cross-examined. Sometimes a witness may be tendered as a witness simply for the purpose of being cross-examined.

A defendant has the right to cross-examine a co-defendant regardless of whether or not the co-defendant has given evidence against the defendant: *R. v Hadwen* [1902] 1 K.B. 882; *R. v Paul* [1920] 2 K.B. 183; *R. v Hilton* [1972] 1 Q.B. 421; *Murdoch v Taylor* [1965] A.C. 574.

B. Form of Questioning

20–83   Cross-examination should be conducted with restraint and with the courtesy and consideration which a witness is entitled to expect in a court of law: *Mechanical and General Inventions Co Ltd v Austin* [1935] A.C. 346. Questions should be framed to elicit answers as to matters of fact: see *Randall v The Queen* [2002] 1 W.L.R. 2237. Leading questions may be used: *Parkin v Moon* (1836) 7 C & P 409.

Cross-examination is not confined to the issues that were raised in evidence-in-chief however questions must relate either to the issues in the case or to the credibility of the witness: *R. v Treacey* [1944] 2 All E.R. 229.

A witness may not be asked about inadmissible evidence: *R. v Thompson* [1912] 3 K.B. 19; *R. v Treacey* (above); *R. v Rice* [1963] 1 Q.B. 857. A defendant may however be cross-examined by a co-defendant as to the contents of an inadmissible statement made by the defendant if he or she gives evidence which is inconsistent with the statement: *R. v Rowson*, 80 Cr.App.R. 218; *Lui Mei Lin v R* [1989] 2 W.L.R. 175.

As to previous inconsistent statements see § 20–103, below.

If a party intends to call evidence to contradict that given by the witness, the party   **20–84**
should put his version of events to the witness in cross-examination so that the witness
may explain the contradiction: *Brown v Dunn* (1869) 6 R 67; *R. v Hart*, 23 Cr.App.R.
202.

The court does not have to accept the evidence of a witness just because it has not
been challenged: *O'Connell v Adams* [1973] R.T.R. 150. This was confirmed in *R. (on
the application of Wilkinson) v DPP* (2003) 167 J.P. 229, QBD, where Burton J.
stated that it is the professional obligation of an advocate acting for the defence to put to
prosecution witnesses conflicts between the defence case and the evidence given by the
prosecution witness in question in order to give the prosecution witness an opportunity
to comment on what is put: whether it is the possibility of a mistake or whether the
prosecution witness is lying, whether his recollection is incorrect, whether he has been
confused or whatever. The position in relation to the defence case is somewhat different.
By the time the defence comes to give evidence, the prosecution evidence has been
given, the defence is aware of what evidence has been given and is able, therefore, in
chief, to ask witnesses whether or not they agree with the prosecution evidence and to
comment on it. It is nonetheless the professional duty of the advocate acting for the
defence to make it clear what evidence is rejected or disputed.

The court should disallow questions which are irrelevant or vexatious and keep cross-   **20–85**
examination to the points in issue: *R. v Kalia*, 60 Cr.App.R. 200, *R. v Simmonds*
[1969] 1 Q.B. 685; *R. v Maynard*, 69 Cr.App.R. 309. It is the duty of the legal adviser
to assist an unrepresented defendant in putting succinct questions to witnesses. Where
the offence is of a sexual nature and the defendant is unrepresented, the court is under
a duty to protect the complainant from intimidation or abuse by the manner of the
defendant's questioning: *R. v Brown* [1998] 2 Cr.App.R. 364.

For restrictions on cross-examination of such witnesses, see § 20–88 below.

Where more than one defendant is being tried and each is defended by different
legal representatives, the rule is that in the absence of agreement between the
representatives the court will call upon them to cross-examine in the order in which the
names of the defendants appear on the court list.

C. The Duty of Legal Representatives

The duties of counsel in conducting cross-examination are contained in the Code of   **20–86**
Conduct for the Bar of England and Wales, pronouncements made to the profession by
or on behalf of the Bar Council and judicial statements.

In *R. v O'Neill*, 34 Cr.App.R. 105 Lord Goddard C.J. stated:

> In this case a violent attack was made on the police. It was suggested that they had done
> improper things …The applicants had the opportunity of going into the box at the trial and
> explaining and supporting what they had instructed their counsel to say. They did not dare go
> into the box and therefore counsel, who knew they were not going into the box, ought not to
> have made these suggestions against the police … It is … entirely wrong to make such sugges-
> tions as were made in this case, namely that the police beat the prisoners until they made confes-
> sions, and then, when there is the chance for the prisoners to substantiate what has been said by
> going into the box, for counsel not to call them …

This was endorsed in *R. v Callaghan* (1979) 69 Cr.App.R. 88, CA. The effect of   **20–87**
such comments is that the defendant may be forced to relinquish the right to refuse to
give evidence: see above.

Where a client requires police evidence to be challenged in the manner considered in
R. v O'Neill and *R. v Callaghan* but refuses to give evidence because of his bad record, it is an advocate's duty to warn his client that the court will probably view the failure to give evidence adversely.

D. Restrictions on Cross Examination

Generally the defendant is entitled to cross-examine in person any witness called by   **20–88** the prosecution. This rule is subject to the common law and statutory exceptions. See *Archbold Crown*, § 8–123.

20–89 In *R. v Brown (Milton)* [1998] 2 Cr.App.R. 364, the Court of Appeal stated that a trial is not fair if an unrepresented defendant gains an advantage he would not have otherwise have had by abusing the rules in relation to relevance and repetition when cross-examining. While it was vital that the judge did his utmost to ensure that such a defendant received a fair trial and was seen by the jury to have done so, the judge was also under a duty to protect the interests of other parties to the proceedings, particularly witnesses who were required to describe a traumatic incident which was alleged to have occurred. In those circumstances, it was preferable for the judge to meet with the defendant in the jury's absence to discuss the nature of the evidence the defendant wished to elicit from the complainant and from any defence witnesses.

In the magistrates' courts the duty to elicit the nature of the evidence lies with the legal adviser.

Youth Justice and Criminal Evidence Act 1999, ss.34–38

Complainants in proceedings for sexual offences

20–90 **34.** No person charged with a sexual offence may in any criminal proceedings cross— examine in person a witness who is the complainant, either—

 (a) in connection with that offence, or

 (b) in connection with any other offence (of whatever nature) with which that person is charged in the proceedings.

Child complainants and other child witnesses

20–91 **35.**—(1) No person charged with an offence to which this section applies may in any criminal proceedings cross-examine in person a protected witness, either—

 (a) in connection with that offence, or

 (b) in connection with any other offence (of whatever nature) with which that person is charged in the proceedings.

 (2) For the purposes of subsection (1) a "protected witness" is a witness who—

 (a) either is the complainant or is alleged to have been a witness to the commission of the offence to which this section applies, and

 (b) either is a child or falls to be cross-examined after giving evidence in chief (whether wholly or in part)—

 (i) by means of a video recording made (for the purposes of section 27) at a time when the witness was a child, or

 (ii) in any other way at any such time.

 (3) The offences to which this section applies are—

 (a) any offence under—

 (i) the *Sexual Offences Act* 1956,

 (ii) the *Indecency with Children Act* 1960,

 (iii) the *Sexual Offences Act* 1967,

 (iv) section 54 of the *Criminal Law Act* 1977, or

 (v) the *Protection of Children Act* 1978;

 (b) kidnapping, false imprisonment or an offence under section 1 or 2 of the *Child Abduction Act* 1984;

 (c) any offence under section 1 of the *Children and Young Persons Act* 1933;

 (d) any offence (not within any of the preceding paragraphs) which involves an assault on, or injury or a threat of injury to, any person.

 (4) In this section "child" means—

 (a) where the offence falls within subsection (3)(a), a person under the age of 17; or

 (b) where the offence falls within subsection (3)(b), (c) or (d), a person under the age of 14.

 (5) For the purposes of this section "witness" includes a witness who is charged with an offence in the proceedings.

Direction prohibiting accused from cross-examining particular witness

36.—(1) This section applies where, in a case where neither of sections 34 and 35 operates to **20–92** prevent an accused in any criminal proceedings from cross— examining a witness in person—

    (a) the prosecutor makes an application for the court to give a direction under this section in relation to the witness, or

    (b) the court of its own motion raises the issue whether such a direction should be given.

  (2) If it appears to the court—

    (a) that the quality of evidence given by the witness on cross-examination—

        (i) is likely to be diminished if the cross-examination (or further cross-examination) is conducted by the accused in person, and

        (ii) would be likely to be improved if a direction were given under this section, and

    (b) that it would not be contrary to the interests of justice to give such a direction,

the court may give a direction prohibiting the accused from cross-examining (or further cross-examining) the witness in person.

  (3) In determining whether subsection (2)(a) applies in the case of a witness the court must have regard, in particular, to—

    (a) any views expressed by the witness as to whether or not the witness is content to be cross-examined by the accused in person;

    (b) the nature of the questions likely to be asked, having regard to the issues in the proceedings and the defence case advanced so far (if any);

    (c) any behaviour on the part of the accused at any stage of the proceedings, both generally and in relation to the witness;

    (d) any relationship (of whatever nature) between the witness and the accused;

    (e) whether any person (other than the accused) is or has at any time been charged in the proceedings with a sexual offence or an offence to which section 35 applies, and (if so) whether section 34 or 35 operates or would have operated to prevent that person from cross-examining the witness in person;

    (f) any direction under section 19 which the court has given, or proposes to give, in relation to the witness.

  (4) For the purposes of this section—

    (a) "witness", in relation to an accused, does not include any other person who is charged with an offence in the proceedings; and

    (b) any reference to the quality of a witness's evidence shall be construed in accordance with section 16(5).

Further provisions about directions under 36

37.—(1) Subject to subsection (2), a direction has binding effect from the time it is made until **20–93** the witness to whom it applies is discharged.

In this section "direction" means a direction under section 36.

  (2) The court may discharge a direction if it appears to the court to be in the interests of justice to do so, and may do so either—

    (a) on an application made by a party to the proceedings, if there has been a material change of circumstances since the relevant time, or

    (b) of its own motion.

  (3) In subsection (2) "the relevant time" means—

    (a) the time when the direction was given, or

    (b) if a previous application has been made under that subsection, the time when the application (or last application) was made.

  (4) The court must state in open court its reasons for—

    (a) giving, or

    (b) refusing an application for, or for the discharge of, or

    (c) discharging,

a direction and, if it is a magistrates' court, must cause them to be entered in the register of its proceedings.

  (5) Rules of court may make provision—

    (a) for uncontested applications to be determined by the court without a hearing;

    (b) for preventing the renewal of an unsuccessful application for a direction except where there has been a material change of circumstances;

(c) for expert evidence to be given in connection with an application for, or for discharging, a direction;

(d) for the manner in which confidential or sensitive information is to be treated in connection with such an application and in particular as to its being disclosed to, or withheld from, a party to the proceedings.

Defence representation for purposes of cross-examination

20–94   **38.**—(1) This section applies where an accused is prevented from cross-examining a witness in person by virtue of section 34, 35 or 36.

(2) Where it appears to the court that this section applies, it must—

(a) invite the accused to arrange for a legal representative to act for him for the purpose of cross-examining the witness; and

(b) require the accused to notify the court, by the end of such period as it may specify, whether a legal representative is to act for him for that purpose.

(3) If by the end of the period mentioned in subsection (2)(b) either—

(a) the accused has notified the court that no legal representative is to act for him for the purpose of cross-examining the witness, or

(b) no notification has been received by the court and it appears to the court that no legal representative is to so act,

the court must consider whether it is necessary in the interests of justice for the witness to be cross-examined by a legal representative appointed to represent the interests of the accused.

(4) If the court decides that it is necessary in the interests of justice for the witness to be so cross-examined, the court must appoint a qualified legal representative (chosen by the court) to cross-examine the witness in the interests of the accused.

(5) A person so appointed shall not be responsible to the accused.

(6) Rules of court may make provision—

(a) as to the time when, and the manner in which, subsection (2) is to be complied with;

(b) in connection with the appointment of a legal representative under subsection (4), and in particular for securing that a person so appointed is provided with evidence or other material relating to the proceedings.

(7) Rules of court made in pursuance of subsection (6)(b) may make provision for the application, with such modifications as are specified in the rules, of any of the provisions of—

(a) Part I of the *Criminal Procedure and Investigations Act* 1996 (disclosure of material in connection with criminal proceedings), or

(b) the *Sexual Offences (Protected Material) Act* 1997.

(8) For the purposes of this section—

(a) any reference to cross-examination includes (in a case where a direction is given under section 36 after the accused has begun cross-examining the witness) a reference to further cross-examination; and

(b) "qualified legal representative" means a legal representative who has a right of audience (within the meaning of the *Courts and Legal Services Act* 1990) in relation to the proceedings before the court.

20–95   The court may direct, in particular cases, that a defendant may not cross-examine a child or a complainant in proceedings for a sexual offence. It may also prevent cross-examination in person of any other witness if the quality of the evidence is likely to be diminished in those circumstances and that it would be improved if a direction were given and it is in the interests of justice.

The court will invite the defendant to be represented for the purposes of cross-examination and, in the event that the defendant chooses not to be, will arrange representation for him.

Youth Justice and Criminal Evidence Act 1999, ss.41–43

Restriction on evidence or questions about complainant's sexual history

20–96   **41.**—(1) If at a trial a person is charged with a sexual offence, then, except with the leave of the court—

(a) no evidence may be adduced, and

(b) no question may be asked in cross-examination,

by or on behalf of any accused at the trial, about any sexual behaviour of the complainant.

(2) The court may give leave in relation to any evidence or question only on an application made by or on behalf of an accused, and may not give such leave unless it is satisfied—

(a) that subsection (3) or (5) applies, and

(b) that a refusal of leave might have the result of rendering unsafe a conclusion of the jury or (as the case may be) the court on any relevant issue in the case.

(3) This subsection applies if the evidence or question relates to a relevant issue in the case and either—

(a) that issue is not an issue of consent; or

(b) it is an issue of consent and the sexual behaviour of the complainant to which the evidence or question relates is alleged to have taken place at or about the same time as the event which is the subject matter of the charge against the accused; or

(c) it is an issue of consent and the sexual behaviour of the complainant to which the evidence or question relates is alleged to have been, in any respect, so similar—

(i) to any sexual behaviour of the complainant which (according to evidence adduced or to be adduced by or on behalf of the accused) took place as part of the event which is the subject matter of the charge against the accused, or

(ii) to any other sexual behaviour of the complainant which (according to such evidence) took place at or about the same time as that event,

that the similarity cannot reasonably be explained as a coincidence.

(4) For the purposes of subsection (3) no evidence or question shall be regarded as relating to a relevant issue in the case if it appears to the court to be reasonable to assume that the purpose (or main purpose) for which it would be adduced or asked is to establish or elicit material for impugning the credibility of the complainant as a witness.

(5) This subsection applies if the evidence or question—   **20–97**

(a) relates to any evidence adduced by the prosecution about any sexual behaviour of the complainant; and

(b) in the opinion of the court, would go no further than is necessary to enable the evidence adduced by the prosecution to be rebutted or explained by or on behalf of the accused.

(6) For the purposes of subsections (3) and (5) the evidence or question must relate to a specific instance (or specific instances) of alleged sexual behaviour on the part of the complainant (and accordingly nothing in those subsections is capable of applying in relation to the evidence or question to the extent that it does not so relate).

(7) Where this section applies in relation to a trial by virtue of the fact that one or more of a number of persons charged in the proceedings is or are charged with a sexual offence—

(a) it shall cease to apply in relation to the trial if the prosecutor decides not to proceed with the case against that person or those persons in respect of that charge; but

(b) it shall not cease to do so in the event of that person or those persons pleading guilty to, or being convicted of, that charge.

(8) Nothing in this section authorises any evidence to be adduced or any question to be asked which cannot be adduced or asked apart from this section.

Interpretation and application of section 41

42.—(1) In section 41—   **20–98**

(a) "relevant issue in the case" means any issue falling to be proved by the prosecution or defence in the trial of the accused;

(b) "issue of consent" means any issue whether the complainant in fact consented to the conduct constituting the offence with which the accused is charged (and accordingly does not include any issue as to the belief of the accused that the complainant so consented);

(c) "sexual behaviour" means any sexual behaviour or other sexual experience, whether or not involving any accused or other person, but excluding (except in section 41(3)(c)(i) and (5)(a)) anything alleged to have taken place as part of the event which is the subject matter of the charge against the accused; and

(d) subject to any order made under subsection (2), "sexual offence" shall be construed in accordance with section 62.

(2) The Secretary of State may by order make such provision as he considers appropriate for adding or removing, for the purposes of section 41, any offence to or from the offences which are sexual offences for the purposes of this Act by virtue of section 62.

(3) Section 41 applies in relation to the following proceedings as it applies to a trial, namely—

(a) proceedings before a magistrates' court inquiring into an offence as examining justices,

(b) the hearing of an application under paragraph 5(1) of Schedule 6 to the *Criminal Justice Act* 1991 (application to dismiss charge following notice of transfer of case to Crown Court),

(c) the hearing of an application under paragraph 2(1) of Schedule 3 to the *Crime and Disorder Act* 1998 (application to dismiss charge by person sent for trial under section 51 of that Act),

(d) any hearing held, between conviction and sentencing, for the purpose of determining matters relevant to the court's decision as to how the accused is to be dealt with, and

(e) the hearing of an appeal,

and references (in section 41 or this section) to with an offence accordingly include a person convicted of an offence.

Procedure on applications under section 41

20–99　　43.—(1) An application for leave shall be heard in private and in the absence of the complainant.

In this section "leave" means leave under section 41.

(2) Where such an application has been determined, the court must state in open court (but in the absence of the jury, if there is one)—

(a) its reasons for giving, or refusing, leave, and

(b) if it gives leave, the extent to which evidence may be adduced or questions asked in pursuance of the leave,

and, if it is a magistrates' court, must cause those matters to be entered in the register of its proceedings.

(3) Rules of court may make provision—

(a) requiring applications for leave to specify, in relation to each item of evidence or question to which they relate, particulars of the grounds on which it is asserted that leave should be given by virtue of subsection (3) or (5) of section 41;

(b) enabling the court to request a party to the proceedings to provide the court with information which it considers would assist it in determining an application for leave;

(c) for the manner in which confidential or sensitive information is to be treated in connection with such an application, and in particular as to its being disclosed to, or withheld from, parties to the proceedings.

20–100　　No questions about a complainant's sexual behaviour may be asked in cross-examination without the leave of the court. An application will be heard "in camera" with the reasons for any ruling being given in open court and entered in the court's register.

The sectionitself has been held to be incompatible with ECHR in that it renders inadmissible, evidence which might be relevant to the charge concerned. The court will have to decide whether the evidence and the questioning in relation to it is so relevant that to exclude it would endanger a fair trial: *R. v A (No.2)* [2002] 1 A.C. 45. In that case, which concerned the issue of consent, Lord Hope gave examples of what might fall within s.41(3)(a):

— Honest belief in consent;

— Bias on the part of the complainant against the accused or a motive to fabricate the evidence;

— An alternative explanation for the physical conditions on which the prosecution relies;

— The detail of the complainant's account (especially where the complainant is young) must have come from other sexual activity which provides an explanation for knowledge of that activity.

In *R. v R.T.; R. v M.H.* [2002] 1 W.L.R. 632, CA it was held that, for the purposes **20–101** of s.41, a distinction is to be drawn between questions about sexual behaviour itself and questions concerning statements about such behaviour by the complainant, even if the questions concerned the credibility of the complainant they were not automatically barred by s.41. See also *R. v Mokrecovas* [2002] 1 Cr.App.R. 20, CA.

Other restrictions

A witness may not be cross-examined if he has not been sworn and has been called **20–102** merely to produce a document: *Sumners v Moseley* (1834) 2 Cr & M 477. A witness who is called by mistake where matters are not within his knowledge is not liable to be cross-examined, provided that the mistake is discovered after the witness has been sworn but before examination in chief: *Wood v Mackinson* (1840) 2 Mood & R 273. A witness called by the court may only be cross-examined with leave of the court. Leave should be given if the witness's evidence has been adverse to either party: *Coulson v Disborough* [1894] 2 Q.B. 316; *R. v Cliburn* (1898) 62 J.P. 232.

E.　PREVIOUS INCONSISTENT STATEMENTS

Criminal Procedure Act 1865, s.4

As to proof of contradictory statements of adverse witness
   4. If a witness, upon cross-examination as to a former statement made by him relative to the **20–103** subject matter of the indictment or proceeding, and inconsistent with his present testimony, does not distinctly admit that he has made such statement, proof may be given that he did in fact make it; but before such proof can be given the circumstances of the supposed statement, sufficient to designate the particular occasion, must be mentioned to the witness, and he must be asked whether or not he has made such statement.

A witness may, when giving evidence, make a statement which contradicts what the witness has said before thus undermining the witness in a material particular or credibility. It usually happens in cross-examination. The inconsistency should be put to the witness so that he has a chance of stating which facts are true. If the witness denies the statement evidence may be called to show that he did make the statement.

In *R. v Derby Magistrates' Court Ex p. B* [1996] A.C. 487, HL, it was said that s.4 applies to written as well as oral statements.

Criminal Procedure Act 1865, s.5

Cross-examinations as to previous statements in writing
   5. A witness may be cross-examined as to previous statements made by him in writing, or **20–104** reduced into writing, relative to the subject matter of the indictment or proceeding, without such writing being shown to him; but if it is intended to contradict such witness by the writing, his attention must, before such contradictory proof can be given, be called to those parts of the writing which are to be used for the purpose of so contradicting him:
   Provided always, that it shall be competent for the judge, at any time during the trial, to require the production of the writing for his inspection, and he may thereupon make such use of it for the purposes of the trial as he may think fit.

A previous inconsistent statement in writing should be put to the witness who should be asked whether he made the statement.

It is for the court to determine whether the statement relates to the subject matter of **20–105** the proceedings: *R. v Bashir* (1970) 54 Cr.App.R. 1.

In *R. v Clarke and Hewins* [1999] *Archbold News* 2, CA, it was stated that when a witness is cross-examined on a previous statement, the questioning should be selective and done with precision; it is inappropriate to read long extracts from the statement and then merely to ask one or two short questions; such a method lengthens the proceedings, makes cross-examination difficult to follow and creates the risk that the witness's evidence will become confused with what was said on the previous occasion. The statement need not be shown to the witness but it must be available in court even if the advocate does not intend to use it: *R. v Anderson*, 21 Cr.App.R. 178. The witness's answers may not be contradicted by putting the document in evidence unless the witness has been shown the document and has been given the opportunity of explaining its contents.

The inconsistency is relevant to the witness's credibility and the earlier statement cannot be regarded as evidence of its truth: *R. v O'Neill* [1969] Crim.L.R. 260, CA; *R. v Golder* (1961) 45 Cr.App.R. 5.

The *Criminal Justice Act* 2003, when in force, makes provision for inconsistent statements.

Criminal Justice Act 2003, s.119

20–106   119.—(1) If in criminal proceedings a person gives oral evidence and—
         (a) he admits making a previous inconsistent statement, or
         (b) a previous inconsistent statement made by him is proved by virtue of section 3, 4 or 5 of the *Criminal Procedure Act* 1865,
the statement is admissible as evidence of any matter stated of which oral evidence by him would be admissible.

     (2) If in criminal proceedings evidence of an inconsistent statement by any person is given under section 124(2)(c), the statement is admissible as evidence of any matter stated in it of which oral evidence by that person would be admissible.

F. Cross Examination as to Credibility

20–107   The credibility of a witness depends on: (a) his knowledge of the facts to which he testifies; (b) independence; (c) integrity; (d) veracity; and (e) being bound to speak the truth either on oath or by affirmation. Questions may be put to a witness in relation to any improper conduct of which he may be guilty in order to show that the witness should not be believed: *R. v Edwards*, 93 Cr.App.R. 48.

A witness can be compelled to answer questions about his credibility: *Cundell v Pratt* (1827) M & M 108. The court has a discretion to direct that a witness should not answer where the court is of the opinion that an answer verifying the truth of the matter suggested would not in fact affect the credibility of the witness: *R. v Sweet-Escott*, 55 Cr.App.R. 316. In *R. v Malik* [2000] 2 Cr. App.R. 8, CA cross-examination of a police officer whose evidence in a previous case had been disbelieved resulting in an acquittal was allowed even though the misconduct alleged was of a different nature from that alleged in the earlier case

A witness may not be asked to draw an inference of fact which is discreditable to him: *R. v Bernard* (1858) 1 F & F 240. A witness may not be asked questions about his religious beliefs for the purposes of discrediting him: *Darby v Ouseley* (1856) 1 H & N 1.

20–108   Where particular allegations of misconduct are put to a witness, it is not open to the party calling the witness to call evidence of the good character of the witness for the purpose of rebutting the allegations. The character of the witness not being itself in issue, such evidence is excluded on the grounds of being collateral: *R. v Hamilton, The Times*, July 25, 1998; *R. v Beard* [1998] Crim.L.R. 585, CA.

Witnesses may be called to speak about a witness's general character, although not in relation to any particular offence of which he may be guilty: *R. v Watson* (1817) 32 St.Tr 1. Evidence is not admissible to contradict answers given on cross-examination as to credit: *R. v Mendy*, 64 Cr.App.R. 4, CA. The following instances are however exceptions and the list is not closed:

Bias

20–109   Facts showing that a witness is biased in relation to the party calling him may be elicited in cross-examination and, if denied, independently proved. *Att.-Gen v Hitchcock* (1847) 1 Ex. 91; *R. v Denley* [1970] Crim.L.R. 583; *R. v Phillips*, 26 Cr.App.R. 17; *R. v Mendy*, 64 Cr.App.R. 4.

In *R. v Busby*, 75 Cr.App.R. 79, police officers were cross-examined to the effect that they had fabricated statements attributed to the defendant and indicative of his guilt and had threatened a potential defence witness to stop him from giving evidence. The judge ruled that the defence could not call that potential witness to give evidence that he had been threatened by the police officers because it would go solely to their credibility. The Court of Appeal held that the judge had been incorrect because, if the allegations were true, it showed that the police were prepared to go to improper lengths to secure a conviction, which would have supported the defence case that the statements attributed to the defendant had been fabricated.

In *R. v Funderburk*, 90 Cr.App.R. 466, [1990] 1 W.L.R. 587 it was said that the decision in *Busby* provided an exception to the general rule. In *R. v Edwards* [1991] 1 W.L.R. 207, however, it was said that *Busby* related to the question of bias. Cross-examination is permissible to show that a witness was biased.

Previous convictions

Criminal Procedure Act 1865, s.6

Proof of previous conviction of witness may be given

6.—(1) A witness may be questioned as to whether he has been convicted of any felony or   **20–110**
misdemeanor, and upon being so questioned, if he either denies or does not admit the fact, or refuses to answer, it shall be lawful for the cross-examining party to prove such conviction; and a certificate containing the substance and effect only (omitting the formal part) of the indictment and conviction for such offence, purporting to be signed by the proper officer of the court where the offender was convicted (for which certificate a fee of 25 p and no more shall be demanded or taken,) shall, upon proof of the identity of the person, be sufficient evidence of the said conviction, without proof of the signature or official character of the person appearing to have signed the same.

(2) In subsection (1) "proper officer" means—

    (a) in relation to a magistrates' court in England and Wales, the justices' chief executive for the court; and

    (b) in relation to any other court, the clerk of the court or other officer having the custody of the records of the court, or the deputy of such clerkor other officer.

[This section is reprinted as amended by the *Police and Criminal Evidence Act* 1999, Sch.7 and the *Access to Justice Act* 1999, Sch.13, para.4.]

If a witness, who is cross-examined regarding a previous conviction, denies it or re-   **20–111**
fuses to answer, the previous conviction may be proved under the *Criminal Procedure Act* 1865, s.6. The section does not however confer an absolute right to cross-examine a witness on any previous convictions as that sort of cross-examination is subject to a degree of judicial control and the court may prevent it if is unnecessary, improper or oppressive: *R. v Sweet-Escott*, 55 Cr.App.R. 316

A police officer may be questioned about any relevant criminal offences or disciplinary charges found proved against him, but charges which have not yet been adjudicated upon should not be put in cross-examination, and nor should allegedly discreditable conduct of other officers, whether or not they happened to be serving in the same squad: *R. v Edwards* above.

The *Children and Young Persons Act* 1963, s.16(2) and (3) and the *Rehabilitation of Offenders Act* 1974 apply.

The *Criminal Justice Act* 2003 makes provision for bad character—see § 21–104, below.

A reputation for untruthfulness

The other party may call witnesses to prove that a witness's general reputation is such   **20–112** that they would not believe him upon oath: *R. v Brown and Hedley* (1867) LR ICCR 70. They need not have heard the witness on oath: *R. v Bisphan* (1830) 4 C & P 392.

Medical issues

20–113   It is admissible to show that a witness suffers from a disease, defect or abnormality of mind which affects the reliability of his evidence: *Toohey v Metropolitan Police Commissioner* [1965] A.C. 595, HL.

Evidence is not admissible to contradict answers given by a witness to questions put in cross-examination which concern collateral matters, *i.e.* matters which go to credit but not the facts in issue: *Palmer v Trower* (1852) 8 Exch 247.

G. CROSS EXAMINATION OF THE DEFENDANT

Criminal Evidence Act 1898, s.1

Competency of witnesses in criminal cases

20–114   **1.**—(1) A person charged in criminal proceedings shall not be called as a witness in the proceedings except upon his own application.

(2) A person charged in criminal proceedings who is called as a witness in the proceedings may be asked any question in cross-examination notwithstanding that it would tend to criminate him as to any offence with which he is charged in the proceedings.

(3) A person charged in criminal proceedings who is called as a witness in the proceedings shall not be asked, and if asked shall not be required to answer, any question tending to show that he has committed or been convicted of or been charged with any offence other than one with which he is then charged, or is of bad character, unless—

    (i)   the proof that he has committed or been convicted of such other offence is admissible evidence to show that he is guilty of an offence with which he is then charged; or

    (ii) he has personally or by his advocate asked questions of the witnesses for the prosecution with a view to establish his own good character, or has given evidence of his good character, or the nature or conduct of the defence is such as to involve imputations on the character of the prosecutor or the witnesses for the prosecution, or the deceased victim of the alleged crime; or

    (iii) he has given evidence against any other person charged in the same proceedings.

(4) Every person charged in criminal proceedings who is called as a witness in the proceedings shall, unless otherwise ordered by the court, give his evidence from the witness box or other place from which the other witnesses give their evidence.

[This section is reprinted as amended by the *Youth Justice and Criminal Evidence Act* 1999, Sch.4, para.1.]

20–115   If the defendant admits his guilt in the witness box, the prosecution is still entitled to elicit evidence which incriminates co-defendants: *R. v Paul and McFarlane* [1920] 2 K.B. 193, 14 Cr.App.R. 155; *R. v O'Neill* [1969] Crim.L.R. 260, CA.

If a defendant testifies to his own good character he may be cross-examined on that fact as the court is entitled to know the true position: *R. v Marsh* [1994] Crim.L.R. 52.

In *R. v Nye*, 75 Cr.App.R. 247 the Court of Appeal rejected the submission that when a person, who has previously been convicted, has reached the stage where those convictions are spent, he or she should as of right be entitled to present him or herself as a person of good character. Talbot J. said at 250–251:

> It is entirely a question for the discretion of the judge. It may well be that the past spent conviction happened when the defendant being tried was a juvenile, for instance for stealing apples, a conviction of many years before. In those circumstances quite plainly a trial judge would rule that such a person ought to be permitted to present himself as a man of good character. At the other end of the scale, if a defendant is a man who has been convicted of some offence of violence and his conviction has only just been spent and the offence for

which he is then standing trial involves some violence, then it would be plain that a trial judge would rule that it would not be right for such a person to present himself as a man of good character.

A defendant may be cross-examined on his character with the leave of the court **20–116** where he has made imputations on the character of any prosecution witness. An imputation is more than an emphatic denial of the offence. It could be an allegation that the prosecution witness has previous convictions or a serious suggestion of immorality or a claim that the evidence has been fabricated: *Selvey v DPP* [1970] A.C. 304.

In *R. v McLeod* [1994] 3 All E.R. 254 the Court of Appeal laid down guidelines on when to allow such cross-examination so as to ensure a fair trial to both parties. The court must weigh the prejudicial effect of the questions against the damage done by the attack on the prosecution witnesses

See § 21–102 below.

IX. RE-EXAMINATION

After cross-examination a witness may be re-examined by the party who called him. **20–117** Unless the court gives leave, questions in re-examination are confined to matters arising out of cross-examination.

It is unclear whether a hostile witness may be re-examined after cross-examination: *R. v Booth*, above; *R. v Wong* [1986] Crim.L.R. 683. In the latter case the prosecution was allowed to treat a witness as hostile and to examine him on previous inconsistent statements and following cross-examination by the defence, was allowed to re-examine the witness but only upon completely and genuinely new matters which had arisen from defence cross-examination where those matters were defined beforehand.

A witness may be treated as hostile during re-examination when he has shown hostility to the party calling him during cross-examination: *R. v Powell* [1985] Crim.L.R. 592. In *R. v Norton and Driver* [1987] Crim.L.R. 687 a prosecution witness said that he could not remember incidents relating to the offence charged however during cross-examination he gave evidence exculpating the defendants. The prosecution was permitted to treat him as hostile during re-examination.

X. RECALL OF A WITNESS

Once a party has closed his case, further evidence other than rebuttal evidence may **20–118** not be called: *Magistrates' Courts Rules* 1981, rr.13–14. The court has a limited discretion to reopen a case at any time before final adjudication. The court should look carefully at the interests of justice and the risk of any prejudice to the defendant: *Jolly v DPP* [2000] Crim.L.R. 471; *Cook v DPP* [2001] Crim.L.R. 321.

Magistrates should not allow evidence to be called once they have retired: *Webb v Leadbetter* [1966] 2 All E.R. 114. A witness may be recalled to present evidence of a formal nature but not to remedy a deficiency which goes to the merits of the case: *R. v Day* [1940] 1 All E.R. 402; *Middleton v Rowlett* [1954] 2 All E.R. 277; *R. v Tate* [1977] R.T.R. 17.

XI. ILLNESS OR DEATH OF A WITNESS

If a witness becomes incapable of giving further evidence the court may allow the **20–119** trial to continue on the basis of the evidence already given: *R. v Stretton*, 86 Cr.App.R. 7, CA. The evidence of such a witness remains admissible although little weight may attach to it: *R. v Doolin*, 1 Jebb CC 123.

Statements of those who die before trial are usually inadmissible because they offend the rule against hearsay. This rule is subject to several exceptions:

1. Written or verbal declarations contemporaneously made in the course of a person's business, provided it was made as part of his duty and limited to the

precise facts which it was his duty to state or record: *R. v Buckley* (1873) 13 Cox CC 293.

2. Declarations knowingly made against a person's pecuniary or proprietary interests: *R. v Rodgers* [1995] 1 Cr.App.R. 374.

3. Declarations as to public and general rights or interests: *Weeks v Sparke* (1813) 1 M & S 679.

XII. THE POWER OF THE COURT TO CALL WITNESSES

20–120　The court has a residuary discretion to call witnesses where either party has not called them. The discretion should be exercised sparingly and in the interests of justice and fairness: *R. v Grafton* [1992] 3 W.L.R. 532.

This discretion may not usually be exercised after the defence has closed its case, nor after the magistrates have retired to deliberate: *Webb v Leadbetter* [1966] 1 W.L.R. 245. Once the justices have retired to consider their verdict further evidence should only be called in exceptional circumstances: *French Dairies (Sevenoaks) Ltd v Davis* [1973] Crim.L.R. 630; *Phelan v Back* (1972) 56 Cr.App.R. 257.

In *R. v Haringey Justices Ex p. DPP* [1996] 1 W.L.R. 114, the defendant was charged with threatening behaviour and assaulting a police officer following an attack on two officers. One police officer was subsequently suspended following accusations concerning his honesty on an unrelated matter. The CPS, in accordance with its policy of not calling suspended officers if it could be avoided, gave notice that it would not be calling the suspended officer, and refused the defendant's request to tender him for cross examination. The justices dismissed the case on the grounds that it was an abuse of process, and the CPS sought judicial review of that decision. The application was granted on the basis that the prosecution has an unfettered discretion as to which witnesses to call. Where there were special reasons for not calling an important witness these should be disclosed to the defence and where the prosecution chose not to call a witness whose evidence was central to the case, and the justices were satisfied that the interests of justice required he be called, they should so rule. If the prosecution refused to call the witness the justices could do so.

20–121　The court's permission is required before the prosecution or defence may question a witness called by the court:

The court has the power to recall a witness at any stage of the trial to put such questions as may be required in the interests of justice: *R. v Sullivan* [1923] 1 K.B. 47.

The court may also question witnesses during the course of their examination by counsel however it should not actively interfere with counsel's examination: *R. v Leggatt* [1970] 1 Q.B. 67; *R. v Hulusi and Purvis* (1974) 58 Cr.App.R. 378. Questions should be for clarification purposes only.

XIII. EXHIBITS

20–122　Where a witness produces an exhibit, the court will list the exhibit and identify it by name and number, for example, where Ann Smith produces an exhibit it becomes AS1.

At the conclusion of thecase the exhibits are generally not retained by the court but are returned to the producing party who then signs for them. The court may retain documentary exhibits. See *Archbold Crown*, § 9–154.

CHAPTER 21

EVIDENCE

I. THE ROLE OF THE JUDICIARY IN MAGISTRATES' COURTS

In magistrates' courts, the judiciary decide both law and fact and will, therefore, **21–1** determine the admissibility of evidence. On questions of law, including the law of evidence, it is accepted that magistrates should accept the advice of the legal adviser. District judges (magistrates' courts) may also seek the advice of the legal adviser. Where the court decides that evidence is inadmissible it will put that evidence out of its mind when determining the facts in issue.

The judiciary should keep interventions to a minimum. They should clarify evidence if an answer is ambiguous or inaudible and to curb repetition and irrelevance.

II. FACTS IN ISSUE

21–2   The facts in issue are: (a) the facts which the prosecution bears the burden of proving or disproving in order to establish the guilt of the defendant and (b) the facts which the defendant bears the burden of proving in order to succeed in his defence. Where the defendant has pleaded not guilty then "everything is in issue and the prosecution has to prove the whole of its case, including the identity of the accused, the nature of the act and the existence of any necessary knowledge or intent": *R. v Sims* [1946] K.B. 531 at 539.

III. FORMAL ADMISSIONS

21–3   Section 10 of the *Criminal Justice Act* 1967 provides for a party to admit certain facts and that formal admission becomes conclusive evidence of those facts.

IV. RELEVANCE

21–4   Evidence is admissible only where it is relevant and this depends on the individual circumstances of each particular case. Evidence is relevant if it is logically probative of a matter which must be proved: *DPP v Kilbourne* [1973] 1 All E.R. 440. It is also admissible if it relates to circumstantial facts which if proved make the facts in issue probable or not. In *R. v Guney* [1998] 2 Cr.App.R., evidence that a large sum of cash was found in the same place as guns and drugs was held to be relevant in a case of possession of drugs with intent to supply. Where the offence is one of strict liability, evidence of motive, intention or knowledge is irrelevant and therefore inadmissible: *R. v Sandhu* [1997] Crim.L.R. 288; *R. v Byrne* [2002] 2 Cr.App.R. 311. In *R. v Nethercott* [2002] Cr.App.R. 117 the defence was that the defendant had acted under duress as a result of threats made by his co-defendant. Evidence of the fact that the co-defendant had subsequently attacked him with a knife was relevant to the defence because it made it more likely that the defendant, at the time of the offence, had genuinely feared for his safety.

V. BURDEN AND STANDARD OF PROOF

21–5   In criminal trials the legal burden of proving the guilt of the defendant is on the prosecution and remains so throughout the trial: *Woolmington v DPP* [1935] A.C. 462; *R. v Hunt* [1987] A.C. 352. The standard of proof is that of beyond reasonable doubt: *R. v Ewing* 77 Cr.App.R. 47, CA. This does not mean proof beyond a shadow of a doubt. It is less than absolute certainty. In *Walters v R* [1969] 2 A.C. 26 at 30 the words referring to a jury "satisfied so they are sure " were approved.

In *R. v Edwards* [1975] Q.B. 27 the Court of Appeal held that there was an exception to the fundamental rule that the prosecution must prove every element of the offence charged. The exception was "limited to offences arising under enactments which prohibit the doing of an act save in specified circumstances or by persons of specified classes or with specified qualifications or with the licence or permission of specified authorities". The court rejected the view that only the evidential burden and not the legal burden shifted to the defendant. In that particular case, the onus was on the defendant to show that he had a licence when charged with the offence of selling liquor without a licence.

So, the legal burden lies on the defendant only where the defence is one of insanity and in the case of statutory exceptions: *R. v Mancini* [1963] A.C. 386, *i.e.* s.30 *Sexual Offences Act* 1956 (living off the earnings of prostitution); repealed as of May 1, 2004 and s.101 *Magistrates' Courts Act* 1980, see § 21–6 below. In those situations the standard of proof is on the balance of probabilities: *R. v Carr-Briant* [1943] K.B. 607, 29 Cr.App.R. 76; *Islington London Borough v Panico* [1973] 3 All E.R. 483. This means more probable than not.

Magistrates' Courts Act 1980, s.101

Onus of proving exceptions, etc
101. Where the defendant to an information or complaint relies for his defence on any   **21–6**
exception, exemption, proviso, excuse or qualification, whether or not it accompanies the description of the offence or matter of complaint in the enactment creating the offence or on which
the complaint is founded, the burden of proving the exception, exemption, proviso, excuse or
qualification shall be on him; and this notwithstanding that the information or complaint contains
an allegation negativing the exception, exemption, proviso, excuse or qualification.

In the case of driving without a licence, for example, it is for the driver to prove that
he has a current driving licence: *John v Humphreys* [1955] 1 W.L.R. 325. The same applies to driving without insurance: *Williams v Russell* (1933) 149 LT 190; *Philcox v
Carberry* [1960] Crim.L.R. 563.

In *Gatland v Metropolitan Police Commissioner* [1968] 2 Q.B. 279 the defendant
had been charged with leaving a skip on a road contrary to the *Highways Act* 1959,
which provided that "if a person, without lawful authority or excuse, deposits anything
whatsoever on a highway ... that person shall be guilty of an offence". It was held that
the prosecution had to prove that the skip had been deposited on the highway but that
the defendant had to prove lawful authority or excuse.

The House of Lords considered *R. v Edwards* in *R. v Hunt*, above. It held that   **21–7**
there is no rule of law that the burden of proving a statutory defence lies on the defendant only where the statute specifically so provides. Such exceptions might be express or
implied. The exception might be in the same clause that created the offence or in a
subsequent proviso and that where a linguistic construction of the legislation did not
indicate clearly on whom the burden of proof should be, the court might look to other
considerations to determine the intention of Parliament. Each case turns on its own
construction of the particular legislation, but a court should be slow to infer that Parliament intended to impose an onerous duty on the defendant to prove his innocence in a
criminal case. In that case it was held that it was for the prosecution to prove that the
compound in the defendant's possession contained morphine contrary to the *Misuse of
Drugs Act* 1971. The defendant would have had difficulty in proving that there was either no morphine or that the level was within the permissible level as he had no ready
access to scientific facilities for analysis.

The duty of a party to adduce sufficient evidence either by calling evidence or by
cross-examination to put a matter in issue is called the evidential burden. This arises in
cases of alibi, duress, provocation and self defence.

Article 6(2) of the European Convention on Human Rights (above) does not prohibit   **21–8**
rules which transfer an evidential burden provided the overall burden of proving guilt
remains with the prosecution: *Lingens v Leitgens v Austria*, 4 E.H.R.R. 373 at para.4.

Barbera, Messegue and Jabardo v Spain (1988) 11 E.H.R.R. 360; *Salabiaku v
France* (1988) 13 E.H.R.R. 379. See *Archbold Crown*, § 16–77.

In *R. v DPP Ex p. Kebilene* [2000] 2 A.C. 326, HL the court advised that in order
to establish whether a statutory reverse burden provision is vulnerable to challenge
under Art.6(2) is to determine its nature and whether it is an evidential burden requiring a defendant to adduce sufficient evidence to raise an issue or whether it is a
persuasive burden requiring him to prove a fact essential to his guilt or innocence. A
mandatory presumption of guilt would not necessarily be incompatible so long as it was
confined within reasonable limits. In order to decide reasonableness in that context
three questions should be asked:

1. What does the prosecution have to prove in order to transfer the onus to the
   defence?
2. Does the burden on the defendant relate to something which is likely to be difficult for him to prove or is it within his knowledge or to which he has ready access?
3. What is the nature of the threat faced by society which the provision is designed
   to combat?

21–9   In *R. v Lambert* [2001] 3 W.L.R. the House of Lords applied these principles to s.28(2) and (3) of the *Misuse of Drugs Act* 1971 which created "knowledge" defences to charges of possession. It was decided that the provisions could be read as imposing an evidential burden only. In this particular case, once the defendant raised the issue of knowledge, it was for the prosecution to prove the requisite knowledge beyond reasonable doubt.

In *Sheldrake v DPP* [2003] 2 W.L.R. 1629 it was held that the defence had an evidential but not a legal burden to prove that there was no likelihood of the defendant driving the vehicle while over the prescribed limit of alcohol (s.5(2) of the *Road Traffic Act* 1988). This was followed in *R. v Carass* [2002] 1 W.L.R. 1714, a case under the *Insolvency Act* 1986 where there was a defence if the defendant could prove that he had no intention to defraud, see also *R. v Drummond* [2002] 2 Cr.App.R. 25— consumption of alcohol before providing a specimen; *L v DPP* [2003] Q.B. 137— possession of a lock knife.

In *Att.-Gen.'s Reference (No.4 of 2002)* [2003] 2 Cr.App.R. 22, a case under the *Terrorism Act* 2000, the court found that a legal burden had passed to the defendant and that was the intention of Parliament. It was in any event proportionate in an Act intended to suppress terrorism. In *R. v Johnstone* [2003] 1 W.L.R. 1736 too, an offence under the *Trade Marks Act* 1994, the legal burden was said to have passed to the defendant. Lord Nicholls stated that:

> "The extent and nature of the factual matters required to be proved by the accused, and their importance relative to the matters required to be proved by the prosecution, have to be taken into account. So also does the extent to which the burden on the accused relates to facts which, if they exist, are readily provable by him as matters within his own knowledge or to which he has ready access."

In this case counterfeiting was considered to be a serious matter and there was a need to protect consumers, honest traders and manufacturers.

21–10   In *R. (on the application of Grundy & Co. Excavations Ltd) v Halton Division Magistrates' Court* [2003] EWHC 272, 167 J.P. 387, it was held that, as the offence of felling trees without a licence under the *Forestry Act* 1967, was an absolute one and the onus of proving an exception, *i.e.* that a licence was either in existence or was unnecessary was on the defence, this derogated from the presumption of innocence in Art.6(2) but was justified as necessary and proportionate.

VI. PRESUMPTIONS

21–11   A court may be required to make assumptions and those may relate to law or fact.

A. PRESUMPTIONS OF FACT

21–12   These are inferences which the court may or may not draw from the facts which are established, for example, that a person is alive on a given day may be presumed from proof of his or her being alive on an antecedent day. If that fact is in issue, however, evidence will have to be called and the matter decided by the court

Other facts may be presumed from circumstantial evidence. So, for example, where a defendant charged with handling stolen goods is found to be in possession of those goods without any explanation, this circumstantial evidence may give rise to a provisional conclusion that the defendant is the handler of those goods.

Lord Normand in *Teper v R* [1952] A.C. 480 at 489, PC, stated in relation to circumstantial evidence that " It must always be narrowly examined, if only because evidence of this kind may be fabricated to cast suspicion on another....It is also necessary before drawing the inference of the accused's guilt from circumstantial evidence to be sure that there are no other co-existing circumstances which would weaken or destroy the inference". On the other hand it has been said that circumstantial evidence is often the best evidence. It is no derogation of evidence to say that it is circumstantial: *R. v Taylor, Weaver and Donovan*, 21 Cr.App.R. 20, CCA.

B. PRESUMPTIONS OF LAW

Presumptions of law may be rebuttable or irrebutable. Some presumptions do not **21–13** depend upon proof of a basic fact, for example, the presumptions of innocence and sanity. Others depend upon proof of a basic fact

A presumption would be irrebuttable where on the proof or admission of a basic or primary fact, another fact could not be rebutted, for example, if a court were satisfied that a child appearing before it were nine years of age then, under s.50 of the *Children and Young Persons Act* 1933, "it shall be conclusively presumed that no child under the age of 10 years can be guilty of an offence". See *Walters v Lunt* [1951] 2 All E.R. 645.

Most presumptions of law, however, are rebuttable, *i.e.* evidence can be brought to show that the presumption is incorrect. If the defence relies on a rebuttable presumption, the prosecution must prove the presumed fact beyond reasonable doubt. If the prosecution relies on a rebuttable presumption, an evidential burden is placed on the defence to adduce evidence which might create a reasonable doubt. The prosecution is still required to prove the disputed fact beyond reasonable doubt: *R. v Kay* (1887) 16 Cox CC 292.

It can be presumed that a police officer has been lawfully appointed *R. v Gordon* **21–14** (1789) 1 Leach 515, that a solicitor has been admitted: *Berryman v Wise* (1791) 4 Term, Rep. 366, that a limited company has been incorporated: *R. v Langton* (1876) 2 Q.B.D. 296, or that a police officer requiring a breath test was in uniform: *Gage v Jones* [1983] R.T.R. 508. A document can be presumed to have been made on the date it bears, and a signed deed to have been sealed and delivered: *Hall v Bainbridge and Enderby* [1848] 12 Q.B. 699 (although a deed no longer needs to be sealed). Evidence of a ceremony of marriage presumes a valid marriage: *Mahadervan v Mahadervan* [1964] P 233.

Presumptions of law must be drawn unless rebutted: presumptions of fact may be drawn. When presumptions conflict they cancel each other out and the issue is decided without reference to the presumptions: *R. v Willshire* (1881) 6 Q.B.D. 366.

VII. DOCUMENTARY EVIDENCE

A. GENERAL

Statements contained in documents are subject to the general rules of the admissibil- **21–15** ity of evidence, particularly those relating to hearsay, opinion and privilege. Two issues arise (a) how may the document be proved and (b) what use may be made of its contents. It is only in relation to the second issue that the rule of hearsay arises. In that case the purpose for which the document is tendered must be identified

B. PUBLIC DOCUMENTS

Generally it is unnecessary to produce the original of any document made by a pub- **21–16** lic officer. Special provisions are made for the production of public documents such as Acts of Parliament, byelaws, judgements, treaties, previous convictions, court registers, marriage or death certificates etc. These can be regarded as exceptions to the hearsay rule and can prove the facts stated therein: *Sturla v Freccia* (1880) 5 App. Cas. 623, HL; *Wilton & Co v Phillips* [1903] T.L.R. 390

Evidence Act 1845, s.1

Certain documents to be received in evidence without proof of seal or signature, &c. of person signing the same

    1. Whenever by any Act now in force or hereafter to be in force any certificate, official or pub- **21–17** lic document, or document or proceeding of any corporation or joint stock or other company, or any certified copy of any document, bye law, entry in any register or other book, or of any

other proceeding, shall be receivable in evidence of any particular in any court of justice, or before any legal tribunal, or either House of Parliament, or any committee of either House, or in any judicial proceeding, the same shall respectively be admitted in evidence, provided they respectively purport to be sealed or impressed with a stamp or sealed and signed, or signed alone, as required, or impressed with a stamp and signed, as directed by the respective Acts made or to be hereafter made, without any proof of the seal or stamp, where a seal or stamp is necessary, or of the signature or of the official character of the person appearing to have signed the same, and without any further proof thereof, in every case in which the original record could have been received in evidence.

Evidence Act 1845, s.3

Copies of private Acts, printed by Queen's printer, journals of Parliament, and proclamations, admissible as evidence

21–18   3. All copies of private and local and personal Acts of Parliament not public Acts, if purporting to be printed by the Queen's printers, and all copies of the journals of either House of Parliament, and of royal proclamations, purporting to be printed by the printers to the crown or by the printers to either House of Parliament, or by any or either of them, shall be admitted as evidence thereof by all courts, judges, justices, and others without any proof being given that such copies were so printed.

Documentary Evidence Act 1882, s.2

Documents printed under superintendence of Stationery Office receivable in evidence

21–19   2. Where any enactment, whether passed before or after the passing of this Act, provides that a copy of any Act of Parliament, proclamation, order, regulation, rule, warrant, circular, list, gazette, or document shall be conclusive evidence, or be evidence, or have any other effect, when purporting to be printed by the Government Printer, or the Queen's Printer, or a printer authorised by Her Majesty, or otherwise under Her Majesty's authority, whatever may be the precise expression used, such copy shall also be conclusive evidence, or evidence, or have the said effect (as the case may be) if it purports to be printed under the superintendence or authority of Her Majesty's Stationery Office.

Documentary Evidence Act 1868, ss.2, 3, 5 and 6

Mode of proving certain documents

21–20   2. Prima facie evidence of any proclamation, order, or regulation issued before or after the passing of this Act by Her Majesty, or by the Privy Council, also of any proclamation, order, or regulation issued before or after the passing of this Act by or under the authority of any such department of the Government or officer as is mentioned in the first column of the schedule hereto, may be given in all courts of justice, and in all legal proceedings whatsoever, in all or any of the modes herein-after mentioned; that is to say:

(1) By the production of a copy of the Gazette purporting to contain such proclamation, order, or regulation.

(2) By the production of a copy of such proclamation, order, or regulation, purporting to be printed by the Government printer, or, where the question arises in a court in any British colony or possession, of a copy purporting to be printed under the authority of the legislature of such British colony or possession.

(3) By the production, in the case of any proclamation, order or regulation issued by Her Majesty or by the Privy Council, of a copy or extract purporting to be certified to be true by the clerk of the Privy Council, or by any one of the lords or others of the Privy Council, and, in the case of any proclamation, order, or regulation issued by or under the authority of any of the said departments or officers, by the production of a copy or extract purporting to be certified to be true by the person or persons specified in the second column of the said schedule in connexion with such department or officer.

Any copy or extract made in pursuance of this Act may be in print or in writing, or partly in print and partly in writing.

No proof shall be required of the handwriting or official position of any person certifying, in pursuance of this Act, to the truth of any copy of or extract from any proclamation, order, or regulation.

Act to be in force in colonies
3. Subject to any law that may be from time to time made by the legislature of any British colony or possession, this Act shall be in force in every such colony and possession.

Definition of terms
5. The following words shall in this Act have the meaning herein-after assigned to them, unless there is something in the context repugnant to such construction; (that is to say),
　　"British colony and possession" shall for the purposes of this Act include the Channel Islands, the Isle of Man and all other Her Majesty's dominions.
　　"Legislature" shall signify any authority, other than the Imperial Parliament or Her Majesty in Council, competent to make laws for any colony or possession.
　　"Privy Council" shall include Her Majesty in Council and the lords and others of Her Majesty's Privy Council, or any of them, and any committee of the Privy Council that is not specially named in the schedule hereto.
　　"Government printer" shall mean and include the printer to Her Majesty, the Queen's Printer for Scotland, and any printer purporting to be the printer authorized to print the statutes, ordinances, acts of state, or other public acts of the legislature of any British colony or possession, or otherwise to be the Government printer of such colony or possession.
　　"Gazette" shall include the London Gazette, the Edinburgh Gazette, and the Belfast Gazette, or any of such Gazettes.

Act to be cumulative
6. The provisions of this Act shall be deemed to be in addition to, and not in derogation of, any powers of proving documents given by any existing statute, or existing at common law.

In *R. v Clarke* [1969] 2 Q.B. 91 the Court of Appeal said that the word "order" in **21–21** the 1868 Act should be given a wide meaning, covering "any executive act of government performed by the bringing into existence of a public document for the purposes of giving effect to an Act of Parliament". It held that the *Breath Test (Approval) (No.1) Order* 1968, although not a statutory instrument, was an order within the meaning of the Act.

Evidence Act 1851, s.7

Foreign and colonial acts of state, judgments, etc.provable by certified copies, without proof of seal or signature or judicial character of person signing the same
7. All proclamations, treaties, and other acts of state of any foreign state or of any British colony, and all judgments, decrees, orders, and other judicial proceedings of any court of justice in any foreign state or in any British colony, and all affidavits, pleadings, and other legal documents filed or deposited in any such court, may be proved in any court of justice, or before any person having by law or by consent of parties authority to hear, receive, and examine evidence, either by examined copies or by copies authenticated as herein-after mentioned; that is to say, if the document sought to be proved be a proclamation, treaty, or other act of state, the authenticated copy to be admissible in evidence must purport to be sealed with the seal of the foreign state or British colony to which the original document belongs; and if the document sought to be proved be a judgment, decree, order, or other judicial proceeding of any foreign or colonial court, or an affidavit, pleading, or other legal document filed or deposited in any such court, the authenticated copy to be admissible in evidence must purport either to be sealed with the seal of the foreign or colonial court to which the original document belongs, or, in the event of such court having no seal, to be signed by the judge, or, if there be more than one judge, by any one of the judges of the said court, and such judge shall attach to his signature a statement in writing on the said copy that the court whereof he is a judge has no seal; but if any of the aforesaid authenticated copies shall purport to be sealed or signed as hereinbefore respectively directed, the same shall respectively be admitted in evidence in every case in which the original document could have been received in evidence, without any proof of the seal where a seal is necessary, or of the signature, or of the truth of the statement attached thereto, where such signature and statement are necessary, or of the judicial character of the person appearing to have made such signature and statement.

Authenticated or examined copies may be used to prove foreign law or judgments.

21–22

Births and Deaths Registration Act 1953, s.34

Entry in register as evidence of birth or death

21–23   **34.**—(1) The following provisions of this section shall have effect in relation to entries in registers under this Act or any enactment repealed by this Act.

(2) An entry or a certified copy of an entry of a birth or death in a register, or in a certified copy of a register, shall not be evidence of the birth or death unless the entry purports to be signed by some person professing to be the informant and to be such a person as might be required or permitted by law at the date of the entry to give to the registrar information concerning that birth or death:

Provided that this subsection shall not apply—

(a) in relation to an entry of a birth which, not being an entry signed by a person professing to be a superintendent registrar, purports to have been made with the authority of the Registrar General; or

(b) in relation to an entry of a death which purports to have been made upon a certificate from a coroner; or

(c) in relation to an entry of a birth or death which purports to have been made in pursuance of the enactments with respect to the registration of births and deaths at sea;

(d) in relation to the re-registration of a birth under section (5) of this Act.

(3) Where more than three months have intervened between the date of the birth of any child or the date when any living new-born child or still-born child was found exposed and the date of the registration of the birth of that child, the entry or a certified copy of the entry of the birth of the child in the register, or in a certified copy of the register, shall not be evidence of the birth unless—

(a) if it appears that not more than twelve months have so intervened, the entry purports either to be signed by the superintendent registrar as well as by the registrar or to have been made with the authority of the Registrar General;

(b) if more than twelve months have so intervened, the entry purports to have been made with the authority of the Registrar General:

Provided that this subsection shall not apply in any case where the original entry in the register was made before the first day of January, eighteen hundred and seventy-five.

21–24   (4) Where more than twelve months have intervened between the date of the death or of the finding of the dead body of any person and the date of the registration of that person's death, the entry or a certified copy of the entry of the death in the register, or in a certified copy of the register, shall not be evidence of the death unless the entry purports to have been made with the authority of the Registrar General:

Provided that this subsection shall not apply in any case where the original entry in the register was made before the first day of January, eighteen hundred and seventy-five.

(5) A certified copy of an entry in a register or in a certified copy of a register shall be deemed to be a true copy notwithstanding that it is made on a form different from that on which the original entry was made if any differences in the column headings under which the particulars appear in the original entry and the copy respectively are differences of form only and not of substance.

(6) The Registrar General shall cause any certified copy of an entry given in the General Register Office to be sealed or stamped with the seal of that Office; and, subject to the foregoing provisions of this section, any certified copy of an entry purporting to be sealed or stamped with the said seal shall be received as evidence of the birth or death to which it relates without any further or other proof of the entry, and no certified copy purporting to have been given in the said Office shall be of any force or effect unless it is sealed or stamped as aforesaid.

Local Government Act 1972, s.238

Evidence of byelaws

21–25   **238.** The production of a printed copy of a byelaw purporting to be made by a local authority, the Greater London Authority or a metropolitan county passenger transport authority upon which is endorsed a certificate purporting to be signed by the proper officer of the authority stating—

(a) that the byelaw was made by the authority;

(b) that the copy is a true copy of the byelaw;

(c) that on a specified date the byelaw was confirmed by the authority named in the certificate or, as the case may require, was sent to the Secretary of State and has not been disallowed;

(d) the date, if any, fixed by the confirming authority for the coming into operation of the byelaw;

shall be prima facie evidence of the facts stated in the certificate, and without proof of the handwriting or official position of any person purporting to sign the certificate.

Public Records Act 1958, s.9

Legal validity of public records and authenticated copies

9.—(1) The legal validity of any record shall not be affected by its removal under the provi- **21–26** sions of this Act, or of the *Public Record Office Acts* 1838 to 1898, or by any provisions in those Acts with respect to its legal custody.

(2) A copy of or extract from a public record in the Public Record Office purporting to be examined and certified as true and authentic by the proper officer and to be sealed or stamped with the seal of the Public Record Office shall be admissible as evidence in any proceedings without any further or other proof thereof if the original record would have been admissible as evidence in those proceedings.

(3) An electronic copy of or extract from a public record in the Public Record Office which—

(a) purports to have been examined and certified as true and authentic by the proper officer; and

(b) appears on a website purporting to be one maintained by or on behalf of the Public Record Office,;

shall, when viewed on that website, be admissible as evidence in any proceedings without further or other proof if the original record would have been admissible as evidence in those proceedings.

(4) In this section any reference to the proper officer is a reference to the Keeper of Public Records or any other officer of the Public Record Office authorised in that behalf by the Keeper of Public Records, and, in the case of copies and extracts made before the commencement of this Act, the deputy keeper of the records or any assistant record keeper appointed under the *Public Record Office Act* 1838.

Magistrates' Court Rules 1981, r.68

Proof of proceedings

68. The register of a magistrates' court, or any document purporting to be an extract from **21–27** the register certified by the justices' chief executive as a true extract, shall be admissible in any legal proceedings as evidence of the proceedings of the court entered in the register.

Police and Criminal Evidence Act 1984, ss.73–75

Proof of convictions and acquittals.

73.—(1) Where in any proceedings the fact that a person has in the United Kingdom been **21–28** convicted or acquitted of an offence otherwise than by a Service court is admissible in evidence, it may be proved by producing a certificate of conviction or, as the case may be, of acquittal relating to that offence, and proving that the person named in the certificate as having been convicted or acquitted of the offence is the person whose conviction or acquittal of the offence is to be proved.

(2) For the purposes of this section a certificate of conviction or of acquittal—

(a) shall, as regards a conviction or acquittal on indictment, consist of a certificate, signed by the proper officer of the court where the conviction or acquittal took place, giving the substance and effect (omitting the formal parts) of the indictment and of the conviction or acquittal; and

(b) shall, as regards a conviction or acquittal on a summary trial, consist of a copy of the conviction or of the dismissal of the information, signed by the of the court where the conviction or acquittal took place or by the proper officer of the court, if any, to which a memorandum of the conviction or acquittal was sent;

and a document purporting to be a duly signed certificate of conviction or acquittal under this section shall be taken to be such a certificate unless the contrary is proved.

(3) In subsection (2) above "proper officer" means—

(a) in relation to a magistrates' court in England and Wales, the justices' chief executive for the court; and

(b) in relation to any other court, the clerk of the court, his deputy or any other person having custody of the court record.

(4) The method of proving a conviction or acquittal authorised by this section shall be in addition to and not to the exclusion of any other authorised manner of proving a conviction or acquittal.

[This section is printed as amended by the *Access to Justice Act* 1999, s.90(1) and Sch.13, para.12.]

Conviction as evidence of commission of offence

21–29   **74.**—(1) In any proceedings the fact that a person other than the accused has been convicted of an offence by or before any court in the United Kingdom or by a Service court outside the United Kingdom shall be admissible in evidence for the purpose of proving, where to do so is relevant to any issue in those proceedings, that that person committed that offence, whether or not any other evidence of his having committed that offence is given.

(2) In any proceedings in which by virtue of this section a person other than the accused is proved to have been convicted of an offence by or before any court in the United Kingdom or by a Service court outside the United Kingdom, he shall be taken to have committed that offence unless the contrary is proved.

(3) In any proceedings where evidence is admissible of the fact that the accused has committed an offence, in so far as that evidence is relevant to any matter in issue in the proceedings for a reason other than a tendency to show in the accused a disposition to commit the kind of offence with which he is charged, if the accused is proved to have been convicted of the offence—

(a) by or before any court in the United Kingdom; or

(b) by a Service court outside the United Kingdom,

he shall be taken to have committed that offence unless the contrary is proved.

(4) Nothing in this section shall prejudice—

(a) the admissibility in evidence of any conviction which would be admissible apart from this section; or

(b) the operation of any enactment whereby a conviction or a finding of fact in any proceedings is for the purposes of any other proceedings made conclusive evidence of any fact.

Provisions supplementary to section 74.

21–30   **75.**—(1) Where evidence that a person has been convicted of an offence is admissible by virtue of section 74 above, then without prejudice to the reception of any other admissible evidence for the purpose of identifying the facts on which the conviction was based—

(a) the contents of any document which is admissible as evidence of the conviction; and

(b) the contents of the information, complaint, indictment or charge-sheet on which the person in question was convicted,

shall be admissible in evidence for that purpose.

(2) Where in any proceedings the contents of any document are admissible in evidence by virtue of subsection (1) above, a copy of that document, or of the material part of it, purporting to be certified or otherwise authenticated by or on behalf of the court or authority having custody of that document shall be admissible in evidence and shall be taken to be a true copy of that document or part unless the contrary is shown.

(3) Nothing in any of the following—

(a) section 14 of the *Powers of Criminal Courts (Sentencing) Act* 2000 (under which a conviction leading to probation or discharge is to be disregarded except as mentioned in that section);

(b) section 247 of the *Criminal Procedure (Scotland) Act* 1995 (which makes similar provision in respect of convictions on indictment in Scotland); and

(c) section 8 of the *Probation Act (Northern Ireland)* 1950 (which corresponds to section 13 of the *Powers of Criminal Courts Act* 1973) or any legislation which is in force in Northern Ireland for the time being and corresponds to that section, shall affect the operation of section 74 above; and for the purposes of that section any order made by a court of summary jurisdiction in Scotland under section 228 or section 246(3) of the said Act of 1995 shall be treated as a conviction.

(4) Nothing in section 74 above shall be construed as rendering admissible in any proceedings evidence of any conviction other than a subsisting one.

[This section is printed as amended by the *PCC(S)A* 2000, s.165(1) and Sch.9, para.98.]

There are other official documents which are not admissible or do not constitute **21–31** *prima facie* evidence, for example, circulars from government departments: *Peagram v Peagram* [1926] 2 K.B. 165, a motor vehicle registration book is not evidence as to its contents: *R. v Sealby* [1965] 1 All E.R. 701, and regimental records: *Andrews v Cordiner* [1947] 1 All E.R. 777.

C. PRIVATE DOCUMENTS

Usually the original must be produced but secondary evidence may be given where: **21–32**
— the other party has the evidence and refuses to produce it after proper notice (a defendant is not generally required to produce evidence against himself): *R. v Sanders* [1919] 1 K.B. 550; *R. v Worsenham* (1701) 1 Ld Raym 705; *Spokes v Grosvenor Hotel Co.* [1897] 2 Q.B. 124.
— a third person has the document and refuses to produce it, *e.g.* because of privilege
— the original is lost or destroyed: *R. v Wayte* (1982) 76 Cr.App.R. 110
— the original is not physically or conveniently removable or may not be lawfully moved: *Owner v Bee Hive Spinning Co. Ltd* [1914] 1 K.B. 105.

D. PROOF

Criminal Justice Act 1988, s.27

Proof of statements contained in documents
27. Where a statement contained in a document is admissible as evidence in criminal proceed-   **21–33** ings, it may be proved—
   (a) by the production of that document; or
   (b) (whether or not that document is still in existence) by the production of a copy of that document, or of the material part of it,
authenticated in such manner as the court may approve; and it is immaterial for the purposes of this subsection how many removes there are between a copy and the original.
   This section shall not apply to proceedings before a magistrates' court inquiring into an offence as examining justices.

[This section is reprinted as amended by the *Criminal Procedure and Investigations Act* 1996, s.47 and Sch.1, para.31.]

A witness who has attested a document may be called to prove it. A document which   **21–34** is more that 20 years old and comes from proper custody, however, is presumed to have been duly executed. It is also presumed that: a document was made on the date which it bears: *Re Adamson* (1875) LR 3 P& D 253; a deed was duly sealed: *Re Sandilands* (1871) L.R. 6 C.P. 411; an alteration or erasure in a deed was made before execution, but that an alteration or erasure in a will was made after execution: *Doe d Tatum v Catomore* [1851] 16 Q.B. 745. Where one deed is recited in another the proof of the deed is proof of the one recited.

Where a document, which is found by a police officer in the possession of the defendant, aids the prosecution case it may be produced by the officer who must explain how he found it. Evidence must also be given about how it came into existence.

The purpose of introducing the document must be identified. The purpose may be to show that the document was written as opposed to proving the facts contained therein.

21–35   Those facts would be hearsay and are inadmissible unless the exceptions to the hearsay rule apply. In order to prove the facts the document must be linked to the defendant. There must be *prima facie* evidence that he was the author of the document, or that he was in, or had been in possession or control of the document, or that he knew of the document or was in some other way connected to the document: *Howey v Bradley* [1970] Crim.L.R. 223, DC; *R. v Horne* [1992] Crim.L.R. 304; *R. v Podmore*, 22 Cr.App.R. 36, CCA.

Where the prosecution cannot prove the contents of an incriminating document, it can prove the finding of the document and if the defendant gives evidence he may be asked if he was aware of the document and of its contents. If he answers in the affirmative he may be asked about the meaning of it: *R. v Gillespie and Simpson*, 51 Cr.App.R. 172, CA; *R. v Cooper (W.J.)*, 82 Cr.App.R. 74, CA; *R. v Cross*, 91 Cr.App.R. 115, CA.

(1) Handwriting

21–36   Handwriting may be proved by someone who has knowledge of the handwriting: *R. v McCartney and Hansen* (1928) 20 Cr.App.R. 179; *R. v O'Brien* (1911) 7 Cr.App.R. 29.

(2) Bankers Books

21–37   An entry in a banker's book may be proved by a copy produced by a witness in person or by affidavit and examined as correct as being one of the ordinary books of the bank which is in that bank's custody or control and has been made in the usual course of business

(3) Absence of an entry in a record

21–38   The record must be produced by a person responsible for maintaining it who can explain the significance of the entries and omissions: *R. v Patel*, 73 Cr.App.R. 117, CA; *R. v Shone*, 76 Cr.App.R. 72, CA.

(4) Microfilm

Police and Criminal Evidence Act 1984, s.71

Microfilm copies

21–39   71. In any proceedings the contents of a document may (whether or not the document is still in existence) be proved by the production of an enlargement of a microfilm copy of that document or of the material part of it, authenticated in such manner as the court may approve.

Where the proceedings concerned are proceedings before a magistrates' court inquiring into an offence as examining justices this section shall have effect with the omission of the words "authenticated in such manner as the court may approve".

[This section is reprinted as amended by the *Criminal Procedure and Investigation Act* 1996, s.47, Sch.1, para.24.]

(5) General Documents

Criminal Justice Act 1988, s.23

21–40   23.—(1) Subject—
      (a) to subsection (4) below; and
      (b) to paragraph 1A of Schedule 2 to the *Criminal Appeal Act* 1968 (evidence given orally at original trial to be given orally at retrial);
a statement made by a person in a document shall be admissible in criminal proceedings as evidence of any fact of which direct oral evidence by him would be admissible if—

    (i) the requirements of one of the paragraphs of subsection (2) below are satisfied; or

    (ii) the requirements of subsection (3) below are satisfied.

  (2) The requirements mentioned in subsection (1)(i) above are—

    (a) that the person who made the statement is dead or by reason of his bodily or mental condition unfit to attend as a witness;

    (b) that—

      (i) the person who made the statement is outside the United Kingdom; and

      (ii) it is not reasonably practicable to secure his attendance; or

    (c) that all reasonable steps have been taken to find the person who made the statement, but that he cannot be found.

  (3) The requirements mentioned in subsection (1)(ii) above are—   **21–41**

    (a) that the statement was made to a police officer or some other person charged with the duty of investigating offences or charging offenders; and

    (b) that the person who made it does not give oral evidence through fear or because he is kept out of the way.

  (4) Subsection (1) above does not render admissible a confession made by an accused person that would not be admissible under section 76 of the *Police and Criminal Evidence Act* 1984.

  (5) This section shall not apply to proceedings before a magistrates' court inquiring into an offence as examining justices.

[This section is printed as amended and repealed in part by the *YJCEA* 1999, s.67 (1) and (3) and Schs 4, paras 15 and 16, and 6. Subsection (5) was inserted by the *CPIA* 1996, s. 47 and Sch.1, para.28. It applies only in relation to alleged offences into which no criminal investigation had begun before April 1, 1997, SI 1997/682 and 683.]

(6) Business and Computer records

Criminal Justice Act 1988, ss.24, 25, 26

24.—(1) Subject—   **21–42**

    (a) to subsections (3) and (4) below; and

    (b) to paragraph 1A of Schedule 2 to the *Criminal Appeal Act* 1968;

a statement in a document shall be admissible in criminal proceedings as evidence of any fact of which direct oral evidence would be admissible, if the following conditions are satisfied—

    (i) the document was created or received by a person in the course of a trade, business, profession or other occupation, or as the holder of a paid or unpaid office; and

    (ii) the information contained in the document was supplied by a person (whether or not the maker of the statement) who had, or may reasonably be supposed to have had, personal knowledge of the matters dealt with.

  (2) Subsection (1) above applies whether the information contained in the document was supplied directly or indirectly but, if it was supplied indirectly, only if each person through whom it was supplied received it—

    (a) in the course of a trade, business, profession or other occupation; or

    (b) as the holder of a paid or unpaid office.

  (3) Subsection (1) above does not render admissible a confession made by an accused person that would not be admissible under section 76 of the *Police and Criminal Evidence Act* 1984.

  (4) A statement prepared otherwise than in accordance with section 3 of the *Criminal Justice (International Co-operation) Act* 1990 or an order under paragraph 6 of Schedule 13 to this Act or under section 30 or 31 below for the purposes—

    (a) of pending or contemplated criminal proceedings; or

    (b) of a criminal investigation,

shall not be admissible by virtue of subsection (1) above unless—

    (i) the requirements of one of the paragraphs of subsection (2) of section 23 above are satisfied; or

    (ii) the requirements of subsection (3) of that section are satisfied; or

      (iii) the person who made the statement cannot reasonably be expected (having regard to the time which has elapsed since he made the statement and to all the circumstances) to have any recollection of the matters dealt with in the statement.

(5) This section shall not apply to proceedings before a magistrates' court inquiring into an offence as examining justices.

[This section is printed as amended by the *Criminal Justice (International Cooperation) Act* 1990, s.31(1) and Sch.4, para.6(2); and (insertion of subs.(5)) by the *CIPA* 1996, s.47 and Sch.1, para.29; and as amended and repealed in part by the *YJCEA* 1999 s.67(1) and (3) and Schs 4, paras 15 and 16, and 6. As amended by the 1996 Act it applies only in relation to alleged offences into which no criminal investigation had begun before April 1, 1997; SI 1997/682 and 683.]

21–43   **25.**—(1) If, having regard to all the circumstances—

      (a) the Crown Court—

          (i) on a trial on indictment;

          (ii) on an appeal from a magistrates' court;

          (iii) on the hearing of an application under section 6 of the *Criminal Justice Act* 1987 (applications for dismissal of charges of fraud transferred from magistrates' court to Crown Court); or

          (iv) on the hearing of an application under paragraph 5 of Schedule 6 to the *Criminal Justice Act* 1991 (applications for dismissal of charges in certain cases involving children transferred from magistrates' court to Crown Court); or

      (b) the criminal division of the Court of Appeal; or

      (c) a magistrates' court on a trial of an information,

is of the opinion that in the interests of justice a statement which is admissible by virtue of section 23 or 24 above nevertheless ought not to be admitted, it may direct that the statement shall not be admitted.

(2) Without prejudice to the generality of subsection (1) above, it shall be the duty of the court to have regard—

      (a) to the nature and source of the document containing the statement and to whether or not, having regard to its nature and source and to any other circumstances that appear to the court to be relevant, it is likely that the document is authentic;

      (b) to the extent to which the statement appears to supply evidence which would otherwise not be readily available;

      (c) to the relevance of the evidence that it appears to supply to any issue which is likely to have to be determined in the proceedings; and

      (d) to any risk, having regard in particular to whether it is likely to be possible to controvert the statement if the person making it does not attend to give oral evidence in the proceedings, that its admission or exclusion will result in unfairness to the accused or, if there is more than one, to any of them.

[This section is printed as amended by the *CJPOA* 1994, s.168(1) and Sch.9, para.31.]

21–44   **26.** Where a statement which is admissible in criminal proceedings by virtue of section 23 or 24 above appears to the court to have been prepared, otherwise than in accordance with section 3 of the *Criminal Justice (International Co-operation) Act* 1990 or an order under paragraph 6 of Schedule 13 to this Act or under section 30 or 31 below, for the purposes—

      (a) of pending or contemplated criminal proceedings; or

      (b) of a criminal investigation,

the statement shall not be given in evidence in any criminal proceedings without the leave of the court, and the court shall not give leave unless it is of the opinion that the statement ought to be admitted in the interests of justice; and in considering whether its admission would be in the interests of justice, it shall be the duty of the court to have regard—

          (i) to the contents of the statement;

          (ii) to any risk, having regard in particular to whether it is likely to be possible to controvert the statement if the person making it does not attend to give oral evidence in the proceedings, that its admission or exclusion will result in unfairness to the accused or, if there is more than one, to any of them; and

          (iii) to any other circumstances that appear to the court to be relevant.

This section shall not apply to proceedings before a magistrates' court inquiring into an offence as examining justices.

[This section is printed as amended by the *Criminal Justice (International Cooperation) Act* 1990, s.31(1) and Sch.4, para.6(2) and (insertion of last paragraph) by the *CIPA* 1996, s.47 and Sch.1, para.30. As amended by the 1996 Act it applies only in relation to alleged offences into which no criminal investigation had begun before April 1, 1997, SI 1997/682 and 683.]

Information obtained from a computer, whether printed out or read from a display, **21–45** may be divided into three categories:

— where the computer was used to calculate or process information: *R. v Wood*, 76 Cr.App.R. 23; *Sophocleous v Ringer* [1988] R.T.R. 52, DC.
— where the computer was programmed to record information: *R. v Pettigrew*, 71 Cr.App.R. 186; *R. v Spiby*, 91 Cr.App.R. 186, CA.
— where the information recorded and processed by the computer has been entered by a person, directly or indirectly. Information in this category is hearsay.

The court has a general discretion to refuse to admit such documents: s.25(1)(c).

(7) Medical records

Records are admissible to show that a witness suffers from some disease or defect or **21–46** abnormality of mind that affects his reliability as a witness: *Toohey v Metropolitan Police Comr.* [1965] 1 All E.R. 506.

(8) Tape and Video recordings

These are treated in the same way as other documents.　　　**21–47**

(9) Photographs and sketches

A photograph or sketch is admissible provided it is verified on oath by a person able **21–48** to speak to its accuracy, not necessarily the photographer: *R. v Tolson* (1864) 4 F & F 103; *Mille v Lamson, The Times*, October 29, 1892.

(10) Maps and plans

A map or a plan may be produced by its maker or authenticated by a witness pro- **21–49** ducing it. A map or plan prepared for the trial and containing any references to occurrences which are the subject matter of the trial, but which did not exist when the map was prepared, is inadmissible if objection is made. In *R. v Mitchell* (1852) 6 Cox CC 82, for example, a skid mark which was visible on the road when the map was prepared is admissible whereas the position of a car which had been moved since the accident had occurred was not.

(11) Certificates and statutory declarations

Various matters are by statute provable by certificate.　　　**21–50**

Criminal Justice Act 1948, s.41

Evidence by certificate

41.—(1) In any criminal proceedings, a certificate purporting to be signed by a constable, or **21–51** by a person having the prescribed qualifications, and certifying that a plan or drawing exhibited thereto is a plan or drawing made by him of the place or object specified in the certificate, and that the plan or drawing is correctly drawn to a scale so specified, shall be evidence of the relative position of the things shown on the plan or drawing.

(4) Nothing in this section shall be deemed to make a certificate admissible as evidence in proceedings for an offence except in a case where and to the extent to which oral evidence to the like effect would have been admissible in those proceedings.

(5) Nothing in this section shall be deemed to make a certificate admissible as evidence in proceedings for any offence—

   (a) unless a copy thereof has, not less than seven days before the hearing of trial, been served in the prescribed manner on the person charged with the offence; or

   (b) if that person, not later than three days before the hearing or trial or within such further time as the court may in special circumstances allow, serves notice in the prescribed from and manner on the prosecutor requiring the attendance at the trial of the person who signed the certificate

[(5A) Where the proceedings mentioned in subsection (1) above are proceedings before a magistrates' court inquiring into an offence as examining justices this section shall have effect with the omission of—

   (a) subsection (4), and

   (b) in subsection (5), paragraph (b) and the word "or" immediately preceding it.]

(6) In this section the expression "prescribed" means prescribed by rules made by the Secretary of State.

[This section is reprinted as amended by the *Road Traffic Act* 1960, s.267 and Sch.18, the *Theft Act* 1968, s.33(3) and Sch.3, and the *Criminal Proceedings and Investigations Act* 1996, s.47.]

Evidence by Certificate Rules 1961 (SI 1962/2319), rr.1–3

21–52   **1.** The prescribed qualifications for the purpose of subsection (1) of section forty-one of the *Criminal Justice Act,* 1948 (which relates to the admissibility of certified plans and drawings in criminal proceedings), shall be—

   (a) registration as an architect under the Architects (Registration) Acts, 1931 to 1938, or

   (b) membership of any of the following bodies, that is to say, the Royal Institution of Chartered Surveyors, the Institution of Civil Engineers, the Institution of Municipal Engineers and the Land Agents Society.

21–53   **2.** A certificate under subsection (1) of section two hundred and forty-two of the *Road Traffic Act,* 1960, shall be in the form numbered 1 in the Schedule hereto or in a form to the like effect and a notice under paragraph (b) of subsection (3) of that section or under paragraph (b) of subsection (5) of section forty-one of the *Criminal Justice Act,* 1948, shall be in the form numbered 2 in the Schedule hereto or in a form to the like effect.

21–54   **3.** Any certificate or other document required to be served by subsection (3) of the said section two hundred and forty-two or by subsection (5) of the said section forty-one shall be served in the following manner, that is to say—

   (a) where the person to be served is a corporation, by addressing it to the corporation and leaving it at, or sending it by registered post or by the recorded delivery service to, the registered office of the corporation or, if there be no such office, its principal office or place at which it conducts its business;

   (b) in any other case, by delivering it personally to the person to be served or by addressing it to him and leaving it at, or sending it by registered post or by the recorded delivery service to, his last or usual place of abode or place of business.

[These rules are printed as amended by the *Evidence by Certificate Rules* 1962 and the *Road Traffic (Consequential Provisions) Act* 1988, s.2(4).]

21–55   Where one subsection of a section of a statute provides that a certificate as to a certain matter "shall be admissible in evidence" as proof of its contents, and the following subsection provides that such certificate "shall not be received in evidence" unless certain steps have been taken, admissibility does not depend upon proof by the prosecution that such steps have been taken; it is for the defence to object to admissibility prior to the end of the trial. It is no ground of appeal against conviction that the requisite steps were not taken. If the defendant was unrepresented at trial, a failure to object should not be held against him on appeal. As to admissibility it would be otherwise where the statutory provision governing admissibility was to the effect that a certificate "is admissible only if" certain steps have been taken: *Att.-Gen. for the Cayman Islands v Roberts* [2002] 1 W.L.R. 1842, PC; *McCormack v DPP* [2002] R.T.R. 20, QBD.

VIII. PHYSICAL OBJECTS

Material objects are produced as exhibits by the person who found them. **21–56**
The prosecution is not obliged to place every item of physical evidence before the
court: *Hockin v Alquist Brothers Ltd* [1944] K.B. 120. Where original exhibits are too
large to be produced conveniently, photographs of them may be admitted: *R. v Uxbridge Justices Ex p. Sofaer* (1987) 85 Cr.App.R. 367.

IX. JUDICIAL NOTICE

Courts may take judicial notice of matters which are so notorious, or clearly **21–57**
established, or susceptible of demonstration by reference to readily obtainable and authoritative source that evidence of their existence is unnecessary: *Mullen v Hackney
LBC* [1997] 1 W.L.R. 1103, CA (Civ. Div).

The court in *Commonwealth Shipping Representative v Peninsular and Oriental
Branch Service* [1923] A.C. 191 at 212 said that:

> Judicial notice refers to facts, which a judge can be called upon to receive and to act upon,
> either from his general knowledge of them, or from inquiries to be made by himself for his
> own information from sources to which it is proper for which it is proper to refer.

Examples of such matters are: Rain falls: *Fay v Prentice* (1845) 14 L.J.C. 298; but-
terfly knives are offensive weapons made or adapted for use for causing injury: *DPP v
Hynde* [1998] Crim.L.R. 72.

When a court takes judicial notice of a fact it finds that the fact exists although its existence has not been established by evidence. The court should be cautious in treating a
factual conclusion as obvious even though the person in the street would unhesitatingly
hold it to be so: *Carter v Eastbourne BC (2000)* 164 J.P. 273, DC.

Although the court may, in arriving at its decision, use general information and a **21–58**
knowledge of the common affairs of life which people of ordinary intelligence possess, it
may not act on its own private knowledge or belief regarding the facts of the particular
case: *R. v Sutton* (1816) 4 M & S 532; *Ingram v Percival* [1969] 1 Q.B. 548, DC. In
Wetherall v Harrison [1976] Q.B. 773, DC, it was held that it was proper for a magistrate with specialised knowledge of the circumstances forming the background to a particular case to draw upon that knowledge in interpreting the evidence, but improper in
effect to give evidence to himself and the other justices which is at variance with the evidence given, for it would offend the fundamental principle that evidence should be
given in the presence of the parties and be subject to cross-examination. Magistrates are
entitled to rely on knowledge of the area in concluding that residents are likely to be
caused nuisance by practice of kerb-crawling: *Paul v DPP* (1990) 90 Cr.App.R. 173,
DC.

The judiciary in magistrates' courts must be circumspect in their use of local knowledge and inform the parties when reliance is being placed upon local knowledge. In
Bowman v DPP [1990] Crim.L.R. 600, DC, the defendant was charged with driving in
a public place having consumed excess alcohol contrary to the *Road Traffic Act* 1972,
s.6. The issue was whether the car park was a public place. There was evidence that
there were other cars in the car park and that there was no barrier present at the time.
The magistrates, using their own local knowledge of the car park, found that the car
park was a public place and convicted. On appeal it was held that the magistrates were
entitled to find as they did on the basis of the evidence before them and their own local
knowledge of the area. Where magistrates do use their own local knowledge they
should make that known to the parties and give the parties an opportunity to comment.

In *Norbrook Laboratories (GB) Ltd v Health and Safety Executive, The Times,* **21–59**
February 23, 1998, DC, it was held that an appeal against a conviction under health and
safety at work legislation would be allowed where magistrates had failed to inform the
parties to the case that they were bringing their own local knowledge to bear in reaching a decision. Although it was perfectly legitimate for local knowledge to be relied upon

by magistrates, both defence and prosecution should be informed so that they might be afforded an opportunity to comment upon the knowledge the magistrates claimed to have.

As lay magistrates are not legally qualified, they are in a unique position compared to judges. In *Wetherall v Harrison* [1976] Q.B. 773 the question was whether the defendant had a reasonable excuse for failing to give a blood sample. The defendant said that he had had a fit but the prosecution alleged that it had not been genuine. One of the magistrates was a medical practitioner and gave his professional opinion to the other magistrates, who drew on their wartime experience of inoculations and the fear that they could create in certain cases. The Divisional Court held that magistrates lack the ability to exclude certain factors from their consideration. If a magistrate is a specialist, such as a doctor, it is not possible for him to approach the case as if he did not have that expertise and it would be a bad thing if that were required. One of the advantages of magistrates is the varied experience that they bring to the magistrates' courts. Although it would be wrong for the magistrate to give evidence personally, he can employ basic knowledge to the benefit of the other magistrates in considering and weighing the evidence.

Every statute passed since 1850 is a public Act to be judicially noted unless the contrary is expressly provided: *Interpretation Act* 1978, s.3, Sch.2, para.2. See *Pillai v Mudanayaka* [1953] A.C. 514, PC.

Evidence Act 1845, s.2

Courts, &c. to take judicial notice of signature of equity or common law judges, &c.

21–60   **2.** All courts, judges, justices, masters in chancery, masters of courts, commissioners judicially acting, and other judicial officers, shall henceforth take judicial notice of the signature of any of the equity or common law judges of the superior courts at the Royal Courts of Justice], provided such signature be attached or appended to any decree, order, certificate, or other judicial or official document.

[This section is reprinted as amended by the *Supreme Court of Judicature (Consolidation) Act* 1925, s.224(1).]

X. HEARSAY

A. GENERAL

21–61   Evidence given by a witness of what someone else said is generally inadmissible to prove the truth of what was said: *Shaw v Roberts* (1818) 2 Stark 455. In *R. v McLean*, 52 Cr.App.R. 80, CA a witness made a mental note of a car's registration number and dictated it to C, who wrote it down. The witness did not check the accuracy of C's note and could not remember the number when giving evidence. It was held that C could not give evidence of what the witness had told him in relation to the number. See also *Jones v Metcalfe* [1967] 1 W.L.R. 1286, DC and *Cattermole v Miller* [1977] Crim.L.R. 553, DC.

Such evidence is admissible, however, to prove that the statement was made: *Subramanian v Public Prosecutor* [1956] 1 W.L.R. 965.

The admissibility of evidence is a matter for regulation by national law. Article 6(3)(d) of the European Convention on Human Rights provides that everyone charged with a criminal offence is entitled to examine witnesses called against him but nothing in that article prevents reliance on hearsay evidence where there are counterbalancing factors which preserve the rights of the defence: *Kostovski v Netherlands* (1989) 12 E.H.R.R. 434.

See *Archbold Crown*, § 16–91

B. EXCEPTIONS

21–62   Where a statement is admissible under an exception to the rule against hearsay, it is admissible as evidence of the truth of its contents.

Confessions

As to the admissibility of confessions see § 21–67 below. **21–63**

Statements of deceased persons

These may be used to prove traditions or custom or public rights where a witness will **21–64** tell the court what he had heard from those who are now dead: *R. v Antrobus* (1835) 3 A7E 788; *R. v Bedfordshire* (1855) 4 E&B 535.

Declarations made by persons against their pecuniary or proprietary interests and who are now dead are admissible: *R. v Rogers* [1995] 1 Cr.App.R. 374, CA.

A statement which it is the duty of a person to make in the ordinary course of his business or professional employment, is admissible after his decease provided it was made contemporaneously with the act to which it relates: *Mercer v Denne* [1905] 2 Ch. 538: see also *R. v McGuire* (1985) 81 Cr.App.R. 323, CA.

Statements in public and certain private documents

See Documents, § 21–16 above. **21–65**

Statements falling within the res gestae principle

Statements or acts which are connected with the facts in issue and occur at the same **21–66** time and are an integral part of what happened are admissible. In *R. v Nye and Loan*, 66 Cr.App.R. 252, CA, the statement of the victim of an assault which had taken place during an altercation after a road traffic accident, identifying one of the appellants as the assailant, was admitted. The statement had been made to a police officer shortly after the event. The Court of Appeal said it was difficult to imagine a more spontaneous identification.

The case of *R. v Andrews* [1987] A.C. 281 set guidelines for the admissibility of *res* **21–67** *gestae*.

"1. The primary question which the judge must ask himself is—can the possibility of concoction or distortion be disregarded?

2. To answer that question the judge must first consider the circumstances in which the particular statement was made, in order to satisfy himself that the event was so unusual or startling or dramatic as to dominate the thoughts of the victim, so that his utterance was an instinctive reaction to that event thus giving no real opportunity for reasoned reflection. In such a situation the judge would be entitled to conclude that the involvement or the pressure of the event would exclude the possibility of concoction or distortion, providing that the statement was made in conditions of approximate but not exact contemporaneity.

3. in order for the statement to be sufficiently 'spontaneous' it must be so closely associated with the event which has excited the statement, that it can be fairly stated that the mind of the declarant was still dominated by the event. Thus the judge must be satisfied that the event, which provided the trigger mechanism for the statement, was still operative. The fact that the statement was made in answer to a question is but one factor to consider under this heading.

4.Quite apart from the time factor, there may be special features in the case, which relate to the possibility of concoction or distortion ... The judge must be satisfied that the circumstances were such that having regard to the special feature of malice there was no possibility of any concoction or distortion to the advantage of the maker or the disadvantage of the accused

5.As to the possibility of error in the facts narrated in the statement, if only the ordinary fallibility of human recollection is relied upon, this goes to the weight to be attached to and not to the admissibility of the statement ... However ... here there may be special features that may give rise to the possibility of error. In the instant case there was evidence that the deceased had drunk to excess...Another example would be where the identification was made in circumstances of particular difficulty or where the declarant suffered from defective eyesight. In such circumstances the trial judge must consider whether he can exclude the possibility of error.

Statements of health or feelings are admissible as original evidence and are not exceptions to the hearsay rule: *Gilbey v Great Western RyCo.* (1910) 102 L.T. 202.

C. CRIMINAL JUSTICE ACT 2003

21–68　　The *Criminal Justice Act* 2003, when in force, will change the position with regard to admissibility.

Criminal Justice Act 2003, s.114

Admissibility of hearsay evidence

21–69　　**114.**—(1) In criminal proceedings a statement not made in oral evidence in the proceedings is admissible as evidence of any matter stated if, but only if—

(a) any provision of this Chapter or any other statutory provision makes it admissible,

(b) any rule of law preserved by section 118 makes it admissible,

(c) all parties to the proceedings agree to it being admissible, or

(d) the court is satisfied that it is in the interests of justice for it to be admissible.

(2) In deciding whether a statement not made in oral evidence should be admitted under subsection (1)(d), the court must have regard to the following factors (and to any others it considers relevant)—

(a) how much probative value the statement has (assuming it to be true) in relation to a matter in issue in the proceedings, or how valuable it is for the understanding of other evidence in the case;

(b) what other evidence has been, or can be, given on the matter or evidence mentioned in paragraph (a);

(c) how important the matter or evidence mentioned in paragraph (a) is in the context of the case as a whole;

(d) the circumstances in which the statement was made;

(e) how reliable the maker of the statement appears to be;

(f) how reliable the evidence of the making of the statement appears to be;

(g) whether oral evidence of the matter stated can be given and, if not, why it cannot;

(h) the amount of difficulty involved in challenging the statement;

(i) the extent to which that difficulty would be likely to prejudice the party facing it.

(3) Nothing in this Chapter affects the exclusion of evidence of a statement on grounds other than the fact that it is a statement not made in oral evidence in the proceedings.

21–70　　Hearsay evidence, *i.e.* a statement not made in oral testimony will be admissible if:

— it falls within the following statutory provisions

— the parties agree

— the court is satisfied, in the interests of justice, that it should be admitted.

In the latter case, the court will have regard to:

— its probative value to matters in issue or its value to the understanding of other evidence

— what other evidence has or can be given on the matter

— the importance of the matter or the other evidence which needs to be understood

— the circumstances in which it was made

— the reliability of its maker

— the reliability of the making of the statement

— whether oral evidence can be given and, if not, why not

— difficulties in challenging the statement

— the extent that those difficulties would prejudice the defendant.

Criminal Justice Act 2003, s.116

21–71　　**116.**—(1) In criminal proceedings a statement not made in oral evidence in the proceedings is admissible as evidence of any matter stated if—

(a) oral evidence given in the proceedings by the person who made the statement would be admissible as evidence of that matter,

(b) the person who made the statement (the relevant person) is identified to the court's satisfaction, and

(c) any of the five conditions mentioned in subsection (2) is satisfied.

(2) The conditions are—

(a) that the relevant person is dead;

(b) that the relevant person is unfit to be a witness because of his bodily or mental condition;

(c) that the relevant person is outside the United Kingdom and it is not reasonably practicable to secure his attendance;

(d) that the relevant person cannot be found although such steps as it is reasonably practicable to take to find him have been taken;

(e) that through fear the relevant person does not give (or does not continue to give) oral evidence in the proceedings, either at all or in connection with the subject matter of the statement, and the court gives leave for the statement to be given in evidence.

(3) For the purposes of subsection (2)(e) "fear" is to be widely construed and (for **21–72** example) includes fear of the death or injury of another person or of financial loss.

(4) Leave may be given under subsection (2)(e) only if the court considers that the statement ought to be admitted in the interests of justice, having regard—

(a) to the statement's contents,

(b) to any risk that its admission or exclusion will result in unfairness to any party to the proceedings (and in particular to how difficult it will be to challenge the statement if the relevant person does not give oral evidence),

(c) in appropriate cases, to the fact that a direction under section 19 of the *Youth Justice and Criminal Evidence Act* 1999 (c. 23) (special measures for the giving of evidence by fearful witnesses etc) could be made in relation to the relevant person, and

(d) to any other relevant circumstances.

(5) A condition set out in any paragraph of subsection (2) which is in fact satisfied is to be treated as not satisfied if it is shown that the circumstances described in that paragraph are caused—

(a) by the person in support of whose case it is sought to give the statement in evidence, or

(b) by a person acting on his behalf,

In order to prevent the relevant person giving oral evidence in the proceedings (whether at all or in connection with the subject matter of the statement).

Where a person is dead, mentally or physically unfit, outside the UK and it is not rea- **21–73** sonably practicable for him to attend, unable to be found or afraid then his statement may be admissible if his oral evidence would have been admissible and his identity is confirmed. In the case of fear the court must also give leave: s.116(4).

Criminal Justice Act 2003, s.117

117.—(1) In criminal proceedings a statement contained in a document is admissible as evi- **21–74** dence of any matter stated if—

(a) oral evidence given in the proceedings would be admissible as evidence of that matter,

(b) the requirements of subsection (2) are satisfied, and

(c) the requirements of subsection (5) are satisfied, in a case where subsection (4) requires them to be.

(2) The requirements of this subsection are satisfied if—

(a) the document or the part containing the statement was created or received by a person in the course of a trade, business, profession or other occupation, or as the holder of a paid or unpaid office,

(b) the person who supplied the information contained in the statement (the relevant person) had or may reasonably be supposed to have had personal knowledge of the matters dealt with, and

(c) each person (if any) through whom the information was supplied from the relevant person to the person mentioned in paragraph (a) received the information in the course of a trade, business, profession or other occupation, or as the holder of a paid or unpaid office.

(3) The persons mentioned in paragraphs (a) and (b) of subsection (2) may be the same person.

21–75   (4) The additional requirements of subsection (5) must be satisfied if the statement—

(a) was prepared for the purposes of pending or contemplated criminal proceedings, or for a criminal investigation, but

(b) was not obtained pursuant to a request under section 7 of the *Crime (International Co-operation) Act* 2003 or an order under paragraph 6 of Schedule 13 to the *Criminal Justice Act* 1988 (which relate to overseas evidence).

(5) The requirements of this subsection are satisfied if—

(a) any of the five conditions mentioned in section 116(2) is satisfied (absence of relevant person etc), or

(b) the relevant person cannot reasonably be expected to have any recollection of the matters dealt with in the statement (having regard to the length of time since he supplied the information and all other circumstances).

(6) A statement is not admissible under this section if the court makes a direction to that effect under subsection (7).

(7) The court may make a direction under this subsection if satisfied that the statement's reliability as evidence for the purpose for which it is tendered is doubtful in view of—

(a) its contents,

(b) the source of the information contained in it,

(c) the way in which or the circumstances in which the information was supplied or received, or

(d) the way in which or the circumstances in which the document concerned was created or received.

21–76   Documents will be admissible if:

— created or received in the course of a business etc.

— the person supplying the information had personal knowledge

— each person handling the information received it in the course of a business etc.

— oral evidence of the fact would have been admissible

— where the document was made for criminal proceedings or an investigation in UK the maker is dead, physically or mentally unfit, outside UK and impracticable for him to attend, unable to be found or afraid or he cannot be expected to have any recollection.

The court may direct that the statement may not be introduced if it believes that its reliability is doubtful: s.117(7).

The rules of public information, reputation, *res gestae*, confessions, admissions by agents, common enterprise and expert evidence are preserved: s.118.

If a witness admits a previous inconsistent statement or the admission is proved that inconsistent statement is admissible:s.119.

A statement will not be admissible to prove an earlier hearsay statement was made unless all parties agree, the statement would admissible under ss.117, 119, or 120 above or the court is satisfied that, taking into account the reliability of the statement, that its value is so high that the interests of justice require its admissibility: s.121.

Criminal Justice Act 2003, ss.124, 125, 126

Credibility

21–77   124.—(1) This section applies if in criminal proceedings—

(a) a statement not made in oral evidence in the proceedings is admitted as evidence of a matter stated, and

(b) the maker of the statement does not give oral evidence in connection with the subject matter of the statement.

(2) In such a case—

(a) any evidence which (if he had given such evidence) would have been admissible as relevant to his credibility as a witness is so admissible in the proceedings;

(b) evidence may with the court's leave be given of any matter which (if he had given such evidence) could have been put to him in cross-examination as relevant to his credibility as a witness but of which evidence could not have been adduced by the cross-examining party;

(c) evidence tending to prove that he made (at whatever time) any other statement inconsistent with the statement admitted as evidence is admissible for the purpose of showing that he contradicted himself.

(3) If as a result of evidence admitted under this section an allegation is made against the maker of a statement, the court may permit a party to lead additional evidence of such description as the court may specify for the purposes of denying or answering the allegation.

(4) In the case of a statement in a document which is admitted as evidence under section 117 each person who, in order for the statement to be admissible, must have supplied or received the information concerned or created or received the document or part concerned is to be treated as the maker of the statement for the purposes of subsections (1) to (3) above.

Stopping the case where evidence is unconvincing

125.—(1) If on a defendant's trial before a judge and jury for an offence the court is satisfied **21–78** at any time after the close of the case for the prosecution that—

(a) the case against the defendant is based wholly or partly on a statement not made in oral evidence in the proceedings, and

(b) the evidence provided by the statement is so unconvincing that, considering its importance to the case against the defendant, his conviction of the offence would be unsafe,

the court must either direct the jury to acquit the defendant of the offence or, if it considers that there ought to be a retrial, discharge the jury.

(2) Where—

(a) a jury is directed under subsection (1) to acquit a defendant of an offence, and

(b) the circumstances are such that, apart from this subsection, the defendant could if acquitted of that offence be found guilty of another offence,

the defendant may not be found guilty of that other offence if the court is satisfied as mentioned in subsection (1) in respect of it.

(3) If—

(a) a jury is required to determine under section 4A(2) of the *Criminal Procedure (Insanity) Act* 1964 (c. 84) whether a person charged on an indictment with an offence did the act or made the omission charged, and

(b) the court is satisfied as mentioned in subsection (1) above at any time after the close of the case for the prosecution that—

(i) the case against the defendant is based wholly or partly on a statement not made in oral evidence in the proceedings, and

(ii) the evidence provided by the statement is so unconvincing that, considering its importance to the case against the person, a finding that he did the act or made the omission would be unsafe,

the court must either direct the jury to acquit the defendant of the offence or, if it considers that there ought to be a rehearing, discharge the jury.

(4) This section does not prejudice any other power a court may have to direct a jury to acquit a person of an offence or to discharge a jury.

Court's general discretion to exclude evidence

126.—(1) In criminal proceedings the court may refuse to admit a statement as evidence of a **21–79** matter stated if—

(a) the statement was made otherwise than in oral evidence in the proceedings, and

(b) the court is satisfied that the case for excluding the statement, taking account of the danger that to admit it would result in undue waste of time, substantially outweighs the case for admitting it, taking account of the value of the evidence.

(2) Nothing in this Chapter prejudices—

(a) any power of a court to exclude evidence under section 78 of the *Police and Criminal Evidence Act* 1984 (c. 60) (exclusion of unfair evidence), or

(b) any other power of a court to exclude evidence at its discretion (whether by preventing questions from being put or otherwise).

XI. SIMILAR FACT EVIDENCE

21–80   This is evidence which does not directly implicate the accused in the offence charged but which suggests, directly or indirectly, from his previous conduct, either behaviour, previous convictions or acquittals,that he has committed one or more other offences. The issue is when can evidence suggestive of discreditable conduct, whether or not criminal, or of the disreputable character of the defendant be admitted as evidence that he is guilty of the offence charged albeit the evidence has no connection with that offence. In *R. v Smith* (1915) 11 Cr.App.R. 229, the brides in the Bath case, there were no less than thirteen sinister points of resemblance linking two previous "accidental drownings" to the case.

In *DPP v P* [1991] 2 A.C. 447 it was stated that the essential feature of evidence to be admitted under the 'similar fact' rule is that its probative force in support of the allegation being tried is sufficiently great to make it just to admit the evidence, notwithstanding that it is prejudicial to the defendant in tending to show that he was guilty of another crime. Such probative force may be derived from striking similarities in the evidence about the manner in which the crime was committed. The degree of similarity will vary according to the issues in the case and the nature of the other evidence.

21–81   Evidence will be admissible if explanation of it on the basis of coincidence would be an "affront to common sense" or would be "against all probabilities": *DPP v Boardman* [1975] A.C. 421.

There must be a high degree of relevance and a strong degree of probative force. There are two tests to determine how strong that probative force needs to be:

— Does the evidence point so strongly to guilt that only an ultra cautious jury, if thy accepted it as true, would acquit in the face of it?

— Is the evidence capable of tending to persuade a reasonable jury of the accused's guilt on some ground other than his bad character and disposition to commit the sort of crime with which he is charged.

In *R. v West* [1996] 2 Cr.App.R. 374, evidence was admitted in the murder trial that Rosemary West was an energetic and committed participator, together with her husband, in acts of sexual violence and that she had derived sexual gratification from such acts. It had sufficient probative force.

21–82   In *R. v Z* [2000] 2 A.C. 483 HL, it was held that, provided it was relevant, evidence which also proves guilt in prior acquittals is admissible so long as it is fair. Lord Hobhouse stated that an accused may be acquitted a number of times but after a time it becomes implausible and the case against him becomes overwhelming.

In order to understand a situation, background evidence may be allowed. In *R. v Sawoniuk* [2000] 2 Cr.App.R. 220, on charges of war crimes, the prosecutor was allowed to prove Nazi policy and the extent of the local police force's participation in that policy and that the defendant had participated in search and kill missions to mop up survivors of an earlier massacre.

See *Archbold Crown*, §§ 13–1—13–4.

XII. IDENTIFICATION EVIDENCE

A. General

21–83   Where the identity of the defendant is in issue the prosecution must call identification evidence. Code D of the Police Code of Practice issued under the *Police and Criminal Evidence Act* 1984 applies.

The House of Lords held in *R. v Forbes* [2001] 1 All E.R. 686 that in the case of a disputed identification, the police must hold an identification parade if the suspect consents unless one of the savings made by Code D applies or a parade would be futile because the witness makes it plain that he cannot identify the culprit or can only identify his clothing; or where the case is one of "pure recognition" of someone well known to the victim; or there exists "other exceptional circumstances". In *R. v H* [2003] EWCA Crim 174, a recognition case, the Court of Appeal held that Code D now requires an ID parade where a dispute as to identity might reasonably be expected.

When a witness has failed to make a positive identification in an identification parade the witness may still be called as a witness to describe the offender and what had occurred on the identification parade: *R. v George* [2003] Crim.L.R. 282.

In summary proceedings it is permissible for the prosecution to seek and rely upon a **21–84** dock identification of the defendant in circumstances where there has been no prior notification that identity is in issue. It is not a violation of the right to a fair trial for the court to expect, and in that sense require, an accused person to indicate prior to trial that identification is in issue: *Karia v DPP* (2002) 166 J.P. 753, QBD.

The *Att.-Gen.'s Reference (No. 2 of 2002)* [2003] 1 Cr.App.R. 21, CA, gave at least **21–85** four circumstances where the court can conclude that the defendant is shown on a photographic image from the scene of the crime:

1. where the photographic image was sufficiently clear it could be compared to the defendant in the dock
2. where the witness knew then defendant sufficiently well to recognise him as the offender depicted in the photograph image, he could give evidence of that
3. where a witness did not know the defendant but had spent a substantial time viewing and analysing the photographic images from the scene and had therefore acquired special knowledge, he could give evidence of identification based upon a comparison between those images and a reasonably contemporary photograph of the defendant, provided the images and the photograph were available to the jury
4. a suitably qualified expert with facial mapping skills could give opinion evidence of identification from a comparison between images from the scene, whether expertly enhanced or not, and a reasonably contemporary photograph of the defendant, provided both were available to the court.

When identity is in issue the court will follow the *Turnbull* guidelines: *R. v Turn-* **21–86** *bull* [1977] Q.B. 244; (1976) 63 Cr.App.R. 132.

1. whenever the case against an accused depends wholly or substantially on the accuracy of one or more identifications of the accused which the defence alleges to be mistaken, there is a special need for caution before convicting the accused on those identifications
2. the circumstances in which the identification by each witness came to be made should be examined closely. How long did the witness have the accused under observation? At what distance? In what light? Was the observation impeded in any way, for example, by passing traffic or a press of people? Had the witness ever seen the accused before? How often? If only occasionally, had he any special reason to remember? How long elapsed between the original observation and the subsequent identification to the police? Was there any material discrepancy between the description of the accused given to the police by the witness when first seen by him and the actual appearance of the defendant?
3. any special weaknesses in the identification evidence should be considered.

Recognition may be more reliable than identification of a stranger but even then **21–87** mistakes may be made by close friends and relatives.

All these matters relate to the quality of the evidence. Where the quality is poor, the court should find that there is no case to answer: *R. v Fergus (Ivan)* (1994) 98 Cr.App.R. 313, CA. Identification by more than one witness is a factor influencing the quality of the evidence but poor identification is not proved by mere repetition by different witnesses.

Fingerprints etc.

21–88   A person may be identified by fingerprints alone *R. v Castleton*, 3 Cr.App.R. 74, CCA. The prosecution must show that the fingerprints taken from the scene of the crime match those on the fingerprint form, and also identify the fingerprints on the form. Strict proof is required: *Chappell v DPP* (1989) 89 Cr.App.R. 82, DC. Guidance was given in *R. v Buckley* (1999) 163 J.P. 561.

Strict proof is also required for palm and ear prints. The weight to be attached to such evidence is a matter for the court: *R. v Dallagher* [2003] 1 Cr.App.R. 12, *The Times*, August 21, 2002, CA.

For voice identification see *R. v O'Doherty* [2002] Crim.L.R. 761.

DNA profiles

21–89   Where the perpetrator of a crime leaves a stain of blood or semen at the scene it may prove possible to extract sufficient sections of DNA to enable a comparison to be drawn with the same sections extracted for a sample of blood taken from the defendant. A DNA profile is not unique; it establishes probabilities. Specific guidance is found in *R. v Doheny* [1999] 1 Cr.App.R. 369.

See *Archbold Crown*, § 14–58.

B. OPINION

21–90   The general rule is that opinion evidence is excluded except as evidence of identity, feelings, physical condition, handwriting, impressions or expert evidence.

See *Archbold Crown*, § 10–64.

(a) Non-expert

21–91   Evidence of the opinion of a witness who is not an expert may be admissible if the impression received by the witness is too vague to be otherwise described or if made as a way of conveying relevant facts perceived by him or her. A witness may give evidence of his opinion of the age of a person: *R. v Cox* [1898] 1 Q.B. 179 (a "young woman"), *Wallworth v Balmer* [1966] 1 W.L.R. 16 ("a child of about five"); *R. v Davies* 46 Cr.App.R. 292; *R. v Neal* [1962] Crim.L.R. 698.

(b) Expert

21–92   Where a witness is qualified to express a credible opinion or belief on the subject then evidence of the witness's opinion is admissible: *R. v Silverlock* [1894] 2 Q.B. 766. It is for the court to determine a witness's competence. If the court can form its own conclusions from the facts without help, then the opinion of an expert is unnecessary: *R. v Turner* [1975] Q.B. 834; *R. v Loughran* [1999] Crim.L.R. 404, CA.

An expert is now permitted to give his opinion on what has been called the "ultimate issue" that is the very issue to be determined by the court, for example, on whether the defendant is suffering from diminished responsibility. The ultimate issue is however for the tribunal of fact to decide and the court is not bound to accept the expert's opinion: *R. v Stockwell* (1993) 97 Cr.App.R. 260, CA.

In *R. v Jeffries* [1997] Crim.L.R. 819 it was held that a police officer was able to give evidence as to the values and prices of drugs in order that the jury may interpret lists found at the defendant's premises but the officer could not express an opinion that the lists related to the sale of drugs because that would amount to a statement that the defendant was guilty of the offence charged.

21–93   Before the court can assess the value of an opinion it must know the facts upon which it is based. If the expert has been misinformed or has taken irrelevant facts into account, or has failed to consider relevant ones, the opinion is likely to be of little value. An expert witness should be asked to state the facts upon which the opinion is based: *R. v JP* [1999] Crim.L.R. 401, CA; *R. v Jackson* [1996] 2 Cr.App.R. 420, CA.

The witness need not have conducted any test or examination himself. The opinion may be given on the basis of facts proved in court: *R. v Mason*, 7 Cr.App.R. 67. The fact that a witness did not personally conduct a test or examination will go to the weight to be attached to the opinion.

Expert witnesses may refer not only to their own research, tests and experiments but also to works of authority, learned articles, research papers and other similar materials written by others and forming part of the general body of knowledge falling within their field of expertise: *Davie v Magistrates of Edinburgh*, 1953 SC34; *Seyfang v JD Searle & Co* [1973] Q.B. 148; *H v Schering Chemicals Ltd* [1983] 1 W.L.R. 143.

This principle does not however extent to purely anecdotal evidence. In *R. v Ed-*   **21–94** *wards* [2001] All E.R. (D) 271, [2001] EWCA Crim 2185 the question was whether ecstasy tablets found in the defendant's possession were for personal consumption or supply. The prosecution and defence sought to call persons neither of whom had formal medical or toxicological training to give evidence based on their experience rather than on statistical surveys or reports as to the personal consumption rates of ecstasy tablet users. It was held that the trial judge had properly excluded their evidence as inadmissible hearsay.

An expert witness should give reasons for his conclusions: *R. v Hipson* [1969] Crim.L.R. 85, CA.

Criminal Justice Act 1988, s.30

Expert reports

30.—(1) An expert report shall be admissible as evidence in criminal proceedings, whether or   **21–95** not the person making it attends to give oral evidence in those proceedings.

(2) If it is proposed that the person making the report shall not give oral evidence, the report shall only be admissible with the leave of the court.

(3) For the purpose of determining whether to give leave the court shall have regard—

(a) to the contents of the report;

(b) to the reasons why it is proposed that the person making the report shall not give oral evidence;

(c) to any risk, having regard in particular to whether it is likely to be possible to controvert statements in the report if the person making it does not attend to give oral evidence in the proceedings, that its admission or exclusion will result in unfairness to the accused or, if there is more than one, to any of them; and

(d) to any other circumstances that appear to the court to be relevant.

(4) An expert report, when admitted, shall be evidence of any fact or opinion of which the person making it could have given oral evidence.

(4A) Where the proceedings mentioned in subsection (1) above are proceedings before a magistrates' court inquiring into an offence as examining justices this section shall have effect with the omission of—

(a) in subsection (1) the words "whether or not the person making it attends to give oral evidence in those proceedings", and

(b) subsections (2) to (4).

(5) In this section "expert report" means a written report by a person dealing wholly or mainly with matters on which he is (or would if living be) qualified to give expert evidence.

[This section is reprinted as amended by the *Criminal Procedure and Investigations Act* 1996, s.47 and Sch.1, para.32.]

This section allows for the receipt of reports whether or not the expert gives oral evidence. Notice needs to be given of expert evidence.

(c) *Disclosure*

Magistrates' Courts (Advance Notice of Expert Evidence) Rules 1997, rr.3–5

3.—(1) Where a magistrates' court proceeds to summary trial in respect of an alleged offence   **21–96** and the person charged with that offence pleads not guilty in respect of it, if any party to the proceedings proposes to adduce expert evidence (whether of fact or opinion) in the proceedings (otherwise than in relation to sentence) he shall as soon as practicable after the person charged has so pleaded, unless in relation to the evidence in question he has already done so—

    (a) furnish the other party or parties with a statement in writing of any finding or opinion which he proposes to adduce by way of such evidence; and

    (b) where a request in writing is made to him in that behalf by any other party, provide that party also with a copy of (or if it appears to the party proposing to adduce the evidence to be more practicable, a reasonable opportunity to examine) the record of any observation, test, calculation or other procedure on which such finding or opinion is based and any document or other thing or substance in respect of which any such procedure has been carried out.

(2) A party may by notice in writing waive his right to be furnished with any of the matters mentioned in paragraph (1) above and, in particular, may agree that the statement mentioned in sub-paragraph (a) thereof may be furnished to him orally and not in writing.

(3) In paragraph (1) above, "document" means anything in which information of any description is recorded.

21–97   **4.**—(1) If a party has reasonable grounds for believing that the disclosure of any evidence in compliance with the requirements imposed by rule 3 above might lead to the intimidation, or attempted intimidation, of any person on whose evidence he intends to rely in the proceedings, or otherwise to the course of justice being interfered with, he shall not be obliged to comply with those requirements in relation to that evidence.

(2) Where, in accordance with paragraph (1) above, a party considers that he is not obliged to comply with the requirements imposed by rule 3 above with regard to any evidence in relation to any other party, he shall give notice in writing to that party to the effect that the evidence is being withheld and the grounds therefor.

5. A party who seeks to adduce expert evidence in any proceedings and who fails to comply with rule 3 above shall not adduce that evidence in those proceedings without the leave of the court.

21–98   It is the duty of an expert instructed by the prosecution to act in the interests of justice: *R. v Ward* (1993) 96 Cr.App.R. 1, CA. If an expert has carried out a test which casts doubt on his opinion, or if such a test has been carried out in his laboratory and is known to him, the expert is under a duty to disclose this to the solicitor instructing him, who in turn has a duty to disclose it to the defence.

C. CRIMINAL JUSTICE ACT 2003

21–99   The *Criminal Justice Act* 2003, when in force, makes provision for expert evidence.

Criminal Justice Act 2003, s.127

21–100   **127.**—(1) This section applies if—

    (a) a statement has been prepared for the purposes of criminal proceedings,

    (b) the person who prepared the statement had or may reasonably be supposed to have had personal knowledge of the matters stated,

    (c) notice is given under the appropriate rules that another person (the expert) will in evidence given in the proceedings orally or under section 9 of the *Criminal Justice Act* 1967 (c. 80) base an opinion or inference on the statement, and

    (d) the notice gives the name of the person who prepared the statement and the nature of the matters stated.

(2) In evidence given in the proceedings the expert may base an opinion or inference on the statement.

21–101   (3) If evidence based on the statement is given under subsection (2) the statement is to be treated as evidence of what it states.

(4) This section does not apply if the court, on an application by a party to the proceedings, orders that it is not in the interests of justice that it should apply.

(5) The matters to be considered by the court in deciding whether to make an order under subsection (4) include—

    (a) the expense of calling as a witness the person who prepared the statement;

    (b) whether relevant evidence could be given by that person which could not be given by the expert;

   (c)　whether that person can reasonably be expected to remember the matters stated well enough to give oral evidence of them.

   (6) Subsections (1) to (5) apply to a statement prepared for the purposes of a criminal investigation as they apply to a statement prepared for the purposes of criminal proceedings, and in such a case references to the proceedings are to criminal proceedings arising from the investigation.

   (7) The appropriate rules are rules made—

   (a)　under section 81 of the *Police and Criminal Evidence Act* 1984 (advance notice of expert evidence in Crown Court), or

   (b)　under section 144 of the *Magistrates' Courts Act* 1980 by virtue of section 20(3) of the *Criminal Procedure and Investigations Act* 1996 (advance notice of expert evidence in magistrates' courts).

XIII. CHARACTER

The general rule is that evidence of disposition or character, whether of parties or **21–102** witnesses, is inadmissible. See *Archbold Crown*, §§ 8–166—8–246.

There are exceptions, however:

— similar facts, §§ 21–81—21–82, below.

— statutory exceptions: s.27(3) of the *Theft Act* 1968; s.1(2) of the *Official Secrets Act* 1911; s.1(1) of the *Street Offences Act* 1959. In the latter case, *e.g.*, a person's character is admissible in evidence to prove the fact of being a "common prostitute".

— where the defendant's character has been put in issue by his giving evidence of good character, calling character witnesses or cross-examining prosecution witnesses.

   A defendant is not entitled to put part of his character in only: *R. v Wingfield*, 27 Cr.App.R. 139, CCA. Once his character goes in he is open to enquiry to disprove his good character. In *R. v Nye*, 75 Cr.App.R. 247, it was said that it is in the court's discretion whether a person with spent convictions can hold himself out as being of good character. In any event the court must not be told that he has no previous convictions. Where imputations have been made on the character of a prosecution witness, a defendant may be questioned on his character. If he does not give evidence, however, the prosecution is not entitled to give evidence in chief of the defendant's character: s.1(3)(ii) *Criminal Evidence Act* 1898; *R. v Butterwasser* [1948] 1 K.B. 4; *Selvey v DPP* [1970] A.C. 304.

— if previous convictions are logically probative of the crime charged: *Att.-Gen. of Hong Kong v Siu Yuk-shing* [1989] 1 W.L.R. 236, PC.

— as a result of cross-examination as to credit, see § 20–104 below.

The *Criminal Justice Act* 2003, when in force, will make statutory provision with **21–103** regard to evidence of character. Reasons for rulings will have to be entered in the court register: s.110.

Criminal Justice Act 2003, ss.100–106, 108

Non-defendant's bad character

   100.—(1) In criminal proceedings evidence of the bad character of a person other than the **21–104** defendant is admissible if and only if—

   (a)　it is important explanatory evidence,

   (b)　it has substantial probative value in relation to a matter which—

      (i)　is a matter in issue in the proceedings, and

      (ii)　is of substantial importance in the context of the case as a whole, or

   (c)　all parties to the proceedings agree to the evidence being admissible.

   (2) For the purposes of subsection (1)(a) evidence is important explanatory evidence if—

    (a) without it, the court or jury would find it impossible or difficult properly to understand other evidence in the case, and

    (b) its value for understanding the case as a whole is substantial.

(3) In assessing the probative value of evidence for the purposes of subsection (1)(b) the court must have regard to the following factors (and to any others it considers relevant)—

    (a) the nature and number of the events, or other things, to which the evidence relates;

    (b) when those events or things are alleged to have happened or existed;

    (c) where—

        (i) the evidence is evidence of a person's misconduct, and

        (ii) it is suggested that the evidence has probative value by reason of similarity between that misconduct and other alleged misconduct,

    the nature and extent of the similarities and the dissimilarities between each of the alleged instances of misconduct;

    (d) where—

        (i) the evidence is evidence of a person's misconduct,

        (ii) it is suggested that that person is also responsible for the misconduct charged, and

        (iii) the identity of the person responsible for the misconduct charged is disputed,

    the extent to which the evidence shows or tends to show that the same person was responsible each time.

(4) Except where subsection (1)(c) applies, evidence of the bad character of a person other than the defendant must not be given without leave of the court.

This ensures that, unless both parties agree, the leave of the court is sought before a witness is examined on his bad character. It sets out clear limitations on the introduction of such evidence.

Defendant's bad character

21–105   **101.**—(1) In criminal proceedings evidence of the defendant's bad character is admissible if, but only if—

    (a) all parties to the proceedings agree to the evidence being admissible,

    (b) the evidence is adduced by the defendant himself or is given in answer to a question asked by him in cross-examination and intended to elicit it,

    (c) it is important explanatory evidence,

    (d) it is relevant to an important matter in issue between the defendant and the prosecution,

    (e) it has substantial probative value in relation to an important matter in issue between the defendant and a co-defendant,

    (f) it is evidence to correct a false impression given by the defendant, or

    (g) the defendant has made an attack on another person's character.

(2) Sections 102 to 106 contain provision supplementing subsection (1).

(3) The court must not admit evidence under subsection (1)(d) or (g) if, on an application by the defendant to exclude it, it appears to the court that the admission of the evidence wouldhave such an adverse effect on the fairness of the proceedings that the court ought not to admit it.

(4) On an application to exclude evidence under subsection (3) the court must have regard, in particular, to the length of time between the matters to which that evidence relates and the matters which form the subject of the offence charged.

Important explanatory evidence

21–106   **102.** For the purposes of section 101(1)(c) evidence is important explanatory evidence if—

    (a) without it, the court or jury would find it impossible or difficult properly to understand other evidence in the case, and

    (b) its value for understanding the case as a whole is substantial.

Matter in issue between the defendant and the prosecution

21–107   **103.**—(1) For the purposes of section 101(1)(d) the matters in issue between the defendant and the prosecution include—

(a) the question whether the defendant has a propensity to commit offences of the kind with which he is charged, except where his having such a propensity makes it no more likely that he is guilty of the offence;

(b) the question whether the defendant has a propensity to be untruthful, except where it is not suggested that the defendant's case is untruthful in any respect.

(2) Where subsection (1)(a) applies, a defendant's propensity to commit offences of the kind with which he is charged may (without prejudice to any other way of doing so) be established by evidence that he has been convicted of—

(a) an offence of the same description as the one with which he is charged, or

(b) an offence of the same category as the one with which he is charged.

(3) Subsection (2) does not apply in the case of a particular defendant if the court is satisfied, by reason of the length of time since the conviction or for any other reason, that it would be unjust for it to apply in his case.

(4) For the purposes of subsection (2)—

(a) two offences are of the same description as each other if the statement of the offence in a written charge or indictment would, in each case, be in the same terms;

(b) two offences are of the same category as each other if they belong to the same category of offences prescribed for the purposes of this section by an order made by the Secretary of State.

(5) A category prescribed by an order under subsection (4)(b) must consist of offences of the same type.

(6) Only prosecution evidence is admissible under section 101(1)(d).

Matter in issue between the defendant and a co-defendant

104.—(1) Evidence which is relevant to the question whether the defendant has a propensity **21–108** to be untruthful is admissible on that basis under section 101(1)(e) only if the nature or conduct of his defence is such as to undermine the co-defendant's defence.

(2) Only evidence—

(a) which is to be (or has been) adduced by the co-defendant, or

(b) which a witness is to be invited to give (or has given) in cross-examination by the co-defendant,

is admissible under section 101(1)(e).

Evidence to correct a false impression

105.—(1) For the purposes of section 101(1)(f)— **21–109**

(a) the defendant gives a false impression if he is responsible for the making of an express or implied assertion which is apt to give the court or jury a false or misleading impression about the defendant;

(b) evidence to correct such an impression is evidence which has probative value in correcting it.

(2) A defendant is treated as being responsible for the making of an assertion if—

(a) the assertion is made by the defendant in the proceedings (whether or not in evidence given by him),

(b) the assertion was made by the defendant—

(i) on being questioned under caution, before charge, about the offence with which he is charged, or

(ii) on being charged with the offence or officially informed that he might be prosecuted for it,

and evidence of the assertion is given in the proceedings,

(c) the assertion is made by a witness called by the defendant,

(d) the assertion is made by any witness in cross-examination in response to a question asked by the defendant that is intended to elicit it, or is likely to do so, or

(e) the assertion was made by any person out of court, and the defendant adduces evidence of it in the proceedings.

(3) A defendant who would otherwise be treated as responsible for the making of an as- **20–110** sertion shall not be so treated if, or to the extent that, he withdraws it or disassociates himself from it.

(4) Where it appears to the court that a defendant, by means of his conduct (other than

the giving of evidence) in the proceedings, is seeking to give the court or jury an impression about himself that is false or misleading, the court may if it appears just to do so treat the defendant as being responsible for the making of an assertion which is apt to give that impression.

(5) In subsection (4) "conduct" includes appearance or dress.

(6) Evidence is admissible under section 101(1)(f) only if it goes no further than is necessary to correct the false impression.

(7) Only prosecution evidence is admissible under section 101(1)(f).

Attack on another person's character

21–111   **106.**—(1) For the purposes of section 101(1)(g) a defendant makes an attack on another person's character if—

    (a) he adduces evidence attacking the other person's character,

    (b) he (or any legal representative appointed under section 38(4) of the *Youth Justice and Criminal Evidence Act* 1999 to cross-examine a witness in his interests) asks questions in cross-examination that are intended to elicit such evidence, or are likely to do so, or

    (c) evidence is given of an imputation about the other person made by the defendant—

        (i) on being questioned under caution, before charge, about the offence with which he is charged, or

        (ii) on being charged with the offence or officially informed that he might be prosecuted for it.

(2) In subsection (1) "evidence attacking the other person's character" means evidence to the effect that the other person—

    (a) has committed an offence (whether a different offence from the one with which the defendant is charged or the same one), or

    (b) has behaved, or is disposed to behave, in a reprehensible way;

and "imputation about the other person" means an assertion to that effect.

(3) Only prosecution evidence is admissible under section 101(1)(g).

Offences committed by defendant when a child

21–112   **108.**—(1) Section 16(2) and (3) of the *Children and Young Persons Act* 1963 (offences committed by person under 14 disregarded for purposes of evidence relating to previous convictions) shall cease to have effect.

(2) In proceedings for an offence committed or alleged to have been committed by the defendant when aged 21 or over, evidence of his conviction for an offence when under the age of 14 is not admissible unless—

    (a) both of the offences are triable only on indictment, and

    (b) the court is satisfied that the interests of justice require the evidence to be admissible.

(3) Subsection (2) applies in addition to section 101.

The provisions apply both to propensity or similar fact evidence and to the attacking of a prosecution witness so as to put his own character in issue.

XIV. UNFAIRLY OR ILLEGALLY OBTAINED EVIDENCE

21–113   See also *Archbold Crown*, § 15–452.

A. Unfair Evidence

Police and Criminal Evidence Act 1984, s.78

Exclusion of unfair evidence

21–114   **78.**—(1) In any proceedings the court may refuse to allow evidence on which the prosecution proposes to rely to be given if it appears to the court that, having regard to all the circumstances, including the circumstances in which the evidence was obtained, the admission of the evidence would have such an adverse effect on the fairness of the proceedings that the court ought not to admit it.

(2) Nothing in this section shall prejudice any rule of law requiring a court to exclude evidence.

(3) This section shall not apply in the case of proceedings before a magistrates' court inquiring into an offences as examining justices.

Where an application is made under s.78, a magistrates' court has a discretion either **21-115** to deal with the application by way of a *voire dire* when it arises or to leave the decision until the end of the hearing when all the evidence has been heard. The aim should always be to secure a trial which is fair to both sides: *Vel v Owen* [1987] Crim.L.R. 496, DC. In *Halawa v Federation Against Copyright Theft* [1995] 1 Cr.App.R. 21, DC, the court said:

— A proper understanding of what is fair will lead in some cases to the conclusion that, if the defendant wishes to proceed by way of a *voire dire*, he or she should be allowed to do so because, unless there is good reason to take a different course, he or she should have the opportunity to secure the exclusion of unfair evidence before he or she decides whether to give evidence. If he or she is unfairly denied that opportunity, the right to silence is impaired.

— If the application is made as alternative to a submission under section 76 of the 1984 Act, it should be examined at the same time in accordance with the procedure set out in *R. v Liverpool Juvenile Court Ex p. R* [1988] Q.B. 1.

— If the point is raised only under section 78 in most cases the better course will be for the whole of the prosecution case to be heard, including the disputed evidence, before any *voire dire* is held.

— In order to decide which course to take, the court may ask the defence the extent of the issues to be address by the defendant's evidence on the *voire dire*. If the issues are limited to the circumstances in which the evidence was obtained, there would in most cases be no apparent reason why the defendant should be heard as on a *voire dire*. If however the defendant intends to contradict some part of the prosecution's account of "all the circumstances" it would be open to the court to conclude that the proceedings on the *voire dire* might be protracted and would introduce issues which would have to be re-examined in the remaining stages of the trial if a *prima facie* case is held to be established, in which case the securing of a fair trial to both sides would not require a *voire dire*. For this purpose the court would be entitled to take account of the nature and extent of the cross-examination of the prosecution witnesses for an understanding of the extent of any dispute as to "all the circumstances".

In extradition proceedings, where the judge is concerned with the fairness of admit- **21-116** ting evidence, he must have regard to the extradition context in which the issue arises; his decision is in, and solely for the purpose of, his determination on the issue of extradition and he should only exclude evidence where to admit it would outrage civilised values: *R. v Bow Street Magistrates' Court Ex p. Proulx* [2001] 1 All E.R. 57; *R. v Saifi* [2001] 4 All E.R. 168. The concept of the burden of proof has no part to play in the exercise of the discretion.

Exclusion is not automatic where there has been a breach of the Act or the Codes of practice *R. v Walsh* (1989) 91 Cr.App.R. 161. Case law has suggested that the breach should be significant and substantial before discretion is exercised: *R. v Absalom* 88 Cr.App.R. 332. In *R. v Stewart* [1995] Crim.L.R. 500, CA it was pointed out that it was the nature and not the number of breaches that was the important factor.

There is no requirement of bad faith on the part of police officers before evidence is excluded although case law in breath test cases suggests that evidence will not be excluded unless there is bad faith: *Matto v Wolverhampton Crown Court* [1987] R.T.R. 337, DC; *Fox v Chief Constable of Gwent* [1986] A.C. 281, HL. In other cases bad faith means that evidence is usually excluded: *R. v Alladice* 87 Cr.App.R. 380, CA. Good faith, on the other hand, will not excuse serious breaches: *R v Samuel* [1988] Q.B. 615.

In entrapment cases, proceedings may be stayed or evidence may be excluded under s.78: *R. v Loosely* [2001] 1 W.L.R. 2060. The issue is whether the proceedings as a whole are fair: *Khan v United Kingdom* (2001) 31 E.H.R.R. 1066; *Allan v United Kingdom* (2002) 36 E.H.R.R. 143.

B. Admissions

21–117 An admission made in the course of judicial proceedings, whether at an earlier stage of proceedings for the same offence or in separate proceedings will come within the definition of "confession" in s.82(1) of the *Police and Criminal Evidence Act* 1984. An admission made during the course of a trial is admissible in the event of a retrial: *R. v McGregor* [1968] 1 Q.B. 372.

Admissions by a person in a former trial or enquiry are excluded by certain statutes, for example, the *Explosive Substances Act* 1883, s.6(2)

C. Confessions

Police and Criminal Evidence Act 1984, s.76

Confessions

21–118   76.—(1) In any proceedings a confession made by an accused person may be given in evidence against him in so far as it is relevant to any matter in issue in the proceedings and is not excluded by the court in pursuance of this section.

(2) If, in any proceedings where the prosecution proposes to give in evidence a confession made by an accused person, it is represented to the court that the confession was or may have been obtained—

    (a) by oppression of the person who made it; or

    (b) in consequence of anything said or done which was likely, in the circumstances existing at the time, to render unreliable any confession which might be made by him in consequence thereof.

the court shall not allow the confession to be given in evidence against him except in so far as the prosecution proves to the court beyond reasonable doubt that the confession (notwithstanding that it may be true) was not obtained as aforesaid.

(3) In any proceedings where the prosecution proposes to give in evidence a confession made by an accused person, the court may of its own motion require the prosecution, as a condition of allowing it to do so, to prove that the confession was not obtained as mentioned in subsection (2) above.

(4) The fact that a confession is wholly or partly excluded in pursuance of this section shall not affect the admissibility in evidence—

    (a) of any facts discovered as a result of the confession; or

    (b) where the confession is relevant as showing that the accused speaks, writes or expresses himself in a particular way, of so much of the confession as is necessary to show that he does so.

(5) Evidence that a fact to which this subsection applies was discovered as a result of a statement made by an accused person shall not be admissible unless evidence of how it was discovered is given by him or on his behalf.

(6) Subsection (5) above applies—

    (a) to any fact discovered as a result of a confession which is wholly excluded in pursuance of this section; and

    (b) to any fact discovered as a result of a confession which is partly so excluded, if the fact is discovered as a result of the excluded part of the confession.

(7) Nothing in Part VII of this Act shall prejudice the admissibility of a confession made by an accused person.

(8) In this section "oppression" includes torture, inhuman or degrading treatment, and the use or threat of violence (whether or not amounting to torture).

(9) Where the proceedings mentioned in subsection (1) above are proceedings before a magistrates' court inquiring into an offence as examining justices this section shall have effect with the omission of—

    (a) in subsection (1) the words "and is not excluded by the court in pursuance of this section", and

(b) subsections (2) to (6) and (8).

Where an objection to evidence is based on s.76, the court shall not admit the confes- **21–119**
sion unless it is satisfied that it was not obtained by oppression or by words or conduct
likely to render it unreliable: *Police and Criminal Evidence Act* 1984, s.76(2). The
court must determine the question as soon as it is raised and, if it is necessary to hear
evidence, to do so upon a *voire dire*: *R. v Liverpool Juvenile Court Ex p. R* [1988]
Q.B. 1. In *R. v Fulling* [1987] Q.B. 426 it was held that "oppression" was to be given
its ordinary dictionary meaning. In making a judgement about what is oppressive or
likely to make a confession unreliable, the court may have regard to the character and
experience of the suspect: *R. v Seelig*, 94 Cr.App.R.17, CA.

Hostile and aggressive questioning which puts pressure on a defendant will not necessarily render the confession unreliable. The length of the interviews and the nature of
the questioning are the important considerations: *R. v L* [1994] Crim.L.R. 839, CA.

Police and Criminal Evidence Act 1984, s.77

Confessions by mentally handicapped persons
   77.—(1) Without prejudice to the general duty of the court at a trial on indictment to direct   **21–120**
the jury on any matter on which it appears to the court appropriate to do so, where at such a
trial—
   (a) the case against the accused depends wholly or substantially on a confession by
       him; and
   (b) the court is satisfied—
       (i) that he is mentally handicapped; and
       (ii) that the confession was not made in the presence of an independent
            person,
       the court shall warn the jury that there is special need for caution before convicting
       the accused in reliance on the confession, and shall explain that the need arises because
       of the circumstances mentioned in paragraphs (a) and (b) above.
   (2) In any case where at the summary trial of a person for an offence it appears to the
court that a warning under subsection (1) above would be required if the trial were on
indictment, the court shall treat the case as one in which there is a special need for caution
before convicting the accused on his confession.
   (3) In this section—
       "independent person" does not include a police officer or a person employed for, or
           engaged on, police purposes;
       "mentally handicapped", in relation to a person, means that he is in a state of ar-
           rested or incomplete development of mind which includes significant impairment
           of intelligence and social functioning; and
       "police purposes" has the meaning assigned to it by section 101(2) of the *Police Act*
           1996.

[This section is reprinted as amended by the *Summary Appeal Court (Navy) Rules*
2000, Sch.3(III), para.18(d).]

Section 128 of the *Criminal Justice Act* 2003, when in force, makes statutory provision for confessions to be given in evidence for a co-accused.

Criminal Justice Act 2003, s.128

   128.—(1) In the *Police and Criminal Evidence Act* 1984 (c. 60) the following section is   **21–121**
inserted after section 76—

Confessions may be given in evidence for co-accused
   "**76A**—(1) In any proceedings a confession made by an accused person may be given in
evidence for another person charged in the same proceedings (a co-accused) in so far as it is
relevant to any matter in issue in the proceedings and is not excluded by the court in pursuance of this section.
   (2) If, in any proceedings where a co-accused proposes to give in evidence a confession

made by an accused person, it is represented to the court that the confession was or may have been obtained—

    (a) by oppression of the person who made it; or

    (b) in consequence of anything said or done which was likely, in the circumstances existing at the time, to render unreliable any confession which might be made by him in consequence thereof,

the court shall not allow the confession to be given in evidence for the co-accused except in so far as it is proved to the court on the balance of probabilities that the confession (notwithstanding that it may be true) was not so obtained.

21–122   (3) Before allowing a confession made by an accused person to be given in evidence for a co-accused in any proceedings, the court may of its own motion require the fact that the confession was not obtained as mentioned in subsection (2) above to be proved in the proceedings on the balance of probabilities.

(4) The fact that a confession is wholly or partly excluded in pursuance of this section shall not affect the admissibility in evidence—

    (a) of any facts discovered as a result of the confession; or

    (b) where the confession is relevant as showing that the accused speaks, writes or expresses himself in a particular way, of so much of the confession as is necessary to show that he does so.

(5) Evidence that a fact to which this subsection applies was discovered as a result of a statement made by an accused person shall not be admissible unless evidence of how it was discovered is given by him or on his behalf.

(6) Subsection (5) above applies—

    (a) to any fact discovered as a result of a confession which is wholly excluded in pursuance of this section; and

    (b) to any fact discovered as a result of a confession which is partly so excluded, if the fact is discovered as a result of the excluded part of the confession.

(7) In this section "oppression" includes torture, inhuman or degrading treatment, and the use or threat of violence (whether or not amounting to torture)."

(2) Subject to subsection (1), nothing in this Chapter makes a confession by a defendant admissible if it would not be admissible under section 76 of the *Police and Criminal Evidence Act* 1984 (c. 60).

(3) In subsection (2) "confession" has the meaning given by section 82 of that Act.

XV. ADVERSE INFERENCES

21–123   At common law a statement made in the presence of the defendant, which accuses him of having committed a crime, upon an occasion which may be expected reasonably to call for some explanation or denial, is not evidence against him of the facts stated, save except in so far as he accepts the statement so as to make it in effect his own. Statute has, however, created restrictions.

See also *Archbold Crown*, §§ 15–316 *et seq.*

Criminal Justice and Public Order Act 1994, ss.34–37

Effect of accused's failure to mention facts when questioned or charged.

21–124   **34.**—(1) Where, in any proceedings against a person for an offence, evidence is given that the accused—

    (a) at any time before he was charged with the offence, on being questioned under caution by a constable trying to discover whether or by whom the offence had been committed, failed to mention any fact relied on in his defence in those proceedings; or

    (b) on being charged with the offence or officially informed that he might be prosecuted for it, failed to mention any such fact,

being a fact which in the circumstances existing at the time the accused could reasonably have been expected to mention when so questioned, charged or informed, as the case may be, subsection (2) below applies.

(2) Where this subsection applies—

    (a) a magistrates' court inquiring into the offence as examining justices;

(b) a judge, in deciding whether to grant an application made by the accused under—

  (i) section 6 of the *Criminal Justice Act* 1987 (application for dismissal of charge of serious fraud in respect of which notice of transfer has been given under section 4 of that Act; or

  (ii) paragraph 5 of Schedule 6 to the *Criminal Justice Act* 1991 (application for dismissal of charge of violent or sexual offence involving child in respect of which notice of transfer has been given under section 53 of that Act);

(c) the court, in determining whether there is a case to answer; and

(d) the court or jury, in determining whether the accused is guilty of the offence charged,

may draw such inferences from the failure as appear proper.

21–125 (2A) Where the accused was at an authorised place of detention at the time of the failure, subsections (1) and (2) above do not apply if he had not been allowed an opportunity to consult a solicitor prior to being questioned, charged or informed as mentioned in subsection (1) above.

(3) Subject to any directions by the court, evidence tending to establish the failure may be given before or after evidence tending to establish the fact which the accused is alleged to have failed to mention.

(4) This section applies in relation to questioning by persons (other than constables) charged with the duty of investigating offences or charging offenders as it applies in relation to questioning by constables; and in subsection (1) above "officially informed" means informed by a constable or any such person.

(5) This section does not—

(a) prejudice the admissibility in evidence of the silence or other reaction of the accused in the face of anything said in his presence relating to the conduct in respect of which he is charged, in so far as evidence thereof would be admissible apart from this section; or

(b) preclude the drawing of any inference from any such silence or other reaction of the accused which could properly be drawn apart from this section.

(6) This section does not apply in relation to a failure to mention a fact if the failure occurred before the commencement of this section.

[This section is reprinted as amended by the *Youth Justice and Criminal Evidence Act* 1999, s.58(2). Subsection 2A is not yet in force]

21–126 The European Court has confirmed that the right to silence is not an absolute right but is at the heart of the notion of a fair trial. Caution must therefore be exercised before drawing adverse inferences.

In *Averill v UK* (2001) 31 E.H.R.R. 839 it was said that the extent to which adverse inferences may be drawn in this context should be limited.

21–127 In *R. v Argent* [1997] 2 Cr.App.R. 27 Lord Bingham defined the six conditions which had to be met before adverse inferences could be drawn:

— Proceedings for an offence must be in existence

— Failure to answer must have occurred before charge

— Failure to answer must have occurred during questioning under caution by a police officer or relevant person

— The questioning was intended to discover whether or by whom the offence was committed

— The failure had to be with regard to the mention of a fact which was then relied upon in the proceedings

— The fact concerned and the one which the defendant had failed to mention must have been one which he could reasonably have been expected to mention at the time of questioning, given the circumstances of the interview.

21–128 In *Condron and Condron* [1997] 1 Cr.App.R. 185 it was said that legal advice to remain silence cannot of itself prevent an adverse inference being drawn. The defendant and his solicitor may have to state the basis or the reason for the advice given. There may be good reason for such advice. In *R. v Roble* [1997] Crim.L.R. 449, CA it was suggested that good reasons might be that the interviewing officer had not disclosed the nature of the case or the offence or the evidence was so complex or old that an immediate response cannot be given. See also *R. v Beard* [2002] Crim.L.R. 684, CA. In *Howell* [2003] EWCA Crim. 1169 it was also said that the kind of circumstances which may most likely justify silence are ill health, in particular mental disability, confusion, shock, intoxication, inability to recollect events without documents to hand or speaking to others. There must always be soundly based reasons for silence.

The court may draw inferences upon a submission of no case to answer: s.34(2)(c) but s.38(3) states that a case to answer shall not be based solely on an adverse inference. In *R. v Hart and McLean* [1998] 6 *Archbold News* 1 it was said that this could apply where the defence is putting a positive case which might include documentation.

21-129   In *R. v Webber* [2004] 1 Cr.App.R. 40 it was held that a positive suggestion put to a witness by or on behalf of a defendant might amount to a fact relied on in his defence even if that suggestion was not adopted by the witness. The word "fact" should be given a wide meaning. It covered any fact in issue and which was put forward as part of the defence case. A defendant relied on a fact not only when he have or adduced evidence of it but also when his advocate put a specific and positive case to prosecution witnesses.

In *Brizzalari* [2004] EWCA Crim 310, the Court of Appeal discouraged prosecutors from too readily seeking to activate the provisions under s.34 unless the merits of the individual case required that that should be done.

Effect of accused's silence at trial

21-130   **35.**—(1) At the trial of any person for an offence, subsections (2) and (3) below apply unless—

     (a) the accused's guilt is not in issue; or

     (b) it appears to the court that the physical or mental condition of the accused makes it undesirable for him to give evidence;

but subsection (2) below does not apply if, at the conclusion of the evidence for the prosecution, his legal representative informs the court that the accused will give evidence or, where he is unrepresented, the court ascertains from him that he will give evidence.

     (2) Where this subsection applies, the court shall, at the conclusion of the evidence for the prosecution, satisfy itself (in the case of proceedings on indictment, in the presence of the jury) that the accused is aware that the stage has been reached at which evidence can be given for the defence and that he can, if he wishes, give evidence and that, if he chooses not to give evidence, or having been sworn, without good cause refuses to answer any question, it will be permissible for the court or jury to draw such inferences as appear proper from his failure to give evidence or his refusal, without good cause, to answer any question.

     (3) Where this subsection applies, the court or jury, in determining whether the accused is guilty of the offence charged, may draw such inferences as appear proper from the failure of the accused to give evidence or his refusal, without good cause, to answer any question.

     (4) This section does not render the accused compellable to give evidence on his own behalf, and he shall accordingly not be guilty of contempt of court by reason of a failure to do so.

     (5) For the purposes of this section a person who, having been sworn, refuses to answer any question shall be taken to do so without good cause unless—

         (a) he is entitled to refuse to answer the question by virtue of any enactment, whenever passed or made, or on the ground of privilege; or

         (b) the court in the exercise of its general discretion excuses him from answering it.

[repealed]

     (7) This section applies—

         (a) in relation to proceedings on indictment for an offence, only if the person charged with the offence is arraigned on or after the commencement of this section;

         (b) in relation to proceedings in a magistrates' court, only if the time when the court begins to receive evidence in the proceedings falls after the commencement of this section.

[This section is reprinted as amended by the *Crime and Disorder Act* 1998, Sch.10, para.1.]

The legal adviser will ensure that the defendant is aware of this provision: *Practice* **21–131**
Direction (Criminal Proceedings: Consolidation) [2002] 1 W.L.R. 2870, para.IV.44
above. Section 38(3) of the Act prohibits a conviction on an inference alone. In *Murray*
v UK (1996) 22 E.H.R.R. 29, it was said that it would be incompatible with the rights of
the defendant to base a conviction solely or mainly on his silence or on a refusal to
answer questions or give evidence himself. A defendant does not need to give evidence
where the prosecution case is weak. The principle in *Murray* was confirmed in *Beccles*
v UK [2002] 36 E.H.R.R. 162; see also *R. v Milford* [2001] Crim.L.R. 330; *R. v Che-*
nia [2003] 2 Cr.App.R. 6.

Effect of accused's failure or refusal to account for objects, substances or marks
    36.—(1) Where—   **21–132**
      (a) a person is arrested by a constable, and there is—
         (i) on his person; or
        (ii) in or on his clothing or footwear; or
        (iii) otherwise in his possession; or
        (iv) in any place in which he is at the time of his arrest,
      any object, substance or mark, or there is any mark on any such object; and
      (b) that or another constable investigating the case reasonably believes that the pres-
        ence of the object, substance or mark may be attributable to the participation of
        the person arrested in the commission of an offence specified by the constable;
        and
      (c) the constable informs the person arrested that he so believes, and requests him to
        account for the presence of the object, substance or mark; and
      (d) the person fails or refuses to do so,
then if, in any proceedings against the person for the offence so specified, evidence of those matters is given, subsection (2) below applies.
    (2) Where this subsection applies—
      (a) a magistrates' court inquiring into the offence as examining justices;
      (b) a judge, in deciding whether to grant an application made by the accused
        under—
        (i) section 6 of the *Criminal Justice Act* 1987 (application for dismissal of charge
         of serious fraud in respect of which notice of transfer has been given under sec-
         tion 4 of that Act); or
        (ii) paragraph 5 of Schedule 6 to the *Criminal Justice Act* 1991 (application for
         dismissal of charge of violent or sexual offence involving child in respect of
         which notice of transfer has been given under section 53 of that Act);
      (c) the court, in determining whether there is a case to answer; and
      (d) the court or jury, in determining whether the accused is guilty of the offence
        charged,
may draw such inferences from the failure or refusal as appear proper.
    (3) Subsections (1) and (2) above apply to the condition of clothing or footwear as they
apply to a substance or mark thereon.
    (4) Subsections (1) and (2) above do not apply unless the accused was told in ordinary
language by the constable when making the request mentioned in subsection (1)(c) above
what the effect of this section would be if he failed or refused to comply with the request.
    (4A) Where the accused was at an authorised place of detention at the time of the fail-
ure or refusal, subsections (1) and (2) above do not apply if he had not been allowed an
opportunity to consult a solicitor prior to the request being made.
    (5) This section applies in relation to officers of customs and excise as it applies in rela-
tion to constables.
    (6) This section does not preclude the drawing of any inference from a failure or refusal
of the accused to account for the presence of an object, substance or mark or from the
condition of clothing or footwear which could properly be drawn apart from this section.
    (7) This section does not apply in relation to a failure or refusal which occurred before
the commencement of this section.

[This section is reprinted as amended by the *Youth Justice and Criminal Evidence*
Act 1999, s.58(3). Subsection 4A is not yet in force.]

Effect of accused's failure or refusal to account for presence at a particular place

21–133   **37.**—(1) Where—

    (a) a person arrested by a constable was found by him at a place at or about the time the offence for which he was arrested is alleged to have been committed; and

    (b) that or another constable investigating the offence reasonably believes that the presence of the person at that place and at that time may be attributable to his participation in the commission of the offence; and

    (c) the constable informs the person that he so believes, and requests him to account for that presence; and

    (d) the person fails or refuses to do so,

then if, in any proceedings against the person for the offence, evidence of those matters is given, subsection (2) below applies.

    (2) Where this subsection applies—

    (a) a magistrates' court inquiring into the offence as examining justices;.

    (b) a judge, in deciding whether to grant an application made by the accused under—

        (i) section 6 of the *Criminal Justice Act* 1987 (application for dismissal of charge of serious fraud in respect of which notice of transfer has been given under section 4 of that Act); or

        (ii) paragraph 5 of Schedule 6 to the *Criminal Justice Act* 1991 (application for dismissal of charge of violent or sexual offence involving child in respect of which notice of transfer has been given under section 53 of that Act);

    (c) the court, in determining whether there is a case to answer; and

    (d) the court or jury, in determining whether the accused is guilty of the offence charged,

may draw such inferences from the failure or refusal as appear proper.

    (3) Subsections (1) and (2) do not apply unless the accused was told in ordinary language by the constable when making the request mentioned in subsection (1)(c) above what the effect of this section would be if he failed or refused to comply with the request.

    (3A) Where the accused was at an authorised place of detention at the time of the failure or refusal, subsections (1) and (2) do not apply if he had not been allowed an opportunity to consult a solicitor prior to the request being made.

    (4) This section applies in relation to officers of customs and excise as it applies in relation to constables.

    (5) This section does not preclude the drawing of any inference from a failure or refusal of the accused to account for his presence at a place which could properly be drawn apart from this section.

    (6) This section does not apply in relation to a failure or refusal which occurred before the commencement of this section.

[This section is reprinted as amended by the *Youth Justice and Criminal Evidence Act* 1999, s.58(4). Subsection 4A is not yet in force.]

21–134   The above two sections are concerned with failures to provide explanations when asked to do so after arrest. A court must be satisfied that a defendant has failed to account for the relevant matter before drawing proper inferences: *R. v Compton* [2002] All E.R. 149.

XVI. PRIVILEGE

A. GENERAL

21–135   A witness may refuse to produce documentary evidence or give oral testimony on the ground that the information sought is privileged. In respect of documents he is protected from giving oral evidence as to their content, or his knowledge or belief founded thereupon. Privilege prevents the production of evidence. It is not concerned with its admissibility, which depends upon its relevance: *R. v Governor of Pentonville Prison Ex p. Osman* (1990) 90 Cr.App.R. 281, DC.

See *Archbold Crown*, § 12–22.

B. LEGAL PROFESSIONAL PRIVILEGE

The right to consult legal advisers without fear of the communication's being re- **21-136**
vealed is a fundamental condition on which the administration of justice rests: *R. v
Derby Magistrates' Court Ex p. B* [1996] A.C. 487, HL.

This privilege covers confidential written or oral communications made between a
professional legal adviser and his client or any person representing the client in connection with the giving of legal advice to the client and in connection with or contemplation
of litigation: *Greenough v Gaskell* (1833) 1 M & K 98. The second limb, know as litigation privilege, includes communications between the professional adviser, the client and
any other person.

The privilege is strictly confined to counsel and solicitors, their clerks, agents and
interpreters between them and their clients: *R. v Thames Magistrates' Courts Ex p.
Bozkurt* [2002] R.T.R. 15, DC.

In *R. (Howe) v South Durham Magistrates' Court, The Times*, February 26, 2004, **21-137**
CA, it was held that it is not a breach of legal professional privilege for the defendant's
solicitor to be summoned to give evidence at his trial for allegedly driving whilst disqualified where no other means or proving disqualification is available.

The privilege does not extend to communications which are made for the purposes
of obtaining advice on the commission of a future crime or which are themselves part of
a crime: *R. v Cox and Railton* (1884) 14 Q.B.D. 153. Documents or information
obtained in contravention of domestic or foreign law cannot be privileged: *Dubai Alu-
minium Co Ltd v Al-Alwai* [1999] 1 W.L.R. 1964, QBD. There must be *prima facie*
evidence that it was the client's intention to obtain advice in furtherance of his criminal
purposes: *O'Rourke v Darbishire* [1920] A.C. 581, HL. In deciding whether a document came into existence in furtherance of a crime the court may be entitled to look at
the document itself: *R. v Governor of Pentonville Prison Ex p. Osman*, above.

A document does not become privileged simply by being handed to a lawyer. A solicitor who holds a document for or relating to his or her client can assert in respect of its
seizure no greater authority than the client possesses: *R. v Peterborough Justices Ex p.
Hicks* [1977] 1 W.L.R. 1371, DC. If an unprivileged document in counsel's possession is
called for in court, it must be produced: *Bursill v Tanner* (1885) 16 Q.B.D. 1. Privilege
does not attach to documents obtained by a client or his legal adviser for the purpose of
litigation unless the document has been created for the purpose of litigation: *Ventouris
v Mountain* [1991] 1 W.L.R. 607, CA (Civ Div). Copies of non-privileged documents
are privileged only if (a) the copy was made for the purpose of litigation and (b) the
original document is not and has not at any time been in the control of the party claiming privilege: *The Palermo* (1884) L.R. 9 P.D. 6; *Watson v Cammel Laird & Co Ltd*
[1959] 1 W.L.R. 702, CA. Copy documents sent to a lawyer for legal advice do not
thereby become privileged where the original in the hands of the maker of the copy is
not privileged: *Dubai Bank Ltd v Galadari* [1990] Ch 98, CA (Civ Div).

Where the selection of documents copied or assembled by a solicitor betrays the **21-138**
trend of the advice given to his client, the documents so selected are privileged: *Lyell v
Kennedy (No.3)* (1884) 27 ChD 1.

Translations of documents should be treated in the same way as copies: *Sumitomo
Corporation v Credit Lyonnais Rouse Ltd* [2002] 1 W.L.R. 479, CA (Civ Div).

A document or communication is always privileged once it becomes privileged: *Cal-
craft v Guest* [1898] 1 Q.B. 759. Legal professional privilege must be upheld in the
public interest, even where the witness no longer has any recognisable interest in
preserving the confidentiality: *R. v Derby Magistrates' Court Ex p. B* [1996] A.C. 487,
HL.

Where the expert's opinion is to an extent based on privileged material, the opinion **21-139**
itself is also privileged. Consequently the defence can object if the prosecution seeks to
elicit evidence from an expert who has been abandoned and not relied upon by the
defence: *R. v Davies* (2002) 166 J.P. 243, CA. A person interviewed by a doctor at the
instigation of his own lawyers for the purpose of his defence is entitled to assume that

what he says to the doctor has the same status as communications with his lawyers. Both the interview and the opinion based upon it are privileged: *Davies* above. An expert's opinion on DNA is privileged where it is based upon a blood sample taken form the defendant and sent to the expert by his solicitors in contemplation of criminal proceedings because the blood sample itself is an item subject to the legal professional privilege within the meaning of the *Police and Criminal Evidence Act* 1984, s.10: *R. v R* [1995] 1 Cr.App.R. 183, CA.

C. PRIVILEGE AGAINST SELF INCRIMINATION

21–140   A witness is entitled to claim the privilege against self-incrimination in respect of any piece of information or evidence on the basis of which the prosecution might wish to establish guilt or decide to prosecute under English law: *Den Norske Bank ASA v Antonatos* [1999] Q.B. 271 at 287, CA (Civ Div).

Although it has been held that a witness must object personally on oath: *Downie v Doe, The Times*, November 28, 1997, it is the legal adviser who will normally warn of self incrimination. If the witness is wrongly compelled to answer and the defendant is convicted, the defendant cannot use the witness's compulsion to answer as a ground for appeal: *R. v Kinglake* (1870) 11 Cox 499.

If the witness does not object, his replies once given will be admissible evidence in any proceedings brought against him: *Sloggett* (1865) Dears 656. If the witness objects but is compelled to answer the answers are not admissible in evidence in later proceedings: *R. v Garbett* (1847) 1 Den 236.

There must be reasonable grounds for claiming the privilege: *R. v Boyes* (1861) 1 B & S 311.

The privilege may be expressly removed by statute. Statutory exceptions include the *Criminal Evidence Act* 1898, s.1(e) and the *Theft Act* 1968, s.31. See *Khan v Khan* [1982] 1 W.L.R. 513 in respect of the *Theft Act* 1968.

21–141   In *Saunders* [1996] 1 Cr.App.R. 463 the Court of Appeal rejected an argument that the trial judge should have excluded the transcript of interviews with DTI inspectors because the questioning under s.434 of the *Companies Act* 1985 was outside the safeguards of an interview under caution and the defendants were deprived of their protection against self-incrimination. Lord Taylor C.J. said that Parliament's intention was clear in s.434(5) and it could not be right for a judge to exercise his or her discretion to exclude evidence of interviews simply on the basis that Parliament ought not to countenance the possibility of self-incrimination. The European Court of Human Rights held that Saunders had been denied a fair trial because the use of statements obtained from him by the DTI inspectors amounted to an unjustifiable infringement of the right to silence and the right not to incriminate oneself: *Saunders v UK* (1997) 23 E.H.R.R. 313. The court said that the question whether the use made by the prosecution of the statements obtained by the inspectors amounted to such an infringement must be examined in the light of all the circumstances in particular whether the applicant had been subject to compulsion to give principles of a fair procedure inherent in art.6(1). See also *Heaney and McGovern v Ireland* (2001) 33 E.H.R.R. 12.

21–142   The privilege relates to any risk of prosecution under English law: *Den Norske Bank ASA v Antonatos*, above. No privilege arises where matters are covered by a pardon: *R. v Boyes* (1861) 1 B & S 311, by undertakings and immunities from prosecution given by the DPP, or where the risk relates to liability for debt in civil proceedings. The privilege does not extend to incrimination under foreign law however the court has a discretion to excuse a witness from giving evidence or producing documents which may so incriminate him: *Brannigan v Davidson* [1997] A.C. 238, PC. A remote possibility of prosecution is not enough. The danger must be "real and appreciable, with reference to the ordinary operation of law and in the ordinary course of things": *R. v Boyes*, above. Provided that the risk of proceedings being taken against the witness is real and not remote or insubstantial, the witness does not have to show that proceedings are likely or could probably be taken against him: *Re Westinghouse Electric Corp* [1977] 3 All E.R. 703.

D. CONFIDENTIAL COMMUNICATIONS

No legal privilege arises out of the relationship between doctor and patient: *R. v* **21–143** *McDonald* [1991] Crim.L.R. 122, CA. It does not arise between journalist and informer: *Att.-Gen. v Mulholland and Foster* [1963] 2 Q.B. 477. See however the *Contempt of Court Act* 1981, s.10. The position of priest and penitent has not been authoritively decided but the tendency of judicial dicta is that while in strict law the privilege does not exist, a minister of religion should not be required to give evidence as to a confession made to him: *R. v Griffin* (1853) 6 Cox 219; *R. v Hay* (1896) 2 F & F 4.

The court has a discretion to excuse a witness from answering a question where to do so would involve a breach of confidence. In *Hunter v Mann* [1974] Q.B. 767, 59 Cr.App.R 37, DC, Lord Widgery C.J. said (*obiter*):

> If a doctor, giving evidence ... is asked a question which he finds embarrassing because it involves him talking about things which he would normally regard as confidential, he can seek the protection of the judge and ask the judge if it is necessary for him to answer. The judge, by virtue of the overriding discretion to control his court which all English judges have, can, if he thinks fit, tell the doctor that he need not answer the question. Whether or not the judge would take that line, of course, depends largely on the importance of the potential answer to the issues being tried.

Before compelling disclosure the court should be satisfied that the potential answer is relevant and will serve a useful purpose in relation to the proceedings, and then weigh the conflicting interests to determine whether confidentiality should be overridden or respected: *Att.-Gen. v Mulholland and Foster*, above.

The *Police and Criminal Evidence Act* 1984 imposed restrictions on the extent to which access may be obtained to confidential information for the purposes of a criminal investigation: *PACE* 1984, ss.8–13.

XVII. CORROBORATION

Corroboration is evidence which supports a witness's testimony. Where one piece of **21–144** evidence confirms and supports another, corroboration takes place if both pieces of evidence are accepted by the tribunal of fact.

A definition of corroboration was found in *R. v Baskerville* [1916] 2 K.B. 658. Lord Reid said at 667:

> Evidence in corroboration must be independent testimony which affects the accused by connecting or tending to connect him with the crime. In other words, it must be evidence which implicates him, that is, which confirms in some material particular not only the evidence that the crime has been committed, but also that the prisoner committed it. The test applicable to determine the nature and extent of the corroboration is thus the same whether the case falls within the rule of practice at common law or within that class of offences for which corroboration is required by statute.

Some statutes require corroboration. In the magistrates' courts this applies to speeding offences: *Road Traffic Regulation Act* 1984, s.89(2). In certain cases it has been considered dangerous to convict on the evidence of a single person unless the court was convinced of the guilt of the defendant:

— Evidence of a complaint in any allegation of a sexual offence
— Evidence of an accomplice when called by the prosecutor
— Evidence of children.

Legislation has abolished the requirement to warn juries of the danger in the above **21–145** cases. Sections 32 and 33 of the *Criminal Justice and Public Order Act* 1994 abolished the rule requiring a corroboration warning to be given in relation to the evidence of accomplices and the evidence of complainants in sexual offences and the requirement for corroboration in offences under the *Sexual Offences Act* 1956 in trials on indictment.

In the magistrates' courts, the judiciary will exercise caution in convicting without corroboration in certain circumstances, for example, where a witness is considered unreliable, is shown to have lied, to have made previous false complaints, is of bad character, is a co-defendant, bears the defendant a grudge or has an improper motive: *R. v Makanjuola*; *R. v Easton* [1995] 2 Cr.App.R. 469, CA; *R. v Knowlden and Knowlden* (1983) 77 Cr.App.R. 94, CA; *R. v Beck* (1982) 74 Cr.App.R. 221; *R. v Witts and Witts* [1991] Crim.L.R 562, CA; *Chan Wei-Keung v R* [1995] 2 Cr.App.R. 194.

XVIII. PROCEDURE FOR CHALLENGING ADMISSIBILITY

21–146   Since the judiciary in magistrates' courts are judges of both fact and law they must rule on the admissibility of evidence and decide the question of the defendant's guilt. If they rule evidence inadmissible they must ignore that evidence when deciding whether to convict or acquit the defendant.

The magistrates' court has an overall responsibility for ensuring that the defendant receives a fair trial according to law: *R. v Sang* [1980] A.C. 402. It should not wait for an objection to be taken to the admissibility of evidence but should itself stop questions likely to elicit such evidence: *R. v Ellis* [1910] 2 K.B. 746; *Stirland v DPP* [1944] A.C. 315.

The point at which the magistrates' court should rule upon a question of admissibility is a matter for its discretion: *F (an infant) v Chief Constable of Kent* [1982] Crim.L.R. 682. The Divisional Court held that a trial within a trial is not an appropriate procedure in the magistrates' court. This is because the purpose of a *voire dire* is to allow the judge to determine a question of law in the absence of the jury. Incidental matters, such as the admissibility of evidence, should be decided as separate issues from that of guilt.

21–147   In *R. v Epping and Ongar Justices Ex p. Manby* [1986] Crim.L.R. 666, the defendant had been charged with driving an overweight vehicle. The prosecution relied upon a police officer's certificate that the defendant had admitted responsibility for the vehicle pursuant to the *Road Traffic Act* 1972, s.181. The defendant's solicitor wished to challenge the admissibility of the certificate but did not require the officer to be called to give evidence. The justices refused to hear evidence from the defendant on the point as a preliminary issue and proceeded with the prosecution case. No defence evidence was called. The application for review of the decision to refuse to decide the issue of admissibility as a preliminary issue was dismissed since, within statutory restraints, justices determine their own procedure. Since the defendant had not required the officer to be called, the justices were entitled to accept the prosecution evidence as providing a prima facie case on the point.

It has also been said, however, that the court should not rule on the admissibility of evidence until the evidence has been tendered and objection taken: *R. v Sang*, 69 Cr.App.R. 282; *Williams v Mohamed* [1977] R.T.R. 12.

Where the court is determining the admissibility of a confession under s.76 of the *Police and Criminal Evidence Act* 1984 then it has been held that admissibility should be determined by way of *voire dire*: *R. v Liverpool Juvenile Court Ex p. R* [1988] Q.B. 1. Section 76(2) of the same Act provides that if it is represented that the confession has or may have been obtained in either of the two ways set out in that subsection, the court shall not allow it to be given in evidence except insofar as the prosecution proves beyond reasonable doubt that it was not so obtained. Section 76(2) accordingly obliges a magistrates' court to hold a trial within a trial in such cases. This rule also applies to committal proceedings: *R. v Oxford City Justices Ex p. Berry* [1988] Q.B. 507.

21–148   If an application to exclude evidence is made under s.78 of the *Police and Criminal Evidence Act* 1984 the court is not obliged to hold a trial within a trial: *Vel v Owen* [1987] Crim.L.R. 496. The defendant has no right to have the admissibility of evidence determined under s.78 in advance of evidence being given because the court under s.78 has a discretion to exclude evidence if it would bear unfairly on the proceedings and there is no burden on the prosecution to disprove unfairness.

The court does not have the power to delegate the function of determining the admissibility of evidence to another bench: *R. v Ormskirk Justices Ex p. Davies* (1994)

158 J.P. 1145. After the court rules that evidence is inadmissible it must then ignore that evidence when determining the issue of guilt. If a court hears of a defendant's convictions or pending charges, it may be necessary to adjourn the case to be heard by another bench. In *R. v Liverpool Justices Ex p. Tapping* (1983) 76 Cr.App.R. 170 the court said that the test in such circumstances is "would a reasonable and fair-minded person sitting in court and knowing all the relevant facts have a reasonable suspicion that a fair trial for the [defendant] was not possible?"

The court may reverse a previous decision as to inadmissibility provided that there is good reason to do so and that no injustice is caused. Such reversals should, however, be exceptional: *R. v Sittingbourne Justices Ex p. Stickings* (1996) 160 J.P. 801.

There is no need for evidence to be repeated after the question of admissibility has been determined: *F (an infant) v Chief Constable of Kent*, above.

CHALLENGING DECISIONS

I. RE-OPENING A CASE

Magistrates' Courts Act 1980, s.142

Power of magistrates' court to re-open cases to rectify mistakes etc.

142.—(1) A magistrates' court may vary or rescind a sentence or other order imposed or **22–1** made by it when dealing with an offender if it appears to the court to be in the interests of justice to do so, and it is hereby declared that this power extends to replacing a sentence or order which for any reason appears to be invalid by another which the court has power to impose or make.

(1A) The power conferred on a magistrates' court by subsection (1) above shall not be exercisable in relation to any sentence or order imposed or made by it when dealing with an offender if—

(a) the Crown Court has determined an appeal against—
  (i) that sentence or order;
  (ii) the conviction in respect of which that sentence or order was imposed or made; or
  (iii) any other sentence or order imposed or made by the magistrates' court when dealing with the offender in respect of that conviction (including a sentence or order replaced by that sentence or order); or

(b) the High Court has determined a case stated for the opinion of that court on any question arising in any proceeding leading to or resulting from the imposition or making of the sentence or order.

(2) Where a person is convicted by a magistrates' court and it subsequently appears to the court that it would be in the interests of justice that the case should be heard again by different justices, the court may so direct.

(2A) The power conferred on a magistrates' court by subsection (2) above shall not be exercisable in relation to a conviction if—

    (a) the Crown Court has determined an appeal against—

        (i) the conviction; or

        (ii) any sentence or order imposed or made by the magistrates' court when dealing with the offender in respect of the conviction; or

    (b) the High Court has determined a case stated for the opinion of that court on any question arising in any proceeding leading to or resulting from the conviction.

(3) Where a court gives a direction under subsection (2) above—

    (a) the conviction and any sentence or other order imposed or made in consequence thereof shall be of no effect; and

    (b) section 10(4) above shall apply as if the trial of the person in question had been adjourned.

[(4) ...repealed]

(5) Where a sentence or order is varied under subsection (1) above, the sentence or other order, as so varied, shall take effect from the beginning of the day on which it was originally imposed or made, unless the court otherwise directs.

[This section is reprinted as amended by the *Criminal Appeal Act* 1995, Sch.3, para.1.]

22–2   The provisions are wide. They should be used to rectify obvious mistakes. In *R. v Croydon Youth Court Ex p. DPP* [1997] 2 Cr.App.R. 411 it was said that it is wrong to employ s.142(2) as a method by which a defendant could obtain a rehearing in circumstances where he could not appeal to the Crown Court by reason of his unequivocal plea of guilty, nor was it in the interests of justice. The interests of justice were defined as including the interests of the courts and the public, that people who had pleaded guilty with the advice of counsel should continue to be regarded as guilty, and that there should be certainty and an end to litigation.

The power is not available where the prosecutor has withdrawn the charge: *Coles v East Penwith Justices* (1998) 162 J.P. 687. The power extends only to cases where the defendant has been found guilty and not where he has been acquitted: *R. v Gravesend Justices Ex p. Dexter* [1977] Crim.L.R. 298.

22–3   A court may rescind a hospital order under s.37(3) of the *Mental Health Act* 1983 where the court was satisfied that he "did the act": *R. v Thames Magistrates' Court Ex p. Ramadan* [1999] 1 Cr.App.R. 386, [1999] Crim.L.R. 498, DC.

A court may review orders including the issue of a warrant for detention under s.136 of the *MCA* 1980 following non-payment of a fine: *R. v Sheffield City JJ Ex p. Foster, The Times*, November 2, 1999, DC. A court may review an incorrect sentence and increase it: *Jane v Broome, The Times*, November 2, 1987, DC. It may not increase a sentence for misbehaviour in the court: *R. v Powell* (1985) 7 Cr.App.R.(S.) 247.

22–4   There is no time limit for making an application under this section. Mere delay in making an application is not a ground for refusing the application, however it is a factor for the court to take into account along with all other relevant circumstances: *R. v Ealing Justices Ex p. Sahota* (1998) 162 J.P. 73. This was confirmed in *R. (on the application of Dunlop) v DPP* [2004] EWHC 225. In that case informations alleging offences of using a motor vehicle without insurance, driving without a licence and having no test certificate were laid in March 2001. The defendant did not appear in court in April 2001 to answer the summonses. In May 2001, he was sentenced in his absence. When he appeared voluntarily after a warrant had been issued for his arrest, he said that he had not received the summonses and had not owned a car or held a licence. He had first known about the convictions in March 2002. The magistrates' court refused to re-open under s.142 in view of the length of time which had elapsed. The appeal was allowed.

In *R. v Gwent Magistrates' Court Ex p. Carey* (1996) 160 J.P. 613 on review of the magistrates' decision not to reopen the matter under s.142, the court said that the magistrates are entitled to emphasise the inconvenience to witnesses when defendants do not attend due to their own conduct. They should also weigh the strength of the prosecution case.

The court must exercise its discretion judicially. The late arrival at court of a defendant was not a proper ground for refusing a rehearing: *R. v Camberwell Green Magistrates' Court Ex p. Ibrahim* (1984) 148 J.P. 400.   **22–5**

II. APPEAL TO CROWN COURT

A. GENERAL

Magistrates' Courts Act 1980, s.108

Right of appeal to the Crown Court
108.—(1) A person convicted by a magistrates' court may appeal to the Crown Court—   **22–6**
(a) if he pleaded guilty, against his sentence;
(b) if he did not, against the conviction or sentence.
(1A) [Section 14 of the *Powers of Criminal Courts (Sentencing) Act* 2000] (under which a conviction of an offence for which an order for conditional or absolute discharge is made is deemed not to be a conviction except for certain purposes) shall not prevent an appeal under this Act, whether against conviction or otherwise.
(2) A person sentenced by a magistrates' court for an offence in respect of which an order for conditional discharge has been previously made may appeal to the Crown Court against the sentence.
(3) In this section "sentence" includes any order made on conviction by a magistrates' court, not being—
(b) an order for the payment of costs;
(c) an order under section 2 of the *Protection of Animals Act* 1911 (which enables a court to order the destruction of an animal); or
(d) an order made in pursuance of any enactment under which the court has no discretion as to the making of the order or its terms and also includes a declaration of relevance under the *Football Spectators Act* 1989.

[This section is reprinted as amended by the *Powers of Criminal Courts (Sentencing) Act* 2000, Sch.9, para.71.]

Where a defendant pleaded guilty he may only appeal against the sentence imposed. Where a defendant pleaded not guilty he may appeal against both conviction and sentence. Appeals by young persons against conviction and/or sentence in the Youth Court are governed by these provisions, since Youth Courts are magistrates' courts: *Magistrates' Courts Act* 1980, ss.148, 152; *Children and Young Persons Act* 1933, ss.45, 46 and the *Powers of Criminal Courts (Sentencing) Act* 2000, s.137.

B. AGAINST CONVICTION

A plea of guilty in the magistrates' court usually means that the defendant cannot appeal against conviction to the Crown Court: *Magistrates' Courts Act* 1980, s.108. In *R. v Birmingham Crown Court Ex p. Sharma* [1988] Crim.L.R. 741 the defendant pleaded guilty by post to failing to stop at a traffic light and driving without insurance. He sought leave to appeal to the Crown Court out of time against conviction on the grounds that he had not intended to plead guilty to driving without insurance, and had in fact been insured. On review of the decision to refuse leave it was held that the defendant was not within any exception to the rule that a plea of guilty in the magistrates' court was final. It made no difference that he had pleaded guilty by post.   **22–7**
The Crown Court has no jurisdiction to entertain an application, set aside the convic-

tion or remit the case to the magistrates simply because the defendant has subsequently regretted pleading guilty and thinks that he has an arguable defence: *R. v Marylebone Justices Ex p. Westminster City Council* [1971] 1 W.L.R. 567, [1971] 1 All E.R. 1025.

The Crown Court has a limited jurisdiction to hear appeals against conviction where the defendant has pleaded guilty. This will arise when there has been an equivocal plea or where a plea has been made under duress: *R. v Durham Quarter Sessions Ex p. Virgo*; *R. v Huntingdon Crown Court Ex p. Jordan*, 73 Cr.App.R. 194.

22–8   If a defendant pleads guilty but is then committed to the Crown Court for sentence, the Crown Court has a general discretion to remit to the lower court whenever it considers it just to do so: *R. v Inner London Crown Court Ex p. Sloper* (1979) 69 Cr.App.R. 1.

The duties of the Crown Court and the magistrates whose conviction following a guilty plea is being challenged were examined in *R. v Plymouth Justices Ex p. Hart* [1986] Q.B. 950. If the Crown Court conducts a proper inquiry into whether the defendant's plea was equivocal and it has sufficient evidence before it to conclude that it was, the Crown Court's direction that a not guilty plea be entered and a summary trial be held is binding on the magistrates. The magistrates should assist the Crown Court in its inquiry into equivocality of the plea by supplying affidavits.

The Crown Court must make proper inquiry as to what happened in the magistrates' court before considering remitting the case: *R. v Marylebone Justices Ex p. Westminster City Council*, above. It is not under such a duty, however, unless something indicates that the magistrates should have considered permitting a change of plea: *R. v Coventry Crown Court Ex p. Manson* (1978) 67 Cr.App.R. 315.

Where equivocality of plea is raised on appeal, the Crown Court should first decide if there is *prima facie* evidence of equivocality. If there is, it should request affidavit evidence from the Bench, the clerk or both. Only if it is then satisfied that the plea was equivocal should the case be remitted for a fresh plea to be taken: *R. v Rochdale Justices Ex p. Allwork* (1981) 73 Cr.App.R. 319.

22–9   If the Crown Court finds the defendant not guilty of the offence charged, it may not convict the defendant of an attempt to commit the offence as that was not within the powers of the magistrates' court: *R. v Manchester Crown Court Ex p. Hill* (1985) 149 J.P.N. 29.

There is no power to appeal against acquittal or dismissal unless provided for by statute: *R. v London Keepers of the Peace and Justices* [1945] K.B. 528.

C. AGAINST SENTENCE

22–10   There is no appeal against the making of a costs order, the destruction of an animal or a non-discretionary order.

Where a defendant appeals against a sentence imposed by a magistrates' court, the Crown Court should not review the decision reached by the magistrates but should carry out a complete rehearing of the issues and form an independent view, on all the evidence, of the correct sentence: *R. v Swindon Crown Court Ex p. Murray* (1998) 162 J.P. 36.

The Crown Court is not bound by findings of fact made by a magistrates' court in a way that could limit its sentencing powers. Where a defendant appeals against sentence to the Crown Court, the court is entitled to decide the appeal on a different factual basis from that accepted by the magistrates' court. Where the Crown Court rejects the view taken by the magistrates' court, the court should make the position plain to the appellant and give him an opportunity, under the *Newton* principle, to challenge the factual basis adopted by the court: *Bussey v DPP* [1999] 1 Cr.App.R. 125.

22–11   The Crown Court has no power to order that the sentence, which was the subject of the appeal, should be consecutive to a sentence passed after the justices had imposed the sentence in question: *R. v Portsmouth Crown Court Ex p. Ballard* (1990) 154 J.P. 109.

In *R. v Isleworth Crown Court Ex p. Irvin* [1992] R.T.R. 281, the court adjourned the matter for inquiries before sentencing in such a way that the defendant formed the opinion that he would not receive a custodial sentence if the reports were favourable. In such circumstances it was held that where the reports are favourable then the Crown Court may not impose or uphold a custodial sentence.

There is no right to appeal against committal to the Crown Court for sentencing: *R. v London Sessions Ex p. Rogers* [1951] 2 K.B. 74.

D. Against Binding Over Order

Magistrates' Courts (Appeals from Binding Over Orders) Act 1956, s.1

Right of appeal to quarter sessions

1.—(1) Where, under the *Justices of the Peace Act* 1361, or otherwise, a person is ordered **22–12** by a magistrates' court (as defined in the *Magistrates' Courts Act* 1952) to enter into a recognisance with or without sureties to keep the peace or to be of good behaviour, he may appeal to [the Crown Court]

(2) In the case of an appeal under this section—

(a) the other party to the proceedings which were the occasion of the making of the order shall be the respondent to the appeal;

(b) [...] in relation to an appellant in custody for failure to comply with the order, so much of section [twenty-two of the *Criminal Justice Act* 1967], as relates to the release of convicted persons from custody pending an appeal to [the Crown Court] shall, with the necessary adaptations, apply as if the appeal were an appeal against a conviction.

(3) Nothing in this section shall apply in relation to any order an appeal from which lies to [the Crown Court] apart from the provisions of this section.

(4) This section shall not apply to any order made before the expiration of a period of one month beginning with the date of the passing of this Act.

[This section is reprinted as amended by the *Courts Act* 1971, s.56(2), Sch.9, Pt I, the *Criminal Justice Act* 1967, Sch.7, Pt I, and the *Interpretation Act* 1978, s.17(2)(a).]

An appeal against a binding over order is by way of rehearing. Unless the appellant **22–12.1** admits the facts upon which the order was based, sworn evidence must be adduced and will be open to cross-examination: *Shaw v Hamilton* [1982] 1 W.L.R. 1308.

E. Constitution of Crown Court on Appeal

Supreme Court Act 1981, s.74

Appeals and committals for sentence

74.—(1) On any hearing by the Crown Court— **22–13**

(a) of any appeal;

the Crown Court shall consist of a judge of the High Court or a Circuit judge or a Recorder who, subject to the following provisions of this section, shall sit with not less than two nor more than four justices of the peace.

(2) *Crown Court Rules* may, with respect to hearings falling within subsection (1)—

(a) prescribe the number of justices of the peace constituting the court (within the limits mentioned in that subsection); and

(b) prescribe the qualifications to be possessed by any such justices of the peace;

and the rules may make different provision for different descriptions of cases, different places of sitting or other different circumstances.

(3) *Crown Court Rules* may authorise or require a judge of the High Court, Circuit judge or Recorder, in such circumstances as are specified by the rules, to enter on, or at any stage to continue with, any proceedings with a court not comprising the justices required by subsections (1) and (2).

(4) The Lord Chancellor may from time to time, having regard to the number of justices, or the number of justices with any prescribed qualifications, available for service in the Crown Court, give directions providing that, in such descriptions of proceedings as may be specified by the Lord Chancellor, the provisions of subsections (1) and (2) shall not apply.

(5) Directions under subsection (4) may frame descriptions of proceedings by reference to the place of trial, or by reference to the time of trial, or in any other way.

(6) No decision of the Crown Court shall be questioned on the ground that the court was not constituted as required by or under subsections (1) and (2) unless objection was taken by or on behalf of a party to the proceedings not later than the time when the proceedings were entered on, or when the alleged irregularity began.

(7) *Crown Court Rules* may make provision as to the circumstances in which—

    (a) a person concerned with a decision appealed against is to be disqualified from hearing the appeal;

    (c) proceedings on the hearing of an appeal [...] are to be valid notwithstanding that any person taking part in them is disqualified.

[This section is reprinted as amended by the *Access to Justice Act* 1999, Sch.15(V)(4), para.1.]

22–14   On an appeal to the Crown Court a judge will sit with magistrates who have not adjudicated at the hearing in the magistrates' court: *Crown Court Rules* 1982, r.5. The following dispensations apply.

Crown Court Rules 1982, r.4

Dispensations for special circumstances

22–15   **4.**—(1) The Crown Court may enter on any appeal notwithstanding that the Court is not constituted as required by section 74(1) of the *Supreme Court Act* 1981 or Rule 3 if it appears to the judge that the Court could not be so constituted without unreasonable delay and the Court includes—

    (a) in a case to which paragraph (2) of that Rule applies, at least two justices each of whom is a member of a committee specified in that paragraph, provided that the Court includes a justice for the petty sessions area so specified and a justice for some other area;

    (b) in a case to which paragraph (3) of that Rule applies, at least two justices including a justice for the petty sessions area so specified and a justice for some other area;

    (c) in a case to which paragraph (4) of that Rule applies, one justice who is a member of a juvenile court panel;

    (d) in a case to which paragraph (5) of that Rule applies, one justice who is a member of a domestic court panel;

    (e) in any other case, one justice:

Provided that the judge may sit without one or both of the justices required by sub-paragraphs (a) and (b) above if the parties appearing at the hearing of the appeal agree.

[...]

(3) The Crown Court may at any stage continue with any proceedings with a Court from which any one or more of the justices initially comprising the Court has withdrawn, or is absent for any reason.

[This rule is reprinted as amended by the *Crown Court (Amendment) Rules* 1999, r.2(3).]

F. PROCEDURE

Crown Court Rules 1982, r.7

Notice of appeal

22–16   **7.**—(1) An appeal shall be commenced by the appellant's giving notice of appeal in accordance with the following provisions of this Rule.

(2) The notice required by the preceding paragraph shall be in writing and shall be given—

    (a) in a case where the appeal is against a decision of a magistrates' court, to the justices' chief executive for the magistrates' court;

...

(e) in any case, to any other party to the appeal.

(3) Notice of appeal shall be given not later than 21 days after the day on which the decision appealed against is given and, for this purpose, where the court has adjourned the trial of an information after conviction, that day shall be the day on which the court sentences or otherwise deals with the offender:

Provided that, where a court exercises its power to defer sentence under section 1(1) of the *Powers of Criminal Courts (Sentencing) Act* 2000, that day shall, for the purposes of an appeal against conviction, be the day on which the court exercises that power.

(4) A notice of appeal shall state—

(a) in the case of an appeal arising out of a conviction by a magistrates' court, whether the appeal is against conviction or sentence or both; and

(b) in the case of an appeal under an enactment listed in Part III of Schedule 3, the grounds of appeal.

(5) The time for giving notice of appeal (whether prescribed under paragraph (3), or under an enactment listed in Part 1 of Schedule 3) may be extended, either before or after it expires, by the Crown Court, on an application made in accordance with paragraph (6)

(6) An application for an extension of time shall be made in writing, specifying the grounds of the application and sent to the appropriate officer of the Crown Court

(7) Where the Crown Court extends the time for giving notice of appeal, the appropriate officer of the Crown Court shall give notice of the extension to—

(a) the appellant;

(b) in the case of an appeal from a decision of the magistrates' court, to the justices' chief executive for that court;

A notice of appeal to the Crown Court must be given in writing within 21 days of the **22–17** adjudication. Forms are available in courthouses for this purpose. A magistrates' court will accept notice of appeal out of time and will forward it to the Crown Court while at the same time notifying the appellant that it is out of time. The Crown Court should give brief reasons to the appellant of any refusal of an extension: *Re Worth (application for judicial review)* (1979) 1 F.L.R. 159, (1979) 10 Fam. Law 54. Where an extension is given the appellant must give notice to any other party to the appeal. The Crown Court will give notice of the hearing to the parties and the magistrates' court: r.8, *Crown Court Rules* 1982. The appeal will be by way of a rehearing: *Supreme Court Act* 1981, s.79(3).

The court may deal with a procedural irregularity: *R. v Teeside Magistrates' Court Ex p. Bujinowski* [1997] Crim.L.R. 51. In that case, it was held that, on appeal against conviction for failing to surrender to bail, the Crown Court had jurisdiction to determine the matter on the basis that the magistrates had acted in breach of the relevant practice direction.

Where a defendant appeals to the Crown Court against conviction, the justices' clerk **22–18** is not under a duty to provide the defendant with any notes of evidence unless the defendant is legally aided. There is no rule at common law which entitles the defendant to a copy of the clerk's notes and the *Magistrates' Courts Rules* 1981, r.17 do not require the clerk to send any notes of evidence to the Crown Court when a defendant appeals against conviction, unlike r.74, which requires such notes to be sent to a Crown Court if the defendant is committed to the Crown Court for sentence after conviction. It is desirable that there should be no difference in procedure as far as possible between appeals by legally-aided defendants and non-legally aided defendants and therefore, requests for copies of notes of evidence should be viewed sympathetically by justices' clerks: *R. v Clerk to Highbury Justices Ex p. Hussein* [1986] 1 W.L.R. 1266.

Where a judge sitting with magistrates in the Crown Court fails to give reasons when dismissing an appeal from the magistrates' court, he may prepare a note of the reasons subsequently; there is no need for the justices to provide supporting affidavits or to sign the judge's note: *R. v Snaresbrook Crown Court Ex p. Input Management Ltd* (1999) 163 J.P. 533. In order to reassure an appellant that there has been no after-the-event rationalisation, reasons for the ruling should be given contemporaneously. Reasons will enable a defendant to understand the findings and to consider whether there are grounds for a further appeal to the Divisional Court by way of case stated. The failure to provide reasons is not always fatal to the Crown Court's decision since the reasons may be obvious, the decision is simple or the subject matter of the appeal is unimportant: *R. v Kingston Crown Court Ex p. Bell* (2000) 164 J.P. 633.

22–19   The magistrates whose decision is under appeal have a right to appear and to call evidence: *R. v Kent Justices Ex p. Metropolitan Police Commissioner* [1936] 1 K.B. 547. In these circumstances they do not make themselves a party to the appeal and so incur no liability for costs: *R. v Davidson, Nanson and Marley* (1871) 35 J.P. 500. This practice is highly unusual in criminal matters.

G. POWERS OF CROWN COURT ON APPEAL

Supreme Court Act 1981, s.48

Appeals to Crown Court

22–20   **48.**—(1) The Crown Court may, in the course of hearing any appeal, correct any error or mistake in the order or judgment incorporating the decision which is the subject of the appeal.

(2) On the termination of the hearing of an appeal the Crown Court—

      (a) may confirm, reverse or vary the decision appealed against or any part of the decision appealed against, including a determination not to impose a separate penalty in respect of an offence ; or

      (b) may remit the matter with its opinion thereon to the authority whose decision is appealed against; or

      (c) may make such other order in the matter as the court thinks just, and by such order exercise any power which the said authority might have exercised.

(3) Subsection (2) has effect subject to any enactment relating to any such appeal which expressly limits or restricts the powers of the court on the appeal.

(4) [Subject to section 11(6) of the *Criminal Appeal Act* 1995, if] the appeal is against a conviction or a sentence, the preceding provisions of this section shall be construed as including power to award any punishment, whether more or less severe than that awarded by the magistrates' court whose decision is appealed against, if that is a punishment which that magistrates' court might have awarded.

(5) This section applies whether or not the appeal is against the whole of the decision.

(6) In this section "sentence" includes any order made by a court when dealing with an offender, including—

      (a) a hospital order under Part III of the *Mental Health Act* 1983, with or without a restriction order, and an interim hospital order under that Act; and

      (b) a recommendation for deportation made when dealing with an offender.

(7) The fact that an appeal is pending against an interim hospital order under the said Act of 1983 shall not affect the power of the magistrates' court that made it to renew or terminate the order or to deal with the appellant on its termination; and where the Crown Court quashes an order but does not pass any sentence or make any other order in its place the Court may direct the appellant to be kept in custody or released on bail pending his being dealt with by that magistrates' court.

(8) Where the Crown Court makes an interim hospital order by virtue of subsection (2)—

      (a) the power of renewing or terminating the order and of dealing with the appellant on its termination shall be exercisable by the magistrates' court whose decision is appealed against and not by the Crown Court; and

      (b) that magistrates' court shall be treated for the purposes of section 38(7) of the said Act of 1983 (absconding offenders) as the court that made the order.

[This section is reprinted as amended by the *Criminal Appeal Act* 1995, Sch.2, para.14 and the *Criminal Justice Act* 1988, s.156.]

22–21   The Crown Court has no power to amend an information on appeal: *R. v Swansea Crown Court Ex p. Stacey* [1990] R.T.R. 183, see above. It may not hear an appeal against a magistrate's amendment of an information: *Fairgrieve v Newman* (1986) 82 Cr.App.R. 60, [1986] R.T.R. 47.

H. Abandonment of Appeal

Magistrates' Courts Act 1980, s.109

Abandonment of appeal
    109.—(1) Where notice to abandon an appeal has been duly given by the appellant—   **22-22**
    (a) the court against whose decision the appeal was brought may issue process for enforcing that decision, subject to anything already suffered or done under it by the appellant; and
    (b) the said court may, on the application of the other party to the appeal, order the appellant to pay to that party such costs as appear to the court to be just and reasonable in respect of expenses properly incurred by that party in connection with the appeal before notice of the abandonment was given to that party.
    (2) In this section "appeal" means an appeal from a magistrates' court to the Crown Court, and the reference to a notice to abandon an appeal is a reference to a notice shown to the satisfaction of the magistrates' court to have been given in accordance with Crown Court rules.

    An appeal may be abandoned by giving notice in writing to the other party and to   **22-23** the magistrates' court no later than the third day before the date set for the hearing:r.11, *Crown Court Rules* 1982. The magistrates' court's decision may then be enforced.
    If the appellant fails to attend the Crown Court hearing but has not give notice of withdrawal then the Crown Court is entitled to hear the appeal in his absence as it is a rehearing: *R. v Guildford Crown Court Ex p. Brewer* (1988) 87 Cr.App.R. 265.
    Where a person appealing to the Crown Court is represented at the hearing by counsel there is no obligation upon him to be present in person: *R. v Croydon Crown Court Ex p. Clair* [1986] 1 W.L.R. 746.
    Where neither party appears the court should dismiss the appeal.

I. Enforcement of Crown Court Orders on Appeal

Magistrates' Courts Act 1980, s.110

Enforcement of decision of the Crown Court
    110. After the determination by the Crown Court of an appeal from a magistrates' court the   **22-24** decision appealed against as confirmed or varied by the Crown Court, or any decision of the Crown Court substituted for the decision appealed against, may, without prejudice to the powers of the Crown Court to enforce the decision, be enforced—
    (a) by the issue by the court by which the decision appealed against was given of any process that it could have issued if it had decided the case as the Crown Court decided it;
    (b) so far as the nature of any process already issued to enforce the decision appealed against permits, by that process;
and the decision of the Crown Court shall have effect as if it had been made by the magistrates' court against whose decision the appeal is brought.

    [This section is reprinted as amended by the *Access to Justice Act* 1999, Sch.4, para.22.]

    Any order made by the Crown Court on appeal may be enforced by the magistrates' court.

III. APPEAL BY WAY OF CASE STATED

A. Application to State Case

Magistrates' Courts Act 1980, s.111

Statement of case by magistrates' court
    111.—(1) Any person who was a party to any proceeding before a magistrates' court or is ag-   **22-25**

grieved by the conviction, order, determination or other proceeding of the court may question the proceeding on the ground that it is wrong in law or is in excess of jurisdiction by applying to the justices composing the court to state a case for the opinion of the High Court on the question of law or jurisdiction involved; but a person shall not make an application under this section in respect of a decision against which he has a right of appeal to the High Court or which by virtue of any enactment passed after 31st December 1879 is final.

(2) An application under subsection (1) above shall be made within 21 days after the day on which the decision of the magistrates' court was given.

(3) For the purpose of subsection (2) above, the day on which the decision of the magistrates' court is given shall, where the court has adjourned the trial of an information after conviction, be the day on which the court sentences or otherwise deals with the offender.

(4) On the making of an application under this section in respect of a decision any right of the applicant to appeal against the decision to the Crown Court shall cease.

(5) If the justices are of opinion that an application under this section is frivolous, they may refuse to state a case, and, if the applicant so requires, shall give him a certificate stating that the application has been refused; but the justices shall not refuse to state a case if the application is made by or under the direction of the Attorney General.

(6) Where justices refuse to state a case, the High Court may, on the application of the person who applied for the case to be stated, make an order of mandamus requiring the justices to state a case.

22–26 If a party is aggrieved by a magistrates court's finding of fact the proper course is to appeal to the Crown Court: *James v Chief Constable of Kent, The Times*, June 7, 1986. If a person wishes to complain about the harshness of the sentence passed, the appeal should also be to the Crown Court, despite the risk that the Crown Court might take a decision to his disadvantage: *Tucker v DPP* (1992) 13 Cr.App.R. 495; *Allen v West Yorkshire Probation Service* [2001] EWCA Admin 2, 165 J.P. 313, DC, *The Times*, February 20, 2001.

Where the final determination is a decision on an application for costs the 21-day time limit starts to run from the date of the decision on costs: *Liverpool City Council v Worthington, The Times*, June 16, 1998. The time limit cannot be varied by the High Court: *Michael v Garland* [1977] 1 W.L.R. 296; *R. v Clerkenwell Magistrates' Court Ex p. DPP* [1984] Q.B. 821. Where an application which does not comply with the requirements of the *Magistrates' Courts Rules* 1981, r.76, is laid within time, the Divisional Court will still accept jurisdiction even if the defect is remedied outside the 21-day time limit: *Parsons v FW Woolworth and Co Ltd* [1980] 1 W.L.R. 1472; *R. v Croydon Justices Ex p. Lefore Holdings Ltd* [1980] 1 W.L.R. 1465.

The case must be concluded before the magistrates' court may state a case: *Streames v Copping* [1985] Q.B. 920; *Loade v DPP* [1990] 1 Q.B. 1052. There is no jurisdiction to state a case in respect of interlocutory matters: *R. v Greater Manchester Justices Ex p. Aldi GmbH and Co KG* (1995) 159 J.P. 717. Mistakes of law in committal proceedings nor the decision of committal itself can be challenged by way of case stated: *Dewing v Cummings* [1971] R.T.R. 1295.

22–27 If a magistrates' court considers that the application to state a case is frivolous it may refuse to do so and certify that fact to the applicant: *Magistrates' Courts Act* 1980, s.111(5). "Frivolous" in this context means that the magistrates' court considers the application to be futile, misconceived, hopeless or academic. Although it is not a conclusion which a court should often or easily reach, it is entitled to do so in appropriate circumstances, and should briefly state the reasons for doing so: *Mildenhall Magistrates' Court Ex p. Forest Heath District Council* (1997) 161 J.P. 401.

22–28 If a court refuses to state a case then the applicant may apply for judicial review and seek a mandatory order to compel the stating of a case: *R. v Blackfriars Crown Court Ex p. Sunworld Ltd* [2000] 1 W.L.R. 2102, [2000] 2 All E.R. 837. In that case the court gave some guidance on the approach for the Divisional Court. The aggrieved party should immediately apply for permission to bring an application for judicial review. If the court below has already given a reasoned judgment which contains all the necessary factual findings and has explained why it has refused to state a case in a manner which clearly raises the true point of law in question, the single judge should grant permission for judicial review which challenges the order in question. It may be possible then to proceed immediately to a substantive determination of the merits however this will depend on whether the interested parties are represented and prepared and on the availability of court time: *R. v Thames Magistrates' Court Ex p. Levy, The Times*, July 17, 1997.

If the court refuses to state a case having been ordered to do so following judicial review the members of the court are liable to pay costs: *R. v Huntingdon Magistrates' Court Ex p. Percy, The Times*, March 4, 1994.

Magistrates' Courts Act 1980, s.112

Effect of decision of High Court on case stated by magistrates' court

112. Any conviction, order, determination or other proceeding of a magistrates' court varied **22–29** by the High Court on an appeal by case stated, and any judgment or order of the High Court on such an appeal, may be enforced as if it were a decision of the magistrates' court from which the appeal was brought.

Magistrates' Courts Act 1980, s.114

Recognizances and fees on case stated

114. Justices to whom application has been made to state a case for the opinion of the High **22–30** Court on any proceeding of a magistrates' court shall not be required to state the case until the applicant has entered into a recognizance, with or without sureties, before the magistrates' court, conditioned to prosecute the appeal without delay and to submit to the judgment of the High Court and pay such costs as that Court may award; and (except in any criminal matter) the clerk of a magistrates' court shall not be required to deliver the case to the applicant until the applicant has paid [the fees payable for the case and for the recognizances to the justices' chief executive for the court].

[This section is reprinted as amended by the *Access to Justice Act* 1999, Sch.13, para.113.]

A magistrates' court may make the stating of a case conditional on the applicant's entering into a recognisance in order to discourage the waste of resources and to ensure that the applicant fully intends to pursue his claim.

Constitution of High Court

An appeal by way of case stated is heard by the Divisional Court of the Queen's **22–31** Bench Division. At least two judges of the division must sit on the appeal: *Supreme Court Act* 1981, s.66(3). If the opinion of a two-judge court is divided then the appeal fails: *Flanagan v Shaw* [1920] 3 K.B. 96.

B. Procedure

Magistrates' Courts Rules 1981, rr.76–81

Application to state case

76.—(1) An application under section 111(1) of the Act of 1980 shall be made in writing and **22–32** signed by or on behalf of the applicant and shall identify the question or questions of law or jurisdiction on which the opinion of the High Court is sought.

(2) Where one of the questions on which the opinion of the High Court is sought is whether there was evidence on which the magistrates' court could come to its decision, the particular finding of fact made by the magistrates' court which it is claimed cannot be supported by the evidence before the magistrates' court shall be specified in such application.

(3) Any such application shall be sent to the [justices' chief executive for] the magistrates' court whose decision is questioned.

[This rule is reprinted as amended by *Magistrates' Courts (Amendment) Rules*

2001, r.3.]

Consideration of draft case

22–33   **77.**—(1) Within 21 days after receipt of an application made in accordance with rule 76, the justices' chief executive for the magistrates' court whose decision is questioned shall, unless the justices refuse to state a case under section 111(5) of the Act of 1980, send a draft case in which are stated the matters required under rule 81 to the applicant or his solicitor and shall send a copy thereof to the respondent or his solicitor.

(2) Within 21 days after receipt of the draft case under paragraph (1), each party may make representations thereon. Any such representations shall be in writing and signed by or on behalf of the party making them and shall be sent to the justices' chief executive.

(3) Where the justices refuse to state a case under section 111(5) of the Act and they are required by the High Court by order of mandamus under section 111(6) to do so, this rule shall apply as if in paragraph (1)—

    (a) for the words "receipt of an application made in accordance with rule 76" there were substituted the words "the date on which an order of mandamus under section 111(6) of the Act of 1980 is made"; and

    (b) the words "unless the justices refuse to state a case under section 111(5) of the Act of 1980" were omitted.

[This section is printed as amended by the *Magistrates' Courts (Amendment) Rules* 2001, r.5.]

Preparation and submission of final case

22–34   **78.**—(1) Within 21 days after the latest day on which representations may be made under rule 77, the justices whose decision is questioned shall make such adjustments, if any, to the draft case prepared for the purposes of that rule as they think fit, after considering any such representations, and shall state and sign the case.

(2) A case may be stated on behalf of the justices whose decision is questioned by any 2 or more of them and may, if the justices so direct, be signed on their behalf by their clerk.

(3) Forthwith after the case has been stated and signed the justices' chief executive for the court shall send it to the applicant or his solicitor, together with any statement required by rule 79.

[This rule is reprinted as amended by *Magistrates' Courts (Amendment) Rules* 2001, r.3.]

Extension of time limits

22–35   **79.**—(1) If the justices' chief executive shall a magistrates' court is unable to send to the applicant a draft case under paragraph (1) of rule 77 within the time required by that paragraph, he shall do so as soon as practicable thereafter and the provisions of that rule shall apply accordingly; but in that event the clerk shall attach to the draft case, and to the final case when it is sent to the applicant or his solicitor under rule 78(3), a statement of the delay and the reasons therefor.

(2) If the justices' chief executive shall a magistrates' court receives an application in writing from or on behalf of the applicant or the respondent for an extension of the time within which representations on the draft case may be made under paragraph (2) of rule 77, together with reasons in writing therefor, the clerk of the magistrates' court may by notice in writing sent to the applicant or respondent as the case may be by the justices' chief executive extend the time and the provisions of that paragraph and of rule 78 shall apply accordingly; but in that event the clerk shall attach to the final case, when it is sent to the applicant or his solicitor under rule 78(3), a statement of the extension and the reasons therefor.

(3) If the justices are unable to state a case within the time required by paragraph (1) of rule 78, they shall do so as soon as practicable thereafter and the provisions of that rule shall apply accordingly; but in that event the justices' chief executive shall attach to the final case, when it is sent to the applicant or his solicitor under rule 78(3), a statement of the delay and the reasons therefor.

[This section is printed as amended by the *Magistrates' Courts (Amendment) Rules*

Service of documents

80. Any document required by rules 76 to 79 to be sent to any person shall either be delivered **22–36**
to him or be sent by post in a registered letter or by recorded delivery service and, if sent by post
to an applicant or respondent, shall be addressed to him at his last known or usual place of
abode

Content of case

81.—(1) A case stated by the magistrates' court shall state the facts found by the court and the **22–37**
question or questions of law or jurisdiction on which the opinion of the High Court is sought.

(2) Where one of the questions on which the opinion of the High Court is sought is
whether there was evidence on which the magistrates' court could come to its decision, the
particular finding of fact which it is claimed cannot be supported by the evidence before
the magistrates' court shall be specified in the case.

(3) Unless one of the questions on which the opinion of the High Court is sought is
whether there was evidence on which the magistrates' court could come to its decision, the
case shall not contain a statement of evidence.

The above rules outline the exact procedure and timetables to be followed in an ap- **22–38**
plication to state a case. A case stated should be succinct. It is usual for the court to draft
its own case but there is no reason why the court could not invite the parties to submit
the first draft, indicating any areas of disagreement: *Vehicle Inspectorate v George Jenkins Transport Ltd, The Times*, December 5, 2003. The question stated for the High
Court should be one the answer to which will resolve the issue in dispute: *Corcoran v
Anderton* (1980) 71 Cr.App.R. 104. It should be drafted as simply as possible and
directed to the crucial issues upon which the case turns.

Where a document forms a material part of the case stated, it or a copy should be appended: *Gainster v Marlow* [1984] Q.B. 218; *Kent County Council v Multi Media
Marketing (Canterbury) Ltd, The Times*, December 7, 1994.

Below is a form of case stated.

CASE STATED

In the High Court of Justice
Queen's Bench Division

Between (insert name)   Appellant
                 And
(insert name)   Respondent

Case stated by Justices [District Judge (name)] for the ....Commission Area of
............, acting in and for the Petty Sessional Area of........., in respect of their (his)
adjudication as a magistrates' court sitting at...............

Case

1. On the ......day of......20..., an information was laid by the appellant (or respondent) against the respondent (or appellant) that he/she (insert offence and statute)
2. We heard the said information on the.... ......(insert date) and found the following facts:- (here the findings but not the evidence should be set out in numbered paragraphs)
3. The following is a short statement of the evidence:- (this paragraph should only be inserted where the question asks whether there was evidence upon which the court could convict)
4. It was contended by the appellant that (here the argument should be summarised briefly)
5. It was contended by the respondent that (here the opposing argument should be summarised briefly)
6. We were referred to the following cases:-
7. We were (I was) of the opinion that (insert the grounds upon which the decision was made) and accordingly (insert either convicted or acquitted together with any sentence or order).

Question

8. The question for the opinion of the High Court is............

Dated the ....day of..........20..

(Insert signatures of the Justices/ one of them on
behalf of all/District Judge/ Justices' Clerk on behalf of the Justices)

Magistrate
District Judge
Justices' Clerk.

The appellant may withdraw the appeal by way of case stated without having to obtain the leave of the court: *Collett v Broomsgrove District Council* (1996) 160 J.P. 593.

Upon an application being made to a magistrates' court to state a case the applicant loses the right to appeal to the Crown Court: Magistrates' Courts Act 1980, s.111(4). This rule is still effective even if the application to state a case does not arrive within the statutory twenty one days, provided that it was made within the prescribed time and would have in the normal course of events arrived within the prescribed time: *P and M Supplies (Essex) Ltd v Hackney London Borough Council* (1990) 154 J.P. 814.

C. POWERS OF HIGH COURT ON CASE STATED

Supreme Court Act 1981, s.28A

Proceedings on case stated by magistrates' court or Crown Court

28A.—(1) This section applies where a case is stated for the opinion of the High Court—　　**22–39**

(a) by a magistrates' court under section 111 of the *Magistrates' Courts Act* 1980; or

(b) by the Crown Court under section 28(1) of this Act.

(2) The High Court may, if it thinks fit, cause the case to be sent back for amendment and, where it does so, the case shall be amended accordingly.

(3) The High Court shall hear and determine the question arising on the case (or the case as amended) and shall—

(a) reverse, affirm or amend the determination in respect of which the case has been stated; or

(b) remit the matter to the magistrates' court, or the Crown Court, with the opinion of the High Court,

and may make such other order in relation to the matter (including as to costs) as it thinks fit.

(4) Except as provided by the *Administration of Justice Act* 1960 (right of appeal to House of Lords in criminal cases), a decision of the High Court under this section is final.

[This section is reprinted as amended by the *Access to Justice Act* 1999, s.61.]

The appeal takes the form of legal argument and no evidence is called.

On an appeal by way of case stated, the High Court cannot refuse to determine a pure point of law simply because that point of law was only first appreciated after the conviction of the defendant: *Whitehead v Haines* [1965] 1 Q.B. 200, QBD.

The High Court has the power to order a rehearing: *Griffith v Jenkins* [1992] 2 A.C. 76, 95 Cr.App.R. 35.

IV. JUDICIAL REVIEW

A. GENERAL

The purpose of judicial review is to prevent magistrates' courts exceeding their juris-　**22–40** diction and to compel them to exercise their correct jurisdiction. It is a review of the way in which the court's decision was made: *Chief Constable of North Wales v Evans* [1982] 1 W.L.R. 1155, HL. It is the most appropriate procedure for challenging a magistrates' court decision, where the issue is the extent of that court's jurisdiction: *North Essex Justices Ex p. Lloyd* [2001] 2 Cr.App.R.(S.) 15.

The proceedings in the magistrates' court must be complete before the Administrative Court will consider a quashing order: *R.(on the application of Hoar-Stevens) v Richmond upon Thames Magistrates' Court* [2003] EWHC 2660. The case concerned the adequacy of disclosure of material to the defence. The court stated that it was of the utmost importance that the course of a criminal trial in the magistrates' court should not be punctuated by applications for adjournments to test a ruling in the Divisional Court, especially when in reality if the case proceeded, the ruling might turn out to be of little or no importance. That was so even where there was an important substantive point which arose during a trial. The proper course was to proceed to the end of the trial in the lower court and then to test the matter, almost certainly by way of case stated.

Where case stated is available it is the preferred procedure: *R. v Oldbury Justices Ex p. Smith* (1995) 159 J.P. 316 but that is not to say that judicial review cannot be used: *R. v Hereford Magistrates' Court Ex p. Rowlands* [1998] Q.B. 110. In *R. v Morpeth Ward Justices Ex p. Ward* (1992) 95 Cr.App.R. 215 it was stated that where the identification of facts as found is critical to challenging the decision, the better course is to appeal by way of case stated. Applications for judicial review are made in accordance with the procedures set out in the *Supreme Court Act* 1981, ss.29 and 31 and Pt 54 of the *Civil Procedure Rules* 1998.

B. PROCEDURE FOR BRINGING CLAIM

Supreme Court Act 1981, s.29

Orders of mandamus, prohibition and certiorari

22–41   **29.**—(1) Subject to subsection (3A), the High Court shall have jurisdiction to make orders of mandamus, prohibition and certiorari in those classes of cases in which it had power to do so immediately before the commencement of this Act.

(2) Every such order shall be final, subject to any right of appeal therefrom.

(3) In relation to the jurisdiction of the Crown Court, other than its jurisdiction in matters relating to trial on indictment, the High Court shall have all such jurisdiction to make orders of mandamus, prohibition or certiorari as the High Court possesses in relation to the jurisdiction of an inferior court.

(3A) The High Court shall have no jurisdiction to make orders of mandamus, prohibition or certiorari in relation to the jurisdiction of a court-martial in matters relating to—

(a) trial by court-martial for an offence, or

(b) appeals from a Standing Civilian Court;

and in this subsection "court-martial" means a court-martial under the *Army Act* 1955, the *Air Force Act* 1955 or the *Naval Discipline Act* 1957.

(4) The power of the High Court under any enactment to require justices of the peace or a judge or officer of a county court to do any act relating to the duties of their respective offices, or to require a magistrates' court to state a case for the opinion of the High Court, in any case where the High Court formerly had by virtue of any enactment jurisdiction to make a rule absolute, or an order, for any of those purposes, shall be exercisable by order of mandamus.

(5) In any enactment—

(a) references to a writ of mandamus, of prohibition or of certiorari shall be read as references to the corresponding order; and

(b) references to the issue or award of any such writ shall be read as references to the making of the corresponding order.

(6) In subsection (3) the reference to the Crown Court's jurisdiction in matters relating to trial on indictment does not include its jurisdiction relating to orders under section 17 of the *Access to Justice Act* 1999.

22–42   [This section is reprinted as amended by the *Access to Justice Act* 1999, and the *Armed Forces Act* 2001, s.23(3).]

22–43   By virtue of the *Practice Direction (Administrative Court: Establishment)* [2001] 1 W.L.R. 1654 the names of *mandamus*, prohibition and *certiorari* were changed to mandatory order, prohibiting order and quashing order respectively.

Supreme Court Act 1981, s.31

Application for judicial review

22–44   **31.**—(1) An application to the High Court for one or more of the following forms of relief, namely—

(a) an order of mandamus, prohibition or certiorari;

(b) a declaration or injunction under subsection (2); or

(c) an injunction under section 30 restraining a person not entitled to do so from acting in an office to which that section applies,

shall be made in accordance with rules of court by a procedure to be known as an application for judicial review.

(2) A declaration may be made or an injunction granted under this subsection in any case where an application for judicial review, seeking that relief, has been made and the High Court considers that, having regard to—

(a) the nature of the matters in respect of which relief may be granted by orders of mandamus, prohibition or certiorari;

(b) the nature of the persons and bodies against whom relief may be granted by such orders; and

(c) all the circumstances of the case,

it would be just and convenient for the declaration to be made or the injunction to be granted, as the case may be.

(3) No application for judicial review shall be made unless the leave of the High Court has been obtained in accordance with rules of court; and the court shall not grant leave to make such an application unless it considers that the applicant has a sufficient interest in the matter to which the application relates.

(4) On an application for judicial review the High Court may award damages to the applicant if—

    (a) he has joined with his application a claim for damages arising from any matter to which the application relates; and

    (b) the court is satisfied that, if the claim had been made in an action begun by the applicant at the time of making his application, he would have been awarded damages.

(5) If, on an application for judicial review seeking an order of certiorari, the High Court quashes the decision to which the application relates, the High Court may remit the matter to the court, tribunal or authority concerned, with a direction to reconsider it and reach a decision in accordance with the findings of the High Court.

(6) Where the High Court considers that there has been undue delay in making an application for judicial review, the court may refuse to grant—

    (a) leave for the making of the application; or

    (b) any relief sought on the application,

if it considers that the granting of the relief sought would be likely to cause substantial hardship to, or substantially prejudice the rights of, any person or would be detrimental to good administration.

(7) Subsection (6) is without prejudice to any enactment or rule of court which has the effect of limiting the time within which an application for judicial review may be made.

Civil Procedure Rules 1998, Pt 54, rr.1–3

Scope and interpretation

54.1.—(1) This Section of this Part contains rules about judicial review.　　　　**22–45**

(2) In this Section—

    (a) a "claim for judicial review" means a claim to review the lawfulness of—

        (i) an enactment; or

        (ii) a decision, action or failure to act in relation to the exercise of a public function.

    (b) an order of mandamus is called a "mandatory order";

    (c) an order of prohibition is called a "prohibiting order;

    (d) an order of certiorari is called a "quashing order";

    (e) "the judicial review procedure" means the Part 8 procedure as modified by [this Section];

    (f) "interested party" means any person (other than the claimant and defendant) who is directly affected by the claim; and

    (g) "court" means the High Court, unless otherwise stated.

(Rule 8.1(6)(b) provides that a rule or practice direction may, in relation to a specified type of proceedings, disapply or modify any of the rules set out in Part 8 as they apply to those proceedings)

When this Section must be used

54.2. The judicial review procedure must be used in a claim for judicial review where the **22–46** claimant is seeking—

    (a) a mandatory order;

    (b) a prohibiting order;

    (c) a quashing order; or

    (d) an injunction under section 30 of the *Supreme Court Act* 1981 (restraining a person from acting in any office in which he is not entitled to act).

When this Section may be used

54.3.—(1) The judicial review procedure may be used in a claim for judicial review where **22–47** the claimant is seeking—

(a) a declaration; or

(b) an injunction.

(Section 31(2) of the *Supreme Court Act* 1981 sets out the circumstances in which the court may grant a declaration or injunction in a claim for judicial review)

(Where the claimant is seeking a declaration or injunction in addition to one of the remedies listed in rule 54.2, the judicial review procedure must be used)

(2) A claim for judicial review may include a claim for damages but may not seek damages alone.

(Section 31(4) of the *Supreme Court Act* 1981 sets out the circumstances in which the court may award damages on a claim for judicial review).

Civil Procedure Rules 1998, Pt 54, rr.5–9

Time limit for filing claim form

22–48   **54.5.**—(1) The claim form must be filed—

(a) promptly; and

(b) in any event not later than 3 months after the grounds to make the claim first arose.

(2) The time limit in this rule may not be extended by agreement between the parties.

(3) This rule does not apply when any other enactment specifies a shorter time limit for making the claim for judicial review.

[This section is reprinted as amended by the *Civil Procedure Rules* 2003, Sch.1(1), para.1.]

Claim form

22–49   **54.6.**—(1) In addition to the matters set out in rule 8.2 (contents of the claim form) the claimant must also state—

(a) the name and address of any person he considers to be an interested party;

(b) that he is requesting permission to proceed with a claim for judicial review; and

(c) any remedy (including any interim remedy) he is claiming.

(Part 25 sets out how to apply for an interim remedy)

(2) The claim form must be accompanied by the documents required by the relevant practice direction.

Service of claim form

22–50   **54.7.** The claim form must be served on—

(a) the defendant; and

(b) unless the court otherwise directs, any person the claimant considers to be an interested party, within 7 days after the date of issue.

[This section is reprinted as amended by the *Civil Procedure (Amendment) Rules 2003*, Sch.1(1), para.1.]

Acknowledgment of service

22–51   **54.8.**—(1) Any person served with the claim form who wishes to take part in the judicial review must file an acknowledgment of service in the relevant practice form in accordance with the following provisions of this rule.

(2) Any acknowledgment of service must be—

(a) filed not more than 21 days after service of the claim form; and

(b) served on—

(i) the claimant; and

(ii) subject to any direction under rule 54.7(b), any other person named in the claim form,

as soon as practicable and, in any event, not later than 7 days after it is filed.

(3) The time limits under this rule may not be extended by agreement between the parties.

(4) The acknowledgment of service—

(a) must—
  (i)   where the person filing it intends to contest the claim, set out a summary of his grounds for doing so; and
  (ii) state the name and address of any person the person filing it considers to be an interested party; and
(b) may include or be accompanied by an application for directions.
(5) Rule 10.3(2) does not apply.

Failure to file acknowledgment of service
54.9.—(1) Where a person served with the claim form has failed to file an acknowledgment   **22–52**
of service in accordance with rule 54.8, he—
  (a) may not take part in a hearing to decide whether permission should be given unless the court allows him to do so; but
  (b) provided he complies with rule 54.14 or any other direction of the court regarding the filing and service of—
    (i)   detailed grounds for contesting the claim or supporting it on additional grounds; and
    (ii) any written evidence,
  may take part in the hearing of the judicial review.
(2) Where that person takes part in the hearing of the judicial review, the court may take his failure to file an acknowledgment of service into account when deciding what order to make about costs.
(3) Rule 8.4 does not apply.

Upon receipt of a claim form, a party must acknowledge it within the required   **22–53**
timescale. Failure to do so may result in not being able to take part in the hearing which decides whether to give the applicant permission to proceed with the judicial review. As permission is often refused where sufficient information is given, a party on whom a claim form is served must act swiftly. In any event, the position with regard to costs at a full hearing needs to be borne in mind.

C. Response to Claim

Civil Procedure Rules 1998, Pt 54, r.14

Response
54.14.—(1) A defendant and any other person saved with the claim form who wishes to   **22–54**
contest the claim or support it on additional grounds must file and serve—
  (a) detailed grounds for contesting the claim or supporting it on additional grounds; and
  (b) any written evidence,
within 35 days after service of the order giving permission.
(2) The following rules do not apply—
  (a) rule 8.5(3) and 8.5(4) (defendant to file and serve written evidence at the same time as acknowledgment of service); and
  (b) rule 8.5(5) and 8.5(6) (claimant to file and serve any reply within 14 days).

A magistrates' court which is in the position of having to respond to a claim may wish to instruct solicitors on its behalf.

D. Leave to Proceed

Pursuant to s.31(3) of the *Supreme Court Act* 1981 requires that an applicant for   **22–55**
judicial review obtain leave from the High Court before bringing an application.

Civil Procedure Rules 1998, Pt 54, rr.4, 10–13

Permission required
54.4. The court's permission to proceed is required in a claim for judicial review whether   **22–56**
started under this [Section] or transferred to the Administrative Court.

[This rule is reprinted as amended by the *Civil Procedure Amendment Rules* 2003, r.5(d).]

Permission given

22–57   **54.10.**—(1) Where permission to proceed is given the court may also give directions.

(2) Directions under paragraph (1) may include a stay of proceedings to which the claim relates.

(Rule 3.7 provides a sanction for the non-payment of the fee payable when permission to proceed has been given)

Service of order giving or refusing permission

22–58   **54.11.** The court will serve—

    (a) the order giving or refusing permission; and

    (b) any directions,

on—

        (i) the claimant;

        (ii) the defendant; and

        (iii) any other person who filed an acknowledgment of service.

Permission decision without a hearing

22–59   **54.12.**—(1) This rule applies where the court, without a hearing—

    (a) refuses permission to proceed; or

    (b) gives permission to proceed—

        (i) subject to conditions; or

        (ii) on certain grounds only.

(2) The court will serve its reasons for making the decision when it serves the order giving or refusing permission in accordance with rule 54.11.

(3) The claimant may not appeal but may request the decision to be reconsidered at a hearing.

(4) A request under paragraph (3) must be filed within 7 days after service of the reasons under paragraph (2).

(5) The claimant, defendant and any other person who has filed an acknowledgment of service will be given at least 2 days' notice of the hearing date.

Defendant etc. may not apply to set aside

22–60   **54.13.** Neither the defendant nor any other person served with the claim form may apply to set aside an order giving permission to proceed.

Civil Procedure Rules 1998, Pt 54, r.15

Where claimant seeks to rely on additional grounds

22–61   **54.15.** The court's permission is required if a claimant seeks to rely on grounds other than those for which he has been given permission to proceed.

See *R. v Blackfriars Crown Court Ex p. Sunworld Ltd* [2000] 1 W.L.R. 2102, above.

E. HEARING

Civil Procedure Rules 1998, Pt 54, rr.16–18

Evidence

22–62   **54.16.**—(1) Rule 8.6(1) does not apply.

(2) No written evidence may be relied on unless—

    (a) it has been served in accordance with any—

        (i) rule under this [Section]; or

        (ii) direction of the court; or

(b) the court gives permission.

Court's powers to hear any person
　54.17.—(1) Any person may apply for permission—　　　　　　　　　　**22–63**
　　(a) to file evidence; or
　　(b) make representations at the hearing of the judicial review.
　(2) An application under paragraph (1) should be made promptly.

Judicial review may be decided without a hearing
　54.18. The court may decide the claim for judicial review without a hearing where all the　**22–64**
parties agree.

F. STANDING

The High Court will not grant leave to bring a claim for judicial review unless it　**22–65**
considers that the applicant has a sufficient interest in the matter to which the application relates.

G. GROUNDS FOR REVIEW

Lord Diplock in the case of *CCSU v Minister for the Civil Service* [1985] A.C. 374　**22–66**
outlined the main grounds for review:
　— illegality—has the decision maker understood the law
　— procedural impropriety—failure to observe procedural rules, basic rules of natural justice or a failure to act with procedural fairness
　— irrationality—"Wednesbury unreasonableness", *i.e.* a decision which is so outrageous in its defiance of logic or of accepted moral standards that no sensible person who had applied his mind to the question to be decided could have arrived at it: *Associated Picture Houses Ltd v Wednesbury Corporation* [1948] 1 K.B. 223.
The question of proportionality was left open.

The Divisional Court may intervene if police procedures are shown to be manifestly　**22–67**
producing a result which induces a plea of guilty: *R. v Bolton Magistrates' Court Ex p. Scally* [1991] 1 Q.B. 537; *R. v Kingston-Upon-Thames Justices Ex p. Khana* [1986] R.T.R. 364. In the former case the defendants applied to have their convictions for drink driving quashed. They had been arrested on suspicion of drink driving and when blood tests had revealed excessive alcohol levels they had been obliged to plead guilty. That the swabs used were impregnated with alcohol was not known at the time by the prosecution authorities, the magistrates or the defendants. It was held that the prosecutor had unwittingly corrupted the process leading to conviction in a way which was detrimental to the defendants because it left them with no choice but to plead guilty and denied them a complete defence. The police had failed in their duty to exercise care when supplying blood-sampling kits. The prosecution case was tantamount to "fraud, collusion or perjury" and the convictions were quashed.

It is a denial of natural justice for a prosecutor to fail to disclose witnesses' statements favourable to the defence: *R. v Leyland Justices Ex p. Hawthorn* [1979] Q.B. 283.

Mere procedural impropriety on the part of the bench or a plea of guilty resulting from poor advice from the defendant's solicitors does not confer jurisdiction on the Divisional Court to quash the resultant conviction: *R. v Home Secretary Ex p. Al-Mehdawi* [1990] 1 A.C. 876.

The jurisdiction of the Divisional Court to quash convictions following a plea of guilty　**22–68**
is confined to cases where the plea was obtained by fraud, collusion or perjury on the part of the prosecution: *R. v Burton-Upon-Trent Justices Ex p. Woolley* (1995) 159 J.P. 183, [1995] R.T.R. 139, [1996] R.T.R. 340.

H. REVIEW OF COMMITTAL PROCEEDINGS

These proceedings are now rare.　　　　　　　　　　　　　　　　　　　**22–69**

It is not the practice of the Divisional Court to review committal proceedings which have not been concluded: *R. v Wells Street Stipendiary Magistrate Ex p. Seillon* 69 Cr.App.R. 77, DC; *R. v Horsham Justices Ex p. Bukhari* (1982) 74 Cr.App.R. 291, DC.

Judicial review lies in respect of committal proceedings where there has been a procedural flaw: *R. v Oxford City Justices Ex p. Berry* [1988] Q.B. 507, 85 Cr.App.R. 89, DC; *R. v Horseferry Road Magistrates' Court Ex p. Doung, The Times*, March 22, 1996; *R. v Wigan Justices Ex p. Sullivan* [1999] C.O.D. 21, DC. The remedy is discretionary, and is unlikely to be granted if the defendant's own conduct has contributed to the procedural failure or if an application to quash the indictment is an adequate alternative remedy.

Judicial review may be available to quash a committal on the ground of inadmissibility or insufficiency of the evidence: *Neill v North Antrim Magistrates' Court* 97 Cr.App.R. 121, HL; *R. v Bedwelty Justices Ex p. Williams* [1997] A.C. 225, HL. It is a misuse of judicial review to challenge a committal for trial on the basis of insufficiency of evidence except in the clearest cases: *R. v Whitehaven Justices Ex p. Thompson* [1999] C.O.D. 15, DC.

I. REMEDIES

22–70   The most common remedy sought by way of judicial review is the quashing order—the defendant seeks to have the conviction quashed.

Civil Procedure Rules 1998, Pt 54, r.19

Court's powers in respect of quashing orders

22–71   **54.19.**—(1) This rule applies where the court makes a quashing order in respect of the decision to which the claim relates.

(2) The court may—

    (a) remit the matter to the decision-maker; and

    (b) direct it to reconsider the matter and reach a decision in accordance with the judgment of the court.

(3) Where the court considers that there is no purpose to be served in remitting the matter to the decision-maker it may, subject to any statutory provision, take the decision itself.

(Where a statutory power is given to a tribunal, person or other body it may be the case that the court cannot take the decision itself).

22–72   Remedies in judicial review are discretionary. In deciding whether to grant a remedy the court will take into account a variety of factors including waiver, bad faith, the premature nature of the application, the absence of any injustice, and whether the decision would have been the same regardless of the error.

22–73   In *R. v Hereford Magistrates' Court Ex p. Rowlands* [1997] 2 W.L.R. 854, CA, Lord Bingham C.J. confirmed the court's supervisory jurisdiction over magistrates' courts as a guarantee of the integrity of proceedings in those courts which ensures that high standards of procedural fairness and impartiality are maintained. He outlined the approach of the court:

'First, leave to move should not be granted unless the applicant advances an apparently plausible complaint which, if made good, might arguably be held to vitiate the proceedings in the magistrates court. Immaterial and minor deviations from best practice would not have that effect, and the court should be respectful of discretionary decisions of magistrates' courts as of all other courts. This court should be generally slow to intervene, and should do so only where good (or arguably good) grounds for doing so are shown. Secondly, the decision whether or not to grant relief by way of judicial review is always, in the end, a discretionary one. Many factors may properly influence the exercise of discretion, and it would be both foolish and impossible to seek to anticipate them all. The need for an applicant to make full disclosure of all matters relevant to the exercise of discretion should require no emphasis. We do not, however, consider that the existence of a right of appeal to the Crown Court, particularly if unexercised, should ordinarily weigh against the grant of leave to move for judicial review, or the grant of substantive relief, in a proper case.

In *R. v DPP Ex p. Kebilene* [1999] 3 W.L.R. 175 Lord Bingham C.J. went on to **22–74** say at p.183:

> "Where the grant of leave to move judicial review would delay or obstruct the conduct of criminal proceedings which ought, in the public interest, to be resolved with all appropriate expedition, the court will always scrutinise the application with greatest care, both to satisfy itself that there are sound reasons for making the application and satisfy itself that there are no discretionary grounds (such as delay or the availability of alternative remedies or vexatious conduct by the applicant) which should lead it to refuse leave. The court would be very slow to intervene where the applicant's complaint is one that can be met by appropriate orders or directions in the criminal proceedings ..."

V. SUSPENDING DECISIONS PENDING OUTCOME

A. Bail

Magistrates' Courts Act 1980, s.113

Bail on appeal or case stated

113.—(1) Where a person has given notice of appeal to the Crown Court against the decision **22–75** of a magistrates' court or has applied to a magistrates' court to state a case for the opinion of the High Court, then, if he is in custody, the magistrates' court may, subject to section 25 of the *Criminal Justice and Public Order Act* 1994 grant him bail.

(2) If a person is granted bail under subsection (1) above, the time and place at which he is to appear (except in the event of the determination in respect of which the case is stated being reversed by the High Court) shall be—

(a) if he has given notice of appeal, the Crown Court at the time appointed for the hearing of the appeal;

(b) if he has applied for the statement of a case, the magistrates' court at such time within 10 days after the judgment of the High Court has been given as may be specified by the magistrates' court;

and any recognizance that may be taken from him or from any surety for him shall be conditioned accordingly.

(3) Subsection (1) above shall not apply where the accused has been committed to the Crown Court for sentence under [sentence 37] [above or section 3 of the *Powers of Criminal Court (Sentencing) Act* 2000].

(4) Section 37(6) of the *Criminal Justice Act* 1948 (which relates to the currency of a sentence while a person is released on bail by the High Court) shall apply to a person released on bail by a magistrates' court under this section pending the hearing of a case stated as it applies to a person released on bail by the High Court under section 22 of the *Criminal Justice Act* 1967.

[This section is reprinted as amended by *Powers of Criminal Courts (Sentencing) Act* 2000, Sch.9, para.72.]

A magistrates' court has the power to grant bail where the defendant, being in **22–76** custody, challenges its decision by way of appeal or case stated. It does not, however, have the power to grant bail where the challenge is by way of judicial review.

B. Sentence

A sentence is in force and enforceable once it has been passed. The lodging of an ap- **22–77** peal against conviction does not prevent the sentence from being enforced: *Greater Manchester Probation Service v Bent* (1996) 160 J.P. 297. There is statutory provision for the suspension of a driving disqualification pending appeal—see *Road Traffic Offenders Act* 1988, s.39.

Part IV

Sentencing

CHAPTER 23

GENERAL PRINCIPLES OF SENTENCING

I. THE PURPOSES OF SENTENCING

Sentencing can range from a relatively complex task to a relatively straightforward **23–1** one. At its most difficult, it is a complex balance in which conflicting goals have to be addressed. The main sentencing statute currently in force is the *Powers of Criminal Courts (Sentencing) Act* 2000 (*PCC(S)A* 2000).

This Act does not expressly state the purposes of sentencing, which have traditionally been said to be retribution, deterrence and rehabilitation (*per* Lord Bingham C.J., address to the Police Foundation, July 10, 1997). When in force, s.142 of the *Criminal Justice Act* 2003 will require every court to have regard to five specified purposes—punishment, reduction of crime, reform and rehabilitation, protection of the public and the making of reparation to those affected by the offence. Sentencing of youths (those aged under 18 at the time of conviction) is excluded from this obligation: s.142(2)(a). For adults, reduction of crime is simply listed as one of the five; for youths, there is a clear obligation to treat preventing of offending by young people as the primary goal (s.37 of the *Crime and Disorder Act* 1998) supported by the obligation to have regard to the welfare of the youth: s.44 of the *Children and Young Persons Act* 1933.

Criminal Justice Act 2003, s.142

Purposes of sentencing

142.—(1) Any court dealing with an offender in respect of his offence must have regard to **23–2** the following purposes of sentencing—
(a) the punishment of offenders,
(b) the reduction of crime (including its reduction by deterrence),
(c) the reform and rehabilitation of offenders,
(d) the protection of the public, and
(e) the making of reparation by offenders to persons affected by their offences.
(2) Subsection (1) does not apply—
(a) in relation to an offender who is aged under 18 at the time of conviction,
(b) to an offence the sentence for which is fixed by law,
(c) to an offence the sentence for which falls to be imposed under section 51A(2) of the *Firearms Act* 1968 (minimum sentence for certain firearms offences), under subsection (2) of section 110 or 111 of the *Sentencing Act* (required custodial sentences) or under any of sections 225 to 228 of this Act (dangerous offenders), or
(d) in relation to the making under Part 3 of the *Mental Health Act* 1983 of a hospital order (with or without a restriction order), an interim hospital order, a hospital direction or a limitation direction.
(3) In this Chapter "sentence", in relation to an offence, includes any order made by a court when dealing with the offender in respect of his offence; and "sentencing" is to be

construed accordingly

23–3   The central concept of the current sentencing framework is the seriousness of the offence, with the *PCC(S)A* 2000 providing threshold criteria for the imposition of both custodial and community penalties which are based on the seriousness of the offence committed: *PCC(S)A* 2000, s.79 (custodial sentences) and s.35 (community sentences). In addition, the sentence must not be more severe than can be said to be commensurate with the seriousness of the offence.

When in force, s.148 of the 2003 Act will provide that a court must not pass a community sentence on an offender unless it is of the opinion that the offence, or the combination of the offence and one or more offences associated with it, was *serious enough* to warrant such a sentence. Section 152 will provide that the court must not pass a custodial sentence unless it is of the opinion that the offence, or the combination of the offence and one or more offences associated with it, was *so serious* that neither a fine alone nor a community sentence can be justified for the offence (though see further at § 26–34 below)—whilst this is the same basic criterion as the *PCC(S)A* 2000, it is articulated a little differently.

23–4   The *Magistrates' Courts Sentencing Guidelines* (2003), p.81, provide that in determining the question of seriousness, courts should:

— make sure that all factors which aggravate or mitigate the offence are considered. (The lists which are contained in the Guidelines themselves should not be seen as being either exhaustive or a substitute for the personal judgment of the member(s) of the court).

— consider the various seriousness indicators, remembering that some will carry more weight than others;

— take into account the impact of the offence upon the victim

— note that, by statute, racial and religious aggravation increase the seriousness of any offence (there is a note on specific racially aggravated offences in the body of the Guidelines)

— always bear in mind that, by statute, the commission of an offence on bail aggravates its seriousness;

— consider the effect of using previous convictions, or any failure to respond to previous sentences, in assessing seriousness. Courts should identify any convictions relevant for this purpose and then consider to what extent they affect the seriousness of the present offence;

— note that when there are several offences to be sentenced, the court must have regard to the totality principle—the overall effect of the sentence must be commensurate with the total criminality involved.

23–5   The creation of the Sentencing Guidelines Council by s.167 of the *Criminal Justice Act* 2003 (see § 23–8 below) will provide an opportunity for greater clarity on this issue.

The *PCC(S)A* 2000 offers little guidance on the determination of seriousness but the 2003 Act seeks to assist by identifying issues for the court to consider.

Criminal Justice Act 2003, s.143

Determining the seriousness of an offence

23–6   **143.**—(1) In considering the seriousness of any offence, the court must consider the offender's culpability in committing the offence and any harm which the offence caused, was intended to cause or might forseeably have caused.

(2) In considering the seriousness of an offence ("the current offence") committed by an offender who has one or more previous convictions, the court must treat each previous conviction as an aggravating factor if (in the case of that conviction) the court considers that it can reasonably be so treated having regard, in particular, to—

(a) the nature of the offence to which the conviction relates and its relevance to the current offence, and

(b) the time that has elapsed since the conviction.

(3) In considering the seriousness of any offence committed while the offender was on bail, the court must treat the fact that it was committed in those circumstances as an aggravating factor.

(4) Any reference in subsection (2) to a previous conviction is to be read as a reference to—

(a) a previous conviction by a court in the United Kingdom, or

(b) a previous finding of guilt in service disciplinary proceedings.

(5) Subsection (2) and (4) do not prevent the court from treating a previous conviction by a court outside the United Kingdom as an aggravating factor in any case where the court considers it appropriate to do so.

A court must take into account two aspects directly relevant to the offence itself—the **23–7** culpability of the offender and the harm which was caused, intended or could have been caused. No guidance is given as to different types of harm or the people by whom the harm has been/could have been suffered. A person damaging property in a minor way as part of a campaign by activists against certain (lawful) activity may be playing a part in a chain of events that causes serious financial harm to the country as a whole by deterring inward investment. To incorporate that level of harm is likely to be seen as stretching the chain too far. However, those sentenced for importing illegal drugs will be sentenced on the basis of the harm those drugs will have the potential to do to people far removed in the chain of events from the importer. Perhaps the link then is generally the extent to which the harm is an inevitable consequence of the conduct. Again, it may be that the Sentencing Guidelines Council will consider this issue and offer guidance.

A more radical proposal is set out in s.143(2). There has long been an issue about the significance of previous convictions given the obligation to ensure that a sentence is not greater than is commensurate with the seriousness of the offence. This provision seeks to circumvent that by causing a previous conviction to aggravate the seriousness of the current offence, presumably because it influences the decision as to culpability. Further guidance will no doubt be available when this provision is brought into force.

II. ESTABLISHMENT OF SENTENCING GUIDELINES COUNCIL

The *Criminal Justice Act* 2003 establishes a Sentencing Guidelines Council to issue **23–8** guidelines for any issue that affects sentencing decisions. The Council was established in March 2004 and will gradually develop a body of guidelines to which each magistrates' court will have regard when passing sentence.

As well as dealing with individual offences, the guidelines will deal with more general issues such as the extent of the reduction in sentence following a guilty plea and the significance of previous convictions. Information on the Council and any guidelines can be found at *www.sentencing-guidelines.gov.uk*.

CHAPTER 24

INFORMATION GATHERING

I. FUNCTION OF THE PROSECUTION IN RELATION TO SENTENCE

There is a substantial difference in the range and the volume of the workload be- **24–1** tween the Crown Court and the magistrates' courts. Not every prosecutor in a magistrates' court is a solicitor or barrister; in addition to the lay presenters appearing on behalf of the Crown Prosecution Service, other prosecutors can authorise suitable individuals to prosecute on their behalf. In addition, the volume of cases and the speed of throughput is much greater in a magistrates' court. The existing guidelines are published more systematically. The case law tends to come from proceedings in the Crown Court and needs to be read in the light of these differences. The principles that can be deduced from the cases are as follows.

1. In *Att.-Gen.'s Reference (No.7 of 1997) (R. v Fearon)* [1998] 1 Cr.App.R.(S.) **24–2** 268 it was clearly stated that the role of the prosecution as regards sentencing includes providing assistance and guidance. Judges should not be slow to invite assistance from prosecuting counsel in these matters and counsel should be ready to offer assistance if asked. The Court hoped that judges would not be affronted if prosecuting counsel did offer to give guidance on the relevant provisions and appropriate authorities.

2. This approach was developed further by Lord Woolf C.J. in *Att.-Gen.'s Reference (No.52 of 2003)(R. v Webb)* [2003] EWCA Crim 3731. It was emphasised that prosecuting counsel had a duty to draw relevant guideline cases to the attention of the court and it would be wrong for a Judge to suggest that counsel should not do his duty. Prosecuting counsel, it was said, should be meticulous in drawing relevant guidelines to the attention of the Judge and in having copies available if required.

Whilst this is a desirable situation also in the magistrates' court, it is legitimate to expect the legal adviser to the magistrates to fulfil that function in normal circumstances. However, prosecution and defence advocates should always be aware of the existence of relevant guidance and be prepared to draw it to the attention of the court should the court seem to be unaware of it.

See also *R. v Blight* [1999] Crim.L.R. 426 for the duty on counsel to be ready to assist the court and *R. v Hartery* [1993] Crim.L.R. 230 emphasising the duty of counsel to inform themselves of the extent of the court's powers, to know what options are open to the judge, and to correct the judge if a mistake is made.

24–3   3. Prosecution Counsel should be able to present the court with sufficient information about the offence to enable the court to assess its seriousness. It is not part of the function to influence the court with regard to that assessment. However, if a defendant is not legally represented it is proper to inform the judge of any mitigating circumstances about which counsel is instructed.

      4. Counsel should also be in a position to assist the Court, if requested, as to any statutory provisions relevant to the offence or the offender. Counsel should be prepared to bring to the attention of the court any matters referred to above in which he feels the Court has erred and should also bring to the attention of the Court any appropriate compensation, forfeiture and restitution matters which arise on conviction.

      5. Counsel should draw the attention of the Court to any assertion of material fact put forward in mitigation which prosecuting counsel believes to be untrue: if the defence persist in this assertion, prosecuting counsel should invite the Court to consider requiring the issue to be determined through a *Newton* hearing (described below § 25–2): para.11.8(e) of the *Code of Conduct of the Bar Written Standards* (7th Ed.).

24–4   6. For defence counsel, the same rules apply to mitigation as to any other court proceedings. Defence counsel should notify the prosecution of anything which counsel is instructed to submit in mitigation which casts aspersions on the conduct or character of a victim or witness in the case. The purpose of this is to give prosecuting counsel sufficient opportunity to consider whether or not to challenge these assertions.

      7. Para.708(g) of the Code of Conduct of the Bar provides that a barrister must not make statements or ask questions which are merely scandalous or intended or calculated only to vilify insult or annoy either a witness or some other person. The barrister must also, if possible, avoid naming in open court a third party whose conduct would be impugned thereby (para.708(h)).

24–5   The *Criminal Proceedings and Investigations Act* 1996, ss.58 to 60 give the court power to restrict the reporting of false or irrelevant assertions made during a speech in mitigation. Where there are substantial grounds for concluding that an assertion is both derogatory and either false or irrelevant to sentence (s.58(4)), the court may make an order which makes it an offence to publish that assertion: ss.59 and 60. An order may be made before the court determines sentences (s.58(7)), in which case it ceases on sentence being passed, or it may be made as soon as reasonably practicable after sentence in which case, unless earlier revoked, it will cease to be effective after 12 months: s.58(8).

Criminal Procedure and Investigations Act 1996, ss.58–60

Orders in respect of certain assertions

24–6   58.—(1) This section applies where a person has been convicted of an offence and a speech in mitigation is made by him or on his behalf before—

      (a) a court determining what sentence should be passed on him in respect of the offence, or

      (b) a magistrates' court determining whether he should be committed to the Crown Court for sentence.

      (2) This section also applies where a sentence has been passed on a person in respect of an offence and a submission relating to the sentence is made by him or on his behalf before—

      (a) a court hearing an appeal against or reviewing the sentence, or

      (b) a court determining whether to grant leave to appeal against the sentence.

      (3) Where it appears to the court that there is a real possibility that an order under subsection (8) will be made in relation to the assertion, the court may make an order under subsection (7) in relation to the assertion.

      (4) Where there are substantial grounds for believing—

      (a) that an assertion forming part of the speech or submission is derogatory to a person's character (for instance, because it suggests that his conduct is or has been criminal, immoral or improper), and

(b) that the assertion is false or that the facts asserted are irrelevant to the sentence, the court may make an order under subsection (8) in relation to the assertion.

(5) An order under subsection (7) or (8) must not be made in relation to an assertion if it appears to the court that the assertion was previously made—

(a) at the trial at which the person was convicted of the offence, or

(b) during any other proceedings relating to the offence.

(6) Section 59 has effect where a court makes an order under subsection (7) or (8).

(7) An order under this subsection—

(a) may be made at any time before the court has made a determination with regard to sentencing;

(b) may be revoked at any time by the court;

(c) subject to paragraph (b), shall cease to have effect when the court makes a determination with regard to sentencing.

(8) An order under this subsection—

(a) may be made after the court has made a determination with regard to sentencing, but only if it is made as soon as is reasonably practicable after the making of the determination;

(b) may be revoked at any time by the court;

(c) subject to paragraph (b), shall cease to have effect at the end of the period of 12 months beginning with the day on which it is made;

(d) may be made whether or not an order has been made under subsection (7) with regard to the case concerned.

(9) For the purposes of subsection (7) and (8) the court makes a determination with regard to sentencing—

(a) when it determines what sentence should be passed (where this section applies by virtue of subsection (1)(a);

(b) when it determines whether the person should be committed to the Crown Court for sentence (where this section applies by virtue of subsection (1)(b));

(c) when it determines what the sentence should be (where this section applies by virtue of subsection (2)(a));

(d) when it determines whether to grant leave to appeal (where this section applies by virtue of subsection (2)(b).

Restriction on reporting of assertions

59.—(1) Where a court makes an order under section 58(7) or (8) in relation to any assertion, **24–7** at any time when the order has effect the assertion must not—

(a) be published in Great Britain in a written publication available to the public, or

(b) be included in a relevant programme for reception in Great Britain.

(2) In this section—

"relevant programme" means a programme included in a programme service, within the meaning of the *Broadcasting Act* 1990;

"written publication" includes a film, a soundtrack and any other record in permanent form but does not include an indictment or other document prepared for use in particular legal proceedings.

(3) For the purposes of this section an assertion is published or included in a programme if the material published or included—

(a) names the person about whom the assertion is made or, without naming him, contains enough to make it likely that members of the public will identify him as the person about whom it is made, and

(b) reproduces the actual wording of the matter asserted or contains its substance.

Reporting of assertions: offences

60.—(1) If an assertion is published or included in a relevant programme in contravention of **24–8** section 59, each of the following persons is guilty of an offence—

(a) in the case of publication in a newspaper or periodical, any proprietor, any editor and any publisher of the newspaper or periodical;

(b) in the case of publication in any other form, the person publishing the assertion;

(c) in the case of an assertion included in a relevant programme, any body corporate engaged in providing the service in which the programme is included and any person having functions in relation to the programme corresponding to those of an editor of a newspaper.

(2) A person guilty of an offence under this section is liable on summary conviction to a fine of an amount not exceeding level 5 on the standard scale.

(3) Where a person is charged with an offence under this section it is a defence to prove that at the time of the alleged offence—

    (a) he was not aware, and neither suspected nor had reason to suspect, that an order under section 58(7) or (8) had effect at that time, or

    (b) he was not aware, and neither suspected nor had reason to suspect, that the publication or programme in question was of, or (as the case may be) included, the assertion in question.

(4) Where an offence under this section committed by a body corporate is proved to have been committed with the consent or connivance of, or to be attributable to any neglect on the part of—

    (a) a director, manager, secretary or other similar officer of the body corporate, or

    (b) a person purporting to act in any such capacity,

he as well as the body, corporate is guilty of the offence and liable to be proceeded against and punished accordingly.

(5) In relation to a body corporate whose affairs are managed by its members "director" in subsection (4) means a member of the body corporate.

(6) Subsection (2) and (3) of section 59 apply for the purposes of this section as they apply for the purposes of that.

II. LEGAL REPRESENTATION

24–9　　There is no obligation on a person to be legally represented (although there are certain things that an unrepresented defendant cannot do). However, the court must not impose a custodial sentence on an offender who is not legally represented unless an opportunity to apply for legal representation at public expense has been given and not taken or, though taken, has been withdrawn on the ground of the conduct of the defendant: s.83(1)–(3) of the *PCC(S)A* 2000.

For magistrates' courts, this additional requirement applies where a defendant aged 21 or over on conviction who is liable to receive imprisonment has not previously been so sentenced and is not legally represented: s.83(1) and (2). For other defendants, it applies regardless of whether a custodial sentence has previously been imposed—the only criterion is lack of legal representation: s.83(2).

Powers of Criminal Court (Sentencing) Act 2000, s.83

Restriction on imposing custodial sentences on persons not legally represented

24–10　　83.—(1) A magistrates' court on summary conviction, or the Crown Court on committal for sentence or on conviction on indictment, shall not pass a sentence of imprisonment on a person who—

    (a) is not legally represented in that court, and

    (b) has not been previously sentenced to that punishment by a court in any part of the United Kingdom,

unless he is a person to whom subsection (3) below applies.

(2) A magistrates' court on summary conviction, or the Crown Court on committal for sentence or on conviction on indictment, shall not—

    (a) pass a sentence of detention under section 90 or 91 below,

    [(aa) pass a sentence of imprisonment on a person who, when convicted, was aged at least 18 but under 21,]

    (b) pass a sentence of custody for life under section 93 or 94 below,

    (c) pass a sentence of detention in a young offender institution, or

    (d) make a detention and training order,

on or in respect of a person who is not legally represented in that court unless he is a person to whom subsection (3) below applies.

(3) This subsection applies to a person if either—

(a) he was granted a right to representation funded by the Legal Services Commission as part of the Criminal Defence Service but the right was withdrawn because of his conduct; or

(b) having been informed of his right to apply for such representation and having had the opportunity to do so, he refused or failed to apply.

(4) For the purposes of this section a person is to be treated as legally represented in a court if, but only if, he has the assistance of counsel or a solicitor to represent him in the proceedings in that court at some time after he is found guilty and before he is sentenced.

(5) For the purposes of subsection (1)(b) above a previous sentence of imprisonment which has been suspended and which has not taken effect under section 119 below or under section 19 of the *Treatment of Offenders Act (Northern Ireland)* 1968 shall be disregarded.

(6) In this section "sentence of imprisonment" does not include a committal for contempt of court or any kindred offence.

[Subs.(2): paras (b), (c) substituted, by subsequent para.(aa), by the *Criminal Justice and Court Services Act* 2000, s.74, Sch.7, Pt II, paras 160, 178 from a date to be appointed: see the *Criminal Justice and Court Services Act* 2000, s.80(1).]

III. FUNCTION OF THE LEGAL ADVISER (COURT CLERK) IN RELATION TO SENTENCE

24–11 The *Practice Direction (Criminal Proceedings: Consolidation)* [2002] 1 W.L.R. 2870 at para.55 (clerk retiring with justices) makes it clear that the justices' clerk is responsible for the advice tendered to justices in the area either directly or through a legal adviser. Job titles will vary but the term "legal adviser" has generally superseded that of "court clerk". Both Direction 55 and the Legal Adviser competences (published by the Justices' Clerks' Society) make it clear that sentencing advice should be given and that it is the responsibility of the legal adviser to do so whether or not that advice is requested. Advice on sentencing will be required:

— where the plea before venue procedure is adopted, and the court is unsure of its sentencing powers,

— when the court is considering the issue of mode of trial and it needs to decide whether the sentencing powers would be sufficient should the defendant be convicted, and

— when passing sentence.

24–12 Direction 55.3 provides that it is the responsibility of the legal adviser to provide the justices with any advice they require to properly perform their functions whether or not the justices have requested that advice, on, amongst other matters, the range of penalties available, the relevant decisions of the superior courts or other guidelines, other issues relevant to the matter before the court and the appropriate decision making structure to be applied in any given case. Paragraph 7 confirms that any legal advice given to justices other than in open court should clearly be stated to be provisional, and the adviser should subsequently repeat the substance of the advice in open court and give the parties an opportunity to make any representations they wish on that provisional advice. This procedure will ensure that any party can challenge the advice given where necessary.

IV. PRE-SENTENCE REPORTS

24–13 The court must obtain and consider a pre-sentence report (PSR) before imposing certain types of sentence: see *PCC(S)A* 2000, ss.36(4) (community sentences) and 81(1) (custodial sentences). This does not apply where the court considers that such a report is "unnecessary": s.36(5)–(6). Although there is authority that indicates that a pre-sentence report may be unnecessary where the court is willing to make every possible assumption in favour of the defendant: *R. v Armsaramah* [2001] 1 Cr.App.R.(S.) 133; this is unlikely to be applicable in a magistrates' court which is dealing with relatively short sentences. For an offender under 18 in a case where the offence is not one triable only on indictment, a court may only find it unnecessary to have a report where there is an earlier pre-sentence report which the court has considered.

Powers of Criminal Courts (Sentencing) Act 2000, s.36(3)–(10)

Procedural requirements for community sentences: pre-sentence reports etc.

24–14   **36.**—(3) The following provisions of this section apply in relation to—

     (a) a probation order which includes additional requirements authorised by Schedule 2 to this Act;

     (b) a community punishment order;

     (c) a community punishment and rehabilitation order;

     (d) a drug treatment and testing order;

     (e) a supervision order which includes requirements authorised by Schedule 6 to this Act.

(4) Subject to subsection (5) below, a court shall obtain and consider a pre-sentence report before forming an opinion as to the suitability for the offender of one or more of the orders mentioned in subsection (3) above.

(5) Subsection (4) above does not apply if, in the circumstances of the case, the court is of the opinion that it is unnecessary to obtain a pre-sentence report.

(6) In a case where the offender is aged under 18 and the offence is not triable only on indictment and there is no other offence associated with it that is triable only on indictment, the court shall not form such an opinion as is mentioned in subsection (5) above unless—

     (a) there exists a previous pre-sentence report obtained in respect of the offender; and

     (b) the court has had regard to the information contained in that report, or, if there is more than one such report, the most recent report.

(7) No community sentence which consists of or includes such an order as is mentioned in subsection (3) above shall be invalidated by the failure of a court to obtain and consider a pre-sentence report before forming an opinion as to the suitability of the order for the offender, but any court on an appeal against such a sentence—

     (a) shall, subject to subsection (8) below, obtain a pre-sentence report if none was obtained by the court below; and

     (b) shall consider any such report obtained by it or by that court.

(8) Subsection (7)(a) above does not apply if the court is of the opinion—

     (a) that the court below was justified in forming an opinion that it was unnecessary to obtain a pre-sentence report; or

     (b) that, although the court below was not justified in forming that opinion, in the circumstances of the case at the time it is before the court, it is unnecessary to obtain a pre-sentence report.

(9) In a case where the offender is aged under 18 and the offence is not triable only on indictment and there is no other offence associated with it that is triable only on indictment, the court shall not form such an opinion as is mentioned in subsection (8) above unless—

     (a) there exists a previous pre-sentence report obtained in respect of the offender; and

     (b) the court has had regard to the information contained in that report, or, if there is more than one such report, the most recent report.

(10) Section 156 below (disclosure of pre-sentence report to offender etc.) applies to any pre-sentence report obtained in pursuance of this section.

24–15   A PSR is a written report; it is written to help the court decide the most suitable way of dealing with an offender; it is a report of an "appropriate officer" (normally an officer of a local probation board or a member of a youth offending team). Its content and style are prescribed by rules made by the Secretary of State and contained in National Standards at paragraphs B5–B10. It is written for the benefit of the court and the court will weigh carefully the content as part of the decision making process.

Powers of Criminal Courts (Sentencing) Act 2000, s.162

Meaning of "pre-sentence report"

162.—(1) In this Act "pre-sentence report" means a report in writing which— **24–16**
(a) with a view to assisting the court in determining the most suitable method of dealing with an offender, is made or submitted by an appropriate officer; and
(b) contains information as to such matters, presented in such manner, as may be prescribed by rules made by the Secretary of State.

(2) In subsection (1) above "an appropriate officer" means—
(a) where the offender is aged 18 or over, an officer of a local probation board or a social worker of a local authority social services department;
(b) where the offender is aged under 18, an officer of a local probation board a social worker of a local authority social services department or a member of a youth offending team.

(1) Probation Service National Standards

Pre-Sentence Reports

B5. The purpose of a pre-sentence report (PSR) is to provide information to the sentencing **24–17** court about the offender and the offence(s) committed and to assist the court to decide on suitable sentence. A PSR shall:
— be objective, impartial, free from discriminatory language and stereotype, balanced, verified and factually accurate;
— be based on the use of the Offender Assessment System (OASys), when implemented, to provide a systematic assessment of the nature and the causes of the offender's offending behaviour, the risk of harm the offender poses to the public and the action which can be taken to reduce the likelihood of re-offending;
— be based on at least one face-to-face interview with the offender (which can be made via a video link where this is available);
— specify information available from the CPS, any approved premises placement or from any other relevant source;
— be written, and a copy provided to the court, the defence, the offender and (where required by s.156 of the *Powers of Criminal Courts (Sentencing) Act* 2000) the prosecution;
— be prepared within, at most, 15 working days of request; or such shorter timescale as has been agreed in protocols with the court;
— contain the sections indicated in italics below.
(These sections are a front sheet (B6), offence analysis (B7), offender assessment (B8), assessment of risk of harm to the public and the likelihood of reoffending (B9) and a conclusion (B10)).

B10. Conclusion

B10. Every PSR shall contain a conclusion which: **24–18**
— evaluates the offender's motivation and ability to change and identifies, where relevant, action required to improve motivation;
— explicitly states whether or not an offender is suitable for a community sentence;
— makes a clear and realistic proposal for sentence designed to protect the public and reduce reoffending, including for custody where this is necessary;
— where the proposal is for a community rehabilitation order or community punishment and rehabilitation order, includes an outline supervision plan containing:
　— a description of the purposes and desired outcomes of the proposed sentence;
　— the methods envisaged and interventions likely to be undertaken, including attendance at accredited programmes where appropriate;
　— the level of supervision envisaged (which for offenders at high risk of causing serious harm to the public is likely to be higher than the minimum required by the Standards);
— where a specific condition is proposed, sets out the requirement precisely as it is proposed to appear in any order, and gives a likely start date;
— where the proposal is for a curfew order, includes details of the suitability of the proposed curfew address and its likely effects on others living at the offender's address;

— for all serious sexual or violent offences, provides advice on the appropriateness of extended supervision;
— where custody is a likely option, identifies any anticipated effects on the offender's family circumstances, current employment or education.

Specific Sentence Reports

24–19   B11. The purpose of a specific sentence report (SSR) is to provide information about the offender and offence(s) so as to assist the sentencing court to determine the offender's suitability for a specific sentence envisaged by the court. It is a PSR for the formal purposes of section 162 of the *Powers of Criminal Courts (Sentencing) Act* 2000 and is used to speed up the provision of information to the court to allow sentencing without delay and is most likely to be used where the court envisages a community punishment order of up to 100 hours or community rehabilitation order without additional requirements. An SSR shall:
— be based on an initial assessment of risk of serious harm and likelihood of reoffending;
— be a written report, even where presented orally to the court. An approved format is at Annex C;
— clearly set out the offender's suitability for a particular penalty as requested by the court;
— other than in exceptional circumstances, be available to the court on the day requested;
— recommend an adjournment for a full PSR if the writer believes that further investigation is required.

Where it has not been possible to complete a PSR or an SSR, for whatever reason, including non-attendance by the offender at interview, the report writer shall submit written notice to the court giving reasons why the report has not been completed.

24–20   The expectation is that a report will be prepared within 15 working days for a defendant on bail and 10 working days for a defendant in custody. However, it may be possible for sufficient information to be gained on the day of the court and a specific sentence report (SSR) (sometimes called a stand-down report) may be requested—this report will comply with all the requirements regarding a PSR and enable a court to proceed to sentence on the same day as the day on which the report was requested: see *Probation Service National Standards*, para.B11. If such a report is requested but the report writer discovers issues that require more investigation than could occur within the day, a request should be made for an adjournment and for the preparation of a full PSR.

If an SSR is not possible, the court may adjourn for up to four weeks after conviction (three weeks if the defendant is kept in custody) to enable the preparation of reports as to the most suitable way of dealing with the defendant: s.10(3) of the *Magistrates' Courts Act* 1980. If the offence is imprisonable, the defendant must be granted bail unless one of the general exceptions to the right to bail applies (see Chapter 7 above), or that it would be impracticable to complete the inquiries or make the report without keeping the defendant in custody. If the offence is not imprisonable, bail may only be withheld if one of the exceptions specified in paras 2–5 of Pt II of Sch.1 to the 1976 Act applies (see Chapter 7 above).

24–21   Once a report is prepared and delivered to the court, the court is under an obligation to give a copy of that report to the people specified in ss.156 and 157 of the *PCC(S)A* 2000 (see below). A relatively recent addition to the list is the group of approved prosecutors (s.156(2) and (4))—this is designed to ensure that any assertions made in the report that may have a bearing on the allegations concerning the nature of the offence (and often the conduct of the victim) are known to the prosecutor who can decide whether to challenge them.

The court should arrange for a copy of the PSR to be given to such a prosecutor: s.156(2). However, unless the prosecutor falls within a description specified by order, the court retains a discretion not to do so if giving the report would be inappropriate: s.156(4). This is most likely in a private prosecution. The *Pre-Sentence Report Disclosure (Description of Prosecutors) Order* 1998 (SI 1998/191) prescribes the following descriptions of prosecutors for the purposes of s.156(4): a Crown Prosecutor, any other person acting on behalf of the Crown Prosecution Service, a person acting on behalf of the Commissioners of Customs and Excise, the Secretary of State for Social Security, the Commissioners of Inland Revenue or the Director of the Serious Fraud Office. For these prosecutors, the court does not have a discretion and must give the prosecutor a copy of the report.

In an ideal world, the report will be delivered to the court and to the parties at least a **24–22** day ahead of the court hearing which will give all parties the opportunity to consider its contents. This can be done by electronic means but it is a process which must be under the control of the court—the report is to the court; the statutory obligation to ensure copies are given out is also placed on the court.

However, in reality, the report will almost always be delivered to a magistrates' court on the day of the hearing and there will be local arrangements to ensure that copies get to the appropriate parties.

A report is a key element in assisting a court to decide the appropriate sentence; it also enables the commencement of post sentence planning and so needs to be done thoroughly and effectively. At its heart is the assessment of the risk of the offender reoffending and an analysis of ways in which any risk can be reduced.

In a magistrates' court, the court that passes sentence will often consist of different people from those who ordered the pre-sentence report. It is highly desirable that the court ordering the report identifies clearly what it sees as the issues both in terms of the assessment of seriousness of the offences committed and in terms of the offender's personal circumstances.

When proceeding to sentence after a PSR has been prepared, the normal sequence **24–23** will be for the court to hear from the prosecutor setting out the circumstances of the offence and any previous criminal activity of the defendant, for the court to consider the pre-sentence report (though it may have taken an opportunity to read the report in advance of hearing from the prosecution) and then for the court to hear from the defendant or his legal representative.

After hearing from the prosecution and reading the report, the court may wish to consider certain issues in detail—for instance, the report may have suggested a community sentence with certain requirements which seem to the court to be highly commendable or the court may have taken a completely different view from the report writer on either sentence or the seriousness of certain events. It is quite legitimate to put the defence on notice before the court is addressed, perhaps by way of "The court has read the report and heard from the prosecution. On what we know so far we can see merit in following the proposal in the pre-sentence report—do you wish to persuade us otherwise?" Where there is agreement, that can readily be identified. Where there is disagreement, the defence knows clearly what the issues are for the court and this enables the defence advocate to address those issues directly rather than having to try to guess what the court is thinking.

Regarding the facts of the offence given to the probation officer for the preparation **24–24** of a PSR, the offender may sometimes give an account which differs from that given by the prosecution. Guidance as to the approach of the court was given in *R. v Tolera* [1999] 1 Cr.App.R. 29. Whilst this part of the pre-sentence report would, of course, be read by the court, it was not ordinarily to form part of the factual basis for the passing of sentence. If a defendant wishes to rely on this part of the pre-sentence report for the purposes of sentence, the defence should make this clear, and the prosecution should be forewarned. The issue could then be resolved, if necessary by the calling of evidence.

Powers of Criminal Court (Sentencing) Act 2000, s.156

Disclosure of pre-sentence reports
156.—(1) This section applies where a court obtains a pre-sentence report.   **24–25**
(2) Subject to subsection (3) and (4) below, the court shall give a copy of the report—
    (a) to the offender or his counsel or solicitor; and
    (b) to the prosecutor, that is to say, the person having the conduct of the proceedings in respect of the offence.

(3) If the offender is aged under 17 and is not represented by counsel or a solicitor, a copy of the report need not be given to him but shall be given to his parent or guardian if present in court.

(4) If the prosecutor is not of a description prescribed by order made by the Secretary of State, a copy of the report need not be given to the prosecutor if the court considers that it would be inappropriate for him to be given it.

(5) No information obtained by virtue of subsection (2)(b) above shall be used or disclosed otherwise than for the purpose of—

    (a) determining whether representations as to matters contained in the report need to be made to the court; or

    (b) making such representations to the court.

V. OTHER REPORTS

24–26   Other reports may be obtained or are required to be obtained in certain other circumstances. Whenever a report is obtained which, although from an officer of a local probation board or a member of a Youth Offending Team, is not a PSR, the court is obliged to ensure that a copy of the report is given to the offender or to his legal representative. If the offender is under 17 years of age and not legally represented, the court is not obliged to give the offender a copy (but may do so if it wishes) but must give a copy to a parent or guardian if they are at court: s.157(3).

Powers of Criminal Court (Sentencing) Act 2000, s.157

Other reports of probation officers and members of youth offending teams

24–27   **157.**—(1) This section applies where—

    (a) a report by an officer of a local probation board or a member of a youth offending team is made to any court (other than a youth court) with a view to assisting the court in determining the most suitable method of dealing with any person in respect of an offence; and

    (b) the report is not a pre-sentence report (as defined by section 162 below).

(2) Subject to subsection (3) below, the court shall give a copy of the report to the offender or his counsel or solicitor.

(3) If the offender is aged under 17 and is not represented by counsel or a solicitor, a copy of the report need not be given to him but shall be given to his parent or guardian if present in court.

VI. PRE-SENTENCE DRUG TESTING

24–28   When in force, there will be a further power to require a person to provide samples to find out whether there are traces of certain illegal drugs present in the body. The offender must be aged 14 years or over and the court must be considering a community sentence or a suspended sentence.

Criminal Justice Act 2003, s.161

Pre-sentence drug testing

24–29   **161.**—(1) Where a person aged 14 or over is convicted of an offence and the court is considering passing a community sentence or a suspended sentence, it may make an order under subsection (2) for the purpose of ascertaining whether the offender has any specified Class A drug in his body.

(2) The order requires the offender to provide, in accordance with the order, samples of any description specified in the order.

(3) Where the offender has not attained the age of 17, the order must provide for the samples to be provided in the presence of an appropriate adult.

(4) If it is proved to the satisfaction of the court that the offender has, without reasonable excuse, failed to comply with the order it may impose on him a fine of an amount not exceeding level 4.

(5) In subsection (4) "level 4" means the amount which, in relation to a fine for a summary offence, is level 4 on the standard scale.

(6) The court may not make an order under subsection (2) unless it has been notified by the Secretary of State that the power to make such orders is exercisable by the court and the notice has not been withdrawn.

(7) The Secretary of State may by order amend subsection (1) by substituting for the age for the time being specified there a different age specified in the order.

(8) In this section—

"appropriate adult", in relation to a person under the age of 17, means—

> (a) his parent or guardian or, if he is in the care of a local authority or voluntary organisation, a person representing that authority or organisation,
>
> (b) a social worker of a local authority social services department, or
>
> (c) if no person falling within paragraph (a) or (b) is available, any responsible person aged 18 or over who is not a police officer or a person employed by the police;

"specified Class A drug" has the same meaning as in Part 3 of the *Criminal Justice and Court Services Act* 2000 (c. 43).

See also ss.35, 36 of the *Mental Health Act* 1983 for the power to remand a mentally disordered offender to hospital for a report on his medical condition, §§ 35–9—35–14 below.

VII. ADJOURNMENTS AFTER CONVICTION AND BEFORE SENTENCE

24–30 As stated above § 24–20, a court may need toadjourn the proceedings to allow for the preparation of reports. This power is contained in s.10(3) of the *Magistrates' Courts Act* 1980.

Magistrates' Courts Act 1980, s.10

Adjournment of trial

24–31 **10.**—(1) A magistrates' court may at any time, whether before or after beginning to try an information, adjourn the trial, and may do so, notwithstanding anything in this Act, when composed of a single justice.

(2) The court may when adjourning either fix the time and place at which the trial is to be resumed, or, unless it remands the accused, leave the time and place to be determined later by the court; but the trial shall not be resumed at that time and place unless the court is satisfied that the parties have had adequate notice thereof.

(3) A magistrates' court may, for the purpose of enabling inquiries to be made or of determining the most suitable method of dealing with the case, exercise its power to adjourn after convicting the accused and before sentencing him or otherwise dealing with him; but, if it does so, the adjournment shall not be for more than 4 weeks at a time unless the court remands the accused in custody, and, where it so remands him, the adjournment shall not be for more than 3 weeks at a time.

(3A) A youth court shall not be required to adjourn any proceedings for an offence at any stage by reason only of the fact—

> (a) that the court commits the accused for trial for another offence; or
>
> (b) that the accused is charged with another offence.

(4) On adjourning the trial of an information the court may remand the accused and, where the accused has attained the age of 18 years, shall do so if the offence is triable either way and—

> (a) on the occasion on which the accused first appeared, or was brought, before the court to answer to the information he was in custody or, having been released on bail, surrendered to the custody of the court; or
>
> (b) the accused has been remanded at any time in the course of proceedings on the information;

and, where the court remands the accused, the time fixed for the resumption of the trial shall be that at which he is required to appear or be brought before the court in pursuance of the remand or would be required to be brought before the court but for section 128(3A) below.

24–32   Where a magistrates' court adjourns for reports after conviction, what is said at the time can restrict the options of the court that passes sentence. Great care, therefore, needs to be taken to ensure that justice is done. The defendant should invariably be told clearly that he must not assume from the fact that the court has ordered an assessment or investigation, that he is likely to receive any particular form of sentence or that a custodial sentence is ruled out: *R. v Chamberlain* (1995) 16 Cr.App.R.(S.) 473, CA.

Where the court fails to warn the offender that all sentencing options remain open to the court, a legitimate expectation may be created in the mind of the offender that a non-custodial sentence may be imposed by the sentencing court. In *R. v Inner London Crown Court Ex p. Mentesh* [2001] 1 Cr.App.R.(S.) 94, the offender submitted that the magistrates' actions in adjourning sentence to permit preparation of a further report in addition to the pre-sentence report had created a legitimate expectation that, if all went well, he would receive a non-custodial sentence and that the expectation should have been honoured by the sentencing court. The questions were:

a) whether, when the magistrates adjourned the case, they created an expectation on the part of the applicant that if all went well he would receive a non-custodial sentence

b) whether it was legitimate, if there were such an expectation, that it should have been honoured by the sentencing court, and

c) whether anything had intervened to change the position.

24–33   Following *R. v Gillam* (1980) 2 Cr.App.R.(S.) 267 and *R. v Chamberlain* (above), the Court held that this case was squarely within the situations envisaged by previous authorities as giving rise to a legitimate expectation of a non-custodial sentence and the appeal against sentence was allowed. In *R. v Southampton Magistrates' Court Ex p. Sansome* [1999] 1 Cr.App.R.(S.) 112, CA, the offender was tried summarily, despite representations by the prosecutor that the case should be heard by the Crown Court. The matter was then adjourned for a pre-sentence report which recommended a probation order. After considering the pre-sentence report, the Court decided to commit the offender to the Crown Court for sentence. Upholding this order, Schiemann L.J. said that nothing in the case constituted the breaking of a promise by the court, hence the decision to commit to the Crown Court for sentence could not be interfered with. However, in circumstances in which a reasonable expectation of a non-custodial sentence is created in the mind of the offender, and a favourable report is received, then, should the magistrates' court commit the offender to the Crown Court for sentence, the Crown Court should not impose a custodial sentence: *R. v Rennes* (1985) 7 Cr.App.R.(S.) 343, CA. See also *Gutteridge v DPP* (1987) 9 Cr.App.R.(S.) 279, DC.

24–34   It is an improper exercise of power for a court to adjourn solely to enable an offender to be sentenced as an adult. The date of conviction is taken to be the date of the finding of guilt or plea of guilty, not the date sentence is passed: *R. v Danga* [1992] Q.B. 476, CA. When approaching sentence for an individual who has crossed a significant threshold between the date of the commission of the offence and the date of sentence, the court should start from a sentence appropriate if sentencing had taken place at the date of the commission of the offence: *R. v Ghafoor* [2003] 1 Cr.App.R.(S.) 84.

VIII. POWERS OF YOUTH COURT TO REMIT TO ADULT COURT, AND SENTENCING POWERS OF ADULT COURT DEALING WITH YOUTH

24–35   An adult court has limited sentencing powers in respect of young offenders convicted in an adult court: see Chapter 32 below. Where a youth appearing in a youth court becomes 18 years old before sentence is passed, the youth court has the additional option of remitting the case to the adult court for sentence and that court will have its usual range of sentencing options. However, see *R. v Ghafoor*, above, emphasising that the starting point for sentence should be that which would have been passed if the defendant had been sentenced on the date on which the offence was committed.

Powers of Criminal Courts (Sentencing) 2000, s.9

Power of youth court to remit offender who attains age of 18 to magistrates' court other than youth court for sentence

9.—(1) Where a person who appears or is brought before a youth court charged with an of- **24–36** fence subsequently attains the age of 18, the youth court may, at any time after conviction and before sentence, remit him for sentence to a magistrates' court (other than a youth court) acting for the same petty sessions area as the youth court.

(2) Where an offender is remitted under subsection (1) above, the youth court shall adjourn proceedings in relation to the offence, and—

    (a) section 128 of the *Magistrates' Courts Act* 1980 (remand in custody or on bail) and all other enactments, whenever passed, relating to remand or the granting of bail in criminal proceedings shall have effect, in relation to the youth court's power or duty to remand the offender on that adjournment, as if any reference to the court to or before which the person remanded is to be brought or appear after remand were a reference to the court to which he is being remitted; and

    (b) subject to subsection (3) below, the court to which the offender is remitted ("the other court") may deal with the case in any way in which it would have power to deal with it if all proceedings relating to the offence which took place before the youth court had taken place before the other court.

(3) Where an offender is remitted under subsection (1) above, section 8(6) above (duty of adult magistrates' court to remit young offenders to youth court for sentence) shall not apply to the court to which he is remitted.

(4) Where an offender is remitted under subsection (1) above he shall have no right of appeal against the order of remission (but without prejudice to any right of appeal against an order made in respect of the offence by the court to which he is remitted).

(5) In this section—

    (a) "enactment" includes an enactment contained in any order, regulation or other instrument having effect by virtue of an Act; and

    (b) "bail in criminal proceedings" has the same meaning as in the *Bail Act* 1976.

IX. POWERS TO REMIT A YOUTH WHO APPEARS IN THE ADULT COURT TO THE YOUTH COURT FOR SENTENCE

The presumption is that a youth convicted in the adult court will be remitted to a **24–37** youth court (usually the one for the area in which the youth resides) for sentence. The only circumstance in which a youth can be sentenced in an adult magistrates' court is where the sentence to be passed comes within s.8(7) or (8), that is, a referral order, a fine (note lower maximum penalties for youths), an absolute or conditional discharge or an order binding over parents to take proper control of the youth. If one of these sentences is being used, ancillary orders (such as endorsement or disqualification from driving) can also be made.

Powers of Criminal Courts (Sentencing) Act 2000, s.8

Power and duty to remit young offenders to youth courts for sentence

8.—(1) Subsection (2) below applies where a child or young person (that is to say, any person **24–38** aged under 18) is convicted by or before any court of an offence other than homicide.

(2) The court may and, if it is not a youth court, shall unless satisfied that it would be undesirable to do so, remit the case—

    (a) if the offender was committed for trial or sent to the Crown Court for trial under section 51 of the *Crime and Disorder Act* 1998, to a youth court acting for the place where he was committed for trial or sent to the Crown Court for trial;

    (b) in any other case, to a youth court acting either for the same place as the remitting court or for the place where the offender habitually resides;

but in relation to a magistrates' court other than a youth court this subsection has effect subject to subsection (6) below.

(3) Where a case is remitted under subsection (2) above, the offender shall be brought before a youth court accordingly, and that court may deal with him in any way in which it might have dealt with him if he had been tried and convicted by that court.

(4) A court by which an order remitting a case to a youth court is made under subsection (2) above—

    (a) may, subject to section 25 of the *Criminal Justice and Public Order Act* 1994 (restrictions on granting bail), give such directions as appear to be necessary with respect to the custody of the offender or for his release on bail until he can be brought before the youth court; and

    (b) shall cause to be transmitted to the justices' chief executive for the youth court a certificate setting out the nature of the offence and stating—

        (i) that the offender has been convicted of the offence; and

        (ii) that the case has been remitted for the purpose of being dealt with under the preceding provisions of this section.

(5) Where a case is remitted under subsection (2) above, the offender shall have no right of appeal against the order of remission, but shall have the same right of appeal against any order of the court to which the case is remitted as if he had been convicted by that court.

(6) Without prejudice to the power to remit any case to a youth court which is conferred on a magistrates' court other than a youth court by subsection (1) and (2) above, where such a magistrates' court convicts a child or young person of an offence it must exercise that power unless the case falls within subsection (7) or (8) below.

(7) The case falls within this subsection if the court would, were it not so to remit the case, be required by section 16(2) below to refer the offender to a youth offender panel (in which event the court may, but need not, so remit the case).

(8) The case falls within this subsection if it does not fall within subsection (7) above but the court is of the opinion that the case is one which can properly be dealt with by means of—

    (a) an order discharging the offender absolutely or conditionally, or

    (b) an order for the payment of a fine, or

    (c) an order (under section 150 below) requiring the offender's parent or guardian to enter into a recognizance to take proper care of him and exercise proper control over him, with or without any other order that the court has power to make when absolutely or conditionally discharging an offender.

(9) In subsection (8) above "care" and "control" shall be construed in accordance with section 150(11) below.

(10) A document purporting to be a copy of an order made by a court under this section shall, if it purports to be certified as a true copy by the justices' chief executive for the court, be evidence of the order.

CHAPTER 25

APPROACH TO SENTENCE

I. APPROACH TO SENTENCE

A. STRUCTURE OF DECISION

The standard approach to sentencing on which magistrates have been trained for **25–1** many years commences with an assessment of the seriousness of the offences (which sets the ceiling above which the sentence imposed should never rise) and then considers circumstances relevant to the offender which may mitigate the level of penalty that the offence would otherwise deserve. The *Magistrates' Courts Sentencing Guidelines* (2003), pp.9/10, explain the structure of the Guidelines by reference to that approach. The court will first assess the seriousness of the offence itself, ensuring that it takes into account all factors which make this particular offence more or less serious. This will include statutory aggravating factors such as racial or religious aggravation or the fact that the offence was committed whilst the offender was on bail. The existence of previous convictions may make the offence more serious because they indicate that the offender was more culpable since they demonstrate that he was clearly aware that what was being done was wrong.

Having formed a view of the seriousness of the offence, personal mitigation is considered and the sentence may be reduced accordingly. The absence of relevant previous convictions may assist a defendant by showing good character. Sentence is then determined taking account of other relevant factors such as credit for entering a timely guilty plea and periods spent in custody on remand.

B. FACTUAL BASIS FOR SENTENCE

A defendant wishing to ask the court to pass sentence on a basis other than that **25–2** disclosed in the prosecution case has to make that quite clear. Where a plea of guilty is tendered on the basis of facts which the Crown could not accept, and the discrepancy between the two accounts is such that the choice between them will potentially have a significant effect on the level of sentence, then the court has to consider resolving the issue by hearing evidence—a *Newton* hearing (see *R. v Newton* (1983) 77 Cr.App.R. 13). When faced with differing versions of the facts of the offence, the choices available to the court are:

(a) to hear evidence and come to a conclusion or

(b) to hear no evidence, though, in the event of a substantial conflict between the versions of events, the version of the defendant must 'so far as possible be accepted.'

If the court does hear evidence, the normal rules of procedure apply, the court should apply the criminal standard of proof and must announce that it has done so when passing sentence: *R. v Kerrigan* (1993) 14 Cr.App.R.(S.) 179, CA.

25–3   The procedure to be adopted following a guilty plea in such circumstances was further examined by Lord Bingham C.J. in *R. v Tolera* [1999] 1 Cr.App.R. 29:

   'a) where a defendant pleads guilty and gives an account of the offence which the *prosecution* does not challenge, but which the *court* feels unable to accept, the court should make it clear before sentence that it did not accept the defence account. Failing any other resolution, evidence can be called and the prosecution can explore matters which the court wishes to explore.

   b) regarding the facts of the offence given to the probation officer for the preparation of a pre-sentence report, an offender may sometimes give an account which differs from that which emerged in the prosecution case. Whilst this part of the pre-sentence report would, of course, be read by the court, it was not ordinarily to form part of the factual basis for the passing of sentence. If the defendant wished to rely on this part of the pre-sentence report for the purposes of sentence, the defence should make this clear, and the prosecution should be forewarned. The issue could then be resolved, if necessary, by the calling of evidence.'

25–4   In *Tolera*, the Court held that there was an onus on the prosecution to rebut an allegation that the defendant had been subject to a degree of compulsion, falling short of duress, to act as a drug courier. *Tolera* was followed in *R. v Artwell* [2001] EWCA Crim 1387, CA where the offender appealed against his sentence of six years' imprisonment imposed for being concerned in the supply of heroin. He contended that there had been a large discrepancy between his basis of plea and the prosecution's case that he was the main organiser. The judge had not held a *Newton* hearing on this matter and had not clarified why he did not accept the defence account of the facts. The Court of Appeal held that the judge should have clarified why he did not accept the defence account and, failing a solution, should have a held a *Newton* hearing. The offender's sentence was reduced from six years' imprisonment to three. If there is a meaningful discrepancy between the way in which the Crown put the case and the way in which the defence asked the court to sentence, there should either be a *Newton* hearing or the court has to be faithful to the basis of the plea.

Following the holding of a *Newton* hearing, the accused may still be entitled to receive some credit for his guilty plea in the form of a reduction of sentence: *R. v Williams (Timothy)* (1990) 12 Cr.App.R.(S.) 415 (though see the *Consultation Paper Reductions for Guilty Pleas*, issued by the Sentencing Advisory Panel (2003) on this). However, the court may properly withhold some part of the discount which the defendant would normally receive in recognition of his plea of guilty: *R. v Hassell* [2000] 1 Cr.App.R.(S.) 67, CA.

25–5   A *Newton* hearing will not be necessary:

i) where the difference in the two versions of the facts of the case is immaterial to the sentence. In *R. v Hall* (1984) 6 Cr.App.R.(S.) 321, the Court of Appeal held that the additional facts which the defendant disputed would not have affected the sentence, and in such a case the judge should proceed only on the defendant's version of events.

ii) where the defence version can be described as 'manifestly false' or 'wholly implausible': *R. v Walton* (1987) 9 Cr.App.R.(S.) 107, *Att.-Gen.'s Ref Nos. 3 and 4 of 1996 (Alan Anthony Healy and Robert William Taylor)* [1997] 1 Cr.App.R.(S.) 29, CA.

iii) where the matters put forward do not challenge the prosecutor's version of events, but rather challenge extraneous matters, such as the background of the offence. These matters are likely to be outside the knowledge of the prosecution: *R. v Broderick* (1994) 15 Cr.App.R.(S.) 476, CA.

C. General Aggravating Factors

(1) Previous convictions

25–6   The significance of previous convictions in assessing sentence has been the subject of debate for many years. At one extreme, the argument is that, once a person has been punished and that punishment completed, then the significance of the offence should be at an end. At the other, is the argument now contained in the *Criminal Justice Act* 2003 (though not in force) that each previous conviction should aggravate the seriousness of the current offence. The existence of a previous conviction for the same offence prevents any argument that the defendant was unaware of the significance of what was being done.

In practice, courts tend to treat the absence of previous convictions as mitigating factor rather than the existence as an aggravating factor. There will be some circumstances where statute prescribes a minimum sentence where there have been previous convictions—for magistrates' courts, this tends to be for road traffic offences where, for instance, disqualification generally follows the acquisition of 12 penalty points and higher periods of disqualification become the minimum where previous disqualifications have been imposed.

(2) Offence committed whilst on bail

If the offence is committed whilst the offender was on bail for some other matter, the **25–7** court has to treat that fact as a factor that aggravates the seriousness of the present offence: s.151(2) and *Criminal Justice Act* 2003, s.143(3). (Note the wording of s.151(2) is stronger than that relating to previous convictions, where it is simply stated that the court *may* take that into account in assessing the seriousness of the offence.)

Powers of Criminal Courts (Sentencing) Act 2000, s.151

Effect of previous convictions and of offending while on bail
 151.—(1) In considering the seriousness of any offence, the court may take into account any **25–8** previous convictions of the offender or any failure of his to respond to previous sentences.
 (2) In considering the seriousness of any offence committed while the offender was on bail, the court shall treat the fact that it was committed in those circumstances as an aggravating factor.
 (3) A probation order or conditional discharge order made before 1st October 1992 (which by virtue of section 2 or 7 of the *Powers of Criminal Courts Act* 1973 would otherwise not be a sentence for the purposes of this section) is to be treated as a sentence for those purposes.
 (4) A conditional discharge order made after 30th September 1992 (which by virtue of section 1A of the *Powers of Criminal Courts Act* 1973 or section 12 above would otherwise not be a sentence for the purposes of this section) is to be treated as a sentence for those purposes.
 (5) A conviction in respect of which a probation order was made before 1st October 1992 (which by virtue of section 13 of the *Powers of Criminal Courts Act* 1973 would otherwise not be a conviction for the purposes of this section) is to be treated as a conviction for those purposes.
 (6) A conviction in respect of which an order discharging the offender absolutely or conditionally was made at any date (which by virtue of section 14 above would otherwise not be a conviction for the purposes of this section) is to be treated as a conviction for those purposes.

(3) Religious or racial aggravation

The existence of an element of racial or religious aggravation may cause a particular **25–9** offence to be committed in an aggravated fashion with a higher maximum penalty. Even where that is not the case, the existence of racial or religious aggravation (as defined in s.28 of the *Crime and Disorder Act* 1998) will make the offence more serious. This approach is continued in s.145 of the *Criminal Justice Act* 2003 and extended by s.146, when in force, to aggravation related to disability or sexual orientation.

(4) Antecedents

Courts rely heavily on information regarding previous convictions provided through **25–10** the prosecution. Drawn from national records, there are times when the information is not as current as it ought to be and courts need to be on their guard in case there are apparent disparities between information sources. The prosecution will tender a list of previous convictions at the conclusion of its presentation once a defendant has been found guilty. Alternatively, for road traffic offenders, this information may come form the defendant's driving licence or from a copy of the driving record.

Practice Direction (Criminal Proceedings: Consolidation) [2002] 1 W.L.R. 2870

25–11   **27.** Antecedents Standard for the provision of information of antecedents in the Crown Court and magistrates' courts.

27.1 In the Crown Court the police will provide brief details of the circumstances of the last three similar convictions and/or of convictions likely to be of interest to the court, the latter being judged on a case by case basis. This information should be provided separately and attached to the antecedents as set out below.

27.2 Where the current alleged offence could constitute a breach of an existing community order, *e.g.* community rehabilitation order, and it is known that that order is still in force then, to enable the court to consider the possibility of revoking that order, details of the circumstances of the offence leading to the community order should be included in the antecedents as set out below.

Preparation of antecedents and standard formats to be used

27.3 In magistrates' courts and the Crown Court:

- Personal details and summary of convictions and cautions—Police National Computer ["PNC"] Court/Defence/Probation Summary Sheet;
- Previous convictions—PNC Court/Defence/Probation printout, supplemented by Form MG16 if the police force holds convictions not shown on PNC;
- Recorded cautions—PNC Court/Defence/Probation printout, supplemented by Form MG17 if the police force holds cautions not shown on PNC.
  and, in addition, in the Crown Court:
- Circumstances of the last three similar convictions;
- Circumstances of offence leading to a community order still in force;
- Form MG(c). The detail should be brief and include the date of the offence.

Provision of antecedents to the court and parties

(a) Crown Court
    27.4 ...

(b) Magistrates' courts
25–12   **27.8** The magistrates' court antecedents will be prepared by the police and submitted to the CPS with the case file.

27.9 Five copies of the antecedents will be prepared in respect of each defendant and provided to the CPS who will be responsible for distributing them to others at the sentencing hearing. Normally two copies will be provided to the court, one to the defence and one to the Probation Service when appropriate. Where following conviction a custodial order is made, one of the court's copies is to be attached to the order sent to the prison.

27.10 In instances where antecedents have been provided to the court some time before the hearing the police will, if requested to do so by the CPS, check the record of convictions. Details of any additional convictions will be provided using the standard format above. These will be provided as above and attached to the documents already supplied. Details of any additional outstanding cases will also be provided at this stage.

27.11 The above arrangements whereby the police provide the antecedents to the CPS for passing on to others will apply unless there is a local agreement between the CPS and the court that alters that arrangement.

25–13   An antecedents statement should not refer to the fact that the offender has been acquitted on a previous occasion. Where an offender disputes a statement of fact contained in an antecedents statement, it must be proved by admissible evidence or omitted from the evidence placed before the court: *R. v Sargeant* (1974) 60 Cr.App.R. 74, CA. Particular care must be taken where the defendant denies that the record of a particular conviction relates to him.

(5) Rehabilitation of offenders

One aspect of the approach to the rehabilitation of offenders is that many sentences **25–14** will become "spent" after a specified period. This means that the conviction does not have to be declared except in certain prescribed circumstances. The time scales for youths are less than for adults. One exception relates to criminal proceedings before a magistrates' court. A court is entitled to take into account convictions that are spent under the *Rehabilitation of Offenders Act* 1974. However, a court does not have an unfettered discretion, it must be demonstrated that justice cannot be done without the admission of such evidence for spent convictions to be admitted: *R. v Hastings Magistrates' Court Ex p. McSpirit* (1998) 162 J.P. 44. In practice, the normal approach will be to ignore spent convictions.

Rehabilitation of Offenders Act 1974, s.5

Rehabilitation periods for particular sentences

5.—(1) The sentences excluded from rehabilitation under this Act are— **25–15**

    (a) a sentence of imprisonment for life;

    (b) a sentence of imprisonment, youth custody or corrective training for a term exceeding thirty months;

    (c) a sentence of preventive detention;

    (d) a sentence of detention during Her Majesty's pleasure or for life under section 90 or 91 of the *Powers of Criminal Courts (Sentencing) Act* 2000 or under section 205(2) or (3) of the *Criminal Procedure (Scotland) Act* 1975,, or a sentence of detention for a term exceeding thirty months passed under section 91 of the said Act of 2000 (young offenders convicted of grave crimes) or under section 206 of the said Act of 1975 (detention of children convicted on indictment) or a corresponding court-martial punishment;

and

    (e) a sentence of custody for life

and any other sentence is a sentence subject to rehabilitation under this Act.

    (1A) In subsection (1)(d) above "corresponding court-martial punishment" means a punishment awarded under section 71A(3) or (4) of the *Army Act* 1955, section 71A(3) or (4) of the *Air Force Act* 1955 or section 43A(3) or (4) of the *Naval Discipline Act* 1957.

    (2) For the purposes of this Act—

    (a) the rehabilitation period applicable to a sentence specified in the first column of Table A below is the period specified in the second column of that Table in relation to that sentence, or, where the sentence was imposed on a person who was under eighteen years of age at the date of his conviction, half that period; and

    (b) the rehabilitation period applicable to a sentence specified in the first column of Table B below is the period specified in the second column of that Table in relation to that sentence;

reckoned in either case from the date of the conviction in respect of which the sentence was imposed.

REHABILITATION PERIODS SUBJECT TO REDUCTION BY HALF FOR PERSONS UNDER 18

TABLE A	*Rehabilitation*	**25–16**
Sentence	*period*	
A sentence of imprisonment or youth custody or corrective training for a term exceeding six months but not exceeding thirty months.[1]	Ten years	

25–16

TABLE A *Sentence*	*Rehabilitation period*
A sentence of cashiering, discharge with ignominy or dismissal with disgrace from Her Majesty's service.	Ten years
A sentence of imprisonment or youth custody for a term not exceeding six months.	Seven years
A sentence of dismissal from Her Majesty's service.	Seven years
Any sentence of detention in respect of a conviction in service disciplinary proceedings.	Five years
A fine or any other sentence subject to rehabilitation under this Act, not being a sentence to which Table B below or any of subsection (3) to (8) below applies.	Five years
[1]In relation to England and Wales: A sentence of imprisonment, detention in a young offender institution or youth custody or corrective training for a term exceeding six months but not exceeding thirty months. [2]In relation to England and Wales: A sentence of imprisonment, detention in a young offender institution or youth custody for a term not exceeding six months.	

REHABILITATION PERIODS FOR CERTAIN SENTENCES CONFINED TO YOUNG OFFENDERS

25–17

TABLE B *Sentence*	*Rehabilitation period*
A sentence of Borstal training.	Seven years
A custodial order under section 71AA of the *Army Act* 1955 or the *Air Force Act* 1955, or under section 43AA of the *Naval Discipline Act* 1957, where the maximum period of detention specified in the order is more than six months.	Seven years
A custodial order under Schedule 5A to the *Army Act* 1955 or the *Air Force Act* 1955, or under Schedule 4A to the *Naval Discipline Act* 1957, where the maximum period of detention specified in the order is more than six months.	Seven years
A sentence of detention for a term exceeding six months but not exceeding thirty months passed under section 91 of the *Powers of Criminal Courts (Sentencing) Act* 2000 or under 206 of the *Criminal Procedure (Scotland) Act* 1975.	Five years
A sentence of detention for a term not exceeding six months passed under either of those provisions.	Three years
An order for detention in a detention centre made under section 4 of the *Criminal Justice Act* 1982, section 4 of the *Criminal Justice Act* 1961.	Three years

TABLE B	Rehabilitation	25–17
Sentence	period	
A custodial order under any of the Schedules to the said Acts of 1955 and 1957 mentioned above, where the maximum period of detention specified in the order is six months or less.	Three years	
A custodial order under section 71AA of the said Acts of 1955, or section 43AA or the said act of 1957, where the maximum period of detention specified in the order is six months or less.	Three years	

(3) The rehabilitation period applicable—   **25–18**
    (a) to an order discharging a person absolutely for an offence; and
    (b) to the discharge by a children's hearing under section 69(1)(b) and (12) of the *Children (Scotland) Act* 1995 of the referral of a child's case;
shall be six months from the date of conviction.

(4) Where in respect of a conviction a person was conditionally discharged, bound over to keep the peace or be of good behaviour, the rehabilitation period applicable to the sentence shall be one year from the date of conviction or a period beginning with that date and ending when the order for conditional discharge or (as the case may be) the recognizance or bond of caution to keep the peace or be of good behaviour ceases or ceased to have effect, whichever is the longer.

(4A) Where in respect of a conviction a probation order was made, the rehabilitation period applicable to the sentence shall be—
    (a) in the case of a person aged eighteen years or over at the date of his conviction, five years from the date of conviction;
    (b) in the case of a person aged under the age of eighteen years at the date of his conviction, two and a half years from the date of conviction or a period beginning with the date of conviction and ending when the order in question ceases or ceased to have effect, whichever is the longer.

(4B) Where in respect of a conviction a referral order (within the meaning of the *Powers of Criminal Courts (Sentencing) Act* 2000) is made in respect of the person convicted, the rehabilitation period applicable to the sentence shall be—
    (a) if a youth offender contract takes effect under section 23 of that Act between him and a youth offender panel, the period beginning with the date of conviction and ending on the date when (in accordance with section 24 of that Act) the contract ceases to have effect;
    (b) if no such contract so takes effect, the period beginning with the date of conviction and having the same length as the period for which such a contract would (ignoring any order under paragraph 11 or 12 of Schedule 1 to that Act) have had effect had one so taken effect.

(4C) Where in respect of a conviction an order is made in respect of the person convicted under paragraph 11 or 12 of Schedule 1 to the *Powers of Criminal Courts (Sentencing) Act* 2000 (extension of period for which youth offender contract has effect), the rehabilitation period applicable to the sentence shall be—
    (a) if a youth offender contract takes effect under section 23 of that Act between the offender and a youth offender panel, the period beginning with the date of conviction and ending on the date when (in accordance with section 24 of that Act) the contract ceases to have effect;
    (b) if no such contract so takes effect, the period beginning with the date of conviction and having the same length as the period for which, in accordance with the order, such a contract would have had effect had one so taken effect.

(5) Where in respect of a conviction any of the following sentences was imposed, that is   **25–19**
to say—
    (a) an order under section 57 of the *Children and Young Persons Act* 1933 or section 61 of the *Children and Young Persons (Scotland) Act* 1937 committing the person convicted to the care of a fit person;

   (b) a supervision order under any provision of either of those Acts or of the 5;

   (c) an order under section 413 of the *Criminal Procedure (Scotland) Act* 1975 committing a child for the purpose of his undergoing residential training:

   (d) an approved school order under section 61 of the said Act of 1937;

   (e) a supervision order under section 63(1) of the *Powers of Criminal Courts (Sentencing) Act* 2000; or

   (f) a supervision requirement under any provision of the *Children (Scotland) Act* 1995;

   (g) a community supervision order under Schedule 5A to the *Army Act* 1955 or the *Air Force Act* 1955, or under Schedule 4A to the *Naval Discipline Act* 1957;

the rehabilitation period applicable to the sentence shall be one year from the date of conviction or a period beginning with that date and ending when the order or requirement ceases or ceased to have effect, whichever is the longer.

(6) Where in respect of a conviction any of the following orders was made, that is to say—

   (a) an order under section 54 of the said Act of 1933 committing the person convicted to custody in a remand home;

   (b) an approved school order under section 57 of the said Act of 1933; or

   (c) an attendance centre order under section 60 of the *Powers of Criminal Courts (Sentencing) Act* 2000;

   (d) a secure training order under section 1 of the *Criminal Justice and Public Order Act* 1994;

the rehabilitation period applicable to the sentence shall be a period beginning with the date of conviction and ending one year after the date on which the order ceases or ceased to have effect.

(6A) Where in respect of a conviction a detention and training order was made under section 100 of the *Powers of Criminal Courts (Sentencing) Act* 2000, the rehabilitation period applicable to the sentence shall be—

   (a) in the case of a person aged fifteen years or over at the date of his conviction, five years if the order was, and three and a half years if the order was not, for a term exceeding six months;

   (b) in the case of a person aged under fifteen years at the date of his conviction, a period beginning with that date and ending one year after the date on which the order ceases to have effect.

(7) Where in respect of a conviction a hospital order under Part III of the *Mental Health Act* 1983 or under Part VI of the *Mental Health (Scotland) Act* 1984 (with or without a restriction order) was made, the rehabilitation period applicable to the sentence shall be the period of five years from the date of conviction or a period beginning with that date and ending two years after the date on which the hospital order ceases or ceased to have effect, whichever is the longer.

25–20   (8) Where in respect of a conviction an order was made imposing on the person convicted any disqualification, disability, prohibition or other penalty, the rehabilitation period applicable to the sentence shall be a period beginning with the date of conviction and ending on the date on which the disqualification, disability, prohibition or penalty (as the case may be) ceases or ceased to have effect.

(9) For the purposes of this section—

   (a) "sentence of imprisonment" includes a sentence of detention under section 207 or 415 of the *Criminal Procedure (Scotland) Act* 1975 and a sentence of penal servitude, and "term of imprisonment" shall be construed accordingly;

   (b) consecutive terms of imprisonment or of detention under section 91 of the *Powers of Criminal Courts (Sentencing) Act* 2000 or section 206 of the said Act of 1975, and terms which are wholly or partly concurrent (being terms of imprisonment or detention imposed in respect of offences of which a person was convicted in the same proceedings) shall be treated as a single term;

   (c) no account shall be taken of any subsequent variation, made by a court in dealing with a person in respect of a suspended sentence of imprisonment, of the term originally imposed; and

   (d) a sentence imposed by a court outside Great Britain shall be treated as a sentence of that one of the descriptions mentioned in this section which most nearly corresponds to the sentence imposed.

(10) References in this section to the period during which a probation order, or a

supervision order under the *Powers of Criminal Courts (Sentencing) Act* 2000, or a supervision requirement under the *Children (Scotland) Act* 1995, is or was in force include references to any period during which any order or requirement to which this subsection applies, being an order or requirement made or imposed directly or indirectly in substitution for the first-mentioned order or requirement, is or was in force.

This subsection applies—

(a) to any such order or requirement as is mentioned above in this subsection;

(b) to any order having effect under section 25(2) of the *Children and Young Persons Act* 1969 as if it were a training school order in Northern Ireland; and

(c) to any supervision order made under section 72(2) of the said Act of 1968 and having effect as a supervision order under the *Children and Young Persons Act (Northern Ireland)* 1950.

(11) The Secretary of State may by order—

(a) substitute different periods or terms for any of the periods or terms mentioned in subsection (1) to (8) above; and

(b) substitute a different age for the age mentioned in subsection (2)(a) above.

Rehabilitation of Offenders Act 1974, s.6

The rehabilitation period applicable to a conviction

6.—(1) Where only one sentence is imposed in respect of a conviction (not being a sentence **25–21** excluded from rehabilitation under this Act) the rehabilitation period applicable to the conviction is, subject to the following provisions of this section, the period applicable to the sentence in accordance with section 5 above.

(2) Where more than one sentence is imposed in respect of a conviction (whether or not in the same proceedings) and none of the sentences imposed is excluded from rehabilitation under this Act, then, subject to the following provisions of this section, if the periods applicable to those sentences in accordance with section 5 above differ, the rehabilitation period applicable to the conviction shall be the longer or the longest (as the case may be) of those periods.

(3) Without prejudice to subsection (2) above, where in respect of a conviction a person was conditionally discharged or a probation order was made and after the end of the rehabilitation period applicable to the conviction in accordance with subsection (1) or (2) above he is dealt with, in consequence of a breach of conditional discharge or a breach of the order, for the offence for which the order for conditional discharge or a breach of the order was made, then, if the rehabilitation period applicable to the conviction in accordance with subsection (2) above (taking into account any sentence imposed when he is so dealt with) ends later than the rehabilitation period previously applicable to the conviction, he shall be treated for the purposes of this Act as not having become a rehabilitated person in respect of that conviction, and the conviction shall for those purposes be treated as not having become spent, in relation to any period falling before the end of the new rehabilitation period.

(4) Subject to subsection (5) below, where during the rehabilitation period applicable to a conviction—

(a) the person convicted is convicted of a further offence; and

(b) no sentence excluded from rehabilitation under this Act is imposed on him in respect of the later conviction;

if the rehabilitation period applicable in accordance with this section to either of the convictions would end earlier than the period so applicable in relation to the other, the rehabilitation period which would (apart from this subsection) end the earlier shall be extended so as to end at the same time as the other rehabilitation period.

(5) Where the rehabilitation period applicable to a conviction is the rehabilitation period **25–22** applicable in accordance with section 5(8) above to an order imposing on a person any disqualification, disability, prohibition or other penalty, the rehabilitation period applicable to another conviction shall not by virtue of subsection (4) above be extended by reference to that period; but if any other sentence is imposed in respect of the first-mentioned conviction for which a rehabilitation period is prescribed by any other provision of section 5 above, the rehabilitation period applicable to another conviction shall, where appropriate, be extended under subsection (4) above by reference to the rehabilitation period applicable in accordance with that section to that sentence or, where more than one such

sentence is imposed, by reference to the longer or longest of the periods so applicable to those sentences, as if the period in question were the rehabilitation period applicable to the first-mentioned conviction.

(6) For the purposes of subsection (4)(a) above there shall be disregarded—

(a) any conviction in England and Wales of a summary offence or of a scheduled offence (within the meaning of section 22 of the *Magistrates' Courts Act* 1980) tried summarily in pursuance of subsection (2) of that section (summary trial where value involved is small);

(b) any conviction in Scotland of an offence which is not excluded from the jurisdiction of inferior courts of summary jurisdiction by virtue of section 4 of the *Summary Jurisdiction (Scotland) Act* 1954 (certain crimes not to be tried in inferior courts of summary jurisdiction);

(bb) any conviction in service disciplinary proceedings for an offence listed in the Schedule to this Act; and

(c) any conviction by or before a court outside Great Britain of an offence in respect of conduct which, if it had taken place in any part of Great Britain, would not have constituted an offence under the law in force in that part of Great Britain.

D. Mitigation

25–23   A court has a wide discretion concerning what it chooses to take into account as mitigation. Factors that mitigate the seriousness of an offence may relate to the offence itself or to the offender. In relation to the sentences for individual offences, they are set out in earlier chapters that relate to those offences.

There may be times when a court has some difficulty in accepting what is put forward either as a description of the circumstances of the offence or as the circumstances of the offender. If a significant issue is put forward by the defence which the prosecution or the court is not prepared to accept as accurate, this will normally need to be resolved by the hearing of evidence—a *Newton* hearing (see § 25–2 above, for a general discussion of the approach where there is a dispute about the factual basis on which sentence is to be passed).

However, situations are not always so straight forward to identify and defence advocates will often be instructed to put forward versions of events or the conduct of the defendant that it would not be appropriate to spend large amounts of court time disputing.

The offender or his/her legal representative should be able to address the court in mitigation, notwithstanding that the offender has been convicted by a jury after having denied the charge led against him: *R. v Jones*, unreported, August 6, 1979, CA. The same principle applies where a defendant is convicted after a trial in a magistrates' court. The judge is also under a duty of fairness to alert defence counsel to the possibility that he may impose a sentence which the defence counsel is not anticipating. This is to allow defence counsel to make submissions on this issue: *R. v Scott* (1989) 11 Cr.App.R.(S.) 249.

(1) General Mitigating Circumstances

Powers of Criminal Courts (Sentencing) Act 2000, s.158

Savings for powers to mitigate sentences and deal appropriately with mentally disordered offenders

25–24   158.—(1) Nothing in—

(a) sections 35 and 36 above (imposing community sentences),

(b) sections 79 to 82 above (imposing custodial sentences), or

(c) section 128 above (fixing of fines),

shall prevent a court from mitigating an offender's sentence by taking into account any such matters as, in the opinion of the court, are relevant in mitigation of sentence.

(2) Without prejudice to the generality of subsection (1) above, nothing in those sections shall prevent a court—

(a) from mitigating any penalty included in an offender's sentence by taking into account any other penalty included in that sentence; or

(b) in a case of an offender who is convicted of one or more other offences, from mitigating his sentence by applying any rule of law as to the totality of sentences.

(3) Nothing in those sections shall be taken—

(a) as requiring a court to pass a custodial sentence, or any particular custodial sentence, on a mentally disordered offender; or

(b) as restricting any power (whether under the *Mental Health Act* 1983 or otherwise) which enables a court to deal with such an offender in the manner it considers to be most appropriate in all the circumstances.

(4) In subsection (3) above, "mentally disordered", in relation to any person, means suffering from a mental disorder within the meaning of the *Mental Health Act* 1983.

(2) Mitigation for assistance

An offender who materially assists the police, perhaps by disclosing information of **25–25** value to an investigation of offences committed by others, or relating to the involvement of others in the offence for which he is charged, may expect some degree of discount from the court: *R. v Sinfield* (1981) 3 Cr.App.R.(S.) 258, CA. The size of the discount depends on the individual facts of the case: *R. v Rose and Sapiano* (1980) 2 Cr.App.R.(S.) 239, CA. There is no 'tariff' for people who give evidence against co-defendants, each case must be approached on its own particular facts, weighing up the criminality of the admitted offences against the offender's assistance to and co-operation with the police, and taking into account the public interest in encouraging others to come forward. Whilst most cases of this type will be dealt with in the Crown Court, there will be occasions when they will appear for sentence in a magistrates' court, perhaps with the additional complication that a lesser (summary only) charge has been preferred as a part of the response to the assistance given.

The discount should be calculated by deciding what would have been the appropriate sentence had the offence not been admitted by the defendant and been contested at trial. The judge should then make an appropriate reduction which adequately reflects the nature and importance of the information and assistance actually given: *R. v Sehitoglu and Ozakan* [1998] 1 Cr.App.R.(S.) 89, CA.

In *R. v King* (1985) 7 Cr.App.R.(S.) 227 it was held that the correct approach is for **25–26** the court first to assess the gravity and number of the offences committed by the defendant, which should result in what might be called a starting figure. The amount by which that figure should be reduced would depend on a number of variable features including the quality and quantity of the material disclosed by the informer, its accuracy and his willingness to confront other criminals or give evidence against them and the degree to which the offender had put himself and his family at risk of reprisal. The amount of that mitigation would vary from about one half to two thirds, according to the circumstances. The sentence must be tailored to punish the defendant, but at the same time reward him as possible for the help he has given and to demonstrate to offenders that it is worth their while to disclose the criminal activities of others for the benefit of the law-abiding public in general: *R. v Sivan* (1988) 10 Cr.App.R.(S.) 282, CA.

Further guidance on how to assess the accuracy of the information offered, given the **25–27** defendant's desire to preserve anonymity, was stated in *R. v Sivan*, above. Lord Lane C.J. stated that, in important cases, it might be desirable for the court to have a letter from a senior officer in the investigating agency, unconnected with the case, who has examined all the facts and is able to certify that the facts are as reported by the officers conducting the investigation. There should be a statement in writing from the officer in charge of the investigation setting out those facts which will be certified by the senior unconnected officer. It would also be advisable in the more important cases to have the officer in charge of the investigation available to give evidence if necessary, whether in court or in the judge's chambers as the situation may demand. The shorthand writer should also be present taking a note of what transpires in the judge's private room.

Credit should only be given if the information is offered early enough for it to be potentially useful: *R. v Debbag and Izzet* (1991) 12 Cr.App.R.(S.) 733, CA. This aversion to encouraging a system of negotiation is particularly so where the information offered proves to be of no practical assistance to the authorities. See also *R. v A and B* [1999] 1 Cr.App.R.(S.) 52, CA and *R. v X* (1994) 15 Cr.App.R.(S.) 750, CA.

In *R. v X (No. 2)* [1999] 2 Cr.App.R.(S.) 294, CA, guidance was given on the appropriate approach when the defendant disagrees with the police account of the assistance he has given to the investigation of the case. Hughes J. stated:

25–28   'We consider that the proper principles to be followed in a case of this kind are as follows:

1. It is convenient to remember that a document of this kind, although supplied by a police officer, is supplied at the request of the defendant.

2. Except to the extent that the defendant's contention that he has given assistance is supported by the police, it will not generally be likely that the sentencing judge will be able to make any adjustment in sentence. A defendant's unsupported assertion to that effect is not normally likely to be a reliable basis for mitigation.

3. It follows from that, that courts must rely very heavily upon the greatest possible care being taken, in compiling such a document for the information of the judge. The judge will have to rely upon it, without investigation, if police inquiries are not to be damaged or compromised and other suspects, guilty or innocent, are not to be affected.

We have to express our regret that the document in the present case had not been prepared with sufficient care. Those who prepare such documents, and senior officers who verify them, must realise the importance of ensuring that they are complete and accurate.

25–29   4. Except in very unusual circumstances, it will not be necessary, nor will it be desirable for a document of this kind to contain the kind of details which would attract a public interest immunity application. We should observe that, as it seems to us, the document in the present case did not do so.

5. If very exceptionally such a document does contain information attracting a public interest immunity consideration, then the usual rules about the conduct of such an application will apply. In particular, the *Crown Court (Criminal Procedure and Investigations Act 1996) (Disclosure) Rules* 1997, will apply. It will of course be a case in which the defence can and should be told of the public interest immunity application.

6. Absent any consideration of public interest immunity, which we take to be the general position, a document of this kind should be shown to counsel for the defence, who will no doubt discuss its contents with the defendant. That is not, we emphasise, because it will be necessary to debate its contents, but it is so that there should be no room for any unfounded suspicion that the judge has been told something potentially adverse to the defendant without his knowing about it. On general principles, a defendant is entitled to see documents put before the trial judge on which he is to be sentenced. Expeditions to the judge's chambers should not be necessary in these cases. There should never normally be any question of evidence being given, nor of an issue being tried upon the question of the extent of the information provided. To that extent, we entirely agree with the learned judge.

25–30   7. If the defendant wishes to disagree with the contents of such a document, it is not appropriate for there to be cross-examination of the policeman, whether in court or in chambers. The policeman is not a Crown witness, he has simply supplied material for the judge, at the request of the defendant. It would no doubt be possible, in an appropriate case, for a defendant to ask for an adjournment to allow any opportunity for further consideration to be given to the preparation of the document. Otherwise, if the defendant does not accept what the document says, his remedy is not to rely upon it.

Quite apart from the position of the police officer as an officer reporting at the request of the defendant, cross-examination on the usefulness of the information would almost inevitably be contrary to the public interest. It would be likely to damage inquiries still in train, trials yet to come, suspects guilty or innocent and quite possibly the defendant in the instant case. In a limited number of cases, such a request for cross-examination might even have been set up deliberately for such purpose, although we do not, for a moment, say that would have been the position here.

8. No doubt, the learned judge should ordinarily disregard such a document, if asked by the defendant to do so. In such case, he will no doubt not then be minded to entertain any submission that the defendant has given valuable assistance to the police.

9. If the judge does take the document into consideration he will, no doubt, say no more

than is in accordance with the present practice, namely that he has taken into consideration all the information about the defendant, with which he has been provided.'

(3) Mitigation where the offender avoids apprehension for a substantial period of time

Where the offender avoids apprehension for a substantial period of time, the sen- **25–31** tencer may make such allowance in mitigation as he feels proper: *R. v Bird* (1987) 9 Cr.App.R.(S.) 77, CA.

However, this principle does not extend to cases involving sexual abuse within a family, which are very likely to remain undetected for substantial periods: *R. v Tiso* (1990) 12 Cr.App.R.(S.) 122, CA.

(4) Mitigation where the offender committed the offence as a young person but convicted of them as an adult

In cases where an offender has committed offences as a youth but is not convicted of **25–32** them for many years, the proper approach for the sentencing judge is to identify the sentence which would have been passed if the defendant had been sentenced within a reasonable period after committing the offences and to take that sentence as a starting point in determining the proper sentence to be imposed: *R. v Fowler (Alan)* [2002] 2 Cr.App.R.(S.) 99. See also *R. v Dashwood* (1995) 16 Cr.App.R.(S.) 733, CA.

Similarly, where an offence is committed by an offender under eighteen, who is convicted after attaining the age of eighteen the starting point for consideration of the appropriate sentence is the sentence that the offender would have been likely to receive if he had been sentenced at the date of the commission of the offence: *R. v Ghafoor* [2003] 1 Cr.App.R.(S.) 84. See also *R. v M* (2002) J.P.N. 963, where an offender who attained the age of fifteen between the date of offence and date of conviction should normally receive the same sentence as he would at the earlier date. A sentence may also be discounted to reflect the youth of the offender, see *R. v Pinnock* (1979) 1 Cr.App.R.(S.) 169.

(5) Mitigation due to personal characteristics of the offender

A sentencer may give credit for meritorious conduct that is unrelated to the offence **25–33** for which he is to be sentenced: *R. v Alexander* [1997] 2 Cr.App.R.(S.) 74; but great care needs to be paid to whether that is appropriate. Whilst such credit may be acceptable in relation to non violent offences, it may be less so where the offender has inflicted injury on another person. So, for instance, a person with a good record of public service who is convicted of assaults taking place in a domestic context may not merit any reduction in sentence whereas such a person convicted of theft may do.

The hardship inflicted on the offender's family may be a mitigating factor in exceptional cases: *R. v Summers* (1979) 1 Cr.App.R.(S.) 13. In *R. v Whitehead* [1996] 1 Cr.App.R.(S.) 111, CA the case was described as 'finely balanced as to whether a custodial sentence was required or not.' The matter tipping the balance in favour of a non-custodial sentence was the position of the three children, aged nine, seven and five. As a result of both parents being sent to prison, they were deprived of the care of both father and mother. The factor relating to the children was decisive in coming to the conclusion that the imprisonment was inappropriate and a 50–hour community service order was imposed.

Ill-health should not affect the length of the sentence imposed, but in exceptional cases the court could reduce the sentence imposed as an act of mercy: *R. v Moore* (1994) 15 Cr.App.R.(S.) 97. Asperger's syndrome, an abnormality of development related to autism, characterised by subtle abnormalities of social interaction, preoccupation with special interests and abnormalities of personality may persuade the court to take an exceptional course: *R. v Gibson* [2001] EWCA 656. A short life expectancy may also persuade the court to reduce the sentence it would otherwise impose: *R. v Lewis* [2001] EWCA Crim 935.

(6) Mitigation relating to the circumstances of the offence

25–34 The fact that the offence was committed under the influence of alcohol is not normally a mitigating factor: *R. v Bradley* (1980) 2 Cr.App.R.(S.) 12 nor is the fact that the offence was committed to provide money to support an addiction: *R. v Lawrence* (1988) 10 Cr.App.R.(S.) 463, CA.

The use of an agent provocateur to facilitate commission of the offence will not be a mitigating factor unless the officer concerned has acted improperly: *R. v Underhill* (1979) 1 Cr.App.R.(S.) 270, CA; *R. v Springer* [1999] 1 Cr.App.R.(S.) 217, CA. Entrapment as a result of the conduct of journalists rather than police officers will also result in mitigation of sentence: *R. v Tonnessen* [1998] 2 Cr.App.R.(S.) 328, CA.

(7) Mitigation relating to mentally disordered offenders

25–35 Section 158(3) of the *PCC(S)A* 2000 makes it clear that the court is not fettered in regard to making appropriate orders regarding mentally disordered offenders by the criteria for other sentences. An offender is mentally disordered if suffering from a mental disorder within the meaning of the *Mental Health Act* 1983: s.158(4). See further in Chapter 35 above.

(8) The totality principle

25–36 A defendant will often face more than one offence, sometimes arising out of the same circumstances, sometimes arising out of different circumstances. Each offence must receive a sentence (even if it is "no separate penalty"). As well as looking at the appropriate sentence for each offence, the court must also consider the appropriate sentence for the totality of the offending before it. When the court has calculated the sentence appropriate for each offence, it should then consider the aggregate sentence and decide whether the total sentence is just and appropriate: *R. v Hewitt* [1980] Crim.L.R. 116, *R. v Jones* [1996] 1 Cr.App.R.(S.) 153.

The effect of this is confirmed in s.158(2)(b) of the *PCC(S)A* 2000.

Powers of Criminal Courts (Sentencing) Act 2000, s.158(2)

Savings for powers to mitigate sentences and deal appropriately with mentally disordered offenders

25–37 **158.**—(2) Without prejudice to the generality of subsection (1) above, nothing in those sections shall prevent a court—

    (a) from mitigating any penalty included in an offender's sentence by taking into account any other penalty included in that sentence; or

    (b) in a case of an offender who is convicted of one or more other offences, from mitigating his sentence by applying any rule of law as to the totality of sentences.

This principle applies to community penalties and financial orders as well as to custodial sentences. In magistrates' courts, the issue is more likely to arise in relation to financial penalties than to custodial or community sentences with the additional obligation to set the penalty in the light of the resources available to the defendant.

Generally, financial penalties are in addition to other financial penalties imposed whereas community penalties will each start from the day of imposition. Custodial penalties are either concurrent with each other or consecutive to others as specified by the court at the time of sentence.

E. Taking Offences into Consideration and Specimen Charges

25–38 When passing sentence for the principal offence, the court may take into consideration other offences admitted by the defendant but with which he has not been charged, and in respect of which he will not receive a conviction. The practice of taking offences into consideration has no statutory foundation, and has been described as 'a convention under which if a court is informed that there are outstanding charges against a prisoner who is before it for a particular offence the court can, if the prisoner admits the offences and asks that they should be taken into account, take them into account.' Lord Goddard C.J. in *R. v Batchelor* (1952) 36 Cr.App.R. 64.

However, a charge should not be taken into consideration if the public interest requires that it should be the subject of a separate trial: *R. v McClean*, 6 Cr.App.R.(S.), CA.

A court should also not take into consideration an offence which it is not empowered to try, hence a magistrates' court could not take into consideration a charge triable only on indictment: *R. v Simons* (1953) 37 Cr.App.R. 120, CA.

An offence should not be taken into consideration where the court is required to **25–39** disqualify the offender from driving or to endorse his driving licence in the event of conviction, as such measures cannot be taken where the offence is taken into consideration.

In *DPP v Anderson* (1978) 142 J.P. 391, it was held that if justice is to be done the practice of taking cases into consideration should not be followed except with the express and unequivocal assent of the offender. Hence he should be informed explicitly of each offence which the judge proposes to be taken into consideration and should explicitly admit that he committed them and should state his desire that they should be taken into consideration in determining the sentence passed upon him.

A similar practice has grown up in relation to specimen charges. The prosecution may select a small number of occasions where an offence has been committed knowing that similar offences have taken place on other occasions. Providing the defendant clearly accepts responsibility for all offences, the court can sentence on the basis of the whole course of conduct.

F. Credit for Guilty Plea

Powers of Criminal Court (Sentencing) Act 2000, s.152

Reduction in sentences for guilty pleas

152.—(1) In determining what sentence to pass on an offender who has pleaded guilty to an **25–40** offence in proceedings before that or another court, a court shall take into account—

(a) the stage in the proceedings for the offence at which the offender indicated his intention to plead guilty; and

(b) the circumstances in which this indication was given.

(2) If, as a result of taking into account any matter referred to in subsection (1) above, the court imposes a punishment on the offender which is less severe than the punishment it would otherwise have imposed, it shall state in open court that it has done so.

(3) In the case of an offence the sentence for which falls to be imposed under subsection (2) of section 110 or 111 above, nothing in that subsection shall prevent the court, after taking into account any matter referred to in subsection (1) above, from imposing any sentence which is not less than 80 per cent of that specified in that subsection.

Section 152 does not confer a statutory discount, the issue remains one in the discre- **25–41** tion of the court. Where a court takes a guilty plea into account, it is important that it states that it has done so, for the benefit of the defendant and a later appeal court: *R. v Fearon* [1996] 2 Cr.App.R.(S.) 25, CA; *R. v Aroride* [1999] 2 Cr.App.R.(S.) 406, CA. However, there are two main justifications for providing a reduction in these circumstances. One is the benefit to the administration of justice both by saving the time and expense of a trial and by saving witnesses from the ordeal of giving evidence. The second is the extent to which it reflects remorse for the offence. It appears to be more generally accepted that it is the first of these justifications that should be followed— remorse is an issue of personal mitigation which can be shown in other, less ambiguous ways and which should be taken account of as a separate issue. This approach has been accepted in other jurisdictions—see, for instance, *Cameron v The Queen* (2002) 187 A.L.R. 65, a decision of the High Court of Australia and *R. v Thomson; R. v Houlton* (2000) 49 N.S.W.L.R. 383, a decision of the New South Wales Court of Appeal.

25–42   It is likely that the approach in England and Wales will follow that recently enunciated in Scotland by the High Court of Judiciary in *Du Plooy* [2003] S.L.T. 1237. Emphasising the importance of the system benefit approach, the Appeal Court emphasised the importance of a court stating clearly the extent of the reduction given and that, whilst the degree should be left to the discretion of the court, it should rarely exceed one third.

At present, English authorities suggest that there is no fixed discount that it is considered appropriate to give, but between one third and one fifth of the sentence is the range which would be used: *R. v Buffrey* (1993) 14 Cr.App.R.(S.) 511. Where an offender surrenders voluntarily to the police and admits an offence which could otherwise not be proved against him he may be allowed a greater discount than would normally be appropriate when the court is dealing with a guilty plea: *R. v Claydon* (1994) 15 Cr.App.R.(S.) 526. For a full review of the authorities, see the Consultation Paper published by the Sentencing Advisory Panel in 2003 at *www.sentencing-guidelines.gov.uk*.

25–43   In *R. v Okee* [1998] 2 Cr.App.R.(S.) 199, the court stated that it was vital that offenders should know that if they pleaded guilty their sentences would be discounted, and that they should see the discount. It was likewise right that those who delayed their pleas until the last moment should know that the discount would be substantially and visibly reduced from that which they would otherwise have earned.

25–44   Defendants who initially plead not guilty, and then change their plea to guilty when finally arraigned cannot expect to get the same discount when sentenced as they would have received had they pleaded guilty at the beginning: *R. v Hollington and Emmens* (1985) 7 Cr.App.R.(S.) 364. There is some authority for the suggestion that only a small discount will be appropriate when the offender is caught 'red handed', or where the defendant pleads guilty in the face of overwhelming evidence: *R. v Fearon* [1996] 2 Cr.App.R.(S.) 25, CA; *R. v Williams* (2001) 165 J.P.N. 735; *R. v Hastings* [1996] 1 Cr.App.R.(S.) 167, CA. However, since the primary purpose of the giving of credit is to encourage as many guilty people as possible to plead guilty at the earliest opportunity and since any defendant can seek to prolong the proceedings in the hope that something will go wrong, there seems no logical reason why credit should be refused or reduced for this purpose.

The discount may be reduced where there has been a *Newton* hearing and the defence account has been disbelieved. However, withholding all the discount in such a case may be inappropriate: *R. v Hassall* [2000] 1 Cr.App.R.(S.) 67, CA.

G. Explanations of Sentence

25–45   Giving reasons for a decision is now widely accepted as important both for the benefit of those directly involved in a case and for the wider understanding of the court process. Whilst there is no general statutory duty, there are a number of individual obligations to give information to support specific decisions. In addition, giving of reasons helps to fulfil obligations under the European Convention on Human Rights to ensure a fair trial. Reasons should enable an interested observer to understand the significant factors in a decision. The more the decision differs from what might be considered a normal sentence in the circumstances, the more extensive the reasons should be. A court will also need to be aware of the anxiety being experienced by the defendant and that what is said is tempered to the occasion.

The requirements were previously contained in a range of provisions (primarily in the *PCC(S)A* 2000) but are now brought together in s.174 of the *Criminal Justice Act* 2003.

Criminal Justice Act 2003, s.174

Duty to give reasons for, and explain effect of, sentence

25–46   **174.**—(1) Subject to subsections (3) and (4), any court passing sentence on an offender—

    (a) must state in open court, in ordinary language and in general terms, its reasons for deciding on the sentence passed, and

    (b) must explain to the offender in ordinary language—

        (i) the effect of the sentence,

        (ii) where the offender is required to comply with any order of the court forming part of the sentence, the effects of non-compliance with the order,

        (iii) any power of the court, on the application of the offender or any other person, to vary or review any order of the court forming part of the sentence, and

        (iv) where the sentence consists of or includes a fine, the effects of failure to pay the fine.

(2) In complying with subsection (1)(a), the court must—

    (a) where guidelines indicate that a sentence of a particular kind, or within a particular range, would normally be appropriate for the offence and the sentence is of a different kind, or is outside that range, state the court's reasons for deciding on a sentence of a different kind or outside that range,

    (b) where the sentence is a custodial sentence and the duty in subsection (2) of section 152 is not excluded by subsection (1)(a) or (b) or (3) of that section, state that it is of the opinion referred to in section 152(2) and why it is of that opinion,

    (c) where the sentence is a community sentence and the case does not fall within section 151(2), state that it is of the opinion that section 148(1) applies and why it is of that opinion,

    (d) where as a result of taking into account any matter referred to in section 144(1), the court imposes a punishment on the offender which is less severe than the punishment it would otherwise have imposed, state that fact, and

    (e) in any case, mention any aggravating or mitigating factors which the court has regarded as being of particular importance.

(3) Subsection (1)(a) does not apply—

    (a) to an offence the sentence for which is fixed by law (provision relating to sentencing for such an offence being made by section 270), or

    (b) to an offence the sentence for which falls to be imposed under section 51A(2) of the *Firearms Act* 1968 (c 27) or under subsection (2) of section 110 or 111 of the Sentencing Act (required custodial sentences).

(4) The Secretary of State may by order—

    (a) prescribe cases in which subsection (1)(a) or (b) does not apply, and

    (b) prescribe cases in which the statement referred to in subsection (1)(a) or the explanation referred to in subsection (1)(b) may be made in the absence of the offender, or may be provided in written form.

(5) Where a magistrates' court passes a custodial sentence, it must cause any reason stated by virtue of subsection (2)(b) to be specified in the warrant of commitment and entered on the register.

(6) In this section—

"guidelines" has the same meaning as in section 172;

"the register" has the meaning given by section 163 of the Sentencing Act.

There is a general obligation to state in ordinary language the reasons for deciding **25–47** on the sentence to be passed and to explain to the offender the effect of the sentence, including what might happen if he fails to comply with the order of the court: s.174(1). Where a relevant guideline has been issued by the Sentencing Guidelines Council and the sentence is outside the range suggested in that guideline, the reasons must also show why that decision has been made: s.174(2)(a).

More specific obligations require a court:

    — when passing a custodial sentence to state why the offence is so serious than nothing other than custody is justified

    — when passing a community sentence, to state why the offence was serious enough to warrant such a sentence (unless it was based on some other rationale such as that contained in s.151(2) of the *Criminal Justice Act* 2003 when in force)

    — when reducing a sentence on account of the defendant's guilty plea, to state that that has been done

— always to draw attention to any aggravating or mitigating factors that were of particular importance in determining sentence.

When the court has taken other offences into consideration when passing sentence, it should expressly state that it has done so.

25–48　　The *Magistrates' Courts Sentencing Guidelines*(2003), p.84, state that reasons for findings and decisions should normally be given. Victims are likely to want to know the reasons for the decision, the public are entitled to know what is going on in the criminal justice system and to have confidence in it and ill-informed criticism in the media may be reduced if reasons have been given in public and recorded.

In preparing a SSR or a PSR (see §§ 24–12—24–19 above), or in implementing a community sentence, the probation service will better be able to respond to the wishes of the court if it is known what the court had in mind.

If a case has to be adjourned, and a differently constituted court sits on the next occasion, the later court must know the reasons for the decision of the earlier court.

The guidelines also list occasions where the giving of reasons is required by law including why bail is refused, why a compensation order is not made and why a court is not disqualifying from driving or endorsing a licence for 'special reasons'.

I SPECIFIC ASPECTS OF SENTENCING

A. DEFERMENT OF SENTENCE

Powers of Criminal Courts (Sentencing) Act 2000, ss.1, 2

Deferment of sentence

1.—(1) The Crown Court or a magistrates' court may defer passing sentence on an offender **26–1** for the purpose of enabling the court, or any other court to which it falls to deal with him, to have regard in dealing with him to—

(a) his conduct after conviction (including, where appropriate, the making by him of reparation for his offence); or

(b) any change in his circumstances;

but this is subject to subsection (2) and (3) below.

(2) The power conferred by subsection (1) above shall be exercisable only if—

(a) the offender consents; and

(b) the court is satisfied, having regard to the nature of the offence and the character and circumstances of the offender, that it would be in the interests of justice to exercise the power.

(3) Any deferment under this section shall be until such date as may be specified by the court, not being more than six months after the date on which the deferment is announced by the court; and, subject to section 2(7) below, where the passing of sentence has been deferred under this section it shall not be further so deferred.

(4) Notwithstanding any enactment, a court which under this section defers passing sentence on an offender shall not on the same occasion remand him.

(5) Where the passing of sentence on an offender has been deferred by a court under this section, the court's power under this section to deal with the offender at the end of the period of deferment—

    (a) is power to deal with him, in respect of the offence for which passing of sentence has been deferred, in any way in which it could have dealt with him if it had not deferred passing sentence; and

    (b) without prejudice to the generality of paragraph (a) above, in the case of a magistrates' court includes the power conferred by section 3 below to commit him to the Crown Court for sentence.

(6) Nothing in this section or section 2 below shall affect—

    (a) the power of the Crown Court to bind over an offender to come up for judgment when called upon; or

    (b) the power of any court to defer passing sentence for any purpose for which it may lawfully do so apart from this section.

Further powers of courts where sentence deferred under section 1

26–2   **2.**—(1) A court which under section 1 above has deferred passing sentence on an offender may deal with him before the end of the period of deferment if during that period he is convicted in Great Britain of any offence.

(2) Subsection (3) below applies where a court has under section 1 above deferred passing sentence on an offender in respect of one or more offences and during the period of deferment the offender is convicted in England or Wales of any offence ("the later offence").

(3) Where this subsection applies, then (without prejudice to subsection (1) above and whether or not the offender is sentenced for the later offence during the period of deferment), the court which passes sentence on him for the later offence may also, if this has not already been done, deal with him for the offence or offences for which passing of sentence has been deferred, except that—

    (a) the power conferred by this subsection shall not be exercised by a magistrates' court if the court which deferred passing sentence was the Crown Court; and

    (b) the Crown Court, in exercising that power in a case in which the court which deferred passing sentence was a magistrates' court, shall not pass any sentence which could not have been passed by a magistrates' court in exercising that power.

(4) Where—

    (a) a court which under section 1 above has deferred passing sentence on an offender proposes to deal with him, whether on the date originally specified by the court or by virtue of subsection (1) above before that date, or

    (b) the offender does not appear on the date so specified,

the court may issue a summons requiring him to appear before the court, or may issue a warrant for his arrest.

(5) In deferring the passing of sentence under section 1 above a magistrates' court shall be regarded as exercising the power of adjourning the trial conferred by section 10(1) of the *Magistrates' Courts Act* 1980, and accordingly sections 11(1) and 13(1) to (3A) and (5) of that Act (non-appearance of the accused) apply (without prejudice to subsection (4) above) if the offender does not appear on the date specified under section 1(3) above.

(6) Any power of a court under this section to deal with an offender in a case where the passing of sentence has been deferred under section 1 above—

    (a) is power to deal with him, in respect of the offence for which passing of sentence has been deferred, in any way in which the court which deferred passing sentence could have dealt with him; and

    (b) without prejudice to the generality of paragraph (a) above, in the case of a magistrates' court includes the power conferred by section 3 below to commit him to the Crown Court for sentence.

26–3   (7) Where—

    (a) the passing of sentence on an offender in respect of one or more offences has been deferred under section 1 above, and

    (b) a magistrates' court deals with him in respect of the offence or any of the offences by committing him to the Crown Court under section 3 below,

the power of the Crown Court to deal with him includes the same power to defer passing sentence on him as if he had just been convicted of the offence or offences on indictment before the court.

(1) Purpose and Effect

The purpose of deferring sentence is to enable the offender to do (or refrain from **26–4** doing) something where his success will significantly influence the sentence to be passed. However, it has a number of problems, not least the inability to take action earlier than the end of the period of deferment where the offender does not comply with the terms of the deferment but does not commit any further offences. Generally, the power to defer sentence has been used infrequently. However, when s.278 of, and Sch.23 to the *Criminal Justice Act* 2003 come into force replacing these two sections, the power may well start to be used more extensively because of the greater enforcement powers given to the court and the changes in the way the terms imposed on the defendant will be set. In essence, under the new provisions, a court may require the defendant to enter into undertakings and to be under supervision during the period of the deferment. The supervisor may (but need not) be an officer of a local probation board. If the undertakings are not being complied with, the court may require the defendant to attend court before the end of the period of deferment.

(2) General

When deferring sentence, the court must make clear to the defendant why sentence **26–5** is being deferred and what is expected of him during the deferment. Ideally, the defendant himself should be given notice in writing of what he is expected to do or refrain from doing, so that there can be no doubt what is expected.

Deferment is only appropriate where what is expected of the defendant is not sufficiently specific to be made the subject of a condition imposed as part of a community rehabilitation order or where the steps to be taken by the defendant could not of their nature be the subject of a condition. Consider carefully whether the intentions of the court could not best be achieved by other means. If sentence is deferred, care must be taken to avoid the risk of misunderstanding and a sense of injustice when the defendant returns before the court: *R. v George* (1984) 79 Cr.App.R. 26.

An order can only be made if the defendant consents. This consent should be **26–6** obtained from the defendant directly rather than through his counsel: *R. v Fairhead* [1975] 2 All E.R. 737. Where a court defers sentence without obtaining consent, any sentence passed at the end of the period of deferment will be invalid, though the Court of Appeal will have power to deal with the matter as if a valid sentence had been passed.

Sentence may be deferred for any period up to six months: s.1(3). The period should be closely matched to the expectations placed upon the defendant. Once sentence has been deferred, the defendant may not be sentenced until the period of deferment expires or the offender is convicted of another offence.

(3) Convictions during period of deferment

If the defendant is convicted anywhere in Great Britain (*i.e.* England, Wales and **26–7** Scotland) of another offence committed during the period of deferral, the *court that has deferred sentence* may deal with the defendant before the end of the period of deferment: s.2(1). In order to bring the defendant before the court, a summons or a warrant may be issued: s.2(4)(a).

If a defendant subject to a deferred sentence is convicted in England and Wales of an offence, then *the court dealing with the later offence* may be able to deal with the offence on which sentence was deferred even though it was not the court which deferred sentence: s.2(2), (3). However, a magistrates' court may not sentence for an offence that is subject to a deferred sentence imposed by the Crown Court: s.2(3)(a). A Crown Court sentencing for an offence on which a magistrates' court has deferred sentence is limited to the maximum sentence that a magistrates' court could have passed: s.2(3)(b). This limit applies even though one of the options available to a magistrates' court at the end of the period of deferment is to commit the defendant to the Crown Court for sentence: s.2(6)(b).

(4) Sentence after deferment

26–8   The approach to sentence at the end of the period of deferment was also considered in *R. v George* (above).

    i) be clear about the purpose of the deferment and any requirement imposed by the deferring court

   ii) decide whether the defendant has substantially conformed or attempted to conform with the expectations of the deferring court.

  iii) if he has, then the defendant may legitimately expect that an immediate custodial sentence will not be imposed: *R. v Smith* (1979) 1 Cr.App.R.(S.) 339.

  iv) if he has not, then the court should state clearly how the defendant has failed to do what the court required.

B. ABSOLUTE AND CONDITIONAL DISCHARGE

Powers of Criminal Courts (Sentencing) Act 2000, s.12

Absolute and conditional discharge

26–9   **12.**—(1) Where a court by or before which a person is convicted of an offence (not being an offence the sentence for which is fixed by law or falls to be imposed under section 109(2), 110(2) or 111(2) below) is of the opinion, having regard to the circumstances including the nature of the offence and the character of the offender, that it is inexpedient to inflict punishment, the court may make an order either—

    (a) discharging him absolutely; or

    (b) if the court thinks fit, discharging him subject to the condition that he commits no offence during such period, not exceeding three years from the date of the order, as may be specified in the order.

    (2) Subsection (1)(b) above has effect subject to section 66(4) of the *Crime and Disorder Act* 1998 (effect of reprimands and warnings).

    (3) An order discharging a person subject to such a condition as is mentioned in subsection (1)(b) above is in this Act referred to as an "order for conditional discharge"; and the period specified in any such order is in this Act referred to as "the period of conditional discharge".

    (4) Before making an order for conditional discharge, the court shall explain to the offender in ordinary language that if he commits another offence during the period of conditional discharge he will be liable to be sentenced for the original offence.

    (5) If (by virtue of section 13 below) a person conditionally discharged under this section is sentenced for the offence in respect of which the order for conditional discharge was made, that order shall cease to have effect.

    (6) On making an order for conditional discharge, the court may, if it thinks it expedient for the purpose of the offender's reformation, allow any person who consents to do so to give security for the good behaviour of the offender.

    (7) Nothing in this section shall be construed as preventing a court, on discharging an offender absolutely or conditionally in respect of any offence, from making an order for costs against the offender or imposing any disqualification on him or from making in respect of the offence an order under section 130, 143 or 148 below (compensation orders, deprivation orders and restitution orders).

(1) Purpose and Effect

26–10   An offender suffers no penalty for the offence providing (in the case of a conditional discharge) that he commits no further offence during the period specified. If he does, the court that deals with him for the later offence may also sentence him for the offence subject to the discharge.

(2) General

26–11   When making an order of conditional discharge, the court must explain to the offender, in ordinary language, that, if he commits another offence during the period of the conditional discharge, he will be liable to be sentenced for the original offence. This task does not have to be undertaken by the court; an undertaking from the defendant's counsel that they will explain the effect of the order will suffice: *R. v Wehner* [1977] 3 All E.R. 553.

A discharge may not be combined with a fine for the same offence: *R. v Sanck* (1990) 12 Cr.App.R.(S.) 155. A conditional discharge may be combined with an ancillary order such as a compensation order, a restitution order, an order to pay the costs of the prosecution, or a order depriving the offender of his rights in property under s.143 of the 2000 Act, or a recommendation for deportation order. A court which makes an order of discharge may exercise any power arising out of the *Road Traffic Offenders Act* 1988, ss.34, 35, 36 or 44 and must comply with any mandatory requirement of those sections: s.46 of the 1988 Act.

Magistrates' courts should not make an order of discharge in respect of an offence committed during the currency of a suspended sentence of imprisonment imposed by the Crown Court, the offender should be committed to the Crown Court so that both elements can be dealt with together: *R. v Moore* [1995] Q.B. 353.

Powers of Criminal Courts (Sentencing) Act 2000, ss.13–15

Commission of further offence by person conditionally discharged
13.—(1) If it appears to the Crown Court, where that court has jurisdiction in accordance **26–12** with subsection (2) below, or to a justice of the peace having jurisdiction in accordance with that subsection, that a person in whose case an order for conditional discharge has been made—
    (a) has been convicted by a court in Great Britain of an offence committed during the period of conditional discharge, and
    (b) has been dealt with in respect of that offence,
that court or justice may, subject to subsection (3) below, issue a summons requiring that person to appear at the place and time specified in it or a warrant for his arrest.

(2) Jurisdiction for the purposes of subsection (1) above may be exercised—
    (a) if the order for conditional discharge was made by the Crown Court, by that court;
    (b) if the order was made by a magistrates' court, by a justice acting for the petty sessions area for which that court acts.

(3) A justice of the peace shall not issue a summons under this section except on information and shall not issue a warrant under this section except on information in writing and on oath.

(4) A summons or warrant issued under this section shall direct the person to whom it relates to appear or to be brought before the court by which the order for conditional discharge was made.

(5) If a person in whose case an order for conditional discharge has been made by the Crown Court is convicted by a magistrates' court of an offence committed during the period of conditional discharge, the magistrates' court—
    (a) may commit him to custody or release him on bail until he can be brought or appear before the Crown Court; and
    (b) if it does so, shall send to the Crown Court a copy of the minute or memorandum of the conviction entered in the register, signed by the justices' chief executive by whom the register is kept.

(6) Where it is proved to the satisfaction of the court by which an order for conditional **26–13** discharge was made that the person in whose case the order was made has been convicted of an offence committed during the period of conditional discharge, the court may deal with him, for the offence for which the order was made, in any way in which it could deal with him if he had just been convicted by or before that court of that offence.

(7) If a person in whose case an order for conditional discharge has been made by a magistrates' court—
    (a) is convicted before the Crown Court of an offence committed during the period of conditional discharge, or
    (b) is dealt with by the Crown Court for any such offence in respect of which he was committed for sentence to the Crown Court,

the Crown Court may deal with him, for the offence for which the order was made, in any way in which the magistrates' court could deal with him if it had just convicted him of that offence.

(8) If a person in whose case an order for conditional discharge has been made by a magistrates' court is convicted by another magistrates' court of any offence committed during the period of conditional discharge, that other court may, with the consent of the court which made the order, deal with him, for the offence for which the order was made, in any way in which the court could deal with him if it had just convicted him of that offence.

(9) Where an order for conditional discharge has been made by a magistrates' court in the case of an offender under 18 years of age in respect of an offence triable only on indictment in the case of an adult, any powers exercisable under subsection (6), (7) or (8) above by that or any other court in respect of the offender after he attains the age of 18 shall be powers to do either or both of the following—

> (a) to impose a fine not exceeding £5,000 for the offence in respect of which the order was made;
>
> (b) to deal with the offender for that offence in any way in which a magistrates' court could deal with him if it had just convicted him of an offence punishable with imprisonment for a term not exceeding six months.

(10) The reference in subsection (6) above to a person's having been convicted of an offence committed during the period of conditional discharge is a reference to his having been so convicted by a court in Great Britain.

Effect of discharge

26–14　　**14.**—(1) Subject to subsection (2) below, a conviction of an offence for which an order is made under section 12 above discharging the offender absolutely or conditionally shall be deemed not to be a conviction for any purpose other than the purposes of the proceedings in which the order is made and of any subsequent proceedings which may be taken against the offender under section 13 above.

(2) Where the offender was aged 18 or over at the time of his conviction of the offence in question and is subsequently sentenced (under section 13 above) for that offence, subsection (1) above shall cease to apply to the conviction.

(3) Without prejudice to subsections (1) and (2) above, the conviction of an offender who is discharged absolutely or conditionally under section 12 above shall in any event be disregarded for the purposes of any enactment or instrument which—

> (a) imposes any disqualification or disability upon convicted persons; or
>
> (b) authorises or requires the imposition of any such disqualification or disability.

(4) Subsections (1) to (3) above shall not affect—

> (a) any right of an offender discharged absolutely or conditionally under section 12 above to rely on his conviction in bar of any subsequent proceedings for the same offence;
>
> (b) the restoration of any property in consequence of the conviction of any such offender; or
>
> (c) the operation, in relation to any such offender, of any enactment or instrument in force on 1st July 1974 which is expressed to extend to persons dealt with under section 1(1) of the *Probation of Offenders Act* 1907 as well as to convicted persons.

(5) In subsections (3) and (4) above—

"enactment" includes an enactment contained in a local Act; and

"instrument" means an instrument having effect by virtue of an Act.

(6) Subsection (1) above has effect subject to section 50(1A) of the *Criminal Appeal Act* 1968 and section 108(1A) of the *Magistrates' Courts Act* 1980 (rights of appeal); and this subsection shall not be taken to prejudice any other enactment that excludes the effect of subsection (1) or (3) above for particular purposes.

(7) Without prejudice to paragraph 1(3) of Schedule 11 to this Act (references to provisions of this Act to be construed as including references to corresponding old enactments), in this section—

> (a) any reference to an order made under section 12 above discharging an offender absolutely or conditionally includes a reference to an order which was made under any provision of Part I of the *Powers of Criminal Courts Act* 1973 (whether or not reproduced in this Act) discharging the offender absolutely or conditionally;

(b) any reference to an offender who is discharged absolutely or conditionally under section 12 includes a reference to an offender who was discharged absolutely or conditionally under any such provision.

Discharge: Supplementary

15.—(1) The Secretary of State may by order direct that subsection (1) of section 12 above **26-15** shall be amended by substituting, for the maximum period specified in that subsection as originally enacted or as previously amended under this subsection, such period as may be specified in the order.

(2) Where an order for conditional discharge has been made on appeal, for the purposes of section 13 above it shall be deemed—

(a) if it was made on an appeal brought from a magistrates' court, to have been made by that magistrates' court;

(b) if it was made on an appeal brought from the Crown Court or from the criminal division of the Court of Appeal, to have been made by the Crown Court.

(3) In proceedings before the Crown Court under section 13 above, any question whether any person in whose case an order for conditional discharge has been made has been convicted of an offence committed during the period of conditional discharge shall be determined by the court and not by the verdict of a jury.

C. Financial Penalties

(1) Purpose and Effect

A financial penalty is the sanction most often imposed in magistrates' courts. There **26-16** are three main types—the fine itself, a compensation order (which can be a sentence in itself or an ancillary order) and an order to pay the costs of the prosecution. A fine is primarily a punishment for the current offence and a deterrent to future offending and so is designed to make sufficient impact on the spending power of the defendant to cause a degree of hardship commensurate with the seriousness of the offence.

A compensation order is primarily concerned with reparation, making financial compensation for the harm or loss caused by the offence. Where there is not enough money to pay a fine and compensation, then it is the compensation that must take priority. Where both a fine and compensation are ordered, money paid by the defendant is allocated first to paying off the compensation and then to any fines.

An order for costs reimburses, or contributes to, the costs incurred by the prosecution in bringing the case to court. Such an order takes priority over a fine but not over compensation.

(2) Assessment of amount

Fines are in the lowest tier of sanctions and there is no threshold criteria that need to **26-17** be passed before a financial penalty can be imposed. However, any amount imposed must be balanced by the resources available to the defendant. In most circumstances, a fine must be capable of being paid within one year, compensation within no more than three years. Even where an offence is serious enough to justify a community sentence, a court may still impose a financial penalty instead where appropriate: s.127 of the *PCC(S)A* 2000.

Balancing the seriousness of the offence with the financial resources available to the offender is often a difficult task. The amount of the fine will, therefore, be determined by reference to the gravity of the offence with the court also taking into account the whole of the circumstances of the case including the financial circumstances of the offender. In *R. v Cleminson* (1985) 7 Cr.App.R.(S.) 128, the Court of Appeal said that the correct approach was to decide the appropriate sentence for the offence and the offender and then to consider the offender's resources. The *Magistrates' Courts Sentencing Guidelines* (2003) approaches the task by setting three levels of fine which relate to the weekly income of the offender. The sentencer must ensure that the fine imposed is such that the offender can afford to pay: *R. v Chelmsford Crown Court Ex p. Birchall*

(1989) 11 Cr.App.R.(S.) 510, DC. The sentencer may have regard to the earning capacity of the defendant as well as current savings: *R. v Little*, unreported, April 14, 1976. A fine should not be imposed on the assumption that someone else will pay: *R. v Charalambous* (1984) 6 Cr.App.R.(S.) 389.

The normal process followed by a court will be:

— Is a fine appropriate?
— What level of fine reflects the seriousness of the offence?
— What are the financial resources available to the offender?
— What is a suitable balance between the two?

26–18　　A court is obliged to inquire into the financial circumstances of the offender before fixing the amount of a fine: s.128 of the *PCC(S)A* 2000. The onus is on the offender to disclose evidence of his financial situation; if he does not, the court is entitled to draw whatever inferences it sees fit, and may conclude that the offender is being evasive about his financial circumstances and has the means to pay: *R. v Higgins* (1988) 10 Cr.App.R.(S.) 144. In certain limited circumstances, where there are insufficient financial resources to pay a fine that properly reflects the serious of the offence, a court may be able to impose a community sentence where a fine would otherwise be appropriate and the threshold criterion is not passed, see § 26–34 below.

There is nothing wrong in principle with the fine being paid in instalments. Where a compensation order is being paid, the instalment period may quite properly be longer than one year, provided that it is not an undue burden and too severe a punishment for the offender, having regard to the nature of the offence and the offender. There is authority that a two year period will seldom be too long and in exceptional circumstances, a three year period might prove unassailable: *R. v Olliver and Olliver* (1989) 11 Cr.App.R.(S.) 10, CA. However, a court will always need to ensure that there is a realistic prospect of the order being paid and will be conscious of the impact on the victim also where payments received from a court extend over a lengthy period. When in force, Sch.5, Pt 3 to the *Courts Act* 2003 will require a court (when allowing time for payment on imposition) to make an attachment of earnings order or a deduction from benefit order in respect of an "existing defaulter" (as defined) unless that is impracticable and, for others, to make such an order with the consent of the person on whom the financial penalty has been imposed.

26–19　　Where an offender has spent time in custody on remand before a fine is imposed, credit should be given for that time when the amount of the fine is determined: *R. v Warden* [1996] 2 Cr.App.R.(S.) 269, CA.

A fine cannot be imposed at the same time as a discharge (*PCC(S)A* 2000, s.12(1)) unless the offender is being sentenced for two or more offences: *R. v Sanck* (1990) 12 Cr.App.R.(S.) 155. It will only rarely be appropriate to combine a fine with a custodial sentence in a magistrates' court. One of the effects of a custodial sentence is to reduce the employability of the offender and it is unlikely to aid the objective of reducing crime by having an offender released from custody with a continuing obligation to pay fines to the court. This may be different where a defendant has substantial savings or where the order seeks to reclaim the proceeds of the crime.

The *Magistrates' Courts Sentencing Guidelines* (2003) suggest appropriate fines for particular circumstances, but emphasise that the guidance should not be used as a tariff and every offender's means should be individually considered. These suggestions are noted in the appropriate chapters above in this work or can be found in the Guidelines themselves.

Powers of Criminal Courts (Sentencing) Act 2000, s.128

Fixing of fines

26–20　　**128.**—(1) Before fixing the amount of any fine to be imposed on an offender who is an individual, a court shall inquire into his financial circumstances.

(2) The amount of any fine fixed by a court shall be such as, in the opinion of the court, reflects the seriousness of the offence.

(3) In fixing the amount of any fine to be imposed on an offender (whether an individual or other person), a court shall take into account the circumstances of the case including, among other things, the financial circumstances of the offender so far as they are known, or appear, to the court.

(4) Subsection (3) above applies whether taking into account the financial circumstances of the offender has the effect of increasing or reducing the amount of the fine.

(5) Where—

    (a) an offender has been convicted in his absence in pursuance of section 11 or 12 of the *Magistrates' Courts Act* 1980 (non-appearance of accused), or

    (b) an offender—

        (i) has failed to comply with an order under section 126(1) above, or

        (ii) has otherwise failed to co-operate with the court in its inquiry into his financial circumstances,

and the court considers that it has insufficient information to make a proper determination of the financial circumstances of the offender, it may make such determination as it thinks fit.

Powers to order statement as to offender's financial circumstances

126.—(1) Where an individual has been convicted of an offence, the court may, before **26–21** sentencing him, make a financial circumstances order with respect to him.

(2) Where a magistrates' court has been notified in accordance with section 12(4) of the *Magistrates' Courts Act* 1980 that an individual desires to plead guilty without appearing before the court, the court may make a financial circumstances order with respect to him.

(3) In this section "a financial circumstances order" means, in relation to any individual, an order requiring him to give to the court, within such period as may be specified in the order, such a statement of his financial circumstances as the court may require.

(4) An individual who without reasonable excuse fails to comply with a financial circumstances order shall be liable on summary conviction to a fine not exceeding level 3 on the standard scale.

(5) If an individual, in furnishing any statement in pursuance of a financial circumstances order—

    (a) makes a statement which he knows to be false in a material particular,

    (b) recklessly furnishes a statement which is false in a material particular, or

    (c) knowingly fails to disclose any material fact,

he shall be liable on summary conviction to imprisonment for a term not exceeding three months or a fine not exceeding level 4 on the standard scale or both.

(6) Proceedings in respect of an offence under subsection (5) above may, notwithstanding anything in section 127(1) of the *Magistrates' Courts Act* 1980 (limitation of time), be commenced at any time within two years from the date of the commission of the offence or within six months from its first discovery by the prosecutor, whichever period expires the earlier.

Criminal Justice Act 1982, s.37

The standard scale of fines for summary offences

37.—(1) There shall be a standard scale of fines for summary offences, which shall be known **26–22** as "the standard scale".

(2) The standard scale is shown below—

Level on the scale	Amount of fine
1	£200
2	£500
3	£1,000
4	£2,500
5	£5,000.

(3) Where any enactment (whether contained in an Act passed before or after this Act) provides—

    (a) that a person convicted of a summary offence shall be liable on conviction to a fine or a maximum fine by reference to a specified level on the standard scale; or

(b) confers power by subordinate instrument to make a person liable on conviction of a summary offence (whether or not created by the instrument) to a fine or maximum fine by reference to a specified level on the standard scale,

it is to be construed as referring to the standard scale for which this section provides as that standard scale has effect from time to time by virtue either of this section or of an order under section 143 of the *Magistrates' Courts Act* 1980.

Magistrates' Courts Act 1980, s.32

Penalties on summary conviction for offences triable either way

26–23   **32.**—(1) On summary conviction of any of the offences triable either way listed in Schedule 1 to this Act a person shall be liable to imprisonment for a term not exceeding 6 months or to a fine not exceeding the prescribed sum or both, except that—

    (a) a magistrates' court shall not have power to impose imprisonment for an offence so listed if the Crown Court would not have that power in the case of an adult convicted of it on indictment;

    (b) on summary conviction of an offence consisting in the incitement to commit an offence triable either way a person shall not be liable to any greater penalty than he would be liable to on summary conviction of the last-mentioned offence: and

(2) For any offence triable either way which is not listed in Schedule 1 to this Act, being an offence under a relevant enactment, the maximum fine which may be imposed on summary conviction shall be virtue of this subsection be the prescribed sum unless the offence is one for which by virtue of an enactment other than this subsection a larger fine may be imposed on summary conviction.

(3) Where, by virtue of any relevant enactment, a person summarily convicted of an offence triable either way would, apart from this section, be liable to a maximum fine of one amount in the case of a first conviction and of a different amount in the case of a second or subsequent conviction, subsection (2) above shall apply irrespective of whether the conviction is a first, second or subsequent one.

(4) Subsection (2) above shall not affect so much of any enactment as (in whatever words) makes a person liable on summary conviction to a fine not exceeding a specified amount for each day on which a continuing offence is continued after conviction or the occurrence of any other specified event.

(5) Subsection (2) above shall not apply on summary conviction of any of the following offences—

    (a) offences under section 5(2) of the *Misuse of Drugs Act* 1971 (having possession of a controlled drug) where the controlled drug in relation to which the offence was committed was a Class B or Class C drug;

    (b) offences under the following provisions of that Act, where the controlled drug in relation to which the offence was committed was a Class C drug, namely—

       (i) section 4(2) (production, or being concerned in the production, of a controlled drug);

       (ii) section 4(3) (supplying or offering a controlled drug or being concerned in the doing of either activity by another);

       (iii) section 5(3) (having possession of a controlled drug with intent to supply it to another);

       (iv) section 8 (being the occupier, or concerned in the management, of premises and permitting or suffering certain activities to take place there);

       (v) section 12(6) (contravention of direction prohibiting practitioner etc. from possessing, supplying etc. controlled drugs); or

       (vi) section 13(3) (contravention of direction prohibiting practitioner etc. from prescribing, supplying etc. controlled drugs).

26–24   (6) Where, as regards any offence triable either way, there is under any enactment (however framed or worded) a power by subordinate instrument to restrict the amount of the fine which on summary conviction can be imposed in respect of that offence—

    (a) subsection (2) above shall not affect that power or override any restriction imposed in the exercise of that power; and

    (b) the amount to which that fine may be restricted in the exercise of that power shall be any amount less than the maximum fine which could be imposed on summary conviction in respect of the offence apart from any restriction so imposed.

(8) In subsection (5) above "controlled drug", "Class B drug" and "Class C drug" have the same meaning as in the *Misuse of Drugs Act* 1971.

(9) In this section—

"fine" includes a pecuniary penalty but does not include a pecuniary forfeiture or pecuniary compensation;

"the prescribed sum" means £5,000 or such sum as is for the time being substituted in this definition by an order in force under section 143(1) below;

"relevant enactment" means an enactment contained in the *Criminal Law Act* 1977 or in any Act passed before, or in the same Session as, that Act.

Magistrates' Courts Act 1980, ss.36, 75, 82 (1), (6)

Restriction on fines in respect of young persons

26–25

36.—(1) Where a person under 18 years of age is found guilty by a magistrates' court of an offence for which, apart from this section, the court would have power to impose a fine of an amount exceeding £1,000, the amount of any fine imposed by the court shall not exceed £1,000.

(2) In relation to a person under the age of 14 subsection (1) above shall have effect as if for the words "£1,000", in both the places where they occur, there were substituted the words "£250"

Power to dispense with immediate payment

26–26

75.—(1) A magistrates' court by whose conviction or order a sum is adjudged to be paid may, instead of requiring immediate payment, allow time for payment, or order payment by instalments.

(2) Where a magistrates' court has allowed time for payment, the court may, on application by or on behalf of the person liable to make the payment, allow further time or order payment by instalments.

(2A) An order under this section that a lump sum required to be paid under a maintenance order shall be paid by instalments (a "maintenance instalments order") shall be treated for the purposes of sections 59, 59B and 60 above as a maintenance order.

(2B) Subsections (5) and (7) of section 59 above (including those subsections as they apply for the purposes of section 60 above) shall have effect in relation to a maintenance instalments order—

(a) as if in subsection (5), paragraph (c) and the word "and" immediately preceding it were omitted; and

(b) as if in subsection (7)—

(i) the reference to the maintenance order were a reference to the maintenance order in respect of which the maintenance instalments order in question is made;

(ii) for the words "the person who applied for the maintenance order" there were substituted "the debtor".

(2C) Section 60 above shall have effect in relation to a maintenance instalments order as if in subsection (7), paragraph (c) and the word "and" immediately preceding it were omitted.

(3) Where a court has ordered payment by instalments and default is made in the payment of any one instalment, proceedings may be taken as if the default had been made in the payment of all the instalments then unpaid.

Restriction on power to impose imprisonment for default

26–27

82.—(1) A magistrates' court shall not on the occasion of convicting an offender of an offence issue a warrant of commitment for a default in paying any sum adjudged to be paid by the conviction unless—

(a) in the case of an offence punishable with imprisonment, he appears to the court to have sufficient means to pay the sum forthwith;

(b) it appears to the court that he is unlikely to remain long enough at a place of abode in the United Kingdom to enable payment of the sum to be enforced by other methods; or

(c) on the occasion of that conviction the court sentences him to immediate imprisonment, youth custody or detention in a detention centre for that or another offence or he is already serving a sentence of custody for life, or a term of imprisonment, youth custody, detention under section 9 of the *Criminal Justice Act* 1982 or detention in a detention centre.

(6) Where a magistrates' court issues a warrant of commitment on the ground that one of the conditions mentioned in subsection (1) ... above is satisfied, it shall state that fact, specifying the ground, in the warrant.

Magistrates' Courts Act 1980, ss.88, 89

Supervision pending payment

26–28   **88.**—(1) Where any person is adjudged to pay a sum by a summary conviction and the convicting court does not commit him to prison forthwith in default of payment, the court may, either on the occasion of the conviction or on a subsequent occasion, order him to be placed under the supervision of such person as the court may from time to time appoint.

(2) An order placing a person under supervision in respect of any sum shall remain in force so long as he remains liable to pay the sum or any part of it unless the order ceases to have effect or is discharged under subsection (3) below.

(3) An order under this section shall cease to have effect on the making of a transfer of fine order under section 89 below with respect to the sum adjudged to be paid and may be discharged by the court that made it, without prejudice in either case to the making of a new order.

(4) Where a person under 21 years old has been adjudged to pay a sum by a summary conviction and the convicting court does not commit him to detention under section 108 of the *Powers of Criminal Courts (Sentencing) Act* 2000 forthwith in default of payment, the court shall not commit him to such detention in default of payment of the sum, or for want of sufficient distress to satisfy the sum, unless he has been placed under supervision in respect of the sum or the court is satisfied that it is undesirable or impracticable to place him under supervision.

(5) Where a court, being satisfied as aforesaid, commits a person under 21 years old to such detention without an order under this section having been made, the court shall state the grounds on which it is so satisfied in the warrant of commitment.

(6) Where an order placing a person under supervision with respect to a sum is in force, a magistrates' court shall not commit him to prison in default of payment of the sum, or for want of sufficient distress to satisfy the sum, unless the court has before committing him taken such steps as may be reasonably practicable to obtain from the person appointed for his supervision an oral or written report on the offender's conduct and means and has considered any report so obtained, in addition, in a case where an inquiry is required by section 82 above, to that inquiry.

Transfer of fine order

26–29   **89.**—(1) Where a magistrates' court has, or is treated by any enactment as having, adjudged a person by a conviction to pay a sum and it appears to the court that the person is residing in any petty sessions area other than that for which the court acted, the court may make a transfer of fine order, that is to say, an order making payment enforceable in the petty sessions area in which it appears to the court that he is residing; and that area shall be specified in the order.

(2) As from the date on which a transfer of fine order is made with respect to any sum, all functions under this Part of this Act relating to that sum which, if no such order had been made, would have been exercisable by the court which made the order, or the justices' chief executive for that court, shall be exercisable by a court acting for the petty sessions area specified in the order, or the justices' chief executive for that court, as the case may be, and not otherwise.

(2A) The functions of the court to which subsection (2) above relates shall be deemed to include the court's power to apply to the Secretary of State under any regulations made by him under section 24(1)(a) of the *Criminal Justice Act* 1991 (power to deduct fines etc. from income support).

(3) Where it appears to a court by which functions in relation to any sum are for the time being exercisable by virtue of a transfer of fine order that the person liable to pay the sum is residing in a petty sessions area other than that for which the court is acting, the court may make a further transfer of fine order with respect to that sum.

(4) In this section and sections 90 and 91 below, references to this Part of this Act do not include references to section 81(1) above.

D. Power to Order Periodical Payments

Magistrates' Courts Act 1980, s.75

Power to dispense with immediate payment

75.—(1) A magistrates' court by whose conviction or order a sum is adjudged to be paid may, **26–30** instead of requiring immediate payment, allow time for payment, or order payment by instalments.

(2) Where a magistrates' court has allowed time for payment, the court may, on application by or on behalf of the person liable to make the payment, allow further time or order payment by instalments.

(3) Where a court has ordered payment by instalments and default is made in the payment of any one instalment, proceedings may be taken as if the default had been made in the payment of all the instalments then unpaid.

E. Power to Order Appearance Before the Court if Any Part of the Sum Remains Unpaid

Magistrates' Courts Act 1980, s.86

Power of magistrates' court to fix day for appearance of offender at means inquiry etc.

86.—(1) A magistrates' court which has exercised in relation to a sum adjudged to be paid by **26–31** a conviction either of the powers conferred by section 75(1) above shall have power, either then or later, to fix a day on which, if the relevant condition is satisfied, the offender must appear in person before the court for either or both of the following purposes, namely—

(a) to enable an inquiry into his means to be made under section 82 above;

(b) to enable a hearing required by subsection (5) of the said section 82 to be held.

(1A) Where the power which the court has exercised is the power to allow time for payment of a sum ("the adjudged sum"), the relevant condition is satisfied if any part of that sum remains unpaid on the day fixed by the court.

(1B) Where the power which the court has exercised is the power to order payment by instalments, the relevant condition is satisfied if an instalment which has fallen due remains unpaid on the day fixed by the court.

(2) Except as provided in subsection (3) below, the power to fix a day under this section shall be exercisable only in the presence of the offender.

(3) Where a day has been fixed under this section, the court may fix a later day in subsection for the day previously fixed, and may do so—

(a) when composed of a single justice; and

(b) whether the offender is present or not.

(4) Subject to subsection (5) below, if on the day fixed under this section—

(a) the relevant condition is satisfied; and

(b) the offender fails to appear in person before the court,

the court may issue a warrant to arrest him and bring him before the court; and subsection (3) of section 83 above shall apply in relation to a warrant issued under this section.

(5) Where under subsection (3) above a later day has in the absence of the offender been fixed in substitution for a day previously fixed under this section, the court shall not issue a warrant under this section unless it is proved to the satisfaction of the court, on oath or in such other manner as may be prescribed, that notice in writing of the substituted day was served on the offender not less than what appears to the court to be a reasonable time before that day.

F. Community Sentences

A community sentence is a sentence which consists of one or more community orders: **26–32** s.33(2) of the *PCC(S)A* 2000. The "community orders" are set out in s.33(1) of the Act and include, for example, curfew orders, community rehabilitation orders and attendance centre orders. Some orders are available only in prescribed circumstances (such as for offenders of a certain age) and some are not available in combination with other orders (for instance, a community rehabilitation order and a community punishment order—the order that would need to be made is a combination order which provides for different limits for some of the elements).

Section 35(1) of the *PCC(S)A* 2000 provides that a court may not make a community sentence unless, in its view, the offence was *serious enough* to justify such a sentence. This level contrasts with the threshold for a custodial sentence which requires that the offence is *so serious* that only custody is justified (see § 26–113 below). There a few exceptions to this (see below at § 26–34).

In considering whether the threshold has been crossed, the court may take into account both the offence itself and any other offence "associated with it".

26–33   The fact that the threshold has been crossed does not require the court to pass a community sentence. That decision simply sets an upper limit on the most severe type of sentence that can be imposed. Prior to deciding on the sentence to be imposed, the court will:

— first decide whether the threshold has been crossed (s.35(1)) and

— then decide which order is most suitable for the offender (s.35(3)(a)) whilst

— ensuring that the restrictions on liberty that result from the imposition of the order(s) are commensurate with the seriousness of the offence(s) (s.35(3)(b)).

There are two circumstances where a community order may be made without this threshold being crossed.

26–34   *In relation to enforcement of financial penalties,* powers exist enabling an attendance centre order or a community punishment order to be made in certain circumstances.

In relation to "persistent petty offenders", there is provision removing the need for the threshold to be crossed prior to imposing a community sentence: s.59. Inevitably, there will be offenders who continue to commit relatively minor offences for which a financial penalty would normally follow. However, the financial resources of the offender are such that existing fines are not paid and the court could not impose a realistic fine for the current offence and expect it to be paid within a reasonable time. In such circumstances, the court may make a curfew order or a community punishment order (s.59(3)) instead of imposing a fine. Four criteria must first be met:

     a) the defendant must be aged 16 or over when convicted (*i.e.* the critical date is not the date of the offence or the date of sentence)

     b) one or more fines previously imposed have not been paid (presumably this means paid in full)

     c) if a court imposed a fine for the current offence that matched the seriousness of the offence, the defendant would not have the financial resources to pay it (presumably within a reasonable time rather than forthwith) and

     d) if b) or c) had not been satisfied, the court would have been likely to have imposed a fine for the current offence (*i.e.* not, for instance, a conditional discharge).

26–35   Where these four criteria are met, the court may make a curfew order or a community punishment order for the offence (s.59(3)) and the empowering provisions are suitably modified (see s.59(5), (6) and paragraphs below relating to these two orders).

The power to make these orders in these circumstances only applies where the court has been notified that such an order can be implemented in the relevant area (*i.e.* where the defendant is going to be: s.59(7), (8)).

The *Magistrates' Courts Sentencing Guidelines* (2003) provide that a community penalty has three principal elements: restriction of liberty, reparation and the prevention of re-offending.

It is in making a community sentence that the conflict is often most apparent between the needs of the offender in order to reduce the likelihood of re-offending and the need to maintain the balance between the seriousness of the offence and the severity of the sanction. This can be seen in the shift away from financial penalties towards a community sentence. It may also be a factor in the increased use of custody since a person who has offended again after (or during) such a sentence is more likely to receive a custodial sentence.

Prior to making a community sentence, a court will consider what information it has **26–36** and what else is needed. Information about the offence will assist the court particularly in relation to the threshold of seriousness: s.35(1) and the extent to which any order(s) need to restrict the liberty of the defendant: ss.35(3)(b) and 36(1). Information about the offender will particularly assist in relation to deciding the most suitable order for the offender: ss.35(3)(a) and 36(2).

In relation to some community orders, a court will normally expect to consider a pre-sentence report before determining sentence (see also §§ 24–15 *et seq.*, above): s.39(4). Those orders are a community rehabilitation order or supervision order with additional requirements, orders containing a community punishment order and drug treatment and testing orders: s.36(3). Although this requirement can be ignored (s.36(5)), this can only happen if the court considers that such a report would be unnecessary. This should mean only where the court has enough information to enable it to assess the suitability of the order for the offender: see s.36(4).

Where the offender is under 18, there is an additional restraint on the power to **26–37** dispense with a pre-sentence report where the offence is not one that is triable only on indictment. In those circumstances, a pre-sentence report is unnecessary only where there is a previous pre-sentence report which the court has considered: s.36(6). However, if an order is made without a pre-sentence report where one should have been obtained, the order is not invalid though any appeal court should normally have access to a pre-sentence report: s.37(7)–(9).

Further information can be obtained by a court where the fact that a defendant has taken Class A drugs is relevant to the decision to make a community sentence. Where the defendant is aged 14 or more, the court may order the defendant to provide samples to enable them to know whether there are Class A drugs present in the body: *PCC(S)A* 2000, s.36A.

Where it is intended to require that compliance with a community order is monitored electronically and that requires the co-operation of another person, that person's consent must also be secured: *PCC(S)A* 2000, s.36B.

Powers of Criminal Courts (Sentencing) Act 2000, s.33

Meaning of "community order" and "community sentence"

33.—(1) In this Act, "community order" means any of the following orders—   **26–38**
    (a) a curfew order;
    (b) a community rehabilitation order;
    (c) a community punishment order;
    (d) a community punishment and rehabilitation order;
    (e) a drug treatment and testing order;
   (ee) a drug abstinence order
    (f) an attendance centre order;
    (g) a supervision order;
    (h) an action plan order.

    (2) In this Act, "community sentence" means a sentence which consists of or includes one or more community orders.

[This section is printed as amended by the *Criminal Justice and Court Services Act* 2000, Sch.7, Pt II, para.161(b)].

Powers of Criminal Courts (Sentencing) Act 2000, ss.35, 36

Restrictions on imposing community sentences

    35.—(1) A court shall not pass a community sentence on an offender unless it is of the **26–39** opinion that the offence, or the combination of the offence and one or more offences associated with it, was serious enough to warrant such a sentence.

    (2) In consequence of the provision made by section 51 below with respect to community punishment and rehabilitation orders, a community sentence shall not consist of or include both a community rehabilitation order and a community punishment order.

(3) Subject to subsection (2) above and to section 69(5) below (which limits the community orders that may be combined with an action plan order), where a court passes a community sentence—

    (a) the particular order or orders comprising or forming part of the sentence shall be such as in the opinion of the court is, or taken together are, the most suitable for the offender; and

    (b) the restrictions on liberty imposed by the order or orders shall be such as in the opinion of the court are commensurate with the seriousness of the offence, or the combination of the offence and one or more offences associated with it.

(4) Subsections (1) and (3)(b) above have effect subject to section 59 below (curfew orders and community service orders for persistent petty offenders).

Procedural requirements for community sentences: pre-sentence reports etc.

26–40   **36.**—(1) In forming any such opinion as is mentioned in subsection (1)or (3)(b) of section 35 above, a court shall take into account all such information as is available to it about the circumstances of the offence or (as the case may be) of the offence and the offence or offences associated with it, including any aggravating or mitigating factors.

(2) In forming any such opinion as is mentioned in subsection (3)(a) of that section, a court may take into account any information about the offender which is before it.

(3) The following provisions of this section apply in relation to—

    (a) a probation order which includes additional requirements authorised by Schedule 2 to this Act;

    (b) a community punishment order;

    (c) a community punishment and rehabilitation order;

    (d) a drug treatment and testing order;

    (e) a supervision order which includes requirements authorised by Schedule 6 to this Act.

(4) Subject to subsection (5) below, a court shall obtain and consider a pre-sentence report before forming an opinion as to the suitability for the offender of one or more of the orders mentioned in subsection (3) above.

(5) Subsection (4) above does not apply if, in the circumstances of the case, the court is of the opinion that it is unnecessary to obtain a pre-sentence report.

26–41   (6) In a case where the offender is aged under 18 and the offence is not triable only on indictment and there is no other offence associated with it that is triable only on indictment, the court shall not form such an opinion as is mentioned in subsection (5) above unless—

    (a) there exists a previous pre-sentence report obtained in respect of the offender; and

    (b) the court has had regard to the information contained in that report, or, if there is more than one such report, the most recent report.

(7) No community sentence which consists of or includes such an order as is mentioned in subsection (3) above shall be invalidated by the failure of a court to obtain and consider a pre-sentence report before forming an opinion as to the suitability of the order for the offender, but any court on an appeal against such a sentence—

    (a) shall, subject to subsection (8) below, obtain a pre-sentence report if none was obtained by the court below; and

    (b) shall consider any such report obtained by it or by that court.

(8) Subsection (7)(a) above does not apply if the court is of the opinion—

    (a) that the court below was justified in forming an opinion that it was unnecessary to obtain a pre-sentence report; or

    (b) that, although the court below was not justified in forming that opinion, in the circumstances of the case at the time it is before the court, it is unnecessary to obtain a pre-sentence report.

(9) In a case where the offender is aged under 18 and the offence is not triable only on indictment and there is no other offence associated with it that is triable only on indictment, the court shall not form such an opinion as is mentioned in subsection (8) above unless—

    (a) there exists a previous pre-sentence report obtained in respect of the offender; and

(b) the court has had regard to the information contained in that report, or, if there is more than one such report, the most recent report.

(10) Section 156 below (disclosure of pre-sentence report to offender etc.) applies to any pre-sentence report obtained in pursuance of this section.

G. Electronic Monitoring Requirement

Powers of Criminal Courts (Sentencing) Act 2000, s.36B

Electronic monitoring of requirements in community orders

26-42 36B.—(1) Subject to subsections (2) to (4) below, a community order may include requirements for securing the electronic monitoring of the offender's compliance with any other requirements imposed by the order.

(2) A court shall not include in a community order a requirement under subsection (1) above unless the court—

(a) has been notified by the Secretary of State that electronic monitoring arrangements are available in the relevant areas specified in subsections (7) to (10) below; and

(b) is satisfied that the necessary provision can be made under those arrangements.

(3) Where—

(a) it is proposed to include in an exclusion order a requirement for securing electronic monitoring in accordance with this section; but

(b) there is a person (other than the offender) without whose co-operation it will not be practicable to secure the monitoring,

the requirement shall not be included in the order without that person's consent.

(4) Where—

(a) it is proposed to include in a community rehabilitation order or a community punishment and rehabilitation order a requirement for securing the electronic monitoring of the offender's compliance with a requirement such as is mentioned in paragraph 8(1) of Schedule 2 to this Act; but

(b) there is a person (other than the offender) without whose co-operation it will not be practicable to secure the monitoring,

the requirement shall not be included in the order without that person's consent.

(5) An order which includes requirements under subsection (1) above shall include pro-
vision for making a person responsible for the monitoring; and a person who is made so responsible shall be of a description specified in an order made by the Secretary of State.

(6) The Secretary of State may make rules for regulating—   **26-43**

(a) the electronic monitoring of compliance with requirements included in a community order; and

(b) without prejudice to the generality of paragraph (a) above, the functions of persons made responsible for securing the electronic monitoring of compliance with requirements included in the order.

(7) In the case of a curfew order or an exclusion order, the relevant area is the area in which the place proposed to be specified in the order is situated.

In this subsection, "place", in relation to an exclusion order, has the same meaning as in section 40A below.

(8) In the case of a community rehabilitation order or a community punishment and rehabilitation order, the relevant areas are each of the following—

(a) where it is proposed to include in the order a requirement for securing compli-
ance with a requirement such as is mentioned in sub-paragraph (1) of paragraph 7 of Schedule 2 to this Act, the area mentioned in sub-paragraph (5) of that paragraph;

(b) where it is proposed to include in the order a requirement for securing compli-
ance with a requirement such as is mentioned in sub-paragraph (1) of paragraph 8 of that Schedule, the area mentioned in sub-paragraph (5) of that paragraph;

(c) where it is proposed to include in the order a requirement for securing compliance with any other requirement, the area proposed to be specified under section 41(3) below.

(9) In the case of a community punishment order, a drug treatment and testing order,

a drug abstinence order, a supervision order or an action plan order, the relevant area is the petty sessions area proposed to be specified in the order.

(10) In the case of an attendance centre order, the relevant area is the petty sessions area in which the attendance centre proposed to be specified in the order is situated.

H. COMMUNITY REHABILITATION ORDERS

(1) Purpose and effect

26–44   The purposes of a community rehabilitation order are set out in s.41(1) of the 2000 Act. It is for the court to decide that such an order is desirable in order to:

— secure the rehabilitation of the offender

— protect the public from harm from the offender or

— prevent the commission of further offences by the offender

Orders can be made on any offender (whose offence passes the threshold criterion, see above at §§ 26–32—26–34) aged 16 or more. Offenders aged 18 or over will be supervised by an officer of the local probation board; offenders aged 16 or 17 will be supervised either by such an officer or by a member of a Youth Offending Team.

A community rehabilitation order primarily places obligations on the offender but it is also possible (though rare) for another person to give a security for the good behaviour of the offender: s.41(8). The criterion for the court is that a security would be "expedient for the purpose of the offender's reformation". The person giving the security must consent to do so—there is no guidance on the amount of the security that should be sufficient to encourage the offender not to misbehave. It must be clear what behaviour would cause the security to be forfeited—in the context of bind over, the phrase "to be of good behaviour" has been held to be too imprecise.

26–45   The consequence of a community rehabilitation order is that the offender is under supervision for the period specified, which will be between six months and three years. Generally, the greatest effect is seen in the first months of an order and so orders of 12–18 months are likely to be the most effective since they give sufficient time for the supervision to be effective and sufficient to ensure that the effect gained under the order is consolidated.

The court must explain to the offender what is the effect of the order, what might happen if the offender fails to comply with the order and the power to review the order in due course, either on the application of the offender or on that of the supervisor: s.41(7).

(2) Content

26–46   In addition to the basic requirement of the order, additional conditions may be included where they are appropriate to meet the three criteria set out above (see § 26–33): s.42(1). The effect of the order with these conditions must continue to comply with the criteria that apply to all community sentences regarding suitability for the offender and the extent of deprivation of liberty, see § 26–161 above. The range of options is not limited (except by the need to meet those general criteria) but further details and restrictions on certain conditions are set out in s.42(2)–(2F) (drug abstinence) and in Sch.2 (residence, activities, treatment for a mental condition, treatment for drug or alcohol dependency).

The requirement that an offender express his willingness to comply with the requirements of a probation order was abolished by the *Crime (Sentences) Act* 1997, s.38(2), regarding Probation Orders made after October 1, 1997. Where a court proposes to make a community rehabilitation order for an offence committed before that date the requirement remains, see Sch.11, para.4(1)(b) to the 2000 Act. An offender must still express his willingness to comply with psychiatric treatment, or with treatment for drug and alcohol dependency: Sch.2, paras 5(4) and 6(5). See also *R. v Barnett* (1986) 8 Cr.App.R.(S.) 200, CA.

(3) Interaction with Other Sentences

A community rehabilitation order should not be made when the offender is the **26–47** subject of a suspended sentence for another offence: s.118(6) of the *PCC(S)A* 2000.

As regards the imposition of a community rehabilitation order where the offender is already serving a custodial sentence, the Divisional Court in *Fonteneau v DPP* [2001] 1 Cr.App.R.(S.) 15 stated that whilst ordinarily it would doubtless be futile and thoroughly undesirable to impose community penalties and custodial sentences on the same occasion, there was nothing in statute, authority or principle which precluded such action being taken; there was nothing to prevent a community order being made in addition to a custodial sentence if it was justified on the merits as serving a proper penal purpose, if the court was satisfied that the statutory criteria for imposing such a sentence were met and if the delay before the community order could take effect was so short as in practice to be minimal. This is contrary to the approach of the Court of Appeal in *R. v Carr-Thompson* [2000] 2 Cr.App.R.(S.) 335, where a probation order made on the same occasion as the dismissal of an appeal against a custodial sentence was quashed.

As regards enforcement of a community rehabilitation order, see below at § 29–25.

Powers of Criminal Courts (Sentencing) Act 2000, ss.41, 42

Community rehabilitation orders

41.—(1) Where a person aged 16 or over is convicted of an offence and the court by or **26–48** before which he is convicted is of the opinion that his supervision is desirable in the interests of—

(a) securing his rehabilitation, or

(b) protecting the public from harm from him or preventing the commission by him of further offences,

the court may (subject to sections 34 to 36 above) make an order requiring him to be under supervision for a period specified in the order of not less than six months nor more than three years.

(2) An order under subsection (1) above is in this Act referred to as a "community rehabilitation order".

(3) A community rehabilitation order shall specify the petty sessions area in which the offender resides or will reside.

(4) If the offender is aged 18 or over at the time when the community rehabilitation order is made, he shall, subject to paragraph 18 of Schedule 3 to this Act (offender's change of area), be required to be under the supervision of an officer of a local probation board appointed for or assigned to the petty sessions area specified in the order.

(5) If the offender is aged under 18 at that time, he shall, subject to paragraph 18 of Schedule 3, be required to be under the supervision of—

(a) an officer of a local probation board appointed for or assigned to the petty sessions area specified in the order; or

(b) a member of a youth offending team established by a local authority specified in the order;

and if an order specifies a local authority for the purposes of paragraph (b) above, the authority specified must be the local authority within whose area it appears to the court that the offender resides or will reside.

(6) In this Act, "responsible officer", in relation to an offender who is subject to a com- **26–49** munity rehabilitation order, means the officer of a local probation board or member of a youth offending team responsible for his supervision.

(7) Before making a community rehabilitation order, the court shall explain to the offender in ordinary language—

(a) the effect of the order (including any additional requirements proposed to be included in the order in accordance with section 42 below);

(b) the consequences which may follow (under Part II of Schedule 3 to this Act) if he fails to comply with any of the requirements of the order; and

(c) that the court has power (under Parts III and IV of that Schedule) to review the order on the application either of the offender or of the responsible officer.

(8) On making a community rehabilitation order, the court may, if it thinks it expedient

for the purpose of the offender's reformation, allow any person who consents to do so to give security for the good behaviour of the offender.

(9) The court by which a community rehabilitation order is made shall forthwith give copies of the order to—

    (a) if the offender is aged 18 or over, an officer of a local probation board assigned to the court, or

    (b) if the offender is aged under 18, an officer of a local probation board or member of a youth offending team so assigned,

and he shall give a copy to the offender, to the responsible officer and to the person in charge of any institution in which the offender is required by the order to reside.

(10) The court by which such an order is made shall also, except where it itself acts for the petty sessions area specified in the order, send to the justices' chief executive for that area—

    (a) a copy of the order; and

    (b) such documents and information relating to the case as it considers likely to be of assistance to a court acting for that area in the exercise of its functions in relation to the order.

(11) An offender in respect of whom a community rehabilitation order is made shall keep in touch with the responsible officer in accordance with such instructions as he may from time to time be given by that officer, and shall notify him of any change of address.

[(12) For the purposes of this Act, a person is an affected person in relation to a community rehabilitation order if—

    a requirement under section 36B(1) above is included in the order by virtue of his consent; or

    a requirement is included in the order under paragraph 8 (1) of Schedule 2 to this Act for the purpose (or partly for the purpose) of protecting him from being approached by the offender.]

Additional requirements which may be included in probation orders

26–50   **42.**—(1) Subject to subsection (3) below, a community rehabilitation order may in addition require the offender to comply during the whole or any part of the probation period with such requirements as the court, having regard to the circumstances of the case, considers desirable in the interests of—

    (a) securing the rehabilitation of the offender; or

    (b) protecting the public from harm from him or preventing the commission by him of further offences.

(2) Without prejudice to the generality of subsection (1) above

    (a) the additional requirements which may be included in a community rehabilitation order shall include the requirements which are authorised by Schedule 2 to this Act.

    (b) subject to subsections (2D) and (2F) below, the order shall, if the first set of conditions is satisfied, include a drug abstinence requirement and may include such a requirement if the second set of conditions is satisfied.

(2A) For the purposes of this Part of this Act, a drug abstinence requirement is a requirement for the offender—

    (a) to abstain from misusing specified Class A drugs; and

    (b) to provide, when instructed to do so by the responsible officer, any sample mentioned in the instruction for the purpose of ascertaining whether he has any specified Class A drug in his body.

(2B) The first set of conditions is—

    (a) that the offender was aged 18 or over on the date of his conviction for the offence;

    (b) that, in the opinion of the court, the offender is dependent on or has a propensity to misuse specified Class A drugs; and

    (c) that the offence is a trigger offence.

(2C) The second set of conditions is—

    (a) that the offender was aged 18 or over on the date of his conviction for the offence; and

    (b) that, in the opinion of the court—

(i) the offender is dependent on or has a propensity to misuse specified Class A drugs; and

(ii) the misuse by the offender of any specified Class A drug caused or contributed to the offence.

(2D) The order may not include a drug abstinence requirement if— **26–51**

(a) the community rehabilitation order includes any requirement in respect of drugs under paragraph 6 of Schedule 2 to this Act; or

(b) the community sentence includes a drug treatment and testing order or a drug abstinence order.

(2E) The function of giving instructions for the purposes of subsection (2A)(b) above shall be exercised in accordance with guidance given from time to time by the Secretary of State; and the Secretary of State may make rules for regulating the provision of samples in pursuance of such instructions.

(2F) The court shall not include a drug abstinence requirement in the order unless the court has been notified by the Secretary of State that arrangements for implementing such requirements are available in the area proposed to be specified under section 41(3) above and the notice has not been withdrawn.

(3) Without prejudice to the power of the court under section 130 below to make a compensation order, the payment of sums by way of damages for injury or compensation for loss shall not be included among the additional requirements of a community rehabilitation order.

Powers of Criminal Courts (Sentencing) Act 2000, Sch.2

SCHEDULE 2

[Additional Requirements which may be Included in Community Rehabilitation Orders]

Requirements as to residence

1.—(1) Subject to sub-paragraphs (2) and (3) below, a [community rehabilitation order] **26–52** may include requirements as to the residence of the offender.

(2) Before making a [community rehabilitation order] containing any such requirement, the court shall consider the home surroundings of the offender.

(3) Where a [community rehabilitation order] requires the offender to reside in an approved hostel or any other institution, the period for which he is required to reside there shall be specified in the order.

Requirements as to activities etc.

2.—(1) Subject to the provisions of this paragraph, a [community rehabilitation order] **26–53** may require the offender—

(a) to present himself to a person or persons specified in the order at a place or places so specified;

(b) to participate or refrain from participating in activities specified in the order—

(i) on a day or days so specified; or

(ii) during the [community rehabilitation period] or such portion of it as may be so specified.

(2) A court shall not include in a [community rehabilitation order] a requirement such as is mentioned in sub-paragraph (1) above unless—

(a) it has consulted—

(i) in the case of an offender aged 18 or over, [an officer of a local probation board]; or

(ii) in the case of an offender aged under 18, either [an officer of a local probation board] or a member of a youth offending team; and

(b) it is satisfied that it is feasible to secure compliance with the requirement.

(3) A court shall not include a requirement such as is mentioned in sub-paragraph (1)(a) above or a requirement to participate in activities if it would involve the co-operation of a person other than the offender and the offender's responsible officer, unless that other person consents to its inclusion.

(4) A requirement such as is mentioned in sub-paragraph (1)(a) above shall operate to require the offender—

    (a) in accordance with instructions given by his responsible officer, to present himself at a place or places for not more than 60 days in the aggregate; and

    (b) while at any place, to comply with instructions given by, or under the authority of, the person in charge of that place.

(5) A place specified in an order shall have been approved by the [local probation board] for the area in which the premises are situated as providing facilities suitable for persons subject to [community rehabilitation orders].

(6) A requirement to participate in activities shall operate to require the offender—

    (a) in accordance with instructions given by his responsible officer, to participate in activities for not more than 60 days in the aggregate; and

    (b) while participating, to comply with instructions given by, or under the authority of, the person in charge of the activities.

(7) Instructions given by the offender's responsible officer under sub-paragraph (4) or (6) above shall, as far as practicable, be such as to avoid—

    (a) any conflict with the offender's religious beliefs or with the requirements of any other community order to which he may be subject; and

    (b) any interference with the times, if any, at which he normally works or attends school or any other educational establishment.

Requirements as to attendance at community rehabilitation centres

26–54   3.—(1) Subject to the provisions of this paragraph, a [community rehabilitation order] may require the offender during the [community rehabilitation period] to attend at a [community rehabilitation centre] specified in the order.

(2) A court shall not include in a [community rehabilitation order] such a requirement as is mentioned in sub-paragraph (1) above unless it has consulted—

    (a) in the case of an offender aged 18 or over, [an officer of a local probation board]; or

    (b) in the case of an offender aged under 18, either [an officer of a local probation board] or a member of a youth offending team.

(3) A court shall not include such a requirement in a [community rehabilitation order] unless it is satisfied—

    (a) that arrangements can be made for the offender's attendance at a centre; and

    (b) that the person in charge of the centre consents to the inclusion of the requirement.

26–55   (4) A requirement under sub-paragraph (1) above shall operate to require the offender—

    (a) in accordance with instructions given by his responsible officer, to attend on not more than 60 days at the centre specified in the order; and

    (b) while attending there to comply with instructions given by, or under the authority of, the person in charge of the centre.

(5) Instructions given by the offender's responsible officer under sub-paragraph (4) above shall, as far as practicable, be such as to avoid—

    (a) any conflict with the offender's religious beliefs or with the requirements of any other community order to which he may be subject; and

    (b) any interference with the times, if any, at which he normally works or attends school or any other educational establishment.

(6) References in this paragraph to attendance at a [community rehabilitation centre] include references to attendance elsewhere than at the centre for the purpose of participating in activities in accordance with instructions given by, or under the authority of, the person in charge of the centre.

(7) The Secretary of State may make rules for regulating the provision and carrying on of [community rehabilitation centres] and the attendance at such centres of persons subject to [community rehabilitation orders]; and such rules may in particular include provision with respect to hours of attendance, the reckoning of days of attendance and the keeping of attendance records.

(8) In this paragraph "[community rehabilitation centre]" means premises—

    (a) at which non-residential facilities are provided for use in connection with the rehabilitation of offenders; and

    (b) which are for the time being approved by the Secretary of State as providing facilities suitable for persons subject to [community rehabilitation orders].

Extension of requirements for sexual offenders

4. If the court so directs in the case of an offender who has been convicted of a sexual **26–56** offence—

　(a) sub-paragraphs (4) and (6) of paragraph 2 above, and

　(b) sub-paragraph (4) of paragraph 3 above,

shall each have effect as if for the reference to 60 days there were substituted a reference to such greater number of days as may be specified in the direction.

Requirements as to treatment for mental condition etc.

5.—(1) This paragraph applies where a court proposing to make a [community rehabil- **26–57** itation order] is satisfied, on the evidence of a registered medical practitioner approved for the purposes of section 12 of the *Mental Health Act* 1983, that the mental condition of the offender—

　(a) is such as requires and may be susceptible to treatment; but

　(b) is not such as to warrant the making of a hospital order or guardianship order within the meaning of that Act.

(2) Subject to sub-paragraph (4) below, the [community rehabilitation order] may include a requirement that the offender shall submit, during the whole of the [community rehabilitation period] or during such part or parts of that period as may be specified in the order, to treatment by or under the direction of a registered medical practitioner or a chartered psychologist (or both, for different parts) with a view to the improvement of the offender's mental condition.

(3) The treatment required by any such order shall be such one of the following kinds of treatment as may be specified in the order, that is to say—

　(a) treatment as a resident patient in [an independent hospital or care home within the meaning of the *Care Standards Act* 2000 or a hospital] within the meaning of the *Mental Health Act* 1983, but not hospital premises at which high security psychiatric services within the meaning of that Act are provided;

　(b) treatment as a non-resident patient at such institution or place as may be specified in the order;

　(c) treatment by or under the direction of such registered medical practitioner or chartered psychologist (or both) as may be so specified;

but the nature of the treatment shall not be specified in the order except as mentioned in paragraph (a), (b) or (c) above.

(4) A court shall not by virtue of this paragraph include in a [community rehabilitation **26–58** order] a requirement that the offender shall submit to treatment for his mental condition unless—

　(a) it is satisfied that arrangements have been or can be made for the treatment intended to be specified in the order (including arrangements for the reception of the offender where he is to be required to submit to treatment as a resident patient); and

　(b) the offender has expressed his willingness to comply with such a requirement.

(5) While the offender is under treatment as a resident patient in pursuance of a requirement of the [community rehabilitation order], his responsible officer shall carry out the supervision of the offender to such extent only as may be necessary for the purpose of the revocation or amendment of the order.

(6) Where the medical practitioner or chartered psychologist by whom or under whose direction an offender is being treated for his mental condition in pursuance of a [community rehabilitation order] is of the opinion that part of the treatment can be better or more conveniently given in or at an institution or place which—

　(a) is not specified in the order, and

　(b) is one in or at which the treatment of the offender will be given by or under the direction of a registered medical practitioner or chartered psychologist,

he may, with the consent of the offender, make arrangements for him to be treated accordingly.

(7) Such arrangements as are mentioned in sub-paragraph (6) above may provide for **26–59** the offender to receive part of his treatment as a resident patient in an institution or place

notwithstanding that the institution or place is not one which could have been specified for that purpose in the [community rehabilitation order].

(8) Where any such arrangements as are mentioned in sub-paragraph (6) above are made for the treatment of an offender—

    (a) the medical practitioner or chartered psychologist by whom the arrangements are made shall give notice in writing to the offender's responsible officer, specifying the institution or place in or at which the treatment is to be carried out; and

    (b) the treatment provided for by the arrangements shall be deemed to be treatment to which he is required to submit in pursuance of the [community rehabilitation order].

(9) Subsections (2) and (3) of section 54 of the *Mental Health Act* 1983 shall have effect with respect to proof for the purposes of sub-paragraph (1) above of an offender's mental condition as they have effect with respect to proof of an offender's mental condition for the purposes of section 37(2)(a) of that Act.

(10) In this paragraph, "chartered psychologist" means a person for the time being listed in the British Psychological Society's Register of Chartered Psychologists.

Requirements as to treatment for drug or alcohol dependency

26–60   6.—(1) Subject to sub-paragraph (2) below, this paragraph applies where a court proposing to make a [community rehabilitation order] is satisfied—

    (a) that the offender is dependent on drugs or alcohol;

    (b) that his dependency caused or contributed to the offence in respect of which the order is proposed to be made; and

    (c) that his dependency is such as requires and may be susceptible to treatment.

(2) If the court has been notified by the Secretary of State that arrangements for implementing drug treatment and testing orders are available in the area proposed to be specified in the [community rehabilitation order], and the notice has not been withdrawn, this paragraph shall have effect as if the words "drugs or", in each place where they occur, were omitted.

(3) Subject to sub-paragraph (5) below, the [community rehabilitation order] may include a requirement that the offender shall submit, during the whole of the [community rehabilitation period] or during such part of that period as may be specified in the order, to treatment by or under the direction of a person having the necessary qualifications or experience with a view to the reduction or elimination of the offender's dependency on drugs or alcohol.

(4) The treatment required by any such order shall be such one of the following kinds of treatment as may be specified in the order, that is to say—

    (a) treatment as a resident in such institution or place as may be specified in the order;

    (b) treatment as a non-resident in or at such institution or place as may be so specified;

    (c) treatment by or under the direction of such person having the necessary qualifications or experience as may be so specified;

but the nature of the treatment shall not be specified in the order except as mentioned in paragraph (a), (b) or (c) above.

(5) A court shall not by virtue of this paragraph include in a [community rehabilitation order] a requirement that the offender shall submit to treatment for his dependency on drugs or alcohol unless—

    (a) it is satisfied that arrangements have been or can be made for the treatment intended to be specified in the order (including arrangements for the reception of the offender where he is to be required to submit to treatment as a resident); and

    (b) the offender has expressed his willingness to comply with such a requirement.

26–61   (6) While the offender is under treatment as a resident in pursuance of a requirement of the [community rehabilitation order], his responsible officer shall carry out the offender's supervision to such extent only as may be necessary for the purpose of the revocation or amendment of the order.

(7) Where the person by whom or under whose direction an offender is being treated for dependency on drugs or alcohol in pursuance of a [community rehabilitation order] is of the opinion that part of the treatment can be better or more conveniently given in or at an institution or place which—

(a) is not specified in the order, and

(b) is one in or at which the treatment of the offender will be given by or under the direction of a person having the necessary qualifications or experience,

he may, with the consent of the offender, make arrangements for him to be treated accordingly.

(8) Where any such arrangements as are mentioned in sub-paragraph (7) above are made for the treatment of an offender—

(a) the person by whom the arrangements are made shall give notice in writing to the offender's responsible officer, specifying the institution or place in or at which the treatment is to be carried out; and

(b) the treatment provided for by the arrangements shall be deemed to be treatment to which he is required to submit in pursuance of the [community rehabilitation order].

(9) In this paragraph, the reference to the offender, being dependent on drugs or alcohol includes a reference to his having a propensity towards the misuse of drugs or alcohol; and references to his dependency on drugs or alcohol shall be construed accordingly.

Curfew requirements

7.—(1) Subject to the provisions of this paragraph, a community rehabilitation order **26–62** may include a requirement that the offender remain, for periods specified in the requirement, at a place so specified.

(2) A requirement under sub-paragraph (1) above may specify different places or different periods for different days, but shall not specify—

(a) periods which fall outside the period of six months beginning with the day on which the order is made; or

(b) periods which amount to less than two hours or more than twelve hours in any one day.

(3) A requirement under sub-paragraph (1) above shall, as far as practicable, be such as to avoid—

(a) any conflict with the offender's religious beliefs or with the requirements of any other community order to which he may be subject; and

(b) any interference with the times, if any, at which he normally works or attends school or any other educational establishment.

(4) An order which includes a requirement under sub-paragraph (1) above shall include provision for making a person responsible for monitoring the offender's whereabouts during the curfew periods specified in the requirement; and a person who is made so responsible shall be of a description specified in an order made by the Secretary of State.

(5) A court shall not include in a community rehabilitation order such a requirement as **26–63** is mentioned in sub-paragraph (1) above unless the court has been notified by the Secretary of State that arrangements for monitoring the offender's whereabouts are available in the area in which the place proposed to be specified in the requirement is situated and the notice has not been withdrawn.

(6) A court shall not include in a community rehabilitation order such a requirement as is mentioned in sub-paragraph (1) above if the community sentence includes a curfew order.

(7) Before including in a community rehabilitation order such a requirement as is mentioned in sub-paragraph (1) above, the court shall obtain and consider information about the place proposed to be specified in the requirement (including information as to the attitude of persons likely to be affected by the enforced presence there of the offender).

(8) The Secretary of State may make rules for regulating—

(a) the monitoring of the whereabouts of an offender who is subject to a requirement under sub-paragraph (1) above; and

(b) without prejudice to the generality of paragraph (a) above, the functions of any person responsible for monitoring the offender's whereabouts during the curfew periods specified in the requirement.

(9) The Secretary of State may by order direct that sub-paragraph (3) above shall have effect with such additional restrictions as may be specified in the order.]

Exclusion requirements

8.—(1) Subject to the provisions of this paragraph, a community rehabilitation order **26–64** may include a requirement prohibiting the offender from entering a place specified in the requirement for a period so specified of not more than two years.

(2) A requirement under sub-paragraph (1) above—

(a) may provide for the prohibition to operate only during the periods specified in the order;

(b) may specify different places for different periods or days.

(3) A requirement under sub-paragraph (1) above shall, as far as practicable, be such as to avoid—

(a) any conflict with the offender's religious beliefs or with the requirements of any other community order to which he may be subject; and

(c) any interference with the times, if any, at which he normally works or attends school or any other educational establishment.

(4) An order which includes a requirement under sub-paragraph (1) above shall include provision for making a person responsible for monitoring the offender's whereabouts during the periods when the prohibition operates; and a person who is made so responsible shall be of a description specified in an order made by the Secretary of State.

26–65   (5) A court shall not include in a community rehabilitation order such a requirement as is mentioned in sub-paragraph (1) above unless the court has been notified by the Secretary of State that arrangements for monitoring the offender's whereabouts are available in the area in which the place proposed to be specified in the order is situated and the notice has not been withdrawn.

(6) A court shall not include in a community rehabilitation order such a requirement as is mentioned in sub-paragraph (1) above if the community sentence includes an exclusion order.

(7) The Secretary of State may make rules for regulating—

(a) the monitoring of the whereabouts of an offender who is subject to a requirement under sub-paragraph (1) above; and

(b) without prejudice to the generality of paragraph (a) above, the functions of any person responsible for monitoring the offender's whereabouts during the periods when the prohibition operates.

(8) The Secretary of State may by order direct that sub-paragraph (3) above shall have effect with such additional restrictions as may be specified in the order.

(9) In this paragraph, "place" includes an area.

I. Community Punishment Orders

(1) Purpose and effect

26–66   A community punishment order requires the offender to undertake unpaid work. The work will generally be for the benefit of the community though this may be to the community as a whole or to an individual or smaller group within the community. Although primarily designed as an order with a large element of punishment and of reparation to the community, it is quite common for the involvement of the offender to lead on to continuing beneficial contact with the community group initially involved.

The only criterion specific to this order is that the offence must be punishable with imprisonment: s.46(1). This means that the offence committed must have imprisonment as a punishment available (not necessarily in the court passing sentence) not that the particular offence must be so serious that imprisonment could be justified for it.

The court will need to be satisfied that provision for this offender to perform unpaid work can be made in the area where she/he will reside. The court will not need to know (nor can it specify) what work is to be done, simply that provision can be made for work to be undertaken.

It must also be satisfied that the offender is suitable to perform work. In reaching that conclusion, the court may hear from an "appropriate officer", that is an officer of a probation board, a social worker or (for offenders aged 16 or 17) a member of a Youth Offending Team: s.46(4), (5).

An order can be made in relation to an offender aged 16 or over. For offenders aged

18 or over, supervision is exercised by an officer of a local probation board; for those aged 16 or 17, supervision is either by such an officer or by a member of a Youth Offending Team: s.47(4), (5).

(2) Content

The court will specify the number of hours to be completed. In total, there has to be **26–67** not less than 40 hours nor more than 240 hours: s.46(3). Those hours will normally be completed within a maximum of 12 months (s.47(3)) though this period may be extended by the court (Sch.3, para.22—see further in Enforcement at §§ 29–25 *et seq.* below).

If the court is making several orders on the same occasion, it is possible to make the hours in each order consecutive to each other: s.46(8). Individual orders may be for less than 40 hours as long as the minimum in total is at least 40 hours. The maximum may not exceed 240 hours. In practice, making concurrent orders is usually simpler both for the defendant and the public to understand and also for the management of the orders. This is permissible because of the power of the court in assessing both the seriousness of the offence and the extent of restriction on liberty to consider both the offence and other offences associated with it: s.35. Where an offender who is subject to a community punishment order is convicted of a further offence and a further community punishment order is made in respect of that offence, the second order may be made consecutive to the first, but the total number of hours the offender has to perform must not exceed 240: *R. v Evans* (1976) 64 Cr.App.R. 127, CA; *R. v Siha* (1992) 13 Cr.App.R.(S.) 588.

The court must explain to the offender what is the effect of the order, what might happen if the offender fails to comply with the order and the power to review the order in due course, either on the application of the offender or on that of the supervisor: s.41(7).

(3) Interaction with other sentences

It is not possible to impose a community rehabilitation order and a community **26–68** punishment order at the same time other than as a combination order (see below at § 26–72) which has different restrictions on the length of each element. Some other community orders can be included with a community punishment order (*e.g.* a drug abstinence requirement) and some may be made as additional orders at the same time.

A community punishment order cannot be made at the same time as a suspended sentence is imposed: *PCC(S)A* 2000, s.118(6). An offender convicted at a magistrates' court of an offence committed during the currency of a suspended sentence imposed by the Crown Court should be committed to the Crown Court for sentence for the new offence and for the failure to comply with the terms of the suspended sentence: *R. v Stewart* (1984) 6 Cr.App.R.(S.) 166, CA.

The fact that an offender has received a community punishment order shortly before he is sentenced for offences committed before the community punishment order was made does not necessarily render imposition of a custodial sentence for the earlier offences inappropriate: *R. v Bennet* (1980) 2 Cr.App.R.(S.) 96.

As regards the enforcement of community punishment orders, see §§ 29–25 *et seq.* below.

Powers of Criminal Courts (Sentencing) Act 2000, ss.46, 47

Community punishment orders

    46.—(1) Where a person aged 16 or over is convicted of an offence punishable with imprison- **26–69** ment, the court by or before which he is convicted may (subject to sections 34 to 36 above) make an order requiring him to perform unpaid work in accordance with section 47 below.

    (2) An order under subsection (1) above is in this Act referred to as a "community punishment order".

(3) The number of hours which a person may be required to work under a community punishment order shall be specified in the order and shall be in the aggregate—

(a) not less than 40; and

(b) not more than 240.

(4) A court shall not make a community punishment order in respect of an offender unless, after hearing (if the court thinks it necessary) an appropriate officer, the court is satisfied that the offender is a suitable person to perform work under such an order.

(5) In subsection (4) above "an appropriate officer" means—

(a) in the case of an offender aged 18 or over, an officer of a local probation board or social worker of a local authority social services department; and

(b) in the case of an offender aged under 18, an officer of a local probation board, a social worker of a local authority social services department or a member of a youth offending team.

(6) A court shall not make a community punishment order in respect of an offender unless it is satisfied that provision for him to perform work under such an order can be made under the arrangements for persons to perform work under such orders which exist in the petty sessions area in which he resides or will reside.

(7) Subsection (6) above has effect subject to paragraphs 3 and 4 of Schedule 4 to this Act (transfer of order to Scotland or Northern Ireland).

(8) Where a court makes community punishment orders in respect of two or more offences of which the offender has been convicted by or before the court, the court may direct that the hours of work specified in any of those orders shall be concurrent with or additional to those specified in any other of those orders, but so that the total number of hours which are not concurrent shall not exceed the maximum specified in subsection (3)(b) above.

26–70 (9) A community punishment order—

(a) shall specify the petty sessions area in which the offender resides or will reside; and

(b) where the offender is aged under 18 at the time the order is made, may also specify a local authority for the purposes of section 47(5)(b) below (cases where functions are to be discharged by member of a youth offending team);

and if the order specifies a local authority for those purposes; the authority specified must be the local authority within whose area it appears to the court that the offender resides or will reside.

(10) Before making a community punishment order, the court shall explain to the offender in ordinary language—

(a) the purpose and effect of the order (and in particular the requirements of the order as specified in section 47(1) to (3) below);

(b) the consequences which may follow (under Part II of Schedule 3 to this Act) if he fails to comply with any of those requirements; and

(c) that the court has power (under Parts III and IV of that Schedule) to review the order on the application either of the offender or of the responsible officer.

(11) The court by which a community punishment order is made shall forthwith give copies of the order to—

(a) if the offender is aged 18 or over, an officer of a local probation board assigned to the court, or

(b) if the offender is aged under 18, an officer of a local probation board or member of a youth offending team so assigned,

and he shall give a copy to the offender and to the responsible officer.

(12) The court by which such an order is made shall also, except where it itself acts for the petty sessions area specified in the order, send to the justices' chief executive for that area—

(a) a copy of the order; and

(b) such documents and information relating to the case as it considers likely to be of assistance to a court acting for that area in the exercise of its functions in relation to the order.

(13) In this section and Schedule 3 to this Act "responsible officer", in relation to an offender subject to a community punishment order, means the person mentioned in subsection (4) or (5)(b) of section 47 below who, as respects the order, is responsible for discharg-

ing the functions conferred by that section.

Obligations of person subject to community punishment order.
    47.—(1) An offender in respect of whom a community punishment order is in force shall—   **26–71**
      (a) keep in touch with the responsible officer in accordance with such instructions as he may from time to time be given by that officer and notify him of any change of address; and
      (b) perform for the number of hours specified in the order such work at such times as he may be instructed by the responsible officer.
    (2) The instructions given by the responsible officer under this section shall, as far as practicable, be such as to avoid—
      (a) any conflict with the offender's religious beliefs or with the requirements of any other community order to which he may be subject; and
      (b) any interference with the times, if any, at which he normally works or attends school or any other educational establishment.
    (3) Subject to paragraph 22 of Schedule 3 to this Act (power to extend order), the work required to be performed under a community punishment order shall be performed during the period of twelve months beginning with the date of the order; but, unless revoked, the order shall remain in force until the offender has worked under it for the number of hours specified in it.
    (3A) Subject to subsection (3B) below, the community punishment order shall, if the set of conditions in section 42(2B) above is satisfied, include a drug abstinence requirement and may include such a requirement if the set of conditions in section 42(2C) above is satisfied,
    (3B) The order may not include a drug abstinence requirement if the community sentence includes a drug treatment and testing order or a drug abstinence order.
    (3C) Subsections (2E) and (2F) of section 42 above apply for the purposes of this section as they apply for the purposes of that.
    (4) If the offender is aged 18 or over at the time when the order is made, the functions conferred by this section on "the responsible officer" shall be discharged by an officer of a local probation board appointed for or assigned to the petty sessions area specified in the order.
    (5) If the offender is aged under 18 at that time, those functions shall be discharged by—
      (a) a person mentioned in subsection (4) above; or
      (b) a member of a youth offending team established by a local authority specified in the order.
    (6) The reference in subsection (4) above to the petty sessions area specified in the order and the reference in subsection (5) above to a local authority so specified are references to the area or an authority for the time being so specified, whether under section 46(9) above or by virtue of Part IV of Schedule 3 to this Act (power to amend orders).

J. COMMUNITY PUNISHMENT AND REHABILITATION ORDERS

    It is possible to combine a community rehabilitation order and a community punish- **26–72**
ment order where the general criteria for a community sentence are met and the offence is punishable by imprisonment. In such a case, because the demands being made on the offender are potentially greater, the period of supervision must be for not less than 12 months (six months where community rehabilitation order made on its own) and not more than three years; the community punishment order must be for not less than 40 hours nor more than 100 hours (240 hours where community punishment order made on its own). It will be for the court to judge whether this is suitable for the offender and the offence and whether the deprivation of liberty is commensurate with the seriousness of the offence.

Powers of Criminal Courts (Sentencing) Act 2000, s.51

Community punishment and rehabilitation orders
    51.—(1) Where a person aged 16 or over is convicted of an offence punishable with impris- **26–73**

ment and the court by or before which he is convicted is of the opinion mentioned in subsection (3) below, the court may (subject to sections 34 to 36 above) make an order requiring him both—

   (a) to be under supervision for a period specified in the order, being not less than twelve months nor more than three years; and
   (b) to perform unpaid work for a number of hours so specified, being in the aggregate not less than 40 nor more than 100.

(2) An order under subsection (1) above is in this Act referred to as a "community punishment and rehabilitation order".

(3) The opinion referred to in subsection (1) above is that the making of a community punishment and rehabilitation order is desirable in the interests of—

   (a) securing the rehabilitation of the offender; or
   (b) protecting the public from harm from him or preventing the commission by him of further offences.

(4) Subject to subsection (1) above, sections 41, 42, 46 and 47 above and Schedule 2 to this Act shall apply in relation to community punishment and rehabilitation orders—

   (a) in so far as those orders impose such a requirement as is mentioned in paragraph (a) of subsection (1) above, as if they were community rehabilitation orders; and
   (b) in so far as they impose such a requirement as is mentioned in paragraph (b) of that subsection, as if they were community punishment orders.

(5) Schedule 3 to this Act (which makes provision for dealing with failures to comply with the requirements of certain community orders, for revoking such orders with or without the substitution of other sentences and for amending such orders) shall have effect so far as relating to community punishment and rehabilitation orders.

(6) Schedule 4 to this Act (which makes provision for and in connection with the making and amendment in England and Wales of certain community orders relating to persons residing in Scotland or Northern Ireland) shall have effect so far as relating to community punishment and rehabilitation orders.

The performance of work under combination orders and the arrangements for persons to perform such work are regulated by the *Community Service and Combination Orders Rules* 1992.

K. Curfew Orders

(1) Purpose and effect

26–74   A curfew order is designed to keep a person in a certain place at specified times. Although it may have an element that helps reduce the likelihood of the offender committing further offences, its primary purpose is to impose punishment by restricting the liberty of the offender.

Subject to the general criteria for community sentences (see § 26–32 above), an order may be made for any offence.

(2) Content

26–75   The obligation on the offender is to remain at a specified place for the periods specified in the order. Those periods must add up to no less than two hours and no more than 12 hours in any one day: s.37(3)(b). The order must not continue for more than six months: s.37(3)(a)—maximum of three months if the offender is 16 or below when the order is made.

The hours and the place may vary from time to time: s.37(3). Compliance with the order will often be monitored electronically; in these circumstances, the consent of anyone other than the offender who is involved in the monitoring will need to be obtained: *PCC(S)A* 2000, s.36B (see § 26–42 above) although blanket contracts will have been made for this purpose.

The court must explain to the offender what is the effect of the order, what might happen if the offender fails to comply with the order and the power to review the order in due course, either on the application of the offender or on that of the supervisor: s.41(7).

Powers of Criminal Courts (Sentencing) Act 2000, s.37

Curfew orders

37.—(1) Where a person is convicted of an offence, the court by or before which he is **26–76** convicted may (subject to sections 34 to 36 above) make an order requiring him to remain, for periods specified in the order, at a place so specified.

(2) An order under subsection (1) above is in this Act referred to as a "curfew order".

(3) A curfew order may specify different places or different periods for different days, but shall not specify—

    (a) periods which fall outside the period of six months beginning with the day on which it is made; or

    (b) periods which amount to less than two hours or more than twelve hours in any one day.

(4) In relation to an offender aged under 16 on conviction, subsection (3)(a) above shall have effect as if the reference to six months were a reference to three months.

(5) The requirements in a curfew order shall, as far as practicable, be such as to avoid—

    (a) any conflict with the offender's religious beliefs or with the requirements of any other community order to which he may be subject; and

    (b) any interference with the times, if any, at which he normally works or attends school or any other educational establishment.

(6) A curfew order shall include provision for making a person responsible for monitoring the offender's whereabouts during the curfew periods specified in the order; and a person who is made so responsible shall be of a description specified in an order made by the Secretary of State.

(7) A court shall not make a curfew order unless the court has been notified by the Secretary of State that arrangements for monitoring the offender's whereabouts are available in the area in which the place proposed to be specified in the order is situated and the notice has not been withdrawn.

(8) Before making a curfew order, the court shall obtain and consider information **26–77** about the place proposed to be specified in the order (including information as to the attitude of persons likely to be affected by the enforced presence there of the offender).

(9) Before making a curfew order in respect of an offender who on conviction is under 16, the court shall obtain and consider information about his family circumstances and the likely effect of such an order on those circumstances.

(10) Before making a curfew order, the court shall explain to the offender in ordinary language—

    (a) the effect of the order (including any additional requirements proposed to be included in the order in accordance with section 36B above below (electronic monitoring));

    (b) the consequences which may follow (under Part II of Schedule 3 to this Act) if he fails to comply with any of the requirements of the order; and

    (c) that the court has power (under Parts III and IV of that Schedule) to review the order on the application either of the offender or of the responsible officer.

(11) The court by which a curfew order is made shall give a copy of the order to the offender and to the responsible officer.

(12) In this Act, "responsible officer", in relation to an offender subject to a curfew order, means the person who is responsible for monitoring the offender's whereabouts during the curfew periods specified in the order.

L. Attendance Centre Order

(1) Purpose and effect

This order is available for youths and adults. In relation to youths, see chapter 34 **26–78** later earlier in this work. For adults, there are a small number of centres available. An order will require the offender to attend at the centre as required until the hours fixed by the court are completed. Attendance is designed both to be a punishment (by intruding into the offender's time, and by requiring them to be at a certain place for a certain period and to obey the requirements of the centre) and to offer an opportunity for a positive challenge to continuing criminality. A Centre is generally run by the Police or by the Youth Offending Team.

As a sentence, it is available for those under 21 convicted of offences punishable by imprisonment. It can also be ordered in relation to fine default for those up to 25 (see § 29–18 below).

(2) Content

26–79   The court has the power to require a minimum of 12 hours attendance and a maximum of 36 hours for this age range (18 years and above). The court will specify the Centre to be attended and will fix the date and time of the offender's first attendance. Attendance on any one day must not exceed three hours; in practice, it tends to be two hours on each attendance.

The court must be satisfied that the specified Centre is reasonably accessible to the offender given his age, the means of transport available and any other relevant circumstance. As far as practicable, the court should also seek to ensure that attendance at the centre will not conflict with the defendant's religious beliefs, the requirements of any other community penalties to which the defendant may be subject or interfere with normal work or education.

Although it is a Community Penalty, an Attendance Centre Order does not require the preparation of a written report before it is imposed.

Powers of Criminal Courts (Sentencing) Act 2000, s.60

Attendance centre orders

26–80   **60.**—(1) Where—

     (a) (subject to sections 34 to 36 above) a person aged under 21 is convicted by or before a court of an offence punishable with imprisonment, or

     (b) a court [has power or] would have power, but for section 89 below (restrictions on imprisonment of young offenders and defaulters), to commit a person aged under 21 to prison in default of payment of any sum of money or for failing to do or abstain from doing anything required to be done or left undone, or

     (c) a court has power to commit a person aged at least 21 but under 25 to prison in default of payment of any sum of money,

the court may, if it has been notified by the Secretary of State that an attendance centre is available for the reception of persons of his description, order him to attend at such a centre, to be specified in the order, for such number of hours as may be so specified.

(2) An order under subsection (1) above is in this Act referred to as an "attendance centre order".

(3) The aggregate number of hours for which an attendance centre order may require a person to attend at an attendance centre shall not be less than 12 except where—

     (a) he is aged under 14; and

     (b) the court is of the opinion that 12 hours would be excessive, having regard to his age or any other circumstances.

(4) The aggregate number of hours shall not exceed 12 except where the court is of the opinion, having regard to all the circumstances, that 12 hours would be inadequate, and in that case—

     (a) shall not exceed 24 where the person is aged under 16; and

     (b) shall not exceed 36 where the person is aged 16 or over but under 21 or (where subsection (1)(c) above applies) under 25.

26–81   (5) A court may make an attendance centre order in respect of a person before a previous attendance centre order made in respect of him has ceased to have effect, and may determine the number of hours to be specified in the order without regard—

     (a) to the number specified in the previous order; or

     (b) to the fact that order is still in effect.

(6) An attendance centre order shall not be made unless the court is satisfied that the attendance centre to be specified in it is reasonably accessible to the person concerned, having regard to his age, the means of access available to him and any other circumstances.

(7) The times at which a person is required to attend at an attendance centre shall, as for as practicable, be such as to avoid—
  (a) any conflict with his religious beliefs or with the requirements of any other community order to which he may be subject; and
  (b) any interference with the times, if any, at which he normally works or attends school or any other educational establishment.

(8) The first time at which the person is required to attend at an attendance centre shall be a time at which the centre is available for his attendance in accordance with the notification of the Secretary of State, and shall be specified in the order.

(9) The subsequent times shall be fixed by the officer in charge of the centre, having regard to the person's circumstances.

(10) A person shall not be required under this section to attend at an attendance centre on more than one occasion on any day, or for more than three hours on any occasion.

(11) Where a court makes an attendance centre order, the clerk of the court shall—
  (a) deliver or send a copy of the order to the officer in charge of the attendance centre specified in it; and
  (b) deliver a copy of the order to the person in respect of whom it is made or send a copy by registered post or the recorded delivery service addressed to his last or usual place of abode.

(12) Where a person ("the defaulter") has been ordered to attend at an attendance cen- **26–82** tre in default of the payment of any sum of money—
  (a) on payment of the whole sum to any person authorised to receive it, the attendance centre order shall cease to have effect;
  (b) on payment of a part of the sum to any such person, the total number of hours for which the defaulter is required to attend at the centre shall be reduced proportionately, that is to say by such number of complete hours as bears to the total number the proportion most nearly approximating to, without exceeding, the proportion which the part bears to the whole sum.

[This section is printed as amended, as from a day to be appointed, by the *CJCSA* 2000, s.74 and Sch.7, para.96 (insertion of words in square brackets).]

M. Drug Treatment and Testing Order

(1) Purpose and effect

The aim of a drug treatment and testing order (DTTO) is to provide a chance for an **26–83** offender to break his drug addiction and thereby cease offending: *R. v Kelly* [2003] 1 Cr.App.R.(S.) 89. An order will consist of three elements, treatment by a suitably qualified person (s.53), general supervision by the probation service (s.54) and reviews of progress by the court: s.55.

An order can be made for not less than six months and not more than three years. A court must first be satisfied both that the offender is either dependent on drugs or has a tendency to misuse them and that this dependency or propensity both requires treatment and is susceptible to treatment.

A drug treatment and testing order may not be made unless the offender expresses his willingness to comply with the requirements of the order after they have been explained to him.

The court must explain to the offender in ordinary language the effect of the order and its requirements as well as the consequences of failure to comply and need for periodical reviews. The offender has to express willingness to comply with the requirements of the order.

There must also be notification by the Secretary of State of arrangements to implement drug treatment and testing orders in the area and the court must be satisfied that arrangements have or can be made for the treatment to be specified in the order.

(2) When to make orders

This is often an even more complex balancing exercise than usual since those most **26–84** needing treatment will often have committed offences that are both serious and prolific. A spate of judicial consideration led to the Court of Appeal (Criminal Division) reviewing the authorities and identifying some of the most relevant factors: *Att.-Gen.'s Reference (No. 64 of 2003) (Boujettif, Harrison)* [2004] 2 Cr.App.R.(S.) 22. It concluded that although a DTTO may well be suitable where a substantial number of offences have been committed, such an order is not likely to be appropriate for an offender who has committed a substantial number of serious offences which either involve minor violence or have had a particularly damaging effect on the victim(s)—"excessive weight must not be given to the prospect of rehabilitation at the expense of proper regard for the criminality of the offender": Rose V.P. at para.14. It was also noted that a DTTO is more likely to be effective early in a criminal career but that there will be exceptional cases justifying such orders at other times. There must be clear evidence that the offender is determined to be free from drugs.

Referring to the complexity in this area, and to the considerable pressure on District Judges and magistrates, Lord Woolf C.J. has emphasised the need for the court to be able to rely on the prosecutor for assistance as to the appropriate steps to be taken whilst sentencing. It is the duty of prosecutors to draw a court's attention to any relevant guideline cases and to have copies of those cases available so the court could look at them if it so wishes. He emphasised that even experienced judges could be unfamiliar with guidelines cases, and in consequence impose inappropriate sentences, which did not help the administration of justice: *Att.-Gen.'s Reference (No. 52 of 2003)(R. v Webb)* [2003] EWCA Crim 3731, see also § 24–2 above.

(3) Review of orders

26–85   In *R. v Robinson* [2002] 2 Cr.App.R.(S.) 95, guidance was issued as to the treatment of offenders who commit further offences whilst the subject of a drug treatment and testing order.

There might be circumstances in which it was necessary for a sentence of imprisonment to be passed even though a drug treatment and testing order had been made only a matter of days before. Whether a custodial sentence should be passed when a recently imposed drug treatment and testing order had been breached must be a matter for the exercise of judicial discretion, according to the circumstances of the particular case. If a sentencing judge decided not to impose a custodial sentence, and was minded to permit the drug treatment and testing procedures to continue, the court considered that there were five possible options.

First, he could make no order; secondly he could defer sentence; thirdly, he could grant a conditional discharge; fourthly, he could make a community rehabilitation order; fifthly he could make a new and further drug treatment and testing order.

26–86   The option of making no order might be appropriate where the original order had been made such a short time before but, save in such cases, it was generally undesirable to make no order. It was generally undesirable to proceed by way of deferment of sentence or conditional discharge, because the ultimate sentencing powers of the court, if such courses were followed, would be to some extent limited.

In most cases, if a custodial sentence was not imposed, it would be desirable to make a further drug treatment and testing order, a community rehabilitation order or both. If a community rehabilitation order was imposed, additional requirements over and above those in relation to the drug treatment and testing order could be imposed. In the event of the commission of further offences, the court dealing with an offender for those offences would have the power to revoke the community rehabilitation order under the *PCC(S)A* 2000, Sch.3, provided that the defendant was convicted or appeared for sentence while the community rehabilitation order was in existence.

There was no apparent statutory restriction on making a community rehabilitation order in respect of a person who was subject to an existing drug treatment and testing order. The option of making a further drug treatment and testing order could properly be taken, provided that the court was satisfied that the offender was still dependent on, or had a propensity to misuse, drugs, and his dependency or propensity was such as to require or be susceptible to treatment.

Where the court had to deal with an offender convicted of offences committed shortly **26–87** before or shortly after the making of a drug treatment and testing order and the court wished to allow that order to continue in force without interruption, the best course would be to make a further drug treatment and testing order in terms which were identical to the first order, unless it was decided that some further requirement was necessary, in which case a community rehabilitation order might be a better option.

If the sentencing court took the view that there was no alternative to a custodial sentence for the offence committed during the currency of the original drug treatment and testing order, there were three possible options in relation to the existing order.

The first option would be to revoke the drug treatment and testing order and pass in its place a custodial sentence for the original offence as well as for the new offence.

The second possible option would be to leave the drug treatment and testing order in force while the offender was in custody. Generally speaking, the court had disapproved of community sentences running at the same time as custodial sentences. There were likely to be few cases where it would be both appropriate and feasible to allow the drug treatment and testing order to continue when a sentence of custody was being imposed.

The third possible option would be to revoke the drug treatment and testing order **26–88** and replace it with a drug abstinence order under the *PCC(S)A* 2000, s.58A, though, as the court noted, the magistrates' court has more limited powers to revoke a drug treatment and testing order than the Crown Court by virtue of Sch.3, paras 10 and 13 to the *PCC(S)A* 2000. The court was also doubtful whether a drug abstinence order could sensibly be made at the same time as the imposition of a period of custody. There would be a danger of overlap in relation to prison discipline on the one hand and the requirements of such an order on the other.

Powers of Criminal Courts (Sentencing) Act 2000, s.52–55

Drug treatment and testing orders

52.—(1) Where a person aged 16 or over is convicted of an offence, the court by or before **26–89** which he is convicted may (subject to ssection 34 to 36 above) make an order which—

(a) has effect for a period specified in the order of not less than six months nor more than three years ("the treatment and testing period"); and

(b) includes the requirements and provisions mentioned in ssection 53 and 54 below;

but this section does not apply in relation to an offence committed before 30th September 1998.

(2) An order under subsection (1) above is in this Act referred to as a "drug treatment and testing order".

(3) A court shall not make a drug treatment and testing order in respect of an offender unless it is satisfied—

(a) that he is dependent on or has a propensity to misuse drugs; and

(b) that his dependency or propensity is such as requires and may be susceptible to treatment.

(4) For the purpose of ascertaining for the purposes of subsection (3) above whether the offender has any drug in his body, [(in a case where, at the time of conviction, he was aged under 18)] the court may by order require him to provide samples of such description as it may specify; but the court shall not make such an order unless the offender expresses his willingness to comply with its requirements.

(5) A court shall not make a drug treatment and testing order unless it has been notified by the Secretary of State that arrangements for implementing such orders are available in the area proposed to be specified in the order under section 54(1) below and the notice has not been withdrawn.

(6) Before making a drug treatment and testing order, the court shall explain to the offender in ordinary language—

(a) the effect of the order and of the requirements proposed to be included in it;

(b) the consequences which may follow (under Part II of Schedule 3 to this Act) if he fails to comply with any of those requirements;

    (c) that the order will be periodically reviewed at intervals as provided for in the order (by virtue of section 54(6) below); and

    (d) that the order may be reviewed (under Parts III and IV of Schedule 3) on the application either of the offender or of the responsible officer;

and "responsible officer" here has the meaning given by section 54(3) below.

(7) A court shall not make a drug treatment and testing order unless the offender expresses his willingness to comply with its requirements.

The treatment and testing requirements

26–90   53.—(1) A drug treatment and testing order shall include a requirement ("the treatment requirement") that the offender shall submit, during the whole of the treatment and testing period, to treatment by or under the direction of a specified person having the necessary qualifications or experience ("the treatment provider") with a view to the reduction or elimination of the offender's dependency on or propensity to misuse drugs.

(2) The required treatment for any particular period shall be—

    (a) treatment as a resident in such institution or place as may be specified in the order; or

    (b) treatment as a non-resident in or at such institution or place, and at such intervals, as may be so specified;

but the nature of the treatment shall not be specified in the order except as mentioned in paragraph (a) or (b) above.

(3) A court shall not make a drug treatment and testing order unless it is satisfied that arrangements have been or can be made for the treatment intended to be specified in the order (including arrangements for the reception of the offender where he is to be required to submit to treatment as a resident).

(4) A drug treatment and testing order shall include a requirement ("the testing requirement") that, for the purpose of ascertaining whether he has any drug in his body during the treatment and testing period, the offender shall during that period, at such times or in such circumstances as may (subject to the provisions of the order) be determined by the treatment provider, provide samples of such description as may be so determined.

(5) The testing requirement shall specify for each month the minimum number of occasions on which samples are to be provided.

Provisions of order as to supervision and periodic review

26–91   54.—(1) A drug treatment and testing order shall include a provision specifying the petty sessions area in which it appears to the court making the order that the offender resides or will reside.

(2) A drug treatment and testing order shall provide that, for the treatment and testing period, the offender shall be under the supervision of an officer of a local probation board appointed for or assigned to the petty sessions area specified in the order.

(3) In this Act "responsible officer", in relation to an offender who is subject to a drug treatment and testing order, means the officer of a local probation board responsible for his supervision.

(4) A drug treatment and testing order shall—

    (a) require the offender to keep in touch with the responsible officer in accordance with such instructions as he may from time to time be given by that officer, and to notify him of any change of address; and

    (b) provide that the results of the tests carried out on the samples provided by the offender in pursuance of the testing requirement shall be communicated to the responsible officer.

26–92   (5) Supervision by the responsible officer shall be carried out to such extent only as may be necessary for the purpose of enabling him—

    (a) to report on the offender's progress to the court responsible for the order;

    (b) to report to that court any failure by the offender to comply with the requirements of the order; and

    (c) to determine whether the circumstances are such that he should apply to that court for the revocation or amendment of the order.

(6) A drug treatment and testing order shall—

    (a) provide for the order to be reviewed periodically at intervals of not less than one month;

(b) provide for each review of the order to be made, subject to section 55(6) below, at a hearing held for the purpose by the court responsible for the order (a "review hearing");

(c) require the offender to attend each review hearing;

(d) provide for the responsible officer to make to the court responsible for the order, before each review, a report in writing on the offender's progress under the order; and

(e) provide for each such report to include the test results communicated to the responsible officer under subsection (4)(b) above and the views of the treatment provider as to the treatment and testing of the offender.

(7) In this section references to the court responsible for a drug treatment and testing order are references to—

(a) where a court is specified in the order in accordance with subsection (8) below, that court;

(b) in any other case, the court by which the order is made.

(8) Where the area specified in a drug treatment and testing order made by a magistrates' court is not the area for which the court acts, the court may, if it thinks fit, include in the order provision specifying for the purposes of subsection (7) above a magistrates' court which acts for the area specified in the order.

(9) Where a drug treatment and testing order has been made on an appeal brought from the Crown Court or from the criminal division of the Court of Appeal, for the purposes of subsection (7)(b) above it shall be deemed to have been made by the Crown Court.

Periodic reviews

55.—(1) At a review hearing (within the meaning given by subsection (6) of section 54 above) **26–93** the court may, after considering the responsible officer's report referred to in that subsection, amend any requirement or provision of the drug treatment and testing order.

(2) The court—

(a) shall not amend the treatment or testing requirement unless the offender expresses his willingness to comply with the requirement as amended;

(b) shall not amend any provision of the order so as to reduce the treatment and testing period below the minimum specified in section 52(1) above, or to increase it above the maximum so specified; and

(c) except with the consent of the offender, shall not amend any requirement or provision of the order while an appeal against the order is pending.

(3) If the offender fails to express his willingness to comply with the treatment or testing requirement as proposed to be amended by the court, the court may—

(a) revoke the order; and

(b) deal with him, for the offence in respect of which the order was made, in any way in which it could deal with him if he had just been convicted by the court of the offence.

(4) In dealing with the offender under subsection (3)(b) above, the court—

(a) shall take into account the extent to which the offender has complied with the requirements of the order; and

(b) may impose a custodial sentence (where the order was made in respect of an offence punishable with such a sentence) notwithstanding anything in section 79(2) below.

(5) Where the order was made by a magistrates' court in the case of an offender under **26–94** 18 years of age in respect of an offence triable only on indictment in the case of an adult, any powers exercisable under subsection (3)(b) above in respect of the offender after he attains the age of 18 shall be powers to do either or both of the following—

(a) to impose a fine not exceeding £5,000 for the offence in respect of which the order was made;

(b) to deal with the offender for that offence in any way in which the court could deal with him if it had just convicted him of an offence punishable with imprisonment for a term not exceeding six months.

(6) If at a review hearing the court, after considering the responsible officer's report, is of the opinion that the offender's progress under the order is satisfactory, the court may so

amend the order as to provide for each subsequent review to be made by the court without a hearing.

(7) If at a review without a hearing the court, after considering the responsible officer's report, is of the opinion that the offender's progress under the order is no longer satisfactory, the court may require the offender to attend a hearing of the court at a specified time and place.

(8) At that hearing the court, after considering that report, may—

(a) exercise the powers conferred by this section as if the hearing were a review hearing; and

(b) so amend the order as to provide for each subsequent review to be made at a review hearing.

(9) In this section any reference to the court, in relation to a review without a hearing, shall be construed—

(a) in the case of the Crown Court, as a reference to a judge of the court;

(b) in the case of magistrates' court, as a reference to a justice of the peace acting for the commission area for which the court acts.

Powers of Criminal Courts (Sentencing) Act 2000, s.57

Copies of orders

26–95   **57.**—(1) Where a drug treatment and testing order is made, the court making the order shall (subject to subsection (3) below) forthwith give copies of the order to an officer of a local probation board assigned to the court.

(2) Where such an order is amended under section 55(1) above, the court amending the order shall (subject to subsection (3A) below) forthwith give copies of the order as amended to an officer of a local probation board so assigned.

(3) Where a drug treatment and testing order is made by a magistrates' court and another magistrates' court is responsible for the order (within the meaning given by section 54(7) above) by virtue of being specified in the order in accordance with section 54(8)—

(a) the court making the order shall not give copies of it as mentioned in subsection (1) above but shall forthwith send copies of it to the court responsible for the order; and

(b) the court shall, as soon as reasonably practicable after the order is made, give copies of it to an officer of a local probation board assigned to that court.

(3A) Where—

(a) a magistrates' court amends a drug treatment and testing order under section 55(1) above; and

(b) the order as amended provides for a magistrates' court other than that mentioned in paragraph (a) above to be responsible for the order;

the court amending the order shall not give copies of the order as amended as mentioned in subsection (2) above but shall forthwith send copies of it to the court responsible for the order and that court shall, as soon as reasonably practicable after the order is amended, give copies to an officer of a local probation board assigned to that court.

(4) An officer of a local probation board to whom copies of an order are given under this section shall give a copy to—

(a) the offender;

(b) the treatment provider; and

(c) the responsible officer.

N. DRUG ABSTINENCE ORDERS

(1) Purpose and effect

26–96   This order is designed to assist an offender to stop using Class A drugs. This may enable a court to pass a lesser sentence than it would otherwise have felt able to.

The order requires the offender to not misuse Class A drugs and empowers the responsible officer to require samples to enable compliance to be tested. The responsible person is the person supervising the offender.

(2) When can the order be made?

26–97   The offence committed must be a "trigger offence"—one of the small number of more serious offences most likely to be committed by those misusing Class A drugs (see list at § 26–101 below). There must be a dependency on or a propensity to misuse Class A drugs or the misuse of any Class A drug caused or contributed to the commission of the offence in the opinion of the court.

The court must have been notified by the Secretary of State that such orders are possible in their area.

The effect of the order, and the consequences of failing to comply with it, must be explained to the offender by the court.

Powers of Criminal Courts (Sentencing) Act 2000, ss.58A, 58B

Drug abstinence orders

58A.—(1) Where a person aged 18 or over is convicted of an offence, the court by or before **26–98** which he is convicted may (subject to sections 34 to 36 above) make an order which requires the offender—

(a) to abstain from misusing specified Class A drugs; and

(b) to provide, when instructed to do so by the responsible officer, any sample mentioned in the instruction for the purpose of ascertaining whether he has any specified Class A drug in his body.

(2) An order under subsection (1) above is in this Act referred to as a "drug abstinence order".

(3) The court shall not make a drug abstinence order in respect of an offender unless—

(a) in the opinion of the court, the offender is dependent on, or has a propensity to misuse, specified Class A drugs; and

(b) the offence in question is a trigger offence or, in the opinion of the court, the misuse by the offender of any specified Class A drug caused or contributed to the offence in question.

(4) A drug abstinence order shall provide that, for the period for which the order has effect, the offender shall be under the supervision of a person, being a person of a description specified in an order made by the Secretary of State.

(5) In this Act, "responsible officer", in relation to an offender who is subject to a drug abstinence order, means the person who is responsible for his supervision.

(6) The function of giving instructions for the purposes of subsection (1)(b) above shall be exercised in accordance with guidance given from time to time by the Secretary of State.

(7) A drug abstinence order shall have effect for a period specified in the order of not less than six months nor more than three years.

(8) The Secretary of State may make rules for regulating the provision of samples in pursuance of such instructions.

(9) A court shall not make a drug abstinence order unless the court has been notified by the Secretary of State that arrangements for implementing such orders are available in the area proposed to be specified in the order under section 54(1) above (as applied by section 58B(2) below) and the notice has not been withdrawn.

Drug abstinence orders: supplementary

58B.—(1) Before making a drug abstinence order, the court shall explain to the offender in **26–99** ordinary language—

(a) the effect of the order and of the requirements proposed to be included in it;

(b) the consequences which may follow (under Part II of Schedule 3 to this Act) if he fails to comply with any of those requirements; and

(c) that the order may be reviewed (under Parts III and IV of that Schedule) on the application either of the offender or of the responsible officer.

(2) Section 54 above (except subsections (2), (3) and (6) and section 57 above (except subsections (2), (3A) and (4)(b)) shall apply for the purposes of section 58A above and this section as if references to drug treatment and testing orders were references to drug abstinence orders.

(3) Schedule 3 to this Act (which makes provision for dealing with failures to comply with the requirements of certain community orders, for revoking such orders with or without the substitution of other sentences and for amending such orders) shall have effect

so far as relating to drug abstinence orders.

Section 163 of the *PCC(S)A* 2000 defines the expression 'specified Class A offence' and 'trigger offence' by reference to their meanings on Pt III of the *CJCSA* 2000. The interpretation section for Pt III is s.70.

Criminal Justice and Court Services Act 2000, s.70

Interpretation, etc.

26–100   70.—(1) In this Part—
"Class A drug" has the same meaning as in the *Misuse of Drugs Act* 1971,
"specified", in relation to a Class A drug, means specified by an order made by the Secretary of State,
"trigger offence" has the meaning given by Schedule 6.

(2) The Secretary of State may by order amend Schedule 6 so as to add, modify or omit any description of offence.

(3) In this Part (except in section 69), references to release include temporary release.

(4) In section 163 of the *Powers of Criminal Courts (Sentencing) Act* 2000 (general definitions), at the appropriate places there are inserted—

""specified Class A drug" has the same meaning as in Part III of the *Criminal Justice and Court Services Act* 2000",
""trigger offence" has the same meaning as in Part III of the *Criminal Justice and Court Services Act* 2000".

(5) Section 53 does not apply in relation to any community order made before that section comes into force.

Criminal Justice and Court Services Act 2000, Sch.6

SCHEDULE 6

TRIGGER OFFENCES

26–101   1. Offences under the following provisions of the *Theft Act* 1968 are trigger offences:
section 1 (theft)
section 8 (robbery)
section 9 (burglary)
section 10 (aggravated burglary)
section 12 (taking motor vehicle or other conveyance without authority)
section 12A (aggravated vehicle-taking)
section 15 (obtaining property by deception)
section 25 (going equipped for stealing, etc.)
2. Offences under the following provisions of the *Misuse of Drugs Act* 1971 are trigger offences, if committed in respect of a specified Class A drug:
section 4 (restriction on production and supply of controlled drugs)
section 5(2) (possession of controlled drug)
section 5(3) (possession of controlled drug with intent to supply)

O. COMMITTAL FOR SENTENCE

26–102   If a magistrates' court has convicted a person aged 18 or over of an offence triable either way, it may form the view that the defendant requires a sentence that only the Crown Court has the power to impose. In those circumstances, the magistrates' court may have the power to commit the defendant to the Crown Court for sentence. The decision will be accompanied by a decision on whether the defendant should be remanded in custody or on bail. There have been suggestions that, since the committal is for a sentence beyond the powers of the magistrates' court, that committal should be in custody in most circumstances. However, that approach confuses two distinct decisions—that on the appropriate sentence and that on what is necessary to ensure the defendant attends court, etc. The better approach is to start from the basis of the status of the defendant before committal. Generally speaking, a defendant on bail up to committal would remain on bail pending sentence in the Crown Court whereas a defendant in custody would remain in custody: *R. v Rafferty* [1999] 1 Cr.App.R. 235.

The decision on mode of trial and that on committal for sentence are different deci- **26–103** sions and acceptance of summary trial does not imply that there should not be a committal for sentence: *R. v North Sefton Magistrates' Court Ex p. Marsh* (1995) 16 Cr.App.R.(S.) 401, DC, see also *R. v Dover Magistrates' Court Ex p. Pamment* (1994) 15 Cr.App.R.(S.) 778, CA. Mode of trial is primarily about the most suitable venue for the determination of guilt or innocence; committal is concerned with the most suitable venue for sentence. This distinction has allowed the development of the "plea before venue" procedure (see Chapter 7 above) and s.4 of the *PCC(S)A* 2000 below. However, if a court adjourns a case after conviction and before sentence, care needs to be taken to avoid raising a legitimate expectation that prevents a later court from committing for sentence, see § 26–108 below.

A defendant committed to the Crown Court for sentence in relation to an either way offence will generally be susceptible to the whole range of sentencing powers available to the Court but other cases may in certain circumstances also be committed and then the Crown Court will be restricted to the powers available to a magistrates' court. Where a defendant is committed for sentence for an either way offence, the court may also commit for sentence any other offence that is imprisonable or endorsable of which the court has convicted the defendant: s.6.

For the power of committal for sentence to be used, the offence must be an either **26–104** way offence, the defendant must be 18 years old or over and the court must consider either that the offence (or the combination of the offence and one or more offences associated with it) is so serious that greater punishment should be imposed than it has power to impose or (in the case of a violent or sexual offence) a longer custodial sentence is necessary in order to protect the public from serious harm from the defendant. A violent offence is one which leads to (or is intended or likely to lead to) death or physical injury to a person; this includes arson: s.161(3). For these purposes, a sexual offence is one of those set out in s.161(2) of the *PCC(S)A* 2000.

Powers of Criminal Court (Sentencing) Act 2000, ss.3–6

Committal for sentence on summary trial of offence triable either way

3.—(1) Subject to subsection (4) below, this section applies where on the summary trial of an **26–105** offence triable either way a person aged 18 or over is convicted of the offence.

(2) If the court is of the opinion—

    (a) that the offence or the combination of the offence and one or more offences associated with it was so serious that greater punishment should be inflicted for the offence than the court has power to impose, or

    (b) in the case of a violent or sexual offence, that a custodial sentence for a term longer than the court has power to impose is necessary to protect the public from serious harm from him,

the court may commit the offender in custody or on bail to the Crown Court for sentence in accordance with section 5(1) below.

(3) Where the court commits a person under subsection (2) above, section 6 below (which enables a magistrates' court, where it commits a person under this section in respect of an offence, also to commit him to the Crown Court to be dealt with in respect of certain other offences) shall apply accordingly.

(4) This section does not apply in relation to an offence as regards which this section is excluded by section 33 of the *Magistrates' Courts Act* 1980 (certain offences where value involved is small).

(5) The preceding provisions of this section shall apply in relation to a corporation as if—

    (a) the corporation were an individual aged 18 or over; and

    (b) in subsection (2) above, paragraph (b) and the words "in custody or on bail" were omitted.

Committal for sentence on indication of guilty plea to offence triable either way

26–106   **4.**—(1) This section applies where—

     (a) a person aged 18 or over appears or is brought before a magistrates' court ("the court") on an information charging him with an offence triable either way ("the offence");

     (b) he or his representative indicates that he would plead guilty if the offence were to proceed to trial; and

     (c) proceeding as if section 9(1) of the *Magistrates' Courts Act* 1980 were complied with and he pleaded guilty under it, the court convicts him of the offence.

(2) If the court has committed the offender to the Crown Court for trial for one or more related offences, that is to say, one or more offences which, in its opinion, are related to the offence, it may commit him in custody or on bail to the Crown Court to be dealt with in respect of the offence in accordance with section 5(1) below.

(3) If the power conferred by subsection (2) above is not exercisable but the court is still to inquire, as examining justices, into one or more related offences—

     (a) it shall adjourn the proceedings relating to the offence until after the conclusion of its inquiries; and

     (b) if it commits the offender to the Crown Court for trial for one or more related offences, it may then exercise that power.

(4) Where the court—

     (a) under subsection (2) above commits the offender to the Crown Court to be dealt with in respect of the offence, and

     (b) does not state that, in its opinion, it also has power so to commit him under section 3(2) above,

section 5(1) below shall not apply unless he is convicted before the Crown Court of one or more of the related offences.

(5) Where section 5(1) below does not apply, the Crown Court may deal with the offender in respect of the offence in any way in which the magistrates' court could deal with him if it had just convicted him of the offence.

(6) Where the court commits a person under subsection (2) above, section 6 below (which enables a magistrates' court, where it commits a person under this section in respect of an offence, also to commit him to the Crown Court to be dealt with in respect of certain other offences) shall apply accordingly.

(7) For the purposes of this section one offence is related to another if, were they both to be prosecuted on indictment, the charges for them could be joined in the same indictment.

[Power of Crown Court]

      5. [...]

Committal for sentence in certain cases where offender committed in respect of another offence

26–107   **6.**—(1) This section applies where a magistrates' court ("the committing court") commits a person in custody or on bail to the Crown Court under any enactment mentioned in subsection (4) below to be sentenced or otherwise dealt with in respect of an offence ("the relevant offence").

(2) Where this section applies and the relevant offence is an indictable offence, the committing court may also commit the offender, in custody or on bail as the case may require, to the Crown Court to be dealt with in respect of any other offence whatsoever in respect of which the committing court has power to deal with him (being an offence of which he has been convicted by that or any other court).

(3) Where this section applies and the relevant offence is a summary offence, the committing court may commit the offender, in custody or on bail as the case may require, to the Crown Court to be dealt with in respect of—

     (a) any other offence of which the committing court has convicted him, being either—

          (i) an offence punishable with imprisonment; or

          (ii) an offence in respect of which the committing court has a power or duty to order him to be disqualified under section 34, 35 or 36 of the *Road Traffic Offenders Act* 1988 (disqualification for certain motoring offences); or

(b) any suspended sentence in respect of which the committing court has under section 120(1) below power to deal with him.

(4) The enactments referred to in subsection (1) above are—

(a) the *Vagrancy Act* 1824 (incorrigible rogues);

(b) sections 3 and 4 above (committal for sentence for offences triable either way);

(c) section 13(5) below (conditionally discharged person convicted of further offence);

(d) section 116(3)(b) below (offender convicted of offence committed during currency of original sentence); and

(e) section 120(2) below (offender convicted during operational period of suspended sentence).

Where a court adjourns a case after conviction, care needs to be taken to avoid **26–108** restricting the power of the next court to commit for sentence by raising a legitimate expectation in the mind of the defendant that he will not be committed. In *R. v Feltham Justices Ex p. Rees* [2001] 2 Cr.App.R.(S.) 1, DC Rose L.J. outlined the circumstances leading to a finding of a legitimate expectation which may fetter the power of the Court to commit for sentence. In that case, the critical factors leading to a finding that there was a legitimate expectation were that:

— the justices had been addressed as to the adequacy of their sentencing powers on behalf of the applicant,

— the justices had specifically invited the applicant's solicitor to mitigate before them,

— the solicitor had proceeded to mitigate before them,

— the justices had then adjourned, apparently to consider the impact of that sentence, and that adjournment lasted some ten minutes.

— when the justices returned to court, they said that "they" were unable to sentence him on that date as "they" would require more information in the form of a pre-sentence report.

The justices had stated that they were "leaving all options open" but, in the light of **26–109** the events listed above, something more specific was needed if anything other than sentencing in the magistrates' court was envisaged. If justices have in mind that one of the options which is open to them is to commit for sentence, they should specifically say so.

See also Bingham L.J. in *R. v Nottingham Magistrates' Court Ex p. Davidson* [2000] 1 Cr.App.R.(S.) 167, CA and Potts J. in *R. v Horseferry Road Magistrates' Court Ex p. Rugless* [2000] 1 Cr.App.R.(S.) 484, CA.

When the Court adjourns sentence after specifically indicating to the defendant that **26–110** he will not be committed for sentence, unless there is a change in the relevant circumstances, the offender may not be committed for sentence: *R. v Norwich Magistrates' Court Ex p. Elliot* [2000] 1 Cr.App.R.(S.) 152, CA, where Otton L.J. referred to the 'seminal judgment' of Kennedy L.J. in *R. v Warley Justices Ex p. DPP* [1999] 1 Cr.App.R.(S.) 156, QBD, where he summarised the position as regards triable either way offences, following a guilty plea by the defendant:

"If, after allowance has been made for the plea of guilty, it appears to the court that it will or may be possible for the court to sentence properly by deploying its statutory power—if necessary to the full—then, as it seems to me, the court should proceed to hear the case in the normal way, and, so long as a committal for sentence remains a possibility, care should be taken to ensure that nothing is said or done which might indicate to an accused that that option has been ruled out.

If a court, initially minded to commit at an early stage of the proceedings, is persuaded not to adopt that course at that stage it can keep the option open by saying that is what it is going to do, and then for example, arranging for the preparation of a pre-sentence report. But if it says that it is satisfied that the case is not one in which it will be necessary for it to commit to the Crown Court for sentence, and then adjourns for the pre-sentence report, when the matter comes back before a differently constituted bench that second bench is likely to consider that so far as committal for sentence is concerned its hands are tied."

26–111   Where the 'plea before venue' procedure is adopted, the decision to commit for sentence must be based on the assessment of the adequacy of the magistrates' sentencing powers to deal with the offence, not whether the offence would have been triable on indictment had the 'plea before venue' procedure not been adopted. In making this assessment, the appropriate allowance should be made for the guilty plea. Where this discount results in sentence being able to be imposed in the magistrates' court, it would be helpful if this could be stated: *R. v Warley Magistrates' Court Ex p. DPP*, above.

Subject to the strictures about raising a legitimate expectation of sentence in the magistrates' court, a magistrates' court may still commit for sentence if it has adjourned sentence for the purposes of obtaining a pre-sentence report.

A magistrates' court may also commit for sentence if it considers that, although a financial penalty is appropriate, the limits on the level of financial penalties it can impose is too low to deal with the offence: *R. v North Essex Justices Ex p. Lloyd* [2001] 2 Cr.App.R.(S.) 86.

26–112   Where the Court is dealing with an offender who has breached a community order by revoking the order, the Court may not commit him to the Crown Court for sentence for the offence in relation to which the order was made: *R. v Jordan* [1998] 2 Cr.App.R.(S.) 83, DC. The magistrates may still deal with an offender who has been unlawfully committed: *R. v Norfolk JJ Ex p. DPP* [1950] 2 K.B. 558, DC.

P. Sentences of Imprisonment

(1) Purpose and effect

26–113   Committing a person to a custodial sentence is the most severe punishment available and is hedged around by a number of conditions that need to be fulfilled:

— the offence (or combination of the offence and one or more other associated with it) must be so serious that no other sentence is justified (with a few exceptions),

— the defendant must be legally represented (or have not taken the opportunity to be),

— in most circumstances, a pre-sentence report will be required and

— the length of the sentence must be no more than is commensurate with the seriousness of the offence.

Subject to a lower maximum for an individual offence, a magistrates' court may only impose a custodial sentence on an adult of up to six months unless the defendant is convicted of two or more either way offences. In those circumstances, the maximum becomes 12 months. The minimum sentence is five days. (However, see the power to impose detention for one day either as a sentence or in default of payment of a fine: s.135, *Magistrates' Courts Act* 1980 below, at § 29–21). Although it is common practice to express a sentence in months, expressing it in weeks is the better practice and will become the required practice on implementation of the relevant provisions in the *Criminal Justice Act* 2003.

Custodial sentences in the magistrates' court are primarily about punishment. There will sometimes be an element of protection of the public but the maximum length available is so short that this will rarely be the case. A custodial sentence may also open the door to effective rehabilitation but, again, the period is so short as to make this less likely.

Powers of Criminal Courts (Sentencing) Act 2000, s.78

General limit on magistrates' court's power to impose imprisonment or detention in a young offender institution

26–114   78.—(1) A magistrates' court shall not have power to impose imprisonment, or detention in a young offender institution, for more than six months in respect of any one offence.

(2) Unless expressly excluded, subsection (1) above shall apply even if the offence in

question is one for which a person would otherwise be liable on summary conviction to imprisonment or detention in a young offender institution for more than six months.

(3) Subsection (1) above is without prejudice to section 133 of the *Magistrates' Courts Act* 1980 (consecutive terms of imprisonment).

(4) Any power of a magistrates' court to impose a term of imprisonment for non-payment of a fine, or for want of sufficient distress to satisfy a fine, shall not be limited by virtue of subsection (1) above.

(5) In subsection (4) above "fine" includes a pecuniary penalty but does not include a pecuniary forfeiture or pecuniary compensation.

(6) In this section "impose imprisonment" means pass a sentence of imprisonment or fix a term of imprisonment for failure to pay any sum of money, or for want of sufficient distress to satisfy any sum of money, or for failure to do or abstain from doing anything required to be done or left undone.

(7) Section 132 of the *Magistrates' Courts Act* 1980 contains provision about the minimum term of imprisonment which may be imposed by a magistrates' court.

Magistrates' Courts Act 1980, ss.132, 133

Minimum term
 132. A magistrates' court shall not impose imprisonment for less than 5 days.   **26–115**

Consecutive terms of imprisonment
 133.—(1) Subject to section 84 of the *Powers of Criminal Courts (Sentencing) Act* 2000, a **26–116** magistrates' court imposing imprisonment or youth custody on any person may order that the term of imprisonment or youth custody shall commence on the expiration of any other term of imprisonment or youth custody imposed by that or any other court; but where a magistrates' court imposes two or more terms of imprisonment or youth custody to run consecutively the aggregate of such terms shall not, subject to the provisions of this section, exceed 6 months.

(2) If two or more of the terms imposed by the court are imposed in respect of an offence triable either way which was tried summarily otherwise than in pursuance of section 22(2) above, the aggregate of the terms so imposed and any other terms imposed by the court may exceed 6 months but shall not, subject to the following provisions of this section, exceed 12 months.

(2A) In relation to the imposition of terms of detention in a young offender institution subsection (2) above shall have effect as if the reference to an offence triable either way were a reference to such an offence or an offence triable only on indictment.

(3) The limitations imposed by the preceding subsections shall not operate to reduce the aggregate of the terms that the court may impose in respect of any offences below the term which the court has power to impose in respect of any one of those offences.

(4) Where a person has been sentenced by a magistrates' court to imprisonment and a fine for the same offence, a period of imprisonment imposed for non-payment of the fine, or for want of sufficient distress to satisfy the fine, shall not be subject to the limitations imposed by the preceding subs.s.

(5) For the purposes of this section a term of imprisonment shall be deemed to be imposed in respect of an offence if it is imposed as a sentence or in default of payment of a sum adjudged to be paid by the conviction or for want of sufficient distress to satisfy such a sum.

[The references to 'youth custody' in sub.(1) should be read as references to 'detention in a young offender institution' by virtue of the *CJA* 1988, s.123 and Sch.8, para.2. The first second and fourth of those references are repealed together with subs.(2A) as from a day to be appointed by the *CJCSA* 2000, s.74 and Sch.7, para.66.]

Powers of Criminal Courts (Sentencing) Act 2000, s.79

General restrictions on imposing discretionary custodial sentences
 79.—(1) This section applies where a person is convicted of an offence punishable with a **26–117** custodial sentence other than one—
  (a) fixed by law; or
  (b) falling to be imposed under section 109(2), 110(2) or 111(2) below.

(2) Subject to subsection (3) below, the court shall not pass a custodial sentence on the offender unless it is of the opinion—

    (a) that the offence, or the combination of the offence and one or more offences associated with it, was so serious that only such a sentence can be justified for the offence; or

    (b) where the offence is a violent or sexual offence, that only such a sentence would be adequate to protect the public from serious harm from him.

(3) Nothing in subsection (2) above shall prevent the court from passing a custodial sentence on the offender if he fails to express his willingness to comply with—

    (a) a requirement which is proposed by the court to be included in a community rehabilitation order or supervision order and which requires an expression of such willingness; or

    (b) a requirement which is proposed by the court to be included in a drug treatment and testing order or an order under section 52(4) above (order to provide samples).

(4) Where a court passes a custodial sentence, it shall—

    (a) in a case not falling within subsection (3) above, state in open court that it is of the opinion that either or both of paragraphs (a) and (b) of subsection (2) above apply and why it is of that opinion; and

    (b) in any case, explain to the offender in open court and in ordinary language why it is passing a custodial sentence on him.

(5) A magistrates' court shall cause a reason stated by it under subsection (4) above to be specified in the warrant of commitment and to be entered in the register.

Length of discretionary custodial sentences: general provision

26–118   **80.**—(1) This section applies where a court passes a custodial sentence other than one fixed by law or falling to be imposed under section 109(2) below.

(2) Subject to sections 110(2) and 111(2) below, the custodial sentence shall be—

    (a) for such term (not exceeding the permitted maximum) as in the opinion of the court is commensurate with the seriousness of the offence, or the combination of the offence and one or more offences associated with it; or

    (b) where the offence is a violent or sexual offence, for such longer term (not exceeding that maximum) as in the opinion of the court is necessary to protect the public from serious harm from the offender.

(3) Where the court passes a custodial sentence for a term longer than is commensurate with the seriousness of the offence, or the combination of the offence and one or more offences associated with it, the court shall—

    (a) state in open court that it is of the opinion that subsection (2)(b) above applies and why it is of that opinion; and

    (b) explain to the offender in open court and in ordinary language why the sentence is for such a term.

(4) A custodial sentence for an indeterminate period shall be regarded for the purposes of subsections (2) and (3) above as a custodial sentence for a term longer than any actual term.

(5) Subsection (3) above shall not apply in any case where the court passes a custodial sentence falling to be imposed under subsection (2) of section 110 or 111 below which is for the minimum term specified in that subsection.

(a) *Procedural requirements for imposing discretionary custodial sentences*

Powers of Criminal Courts (Sentencing) Act 2000, ss.81, 82

Pre-sentence reports and other requirements

26–119   **81.**—(1) Subject to subsection (2) below, a court shall obtain and consider a pre-sentence report before forming any such opinion as is mentioned in subsection (2) of section 79 or 80 above.

(2) Subsection (1) above does not apply if, in the circumstances of the case, the court is of the opinion that it is unnecessary to obtain a pre-sentence report.

(3) In a case where the offender is aged under 18 and the offence is not triable only on

indictment and there is no other offence associated with it that is triable only on indictment, the court shall not form such an opinion as is mentioned in subsection (2) above unless—

    (a) there exists a previous pre-sentence report obtained in respect of the offender; and

    (b) the court has had regard to the information contained in that report, or, if there is more than one such report, the most recent report.

(4) In forming any such opinion as is mentioned in subsection (2) of section 79 or 80 **26–120** above, a court—

    (a) shall take into account all such information as is available to it about the circumstances of the offence or (as the case may be) of the offence and the offence or offences associated with it, including any aggravating or mitigating factors; and

    (b) in the case of any such opinion as is mentioned in paragraph (b) of that subsection, may take into account any information about the offender which is before it.

(5) No custodial sentence shall be invalidated by the failure of a court to obtain and consider a pre-sentence report before forming an opinion referred to in subsection (1) above, but any court on an appeal against such a sentence—

    (a) shall, subject to subsection (6) below, obtain a pre-sentence report if none was obtained by the court below; and

    (b) shall consider any such report obtained by it or by that court.

(6) Subsection (5)(a) above does not apply if the court is of the opinion—

    (a) that the court below was justified in forming an opinion that it was unnecessary to obtain a pre-sentence report; or

    (b) that, although the court below was not justified in forming that opinion, in the circumstances of the case at the time it is before the court, it is unnecessary to obtain a pre-sentence report.

(7) In a case where the offender is aged under 18 and the offence is not triable only on indictment and there is no other offence associated with it that is triable only on indictment, the court shall not form such an opinion as is mentioned in subsection (6) above unless—

    (a) there exists a previous pre-sentence report obtained in respect of the offender; and

    (b) the court has had regard to the information contained in that report, or, if there is more than one such report, the most recent report.

(8) Section 156 below (disclosure of pre-sentence report to offender etc.) applies to any pre-sentence report obtained in pursuance of this section.

Additional requirements in case of mentally disordered offender

82.—(1) Subject to subsection (2) below, in any case where the offender is or appears to be **26–121** mentally disordered, the court shall obtain and consider a medical report before passing a custodial sentence other than one fixed by law or falling to be imposed under section 109(2) below.

(2) Subsection (1) above does not apply if, in the circumstances of the case, the court is of the opinion that it is unnecessary to obtain a medical report.

(3) Before passing a custodial sentence, other than one fixed by law or falling to be imposed under section 109(2) below, on an offender who is or appears to be mentally disordered, a court shall consider—

    (a) any information before it which relates to his mental condition (whether given in a medical report, a pre-sentence report or otherwise); and

    (b) the likely effect of such a sentence on that condition and on any treatment which may be available for it.

(4) No custodial sentence which is passed in a case to which subsection (1) above applies shall be invalidated by the failure of a court to comply with that subsection, but any court on an appeal against such a sentence—

    (a) shall obtain a medical report if none was obtained by the court below; and

    (b) shall consider any such report obtained by it or by that court.

(5) In this section, "mentally disordered", in relation to any person, means suffering from a mental disorder within the meaning of the *Mental Health Act* 1983.

(6) In this section, "medical report" means a report as to an offender's mental condition made or submitted orally or in writing by a registered medical practitioner who is approved for the purposes of section 12 of the *Mental Health Act* 1983 by the Secretary of State as having special experience in the diagnosis or treatment of mental disorder.

(7) Nothing in this section shall be taken as prejudicing the generality of section 81 above.

26–122   Custody is primarily for those convicted of violent offences, serious sexual offences and, perhaps, for persistent petty offenders. Considerable judicial and Parliamentary scrutiny has been given to the circumstances in which a custodial sentence is justified. The starting point is the seriousness of the offence. In considering that, the Court may take into account any previous convictions of the offender of any failure to respond to previous sentences (*PCC(S)A* 2000, s.151(1)) and must treat it as an aggravating factor if the offence was committed while the offender was on bail (*PCC(S)A* 2000, s.151(2)) or was racially or religiously aggravated, see also §§ 25–7—25–9 above.

An offence which is deliberate and premeditated or which involves an excessive response to provocation; an offence which inflicts personal injury or mental trauma, particularly if permanent, will usually be more serious than one which inflicts financial loss only: *R. v Howells* [1999] 1 Cr.App.R. 98, CA.

Where offending has been fuelled by addiction to drink or drugs, the Court may be inclined to look more favourably on an offender who has already demonstrated (by taking practical steps to that end) a genuine, self-motivated determination to address his addiction: see further at § 26–84 above in relation to Drug Treatment and Testing Orders.

Youth and immaturity, while affording no defence, will often justify a less rigorous penalty than would be appropriate for an adult.

26–123   Some leniency will often be given to an offender of previous good character, the more so if there is evidence of positive good character (such as solid employment record or faithful discharge of family duties) as opposed to a mere absence of previous convictions. It will sometimes be appropriate to take account of family responsibilities, or physical or mental disability. However, care will be need to be taken to ensure that it is appropriate to do so. Where the primary purpose of the sentence is to show society's disapproval of the conduct (such as offences of violence in a domestic context), previous good character may be less significant. Similarly where offences are serious but likely to be committed by first offenders (for example, serious fraud on an employer).

Particular care should be taken when considering whether to impose a custodial sentence on a woman or on anyone on whom other people are dependent for their physical care.

While the Court will never impose a custodial sentence unless satisfied that it is necessary to do so, there will be even greater reluctance to impose a custodial sentence on an offender who has never before served such a sentence.

26–124   Where the Court is of the opinion that an offence, or the combination of an offence and one or more offences associated with it, is so serious that only a custodial sentence can be justified and that such a sentence should be passed, the sentence imposed should be no longer than is necessary to meet the penal purpose which the Court has in mind: *R. v Ollerenshaw* [1999] 1 Cr.App.R.(S.) 65, CA. In any case, it must be no longer than is commensurate with the seriousness of the offence or, in the case of a violent or sexual offence, is necessary to protect the public from serious harm: s.80(2),

The need for caution in the selection of a custodial sentence was emphasised in *R. v Kefford* [2002] Crim.L.R. 432 where Lord Woolf C.J. stated that those who are responsible for imposing sentences have to take into account the impact on the prison system of the number of prisoners the prison estate is being required to accommodate at the present time. Whilst, the Court did not intend to deter courts from sending to prison for the appropriate period those who commit offences involving violence or intimidation or other grave crimes, there were other categories of offence where a community punishment or a fine can sometimes be a more appropriate form of sentence than imprisonment. Lord Woolf gave the example of economic crimes, such as obtaining undue credit by fraud, which may not, especially in the case of an offender of hitherto good character, require a custodial sentence.

In assessing the seriousness of an offence, the court may take into account the preva- **26–125** lence of the offence: *R. v Cox* (1993) 14 Cr.App.R.(S.) 479, CA. The court is also not precluded from imposing a custodial sentence when it originally dealt with the offence through the imposition of a community sentence: *R. v Oliver and Little* (1993) 14 Cr.App.R.(S.) 479, CA.

The maximum sentence of imprisonment provided should be reserved for the worst forms of that offence: *R. v Byrne* (1975) 62 Cr.App.R. 159, CA. When the sentencer is considering whether an offence is one of the worst examples of its kind, he should have regard to cases that have been encountered in practice, rather than unlikely or imaginary examples: *R. v Ambler* [1976] Crim.L.R. 266. The maximum penalty for an offence should not normally be imposed where there is substantial mitigation: *R. v Cade* (1984) 6 Cr.App.R.(S.) 28, CA. Most imprisonable offences are triable either way and so a magistrates' court will have the option of committing for sentence for the more serious offences. However, for those summary offences that are imprisonable, a court will give credit for any guilty plea and also bear in mind that the longest sentence available should be reserved for the worst type of offending.

(b) *Consecutive sentences*

Magistrates' Courts Act 1980, s.133

Consecutive terms of imprisonment
133.—(1) Subject to section 84 of the *Powers of Criminal Courts (Sentencing) Act* 2000, a **26–126** magistrates' court imposing imprisonment or youth custody on any person may order that the term of imprisonment or youth custody shall commence on the expiration of any other term of imprisonment or youth custody imposed by that or any other court; but where a magistrates' court imposes two or more terms of imprisonment or youth custody to run consecutively the aggregate of such terms shall not, subject to the provisions of this section, exceed 6 months.

(2) If two or more of the terms imposed by the court are imposed in respect of an offence triable either way which was tried summarily otherwise than in pursuance of section 22(2) above, the aggregate of the terms so imposed and any other terms imposed by the court may exceed 6 months but shall not, subject to the following provisions of this section, exceed 12 months.

(2A) In relation to the imposition of terms of detention in a young offender institution subsection (2) above shall have effect as if the reference to an offence triable either way were a reference to such an offence or an offence triable only on indictment.

(3) The limitations imposed by the preceding subsections shall not operate to reduce the aggregate of the terms that the court may impose in respect of any offences below the term which the court has power to impose in respect of any one of those offences.

(4) Where a person has been sentenced by a magistrates' court to imprisonment and a fine for the same offence, a period of imprisonment imposed for non-payment of the fine, or for want of sufficient distress to satisfy the fine, shall not be subject to the limitations imposed by the preceding subsections.

(5) For the purposes of this section a term of imprisonment shall be deemed to be imposed in respect of an offence if it is imposed as a sentence or in default of payment of a sum adjudged to be paid by the conviction or for want of sufficient distress to satisfy such a sum.

An offender who is convicted of more than one offence must be given separate sen- **26–127** tences on each. These sentences may run concurrently or consecutively, or there may be a mixture of concurrent and consecutive sentences. If the court fails to make clear whether the sentences are concurrent or consecutive, it is presumed that the sentences are concurrent.

Where a prison sentence is passed on an offender already serving a prison sentence, the court must make it clear whether this sentence is to be served consecutively or concurrently with the existing sentence. The court cannot direct that a new prison sentence shall commence on the expiration of any other prison sentence from which the offender has been released under the *CJA* 1991, Pt II *(PCC(S)A* 2000, s.84): *R. v Cawthorn* [2001] 1 Cr.App.R.(S.) 136.

The restriction on maximum sentences only applies to terms of imprisonment imposed on the same occasion, and the court may order that the sentence of imprisonment is to commence on the expiration of a term imposed by another court even though the offender will serve longer than the statutory maximum: *Prime* (1983) 5 Cr.App.R.(S.) 127, CA. However, this is subject to the totality principle: *R. v Watts* [2000] 1 Cr.App.R.(S.) 460, CA, see § 25–36 above.

26–128　　Consecutive sentences should not generally be imposed for offences which arise out of the same transaction: *R. v Jones* (1980) 2 Cr.App.R.(S.) 152, CA; *R. v Noble* [2003] 1 Cr.App.R.(S.) 65, CA. The fact that this is not an absolute principle was emphasised in *Noble*, where it was said that the principle may admit of exceptions in exceptional circumstances. Consecutive sentences may be inappropriate where the offences concerned form a series of similar offences against the same victim, and are committed over a short period of time: *R. v Paddon*, March 3, 1971, CA (Crim Div); however, care must be taken to avoid undue lenience—it is not necessarily less serious, for example, to assault the same person three times over a week period than it is to assault three different people.

Consecutive sentences may be appropriate where the offender uses violence to escape: *R. v Bunch*, November 6, 1971, or where violence is used to resist arrest: *R. v Wellington* (1988) 10 Cr.App.R.(S.) 384.

(c) *Time served prior to imposition of sentence*

Criminal Justice Act 1967, s.67

Computation of sentences of imprisonment passed in England and Wales

26–129　　**67.**—(1) The length of any sentence of imprisonment imposed on an offender by a court shall be treated as reduced by any relevant period, but where he was previously subject to a probation order, a community service order, an order for conditional discharge or a suspended sentence in respect of that offence, any such period falling before the order was made or suspended sentence passed shall be disregarded for the purposes of this section.

(1A) In subsection (1) above "relevant period" means—

(a) any period during which the offender was in police detention in connection with the offence for which the sentence was passed; or

(b) any period during which he was in custody—

(i) by reason only of having been committed to custody in connection with any proceedings relating to that sentence or the offence for which it was passed or any proceedings from which those proceedings arose; or

(ii) by reason of his having been so committed and having been concurrently detained otherwise than by order of a court. or—

(c) any period during which, in connection with the offence for which the sentence was passed, he was remanded or committed to local authority accommodation by virtue of an order under section 23 of the *Children and Young Persons Act* 1969 or section 37 of the *Magistrates' Courts Act* 1980 and in accommodation provided for the purpose of restricting liberty.

(2) For the purposes of this section a suspended sentence shall be treated as a sentence of imprisonment when it takes effect under section 119 of the *Powers of Criminal Courts (Sentencing) Act* 2000 and as being imposed by the order under which it takes effect.

(3) No period of custody, other than a period which would have been taken into account before the commencement of this Act under section 17(2) of the *Criminal Justice Administration Act* 1962 (duration of sentence) for the purpose of reducing a term of imprisonment, shall be taken into account for the like purpose under this section unless it falls after the commencement of this Act.

26–130　　(4) Any reference in this Act or any other enactment (whether passed before or after the commencement of this Act) to the length of any sentence of imprisonment shall, unless the context otherwise requires, be construed as a reference to the sentence pronounced by the court and not the sentence as reduced by this section.

(5) This section applies—
(a) to sentences of detention in a young offender institution;
(b) to determinate sentences of detention passed under section 91 of the *Powers of Criminal Courts (Sentencing) Act* 2000 (sentences for serious indictable offences),

as it applies to sentences of imprisonment.

(6) The reference in subsection (1A) above to an offender being committed to custody by an order of a court includes a reference to his being committed to a remand centre or to prison under section 37 of the *Magistrates' Courts Act* 1980 but does not include a reference to his being remanded or committed to local authority accommodation under the said section 23 or 37.

(7) A person is in police detention for the purposes of this section—
(a) at any time when he is in police detention for the purposes of the *Police and Criminal Evidence Act* 1984; and
(b) at any time when he is detained under section 41 of the *Terrorism Act* 2000.

(8) No period of police detention shall be taken into account under this section unless it falls after the coming into force of section 49 of the *Police and Criminal Evidence Act* 1984.

[The references in subs.(1) to a 'probation order' and a 'community service order' include references to a 'community rehabilitation order' and a 'community punishment order' respectively: see the *PCC(S)A* 2000, ss.43(4)(b) and 44(4)(b).]

Where an offender has spent time in custody before being made subject to a com- **26–131** munity rehabilitation or punishment order, and is later sentenced to custody for the same offence under the *PCC(S)A* 2000, Sch.3, para.11, the sentence should be reduced to allow for the time spent in custody on remand before the order was made, since that will not be automatically credited to the time to be served under the sentence: s.67(1).

Section 67 also disregards time spent in custody on remand for an offence which is subsequently taken into consideration. However such circumstances are likely to warrant a reduction in sentence as an 'act of mercy'.

Where an offender is sentenced for a combination of different offences, time spent in custody in connection with any one of the offences will be deductable from the aggregate sentence, subject to the rule that such periods of time can only be counted once: *R. v Governor of Brockhill Prison Ex p. Evans*; *R. v Governor of Onley Young Offender Institution Ex p. Reid* [1997] Q.B. 443, DC.

Q. SUSPENDED SENTENCES OF IMPRISONMENT

(1) Purpose and effect

This is an order that a period of imprisonment imposed by the court will not need to **26–132** be served by the defendant unless he commits another imprisonable offence during the "operational period". This order can be made for any sentence of not more than two years; the operational period will be between one and two years. A court must first decide that it would have passed a sentence of imprisonment if there had been no power to suspend it and, then, that there are exceptional circumstances (see § 26–137 below) enabling the sentence to be suspended. It is a power that is rarely used in a magistrates' court.

If a person subject to a suspended sentence is convicted of a further imprisonable offence committed during the operational period, a court may order the sentence to have effect (possibly with a shorter period of imprisonment), vary the length of the operational period or make no order. The presumption is that the suspended sentence will be implemented in full: s.119(2) (see § 26–138 below). If the suspended sentence had been imposed by a magistrates' court, any magistrates' court can deal with the suspended sentence. If it had been imposed by the Crown Court, then only the Crown Court can deal with any breach. If the conviction for the later offence is in a magistrates' court but the suspended sentence was imposed in the Crown Court, then the magistrates' court may commit the defendant to the Crown Court for sentence: s.120(2).

Powers of Criminal Courts (Sentencing) Act 2000, ss.118–121

Suspended sentences of imprisonment

26–133   **118.**—(1) A court which passes a sentence of imprisonment for a term of not more than two years for an offence may (subject to subsection (4) below) order that the sentence shall not take effect unless, during a period specified in the order, the offender commits in Great Britain another offence punishable with imprisonment and thereafter a court having power to do so orders under section 119 below that the original sentence shall take effect.

(2) The period specified in an order under subsection (1) above must be a period of not less than one year nor more than two years beginning with the date of the order.

(3) In this Act—

> "suspended sentence" means a sentence to which an order under subsection (1) above relates; and

> "operational period", in relation to such a sentence, means the period specified in the order under subsection (1).

(4) A court shall not deal with an offender by means of a suspended sentence unless it is of the opinion—

> (a) that the case is one in which a sentence of imprisonment would have been appropriate even without the power to suspend the sentence; and

> (b) that the exercise of that power can be justified by the exceptional circumstances of the case.

(5) A court which passes a suspended sentence on any person for an offence shall consider whether the circumstances of the case are such as to warrant in addition the imposition of a fine or the making of a compensation order.

(6) A court which passes a suspended sentence on any person for an offence shall not impose a community sentence in his case in respect of that offence or any other offence of which he is convicted by or before the court or for which he is dealt with by the court.

(7) On passing a suspended sentence the court shall explain to the offender in ordinary language his liability under section 119 below if during the operational period he commits an offence punishable with imprisonment.

(8) Subject to any provision to the contrary contained in the *Criminal Justice Act* 1967, this Act or any other enactment passed or instrument made under any enactment after 31st December 1967—

> (a) a suspended sentence which has not taken effect under section 119 below shall be treated as a sentence of imprisonment for the purposes of all enactments and instruments made under enactments except any enactment or instrument which provides for disqualification for or loss of office, or forfeiture of pensions, of persons sentenced to imprisonment; and

> (b) where a suspended sentence has taken effect under section 119, the offender shall be treated for the purposes of the enactments and instruments excepted by paragraph (a) above as having been convicted on the ordinary date on which the period allowed for making an appeal against an order under that section expires or, if such an appeal is made, the date on which it is finally disposed of or abandoned or fails for non-prosecution.

Power of court on conviction of further offence to deal with suspended sentence

26–134   **119.**—(1) Where an offender is convicted of an offence punishable with imprisonment committed during the operational period of a suspended sentence and either he is so convicted by or before a court having power under section 120 below to deal with him in respect of the suspended sentence or he subsequently appears or is brought before such a court, then, unless the sentence has already taken effect, that court shall consider his case and deal with him by one of the following methods—

> (a) the court may order that the suspended sentence shall take effect with the original term unaltered;

> (b) the court may order that the sentence shall take effect with the substitution of a lesser term for the original term;

> (c) the court may by order vary the original order under section 118(1) above by substituting for the period specified in that order a period ending not later than two years from the date of the variation; or

> (d) the court may make no order with respect to the suspended sentence.

(2) The court shall make an order under paragraph (a) of subsection (1) above unless it is of the opinion that it would be unjust to do so in view of all the circumstances, including the facts of the subsequent offence; and where it is of that opinion the court shall state its reasons.

(3) Where a court orders that a suspended sentence shall take effect, with or without any variation of the original term, the court may order that sentence shall take effect immediately or that the term of that sentence shall commence on the expiry of another term of imprisonment passed on the offender by that or another court.

(4) The power to make an order under subsection (3) above has effect subject to section 84 above (restriction on consecutive sentences for released prisoners).

(5) In proceedings for dealing with an offender in respect of a suspended sentence which take place before the Crown Court, any question whether the offender has been convicted of an offence punishable with imprisonment committed during the operational period of the suspended sentence shall be determined by the court and not by the verdict of a jury.

(6) Where a court deals with an offender under this section in respect of a suspended sentence, the appropriate officer of the court shall notify the appropriate officer of the court which passed the sentence of the method adopted.

(7) Where on consideration of the case of an offender a court makes no order with respect to a suspended sentence, the appropriate officer of the court shall record that fact.

(8) For the purposes of any enactment conferring rights of appeal in criminal cases, any order made by a court with respect to a suspended sentence shall be treated as a sentence passed on the offender by that court for the offence for which the suspended sentence was passed.

Court by which suspended sentence may be dealt with

120.—(1) An offender may be dealt with in respect of a suspended sentence by the Crown **26–135** Court or, where the sentence was passed by a magistrates' court, by any magistrates' court before which he appears or is brought.

(2) Where an offender is convicted by a magistrates' court of an offence punishable with imprisonment and the court is satisfied that the offence was committed during the operational period of a suspended sentence passed by the Crown Court—

(a) the court may, if it thinks fit, commit him in custody or on bail to the Crown Court; and

(b) if it does not, shall give written notice of the conviction to the appropriate officer of the Crown Court.

(3) For the purposes of this section and of section 121 below, a suspended sentence passed on an offender on appeal shall be treated as having been passed by the court by which he was originally sentenced.

Procedure where court convicting of further offence does not deal with suspended sentence

121.—(1) If it appears to the Crown Court, where that court has jurisdiction in accordance **26–136** with subsection (2) below, or to a justice of the peace having jurisdiction in accordance with that subsection—

(a) that an offender has been convicted in Great Britain of an offence punishable with imprisonment committed during the operational period of a suspended sentence, and

(b) that he has not been dealt with in respect of the suspended sentence,

that court or justice may, subject to the following provisions of this section, issue a summons requiring the offender to appear at the place and time specified in it, or a warrant for his arrest.

(2) Jurisdiction for the purposes of subsection (1) above may be exercised—

(a) if the suspended sentence was passed by the Crown Court, by that court;

(b) if it was passed by a magistrates' court, by a justice acting for the area for which that court acted.

(3) Where—

(a) an offender is convicted by a court in Scotland of an offence punishable with imprisonment, and

(b) the court is informed that the offence was committed during the operational period of a suspended sentence passed in England or Wales,

the court shall give written notice of the conviction to the appropriate officer of the court by which the suspended sentence was passed.

(4) Unless he is acting in consequence of a notice under subsection (3) above, a justice of the peace shall not issue a summons under this section except on information and shall not issue a warrant under this section except on information in writing and on oath.

(5) A summons or warrant issued under this section shall direct the offender to appear or to be brought before the court by which the suspended sentence was passed.

(6) In relation to a suspended sentence passed on appeal, this section is to be construed in accordance with section 120(3) above.

26–137   What constitutes 'exceptional circumstances' for these purposes was considered in *R. v Okinikan* [1993] 1 W.L.R. 173. The Court held that there could be no definition of 'exceptional circumstances' as everything depends on the facts of each individual case. However, matters such as good character, youth and an early plea were not exceptional circumstances justifying a suspended sentence as they were common features of many cases. See also *R. v Murti* [1996] 2 Cr.App.R.(S.) 152, CA and *Att.-Gen.'s Reference (No. 5 of 1993)(R. v Hartland)* (1994) 15 Cr.App.R.(S.) 201, CA.

26–138   As regards activation of the suspended sentence, s.119(1) and (2) requires the court dealing with a suspended sentence to activate the suspended sentence in full unless it would be unjust to do so. Reasons for not activating the suspended sentence include the relative triviality of the subsequent offence, especially if the subsequent offence is not so serious as to warrant a custodial sentence: *R. v Bee* (1993) 14 Cr.App.R.(S.) 703, CA. Activation of the suspended sentence may also be unjust where the subsequent offence is of a different character to the offence in respect of which the suspended sentence was imposed: *R. v Moylan* [1970] 1 Q.B. 143, CA.

The suspended sentence may be ordered to take effect immediately, or consecutive to some other sentence of imprisonment. In the absence of exceptional circumstances warranting an alternative course, the normal practice of activating the sentence consecutively to any new sentence of imprisonment imposed for the later offence should be followed: *R. v May* (1979) 1 Cr.App.R.(S.) 124, CA. The activation of a suspended sentence is not subject to the restrictions imposed on aggregate sentences by the *MCA* 1980, s.133 so it would be possible to impose the maximum 12 months for two or more either way offences and then activate a suspended sentence consecutively to that 12 months.

A court may only activate a suspended sentence when dealing with the offender for another offence, it may not activate the sentence for breach of a community service order: *R. v Peterborough Justices Ex p. Casey* (1979) 1 Cr.App.R.(S.) 268, CA. Due to the operation of the exception in s.14(1) of the *PCC(S)A* 2000, a person convicted during the operational period of a suspended sentence, who receives a conditional or an absolute discharge may still face activation of the suspended sentence, as such disposals count as convictions for the purposes of s.119(1) of the 2000 Act: *R. v Barnes* (1986) 83 Cr.App.R. 58, CA.

R. RELEASE FROM CUSTODY

(1) Purpose and effect

26–139   A defendant will be released before the end of the period ordered by the court. There are rules that govern the earliest date of release which can be a complex blend of periods spent in custody on remand, the length of the sentence ordered by the court, and the availability of home detention curfew. In terms of sentencing in a magistrates' court, the critical distinction is that a person sentenced to under 12 months will be released unconditionally on serving one half of the sentence, a person sentenced to 12 months will be released on licence at the same point: s.33. There is also a discretionary power to release earlier on licence: s.34A.

A person released early in these ways may be recalled; in particular, conviction of a further imprisonable offence may enable the court sentencing for the new offence to cause the defendant to serve further parts of the original sentence: see § 26–147 below.

Criminal Justice Act 1991, ss.33(1), 34A

Duty to release short-term and long-term prisoners

33.—(1) As soon as a short-term prisoner has served one-half of his sentence, it shall be the   **26–140**
duty of the Secretary of State—

  (a) to release him unconditionally if that sentence is for a term of less than twelve
     months; and

  (b) to release him on licence if that sentence is for a term of twelve months or more.

Power to release short-term prisoners on licence

34A.—(1) Subject to subsection (2) below, subsection (3) below applies where a short-term   **26–141**
prisoner is serving a sentence of imprisonment for a term of three months or more.

  (2) Subsection (3) below does not apply where—

  (a) the sentence is an extended sentence within the meaning of section 85 of the
     Powers of Criminal Courts (Sentencing) Act 2000;

  (b) the sentence is for an offence under section 1 of the *Prisoners (Return to Custody)
     Act* 1995;

  (c) the sentence was imposed under paragraph 4(1)(d) or 5(1)(d) of Schedule 3 to
     the *Powers of Criminal Courts (Sentencing) Act* 2000 in a case where the prisoner
     had failed to comply with a requirement of a curfew order;

  (d) the prisoner is subject to a hospital order, hospital direction or transfer direction
     under section 37, 45A or 47 of the *Mental Health Act* 1983;

  (da) the prisoner is subject to the notification requirements of Part I of the *Sex Of-
     fenders Act* 1997;

  (e) the prisoner is liable to removal from the United Kingdom for the purposes of
     section 46 below;

  (f) the prisoner has been released on licence under this section at any time and has
     been recalled to prison under section 38A(1)(a) below;

  (g) the prisoner has been released on licence under this section or section 36 below
     during the currency of the sentence, and has been recalled to prison under sec-
     tion 39(1) or (2) below;

  (h) the prisoner has been returned to prison under section 116 of the *Powers of
     Criminal Courts (Sentencing) Act* 2000 at any time; or

  (j) the interval between—

      (i) the date on which the prisoner will have served the requisite period for the
          term of the sentence; and

      (ii) the date on which he will have served one-half of the sentence,

     is less than 14 days.

  (3) After the prisoner has served the requisite period for the term of his sentence, the   **26–142**
Secretary of State may, subject to section 37A below, release him on licence.

  (4) In this section "the requisite period" means—

  (a) for a term of three months or more but less than four months, a period of
     30 days;

  (b) for a term of four months or more but less than eighteen months, a period
     equal to one-quarter of the term;

  (c) for a term of eighteen months or more, a period that is 135 days less than
     one-half of the term.

  (5) The Secretary of State may by order made by statutory instrument—

  (a) repeal the words "aged 18 or over" in subsection (1) above;

  (b) amend the definition of "the requisite period" in subsection (4) above; and

  (c) make such transitional provision as appears to him necessary or expedient in
     connection with the repeal or amendment.

  (6) No order shall be made under subsection (5) above unless a draft of the order has
been laid before and approved by a resolution of each House of Parliament.

Criminal Justice Act 1991, s.37

Duration and conditions of licences

37.—(1) Subject to subsections (1A), (1B) and (2) below, where a short-term or long-term   **26–143**

prisoner is released on licence, the licence shall, subject to any revocation under section 39(1) or (2) below, remain in force until the date on which he would (but for his release) have served three-quarters of his sentence.

(1A) Where a prisoner is released on licence under section 33(3) or (3A) above, subsection (1) above shall have effect as if for the reference to three-quarters of his sentence there were substituted a reference to the whole of that sentence.

(1B) Where a prisoner whose sentence is for a term of twelve months or more is released on licence under section 33A(2) or 34A(3) above, subsection (1) above shall have effect as if for the reference to three-quarters of his sentence there were substituted a reference to the difference between—

    (a) that proportion of his sentence; and

    (b) the duration of the curfew condition to which he is or was subject.

26–144   (2) Where a prisoner whose sentence is for a term of less than twelve months is released on licence under section 34A(3) or 36(1) above, subsection (1) above shall have effect as if for the reference to three-quarters of his sentence there were substituted a reference to one-half of that sentence.

(3) [...]

(4) A person subject to a licence under this Part shall comply with such conditions as may for the time being be specified in the licence; and the Secretary of State may make rules for regulating the supervision of any description of such persons.

(4A) The conditions so specified may in the case of a person released on licence under section 34A above whose sentence is for a term of less than twelve months, and shall in any other case, include on the person's release conditions as to his supervision by—

    (a) an officer of a local probation board appointed for or assigned to the petty sessions area within which the person resides for the time being; or

    (b) where the person is under the age of 18 years, a member of a youth offending team established by the local authority within whose area the person resides for the time being.

26–145   (5) The Secretary of State shall not include on release, or subsequently insert, a condition in the licence of a long-term prisoner, or vary or cancel any such condition, except after consultation with the Board.

(6) For the purposes of subsection (5) above, the Secretary of State shall be treated as having consulted the Board about a proposal to include, insert, vary or cancel a condition in any case if he has consulted the Board about the implementation of proposals of that description generally or in that class of case.

(7) The power to make rules under this section shall be exercisable by statutory instrument which shall be subject to annulment in pursuance of a resolution of either House of Parliament

[Subsection (3) was repealed by Sch.6 to the *C(S)A* 1997.]

(2) Order for return to custody

Criminal Justice Act 1991, s.40A

Release on licence following return to prison

26–146   **40A.**—(1) This section applies (in place of sections 33, 33A, 37(1) and 39 above) where a court passes on a person a sentence of imprisonment which—

    (a) includes, or consists of, an order under section 116 of the *Powers of Criminal Courts (Sentencing) Act* 2000; and

    (b) is for a term of twelve months or less.

(2) As soon as the person has served one-half of the sentence, it shall be the duty of the Secretary of State to release him on licence.

(3) Where the person is so released, the licence shall remain in force for a period of three months.

(4) If the person fails to comply with such conditions as may for the time being be specified in the licence, he shall be liable on summary conviction—

    (a) to a fine not exceeding level 3 on the standard scale; or

    (b) to a sentence of imprisonment for a term not exceeding the relevant period, but not liable to be dealt with in any other way.

(5) In subsection (4) above "the relevant period" means a period which is equal in length to the period between the date on which the failure occurred or began and the date of the expiry of the licence.

(6) As soon as a person has served one-half of a sentence passed under subsection (4) above, it shall be the duty of the Secretary of State to release him, subject to the licence if it is still subsisting.

In *R. v Taylor* [1998] 1 Cr.App.R.(S.) 312, QBD, the Court of Appeal considered **26–147** the principles on which the court should act when deciding whether to make an order for return to custody. The sentencer should first decide the appropriate sentence for the new offence. The possibility of an order under s.116 should be disregarded at this stage, as required by s.116(6)(c). In considering whether an order ought to be made under s.116, the court should have regard to the nature and extent of any progress made by the defendant since his release and the nature and gravity of the new offence and whether it called for a custodial sentence. Regard should be had to the totality of the sentence both in determining whether a return to prison should be ordered and whether such a period should be served before or concurrently with the sentence for the new offence and in determining how long the return period should be.

It has been held that where an offender is convicted of a summary offence during the term of a sentence imposed by the Crown Court, the whole matter should be dealt with in the magistrates' court or the Crown Court. Section 116(3) of the 2000 Act provides that a magistrates' court shall not have power to order return to custody for a period of more than six months, but may commit him in custody or on bail to the Crown Court for sentence. The magistrates should commit the question of sentence and the question of return to the Crown Court if there was a significant period of the whole term of sentence unexpired and the new offence was of any gravity.

The return period is not a sentence of imprisonment for the purposes of s.133 of the *Magistrates' Courts Act* 1980 and the limitations as to aggregate periods of imprisonment do not apply to the return period: *R. v Worthing Justices Ex p. Varley* [1998] 1 W.L.R. 819, CA.

The return period is also not a sentence of imprisonment for the purposes of s.102 of **26–148** the *Crime and Disorder Act* 1998, and the court is not precluded from imposing a sentence for the new offence to run consecutively to the period of return: *R. v Lowe* [1999] 3 All E.R. 762, CA. The return period must be served before and followed by, or served concurrently with any other period of imprisonment imposed for the new offence: *R. v Jones* [1996] Crim.L.R. 524 .

Where a court passes a custodial sentence including a period of return under s.116 of the 2000 Act, and the sentence is for 12 months or less, the prisoner must be released on licence after he has served half of the term: *Criminal Justice Act* 1991, s.40A. If he then commits a further offence during this licence period, he is liable on summary conviction to a fine not exceeding level three on the standard scale or to a sentence of imprisonment for a term not exceeding the relevant period, this being the period between the breach of the licence conditions and the date at which the licence would have expired: *Criminal Justice Act* 1991, s.40A(4) and (5).

S. INTERMITTENT CUSTODY

(1) Purpose and effect

A custodial sentence can disrupt employment, family ties or caring responsibilities in **26–149** a way that makes it less likely that a defendant will avoid re-offending after release. A further option has been made available to courts and is currently being piloted. Where a court considers that a custodial sentence is necessary and all the necessary criteria have been fulfilled, it can direct that that sentence will be served intermittently, that is, shorts periods in custody interspersed with short periods on licence, under supervision, in the community: ss.183 to 186 of the *Criminal Justice Act* 2003. The offender must consent.

Where an order is made, the custodial periods will be served in short blocks of a few days at a time, with the licence period running between the blocks of custody. If an offender fails to comply with the terms of the community part of the sentence he will be returned to custody.

Criminal Justice Act 2003, ss.183–186

Intermittent custody

26–150　　　**183.**—(1) A court may, when passing a sentence of imprisonment for a term complying with subsection (4)—

　　(a) specify the number of days that the offender must serve in prison under the sentence before being released on licence for the remainder of the term, and

　　(b) by order—

　　　　(i) specify periods during which the offender is to be released temporarily on licence before he has served that number of days in prison, and

　　　　(ii) require any licence to be granted subject to conditions requiring the offender's compliance during the licence periods with one or more requirements falling within section 182(1) and specified in the order.

(2) In this Part "intermittent custody order" means an order under subsection (1)(b).

(3) In this Chapter—

　　"licence period", in relation to a term of imprisonment to which an intermittent custody order relates, means any period during which the offender is released on licence by virtue of subsection (1)(a) or (b)(i);

　　"the number of custodial days", in relation to a term of imprisonment to which an intermittent custody order relates, means the number of days specified under subsection (1)(a).

(4) The term of the sentence—

　　(a) must be expressed in weeks,

　　(b) must be at least 28 weeks,

　　(c) must not be more than 51 weeks in respect of any one offence, and

　　(d) must not exceed the maximum term permitted for the offence.

(5) The number of custodial days—

　　(a) must be at least 14, and

　　(b) in respect of any one offence, must not be more than 90.

(6) A court may not exercise its powers under subsection (1) unless the offender has expressed his willingness to serve the custodial part of the proposed sentence intermittently, during the parts of the sentence that are not to be licence periods.

(7) Where a court exercises its powers under subsection (1) in respect of two or more terms of imprisonment that are to be served consecutively—

　　(a) the aggregate length of the terms of imprisonment must not be more than 65 weeks, and

　　(b) the aggregate of the numbers of custodial days must not be more than 180.

(8) The Secretary of State may by order require a court, in specifying licence periods under subsection (1)(b)(i), to specify only—

　　(a) periods of a prescribed duration,

　　(b) periods beginning or ending at prescribed times, or

　　(c) periods including, or not including, specified parts of the week.

(9) An intermittent custody order which specifies two or more requirements may, in relation to any requirement, refer to compliance within such licence period or periods, or part of a licence period, as is specified in the order.

Restrictions on power to make intermittent custody order

26–151　　　**184.**—(1) A court may not make an intermittent custody order unless it has been notified by the Secretary of State that arrangements for implementing such orders are available in the area proposed to be specified in the intermittent custody order and the notice has not been withdrawn.

(2) The court may not make an intermittent custody order in respect of any offender unless—

　　(a) it has consulted an officer of a local probation board,

(b) it has received from the Secretary of State notification that suitable prison accommodation is available for the offender during the custodial periods, and

(c) it appears to the court that the offender will have suitable accommodation available to him during the licence periods.

(3) In this section "custodial period", in relation to a sentence to which an intermittent custody order relates, means any part of the sentence that is not a licence period.

Intermittent custody: licence conditions

185.—(1) Section 183(1)(b) has effect subject to section 218 and to the following provisions of **26–152** Chapter 4 limiting the power to require the licence to contain particular requirements—

(a) section 199(3) (unpaid work requirement),

(b) section 201(3) and (4) (activity requirement),

(c) section 202(4) and (5) (programme requirement), and

(d) section 203(2) (prohibited activity requirement).

(2) Subsections (3) to (5) of section 182 have effect in relation to an intermittent custody order as they have effect in relation to a custody plus order.

Further provisions relating to intermittent custody

186.—(1) Section 21 of the 1952 Act (expenses of conveyance to prison) does not apply in re- **26–153** lation to the conveyance to prison at the end of any licence period of an offender to whom an intermittent custody order relates.

(2) The Secretary of State may pay to any offender to whom an intermittent custody order relates the whole or part of any expenses incurred by the offender in travelling to and from prison during licence periods.

(3) In section 49 of the 1952 Act (persons unlawfully at large) after subsection (4) there is inserted—

"(4A) For the purposes of this section a person shall also be deemed to be unlawfully at large if, having been temporarily released in pursuance of an intermittent custody order made under section 183 of the *Criminal Justice Act* 2003, he remains at large at a time when, by reason of the expiry of the period for which he was temporarily released, he is liable to be detained in pursuance of his sentence."

(4) In section 23 of the *Criminal Justice Act* 1961 (c. 39) (prison rules), in subsection (3) for "The days" there is substituted "Subject to subsection (3A), the days" and after subsection (3) there is inserted—

"(3A) In relation to a prisoner to whom an intermittent custody order under section 183 of the *Criminal Justice Act* 2003relates, the only days to which subsection (3) applies are Christmas Day, Good Friday and any day which under the *Banking and Financial Dealings Act* 1971 is a bank holiday in England and Wales."

(5) In section 1 of the *Prisoners (Return to Custody) Act* 1995 (c. 16) (remaining at large after temporary release) after subsection (1) there is inserted—

"(1A) A person who has been temporarily released in pursuance of an intermittent custody order made under section 183 of the *Criminal Justice Act* 2003 is guilty of an offence if, without reasonable excuse, he remains unlawfully at large at any time after becoming so at large by virtue of the expiry of the period for which he was temporarily released."

(6) In this section "the 1952 Act" means the *Prison Act* 1952 (c. 52).

T. Compensation Orders

(1) Purpose and effect

A compensation order enables a court to require an offender to provide financial **26–154** compensation for loss or harm caused by the offence. It is designed for use in simple, straightforward circumstances. It can either be a sentence in its own right or an ancillary order. If no order is made in circumstances where the court has the power to make such an order, then the court must give its reasons for not making the compensation order. This emphasises the importance of this part of the sentencing task which directly recognises the impact of the crime on any victim.

Powers of Criminal Courts (Sentencing) Act 2000, ss.130, 131

Compensation orders against convicted persons

26–155   **130.**—(1) A court by or before which a person is convicted of an offence, instead of or in addition to dealing with him in any other way, may, on application or otherwise, make an order (in this Act referred to as a "compensation order") requiring him—

    (a) to pay compensation for any personal injury, loss or damage resulting from that offence or any other offence which is taken into consideration by the court in determining sentence; or

    (b) to make payments for funeral expenses or bereavement in respect of a death resulting from any such offence, other than a death due to an accident arising out of the presence of a motor vehicle on a road;

but this is subject to the following provisions of this section and to section 131 below.

(2) Where the person is convicted of an offence the sentence for which is fixed by law or falls to be imposed under section 109(2), 110(2) or 111(2) above, subsection (1) above shall have effect as if the words "instead of or" were omitted.

(3) A court shall give reasons, on passing sentence, if it does not make a compensation order in a case where this section empowers it to do so.

(4) Compensation under subsection (1) above shall be of such amount as the court considers appropriate, having regard to any evidence and to any representations that are made by or on behalf of the accused or the prosecutor.

(5) In the case of an offence under the *Theft Act* 1968, where the property in question is recovered, any damage to the property occurring while it was out of the owner's possession shall be treated for the purposes of subsection (1) above as having resulted from the offence, however and by whomever the damage was caused.

(6) A compensation order may only be made in respect of injury, loss or damage (other than loss suffered by a person's dependants in consequence of his death) which was due to an accident arising out of the presence of a motor vehicle on a road, if—

    (a) it is in respect of damage which is treated by subsection (5) above as resulting from an offence under the *Theft Act* 1968; or

    (b) it is in respect of injury, loss or damage as respects which—

        (i) the offender is uninsured in relation to the use of the vehicle; and

        (ii) compensation is not payable under any arrangements to which the Secretary of State is a party.

26–156   (7) Where a compensation order is made in respect of injury, loss or damage due to an accident arising out of the presence of a motor vehicle on a road, the amount to be paid may include an amount representing the whole or part of any loss of or reduction in preferential rates of insurance attributable to the accident.

(8) A vehicle the use of which is exempted from insurance by section 144 of the *Road Traffic Act* 1988 is not uninsured for the purposes of subsection (6) above.

(9) A compensation order in respect of funeral expenses may be made for the benefit of any one who incurred the expenses.

(10) A compensation order in respect of bereavement may be made only for the benefit of a person for whose benefit a claim for damages for bereavement could be made under section 1A of the *Fatal Accidents Act* 1976; and the amount of compensation in respect of bereavement shall not exceed the amount for the time being specified in section 1A(3) of that Act.

(11) In determining whether to make a compensation order against any person, and in determining the amount to be paid by any person under such an order, the court shall have regard to his means so far as they appear or are known to the court.

(12) Where the court considers—

    (a) that it would be appropriate both to impose a fine and to make a compensation order, but

    (b) that the offender has insufficient means to pay both an appropriate fine and appropriate compensation,

the court shall give preference to compensation (though it may impose a fine as well).

Limit on amount payable under compensation order of magistrates' court.

26–157   **131.**—(1) The compensation to be paid under a compensation order made by a magistrates' court in respect of any offence of which the court has convicted the offender shall not exceed £5,000.

(2) The compensation or total compensation to be paid under a compensation order or compensation orders made by a magistrates' court in respect of any offence or offence taken into consideration in determining sentence shall not exceed the difference (if any) between—

(a) the amount or total amount which under subsection (1) above is the maximum for the offence or offences of which the offender has been convicted; and

(b) the amount or total amounts (if any) which are in fact ordered to be paid in respect of that offence or those offences.

Where there are limited financial resources, compensation takes priority over a fine **26–158** (see § 26–16 above). Similarly, where both compensation and confiscation are available sentences, compensation is the first priority. If it is possible to impose both penalties, that course may be followed. If not the court can reduce the amount of the confiscation order by virtue of s.71(1C) of the *Criminal Justice Act* 1988, or make no confiscation order, or make both confiscation and compensation orders and add a direction under s.72(7) of the 1988 Act: *R. v Mitchell and Mitchell* [2001] 2 Cr.App.R.(S.) 29, CA.

It is rarely appropriate to attach a compensation order to a custodial sentence as this may tempt the offender to commit further crimes upon his release: *R. v Wilkinson* (1979) 1 Cr.App.R.(S.) 69, CA.

A compensation order may not be made in respect of admitted offences which have not been charged or formally taken into consideration: *R. v Hose* (1995) 16 Cr.App.R.(S.) 682, CA.

The amount of the order will be such as the court considers appropriate having regard to any evidence and to any representations that are made by or on behalf of the accused or the prosecutor up to the maximum of £5000 for each offence of which the defendant is convicted. Where the defendant challenges the basis on which any compensation order is made and real issues are raised as to whether the claimants have suffered any, and if so what loss, evidence must be received to establish the defendant's liability to pay compensation: *R. v Horsham Justices Ex p. Richards* [1985] 2 All E.R. 1114, DC.

A compensation order must not be made on the basis of pure speculation as to the offender's future prospects: *R. v Ellis* (1994) 158 J.P. 386, though when considering the defendant's means the court may have regard to possible future income: *R. v Ford* [1977] Crim.L.R. 114.

The existence of civil liability is not a precondition to the making of a compensation **26–159** order: *R. v Chappel* (1985) 80 Cr.App.R. 31, CA. Causation must be established before a compensation order is made, though the court does not need to apply the strict test of causation applied in the field of tort: *R. v Derby* (1990) 12 Cr.App.R.(S.) 502, CA.

The *Magistrates' Courts Sentencing Guidelines* (2003), at pp.89–90, provide that in calculating the gross amount of compensation, courts should consider compensating the victim for two types of loss. The first, sometimes called 'special damages', includes compensation for financial loss sustained as a result of the offence. The second type of loss, sometimes called 'general damages', covers compensation for the pain and suffering of the injury itself and for any loss of facility. General guidance is given to assist in identifying starting points for damages for common personal injuries such as a graze, bruise or wrist fracture.

The guidelines add that the amount of compensation should be determined in the light of medical evidence, the victim's sex and age, and any other factors which appear to the court to be relevant in the particular case. If there is insufficient evidence, a court will expect to adjourn the proceedings in order that it can be obtained.

Once the court has made a preliminary calculation of the appropriate compensation, **26–160** it will then consider the means of the offender before making an order. Ideally, orders should be capable of being paid within one year but periods of up to two or even three years have been accepted where there is a real likelihood of the order being paid.

II. ANCILLARY ORDERS

A. Deprivation and Confiscation Orders

(1) Purpose and effect

26–161   These are part of a package of powers to enable the court to remove property from an offender where that property was used to assist the commission of the crime or is part of the proceeds of the crime. It is a potentially complex area of the law and this section briefly summarises the key points that a busy practitioner will need.

Where property was lawfully seized from a defendant or in his possession or under his control at the time he was apprehended, on conviction (or on the offence being taken into consideration), the court can order that he be deprived of any rights over that property if satisfied that the property had been used (or intended to be used) to assist the commission of any offence, not just the offence for which the defendant was apprehended or subsequently convicted.

Where the offence is punishable by imprisonment under the Road Traffic Acts and consists of driving (or attempting to drive or being in charge of) a motor vehicle or failing to provide a specimen for analysis or of failing to stop after and/or report an accident, then the vehicle being used is deemed to have been used for the purpose of committing the offence: s.143(6) and (7).

In deciding whether or not to make an order, the court must consider the value of the property and the likely effect on the offender of making the order—the higher the value, the more careful the court will need to be in deciding whether the order is appropriate.

Powers of Criminal Courts (Sentencing) Act 2000, ss.143–145

Powers to deprive offender of property used etc. for purposes of crime

26–162   **143.**—(1) Where a person is convicted of an offence and the court by or before which he is convicted is satisfied that any property which has been lawfully seized from him, or which was in his possession or under his control at the time when he was apprehended for the offence or when a summons in respect of it was issued—

     (a) has been used for the purpose of committing, or facilitating the commission of, any offence, or

     (b) was intended by him to be used for that purpose,

the court may (subject to subsection (5) below) make an order under this section in respect of that property.

    (2) Where a person is convicted of an offence and the offence, or an offence which the court has taken into consideration in determining his sentence, consists of unlawful possession of property which—

     (a) has been lawfully seized from him, or

     (b) was in his possession or under his control at the time when he was apprehended for the offence of which he has been convicted or when a summons in respect of that offence was issued,

the court may (subject to subsection (5) below) make an order under this section in respect of that property.

    (3) An order under this section shall operate to deprive the offender of his rights, if any, in the property to which it relates, and the property shall (if not already in their possession) be taken into the possession of the police.

    (4) Any power conferred on a court by subsection (1) or (2) above may be exercised—

     (a) whether or not the court also deals with the offender in any other way in respect of the offence of which he has been convicted; and

     (b) without regard to any restrictions on forfeiture in any enactment contained in an Act passed before 29th July 1988.

    (5) In considering whether to make an order under this section in respect of any property, a court shall have regard—

     (a) to the value of the property; and

(b) to the likely financial and other effects on the offender of the making of the order (taken together with any other order that the court contemplates making).

(6) Where a person commits an offence to which this subsection applies by— **26–163**

(a) driving, attempting to drive, or being in charge of a vehicle, or

(b) failing to comply with a requirement made under section 7 or 7A of the *Road Traffic Act* 1988 (failure to provide specimen for analysis or laboratory test or to give permission for such a test in the course of an investigation into whether the offender had committed an offence while driving, attempting to drive or being in charge of a vehicle, or

(c) failing, as the driver of a vehicle, to comply with subsection (2) or (3) of section 170 of the *Road Traffic Act* 1988 (duty to stop and give information or report accident),

the vehicle shall be regarded for the purposes of subsection (1) above (and section 144(1)(b) below) as used for the purpose of committing the offence (and for the purpose of committing any offence of aiding, abetting, counselling or procuring the commission of the offence).

(7) Subsection (6) above applies to—

(a) an offence under the *Road Traffic Act* 1988 which is punishable with imprisonment;

(b) an offence of manslaughter; and

(c) an offence under section 35 of the *Offences Against the Person Act* 1861 (wanton and furious driving).

(8) Facilitating the commission of an offence shall be taken for the purposes of subsection (1) above to include the taking of any steps after it has been committed for the purpose of disposing of any property to which it relates or of avoiding apprehension or detection.

Property which is in possession of police by virtue of section 143

144.—(1) The *Police (Property) Act* 1897 shall apply, with the following modifications, to **26–164**
property which is in the possession of the police by virtue of section 143 above—

(a) no application shall be made under section 1(1) of that Act by any claimant of the property after the end of six months from the date on which the order in respect of the property was made under section 143 above; and ·

(b) no such application shall succeed unless the claimant satisfies the court either—

(i) that he had not consented to the offender having possession of the property; or

(ii) where an order is made under subsection (1) of section 143 above, that he did not know, and had no reason to suspect, that the property was likely to be used for the purpose mentioned in that subsection.

(2) In relation to property which is in the possession of the police by virtue of section 143 above, the power to make regulations under section 2 of the *Police (Property) Act* 1897 (disposal of property in cases where the owner of the property has not been ascertained and no order of a competent court has been made with respect to it) shall, subject to subsection (3) below, include power to make regulations for disposal (including disposal by vesting in the relevant authority) in cases where no application by a claimant of the property has been made within the period specified in subsection (1)(a) above or no such application has succeeded.

(3) The regulations may not provide for the vesting in the relevant authority of property in relation to which an order has been made under section 145 below (court order as to application of proceeds of forfeited property).

(4) Nothing in subsection (2A)(a) or (3) of section 2 of the *Police (Property) Act* 1897 limits the power to make regulations under that section by virtue of subsection (2) above.

(5) In this section "relevant authority" has the meaning given by section 2(2B) of the *Police (Property) Act* 1897.

Application of proceeds of forfeited property.

145.—(1) Where a court makes an order under section 143 above in a case where— **26–165**

(a) the offender has been convicted of an offence which has resulted in a person suffering personal injury, loss or damage, or

(b) any such offence is taken into consideration by the court in determining sentence,

the court may also make an order that any proceeds which arise from the disposal of the property and which do not exceed a sum specified by the court shall be paid to that person.

(2) The court may make an order under this section only if it is satisfied that but for the

inadequacy of the offender's means it would have made a compensation order under which the offender would have been required to pay compensation of an amount not less than the specified amount.

(3) An order under this section has no effect—

    (a) before the end of the period specified in section 144(1)(a) above; or

    (b) if a successful application under section 1(1) of the *Police (Property) Act* 1897 has been made.

The power does not extend to real property: *R. v Khan (Sultan Ashraf)* [1984] 1 W.L.R. 1405, CA.

26–166   As noted above, the power under s.143(1) is widely drawn and is not restricted to property used in the offences currently before the court and an order may be made in respect of property intended to be used by the offender to commit any offence. In *R. v O'Farrell* [1988] Crim.L.R. 387, the court ordered the forfeiture of a large sum of money found on a person convicted of supplying illegal drugs. The defendant sought to argue that the order could not be made as there was no evidence that the money was the proceeds of the current offence and that it was intended for use to fund future offences but the Court of Appeal agreed that the order had been rightly made.

An order should not be made unless the court has information before it relating to the value of the property concerned and the effect on the offender of making the order: *R. v Ball* [2003] 2 Cr.App.R.(S.) 18, CA. A deprivation order made against one offender, where several offenders are responsible for a single offence may give rise to an objectionable disparity: *R. v Burgess* [2001] 2 Cr.App.R.(S.) 5, CA.

26–167   A deprivation order may be made in addition to other sentences imposed in respect of the same offence. The order should be seen as part of the overall penalty, and the other sentences imposed should be adjusted accordingly: *R. v Joyce* [1991] R.T.R. 241, CA. In *R. v Highbury Corner Stipendiary Magistrate Ex p. Di Matteo* [1992] 1 All E.R. 102, DC, Watkins L.J. said that a court considering whether to make an order under s.143 should have regard to the totality principle and to the two matters specifically set out in subs.(5)—the value of the property concerned and the likely financial and other effects on the offender of making the order—taken together with any other order that the court was considering making.

In *R. v Priestly* [1996] 2 Cr.App.R.(S.) 144, CA, a sentence of four years' imprisonment for applying false trademarks to perfumes and clothing so as to resemble goods manufactured by famous manufacturers was reduced to three years, to take account of an order made under the *Powers of Criminal Courts Act* 1973, s.43 (now PCC(S)A 2000, s.143). The Court held that the sentencer had failed to take into account the effect of the order as part of the total sentence, as was required by *Joyce* (1989) 11 Cr.App.R.(S.) 253, CA, and the sentence of four years imprisonment should be reduced to one of three.

26–168   A deprivation order will only be suitable in cases where it will not be difficult to implement. In *R. v Troth* [1980] Crim.L.R. 249, a case concerning partnership property, it was held that difficulties would arise in the implementation of a deprivation order where the property was subject to encumbrances, and it might be appropriate to impose 'an increased financial penalty…in lieu of making a forfeiture order'.

The power to order forfeiture of particular objects is also provided by various statutes. See the *Misuse of Drugs Act* 1971, s.27; *Firearms Act* 1968, s.52; *Salmon and Freshwater Fisheries Act* 1975, Sch.4, para.5 (fish and fishing tackle); *Licensing Act* 1964, ss.161, 162 (intoxicating liquor); *Obscene Publications Act* 1959, s.3 (obscene articles); *Prevention of Crime Act* 1953, s.1 (offensive weapons) and *Wireless Telegraphy Act* 1949, s.14 (wireless telegraphy apparatus).

B. Confiscation Orders under the Criminal Justice Act 1988

26–169   The provisions of the *Criminal Justice Act* 1988 (ss.71 to 102) are repealed with effect from March 24, 2003 by the *Proceeds of Crime Act* 2002. The repeal does not apply to offences committed before that date and so the provisions of the *CJA* 1988 will continue to apply. However, orders under the 2002 Act can only be made in the Crown Court.

Confiscation orders may be made by a magistrates' court in respect of a limited number of summary offences, which are listed in Sch.4 to the 1988 Act.

CHAPTER 27

EXCLUSIONS AND DISQUALIFICATIONS

I. BANNING ORDERS UNDER THE FOOTBALL SPECTATORS ACT 1989

(1) Purpose and effect

Disorder at and around professional football matches had become a major source of **27–1** public disorder. As part of the response to that, courts were given powers under the 1989 Act to restrict the activities of those considered likely to cause trouble. This was refined and developed by the *Football (Disorder) Act* 2000, in particular Sch.1 which makes a series of amendments to Pt II of, and the Schedule to, the 1989 Act.

An order may be made either on conviction of a "relevant offence" or after a specific complaint seeking simply an order under these provisions. Where a person is convicted of a relevant offence (see s.14(8)—an offence to which Sch.1 to the 1989 Act applies) and the court is satisfied that there are reasonable grounds for believing that making a banning order will help to prevent violence or disorder (defined in s.14C), then that order can be made in addition to the sentence for the offence: s.14A(4).

The main effects of the order are to require the subject of the order to report to a po- **27–2** lice station within five days, prohibit the subject from entering premises to attend regulated football matches (s.14(4)), make arrangements for the surrender of the subject's passport when certain matches outside the UK are imminent (s.14E(3)) and make whatever additional requirements are necessary. Minimum and maximum periods for the order are specified: s.14F.

A court may order that the subject attend a specified police station and be required to have his photograph taken to assist in the enforcement of an order under these provisions: s.35 of the *Public Order Act* 1986.

Football Spectators Act 1989, s.1

Scope and interpretation of this Part.

1.—(1) This Part of this Act applies in relation to association football matches played in **27–3** England and Wales which are designated football matches and the following provisions have effect for its interpretation.

(2) "Designated football match" means any such match of a description for the time being designated for the purposes of this Part by order made by the Secretary of State or a particular such match so designated.

(3) The Secretary of State shall not make a designation under subsection (2) above without giving the Football Membership Authority an opportunity to make representations about the proposed designation, and taking any representations he receives into account.

(4) An order under subsection (2) above—

973

(a) may designate descriptions of football matches wherever played or when played at descriptions of ground or in any area specified in the order; and

(b) may provide, in relation to the match or description of match designated by the order or any description of match falling within the designation, that spectators admitted to the ground shall be authorised spectators to the extent, and subject to any restrictions or conditions, determined in pursuance of the order by the licensing authority under this Part of this Act.

(8) Each of the following periods is "relevant to" a designated football match, that is to say—

(a) the period beginning—
    (i) two hours before the start of the match, or
    (ii) two hours before the time at which it is advertised to start, or
    (iii) with the time at which spectators are first admitted to the premises,
    whichever is the earliest, and ending one hour after the end of the match;

(b) where a match advertised to start at a particular time on a particular day is postponed to a later day, or does not take place, the period in the advertised day beginning two hours before and ending one hour after that time.

(8A) In its application to an offence specified in paragraph 1(q), (r), (s) or (t) of Schedule 1 to this Act, subsection (8) above shall have effect as if—

(a) the reference to a designated football match included a reference to a [regulated football matches (within the meaning of Part II of this Act),

(b) for "two hours", wherever occurring, there were substituted "24 hours",

(c) for "one hour", wherever occurring, there were substituted "24 hours", and

(d) paragraph (a)(iii) were omitted.

(9) A person is a "responsible person" in relation to any designated football match at any premises if he is a person concerned in the management of the premises or in the organisation of the match.

(10) The power to make an order under subsection (2) above is exercisable by statutory instrument which shall be subject to annulment in pursuance of a resolution of either House of Parliament.

(11) The imposition under this Part of this Act of restrictions on the persons who may attend as spectators at any designated football match does not affect any other right of any person to exclude persons from admission to the premises at which the match is played.

Football Spectators Act 1989, s.14

Main definitions

27–4   14.—(1) This section applies for the purposes of this Part.

(2) "Regulated football match" means an association football match (whether in England and Wales or elsewhere) which is a prescribed match or a match of a prescribed description.

(3) "External tournament" means a football competition which includes regulated football matches outside England and Wales.

(4) "Banning order" means an order made by the court under this Part which—

(a) in relation to regulated football matches in England and Wales, prohibits the person who is subject to the order from entering any premises for the purpose of attending such matches, and

(b) in relation to regulated football matches outside England and Wales, requires that person to report at a police station in accordance with this Part.

(5) "Control period", in relation to a regulated football match outside England and Wales, means the period—

(a) beginning five days before the day of the match, and

(b) ending when the match is finished or cancelled.

(6) "Control period", in relation to an external tournament, means any period described in an order made by the Secretary of State—

(a) beginning five days before the day of the first football match outside England and Wales which is included in the tournament, and

(b) ending when the last football match outside England and Wales which is included in the tournament is finished or cancelled,

but, for the purposes of paragraph (a), any football match included in the qualifying or pre-qualifying stages of the tournament is to be left out of account.

(7) References to football matches are to football matches played or intended to be played.

(8) "Relevant offence" means an offence to which Schedule 1 to this Act applies.

See the *Football Spectators (Prescription) Order* 2000 (SI 2000/2126) for football **27–5** matches in England and Wales and outside England and Wales that are regulated football matches for the purposes of Pt II of the 1989 Act.

Football Spectators Act 1989, ss.14A–14H

Banning orders made on conviction of an offence.

14A.—(1) This section applies where a person (the "offender") is convicted of a relevant **27–6** offence.

(2) If the court is satisfied that there are reasonable grounds to believe that making a banning order would help to prevent violence or disorder at or in connection with any regulated football matches, it must make such an order in respect of the offender.

(3) If the court is not so satisfied, it must in open court state that fact and give its reasons.

(4) A banning order may only be made under this section—

 (a) in addition to a sentence imposed in respect of the relevant offence, or

 (b) in addition to an order discharging him conditionally.

(5) A banning order may be made as mentioned in subsection (4)(b) above in spite of anything in sections 12 and 14 of the *Powers of the Criminal Courts (Sentencing) Act* 2000 (which relate to orders discharging a person absolutely or conditionally and their effect).

(6) In this section, "the court" in relation to an offender means—

 (a) the court by or before which he is convicted of the relevant offence, or

 (b) if he is committed to the Crown Court to be dealt with for that offence, the Crown Court.

Banning orders made on a complaint.

14B.—(1) An application for a banning order in respect of any person may be made by the **27–7** chief officer of police for the area in which the person resides or appears to reside, if it appears to the officer that the condition in subsection (2) below is met.

(2) That condition is that the respondent has at any time caused or contributed to any violence or disorder in the United Kingdom or elsewhere.

(3) The application is to be made by complaint to a magistrates' court.

(4) If—

 (a) it is proved on the application that the condition in subsection (2) above is met, and

 (b) the court is satisfied that there are reasonable grounds to believe that making a banning order would help to prevent violence or disorder at or in connection with any regulated football matches,

the court must make a banning order in respect of the respondent.

Banning orders: supplementary.

14C.—(1) In this Part, "violence" means violence against persons or property and includes **27–8** threatening violence and doing anything which endangers the life of any person.

(2) In this Part, "disorder" includes—

 (a) stirring up hatred against a group of persons defined by reference to colour, race, nationality (including citizenship) or ethnic or national origins, or against an individual as a member of such a group,

 (b) using threatening, abusive or insulting words or behaviour or disorderly behaviour,

 (c) displaying any writing or other thing which is threatening, abusive or insulting.

(3) In this Part, "violence" and "disorder" are not limited to violence or disorder in connection with football.

(4) The magistrates' court may take into account the following matters (among others), so far as they consider it appropriate to do so, in determining whether to make an order under section 14B above—

(a) any decision of a court or tribunal outside the United Kingdom,

(b) deportation or exclusion from a country outside the United Kingdom,

(c) removal or exclusion from premises used for playing football matches, whether in the United Kingdom or elsewhere,

(d) conduct recorded on video or by any other means.

(5) In determining whether to make such an order—

(a) the magistrates' court may not take into account anything done by the respondent before the beginning of the period of ten years ending with the application under section 14B(1) above, except circumstances ancillary to a conviction,

(b) before taking into account any conviction for a relevant offence, where a court made a statement under section 14A(3) above (or section 15(2A) below or section 30(3) of the *Public Order Act* 1986), the magistrates' court must consider the reasons given in the statement,

and in this subsection "circumstances ancillary to a conviction" has the same meaning as it has for the purposes of section 4 of the *Rehabilitation of Offenders Act* 1974 (effect of rehabilitation).

(6) Subsection (5) does not prejudice anything in the *Rehabilitation of Offenders Act* 1974.

Banning orders: general

27–9   **14E.**—(1) On making a banning order, a court must in ordinary language explain its effect to the person subject to the order.

(2) A banning order must require the person subject to the order to report initially at a police station in England and Wales specified in the order within the period of five days beginning with the day on which the order is made.

(3) A banning order must, unless it appears to the court that there are exceptional circumstances, impose a requirement as to the surrender in accordance with this Part, in connection with regulated football matches outside the United Kingdom, of the passport of the person subject to the order.

(4) If it appears to the court that there are such circumstances, it must in open court state what they are.

(5) In the case of a person detained in legal custody—

(a) the requirement under this section to report at a police station, and

(b) any requirement imposed under section 19 below,

is suspended until his release from custody.

(6) If—

(a) he is released from custody more than five days before the expiry of the period for which the order has effect, and

(b) he was precluded by his being in custody from reporting initially,

the order is to have effect as if it required him to report initially at the police station specified in the order within the period of five days beginning with the date of his release.

Period of banning orders

27–10   **14F.**—(1) Subject to the following provisions of this Part, a banning order has effect for a period beginning with the day on which the order is made.

(2) The period must not be longer than the maximum or shorter than the minimum.

(3) Where the order is made under section 14A above in addition to a sentence of imprisonment taking immediate effect, the maximum is ten years and the minimum is six years; and in this subsection "imprisonment" includes any form of detention.

(4) In any other case where the order is made under section 14A above, the maximum is five years and the minimum is three years.

(5) Where the order is made under section 14B above, the maximum is three years and the minimum is two years.

Additional requirements of orders

27–11   **14G.**—(1) A banning order may, if the court making the order thinks fit, impose additional requirements on the person subject to the order in relation to any regulated football matches.

(2) The court by which a banning order was made may, on an application made by—

(a) the person subject to the order, or

(b) the person who applied for the order or who was the prosecutor in relation to the order, vary the order so as to impose, replace or omit any such requirements.

(3) In the case of a banning order made by a magistrates' court, the reference in subsection (2) above to the court by which it was made includes a reference to any magistrates' court acting for the same petty sessions area as that court.

Termination of orders

14H.—(1) If a banning order has had effect for at least two-thirds of the period determined **27–12** under section 14F above, the person subject to the order may apply to the court by which it was made to terminate it.

(2) On the application, the court may by order terminate the banning order as from a specified date or refuse the application.

(3) In exercising its powers under subsection (2) above, the court must have regard to the person's character, his conduct since the banning order was made, the nature of the offence or conduct which led to it and any other circumstances which appear to it to be relevant.

(4) Where an application under subsection (1) above in respect of a banning order is refused, no further application in respect of the order may be made within the period of six months beginning with the day of the refusal.

(5) The court may order the applicant to pay all or any part of the costs of an application under this section.

(6) In the case of a banning order made by a magistrates' court, the reference in subsection (1) above to the court by which it was made includes a reference to any magistrates' court acting for the same petty sessions area as that court.

Football Spectators Act 1989, s.14J

Offences

14J.—(1) A person subject to a banning order who fails to comply with—   **27–13**
  (a) any requirement imposed by the order, or
  (b) any requirement imposed under section 19(2B) or (2C) below,
is guilty of an offence.

(2) A person guilty of an offence under this section is liable on summary conviction to imprisonment for a term not exceeding six months, or a fine not exceeding level 5 on the standard scale, or both.

Football Spectators Act 1989, s.18

Information

18.—(1) Where a court makes a banning order, the justices' chief executive for the court (in **27–14** the case of a magistrates' court) or the appropriate officer (in the case of the Crown Court)—
  (a) shall give a copy of it to the person to whom it relates;
  (b) shall (as soon as reasonably practicable) send a copy of it to the enforcing authority and to any prescribed person;
  (c) shall (as soon as reasonably practicable) send a copy of it to the police station (addressed to the officer responsible for the police station) at which the person subject to the order is to report initially; and
  (d) in a case where the person subject to the order is detained in legal custody, shall (as soon as reasonably practicable) send a copy of it to the person in whose custody he is detained.

(2) Where a court terminates a banning order under section 14H above, the clerk of the court (in the case of a magistrates' court) or the appropriate officer (in the case of the Crown Court)—
  (a) shall give a copy of the terminating order to the person to whom the banning order relates;
  (b) shall (as soon as reasonably practicable) send a copy of it to the enforcing authority; and
  (c) in a case where the person subject to the banning order is detained in legal custody, shall (as soon as reasonably practicable) send a copy of the terminating order to the person in whose custody he is detained.

(3) Where a person subject to a banning order is released from custody and, in the case of a person who has not reported initially to a police station, is released more than five days before the expiry of the banning order, the person in whose custody he is shall (as soon as reasonably practicable) give notice of his release to the enforcing authority.

(4) References in this section to the clerk of a magistrates' court shall be construed in accordance with section 141 of the *Magistrates' Courts Act* 1980, reading references to that Act as references to this section.

27–15   Article 5 of SI 2000/2126 prescribes the Football Banning Orders Authority as the enforcing authority for the purposes of Pt II of the 1989 Act, and the Chief Executive of the Football Association for the purposes of s.18(1) and (2) of that Act.

For banning orders arising out of offences outside England and Wales, see s.22 of the 1989 Act and a series of orders made thereunder.

Football Spectators Act 1989, s.22A

Other interpretation, etc.

27–16   **22A.**—(1) In this Part—

"British citizen" has the same meaning as in the *British Nationality Act* 1981,

"country" includes territory,

"declaration of relevance" has the same meaning as in section 7,

"enforcing authority" means a prescribed organisation established by the Secretary of State under section 57 of the *Police Act* 1996 (central police organisations),

"passport" means a United Kingdom passport within the meaning of the *Immigration Act* 1971,

"prescribed" means prescribed by an order made by the Secretary of State.

(2) The Secretary of State may, if he considers it necessary or expedient to do so in order to secure the effective enforcement of this Part, by order provide for section 14(5) and (6) above to have effect in relation to any, or any description of, regulated football match or external tournament as if, for any reference to the number of days (not exceeding ten) specified in the order.

(3) Any power of the Secretary of State to make an order under this Part is exercisable by statutory instrument.

(4) An instrument containing an order made by the Secretary of State under this Part shall be subject to annulment in pursuance of a resolution of either House of Parliament.

Football Spectators Act 1989, s.23

Further provision about, and appeals against, declarations of relevance

27–17   **23.**—(1) Subject to subsection (2) below, a court may not make a declaration of relevance as respects any offence unless it is satisfied that the prosecutor gave notice to the defendant, at least five days before the first day of the trial, that it was proposed to show that the offence related to football matches, to a particular football match or to particular football matches (as the case may be).

(2) A court may, in any particular case, make a declaration of relevance notwithstanding that notice to the defendant as required by subsection (1) above has not been given if he consents to waive the giving of full notice or the court is satisfied that the interests of justice do not require more notice to be given.

(3) A person convicted of an offence as respects which the court makes a declaration of relevance may appeal against the making of the declaration of relevance as if the declaration were included in any sentence passed on him for the offence, and accordingly—

     (a) in section 10(3) of the *Criminal Appeal Act* 1968 (appeals against sentence by Crown Court), in paragraph (c), after the sub-paragraph (iv) inserted by section 15(7) above there shall be inserted

"or

         (v) a declaration of relevance under the *Football Spectators Act* 1989;";

     (b) in section 50(1) of that Act (meaning of "sentence"), at the end there shall be inserted the words "and a declaration of relevance under the *Football Spectators Act* 1989"; and

(c) in section 108(3) of the *Magistrates' Courts Act* 1980 (right of appeal to the Crown Court), at the end there shall be inserted the words "and also includes a declaration of relevance under the *Football Spectators Act* 1989"

(4) A banning order made upon a person's conviction of a relevant offence shall be quashed if the making of a declaration of relevance as respects that offence is reversed on appeal.

Football Spectators Act 1989, Sch.1

SCHEDULE 1

RELEVANT OFFENCES

Offences

1. This Schedule applies to the following offences: **27–18**

(a) any offence under section 2(1), 5(7), 14J(1) or 21C(2) of this Act,

(b) any offence under section 2 or 2A of the *Sporting Events (Control of Alcohol etc.) Act* 1985 (alcohol, containers and fireworks) committed by the accused at any football match to which this Schedule applies or while entering or trying to enter the ground,

(c) any offence under section 5 of the *Public Order Act* 1986 (harassment, alarm or distress) or any provision of Part III of that Act (racial hatred) committed during a period relevant to a football match to which this Schedule applies at any premises while the accused was at, or was entering or leaving or trying to enter or leave, the premises,

(d) any offence involving the use or threat of violence by the accused towards another person committed during a period relevant to a football match to which this Schedule applies at any premises while the accused was at, or was entering or leaving or trying to enter or leave, the premises,

(e) any offence involving the use or threat of violence towards property committed during a period relevant to a football match to which this Schedule applies at any premises while the accused was at, or was entering or leaving or trying to enter or leave, the premises,

(f) any offence involving the use, carrying or possession of an offensive weapon or a firearm committed during a period relevant to a football match to which this Schedule applies at any premises while the accused was at, or was entering or leaving or trying to enter or leave, the premises,

(g) any offence under section 12 of the *Licensing Act* 1872 (persons found drunk in public places, etc.) of being found drunk in a highway or other public place committed while the accused was on a journey to or from a football match to which this Schedule applies being an offence as respects which the court makes a declaration that the offence related to football matches,

(h) any offence under section 91(1) of the *Criminal Justice Act* 1967 (disorderly behaviour while drunk in a public place) committed in a highway or other public place while the accused was on a journey to or from a football match to which this Schedule applies being an offence as respects which the court makes a declaration that the offence related to football matches,

(j) any offence under section 1 of the *Sporting Events (Control of Alcohol etc.) Act* 1985 (alcohol on coaches or trains to or from sporting events) committed while the accused was on a journey to or from a football match to which this Schedule applies being an offence as respects which the court makes a declaration that the offence related to football matches,

(k) any offence under section 5 of the *Public Order Act* 1986 (harassment, alarm or distress) or any provision of Part III of that Act (racial hatred) committed while the accused was on a journey to or from a football match to which this Schedule applies being an offence as respects which the court makes a declaration that the offence related to football matches,

(l) any offence under section 4 or 5 of the *Road Traffic Act* 1988 (driving etc. when under the influence of drink or drugs or with an alcohol concentration above the prescribed limit) committed while the accused was on a journey to or from a football match to which this Schedule applies being an offence as respects which the court makes a declaration that the offence related to football matches,

(m) any offence involving the use or threat of violence by the accused towards another person committed while one or each of them was on a journey to or from a football match to which this Schedule applies being an offence as respects which the court makes a declaration that the offence related to football matches,

(n) any offence involving the use or threat of violence towards property committed while the accused was on a journey to or from a football match to which this Schedule applies being an offence as respects which the court makes a declaration that the offence related to football matches,

(o) any offence involving the use, carrying or possession of an offensive weapon or a firearm committed while the accused was on a journey to or from a football match to which this Schedule applies being an offence as respects which the court makes a declaration that the offence related to football matches,

(p) any offence under the *Football (Offences) Act* 1991,

(q) any offence under section 5 of the *Public Order Act* 1986 (harassment, alarm or distress) or any provision of Part III of that Act (racial hatred)—

    (i) which does not fall within paragraph (c) or (k) above,

    (ii) which was committed during a period relevant to a football match to which this Schedule applies, and

    (iii) as respects which the court makes a declaration that the offence related to that match or to that match and any other football match which took place during that period,

(r) any offence involving the use or threat of violence by the accused towards another person—

    (i) which does not fall within paragraph (d) or (m) above,

    (ii) which was committed during a period relevant to a football match to which this Schedule applies, and

    (iii) as respects which the court makes a declaration that the offence related to that match or to that match and any other football match which took place during that period,

(s) any offence involving the use or threat of violence towards property—

    (i) which does not fall within paragraph (e) or (n) above,

    (ii) which was committed during a period relevant to a football match to which this Schedule applies, and

    (iii) as respects which the court makes a declaration that the offence related to that match or to that match and any other football match which took place during that period,

(t) any offence involving the use, carrying or possession of an offensive weapon or a firearm—

    (i) which does not fall within paragraph (f) or (o) above,

    (ii) which was committed during a period relevant to a football match to which this Schedule applies, and

    (iii) as respects which the court makes a declaration that the offence related to that match or to that match and any other football match which took place during that period,

(u) any offence under section 166 of the *Criminal Justice and Public Order Act* 1994 (sale of tickets by unauthorised persons) which relates to tickets for a football match.

27–19   2. Any reference to an offence in paragraph 1 above includes—

(a) a reference to any attempt, conspiracy or incitement to commit that offence, and

(b) a reference to aiding and abetting, counselling or procuring the commission of that offence.

27–20   3. For the purposes of paragraphs 1(g) to (o) above—

(a) a person may be regarded as having been on a journey to or from a football match to which this Schedule applies whether or not he attended or intended to attend the match, and

(b) a person's journey includes breaks (including overnight breaks).

4.—(1) In this Schedule, "football match" means a match which is a regulated football match for the purposes of Part II of this Act.

(2) Section 1(8) and (8A) above apply for the interpretation of references to periods rel-

evant to football matches.

Public Order Act 1986, s.35

Photographs

35.—(1) The court by which a domestic football banning order is made may make an order   **27–21**
which—

    (a) requires a constable to take a photograph of the person to whom the domestic
football banning order relates or to cause such a photograph to be taken, and

    (b) requires that person to go to a specified police station not later than 7 clear days
after the day on which the order under this section is made, and at a specified
time of day or between specified times of day, in order to have his photograph
taken.

(2) In subsection (1) "specified" means specified in the order made under this section
and 'banning order' has the same meaning as in Part II of the *Football Spectators Act* 1989.

(3) No order may be made under this section unless an application to make it is made
to the court by or on behalf of the person who is the prosecutor in respect of the offence
leading to the banning order (or in the case of a banning order made under section 14B of
the *Football Spectators Act* 1989, the complainant)

(4) If the person to whom the exclusion order relates fails to comply with an order
under this section a constable may arrest him without warrant in order that his photograph
may be taken.

In *Gough v Chief Constable of the Derbyshire Constabulary* [2002] 3 W.L.R. 289,   **27–22**
CA, it was held that in order to justify the restriction on freedom of movement imposed
by the banning order, an order should only be made where there are strong grounds
for concluding that the individual who is the subject of the order has a propensity for
taking part in football hooliganism. The principle of proportionality requires that the
restraints on the individual's freedom of movement should be imposed following individual consideration of the case, should not be based simply on the individual's criminal
record, should be rationally connected to the objective of preventing English football
hooliganism abroad and should be the minimum necessary to achieve that legitimate
objective.

When considering the conditions in s.14B, the appropriate standard of proof must
also be applied, this standard being practically indistinguishable from the criminal standard of proof, given the consequences that will follow if the conditions for the banning
order are made out. This follows the approach adopted regarding an application for an
anti-social behaviour order and recommended in relation to an application for a Bind
Over, see §§ 27–53 and 27–60 below.

II. DISQUALIFICATION FROM DRIVING WHEN VEHICLE USED FOR PURPOSES OF CRIME

Powers of Criminal Courts (Sentencing) Act 2000, ss.146, 147

Driving disqualification for any offence

146.—(1) The court by or before which a person is convicted of an offence committed after   **27–23**
31st December 1997 may, instead of or in addition to dealing with him in any other way, order
him to be disqualified, for such period as it thinks fit, for holding or obtaining a driving licence.

(2) Where the person is convicted of an offence the sentence for which is fixed by law or
falls to be imposed under section 109(2), 110(2) or 111(2) above, subsection (1) above shall
have effect as if the words "instead of or" were omitted.

(3) A court shall not make an order under subsection (1) above unless the court has
been notified by the Secretary of State that the power to make such orders is exercisable by
the court and the notice has not been withdrawn.

(4) A court which makes an order under this section disqualifying a person for holding
or obtaining a driving licence shall require him to produce—

    (a) any such licence held by him together with its counterpart; or

    (b) in the case where he holds a Community licence (within the meaning of Part III of the *Road Traffic Act* 1988), his Community licence and its counterpart (if any).

    (5) In this section—

"driving licence" means a licence to drive a motor vehicle granted under Part III of the *Road Traffic Act* 1988;

"counterpart" —

    (a) in relation to a driving licence, has the meaning given in relation to such a licence by section 108(1) of that Act; and

    (b) in relation to a Community licence, has the meaning given by section 99B of that Act.

Driving disqualification where vehicle used for purposes of crime

27–24   **147.**—(1) This section applies where a person—

    (a) is convicted before the Crown Court of an offence punishable on indictment with imprisonment for a term of two years or more; or

    (b) having been convicted by a magistrates' court of such an offence, is committed under section 3 above to the Crown Court for sentence.

(2) This section also applies where a person is convicted by or before any court of common assault or of any other offence involving an assault (including an offence of aiding, abetting, counselling or procuring, or inciting to the commission of, an offence).

(3) If, in a case to which this section applies by virtue of subsection (1) above, the Crown Court is satisfied that a motor vehicle was used (by the person convicted or by anyone else) for the purpose of committing, or facilitating the commission of, the offence in question, the court may order the person convicted to be disqualified, for such period as the court thinks fit, for holding or obtaining a driving licence.

(4) If, in a case to which this section applies by virtue of subsection (2) above, the court is satisfied that the assault was committed by driving a motor vehicle, the court may order the person convicted to be disqualified, for such period as the court thinks fit, for holding or obtaining a driving licence.

(5) A court which makes an order under this section disqualifying a person for holding or obtaining a driving licence shall require him to produce—

    (a) any such licence held by him together with its counterpart; or

    (b) in the case where he holds a Community licence (within the meaning of Part III of the *Road Traffic Act* 1988), his Community licence and its counterpart (if any).

(6) Facilitating the commission of an offence shall be taken for the purposes of this section to include the taking of any steps after it has been committed for the purpose of disposing of any property to which it relates or of avoiding apprehension or detection.

(7) In this section "driving licence" and "counterpart" have the meanings given by section 146(5) above.

27–25   Section 146 is significantly wider than the power under s.147 in that it is available to both the Crown Court and magistrates' courts, it is not limited to any particular offence, and it is not necessary that the offence should be connected in any way with the use of a motor vehicle. The s.147 power is, therefore, only likely to be used for offences committed before the powers under s.146 became available.

Home Office guidance that accompanied the extension of s.146 suggests that the power should be used where the offence is in some way linked to the use of a vehicle although that is not necessary under the terms of the section. Any order needs to be proportionate to the offence and it may be that any disqualification for an offence where no vehicle or driving is involved would fall on that ground.

An offender who receives a custodial sentence should not be disqualified from driving for such a term that he will be prevented from securing employment upon his release from prison: *R. v Wright* (1979) 1 Cr.App.R.(S.) 82, CA. However, there is no absolute principle that an offender's period of disqualification should come to an end before he is released from prison: *R. v Arif* (1985) 7 Cr.App.R.(S.) 92, CA. As the nature of custodial sentences changes with the implementation of the *Criminal Justice Act* 2003, so orders such as these need to be seen in the context of the purpose and effect of the licence conditions that are imposed to apply for the remainder of the sentence after release from custody.

III. DISQUALIFICATION OF COMPANY DIRECTORS

(1) Purpose and Effect

Where a person is convicted of certain offences concerned with the management of a **27–26** company, the court may disqualify that person for a maximum of five years from being a company director, from acting as a receiver of the property of a company or of being directly or indirectly involved in the promotion, formation or management of a company or of acting as an insolvency practitioner.

The power arises on conviction for the offences described in s.5(1) of the 1986 Act. If it is an either way offence, the disqualification can follow any conviction of a qualifying offence. If it is a summary only offence, disqualification can follow only where there have been at least three default orders or convictions in the five years preceding the date of conviction: s.5(2) and (3).

Company Directors Disqualification Act 1986, ss.1, 5

Disqualification orders: general.

1.—(1) In the circumstances specified below in this Act a court may, and under sections 6 and **27–27** 9A shall, make against a person a disqualification order, that is to say an order that for a period specified in the order—

    (a) he shall not be a director of a company, act as receiver of a company's property or in any way, whether directly or indirectly, be concerned or take part in the promotion, formation or management of a company unless (in each case) he has the leave of the court, and

    (b) he shall not act as an insolvency practitioner.

(2) In each section of this Act which gives to a court power or, as the case may be, imposes on it the duty to make a disqualification order there is specified the maximum (and, in section 6, the minimum) period of disqualification which may or (as the case may be) must be imposed by means of the order and, unless the court otherwise orders, the period of disqualification so imposed shall begin at the end of the period of 21 days beginning with the date of the order.

(3) Where a disqualification order is made against a person who is already subject to such an order or to a disqualification undertaking, the periods specified in those orders or, as the case may be, in the order and the undertaking shall run concurrently.

(4) A disqualification order may be made on grounds which are or include matters other than criminal convictions, notwithstanding that the person in respect of whom it is to be made may be criminally liable in respect of those matters.

Disqualification on summary conviction

5.—(1) An offence counting for the purposes of this section is one of which a person is **27–28** convicted (either on indictment or summarily) in consequence of a contravention of, or failure to comply with, any provision of the companies legislation requiring a return, account or other document to be filed with, delivered or sent, or notice of any matter to be given, to the registrar of companies (whether the contravention or failure is on the person's own part or on the part of any company).

(2) Where a person is convicted of a summary offence counting for those purposes, the court by which he is convicted (or, in England and Wales, any other magistrates' court acting for the same petty sessions area) may make a disqualification order against him if the circumstances specified in the next subsection are present.

(3) Those circumstances are that, during the 5 years ending with the date of the conviction, the person has had made against him, or has been convicted of, in total not less than 3 default orders and offences counting for the purposes of this section; and those offences may include that of which he is convicted as mentioned in subsection (2) and any other offence of which he is convicted on the same occasion.

(4) For the purposes of this section—

    (a) the definition of "summary offence" in Schedule 1 to the *Interpretation Act* 1978 applies for Scotland as for England and Wales, and

    (b) "default order" means the same as in section 3(3)(b).

(5) The maximum period of disqualification under this section is 5 years.

27–29   The 'management' of a company has been held to apply to cases of obtaining by deception and similar activities committed during the course of trading by the company: *R. v Corbin* (1984) 6 Cr.App.R.(S.) 17, DC; *R. v Austen* (1985) 7 Cr.App.R.(S.) 214, CA and *R. v Georgiou*, 87 Cr.App.R. 207, CA.

A disqualification order should not be combined with a compensation order, if the effect of the order would be to deprive the offender of his means to earn money with which to pay compensation: *R. v Holmes* (1992) 13 Cr.App.R.(S.) 29, CA.

IV. EXCLUSION FROM LICENSED PREMISES

(1) Purpose and Effect

27–30   This power enables a court to give additional protection to licensees and others in licensed premises where a defendant has shown an inclination to commit offences or otherwise misbehave in such areas.

In order for an order to be made, the defendant must be convicted of an offence committed on licensed premises during which he used, offered or threatened violence. In those circumstances, in addition to sentence, the court may prohibit the defendant from entering the premises on which the offence was committed or any other premises that the court specifies unless he obtains the express consent of the licensee, his servant or his agent before doing so. The court will specify the length of the order which must be at least three months but no more than two years.

Licensed Premises (Exclusion of Certain Persons) Act 1980, ss.1, 2, 4

Exclusion orders

27–31   **1.**—(1) Where a court by or before which a person is convicted of an offence committed on licensed premises is satisfied that in committing that offence he resorted to violence or offered or threatened to resort to violence, the court may, subject to subsection (2) below, make an order (in this Act referred to as an "exclusion order") prohibiting him from entering those premises or any other specified premises, without the express consent of the licensee of the premises or his servant or agent.

(2) An exclusion order may be made either—

(a) in addition to any sentence which is imposed in respect of the offence of which the person is convicted; or

(b) where the offence was committed in England and Wales, notwithstanding the provisions of section 12 and 14 of the *Powers of Criminal Courts (Sentencing) Act* 2000 (cases in which absolute and conditional discharges may be made, and their effect), in addition to an order discharging him absolutely or conditionally;

(c) [Scotland]

but not otherwise.

(3) An exclusion order shall have effect for such period, not less than three months or more than two years, as is specified in the order, unless it is terminated under section 2(2) below.

Penalty for non-compliance with exclusion order

27–32   **2.**—(1) A person who enters any premises in breach of an exclusion order shall be guilty of an offence and shall be liable on summary conviction or, in Scotland, on conviction in a court of summary jurisdiction to a fine not exceeding level 4 on the standard scale or to imprisonment for a term not exceeding one month or both.

(2) The court by which a person is convicted of an offence under subsection (1) above shall consider whether or not the exclusion order should continue in force, and may, if it thinks fit, by order terminate the exclusion order or vary it by deleting the name of any specified premises, but an exclusion order shall not otherwise be affected by a person's conviction for such an offence.

Supplemental

27–33   **4.**—(1) In this Act—

"licensed premises", in relation to England and Wales, means premises in respect of which there is in force a justices' on-licence (within the meaning of section 1 of the *Licensing Act* 1964) and, in relation to Scotland, means premises in respect of which a licence under the *Licensing (Scotland) Act* 1976, other than an off-sales licence or a licence under Part III of that Act (licences for seamen's canteens), is in force; and

"licensee" in relation to any licensed premises means the holder of the licence granted in respect of those premises; and

"specified premises", in relation to an exclusion order, means any licensed premises which the court may specify by name and address in the order.

(2) In the application of section 1 above to Scotland, the reference in subsection (1) of that section to a person's being convicted of an offence shall, in relation to proceedings in a court of summary jurisdiction in which the court, without proceeding to conviction, discharges him absolutely under section 383 of the *Criminal Procedure (Scotland) Act* 1975 or makes a probation order under section 384 of that Act, shall be construed as a reference to the court's being satisfied that he committed the offence.

(3) Where a court makes an exclusion order or an order terminating or varying an exclusion order, the proper officer of the court shall send a copy of the order to the licensee of the premises to which the order relates.

(4) For the purposes of subsection (3) above—

   (a) the proper officer of a magistrates' court in England and Wales is the justices' chief executive for the court;

   (b) the proper officer of the Crown Court is the appropriate officer; and

   (c) the proper officer of a court in Scotland is the clerk of the court.

V. RECOMMENDATION FOR DEPORTATION

(1) Purpose and Effect

Subject to various limitations, a court which sentences a person aged 17 or over who **27–34** is not a British citizen may, where the offence is one that is punishable with imprisonment, recommend to the Home Secretary that the defendant be deported from the United Kingdom. This order is additional to any sentence passed and must be preceded by formal notice of the possibility of the order being made. That notice must be given at least seven days before the making of the order is considered: s.6(2).

There is a further restriction on the court that limits the exercise of the power in relation to citizens of the European Community exercising their right to free movement under the Treaty of Rome. Such citizens may only be recommended for deportation if the court considers that the continued presence of the defendant in the UK represents a "genuine and sufficiently serious threat to the requirements of public policy affecting one of the fundamental interests of society". In such a case, reasons must be given for that view: *Nazari* [1980] 1 W.L.R. 1366.

There are also exceptions provided in ss.7 and 8 protecting long standing residents and also seamen, aircrews and other special cases such as members of diplomatic missions.

The Home Secretary will consider any recommendation but is not bound to order **27–35** deportation.

Immigration Act 1971, ss.3(6), (8), 6, 7

General provisions for regulation and control

   3.—(6) Without prejudice to the operation of subsection (5) above, a person who is not a Brit- **27–36** ish citizen shall also be liable to deportation from the United Kingdom if, after he has attained the age of seventeen, he is convicted of an offence for which he is punishable with imprisonment and on his conviction is recommended for deportation by a court empowered by this Act to do so.

   (8) When any question arises under this Act whether or not a person is a British citizen, or is entitled to any exemption under this Act, it shall lie on the person asserting it to prove that he is.

Recommendations by court for deportation

27–37   **6.**—(1) Where under section 3(6) above a person convicted of an offence is liable to deportation on the recommendation of a court, he may be recommended for deportation by any court
having power to sentence him for the offence unless the court commits him to be sentenced or
further dealt with for that offence by another court...

(2) A court shall not recommend a person for deportation unless he has been given not
less than seven days notice in writing stating that a person is not liable to deportation if he
is a British citizen, describing the persons who are British citizens and stating (so far as material) the effect of section 3(8) above and section 7 below; but the powers of adjournment
conferred by section 10(3) of the *Magistrates' Courts Act* 1980, section 179 or 380 of the
Criminal Procedure (Scotland) Act 1975 or any corresponding enactment for the time being in
force in Northern Ireland shall include power to adjourn, after convicting an offender, for the
purpose of enabling a notice to be given to him under this subsection or, if a notice was so given
to him less than seven days previously, for the purpose of enabling the necessary seven days to
elapse.

(3) For purposes of section 3(6) above—

   (a) a person shall be deemed to have attained the age of seventeen at the time of his
       conviction if, on consideration of any available evidence, he appears to have done
       so to the court making or considering a recommendation for deportation; and
   (b) the question whether an offence is one for which a person is punishable with
       imprisonment shall be determined without regard to any enactment restricting
       the imprisonment of young offenders or persons who have not previously been
       sentenced to imprisonment;

and for purposes of deportation a person who on being charged with an offence is found to
have committed it shall, notwithstanding any enactment to the contrary and notwithstanding
that the court does not proceed to conviction, be regarded as a person convicted of the offence,
and references to conviction shall be construed accordingly.

(4) Notwithstanding any rule of practice restricting the matters which ought to be taken
into account in dealing with an offender who is sentenced to imprisonment, a recommendation for deportation may be made in respect of an offender who is sentenced to imprisonment for life.

(5) Where a court recommends or purports to recommend a person for deportation,
the validity of the recommendation shall not be called in question except on an appeal
against the recommendation or against the conviction on which it is made; but—

   (a) the recommendation shall be treated as a sentence for the purpose of any enact-
       ment providing an appeal against sentence
   (b) [Scotland]

(6) A deportation order shall not be made on the recommendation of a court so long as
an appeal or further appeal is pending against the recommendation or against the conviction on which it was made; and for this purpose an appeal or further appeal shall be
treated as pending (where one is competent but has not been brought) until the expiration
of the time for bringing that appeal or, in Scotland, until the expiration of twenty-eight
days from the date of the recommendation.

(7) [Scotland]

Exemption from deportation for certain existing residents

27–38   **7.**—(1) Notwithstanding anything in section 3(5) or (6) above but subject to the provisions of
this section, a Commonwealth citizen or citizen of the Republic of Ireland who was such a citizen
at the coming into force of this Act and was then ordinarily resident in the United Kingdom—

   (a) shall not be liable under section 3(5)(a) if at the time of the Secretary of State's de-
       cision he had at all times since the coming into force of this Act been ordinarily
       resident in the United Kingdom and Islands;
   (b) shall not be liable to deportation under section 3(5)(a) or (b) or 10 of the *Im-
       migration and Asylum Act* 1999 if at the time of the Secretary of State's decision he
       had for the last five years been ordinarily resident in the United Kingdom and Islands;
   (c) shall not on conviction of an offence be recommended for deportation under sec-
       tion 3(6) if at the time of the conviction he had for the last five years been
       ordinarily resident in the United Kingdom and Islands.

(2) A person who has at any time become ordinarily resident in the United Kingdom or
in any of the Islands shall not be treated for the purposes of this section as having ceased
to be so by reason only of his having remained there in breach of the immigration laws.

(3) The "last five years" before the material time under subsection (1)(b) or (c) above is to be taken as a period amounting in total to five years exclusive of any time during which the person claiming exemption under this section was undergoing imprisonment or detention by virtue of a sentence passed for an offence on a conviction in the United Kingdom and Islands, and the period for which he was imprisoned or detained by virtue of the sentence amounted to six months or more.

(4) For purposes of subsection (3) above—

(a) "sentence" includes any order made on conviction of an offence; and

(b) two or more sentences for consecutive (or partly consecutive) terms shall be treated as a single sentence; and

(c) a person shall be deemed to be detained by virtue of a sentence—

(i) at any time when he is liable to imprisonment or detention by virtue of the sentence, but is unlawfully at large; and

(ii) (unless the sentence is passed after the material time) during any period of custody by which under any relevant enactment the term to be served under the sentence is reduced.

In paragraph (c)(ii) above "relative enactment" means section 67 of the *Criminal Justice Act* 1967 [section 87 of the *Powers of Criminal Courts (Sentencing) Act* 2000] (or, before that section operated, section 17(2) of the *Criminal Justice Administration Act* 1962) and any similar enactment which is for the time being or has (before or after the passing of this Act) been in force in any part of the United Kingdom and Islands.

(5) Nothing in this section shall be taken to exclude the operation of section 3(8) above in relation to an exemption under this section.

Immigration Act 1971, s.8(2), (3), (3A)

Exceptions for seamen, aircrews and other special cases

8.—(2) The Secretary of State may by order exempt any person or class of persons, either **27–39** unconditionally or subject to such conditions as may be imposed by or under the order, from all or any of the provisions of this Act relating to those who are not British citizens.

An order under this subsection, if made with respect to a class of persons, shall be made by statutory instrument, which shall be subject to annulment in pursuance of a resolution of either House of Parliament.

(3) Subject to subsection (3A) below, the provisions of this Act relating to those who are not British citizens shall not apply to any person so long as he is a member of a mission (within the meaning of the *Diplomatic Privileges Act* 1964), a person who is a member of the family and forms part of the household of such a member, or a person otherwise entitled to the like immunity from jurisdiction as is conferred by that Act on a diplomatic agent.

(3A) For the purposes of subsection (3), a member of a mission other than a diplomatic agent (as defined by the 1964 Act) is not to count as a member of a mission unless—

(a) he was resident outside the United Kingdom, and was not in the United Kingdom, when he was offered a post as such a member; and

(b) he has not ceased to be such a member after having taken up the post.

For the definition of 'British Citizen' see the *British Nationality Act* 1981, Pt I. For **27–40** the definition of a Commonwealth Citizen see the *British Nationality Act* 1981, s.37 and Sch.3.

As regards citizens of the European Union, Art.48 of the EC Treaty and Council Directive 64/221 restrict the authority of member states to exclude nationals of other member states who are workers, spouses or dependants of workers. Exclusion may only be justified on grounds of public policy which has been held to mean 'in addition to the perturbation of the social order which any infringement of the law involves...a genuine and sufficiently serious threat to the requirements of public policy affecting one of the fundamental interests of society': *R. v Boucherau* [1978] Q.B. 732, ECJ.

In *R. v Secretary of State for the HD Ex p. Santillo* [1981] Q.B. 778, CA, the **27–41** Court held that the existence of previous criminal convictions is not of itself a basis for making a recommendation. However, if the court considers that the previous record, including the offence with which the court is directly concerned, renders it likely that the person before them will offend again, the court may take account of the previous convictions since the possibility of re-offending is a very important factor in deciding whether to recommend deportation and taking account of it is permitted by the Council Directive. The Court also held that the sentencer should give reasons if a recommendation is to be made and that the reasons should include 'some indication of the extent to which the current and previous criminal convictions of the accused have been taken into account and, in so far as this has been done, the light which in the view of the court, such conviction or convictions throw on the likely nature of the accused's personal conduct in the future.'

27–42   The most important issue in the determination of whether the requirements of Art.48 are satisfied is the defendant's likely future conduct, rather than his criminal history: *R. v Kraus* (1982) 4 Cr.App.R.(S.) 113, CA.

Where a sentencer is considering making a deportation order, he should alert the offender or his counsel, so that mitigation can be advanced in relation to the making of an order: *R. v Omojudi* (1992) 13 Cr.App.R.(S.) 346, CA. There is a formal obligation (s.6(2)) to ensure that the person concerned has received written notice setting out that a British citizen is not liable to deportation with information on who is a British citizen. This notice must be given at least seven days before making a recommendation

When a court makes a recommendation for deportation, it should give its reasons for doing so in adequate detail: *R. v Rodney* [1996] 2 Cr.App.R.(S.) 230, CA.

General guidance as to the making of deportation orders was given in *R. v Nazari* [1980] 1 W.L.R. 1366, CA, where Lawton L.J. said:

27–43   "We now indicate some guidelines which Courts should keep in mind when considering whether to make an order recommending deportation. But we stress that these are guidelines, not rigid rules. There may well be considerations which take a particular case out of the guidelines; that is a matter which will depend on the evidence.

First, the Court must consider ... whether the accused's continued presence in the United Kingdom is to its detriment. This country has no use for criminals of other nationalities, particularly if they have committed serious crimes or have long criminal records ... The more serious the crime and the longer the record the more obvious it is that there should be an order recommending deportation. On the other hand, a minor offence would not merit an order recommending deportation. In the Greater London area, for example, shoplifting is an offence which is frequently committed by visitors to this country. Normally an arrest for shoplifting followed by conviction, even if there were more than one offence being dealt with, would not merit a recommendation for deportation. But a series of shoplifting offences on different occasions may justify a recommendation for deportation. Even a first offence of shoplifting might merit a recommendation if the offender were a member of a gang carrying out a planned raid on a departmental store.

Secondly, the Courts are not concerned with the political systems which operate in other countries ... The Court has no knowledge of those matters over and above that which is common knowledge; and that may he wrong. In our judgment it would be undesirable for this Court or any other Court to express views about regimes which exist outside the United Kingdom...It is for the Home Secretary to decide in each case whether an offender's return to his country of origin would have consequences which would make his compulsory return unduly harsh.

The next ... is the effect that an order recommending deportation will have upon others who are not before the Court and who are innocent persons. This Court and all other Courts would have no wish to break up families or impose hardship on innocent people.

We wish to state clearly and firmly that all a Court does when it makes a recommendation for deportation is to indicate to the Secretary of State that in the opinion of the Court it is to the detriment of this country that the accused should remain here ... No doubt he will take into account the personal circumstances of each person whose case he is considering, and that will include the political situation in the country to which he will have to go if an order of deportation is made. These are matters solely for the Secretary of State."

27–44   In deciding whether to make an order recommending deportation, the key issue for the sentencer is whether the continued presence of the defendant in the UK would be to the detriment of the community: *R. v Cravioto* (1990) 12 Cr.App.R.(S.) 71, CA.

Where the offender has dependants who are resident in the UK, the detriment caused to them by his removal must be balanced against the potential detriment that will arise from his continued presence in the country: *Cravioto* (above).

Where a person enters the UK illegally, a recommendation for deportation may be appropriate, but the sentencer is not obliged to make a recommendation for deportation in every case involving an infringement of the Act: *R. v Akan* (1972) 56 Cr.App.R. 716, CA.

The sentencer should not consider circumstances of a personal nature which make it **27–45** difficult for the offender to return to his country of origin when considering whether to make a recommendation for deportation: *R. v Bali* [2001] 2 Cr.App.R.(S.) 104, CA.

VI. COSTS

The court has the power to compensate a party for costs incurred in relation to the **27–46** prosecution: see Ch.41.

VII. BINDING OVER

(1) Purpose and Effect

A requirement to be bound over is an order designed to prevent future misconduct. **27–47** It is an ancient power deriving statutory authority from one of the oldest statutes still in force as well as being provided for in more recent legislation. As with many crime prevention powers, it is designed to be flexible and easy to use. No formal procedure is required under the 1361 Act (though anyone who a court is proposing to be bound over must have proper opportunity to resist such an order if they wish); the 1980 Act requires a formal commencement though this can be done orally.

The order requires the person against whom it is made to enter into a recognisance to guarantee future conduct. In essence, this is a promise to pay a specified sum of money if the terms of the order are breached. It is a useful power made on over 20,000 occasions each year in magistrates' courts. Its use has come before the European Court of Human Rights, primarily because it can be used even where a person is acquitted of any offence and because of the lack of clarity in defining the conduct that will cause a court to consider whether the recognisance should be forfeited: *Steel v United Kingdom* [1998] E.H.R.R. 603. A recommendation by the Law Commission that the power be abolished (Binding Over, Law Com. No. 222 (Cm. 2439)) was not widely supported and the Home Office has consulted on ways in which the power can be used in ways that comply with obligations on fairness, certainty and proportionality (*Binding Over; A Power for the 21*[st] *Century*: HO 2002).

Pending action following that consultation, courts may be well advised to specify with **27–48** as much precision as possible the type of conduct that it requires that comes within the category of keeping the peace or being of good behaviour. If a court orders a person to enter into a recognisance and they decline to do so, then, if the order is being made under the 1361 Act, the court has no sanction and cannot require the recognisance to be entered into. If the order is being made under the 1980 Act, then the court has the power to commit to custody for up to six months in default of entering into the recognisance; however, it is likely that the exercise of this power would be held to be out of proportion to the nature of the order being made. Clearly, if a person misbehaves in a way that contravenes the criminal law they can in any case be prosecuted for that offence; a bind over is designed for lower levels of misconduct and may gradually be superseded by the Anti-Social Behaviour Order (see §§ 27–54 *et seq.* below).

Justices of the Peace Act 1361

First, that in every county of England shall be assigned for the keeping of the peace, one lord, **27–49** and with him three or four of the most worthy in the county, with some learned in the law, and they shall have power to restrain the offenders, rioters, and all other barators and to pursue, arrest, take, and chastise them according their trespass or offence; and to cause them to be imprisoned and duly punished according to the law and customs of the realm, and according to that which to them shall seem best to do by their discretions and good advisement; ... and to take of all them that they may find by indictment, or by suspicion, and put them in prison; and to take of all them that be [not] of good fame, where they shall be found, sufficient surety and mainprise of their good behaviour towards the King and his people, and the other duly to punish; to the intent that the people be not by such rioters or rebels troubled nor endamaged, nor the peace blemished, nor merchants nor other passing by the highways of the realm disturbed, nor [put in the peril which may happen] of such offenders ...

Magistrates' Courts Act 1980, s.115

Binding over to keep the peace or be of good behaviour

27–50   **115.**—(1) The power of a magistrates' court on the complaint of any person to adjudge any other person to enter into a recognizance, with or without sureties, to keep the peace or to be of good behaviour towards the complainant shall be exercised by order on complaint.

(2) Where a complaint is made under this section, the power of the court to remand the defendant under subsection (5) of section 55 above shall not be subject to the restrictions imposed by subsection (6) of that section.

(3) If any person ordered by a magistrates' court under subsection (1) above to enter into a recognizance, with or without sureties, to keep the peace or to be of good behaviour fails to comply with the order, the court may commit him to custody for a period not exceeding 6 months or until he sooner complies with the order.

27–51   The use of the power to bind over to keep the peace does not depend on conviction: it may be used against any person where a future breach of the peace is apprehended including a witness who has given evidence: *Sheldon v Broomfield JJ.* [1964] 2 Q.B. 573, DC. Previous authorities stated that it is not possible to include specific conditions in an order binding over a person to keep the peace: *R. v Randall* (1986) 8 Cr.App.R.(S.) 433, CA. However, considerable concerns have been expressed about the uncertainty contained in being bound over to keep the peace and/or be of good behaviour. If a person is to be sanctioned for conduct, then it needs to be clear what conduct will lead to the sanction being invoked. In future, therefore, a court, although limited to conditions that come within the scope of "keeping the peace" or "being of good behaviour", may need to state more precisely what that entails.

Where a court is considering binding over a person who is not the defendant in the proceedings before them, clear warning should be given and an opportunity to make representations. Where it is proposed to bind someone over in a substantial sum, it will be a breach of the rules of natural justice for a court to bind a person over without inquiring into his means or giving him an opportunity to make representations on the size of the sum: *R. v Central Criminal Court Ex p. Boulding* (1984) 79 Cr.App.R. 100, DC; *R. v Atkinson* (1988) 10 Cr.App.R.(S.) 470, CA.

27–52   A person who refuses to be bound over to keep the peace may be committed to prison by the magistrates' court: *Magistrates' Courts Act* 1980, s.115(3). A person under 21 and over 18 who refuses to be bound over by a magistrates' court may be detained under the *PCC(S)A* 2000, s.108. An offender under the age of 18 who refuses to be bound over by the magistrates' court may be ordered to attend at an attendance centre: *PCC(S)A* 2000, s.60(1)(b).

In *Steel v United Kingdom* (1999) 38 E.H.R.R. 603, the European Court of Human Rights determined that the committal to prison of two protesters who refused to be bound over to keep the peace fell within the scope of Art.5(1)(b) for non-compliance with the order of a court, and that whilst binding orders are in rather vague and general terms, they were specific enough for the purposes of Art.5(1)(b). However, use of this sanction to secure compliance with this type of order is likely to be seen as disproportionate and, in practice, the order is made with the consent, or at least acquiescence, of the subject of the order.

27–53   The court will need to be satisfied that there is a risk of future conduct which ought to be prevented. This information can come from many sources. Although the proceedings are civil in character, since the outcome of failure to comply is a criminal sanction, the standard of proof should follow the line developed in relation to an anti-social behaviour order. In *R. (McCann) v Manchester Crown Court* [2003] 1 A.C. 787, the House of Lords considered the standard of proof to be applied when the court was considering imposing an anti-social behaviour order. Given that the behaviour leading to the making of an anti-social behaviour order are likely to be similar to the circumstances leading to the application for a bind over order, it appears the standard of proof applicable to the making of each order should be the same. In *McCann* (above), the House of Lords held that the proceedings for the making of an ASBO were civil under domestic law and since the proceedings did not involve the determination of a criminal charge and could not result in the imposition of an immediate penalty on the defendant, they therefore could not be classified as criminal. However, given the seriousness of the matter involved, the court should be satisfied to the criminal standard of proof that a defendant had acted in an anti-social manner before making such an order. Given the similarity between the ASBO and binding over orders, it is submitted that the same standard of proof should apply to the making of the binding over order, and the court should be satisfied to the criminal standard of proof that the defendant's conduct will cause a breach of the peace or is likely to do so if the order is not made.

Where a person who has been bound over has been proved to have broken the terms of the recognisance, the court has power to order the person to pay the amount of the recognisance, but there is no power to order a sentence of imprisonment or otherwise for the breach itself.

VIII. ANTI-SOCIAL BEHAVIOUR ORDERS

(1) Purpose and Effect

This is an order with a potentially very wide scope that may be made to control a **27–54** wide range of behaviour that is deemed to be anti-social. An order can be made as a result of a specific application (*Crime and Disorder Act* 1998, s.1) or by a court that has convicted a defendant of an offence (*ibid.* s.1C) in which case no application is needed though the prosecutor can apply: s.1C(3). Evidence can be led by either the prosecution or the defence and is not restricted to that which would be admissible in relation to the offence itself: s.1C(3A) and (3B) as inserted by the *Anti-Social Behaviour Act* 2003. The order will be additional to the sentence passed for the offence: s.1C(4).

The order will prohibit the offender from doing anything described in the order: s.1C(2). The order will last for the period specified in the order which must be at least two years: s.1(7) as applied by s.1C(9).

A person who does not comply with the order commits an offence punishable by up **27–55** to six months imprisonment or the statutory maximum fine on summary conviction or to imprisonment for up to five years or an unlimited fine on conviction on indictment.

Crime and Disorder Act 1998, s.1C

Orders on conviction in criminal proceedings
 1C. 1C Orders on conviction in criminal proceedings   **27–56**
 (1) This section applies where a person (the 'offender') is convicted of a relevant offence.
 (2) If the court considers—
  (a) that the offender has acted, at any time since the commencement date, in an antisocial manner, that is to say in a manner that caused or was likely to cause harassment, alarm or distress to one or more persons not of the same household as himself, and
  (b) that an order under this section is necessary to protect persons in any place in England and Wales from further anti-social acts by him,
 it may make an order which prohibits the offender from doing anything described in the order.
 (3) The court may make an order under this section

(a) if the prosecutor asks it to do so, or

(b) if the court thinks it is appropriate to do so

(3A) For the purpose of deciding whether to make an order under this section the court may consider evidence led by the prosecution and the defence.

(3B) It is immaterial whether evidence led in pursuance of subsection (3A) would have been admissible in the proceedings in which the offender was convicted

(4) An order under this section shall not be made except—

(a) in addition to a sentence imposed in respect of the relevant offence; or

(b) in addition to an order discharging him conditionally.

(5) An order under this section takes effect on the day on which it is made, but the court may provide in any such order that such requirements of the order as it may specify shall, during any period when the offender is detained in legal custody, be suspended until his release from that custody.

(6) An offender subject to an order under this section may apply to the court which made it for it to be varied or discharged.

(7) In the case of an order under this section made by a magistrates' court, the reference in subsection (6) to the court by which the order was made includes a reference to any magistrates' court acting for the same petty sessions area as that court.

(8) No application may be made under subsection (6) for the discharge of an order before the end of the period of two years beginning with the day on which the order takes effect.

(9) Subsections (7), (10) and (11) of section 1 apply for the purposes of the making and effect of orders made by virtue of this section as they apply for the purposes of the making and effect of anti-social behaviour orders

(9A) The council for the local government area in which a person in respect of whom an anti-social behaviour order has been made resides or appears to reside may bring proceedings under section 1(10) (as applied by subsection (9) above) for breach of an order under subsection (2) above.

(9B) Subsection (9C) applies in relation to proceedings in which an order under subsection (2) is made against a child or young person who is convicted of an offence.

(9C) In so far as the proceedings relate to the making of the order—

(a) section 49 of the *Children and Young Persons Act* 1933 (restrictions on reports of proceedings in which children and young persons are concerned) does not apply in respect of the child or young person against whom the order is made;

(b) section 39 of that Act (power to prohibit publication of certain matter) does so apply.

(10) In this section—

"child" and "young person" have the same meaning as in the *Children and Young Persons Act* 1933;

'the commencement date' has the same meaning as in section 1 above;

'the court' in relation to an offender means—

(a) the court by or before which he is convicted of the relevant offence; or

(b) if he is committed to the Crown Court to be dealt with for that offence, the Crown Court; and

'relevant offence' means an offence committed after the coming into force of section 64 of the *Police Reform Act* 2002.]

Crime and Disorder Act 1998, s.1(7), (10)–(12)

Anti-social behaviour orders

27–57   **1.**—(7) An anti-social behaviour order shall have effect for a period (not less than two years) specified in the order or until further order.

(10) If without reasonable excuse a person does anything which he is prohibited from doing by an anti-social behaviour order, is guilty of an offence and liable—

(a) on summary conviction, to imprisonment for a term not exceeding six months or to a fine not exceeding the statutory maximum, or to both; or

(b) on conviction on indictment, to imprisonment for a term not exceeding five years or to a fine, or to both.

(10A) The following may bring proceedings for an offence under subsection (10)—

(a) a council which is a relevant authority;

(b) the council for the local government area in which a person in respect of whom an anti-social behaviour order has been made resides or appears to reside.

(10B) If proceedings for an offence under subsection (10) are brought in a youth court section 47(2) of the *Children and Young Persons Act* 1933 has effect as if the persons entitled to be present at a sitting for the purposes of those proceedings include one person authorised to be present by a relevant authority.

(11) Where a person is convicted of an offence under subsection (10) above, it shall not be open to the court by or before which he is so convicted to make an order under subsection (1)(b) (conditional discharge) of section 12 of the *Powers of Criminal Courts (Sentencing) Act* 2000 in respect of the offence.

(12) In this section—

"the commencement date" means the date of the commencement of this section;

"local government area" means—

(a) in relation to England, a district or London borough, the City of London, the Isle of Wight and the Isles of Scilly;

(b) in relation to Wales, a county or county borough.

The criteria that must be fulfilled before a court makes an order in respect of a **27–58** person convicted of an offence is that:

— the offender has acted in an anti-social manner at any time since the commencement of this provision (December 2, 2002) and

— that an order is necessary to protect other people in England and Wales from further anti-social acts from him

An "anti-social manner" is a manner that causes (or is likely to cause) harassment, **27–59** alarm or distress to one or more people who are not of the same household as the offender: s.1C(2).

Once made, an order can be varied or discharged but no application for discharge may be made until two years have elapsed: s.1C(6) and (8). If an order is made in relation to a person who is to remain in custody, then the provisions of the order may be suspended until release: s.1C(5). Although it may not be appropriate to make an order where a defendant is sentenced to a long period in custody, that is unlikely to be an issue in a magistrates' court: see *R. v P* [2004] EWCA Crim 287 below.

For consideration of the standard of proof to be applied when the court is consider- **27–60** ing making an ASBO: *R. (McCann) v Manchester Crown Court* [2003] 1 A.C. 787, HL, see § 27–53 above. More detailed consideration was given to the making of orders under this provision in *C. v Sunderland Youth Court* [2004] 1 Cr.App.R.(S.) 76 and in *R. v P, The Times*, February 19, 2004. In the *Sunderland* case, the Divisional Court was reviewing an order made in a youth court. It emphasised that courts must act fairly and take account of all relevant considerations. Whilst that will vary with each case, the basis for both the order itself and its scope must be absolutely clear and the terms of the order must be clearly and accurately explained to the defendant by the court. The written order must correctly reflect the order made by the court.

In *R. v P*, the Court of Appeal considered a range of issues arising from sentencing in the Crown Court including the making of an order under s.1C. Endorsing the comments in the *Sunderland* case, six key principles emerged:

— the test for making the order is the necessity to protect the public from further anti-social acts by the offender

— the terms of the order must be precise

— the terms of the order must be capable of being understood by the offender

— the findings of fact giving rise to the making of the order must be recorded

— the order must be explained to the offender

— the exact terms of the order must both be pronounced in open court and accurately reproduced in the written order.

The Court considered whether it could be said that an order was "necessary" where a **27–61** person had been sentenced to a substantial period in custody which would be followed by a period on licence in the community. Whilst provisions in the order (such as geographical constraints) may effectively supplement licence conditions, generally it would not be possible for a court to be satisfied that such an order was necessary when it would only become operative after a substantial period in custody — here the Crown Court had been dealing with a youth and the sentence was four years detention (reduced to three on appeal). This is less likely to be the case in a magistrates' court but may be the case in a youth court where the maximum period in custody can be 24 months.

27–62   The Court was also very concerned that parts of the order were both too vague and general and could not readily be understood by a person of the age and educational attainment of the offender. Attention was drawn to the Home Office guide "A Guide to Anti-Social Behaviour Orders and Acceptable Behaviour Courses" which, the Court considered, contains helpful instruction on the drafting of orders.

It was argued that, since part of the order prohibited conduct which was already subject to general prohibition under the *Public Order Act* 1986 and the *Prevention of Crime Act* 1953, that was redundant and should not have been included. The Court did not agree. Certainly as far as minor offences are concerned, the Court was satisfied that there is no harm in reminding offenders that certain matters do amount to criminal conduct.

CHAPTER 28

ALTERATION OF SENTENCE

Power to Rectify Sentence

If a party considers a sentence to be wrong, generally it may only seek to rectify that **28–1** by utilising the appeal procedure, an option more readily open to the defence than to the prosecution. However, there will be circumstances where it is subsequently recognised that a mistake has been made and a power has been provided to magistrates' courts which avoids the necessity for an appeal to be made.

This power exists wherever a courts considers it necessary in the interests of justice. A hearing convened to consider such a change should only take place when notice has been given to all relevant parties and the court should take steps to enable everyone with an interest to be heard before a decision is made. The change could be to replace a sentence or part of a sentence which is wrong in law (*e.g.* one year mandatory disqualification imposed where law requires a minimum of three years) or to change a sentence because of new information becoming available that makes the original sentence less just.

Magistrates' Courts Act 1980, s.142

Power of magistrates' court to re-open cases to rectify mistakes etc.

142.—(1) A magistrates' court may vary or rescind a sentence or other order imposed or **28–2** made by it when dealing with an offender if it appears to the court to be in the interests of justice to do so, and it is hereby declared that this power extends to replacing a sentence or order which for any reason appears to be invalid by another which the court has power to impose or make.

(1A) The power conferred on a magistrates' court by subsection (1) above shall not be exercisable in relation to any sentence or order imposed or made by it when dealing with an offender if—

    (a) the Crown Court has determined an appeal against—

        (i) that sentence or order;

        (ii) the conviction in respect of which that sentence or order was imposed or made; or

        (iii) any other sentence or order imposed or made by the magistrates' court when dealing with the offender in respect of that conviction (including a sentence or order replaced by that sentence or order); or

    (b) the High Court has determined a case stated for the opinion of that court on any question arising in any proceeding leading to or resulting from the imposition or making of the sentence or order.

(2) Where a person is convicted by a magistrates' court and it subsequently appears to the court that it would be in the interests of justice that the case should be heard again by different justices, the court may so direct.

(2A) The power conferred on a magistrates' court by subsection (2) above shall not be exercisable in relation to a conviction if—

    (a) the Crown Court has determined an appeal against—

        (i) the conviction; or

        (ii) any sentence or order imposed or made by the magistrates' court when dealing with the offender in respect of the conviction; or

    (b) the High Court has determined a case stated for the opinion of that court on any question arising in any proceeding leading to or resulting from the conviction.

(3) Where a court gives a direction under subsection (2) above—

    (a) the conviction and any sentence or other order imposed or made in consequence thereof shall be of no effect; and

(b) section 10(4) above shall apply as if the trial of the person in question had been adjourned.

(5) Where a sentence or order is varied under subsection (1) above, the sentence or other order, as so varied, shall take effect from the beginning of the day on which it was originally imposed or made, unless the court otherwise directs.

CHAPTER 29

ENFORCEMENT

I. POWERS OF ENFORCEMENT OTHER THAN IMPRISONMENT

The court has a variety of options when dealing with an offender who has failed to **29–1** pay a sum adjudged to be payable upon conviction:

II. POWER TO REMIT THE FINE

A court has the power to remit a fine that has been ordered. The power under s.85 **29–2** of the 1980 Act requires a change in the circumstances of the defaulter: s.85(1). For these purposes, the definition of a fine is tighter than elsewhere or in common use and care needs to be taken to ensure that the penalty is truly a "fine" for these purposes: s.85(4). The most commonly found exception is an "excise penalty", which is the equivalent of a fine for some offences mainly those arising from use of a vehicle without a vehicle excise licence.

The power under s.129 covers situations where the court has fixed the amount of a fine in the absence of information about means from the offender and, that information having subsequently been provided, the court considers that a lower fine (or no fine) would have been imposed if that had been known. In those circumstances, the court can remit some or all of the fine imposed.

Magistrates' Courts Act 1980, s.85

Power to remit fine

85.—(1) Where a fine has been imposed on conviction of an offender by a magistrates' court, **29–3** the court may at any time remit the whole or any part of the fine, but only if it thinks it just to do so having regard to a change of circumstances which has occurred—

    (a) where the court is considering whether to issue a warrant of commitment after the issue of such a warrant in respect of the fine has been postponed under subsection (2) of section 77 above, since the relevant time as defined in subsection (4) of that section; and

    (b) in any other case, since the date of the conviction.

(2) Where the court remits the whole or part of the fine after a term of imprisonment has been fixed, it shall also reduce the term by an amount which bears the same proportion to the whole term as the amount remitted bears to the whole or, as the case may be, shall remit the whole term.

(2A) Where the court remits the whole or part of the fine after an order has been made under section 35(2)(a) or (b) of the *Crime (Sentences) Act* 1997, it shall also reduce the total number of hours or days to which the order relates by a number which bears the same proportion as the amount remitted bears to the whole sum or, as the case may be, shall revoke the order.

(3) In calculating any reduction required by subsection (2) or (2A) above any fraction of a day or hour shall be left out of account.

(4) Notwithstanding the definition of "fine" in section 150(1) below, references in this section to a fine do not include any other sum adjudged to be paid on conviction, whether as a pecuniary penalty, forfeiture, compensation or otherwise.

29–4   The magistrates may not remit the whole or any part of a fine imposed by the Crown Court, without the consent of the Crown Court: *PCC(S)A*, s.140(5). Neither costs nor compensation can be remitted but, with the consent of the beneficiary of the order, can be written out of the court records.

Powers of Criminal Courts (Sentencing) Act, s.129

Remission of fines
29–5   **129.**—(1) This section applies where a court has, in fixing the amount of a fine, determined the offender's financial circumstances under section 128(5) above.

(2) If, on subsequently inquiring into the offender's financial circumstances, the court is satisfied that had it had the results of that inquiry when sentencing the offender it would—

    (a) have fixed a smaller amount, or

    (b) not have fined him,

it may remit the whole or any part of the fine.

(3) Where under this section the court remits the whole or part of a fine after a term of imprisonment has been fixed under section 139 below (powers of Crown Court in relation to fines) or section 82(5) of the *Magistrates' Courts Act* 1980 (magistrates' powers in relation to default), it shall reduce the term by the corresponding proportion.

(4) In calculating any reduction required by subsection (3) above, any fraction of a day shall be ignored.

III. IMPRISONMENT IN DEFAULT OF PAYMENT

29–6   The power to commit to prison in default of payment of a fine is hedged around by many safeguards—it is the final step to be used only where every other option has been shown to be inappropriate or unsuccessful. This section is not an exhaustive study of this complex area but is designed to assist the busy practitioner in identifying the key points in the enforcement process. It is subject to rapid change as provisions to improve enforcement in the *Courts Act* 2003 and the *Criminal Justice Act* 2003 are introduced, sometimes after being piloted in a limited number of areas.

The conditions in which the court may order imprisonment in default of payment are set out in s.82 of the 1980 Act. A court may impose imprisonment as an alternative to payment on the day of conviction only if the offender has the means to pay immediately or is unlikely to remain at a place of abode in the Untied Kingdom for long enough for the fine to be enforced by other means. The minimum period for committal to prison is five days at the point of imposition (though this can be reduced by part payment) and the maximum is on a sliding scale depending on the amount owed. However, shorter periods can be imposed that are not *imprisonment* but have the same effect—see ss.135 and 136 below.

If commitment was not ordered at the point of sentence, it can only subsequently be ordered if the defaulter is already in custody serving a sentence or following a means inquiry: s.82(3). If the offence was punishable by imprisonment and the offender appears to the court to have the resources to pay straightaway, then the court can commit the person to prison in default of payment. Otherwise, commitment can only follow a decision that the default is due to the offender's wilful refusal or culpable neglect **and** that the court has considered or tried every other means of securing payment and each is inappropriate or unsuccessful: s.82(4). Generally the alternatives include allowing payment by instalments, issuing a distress warrant to seize the goods of the defaulter, making a money payment supervision order to assist the offender to manage their financial affairs in a way that allows the fine to be paid and either an attachment of earnings order or deduction from a qualifying state benefit. Additional initiatives are being taken to provide viable alternatives which increase the likelihood of a fine being paid.

When a means inquiry is conducted, the offender should be examined in detail on **29-7** income, capital or savings, expenditure, circumstances of original failure to pay sums as they come due, failure to pay in accordance with any terms subsequently set by the court, likelihood of paying in the future: *R. v Newport Pagnell Justices Ex p. Smith* (1988) 152 J.P. 475.

Wilful refusal or culpable neglect pursuant to s.82(3) must be demonstrated to the criminal standard of proof: *R. v South Tyneside Justices Ex. p. Martin, The Independent*, September 20, 1995. The terms 'wilful refusal' and 'culpable neglect' denote deliberate defiance or reckless disregard of a court order: *R. v Luton Magistrates' Court Ex p. Sullivan* [1992] 2 F.L.R. 196. The defaulter should be given proper opportunity to put his case, and all relevant factors must have been taken into account before the court concludes that the default is due to 'wilful failure' or 'culpable neglect': *R. v York Magistrates' Court Ex p. Grimes* (1997) 161 J.P. 550. The court has an absolute duty to consider all other means of dealing with the defaulter: *R. v Exeter City Magistrates' Court Ex p. Sugar* (1993) 157 J.P. 766. These other methods are listed in s.82(4A) of the 1980 Act, see below.

The implications of Art.8 of the European Convention on Human Rights must be considered when making a decision as to whether to order imprisonment in default of payment; it appears committal will not be an appropriate response where the case involves a single mother with a large number of children with a very limited income, doing her level best to balance one monetary obligation against another. Whilst there might be a case in which the pursuit of the aim to make a mother comply with her legal obligations overrode the rights of her children to have the benefit of her care at home, committal must be a remedy of final resort if all else has failed: *R. (on the application of Stokes) v Gwent Magistrates' Court* (2001) 165 J.P. 766, *per* Brooke L.J. If the defaulter is employed, the fact that his earnings fluctuate from week to week does not preclude the making of an attachment of earnings order: *R. v Stockport Justices Ex p. Conlon* [1997] 2 All E.R. 204.

Where the offender is already serving a sentence of custody for life, or a term of **29-8** imprisonment or detention under s.108 of the *PCC(S)A* 2000 or detention in a young offenders' institution, the magistrates court may order imprisonment, or detention in the case of offenders aged 18–20, under s.82(3) of the *MCA* 1980. This is often a convenient way of ensuring that a person released from custody is able to start again without debts to the court.

However, some care will need to be taken before proceeding too readily to wiping out debts to the court. In *R. v Clacton Justices Ex p. Commissioners of Customs and Excise* (1988) 152 J.P. 129, DC it was held that in exercising their discretion whether to issue a warrant of commitment or a warrant of distress to enforce payment of a fine, it was essential for the justices to consider the defaulter's means and to ascertain whether the prosecution held any assets belonging to him. The defendant cannot be allowed to choose between payment of his fine and imprisonment. In the instant case, the Customs and Excise Commissioners held, unknown to the magistrates, a substantial sum of money belonging to the defaulter. Bingham L.J. stated that had the magistrates known this, it was difficult to suppose that they would have concluded otherwise than that a warrant of distress would, if necessary, lie.

In *R. v Grimsby and Cleethorpes Justices Ex p. Walters* [1997] 1 W.L.R. 89, it was held that that where an offender had just been sentenced to imprisonment for substantive offences, he was then "already serving a term of imprisonment" within the terms of the *Magistrates' Courts Act* 1980, s.82(3)(a), and it was open to justices to sentence him in the same judgment to a consecutive term for failure to pay fines and a compensation order. Any sentence will take effect immediately after it is pronounced.

Magistrates' Courts Act 1980, s.82(2)–(6)

29–9   **82.**—(2) A magistrates' court shall not in advance of the issue of a warrant of commitment fix a term of imprisonment which is to be served by an offender in the event of a default in paying a sum adjudged to be paid by a conviction, except where it has power to issue a warrant of commitment forthwith, but postpones issuing the warrant under section 77(2) above.

(3) Where on the occasion of the offender's conviction a magistrates' court does not issue a warrant of commitment for a default in paying any such sum as aforesaid or fix a term of imprisonment under the said section 77(2) which is to be served by him in the event of any such default, it shall not thereafter issue a warrant of commitment for any such default or for want of sufficient distress to satisfy such a sum unless—

    (a) he is already serving a sentence of custody for life, or a term of imprisonment, youth custody, detention under section 9 of the *Criminal Justice Act* 1982 or detention in a detention centre; or

    (b) the court has since the conviction inquired into his means in his presence on at least one occasion.

29–10   (4) Where a magistrates' court is required by subsection (3) above to inquire into a person's means, the court may not on the occasion of the inquiry or at any time thereafter issue a warrant of commitment for a default in paying any such sum unless—

    (a) in the case of an offence punishable with imprisonment, the offender appears to the court to have sufficient means to pay the sum forthwith; or

    (b) the court—

        (i) is satisfied that the default is due to the offender's wilful refusal or culpable neglect; and

        (ii) has considered or tried all other methods of enforcing payment of the sum and it appears to the court that they are inappropriate or unsuccessful.

(4A) The methods of enforcing payment mentioned in subsection (4)(b)(ii) above are—

    (a) a warrant of distress under section 76 above;

    (b) an application to the High Court or county court for enforcement under section 87 below;

    (c) an order under section 88 below;

    (d) an attachment of earnings order; and

    (e) if the offender is under the age of 25, an order under section 17 of the *Criminal Justice Act* 1982 (attendance centre orders).

(5) After the occasion of an offender's conviction by a magistrates' court, the court shall not, unless—

    (a) the court has previously fixed a term of imprisonment under section 77(2) above which is to be served by the offender in the event of a default in paying a sum adjudged to be paid by the conviction; or

    (b) the offender is serving a sentence of custody for life, or a term of imprisonment, youth custody, detention under section 9 of the *Criminal Justice Act* 1982 or detention in a detention centre,

issue a warrant of commitment for a default in paying the sum or fix such a term except at a hearing at which the offender is present.

(5A) A magistrates' court may not issue a warrant of commitment under subsection (5) above at a hearing at which the offender is not present unless the justices' chief executive for the court has first served on the offender a notice in writing stating that the court intends to hold a hearing to consider whether to issue such a warrant and giving the reason why the court so intends.

(5B) Where after the occasion of an offender's conviction by a magistrates' court the court holds a hearing for the purpose of considering whether to issue a warrant of commitment for default in paying a sum adjudged to be paid by the conviction, it shall consider such information about the offender's means as is available to it unless it has previously—

    (a) inquired into the offender's means; and

    (b) postponed the issue of the warrant of commitment under section 77(2) above.

(5C) A notice under subsection (5A) above—

    (a) shall state the time and place appointed for the hearing; and

    (b) shall inform the offender that, if he considers that there are grounds why the warrant should not be issued, he may make representations to the court in person or in writing, but the court may exercise its powers in relation to the issue of a warrant whether or not he makes representations.

(5D) Except as mentioned in subsection (5E) below, the time stated in a notice under **29–11** subsection (5A) above shall not be earlier than 21 days after the issue of the notice.

(5E) Where a magistrates' court exercises in relation to an offender the power conferred by section 77(2) above and at the same hearing issues a notice under subsection (5A) above in relation to him, the time stated in the notice may be a time on any day following the end of the period for which the issue of the warrant of commitment has been postponed.

(5F) A notice under subsection (5A) above to be served on any person shall be deemed to be served on that person if it is sent by registered post or the recorded delivery service addressed to him at his last known address, notwithstanding that the notice is returned as undelivered or is for any other reason not received by that person.

(6) Where a magistrates' court issues a warrant of commitment on the ground that one of the conditions mentioned in subsection (1) or (4) above is satisfied, it shall state that fact, specifying the ground, in the warrant.

IV. POWER TO MAKE A MONEY PAYMENTS SUPERVISION ORDER

Magistrates' Courts Act 1980, s.88

Supervision pending payment.

88.—(1) Where any person is adjudged to pay a sum by a summary conviction and the **29–12** convicting court does not commit him to prison forthwith in default of payment, the court may, either on the occasion of the conviction or on a subsequent occasion, order him to be placed under the supervision of such person as the court may from time to time appoint.

(2) An order placing a person under supervision in respect of any sum shall remain in force so long as he remains liable to pay the sum or any part of it unless the order ceases to have effect or is discharged under subsection (3) below.

(3) An order under this section shall cease to have effect on the making of a transfer of fine order under section 89 below with respect to the sum adjudged to be paid and may be discharged by the court that made it, without prejudice in either case to the making of a new order.

(4) Where a person under 21 years old has been adjudged to pay a sum by a summary **29–13** conviction and the convicting court does not commit him to detention under section 108 of the *Powers of Criminal Courts (Sentencing) Act* 2000 forthwith in default of payment, the court shall not commit him to such detention in default of payment of the sum, or for want of sufficient distress to satisfy the sum, unless he has been placed under supervision in respect of the sum or the court is satisfied that it is undesirable or impracticable to place him under supervision.

(5) Where a court, being satisfied as aforesaid, commits a person under 21 years old to such detention without an order under this section having been made, the court shall state the grounds on which it is so satisfied in the warrant of commitment.

(6) Where an order placing a person under supervision with respect to a sum is in force, a magistrates' court shall not commit him to prison in default of payment of the sum, or for want of sufficient distress to satisfy the sum, unless the court has before committing him taken such steps as may be reasonably practicable to obtain from the person appointed for his supervision an oral or written report on the offender's conduct and means and has considered any report so obtained, in addition, in a case where an inquiry is required by section 82 above, to that inquiry.

V. POWER TO ORDER A DISTRESS WARRANT

Magistrates' Courts Act 1980, ss.76–78

Enforcement of sums adjudged to be paid

76.—(1) Subject to the following provisions of this Part of this Act, and to section 132 below, **29–14** where default is made in paying a sum adjudged to be paid by a conviction or order of a magistrates' court, the court may issue a warrant of distress for the purposes of levying the sum or issue a warrant committing the defaulter to prison.

(2) A warrant of commitment may be issued as aforesaid either—

(a) where it appears on the return to a warrant of distress that the money and goods of the defaulter are insufficient to satisfy the sum with the costs and charges of levying the sum; or

(b) instead of a warrant of distress.

(3) The period for which a person may be committed to prison under such a warrant as aforesaid shall not, subject to the provisions of any enactment passed after 31st December 1879, exceed the period applicable to the case under Schedule 4 to this Act.

(4) Where proceedings are brought for the enforcement of a magistrates' court maintenance order under this section, the court may vary the order by exercising one of its powers under paragraphs (a) to (d) of section 59(3) above.

(5) Subsections (4), (5) and (7) of section 59 above shall apply for the purposes of subsection (4) above as they apply for the purposes of that section.

(6) Subsections (4) and (5) above shall not have effect in relation to a maintenance order which is not a qualifying maintenance order (within the meaning of section 59 above).

Postponement of issue of warrant

29–15   **77.**—(1) Where a magistrates' court has power to issue a warrant of distress under this Part of this Act, it may, if it thinks it expedient to do so, postpone the issue of the warrant until such time and on such conditions, if any, as the court thinks just.

(2) Where a magistrates' court has power to issue a warrant of commitment under this Part of this Act, it may, if it thinks it expedient to do so, fix a term of imprisonment or detention under section 108 of the *Powers of Criminal Courts (Sentencing) Act* 2000 (detention of persons aged 18 to 20 for default) and postpone the issue of the warrant until such time and on such conditions, if any, as the court thinks just.

(3) A magistrates' court shall have power at any time to do either or both of the following—

(a) to direct that the issue of the warrant of commitment shall be postponed until a time different from that to which it was previously postponed;

(b) to vary any of the conditions on which its issue is postponed,

but only if it thinks it just to do so having regard to a change of circumstances since the relevant time.

(4) In this section "the relevant time" means—

(a) where neither of the powers conferred by subsection (3) above has been exercised previously, the date when the issue of the warrant was postponed under subsection (2) above; and

(b) in any other case, the date of the exercise or latest exercise of either or both of the powers.

29–16   (5) Without prejudice to the generality of subsection (3) above, if on an application by a person in respect of whom issue of a warrant has been postponed it appears to a justice of the peace acting for the petty sessions area in which the warrant has been or would have been issued that since the relevant time there has been a change of circumstances which would make it just for the court to exercise one or other or both of the powers conferred by that subsection, he shall refer the application to the court.

(6) Where such an application is referred to the court—

(a) the clerk of the court shall fix a time and place for the application to be heard; and

(b) the justices' chief executive for the court shall give the applicant notice of that time and place.

(7) Where such a notice has been given but the applicant does not appear at the time and place specified in the notice, the court may proceed with the consideration of the application in his absence.

(8) If a warrant of commitment in respect of the sum adjudged to be paid has been issued before the hearing of the application, the court shall have power to order that the warrant shall cease to have effect and, if the applicant has been arrested in pursuance of it, to order that he shall be released, but it shall only make an order under this subsection if it is satisfied that the change of circumstances on which the applicant relies was not put before the court when it was determining whether to issue the warrant.

Defect in distress warrant and irregularity in its execution

29–17   **78.**—(1) A warrant of distress issued for the purpose of levying a sum adjudged to be paid by the conviction or order of a magistrates' court shall not, if it states that the sum has been so adjudged to be paid, be held void by reason of any defect in the warrant.

(2) A person acting under a warrant of distress shall not be deemed to be a trespasser from the beginning by reason only of any irregularity in the execution of the warrant.

(3) Nothing in this section shall prejudice the claim of any person for special damages in respect of any loss caused by a defect in the warrant or irregularity in its execution.

(4) If any person removes any goods marked in accordance with the rules as articles impounded in the execution of a warrant of distress, or defaces or removes any such mark, he shall be liable on summary conviction to a fine not exceeding level 1 on the standard scale.

(5) If any person charged with the execution of a warrant of distress wilfully retains from the proceeds of a sale of the goods on which distress is levied, or otherwise exacts, any greater costs and charges than those properly payable, or makes any improper charge, he shall be liable on summary conviction to a fine not exceeding level 1 on the standard scale.

VI. POWER TO MAKE AN ATTENDANCE CENTRE ORDER

The court may order an attendance centre order where a centre is available to the **29–18** court and the offender is under 21 years of age: *PCC(S)A* 2000, s.60.

VII. POWER TO MAKE A COMMUNITY SERVICE ORDER

Where the court has power to issue a warrant of commitment, it may instead make a **29–19** community service order, provided that the Secretary of State has notified the court that measures for the implementation of the order are in place: *Crime (Sentences) Act* 1997, s.35.

VIII. POWER TO MAKE A CURFEW ORDER

Where the court has power to issue a warrant of commitment it may instead make a **29–20** curfew order provided that the Secretary of State has notified the court that measures for the implementation of the order are in place: *Crime (Sentences) Act* 1997, s.35.

IX. POWER TO ORDER DETENTION

A widely used power (both as a sentence in its own right and as an order in respect of **29–21** unpaid fines) is the power to order detention within the precincts of the court (or at any police station) for a specified period not later than 8 p.m. on the day on which the order is made. This is not a period of imprisonment and so does not have to meet the criteria for a custodial sentence or for imprisonment in default of a fine. However, it is a sentence for an offence and, where used in response to default on payment of a fine, it removes liability to pay the fine. It can be used either after time has been allowed for payment of the fine or where immediate payment is required.

Magistrates' Courts Act 1980, s.135

Detention of offender for one day in court-house or police station

    135.—(1) A magistrates' court that has power to commit to prison a person convicted of an **29–22** offence, or would have that power but for section 82 or 88 above, may order him to be detained within the precincts of the court-house or at any police station until such hour, not later than 8 o'clock in the evening of the day on which the order is made, as the court may direct, and, if it does so, shall not, where it has power to commit him to prison, exercise that power.

    (2) A court shall not make such an order under this section as will deprive the offender of a reasonable opportunity of returning to his abode on the day of the order.

    (3) This section shall have effect in relation to a person aged 18 or over but less than 21 as if references in it to prison were references to detention under of the *Powers of Criminal*

Courts (Sentencing) Act 2000 (detention of persons aged 17 to 20 for default).

X. POWER TO ORDER DETENTION OVERNIGHT

29–23   This power enables a defendant aged 18 or over to discharge responsibility for payment of a fine by serving a night in custody. As it is not imprisonment (since it is "detention"), the court does not have to be satisfied of all that it must if ordering imprisonment in default. The effect of the warrant (which can be issued in the absence of the defaulter) is to require the defaulter to be arrested and detained in a police station until the 8 a.m. that follows arrest. However, the police may release the defaulter between 4 a.m. and 8 a.m. in the circumstances set out in s.136(3).

Magistrates' Courts Act 1980, s.136

Committal to custody overnight at police station for non-payment of sum adjudged by conviction

29–24   **136.**—(1) A magistrates' court that has power to commit to prison a person in default of payment of a sum adjudged to be paid by a summary conviction, or would have that power but for section 82 or 88 above, may issue a warrant for his detention in a police station, and, if it does so, shall not, where it has power to commit him to prison, exercise that power.

(2) A warrant under this section—

(a) shall authorise the person executing it,

to arrest the defaulter and take him to a police station, and

(b) shall require the officer in charge of the station to detain him there until 8 o'clock in the morning of the day following that on which he is arrested, or, if he is arrested between midnight and 8 o'clock in the morning, until 8 o'clock in the morning of the day on which he is arrested.

(3) Notwithstanding subsection (2)(b) above, the officer may release the defaulter at any time within 4 hours before 8 o'clock in the morning if the officer thinks it expedient to do so in order to enable him to go to his work or for any other reason appearing to the officer to be sufficient.

(4) This section shall have effect in relation to a person aged 18 or over but less than 21 as if references in it to prison were references to detention under section 108 of the *Powers of Criminal Courts (Sentencing) Act* 2000 (detention of persons aged 18 to 20 for default).

XI. ENFORCEMENT OF COMMUNITY ORDERS

29–25   Section 33(1) of the *PCC(S)A* 2000 provides that a 'community order' means a curfew order, a community rehabilitation order, a community punishment order, a community punishment and rehabilitation order, a drug treatment and testing order, a drug abstinence order, an attendance centre order, a supervision order or an action plan order.

Schedule 3, Pts I–III to the 2000 Act govern the enforcement of community orders. Sch.3, para.1 provides that the enforcement provisions contained in Sch.3 apply when there has been a failure to comply with any one of the requirements of a 'relevant order'; these orders being a curfew order, a probation order, a community service order, a combination order, a drug treatment and testing order. Enforcement of attendance centre orders is dealt with by Sch.5 to the *PCC(S)A* 2000, and enforcement of supervision orders is dealt with by Sch.7 to the *PCC(S)A* 2000.

29–26   Decisions on enforcement of a community sentence are often complex and finely balanced. On the one hand, there is the need to reinforce the authority of the court which made the order and of the supervisor in the knowledge that the prospect of a more severe sentence can be a major incentive assisting the offender to comply with the order. On the other hand, there is a desire to see the order properly completed and the realisation of the benefits that it brings particularly where the life style of the offender makes it more difficult to adjust to the self discipline required to complete an order.

29–27   Where an order has been breached, the options available to the magistrates' court are:

(a) imposition of a fine not exceeding £1,000

(b) making a community punishment order for not more than 60 hours in the aggregate (where the community order was a community punishment order the new order must not exceed 240 hours together with that order, or in the case of the community punishment element of the combination order not exceeding 100 hours together with that), and in accordance with the normal provisions for those orders, this order being enforceable for a failure to comply with the requirements of the relevant order in respect of which the community punishment order was made.

(c) Where the relevant order is a curfew order and the offender is aged under 16, or the relevant order is a probation order or combination order and the offender is aged under 21, the court may make an attendance centre order in respect of him, the provisions which apply to the making of such orders being applicable

(d) where the relevant order was made by a magistrates' court, it may deal with him for the offence in respect of which the order was made, in any way in which it could deal with him if he had just been convicted by the court of the offence.

(e) Where the elevant order was made by the Crown Court and the magistrates could deal with the offender by the imposition of a fine, the making of a community service order or the making of an attendance centre order, the magistrates may instead commit him in custody or on bail to the Crown Court together with a certificate that the offender has failed to comply with the requirements of the relevant order and such other particulars of the case as may be desirable.

29–28 The court will need to be satisfied that the offender has failed to comply with the order without reasonable excuse. It is for the supervisor to prove the failure to comply and for the offender to show the reasonable excuse.

Where an order is not complied with, a supervising probation officer will be guided by National Standards as to the action to be taken.

The *Magistrates' Courts Sentencing Guidelines* (2003), at p.91, refer to the National Standards published by the Probation Service for guidance on the powers of supervisors in the event of breach of a community order, as well as to the inter–agency publication Towards Good Practice—Community Sentences and the Courts.

The National Standards (at para.D21) state that any failure to attend an appointment or any other failure to comply with any other requirement of an order or licence should be deemed unacceptable unless the offender provides an acceptable explanation.

29–29 The supervising officer shall:

— where no explanation is provided within two working days of the apparent failure, send a letter to the offender warning him that if no acceptable explanation is received within a further five working days of the date of the letter (or at the next scheduled appointment where appointments are weekly) the failure will be deemed unacceptable and any further failure could lead to breach action (examples of letters are provided);

— if the offender provides an acceptable explanation within the above timescale, rescind the warning and ensure that the fact that the warning has been withdrawn is properly recorded on the offender's file. If the explanation is unacceptable a further letter should be sent drawing the attention of the offender to the warning already issued (an example letter is provided);

— fully record every apparent failure within seven working days of the failure, including whether or not any explanation was given by the offender, and if so what that explanation was and whether or not it was acceptable;

— if the explanation is not considered acceptable or no explanation is given within seven working days of the failure, record the incident as an unacceptable failure to comply;

— place copies of any written warning on the offender's case records along with a note of the offender's comment on the warning;

— where breach proceedings are required, instigate these proceedings within 10 working days of the relevant failure to comply;
— normally offer offenders further appointments or community punishment work pending breach unless it is clear that the offender is completely uncooperative or disruptive, or that for other similar reasons offering further appointments or work would serve no useful purpose and such a decision has been recorded and endorsed by the designated line manager.

29–30 Breach action may be taken following one unacceptable failure, where appropriate. As regards warning proceedings, for offenders on community sentences the supervising officer shall give only one warning in any 12-month period of supervision before commencing breach action. In the case of community punishment and rehabilitation orders, any unacceptable failures between the two elements of the order must be aggregated and breach action must be taken on or before the second unacceptable failure on either part of the order in a 12-month period (para.D22–24).

It is important that arrangements are made by the court to deal quickly with allegations of failure to comply. This is most likely to require the allocation of an early hearing date for the first hearing and pressure on the parties to resolve outstanding issues quickly.

If the failure to comply with an order is admitted or proved, the options available to a court fall into one of two groups—allowing the order to continue (possibly with varied terms) or revoking the order and sentencing the offender again for the original offence. In each case, the court must first be satisfied that the offender has failed without reasonable excuse to comply with any of the requirements of the order: Sch.3, para.4. The supervising officer (usually an officer of the local probation board) will be responsible for instigating and prosecuting proceedings up to the point where the decision is made to revoke the order. Once the order is revoked and the court intends to deal with the original offence, the original prosecutor (usually the Crown Prosecution Service) will again be responsible for presenting the requisite information to the court, see s.3 of the *Prosecution of Offences Act* 1985. Again, this requires efficient arrangements to be in place to minimise delay whilst not making unnecessary demands on the original prosecutor.

Allowing the order to continue

29–31 The court will be looking to see if there is a reasonable prospect of the order being completed satisfactorily. This will not only require the attendance of the offender as directed under the order but will also require a willingness to participate actively in the obligations placed on the offender by the order.

If the court is prepared to allow that order to continue, it may do one only of the following:

— impose a fine of up to £1000
— make a community punishment order for up to 60 hours (whether or not the original offence was punishable by imprisonment—see Sch.3, para.7(1)
— if the order is a community rehabilitation order/combination order and the offender is under 21, make an attendance centre order.

Bringing the order to an end

29–32 If the order was made by a magistrates' court, the court may sentence the offender again for the original offence. It must then revoke the order (Sch.3, para.4(3)). In practice, many courts will revoke the order after considering the breach and then adjourn the proceedings for re-sentencing. This gives a clear indication of what the court is considering, enables the preparation of a further pre-sentence report if appropriate and also ensures that the prosecution papers for the original offence are available. However, a better arrangement is where the court can proceed to sentence on the same day as when the order is revoked, often utilising the pre-sentence report prepared for the time when sentence was originally passed which will be supplemented by the information relevant to the breach proceedings.

Where the original offence was imprisonable, a custodial sentence may be imposed. **29–33** Where the offender has wilfully and persistently failed to comply with the requirements of the order, a custodial sentence may be imposed for the original offence even though that offence does not pass the threshold criterion for a custodial sentence i.e is not so serious that only a custodial sentence can be justified or, where the offence was a violent or sexual offence, that only a custodial sentence would be adequate to protect the public from serious harm from him: Sch.3, para.4(2)(b) and s.79(2).

In deciding on the sentence to be imposed, the court must take account of how much of the order has been completed: Sch.3, para.4(2)(a).The court should therefore allow an appropriate discount if there has been part-performance of the original order, but non-compliance with the original order should not be treated as an aggravating factor as regards the original offence for which the offender stands to be re-sentenced: *R. v Clarke* [1997] 2 Cr.App.R.(S.) 163, CA.

Magistrates may not commit an offender originally sentenced in the magistrates' court for an either way offence to the Crown Court to be sentenced in respect of the breach of the community order: *R. v Jordan* [1998] Crim.L.R. 353.

If the offender has committed a further offence during the currency of the com- **29–34** munity order, this does not render him liable to be brought before the court for failure to comply with the terms of the relevant order. An application may be made for revocation of the order, and the offender may be re-sentenced for the original offence: *R. v Kenny* [1996] 1 Cr.App.R.(S.) 397, CA.

However, Sch.3, para.11 to the 2000 Act provides that a magistrates' court may only revoke and re-sentence in respect of orders made in a magistrates' court. If the original order was made in the Crown Court, an application for revocation shall be made directly to the Crown Court.

A magistrates' court may also revoke the original order if it appears that due to circumstances arising following the imposition of the order, it would be appropriate to revoke the order or deal with the offender in an alternative way, for example a drug treatment and testing order may be revoked to take account of the offender's good progress or satisfactory response.

Where a custodial sentence is passed following revocation, the court should take ac- **29–35** count of time spent in custody on remand before the imposition of the community order: *R. v Henderson* [1997] 2 Cr.App.R.(S.) 266, CA. Where the community order is revoked due to ill-health or inability to perform the work required, it is inappropriate to impose an immediate custodial sentence or a suspended sentence of imprisonment in its place: *R. v Jackson* [2000] 1 Cr.App.R.(S.) 405. In *R. v Hammond* [1998] 2 Cr.App.R.(S.) 202, CA it was established that where the offender had failed to disclose his condition to the court when the order was made, the fact that he was unable to carry out the community service order could not be used to persuade the court not to impose a custodial sentence in its place.

There is a right of appeal to the Crown Court against a sentence passed in this way: Sch.4(6) .

Unacceptable and violent behaviour exhibited towards a Community Service Officer can amount to a failure, without reasonable excuse, to comply with any of the requirements of the relevant order: *Caton v Community Service Office* (1995) 159 J.P. 444.

Powers of Criminal Courts (Sentencing) Act 2000, Sch.3, paras 1–2A, 4, 6, 6A, 7–10, 12, 13, 15

SCHEDULE 3

Breach, Revocation and Amendment of certain Community Orders

Part I

Preliminary

Definitions

29–36   1.—(1) In this Schedule "relevant order" means any of the following orders—
   (a)   a curfew order;
   (aa) an exclusion order;
   (b)   a community rehabilitation order;
   (c)   a community punishment order;
   (d)   a community punishment and rehabilitation order;
   (e)   a drug treatment and testing order.
   (f)   a drug abstinence order.

[(1A) The orders mentioned in paragraphs (a) to (d) and (f) of sub-paragraph (1) above and, I an order made by the Secretary of State so provides, any other order mentioned in that sub-paragraph are referred to in this Schedule as orders to which the warning provisions apply.]

   (2) In this Schedule "the petty sessions area concerned" means—
   (a)   in relation to a curfew order, the petty sessions area in which the place for the time being specified in the order is situated; and
   (b)   in relation to an exclusion, community rehabilitation, community punishment, community punishment and rehabilitation, drug treatment and testing or drug abstinence order, the petty sessions area for the time being specified in the order.

   (3) In this Schedule, references to the court responsible for a drug treatment and testing order or drug abstinence order shall be construed in accordance with section 54(7) of this Act(or that subsection as applied by section 58B(2) of this Act).

   (4) In this Schedule—
   (a)   references to the probation element of a community punishment and rehabilitation order are references to the order in so far as it imposes such a requirement as is mentioned in section 51(1)(a) of this Act (and in so far as it imposes any additional requirements included in the order by virtue of section 42); and
   (b)   references to the community service element of such an order are references to the order in so far as it imposes such a requirement as is mentioned in section 51(1)(b).

Orders made on appeal

29–37   2.—(1) Where a curfew, exclusion, community rehabilitation, community punishment, community punishment and rehabilitation or drug abstinence order has been made on appeal, for the purposes of this Schedule it shall be deemed—
   (a)   if it was made on an appeal brought from a magistrates' court, to have been made by a magistrates' court;
   (b)   if it was made on an appeal brought from the Crown Court or from the criminal division of the Court of Appeal, to have been made by the Crown Court.

   (2) Where a drug treatment and testing order has been made on an appeal brought from the Crown Court or from the criminal division of the Court of Appeal, for the purposes of this Schedule it shall be deemed to have been made by the Crown Court.

Part II

Breach of Requirement of Order

Functions of responsible officer

29–38   2A.—(1) Sub-paragraphs (2) and (3) below apply if the responsible officer is of the

1008

opinion that a person aged 18 or over ("the offender") has failed without reasonable excuse to comply with any of the requirements of an order to which the warning provisions apply other than a requirement to abstain from misusing specified Class A drugs.

(2) The officer shall give him a warning under this paragraph if—

(a) the offender has not within the specified period been given a warning under this paragraph in respect of a failure to comply with any of the requirements of the order; and

(b) the officer does not cause an information to be laid before a justice of the peace in respect of the failure in question.

(3) If the offender has within the specified period been given such a warning, the officer shall cause an information to be laid before a justice of the peace in respect of the failure in question.

(4) In sub-paragraphs (2) and (3) above, "specified period" means—

(a) in the case of a curfew order, the period of six months;

(b) in any other case, the period of twelve months; ending with the failure in question.

(5) A warning under this paragraph must—

(a) describe the circumstances of the failure;

(b) state that the failure is unacceptable;

(c) inform the offender that if within the next six or (as the case may be) twelve months he again fails to comply with any requirement of the order, he will be liable to be brought before a court;

and the officer shall, as soon as is practicable after the warning has been given, record that fact.

(6) If a community sentence consists of or includes two or more orders to which the **29–39** warning provisions apply, being orders in respect of the same offence—

(a) the preceding provisions of this paragraph shall have effect as if those orders were a single order to which the warning provisions apply; and

(b) where one of those orders is a curfew order that fact shall be disregarded for the purposes of sub-paragraph (4) above.]

Powers of magistrates' court

4.—(1) If it is proved to the satisfaction of a magistrates' court before which an offender **29–40** appears or is brought under paragraph 3 above that he has failed without reasonable excuse to comply with any of the requirements of the relevant order, the court may deal with him in respect of the failure in any one of the following ways—

(a) it may impose on him a fine not exceeding £1,000;

(b) where the offender is aged 16 or over it may, subject to paragraph 7 below, make a community service order in respect of him;

(c) where—

(i) the relevant order is a curfew order and the offender is aged under 16, or

(ii) the relevant order is a probation order or combination order and the offender is aged under 21,

it may, subject to paragraph 8 below, make an attendance centre order in respect of him; or

(d) where the relevant order was made by a magistrates' court, it may deal with him, for the offence in respect of which the order was made, in any way in which it could deal with him if he had just been convicted by the court of the offence.

[(1) This paragraph applies if it is proved to the satisfaction of a magistrates' court before which an offender appears or is brought under paragraph 3 above that he has failed without reasonable excuse to comply with any of the requirements of the relevant order (1A).

In a case where the offender is aged 18 or over and the order is one to which the warning provisions apply, the magistrates' court shall impose a sentence of imprisonment for the offence in respect of which the order was made unless it is of the opinion—

that the offender is likely to comply with the requirements of the order during that period for which it remains in force; or

that the exceptional circumstances of the case justify not imposing a sentence of imprisonment.

29–41   (1B) The sentence of imprisonment—

where the offence was an offence punishable by imprisonment, shall be for the term which, if—

         (i)   he had just been convicted of the offence by the court, and

         (ii)   section 79(2) of this Act did not apply,

         the court would impose on him for that offence and

         in any other case, shall be for a term not exceeding three months;

         taking account of the extent to which he has complied with the requirements of the order.

29–42   (1C) If in a case within sub-paragraph (1A) above the court does not impose a sentence of imprisonment of f the case is not within that subparagraph, the magistrates' court may deal with him in respect of the failure in one of the following ways and must deal with him in one of those ways if the relevant order is on force)—

         (a)   by making a curfew order in respect of him (subject to paragraph 6A below);

         (b)   where the offender is aged 16 or over, by making a community punishment order in respect of him (subject to paragraph 7 below);

         (c)   where the offender is aged under 21 by making an attendance centre order in respect of him, subject to paragraph 8 below); or

         (d)   where the relevant order was made by a magistrates' court, by dealing with him, for the offence in respect of which the order was made in any way in which the court could deal with him if he had just been convicted by it of the offence.]

     (2) In dealing with an offender under sub-paragraph (1)(d) above, a magistrates' court—

         (a)   shall take into account the extent to which the offender has complied with the requirements of the relevant order; and

         (b)   in the case of an offender who has wilfully and persistently failed to comply with those requirements, may impose a custodial sentence (where the relevant order was made in respect of an offence punishable with such a sentence) notwithstanding anything in section 79(2) of this Act.

     (3) Where a magistrates' court deals with an offender under sub-paragraph (1)(d) [(1A) or (1C) (d) above] above, it shall revoke the relevant order if it is still in force.

     (4) Where a relevant order was made by the Crown Court and a magistrates' court has power to deal with the offender under sub-paragraph (1)(a) [(1C) (a)], (b) or (c) above, it may instead commit him to custody or release him on bail until he can be brought or appear before the Crown Court.

     (5) A magistrates' court which deals with an offender's case under sub-paragraph (4) above shall send to the Crown Court—

         (a)   a certificate signed by a justice of the peace certifying that the offender has failed to comply with the requirements of the relevant order in the respect specified in the certificate; and

         (b)   such other particulars of the case as may be desirable;

and a certificate purporting to be so signed shall be admissible as evidence of the failure before the Crown Court.

     (6) A person sentenced under sub-paragraph (1)(d) [(1A) or (1C) (d)] above for an offence may appeal to the Crown Court against the sentence.

Exclusions from paragraphs 4 and 5

29–43   6.—(1) Without prejudice to paragraphs 10 and 11 below, an offender who is convicted of a further offence while a relevant order is in force in respect of him shall not on that account be liable to be dealt with under paragraph 4 or 5 above in respect of a failure to comply with any requirement of the order.

     (2) An offender who—

         (a)   is required by a community rehabilitation order or community punishment and rehabilitation order to submit to treatment for his mental condition, or his dependency on or propensity to misuse drugs or alcohol, or

         (b)   is required by a drug treatment and testing order to submit to treatment for his dependency on or propensity to misuse drugs, shall not be treated for the purposes of paragraph 4 or 5 above as having failed to comply with that requirement on the ground only that he has refused to undergo any surgical, electrical or other treatment if, in the opinion of the court, his refusal was reasonable having regard to all the circumstances.

[(3) Paragraphs 4(1A) and 5(1A) above do not apply in respect of a failure to comply with a requirement to abstain from misusing specified Class A drugs]

Curfew orders imposed for breach of relevant order

6A.—(1) Section 37(1) of this Act (curfew orders) shall apply for the purposes of **29–44** paragraphs 4(1C)(a) and 5(1C)(a) above as if for the words from the beginning to "make" there were substituted "Where a court has power to deal with an offender under Part II of Schedule 3 to this Act for failure to comply with any of the requirements of a relevant order, the court may make in respect of the offender".

(2) In this paragraph—

"secondary order" means a curfew order made by virtue of paragraph 4(1C)(a) or 5(1C)(a) above;

"original order" means the relevant order the failure to comply with which led to the making of the secondary order.

(3) A secondary order—

(a) shall specify a period of not less than 14 nor more than 28 days for which the order is to be in force; and

(b) may specify different places, or different periods (within the period for which the order is in force), for different days, but shall not specify periods which amount to less than two hours or more than twelve hours in any one day.

(4) Part IV of this Act, except sections 35, 36, 37(3) and (4), 39 and 40(2)(a), has effect in relation to a secondary order as it has effect in relation to any other curfew order, but subject to the further modifications made below.

(5) Section 37(9) applies as if the reference to an offender who on conviction is under 16 were a reference to a person who on the date when his failure to comply with the original order is proved to the court is under 16.

(6) Paragraphs 2A, 4(1A) to (2) and 5(1A) to (2) above and 10 and 11 below apply as if, in respect of the period for which the secondary order is in force, the requirements of that order were requirements of the original order.

But in paragraphs 4 and 5 above, sub-paragraph (1C)(c) applies as if references to the relevant order were to the original order or the secondary order.

(7) In paragraphs 4 and 5 above, sub-paragraph (3) applies as if references to the relevant order were to the original order and the secondary order

(8) Paragraph 19(3) below applies as if the reference to six months from the date of the original order were a reference to 28 days from the date of the secondary order.]

Community punishment orders imposed for a breach of relevant order

7.—(1) Section 46(1) of this Act (community punishment orders) shall apply for the **29–45** purposes of paragraphs 4(1)(b) and 5(1)(b) [4(1C) and 5(1C)] above as if for the words from the beginning to "make" there were substituted "Where a court has power to deal with an offender aged 16 or over under Part II of Schedule 3 to this Act for failure to comply with any of the requirements of a relevant order, the court may make in respect of the offender".

(2) In this paragraph a "secondary order" means a community punishment order made by virtue of paragraph 4(1)(b) or 5(1)(b) above [4(1B)(b) or 5(1C)(b) and 'original order' means the relevant order the failure to comply with which led to the making of the secondary order].

(3) The number of hours which an offender may be required to work under a secondary order shall be specified in the order and shall not exceed 60 in the aggregate; and—

(a) where the relevant order is a community punishment order, the number of hours which the offender may be required to work under the secondary order shall not be such that the total number of hours under both orders exceeds the maximum specified in section 46(3) of this Act; and

(b) where the relevant order is a community punishment and rehabilitation order, the number of hours which the offender may be required to work under the secondary order shall not be such that the total number of hours under—

(i) the secondary order, and

(ii) the community service element of the community punishment and rehabilitation order,

exceeds the maximum specified in section 51(1)(b) of this Act.

29–46   (4) Section 46(4) of this Act and, so far as applicable—

         (a) section 46(5) to (7) and (9) to (13), and

         (b) section 47 and the provisions of this Schedule so far as relating to community punishment orders,

have effect in relation to a secondary order as they have effect in relation to any other community punishment order, subject to sub-paragraph (6) below.

(5) Sections 35 and 36 of this Act (restrictions and procedural requirements for community sentences) do not apply in relation to a secondary order.

(6) Where the provisions of this Schedule have effect as mentioned in sub-paragraph (4) above in relation to a secondary order—

         (a) the power conferred on the court by each of paragraphs 4(1)(d) and 5(1)(d) above and paragraph 10(3)(b) below to deal with the offender for the offence in respect of which the order was made shall be construed as a power to deal with the offender, for his failure to comply with the original order, in any way in which the court could deal with him if that failure had just been proved to the satisfaction of the court;

         (b) the references in paragraphs 10(1)(b) and 11(1)(a) below to the offence in respect of which the order was made shall be construed as references to the failure to comply in respect of which the order was made; and

         (c) the power conferred on the Crown Court by paragraph 11(2)(b) below to deal with the offender for the offence in respect of which the order was made shall be construed as a power to deal with the offender, for his failure to comply with the original order, in any way in which a magistrates' court (if the original order was made by a magistrates' court) or the Crown Court (if the original order was made by the Crown Court) could deal with him if that failure had just been proved to its satisfaction;

and in this sub-paragraph "the original order" means the relevant order the failure to comply with which led to the making of the secondary order.

Attendance centre orders imposed for breach of relevant order

29–47   8.—(1) Section 60(1) of this Act (attendance centre orders) shall apply for the purposes of paragraphs 4(1)(c) and 5(1)(c) [4(1C)(c) and 5(1C)(c)] above as if for the words from the beginning to "the court may," there were substituted

         "Where a court—

         (a) has power to deal with an offender aged under 16 under Part II of Schedule 3 to this Act for failure to comply with any of the requirements of a curfew order, or

         (b) has power to deal with an offender aged under 21 under that Part of that Schedule for failure to comply with any of the requirements of a probation or combination order,

the court may, [has power to deal with an offender under Part II of Schedule 3 to this Act for failure to comply with any of the requirements of a relevant order, the court may,]"

(2) The following provisions of this Act, namely—

         (a) subsections (3) to (11) of section 60, and

         (b) so far as applicable, Schedule 5,

have effect in relation to an attendance centre order made by virtue of paragraph 4(1C)(c) or 5(1C)(c) [4(1C)(c) or 5(1C)(c)] above as they have effect in relation to any other attendance centre order, but as if there were omitted from each of paragraphs 2(1)(b), 3(1) and 4(3) of Schedule 5 the words ", for the offence in respect of which the order was made," and "for that offence".

(3) Sections 35 and 36 of this Act (restrictions and procedural requirements for community sentences) do not apply in relation to an attendance centre order made by virtue of paragraph 4(1)(c) or 5(1)(c) [4(1C)(c) or 5(1C)(c)]above.

Supplementary

29–48   9.—(1) Any exercise by a court of its powers under paragraph 4(1)(a), (b) or (c) or 5(1)(a), (b) or (c) [4(1C)(a), (b) or (c) or 5(1C)(a), (b) or (c)] above shall be without prejudice to the continuance of the relevant order.

(2) A fine imposed under paragraph 4(1)(a) or 5(1)(a) above shall be deemed, for the purposes of any enactment, to be a sum adjudged to be paid by a conviction.

(3) Where a relevant order was made by a magistrates' court in the case of an offender

under 18 years of age in respect of an offence triable only on indictment in the case of an adult, any powers exercisable under paragraph 4(1)(d) [4 (1C)(d)] above in respect of the offender after he attains the age of 18 shall be powers to do either or both of the following—

    (a) to impose a fine not exceeding £5,000 for the offence in respect of which the order was made;

    (b) todeal with the offender for that offence in any way in which a magistrates' court could deal with him if it had just convicted him of an offence punishable with imprisonment for a term not exceeding six months.

PART III

Revocation of Order

Revocation of order with or without re-sentencing: powers of magistrates' court

10.—(1) This paragraph applies where a relevant order made by a magistrates' court is **29–49** in force in respect of any offender and on the application of the offender or the responsible officer it appears to the appropriate magistrates' court that, having regard to circumstances which have arisen since the order was made, it would be in the interests of justice—

    (a) for the order to be revoked; or

    (b) for the offender to be dealt with in some other way for the offence in respect of which the order was made.

(2) In this paragraph "the appropriate magistrates' court" means—

    (a) in the case of a drug treatment and testing order or a drug abstinence order, the magistrates' court responsible for the order;

    (b) in the case of any other relevant order, a magistrates' court acting for the petty sessions area concerned.

(3) The appropriate magistrates' court may—

    (a) revoke the order; or

    (b) both—

        (i) revoke the order; and

        (ii) deal with the offender, for the offence in respect of which the order was made, in any way in which it could deal with him if he had just been convicted by the court of the offence.

(4) The circumstances in which a probation, combination or drug treatment and testing order may be revoked under sub-paragraph (3)(a) above shall include the offender's making good progress or his responding satisfactorily to supervision or, as the case may be, treatment.

(5) In dealing with an offender under sub-paragraph (3)(b) above, a magistrates' court shall take into account the extent to which the offender has complied with the requirements of the relevant order.

(6) A person sentenced under sub-paragraph (3)(b) above for an offence may appeal to the Crown Court against the sentence.

(7) Where a magistrates' court proposes to exercise its powers under this paragraph otherwise than on the application of the offender, it shall summon him to appear before the court and, if he does not appear in answer to the summons, may issue a warrant for his arrest.

(8) No application may be made by the offender under sub-paragraph (1) above while an appeal against the relevant order is pending.

Substitution of conditional discharge for community rehabilitation or community punishment and rehabilitation order

12.—(1) This paragraph applies where a probation order or combination order is in **29–50** force in respect of any offender and on the application of the offender or the responsible officer to the appropriate court it appears to the court that, having regard to circumstances which have arisen since the order was made, it would be in the interests of justice—

    (a) for the order to be revoked; and

    (b) for an order to be made under section 12(1)(b) of this Act discharging the offender conditionally for the offence for which the probation or combination order was made.

(2) In this paragraph "the appropriate court" means—
- (a) where the probation or combination order was made by a magistrates' court, a magistrates' court acting for the petty sessions area concerned;
- (b) where the probation or combination order was made by the Crown Court, the Crown Court.

(3) No application may be made under paragraph 10 or 11 above for a community rehabilitation order or community punishment and rehabilitation order to be revoked and replaced with an order for conditional discharge under section 12(1)(b); but otherwise nothing in this paragraph shall affect the operation of paragraphs 10 and 11 above.

29–51 (4) Where this paragraph applies—
- (a) the appropriate court may revoke the probation or combination order and make an order under section 12(1)(b) of this Act discharging the offender in respect of the offence for which the probation or combination order was made, subject to the condition that he commits no offence during the period specified in the order under section 12(1)(b); and
- (b) the period specified in the order under section 12(1)(b) shall be the period beginning with the making of that order and ending with the date when the probation period specified in the probation or combination order would have ended.

(5) For the purposes of sub-paragraph (4) above, subsection (1) of section 12 of this Act shall apply as if—
- (a) for the words from the beginning to "may make an order either" there were substituted the words "Where paragraph 12 of Schedule 3 to this Act applies, the appropriate court may (subject to the provisions of sub-paragraph (4) of that paragraph) make an order in respect of the offender"; and
- (b) paragraph (a) of that subsection were omitted.

(6) An application under this paragraph may be heard in the offender's absence if—
- (a) the application is made by the responsible officer; and
- (b) that officer produces to the court a statement by the offender that he understands the effect of an order for conditional discharge and consents to the making of the application;

and where the application is so heard section 12(4) of this Act shall not apply.

(7) No application may be made under this paragraph while an appeal against the probation or combination order is pending.

(8) Without prejudice to paragraph 15 below, on the making of an order under section 12(1)(b) of this Act by virtue of this paragraph the court shall forthwith give copies of the order to the responsible officer, and the responsible officer shall give a copy to the offender.

(9) Each of sections 1(11), 2(9) and 66(4) of the *Crime and Disorder Act* 1998 (which prevent a court from making an order for conditional discharge in certain cases) shall have effect as if the reference to the court by or before which a person is convicted of an offence there mentioned included a reference to a court dealing with an application under this paragraph in respect of the offence.

Revocation following custodial sentence by magistrates' court unconnected with order

29–52 13.—(1) This paragraph applies where—
- (a) an offender in respect of whom a relevant order is in force is convicted of an offence by a magistrates' court unconnected with the order;
- (b) the court imposes a custodial sentence on the offender; and
- (c) it appears to the court, on the application of the offender or the responsible officer, that it would be in the interests of justice to exercise its powers under this paragraph, having regard to circumstances which have arisen since the order was made.

(2) In sub-paragraph (1) above "a magistrates' court unconnected with the order" means—
- (a) in the case of a drug treatment and testing order or a drug abstinence order, a magistrates' court which is not responsible for the order;
- (b) in the case of any other relevant order, a magistrates' court not acting for the petty sessions area concerned.

(3) The court may—

(a) if the order was made by a magistrates' court, revoke it;

(b) if the order was made by the Crown Court, commit the offender in custody or release him on bail until he can be brought or appear before the Crown Court.

(4) Where the court deals with an offender's case under sub-paragraph (3)(b) above, it shall send to the Crown Court such particulars of the case as may be desirable.

Supplementary

15.—(1) On the making under this Part of this Schedule of an order revoking a relevant **29–53** order, the proper officer of the court shall forthwith give copies of the revoking order to the responsible officer.

(2) In sub-paragraph (1) above "proper officer" means—

(a) in relation to a magistrates' court, the justices' chief executive for the court; and

(b) in relation to the Crown Court, the appropriate officer.

(3) A responsible officer to whom in accordance with sub-paragraph (1) above copies of a revoking order are given shall give a copy to the offender and to the person in charge of any institution in which the offender was required by the order to reside.

[Paragraphs 1 to 17 (3, 5 11, 14, 16 and 17 ommited here) are printed as amended as from a day to be appointed, by the *CJCSA* 2000, ss.53, 54 and 74 and Sch.7, paras 1 to 3 and 199(1) to (19) (italicised words are omitted and words in square brackets are inserted as from a day to be appointed). The amendments effected by s.53 (insertion of paras 1(1A), 2A and 6(3) and the substitution of new paras 4(1) to (1C) for 4(1) have no application in relation to any community order made before the commencement date of that section *CJCSA* 2000, s.70(5).]

In relation to an offence committed before October 1, 1997, see the transitional provision (applicable to paras 4(2) and 5(2)) in Sch.11, para.4(2)). As to the transitory modification of para.15, see Sch.10, para.12.

(1) Orders made after the commencement of the CJCSA 2000 s.53

The amendments made by s.53 apply only to orders made after the commencement **29–54** of s.53: *CJCSA* 2000, s.70(5) . The amendments are also affected by a series of amendments to Sch.3 to the *PCC(S)A* 2000, which will continue to exist until in two versions until the last of the pre-commencement orders has been served. The new scheme dictates that an offender over 18 who fails for a second time to comply with the requirements of a community order, other than a drug treatment and testing order or a requirement not to misuse specified Class A drugs, must be brought before the appropriate court; if the court finds that the failure is proved the court must impose a sentence of imprisonment unless it considers the offender is likely to comply with the order during the remaining period of the order, or that there are 'exceptional circumstances.' In imposing a prison sentence, the court is not bound by s.79 of the *PCC(S)A*, though it is bound by s.80. If a court imposes such a mandatory sentence of imprisonment, it must revoke the community order. If the court finds that there are grounds for not imposing the mandatory sentence of imprisonment, the court may deal with the case in one of the ways set out in paras 4(1C) or 5(1C). The power to deal with breach of a requirement by a fine is abolished.

(2) Breach of requirements of an Attendance Centre Order

Powers of Criminal Courts (Sentencing) Act 2000, Sch.5

SCHEDULE 5

Breach of order or attendance centre rules

1.—(1) Where an attendance centre order is in force and it appears on information to a **29–55** justice acting for a relevant petty sessions area that the offender—

(a) has failed to attend in accordance with the order, or

(b) while attending has committed a breach of rules made under section 62(3) of this Act which cannot be adequately dealt with under those rules,

the justice may issue a summons requiring the offender to appear at the place and time specified in the summons before a magistrates' court acting for the area or, if the information is in writing and on oath, may issue a warrant for the offender's arrest requiring him to be brought before such a court.

(2) For the purposes of this paragraph a petty sessions area is a relevant petty sessions area in relation to an attendance centre order—

(a) if the attendance centre which the offender is required to attend by the order or by virtue of an order under paragraph 5(1)(b) below is situated in it; or

(b) if the order was made by a magistrates' court acting for it.

29–56   2.—(1) If it is proved to the satisfaction of the magistrates' court before which an offender appears or is brought under paragraph 1 above that he has failed without reasonable excuse to attend as mentioned in sub-paragraph (1)(a) of that paragraph or has committed such a breach of rules as is mentioned in sub-paragraph (1)(b) of that paragraph, that court may deal with him in any one of the following ways—

(a) it may impose on him a fine not exceeding £1,000;

(b) where the attendance centre order was made by a magistrates' court, it may deal with him, for the offence in respect of which the order was made, in any way in which he could have been dealt with for that offence by the court which made the order if the order had not been made; or

(c) where the order was made by the Crown Court, it may commit him to custody or release him on bail until he can be brought or appear before the Crown Court.

(2) Any exercise by the court of its power under sub-paragraph (1)(a) above shall be without prejudice to the continuation of the order.

(3) A fine imposed under sub-paragraph (1)(a) above shall be deemed, for the purposes of any enactment, to be a sum adjudged to be paid by a conviction.

(4) Where a magistrates' court deals with an offender under sub-paragraph (1)(b) above, it shall revoke the attendance centre order if it is still in force.

(5) In dealing with an offender under sub-paragraph (1)(b) above, a magistrates' court—

(a) shall take into account the extent to which the offender has complied with the requirements of the attendance centre order; and

(b) in the case of an offender who has wilfully and persistently failed to comply with those requirements, may impose a custodial sentence notwithstanding anything in section 79(2) of this Act.

(6) A person sentenced under sub-paragraph (1)(b) above for an offence may appeal to the Crown Court against the sentence.

(7) A magistrates' court which deals with an offender's case under sub-paragraph (1)(c) above shall send to the Crown Court—

(a) a certificate signed by a justice of the peace giving particulars of the offender's failure to attend or, as the case may be, the breach of the rules which he has committed; and

(b) such other particulars of the case as may be desirable;

and a certificate purporting to be so signed shall be admissible as evidence of the failure or the breach before the Crown Court.

3. [Crown Court]

Revocation of order with or without re-sentencing

29–57   4.—(1) Where an attendance centre order is in force in respect of an offender, an appropriate court may, on an application made by the offender or by the officer in charge of the relevant attendance centre, revoke the order.

(2) In sub-paragraph (1) above "an appropriate court" means—

(a) where the court which made the order was the Crown Court and there is included in the order a direction that the power to revoke the order is reserved to that court, the Crown Court;

(b) in any other case, either of the following—

(i) a magistrates' court acting for the petty sessions area in which the relevant attendance centre is situated;

(ii) the court which made the order.

(3) Any power conferred by this paragraph—

(a) on a magistrates' court to revoke an attendance centre order made by such a court, or

(b) on the Crown Court to revoke an attendance centre order made by the Crown Court,

includes power to deal with the offender, for the offence in respect of which the order was made, in any way in which he could have been dealt with for that offence by the court which made the order if the order had not been made.

(4) A person sentenced by a magistrates' court under sub-paragraph (3) above for an offence may appeal to the Crown Court against the sentence.

(5) The proper officer of a court which makes an order under this paragraph revoking an attendance centre order shall—

(a) deliver a copy of the revoking order to the offender or send a copy by registered post or the recorded delivery service addressed to the offender's last or usual place of abode; and

(b) deliver or send a copy to the officer in charge of the relevant attendance centre.

(6) In this paragraph "the relevant attendance centre", in relation to an attendance centre order, means the attendance centre specified in the order or substituted for the attendance centre so specified by an order made by virtue of paragraph 5(1)(b) below.

(7) In this paragraph "proper officer" means—

(a) in relation to a magistrates' court, the justices' chief executive for the court; and

(b) in relation to the Crown Court, the appropriate officer.

Amendment of order

5.—(1) Where an attendance centre order is in force in respect of an offender, an appropriate magistrates' court may, on an application made by the offender or by the officer in charge of the relevant attendance centre, by order— **29–58**

(a) vary the day or hour specified in the order for the offender's first attendance at the relevant attendance centre; or

(b) substitute for the relevant attendance centre an attendance centre which the court is satisfied is reasonably accessible to the offender, having regard to his age, the means of access available to him and any other circumstances.

(2) In sub-paragraph (1) above "an appropriate magistrates' court" means—

(a) a magistrates' court acting for the petty sessions area in which the relevant attendance centre is situated; or

(b) (except where the attendance centre order was made by the Crown Court) the magistrates' court which made the order.

(3) The justices' chief executive for a court which makes an order under this paragraph shall—

(a) deliver a copy to the offender or send a copy by registered post or the recorded delivery service addressed to the offender's last or usual place of abode; and

(b) deliver or send a copy—

(i) if the order is made by virtue of sub-paragraph (1)(a) above, to the officer in charge of the relevant attendance centre; and

(ii) if it is made by virtue of sub-paragraph (1)(b) above, to the officer in charge of the attendance centre which the order as amended will require the offender to attend.

(4) In this paragraph "the relevant attendance centre" has the meaning given by paragraph 4(6) above.

Part V

Youth Courts

CHAPTER 30

THE YOUTH COURT

I. INTRODUCTION

The youth court is part of the magistrates' court system. It is a court of summary ju- **30–1** risdiction that hears charges against children and young defendants aged between 10 and 17 years inclusive. It is conclusively presumed that no child under the age of 10 years can be guilty of any offence. Children over this age are subject to the criminal law in the same way as defendants in the adult magistrates' court. Courtroom procedure closely mirrors that of the adult court. However the procedure is modified to reflect the age group that the youth court deals with. The geography of the courtroom is made less formal. The use of ordinary straightforward language is encouraged. Emphasis is put on the necessity of the court communicating and engaging directly with the defendants and their families. In the youth court it is usual to speak and refer to defendants by their first names.

II. THE YOUTH JUSTICE SYSTEM AND THE YOUTH COURT

Crime and Disorder Act 1998, s.37

Aim of the youth justice system
37.—(1) It shall be the principal aim of the youth justice system to prevent offending by chil- **30–2** dren and young persons.

(2) In addition to any other duty to which they are subject, it shall be the duty of all persons and bodies carrying out functions in relation to the youth justice system to have regard to that aim.

Children and Young Persons Act 1933, s.44

General considerations.
44.—(1) Every court in dealing with a child or young person who is brought before it, either **30–3** as an offender or otherwise, shall have regard to the welfare of the child or young person, and shall in a proper case take steps for removing him from undesirable surroundings, and for securing that proper provision is made for his education and training.

Crime and Disorder Act 1998, s.39

It is the duty of each local authority to establish for their area one or more Youth Of- **30–4** fending Teams.

Youth Offending Teams (YOT) play a vital part in the work of the Youth Court. There are now 155 YOTs covering all of England and Wales. The duty of the YOT is to co-ordinate the provision of youth justice services for all those in the authority's area. It is customary for a representative from the YOT to attend each sitting of the Youth Court and the YOT plays a most important part in assisting in the work of the court. More particularly the YOT will assist the court in dealing with the following matters—

(a) investigating and confirming the personal circumstances and antecedents of defendants;

(b) the provision of bail support (with or without an ISSP programme);

(c) the preparation of appropriate written reports required by the court as part of the sentencing process;

(d) the administration of many of the non-custodial penalties imposed by the Youth Court;

(e) the prosecution of defendants who have breached community penalties.

Defence advocates will obtain much important information by conferring with the YOT prior to the hearing of their clients case.

(1) Preliminary Issues

Children and Young Persons Act 1933, s.34A

Attendance at court of parent or guardian

30–5   **34A.**—(1) Where a child or young person is charged with an offence or is for any other reason brought before a court, the court—

(a) may in any case; and

(b) shall in the case of a child or a young person who is under the age of sixteen years,

require a person who is a parent or guardian of his to attend at the court during all the stages of the proceedings, unless and to the extent that the court is satisfied that it would be unreasonable to require such attendance, having regard to the circumstances of the case.

(2) In relation to a child or young person for whom a Local Authority have parental responsibility and who—

(a) is in their care; or

(b) is provided with accommodation by them in the exercise of any functions (in particular those under the *Children Act* 1989) which are social services functions within the meaning of the *Local Authority Social Services Act* 1970,

the reference in subsection (1) above to a person who is a parent or guardian of his shall be construed as a reference to that Authority, where he is allowed to live with such a person, as including such a reference.

In this subsection "local authority" and "parental responsibility" have the same meanings as in the *Children Act* 1989.

30–6   It is essential that parents or guardians of young defendants attend the youth court with them. Section 34A above makes such attendance mandatory where the youth is under 16 years of age unless the court is satisfied that it would be unreasonable to require such attendance in all the circumstances of the case. If a defendant appears without a parent the court must enquire as to why they are unaccompanied, and consider taking steps to ensure attendance. The court may write to the parent or guardian requesting attendance. Alternatively a summons may be issued and, if this does not remedy the situation, a warrant obtained.

Having secured parental attendance the court will be anxious to allow parents to address the court and to contribute to the hearing generally. It is important that the court engages with both the defendant and his family.

(2) Press and Publicity

30–7   Persons who may be present at the sitting of a youth court are—

(a) members and officers of the court;

(b) parties to the case together with their solicitors and counsel, and other persons directly concerned in that case;

(c) accredited representatives of news agencies;

(d) the court may especially authorise other persons to be present who have good cause to be there.

Accredited press representatives are therefore allowed to observe and report on court **30–8** proceedings in the youth court and their presence in the courtroom cannot be objected to by the parties. However the press is restricted in the details it may report. More particularly no report of any proceedings in a youth court should reveal the name, address or school, or include any particulars likely to lead to the identification of any child or young person concerned in those proceedings. This restriction includes details of young witnesses who are concerned in the court proceedings and the publication of pictures.

Children and Young Persons Act 1933, s.49

The Youth Court may order the lifting of press restrictions to any extent that it speci- **30–9** fies in certain specific circumstances—

(1) That it is appropriate to do so for the purpose of avoiding injustice to the child or young person subject to the application.

(2) In respect of a child or young person who has been convicted of an offence and the court is satisfied that it is in the public interest that details of their identity are given in the press.

(3) Where a defendant has been charged with or convicted of a violent or sexual offence or an offence punishable with imprisonment for 14 years or more if he/she is unlawfully at large and the court is satisfied on the application of the DPP that it is necessary to identify him in the press for the purpose of apprehending him to bring him before a court or to return him to the place in which he was held in custody.

The youth court's power to dispense with reporting restrictions under s.49 should be exercised with the greatest care and caution. International law and practice emphasises the necessity of protecting the privacy of children and young persons involved in legal proceedings. In the case of *McKerry v Teesdale and Wear Valley JJ*. [2000] Crim.L.R. 594, the Divisional Court stated that the need for the full and fair reporting of the administration of justice must be balanced against the welfare of the youth involved. It would be wholly wrong to invoke the power by way of additional punishment and it would only be "very rarely" that the statutory criteria for "naming and shaming" would be met.

(3) Legal Representation

A majority of youths who appear before the youth court will be legally represented **30–10** either under the duty solicitor scheme or as a result of instructing their own lawyers. Representation orders are applied for in the youth court in the same way as in the adult magistrates' court. There is no means test. The applications are considered under the Widgery criteria and decided on the basis of the interests of justice. In considering such an application the age of the applicant must be taken into account. In *R. v Scunthorpe Justices Ex p. S, The Times*, March 5, 1998, DC it was held that a refusal to grant legal aid to a 16-year-old defendant who wished to challenge a police constable as to whether he had acted in the execution of his duty was said to be irrational, as the expertise required to cross examine police witnesses and find, select and proof defence witnesses is beyond that of a defendant aged 16 years.

(4) Reprimands and Final Warnings (s.65 of the Crime and Disorder Act 1998)

These have replaced police cautions for young people. They are not court orders **30–11** and cannot be ordered by the court. However they are frequently cited when the court is told about a defendants antecedent history, in dealing with issues relating to bail and sentencing.

A reprimand will be given for first time offenders and for less serious offences. However if the offence is sufficiently serious a final warning may be given instead of a reprimand.

A final warning is given to offenders who have been reprimanded previously. Once a final warning is given the offender cannot receive a further reprimand or final warning except where the new offence has been committed more than two years since the previous warning and is not sufficiently serious to be charged.

When a final warning is given, the YOT will be notified and the young person should be assessed with a view to work being done with him to prevent offending.

Before the police can give a reprimand or final warning the offender must admit the offence.

30–12 Reprimands and final warnings may be relevant in making a bail decision for a youth. They will also be relevant in assessing his/her antecedent history for the purpose of sentencing. It should be noted that a young person who re-offends and is convicted within two years of receiving a final warning cannot be given a conditional discharge (*Crime and Disorder Act* 1998, s.66) unless there are exceptional circumstances relating to the offence itself or the offender. See Conditional Discharge, Sentencing, §§ 26–9— 26–15 below.

After a defendant has been charged the youth court is sometimes asked to adjourn proceedings against him/her to allow a reprimand or final warning to be administered. This situation was considered by the Divisional Court in *F v CPS* (2004) 168 J.P. 93. In that case the court was asked to judicially review the decision of the CPS not to discontinue a prosecution after a decision had been made by the police not to administer a final warning. The Divisional Court emphasised that final warnings are meant to be administered quickly and that it was clearly envisaged that they should be given before charge. It would only be in exceptional circumstances that the police should administer a final warning or reprimand when the defendant had already been charged and had appeared before a court.

CHAPTER 31

JURISDICTION AND AGE

The youth court's jurisdiction is founded upon the age of the defendant. Therefore **31–1** the court is under a duty to establish that the defendant is aged between 10 and 17 years. Additionally, the powers of the youth court in respect of bail, remand, and sentencing vary widely between the different age groups within the court jurisdiction.

In the vast majority of cases coming before the youth court establishing the age of a defendant does not cause any problem, however if an issue as to age does arise it is dealt with by the following statutory procedure—

Children and Young Persons Act 1933, s.99(1)

Presumption and determination of age

99.—(1) Where a person, whether charged with an offence or not, is brought before any **31–2** court otherwise than for the purpose of giving evidence, and it appears to the court that he is a child or young person, the court shall make due inquiry as to the age of that person, and for that purpose shall take such evidence as may be forthcoming at the hearing of the case, but an order or judgment of the court shall not be invalidated by any subsequent proof that the age of that person has not been correctly stated to the court, and the age presumed or declared by the court to be the age of the person so brought before it shall, for the purposes of this Act, be deemed to be the true age of that person, and, where it appears to the court that the person so brought before it has attained the the age of eighteen years, that person shall for the purposes of this Act be deemed not to be a child or young person.

If the youth court is not satisfied that it has been given accurate information regard- **31–3** ing a defendant's age, s.99, above, places a duty on the court to determine the age of the defendant. For the purposes of determining age the court can hear oral evidence and consider both domestic or foreign documentation. The court can also take into account the physical appearance of the defendant in the courtroom. The YOT, with its wide experience of dealing with young people, may also have a valuable part to play in such hearings. At the end of the hearing the court will deem the defendant to be of a certain age or within a certain age group. If new relevant evidence emerges at future hearings of the case, the court may re-open the question of age and alter its original decision. However this must be based on new factors that have emerged.

(1) Crossing the Age Barrier

The situation sometimes arises that a defendant who has been charged with an of- **31–4** fence when under the age of 18 years, attains that age before proceedings against him in the youth court have been concluded. This has important implications for the defendant. It is submitted that the most common situations are as follows:

   (1) If a young person is charged with an offence whilst he is 17 years of age but turns 18 years of age before his first appearance before the court, then the youth court does not have jurisdiction to deal with him: *R. v Uxbridge Youth Court Ex p. H* (1998) 162 J.P. 327.
   (2) If the young person has appeared before the youth court when under 18 years of age but attains 18 during the proceedings then the following rules apply:

If, before summary trial in the youth court or, after conviction in the youth court but before sentence, the youth court may remit the person to the adult magistrates' court for the same petty sessions area as the youth court.

Powers of Criminal Courts (Sentencing) Act 2000, s.9

9.—(1) Where a person who appears or is brought before a Youth Court charged with an offence subsequently attains the age of 18, the Youth Court may, at any time after conviction and before sentence, remit him for sentence to a magistrates' court (other than a Youth Court) acting for the same Petty Sessions Area as the Youth Court.

(2) Where an offender is remitted under subsection (1) above, the Youth Court shall adjourn proceedings in relation to the offence, and—

(a) Section 128 of the *Magistrates' Courts Act* 1980 (remand in custody or on bail) and all other enactments, whenever passed, relating to remand or the granting of bail in criminal proceedings shall have effect, in relation to the Youth Courts power or duty to remand the offender on that adjournment, as if any reference to the court to or before which the person remanded is to be brought or appear after remand were a reference to the court to which he is being remitted; and

(b) subject to subsection (3), the court to which the offender is remitted ("the other court") may deal with the case in any way in which it would have power to deal with it if all proceedings relating to the offence which took place before the Youth Court had taken place before the other court.

Section 9 of the *PCC(S)A* 2000 gives the youth court discretion whether or not to remit to the magistrates' court. If the youth court decides to retain the case the enabling provision to do so is below.

Children and Young Persons Act 1963, s.29

31–5   **29.** Where proceedings in respect of a young person are begun for an offence and he attains the age of 18 before the conclusion of the proceedings, the court may deal with the case and make any order which it could have made if he had not attained that age.

If, during the course of proceedings against a defendant who the court believes to be under 18 years of age, it emerges that the defendant is in fact 18 or over the youth court has discretion to continue to deal with the defendant under the provision below.

Children and Young Persons Act 1933, s.48(1)

31–6   **48.**—(1) A Youth Court sitting for the purpose of hearing a charge against a person who is believed to be a child or young person may, if it thinks fit to do so, proceed with the hearing and determination of the charge, notwithstanding that it is discovered that the person in question is not a child or young person.

If a defendant under 18 appears before the youth court charged with an offence which is "either way" in the case of an adult (not being a grave crime) and he attains the age of 18 years before his plea is taken, he may apply to the youth court to be remitted to the adult court. Once a defendant has attained 18 years of age he has the right to elect trial by jury in respect of either way charges. However, it seems that if a defendant has entered his plea prior to his 18th birthday it is then "too late" for him to elect Crown Court trial although his trial in the youth court will not commence until after his 18th birthday. It is submitted that this is the interpretation to be given to the judgment in *R. v Islington North Juvenile Court Ex p. Daley* [1982] 2 All E.R. 974. During his leading judgment Lord Diplock stated "my Lords, it seems to me that reason and justice combine to indicate that the only appropriate date at which to determine whether an accused person has attained an age which entitles him to elect trial by jury for offences which under s.18 or s.22 are triable either way is the date of his appearance before the court on the occasion when the court makes its decision as to mode of trial".

If the defendant is charged with a "grave crime" under s.24 *Magistrates' Courts Act* 1980 and the youth court decides to retain jurisdiction before the defendant attains 18 years, the matter must remain for summary trial in the youth court. The defendant does not, on attaining 18 years acquire a right of trial before a jury: *R. v Nottingham Justices Ex p. Taylor* [1991] 4 All E.R. 860. If the defendant attains 18 years before the mode of trial decision, then the youth court has no power to proceed, and the case should be remitted to the adult court in accordance with s.9 of the *PCC(S)A* 2000 (see above).

No matter whether the original charges are summary, either way or indictable, the youth court has no jurisdiction to deal with any further fresh charges after the defendant has turned 18 years. This is irrespective of whether the fresh charges arrive from the same circumstances: *R. v Chelsea Justices Ex p. DPP* [1963] 3 All E.R. 657.

(2) Sentencing Across the Age Barrier

In *R. v Ghafoor* [2002] Crim.L.R. 739, the court of appeal considered the approach **31–7** to be adopted where a court sentences a defendant who crosses a relevant age threshold between the date of the commission of an offence and the date of conviction. The judgments of the court made it clear that the starting point for sentencing a defendant in such circumstances is the sentence that the defendant would have been likely to receive if he had been sentenced on the date of the commission of the offence. The "starting point" principle is a powerful factor in deciding sentence although other factors might have to be considered. However a court would have to have good reason for departing from the starting point sentence and passing a sentence higher than would have been passed at the date of the commission of the offence.

In *R. v L.M.* [2003] 2 Cr.App.R.(S.) 26, a 14-year-old defendant who was not a "persistent offender" was convicted when 15 years old of an offence of inflicting grievous bodily harm. He was sentenced to a detention and training order. He could not have received a custodial sentence when 14 but was eligible for such a sentence once he became 15. It was held that it was wrong for a detention and training order to be imposed as applying *Ghafoor* (above) the starting point for sentence should be the sentence which he would have been likely to receive if he had been sentenced at the date of the commission of the offence when only 14 years old.

If an order of conditional discharge was made in respect of a young person, the youth court may deal with a breach of that order even though the person is over 18 years of age: *Children and Young Persons Act* 1933, s.48(2).

If the order of conditional discharge was made by the youth court for an offence which is indictable only in the case of an adult, and the accused has attained 18 years when breached, the re-sentencing courts powers are set out in the *PCC(S)A* 2000, s.13(9)—

(a) to impose a fine not exceeding £5,000 for the offence in respect of which the order was made;

(b) to deal with the offender for that offence in any way in which a magistrates' court could deal with him if it had just convicted him of an offence punishable with imprisonment for a term not exceeding six months.

If, during the duration of a supervision order, breach proceedings are brought, and the offender has attained 18 years, then the proceedings are brought in the adult court. If the breach proceedings are commenced in the youth court whilst the offender is under 18 years, then they remain in the youth court to be concluded there: *PCC(S)A* 2000, Sch.7, para.1.

JURISDICTION AND GRAVE CRIMES

I. MAGISTRATES' COURTS ACT 1980, S.24

Magistrates' Courts Act 1980, s.24(1)

24.—(1) Where a person under the age of 18 appears or is brought before a Magistrates' **32–1** court on an information charging him with an Indictable offence other than homicide he shall be tried summarily unless—

  (a) the offence is such as is mentioned in subsection (1) or (2) of section 91 of the *Powers of Criminal Courts (Sentencing) Act* 2000 (under which a young person convicted on indictment of certain grave crimes may be sentenced to be detained for long periods) and the court considers that if he is found guilty of the offence it ought to be possible to sentence him in pursuance of subsection (3) of that section; or

  (b) he is charged jointly with a person who has attained the age of 18 and the court considers it necessary in the interests of justice to commit them both for trial.

And accordingly in a case falling within paragraph (a) or (b) of this subsection the court shall commit the accused for trial if either it is of the opinion that there is sufficient evidence to put him on trial or it has power under section 6(2) above so to commit him without consider of the evidence.

It should be noted that possession of prohibited weapons and ammunition, contrary to s.5 of the *Firearms Act* 1968, as amended by s.287 of the *Criminal Justice Act* 2003, now requires a minimum 5-year sentence to be imposed if the offence was:

  — committed after January 22, 2004; and

  — at the time of the offence, the defendant was aged 16 years or over.

Section 39 of the *Anti-social Behaviour Act* 2003 extended the list of prohibited weapons contained in s.5, by adding any air rifle, air gun or air pistol which uses or is designed or adapted for use with a self-contained gas cartridge system.

A young person fitting these criteria must be committed to the Crown Court for trial and in the event of conviction, for a sentence of detention to be passed under s.91 of the *PCC(S)A* 2000.

The plea before venue procedure that takes place in the adult court does not apply **32–2** to young people who do not have a right to elect Crown Court trial. The youth court has jurisdiction to try either way and indictable offences other than offences of homicide. However if the offence alleged is one of the grave crimes (see s.91 of the *PCC(S)A* 2000), s.24(1) above must be considered by the youth court.

In such cases the youth court must consider whether it should retain jurisdiction and try the case, or whether it should decline jurisdiction and, if there is a case to answer, commit the defendant to the Crown Court. In such cases the court must consider the seriousness of the allegation and decide whether its own powers of punishment are sufficient or whether the allegation is of such a serious nature that, if found guilty, it ought to be possible to sentence the defendant to detention under s.91 of the *PCC(S)A* 2000.

The decision the youth court makes as to whether to accept jurisdiction is a most **32–3** important one which may have a profound effect on the outcome of the case for the defendant. If the youth court accepts jurisdiction, and the defendant pleads guilty or is convicted, the youth court has no power to commit him/her to the Crown Court for sentence. In such cases the defendant must, therefore, be sentenced in accordance with the powers of the youth court.

The youth court's powers to impose a custodial sentence are limited in the following ways—

(a) In the case of defendants aged 10 or 11 years of age the youth court has no power at all to impose a custodial sentence.

(b) In the case of defendants aged from 12 to 14 years the court has power to impose a detention and training order for a maximum of two years but only if it is of the opinion that the defendant is a persistent offender. If not, the youth court has no power to impose a custodial sentence (persistent offender—see detention and training order—§ 34–99, below).

(c) Defendants aged 15, 16 and 17 years can be sentenced to a detention and training order up to a maximum of two years: *PCC(S)A* 2000, s.103.

If, however, the youth court decline jurisdiction and commit the defendant to the Crown Court for trial, he/she may then be sentenced by the Crown Court under s.91, below.

II. POWERS OF CRIMINAL COURTS (SENTENCING) ACT 2000, S.91

(1) Punishment of Certain Grave Crimes

32–4   Where a young offender is convicted on indictment of certain grave crimes he may be sentenced to long-term detention. This sentence is available:

— where a person of at least 10 but not more than 17 years is convicted on indictment of any offence punishable in the case of an adult with imprisonment of 14 years or more not being an offence the sentence for which is fixed by law; or an offence under s.14 (indecent assault on a woman) or s.15 (indecent assault on a man) of the *Sexual Offences Act* 1956.

— where a young person is convicted of an offence under s.1 of the *Road Traffic Act* 1988 (causing death by dangerous driving); or an offence under s.3A of the *Road Traffic Act* 1988 (causing death by careless driving while under the influence of drink or drugs).

32–5   Section 91 of the *PCC(S)A* 2000 is available to the Crown Court if a young person is convicted on indictment of a grave crime. Detention under s.91 can be imposed upon defendants aged 10 to 17 years.

(2) The Application of s.24

32–6   The application of s.24 by the youth court has been the subject of much litigation, and scrutiny by the higher courts. There is a considerable body of case law. It is submitted that the following are the principles for the court to apply—

(1) The test that the youth court must apply is whether the court considers that if convicted it ought to be possible to sentence the defendant in pursuance of s.91 of the *PCC(S)A* 2000. There must be a real possibility of such a sentence, not a vague or theoretical one. If the court is of a view that such a sentence is a real possibility, the court has no further discretion and must decline jurisdiction: *R. (on the application of D & N) v Sheffield Youth Court* (2003) 167 J.P. 159, QBD.

(2) The youth court will hear the facts of the prosecution case. The defendant's criminal record will be considered: *R. (on the application of Tullet) v Medway Magistrates' Court* (2003) 167 J.P. 541 and 896. The court must also consider defence submissions both on the undisputed facts of the prosecution case and any other factors relating to the defendant, his character, and his personal circumstances. Contentious mitigation should be ignored.

(3) In *R. (on the application of W) v Southampton Youth Court*; *R. (on the application of K) v Wirral Borough Magistrates' Court* [2003] 1 Cr.App.R.(S.) 87, the Lord Chief Justice emphasised the importance of trials for young offenders taking into account the needs of defendants of that age group: "While the

need to impose the appropriate sentence is important, so is the need to ensure that wherever possible the trial should take place in the appropriate setting. That is more satisfactorily achieved in a Youth Court than in a Crown Court." The youth court should start therefore with a strong presumption against sending young offenders to the Crown Court unless satisfied that it is clearly required, notwithstanding the fact that the forum will not be as appropriate as the youth court. The younger the defendant is, so the stronger the presumption that he/she should be tried in the youth court.

(4) A youth court dealing with a defendant charged with rape should never accept **32–7** jurisdiction to deal with the case itself but should commit the case to the Crown Court for trial: *R. v Billam* [1986] 1 All E.R. 985.

(5) In deciding whether it ought to be possible to sentence a defendant to detention **32–8** under s.91 the youth court must consider the sentencing powers of the Crown Court and the guidance given on the exercise of those powers. If there is no real possibility of such a sentence, committal is inappropriate. In assessing a likely sentence, the youth court should take into account the age of the defendant. Youths aged 15 to 17 years will receive a substantially shorter sentence of custody than adults convicted of a similar crime. Those aged between 10 and 12 years are unlikely to receive any custodial sentence unless the crime is extremely grave. The same applies to the 12 to 15 age group unless they are persistent young offenders. Only in exceptional circumstances will it be appropriate to pass a sentence of less than two years detention under s.91 on a defendant would be eligible for a detention and training order were he not too young for such an order to be made. This issue was considered in *R. v Manchester City Youth Court* [2002] 1 Cr.App.R.(S.) 573 and in *W. v Thetford Youth Justices v DPP* [2003] 1 Cr.App.R.(S.) 67. In his judgment Gage J. said "in respect of offenders under 15 a custodial sentence will ordinarily only be available in the form of a detention and training order. If the court is prohibited from making such an order in general an order under s.91 will not be appropriate. I remain of the opinion that where an offence or offences are likely to attract a sentence of less than two years custody the appropriate sentence will be a detention and training order. In the case of an offender under 15, who is not a persistent offender, or a child under 12, the most likely sentence will be non-custodial sentence. It follows that in most cases the appropriate place of trial will be the youth court. I remain of the view that the mere fact that a youth court, unable to make a short detention and training order, considers that the option to pass a short custodial sentence should be available, does not mean that it should decline jurisdiction. It seems to me that Parliament intended that generally a non-custodial sentence should be passed. Perhaps it would be better to say that cases involving offenders under 15 for whom a detention and training order is not available will only rarely attract a period of detention under s.91; the more rarely if the offender is under 12". Also see *R. v Balham Youth Court Ex p. R (Administrative court)* unreported, September 13, 2002.

In *C. v Balham Youth Court* (2003) 167 J.P. 525, QBD the youth court declined ju- **32–9** risdiction in dealing with a 14-year-old charged with robbery. On appeal the court held that where an offender is not able to be made the subject of a custodial sentence in the youth court because of his age, he should only be committed to the Crown Court for trial if a sentence of two years of more could be expected or if there were exceptional circumstances. The court stated that there was a general principle that first time offenders aged 13 or 14 should not be detained in custody and it was only rarely that a youth under 15 should be give a custodial sentence of under two years.

In deciding the issue of jurisdiction in relation to defendants of different age groups it is submitted that the following principles should be applied—

(3) Defendants Aged 10 or 11 Years of Age

Such defendants should only be committed to the Crown Court when charged with **32–10** exceptionally serious offences of such gravity that in spite of his/her age a custodial sentence exceeding two years is a realistic possibility. Committal to the Crown Court in other circumstances will be rare.

(4) Defendants Aged 12, 13 and 14 Years

(a) *Non-Persistent Offenders*

32–11   The youth court has no power to make detention and training orders in respect of this age group unless it finds that the defendant is a persistent offender. For definition of "persistent offender" see detention and training order—sentencing, below.

   If this is not the case there is a very strong presumption that trial should take place in the youth court. If, however the youth court finds that in all the circumstances of the case the sentencing court ought to have available to it power to impose a custodial sentence greater than two years then, in spite of the defendants age, it should commit to the Crown Court.

(b) *Persistent Young Offenders*

32–12   If the defendant is a persistent offender the youth court has power to impose a detention and training order of up to two years. If, in spite of the defendant's young age, the youth court finds that there is a real possibility that a sentence in excess of two years will be imposed, and that therefore the sentencing court ought to have such powers available to it, the youth court should commit for trial.

(5) Defendants Aged 15, 16 and 17 Years

32–13   The youth court has power to make a detention and training order up to a maximum of two years for this age group whether or not they are persistent offenders. In dealing with jurisdiction the youth court must ask itself whether the circumstances of the alleged crime are so serious that the sentencing court ought to have available to it powers of custody exceeding two years and that such a sentence is more than a vague or theoretical possibility.

CHAPTER 33

BAIL IN THE YOUTH COURT

I. INTRODUCTION

The youth court has power to remand a young person on bail, into local authority **33–1** accommodation (with or without a security requirement) or into custody. The powers vary greatly dependant upon the age and gender of the defendant as shown on the flow charts (§§ 33–39—33–41).

The initial decision to be made by the youth court is whether bail, conditional or unconditional, should be granted.

The *Bail Act* 1976 applies to all youths, the only difference being that the accused may be refused bail for his "own welfare" rather than his "own protection", as is the case with adult offenders: *Bail Act* 1976, Sch.1. The presumption in favour of granting unconditional bail contained in s.4 of the *Bail Act* 1976 applies equally to youths. It is only if bail is refused that the complex provisions of s.23 of the *CYPA* 1969 have to be invoked.

In deciding whether to grant bail, with or without conditions, the court must take **33–2** into account its statutory duties to prevent offending and also consider the welfare of the defendant. The Youth Offending Team (YOT) plays a vital role in any application for bail. More especially, the YOT will provide the court with up to date information relating to :

(a) the defendant's antecedents;
(b) his record in complying with previous bail conditions and any community penalties including referral orders;
(c) his home situation, health and welfare;
(d) confirmation of his attendance at school, college or work.

In addition the YOT will investigate the viability of appropriate bail conditions which **33–3** may meet the concerns of the court especially by way of a Bail Support Programme or an Intensive Supervision and Surveillance Programme (ISSP), see § 34–52.

If a remand into custody is contemplated by the court, the YOT will, in the case of 15 and 16 year old males, carry out the "vulnerability" assessment as required by s.23(5A) of the *CYPA* 1969.

A remand into local authority accommodation is a refusal of bail and custody time limits apply in the same way as a remand into custody.

II. THE BAIL APPLICATION

When the defendant is charged with offences that are not imprisonable, bail may **33–4** only be refused in the circumstances specified in Sch.1, Pt II of the 1976 Act. These circumstances are:

(1) The defendant has previously refused to surrender to bail, and in view of that failure, the court believes that the defendant would fail to surrender if released on bail on this occasion: Sch.1, Pt II, para.2.

(2) The court is satisfied that the defendant should be kept in custody for his own welfare: Sch.1, Pt II, para.3.

(3) The defendant is in custody in pursuance of a sentence of a court or of any authority acting under any of the Service Acts: Sch.1, Pt II, para.4.

(4) The defendant has been arrested under the 1976 Act for failing to surrender to the custody of the court or for being in breach of conditions of bail or likely to be in breach of such conditions: Sch.1, Pt II, para.5.

33–5   When the defendant is charged with offences that are punishable with imprisonment in the case of an adult offender, bail may be refused only in the circumstances specified in Sch.1, Pt 1 of the 1976 Act. These circumstances are:

(1) The court is satisfied that there are substantial grounds for believing that the defendant would fail to surrender to custody, commit an offence whilst on bail, or interfere with witnesses or otherwise obstruct the course of justice whether in relation to himself or another person: Sch.1, Pt I, para.2.

(2) The defendant is charged with or convicted of an indictable offence (whether or not triable either way) committed whilst on bail in criminal proceedings: Sch.1, Pt I, para.2A.

(3) The defendant is in custody in pursuance of a sentence of a court or of any authority acting under any of the Service Acts: Sch.1, Pt 1, para.3.

(4) The court is satisfied that it has not been practicable to obtain sufficient information for the purpose of taking the decisions required regarding bail due to lack of time since the proceedings started: Sch.1, Pt I, para.5.

(5) The defendant had been released on bail in or in connection with proceedings for an offence, and had been arrested under s.7 of the 1976 Act for failing to surrender to the custody of the court or being in breach of conditions of bail or likely to be in breach of such conditions: Sch.1, Pt I, para.6.

(6) Where the court is adjourned for enquiries or for a report to be prepared and it a ppears to the court impracticable to complete the inquiries or make the report unless the defendant is kept in custody: Sch.1, Pt I, para.7.

33–6   Conditions may be imposed following a grant of bail in the circumstances described in para.8 of Sch.1, Pt I of the 1976 Act. These circumstances are when the court believes the conditions imposed are necessary to prevent a failure to surrender to custody, the commission of an offence whilst on bail or the interference with witnesses or any other obstruction of justice. Conditions may also be imposed if they are necessary for the purpose of enabling further inquiries to be made or a report to be made to assist the court in dealing with the offence.

Where the defendant is aged 17 years, electronic tagging may be used to monitor his compliance with the relevant conditions: *Bail Act* 1976, s.3.

Where the defendant is aged between 12 and 16 years electronic tagging may be used in accordance with the conditions laid down in s.3AA of the 1976 Act.

Bail Act 1976, s.3AA(1)–(6), (11), (12)

Electronic monitoring of compliance with bail conditions

33–7   **3AA.**—(1) A court shall not impose on a child or young person a requirement under section 3(6ZAA) above (an "electronic monitoring requirement") unless each of the following conditions is satisfied.

(2) The first condition is that the child or young person has attained the age of twelve years.

(3) The second condition is that—

(a) the child or young person is charged with or has been convicted of a violent or sexual offence, or an offence punishable in the case of an adult with imprisonment for a term of fourteen years or more; or

(b) he is charged with or has been convicted of one or more imprisonable offences which, together with any other imprisonable offences of which he has been convicted in any proceedings—

(i)   amount, or

(ii) would, if he were convicted of the offences with which he is charged, amount,

to a recent history of repeatedly committing imprisonable offences while remanded on bail or to local authority accommodation.

(4) The third condition is that the court—   **33–8**

(a) has been notified by the Secretary of State that electronic monitoring arrangements are available in each petty sessions area which is a relevant area; and

(b) is satisfied that the necessary provision can be made under those arrangements.

(5) The fourth condition is that a youth offending team has informed the court that in its opinion the imposition of such a requirement will be suitable in the case of the child or young person.

(6) Where a court imposes an electronic monitoring requirement, the requirement shall include provision for making a person responsible for the monitoring; and a person who is made so responsible shall be of a description specified in an order made by the Secretary of State.

(11) In this section "local authority accommodation" has the same meaning as in the *Children and Young Persons Act* 1969.

(12) For the purposes of this section a petty sessions area is a relevant area in relation to a proposed electronic monitoring requirement if the court considers that it will not be practicable to secure the electronic monitoring in question unless electronic monitoring arrangements are available in that area.

[Inserted by the *Criminal Justice and Police Act* 2001, s.131.]

III. INTENSIVE SUPERVISION AND SURVEILLANCE PROGRAMME (ISSP)

This programme is intended for the most prolific and serious young offenders. **33–9** Complete guidance is set out in relation to Supervision orders (see sentencing—§ 34–52, below) The principal aim, when used as part of a bail package or as part of the conditions relating to a remand into local authority accommodation, is to prevent the commission of further offences. this is achieved by addressing the needs of young offenders by placing a particular emphasis on education and training. The programme is available for 10- to 17-year-olds but eligibility requires that the defendant fulfils the necessary criteria (above).

Electronic tagging is available but not voice verification. The YOT will carry out an assessment as to suitability and make proposals as the content of the ISSP. Advocates and courts should be aware that the ISSP programme is a limited resource. It is a non-statutory scheme funded by the Youth Justice Board and even if a defendant is deemed a suitable candidate there may not be an ISSP programme available within the defendant's local authority.

IV. APPEAL AGAINST REFUSAL OF BAIL

A right of appeal against the refusal of bail gives the defendant the same rights of ap- **33–10** peal as an adult, namely to the High court: *RSC* 1965, Ord.79, r.9 and to the Crown Court where the magistrates' court has issued a Certificate of Full Argument: *Crown Court Rules* 1982, rr.19 and 20.

(1) Remands available following a Refusal of Bail

Options available to the court are entirely dependant on the age and gender of the **33–11** defendant.

Defendants aged 10 or 11 years

Following a refusal of bail, the defendant must be remanded to local authority ac- **33–12** commodation, with or without conditions, under s.23 of the *Children and Young Persons Act* 1969.

Children and Young Persons Act 1969, s.23

Remands and committals to local authority accommodation

33–13   **23.**—(1) Where—

      (a) a court remands a child or young person charged with or convicted of one or more offences or commits him for trial or sentence; and

      (b) he is not released on bail,

the remand or committal shall be to local authority accommodation; and in the following provisions of this section, any reference (however expressed) to a remand shall be construed as including a reference to a committal.

(2) A court remanding a person to local authority accommodation shall designate the local authority who are to receive him; and that authority shall be—

      (a) in the case of a person who is being looked after by a local authority, that authority; and

      (b) in any other case, the local authority in whose area it appears to the court that he resides or the offence or one of the offences was committed.

(3) Where a person is remanded to local authority accommodation, it shall be lawful for any person acting on behalf of the designated authority to detain him.

(4)–(6) [security requirements, see below]

33–14   (7) Subject to section 23AA below, a court remanding a person to local authority accommodation without imposing a security requirement may, after consultation with the designated authority, require that person to comply with

      (a) any such conditions as could be imposed under section 3(6) of the *Bail Act* 1976 if he were then being granted bail; and

      (b) any conditions imposed for the purpose of securing the electronic monitoring of his compliance with any other condition imposed under this subsection.

(7A) [security requirements, see below]

(7B) [security requirements, see below]

(8) Where a court imposes on a person any such conditions as are mentioned in subsection (7) above, it shall be its duty to explain to him in open court and in ordinary language why it is imposing those conditions; and a magistrates' court shall cause a reason stated by it under this subsection to be specified in the warrant of commitment and to be entered in the register.

(9) A court remanding a person to local authority accommodation without imposing a security requirement may, after consultation with the designated authority, impose on that authority requirements—

      (a) for securing compliance with any conditions imposed on that person under subsection (7) above; or

      (b) stipulating that he shall not be placed with a named person.

(10) Where a person is remanded to local authority accommodation, a relevant court—

      (a) may, on the application of the designated authority, impose on that person any such conditions as could be imposed under subsection (7) above if the court were then remanding him to such accommodation; and

      (b) where it does so, may impose on that authority any requirements for securing compliance with the conditions so imposed.

(11) Where a person is remanded to local authority accommodation, a relevant court may, on the application of the designated authority or that person, vary or revoke any conditions or requirements imposed under subsections (7), (9) or (10) above.

33–15   (12) In this section—

    "children's home" has the same meaning as in the *Care Standards Act* 2000;

    "court" and "magistrates' court" include a justice;

    "imprisonable offence" means an offence punishable in the case of an adult with imprisonment;

    "prescribed description" means a description prescribed by reference to age or sex or both by an order of the Secretary of State;

"relevant court", in relation to a person remanded to local authority accommodation, means the court by which he was so remanded, or any magistrates' court having jurisdiction in the place where he is for the time being;

"secure accommodation" means accommodation which is provided in a children's home in respect of which a person is registered under Part II of the *Care Standards Act* 2000 for the purpose of restricting liberty, and is approved for that purpose by the Secretary of State or the National Assembly for Wales;

"sexual offence" and "violent offence" have the same meanings as in the *PCC(S)A* 2000;

"young person" means a person who has attained the age of fourteen years and is under the age of seventeen years.

but, for the purposes of the definition of "secure accommodation", "local authority accommodation" includes any accommodation falling within section 61(2) of the *Criminal Justice Act* 1991.

(13) In this section—   **33–16**

(a) any reference to a person who is being looked after by a local authority shall be construed in accordance with section 22 of the *Children Act* 1989;

(b) any reference to consultation shall be construed as a reference to such consultation (if any) as is reasonably practicable in all the circumstances of the case; and

(c) any reference, in relation to a person charged with or convicted of a violent or sexual offence, to protecting the public from serious harm from him shall be construed as a reference to protecting members of the public from death or serious personal injury, whether physical or psychological, occasioned by further such offences committed by him.

(14) This section has effect subject to—

(b) section 128(7) of that Act (remands to the custody of a constable for periods of not more than three days),

but section 128(7) shall have effect in relation to a child or young person as if for the reference to three clear days there were substituted a reference to twenty-four hours.

Electronic monitoring may not be used to monitor compliance with the local authority remand conditions.

(2) Remand in secure accommodation under s.25 of the Children Act 1989

Power exists under the *Children Act* 1989 to make a Secure Accommodation order. **33–17** This power exists under the civil jurisdiction of the court. If the court indicate to the YOT that the availability of secure accommodation should be investigated and invite the YOT to make enquiries, the YOT *may* subsequently make an application for such an order on behalf of the local authority in which the defendant is ordinarily resident. It is entirely an issue for the local authority as to whether this application is made or not.

Children Act 1989, s.25

Use of accommodation for restricting liberty

25.—(1) Subject to the following provisions of this section, a child who is being looked after **33–18** by a local authority may not be placed, and, if placed, may not be kept, in accommodation provided for the purpose of restricting liberty ("secure accommodation") unless it appears—

(a) that—

(i) he has a history of absconding and is likely to abscond from any other description of accommodation; and

(ii) if he absconds, he is likely to suffer significant harm; or

(b) that if he is kept in any other description of accommodation he is likely to injure himself or other persons.

(2) [powers of Secretary of State]

(3) It shall be the duty of a court hearing an application under this section to determine whether any relevant criteria for keeping a child in secure accommodation are satisfied in his case.

(4) If a court determines that any such criteria are satisfied, it shall make an order authorising the child to be kept in secure accommodation and specifying the maximum period for which he may be so kept.

(5) On any adjournment of the hearing of an application under this section, a court may make an interim order permitting the child to be kept during the period of the adjournment in secure accommodation.

(6) No court shall exercise the powers conferred by this section in respect of a child who is not legally represented in that court unless, having been informed of his right to apply for representation funded by the Legal Services Commission as part of the Community Legal Service or Criminal Defence Service and having had the opportunity to do so, he refused or failed to apply.

(7) [powers of Secretary of State]

(8) The giving of an authorisation under this section shall not prejudice any power of any court in England and Wales or Scotland to give directions relating to the child to whom the authorisation relates.

(9) This section is subject to section 20(8).

33–19　Regulation 4 of the *Children (Secure Accommodation) Regulations* 1991 provides that a child under 13 may only be placed in secure accommodation with the approval of the Secretary of State for Health. Regulation 5(2)(a) provides that 16- and 17-year-olds accommodated under s.20(5) of the *Children Act* 1989 (which allows the local authority to provide accommodation for any person aged 16 to 20 years if they consider that doing so would safeguard or promote his own welfare) may not be placed in secure accommodation. Children detained under any provision of the *Mental Health Act* 1983 may not be the subject of an order under s.25.

Proceedings for a secure accommodation order are not criminal proceedings within the meaning of Art.6 of the ECHR: *Re C (A Child) (Secure Accommodation order: Representation)* (2001) 2 F.L.R 169. However, a child facing such an application is entitled to the minimum rights to a fair trial set out in Art.6(3) of the European Convention. The requirement that the defendant is legally represented may, in exceptional cases, be satisfied where the defendant's solicitor is only served with the application on the day of the hearing. However, the preferred course of action in such circumstances would be the making of an interim order under s.25(5) of the *Children Act* 1989, which would authorise further detention in secure accommodation, and allow the defence adequate time to prepare its case: *Re C* (above) *per* Thorpe and Brooke L.JJ.

33–20　A court may make a secure accommodation order under s.25 of the *Children Act* 1989 where the criteria for detention in secure accommodation in s.23 of the *Children and Young Persons Act* are not satisfied: *Re G (A Child) (Secure Accommodation order)* (2001) 1 F.L.R. 884. However, where a child has been remanded to local authority accommodation under s.23 of the *Children and Young Persons Act* 1969, the court may only make an order for secure accommodation where the criteria in reg.6(2) of the *Children (Secure Accommodation) Regulations* 1991 are satisfied: *Re W and D (Secure Accommodation)* [1995] 2 F.L.R. 807.

(a) *Defendants aged 12, 13 or 14 years, and females aged 15 or 16*

33–21　The court has the same powers to remand to local authority accommodation following refusal of bail as it does in the context of defendants aged 10 or 11 years. The additional powers are:

— The court may, after consultation with the YOT, impose a security requirement requiring the local authority to place and keep the youth in secure accommodation. A security requirement is defined in s.23(4) of the 1969 Act as a requirement that the youth be placed in secure accommodation, which is described in s.23(12) of the 1969 Act as accommodation which is provided in a children's home in respect of which a person is registered under Pt II of the *Care Standards Act* 2000 for the purpose of restricting liberty. The conditions relating to the imposition of a security requirement are contained in s.23 of the 1969 Act.

— The provisions of the *CYPA* 1969, s.23AA can be made as a requirement of a remand into local authority accomodation.

Children and Young Persons Act 1969, s.23AA(1)–(6)

Electronic monitoring of conditions of remand

23AA.—(1) A court shall not impose a condition on a person under section 23(7)(b) above **33–22** (an "electronic monitoring condition") unless each of the following requirements is fulfilled.

(2) The first requirement is that the person has attained the age of twelve years.

(3) The second requirement is that—

    (a) the person is charged with or has been convicted of a violent or sexual offence, or an offence punishable in the case of an adult with imprisonment for a term of fourteen years or more; or

    (b) he is charged with or has been convicted of one or more imprisonable offence which, together with any other imprisonable offences of which he has been convicted in any proceedings—

        (i) amount, or

        (ii) would, if he were convicted of the offences with which he is charged, amount,

    to a recent history of repeatedly committing imprisonable offences while remanded on bail or to local authority accommodation.

(4) The third requirement is that the court—

    (a) has been notified by the Secretary of State that electronic monitoring arrangements are available in each petty sessions area which is a relevant area; and

    (b) is satisfied that the necessary provision can be made under those arrangements.

(5) The fourth requirement is that a youth offending team has informed the court that in its opinion the imposition of such a condition will be suitable in the person's case.

(6) Where a court imposes an electronic monitoring condition, the condition shall include provision for making a person responsible for the monitoring; and a person who is made so responsible shall be of a description specified in an order made by the Secretary of State.

[Inserted by *Criminal Justice and Police Act* 2001, s.132.]

Thus, the court must consider the following questions when considering the use of **33–23** electronic monitoring:

    (1) Is the youth aged 12–16?

    (2) Is the offence a violent or sexual offence OR

    (3) Does it carry a punishment of fourteen years or more in the case of an adult offender, OR

    (4) Is the defendant charged with or convicted of one or more imprisonable offences which together with any other imprisonable offences which relate to the defendant amounts to or would amount to a recent history of repeatedly committing imprisonable offences whilst remanded on bail or remanded to local authority accommodation?

Children and Young Persons Act 1969, s.23(4)–(5A), (6), (7A)–(8)

23.—(4) Subject to subsections (5) and (5A) below, a court remanding a person to local **33–24** authority accommodation may, after consultation with the designated authority, require that authority to comply with a security requirement, that is to say, a requirement that the person in question be placed and kept in secure accommodation.

(5) A court shall not impose a security requirement except in respect of a child who has attained the age of twelve, or a young person, who (in either case) is of a prescribed description, and then only if—

    (a) he is charged with or has been convicted of a violent or sexual offence, or an offence punishable in the case of an adult with imprisonment for a term of fourteen years or more; or

    (b) he is charged with or has been convicted of one or more imprisonable offences which, together with any other imprisonable offences of which he has been convicted in any proceedings—

    (i)   amount, or

    (ii) would, if he were convicted of the offences with which he is charged, amount,

to a recent history of repeatedly committing imprisonable offences while remanded on bail or to local authority accommodation,

and (in either case) the condition set out in subsection (5AA) below is satisfied.

33–25   (5AA) The condition mentioned in subsection (5) above is that the court is of the opinion, after considering all the options for the remand of the person, that only remanding him to local authority accommodation with a security requirement would be adequate—

    (a) to protect the public from serious harm from him; or

    (b) to prevent the commission by him of imprisonable offences.

    (5A) A court shall not impose a security requirement in respect of a child or young person who is not legally represented in the court unless—

    (a) he was granted a right to representation funded by the Legal Services Commission as part of the Criminal Defence Service but the right was withdrawn because of his conduct; or

    (b) having been informed of his right to apply for such representation and had the opportunity to do so, he refused or failed to apply.

    (6) Where a court imposes a security requirement in respect of a person, it shall be its duty—

    (a) to state in open court that it is of such opinion as is mentioned in subsection (5AA) above; and

    (b) to explain to him in open court and in ordinary language why it is of that opinion;

and a magistrates' court shall cause a reason stated by it under paragraph (b) above to be specified in the warrant of commitment and to be entered in the register.

33–26   (7A) Where a person is remanded to local authority accommodation and a security requirement is imposed in respect of him—

    (a) the designated local authority may, with the consent of the Secretary of State, arrange for the person to be detained, for the whole or any part of the period of the remand or committal, in a secure training centre; and

    (b) his detention there pursuant to the arrangements shall be lawful.

    (7B) Arrangements under subsection (7A) above may include provision for payments to be made by the authority to the Secretary of State.

    (8) Where a court imposes on a person any such conditions as are mentioned in subsection (7) above, it shall be its duty to explain to him in open court and in ordinary language why it is imposing those conditions; and a Magistrates' Court shall cause a reason stated by it under this subsection to be specified in the warrant of commitment and to be entered in the register.

33–27   In *R. v H (Steven) (Remand: Violent Offences)* [1999] C.L.Y. 1027 the offender was refused bail pending committal for sentence for the offence of taking a vehicle without consent, aggravated by damage caused to another vehicle. The prosecution submitted that the offender should be remanded to a remand centre on account of his having committed a violent offence. The court held that for an offence to be violent it was not necessary that physical harm should have been caused to a person. A collision with a car with people in it, in the circumstances of the offence, could lead to injury to a person. Hence this was a violent offence and remand to a remand centre was appropriate.

Thus the relevant questions for the court when considering the imposition of a security requirement are:

    (1) Is the youth aged 12–14, or a female aged 15–16?

    (2) Is the offence a violent or sexual offence, OR

    (3) An offence punishable in the case of an adult with a term of imprisonment for fourteen years or more, OR

(4) Is the defendant charged with or convicted of 1 or more imprisonable offences which together with any other imprisonable offences which relate to the defendant amounts to or would amount to a recent history of repeatedly committing imprisonable offences while remanded on bail ore remanded to local authority accommodation, AND

(5) Is the court of the opinion that only remanding the defendant to local authority accommodation with a security requirement would be adequate to protect the public from serious harm from him or to prevent the commission by him of imprisonable offences? AND

(6) Is the defendant legally represented?

The court may only impose a security requirement following consultation with the **33–28** designated local authority, the length of consultation being that which is reasonably practicable in all the circumstances of the case: s.23(13)(b) of the 1969 Act. The court imposing the security requirement must also state in open court and explain to the youth in ordinary language why it is of the opinion that a security requirement is necessary.

(b) Male defendants who are aged 15 or 16 years

The options available to a court dealing with a male youth aged 15 or 16 are the **33–29** same as those available for dealing with defendants aged 12 to 14 and 15 and 16-year-old females. However, s.23 of the *Children and Young Persons Act* 1969 is modified in relation to male youths of 15 or 16 years. The effect of these modifications is that the defendant will be remanded to local authority accommodation unless the court considers him to be an offender to whom s.23(5), as modified, applies.

The modification of s.23 was effected by s.98(2)–(6) of the *Crime and Disorder Act* 1998, as amended by s.130 of the *Criminal Justice and Police Act* 2001. The modified statute reads:

Children and Young Persons Act 1969, s.23

Remands and committals to local authority accommodation
    23.—(1) Where—   **33–30**
       (a) a court remands a child or young person charged with or convicted of one or more offences or commits him for trial or sentence; and
       (b) he is not released on bail,
the remand or committal shall be to local authority accommodation; and in the following provisions of this section, any reference (however expressed) to a remand shall be construed as including a reference to a committal.

    (2) A court remanding a person to local authority accommodation shall designate the local authority who are to receive him; and that authority shall be—
       (a) in the case of a person who is being looked after by a local authority, that authority; and
       (b) in any other case, the local authority in whose area it appears to the court that he resides or the offence or one of the offences was committed.

    (3) Where a person is remanded to local authority accommodation, it shall be lawful for any person acting on behalf of the designated authority to detain him.

    (4) Where a court, after consultation with a probation officer, a social worker of a local **33–31** authority social services department or a member of a youth offending team, declares a person to be one to whom subsection (5) below applies—
       (a) it shall remand him to local authority accommodation and require him to be placed and kept in secure accommodation, if—
          (i) it also, after such consultation, declares him to be a person to whom subsection (5A) below applies; and
          (ii) it has been notified that secure accommodation is available for him;
       (b) it shall remand him to a remand centre, if paragraph (a) above does not apply and it has been notified that such a centre is available for the reception from the court of persons to whom subsection (5) below applies; and

(c) it shall remand him to a prison, if neither paragraph (a) nor paragraph (b) above applies.

(4A) A court shall not declare a person who is not legally represented in the court to be a person to whom subsection (5) below applies unless—

(a) he applied for legal aid and the application was refused on the ground that it did not appear his means were such that he required assistance; or

(b) having been informed of his right to apply for legal aid and had the opportunity to do so, he refused or failed to apply.

(5) This subsection applies to a person who—

(a) is charged with or has been convicted of a violent or sexual offence, or an offence punishable in the case of an adult with imprisonment for a term of fourteen years or more; or

(b) has a recent history of absconding while remanded to local authority accommodation, and is charged with or has been convicted of an imprisonable offence alleged or found to have been committed while he was so remanded,

if (in either case) the court is of the opinion that only remanding him to a remand centre or prison, or to local authority accommodation with a requirement that he be placed and kept in secure accommodation, would be adequate to protect the public from serious harm from him.

33–32   (5AA) The condition mentioned in subsection (5) above is that the court is of the opinion, after considering all the options for the remand of the person, that only remanding him to local authority accommodation with a security requirement would be adequate—

(a) to protect the public from serious harm from him; or

(b) to prevent the commission by him of imprisonable offences.

(5A) This subsection applies to a person if the court is of opinion that, by reason of his physical or emotional immaturity or a propensity of his to harm himself, it would be undesirable for him to be remanded to a remand centre or a prison.

(6) Where a court declares a person to be one to whom subsection (5) above applies, it shall be its duty—

(a) to state in open court that it is of such opinion as is mentioned in subsection (5AA) above; and

(b) to explain to him in open court and in ordinary language why it is of that opinion;

and a Magistrates' Court shall cause a reason stated by it under paragraph (b) above to be specified in the warrant of commitment and to be entered in the register.

33–33   (7) Subject to section 23AA below, a court remanding a person to local authority accommodation without imposing a security requirement (that is to say a requirement imposed under subsection (4)(a) above that the person be placed and kept in secure accommodation) may, after consultation with the designated authority, require that person to comply with

(a) any such conditions as could be imposed under section 3(6) of the *Bail Act* 1976 if he were then being granted bail; and

(b) any conditions imposed for the purpose of securing the electronic monitoring of his compliance with any other condition imposed under this subsection.

(7A) Where a person is remanded to local authority accommodation and a security requirement is imposed in respect of him—

(a) the designated local authority may, with the consent of the Secretary of State, arrange for the person to be detained, for the whole or any part of the period of the remand or committal, in a secure training centre; and

(b) his detention there pursuant to the arrangements shall be lawful.

(7B) Arrangements under subsection (7A) above may include provision for payments to be made by the authority to the Secretary of State.

(8) Where a court imposes on a person any such conditions as are mentioned in subsection (7) above, it shall be its duty to explain to him in open court and in ordinary language why it is imposing those conditions; and a magistrates' court shall cause a reason stated by it under this subsection to be specified in the warrant of commitment and to be entered in the register.

(9) A court remanding a person to local authority accommodation without imposing a **33–34** security requirement may after consultation with the designated authority impose on that authority requirements—

    (a) for securing compliance with any conditions imposed on that person under subsection (7) above; or

    (b) stipulating that he shall not be placed with a named person.

(9A) Where a person is remanded to local authority accommodation without the imposition of a security requirement, a relevant court may, on the application of the designated authority, declare him to be a person to whom subsection (5) above applies; and on its doing so, subsection (4) above shall apply.

[Subsections (10)–(14) unchanged by the modifications.]

Hence the relevant questions for the court when considering whether to remand the **33–35** defendant in local authority accommodation or custody are:

    (1) Is the youth a male aged 15–16?

    (2) Is the offence violent or sexual, OR

    (3) Is the offence punishable in the case of an adult with imprisonment for a term of 14 years or more, OR

    (4) Has thedefendant been charged with or convicted of 1 or more imprisonable offences which together with any other imprisonable offences of which he has been convicted in any proceedings amount to or would if he were convicted of the offences with which he has been charged amount to a recent history of repeatedly committing imprisonable offences while remanded on bail or remanded to local authority accommodation? AND

    (5) Is the court of the opinion that only remanding the defendant to the local authority accommodation with a security requirement would be adequate to protect the public from serious harm from him or prevent the commission by him of imprisonable offences?

In *R. v Croydon Youth Court Ex p. Grinham (A Minor), The Times*, May 3, 1995, **33–36** the Court of Appeal held that under s.23(5) a court has to be satisfied that a young person whom it was considering remanding was liable to cause harm that could sensibly be described as serious, on account of the nature of the offence or offences that might be committed, and not merely the risk of repetition. It is not the case that following commission of an offence punishable in the case of an adult with imprisonment for a term of fourteen years or more, the court can conclude that only remanding the offender to a remand centre would be adequate to protect the public from serious harm from him. Leggatt L.J. cited the example of the offence of burglary of a dwelling, stating that such an offence is "not necessarily calculated to cause serious harm if, *e.g.* the burglar is careful only to enter unoccupied houses in daylight and steal television sets. A series of such offences, if apprehended, could not be aggregated so as to render serious such harm as might be caused by them".

The issue of vulnerability was examined in *R. (on the application of SR) v Notting-* **33–37** *ham Magistrates' Court* (2002) 166 J.P.N. 209. An offender described as emotionally immature, with a limited range of coping strategies such as to render him at greater risk of self-harm should he be placed in a punitive and stressful environment such as a Young Offenders Institution, was found to be vulnerable for the purposes of s.5A of the 1969 Act by the Divisional Court. The court also held that a young person who had been told by Justices that they regarded him as vulnerable for remand purposes, had a legitimate expectation that such a conclusion would subsist up until the time of sentencing unless he was told that his status might change or another compelling reason existed to alter his status.

(c) *Defendants aged 17 years*

A defendant aged 17 will be treated in the same way as an adult, hence refusal of bail **33–38** will lead to remand in custody. Section 128 (6) of the *Magistrates' Courts Act* 1980 gives guidance as to the maximum period of remand.

33–39　　　　　　　**FLOWCHART FOR BAIL DECISION MAKING**

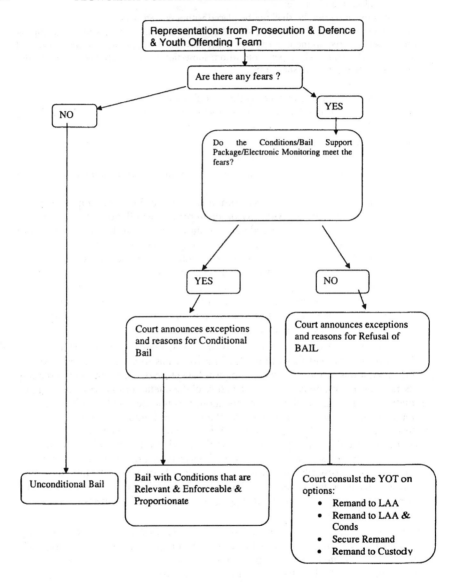

DECISION MAKING PROCESS FOR SECURE REMAND OF 15-16 YR OLDS BOYS UNDER SEC 23(5) CYPA 1969 (AS AMENDED) BY CJPOA 2001

33–40

Is the Youth aged 15-16 ? (BOY)

NO

YES

Secure remand **not** available for children **under 12** For those aged **12-14,** specific rules apply- (see other flowchart)

Is the offence
- Violent or Sexual OR
- Does it carry 14 years or more OR
- is the defendant charged with or convicted of 1 or more imprisonable offences which together with any other imprisonable offences which relate to the defendant amounts to or would amount to a **recent history of repeatedly committing imprisonable offences while remanded on bail or remanded to LAA**

AND :the court is of the opinion that only remanding to LAA with a security requirement would be adequate –
- to protect the public from serious harm from him: OR
- to prevent the commission by him of imprisonable offences

MUST BE LEGALLY REPRESENTED

YES

NO

Is the defendant 'Vulnerable' Court MUST consult the YOT team)

Secure Remand Not Available

YES

NO

Secure Remand to LAA with Security Requirement "Court Ordered Secure Remand"

Remand In Custody to Feltham

33–41

DECISION MAKING PROCESS FOR SECURE REMAND OF 12-14 YR OLDS BOYS AND 12-16 YEAR OLD GIRLS UNDER SEC 23(5) CYPA 1969 (AS AMENDED) BY SEC 130 CJPOA 2001

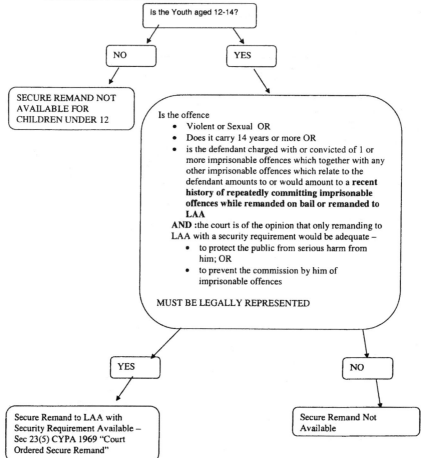

CHAPTER 34

SENTENCING IN THE YOUTH COURT

I. INTRODUCTION

34–1 The youth court is given wide and flexible powers of sentence. Sentencing young offenders is a difficult duty, which involves balancing the seriousness of the offence and offending history, against the welfare needs of young offenders, many of whom have led highly disrupted lives. The availability of the various orders set out in this Chapter partly depend on the age of the offender. In addition some of the orders can be combined with each other to produce a sentencing "package" specifically designed to meet the needs of individual offenders (see the sentence availability and combination charts, below).

The principal aim of the youth justice system is to prevent offending: *Crime and Disorder Act* 1998, s.37, above. This is therefore the youth courts' principal aim in the sentencing process. The court must also have regard to the welfare principle: *Children and Young Persons Act* 1933, s.44, above.

34–2 The aim of "preventing offending" may be given a wide interpretation. In *R. v Inner London Crown Court Ex p. N and S* [2001] 1 Cr.App.R.(S.) 99 the Divisional Court stated (although the point had not been argued before them) that "in the light of s.37 of the Act (*CDA* 1998—see above) in appropriate cases, the need to impose a deterrent sentence in relation to an offender under the age of 18 may take priority over s.44 of the *Children and Young Person Act* 1933, which requires the court to promote the welfare of the individual offender."

The welfare of young offenders remains a vitally important issue for the youth court to consider. However the principal aim of the youth justice system is to "prevent offending." The welfare principal is therefore of relevance and importance to the sentencing court in so far as it is consistent with achieving the prevention of offending by the offender.

34–3 Like the adult magistrates' Court, the youth court sentencing powers fall into the following categories—

1. First Tier Penalties
   — absolute and conditional discharge
   — compensation order
   — fine
   — referral order
   — reparation order
2. Community Penalties
   — attendance centre order
   — action plan order
   — supervision order
   — curfew order
   — community rehabilitation order
   — community punishment order
   — community punishment and rehabilitation order
   — drug treatment and testing order
3. Custodial Sentence
   — The detention and training order
4. Ancillary Orders
   — compensation
   — costs
   — anti-social behaviour order
   — parenting order
   — parental bindover

34–4   Statutory restrictions on imposing community and custodial sentences apply to youths in the same way as they apply to adult offenders.

Powers of Criminal Courts (Sentencing) Act 2000, s.35(1)–(3)

Restrictions on imposing community sentences.

34–5   **35.**—(1) A court shall not pass a community sentence on an offender unless it is of the opinion that the offence, or the combination of the offence and one of more offences associated with it, was serious enough to warrant such a sentence.

(2) In consequence of the provision made by section 51 below with respect to combination orders, a community sentence shall not consist of or include both a Probation order and a Community Service order.

(3) Subject to subsection (2) above and to section 69(5) below (which limits the Community orders that may be combined with an Action Plan order), where a court passes a community sentence—

    (a) the particular order or orders comprising or forming part of the sentence shall be such as in the opinion of the court is, or taken together are, the most suitable for the offender; and

    (b) the restrictions on liberty imposed by the order or orders shall be such as in the opinion of the court are commensurate with the seriousness of the offence or the combination of the offence and one or more offences associated with it.

Powers of Criminal Courts (Sentencing) Act 2000, s.79(1)–(3)(b)

General restrictions on imposing discretionary custodial sentences.

34–6   **79.**—(1) This Section applies where a person is convicted of an offence punishable with a custodial sentence other than—

    (a) fix by law; or

    (b) falling to imposed under section 109(2), 110(2) or 111(2).

(2) Subject to subsection (3) below, the court shall not pass a custodial sentence on the offender unless it is of the opinion—

    (a) that the offence, or the combination of the offence and one or more offences associated with it, was so serious that only such a sentence can be justified for the offence; or

    (b) where the offence is a violent or sexual offence, that only such a sentence would be adequate to protect the public from serious harm from him.

(3) Nothing in subsection (2) above shall prevent the court from passing a custodial sentence on the offender if he fails to express his willing as to comply with—

    (a) a requirement which is proposed by the court to be included in a Community Rehabilitation order or Supervision order and which requires an expression of such willingness; or

    (b) a requirement which is proposed by the court to be included in a Drug Treatment and Testing order or an order under section 52(4) (order to provide samples).

In coming to its decision as to an appropriate sentence therefore, the youth court must take, as its starting point the seriousness of the offence and/or offences associated with it, including any aggravating or mitigating factors. In assessing the seriousness of the offence the court must take into account the offender's criminal record.

Powers of Criminal Courts (Sentencing) Act 2000, s.151(1)–(2)

Effect of previous convictions and of offending while on bail.

34–7

151.—(1) In considering the seriousness of any offence, the court may take into account any previous convictions of the offender or any failure of his to respond to previous sentences.

(2) In considering the seriousness of any offence committed while the offender was on bail, the court shall treat the fact that it was committed in those circumstances as an aggravating factor.

If the offender has pleaded guilty he is entitled to be given credit for his plea and that may be reflected in the sentence he receives:

Powers of Criminal Courts (Sentencing) Act 2000, s.152(1)–(2)

Reduction in sentences for guilty pleas.

34–8

152.—(1) In determining what sentence to pass on an offender who has pleaded guilty to an offence in proceedings before that or another court, a court shall take into account—

    (a) the stage in the proceedings for the offence at which the offender indicated his intention to plead guilty; and

    (b) the circumstances in which this indication was given.

(2) If, as a result of taking into account any matter referred to in subsection (1) above the court imposes a punishment on the offender which is less severe than the punishment it would otherwise have imposed, it shall state in open court that it has done so.

34–9

In *R. v Christopher Pitt* [2002] 1 Cr.App.R.(S.) 46 the court of appeal dealt with an appeal against an 18 months detention and training order made against a 17-year-old defendant. The grounds of the appeal were that insufficient credit had been given to the appellant for his plea of guilty and also time he had spent in custody on remand. The court of appeal reduced the appellant's sentence to 12 months, that being the next "step down" from the 18 month sentence originally imposed.

The court will hear mitigation put forward by the defence. In the youth court, such mitigation will inevitably refer to the contents of a pre-sentence report, or a specific sentence report.

34–10

Written reports on defendants in the youth court are usually prepared by the YOT on the order of the court. Such reports play a vitally important role in the sentencing process. The court will indicate the type of penalty it has in mind on ordering the report. A report dealing with the offender's suitability for community penalties may be requested. Alternatively the court may indicate a specified penalty that it has in mind. If the court is considering a community penalty it must be satisfied that the offence or offences are serious enough to justify that type of penalty.

If the court considers that the offence or offences are so serious that a custodial sentence may be justified a full pre-sentence report will be ordered which must deal with the offender's suitability for such a order.

34–11

The contents of pre-sentence reports are governed by national standards. Such reports should include an analysis of the offence, an assessment of the offender, an assessment of his/her risk of re-offending and risk to the community, and a conclusion which may include a recommendation for the court's consideration. The court will expect the young offender, his parents, and his legal representative to be aware of the contents of any report that the YOT has prepared before the sentencing hearing begins.

This section will now go on to describe each of the various sentences the youth court has power to impose.

34–12

Sentencing Availability Matrix

Order/Age	10 to 11 years	12 to 13 years	14 years	15 years	16 to 17 years
Absolute Discharge	√	√	√	√	√
Referral Order	3 to 12 months	3 to 12 months	3 to 12 months	3 to 12 months	3 to 12 months
Conditional Discharge	Max. 3 year	Max. 3 year	Max. 3 year	Max. 3 year	Max. 3 year
Fine	Max. £250	Max. £250	Max. £1000	Max. £100	Max. £1000
Reparation Order	Max. 24 hours	Max. 24 hours	Max. 24 hours	Max. 24 hours	Max. 24 hours
Action Plan Order	3 months	3 months	3 months	3 months	3 months
Attendance Centre	Max. 12 hours	Max. 12 hours	Max. 24 hours	Max. 24 hours	Max. 36 hours
Supervision Order	Max. 3 year	Max. 3 year	Max. 3 year	Max. 3 year	Max. 3 year
Community Rehabilitation Order	×	×	×	×	6 months to 3 years
Community Punishment Order	×	×	×	×	40 to 240 hours
Community Rehabilitation & Punishment Order	×	×	×	×	1 to 3 years/40 to 100 hours
Curfew Order	3 months; 2 to 12 hours daily	3 months; 2 to 12 hours daily	3 months; 2 to 12 hours daily	3 months; 2 to 12 hours daily	6 months; 2 to 12 hours daily
Drug Treatment & Testing Order	×	×	×	×	6 months to 3 years
Detention & Training Order	×	4, 6, 8, 10, 12, 18, 24 months (if persistent)	4, 6, 8, 10, 12, 18, 24 months (if persistent)	4, 6, 8, 10, 12, 18, 24 months	4, 6, 8, 10, 12, 18, 24 months

34–13

Youth Court Sentence Compatibility Table

	A.D.	C.D.	Fine	Costs	Comp.	Refer Order	Parenting Order	Rep. Order	A.P.O.	Super.	ACO	CRO	CPO	CRO/CPO	Curfew	DTTO	DTO
A.D.				√	√		√										
C.D.				√	√		√										
Fine				√	√		√										
Costs	√	√	√		√	√	√	√	√	√	√	√	√	√	√	√	√
Comp	√	√	√	√		√	√	√	√	√	√	√	√	√	√	√	√
Refer. Order				√	√												
Parenting Order	√	√	√	√				√	√	√	√	√	√	√	√	√	√
Rep. Order				√	√		√										
Action Plan				√	√		√								√		
Super.				√	√		√								√		
ACO				√	√		√								√		
CRO				√	√		√								√		
CPO				√	√		√								√		
CRO/CPO				√	√		√								√		
Curfew				√	√		√		√	√	√	√	√	√		√	
DTTO				√	√		√		√	√	√	√	√	√	√		
DTO				√	√		√										

II. ABSOLUTE AND CONDITIONAL DISCHARGES

Powers of Criminal Courts (Sentencing) Act 2000, s.12

Absolute and conditional discharge

34–14   **12.**—(1) Where a court by or before which a person is convicted of an offence (not being an offence the sentence for which is fixed by law or falls to be imposed under section 109(2), 110(2) or 111(2) below) is of the opinion, having regard to the circumstances including the nature of the offence and the character of the offender, that it is inexpedient to inflict punishment, the court may make an order either—

   (a) discharging him absolutely; or

   (b) if the court thinks fit, discharging him subject to the condition that he commits no offence during such period, not exceeding 3 years from the date of the order as may be specified in the order.

   (2) Subsection (1)(b) above has effect subject to section 66(4) of the *Crime and Disorder Act* 1998 (effect of reprimands and warnings).

(3)–(7) [*omitted*]

Crime and Disorder Act 1998, ss.65, 66

Reprimands and warnings

65.—(1) Subsections (2) to (5) below apply where—   **34–15**
  (a) a constable has evidence that a child or young person (the offender) has commit-
      ted an offence;
  (b) the constable considers that the evidence is such that, if the offender were prose-
      cuted for the offence, there would be a realistic prospect of his being convicted;
  (c) the offender admits to the constable that he committed the offence;
  (d) the offender has not previously been convicted of an offence; and
  (e) the constable is satisfied that it would not be in the public interest for the offender
      to be prosecuted.
  (2) Subject to subsection (4) below, the constable may reprimand the offender if the offender has not previously been reprimanded or warned.
  (3) The constable may warn the offender if—
  (a) the offender has not previously been warned; or
  (b) where the offender has previously been warned, the offence was committed more
      than 2 years after the date of the previous warning and the constable considers
      the offence to be not so serious as to require a charge to be brought;
but no person may be warned under paragraph (b) above more than once.
  (4) Where the offender has not been previously reprimanded, the constable shall warn
rather than reprimand the offender if he considers the offence to be so serious as to
require a warning.
  (5) The constable shall—
  (a) give any reprimand or warning at a police station and, where the offender is
      under the age of 17, in the presence of an appropriate adult; and
  (b) explain to the offender and, where he is under that age, the appropriate adult in
      ordinary language—
      (i) in the case of a reprimand, the effect of subsection (5)(a) of section 66
           below; and
      (ii) in the case of a warning, the effect of subsections (1), (2), (4) and (5)(b) and
           (c) of that section, and any guidance issued under subsection (3) of that
           Section.
  (6)–(9) [*omitted*]

Effect of reprimands and warnings

66.—(1)–(3) [*omitted*]   **34–16**
  (4) Where a person who has been warned under section 65 above is convicted of an of-
fence committed within 2 years of the warning, the court by or before which he is so
convicted—
  (a) shall not make an order under subsection (1) (b) (conditional discharge) of sec-
      tion 12 of the *Powers of Criminal Courts (Sentencing) Act* 2000 in respect of the
      offence unless it is of the opinion that there are exceptional circumstances relating to
      the offence or the offender which justify its doing so; and
  (b) where it does so, shall state in open court that it is of that opinion and why it is.
  (5)–(6) [*omitted*]

The youth court may order the absolute discharge of an offender if, after assessing **34–17**
the seriousness of the case and taking into account personal mitigation, it is of the
opinion that punishment is inappropriate.
    If the youth court is of the view that immediate punishment is inappropriate provid-
ing the offender does not re-offend, it may discharge the offender on condition that he
he/she does not re-offend for a period of a maximum of three years. If the offender
does re-offend within the period of that conditional discharge he will be in breach of
that order and will be liable to be sentenced for the original offence as well as being
sentenced for the new offence that he has committed.
    Conditional discharge orders used to be frequently imposed by the youth court, es- **34–18**

pecially upon those falling to be sentenced by the court for the first time. However this category of offender now usually falls to be dealt with by way of a referral order.

The use of orders of conditional discharge is restricted for young offenders. If the offender commits an offence within two years of receiving a warning under s.65, above, the youth court shall not make an order of conditional discharge unless it is of the opinion that there are exceptional circumstances which either relate to the offence or the offender which justify such an order. There is no definition in statute or case law as to what circumstances might be regarded as "exceptional" under this section.

It should be noted that an order of absolute discharge may be made in respect of an offender who would otherwise be made the subject of a referral order under *PCC(S)A* 2000, s.16.

III. REFERRAL ORDERS

Powers of Criminal Courts (Sentencing) Act 2000, s.16

Duty and power to refer certain young offenders to youth offender panels

34–19   **16.**—(1) This section applies where a Youth Court or other Magistrates' court is dealing with a person aged under 18 for an offence and—

    (a) neither the offence nor any connected offence is one for which the sentence is fixed by law;

    (b) the court is not in respect of the offence or any connected offence, proposing to impose a custodial sentence on the offender or make a hospital order in his case; and

    (c) the court is not proposing to discharge him absolutely in respect of the offence.

    (2) If—

    (a) the compulsory referral conditions are satisfied in accordance with section 17 below; and

    (b) referral is available to the court,

the court shall sentence the offender for the offence by ordering him to be referred to a youth Offender Panel.

    (3) If—

    (a) the discretionary referral conditions are satisfied in accordance with section 17 below; and

    (b) referral is available to the court,

the court may sentence the offender for the offence by ordering him to be referred to a youth Offender Panel.

34–20   (4) For the purposes of this part an offence is connected with another if the offender falls to be dealt with for it at the same time as he is dealt with for the other offence (whether or not he is convicted of the offences at the same time or by or before the same court).

    (5)–(7) [*omitted*]

34–21   Referral orders are a comparatively new provision introducing a mandatory sentence for young offenders appearing before a youth or magistrates' court for the first time. On making such an order, the defendant is referred to a youth offender panel.

The referral order must—

    (a) specify the Youth Offending Team responsible for implementing the order;

    (b) require the offender to attend each meeting of a youth offender panel to be established by the team for the offender; and

    (c) specify the period for which any youth offender contract taking effect between the offender and the panel is to have effect being a period of not less than 3 months nor more than 12 months.

The panel consists of a YOT officer and two community volunteers who are not members of a YOT. It is the defendant's responsibility to attend the panel. One of the main purposes of a referral order is for the panel to engage in a dialogue with the young offender and his parents or guardian. The panel is not a court and formalities are kept to a minimum. To this end, on making a referral order the youth court shall make an order requiring at least one parent or guardian to attend meetings with the YOT unless the court considers that it would be unreasonable to make such an order.

At the meetings members of the panel will speak to the defendant and his family. The aims of the panel are to stop further offending, help the offender right the wrong he did to his victim, and help the offender with any problems he might have. To this end they will discuss with him why he committed the crime in question. They will speak to him about other relevant aspects of his life. The victim may well be present at one or more of the meetings. The panel will then agree with the defendant a youth offender contract, which is a programme of behaviour aimed at preventing re-offending. It is for the sentencing court to specify the length of the contract which can be from 3 to 12 months duration. It is for the panel (and not the court) to agree the terms of the youth offender contract.

If the referral conditions set out in s.17(1) below are satisfied the court must make a **34–22** referral order if the offence is an imprisonable one.

Powers of Criminal Courts (Sentencing) Act 2000, s.17(1)

The referral conditions

17.—(1) For the purposes of section 16(2) above the compulsory referral conditions are satis- **34–23** fied in relation to an offence if the offender—

    (a) pleads guilty to the offence and to any connected offence;

    (b) has never been convicted by or before a court in the United Kingdom of any of-
        fence other than the offence and any connected offence; and

    (c) has never been bound over in criminal proceedings in England and Wales or
        Northern Ireland to keep the peace or be of good behaviour.

A referral order cannot be made unless the offender pleads guilty to the offence with which he is charged. The order is clearly designed to encourage young people to admit their guilt by restricting the courts powers of sentence and allowing the conviction to become "spent" at an earlier stage.

Rehabilitation of Offenders Act 1974, s.5(4B)

5.—(4B) Where in respect of a conviction a referral order (within the meaning of the *Powers* **34–24** *of Criminal Courts (Sentencing) Act* 2000 is made in respect of the person convicted, the reha- bilitation period applicable to the sentence shall be—

    (a) if a youth offender contract takes effect under section 23 of that Act between him
        and a youth Offender Panel, the period beginning with the date of conviction
        and ending on the date when (in accordance with section 24 of that Act) the
        contract ceases to have effect;

    (b) if no such contract so takes effect, the period beginning with the date of convic-
        tion and having the same length as the period for which such a contract would
        (ignoring any order under paragraph 11 or 12 of Schedule 1 to that Act) have
        had any effect had one so taken effect.

If a defendant has been convicted or bound over by or before a court in the United Kingdom he cannot be made the subject of a referral order. It should be noted that the existence of cautions, reprimands or final warnings do not prevent a referral order be- ing made. The only circumstances in which the court may not make a referral order is if it considers the offence to be of such a nature that an absolute discharge is appropriate, or it considers the offence to be so serious that a custodial sentence is appropriate.

If s.17(2) is satisfied, the court has a discretion whether or not to make a referral order.

Powers of Criminal Courts (Sentencing) Act 2000, s.17(2)

The Discretionary Referral Conditions

17.—(2) For the purposes of section 16(3) above the discretionary referral conditions are **34–25** satisfied in relation to an offence if—

   (a) the offender is being dealt with by the court for an offence and one or more connected offences;

   (b) although he pleaded guilty to at least one of the offences mentioned in paragraph (a) above he also pleaded not guilty to at least one of them;

   (c) he has never been convicted by or before a court in the United Kingdom of any offence other than the offences mentioned in paragraph (a) above; and

   (d) he has never been bound over in criminal proceedings in England and Wales or Northern Ireland to keep the peace or be of good behaviour.

This section now also applies if the offender has pleaded guilty to a non-imprisonable offence.

34–26   The distinction between imprisonable and non-imprisonable offences in relation to referral orders applies to those sentenced on and after August 18, 2003. If the court decides not to make a referral order in respect of a non-imprisonable offence it may impose any other sentence which it has the power to impose.

Where the first time offender is charged with a mix of imprisonable and non-imprisonable offences and in other respects qualifies for a referral order and the court make a referral order in respect of the imprisonable offences, it must also make a referral order in respect of the non-imprisonable offences.

On making a referral order the court must nominate the appropriate YOT responsible for the defendant. If the defendant is under 16 years of age the court must include a requirement that at least one of his parents attend the meetings with the youth offender panel.

On making a referral order the court can also make orders for compensation, forfeiture and deprivation and costs. The court may make a parenting order when making a referral order: *CJA* 2003, Sch.34.

(1) Breach of Referral Order

34–27   The youth offender panel may refer an offender back to the youth court on the basis that he/she has failed to comply with the referral order and the subsequent youth offender contract. The court must then cause the offender to appear before it by issuing a summons or, if the report is substantiated on oath, a warrant. If, at the subsequent hearing, the court is satisfied that the offender has breached the referral order, it may revoke that order and go on to deal with the offender in any other way he/she could have been dealt with for that offence by the court that made the order. In such circumstances the court will often be assisted by information from the YOT regarding the extent of the offender's compliance with the referral order and the circumstances of his referral back to the court. A written report from the YOT might also suggest an appropriate order to make on re-sentencing.

(2) Further Convictions during Referral

Powers of Criminal Courts (Sentencing) Act 2000, Sch.1, Pt II, paras 10–12

Extension of referral for further offences

34–28   10.—(1) Paragraphs 11 and 12 below apply where, at a time when an offender aged under 18 is subject to referral, a Youth Court or other magistrates' court is dealing with him for an offence in relation to which paragraphs (a) to (c) of section 16(1) of this Act are applicable.

(2) But paragraphs 11 and 12 do not apply unless the offenders compliance period is less than 12 months.

Extension where further offences committed pre-referral

   11. If—

   (a) the occasion on which the offender was referred back to the Panel is the only other occasion on which it has fallen to a court in the United Kingdom to deal with the offender for any offence or offences, and

(b) the offender committed the offence mentioned in paragraph 10 above, and any
    connected offence, before he was referred to the Panel,
the relevant court many sentence the offender for the offence by making an order extending his compliance period.

Extension where further offence committed after referral

12.—(1) If—

(a) Paragraph 11(a) above applies, but
(b) the offender committed the offence mentioned in paragraph 10 above or any
    connected offence, after he was referred to the Panel,
the relevant court may sentence the offender for the offence by making an order extending his
compliance period but only if the requirements of sub-paragraph (2) below are complied with.

(2) Those requirements are that the court must—

(a) be satisfied, on the basis of a report made to it by the relevant body that there are
    exceptional circumstances which indicate that, even though the offender has re-
    offended since being referred to the Panel, extending his compliance period is
    likely to help prevent further re-offending by him; and
(b) state in open court that it is so satisfied and why it is.

(3) In sub paragraph (2) above "the relevant body" means the Panel to which the offender has been referred, or if no contact has yet taken effect between the offender and the
Panel under section 23 of this Act, the specified Team.

Paragraphs 10, 11 and 12 above deal with the situation where the offender has been
further convicted during the course of his Referral order. These paragraphs allow the
original Referral order to be extended in respect of the new offence. However it should
be noted that orders made under paragraphs 11 or 12 above must not extend the offender's Referral order so as to cause it to exceed 12 months.

There are two scenarios. Under para.11 above, the new offence is committed before   **34–29**
the referral order was made. In such a case, the court has discretion to sentence the offender for the offence by making an order extending the compliance period, as long as
it does not exceed 12 months in total. Under para.12 above a new offence has been
committed after the referral order was made. Under these circumstances the court may
also extend the existing referral order up to the 12 month limit. However before doing
so the court must be satisfied with those matters set out in para.12(2)(a) and (b) above.

In either scenario, the youth court has discretion as to whether to extend the existing
referral order. This will depend on the aggravating and mitigating factors that apply to
the new offence. Additionally the court will wish to have a verbal or written report from
the YOT indicating the offender's progress on the existing referral order. If the court
considers that extending the referral order is inappropriate the offender will be
sentenced in some other way for the new offence. This will have implications for the
original referral order.

Powers of Criminal Courts (Sentencing) Act 2000 Sch.1, Pt II, para.14

Further convictions which lead to revocation of referral

14.—(1) This paragraph applies where, at a time when an offender is subject to referral,   **34–30**
a court in England and Wales deals with him for an offence (whether committed before or
after he was referred to the Panel) by making an order other than—

(a) an order under paragraph 11 or 12 above; or
(b) an order discharging him absolutely.

(2) In such a case the order of the court shall have the effect of revoking—

(a) the referral order (or orders); and
(b) any related order (or orders) under paragraph 11 or 12 above.

(3) Where any order is revoked by virtue of sub-paragraph (2) above, the court may, if
it appears to the court that it would be in the interests of justice to do so, deal with the offender for the offence in respect of which the revoked order was made in any way which
(assuming section 16 of this Act had not applied) he could have been dealt with for that offence by the court which made the order.

(4) When dealing with the offender under sub-paragraph (3) above, the court shall, where a contract has taken effect between the offender and the panel under section 23 of this Act, have regard to the extent of his compliance with the terms of the contract.

IV. FINES AND OTHER FINANCIAL PENALTIES

A. Fines

34–31　　The amount of a fine imposed by the youth court on a young offender must reflect the seriousness of the offence and the defendant's financial circumstances.

The maximum fine which may be imposed on a youth is dependent upon his age: *PCC(S)A* 2000, s.135, Pt III. The amounts are as follows:

(a) 10–13 years of age inclusive—the maximum fine is £250.

(b) 14–17 years of age inclusive—the maximum fine is £1,000.

Where the fine is imposed on a youth under the age of 16 years the court is under a duty to order that the fine, compensation or costs awarded, be paid by the parent or guardian of the youth instead of by the youth himself, unless the court is satisfied that:

(a) the parent or guardian cannot be found;

(b) it would be unreasonable to make an order for payment having regard to the circumstances of the case.

Where the youth has attained the age of 16, the court duty to make an order against the parent or guardian is discretionary: *PCC(S)A* 2000, s.137, Pt III.

Before making an order against a parent or guardian the youth court must give such person the opportunity of being heard. If the parent or guardian has not attended, the court must require their attendance. If they fail to attend an order for payment may be made against them in their absence. When a fine or compensation is ordered to be paid by a parent or guardian, their means or financial circumstances must be taken into consideration. If, having imposed a financial penalty, the parent or guardian fails to pay, then enforcement powers will apply in the Adult court.

Upon imposing a fine against a young offender the youth court may grant time to pay, fix periodical payments, or make a Money Payment Supervision order. If there is default in payment, the court also has power:

(a) to make an Attendance Centre order (Attendance Centre—see §§ 26–78—26–82); or

(b) to order the parent or guardian (who must be given an opportunity to attend) to pay the fine, if the court is satisfied that the offender has had the means to pay the sum or any instalment of it on which he has defaulted and has refused or neglected to pay.

Where the offender is under the age of 18 years the youth court does not have power to fix a term of detention in default of payment of a fine.

B. Compensation

34–32　　A Compensation order may be made against a young offender as a penalty in itself or in addition to other penalties that the court has imposed.

Compensation is governed by s.137 of the *PCC(S)A* 2000. If the youth court decides that the victim of the offence has suffered a loss that deserved to be compensated and that the case would be appropriately dealt with by the imposition of a fine, costs or a Compensation order with or without other punishment the court may make a Compensation order. If the offender is under 16 the order for payment must be made against the parent or guardian. If over 16, such order may be made against the parent or guardian. The principles for payment and enforcement of a Compensation order are similar to those as for a fine.

If a local authority has parental responsibility for a youth who is fined his parent or guardian shall be construed to be a reference to that Authority. Therefore an order for payment of a fine, costs or compensation may be made against such a local authority, unless the court is satisfied that it would be unreasonable to make an order for payment, having regard to the circumstances of the case.

C. Costs

Costs incurred by the prosecution can be awarded against the defendant and his **34–33** parents/guardian may be ordered to pay in the same way as for a financial penalty. There is no maximum figure for costs. However, if a fine is imposed as well as costs, the amount of costs ordered by the court cannot exceed the amount of any fine imposed.

V. REPARATION ORDER

Powers of Criminal Courts (Sentencing) Act 2000, s.73

Reparation orders

73.—(1) Where a child or young person (that is to say any person aged under 18) is convicted **34–34** of an offence other than one for which the sentence is fixed by law, the court by or before which he is convicted may make an order requiring him to make reparation specified in the order—

    (a) to a person or person so specified; or

    (b) to the community at large;

and any person so specified must be a person identified by the court as a victim of the offence or a person otherwise affected by it.

(2)–(4) [*omitted*]

(5) Before making a reparation order, a court shall obtain and consider a written report by an officer of a local probation board, a social worker of a local authority social services department or a member of a youth offending team indicating—

    (a) the type of work that is suitable for the offender

and

    (b) the attitude of the victim or victims to the requirements proposed to be included in the order.

(6)–(8) [*omitted*]

Powers of Criminal Courts (Sentencing) Act 2000, s.73(5)

73.—(5) The Youth Court has power to make a Reparation order that must not require the **34–35** offender to work for more than 24 hours in aggregate or to require the offender to make reparation to any person without the consent of that person (*PCC(S)A* 2000 section 74(1)).

The requirements that the court specifies in a reparation order must be commensurate with the seriousness of the offence or offences that the court is dealing with: *PCC(S)A* 2000, s.74(2).

The work to be done under the order will normally be undertaken under the supervision of the Youth Offending Team, and must be completed within three months.

The requirements specified in a reparation order shall, as far as practicable, be such as to avoid conflict with the offenders religious beliefs or with the requirements of any community order which he may be subject and any interference with the times at which he attends work, school or any other educational establishment: *PCC(S)A* 2000, s.74(3).

The legislation clearly envisages and stresses the importance of victim participation in **34–36** the reparation process. If the victim is unwilling to co-operate or cannot be found the YOT will normally recommend a form of reparation to the community generally.

A reparation order is based on the concept of "restorative justice". Apart from reparation orders, a reparative element is often included as part of an action plan, supervision order, or community rehabilitation order, see §§ 26–44—26–65.

Breach, revocation and amendment of reparation orders are dealt with under Sch.8 of the *PCC(S)A (Sentencing) Act* 2000.

VI. ATTENDANCE CENTRE ORDERS

Powers of Criminal Courts (Sentencing) Act 2000, s.60(1)

34–37   **60.**—(1) The Youth Court has power to make an attendance centre order in the case of a youth who has been found guilty of an offence that would be punishable with imprisonment in the case of an adult, or who has failed to comply with the requirements of a curfew order, a probation order, a supervision order, an action plan order or a reparation order.

An attendance centre order is a community penalty requiring the offender to attend a centre generally run by the police or by the YOT. The aggregate number of hours must not be less than 12 or exceed 36. However this is subject to restrictions relating to different age groups—

     (a) A child under 14 years may be ordered to attend for less than 12 hours if the court is of the opinion having regard to his age or any other circumstances, that 12 hours would be excessive. He may not be ordered to attend for more than 12 hours.

     (b) For a child under 16 years the court's powers start from a minimum of 12 hours to a maximum of 24 hours.

     (c) For a young offender over 16, the court's powers start at 12 hours with a maximum of 36 hours.

34–38   Youths are usually required to attend the centre for two or three hours on alternate Saturdays and participate in a programme of activities. The order cannot be made until the court is satisfied that the specified centre is reasonably accessible to the offender and does not conflict with his religious beliefs, requirements of any other community penalties to which he may be subject and does not interfere with his normal work or education.

The order itself will name the centre and the court will fix the date and time of the offender's first attendance.

Although it is a community penalty, an attendance centre order does not require the preparation of a written report before it is imposed. This means that the court can proceed to sentence in this way with comparative rapidity. However it may well be that more will need to be known about the circumstances of a young offender before a decision is reached as to the appropriate disposal.

Attendance at an attendance centre may also be a requirement of an action plan order made under *PCC(S)A* 2000, s.69, see § 34–40, below. Such a requirement is not an attendance centre order under s.60 above but is part of an action plan order.

Breach of Attendance Centre order

34–39   Breach, revocation and amendment of attendance centre orders is dealt with under Sch.5 of the *PCC(S)A* 2000.

Where an offender is subject to an attendance centre order made by a youth court appears before either the youth court acting for the area where the attendance centre is situated, or before the youth court that made the attendance centre order, and the court is satisfied that he has failed without reasonable excuse to attend or has committed a breach of the attendance centre rules, that court may, without prejudice to the continuance of the order, may impose a fine or may revoke the attendance centre order and deal with the offender for the offence in respect of the order was made in any manner which he could have been dealt with for that offence if the order had not been made.

An attendance centre order may be discharged or varied on an application made by the offender or the officer in charge of the attendance centre, the power to discharge includes the power to deal with the offender in any manner in which he could have been dealt with for the original offence.

VII. ACTION PLAN ORDERS

Powers of Criminal Courts (Sentencing) Act 2000, s.69(1)

34–40   **69.**—(1) Where a child or young person is convicted of an offence and the court by or before which he is convicted is of the opinion mentioned in subsection (3) below, the court may make an order which—

(a) requires the offender for a period of 3 months beginning with the date of the order to comply with an action plan consisting of a series of requirements with respect to his actions and whereabouts during that period;

(b) places the offender under the supervision for that period of the responsible officer; and

(c) requires the offender to comply with any directions given by that officer with a view to the implementation of that plan;

and the requirements included in the order, and any directions given by the responsible officer, may include requirements authorised by section 70 below.

Powers of Criminal Courts (Sentencing) Act 2000, s.70(1)

70.—(1) Requirements included in an action plan order, or directions given by a responsible officer, may require the offender to do all or any of the following things namely—

(a) to participate in activities specified in the requirements or directions at a time or times so specified;

(b) to present himself to a person or persons specified in the requirements or directions at a place or places and at a time so specified;

(c) to attend at an Attendance Centre specified in the requirements or directions for the number of hours so specified (not available to the court unless the offence committed by the offender is punishable with imprisonment in the case of a person aged 21 years or over);

(d) to stay away from a place or places specified in the requirements or directions;

(e) to comply with any arrangements for his education specified in the requirements or directions;

(f) to make reparation specified in the requirements or directions to a person or persons so specified or to the community at large;

(g) to attend any hearing fixed by the court to take place after the making of the order.

Powers of Criminal Courts (Sentencing) Act 2000, s.69(6)

69.—(6) Before making an action plan order the court must obtain and consider—

(a) a written report by a probation officer, a social worker of a local authority social services department or a member of a youth offending team indicating—

   (i) the requirements proposed by that person to be included in the order;

   (ii) the benefit to the offender that the proposed requirements are designed to achieve; and

   (iii) the attitude of a parent or guardian of the offender to the proposed requirements; and

(b) where the offender is under the age of 16 information about the offender's family circumstances and the likely effect of the order on those circumstances.

An action plan order is a community penalty placing the offender under supervision **34–41** for a fixed period of three months duration. During that three months the offender will be subject to intense supervision and will be required to do all or any of the things specified in s.70(1) above.

The purpose of an action plan is that supervision must be intensive, involving regular meetings with the YOT throughout its duration. The court must set out details of its requirements in its order and carefully explain to the offender his/her obligations. Typical requirements would be for an offender to attend school or training, see a drugs counsellor for advice and assistance, and to meet with his victim and make direct reparation to him or the community at large.

Powers of Criminal Courts (Sentencing) Act 2000, s.71

71.—(1) Immediately after making an Action Plan order a court may—   **34–42**

(a) fix a hearing for a date not more than 21 days after the making of the order; and

    (b) direct the responsible officer to make at that hearing a report as to the effectiveness of the order and the extent to which it has been implemented.

(2) At a hearing fixed under this section the court—

    (a) shall consider the responsible officer's report; and

    (b) may on the application of the responsible officer or the offender amend the order—

        (i) by cancelling any provision included in it; or

        (ii) by inserting in it (either in addition to or in substitution for any of its provisions) and provision that the court could have originally included in it.

34–43   This section gives the court power to monitor the progress that the defendant is making under an action plan order by requiring him to attend court on a date within 21 days from the making of the original order. On considering a report on the defendant's progress the court may amend the order.

    The breach, revocation and amendment of action plan orders are dealt with in *Powers of Criminal Courts (Sentencing) Act* 2000, Sch.8.

VIII. SUPERVISION ORDERS

Powers of Criminal Courts (Sentencing) Act 2000, s.63(1)

34–44   **63.**—(1) Where a child or young person is convicted of an offence, the court by or before which he is convicted may make an order placing him under the supervision of—

    (a) a local authority designated by the order;

    (b) a probation officer; or

    (c) a member of a youth offending team.

34–45   A supervision order is a community penalty and is available for all youths and for all offences.

    A pre-sentence report is required before such an order can be made. The order lasts for a maximum period of three years. There is no minimum period. The effect of the order is to place the offender under the supervision of the Youth Offending Team or a probation officer. The supervising officer shall "advise, assist and befriend the offender". The emphasis of such orders is clearly on preventing offending by securing the rehabilitation of the offender. In order to assist in this process the court is given powers to impose a variety of conditions and requirements.

Powers of Criminal Courts (Sentencing) Act 2000, Sch.6

34–46   1. A Supervision order may require the offender to reside with an individual named in the order who agrees to the requirement, but a requirement imposed by a Supervision order in pursuance or this paragraph shall be subject to any requirement of the order as is authorised by paragraph 2, 3, 6 or 7 below.

    2.—(1) Subject to paragraph (2) below, a Supervision order may require the offender to comply with any directions given from time to time by the supervisor and requiring him to do all or any of the following things—

    (a) to live at a place or places specified in the directions for a period or periods so specified;

    (b) to present himself to a person or persons specified in the directions at a place or places on a day or days so specified;

    (c) to participate in activities specified in the directions on a day or days so specified.

    (2) A Supervision order shall not require compliance with directions given by virtue of sub-paragraph (1) above unless the court making it is satisfied that a scheme under section 66 of this Act (Local Authority Schemes) is in force for the area where the offender resides or will reside; and no such directions may involve the use of facilities which are not for the time being specified in a scheme in force under that section for that area.

    (3) A requirement imposed by a Supervision order in pursuance of sub-paragraph (1) above shall be subject to any requirement of the order as is authorised by paragraph 6 below (treatment for offender's mental condition).

(4) It shall be for the supervisor to decide—   **34–47**

    (a) whether and to what extent he exercises any power to give directions conferred on him by virtue of sub-paragraph (1) above; and

    (b) the form of any directions.

(5) The total number of days in respect of which an offender may be required to comply with directions given by virtue of paragraphs (a), (b), or (c), of sub-paragraph (1) above shall not exceed 90 or such lesser number, if any, as the order may specify for the purposes of this sub-paragraph.

(6) For the purpose of calculating the total number of days in respect of which such directions may be given the supervisor shall be entitled to disregard any day in respect of which directions were previously given in pursuance of the order and on which the directions were not complied with.

(7) Directions given by the supervisor by virtue of sub-paragraph (1)(b) or (c) above, shall as far as are practicable be such as to avoid—

    (a) any conflict with the offender's religious beliefs or with the requirements of any other Community order to which he may be subject; and

    (b) any interference with the times, if any, at which he normally works or attends school or any other educational establishment.

3.—(1) This paragraph applies to a Supervision order unless the order requires the of- **34–48** fender to comply with directions given by the supervisor under paragraph 2(1) above.

(2) Subject to the following provisions of this paragraph and paragraph 4 below, a Supervision order to which this paragraph applies may require the offender—

    (a) to live at a place or places specified in the order for a period or periods so specified;

    (b) to present himself to a person or person(s) specified in the order at a place or places and on a day or day(s) so specified;

    (c) to participate in activities specified in the order on a day or day(s) so specified;

    (d) to make reparation specified in the order to a person or person(s) so specified or to the community at large;

    (e) to remain for specified periods between 6pm and 6am—

        (i) at a place specified in the order; or

        (ii) at one of several places so specified;

    (f) to refrain from participating in activities specified in the order—

        (i) on a specified day or day(s) during the period for which the Supervision order is in force; or

        (ii) during the whole of that period or a specified portion of it;

    and in this paragraph "make reparation" means make reparation for the offence otherwise than by the payment of compensation.

(3) The total number of days in respect of which an offender may be subject to requirements imposed by virtue of paragraphs (a), (b), (c), (d) or (e) of sub-paragraph (2) above shall not exceed 90.

(4) The court may not include requirements under sub-paragraph (2) above in a Supervision order unless—

    (a) it has first consulted the supervisor as to—

        (i) the offender's circumstances; and

        (ii) the feasibility of securing compliance with the requirements,

    and is satisfied, having regard to the supervisor's report, that it is feasible to secure compliance with them;

    (b) having regard to the circumstances of the case it considers the requirement necessary for securing the good conduct of the offender or for preventing a repetition by him of the same offence or the commission of other offences; and

    (c) if the offender is aged under 16 it has obtained and considered information about his family circumstances and the likely effect of the requirements on those circumstances.

(5) The court shall not by virtue of sub-paragraph (2) above include in a Supervision or- **34–49** der—

    (a) any requirement that would involve the co-operation of a person other than the supervisor and the offender unless that other person consents to its inclusion;

     (b) any requirement to make reparation to any person unless that person—
        (i) is identified by the court as a victim of the offence or a person otherwise affected by it; and
        (ii) consents to the inclusion of the requirement.
     (c) any requirement requiring the offender to reside with a specified individual; or
     (d) any such requirement as is mentioned in paragraph 6(2)(treatment for offender's mental condition).

    (6) Requirements included in a Supervision order by virtue of sub-paragraph (2)(b) or (c) above shall, as far as is practicable be such as to avoid—
     (a) any conflict with the offender's religious beliefs or with the requirements of any other Community order to which he may be subject; and
     (b) any interference with the times, if any, at which he normally works or attends school or any other educational establishment;
and sub-paragraphs (7) and (8) below are without prejudice to this sub-paragraph.

34–50   (7) Subject to sub-paragraph (8) a Supervision order may not by virtue of sub-paragraph (2) above include—
     (a) any requirement that would involve the offender in absence from home—
        (i) for more than 2 consecutive nights, or
        (ii) for more than 2 nights in any one week, or
     (b) if the offender is of compulsory school age any requirement to participate in activities during normal school hours,
unless the court making the order is satisfied that the facilities whose use would be involved are for the time being specialised in a scheme in force under section 66 of this Act for the area in which the defendant resides or will reside.
    (8)–(9) [*omitted*]

34–51   Because of their flexibility supervision orders are used extensively in the youth court for offences of all degrees of gravity. A pre-sentence report is essential not just because it will deal with the offender's personal circumstances, but also because it will set out in detail the precise requirements that the Youth Offending Team will ask the court to impose. These requirements can be complex and it is important that the offender understands precisely what is proposed for him before the hearing begins.

    It should be noted that the requirements set out above of residence, specified activities, specified reparation, and presenting him/herself to a specified person can be imposed for a maximum of 90 days. A night restriction order may not be imposed in respect of more than 30 days in all.

    An order made under s.3(2)(c)—(specified activities) may also involve participation in the Intensive Supervision and Surveillance and Programme (ISSP).

    ISSPs are a recently introduced programme which can be attached to a Supervision order. The ISSP is not a separate court order and is not created by statute. The ISSP programme can be attached to a supervision order, a community rehabilitation order, as a condition of bail, and as a condition of release into the community half of a detention and training order. The ISSP programme is recognised as an effective way of sentencing young people who are prolific young offenders and who commit serious offences. It is financed by the Youth Justice Board and provided by the Youth Offending Team. The programme involves extremely intense supervision, often backed up by a curfew order and electronic tagging. The maximum effect is to monitor an offender's activities on a 24 hour per day basis. For Bail ISSP, see § 33–9, above.

34–52   The programme is available for all youths 10 to 17 years inclusive. Having been piloted in various areas of England and Wales the ISSP is now available nationally. The programme is seen by the Youth Justice Board as offering the court an alternative to a short detention and training order. To qualify for the ISSP programme the offender must:
     (a) be charged with or convicted of an imprisonable offence in the current proceedings;
     (b) have been charged with an offence or warned 4 times in the previous 12 months and must also have been sentenced to a community penalty or custody at any time.

(c) be at risk of a custodial sentence relating to an offence which carries imprisonment of 14 years or more for an adult.

ISSP programmes are limited in availability depending on the resources of each YOT and the demand placed on those resources. Availability, and the offender's suitability for an ISSP programme will be dealt with in the context of a full Pre-Sentence Report ordered by the court.

The ISSP programme may offer the following facilities:

(1) A programme of education or other activities each week day at specified times and places.

(2) 5 hours of contact time with the Youth Offending Team each week day.

(3) Electronic surveillance either by electronic tagging or voice recognition or both.

(4) A tracker will be allocated. It is this person's job to track the whereabouts of offender's throughout the week and accompany them to appointments relating to work, education, or any other activities organised by the YOT.

(5) Weekend contact and supervision with the young person.

(6) A curfew order is often suggested by the YOT reinforced with electronic tagging. It should be noted that this must be done by way of a separate curfew order.

34–53 If the YOT proposes a supervision order coupled with an ISSP it will provide full details to the court in a written report. The ISSP offers the opportunity for very intensive supervision and will therefore be tailored to the needs of the individual offender. If the court wishes to make such an order it must take the following steps:

(1) Make a supervision order for a period commensurate with the seriousness of the offence.

(2) Order a maximum of 90 days of specified activities in accordance with s.63.

(3) Attach to those specified activities the ISSP programme.

(4) If the court is making a community rehabilitation order the maximum number of days of specified activities is 60.

Breach, revocation and amendment of supervision orders are dealt with under the provisions of Sch.7 of the *PCC(S)A* 2000.

IX. COMMUNITY REHABILITATION ORDERS

34–54 A community rehabilitation order is a community penalty available to the youth court for offenders who are 16 years or over on the conviction. The order places an offender under the supervision of a probation officer or a member of a YOT. There is therefore, some overlap between a community rehabilitation order and a supervision order under *PCC(S)A* 2000, s.63, see § 34–44. However the community rehabilitation order is particularly intended for the more mature offender who will benefit from the structured supervision that the community rehabilitation order provides.

Powers of Criminal Courts (Sentencing) Act 2000, ss.41(1)–(6), 42

34–55 **41.**—(1) Where a person aged 16 or over is convicted of an offence and the court by or before which he is convicted is of the opinion that his supervision is desirable in the interests of—

(a) securing his rehabilitation; or

(b) protecting the public from harm from him or preventing the commission by him of further offences,

the court may (subject to sections 34–36) make an order requiring him to be under supervision for a period specified in the order of not less than six months nor more than three years.

(2) An order under subsection (1) above in this Act is referred to as a "community rehabilitation order".

(3) A community rehabilitation order shall specify the petty sessions area in which the offender resides or will reside.

(4) If the offender is aged 18 or over at the time when the community rehabilitation order is made he shall, subject to paragraph 18 of Schedule 3 to this Act (offenders change of

area), be required to be under the supervision of a probation officer appointed for or assigned to the petty sessions area specified in the order.

(5) If the offender is aged under 18 at that time, he shall, subject to paragraph 18 of Schedule 3, be required to be under the supervision of—

(a) a probation officer appointed for or assigned to the petty sessions area specified in the order; or

(b) a member of a Youth Offending Team established by a local authority specified in the order;

and if an order specifies a local authority for the purposes of paragraph (b) above, the authority specified must be the local authority within whose area it appears to the court that the offender resides or will reside.

(6) In this Act, "responsible officer", in relation to an offender who is subject to a probation order, means the probation officer or member of a Youth Offending Team responsible for his supervision.

34–56   42.—(1) Subject to subsection (3) below, a community rehabilitation order may in addition require the offender to comply during the whole or any part of the Probation period which such requirements as the court, having regard to the circumstances of the case, considers desirable in the interests of—

(a) securing the rehabilitation of the offender; or

(b) protecting the public from harm from him or preventing the commission by him of further offences.

(2) Without prejudice to the generality of subsection (1) above, the additional requirements which may be included in the rehabilitation order shall include the requirements which are authorised by Schedule 2 to this Act.

(3) Without prejudice to the power of the court under section 130 of this act to make a compensation order, the payment of sums by way of damages for injury or compensation for loss shall not be included among the additional requirements of a rehabilitation order.

Before making a community rehabilitation order (CRO), the youth court is required to obtain a pre-sentence report, unless it is of the opinion that it is unnecessary to obtain one. Where the offender is under 18 and the offence is not triable only on indictment the court may not draw such a conclusion unless it can establish that a pre-sentence report is unnecessary by referring to a previous report about the offender (*PCC(S)A* 2000, s.36(5) and (6)).

34–57   Schedule 2 of the *PCC(S)A* 2000 set out the additional requirements which may be included in a CRO. The requirements are particularly designed for offenders needing intensive supervision and expert help for specific problems. The court may make requirement that the offender:

(1) Attends a community rehabilitation centre for not more than 60 days and complies with instructions given by the person in charge of the centre.

(2) Attends during the whole of the period of the CRO or a lesser time a registered medical practitioner and/or a chartered psychologist with a view to improvement of his/her mental condition.

(3) Attends during the whole of the rehabilitation period or a lesser time for treatment by or under the direction of a person having necessary qualifications or experience with a view to the reduction or elimination of the offender's dependency on drugs or alcohol.

(4) Remains, for period specified, at a place so specified for not less than 2 hours or more than 12 hours in any one day during a period which must not fall outside six months beginning with the day on which the order is made. This is not the same order as a curfew order made under s.37 of the Act. It is a requirement of a community rehabilitation order.

(5) Resides in an approved hostel or any other institution for the period set out in the order.

Any requirement in a CRO that involves the defendant receiving treatment of any nature requires the defendant's consent before it can be imposed.

Breach of Community Rehabilitation order Powers of Criminal Courts (Sentencing) Act 2000, s.43

Schedule 3 to this Act (which makes provision for dealing with failures to comply with **34–58** the requirements of certain community orders, for revoking such orders with or without the substitution of other sentences and for amending such orders) shall have effect so far as relating to community rehabilitation orders.

X. CURFEW ORDERS

Powers of Criminal Courts (Sentencing) Act 2000, ss.37(1)–(9), 38

Curfew orders.
  37.—(1) Where a person is convicted of an offence the court by or before which is convicted **34–59** may (subject to sections 34–36) make an order requiring him to remain, for periods specified in the order, at a place so specified.
  (2) An order under subsection (1) above is in this Act referred to as a "curfew order".
  (3) A curfew order may specify different places or different periods for different days, but shall not specify—
    (a) periods which fall outside the period of six months beginning with the day on which it is made; or
    (b) periods which amount to less than 2 hours or more than 12 hours in any one day.

  (4) In relation to an offender aged under 16 on conviction, subsection (3)(a) above shall **34–60** have effect as if the reference to six months were a reference to three months.
  (5) The requirement in a curfew order shall, as far as practicable, be such as to avoid—
    (a) any conflict with the offender's religious beliefs or with the requirements of any other community order to which he may be subject; and
    (b) any interference with the times, if any, at which he normally works or attends school or any other educational establishment.
  (6) A curfew order shall include provision for making a person responsible for monitoring the offender's whereabouts during the curfew periods specified in the order; and a person who is made so responsible shall be of a description specified in any order made by the secretary of state.

  (7) A court shall not make a curfew order unless the court has been notified by the sec- **34–61** retary or state that arrangements for monitoring the offender's whereabouts are available in the area in which the place proposed to be specified in the order is situated and the notice has not been withdrawn.
  (8) Before making a curfew order, the court shall obtain and consider information about the placed proposed to be specified in the order (including information as to the attitude of persons likely to be affected by the enforced presence there of the offender).
  (9) Before making a curfew order in respect of an offender who on conviction is under 16, the court shall obtain and consider information about his family circumstances and the likely effect of such an order on those circumstances.

  38.—(1) Subject to subsection (2) below, a curfew order may in addition include require- **34–62** ments for securing the electronic monitoring of the offender's whereabouts during the curfew periods specified in the order.
  (2) A court shall not make a curfew order which includes such requirements unless the court—
    (a) has been notified by the secretary of state that electronic monitoring arrangements are available in the area in which the place proposed to be specified in the order is situated; and
    (b) is satisfied that the necessary provision can be made under those arrangements.
  (3) Electronic monitoring arrangements made by the secretary of state under this section may include entering into contracts with other persons for the electronic monitoring by them of offender's whereabouts.

A curfew order is a community penalty available for offenders of any age.

34–63   The length of the curfew imposed by the youth court may be between 2 and 12 hours per day. The court can specify between one and seven days per week.

If the offender is aged under 16 the maximum length of a curfew order is three months. If he/she is over 16 years of age the maximum sentence is six months.

34–64   A pre-sentence report is not essential before making a curfew order. However the court must obtain "information" regarding the following issues:

     (a) The address or addresses to which the offender will be ordered to remain.

     (b) Information as to the suitability of such addresses and the attitude of others who reside there as to the compulsory presence of the offender during the curfew hours.

     (c) Confirmation that the curfew order does not interfere with the offender's education, employment or religion.

     (d) In the case of an offender who is under 16 on conviction, information about his family circumstances and the effect of the proposed curfew order upon him.

34–65   It should be noted that a curfew order can be combined with other community penalties including an action plan order, a supervision order, a community punishment order and a community rehabilitation order.

A curfew order is considered to be an effective way of punishing young offenders, either in itself or in combination with other community penalties. The effectiveness of the order may be usefully reinforced by electronic tagging. It is a common misconception that curfew orders are only intended for offenders who commit crime at night. This is not so. The order is a restriction of liberty in itself. When used in combination with other community penalties it may be regarded as a way of reinforcing those penalties by stabilising and regulating the offender's lifestyle.

Breach Revocation and Amendment of curfew orders

34–66   Schedule 3 of the *Powers of Criminal Courts (Sentencing) Act* 2000 relates to the breach and variation of curfew orders.

XI. COMMUNITY PUNISHMENT ORDERS

34–67   A community punishment order is a community penalty available to the youth court for offenders who are aged 16 years or over. It requires the offender to do unpaid work for the community at the direction of the Probation Service or Youth Offending Team.

Powers of Criminal Courts (Sentencing) Act 2000, s.46

Community punishment orders.

34–68   **46.**—(1) Where a person aged 16 or over is convicted of an offence punishable with imprisonment, the court by or before which he is convicted may (subject to sections 34 to 36 above) make an order requiring him to perform unpaid work in accordance with section 47 below.

(2) An order under subsection (1) above is in this Act referred to as a "community punishment order".

(3) The number of hours which a person may be required to work under a community punishment order shall be specified in the order and shall be in the aggregate—

     (a) not less than 40; and

     (b) not more than 240.

(4) A court shall not make a community punishment order in respect of an offender unless, after hearing (if the court thinks it necessary) an appropriate officer, the court is satisfied that the offender is a suitable person to perform work under such an order.

(5) In subsection (4) above "an appropriate officer" means—

     (a) in the case of an offender aged 18 or over, an officer of a local probation board or social worker of a local authority social services department; and

     (b) in the case of an offender aged under 18, an officer of a local probation board, a social worker of a local authority social services department or a member of a youth offending team.

(6) A court shall not make a community punishment order in respect of an offender unless it is satisfied that provision for him to perform work under such an order can be made under the arrangements for persons to perform work under such orders which exist in the petty sessions area in which he resides or will reside.

(7) Subsection (6) above has effect subject to paragraphs 3 and 4 of Schedule 4 to this Act (transfer of order to Scotland or Northern Ireland).

(8) Where a court makes community punishment orders in respect of two or more offences of which the offender has been convicted by or before the court, the court may direct that the hours of work specified in any of those orders shall be concurrent with or additional to those specified in any other of those orders, but so that the total number of hours which are not concurrent shall not exceed the maximum specified in subsection (3)(b) above.

(9) A community punishment order—

    (a) shall specify the petty sessions area in which the offender resides or will reside; and

    (b) where the offender is aged under 18 at the time the order is made, may also specify a local authority for the purposes of section 47(5)(b) below (cases where functions are to be discharged by member of a youth offending team);

and if the order specifies a local authority for those purposes; the authority specified must be the local authority within whose area it appears to the court that the offender resides or will reside.

(10) Before making a community punishment order, the court shall explain to the offender in ordinary language—

    (a) the purpose and effect of the order (and in particular the requirements of the order as specified in section 47(1) to (3) below);

    (b) the consequences which may follow (under Part II of Schedule 3 to this Act) if he fails to comply with any of those requirements; and

    (c) that the court has power (under Parts III and IV of that Schedule) to review the order on the application either of the offender or of the responsible officer.

(11) The court by which a community punishment order is made shall forthwith give copies of the order to—

    (a) if the offender is aged 18 or over, an officer of a local probation board assigned to the court, or

    (b) if the offender is aged under 18, an officer of a local probation board or member of a youth offending team so assigned,

and he shall give a copy to the offender and to the responsible officer.

(12) The court by which such an order is made shall also, except where it itself acts for the petty sessions area specified in the order, send to the justices' chief executive for that area—

    (a) a copy of the order; and

    (b) such documents and information relating to the case as it considers likely to be of assistance to a court acting for that area in the exercise of its functions in relation to the order.

(13) In this section and Schedule 3 to this Act "responsible officer", in relation to an offender subject to a community punishment order, means the person mentioned in subsection (4) or (5)(b) of section 47 below who, as respects the order, is responsible for discharging the functions conferred by that section.

The community punishment order requires the defendant to participate in a scheme **34–69** of unpaid work at the direction of a community service officer for the number of hours set by the court. The minimum duration of the order is a period of 40 hours, and the maximum duration of the order is a period of 240 hours: s.46(3). The order is available to all offenders over the age of 16 who are convicted of an offence which would be punishable with imprisonment if tried in the adult court: s.46(1) Before making a community punishment order, the court must hear from an "appropriate officer" regarding the suitability of the offender for community service: s.46(4). Where the offender is aged under 18 "an appropriate officer" means "a probation officer, a social worker of a local authority social services department or a member of a youth offending team": s.46(5)(b). The court is required to obtain a pre-sentence report, unless it is of the opinion that it is unnecessary to obtain one: *PCC(S)A* 2000, s.36(5). Where the offender is under 18 and the offence is not triable only on indictment the court may not draw such a conclusion unless it can establish that a pre-sentence report is unnecessary by referring to a previous report about the offender: s.36(6). The court must also be satisfied that arrangements can be made to provide work for the offender: s.46(6), and must explain the purpose and effect of the order, the consequences which may follow if the order is not complied with and that the court may review the order on application by the offender or responsible officer: s.46(10).

34–70   The community punishment order has been considered appropriate where the offence is of a serious nature but bearing in mind the offender's age, and personal circumstances not so serious as to justify an immediate loss of liberty.

In *R. v Mole* (1990) 12 Cr.App.R.(S.) 371, the young offender was convicted of burglary of a dwelling. The court of appeal concluded that community service was the appropriate penalty, having regard to the offender's minor role in the commission of the offence and his previous good character.

Community service was held to be the appropriate penalty for criminal damage in *R. v Ferreira* (1988) 10 Cr.App.R.(S.) 343, where two youths had sprayed graffiti on train carriages at a London Underground depot, Mr Justice Farquharson stating that "This is the kind of offence for which, in the judgment of this court, a community service order is designed. They have done this wanton damage and therefore it behoves them to do some service to the public to put it right".

34–71   The order may also be appropriate in cases of offences involving violence, where there are unusually strong mitigating circumstances. In *R. v Grant* (1990) 12 Cr.App.R.(S.) 441, the offender pleaded guilty to wounding his ex-cohabitee's new boyfriend by punching him and pushing him down a flight of stairs. The offender was aged 20 and of previous good character. The court of appeal held that the case was tailor-made for a community service order since the offender was of previous good character, in regular employment and had acted out of character. The court also considered the effect of a custodial sentence on the offender's life, wife and family, and imposed a community service order of 80 hours' duration.

34–72   Thefts in breach of trust may also warrant a community punishment order. In *R. v Brown* (1981) 3 Cr.App.R.(S.) 294, CA, the offender was aged 19 and with no previous convictions, pleaded guilty to burglary. He had taken part in a burglary at the premises of his employer, allowing his keys to be used to unlock padlocks securing the door of the stock room. Goods worth a total of about £2,850 were stolen. The court described the case as tailor made for community service, citing the fact that the offender was a first offender (although the position would have been the same if he had had a "light" criminal record), he came from a stable home background, with a wife and young child, had a good work record and had a job available. There was apparently genuine remorse and the risk of re-offending was slight.

The breach, revocation and amendment of community punishment orders is dealt with under Sch.3 of the *PCC(S)A* 2000.

XII. COMMUNITY PUNISHMENT AND REHABILITATION ORDER

Powers of Criminal Courts (Sentencing) Act 2000, s.51(1)–(3)

34–73   51.—(1) Where a person aged 16 or over is convicted of an offence punishable with imprisonment and the court by or before which he is convicted is of the opinion mentioned in subsection (3) below, the court may (subject to sections 34–36 above) make an order requiring him both—

         (a) to be under supervision for a period specified in the order, being not less than 12 months nor more than 3 years; and

         (b) to perform unpaid work for a number of hours so specified being in the aggregate not less than 40 nor more than 100.

(2) An order under subsection (1) above is in this Act referred to as a "community punishment and rehabilitation order".

(3) The opinion referred to in subsection (1) above is that the making of a community punishment and Rehabilitation order is desirable in the interests of—

(a) securing the rehabilitation of the offender; or
(b) protecting the public from harm from him or preventing the commission by him of further offences.

A community punishment and rehabilitation order is a community penalty which **34–74** may place a high level of restriction on the offender's liberty. It is an order designed to combine community rehabilitation with community punishment. The offender will be ordered to perform unpaid work in the community at the same time as being under the supervision of a probation officer, or member of the YOT.

The order is subject to time limits. The community rehabilitation element must be for a minimum of 12 months and a maximum of three years. The community punishment element must be between 40 and 100 hours.

As part of the supervisory element of a community punishment and rehabilitation order the youth court may include additional requirements upon the offender under ss.41, 42, 46 and 47 and Sch.2 of the *PCC(S)A* 2000.

Before making a community punishment and rehabilitation order the youth court is **34–75** required to have before it a written report, usually from the YOT unless it is of the opinion that it is unnecessary to obtain one. Where the offender is under 18 and the offence is not triable only on indictment the court may not draw such a conclusion unless it can establish that a report is unnecessary by referring to a previous report about the offender: *PCC(S)A* 2000, s.36(5) and (6). The report should address the defendant's suitability for such an order and assess his suitability to perform community punishment.

Breach, revocation and amendment of community punishment and rehabilitation orders are dealt with in Sch.3 of the *PCC(S)A* 2000.

XIII. DRUG TREATMENT AND TESTING ORDERS

Powers of Criminal Courts (Sentencing) Act 2000, ss.52–55

Drug treatment and testing orders.
52.—(1) Where a person aged 16 or over is convicted of an offence, the court by or before **34–76** which he is convicted may (subject to sections 34 to 36 above) make an order which—
   (a) has effect for a period specified in the order of not less than six months nor more than three years ("the treatment and testing period"); and
   (b) includes the requirements and provisions mentioned in sections 53 and 54 below;
but this section does not apply in relation to an offence committed before 30th September 1998.

(2) An order under subsection (1) above is in this Act referred to as a "drug treatment and testing order".

(3) A court shall not make a drug treatment and testing order in respect of an offender unless it is satisfied—
   (a) that he is dependent on or has a propensity to misuse drugs; and
   (b) that his dependency or propensity is such as requires and may be susceptible to treatment.

(4) For the purpose of ascertaining for the purposes of subsection (3) above whether the offender has any drug in his body, [(in a case where, at the time of conviction, he was aged under 18)] the court may by order require him to provide samples of such description as it may specify; but the court shall not make such an order unless the offender expresses his willingness to comply with its requirements.

(5) A court shall not make a drug treatment and testing order unless it has been notified **34–77** by the Secretary of State that arrangements for implementing such orders are available in the area proposed to be specified in the order under section 54(1) below and the notice has not been withdrawn.

(6) Before making a drug treatment and testing order, the court shall explain to the offender in ordinary language—
   (a) the effect of the order and of the requirements proposed to be included in it;
   (b) the consequences which may follow (under Part II of Schedule 3 to this Act) if he fails to comply with any of those requirements;

(c) that the order will be periodically reviewed at intervals as provided for in the order (by virtue of section 54(6) below); and

(d) that the order may be reviewed (under Parts III and IV of Schedule 3) on the application either of the offender or of the responsible officer;

and "responsible officer" here has the meaning given by section 54(3) below.

(7) A court shall not make a drug treatment and testing order unless the offender expresses his willingness to comply with its requirements.

[This section is printed as amended as from a day to be appointed, by the *CJCSA* 2000, s.74 and Sch.7, para.170 (insertion of words in square brackets).]

The treatment and testing requirements.

34–78   **53.**—(1) A drug treatment and testing order shall include a requirement ("the treatment requirement") that the offender shall submit, during the whole of the treatment and testing period, to treatment by or under the direction of a specified person having the necessary qualifications or experience ("the treatment provider") with a view to the reduction or elimination of the offender's dependency on or propensity to misuse drugs.

(2) The required treatment for any particular period shall be—

(a) treatment as a resident in such institution or place as may be specified in the order; or

(b) treatment as a non-resident in or at such institution or place, and at such intervals, as may be so specified;

but the nature of the treatment shall not be specified in the order except as mentioned in paragraph (a) or (b) above.

(3) A court shall not make a drug treatment and testing order unless it is satisfied that arrangements have been or can be made for the treatment intended to be specified in the order (including arrangements for the reception of the offender where he is to be required to submit to treatment as a resident).

(4) A drug treatment and testing order shall include a requirement ("the testing requirement") that, for the purpose of ascertaining whether he has any drug in his body during the treatment and testing period, the offender shall during that period, at such times or in such circumstances as may (subject to the provisions of the order) be determined by the treatment provider, provide samples of such description as may be so determined.

(5) The testing requirement shall specify for each month the minimum number of occasions on which samples are to be provided.

Provisions of order as to supervision and periodic review.

34–79   **54.**—(1) A drug treatment and testing order shall include a provision specifying the petty sessions area in which it appears to the court making the order that the offender resides or will reside.

(2) A drug treatment and testing order shall provide that, for the treatment and testing period, the offender shall be under the supervision of an officer of a local probation board appointed for or assigned to the petty sessions area specified in the order.

(3) In this Act "responsible officer", in relation to an offender who is subject to a drug treatment and testing order, means the officer of a local probation board responsible for his supervision.

(4) A drug treatment and testing order shall—

(a) require the offender to keep in touch with the responsible officer in accordance with such instructions as he may from time to time be given by that officer, and to notify him of any change of address; and

(b) provide that the results of the tests carried out on the samples provided by the offender in pursuance of the testing requirement shall be communicated to the responsible officer.

34–80   (5) Supervision by the responsible officer shall be carried out to such extent only as may be necessary for the purpose of enabling him—

(a) to report on the offender's progress to the court responsible for the order;

(b) to report to that court any failure by the offender to comply with the requirements of the order; and

(c) to determine whether the circumstances are such that he should apply to that court for the revocation or amendment of the order.

(6) A drug treatment and testing order shall—

    (a) provide for the order to be reviewed periodically at intervals of not less than one month;

    (b) provide for each review of the order to be made, subject to section 55(6) below, at a hearing held for the purpose by the court responsible for the order (a "review hearing");

    (c) require the offender to attend each review hearing;

    (d) provide for the responsible officer to make to the court responsible for the order, before each review, a report in writing on the offender's progress under the order; and

    (e) provide for each such report to include the test results communicated to the responsible officer under subsection (4)(b) above and the views of the treatment provider as to the treatment and testing of the offender.

(7) In this section references to the court responsible for a drug treatment and testing **34–81** order are references to—

    (a) where a court is specified in the order in accordance with subsection (8) below, that court;

    (b) in any other case, the court by which the order is made.

(8) Where the area specified in a drug treatment and testing order made by a magistrate' court is not the area for which the court acts, the court may, if it thinks fit, include in the order provision specifying for the purposes of subsection (7) above a magistrates' court which acts for the area specified in the order.

(9) [*omitted*]

[This section is printed as amended by the *CJCSA* 2000, s.74, and Sch.7, para.4.]

Periodic reviews.

55.—(1) At a review hearing (within the meaning given by subsection (6) of section 54 above) **34–82** the court may, after considering the responsible officer's report referred to in that subsection, amend any requirement or provision of the drug treatment and testing order.

(2) The court—

    (a) shall not amend the treatment or testing requirement unless the offender expresses his willingness to comply with the requirement as amended;

    (b) shall not amend any provision of the order so as to reduce the treatment and testing period below the minimum specified in section 52(1) above, or to increase it above the maximum so specified; and

    (c) except with the consent of the offender, shall not amend any requirement or provision of the order while an appeal against the order is pending.

(3) If the offender fails to express his willingness to comply with the treatment or testing requirement as proposed to be amended by the court, the court may—

    (a) revoke the order; and

    (b) deal with him, for the offence in respect of which the order was made, in any way in which it could deal with him if he had just been convicted by the court of the offence.

(4) In dealing with the offender under subsection (3)(b) above, the court— **34–83**

    (a) shall take into account the extent to which the offender has complied with the requirements of the order; and

    (b) may impose a custodial sentence (where the order was made in respect of an offence punishable with such a sentence) notwithstanding anything in section 79(2) below.

(5) Where the order was made by a magistrates' court in the case of an offender under 18 years of age in respect of an offence triable only on indictment in the case of an adult, any powers exercisable under subsection (3)(b) above in respect of the offender after he attains the age of 18 shall be powers to do either or both of the following—

    (a) to impose a fine not exceeding £5,000 for the offence in respect of which the order was made;

    (b) to deal with the offender for that offence in any way in which the court could deal with him if it had just convicted him of an offence punishable with imprisonment for a term not exceeding six months.

(6) If at a review hearing the court, after considering the responsible officer's report, is of the opinion that the offender's progress under the order is satisfactory, the court may so amend the order as to provide for each subsequent review to be made by the court without a hearing.

34–84   (7) If at a review without a hearing the court, after considering the responsible officer's report, is of the opinion that the offender's progress under the order is no longer satisfactory, the court may require the offender to attend a hearing of the court at a specified time and place.

(8) At that hearing the court, after considering that report, may—

  (a) exercise the powers conferred by this section as if the hearing were a review hearing; and

  (b) so amend the order as to provide for each subsequent review to be made at a review hearing.

(9) In this section any reference to the court, in relation to a review without a hearing, shall be construed—

  (a) in the case of the Crown Court, as a reference to a judge of the court;

  (b) in the case of magistrates' court, as a reference to a justice of the peace acting for the commission area for which the court acts.

34–85   The court may therefore make a drug treatment and testing order where the offender is dependant on, or has a propensity to misuse drugs, and where this dependency or propensity is such as requires and may be susceptible to treatment: s.52(3). This may be demonstrated by the offender's previous record, or by the current offences for sentence. A full pre-sentence report is required, and to enable the court to determine whether the criteria in s.52(3) are established, s.52(4) allows the court to require the defendant to provide samples, subject to the defendant's consent. The finding that the offender satisfies the conditions specified in s.52(3) must be announced with reasons to support such a conclusion. The offender must also express his willingness to comply with treatment: s.52(7) and the court may only impose a drug treatment and testing order when it has been notified that arrangements for implementing such orders are available in the area to be specified in the order: s.52(5).

The treatment requirement must state whether the treatment is residential or non-residential and the identity of the treatment provider: s.53(2). There must be a testing requirement with a specified frequency of drug testing and the court must set a minimum number of times a month samples should be provided for testing: s.53(4), (5). The court must also set a review period, with the reviews being not more than a month apart: s.54(6).

XIV. DETENTION AND TRAINING ORDER

34–86   The detention and training order is the only custodial sentence for young offenders appearing in the youth court. The court's power to impose a custodial sentence is restricted—

Powers of Criminal Courts (Sentencing) Act 2000, s.79(2)

34–87   79.—(2) The court shall not pass a custodial sentence on the offender unless it is of the opinion—

  (a) that the offence or the combination of the offence and one or more offences associated with it, was so serious that only such a sentence can be justified for the offence; or

  (b) where the offence is a violent or sexual offence, that only such a sentence would be adequate to protect the public from serious harm from him.

(1) Detention and Training Orders

Powers of Criminal Courts (Sentencing) Act 2000, ss.100–103

Offenders under 18: detention and training orders

34–88   100.—(1) Subject to sections 90, 91 and 93 above and subsection (2) below, where—

(a) a child or young person (that is to say any person aged under 18) is convicted of an offence which is punishable with imprisonment in the case of a person aged 21 or over, and

(b) the court is of the opinion that either or both of paragraphs (a) and (b) of section 79 above apply, or the case falls within section 79(3),

the sentence that the court is to pass is a detention and training order.

(2) A court shall not make a detention and training order—

(a) in the case of an offender under the age of 15 at the time of conviction unless it is of the opinion that he is a persistent offender;

(b) In the case of an offender under the age of 12 at that time unless—

(i) it is of the opinion that only a custodial sentence would be adequate to protect the public from further offending by him; and

(ii) the offence was committed on or after such date as the Secretary of State may by order appoint.

(3) A detention and training order is an order that the offender in respect of whom it is made shall be subject, for the term specified in the order, to a period of detention and training followed by a period of supervision.

(4) On making a detention and training order in a case where subsection 2 above applies it shall be the duty of the court to state in open court that it is of the opinion mentioned in section 79(2)(a) or, as the case may be, paragraphs (a) and (b) of that subsection

Term of order, consecutive terms and taking account of remands

101.—(1) Subject to subsection (2) below, the term of a detention and training order made in **34–89** respect of an offence (whether by a magistrates' court or otherwise) shall be 4, 6, 8, 10, 12, 18 or 24 months.

(2) The term of a detention and training order may not exceed the maximum term of imprisonment that the Crown Court could (in the case of an offender aged 21 or over) impose for the offence.

(3) Subject to subsections (4) and (6) below, a court making a detention and training order may order that its term shall commence on the expiry of the term of any other detention and training order made by that or any other court.

(4) A court shall not make in respect of an offender a detention and training order the effect of which would be that he would be subject to detention and training orders for a term which exceeds 24 months.

(5) Where the term of the detention and training order to which an offender would otherwise be subject exceeds 24 months, the excess shall be treated as remitted.

(6) A court making a detention and training order shall not order that its term shall commence on the expiry of the term of a detention and training order under which the period of supervision has already begun under section 103(1).

(7) Where a detention and training order (the new order) is made in respect of an of- **34–90** fender who is subject to a detention and training order under which the period of supervision has begun (the old order), the old order shall be disregarded in determining—

(a) for the purpose of subsection (4) above whether the effect of the new order would be that the offender would be subject to detentionand training orders for a term which exceeds 24 months; and

(b) for the purposes of subsection (5) above whether the term of detention and training orders to which the offender would (apart from the subsection) the subject exceeds 24 months.

(8) In determining the term of the detention and training order for an offence, the court shall take into account any period for which the offender has been remanded in custody in connection with the offence, or any other offence, the charge for which was founded on the same facts or evidence.

(9) Where a court proposes to make a detention and training order in respect of an offender for 2 or more offences

(a) subsection (8) above shall not apply; but

(b) in determining the total term of the detention and training orders it proposes to make in respect of the offender, the court shall take into account of the total period (if any) for which he has been remanded in custody in connection with any of those offences, or any other offence the charge for which was founded on the same facts or evidence.

34–91
(10) Once a period of remand has, under subsection (8) or (9) above been taken account of in relation to a detention and training order made in respect of an offender for any offence or offences, it shall not subsequently be taken into account (under either of those subsections) in relation to such an order made in respect of the offender for any other offence or offences.

(11) Any reference in subsection (8) or (9) above to an offender's being remanded in custody is a reference to his being—

    (a) held in police detention;

    (b) remanded in or committed to custody by order of the court;

    (c) remanded or committed to local authority accommodation under section 23 of the *Children and Young Person Act* 1969 and placed and kept in secure accommodation; or

    (d) remanded, admitted or removed to hospital under sections 35, 36, 38 or 48 of the *Mental Health Act* 1983.

34–92
(12) A person is in police detention for the purposes of subsection (11) above—

    (a) at any time when he is in police detention for the purposes of the *Police and Criminal Evidence Act* 1984; and

    (b) at any time when he is detained under section 14 of the *Prevention of Terrorism (Temporary Provision) Act* 1989

and in that subsection "secure accommodation" has the same meaning as in section 23 of the *Children and Young Person Act* 1969.

(13) For the purpose of any reference in sections 102–105 below to the term of a detention and training order, consecutive terms of such orders and terms of such order which are wholly or partly concurrent shall be treated as a single term if—

    (a) the orders were made on the same occasion; or

    (b) where they were made on different occasions the offender has not been released at any time during the period beginning with the first and ending with the last of those occasions.

The period of Detention and Training

34–93
102.—(1) An offender shall serve the period of detention and training under a detention and training order in such secure accommodation as may be determined by the secretary of state or by such other person as may be authorised by him for that purpose.

(2) Subject to subsections (3)–(5) below, the period of detention and training under a detention and training order shall be one half of the term of the order.

(3) The Secretary of State may at any time release the offender if he is satisfied that if exceptional circumstances exist which justify the offenders release on compassionate grounds.

(4) The Secretary of State may release the offender—

    (a) In the case of an order for a term of 8 months or more, but less than 18 months, one month before the half way point of the term of the order; and

    (b) in the case of an order for a term of 18 months or more, one month or two months before that point.

(5) If a Youth Court so orders on an application made by the Secretary of State for the purpose, the Secretary of State shall release the offender—

    (a) in the case of an order for a term of 8 months or more, but less than 18 months, one month after the half way point of the term of the order; and

    (b) in the case of an order for a term of 18 months or more, one month or two months after that point.

(6) An offender detained in pursuance of a detention and training order shall be deemed to be in legal custody.

The period of supervision

34–94
103.—(1) The period of supervision of an offender who is subject to a detention and training order—

    (a) shall begin with the offender's release whether at the half way point of the term of the order or otherwise; and

(b) subject to subsection (2) below shall end when the term of the order ends.

(2) The secretary of state may by order provide that the period of supervision shall end at such point during the term of a detention and training order as may be specified in the order under this subsection.

(3) During the period of supervision the offender shall be under the supervision of—

(a) a probation officer;

(b) a social worker of a local authority social services department; or

(c) a member of a youth offending team;

and the category of person to supervise the offender shall be determined from time to time by the Secretary of State.

(4) Where the supervision is to be provided by a probation officer, the probation officer **34–95** shall be an officer appointed for or assigned to the petty sessions area within which the offender resides for the time being.

(5) Where the supervision is provided by—

(a) a social worker of a local authority social services department, or

(b) a member of a youth offending team,

the social worker or member shall be a social worker of, or a member of a youth offending team, established by, the local authority within whose area the offender resides for the time being.

(6)–(7) [*omitted*]

A detention and training order may be imposed for fixed periods of 4, 6, 8, 10, 12, **34–96** 18 or 24 months.

If the court having considered the facts of the case and the defendants antecedent history considers that a detention and training order may be appropriate it must first order the preparation of a full written pre-sentence report, unless there exists a previous report: *PCC(S)A* 2000, s.81. The report must specifically address custody as a sentencing option.

The offence itself must be one which is punishable with a minimum of four months **34–97** imprisonment in the adult court and is also so serious that only a custodial sentence of four months or over can be justified. Following the making of a detention and training order the offender is held in a custodial institution for one half of the duration of the order. He is then released into the community under the supervision of the YOT. Such supervision may included electronic tagging and an intensive supervision and surveillance programme. However this is a matter purely for the YOT and does not involve an order of the court.

In determining the appropriate term of a detention and training order the court must take into account any period for which the offender has been remanded in custody. This includes time held in police detention, remand to local authority accommodation and secure accommodation or remanded or admitted to hospital under ss.35, 36, 38 or 48 of the *Mental Health Act* 1983. Although the court must take such periods of custody into account it is not required to discount the sentence on a one to one basis nor is the court required to fine tune the appropriate sentence by taking into account a few days spent in custody: *R. v B* [2000] Crim.L.R. 870, CA. In *R. v Inner London Crown Court Ex p. NS* [2000] Crim.L.R. 871, CA, two offenders had each been sentenced to a detention and training order (DTO) of four months. Each appeal on the basis that the three days that they had both spent in custody on remand had not been taken into account in deciding the term of the DTO. The court held that it was neither appropriate or desirable that any precise reflection should be given, in the making of a DTO, of two or three days spent in custody. If a more substantial time of weeks or months had been spent on remand the proper approach would have been to reduce sentence to reflect that period.

In determining the length of a detention and training order the court must also take **34–98** into account a plea of guilty in accordance with *PCC(S)A* 2000, s.152. In *R. v Marley* [2002] 2 Cr.App.R.(S.) 21 a detention and training order of 24 months was reduced to 18 months on the ground that the appellant had pleaded guilty and it was inappropriate to impose the maximum sentence available. The provisions relating to detention and training orders were restricted as to their length. If the maximum sentence of 24 months was not to be imposed, the next permissible length below that level was 18 months.

(2) Definition of "Persistency"

34–99   Youths aged between 12 and 14 years cannot be given a detention and training order unless they are persistent offenders. In deciding whether a defendant is "persistent" it is appropriate to apply the currently understood meaning of that word. The court should assess whether the defendant's criminal behaviour demonstrates a sufficient degree of persistence. Previous findings of guilt and findings of guilt made after the commission of the offence in question will all count in assessing the defendant's criminal behaviour as will cautions, reprimands and final warnings: *R. v Charlton* (2000) 164 J.P. 685. It is not necessary that a defendant should have committed a string of offences or that he has failed to comply with previous orders of the court: *R. v B* [2001] Crim.L.R. 50. However in *R. v JD* (2001) 165 J.P. 1, a 14-year-old charged with affray was held not to be a persistent offender although he had a previous finding of guilt for handling stolen goods and a caution for a similar offence. The offence of affray was a different type of offence than those he had committed before. In *R. v Smith* [2000] Crim.L.R. 613, a 14-year-old who had pleaded guilty to robbery, offensive weapon and false imprisonment, all committed over a two day period, was held to be a persistent offender although he had no previous convictions.

(3) Consecutive Periods of Detention

34–100   The youth court may impose consecutive detention and training orders for summary offences up to an aggregate of 24 months: *C v DPP* [2002] 1 Cr.App.R.(S.) 45. However in *R. v Norris* (2000) 164 J.P. 689 it was held that in passing a consecutive DTO upon an offender who was already serving such a sentence the aggregate of the two orders did not have to correspond with one of the periods set out in s.101 of the *PCC(S)A* 2000.

Where an offender is already serving a period of detention under s.91 of the *PCC(S)A* 2000 there is no power to impose a consecutive detention and training order for a further offence as the two sentencing regimes are incompatible.

(4) Offenders attaining 18 years during the course of proceedings

34–101   Where an offender attains 18 years of age during the course of proceedings the starting point for sentence is that which he would have been likely to receive had he been sentenced on the date of the commission of the offence: *R. v Ghafoor* [2002] Crim.L.R. 739: see § 31–7. In *Aldis v DPP* [2002] 2 Cr.App.R.(S.) 88 it was held that an 18-year-old offender was correctly sentenced to a detention and training order as he had committed the offence when he was 17 years old. He appealed on the basis that, as an 18-year-old at the time of sentence, he should have received a term of custody in a young offenders institute.

(5) Cases on the length of detention and training orders

34–102   There are a number of decisions giving guidance as to when a sentencing court should impose a detention and training order and the appropriate length of such an order.

Att.-Gen.'s References (Nos 4 and 7 of 2002) (R. v Lobban and Sawyers) (R. v Q) [2002] 2 Cr.App.R.(S.) 77, CA
In this case the court of appeal held that street robberies of mobile phones would be punished severely. Custodial sentences would be the only option available irrespective of the age of the offender or his previous good character, unless there are exceptional circumstances. The sentencing bracket would be 18 months to 3 years where no weapon is used.

R. v L [2003] All E.R. (D) 37 (APR)

In this case the 15-year-old defendants had both pleaded guilty to burglary and each were sentenced to a 12 month DTO. On appeal it was held that the circumstances of the burglary put it at the lower end of the scale. A custodial sentence could have been avoided as both defendants were young and had entered timely pleas. Each defendant had served the equivalent of a four month sentence and the sentence of 12 months was reduced to four months accordingly.

R. v FA [2003] 2 Cr.App.R.(S.)

In this case two applicants of good character had admitted a number of robberies of fellow pupils at their school. Each was sentenced to a DTO of 8 months. On appeal the court held that pupils at school who indulge in a campaign of intimidation and violence could expect to be dealt with severely. The sentences were upheld.

R. v Hahn [2003] Cr.App.R.(S.) 106, CA

In this case it was held that as the appellant was 17 years at the date of conviction the power of the sentencing court was limited to a detention and training order. The power to order detention under s.91 of the *PCC(S)A* 2000 may be exercised only in cases where the offender was convicted of a "grave crime". Before imposing such a sentence the court must be of the opinion that none of the other methods in which the case might be dealt with was suitable. In this particular case it was held that a detention and training order was a suitable sentence and the appeal was allowed accordingly.

(6) Breaches of Supervision Requirements in a detention and training order

Powers of Criminal Courts (Sentencing) Act 2000, s.103(1), (3)

103.—(1) The period of supervision of an offender who is subject to a detention and training **34–103** order—

    (a) shall be given with the offender's release whether at the half way point of the term of the order or otherwise; and

    (b) shall end when the term of the order ends.

(3) During the period of supervision the offender shall be under the supervision of—

    (a) a probation officer;

    (b) a social worker of a local authority social services department; or

    (c) a member of a youth offending team;

and the category of person to supervise the offender shall be determined from time to time by the Secretary of State.

Powers of Criminal Courts (Sentencing) Act 2000, s.104(1), (3)

Breach of supervision requirements

104.—(1) Where a detention and training order is in force in respect of an offender and it **34–104** appears on information to a Justice of the Peace acting for a relevant petty sessions area that the offender has failed to comply with the supervision requirements, the Justice—

    (a) may issue a summons requiring the offender to appear at the place and time specified in the summons before a Youth Court acting for the area; or

    (b) if the information is in writing and on oath may issue a warrant for the offender's arrest requiring him to be brought before such a court.

(3) If it is proved to the satisfaction of the Youth Court before which an offender appears or is brought that he has failed to comply with requirements specified in the notice from the Secretary of State that court may—

    (a) order the offender to be detained in such secure accommodation as the secretary of state may determine, for such period, not exceeding the shorter of three months or the remainder of the term of the detention and training order as the court may specify; or

    (b) impose on the offender a fine not exceeding level 3 on the standard scale.

(7) Committing an offence during the currency of a detention and training order

34–105　　The power to deal with a person for an offence committed during the currency of a detention and training order arises if that person after his release and before the date on which the term of the order ends, commits an offence punishable with imprisonment in the case of a person aged 21 or over, and before or after that date, he is convicted of that offence ("the new offence").

Powers of Criminal Courts (Sentencing) Act 2000, s.105(2), (3)

Offences during currency of order

105.—(2) Subject to section 8(6) above (duty of adult Magistrates' Court to remit young offenders to Youth Court for sentence), the court by or before which a person to whom this section applies is convicted of the new offence may, whether or not it passes any other sentence on him, order him to be detained in such secure accommodation as the Secretary of State may determine for the whole or any part of the period which—

(a) begins with the date of the court's order; and

(b) is equal in length to the period between the date on which the new offence was committed and the date on which the term of the detention and training order ends.

(3) The period for which a person under these provision is ordered to be detained in secure accommodation—

(a) shall, as the court may direct, either be served before and be followed by, or be served concurrently with, any sentence imposed for the new offence; and

(b) in either case, shall be disregarded in determining the appropriate length of that sentence.

XV. PARENTING ORDER

Crime and Disorder Act 1998, ss.8–10

Parenting orders

34–106　　**8.**—(1) This section applies where, in any court proceedings—

(a) a child safety order is made in respect of a child;

(b) an anti-social behaviour order or sex offender order is made in respect of a child or young person;

(c) a child or young person is convicted of an offence; or

(d) a person is convicted of an offence under section 443 (failure to comply with school attendance order) or section 444 (failure to secure regular attendance at school of registered pupil) of the *Education Act* 1996.

(2) Subject to subsection (3) and section 9(1) below and to section 19(5) of, and paragraph 13(5) of Schedule 1 to, the *Powers of Criminal Courts (Sentencing) Act* 2000, if in the proceedings the court is satisfied that the relevant condition is fulfilled, it may make a parenting order in respect of a person who is a parent or guardian of the child or young person or, as the case may be, the person convicted of the offence under section 443 or 444 ("the parent").

(3) A court shall not make a parenting order unless it has been notified by the Secretary of State that arrangements for implementing such orders are available in the area in which it appears to the court that the parent resides or will reside and the notice has not been withdrawn.

(4) A parenting order is an order which requires the parent—

(a) to comply, for a period not exceeding twelve months, with such requirements as are specified in the order; and

(b) subject to subsection (5) below, to attend, for a concurrent period not exceeding three months and not more than once in any week, such counselling or guidance sessions as may be specified in directions given by the responsible officer;

and in this subsection "week" means a period of seven days beginning with a Sunday.

(5) A parenting order may, but need not, include such a requirement as is mentioned **34–107** in subsection (4)(b) above in any case where such an order has been made in respect of the parent on a previous occasion.

(6) The relevant condition is that the parenting order would be desirable in the interests of preventing—

(a) in a case falling within paragraph (a) or (b) of subsection (1) above, any repetition of the kind of behaviour which led to the child safety order, anti-social behaviour order or sex offender order being made;

(b) in a case falling within paragraph (c) of that subsection, the commission of any further offence by the child or young person;

(c) in a case falling within paragraph (d) of that subsection, the commission of any further offence under section 443 or 444 of the *Education Act* 1996.

(7) The requirements that may be specified under subsection (4)(a) above are those which the court considers desirable in the interests of preventing any such repetition or, as the case may be, the commission of any such further offence.

(8) In this section and section 9 below "responsible officer", in relation to a parenting order, means one of the following who is specified in the order, namely—

(a) an officer of a local probation board;

(b) a social worker of a local authority social services department; and

(c) a member of a youth offending team

Parenting orders: supplemental.

9.—(1) Where a person under the age of 16 is convicted of an offence, the court by or before **34–108** which he is so convicted—

(a) if it is satisfied that the relevant condition is fulfilled, shall make a parenting order; and

(b) if it is not so satisfied, shall state in open court that it is not and why it is not.

(1A) Subsection (1) above has effect subject to section 19(5) of, and paragraph 13(5) of Schedule 1 to, the *Powers of Criminal Courts (Sentencing) Act* 2000.

(2) Before making a parenting order—

(a) in a case falling within paragraph (a) of subsection (1) of section 8 above;

(b) in a case falling within paragraph (b) or (c) of that subsection, where the person concerned is under the age of 16; or

(c) in a case falling within paragraph (d) of that subsection, where the person to whom the offence related is under that age,

a court shall obtain and consider information about the person's family circumstances and the likely effect of the order on those circumstances.

(3) Before making a parenting order, a court shall explain to the parent in ordinary language—

(a) the effect of the order and of the requirements proposed to be included in it;

(b) the consequences which may follow (under subsection (7) below) if he fails to comply with any of those requirements; and

(c) that the court has power (under subsection (5) below) to review the order on the application either of the parent or of the responsible officer.

(4) Requirements specified in, and directions given under, a parenting order shall, as far as practicable, be such as to avoid—

(a) any conflict with the parent's religious beliefs; and

(b) any interference with the times, if any, at which he normally works or attends an educational establishment.

(5) If while a parenting order is in force it appears to the court which made it, on the **34–109** application of the responsible officer or the parent, that it is appropriate to make an order under this subsection, the court may make an order discharging the parenting order or varying it—

(a) by cancelling any provision included in it; or

(b) by inserting in it (either in addition to or in substitution for any of its provisions) any provision that could have been included in the order if the court had then had power to make it and were exercising the power.

(6) Where an application under subsection (5) above for the discharge of a parenting order is dismissed, no further application for its discharge shall be made under that subsection by any person except with the consent of the court which made the order.

(7) If while a parenting order is in force the parent without reasonable excuse fails to comply with any requirement included in the order, or specified in directions given by the responsible officer, he shall be liable on summary conviction to a fine not exceeding level 3 on the standard scale.

Appeals against parenting orders.

34–110   **10.**—(1) An appeal shall lie—

(a) to the High court against the making of a parenting order by virtue of paragraph (a) of subsection (1) of section 8 above; and

(b) to the Crown Court against the making of a parenting order by virtue of paragraph (b) of that subsection.

(2) On an appeal under subsection (1) above the High court or the Crown Court—

(a) may make such orders as may be necessary to give effect to its determination of the appeals; and

(b) may also make such incidental or consequential orders as appear to it to be just.

(3) Any order of the High court or the Crown Court made on an appeal under subsection (1) above (other than one directing that an application be re-heard by a magistrates' court) shall, for the purposes of subsections (5) to (7) of section 9 above, be treated as if it were an order of the court from which the appeal was brought and not an order of the High court or the Crown Court.

(4) A person in respect of whom a parenting order is made by virtue of section 8(1)(c) above shall have the same right of appeal against the making of the order as if—

(a) the offence that led to the making of the order were an offence committed by him; and

(b) the order were a sentence passed on him for the offence.

(5) A person in respect of whom a parenting order is made by virtue of section 8(1)(d) above shall have the same right of appeal against the making of the order as if the order were a sentence passed on him for the offence that led to the making of the order.

(6) The Lord Chancellor may by order make provision as to the circumstances in which appeals under subsection (1)(a) above may be made against decisions taken by courts on questions arising in connection with the transfer, or proposed transfer, of proceedings by virtue of any order under paragraph 2 of Schedule 11 (jurisdiction) to the *Children Act 1989* ("the 1989 Act").

(7) Except to the extent provided for in any order made under subsection (6) above, no appeal may be made against any decision of a kind mentioned in that subsection.

34–111   In summary, a parenting order may be imposed where:

(a) a child safety order is made in respect of a child;

(b) an anti-social behaviour order or a sex offender order is made in respect of a child or young person;

(c) a child or young person is convicted of an offence;

(d) a person is convicted of an offence under s.443 (failure to comply with school attendance order) or s.444 (failure to secure regular attendance at school of registered pupil) of the *Education Act* 1996;

(e) a youth court may make a parenting order when making a referral order, see § 34–19.

34–112   The parenting order consists of two elements; compliance with such requirements as are specified in the order and attendance at counselling or guidance sessions. These measures are designed to encourage parents to accept responsibility for their children's offending and to provide appropriate support and discipline to prevent further offending. The order may not be made unless the court has received notification from the Secretary of State that arrangements for implementing such orders are available in the area in which it appears to the court that the parent resides or will reside and the notice has not been withdrawn: *Crime and Disorder Act* 1998, s.8(3). The order may be imposed for a maximum of twelve months, and the requirement to attend counselling or guidance session may last for a maximum period of three months with attendance a maximum of one session a week: *Crime and Disorder Act* 1998, s.8(4).

34–113   The order is mandatory where the offender is under 16 and the court considers that the relevant condition (prevention of re-offending) is satisfied; where the court does not consider the relevant condition to be satisfied, it must state in open court why it has arrived at that conclusion: *Crime and Disorder Act* 1998, s.9(1). The order is discretionary in the case of offenders aged 16 or 17. The court does not have to obtain a pre-sentence report, but the court should obtain and consider information about the person's family circumstances and the likely effect of the order on those circumstances: *Crime and Disorder Act* 1998, s.9(2). Before making the order, the court must explain to the parent in ordinary language:

   (1) The effect of the order and of the requirements proposed to be included in it.

   (2) The consequences which may follow if he fails to comply with any of those requirements.

   (3) That the court has power to review the order on the application either of the parent or of the responsible officer: *Crime and Disorder Act* 1998, s.9(4).

The requirements specified in the order must also be such as to avoid any conflict **34–114** with the parents religious beliefs, and any interference with the times at which he normally works or attends an educational establishment: *Crime and Disorder Act* 1998, s.9(5).

The court may vary or discharge the parenting order following an application made to the court by the responsible officer or the parent: s.9(5). If an application for variation or discharge is made and dismissed, a further such application may not proceed without the consent of the court which refused the original application: s.9(6). A person in respect of whom a parenting order is made by virtue of paras (c) or (d) of s.8 of the 1998 Act will have the same right of appeal against the making of the order as if the order were a sentence passed on him for the offence: *Crime and Disorder Act* 1998, s.10(4).

Breach of a parenting order will result in the parent being liable upon summary conviction to a fine not exceeding level three on the standard scale: s.9(7).

XVI. ANTI-SOCIAL BEHAVIOUR ORDERS

Crime and Disorder Act 1998, s.1C

Orders on conviction in criminal proceedings

   1C.—(1) This section applies where a person (the "offender") is convicted of a relevant **34–115** offence.

   (2) If the court considers—

      (a) that the offender has acted, at any time since the commencement date, in an anti-social manner, that is to say in a manner that caused or was likely to cause harassment, alarm or distress to one or more persons not of the same household as himself, and

      (b) that an order under this section is necessary to protect persons in any place in England and Wales from further anti-social acts by him,

it may make an order which prohibits the offender from doing anything described in the order.

   (3) The court may make an order under this section whether or not an application has been made for such an order.

   (4) An order under this section shall not be made except—

      (a) in addition to a sentence imposed in respect of the relevant offence; or

      (b) in addition to an order discharging him conditionally.

   (5) An order under this section takes effect on the day on which it is made, but the court may provide in any such order that such requirements of the order as it may specify shall, during any period when the offender is detained in legal custody, be suspended until his release from that custody.

   (6) An offender subject to an order under this section may apply to the court which **34–116** made it for it to be varied or discharged.

   (7) In the case of an order under this section made by a magistrates' court, the reference in subsection (6) to the court by which the order was made includes a reference to any magistrates' court acting for the same petty sessions area as that court.

   (8) No application may be made under subsection (6) for the discharge of an order before the end of the period of two years beginning with the day on which the order takes effect.

   (9) Subsections (7), (10) and (11) of section 1 apply for the purposes of the making and

effect of orders made by virtue of this section as they apply for the purposes of the making and effect of anti-social behaviour orders.

(10) In this section—

"the commencement date" has the same meaning as in section 1 above;

"the court" in relation to an offender means—

(a) the court by or before which he is convicted of the relevant offence; or

(b) if he is committed to the Crown Court to be dealt with for that offence, the Crown Court; and

"relevant offence" means an offence committed after the coming into force of section 64 of the *Police Reform Act* 2002.

34–117 The court may make an anti-social behaviour order where an offender is convicted of an offence committed on or after December 2, 2002: *Crime and Disorder Act* 1998, s.1C(2) and (10) and SI 2002/2750. The court must consider the offender to have acted, at any time since April 1, 1999, in a manner that was likely to cause harassment, alarm or distress to one or more persons not of the same household as himself: *Crime and Disorder Act* 1998, s.1C(2) and (10) and SI 1998/3263. The court must also consider that an anti-social behaviour order made on conviction is necessary to protect persons in any place in England and Wales from further anti-social acts committed by him: s.1C(2). Although this is a civil order, the criminal standard of proof applies to the satisfaction of these criteria. The order itself must contain prohibitions rather than positive require-ments: s.1C(2), and the order may take effect immediately, or may be suspended whilst the defendant completes a custodial sentence: s.1C(5). The order may last for a mini-mum of two years and a maximum of five years.

The Anti-Social Behaviour order is a civil proceedings order with criminal penalties if breached; s.1C(9) provides that subss.(10) and (11) of s.1 of the 1998 Act shall apply to s.1C, hence if without reasonable excuse a person does anything which he is prohibited from doing by an anti-social behaviour order, he shall be guilty of an offence which, when tried summarily, carries a penalty of imprisonment for a term not exceeding six months, a fine not exceeding the statutory maximum, or to both. Where a person is convicted of an offence under s.1(10) the court may not make an order of conditional discharge in respect of the offence.

34–118 It should be noted that an order under s.1C is an order on conviction in criminal proceedings. The youth court therefore has power to impose such an order.

Free standing applications against youths for an ASBO are heard in the adult magis-trates' court. They are civil proceedings and the youth court has no jurisdiction to hear them. However, breach of such an order by children and young people is dealt with in the youth court and prosecuted by the CPS.

The youth court may make an ASBO under s.1C upon the application of any agency concerned in the case that would be entitled to apply for such an order. In addition the youth court may make an order of its own volition.

34–119 Section 1C does not prescribe any particular procedure when consideration is given as to whether an ASBO should be made on conviction. However, the youth court must act fairly and have regard to all relevant considerations. In *C v (1) Sunderland Youth Court (2) Northumbria Police and (3) CPS* [2004] 1 Cr.App.R.(S.) 76, DC a youth ap-plied for judicial review of the youth court's decision to impose an ASBO under s.1(c) of the *CDA* 1998. The application was allowed, the court emphasising the importance of fairness, careful consideration of evidence, and clarity as to the reasons for its decision. It was also said to be vital that the terms of an ASBO were clearly and accurately explained to the offender by the court.

In the case of *R. v P*, *The Times*, February 19, 2004, CA a youth was sentenced to detention for four years. In addition an ASBO for two years was made, suspended until his release from custody. On appeal the ASBO was quashed because it was not possible for the court to determine that an ASBO was necessary to protect the public at a future date in view of the length of the sentence coupled with a 12 month period on licence. The court also confirmed the principles set out in *C v Sunderland Youth Court*—above.

Part VI

Mentally Disordered Offenders

CHAPTER 35

MENTALLY DISORDERED OFFENDERS

I. INTRODUCTION

"Mental disorder" is defined by statute (*Mental Health Act* 1983, s.1). The fact that **35–1** an accused person has been diagnosed as suffering from mental disorder (or in some instances appears to be suffering from mental disorder) may affect the way in which that person is dealt with at different stages of the proceedings. In many, but certainly not all cases, the fact that the accused may be mentally disordered will be apparent from the custody record which is often available as part of the papers supplied to the defence at the first hearing in the magistrates' court. Readers will be aware that there has been government consultation on proposals for a wide ranging revision of mental health law. The discussions have not borne fruit: there are no current proposals for the introduction of a Mental Health Bill.

The provisions relevant to mentally disordered offenders (MDOs) are not to be found in any single statute but the law does make special provision for MDOs in relation to charging, whether to prosecute or continue to prosecute, for magistrates to obtain reports on the accused pre and post trial and for remands during the lifetime of the case to be to a hospital rather than on bail. There is provision for the court to find against an MDO without entering a formal conviction and provision for the court to pass a sentence which sends an MDO to hospital rather than to prison. Where appropriate, an MDO may be sentenced to a community rehabilitation order that includes a requirement to accept treatment.

II. DEFINITION OF "MENTAL DISORDER"

Mental Health Act 1983, s.1

Application of Act: "mental disorder"

1.—(1) The provisions of this Act shall have effect with respect to the reception, care and **35–2** treatment of mentally disordered patients, the management of their property and other related matters.

(2) In this Act—
"mental disorder" means mental illness, arrested or incomplete development of mind, psychopathic disorder and any other disorder or disability of mind and "mentally disordered" shall be construed accordingly;

"severe mental impairment" means a state of arrested or incomplete development of mind which includes severe impairment of intelligence and social functioning and is associated with abnormally aggressive or seriously irresponsible conduct on the part of the person concerned and "severely mentally impaired" shall be construed accordingly;

"mental impairment" means a state of arrested or incomplete development of mind (not amounting to severe mental impairment) which includes significant impairment of intelligence and social functioning and is associated with abnormally aggressive or seriously irresponsible conduct on the part of the person concerned and "mentally impaired" shall be construed accordingly;

"psychopathic disorder" means a persistent disorder or disability of mind (whether or not including significant impairment of intelligence) which results in abnormally aggressive or seriously irresponsible conduct on the part of the person concerned;

and other expressions shall have the meanings assigned to them in section 145 below.

(3) Nothing in subsection (2) above shall be construed as implying that a person may be dealt with under this Act as suffering from mental disorder, or from any form of mental disorder described in this section, by reason only of promiscuity or other immoral conduct, sexual deviancy or dependence on alcohol or drugs.

35–3   The term 'mental illness" is not further defined in the 1983 Act, though the term is defined in the Department of Social Security's consultation paper on the *Mental Health Act* 1959 as any disorder having one or more of the following characteristics:

(a) more than temporary impairment of intellectual functions shown by a failure of memory, orientation, comprehension and learning capacity;

(b) more than temporary alteration of mood of such degree as to give rise to the patient having a delusional appraisal of his situation, his past or future or that of others or the lack of any appraisal;

(c) delusional beliefs persecutory, jealous or grandiose;

(d) abnormal perceptions associated with delusional misinterpretation of events;

(e) thinking so disordered as to prevent the patient making a reasonable appraisal of his situation or having reasonable communication with others.

III. DIVERSION FROM THE CRIMINAL JUSTICE SYSTEM

35–4   Two government policy documents encourage the diversion of MDOs away from the criminal justice system in appropriate cases. First, Home Office Circular 66/90 (*Provision for Mentally Disordered Offenders*) provides that government's policy is to divert mentally disordered persons from the Criminal Justice System in cases where the public interest does not require their prosecution. Chief Officers of Police are therefore asked to ensure that, taking into account the public interest, consideration is always given to alternatives to prosecution, including taking no further action where appropriate and that effective arrangements are established with local health and social services authorities to ensure their speedy involvement when mentally disordered persons are taken into police custody. Where a prosecution is considered necessary, non-penal disposals should be used wherever appropriate and the police, courts and probation services should work with their local health and social services to make effective use of the provisions of the *Mental Health Act* 1983 and the services which exist to help the mentally disordered offender.

Secondly, further advice is contained in Home Office Circular 12/95 Mentally Disordered Offenders—Inter-Agency Working, produced jointly by the Home Office and the Department of Health. This includes advice to the police on criteria to apply when considering whether to charge. The existence of a mental disorder should never be the only factor considered in reaching a decision about charging. When assessing the need for action to protect the safety of the public, the police need to enquire into the offender's history of mental disorder and any previous convictions. In appropriate cases the offender can be diverted from being charged if the police either take no further action, give the offender an informal warning or a caution.

In deciding whether a prosecution should be commenced or continued prosecutors **35–5** have regard for The Code for Crown Prosecutors (2000). The Code (at para.6.5) provides some common public interest factors against prosecution, which include: if the prosecution is likely to have a bad effect on the victim's physical or mental health (always bearing in mind the seriousness of the offence) and whether the defendant is, or was at the time of the offence, suffering from significant mental or physical ill heath. The Code identifies the need for prosecutors to "balance the desirability of diverting a defendant who is suffering from significant mental or physical ill health with the need to safeguard the general public." The Code is reproduced in full in *Archbold Crown Supplement, App.E.*

IV. BAIL

(1) Bail from the Police Station

After charge at the police station, the general right to bail for persons accused of of- **35–6** fences in the magistrates' courts applies to the mentally disordered offender. The offender must be granted bail unless one of the conditions specified in s.38(1) of the *Police and Criminal Evidence Act* 1984 applies. Bail may be refused in specifired circumstances, some of which may apply in the case of an accused who is suspected of suffering from mental disorder:

Police and Criminal Evidence Act 1984, s.38(1)

Duties of custody officer after charge

38.—(1) Where a person arrested for an offence otherwise than under a warrant endorsed **35–7** for bail is charged with an offence, the custody officer shall, subject to section 25 of the *Criminal Justice and Public Order Act* 1994, order his release from police detention, either on bail or without bail, unless—

(a) if the person arrested is not an arrested juvenile—

   (i) his name or address cannot be ascertained or the custody officer has reasonable grounds for doubting whether a name or address furnished by him as his name or address is his real name or address;

   (ii) the custody officer has reasonable grounds for believing that the person arrested will fail to appear in court to answer to bail;

   (iii) in the case of a person arrested for an imprisonable offence, the custody officer has reasonable grounds for believing that the detention of the person arrested is necessary to prevent him from committing an offence;

   (iiia) except in a case where (by virtue of subsection (9) of section 63B below) that section does not apply, the custody officer has reasonable grounds for believing that the detention of the person is necessary to enable a sample to be taken from him under that section;

   (iv) in the case of a person arrested for an offence which is not an imprisonable offence, the custody officer has reasonable grounds for believing that the detention of the person arrested is necessary to prevent him from causing physical injury to any other person or from causing loss of or damage to property;

   (v) the custody officer has reasonable grounds for believing that the detention of the person arrested is necessary to prevent him from interfering with the administration of justice or with the investigation of offences or of a particular offence; or

   (vi) the custody officer has reasonable grounds for believing that the detention of the person arrested is necessary for his own protection;

(b) if he is an arrested juvenile—

(i) any of the requirements of paragraph (a) above is satisfied (but, in the case of paragraph (a)(iiia) above, only if the arrested juvenile has attained the minimum age); or

(ii) the custody officer has reasonable grounds for believing that he ought to be detained in his own interests.

(2) Bail at the Magistrates' Court

35–8　　The *Bail Act* 1976 applies to an MDO as to any other offender. Note the exceptions to right to bail where there are grounds for believing that the defendant may abscond, commit an offence or interfere with witnesses. The court may exercise its power to remand in custody for the defendant's own protection (*Bail Act* 1976, Sch.1, Pt 1, para.3).

Post conviction the court may exercise its power to impose a requirement that the offender makes himself available for the purpose of enabling enquiries or a report to be made to assist the court in dealing with him for the offence: *Bail Act* 1976, s.3(6)(d).

If a defendant is remanded in custody, the Home Secretary may direct that the defendant be transferred from prison to a hospital for the purpose of the preparation of medical reports on the accused's psychiatric condition: *Mental Health Act* 1983, s.48(2)(b). A transfer under s.48 may be ordered before or after conviction. It is an administrative alternative to a remand to hospital ordered by a court under s.35 or s.38, see below.

V. REMAND TO HOSPITAL FOR ASSESSMENT

Mental Health Act 1983, s.35

Remand to hospital for report on accused's mental condition.

35–9　　**35.**—(1) Subject to the provisions of this section, the Crown Court or a magistrates' court may remand an accused person to a hospital specified by the court for a report on his mental condition.

(2) For the purposes of this section an accused person is—

(a) in relation to the Crown Court, any person who is awaiting trial before the court for an offence punishable with imprisonment or who has been arraigned before the court for such an offence and has not yet been sentenced or otherwise dealt with for the offence on which he has been arraigned;

(b) in relation to a magistrates' court, any person who has been convicted by the court of an offence punishable on summary conviction with imprisonment and any person charged with such an offence if the court is satisfied that he did the act or made the omission charged or he has consented to the exercise by the court of the powers conferred by this section.

(3) Subject to subsection (4) below, the powers conferred by this section may be exercised if—

(a) the court is satisfied, on the written or oral evidence of a registered medical practitioner, that there is reason to suspect that the accused person is suffering from mental illness, psychopathic disorder, severe mental impairment or mental impairment; and

(b) the court is of the opinion that it would be impracticable for a report on his mental condition to be made if he were remanded on bail;

but those powers shall not be exercised by the Crown Court in respect of a person who has been convicted before the court if the sentence for the offence of which he has been convicted is fixed by law.

(4) The court shall not remand an accused person to a hospital under this section unless satisfied, on the written or oral evidence of the registered medical practitioner who would be responsible for making the report or of some other person representing the managers of the hospital, that arrangements have been made for his admission to that hospital and for his admission to it within the period of seven days beginning with the date of the remand; and if the court is so satisfied it may, pending his admission, give directions for his conveyance to and detention in a place of safety.

(5) Where a court has remanded an accused person under this section it may further remand him if it appears to the court, on the written or oral evidence of the registered medical practitioner responsible for making the report, that a further remand is necessary for completing the assessment of the accused person's mental condition.

(6) The power of further remanding an accused person under this section may be exercised by the court without his being brought before the court if he is represented by counsel or a solicitor and his counsel or solicitor is given an opportunity of being heard.

(7) An accused person shall not be remanded or further remanded under this section for more than 28 days at a time or for more than 12 weeks in all; and the court may at any time terminate the remand if it appears to the court that it is appropriate to do so.

(8) An accused person remanded to hospital under this section shall be entitled to obtain at his own expense an independent report on his mental condition from a registered medical practitioner chosen by him and to apply to the court on the basis of it for his remand to be terminated under subsection (7) above.

(9) Where an accused person is remanded under this section—

    (a) a constable or any other person directed to do so by the court shall convey the accused person to the hospital specified by the court within the period mentioned in subsection (4) above; and

    (b) the managers of the hospital shall admit him within that period and thereafter detain him in accordance with the provisions of this section.

(10) If an accused person absconds from a hospital to which he has been remanded under this section, or while being conveyed to or from that hospital, he may be arrested without warrant by any constable and shall, after being arrested, be brought as soon as practicable before the court that remanded him; and the court may thereupon terminate the remand and deal with him in any way in which it could have dealt with him if he had not been remanded under this section.

Whilst the proceedings remain in the magistrates' court, this power to remand to **35–14** hospital for assessment only arises if the defendant has been convicted of an offence which is punishable with imprisonment on summary conviction or if the defendant is charged with such an offence and the court have made a finding (without convicting) that the defendant did the act or made the admission charged in accordance with s.37(3). The making of a finding under s.37(3) may be desirable in that avoids the stigma that attaches to a formal conviction.

VI. HOSPITAL/GUARDIANSHIP ORDER

Mental Health Act 1983, s.37

Powers of courts to order hospital admission or guardianship

37.—(1) Where a person is convicted before the Crown Court of an offence punishable with **35–15** imprisonment other than an offence the sentence for which is fixed by law or falls to be imposed under section 109(2) of the *Powers of Criminal Courts (Sentencing) Act* 2000, or is convicted by a magistrates' court of an offence punishable on summary conviction with imprisonment, and the conditions mentioned in subsection (2) below are satisfied, the court may by order authorise his admission to and detention in such hospital as may be specified in the order or, as the case may be, place him under the guardianship of a local social services authority or of such other person approved by a local social services authority as may be so specified.

(1A) In the case of an offence the sentence for which would otherwise fall to be imposed under subsection (2) of section 110 or 111 of the *Powers of Criminal Courts (Sentencing) Act* 2000, nothing in that subsection shall prevent a court from making an order under subsection (1) above for the admission of the offender to a hospital.

(1B) For the purposes of subsections (1) and (1A) above, a sentence falls to be imposed under section 109(2), 110(2) or 111(2) of the *Powers of Criminal Courts (Sentencing) Act* 2000 if it is required by that provision and the court is not of the opinion there mentioned.

(2) The conditions referred to in subsection (1) above are that—

    (a) the court is satisfied, on the written or oral evidence of two registered medical practitioners, that the offender is suffering from mental illness, psychopathic disorder, severe mental impairment or mental impairment and that either—

(i) the mental disorder from which the offender is suffering is of a nature or degree which makes it appropriate for him to be detained in a hospital for medical treatment and, in the case of psychopathic disorder or mental impairment, that such treatment is likely to alleviate or prevent a deterioration of his condition; or

(ii) in the case of an offender who has attained the age of 16 years, the mental disorder is of a nature or degree which warrants his reception into guardianship under this Act; and

(b) the court is of the opinion, having regard to all the circumstances including the nature of the offence and the character and antecedents of the offender, and to the other available methods of dealing with him, that the most suitable method of disposing of the case is by means of an order under this section.

(3) Where a person is charged before a magistrates' court with any act or omission as an offence and the court would have power, on convicting him of that offence, to make an order under subsection (1) above in his case as being a person suffering from mental illness or severe mental impairment, then, if the court is satisfied that the accused did the act or made the omission charged, the court may, if it thinks fit, make such an order without convicting him.

(4) An order for the admission of an offender to a hospital (in this Act referred to as "a hospital order") shall not be made under this section unless the court is satisfied on the written or oral evidence of the registered medical practitioner who would be in charge of his treatment or of some other person representing the managers of the hospital that arrangements have been made for his admission to that hospital, and for his admission to it within the period of 28 days beginning with the date of the making of such an order; and the court may, pending his admission within that period, given such directions as it thinks fit for his conveyance to and detention in a place of safety.

(5) If within the said period of 28 days it appears to the Secretary of State that by reason of an emergency or other special circumstances it is not practicable for the patient to be received into the hospital specified in the order, he may give directions for the admission of the patient to such other hospital as appears to be appropriate instead of the hospital so specified; and where such directions are given—

(a) the Secretary of State shall cause the person having the custody of the patient to be informed, and

(b) the hospital order shall have effect as if the hospital specified in the directions were substituted for the hospital specified in the order.

(6) An order placing an offender under the guardianship of a local social services authority or of any other person (in this Act referred to as "a guardianship order") shall not be made under this section unless the court is satisfied that that authority or person is willing to receive the offender into guardianship.

(7) A hospital order or guardianship order shall specify the form or forms of mental disorder referred to in subsection (2)(a) above from which, upon the evidence taken into account under that subsection, the offender is found by the court to be suffering; and no such order shall be made unless the offender is described by each of the practitioners whose evidence is taken into account under that subsection as suffering from the same one of those forms of mental disorder, whether or not he is also described by either of them as suffering from another of them.

(8) Where an order is made under this section, the court shall not—

(a) pass sentence of imprisonment or impose a fine or make a probation order in respect of the offence,

(b) if the order under this section is a hospital order, make a referral order (within the meaning of the *Powers of Criminal Courts (Sentencing) Act* 2000 in respect of the offence, or

(c) make in respect of the offender a supervision order (within the meaning of that Act) or an order under section 150 of that Act (binding over of parent or guardian)

but the court may make any other order which it has power to make apart from this section; and for the purposes of this subsection "sentence of imprisonment" includes any sentence or order for detention.

35–21   The court must be satisfied on the evidence of two registered medical practitioners that the offender is suffering from a mental disorder, as defined in s.1 of the 1983 Act, of a nature or degree which makes it appropriate for him to be detained and treated in hospital for medical treatment and the court is of the opinion that this would be the most suitable method of disposal of the case. The court may make a hospital order without the offender's consent. The order may be made for a maximum of up to one year, and is subject to review.

If the offender is aged over 14, and he has been convicted of a summary offence punishable with imprisonment, if the court considers that all the conditions for the making of a hospital order are satisfied and a restriction order (*Mental Health Act* 1983, s.41) is necessary for the effective punishment of the offender it should commit to the Crown Court for sentence: *Mental Health Act* 1983, s.43.

35–22 Where an offender is committed under s.43(1) and the magistrates' court by which he is committed is satisfied on written or oral evidence that arrangements have been made for admission of the offender to hospital, the court may order the offender to be detained in hospital until the case is disposed of by the Crown Court: *Mental Health Act* 1983, s.44.

35–23 In *R. v Birch* (1989) 11 Cr.App.R.(S.) 202, the Cour of Appeal described the hospital order as having the 'sole purpose' of ensuring 'that the offender receives the medical care and attention which he needs in the hope and expectation of course that the result will be to avoid the commission be the offender of further criminal acts.' The court also outlined the appropriate approach of a court called upon to sentence a mentally disordered offender;

> 'First he should decide whether a period of compulsory detention is apposite. If the answer is that it is not, or may not be, the possibility of a probation order with a condition of out-patient treatment should be considered…
>
> Secondly the judge will ask himself whether the conditions contained in section 37(2)(a) for the making of a hospital order are satisfied. Here the judge acts on the evidence of the doctors. If he is left in doubt, he may wish to avail himself of the valuable provisions of sections 38 and 39.
>
> If the judge concludes that the conditions empowering him to make an order are satisfied, he will consider whether to make such an order, or whether 'the most suitable method of disposing of the case (section 37(2)(b)) is to impose a sentence of imprisonment'.

VII. HOSPITAL ORDERS WITHOUT CONVICTION

Mental Health Act 1983, s.37(3)

35–24 Where a person is tried summarily for an act or omission which would, upon conviction, warrant a hospital order, the court may impose such an order once it is satisfied that the accused did the act or made the omission charged. The court must still have the reports of two registered medical practitioners testifying to the mental state of the accused, and a hospital bed must be available before this power becomes exercisable.

The order is available where the offender is charged with an offence triable either way and he elects trial by indictment: *R. v Ramsgate Justices Ex p. Kazmarek* (1984) 80 Cr.App.R. 366. The order is also available where the offender was unable to consent to summary trial: *R. v Lincolnshire (Kesteven) Justices Ex p. O'Connor* [1983] 1 W.L.R. 335, DC. Because s.37(3) gives the court the power to make a hospital order without convicting the accused, it has been held that it is not necessary that a trial be held: *R. v Lincolnshire (Kesteven) Justices Ex p. O'Connor, ibid.* To satisfy the court that the defendant did the act or made the omission charged, the prosecution need only prove the ingredients which comprise the *actus reus* of the offence: *R. v Antoine* (2000) 2 All E.R.208, HL. Whilst a finding under s.37(3) is not a conviction, a defendant against whom such an order is made has a right of appeal as if it were a conviction: s.45.

The consequence of consensual admission is little different from the consequence of a hospital order under s.37 of the *Mental Health Act* 1983, save that a patient detained under a hospital order may not apply for discharge until six months have elapsed.

(1) Fitness to plead

35–25 The question of fitness to plead is not relevant to proceedings in the magistrates' court. The issue of fitness to plead arises only under the *Criminal Procedure (Insanity) Act* 1964 and the *Criminal Procedure (Insanity and Unfitness to Plead) Act* 1991, which apply only to proceedings in the Crown Court. The magistrates may commit an accused charged with an offence triable either way to the Crown Court, where the issue may be raised, though this power is not available if the accused is charged with an offence triable only summarily: *R. v Metropolitan Stipendiary Magistrate Tower Bridge Ex p. Antifowosi* (1985) 144 J.P. 752.

(2) Insanity

35–26   The *Trial of Lunatics Act* 1883, s.2(1) provides that the special verdict of not guilty by reason of insanity may only be returned by a jury, the defence is not limited to trials on indictment. The legal definition of insanity is that the accused was, at the time of commission of the act in question, labouring under a defect of reason, from disease of the mind as not to know the nature and the quality of the act he was doing, or if he did know it, he did not know it was wrong: *McNaughten's case* (1843) 10 Cl. & Fin 200

A disorder which impairing the accused's mental faculties of reason, memory and understanding so as to render him unaware of what he was doing, or unaware of the fact that what he was doing was wrong will be a "disease of the mind" causing a "defect of reason" within the M'Naghten Rules, whether the aetiology of the impairment was organic or functional and whether it was permanent or transient and intermittent: *R. v Sullivan* (1984) A.C 156.

35–27   Insanity will be a defence to any criminal charge as it operates as to render absent the mens rea element of the crime. Insanity may therefore be raised against a charge tried summarily, though the court may not return the special verdict of 'not guilty by reason of insanity': *Trial of Lunatics Act* 1883, above. In *DPP v Harper* [1997] 1 W.L.R. 1406, the respondent had been acquitted of driving a motor vehicle with an excess of alcohol in his blood, contrary to s.5(1)(a) of the *Road Traffic Act* 1988, on grounds of insanity. The prosecution appealed to the Divisional Court of the Queen's Bench Division, who granted the appeal holding that no defence of insanity is available in cases where the offence is one of strict liability. McCowan L.J. stated:

> '[I]nsanity can be a defence in the magistrates' court, but only if the offence charged is one in which *mens rea* is an element. Every man is assumed to be sane at the time of an alleged offence and, accordingly, the burden is on the accused to establish insanity at the time of the commission of the offence on the balance of probabilities. The defence is based on the absence of *mens rea*, but none is required for the offence of driving with an excess of alcohol. Hence, the defence of insanity has no relevance to such a charge, as it is an offence of strict liability.' [at p.1409]

35–28   In addition to the inability to return the special verdict, the 1983 Act makes no provision for committal to the Crown Court by the magistrates for imposition of a restriction order under s.41 upon a person who has been acquitted of an offence by reason of insanity. The magistrates only have such a power to commit to the Crown Court for that purpose in the case of a person convicted of an imprisonable offence, whether indictable or summary only. This situation has been described as a 'legislative lacuna': *R. v Horseferry Road Magistrates' Court Ex p. K* [1996] Cr.App.R. 574, DC.

VIII. SENTENCING POWERS

Pre-sentence reports

Magistrates' Court Act 1980, s.30

35–29   This section gives the court power to order a medical report on the offender's physical or mental condition when it considers such report necessary for disposal of the case. This power arises when the offence is triable summarily and punishable with imprisonment, and the court is satisfied that the offender did the act or made the omission charged.

When exercising this power, the court must send a statement to the doctor where the offender is to be examined listing reasons for the request and any information before the court about the offender's mental or physical condition: *Magistrates' Courts Rules 1981*, r.24

IX. INTERIM HOSPITAL ORDERS

Mental Health Act 1983, s.38

Interim hospital orders

38.—(1) Where a person is convicted before the Crown Court of an offence punishable with **35–30** imprisonment (other than an offence the sentence for which is fixed by law) or is convicted by a magistrates' court of an offence punishable on summary conviction with imprisonment and the court before or by which he is convicted is satisfied, on the written or oral evidence of two registered medical practitioners—

    (a) that the offender is suffering from mental illness, psychopathic disorder, severe mental impairment or mental impairment; and

    (b) that there is reason to suppose that the mental disorder from which the offender is suffering is such that it may be appropriate for a hospital order to be made in his case,

the court may, before making a hospital order or dealing with him in some other way, make an order (in this Act referred to as "an interim hospital order") authorising his admission to such hospital as may be specified in the order and his detention there in accordance with this section.

(2) In the case of an offender who is subject to an interim hospital order the court may **35–31** make a hospital order without his being brought before the court if he is represented by counsel or a solicitor and his counsel or solicitor is given an opportunity of being heard.

(3) At least one of the registered medical practitioners whose evidence is taken into account under subsection (1) above shall be employed at the hospital which is to be specified in the order.

(4) An interim hospital order shall not be made for the admission of an offender to a **35–32** hospital unless the court is satisfied, on the written or oral evidence of the registered medical practitioner who would be in charge of his treatment or of some other person representing the managers of the hospital, that arrangements have been made for his admission to that hospital and for his admission to it within the period of 28 days beginning with the date of the order; and if the court is so satisfied the court may, pending his admission, given directions for his conveyance to and detention in a place of safety.

(5) An interim hospital order—

    (a) shall be in force for such period, not exceeding 12 weeks, as the court may specify when making the order; but

    (b) may be renewed for further periods of not more than 28 days at a time if it appears to the court, on the written or oral evidence of the responsible medical officer, that the continuation of the order is warranted;

but no such order shall continue in force for more than twelve months in all and the court shall terminate the order if it makes a hospital order in respect of the offender or decides after considering the written or oral evidence of the responsible medical officer to deal with the offender in some other way.

(6) The power of renewing an interim hospital order may be exercised without the of- **35–33** fender being brought before the court if he is represented by counsel or a solicitor and his counsel or solicitor is given an opportunity of being heard.

(7) If an offender absconds from a hospital in which he is detained in pursuance of an interim hospital order, or while being conveyed to or from such a hospital, he may be arrested without warrant by a constable and shall, after being arrested, be brought as soon as practicable before the court that made the order; and the court may thereupon terminate the order and deal with him in any way in which it could have dealt with him if no such order had been made.

X. PROBATION WITH A CONDITION OF MEDICAL TREATMENT

Powers of Criminal Courts (Sentencing) Act 2000, Sch.2, para.5(1)–(3)

Requirements as to treatment for mental condition etc.

35–34   5.—(1) This paragraph applies where a court proposing to make a community rehabilitation order is satisfied, on the evidence of a registered medical practitioner approved for the purposes of section 12 of the *Mental Health Act* 1983, that the mental condition of the offender—

     (a) is such as requires and may be susceptible to treatment; but

     (b) is not such as to warrant the making of a hospital order or guardianship order within the meaning of that Act.

(2) Subject to sub-paragraph (4) below, the community rehabilitation order may include a requirement that the offender shall submit, during the whole of the community rehabilitation period or during such part or parts of that period as may be specified in the order, to treatment by or under the direction of a registered medical practitioner or a chartered psychologist (or both, for different parts) with a view to the improvement of the offender's mental condition.

(3) The treatment required by any such order shall be such one of the following kinds of treatment as may be specified in the order, that is to say—

     (a) treatment as a resident patient in an independent hospital or care home within the meaning of the *Care Standards Act* 2000 or a hospital within the meaning of the *Mental Health Act* 1983, but not hospital premises at which high security psychiatric services within the meaning of that Act are provided;

     (b) treatment as a non-resident patient at such institution or place as may be specified in the order;

     (c) treatment by or under the direction of such registered medical practitioner or chartered psychologist (or both) as may be so specified;

but the nature of the treatment shall not be specified in the order except as mentioned in paragraph (a), (b) or (c) above.

35–36   Before making such an order, the court must be satisfied that arrangements have been or can be made for the treatment intended to be specified in the order (including arrangements for the reception of the offender where he is to be required to submit to treatment as a resident patient) and the offender has consented to the treatment: *PCC(S)A* 2000, Sch.2, para.5(1)(4).

XI. IMPRISONMENT

Powers of Criminal Court (Sentencing) Act 2000, s.82

Additional requirements in case of mentally disordered offender

35–37   82.—(1) Subject to subsection (2) below, in any case where the offender is or appears to be mentally disordered, the court shall obtain and consider a medical report before passing a custodial sentence other than one fixed by law or falling to be imposed under section 109(2) below.

(2) Subsection (1) above does not apply if, in the circumstances of the case, the court is of the opinion that it is unnecessary to obtain a medical report.

(3) Before passing a custodial sentence, other than one fixed by law or falling to be imposed under section 109(2) below, on an offender who is or appears to be mentally disordered, a court shall consider—

     (a) any information before it which relates to his mental condition (whether given in a medical report, a pre-sentence report or otherwise); and

     (b) the likely effect of such a sentence on that condition and on any treatment which may be available for it.

(4) No custodial sentence which is passed in a case to which subsection (1) above applies shall be invalidated by the failure of a court to comply with that subsection, but any court on an appeal against such a sentence—

     (a) shall obtain a medical report if none was obtained by the court below; and

(b) shall consider any such report obtained by it or by that court.

(5) In this section, "mentally disordered", in relation to any person, means suffering from a mental disorder within the meaning of the *Mental Health Act* 1983.

(6) In this section, "medical report" means a report as to an offender's mental condition made or submitted orally or in writing by a registered medical practitioner who is approved for the purposes of section 12 of the *Mental Health Act* 1983 by the Secretary of State as having special experience in the diagnosis or treatment of mental disorder.

(7) Nothing in this section shall be taken as prejudicing the generality of section 81 above.

Section 109(2) concerns automatic life sentences following the commission of a second **35–38** 'serious offence.'

The power to impose extended sentences under s.85 and s.80(2)(b) of the *Powers of* **35–39** *Criminal Courts (Sentencing) Act* 2000 should be considered, and may influence the magistrates in their decision whether or not to commit to the Crown Court for sentence.

XII. HOSPITAL ORDER WITH RESTRICTION ORDER

The magistrates' court has no power to attach to a hospital order an order restricting **35–40** discharge from hospital: s.41 of the *Mental Health Act* 1883.If a restriction order may be necessary the magistrates court should exercise its power in cases triable either way to decline jurisdiction or commit to the Crown Court for sentence.

Part VII

Legal Aid and Costs

LEGAL REPRESENTATION

I. CRIMINAL DEFENCE REPRESENTATION ORDERS

A. GENERAL

The *Access to Justice Act* 1999 established a new framework for the public funding **36–1** of legal representation in the criminal courts. It created the Legal Services Commission to replace the Legal Aid Board, and the Criminal Defence Service, which secures access to legal advice, assistance and representation in criminal matters. The Community Legal Service, also created by the Act, deals with the public funding of civil matters. The Act has been supplemented by regulations.

Legal aid is available to defendants to ensure that legal representation is provided irrespective of the ability to pay for it. Free legal assistance is not automatic in criminal cases in the magistrates' court. The circumstances and impact of the charge will be taken into account in assessing whether it is in the interests of justice that representation should be paid for from public funds. Schedule 3, para.5 of the *Access to Justice Act* 1999 lists the factors that are relevant.

There are standard forms used to make the application for an order for **36–2** representation.

In the magistrates' court the application will be considered by a 'proper officer of the court' who will usually be a trained member of staff to whom the power to grant legal representation orders has been delegated by the justices' clerk. The application must identify fully the reasons why it is in the interests of justice for an order to be granted in accordance with the provisions of Sch.3 of the Act, otherwise the application may be refused. The form must also be signed and dated.

The application should be completed and submitted at the earliest opportunity after charge and certainly by the time of the first court appearance as the order can only be dated from the date of receipt by the proper officer and cannot be issued retrospectively. It is possible for applications to be made orally in court but this may not always be encouraged as a written record has to be made not only of the application but also the reasons for granting or refusing the application. It may not be convenient for this to be done during a busy court list.

The Human Rights Act 1998

Under Art.6(3)(c) of the European Convention on Human Rights everyone charged **36–3** with a criminal offence has the right 'to defend himself in person or through legal assistance of his own choosing or, if he does not have sufficient means to pay for legal assistance, to be given it free when the interests of justice require it.'

In the magistrates' court, applications for legal representation will be granted if the interests of justice require it. The means of a defendant in criminal cases is not relevant at summary level but the Crown Court has power to make an order for the recovery of costs following a Crown Court trial where the defendant had the benefit of a representation order and has the means to pay. The interests of justice tests are included in the *Access to Justice Act* 1999 and European case law also gives an indication of the factors to be taken into account when assessing the interests of justice. The complexity of the case is relevant; *Benham v UK* [1996] 22 E.H.R.R. 293 as is the ability of the defendant to comprehend and present his case: *Hoang v France* [1993] 16 E.H.R.R. 53. The likelihood of a custodial sentence is an important factor: *Benham v UK*, above.

36–4   The legal representation granted must be 'practical and effective' and it is not sufficient for a lawyer to be merely nominated by the state. The system for legal aid must ensure that advice and assistance is given: *Artico v Italy* [1981] 3 E.H.R.R. 1.

The choice of lawyer is not absolute. Where free legal aid is concerned, the wishes of the defendant will be given consideration but the state can override those wishes where necessary. Also the right to conduct a complex case unrepresented may be restricted: *Croissant v Germany* [1993] 16 E.H.R.R. 135. Article 6 requires the hearing to be 'fair' and if the conduct or incompetence of a legal representative assigned under a scheme affects the fairness of the trial, a court may be obliged to intervene: *R. v Nangle* [2001] Crim.L.R. 506.

A defence application for an adjournment of criminal proceedings should normally be granted where the defendant has not had the opportunity to apply for free legal representation. In such circumstances the right to free legal representation (or to a proper opportunity to apply for it) will normally outweigh other considerations, such as the convenience of the other parties and the use of court resources: *Berry Trade Ltd v Moussavi* [2002] 1 W.L.R. 1910.

B. The Legal Services Commission

(1) Constitution of the Commission

Access to Justice Act 1999, s.1

Legal Services Commission

36–5   **1.**—(1) There shall be a body known as the Legal Services Commission (in this Part referred to as "the Commission").

(2) The Commission shall have the functions relating to—

    (a) the Community Legal Service, and

    (b) the Criminal Defence Service,

which are conferred or imposed on it by the provisions of this Act or any other enactment.

(3) The Commission shall consist of—

    (a) not fewer than seven members, and

    (b) not more than twelve members;

but the Lord Chancellor may by order substitute for either or both of the numbers for the time being specified in paragraphs (a) and (b) such other number or numbers as he thinks appropriate.

(4) The members of the Commission shall be appointed by the Lord Chancellor; and the Lord Chancellor shall appoint one of the members to chair the Commission.

(5) In appointing persons to be members of the Commission the Lord Chancellor shall have regard to the desirability of securing that the Commission includes members who (between them) have experience in or knowledge of—

    (a) the provision of services which the Commission can fund as part of the Community Legal Service or Criminal Defence Service,

    (b) the work of the courts,

    (c) consumer affairs,

    (d) social conditions, and

    (e) management.

  (6) Schedule 1 (which makes further provision about the Commission) has effect.

Access to Justice Act 1999, s.2

Power to replace Commission with two bodies

  2.—(1) The Lord Chancellor may by order establish in place of the Commission two bodies— **36–6**

    (a) one to have functions relating to the Community Legal Service, and

    (b) the other to have functions relating to the Criminal Defence Service.

  (2) The order may make any consequential, incidental, supplementary or transitional provisions, and any savings, which appear to the Lord Chancellor to be appropriate.

  (3) The order shall include amendments of—

    (a) any provisions of, or amended by, this Part which refer to the Commission, and

    (b) any other enactments which so refer,

to replace references to the Commission with references to either or both of the bodies established by the order.

(2) Powers of the Commission

Access to Justice Act 1999, s.3

Powers of Commission

  3.—(1) Subject to the provisions of this Part, the Commission may do anything which it **36–7** considers—

    (a) is necessary or appropriate for, or for facilitating, the discharge of its functions, or

    (b) is incidental or conducive to the discharge of its functions.

  (2) In particular, the Commission shall have power—

    (a) to enter into any contract,

    (b) to make grants (with or without conditions),

    (c) to make loans,

    (d) to invest money,

    (e) to promote or assist in the promotion of publicity relating to its functions,

    (f) to undertake any inquiry or investigation which it may consider appropriate in relation to the discharge of any of its functions, and

    (g) to give the Lord Chancellor any advice which it may consider appropriate in relation to matters concerning any of its functions.

  (3) Subsections (1) and (2) do not confer on the Commission power to borrow money.

  (4) The Commission may make such arrangements as it considers appropriate for the discharge of its functions, including the delegation of any of its functions.

  (5) The Lord Chancellor may by order require the Commission—

    (a) to delegate any function specified in the order or to delegate any function so specified to a person (or person of a description) so specified,

    (b) not to delegate any function so specified or not to delegate any function so specified to a person (or person of a description) so specified, or

    (c) to make arrangements such as are specified in the order in relation to the delegation of any function so specified.

  The Commission has made arrangements under s.3(4) of the *Access to Justice Act* **36–8** 1999. The Review Panel Arrangements, which are effective from April 1, 2000, provide for the creation of a Review Panel, the appointment from that Panel of Funding Review Committees and Cost Committees and the regulation of the proceedings of those committees. The Commission has also made the Criminal Defence Service Duty Solicitor Arrangements 2001, which govern the provision of advice and assistance by duty solicitors at police stations and magistrates' courts.

(3) Code of conduct

Access to Justice 1999, s.16

Code of conduct

36–9   **16.**—(1) The Commission shall prepare a code of conduct to be observed by employees of the Commission, and employees of any body established and maintained by the Commission, in the provision of services as part of the Criminal Defence Service.

(2) The code shall include—

    (a) duties to avoid discrimination,

    (b) duties to protect the interests of the individuals for whom services are provided,

    (c) duties to the court,

    (d) duties to avoid conflicts of interest, and

    (e) duties of confidentiality,

and duties on employees who are members of a professional body to comply with the rules of the body.

(3) The Commission may from time to time prepare a revised version of the code.

(4) Before preparing or revising the code the Commission shall consult the Law Society and the General Council of the Bar and such other bodies or persons as it considers appropriate.

(5) After preparing the code or a revised version of the code the Commission shall send a copy to the Lord Chancellor.

(6) If he approves it he shall lay it before each House of Parliament.

(7) The Commission shall publish—

    (a) the code as first approved by the Lord Chancellor, and

    (b) where he approves a revised version, either the revisions or the revised code as appropriate.

(8) The code, and any revised version of the code, shall not come into force until it has been approved by a resolution of each House of Parliament.

The Code of Conduct for Employees of the Legal Services Commission who provide services as part of the Criminal Defence Service was implemented in 2001.

C. CRIMINAL DEFENCE SERVICE

Access to Justice Act 1999, s.12

Criminal Defence Service

36–10   **12.**—(1) The Commission shall establish, maintain and develop a service known as the Criminal Defence Service for the purpose of securing that individuals involved in criminal investigations or criminal proceedings have access to such advice, assistance and representation as the interests of justice require.

(2) In this Part "criminal proceedings" means—

    (a) proceedings before any court for dealing with an individual accused of an offence,

    (b) proceedings before any court for dealing with an individual convicted of an offence (including proceedings in respect of a sentence or order),

    (c) proceedings for dealing with an individual under section 9 of, or paragraph 6 of Schedule 1 to, the *Extradition Act* 1989,

    (d) proceedings for binding an individual over to keep the peace or to be of good behaviour under section 115 of the *Magistrates' Courts Act* 1980 and for dealing with an individual who fails to comply with an order under that section,

    (e) proceedings on an appeal brought by an individual under section 44A of the *Criminal Appeal Act* 1968,

    (f) proceedings for contempt committed, or alleged to have been committed, by an individual in the face of a court, and

    (g) such other proceedings concerning an individual, before any such court or other body, as may be prescribed.

(3) The Commission shall fund services as part of the Criminal Defence Service in accordance with sections 13 to 15.

(4) The Commission may accredit, or authorise others to accredit, persons or bodies providing services which may be funded by the Commission as part of the Criminal Defence Service; and any system of accreditation shall include provision for the monitoring of the services provided by accredited persons and bodies and for the withdrawal of accreditation from any providing services of unsatisfactory quality.

(5) The Commission may charge—
    (a) for accreditation,
    (b) for monitoring the services provided by accredited persons and bodies, and
    (c) for authorising accreditation by others;
and persons or bodies authorised to accredit may charge for accreditation, and for such monitoring, in accordance with the terms of their authorisation.

(6) The Lord Chancellor may by order require the Commission to discharge the functions in subsections (4) and (5) in accordance with the order.

Additional criminal proceedings have been prescribed by the *Criminal Defence Service (General) Regulations (No.2)* 2001. The Rules included here relate specifically to the magistrates' court. For a full version of the *Regulations*, see *Archbold Crown* §§ 6–152 *et seq.* **36–11**

Criminal Defence Service (General) (No.2) Regulations 2001, reg.3(1)&(2)

Criminal proceedings
    3.—(1) For the purposes of this regulation, "the 1998 Act" means the *Crime and Disorder Act* 1998. **36–12**

(2) The following proceedings are criminal proceedings for the purposes of section 12(2)(g) of the Act:
    (a) civil proceedings in a magistrates' court arising from failure to pay a sum due or to obey an order of that court where such failure carries the risk of imprisonment;
    (b) proceedings under [sections 1, 1D, 2, 2A and 4] of the 1998 Act relating to anti-social behaviour orders or sex offender orders;
    (c) proceedings under section 8(1)(b) of the 1998 Act relating to parenting orders made where an anti-social behaviour order or a sex offender order is made in respect of a child;
    (d) proceedings under section 8(1)(c) of the 1998 Act relating to parenting orders made on the conviction of a child;
    (e) proceedings under section 9(5) of the 1998 Act to discharge or vary a parenting order made as mentioned in sub-paragraph (c) or (d);
    (f) proceedings under section 10 of the 1998 Act to appeal against a parenting order made as mentioned in sub-paragraph (c) or (d);
    (g) proceedings under sections 14B, 14D, 14G, 14H, 21B and 21D of the *Football Spectators Act* 1989 (banning orders and references to a court); and
    (h) proceedings under section 137 of the *Financial Services and Markets Act* 2000 to appeal against a decision of the Financial Services and Markets Tribunal.

[This regulation is reprinted as amended by the *Criminal Defence Service (General) (No.2) (Amendment No.2) Regulations* 2002, reg.2(a) and the *Football (Disorder) Act* 2000, Sch.1, paras 2, 21B, 21D, 4.]

Case law under previous legislation clarified the meaning of 'criminal proceedings'. **36–13** In *R. v Recorder of Liverpool Ex p. McCann, The Times*, May 4, 1994, DC the court held that an application for the removal of a driving disqualification under the *Road Traffic Offenders Act* 1988, s.42 qualified as 'criminal proceedings' because they were proceedings 'in respect of a sentence'. In *R. v Redbridge Magistrates' Court Ex p. Guppy* (1995) 159 J.P. 622, it was held that proceedings for the enforcement of a compensation order were criminal proceedings in respect of sentence and so were eligible for legal aid. Applications under s.42(2) of the *Drug Trafficking Act* 1994 for the continued detention of cash seized under s.42(1), or for the forfeiture of that cash did not fall within the definition as the applicant was neither charged with nor convicted of an offence: *R. v Crawley Justices Ex p. Ohakwe, The Times*, May 26, 1994.

Under the regulations the 'hybrid offences' of anti-social behaviour orders and parenting orders introduced by the *Crime and Disorder Act* 1998 qualify for legal representation. Football banning orders are also covered. A surety may be eligible for legal representation under the provision that defines some civil proceedings as criminal for the purposes of legal representation if there is a risk of imprisonment in default of payment of a sum of money: reg.3(2)(a) above.

(a) *Funding of legal services in criminal proceedings*

Access to Justice Act 1999, s.13

Advice and assistance

36–14   13.—(1) The Commission shall fund such advice and assistance as it considers appropriate—

(a) for individuals who are arrested and held in custody at a police station or other premises, and

(b) in prescribed circumstances, for individuals who—

(i) are not within paragraph (a) but are involved in investigations which may lead to criminal proceedings,

(ii) are before a court or other body in such proceedings, or

(iii) have been the subject of such proceedings;

and the assistance which the Commission may consider appropriate includes assistance in the form of advocacy.

(2) The Commission may comply with the duty imposed by subsection (1) by—

(a) entering into contracts with persons or bodies for the provision of advice or assistance by them,

(b) making payments to persons or bodies in respect of the provision of advice or assistance by them,

(c) making grants or loans to persons or bodies to enable them to provide, or facilitate the provision of, advice or assistance,

(d) establishing and maintaining bodies to provide, or facilitate the provision of, advice or assistance,

(e) making grants to individuals to enable them to obtain advice or assistance,

(f) employing persons to provide advice or assistance, or

(g) doing anything else which it considers appropriate for funding advice and assistance.

(3) The Lord Chancellor may by order require the Commission to discharge the function in subsection (2) in accordance with the order.

(4) The Commission may fund advice and assistance by different means—

(a) in different areas in England and Wales, and

(b) in relation to different descriptions of cases.

[This section is reprinted as amended by the *Criminal Defence Service (Advice and Assistance) Act* 2001, s.1(1), which provides that the amendment be retrospective in its effect.]

36–15   The Legal Services Commission is empowered to secure the services referred to in s.12 through contracts with lawyers in private practice or by providing salaried defenders employed directly by the commission. This means that a suspect's choice of legal representation is limited to contracted or salaried defenders although the intention is to provide a choice in all but exceptional cases. This does not offend against the ECHR. The right to have a lawyer of one's own choosing under Art.6(3)(c) is not absolute, particularly where the representation is being publicly funded: *Croissant v Germany* (above). As a general rule the defendant's choice of lawyer should be respected and there must be relevant and sufficient justification to appoint a lawyer against his wishes: *Goddi v Italy* [1984] 6 E.H.R.R. 457. It might be argued that the scheme for control of legal firms supplying defence services by the Legal Services Commission ensures a high standard of service and so is justified. Private solicitors may only undertake publicly funded criminal defence work if they have a contract to provide such services with the Criminal Defence Service: *Criminal Defence Service (General) (No.2) Regulations*

2001, r.11. In 2001 the Legal Services Commission began a four-year trial of its own defender service comprised of six offices staffed by people employed directly by the Commission.

Criminal Defence Service (General) (No.2) Regulations 2001, reg.4

Advice and assistance—scope

4. The Commission shall fund such advice and assistance, including advocacy assistance, as it **36–16** considers appropriate in relation to any individual who:

    (a) is the subject of an investigation which may lead to criminal proceedings;

    (b) is the subject of criminal proceedings;

    (c) requires advice and assistance regarding his appeal or potential appeal against the outcome of any criminal proceedings or an application to vary a sentence;

    (d) requires advice and assistance regarding his sentence;

    (e) requires advice and assistance regarding his application or potential application to the Criminal Cases Review Commission;

    (f) requires advice and assistance regarding his treatment or discipline in prison (other than in respect of actual or contemplated proceedings regarding personal injury, death or damage to property);

    (g) is the subject of proceedings before the Parole Board;

    (h) requires advice and assistance regarding representations to the Home Office in relation to a mandatory life sentence or other parole review;

    (i) is a witness in criminal proceedings and requires advice regarding self-incrimination;[…]

    (j) is a volunteer or

    (k) is detained under Schedule 7 to the *Terrorism Act* 2000.

[This regulation is reprinted as amended by the *Criminal Defence Service (General) (Amendment) (No.2) Regulations* 2002, reg.6.]

A volunteer is any person who voluntarily attends at a police station or elsewhere to **36–17** assist with an investigation without having been arrested. Pursuant to its obligations under this section the Legal Services Commission has established the Police Station Duty Solicitor Scheme and the Magistrates' Courts Duty Solicitor Scheme so that those who require advice and assistance at a police station or court have access to a duty solicitor who is accredited by the Commission. A Duty Solicitor will be available at most courts on a daily basis to provide advice for unrepresented defendants. In busy courts there may well be a 'bail' duty solicitor and a 'custody' duty solicitor.

Criminal Defence Service (General) (No.2) Regulations 2001, reg.5

Advice and assistance—financial eligibility

5.—(1) The following advice and assistance may be granted without reference to the financial **36–18** resources of the individual:

    (a) all advice and assistance provided to an individual who is arrested and held in custody at a police station or other premises;

    (b) all advocacy assistance before a magistrates' court or the Crown Court;

    (c) all advice and assistance provided by a court duty solicitor in accordance with his contract with the Commission;

    (d) all advice and assistance provided to a volunteer during his period of voluntary attendance;

    (e) all advice and assistance provided to an individual being interviewed in connection with a serious service offence; and

    (f) all advice and assistance provided in respect of an individual who is the subject of an identification procedure carried out by means of video recordings in connection with that procedure, notwithstanding the individual's non-attendance at a police station at the time the procedure is carried out.

(2) For the purposes of paragraph (1), a serious service offence is an offence under the *Army Act* 1955, the *Air Force Act* 1955 or the *Naval Discipline Act* 1957 which cannot be dealt with summarily.

(3) Advocacy assistance may be granted to an individual regarding his treatment or discipline in prison (other than in respect of actual or contemplated proceedings regarding personal injury, death or damage to property), or where he is the subject of proceedings before the Parole Board, if his weekly disposable income does not exceed £192 and his disposable capital does not exceed £3,000

[Paragraphs 4–9 cover the financial eligibility tests. This regulation is reprinted as amended by the *Arms Forces Discipline Act* 2000 and the *Criminal Defence Service (General) (No.2) (Amendment) Regulations* 2003, reg.4(2).]

36–19   All advocacy assistance before the magistrates' court is granted without reference to financial resources so there is no means test.

D. Representation

General

Access to Justice Act 1999, s.14

Representation

36–20   **14.**—(1) Schedule 3 (which makes provision about the grant of a right to representation in criminal proceedings) has effect; and the Commission shall fund representation to which an individual has been granted a right in accordance with that Schedule.

(2) Subject to the following provisions, the Commission may comply with the duty imposed by subsection (1) by—

    (a) entering into contracts with persons or bodies for the provision of representation by them,

    (b) making payments to persons or bodies in respect of the provision of representation by them,

    (c) making grants or loans to persons or bodies to enable them to provide, or facilitate the provision of, representation,

    (d) establishing and maintaining bodies to provide, or facilitate the provision of, representation,

    (e) making grants to individuals to enable them to obtain representation,

    (f) employing persons to provide representation, or

    (g) doing anything else which it considers appropriate for funding representation.

(3) The Lord Chancellor—

    (a) shall by order make provision about the payments which may be made by the Commission in respect of any representation provided by non-contracted private practitioners, and

    (b) may by order make any other provision requiring the Commission to discharge the function in subsection (2) in accordance with the order.

(4) For the purposes of subsection (3)(a) representation is provided by a non-contracted private practitioner if it is provided, otherwise than pursuant to a contract entered into by the Commission, by a person or body which is neither—

    (a) a person or body in receipt of grants or loans made by the Commission as part of the Criminal Defence Service, nor

    (b) the Commission itself or a body established or maintained by the Commission.

(5) The provision which the Lord Chancellor is required to make by order under subsection (3)(a) includes provision for reviews of, or appeals against, determinations required for the purposes of the order.

(6) The Commission may fund representation by different means—

    (a) in different areas in England and Wales, and

    (b) in relation to different descriptions of cases.

(1) The right to representation

Access to Justice Act 1999, Sch.3, para.2(1)–(3)

36–21   1.—(1) A right to representation for the purposes of any kind of criminal proceedings before a court may be granted to an individual such as is mentioned in relation to that kind of proceedings in section 12(2).

(2) A right to representation for the purposes of criminal proceedings may also be granted to an individual to enable him to resist an appeal to the Crown Court otherwise than in an official capacity.

(3) In this Schedule "court" includes any body before which criminal proceedings take place.

The Criminal Defence Service must fund representation to an individual who has been granted a right of representation. Legal aid is not available to corporations.

(2) Application for representation order

Criminal Defence Service (General) (No.2) Regulations 2001, reg.6

Representation order
6.—(1) Any application for the grant of a representation order shall be made on form A in **36–22** Schedule 2 to these Regulations and, subject to regulation 10(5) and (6), the date of any representation order shall be the date upon which such form, properly completed, is received in accordance with these Regulations.

(2) Any application for the grant of a representation order in respect of the proceedings mentioned in section 12(2)(a) to (f) of the Act, and those mentioned in regulation 3(2)(h), shall be made in accordance with regulations 8, 9 and 10.

(3) Any application for the grant of a representation order in respect of the proceedings mentioned in regulation 3(2) (criminal proceedings for the purposes of section 12(2)(g) of the Act)[, except those mentioned in regulation 3(2)(h)]:

    (a) shall be made to the Commission; and

    (b) may be granted only by the Commission or a person acting on behalf of the Commission where such function has been delegated in accordance with section 3(4) of the Act.

(4) Where an application under paragraph (3) is refused, the Commission shall provide to the applicant:

    (a) written reasons for the refusal; and

    (b) details of the appeal process.

(5) Where the person who requires representation is aged less than 17, the application for the grant of a representation order may be made by his parent or guardian on his behalf.

(6) The appropriate officer of each court shall keep a record of every application to that court for a representation order, and of its outcome.

(7) The appropriate officer shall send to the Lord Chancellor such information from the record mentioned in paragraph (6) as the Lord Chancellor may request.

[This regulation is reprinted as amended by the *Criminal Defence Service (General) (No.2) (Amendment) Regulations* 2002, reg.8(3).]

The right to representation in respect of criminal proceedings listed in s.12(2) of the **36–23** *Access to Justice Act* 1999 (above) is granted by the court before which the criminal proceedings will take place. The right of representation in respect of criminal proceedings listed in the *Criminal Defence Service (General) (No.2) Regulations* 2001, reg.3(2) is granted by the Commission or a person acting on behalf of the Commission where the task of granting the right has been delegated. A representation order applies from the date that a properly completed application form is received and considered by the court. If there is a delay in a representation order being granted an acquitted defendant may claim costs to cover the pre-order work, see § 37–8.

Criminal Defence Service (General) (No.2) Regulations 2001, reg.7

General power to grant representation
7. The court, [the head of the Civil Appeals Office,] or the registrar of criminal appeals may **36–24**

grant a representation order at any stage of the proceedings in the circumstances set out in these *Regulations* whether or not an application has been made for such an order.

[This regulation is reprinted as amended by the *Criminal Defence Service (General) (No.2) (Amendment) Regulations* 2002, reg.9.]

36–25   This is the delegated power from the Commission for the court to grant representation. The magistrates' court may indicate that an unrepresented defendant should have the benefit of legal representation particularly when there is a possibility of a remand into custody or a custodial disposal. In the first instance the assistance of the Duty Solicitor will be sought who may subsequently assist in the making of an application.

Criminal Defence Service (General) (No.2) Regulations 2001, reg.8

Proceedings in a magistrates' court

36–26   **8.**—(1) Other than where regulation 6(3) applies, an application for a representation order in respect of proceedings in a magistrates' court may be made:

(a) orally or in writing to the court; or

(b) in writing to the appropriate officer.

(2) Where an application is made to the court, it may refer it to the appropriate officer for determination.

(3) Where an application is refused, the appropriate officer shall provide to the applicant:

(a) written reasons for the refusal; and

(b) details of the appeal process.

36–27   Applications for legal aid in a magistrates' court should be made to the justices' clerk on the prescribed form and be lodged at the relevant court. The court may decline to deal with an oral application in court and will direct that a written application be submitted to the 'proper officer' for determination.

Criminal Defence Service (General) (No.2) Regulations 2001, reg.18

36–28   **18.** Where an individual is committed or sent for trial by a lower court to a higher court, or appeals or applies for leave to appeal from a lower court to a higher court, the appropriate officer of the lower court shall send to the appropriate officer of the higher court the following documents:

(a) a copy of any representation order previously made in respect of the same proceedings; and

(b) a copy of any application for a representation order which has been refused.

36–29   A copy of the criminal defence representation order (CDRO) or a notice of refusal will be sent to the Crown Court with the committal documents. The CDRO may be a 'Through order' if the charge is an either way offence and an indication of jury trial is given with the application. Representation will then be granted for both the magistrates and Crown Court proceedings. If the order was not made to cover proceedings right up to the Crown Court it will be necessary for an application to be made at committal for the CDRO to be extended to cover the Crown Court proceedings .In the case of indictable only matters that are sent to the Crown Court, two forms must be completed. Form A covers the interests of justice test and should be completed and submitted at the magistrates' court proceedings. Form B will be served on the defence at the time of sending the case to the Crown Court and requires details of financial circumstances which must be completed and lodged with the Crown Court. A recovery of costs order may be made by the Crown Court at the end of proceedings but the magistrates' court has no power to make such an order: s.17(2) of the *Access to Justice Act* 1999.

Access to Justice Act 1999, Sch.3, para.5

36–30   5.—(1) Any question as to whether a right to representation should be granted shall be determined according to the interests of justice.

(2) In deciding what the interests of justice consist of in relation to any individual, the following factors must be taken into account—

    (a) whether the individual would, if any matter arising in the proceedings is decided against him, be likely to lose his liberty or livelihood or suffer serious damage to his reputation,

    (b) whether the determination of any matter arising in the proceedings may involve consideration of a substantial question of law,

    (c) whether the individual may be unable to understand the proceedings or to state his own case,

    (d) whether the proceedings may involve the tracing, interviewing or expert cross-examination of witnesses on behalf of the individual, and

    (e) whether it is in the interests of another person that the individual be represented.

(3) The Lord Chancellor may by order amend sub-paragraph (2) by adding new factors or varying any factor.

(4) A right to representation shall always be granted in such circumstances as may be prescribed.

A criminal defence representation order will be granted if it is in the interests of **36–31** justice according to these criteria. In the magistrates' court there is no need for a means test to be conducted. The test in Sch.3, para.5 of the *Access to Justice Act* 1999 is similar to that which governed the discretion to grant legal aid in the now-repealed *Legal Aid Act* 1988, s.22(2). Cases concerning that section are of assistance in interpreting the test in the *Access to Justice Act* 1999.

When assessing whether a conviction might lead to deprivation of liberty, loss of livelihood or damage to reputation, the authority asked to grant a representation order should consider the nature of the facts alleged by the prosecution in the particular case rather than the maximum penalty that might theoretically be imposed Although the offence may carry a maximum of five years imprisonment, the court must make a subjective assessment of the likelihood of loss of liberty having regard to the circumstances of the case: *R. v Highgate Justices Ex p. Lewis* [1977] Crim.L.R. 611.

In *R. v Liverpool City Magistrates' Court Ex p. McGhee* (1994) 158 J.P. 275, the court considered that the imposition of a community punishment order could not be regarded as depriving the accused of his liberty but it could still be a relevant factor when deciding whether to grant a right of representation.

In *R. v Chester Magistrates' Court Ex p. Ball* (1999) 163 J.P. 757, DC, the refusal **36–32** to grant legal aid was quashed where justices had considered only the likelihood of loss of liberty in the event of conviction and had failed to have regard to whether a conviction was likely to lead to serious damage to the reputation of the defendant. In *R. v Brigg Justices Ex p. Lynch* (1984) 148 J.P. 214, legal aid was justified because of the serious consequences of a conviction to the reputation and livelihood of a solider who had been charged with indecent exposure.

A defendant who intended to raise a special reason in order to avoid a disqualification from driving on conviction of driving with excess alcohol in his blood was eligible for legal aid in the interests of justice. The suggestion was that his drink had been laced and so the advice and assistance could extend to the instruction of an expert witness. The case was likely to be complex and the obtaining of an expert witness and possible cross-examination of another expert witness meant that the criteria were met: *R. v Gravesend Magistrates' Court Ex p. Baker* (1997) 161 J.P. 765, DC.

In *R. v Scunthorpe Justices Ex p. S, The Times*, March 5, 1998, DC the refusal to grant legal aid to a 16 year old charged with obstruction of a police officer in the execution of his duty was quashed as irrational where there was an issue as to whether the officer was acting in the execution of his duty. The expertise required for the purpose of cross examining the officer and for tracing and taking evidence from defence witnesses and the need to trace and interview them was beyond that of a 16-year-old and a conviction would have damaged a young man of good character on the threshold of his life. If the court is of the view that there is insufficient information about alleged defence witnesses, it should adjourn the matter rather than refuse the application. The inability to understand or follow proceedings may relate to the complexity of the case of individual factors affecting the applicant, such as his age, mental or physical health or language difficulties. These issues may also be relevant as to whether it would be in the interests of another person such as the victim of witnesses for the defendant to be represented so that cross-examination in person by the defendant may be avoided where appropriate. It is generally not sufficient to simply tick or mark "yes" on the form. Full details in the application form indicating which of the criteria apply and the reasons why, should ensure that applications are dealt with expeditiously.

36–33   Where an application for a representation order is made at the conclusion of proceedings in a magistrates' court, the interests of justice test should be applied on the basis of the facts as they appeared at the time when the solicitor was first consulted and not on the basis of hindsight. Where the defendant was charged with an imprisonable offence in relation to which there was a real and practical (not simply a theoretical) risk of imprisonment, an application made at the end of the proceedings should have been granted. It was not open to the appropriate officer to refuse the application on the ground that there was, in the end, no risk of imprisonment because the prosecution had substituted a charge of a non-imprisonable offence to which the defendant had pleaded guilty: *R. v Horseferry Road Magistrates Ex p. Punatar & Co* unreported, May 24, 2002, DC; [2002] EWHC 1196 (Admin).

(3) Selection of the representative

Access to Justice Act 1999, s.15

Selection of representative

36–34   **15.**—(1) An individual who has been granted a right to representation in accordance with Schedule 3 may select any representative or representatives willing to act for him; and, where he does so, the Commission is to comply with the duty imposed by section 14(1) by funding representation by the selected representative or representatives.

(2) Regulations may provide that in prescribed circumstances—

     (a) the right conferred by subsection (1) is not to apply in cases of prescribed descriptions,

     (b) an individual who has been provided with advice or assistance funded by the Commission under section 13 by a person whom he chose to provide it for him is to be taken to have selected that person as his representative pursuant to that right,

     (c) that right is not to include a right to select a representative of a prescribed description,

     (d) that right is to select only a representative of a prescribed description,

     (e) that right is to select not more than a prescribed number of representatives to act at any one time, and

     (f) that right is not to include a right to select a representative in place of a representative previously selected.

(3) Regulations under subsection (2)(b) may prescribe circumstances in which an individual is to be taken to have chosen a person to provide advice or assistance for him.

(4) Regulations under subsection (2) may not provide that only a person employed by the Commission, or by a body established and maintained by the Commission, may be selected.

(5) Regulations may provide that in prescribed circumstances the Commission is not required to fund, or to continue to fund, representation for an individual by a particular representative (but such provision shall not prejudice any right of the individual to select another representative).

(6) The circumstances which may be prescribed by regulations under subsection (2) or (5) include that a determination has been made by a prescribed body or person.

The prescribed description is contained in r.11 and includes an employee in the Criminal Defence Service or a lawyer who is franchised from the Legal Services Commission.

(4) Employment by Legal Services Commission

Criminal Defence Service (General) (No.2) Regulations 2001, reg.11

11.—(1) The right conferred by section 15(1) of the Act, as regards representation in respect **36–35** of any proceedings to which this regulation applies, shall be exercisable only in relation to those representatives who are:

(a) employed by the Commission to provide such representation; or

(b) authorised to provide such representation under a crime franchise contract with the Commission which commences on or after 2nd April 2001 and specifies the rate of remuneration for such representation.

(2) This regulation applies to:

(a) any criminal proceedings in a magistrates' court;

(b) any proceedings in the Crown Court mentioned in regulation 3(2);

(c) any appeal by way of case stated from a magistrates' court; and

(d) any proceedings which are preliminary or incidental to proceedings mentioned in sub-paragraphs (a) to (c).

(3) This regulation does not apply to proceedings referred to in section 12(2)(f) of the Act (proceedings for contempt in the face of a court).

(5) Representation by an advocate

Criminal Defence Service (General) (No.2) Regulations 2001, reg.12

12.—(1) A representation order for the purposes of proceedings before a magistrates' court **36–36** may only include representation by an advocate in the case of:

(a) any indictable offence, including an offence which is triable either way; or

(b) proceedings under section 9 of, or paragraph 6 of Schedule 1 to, the *Extradition Act* 1989

where the court is of the opinion that, because of circumstances which make the proceedings unusually grave or difficult, representation by both a solicitor and an advocate would be desirable.

(2) A representation order for the purposes of proceedings before a magistrates' court may not include representation by an advocate other than as provided in paragraph (1).

Before the court can properly exercise its discretion to assign counsel in a case other **36–37** than a charge of murder, the applicant must show not only that the case is of unusual gravity or difficulty but also that circumstances lead to the conclusion that such representation is desirable in the particular proceedings—whether summary trial or committal proceedings. The proper approach is to recognise that in a large number of cases which might in themselves be grave or difficult it is nevertheless possible at an early stage for any competent solicitor to realise that no useful purpose would be likely to be served in the interests of his client in opposing, for example, a simple committal for trial under s.6(2) of the *Magistrates' Courts Act* 1980. The mere multiplicity of simple, straightforward charges could not make it desirable for counsel to be instructed. The facts in relation to a single charge might be so complex that it is desirable that counsel should at least advise whether there were good grounds for opposing a committal under s.6(2). Assignment of counsel may be justified if a submission of no case to answer is to be made in a case of some gravity and weight: *R. v Guildford Justices Ex p. Scott* [1975] Crim.L.R. 286.

The principle of equality of arms under the ECHR, Art.6 does not require that a de- **36–38** fendant should be represented by leading counsel merely because the prosecution were so represented. What is required is that the defendant be properly represented by an advocate who could ensure that the defendant's case was properly and adequately put before the court: *R. v Lea (Attorney-General's Reference (No.82a of 2000)), R. v Shatwell* [2002] 2 Cr.App.R. 24, CA. Rule 14, para.14 of the regulations makes provision for representation by Queen's Counsel to be ordered in the magistrates court but only at the time when a murder charge is sent to the Crown Court or a case prosecuted by the SFO is transferred.

(6) Representation by advocate only

Criminal Defence Service (General) (No.2) Regulations 2001, reg.15

36–39   **15.** The court may grant a representation order for representation by an advocate alone:

     (a) in any proceedings referred to in section 12(2)(f) of the Act;

     (b) in respect of an appeal to the Court of Appeal or the Courts-Martial Appeal Court; or

     (c) in cases of urgency where it appears to the court that there is no time to instruct a solicitor:

         (i) in respect of an appeal to the Crown Court; or

         (ii) in proceedings in which a person is committed to or appears before the Crown Court for trial or sentence, or appears or is brought before that court to be dealt with.

A CDRO may be granted to a solicitor and it is open to them to brief counsel if they see fit but this rule restricts the circumstances in which an order can specify representation by a barrister.

Criminal Defence Service (General) (No.2) Regulations 2001, reg.22

36–40   **22.** Where a representation order has been made, the assisted person's solicitor or advocate shall not receive or be a party to the making of any payment for work done in connection with the proceedings in respect of which the representation order was made except such payments as may be made:

     (a) by the Lord Chancellor or the Commission; or

     (b) in respect of any expenses or fees incurred in:

         (i) preparing, obtaining or considering any report, opinion or further evidence, whether provided by an expert witness or otherwise; or

         (ii) obtaining any transcripts or recordings

     where an application for an authority to incur such fees or expenses has been refused by the Costs Committee.

(7) High cost cases

Criminal Defence Service (General) (No.2) Regulations 2001, reg.23

36–41   **23.**—(1) This regulation applies to very high cost cases where funded services are provided.

(2) Any solicitor who has conduct of a case which is a very high cost case shall notify the Commission in writing accordingly as soon as is practicable.

(3) Where a solicitor fails to comply with the provisions of this regulation without good reason, and as a result there is a loss to public funds, the court or Costs Committee, as appropriate, may refuse payment of his costs up to the extent of such loss.

(4) No payment under paragraph (3) shall be refused unless the solicitor has been given a reasonable opportunity to show why it should not be refused.

Very high cost cases by definition will rarely be dealt with in the magistrates' court but the original application for legal representation will be made there. The applicant or his solicitor should note the high cost of the case on the application at the earliest opportunity. The Court has a duty to check that the LSC have been notified and will advise that failure to notify may mean costs will not be recovered: *Practice Direction (Costs in Criminal Proceedings)* May, 2004, below.

(8) Expenditure, expert witnesses

36–42   Case law under the previous legislation clarified the situation relating to expert evidence that could be commissioned at public expense. In *R. v Silcott, Braithwaite and Raghip, The Times*, December 9, 1991, the Court of Appeal said that lawyers are under a duty not to involve the legal aid fund in unnecessary expenditure. It was not appropriate to continue to obtain reports until one favourable to the defence case was found. The fund would allow for one or at the most two expert's reports to be commissioned. "Expert shopping" was to be discouraged but in this case there were exceptional circumstances where the need for a further expert opinion could be demonstrated. Counsel should advise on evidence in support of an extension of the representation order to obtain expert's reports and the courts must rely on the proper professional standards being observed by all the lawyers concerned.

The court has no power to authorise the incurring of costs under a representation order for an expert witness, although it may express an opinion as to the desirability of the order being so extended: *R. v Donnelly* [1998] Crim.L.R. 131, CA.

(9) Change of representative

Criminal Defence Service (General) (No.2) Regulations 2001, reg.16

16.—(1) Where a representation order has been granted an application may be made to the   **36–43** court before which the proceedings are heard to select a representative in place of a representative previously selected, and any such application shall state the grounds on which it is made.

(2) The court may:

    (a) grant the application where:

        (i) the representative considers himself to be under a duty to withdraw from the case in accordance with his professional rules of conduct and, in such a case, the representative shall provide details of the nature of such duty;

        (ii) there is a breakdown in the relationship between the assisted person and the representative such that effective representation can no longer be provided and, in such a case, the representative shall provide details of the nature of such breakdown;

        (iii) through circumstances beyond his control, the representative is no longer able to represent the assisted person; or

        (iv) some other substantial compelling reason exists; or

    (b) refuse the application.

When legal advice and assistance is being publicly funded under a CDRO the court has a duty to scrutinise the justification for changing solicitors which may result in a duplication of work and costs. A request for a change of representation should be in writing clearly explaining the reasons for the application. The court will require confirmation that the original solicitor is aware of and consents to the transfer. If there is no consent then representations should be heard.

(10) Withdrawal of representation order

Criminal Defence Service (General) (No.2) Regulations 2001, reg.17

17.—(1) The court before which the proceedings are heard, or, in respect of any proceedings   **36–44** mentioned in [regulation 3(2)(a) to (g)], the Commission, must consider whether to withdraw the representation order in any of the following circumstances:

    (a) where any charge or proceedings against the assisted person are varied, the court or the Commission, as appropriate, must consider whether the interests of justice continue to require that he be represented in respect of the varied charge or proceedings;

    (b) where the assisted person declines to accept a representation order in the terms which are offered;

    (c) at the request of the assisted person; or

    (d) where the representative named on the representation order declines to continue to represent the assisted person.

(2) Where representation is withdrawn, the appropriate officer or the Commission, as appropriate, shall provide written notification to the assisted person and to the solicitor (or, where there was no solicitor assigned, to the advocate), who shall inform any assigned advocate (or, where notification is given to the advocate, any other assigned advocate).

(3) On any subsequent application by the assisted person for a representation order in respect of the same proceedings, he shall declare the previous withdrawal of representation and the reason for it.

36–45   A CDRO may be withdrawn because of a breakdown in the relationship between the defendant and the solicitor. A fresh application for representation may then be made.

(11) Appeal against refusal to grant representation

Criminal Defence Service (Representation Order Appeals) Regulations 2001, reg.3

36–46   3. Appeals against refusals of representation order

(1) A person whose application for the grant of a representation order has been refused may appeal against such refusal by way of a renewed application to the body which refused the application.

(2) Any appeal in writing shall be made on such form as is from time to time specified by the Lord Chancellor.

(3) Subject to the provisions of the *Criminal Defence Service (General) (No. 2) Regulations* 2001, the date of any representation order shall be the date upon which the original application was received in accordance with those Regulations.

[This regulation is reprinted as amended by the *Criminal Defence Service (General) (No.2) (Amendment) Regulations* 2002, reg.13.]

An order will only be refused if the court is of the opinion that the interests of justice do not require representation to be provided. The decision is made on the basis of information in the application and if that is not detailed enough more should be included in any renewed application.

Criminal Defence Service (Representation Order Appeals) Regulations 2001, reg.4

Crown Court and magistrates' court

36–47   4.—(1) A person whose application for the grant of a representation order has been refused by the Crown Court or a magistrates' court may make a renewed application, either orally or in writing to the same court, or in writing to the appropriate officer of that court.

(2) Where a renewed application is made to the appropriate officer, he may:

     (a) grant the order; or

     (b) refer the renewed application:

         (i) in the Crown Court, to a judge of the court; or

         (ii) in a magistrates' court, to the court, a District Judge (magistrates' court) or a single justice

who may grant the order or refuse the application.

(3) The judge hearing the application shall give reasons for the refusal of any application.

(4) Where the application was made in writing, the reasons for any refusal shall be given in writing.

The 'proper officer' cannot refuse the renewed application. If he is not minded to grant the order, the renewed application must be referred to a magistrate or district judge. This will usually be done in writing and the reasons for any further refusal will be given in writing.

Criminal Defence Service (Representation Order Appeals) Regulations 2001, reg.7

Appeals against withdrawals of representation order

36–48   7.—(1) A person whose representation order has been withdrawn may appeal against such withdrawal on one occasion to the body which withdrew the order.

(2) Equivalent provisions to those set out in regulations 4 to 6 shall apply in respect of such appeals.

(3) Any appeal in writing shall be made on such form as is from time to time specified by the Lord Chancellor.

E. Recovery of Defence Costs

Access to Justice Act 1999, s.17(1), (2)

Terms of provision of funded services

36–49 17.—(1) An individual for whom services are funded by the Commission as part of the Criminal Defence Service shall not be required to make any payment in respect of the services except where subsection (2) applies.

(2) Where representation for an individual in respect of criminal proceedings in any court other than a magistrates' court is funded by the Commission as part of the Criminal Defence Service, the court may, subject to regulations under subsection (3), make an order requiring him to pay some or all of the cost of any representation so funded for him (in proceedings in that or any other court).

36–50 The magistrates' court has no power to order that costs of the case be recovered from the legally aided defendant or that he otherwise pays any contribution to the cost of his publicly funded legal representation, irrespective of his means.

Recovery of costs orders may be made in the Crown Court at the conclusion of the case: s.17 of the *Access to Justice Act* 1999.

CHAPTER 37

COSTS

I. INTRODUCTION

The *Prosecution of Offences Act* 1985, Pt II governs the award of costs in criminal **37–1** proceedings. It has been supplemented by the *Costs in Criminal Cases (General) Regulations* 1986 made under ss.19 and 20. The magistrates' court has power to make a defendant's costs order and a prosecution costs order for payment of costs from central or public funds. An order can also be made for the convicted defendant to pay the costs of the prosecution. The court may make a wasted costs order against either the prosecution or defence to cover any costs incurred by a party as a result of an unnecessary or improper act or omission by the other party to the proceedings. The court may also make an order for wasted costs against legal representatives. The *Courts Act* 2003 also adds a power for the court to award costs against third parties. The magistrates' court has no inherent jurisdiction to award the payment of costs in criminal cases. Any party making an application for costs must identify the statutory authority for the court to do so.

General

The *Prosecution of Offences Act* 1985 covers criminal proceedings only. It does not **37–2** extend to applications such as those under the *Police Property Act* 1897 for the release of property being held by the police: *R. v Daventry Justices Ex p. Chief Constable of Northamptonshire Police* [2001] EWCA Admin 446. An application for access orders by Customs and Excise under the *Value Added Tax Act* 1994 were held not to be criminal proceedings as no person had been charged and a wasted costs order could not be made in the course of the application: *Customs and Excise Commissioners v City of London Magistrates' Court* [2000] 4 All E.R. 763. There is power under s.64 of the *Magistrates' Courts Act* 1980 for the court to make an award of costs in civil cases where a complaint is made which may be relevant in some applications.

Human Rights Act 1998

No absolute right to costs or expenses can be read into the European Convention on **37–3** Human Rights: *Lutz v Germany* [1988] 10 E.H.R.R. 182. As a general principle, case law indicates that on acquittal costs should normally be awarded: *Sekanina v Austria* [1993] 17 E.H.R.R. 221. If costs are refused to a defendant where the case has been dismissed or discontinued this could amount to a breach of Art.6 as a violation of the presumption of innocence where the reasons for the refusal amount in substance to a

1111

determination of guilt: *Minelli v Switzerland* [1983] 5 E.H.R.R. 554. Where however a court refers to the state of suspicion against the defendant in support of its exercise of its discretion to refuse costs, there is no violation of the presumption of innocence: *Leutscher v Netherlands* [1997] 24 E.H.R.R. 181. The possibility of the presumption of innocence being violated would appear to be more likely in relation to acquittals as compared to cases where the case is discontinued through a technicality: *Sekanina v Austria*, above.

II. COSTS, ORDERS AND ENFORCEMENT

A. GUIDES TO THE AWARD OF COSTS IN CRIMINAL PROCEEDINGS

37–4   On May 18, 2004, *Practice Directions on Costs in Criminal Proceedings* were issued by the Lord Chief Justice. These replace earlier Practice Notes and apply to magistrates' courts. A clear and detailed explanation of the power to award costs and the procedures is provided. It introduces directions on when costs should be awarded from Central Funds to an acquitted defendant and also gives guidance on the new power brought in by the *Courts Act* 2003 which allows the court to make an order for third party costs. In addition the role of the court in relation to costs is clarified. In Part VII of the directions it is stated—

> "the Judge has a much greater and more direct responsibility for costs in criminal proceedings than in civil and should keep the question of costs at the forefront of his mind at every stage of the case and ought to be prepared to take the initiative himself without any prompting from the parties."

The Justices' Clerks Society has published a Good Practice Guide for the Award of Costs which is directly relevant to the magistrates' courts and will be applied by the court or the appropriate officer when dealing with any claims for costs.

B. DEFENDANT'S COSTS ORDERS

Prosecution of Offences Act 1985, s.16

Defence costs

37–5   **16.**—(1) Where—

    (a) an information laid before a justice of the peace for any area, charging any person with an offence, is not proceeded with;

    (b) a magistrates' court inquiring into an indictable offence as examining justices determines not to commit the accused for trial;

    (c) a magistrates' court dealing summarily with an offence dismisses the information;

that court or, in a case falling within paragraph (a) above, a magistrates' court for that area, may make an order in favour of the accused for a payment to be made out of central funds in respect of his costs (a "defendant's costs order").

(2)–(5) deal with the powers of other courts to order costs.

(6) A defendant's costs order shall, subject to the following provisions of this section, be for the payment out of central funds, to the person in whose favour the order is made, of such amount as the court considers reasonably sufficient to compensate him for any expenses properly incurred by him in the proceedings.

(7) Where a court makes a defendant's costs order but is of the opinion that there are circumstances which make it inappropriate that the person in whose favour the order is made should recover the full amount mentioned in subsection (6) above, the court shall—

    (a) assess what amount would, in its opinion, be just and reasonable; and

    (b) specify that amount in the order.

(9) Subject to subsection (7) above, the amount to be paid out of central funds in pursuance of a defendant's costs order shall—

    (a) be specified in the order, in any case where the court considers it appropriate for the amount to be so specified and the person in whose favour the order is made agrees the amount; and

(b) in any other case, be determined in accordance with regulations made by the Lord Chancellor for the purposes of this section.

(10) Subsection (6) above shall have effect, in relation to any case falling within subsection (1)(a) or (2)(a) above, as if for the words "in the proceedings" there were substituted the words "in or about the defence".

(11) Where a person ordered to be retried is acquitted at his retrial, the costs which may be ordered to be paid out of central funds under this section shall include—

(a) any costs which, at the original trial, could have been ordered to be so paid under this section if he had been acquitted; and

(b) if no order was made under this section in respect of his expenses on appeal, any sums for the payment of which such an order could have been made.

(12) Refers to Crown Court powers.

[This section is reprinted as amended by the *Criminal Justice and Public Order Act* 1994, Sch.9, para.25(a).]

At the end of a case in the magistrates' court where the defendant is found not guilty **37–6** of a charge tried summarily or is discharged on committal or the case is not proceeded with by the prosecution, he may apply for his costs to be paid out of central funds under this section. The application may be made in court immediately. The court may then, if the amount claimed is specified or can be readily assessed make a defendant's costs order for the required amount to be paid out of central funds. The determined total figure must be expressed in the order: *R. v Judd* [1971] 1 All E.R. 127 (Note). If the amount is yet to be properly quantified or cannot be agreed then the court may order that the amount be 'taxed' or assessed by an appropriate officer of the court under the regulations: subs.9. Where a DCO is to be taxed, the claim must be submitted within three months: regs (6) and (12) *Costs in Criminal Cases (General Regulations)*1986. There is no right of appeal to the Crown Court against the decision of the appropriate officer on costs: (s.108 of the *Magistrates' Courts Act* 1980) and any assessment of a claim can only be challenged by way of judicial review.

If an application for a costs order is not made immediately in court it may be made at a later date and be referred to any court in the PSA: *R. v Bolton Justices Ex p. Wildish* (1983) 147 J.P. 309, DC; *R. v Liverpool Magistrates' Court Ex p. Abiaka* [1999] (96) 14 L.S.G. 32, DC. The court must be satisfied that one of the circumstances listed in s.16 above apply. A case is not proceeded with when a notice of discontinuance is served by the prosecution and the court retains the jurisdiction to award costs to the defendant to cover the expense of preparation for the trial: *Denning v DPP* [1991] 2 Q.B. 532. The reason why the case is not proceeded with is irrelevant. Where a case was unable to proceed because the information was found to have been laid out of time it was held that the court still had power to make an award of costs in favour of a defendant: *Patel v Blakely* [1988] R.T.R. 65, DC.

A defendant's costs order may be made in favour of a parent or guardian ordered to **37–7** pay a child or young person's fine, costs or compensation order pursuant to s.137(1) of the *PCC(S)A* 2000. The reference to "the accused" in s.16(5)(a) includes a parent or guardian against whom such an order has been made: *R. v Preston Crown Court Ex p. Lancashire CC*; *R. v Burnley Crown Court Ex p. Same* [1999] 1 W.L.R. 142, DC.

The exception to the entitlement of a defendant's costs order, especially on acquittal is very narrow despite the court's discretion to make such an order: *South West Surrey Magistrates' Court Ex p. James* [2001] Crim.L.R. 690, DC. This is in accordance with European case law. The *Practice Direction on Costs in Criminal Proceedings* (May 2004) covers defence costs orders. In Part III it says that an order for defence costs should normally be made on acquittal unless there are positive reasons for not doing so. An example is given where a defendant's own conduct brings suspicion on him and misleads the prosecution into thinking that the case against him was stronger than it is. The directions also confirm that the court retains a discretion whether to order defence costs or not. It has been held that when an information is dismissed after a trial the fact that a prosecution was properly brought and was not malicious is irrelevant and does not constitute a good reason for a refusal to make a defendant's costs order: *R. v Bir-*

mingham Juvenile Court Ex p. H (1992) 156 J.P. 445. In cases of discontinuance the conduct of the defendant must be carefully considered as it may provide a reason for refusal. The fact that the defendant has brought the prosecution on himself was held to amount to a reason for not making an order: *R. v Spens, The Independent*, March 18, 1992. But the suggestion that the defendant brought the prosecution on himself must be based on strong independent evidence in order to provide a positive reason to refuse costs: *Mooney v Cardiff Magistrates' Court* (1999) 164 J.P. 220. Where a costs order was refused to a defendant whose case was dismissed in the absence of a prosecution witness, it was held that this could interfere with the presumption of innocence under Art.6 as it indicated a determination of guilt: *R. (Barrington) v Preston Crown Court* [2001] EWHC Admin 599.

37–8   The amount ordered to be taxed is for expenses 'properly incurred' by the defendant. The court or the appropriate officer will consider whether the defendant has incurred costs and to what amount.

Under the *Prosecution of Offences Act* 1985, s.21(4A), the costs of a defendant who has the benefit of a criminal defence representation order shall not, for the purposes of a defendant's costs order, be taken to include any expenses incurred on his behalf by the Legal Services Commission or the Lord Chancellor. The costs are paid out of public funds in any event so he incurs no costs. A costs order may be appropriate in limited circumstances, for example, if the defendant was not legally aided until a late stage in the proceedings and paid for early representation personally.

Costs are incurred by a defendant when he is liable to his solicitors for the costs of his defence even if a third party, such as his employer or an insurance company has undertaken or is liable to pay any of the costs. Only if there is an express or implied agreement in binding form that in no circumstances would the solicitor seek to recover costs from the defendant could it be said that the defendant had incurred no costs: *R. v Miller and Glennie* (1984) 78 Cr.App.R. 71, QBD.

37–9   Defence solicitors may be instructed privately with a contract to pay legal expenses but no money actually changing hands until the case is concluded. Difficulties might then arise as to whether costs were actually ' incurred by the defendant.' In the case of *R. (on the application of McCormick) v Liverpool City Magistrates* [2001] 2 All E.R. 705, the precise meaning of 'incurred' was considered in detail. One defendant had entered into a contract with his solicitor that he would not be expected to make any payment not within the ambit of public funds. Another defendant had instructed a solicitor privately but had not made any payment to him during the progression of the case. Both were refused DCOs as the court took the view that in these circumstances no legal costs had been incurred. It was held on appeal against the refusals that in the first case a liability had been incurred because the defendant may have been ordered to pay costs outside the ambit of public funds. In the second case the Act and Regulations were held only to require that costs be incurred and not actually paid by the defendant. In both cases it was held that the financial ability of the defendants to pay any costs incurred was not relevant and in the circumstances the refusals of the DCOs were quashed.

In *R. v Jain, The Times*, December 10, 1987, CA, a defendant's costs order was made in favour of a named person other than the defendant, who had financed the proceedings. However the judgment does not specify how the court dealt with the question of whether the Act allows costs awards in favour of persons other than the defendant.

37–10   A solicitor who represents himself in person in criminal proceedings incurs costs in conducting his own case. He may claim for the fees chargeable by him had he been representing a defendant and not himself: *R. v Stafford, Stone and Eccleshall Magistrates' Court Ex p. Robinson* [1988] 1 W.L.R. 369. A barrister who was represented by counsel in criminal proceedings was entitled to claim costs for his representation and also for the work he had done himself in preparing his own defence. The Code of Conduct prevented him from representing himself in a professional capacity: *Khan v Lord Chancellor* [2003] 1 W.L.R. 2385.

A person in respect of whom a defendant's costs order is made may also be paid subsistence allowance and travelling expenses in relation to his attendances at court under reg.23 of the *Costs on Criminal Cases (General) Regulations* 1986. The rates are fixed by the Lord Chancellor. No claim can be made for loss of earnings or loss of time.

There is no provision in criminal proceedings under the *Prosecution of Offences Act* 1985 or the Regulations to award interest on costs: *Westminster City Council v Wingrove* [1991] 1 Q.B. 652.

Costs in Criminal Cases (General) Regulations 1986, regs.4–8, 12

PART III

COSTS OUT OF CENTRAL FUNDS

Application and definitions

4. This Part of these Regulations applies to costs payable out of central funds in pursuance of **37–11** an order made under or by virtue of Part II of the Act and in this Part of these Regulations—

"applicant" means the person in whose favour a costs order has been made;

"appropriate authority" has the meaning assigned to it by regulation 5;

"costs judge" means a costs judge of the Supreme Court;

"costs order" means an order made under or by virtue of Part II of the Act for the payment of costs out of central funds;

"disbursements" do not include any payment made out of central funds to a witness, interpreter or medical practitioner in accordance with Part V of these Regulations;

"presiding judge" means the judge who presided at the hearing in respect of which the costs are payable; and

The appropriate authority

5.—(1) Costs shall be determined by the appropriate authority in accordance with these **37–12** Regulations.

(2) Subject to paragraph (3), the appropriate authority shall be—

    (a) the registrar of criminal appeals in the case of proceedings in the Court of Appeal,

    (b) the master of the Crown Office in the case of proceedings in a Divisional Court of the Queen's Bench Division,

    (c) an officer appointed by the Lord Chancellor in the case of proceedings in the Crown Court,

    (d) the justices' clerk in the case of proceedings in a magistrates' court.

(3) The appropriate authority may appoint or authorise the appointment of determining officers to act on its behalf under these Regulations in accordance with directions given by it or on its behalf.

Claims for costs

6.—(1) Subject to regulation 12, no claim for costs shall be entertained unless it is submitted **37–13** within three months of the date on which the costs order was made.

(2) Subject to paragraph (3), a claim for costs shall be submitted to the justices' chief executive for the court, in the case of proceedings in a magistrates' court, or to the appropriate authority, in the case of proceedings in any other court specified in regulation 5(2), in such form and manner as he or it may direct and shall be accompanied by receipts or other evidence of the applicant's payment of the costs claimed, and any receipts or other documents in support of any disbursements claimed.

(3) A claim shall—

    (a) summarise the items of work done by a solicitor;

    (b) state, where appropriate, the dates on which items of work were done, the time taken and the sums claimed,

    (c) specify any disbursements claimed, including counsel's fees, the circumstances in which they were incurred and the amounts claimed in respect of them, and

    (d) contain either full particulars, including the date and outcome, of any claim that regulation 44(7) of the *Legal Aid in Criminal and Care Proceedings (General) Regulations* 1989 should be applied in respect of any work comprised in the claim under these Regulations, or a certificate by the solicitor that he has not made, and will not make, any such claim.

(4) Where there are any special circumstances which should be drawn to the attention of the appropriate authority, the applicant shall specify them.

(5) The applicant shall supply such further particulars, information and documents as the appropriate authority may require.

Determination of costs

37–14   **7.**—(1) The appropriate authority shall consider the claim, any further particulars, information or documents submitted by the applicant under regulation 6 and shall allow such costs in respect of—

(a) such work as appears to it to have been actually and reasonably done; and

(b) such disbursements as appear to it to have been actually and reasonably incurred,

as it considers reasonably sufficient to compensate the applicant for any expenses properly incurred by him in the proceedings.

(2) In determining costs under paragraph (1) the appropriate authority shall taken into account all the relevant circumstances of the case including the nature, importance, complexity or difficulty of the work and the time involved.

(3) When determining costs for the purposes of this regulation, there shall be allowed a reasonable amount in respect of all costs reasonably incurred and any doubts which the appropriate authority may have as to whether the costs were reasonably incurred or were reasonable in amount shall be resolved against the applicant.

Payment of costs

37–15   **8.**—(1) When the appropriate authority has determined the costs payable to an applicant in accordance with these Regulations, the justices' chief executive for the court, in the case of proceedings in a magistrates' court, or the appropriate authority, in the case of proceedings in any other court specified in regulation 5(2), shall notify the applicant of the costs payable and authorise payment accordingly.

(2) Where the costs payable under paragraph (1) are varied as a result of a redetermination under regulation 9, an appeal to a costs judge under regulation 10, or an appeal to the High Court under regulation 11, then—

(a) where the costs are increased, the appropriate authority shall authorise payment of the increase;

(b) where the costs are decreased, the applicant shall repay the amount of such decrease; and

(c) where the payment of the costs of an appeal is ordered under regulation 10(14) or 11(8), the appropriate authority shall authorise such payment to the applicant.

Time limits

37–16   **12.**—(1) Subject to paragraph (2), the time limit within which there must be made or instituted—

(a) a claim for costs by an applicant under regulation 6, an application for a redetermination under regulation 9, or a request for an appropriate authority to give reasons for its decision on a redetermination under regulation 9;

(b) an appeal to a costs judge under regulation 10 or an application for a certificate under regulation 11; or

(c) an appeal to the High Court under regulation 11;

may, for good reason, be extended by the appropriate authority, the Senior Costs Judge or the High Court, as the case may be.

(2) Where an applicant without good reason has failed (or, if an extension were not granted, would fail) to comply with a time limit, the appropriate authority, the Senior Costs Judge or the High Court, as the case may be, may, in exceptional circumstances, extend the time limit.

(3) An applicant may appeal to the Senior Costs Judge against a decision made under this regulation by an appropriate authority in respect of proceedings other than proceedings before a magistrates' court and such an appeal shall be instituted within 21 days of the

decision being given by giving notice in writing to the Senior Costs Judge specifying the grounds of appeal.

These regulations outline the procedure to be used when costs awarded under a **37–17** defendant's costs order are assessed. In the magistrates' court the appropriate officer is the justices' clerk who may delegate his powers to tax costs: reg.5 The taxation will be conducted in accordance with the regulations and Practice Notes. The Justices' Clerks Society has also published a Best Practice Guide to Costs which gives detailed guidance on the proper approach to any assessment of claims and has national application. A claim for costs must be submitted within three months of the order for costs being made by the court but the appropriate officer has a discretion to extend that time limit (reg.12). The case file will be provided to the court with a written record of all the work done, including attendance notes for interviews, conferences, telephone calls and correspondence together with a note of time spent on research and preparation. An explanation will be required of the grade of lawyer engaged and the hourly rate charged. There will also be an element of 'care and conduct' which is a percentage increase on the rate to reflect the gravity and complexity of the case. The applicant will then multiply the hourly rate by the time spent to arrive at a global figure to which VAT may be added. The appropriate officer may require that all claims are evidenced in writing and the grade of lawyer chosen must be justified. The figure assessed will include costs for the time spent on the case and for disbursements which are specific payments for identified items. The taxing officer will allow an amount that he considers reasonable to compensate for the expenses incurred. A claimant may dispute the costs allowed and attempt to reach an agreement with the appropriate officer but the final decision of the appropriate officer can only be challenged by way of judicial review as being 'Wednesbury' unreasonable.

In *R. v Leeds Magistrates' Court Ex p. Castle* [1991] Crim.L.R. 770, the court gave consideration to the test to be applied under s.16 and the Regulations. The appellant had been disallowed the claim for representation by two counsel at a lengthy committal. On appeal it was held that there was a two-stage test: first the determination of whether work has been actually and reasonably done and second the consideration of the sum reasonably sufficient to compensate for the expenses incurred. In this case the appropriate officer had exercised his discretion reasonably.

The officer must consider claims objectively and determine whether they were justifiable under reg.7. The fact that solicitors submitted a claim does not automatically prohibit the defendant from submitting his own claim for personal expenses incurred in preparing his case: *R. v Bedlington Magistrates' Court Ex p. Wilkinson* (2000) 164 J.P. 156.

Claims may be disallowed if the grade and cost of the solicitor or counsel instructed is **37–18** considered to be too expensive. The test is not whether a more junior lawyer could have dealt with the case just as competently but whether it was reasonable in all the circumstances to instruct a more senior barrister: *R. v Dudley Magistrates' Court Ex p. Power City Stores Ltd* (1990) 154 J.P. 654. For a defendant charged with common assault and battery the instruction of a solicitor of more than four years' standing was reasonable as was the agreement to incur costs using a flat hourly rate: *R. v Southport Justices Ex p. Hale, The Times,* January 29, 2002, DC.

It may be reasonable to instruct solicitors who are not local and so may be more expensive, but the reasons for doing so must be advanced: *Wraith v Sheffield Forgemasters* (1998) 1 All E.R. 82. Higher rates may be allowed for specialist lawyers if it is reasonable to incur such costs and the rate charged is justifiable in view of higher overheads *etc.*: *Jones v Secretary of State for Wales* [1997] 2 All E.R. 507.

An application to extend the time limit within which a claim should be submitted **37–19** may be made either before or after the limit of three months expires. The appropriate officer will then decide if there is good reason to extend the limit. An extension of time may also be granted if there are 'exceptional circumstances' which led to the delay despite the fact that there was no good reason for it: *R. v Clerk to the North Kent Justices Ex p. McGoldrick & Co.* (1996) 160 J.P. 30.

C. Prosecution Costs

Prosecution of Offences Act 1985, s.17

Prosecution costs

37–20   **17.**—(1) Subject to subsection (2) below, the court may—

(a) in any proceedings in respect of an indictable offence; and

(b) in any proceedings before a Divisional Court of the Queen's Bench Division or the House of Lords in respect of a summary offence;

order the payment out of central funds of such amount as the court considers reasonably sufficient to compensate the prosecutor for any expenses properly incurred by him in the proceedings.

(2) No order under this section may be made in favour of—

(a) a public authority; or

(b) a person acting—

(i) on behalf of a public authority; or

(ii) in his capacity as an official appointed by such an authority.

(3) Where a court makes an order under this section but is of the opinion that there are circumstances which make it inappropriate that the prosecution should recover the full amount mentioned in subsection (1) above, the court shall—

(a) assess what amount would, in its opinion, be just and reasonable; and

(b) specify that amount in the order.

(4) Subject to subsection (3) above, the amount to be paid out of central funds in pursuance of an order under this section shall—

(a) be specified in the order, in any case where the court considers it appropriate for the amount to be so specified and the prosecutor agrees the amount; and

(b) in any other case, be determined in accordance with regulations made by the Lord Chancellor for the purposes of this section.

(5) Where the conduct of proceedings to which subsection (1) above applies is taken over by the Crown Prosecution Service, that subsection shall have effect as if it referred to the prosecutor who had the conduct of the proceedings before the intervention of the Service and to expenses incurred by him up to the time of intervention.

(6) In this section "public authority" means—

(a) a police force within the meaning of section 3 of this Act;

(b) the Crown Prosecution Service or any other government department;

(c) a local authority or other authority or body constituted for purposes of—

(i) the public service or of local government; or

(ii) carrying on under national ownership any industry or undertaking or part of an industry or undertaking; or

(d) any other authority or body whose members are appointed by Her Majesty or by any Minister of the Crown or government department or whose revenues consist wholly or mainly of money provided by Parliament.

37–21   The Crown Prosecution Service and the police are already publicly funded so there is no power to order their costs from central funds. This section refers to private prosecutions for either way offences and does not cover summary only cases. Costs may be awarded irrespective of the outcome of the case but the court has a discretion whether to order costs and to what amount. Expenses for a private prosecutor may include legal expenses, secretarial costs and travel expenses but a claim cannot be made for compensation for lost time: *R. v Stockport Magistrates Ex p. Cooper* (1984) 148 J.P. 261.

D. Award of Costs against Accused

Prosecution of Offences Act 1985, s.18

Award of costs against accused

37–22   **18.**—(1) Where—

(a) any person is convicted of an offence before a magistrates' court;

(b) the Crown Court dismisses an appeal against such a conviction or against the sentence imposed on that conviction; or

(c) any person is convicted of an offence before the Crown Court;

the court may make such order as to the costs to be paid by the accused to the prosecutor as it considers just and reasonable.

(2) Relates to the Court of Appeal...

(3) The amount to be paid by the accused in pursuance of an order under this section shall be specified in the order.

(4) Where any person is convicted of an offence before a magistrates' court and—

(a) under the conviction the court orders payment of any sum as a fine, penalty, forfeiture or compensation; and

(b) the sum so ordered to be paid does not exceed £5;

the court shall not order the accused to pay any costs under this section unless in the particular circumstances of the case it considers it right to do so.

(5) Where any person under the age of eighteen is convicted of an offence before a magistrates' court, the amount of any costs ordered to be paid by the accused under this section shall not exceed the amount of any fine imposed on him.

(6) Relates to the Court of Appeal...

[This section is reprinted as amended by the *Criminal Justice and Public Order Act* 1994, Sch.9, para.26.]

The Crown Prosecution Service may make application to the court for costs of prose- **37–23** cuting the case to be paid by the convicted defendant. The court has a discretion whether to make the order and must specify the amount in accordance with s.18(3). Where a fine is less than £5, the presumption is that no costs will be ordered and for a person under the age of 18, any costs awarded must not be greater than the amount of any fine imposed: ss.18(4) and (5). This must be done in court as there is no provision for prosecution costs to be taxed.

The prosecution will state the amount of costs sought and may be required to submit full details if the amount claimed is high.

Costs payable under such an order were held to be limited to such items as would be payable to the prosecution out of central funds were such an order possible. So counsels' fees, the DPP's costs and witness expenses could be claimed but the jury expenses and cost of security on a trial could not be included: *R. v Maher* [1983] Q.B. 784.

Issues have arisen over whether the costs of the investigation can be included. It was **37–24** held that the order for prosecution costs did not extend to cover the costs of the investigation, particularly when, as in the case, a different body carried out the investigation: *R. v Seymour* (1987) 9 Cr.App.R.(S.) 395. In *Neville (Westminster City Council) v Gardner Merchant Ltd* (1983) 82 L.G.R. 577 it was held that that the court did have the discretion to include the cost of time spent by a salaried Environmental Health Officer in conducting the investigation and inspecting premises under the *Food Safety (General Food Hygiene) Regulations* 1995 (SI 1995/1763). This was especially so if the investigation arose from a specific complaint rather than coming to light through a routine inspection.

More recently in *R. v Associated Octel Ltd* [1997] 1 Cr.App.R. 435, CA, the court said that the costs incurred by the prosecuting authority (the Health and Safety Executive), in investigating a case for prosecution could be recovered under a prosecution costs order. In such a case it was advisable for the prosecution to serve notice on the defence of the full details of the claim so that the defence could consider the claim and make representations.

In cases where a defendant would have paid a fixed penalty if the option had been offered to him but the case ended up in court, it was held to be incumbent upon the court to either not award any costs or to give cogent reasons as to why costs would be awarded: *R. (on the application of Ritson) v County Durham Magistrates' Court* (2002) 166 J.P. 218.

The prosecution will request a specific amount but the court has a discretion as to **37–25** exactly how much it will order to be paid by the defence. In exercising this discretion there are several factors to take into account. The means of the defendant are relevant and it was suggested that an amount that could be paid off within 12 months would be reasonable: *R. v Nottingham Justices Ex p. Fohmann* (1987) 84 Cr.App.R. 316, DC.

The court is obliged when fixing the amount to be paid to investigate the defendant's financial situation with adequate thoroughness and it was held not to be reasonable to make an order for costs that was five times the amount of the fines when the defendant had debts exceeding his savings: *R. v Newham Justices Ex p. Samuels* [1991] C.O.D. 412, DC. Even if the financial situation is investigated with thoroughness the award made may be subject to quashing on appeal if it is considered that no reasonable court could have made such an order on the information obtained: *R. v Croydon Justices Ex p. Summers* [1993] C.O.D. 202, DC. The court however declined to determine whether there ought to be some proportionality between fines and costs awards.

37–26   Where the defendant faces multiple charges it is not appropriate to multiply the costs by the number of summonses which related to offences all resulting from one incident. The defendant was summonsed for 37 offences under the *Food Safety (General Food Hygiene) Regulations* 1995 (SI 1995/1763) and separate costs orders were made in respect of each summons after written pleas of guilty were accepted. The costs ordered were held to be excessive: *R. v Tottenham Justices Ex p. Joshi* (1982) 75 Cr.App.R. 72, DC. In a case of multiple offences it is acceptable to order a global figure of costs more truly reflecting the work done.

37–27   An award of costs should not be made with a view to punishing the defendant for the way in which he chose to conduct his case but if his actions necessarily incur higher costs as for example by electing jury trial then this will inevitably be reflected in the amount ordered: *R. v Hayden* (1964) 60 Cr.App.R. 304, CA. In *R. v Northallerton Magistrates' Court Ex p. Dove* [2000] 1 Cr.App.R. (S.) 136, DC, the court held on appeal that where the costs ordered were almost five times the amount of the fine imposed that this was 'grossly disproportionate'. The court took the opportunity to issue guidelines for the assessment of prosecution costs to be paid by the defendant as follows:

1. The defendant's means and liability for any other financial order should be ascertained so that any order did not exceed a reasonable sum he was able to pay.
2. The sum should never be more than the costs incurred.
3. It was compensation for the prosecutor and not further punishment for the defendant.
4. The costs order should be proportionate to the fine and if the total amount is excessive, the costs should be reduced.
5. The onus was on the defendant to provide details of means and if he failed to do so, the court could deduce his financial circumstances from all available evidence.
6. The defendant must be given the opportunity to produce evidence of his means and should be put on notice of any unusual costs order intended.

37–28   A fine and costs against a company may be payable over a longer period of time than would be regarded as reasonable for an individual defendant. In determining the appropriate amount for directors, the court should consider, on the one hand, the need to avoid the risk of double punishment which may arise where the directors of a small company were also its shareholders, and on the other, that it is important to mark the personal responsibility of the directors: *R. v Rollco Screw and Rivet Co. Ltd* [1999] 2 Cr.App.R. 436, CA.

The court has discretion to make a prosecution costs order whether the defendant pleads guilty or not guilty. On a guilty plea the costs should be greatly reduced because the expense of preparation and conduct of a trial is avoided. The stage at which the guilty plea is tendered will be relevant in assessing the amount of costs to be ordered. The court has a discretion to award costs on a written plea of guilty dealt with under s.12 of the *Magistrates' Courts Act* 1980. The application for costs should be notified to the defendant in the paperwork sent to him but it does not form part of the statement of facts so would not technically need to be read out by the legal adviser in court. It was held to be sufficient for the claim for costs to be drawn to the court's attention by the legal adviser: *R. v Coventry Magistrates' Court Ex p. DPP* [1990] 3 All E.R. 277.

Where there are several defendants and only some of them have the ability to pay, it **37–29** is wrong to divide the total cost of the prosecution between those defendants. If it is not possible to say what part of the total costs is attributable to any defendant, the court should divide the total costs between the total number of defendants, and order those who do have sufficient means to pay their share only: *R. v Ronson and Parnes* (1992) 13 Cr.App.R.(S.) 153, CA; *R. v Harrison* [1993] 14 Cr.App.R.(S.) 419, CA.

In a case where corporate defendants were held to bear a greater responsibility for criminal conduct than the individual co-defendants it was held appropriate for the company to be ordered to pay a greater amount of costs: *R. v Fresha Bakeries* [2003] 1 Cr.App.R.(S.) 44.

E. Wasted Costs Awards

Prosecution of Offences Act 1985, s.19(1), (3)–(4)

Provision for orders as to costs in other circumstances

19.—(1) The Lord Chancellor may by regulations make provision empowering magistrates' **37–30** courts, the Crown Court and the Court of Appeal, in any case where the court is satisfied that one party to criminal proceedings has incurred costs as a result of an unnecessary or improper act or omission by, or on behalf of, another party to the proceedings, to make an order as to the payment of those costs.

(2)–(5) contain the content of Regulations made under subsection (1) above

(3) The Lord Chancellor may by regulations make provision for the payment out of central fund, in such circumstances and in relation to such criminal proceedings as may be specified, of such sums as appear to the court to be reasonably necessary—

   (a) to compensate any witness in the proceedings, and any other person who in the opinion of the court necessarily attends for the purposes of the proceedings otherwise than to give evidence, for the expense, trouble or loss of time properly incurred in or incidental to his attendance,

   (b) to cover the proper expenses of an interpreter who is required because of the accused's lack of English;

   (c) to compensate a duly qualified medical practitioner who—

      (i) makes a report otherwise than in writing for the purposes of section 11 of the *powers of Criminal Courts(Sentencing) Act* 2000 (remand for medical examination); or

      (ii) makes a written report to a court in pursuance of a request to which section 32(2) of the *Criminal Justice Act* 1967 (report by medical practitioner on medical condition of offender) applies;

      for the expenses properly incurred in or incidental to his reporting to the court.

   (d) to cover the proper fee or costs of a person appointed by the Crown Court under section 4A of the *Criminal Procedure (Insanity) Act* 1964 to put the case for the defence.

   (e) To cover the proper fee or costs of a legal representative appointed under section 38(4) of the *Youth Justice and Criminal Evidence Act* 1999 (defence representation for purposes of cross-examination) and any expenses properly incurred in providing such a person with evidence or other material in connection with his appointment.

(3A) In subsection (3)(a) above 'attendance' means attendance at the court or elsewhere.

(4) Court of Appeal.

[This section is reprinted as amended by the *Access to Justice Act* 1999, Sch.4, para.28.]

This section provides for an order to be made for wasted costs between parties and **37–31** also for payments from public funds to witnesses. Pursuant to the power in s.19, the Lord Chancellor has made the *Costs in Criminal Cases (General) Regulations* 1986 which in Pt V sets out the witnesses who are entitled to be paid allowances and the *Costs in Criminal Cases (General) Regulations* 1986— Rates of Allowances which fixes the amounts to be paid. The rates are amended periodically.

Costs in Criminal Cases (General) Regulations 1986, reg.3

Part II

Costs Unnecessarily or Improperly Incurred

Unnecessary or improper acts and omissions

37–32 **3.**—(1) Subject to the provisions of this regulation, where at any time during criminal proceedings—

(a) a magistrates' court,

(b) the Crown Court, or

(c) the Court of Appeal

is satisfied that costs have been incurred in respect of the proceedings by one of the parties as a result of an unnecessary or improper act or omission by, or on behalf of, another party to the proceedings, the court may, after hearing the parties, order that all or part of the costs so incurred by that party shall be paid to him by the other party.

(2) Before making an order under paragraph (1), the court shall take into account any other order as to costs (including any legal aid order) which has been made in respect of the proceedings.

(3) An order made under paragraph (1) shall specify the amount of costs to be paid in pursuance of the order.

(4) Where an order under paragraph (1) has been made, the court may take that order into account when making any other order as to costs in respect of the proceedings.

(5) No order under paragraph (1) shall be made by a magistrates' court which requires a person under the age of seventeen who has been convicted of an offence to pay an amount by way of costs which exceeds the amount of any fine imposed on him.

37–33 An order under s.19, in common with other orders under the Act, may only be made in respect of criminal proceedings. For consideration of this term see above—s.16.The power to award a wasted costs order acts not only as a compensation to any party who incurs extra costs but also as an encouragement to all parties involved in a criminal case to act with diligence and expedition. An application can be made at any time during the proceedings or at the conclusion of the case. The order is made between the parties.

The court must be satisfied that the costs were incurred as a result of 'an unnecessary or improper act or omission.' The word "improper" used in conjunction with 'unnecessary' was held to encompass an act or omission resulting in costs which would not have been incurred in the proper conduct of the party's case: *DPP v Denning* [1991] 2 Q.B. 532. *Per curiam* the court observed that 'improper' did not connote 'grave impropriety'.

37–34 A causal connection must be shown to exist between the unnecessary or improper act or omission and the incurring of the costs or expenses claimed under the order. Where the prosecution was ordered to pay wasted costs which covered the costs of a Crown Court case when no evidence was offered following committal, the court said that inquiries must be made into whether the prosecution's negligence was the cause of the defence costs: *R. v Crown Court at Wood Green Ex p. DPP* [1993] 1 W.L.R. 723.

Where the defendant has the benefit of a criminal defence representation order then for the purposes of s.19 of the *Prosecution of Offences Act* 1985 his costs shall be taken to include the cost of representation publicly funded for him: *Prosecution of Offences Act* 1985, s.21(4A)(b). A wasted costs order may not be appropriate against the prosecution in the case of a legally aided defendant as it simply means the transfer of public funds. Only in extraordinary cases or where the conduct of the police and the Crown Prosecution Service is open to criticism may it be appropriate to make an order. Otherwise the costs of the defence should be borne by the legal aid fund: *R. v Oxford City Justices Ex p. Chief Constable Thames Valley Police, The Times*, April 24, 1987.

This section only allows for orders to be made between the parties. Orders cannot be **37–35** made against solicitors or counsel personally under s.19: *R. v Crown Court at Isleworth Ex p. Montague & Co* [1990] C.O.D. 86, DC. As to costs awarded against representatives personally see below.

F. Orders for Costs against Legal Representatives

Prosecution of Offences Act 1985, s.19A

Costs against legal representatives
   19A.—(1) In any criminal proceedings—   **37–36**
      (a) the Court of Appeal;
      (b) the Crown Court;
      (c) a magistrates' court,
may disallow, or (as the case may be) order the legal or other representative concerned to meet, the whole of any wasted costs or such part of them as may be determined in accordance with regulations.
   (2) Regulations shall provide that a legal or other representative against whom action is taken by a magistrates' court under subsection (1) may appeal to the Crown Court and that a legal or other representative against whom action is taken by the Crown Court under subsection (1) may appeal to the Court of Appeal.
   (3) In this section—
      "legal or other representative" in relation to any proceedings, means a person who is exercising a right of audience, or right to conduct litigation, on behalf of any party to the proceedings;
      "regulations" means regulations made by the Lord Chancellor; and
      "wasted costs" means any costs incurred by a party—
         (a) as a result of any improper, unreasonable or negligent act or omission on the part of any representative or any employee of a representative; or
         (b) which, in the light of any such act or omission occurring after they were incurred, the court considers it is unreasonable to expect that party to pay.

Costs in Criminal Cases (General) Regulations 1986, reg.3A

Part II A

Wasted Costs Orders

Application and definitions
   3A. This Part of these Regulations applies to action taken by a court under section 19A of the   **37–37** Act and in this Part of these regulations—
      "wasted costs order" means any action taken by a court under section 19A of the Act; and
      "interested party" means the party benefiting from the wasted costs order and, where he was legally aided, or an order for the payment of costs out of central funds was made in his favour, shall include the authority responsible for determining costs payable in respect of work done under the legal aid order or out of central funds as the case may be.

Costs in Criminal Cases (General) Regulations 1986, reg.3B

General
   3B.—(1) A wasted costs order may provide for the whole or any part of the wasted costs to be   **37–38** disallowed or ordered to be paid and the court shall specify the amount of such costs.
   (2) Before making a wasted costs order the court shall allow the legal or other representative and any party to the proceedings to make representations.
   (3) When making a wasted costs order the court may take into account any other order as to costs in respect of the proceedings and may take the wasted costs into account when making any other such order.

(4) Where a wasted costs order has been made the court shall notify any interested party of the order and the amount disallowed or ordered to be paid.

Costs in Criminal Cases (General) Regulations 1986, reg.3C

Appeals

37–39   **3C.**—(1) A legal or other representative against whom the wasted costs order is made may appeal—
      (a) in the case of an order made by a magistrates' court, to the Crown Court, and
      (b) in the case of an order made at first instance by the Crown Court, to the Court of Appeal.

(2) Subject to paragraph (4), an appeal shall be instituted within 21 days of the wasted costs order being made by the appellant's giving notice in writing to the court which made the order, stating the grounds of appeal.

(3) The appellant shall serve a copy of the notice of appeal and grounds, including any application for an extension of time in which to appeal, on any interested party.

(4) The time limit within which an appeal may be instituted may, for good reason, be extended before or after it expires—
      (a) in the case of an appeal to the Crown Court, by a judge of that court;
      (b) in the case of an appeal to the Court of Appeal, a judge of the High Court or Court of Appeal,
and in each case the court to which the appeal is made shall give notice of the extension to the appellant, the court which made the wasted costs order and any interested party.

(5) The court shall give notice of the hearing date to the appellant, the court which made the wasted costs order and any interested party and shall allow the interested party to make representations which may be made orally or in writing.

(6) The court may affirm, vary or revoke the order as it thinks fit and shall notify its decision to the appellant, any interested party and the court which made the order.

Costs in Criminal Cases (General) Regulations 1986, reg.3D

Recovery of sums due under a wasted costs order

37–40   **3D.** Where the person required to make a payment in respect of sums due under a wasted costs order fails to do so, the payment may be recovered summarily as a sum adjudged to be paid as a civil debt by order of a magistrates' court by the party benefiting from the order, save that where he was legally aided or an order for the payment of costs out of central funds was made in his favour, the power to recover shall be exercisable by the Lord Chancellor.

37–41   Extra costs may arise when a lawyer is at fault in the conduct of a case before the court. The court has power to order legal representatives to pay personally or be disallowed his own costs when wasted costs are incurred as a result of his actions or omissions. Wasted costs are defined in s.19A. This is a harsh measure and case law provides some guidance on how the Act and regulations should be applied.

In *Re A Barrister (Wasted Costs Order) (No.1 of 1991)* [1993] Q.B. 293, the Court of Appeal gave the following guidance for the making of wasted costs orders against legal representatives.

    1. There is a clear need for any court or judge intending to exercise the wasted costs jurisdiction to formulate carefully and concisely the complaint and the grounds upon which such an order may be sought. The measures are draconian and the grounds must be clear and particular.

    2. Where necessary a transcript of the relevant part of the proceedings under discussion should be available. And in accordance with the Rules, a transcript of a wasted costs hearing must be made.

    3. A defendant involved in a case where such proceedings are contemplated should be present, if after discussion, with counsel, it is thought that his interests may be affected and he should certainly be present and represented if the matter might affect the course of his trial. Regulation 3B(2) of the *Costs in Criminal Cases*

(General) (Amendment) Regulations 1991 furthermore requires that before a wasted costs order is made "the court shall allow the legal or other representative and any party to the proceedings to make representations." There may be cases where it may be appropriate for counsel for the Crown to be present.

4. A three-stage test or approach is recommended when a wasted costs order is contemplated. (i) Has there been an improper, unreasonable or negligent act or omission? (ii) As a result, have any costs been incurred by a party? (iii) If these questions are answered in the affirmative, should the court exercise its discretion to disallow or order the representative to meet the whole or any party of the relevant costs, and if so what specific sum is involved?

5. It is inappropriate to propose any deal or settlement that the representative might forgo fees. The judge should formally state his complaint, in chambers, and invite the representative to make his or her own comments. After any other party has been heard the judge should give a formal ruling. Discursive conversations may be unfair and should certainly not take place.

6. The judge must specify the sum to be disallowed or ordered. Alternatively the relevant available procedure should be substituted, should it be impossible to fix the sum.

In this case the wasted costs order was made against counsel whose unexplained and **37–42** unrefuted remark led the judge to discharge the jury. Because the proper procedure was not followed the order was held invalid. The procedure in the magistrates' court will be slightly different as no full transcripts are taken so the hearing will be recorded only by way of the notes made by the legal adviser. The suggestion of dealing with the matter in chambers is not applicable to the magistrates' court although the court may be cleared in sensitive cases. The general principles enunciated should otherwise be followed. This guidance was approved in *Re Mintz (Wasted Costs Order) The Times*, July 16, 1999, CA, where an order was made against counsel who failed to reach prompt agreement about the removal of certain passages from interview transcripts. The judge did not indicate his complaint in chambers; counsel was not invited to make representations and the amount of costs was not specified. These irregularities led to the order being quashed. Failure to allow representations is in breach of Regulation 3B and failure to specify the amount ordered is a fatal flaw. See also *Re Wiseman Lee (Solicitors) (Wasted Costs Order) (No.5 of 2000), The Times*, April 5, 2001 and *R. v Harry Jagdev & Co. (Wasted Costs Order) (No.2 of 1999), The Times*, August 12, 1999.

Because of the procedural irregularities in these cases, the courts did not go into the **37–43** question of whether the conduct complained of justified the making of such an order. Guidance on this issue is found in *Ridehalgh v Horsefield* [1994] Ch. 205, CA. The court considered a number of applications and reviewed the level of conduct that could be said to give rise to wasted costs. It was stated that 'improper, unreasonable and negligent' were words that bore their established meaning.

1. Improper included conduct that amounted to any significant breach of a substantial duty imposed by a relevant code of professional conduct and included conduct so regarded by the consensus of professional opinion.

2. Unreasonable described conduct which did not permit of a reasonable explanation.

3. Negligent was to be understood in a non-technical way to denote a failure to act with the competence reasonably to be expected of ordinary members of the profession.

It was further said that the conduct so characterised had to be established to be **37–44** directly causative of any wasted costs. From the cases under consideration it was held that such an order was not appropriate for a solicitor pursuing a hopeless case. It was not improper, unreasonable or negligent to act for a defendant whose case was doomed to failure. Also late acceptance of a brief by counsel which led to delay in the case was held to be neither improper nor unnecessary as the 'cab rank' principle applied and counsel was obliged to accept the case.

In *Re P (A Barrister) (Wasted Costs Order)* [2002] 1 Cr.App.R. 207, CA it was held that a judge could decline to deal with an application for a wasted costs order arising from a case he has dealt with but the fact that the judge had expressed views in relation to the conduct of the barrister against whom the order was sought did not of itself amount to bias or the appearance of bias. The appeal court took the view that it was in the interest of both the public and the profession to retain the summary nature of the procedure which was quick, economical and effective so it was acceptable for the trial judge to deal with wasted costs and not adjourn the matter to another court. It was also held that the standard of proof was the normal civil standard unless the allegation was one of serious misconduct or crime. In this case the misconduct complained of was an inference by the defence that the defendant was of good character when in fact he had spent convictions. The jury was discharged as a result of hearing about the convictions and the wasted costs order was upheld.

G. Enforcement

Magistrates' Courts Act 1980, s.76

Enforcement of sums adjudged to be paid

37–45   **76.**—(1) Subject to the following provi sions of this Part of this Act, and to section 132 below, where default is made in paying a sum adjudged to be paid by a conviction or order of a magistrates' court, the court may issue a warrant of distress for the purposes of levying the sum or is- sue a warrant committing the defaulter to prison.

(2) A warrant of commitment may be issued as aforesaid either—

     (a) where it appears on the return to a warrant of distress that the money and goods of the defaulter are insufficient to satisfy the sum with the costs and charges of levying the sum; or

     (b) instead of a warrant of distress.

(3) The period for which a person may be committed to prison under such a warrant as aforesaid shall not, subject to the provisions of any enactment passed after 31st December 1879, exceed the period applicable to the case under Schedule 4 to this Act.

(4)–(6) apply to civil maintenance orders.

[This section is reprinted as amended by the *Criminal Justice Act* 1982, s.78 and Sch.16.]

37–46   Costs may be enforced in the same way as fines, see Chapter 34. A sum adjudged to be paid by a conviction or order includes costs, damages or compensation: s.150(3) of the *Magistrates' Courts Act* 1980. Any period of imprisonment ordered in default of payment cannot be less than five days: s.132 of the *Magistrates' Courts Act* 1980. Maximum periods of imprisonment in default are fixed according to the amount ordered to be paid. There is no power to remit costs, but nominal default orders may be made.

H. Award of Costs against Third Parties

Courts Act 2003, s.93

Award of costs against third parties

37–47   **93.** After section 19A of the *Prosecution of Offences Act* 1985 insert–

Provision for award of costs against third parties

"**19B.**—(1) The Lord Chancellor may by regulations make provision empowering magistrates' courts, the Crown Court and the Court of Appeal to make a third party costs order if the condition in subsection (3) is satisfied.

(2) A "third party costs order" is an order as to the payment of costs incurred by a party to criminal proceedings by a person who is not a party to those proceedings ("the third party").

(3) The condition is that–

    (a) there has been serious misconduct (whether or not constituting a contempt of court) by the third party, and

    (b) the court considers it appropriate, having regard to that misconduct, to make a third party costs order against him.

(4) Regulations made under this section may, in particular–

    (a) specify types of misconduct in respect of which a third party costs order may not be made;

    (b) allow the making of a third party costs order at any time;

    (c) make provision for any other order as to costs which has been made in respect of the proceedings to be varied on, or taken account of in, the making of a third party costs order;

    (d) make provision for account to be taken of any third party costs order in the making of any other order as to costs in respect of the proceedings.

(5) Regulations made under this section in relation to magistrates' courts must provide that the third party may appeal to the Crown Court against a third party costs order made by a magistrates' court.

(6) Regulations made under this section in relation to the Crown Court must provide that the third party may appeal to the Court of Appeal against a third party costs order made by the Crown Court."

This section allows the Lord Chancellor to make regulations giving powers to the courts, including magistrates' courts, to make an order for costs against a person who is not a party to the proceedings, known as a "third party costs order".

The order can only be made if the serious misconduct condition is met and if the court considers such an order to be appropriate. No regulations have yet been published but the order is referred to in the Costs Practice Note of May 2004 and the section came into force in February 2004.

INDEX

⟨LT⟩ *The selection of headings in this index has been informed by Sweet & Maxwell's Legal Taxonomy. Main index entries conform to keywords provided by the Legal Taxonomy. These keywords provide a means of identifying similar concepts in other Sweet & Maxwell publications and online services to which keywords from the Legal Taxonomy have been applied. Using a controlled indexing vocabulary provides a much higher level of quality and consistency in classifying legal materials. Readers may find some minor differences between terms used in the text and those which appear in the index. Suggestions can be made to taxonomy@sweetandmaxwell.co.uk.*